Cases and Materials on
Business Entities

Cases and Materials on
Business Entities

Eric A. Chiappinelli

Associate Dean for Alumni and Professional Relations
Professor of Law
Seattle University School of Law

PUBLISHERS

76 Ninth Avenue, New York, NY 10011
http://lawschool.aspenpublishers.com

© 2006 Aspen Publishers, Inc.
a Wolters Kluwer business
http://lawschool.aspenpublishers.com

Aspen Publishers
Attn: Permissions Department
76 Ninth Avenue, 7th Floor
New York, NY 10011-5201

Printed in the United States of America

1 2 3 4 5 6 7 8 9 0

ISBN 0-7355-2614-1

Library of Congress Cataloging-in-Publication Data

Chiappinelli, Eric A., 1953-
　Cases and materials on business entities / Eric A. Chiappinelli.
　　p. cm.
　ISBN 0-7355-2614-1 (alk. paper)
　1. Corporation law—United States—Cases. 2. Business enterprises—Law and
legislation—United States—Cases. I. Title.

KF1413.C485 2006
346.73′066—dc22

2006003929

About Aspen Publishers

Aspen Publishers, headquartered in New York City, is a leading information provider for attorneys, business professionals, and law students. Written by preeminent authorities, our products consist of analytical and practical information covering both U.S. and international topics. We publish in the full range of formats, including updated manuals, books, periodicals, CDs, and online products.

Our proprietary content is complemented by 2,500 legal databases, containing over 11 million documents, available through our Loislaw division. Aspen Publishers also offers a wide range of topical legal and business databases linked to Loislaw's primary material. Our mission is to provide accurate, timely, and authoritative content in easily accessible formats, supported by unmatched customer care.

To order any Aspen Publishers title, go to *http://lawschool.aspenpublishers.com* or call 1-800-638-8437.

To reinstate your manual update service, call 1-800-638-8437.

For more information on Loislaw products, go to *www.loislaw.com* or call 1-800-364-2512.

For Customer Care issues, e-mail *CustomerCare@aspenpublishers.com*; call 1-800-234-1660; or fax 1-800-901-9075.

Aspen Publishers
a Wolters Kluwer business

Dedication

I've always thought that dedicating a book to family is more than a little propitiatory. While some books might actually atone to the author's loved ones for the time spent away from them, certainly few casebooks fall into that category. I have no illusions that this book is any compensation to my son, Peter, for the hours and hours I spent writing it. I have thanked him, and do so again here, for his willingness to put up with all the time I spent away from him while I was writing. But, in fact, although he was largely cheerful about all of this, he really had no choice. I was the one who decided to write this book and I was the one who decided how much time to spend on it. So this dedication is more in the way of apology than propitiation. I hope it will remind all parents that sometimes the professional choices they make for themselves affect their children in ways that can be rationalized but can't really be remedied.

This book is dedicated to my son, Peter, who is the most wonderful person and who was the most wonderful child. I am sorry that I spent so much time away from you to write it. Thank you, Peter, for sharing so much of your life with me and for letting me be your father. I am grateful to you for far more than you can ever imagine. I love you any time, every time, all the time.

Summary of Contents

Contents   *xi*
Preface   *xxix*
Acknowledgments   *xxxiii*

Part I. THE PRACTICE OF BUSINESS LAW   1

Chapter 1. Practicing Corporate Law   3
Chapter 2. Business and Businesses   19
Chapter 3. Economics   43

Part II. AGENCY   83

Chapter 4. Agency   85

Part III. CORPORATIONS   113

A. Creation

Chapter 5. The Incorporation Process   115

B. The Corporation and Its Finances

Chapter 6. Capital Formation   151
Chapter 7. Cashing Out: Distributing Money to Shareholders   205
Chapter 8. Getting Money to Creditors When the Corporation Can't Pay   275

C. Board Power to Govern the Corporation

Chapter 9. How Corporations Take Actions   313

D. Restrictions on the Board's Power

Chapter 10. Restrictions on the Board's Power   357
Chapter 11. The Duty of Loyalty of Directors (and Officers)   379
Chapter 12. The Duty of Care of Directors (and Officers)   403
Chapter 13. Standards of Review of Board Actions   425
Chapter 14. Do the Restrictions Work?   491

E. Shareholder Power in Public and Private Corporations

Chapter 15. Shareholder Governance Powers: Paradigms and Public
               Companies   543
Chapter 16. Shareholder Governance Questions Most Often Seen in the
               Privately Held Corporation   593

F. Change of Control

Chapter 17. Change of Control   639

Part IV. UNINCORPORATED ENTITIES   685

Chapter 18. Partnerships   687
Chapter 19. Limited Liability Companies   739

Part V. CHOICE OF FORM   771

Chapter 20. Choice of Entity   773

Glossary   793
Table of Cases   809
Index   813

Contents

Preface	*xxix*
Acknowledgments	*xxxiii*

Part I. THE PRACTICE OF BUSINESS LAW   **1**

Chapter 1.   **Practicing Corporate Law**   **3**

    A. What Do Corporate Lawyers Do?   3
        1. A Different Paradigm from Litigators   3
        2. The Typical Roles of the Corporate Lawyer   5
        Notes and Questions   8
    B. Where Do Corporate Lawyers Work?   10
        1. Private Practice   10
        2. Corporations (In-House Lawyers)   11
        3. Other Practice Settings   13
        4. Who Practices Corporate Law?   13
        Notes and Questions   15
    C. What Do Corporate Lawyers Need to Know?   15
        1. Core Areas of Knowledge   15
        2. Secondary Areas of Knowledge   16
        Notes and Questions   17
    D. Federal Securities Regulation   17
    E. Terms of Art in This Chapter   18

Chapter 2.   **Business and Businesses**   **19**

    A. What Is a "Business"?   19
        1. Why Businesses Vary in Size   19
            a. Background and Context—An Example   21
        Fitting In: In Bow to Retailers' New Clout,
        Levi Strauss Makes Alterations   21
        Notes and Questions   24
    B. The Development of Big Business in America   25
        Alfred D. Chandler, Jr., *The Visible Hand: The Managerial*
        Revolution in American Business   25
        Notes and Questions   28
        1. Management Patterns in Large Corporations   28

Alfred D. Chandler, Jr., *The Visible Hand: The Managerial Revolution in American Business*   29

Notes and Questions   31

C. Form Follows Function—Entities for Businesses   32
   1. The Current Setting—From Partnerships to
      Corporations   32

Alfred D. Chandler, Jr., *The Visible Hand: The Managerial Revolution in American Business*   32

Margaret M. Blair, *Locking in Capital: What Corporate Law Achieved for Business Organizers in the Nineteenth Century*   33

Notes and Questions   34
   2. Background and Context—A Vignette   34

Margaret M. Blair, *Locking in Capital: What Corporate Law Achieved for Business Organizers in the Nineteenth Century*   35

Notes and Questions   36
   3. Which State's Law?—The Rise of Delaware   36

William E. Kirk, III, *A Case Study in Legislative Opportunism: How Delaware Used the Federal-State System to Attain Corporate Pre-Eminence*   37

Notes and Questions   38
   4. Which Nation's Law?—Globalization and
      Corporation Law   39

Ronald J. Gilson, *Globalizing Corporate Governance: Convergence of Form or Function*   39

Douglas M. Branson, *The Very Uncertain Prospect of "Global" Convergence in Corporate Governance*   40

Notes and Questions   41

D. Terms of Art in This Chapter   42

Chapter 3. Economics   **43**
A. Risk   43
Notes and Questions   47
B. Valuation   48
   1. Value as Discounted Cash Flow   49
      a. "I'll Gladly Pay You Tuesday, For a Hamburger
         Today"—The Time Value of Money   49
      b. Discounting to Present Value   50
      c. An Example   51
   Notes and Questions   53
   2. A Practical Illustration   54
   Doft & Co. v. Travelocity.Com Inc.   55
   Notes and Questions   59
   3. Background and Context: Options and How to Value
      Them   59
C. Making Economic Decisions   61
   1. Rational Self-Interest: The Classical Paradigm   61
   2. The Myth of Rational Self-Interest: How Humans
      Actually Make Economic Decisions   62

          a. Self-Interest   62

Richard H. Thaler, *The Winner's Curse: Paradoxes and Anomalies of Economic Life*   62

Notes and Questions   63
          b. The Limits of Rationality   63
              i. Heuristics   64

Amos Tversky & Daniel Kahneman, *Judgment Under Uncertainty: Heuristics and Biases*   64

Notes and Questions   66
          c. The Affective Component of Economic Decision Making   67

Notes and Questions   69
          d. The Ethical Component of Economic Decision Making   69

Joseph L. Badaracco, Jr., *The Discipline of Building Character*   69

Notes and Questions   72
    D. Accounting   73
    Notes and Questions   82
    E. Terms of Art in This Chapter   82

Part II. **AGENCY**   83

Chapter 4. Agency   85
    A. Background and Context   85
        1. The Economic Concept of "Agency" and the Problem of Agency Costs   85
        2. Where Do Agency Questions Arise?   88
    Notes and Questions   89
    B. The Current Setting   90
        1. Definition of the Agency Relationship   90
        2. Creation of the Agency Relationship   91

Basile v. H & R Block, Inc.   91

Notes and Questions   94
        3. Relation of the Principal to Third Parties   95
          a. Actual Authority   95
          b. Apparent Authority   96

In the Matter of McDuffie   96

Notes and Questions   97
          c. Principal's Liability to Third Parties for Actions Actually or Apparently Authorized   99
          d. Estoppel   99
          e. Ratification   100
          f. Restitution   100
          g. Principal's Liability for Agent's Torts   100

Fisher v. Townsends, Inc.   101

Notes and Questions   103
          h. Liability of the Third Party to the Principal   105
        4. Relation of the Agent to Third Parties   105

a. Agent's Liability on Contract 105
Benjamin Plumbing, Inc. v. Barnes 106
Notes and Questions 108
b. Other Sources of Agent's Liability to Third Party 109
5. Relation of the Principal to the Agent 109
a. Duties of the Agent 109
b. Duties of the Principal 110
6. Termination of the Agency Relationship 110
a. Termination of Actual and Apparent Authority 110
C. Terms of Art in This Chapter 111

Part III. CORPORATIONS   113

A. Creation

Chapter 5.   The Incorporation Process 115
A. Promoter Liability 115
Moneywatch Companies v. Wilbers 115
Notes and Questions 118
B. Choice of Jurisdiction 119
1. Why the Corporation's Jurisdiction Matters — The Internal Affairs Doctrine 119
a. The Current Setting 119
b. Background and Context 121
Notes and Questions 122
2. The Special Role of Delaware 122
C. Incorporation Mechanics 123
1. Reserving the Name 124
2. The Incorporation Documents 124
3. Filing 125
4. Organizing the New Corporation 126
D. Defective Incorporation 126
1. Background and Context 127
Robert S. Stevens, *Handbook on the Law of Private Corporations* 127
2. The Current Setting 130
a. De Facto Corporations 130
Hill v. County Concrete Company, Inc. 130
Notes and Questions 132
Harris v. Looney 133
Notes and Questions 135
b. Corporations by Estoppel 136
American Vending Services, Inc. v. Morse 136
Notes and Questions 138
E. Lawyer's Professional Responsibility to Multiple Clients and Entity Clients 139
Detter v. Schreiber 140
Notes and Questions 142
Utah Rules of Professional Conduct 144

F. Terms of Art in This Chapter   149

B. The Corporation and Its Finances

Chapter 6. **Capital Formation**   **151**
    A. Financing: Getting Money into the Business   151
      1. Background and Context   151
      2. The Current Setting   153
        a. Corporate Securities   153
          i. (Common) Stock   153
          ii. Preferred Stock   154
          iii. Other Relative Rights   156
        Kaiser Aluminum Corporation v. Matheson   157
        Notes and Questions   159
          iv. Debt   160
          (A) Short-Term Debt   161
          (B) Long-Term Debt   162
          v. More Exotic Securities   164
        b. Planning the Corporate Capital Structure   165
          i. The Consequences of Debt–Leverage   166
          ii. The Economic Risks of Excessive Debt   168
          iii. Other Costs of Debt   170
          iv. The Legal Dangers of Excessive Debt   171
          v. Other Factors That Make Equity Attractive   172
          vi. Choosing a Capital Structure for the Start-Up
             Corporation   174
        Notes and Questions   175
          vii. Background and Context: A Note on Financing
             by Going Public and by Venture Capital   176
        Telcom-SNI Investors, L.L.C. v. Sorrento Networks, Inc. 178
        Notes and Questions   184
        c. The Mechanics of Issuing Stock   185
          i. Statutory Authorization   185
          ii. Issuance of Stock   185
          (A) Board Authorization   186
        Kalageorgi v. Victor Kamkin, Inc.   186
        Notes and Questions   193
            (1) Subscription Agreements   194
          (B) Consideration   194
            (1) The Problem of Ensuring Equal
               Payment by Contemporaneous
               Purchasers (Par Value)   194
            (2) The Problem of Ensuring That the
               Corporation Receives the
               Consideration   195
            (3) The Problem of Later Issuance at an
               Inadequate Price   196
            (4) The Problem of Noncash
               Consideration   196

	iii. The Meaning of *Outstanding*	197
	iv. Preemptive Rights: The Economic Component	197
B.	Federal Securities Regulation	198
	1. Definition of a Security	199
	2. Registration	201
	a. Registration Requirements and Exemptions	201
	b. The Process of Registration — "Going Public"	202
C.	Terms of Art in This Chapter	203

Chapter 7. Cashing Out: Distributing Money to Shareholders — **205**

A.	Making a Profit Part I: Dividends	206
	1. The Current Setting	206
	a. Board Discretion	206
	Notes and Questions	208
	b. Statutory Restrictions	208
	c. The Mechanics of Paying Dividends	210
	McIlvaine v. AmSouth Bank, N.A.	211
	Notes and Questions	213
	d. Stock Splits	213
	Lynam v. Gallagher	214
	Notes and Questions	217
	e. Reverse Stock Splits	217
	Reiss v. Financial Performance Corporation	218
	Reiss v. Financial Performance Corporation	222
	Notes and Questions	223
	2. Background and Context: The Difference Between "Stock Splits" and "Stock Dividends"	224
	In the Matter of the Estate of Dudley B. Dawson	225
	Notes and Questions	227
B.	Making a Profit Part II: Sale of Stock by Shareholders	227
	Harrison v. NetCentric Corp.	229
	Notes and Questions	232
	Man o' War Restaurants, Inc. v. Martin	233
	Notes and Questions	235
	F.B.I. Farms, Inc. v. Moore	237
	Notes and Questions	242
	1. When the Purchaser Is the Corporation That Issued the Shares	243
	a. Limitations on a Corporation's Power to Purchase Its Shares	243
	b. Motivations to Repurchase Shares	244
	c. The Metaphysics of Repurchased Shares	245
C.	Federal Securities Regulation	246
	1. Restrictions on Resale	246
	a. Section 16 (b)	246
	b. Rule 144	247
	2. Rule 10b-5	248
	Dura Pharmaceuticals, Inc. v. Broudo	248

	Notes and Questions	251
	Basic, Inc. v. Levinson	253
	Notes and Questions	258
	a. Insider Trading	259
	In the Matter of Cady, Roberts & Co.	260
	Notes and Questions	261
	Chiarella v. United States	262
	Notes and Questions	264
	Dirks v. SEC	265
	Notes and Questions	268
	United States v. O'Hagan	269
	Notes and Questions	272
	D. Terms of Art in This Chapter	273

Chapter 8. Getting Money to Creditors When the Corporation Can't Pay — 275

	A. The Current Setting	276
	1. Individual Shareholder Liability by Piercing the Corporate Veil	276
	Brevet International, Inc. v. Great Plains Luggage Company	280
	Notes and Questions	282
	2. Enterprise Liability	284
	Smith v. McLeod Distributing, Inc.	285
	Notes and Questions	288
	In re U-Haul International, Inc.	290
	Notes and Questions	291
	Goldberg v. Lee Express Cab Corporation	293
	Notes and Questions	295
	3. Commercial and Bankruptcy Doctrines	296
	In the Matter of Herby's Foods, Inc., Debtor	296
	Notes and Questions	300
	4. Successor Liability	301
	Pancratz v. Monsanto Company	302
	Notes and Questions	305
	B. Background and Context: Direct Liability of Corporate Officers	306
	Saltiel v. GSI Consultants, Inc.	307
	Notes and Questions	310
	C. Terms of Art in This Chapter	311

C. Board Power to Govern the Corporation

Chapter 9. How Corporations Take Actions — 313

	A. The Board of Directors	313
	1. The Role of the Board of Directors	313
	a. The Current Setting	313
	Grimes v. Donald	315
	Notes and Questions	318

      b. Background and Context 320
Victor Morawetz, *A Treatise on the Law of Private Corporations* 320
Notes and Questions 321
    2. Number, Selection, Election, Term, and Removal of
       Directors 322
      a. Number and Selection of Initial Directors 322
      b. Election and Term of Directors 322
      c. Removal of Directors 323
Notes and Questions 325
Hoschett v. TSI International Software, Ltd. 325
Notes and Questions 328
      d. Background and Context 329
Victor Morawetz, *A Treatise on the Law of Private
Corporations* 329
Notes and Questions 330
    3. The Mechanics of Board Action 330
      a. The Current Setting 330
        i.   Call 331
        ii. Notice 331
        iii. Quorum 332
        iv. Sufficient Vote 332
Notes and Questions 333
Adlerstein v. Wertheimer 333
Notes and Questions 339
      b. Background and Context 340
Victor Morawetz, *A Treatise on the Law of Private
Corporations* 340
  B. Officers 340
    1. Officers and Agents 340
      a. Background and Context. Review of Chapter 4 on
        Agency 340
H-D Irrigating, Inc. v. Kimble Properties, Inc. 340
Notes and Questions 342
      b. The Current Setting 343
Peter Bart, *The Studios' Plethora of Presidents* 345
Andrews v. Southwest Wyoming Rehabilitation Center 346
Notes and Questions 347
    2. Power of Officers 348
      a. The Current Setting 348
Snukal v. Flightways Manufacturing, Inc. 349
Notes and Questions 353
      b. Background and Context 354
Notes and Questions 354
  C. Federal Securities Regulation 354
  D. Terms of Art in This Chapter 355

D. Restrictions on the Board's Power

Chapter 10. Restrictions on the Board's Power   357
    A. Legislation That Restricts Board Power   357
    B. Ultra Vires   359
        Harbor Finance Partners v. Huizenga   360
        Notes and Questions   361
    C. Ultimate Beneficiaries   363
        1. The Current Setting   364
        William T. Allen, *Our Schizophrenic Conception of the Business Corporation*   364
        Notes and Questions   367
        2. Background and Context   368
        Adolf A. Berle, Jr., & Gardiner C. Means, *The Modern Corporation and Private Property*   368
        Notes and Questions   370
        Stephen M. Bainbridge, *The Board of Directors as Nexus of Contracts*   370
        Notes and Questions   371
        C.A. Harwell Wells, *The Cycles of Corporate Social Responsibility: An Historical Retrospective for the Twenty-First Century*   372
        Notes and Questions   377
    D. Federal Securities Regulation   377
        1. Foreign Corrupt Practices Act   377
    E. Terms of Art in This Chapter   378

Chapter 11. The Duty of Loyalty of Directors (and Officers)   379
    A. The Current Setting   380
        1. The Corporate Opportunity Doctrine   381
        Northeast Harbor Golf Club, Inc. v. Harris   382
        Notes and Questions   388
        2. Self-Dealing   390
        Tomaino v. Concord Oil of Newport, Inc.   391
        Notes and Questions   394
        3. Trying to Generalize   394
        Geller v. Allied-Lyons plc   396
        Notes and Questions   399
        4. Compensation of Directors and Senior Officers   400
    B. Background and Context   400
        1. Is There a Duty of Good Faith?   400
    C. Terms of Art in This Chapter   402

Chapter 12. The Duty of Care of Directors (and Officers)   403
    A. The Current Setting   403
        Crown v. Hawkins Co., Ltd.   403
        Notes and Questions   408

       In re Caremark International Inc. Derivative Litigation   410
       Notes and Questions   417
  B. Background and Context   419
    1. The Propriety of Analogy to Tort   420
    Notes and Questions   420
    2. Is There a Duty of Care?   421
    Notes and Questions   422
  C. Federal Securities Regulation   422
  D. Terms of Art in This Chapter   423

Chapter 13. Standards of Review of Board Actions   **425**
    Notes and Questions   426
  A. The Duty of Loyalty   427
    Orman v. Cullman   427
    Notes and Questions   433
    1. The Entire Fairness Standard   434
    HMG/Courtland Properties, Inc. v. Gray   434
    Notes and Questions   437
  B. The Duty of Care   437
    In re NCS Healthcare, Inc. Shareholders Litigation   438
    Notes and Questions   442
  C. Prevailing Despite the Application of the Business
    Judgment Rule   444
    Brehm v. Eisner   445
    Notes and Questions   453
  D. Amelioration of Liability for Violations of Fiduciary
    Duties   455
    1. Duty of Loyalty: Statutory Safe Harbor for Conflict of
      Interest Transactions   456
      a. The Current Setting   457
        i. Transactions Eligible to Be Affected   457
        Shapiro v. Greenfield   457
    Notes and Questions   461
        ii. Prerequisites to Being Affected by the CoI
          Safe Harbors   462
        iii. The Effect of Compliance with the CoI Safe
          Harbor   462
    Notes and Questions   463
      b. Background and Context   463
        i. A Note on Shareholder Ratification   463
    2. Duty of Care: Limitations Contained in the Articles
      of Incorporation   465
    Emerald Partners v. Berlin   465
    Notes and Questions   467
    3. Indemnification by the Corporation   468
      a. The Current Setting   468
        i. Advancement of Expenses   468
    Reddy v. Electronic Data Systems Corp.   469
    Notes and Questions   472

	ii.	When Must the Corporation Indemnify?	473
	Notes and Questions		474
	iii.	Procedural and Substantive Prerequisites to Indemnification	474
	4.	Insurance	475
	E.	An Exercise in Synthesis	476
		In re The Walt Disney Co. Deriv. Litig.	476
		Notes and Questions	482
		In re The Walt Disney Co. Deriv. Litig.	482
		Notes and Questions	488
	F.	Terms of Art in This Chapter	489

Chapter 14. Do the Restrictions Work? — 491

A.	Two Twenty-First Century Examples	491
	1. Enron	491
	2. WorldCom	493
	Report of Investigation by the Special Investigative Committee of the Board of Directors of WorldCom, Inc.	493
	Notes and Questions	496
B.	Structural Constraints	497
	1. Board of Directors	498
	a. Enron	498
	Permanent Subcommittee on Investigations of the Committee on Governmental Affairs United States Senate, *The Role of the Board of Directors in Enron's Collapse*	498
	In re Enron Corp. Final Report of Neal Batson, Court-Appointed Examiner	500
	b. WorldCom	504
	Report of Investigation by the Special Investigative Committee of the Board of Directors of WorldCom, Inc.	504
	Notes and Questions	507
	2. Internal Actors Below the Board	507
	a. Officers	508
	In re Enron Corp. Final Report of Neal Batson, Court-Appointed Examiner	508
	Notes and Questions	508
	b. In-House Attorneys and Internal Auditors	509
	In re Enron Corp. Final Report of Neal Batson, Court-Appointed Examiner	509
	Report of Investigation by the Special Investigative Committee of the Board of Directors of WorldCom, Inc.	509
	Notes and Questions	510
	3. Reputational Intermediaries	510
	a. Outside Law Firms	510
	Susan P. Koniak, *Who Gave Lawyers a Pass? We Haven't Blamed the Real Culprits in Corporate Scandals*	510
	Notes and Questions	512
	b. Independent Accountants	512

Jonathan Weil, *Missing Numbers—Behind Wave of Corporate
Fraud: A Change in How Auditors Work*   512

In re WorldCom, Inc. First Interim Report of Dick Thornburgh,
Bankruptcy Court Examiner   514

Report of Investigation by the Special Investigative
Committee of the Board of Directors of WorldCom, Inc.   515

Notes and Questions   516
   c. Credit-Rating Agencies   517

Alec Klein, *Borrowers Find System Open to Conflicts,
Manipulation*   517

Notes and Questions   521
   d. Securities Analysts   521

In re WorldCom, Inc. First Interim Report of Dick Thornburgh,
Bankruptcy Court Examiner   522

Randall Smith, et al., *Wall Street Firms to Pay $1.4 Billion to End
Inquiry—Record Payment Settles Conflict-of-Interest Charges*   526

Notes and Questions   527
4. Intentionality   527

Evelina Shmukler, *Back to School*   527

Notes and Questions   529

Ronald Alsop, *Right and Wrong*   529

Colleen DeBaise, *Corporate-Governance Law Is the Rage*   531

Notes and Questions   531

Lynn A. Stout, *On the Proper Motives of Corporate Directors
(Or, Why You Don't Want to Invite Homo Economicus to
Join Your Board)*   532

Notes and Questions   534
 C. Background and Context   535
   1. Are Reforms Working?   535

Deborah Solomon & Cassell Bryan-Low, *Companies Complain
About Cost of Corporate-Governance Rules*   535

Notes and Questions   536
   2. Systemic Problem or Cyclical Anomalies?   536

Joseph Nocera, et al., *System Failure*   536

E.S. Browning, *Burst Bubbles Often Expose Cooked Books
and Trigger SEC Probes, Bankruptcy Filings*   538

Phyllis Plitch, *When Market Scandals Erupt, Regulation Can
Come in a Flood*   539

 D. Federal Securities Regulation   540
 E. Terms of Art in This Chapter   541

E. Shareholder Power in Public and Private Corporations

**Chapter 15. Shareholder Governance Powers: Paradigms and Public
Companies**   543
 A. Shareholders' Power to Take Action   543
   1. Actions That the Shareholders May Take as a Group   543
   Notes and Questions   545

2. How Shareholders Take Action in a Meeting   545
   a. The Current Setting   545
      i. Call   545
      ii. Notice   545
   McKesson Corp. v. Derdiger   546
   Notes and Questions   552
      iii. Quorum   553
      iv. Sufficient Vote   554
      v. The Importance of Being Present   555
   b. Background and Context — The Annual Meeting of
      the Public Corporation   556
3. How Shareholders Take Action by Consent in
   Lieu of a Meeting   558
4. Tabulating the Votes   559
   a. Whose Vote Counts?   559
   b. Who Counts the Votes?   562
B. Shareholders' Rights to Information   564
   1. Periodic and Transaction Reporting   564
   2. Inspection Right   565
      a. Background and Context   565
      b. The Current Setting   566
   Compaq Computer Corp. v. Horton   567
   Notes and Questions   570
   Parsons v. Jefferson-Pilot Corp.   571
   Notes and Questions   575
C. Shareholders' Power to Redress Harm to the Corporation   575
   1. The Current Setting   575
   Beam v. Stewart   577
   Notes and Questions   582
   2. Background and Context   583
   In re PSE&G Shareholder Litigation   583
   Notes and Questions   587
D. Federal Securities Regulation   588
   1. Matters Requiring Shareholder Vote Under
      Federal Law   588
   2. Regulation of Proxy Solicitations   589
   3. Reporting Requirements   590
   4. Ownership Reporting Requirements   590
E. Terms of Art in This Chapter   591

**Chapter 16. Shareholder Governance Questions Most Often Seen in
the Privately Held Corporation**   **593**
A. Self-Imposed Restrictions on Shareholder Governance
   Rights   593
   1. Preemptive Rights: The Management Component   593
   2. Supermajority Provisions   595
   Whetstone v. Hossfeld Mfg. Co.   595
   Notes and Questions   598
      a. Superquorum Provisions   599

3. Cumulative Voting   599
Notes and Questions   601
4. Agreements Regarding Shareholder Voting   603
   a. The Current Setting   604
     i. Voting Trusts   604
Notes and Questions   605
     ii. Pooling Agreements   606
   b. Background and Context   607
     i Vote Buying   607
Notes and Questions   609
5. Other Shareholder Agreements Affecting Shareholder
   Governance Power   609
Notes and Questions   611
6. The Problem of Deadlock   611
B. External Restrictions on Shareholder Governance Rights   612
   1. Shareholder Fiduciary Duties   613
     a. The Current Setting   613
   Fought v. Morris   613
   Notes and Questions   617
     b. Background and Context   618
     c. The Current Setting   621
   2. Oppression and Unfairness by Shareholders   622
     a. From a New Remedy for Deadlock...   622
     b. ...to a New Cause of Action...   623
   Charles W. Murdock, *The Evolution of Effective Remedies for Minority Shareholders and Its Impact Upon Valuation of Minority Shares*   623
   Notes and Questions   625
   Kiriakides v. Atlas Food Systems & Services, Inc.   626
   Notes and Questions   634
     c. ...to More Remedies   637
   Charles W. Murdock, *The Evolution of Effective Remedies for Minority Shareholders and Its Impact Upon Valuation of Minority Shares*   637
C. Terms of Art in This Chapter   638

F. Change of Control

Chapter 17. Change of Control   639
A. Background and Context   639
B. The Current Setting   641
   1. Motivations for Changing Control   641
   2. Techniques for Combining Entities   642
     a. Purchase of Assets   642
   Hollinger Inc. v. Hollinger International, Inc.   643
   Notes and Questions   650
     b. Purchase of Stock   651
     c. Merger   652
     d. Reverse Triangular Mergers   653

3. Choosing the Appropriate Acquisition Technique 654
Notes and Questions 656
4. The Acquisition Process 656
5. Corporate Law Issues 658
   a. Deal Protective Measures 658
   b. Sale of Control 661
M. Thomas Arnold, *Shareholder Duties Under State Law* 661
Notes and Questions 662
   c. Appraisal 663
      i. Which Transactions Trigger Appraisal Rights? 663
      ii. What Is "Fair Value"? 664
Matthew G. Norton Company v. Smyth 664
Notes and Questions 668
C. Background and Context — Hostile Takeovers 669
   1. Corporate Structures That Deter Hostile Changes of
      Control 670
   2. Standard of Review of a Target Board's Actions When
      Responding to a Hostile Tender Offer 671
Unitrin, Inc. v. American General Corp. 672
Notes and Questions 675
   3. The Target Board's Obligation to Maximize
      Shareholder Value 675
Paramount Communications Inc. v. QVC Network Inc. 676
Notes and Questions 679
   4. State Antitakeover Statutes 680
D. Federal Securities Regulations 681
   1. "Groups" under Section 13(d) 681
   2. Going Private Transactions 681
   3. Tender Offers 682
E. Terms of Art in This Chapter 683

Part IV. UNINCORPORATED ENTITIES

Part IV. **UNINCORPORATED ENTITIES** 685

Chapter 18. Partnerships 687
A. General Partnerships 687
   1. Background and Context 687
   Notes and Questions 690
   2. The Current Setting 690
      a. Formation 691
Tondu v. Akerley 691
Notes and Questions 694
MacArthur Co. v. Stein 695
Notes and Questions 698
Mims, Lyemance & Reich, Inc. v. UAB Research Foundation 699
Notes and Questions 703
      b. Financing and Partners' Ownership Interests 705
         i. Partner Contributions 705
         ii. Partnership Property 706

iii. Partners' Interest in the Partnership   707
iv. Allocations and Distributions to Partners   708
Starr v. Fordham   708
Notes and Questions   710
c. Personal Liability   711
d. Management   712
Kansallis Finance Ltd. v. Fern   713
Notes and Questions   715
e. Fiduciary Duties   717
Meinhard v. Salmon   717
Notes and Questions   722
Baltrusch v. Baltrusch   725
Notes and Questions   727
f. Dissociation   727
g. Dissolution   729
McCormick v. Brevig   730
B. Other Partnership Forms   733
1. Joint Ventures   733
2. Limited Partnerships   735
a. Background and Context   735
b. The Current Setting   736
3. Limited Liability Partnerships and Limited Liability
Limited Partnerships   737
C. Federal Securities Laws   738
D. Terms of Art in This Chapter   738

Chapter 19. Limited Liability Companies   739
A. Background and Context   739
**Susan Pace Hamill, *The Origins Behind the Limited Liability
Company***   739
Notes and Questions   741
B. The Current Setting   742
1. Introduction   742
Elf Atochem North America, Inc. v. Jaffari   742
2. Formation   744
a. Statutory Requirements   744
b. Promoter Liability and Defective Formation   744
P.D. 2000 L.L.C. v. First Financial Planners, Inc.   745
Notes and Questions   747
c. Operating Agreements   747
3. Financing   748
a. Capital Contributions   748
b. Allocations and Distributions to Members   748
4. Members' Interest   750
a. Financial   750
New Horizons Supply Cooperative v. Haack   751
Notes and Questions   753

b. Managerial   753
c. Additional Members, Transferability, and
   Dissociation   754
Five Star Concrete, L.L.C. v. Klink, Inc.   755
Notes and Questions   757
5. Management   758
   a. Statutory Default Rules   758
   b. Manager-Managed Structures   759
6. Fiduciary Duties   759
McConnell v. Hunt Sports Enterprises   760
Notes and Questions   764
7. Dissolution   765
New Horizons Supply Cooperative v. Haack   767
Notes and Questions   768
C. Federal Securities Laws   768
D. Terms of Art in This Chapter   769

Part V. **CHOICE OF FORM**   771

Chapter 20. Choice of Entity   773
A. Variable Characteristics Important in Choosing an Entity   774
   1. Organizational Differences   774
   2. Operational Differences   775
      a. Financial   775
      b. Managerial   775
   3. Differences Regarding Transferred Ownership Interest   776
B. How to Choose the Appropriate Entity   778
C. Fixing the Problem   779
   Harry J. Haynsworth, *The Unified Business Organizations Code:*
   The Next Generation   779
   Notes and Questions   782
   Richard A. Booth, *Form and Function in Business Organizations* 783
   Notes and Questions   790
D. Terms of Art in This Chapter   791

Glossary   *793*
Table of Cases   *809*
Index   *813*

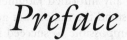

Preface

You have already encountered business entities, even if you are just beginning your second year of law school. Some entities, such as corporations, were parties in cases you read (or were supposed to have read). In other instances the litigants may have been employed by, or dealt with, a business entity, though the entity was not a party. This course is different from the other courses in which you've encountered business entities because it deals with the internal working of business entities. Among other topics, we will look at the ways in which business entities are formed, how they get money from owners and lenders, and how they are governed.

A. HOW TO APPROACH THE COURSE

Your professor will doubtless suggest to you the way in which he or she wants you to think about the course. However, it may be useful to give you my own view as well, in part because I suspect most professors share most of my views in this regard, and in part because sharing my view may help you to understand this casebook better. If there is one big idea that runs through the law of business entities it is *capital formation*. That is, the process of collecting money from more than one person for the purpose of engaging in an enterprise.

The process of capital formation leads, in turn, to three key legal questions. First, what are the economic rights between the money providers? That is, how do the providers share profits? Equally? Proportionally to their investment? Do some providers (e.g., lenders) get paid before others (e.g., owners)? Second, what are the management rights between the money providers? Does each provider have an equal say? Do some providers have no say at all? Finally, what are the rights of outsiders against the business entity and its owners? Obviously contract and tort law provide the answer in many instances. But business entities law also provides answers in many settings. Are the owners liable with the entity? Are the owners liable only after the entity's assets are exhausted? Are the owners not liable at all, even if the entity's assets are gone?

I also want to give you two suggestions for approaching business entities as a law student. First, as you read the cases you should spend the necessary time to understand the transactions and the underlying motivations. Some students find a temptation to ignore those elements (especially if they're not initially interested in the subject) and they resolve to learn only the legal rules. This is a mistake for both high-road and low-road reasons. On the high road, the legal rules are not immutable laws of physics. They're developed in response to business transactions and the motivations behind them. So you can't come to any informed judgment about the propriety of business entities law until you understand the milieu that generates that law. Second, on the low road, it's pretty nearly impossible to succeed in a business entities class simply by trying to learn only the legal rules. There are just too many rules of law in this course and you probably haven't got enough memory to learn them all without knowing the business context that generated those rules. So understanding the transactions will be a way for you to remember and understand more rules and how they relate to one another.

My second suggestion is to pay attention to the *text* of the statutes. For many law students, business entities is their first exposure to an area of law in which the rules are primarily statutory rather than judge-made. You will be repaid many times over for the time you put into reading the statutes.

B. THE PLAN OF THIS CASEBOOK

This casebook is organized into five parts. Part I is about practicing business law. Chapter 1 describes the various practice settings in which business lawyers work. Chapter 2 talks about business itself, and does so largely apart from the question of business entities. Chapter 3 talks about a few of the most central economic concepts that business entities face and also explores the rudiments of accounting. Every lawyer, and especially every business lawyer, needs an exposure to some economic ideas. This exposure is necessary if for no other reasons than that your clients will have this knowledge and you need to be conversant with the basics, at least.

Part II consists of a single chapter. Chapter 4 deals with the law of agency. Agency is not an entity but rather it is a system of relationships and consequences that exist when one person acts for another. Agency problems pervade business entities and other private law areas, as well.

Part III takes up the majority of the book. It deals with the law of corporations, which is the principal business entity. Chapter 5 deals with creating corporations and the difficulties that can be encountered in doing so. Chapters 6, 7, and 8 focus on the "dough-ray-mi," that is, the financial aspects of corporate law. Chapter 6 is about getting money from investors into the corporation; Chapter 7 is about getting it out to them. Chapter 8 is concerned with the ability of creditors to get paid when the entity does not have enough money.

Chapter 9 is about the power of the board of directors to govern a corporation. Chapters 10 through 14 talk about constraints on the board's power to govern. As you intuit, those constraints constitute a significant part of the law of business entities. Chapter 10 looks at external constraints on the board's power. Chapters 11, 12, and 13 are concerned with the directors' duties of loyalty and care, called their fiduciary duties. Finally, Chapter 14 assesses whether the constraints are effective.

Chapters 15 and 16 explore shareholder rights. Chapter 15 mostly concerns publicly held corporations, and Chapter 16 is more focused on privately held companies. Chapter 17 is about changing control of corporations. That subject is typically a separate course in most law schools, so this chapter is primarily an introduction.

Part IV comprises two chapters, and its focus is on business entities other than corporations. They are much briefer than the discussion of corporate law, not because they are less important, but because much of corporate law carries over to these other entities. Chapter 18 looks at partnerships, including limited partnerships. This is an important business entity in large part because it is the default entity. That is, when more than one person owns a business, those owners are usually partners of a partnership unless they've taken specific action to form another entity instead. Chapter 19 involves limited liability companies (LLCs). This is perhaps the most frequently selected business entity for new businesses. From a legal standpoint, LLCs are essentially a blend of corporate law and partnership law. Thus, if you've paid attention from Chapter 5 through Chapter 18, Chapter 19 will be quite easy.

Finally, Part V, Chapter 20, is a look at the way in which lawyers and their clients go about choosing the appropriate entity for a particular business. The placement of this chapter at the end of the book may seem paradoxical, because choosing the appropriate entity is one of the first decisions planners usually make. However, as a student you won't be able to make real sense of Chapter 20 unless you have a detailed knowledge of the business entities from which to select. Hence its placement at the end.

A large number of the chapters have sections entitled "Background and Context" and "The Current Setting." Background and Context material is designed to put the law into some social or historical milieu. These sections provide a richer understanding of the material, but some professors may omit all of them and most professors will omit at least some of them. I've set these sections out separately to make it easier for professors to assign the material and to make the divisions within the material clearer to you. "The Current Setting" is meant to signal to you, and your professor, that the material is not background and context. That is, it focuses mainly on legal, rather than historical or social, ideas and primarily on the law as it exists in the United States currently.

One of the most useful features of this casebook is the way in which the "Notes and Questions" sections are organized. I have divided the notes and questions into five types, labeled each, and set them out in the same order throughout the book. Not every "Notes and Questions" section will have each type. The first type is called, believe it or not, *Notes*. This has factual information, usually about the preceding case, the kind of transaction, or the applicable law. The second type is called *Reality Check*. These questions are designed to make sure you understand the transaction, the dispute, and the resolution. They should be of particular value before class and at the end of the course, when you're preparing for the final exam. The third type is called *Suppose*. These questions ask you to be a bit flexible in your thinking. They ask you to imagine that the facts or the law were slightly different from the actual case. One of a lawyer's most frequent tasks is to analogize or distinguish one set of facts from another. The *Suppose* questions give you practice in doing that. The fourth type is *What Do You Think?* These are policy and theory questions. They ask you for your view of the case's result on the parties, the social effect of the rule in the case, or a more general theoretical question. These may seem a bit divorced from reality at first, but I think law students tend to underestimate the power of theory on the world in which they live.

Finally, some of the "Notes and Questions" sections end with a *You Draft It* exercise. These are, as you see by the name, opportunities to hone your drafting skills. My pedagogical view is that drafting exercises that are simply made up by the professor are not nearly as valuable as those drawn from actual legal practice. Moreover, many drafting assignments that law students undertake require them to draft whole documents or at least extended sections of documents. These are, of course, valuable skills. However, I believe that an underappreciated writing skill is the talent to draft small, very focused, pieces. These pieces are often absolutely critical to the success or failure of a transaction. So, based on those two premises, I have created the *You Draft It* sections. In every instance, the assignment is based on actual language that was important in the case just discussed. Frequently I will ask you to redraft language that was at the center of the case so that first one party and then the other would clearly prevail. Sometimes the drafting involves a statute. In any event, your professors might not assign these exercises (and certainly won't assign all of them to be turned in and evaluated!) but they are quite useful nonetheless. You might find it particularly useful to swap your draft with that of another student in the course to critique one another's work. Another approach is to have the members of a study group take turns so that only one student's draft is critiqued. This approach, incidentally, would replicate a frequent practice setting. That is, a legal issue has arisen, sometimes without warning, and one member of a legal team is given the task of drafting language that solves the problem. The other members then critique that draft as a group.

There's one more element of this casebook that I think sets it apart from other books and that, I'm hoping, will make it more useful to students and their professors. At the end of each chapter is a list of *Terms of Art in This Chapter*. Each term of art is one that is first discussed more than tangentially in the chapter. The term of art is also italicized at its first principal appearance. You might want to preview the chapter by looking at the list before you read the chapter. I think that becoming aware of important terms and then finding the definitions within the chapter context is vital to learning. For that reason I have not placed the definitions with the terms of art at each chapter's end. However, I have assembled them in a glossary at the back along with definitions. So, if you need a quick refresher on a particular term, you can look in the glossary for help. Let me say a word about the footnote conventions in this casebook. Footnotes in my own text are sequentially numbered in each chapter. Footnotes in cases and in other extracts retain their original numbers. Footnotes that I have inserted in a case or extract are indicated both by an asterisk and by ED. at the end of the footnote.

I hope you enjoy using this casebook. It seems to me that students often don't reflect on the book they're using unless it's so problematic that it's a hindrance to their learning. I sincerely hope that this book helps you rather than hinders you as you learn the law of business entities. I also hope you like it.

Eric A. Chiappinelli

February 2006

Acknowledgments

This book would not exist if Lynn Churchill, acquisitions editor at Aspen, hadn't asked me to write it. She first suggested that I might enjoy, and be good at, writing a casebook on business entities. She also shepherded me through the process of submitting a book proposal. As she suspected, I have very much enjoyed writing this book. Thank you, Lynn.

My development editor was Susan Boulanger. Actually, Susan and I have only communicated by e-mail. It is entirely possible that "Susan Boulanger" is someone's *nom de crayon bleu* or that she is a collective person, like Carolyn Keene. Nonetheless, I believe she exists. I had no idea what a development editor was until Susan introduced herself. It turns out that a development editor is sort of a personal coach. She gave me tips for dividing the writing into manageable parts. She also tried to keep me on deadlines that I, myself, had blithely agreed to meet. Nonetheless, I missed (often by a significant margin) every single deadline. She took my drafts and sent them to anonymous reviewers, collected their comments, synthesized them, and helped me to accept and understand them. More than anything else, though, Susan provided enormous support to me during the long writing and rewriting process. That support has been of incalculable help. I am deeply thankful for your help, Susan.

This casebook has been improved a great deal by the anonymous reviewers. I was astonished at the care with which they read the manuscript. They had insights and perspectives that I never would have considered. Thank you, for engaging so thoroughly with me. Lauren Arnest copy edited the manuscript and improved its readability significantly. Thanks, Lauren. The unforgettable Laurel Ibey was the manuscript editor. She answered many of my questions (and posed many more) and ensured that the book sailed through the production process. I appreciate all you've done, Laurel.

A number of my colleagues have helped in this effort. John B. "Jack" Kirkwood used drafts of this book in several of his classes and provided me with much valuable feedback. He also provided a fair bit of help with the economics portions of the text. He was very generous with his time, as well, amounting to hours of conversation on topics large and small. Thank you, Jack. Russell Powell also used this casebook in two of his classes and also gave me his reaction to it. I know the book is much better than it would have been without their help. Annette Clark helped to convince me to accept Lynn Churchill's suggestion that I write this casebook and also provided support during the periods when I was particularly discouraged. My deans, Rudy Hasl and Kellye Testy, provided financial support during the summers, when much of the manuscript was written and edited. I appreciate their support. Finally, my secretary, Laurie Sleeper, coordinated endless details, answered questions from students and colleagues, and obtained all the permissions. Thank you very much, Laurie.

I'm also quite thankful to the Starbucks Corporation and Caffè Ladro in Seattle, Washington. The vast majority of the text was written in their fine establishments and I highly recommend them to other authors and coffee drinkers.

Throughout the entire process of producing this tome one person has been uppermost in my thoughts as the person whose intellect and cast of mind most resemble my own. He is the Reverend Edward Casaubon. I do not blush to say that I have followed his example in the way of pigeonholes. If my small book bears even the faintest resemblance to his book,[1] then I shall have acquitted myself well, indeed.

Finally, I would like to thank the authors, publishers, and copyright holders for their permission to reproduce materials from their publications.

Allen, William T. *Our Schizophrenic Conception of the Business Corporation*. 14 Cardozo Law Review 261 (1992). Reprinted with permission of the Cardozo Law Review.

Alsop, Ronald. *Right and Wrong*. The Wall Street Journal, September 17, 2003, at R9. Reprinted with permission of Dow Jones & Company, Inc., conveyed through Copyright Clearance Center, Inc.

American Bar Association. Model Business Corporation Act. 1984. Reprinted by permission of the American Bar Association.

Arnold, M. Thomas. *Shareholder Duties Under State Law*. 28 Tulsa Law Journal 213, 242-257 (1992). Reprinted with permission of the University of Tulsa College of Law, conveyed through Copyright Clearance Center, Inc.

Bainbridge, Stephen M. *The Board of Directors as Nexus of Contracts*. 88 Iowa Law Review 1, 5-6, 9-11 (2002). Reprinted with permission of the Iowa Law Review, conveyed through Copyright Clearance Center, Inc.

Bart, Peter. *The Studios' Plethora of Presidents*. Variety, March 2, 2003. Reprinted with permission of Reed Business Information, conveyed through Copyright Clearance Center, Inc.

Berle, Adolf A., Jr., and Gardiner C. Means. *The Modern Corporation and Private Property*. 333-338, 343, 353-356 (1933). Reprinted with permission of Commerce Clearing House, conveyed through Copyright Clearance Center, Inc.

Booth, Richard. *Form and Function in Business Organizations*. 58 Business Lawyer 1433 (2003). Reprinted with permission of the American Bar Association.

Branson, Douglas M. *The Very Uncertain Prospect of "Global" Convergence in Corporate Governance*. 34 Cornell International Law Journal 321, 323-327 (2001). Reprinted with permission of the Cornell University International Law Journal, conveyed through Copyright Clearance Center, Inc.

Browning, E. S. *Burst Bubbles Often Expose Cooked Books and Trigger SEC Probes, Bankruptcy Filings*. The Wall Street Journal, February 11, 2002, at C1. Reprinted with permission of Dow Jones & Company, Inc., conveyed through Copyright Clearance Center, Inc.

Chandler, Alfred D. *The Visible Hand: The Managerial Revolution in American Business*. 9-10, 28, 36-37, 50-51, 76-78, 82-86, 87, 497-498 (1977). Reprinted by permission of The Belknap Press of Harvard University Press.

---

1. Edward Casaubon, *The Key to All Mythologies* (forthcoming).

DeBaise, Colleen. *Corporate-Governance Law Is the Rage.* The Wall Street Journal, September 1, 2004, at B7. Reprinted with permission of Dow Jones & Company, Inc., conveyed through Copyright Clearance Center, Inc.

Fitting In: In Bow to Retailers' New Clout, Levi Strauss Makes Alterations. The Wall Street Journal, June 17, 2004, at A1. Reprinted with permission of Dow Jones & Company, Inc., conveyed through Copyright Clearance Center, Inc.

Gilson, Ronald J. *Globalizing Corporate Governance: Convergence of Form or Function.* 49 American Journal of Comparative Law 329, 329-334 (2001). Reprinted with permission of the American Association for the Comparative Study of Law, conveyed through Copyright Clearance Center, Inc.

Hamill, Susan Pace. *The Origins Behind the Limited Liability Company.* 59 Ohio State Law Journal 1459 (1998). Reprinted with the permission of the Ohio State Law Journal.

Haynsworth, Harry J. *The Unified Business Organizations Code: The Next Generation.* 29 Delaware Journal of Corporate Law 83 (2004). Reprinted with permission of the Delaware Journal of Corporate Law, conveyed through Copyright Clearance Center, Inc.

Klein, Alec. *Borrowers Find System Open to Conflicts, Manipulation.* The Washington Post, November 22, 2004, at A01. Reprinted with permission of the Washington Post Writers Group, conveyed through Copyright Clearance Center, Inc.

Koniak, Susan P. *Who Gave Lawyers a Pass? We Haven't Blamed the Real Culprits in Corporate Scandals.* Forbes, August 12, 2002, at 58. Reprinted by permission of Forbes Magazine, Inc.

Murdock, Charles W. *The Evolution of Effective Remedies for Minority Shareholders and Its Impact upon Valuation of Minority Shares.* 65 Notre Dame Law Review 425, 452-470 (1990). Reprinted with permission of the Notre Dame Law Review, conveyed through Copyright Clearance Center, Inc. (The publisher bears responsibility for any errors that have occurred in reprinting or editing.)

Nocera, Joseph, et al. *System Failure.* Fortune, June 24, 2002, at 62. Copyright Time Inc. All rights reserved.

Plitch, Phyllis. *When Market Scandals Erupt, Regulation Can Come in a Flood.* The Wall Street Journal, January 15, 2003. Reprinted with permission of Dow Jones & Company, Inc., conveyed through Copyright Clearance Center, Inc.

Restatement (Second) of Conflict of Law. 1971. Reprinted with permission of the American Law Institute. All rights reserved.

Restatement (Third) of Agency. 2006. Reprinted with permission of the American Law Institute.

Shmukler, Evelina. *Back to School.* The Wall Street Journal, February 24, 2003, at R6. Reprinted with permission of Dow Jones & Company, Inc., conveyed through Copyright Clearance Center, Inc.

Smith, Randall, et al. *Wall Street Firms to Pay $1.4 Billion to End Inquiry-Record Payment Settles Conflict-of-Interest Charges.* The Wall Street Journal, April 29, 2003, at A1. Reprinted with permission of Dow Jones & Company, Inc., conveyed through Copyright Clearance Center, Inc.

Solomon, Deborah, and Cassell Bryan-Low. *Companies Complain About Cost of Corporate-Governance Rules*. The Wall Street Journal, February 10, 2004, at A1. Reprinted with permission of Dow Jones & Company, Inc., conveyed through Copyright Clearance Center, Inc.

Stout, Lynn A. *On the Proper Motives of Corporate Directors (Or, Why You Don't Want to Invite Homo Economicus to Join Your Board)*. 28 Delaware Journal of Corporate Law 1 (2003). Reprinted with permission of the Delaware Journal of Corporate Law, conveyed through Copyright Clearance Center, Inc.

Weil, Jonathan. *Missing Numbers-Behind Wave of Corporate Fraud: A Change in How Auditors Work*. The Wall Street Journal, March 25, 2004, at A1. Reprinted with permission of Dow Jones & Company, Inc., conveyed through Copyright Clearance Center, Inc.

Wells, C. A. Harwell. *The Cycles of Corporate Social Responsibility: An Historical Retrospective for the Twenty-First Century*. 51 University of Kansas Law Review 77 (2002). Reprinted with permission of the Kansas Law Review, conveyed through Copyright Clearance Center, Inc.

Cases and Materials on
Business Entities

Part I.
THE PRACTICE OF BUSINESS LAW

1
Practicing Corporate Law[1]

The subject of this casebook is sometimes loosely called "corporate law." It follows that lawyers who specialize in this subject are "corporate lawyers." We'll start out by defining the term *corporate lawyer*. Then, we'll spend the rest of this chapter exploring three other questions. First, what do corporate lawyers do? Second, where do corporate lawyers work? Third, what substantive legal knowledge do corporate lawyers need?

In the broadest sense, the term *corporate lawyer* means a lawyer whose clients are for-profit or nonprofit entities rather than individuals. The legal work performed by such a corporate lawyer could be in any substantive area, including representing business entities in litigation.

Sometimes the phrase *corporate lawyer* is used to mean a lawyer who is employed by a corporation. When used in this sense, the phrase distinguishes such lawyers from those who are self-employed or who work in law firms, government, or academia.

Corporate lawyer, in its most typical usage within the legal community, denotes a lawyer whose practice is devoted to legal questions that arise under the substantive laws governing business entities. This is the definition we will use throughout this book. Such a lawyer does not litigate nor does he or she deal primarily with other substantive areas such as taxation, labor and employment, intellectual property, or bankruptcy. A corporate lawyer in this sense could be employed in one of several settings and, while he or she probably represents business entities, might represent the government, an interest group, or a charity instead.[2]

A. WHAT DO CORPORATE LAWYERS DO?

1. A Different Paradigm from Litigators

In the first year of law school, the paradigm lawyer is the litigator. Two fundamental assumptions underlie the lawyer-as-litigator idea. First, the lawyer's task is to

---

1. Greg Duff and Alison Ivey, two corporate lawyers who have practiced in a variety of settings, gave me valuable advice about this chapter. My thanks to them.
2. In some ways it might be more accurate to refer to "corporate lawyers" as "transaction lawyers," to better distinguish them from litigators and to reflect the fact that they may represent entities other than corporations. However, the term *corporate lawyer* is so ingrained in legal culture that we're going to use that term throughout this book.

be the client's champion. The lawyer should vindicate the client either by redressing a harm suffered by the client or by defeating a claim that the client has harmed another. Second, in litigation the lawyer is truly the principal actor. The client, while not passive, assists the lawyer in preparing for the conflict. The client rarely decides the legal theory of the case and rarely makes litigational decisions such as whether to move for summary judgment or what discovery to seek.

Corporate lawyers differ from this paradigm in three important ways. As you read about the ways in which corporate lawyers differ from litigators, ask yourself whether your own temperament and preferences might make you better suited to be a corporate lawyer rather than a litigator.

First, corporate lawyers generally deal with prospective matters rather than retrospective ones. The litigator focuses primarily on what happened, not on what will happen. The litigator helps the client pick up the pieces but is not directly concerned with advising the client about the future.[3] The corporate lawyer, by contrast, is looking ahead. The corporate lawyer is enmeshed in effecting future actions on behalf of the business client. This difference in temporal focus may seem small, but it results in an immense difference in the personalities between litigators and corporate lawyers.

The second main difference is that the corporate lawyer's goal is more variegated than vindication. Litigation, in its most abstract, is a zero-sum proposition. Certainly most lawsuits are compromised before trial, and such a settlement is seldom a win-lose result. Further, many lawsuits involve multiple claims or parties such that your client may win even though opposing parties do not entirely lose. Nonetheless, the basic mind-set of the litigator is that doing a good job for the client means defeating someone else.

Corporate lawyers, by contrast, deal with other parties and their lawyers at arm's length, but not adversarially. They recognize that their client will have different interests from the other parties but they also recognize that the ultimate goal of all parties is to effect a particular transaction or business structure. Thus your client does not gain unless others gain as well. Nonetheless, because the parties do have differing interests and a lawyer typically does not represent all parties in a transaction, a corporate lawyer must deal with others at arm's length. This requires the corporate lawyer to work with other parties honestly and candidly, but at the same time understand that the client's interests are paramount. Many lawyers find this approach more challenging and more rewarding than the litigation approach.

Finally, whereas the litigator is in charge of the litigation, the corporate lawyer's client is in charge of the business proposal. Hence, much of the corporate lawyer's professional time is spent talking *with* clients[4] instead of talking *at* them. The corporate lawyer's advice is seldom categorical ("You must do X." "You can't do Y.")[5]

---

3. Obviously the results of litigation over past matters may have an important effect on the client's future, but the litigator's concern is mostly with the past.

4. We're using *client* in this context to mean the actual human or humans who manage the business entity that is the lawyer's true client.

5.   A lawyer shall not counsel a client to engage, or assist a client, in conduct that the lawyer knows is criminal or fraudulent, but a lawyer may discuss the legal consequences of any proposed course of conduct with a client and may counsel or assist a client to make a good faith effort to determine the validity, scope, meaning or application of the law.

Utah R. of Prof. Conduct 1.2(d) (2005). The Utah Rules of Professional Conduct are substantially identical to the ABA's Model Rules of Professional Conduct (MRPC).

but is instead a reflection of the lawyer's own judgment both as to law and, as the lawyer becomes more seasoned, about business and negotiating. This is frequently more nuanced and often more frustrating than controlling litigation. The interpersonal skills required to be an effective corporate lawyer are considerable. One must be able to engage with a wide variety of nonlawyers, to assess their needs and wants, and to communicate one's views clearly. One frustrating element of a corporate lawyer's life is that clients don't always agree with their corporate lawyer's judgment and advice. One inevitable fact is that the corporate lawyer's views don't always prevail and the client moves in a direction the lawyer believes is not the optimal one.

2. The Typical Roles of the Corporate Lawyer

The corporate lawyer serves in four recurring roles in professional life. First, as you no doubt intuited from the discussion above, is the *corporate lawyer as counselor*. The lawyer's job here is to give advice to the client. The context of the advice might involve transactions with others, such as when the client is buying or selling another entity or when the client is entering into a business venture in concert with others. But the context of the lawyer's advice might not involve a business deal. That is, the corporate lawyer may be giving advice about such things as the law surrounding corporate elections or compliance with a regulatory agency's rules.

A second recurring role is the *corporate lawyer as conciliator*. Here the corporate lawyer is called upon to help resolve a conflict between the client and another, often regarding a potential transaction. The corporate lawyer uses analytical powers to assess the source of the conflict, the parties' interests, and the potential solutions. The corporate lawyer typically does not represent more than one party in such a setting and so any proposed solution must be consonant with the lawyer's client's best interests. Nonetheless, the client is often best served when the lawyer is able to find a solution to a conflict that threatens to derail an otherwise viable business opportunity.

A corporate lawyer might also facilitate a transaction between the client and another party. The *corporate lawyer as facilitator* role might comprise three different skills. The corporate lawyer may negotiate the substantive elements of a transaction such as price, quantity, and other essential points. Some clients prefer to do all negotiating themselves; others prefer the lawyer to do much of that work. One consideration in choosing who will be the primary negotiator is the message sent by having the lawyer or the client negotiate. It sometimes happens that the client believes that another party will not react well if the client's lawyer negotiates. Thus the client him- or herself will negotiate even though the client's abstract preference might be for the lawyer to do so.

Whether or not the corporate lawyer negotiates the deal points, the lawyer may facilitate the transaction by ensuring that the transaction complies with applicable regulations. Common examples are Securities and Exchange Commission (SEC) regulations on issuing stock, Federal Trade Commission or Department of Justice antitrust regulations, and Internal Revenue Service regulations on the tax treatment of the proposed transaction. Regulations might also be imposed at the state or local levels. While the corporate lawyer may well call upon lawyers with special expertise in these areas, he or she will doubtless carry the laboring oar in identifying and ensuring compliance with these regulations.

The third essential skill for the corporate lawyer as facilitator is that of drafter. Obviously, few corporate transactions will be effected orally. A transaction must be reduced to writings that both accurately capture the agreed-upon terms and legally effect the anticipated transaction. Frequently, the lawyer must draft documents in addition to the primary, deal-effecting document. Side agreements with other parties are often called for as are documents such as director resolutions and shareholder consents.

Many of these drafting tasks are assigned to more junior lawyers so you might be exposed to this facet of corporate lawyer as facilitator relatively quickly and deeply. Good drafting is a difficult skill in the best of circumstances. In the real world of corporate law, good drafting, especially by junior lawyers, is made more difficult by two common phenomena: the lawyer is relatively inexperienced and the lawyer is frequently not given all the information necessary to make the final documents accurate and advantageous to the client. In this casebook you will find many cases that turn on the drafting of a particular document. Ask yourself how the document likely came to be and how you might have acted differently, which may include more than simply using different words, to avoid the litigation that developed.

A final role, and the most controversial, is the *corporate lawyer as guardian*. Corporate lawyers may be called upon to protect the client and the public against some contemplated actions by persons acting on the client's behalf. This role is sometimes called a "gatekeeper" function, the idea being that the corporate lawyer has the power to deny the corporate client access to the lawyer's skills and reputation. Under the Rules of Professional Conduct (RPC) of most states, a corporate lawyer is required to accept and help implement decisions made by the appropriate corporate managers on behalf of the corporation. See, e.g., Utah R. of Prof. Conduct 1.13.[6] A corporate lawyer is also ordinarily required to keep confidential any client information. See, e.g., Utah R. of Prof. Conduct 1.6. In some situations, though, these norms are superseded by a corporate lawyer's ability and, sometimes, obligation to take other action.

More precisely, the RPC require a corporate lawyer to object when

> [A]n officer, employee or other person associated with the organization is engaged in action, intends to act or refuses to act in a matter related to the representation that is a violation of a legal obligation to the organization, or a violation of law that reasonably might be imputed to the organization, and that is likely to result in substantial injury to the organization....

Utah R. of Prof. Conduct 1.13(b)

---

6. When constituents of the organization make decisions for it, the decisions ordinarily must be accepted by the lawyer even if their utility or prudence is doubtful. Decisions concerning policy and operations, including ones entailing serious risk, are not as such in the lawyer's province. [H]owever, ... when the lawyer knows that the organization is likely to be substantially injured by action of an officer or other constituent that violates a legal obligation to the organization or is in violation of law that might be imputed to the organization, the lawyer must proceed as is reasonably necessary in the best interest of the organization. [K]nowledge can be inferred from circumstances, and a lawyer cannot ignore the obvious.

Utah R. of Prof. Conduct 1.13, cmt. 3

The RPC require the lawyer ordinarily to challenge such an action up to the highest corporate authority, typically the board of directors. See, e.g., Utah R. of Prof. Conduct 1.13(b). This is sometimes called the lawyer's obligation to report "up the ladder." The Comment to Utah Rules of Professional Conduct 1.13 fleshes out a lawyer's role:

> [T]he lawyer should give due consideration to the seriousness of the violation and its consequences, the responsibility in the organization and the apparent motivation of the person involved, the policies of the organization concerning such matters, and any other relevant considerations. Ordinarily, referral to a higher authority would be necessary. In some circumstances, however, it may be appropriate for the lawyer to ask the constituent to reconsider the matter; for example, if the circumstances involve a constituent's innocent misunderstanding of law and subsequent acceptance of the lawyer's advice, the lawyer may reasonably conclude that the best interest of the organization does not require that the matter be referred to higher authority. If a constituent persists in conduct contrary to the lawyer's advice, it will be necessary for the lawyer to take steps to have the matter reviewed by a higher authority in the organization. If the matter is of sufficient seriousness and importance or urgency to the organization, referral to higher authority in the organization may be necessary even if the lawyer has not communicated with the constituent. Any measures taken should, to the extent practicable, minimize the risk of revealing information relating to the representation to persons outside the organization. Even in circumstances where a lawyer is not obligated by Rule 1.13 to proceed, a lawyer may bring to the attention of an organizational client, including its highest authority, matters that the lawyer reasonably believes to be of sufficient importance to warrant doing so in the best interest of the organization.

Utah R. of Prof. Conduct 1.13, cmt. 4

The RPC allow a corporate lawyer to disclose client information to people outside the business in at least two settings. First,

> [I]f
>
> (1) despite the lawyer's efforts [in reporting up the ladder] . . . the highest authority that can act on behalf of the organization insists upon or fails to address in a timely and appropriate manner an action or a refusal to act, that is clearly a violation of law, and
> (2) the lawyer reasonably believes that the violation is reasonably certain to result in substantial injury to the organization, then the lawyer may reveal information relating to the representation whether or not Rule 1.6 permits such disclosure, but only if and to the extent the lawyer reasonably believes necessary to prevent substantial injury to the organization.

Utah R. of Prof. Conduct 1.13(c)

Second, a lawyer may

> (b) [R]eveal information relating to the representation of a client to the extent the lawyer reasonably believes necessary:
> (1) to prevent reasonably certain death or substantial bodily harm;
> (2) to prevent the client from committing a crime or fraud that is reasonably certain to result in substantial injury to the financial interests or property of another and in furtherance of which the client has used or is using the lawyer's services;
> (3) to prevent, mitigate or rectify substantial injury to the financial interests or property of another that is reasonably certain to result or has resulted from the

client's commission of a crime or fraud in furtherance of which the client has used the lawyer's services;

Utah R. of Prof. Conduct 1.6(b)

In response to several corporate scandals in the early 2000s, Congress and the SEC have imposed requirements on corporate lawyers in addition to those of the RPC. See D. Federal Securities Regulation, below.

Notes and Questions

1. Notes

a. In England, the essential difference between litigators and corporate lawyers was captured and institutionalized in the distinction between *barristers* and *solicitors*. Barristers had the exclusive right to appear in court on behalf of clients and derive their title from having been admitted to the bar.[7] Solicitors were not admitted to the bar and could not be heard in court. They undertook all other legal work, however, including what we would today call corporate work. Paradoxically, although barristers were considered to be more elite and more prestigious than solicitors, they were, at least in theory, under the control of solicitors. A barrister could not communicate with a client except with the solicitor's consent, and it was the solicitor who crafted the legal argument that the barrister presented in court. In legal parlance, the solicitor *briefed* the barrister.

b. The RPC *require* a corporate lawyer to disclose client information outside the corporation, "when disclosure is necessary to avoid assisting a criminal or fraudulent act by a client, unless disclosure is prohibited by Rule 1.6." Utah R. of Prof. Conduct 4.1(b).

> Model Rule 4.1(b)'s disclosure mandate only applies to lawyer conduct "in the course of representing a client" — i.e. before representation has ceased. Thus, Comment [3] to Model Rule 4.1(b) points out that "[o]rdinarily, a lawyer can avoid assisting a client's crime or fraud" — and thus avoid the Rule's disclosure obligation — "by withdrawing from the representation." Model Rules Rule 4.1 cmt. 3 (2003)
>
> Lawrence A. Hamermesh, *The ABA Task Force on Corporate Responsibility and the 2003 Changes to the Model Rules of Professional Conduct*, 17 Geo. J. Legal Ethics 35, 54 n.92 (2003)

2. Reality Check

a. How does the mind-set of a trial lawyer — a litigator — differ from that of a corporate lawyer?

b. What roles do corporate lawyers routinely fill?

c. If the authorized decision makers of a corporation disagree with a corporate lawyer's advice, how may the lawyer respond?

d. When may a lawyer present a legal issue to a corporate authority higher than the authority he or she is presently dealing with? Must a lawyer ever do so?

e. When may a lawyer disclose client information to people outside the client without client consent? Must a lawyer ever do so?

---

7. Note that baristas, too, derive their title from their connection with a bar.

3. Suppose

a. Suppose a corporate lawyer in a law firm discovered that a corporate client had overstated its earning in recently published financial statements. How should the corporate lawyer identify the course(s) of action he or she has available? What additional information, if any, would the corporate lawyer need?

b. Assume that the lawyer in question *a* was an in-house lawyer rather than a lawyer in a law firm. Would your analysis of question *a* be different?

c. Suppose that the corporation in questions *a* and *b* intends to publish, next month, financial statements that overstate its earnings. Would your analysis of questions *a* or *b* be different? Suppose publication were scheduled for next week or were scheduled for tomorrow. Would those facts change your analysis?

4. What Do You Think?

a. Do you think the similarities between litigators and corporate lawyers are more important than the differences between them?

b. Are in-house corporate lawyers or law firm corporate lawyers more likely to face hard ethical choices under the RPC?

c. Do you think the RPC's disclosure rules are in tension with the corporate lawyer's other roles? If so, how should that tension be resolved? The current version of MRPC 1.6(b) was adopted by the ABA House of Delegates by a vote of 218 to 201. The principal objections were that the rule would be unlikely to prevent corporate wrongdoing (the Texas ethics rules, which already contained similar disclosure strictures, bound Enron's lawyers yet did not prevent that debacle); that the rule would distort the attorney-client relationship; and that the rule would increase the potential liability of lawyers who could disclose client information but who chose not to do so. See Lawrence A. Hamermesh, *The ABA Task Force on Corporate Responsibility and the 2003 Changes to the Model Rules of Professional Conduct*, 17 Geo. J. Legal Ethics 35, 48-53 (2003).

5. You Draft It

a. Draft disclosure rules that provide the optimum balance between the corporate lawyer's obligations to the client and to society. The text of Utah Rules of Professional Conduct 1.6 and 4.1 follow.

> (a) A lawyer shall not reveal information relating to the representation of a client unless the client gives informed consent, the disclosure is impliedly authorized in order to carry out the representation or the disclosure is permitted by paragraph (b).
> (b) A lawyer may reveal information relating to the representation of a client to the extent the lawyer reasonably believes necessary:
> > (1) to prevent reasonably certain death or substantial bodily harm;
> > (2) to prevent the client from committing a crime or fraud that is reasonably certain to result in substantial injury to the financial interests or property of another and in furtherance of which the client has used or is using the lawyer's services;
> > (3) to prevent, mitigate or rectify substantial injury to the financial interests or property of another that is reasonably certain to result or has resulted from the client's commission of a crime or fraud in furtherance of which the client has used the lawyer's services;

(4) to secure legal advice about the lawyer's compliance with these Rules;

(5) to establish a claim or defense on behalf of the lawyer in a controversy between the lawyer and the client, to establish a defense to a criminal charge or civil claim against the lawyer based upon conduct in which the client was involved, or to respond to allegations in any proceeding concerning the lawyer's representation of the client; or

(6) to comply with other law or a court order.

Utah R. of Prof. Conduct 1.6

In the course of representing a client a lawyer shall not knowingly:

(a) make a false statement of material fact or law to a third person; or

(b) fail to disclose a material fact when disclosure is necessary to avoid assisting a criminal or fraudulent act by a client, unless disclosure is prohibited by Rule 1.6.

Utah R. of Prof. Conduct 4.1

B. WHERE DO CORPORATE LAWYERS WORK?

1. Private Practice

The vast majority of corporate lawyers work in private practice, which means they practice as part of an entity — a law firm — that provides legal services to others. A few corporate lawyers are sole practitioners, but the nature of corporate representation[8] is such that few corporate lawyers are able or inclined to have such a practice. The corporate lawyer in a small firm, say fewer than ten lawyers, probably finds that he or she is called upon to render advice in a wide variety of substantive legal areas. Typically, small firms rely heavily on litigation for much of their revenue. Indeed, nonlitigators in small firms are often thought of as "the business lawyer" and may be called upon to render legal advice in any legal area that isn't connected with litigation.

This kind of practice can be quite fulfilling in at least two respects. First, many lawyers chafe at the idea of becoming too specialized in their practice. Thus they embrace the chance to have a practice that constantly presents new legal areas in which to work but in which they don't have to litigate. Second, the clients of such firms tend to be smaller businesses, which means that the lawyer has the opportunity to make a genuine difference for an entire business.

On the other hand, some lawyers do not like a practice that requires knowledge of a broad array of substantive areas. Further, the legal issues that arise with clients of small firms are often quite routine, which may lead to professional disaffection. Finally, some corporate lawyers in small firms feel isolated because they have no other corporate lawyer colleagues.

Corporate lawyers in medium-sized firms, between 10 and 100 lawyers, still have the opportunity to make an important difference for their corporate clients. They also are able to focus their practice more narrowly on "corporate law," rather than on "non-litigation" areas, because other lawyers in the firm are likely to specialize in tax, labor and employment, environmental, or intellectual property law. Thus a corporate lawyer is likely to be *in* the corporate department rather than to *be* the corporate department. The

---

8. Corporate law practice usually entails a range of legal issues such that the client needs the advice of lawyers in more than one legal specialty. A law firm that can provide such a range of lawyers in one place is typically more attractive to corporate clients than the alternative of seeking out lawyers in separate sole practices for each of their legal needs.

firm's larger size means that it can provide legal services in a range of substantive areas, and so more established business entities are likely to be attracted to such a firm. In turn, these larger and more-established business entities are likely to generate more sophisticated, and hence more interesting, legal problems for the corporate lawyer.

Corporate lawyers in medium-sized firms face professional frustration, however. A medium-sized firm is in constant need of new clients because as their clients get bigger they may migrate to larger law firms. Much of the medium-sized firm lawyer's time is taken up with developing new clients. At the same time, the corporate lawyer is trying to prevent current clients from being snatched away by larger, often more prestigious, law firms that may be perceived as offering more or better services for the client. Even when clients are retained, the corporate lawyer may find him- or herself shunted aside when a large transaction comes along; the client may retain additional counsel from a larger firm to provide particular expertise. These lawyers may squeeze out the lawyer at the mid-sized firm.

Finally, lawyers in large firms, over 100 lawyers, frequently find themselves grappling with extremely sophisticated and complex corporate law issues, often on behalf of the largest corporations in the world. These lawyers are supported by an astonishing array of resources, from support staff to IT equipment, to information services (that's the library to you and me). A corporate lawyer in a large firm will probably find that the corporate department comprises several more focused practice areas and the lawyer probably practices in only one or two of those focused areas. For instance, a typical large firm's corporate department comprises practice areas devoted to mergers and acquisitions[9]; securities (often called public financing or corporate finance)[10]; and venture capital or private equity[11] in addition to a general corporate law practice.

Big firm corporate lawyers may find themselves frustrated by the narrowness of their practice's focus. They may feel that they are simply legal machines rather than productive lawyers. Corporate lawyers in big firms may also feel distanced from clients because they deal with in-house lawyers and corporate managers who are not senior policy makers. Finally, many or most of the corporate lawyer's projects may be very small pieces of very big deals, which may lead to the feeling that the lawyer's efforts are rather superfluous or fruitless.

2. Corporations (In-House Lawyers)

Probably the most typical alternative to practicing corporate law in a law firm is to work directly for a corporation. Here the corporate lawyer works as an employee *of* the client rather than working in a law firm that is hired *by* the client. Obviously, the smaller the business, the more the in-house lawyer is expected to be a general practitioner and possibly a savvy businessperson as well. At the other extreme, a large, well-established, publicly held corporation may have a legal department that resembles a medium-sized firm in terms of both the number of lawyers employed and the division of those lawyers into practice groups.

9. The subject of Chapter 17 and, doubtless, a separate course in law school.
10. *Securities* means the application of the federal securities laws to proposed issuances of stock. This area is certainly a separate course, or courses, in your law school. In this casebook, securities regulation is a separate section at the end of each chapter in which there are significant securities law issues. See, most directly, the Federal Securities Regulation portions of Chapters 6, 7, and 15.
11. See in particular Chapter 6.

The differences between practicing corporate law in a firm and in a corporation can be striking. Having a single client can allow the corporate lawyer to develop a deep knowledge not only of the client but of the whole industry of which the company is a part. This knowledge can allow the corporate lawyer to render advice that is more informed and to apply judgment that is better suited to the client than can a lawyer who practices in a law firm. The in-house lawyer, or at any rate the in-house legal department as a whole, can often have a more direct influence on the corporate client, because the lawyers are permanently connected to the client, than can a law firm that has been retained to provide advice. Further, many times the in-house lawyer will deal with nascent legal issues that are too inchoate or too sensitive to refer to an outside firm. This quality again allows the in-house corporate lawyer to be more effective than a lawyer in private practice might be.

On the other hand, the in-house lawyer runs a risk of being psychologically "captured" by the company. In other words, the in-house corporate lawyer may come to believe that, in effect, the company is always right and the lawyer's advice may come to be less valuable than more dispassionate advice rendered by lawyers in private practice. Also, nonlawyers in the corporation may be required by company policy to deal with in-house lawyers on certain matters. The upshot is that nonlawyers may view in-house lawyers as impediments rather than allies. Further, nonlawyers may discount in-house lawyers' opinions on the ground that, "if they're working for the company, how good can they be?" and may give more credence to advice from outside law firms because, "if we're paying lots of money to outsiders, they must know what they're doing."

Moreover, an in-house lawyer might find him- or herself subjected to increased ratcheting (see Chapter 4) in two ways. First, because the in-house lawyer is paid a salary rather than an hourly rate, there is a temptation to increase the lawyer's work-load because the increased cost is minimal. Second, the in-house lawyer might be consulted by senior executives for advice on the executive's stock portfolio, retirement plan, or employment agreement. These issues may not only be outside the scope of the lawyer's employment but may frequently raise delicate conflict of interest issues if the in-house lawyer could also be considered to have established an attorney-client relationship with the executive.

In terms of the difference in substantive law focus, an in-house lawyer may spend much, or even all, of his or her time supervising legal matters that have been sent to outside law firms rather than spending time working on those legal matters directly. Some lawyers prefer this sort of once-removed contact with corporate law, especially as it often involves working primarily with other lawyers (in the firms to which the legal work has been sent) who are knowledgeable about the subjects. Other corporate lawyers may find such indirect practice frustrating. In-house lawyers usually have the opportunity to undertake three kinds of corporate law work more regularly than lawyers in a law firm. First, if the corporation is publicly held, the in-house lawyer may be involved in ensuring compliance with the periodic reporting requirements of the SEC and stock exchanges. Relatedly, if the corporation does business in a regulated industry such as banking or communications, the in-house lawyer may participate in the corporation's compliance obligations. Finally, the in-house lawyer may be more continuously involved in the corporation's legal and corporate governance compliance and auditing efforts than a lawyer practicing in a law firm.

3. Other Practice Settings

Private practice and in-house employment are by far the most common practice settings for corporate lawyers. Nonetheless, there are other settings for corporate lawyers that may be of interest to you. These practice settings may be thought of as niche practices because, while important, they do not afford employment opportunities for significant numbers of lawyers. First, some corporate lawyers work in not-for-profit organizations devoted in whole or in part to issues of corporate law. These organizations often focus on issues of corporate governance or corporate social responsibility.[12]

Another niche corporate law practice setting is in the government. Intuitively you might think that there are lots of employment opportunities for lawyers in various levels of government. True, but very few of them involve corporate law. The SEC employs many corporate lawyers who focus on the federal securities laws. To some extent these lawyers also deal with state corporate law issues, but such work is essentially ancillary to their focus on the federal securities laws.[13]

Some law students seek judicial clerkships after graduation. Although there's no official "corporation court," much of the most important and sophisticated corporate law cases arise in Delaware.[14] The Delaware Court of Chancery has five jurists and the Supreme Court has five justices. Each of these judges has law clerks selected annually. Your school's career services office can provide you with more information.

Finally, a wonderful niche is in academia. The person teaching this course is a corporate lawyer. It is common knowledge that corporate law scholars occupy the highest level in the legal academic hierarchy — followed, in order, by tax scholars, other law professors, and finally constitutional law profs.

4. Who Practices Corporate Law?

This section shifts to a consideration of the demographics of corporate lawyers. Given that the definition of "corporate lawyer" is imprecise, the statistics that follow are also imprecise. Nonetheless, I suspect they reflect a roughly accurate presentation of the demographics of those who practice corporate law. The numbers focus on lawyers in law firms and in-house lawyers and do not include corporate lawyers working in other practice settings.

The total number of lawyers in the United States is probably around 1 million, of whom around 45,000 (4.5%) are probably corporate lawyers. According to the U.S. Equal Employment Opportunity Commission, there are around 800 law firms in the country with 15 or more lawyers. These law firms doubtless employ the great

---

12. Corporate governance involves issues of the allocation of the power to manage a corporation among various constituencies such as large shareholders, directors, and senior managers. See in particular Chapters 9-14. Other important constituencies include suppliers, customers, and employees. Corporate social responsibility generally refers to the relation between business entities (usually large corporations) and the communities (large or small) in which they do business. Often the emphasis is on the obligations corporations have to the societies in which they operate and the abilities and propriety of governments to enforce those obligations. See in particular Chapters 2 and 10.

13. Every state government also has a securities department. Lawyers in those departments focus on the state's securities laws rather than corporate law, more broadly understood.

14. As you will discover, many of the cases in this casebook are from the Delaware courts and certainly more cases in this book are from Delaware than from any other state. See in particular Chapters 2 and 5 on the importance of Delaware to corporate law.

majority of all corporate lawyers in private practice. In total, these firms employ about 105,000 lawyers. [15] If, speaking quite generally, about one-third of medium-to-large firm lawyers are primarily engaged in corporate work, then there are roughly 35,000 corporate lawyers (about 3.5% of all U.S. lawyers) in private practice.

The number of in-house lawyers is probably around 70,000. Not all of these lawyers practice corporate law, however. In-house lawyers as a whole spend roughly 20 percent of their time on essentially corporate matters. Recognizing, of course, that some in-house lawyers spend all their time on corporate law matters while others spend none, a reasonable estimate might be that 15 percent of in-house lawyers are primarily corporate lawyers. So maybe 10,000 to 12,000 corporate lawyers work in-house.

Let's look separately at the demographics [16] of lawyers in private practice and in-house. For each setting, let's examine all such lawyers and newly hired lawyers. We'll also compare those demographics to all lawyers and to newly graduated lawyers.

First, 60 percent of lawyers working in law firms are male and 40 percent are female. By comparison, among all lawyers the ratio of men to women is 72 percent to 28 percent. Looking to the race or ethnicity of law firm lawyers, we find the breakdown as follows (percentages of all lawyers are in parentheses):

White[17]	87.2% (89.4%)
Asian	5.3% (2.8%)
African American	4.4% (3.6%)
Latino/a	2.9% (4.0%)
Native American	0.2% (0.2%)

Further dividing these figures into partners and associates, the demographics of law firms looks like this: Among partners, 83 percent are men, 17 percent are women; 96 percent are white and 4 percent are people of color. Among associates, 57 percent are men, 43 percent are women; 85 percent are white and 15 percent are people of color.

The demographic breakdown for entry-level hiring in law firms (percentages of all recent law school graduates are in parentheses) looks like this: Demographics by gender: 52 percent (52%) are male and 48 percent (48%) are female. Demographics by race [18]: white 81 percent (80%); people of color 19 percent (20%). On the whole, about one-third of all law graduates initially work for law firms with ten or more lawyers.

For in-house corporate lawyers (again, percentages for all lawyers are in parentheses), 68 percent (72%) are male and 32 percent (28%) are female. Eighty-seven percent (89%) are white and 13 percent (11%) are people of color. The head of a corporation's legal department is usually called the general counsel. Of the general

15. Using the EEOC data results in about 101,000 lawyers in firms of over 100 employees and 15 lawyers. The National Association for Law Placement (NALP) estimates about 115,000 lawyers in private firms of all sizes. Because there are fewer corporate lawyers in smaller firms, the 105,000 number probably captures nearly all corporate lawyers in law firms.

16. Although relatively reliable statistics are available for gender and race or ethnicity, there appear to be no comparable statistics for sexual orientation.

17. In these statistics, white means those lawyers who have not identified themselves as African American, Latino/a, Asian, or Native American.

18. There are no reliable statistics for entry-level hires in which the lawyers' race or ethnicity is further broken down. The breakdown of JDs awarded by race or ethnicity is: white 80%; African American 7.2%; Asian 6.5%; Latino/a 5.6%; Native American 0.7%.

counsels at the 1,000 largest American corporations, 88 percent are men and 12 percent are women. The breakdown by race or ethnicity is:

White	95%
African American	3.1%
Latino/a	0.7%
Asian	0.5%

Among entry-level lawyers at corporations of every size, 57 percent are men and 43 percent are women. Seventy-seven percent of new hires in corporate legal departments are white and 23 percent are people of color. Roughly 11 percent of all law school graduates initially work for corporations. To put the entry-level numbers in some perspective, many corporations, especially medium to large corporations, do not routinely hire lawyers directly from law school. Rather, the large majority of newly hired in-house lawyers have had two to five years of practice experience in law firms or in the public sector.

Notes and Questions

1. What Do You Think?

a. Do you think that law firm corporate lawyers and in-house corporate lawyers encounter roughly comparable ethical issues? If you believe there are differences, what are they?

C. WHAT DO CORPORATE LAWYERS NEED TO KNOW?

This section touches on the substantive areas in which corporate lawyers need to be particularly competent. This discussion certainly isn't meant to suggest that other substantive areas and lawyer skills are unimportant. Rather, the point is to give you a sense of the areas in which corporate lawyers find themselves working on a daily basis so that you can assess whether a career in corporate law is one in which you might be particularly interested.

1. Core Areas of Knowledge

Corporate lawyers need to have a deep knowledge of, and keep current in, five substantive legal areas. Most obviously they need to know the law of business entities. What a good idea it was to take this course and buy this book. Business entities law comprises the law governing corporations, partnerships, and limited liability companies (LLCs). This book covers the law surrounding each of these entities in depth. You will need to know the corporations law of both the state in which you will practice and Delaware, as well. [19] Partnerships are governed by the Uniform Partnership Act, which has been widely adopted. Finally, LLCs are governed by statutes that vary from state

---

19. See Chapter 5 for an explanation of why Delaware law is important to all business entities lawyers.

to state. As with corporations, you will need to be familiar with the LLC law in your own state and probably that of Delaware, too.

The second substantive area is the law of agency. Again, this casebook will provide you with an introduction to agency law. Unlike business entities law, agency law is almost entirely common law. The American Law Institute has issued the *Restatement (Third) of Agency*, which provides an excellent exposition of the workings of agency law. Agency is not itself a business entity but it pervades business life because business entities can act only through humans, and those actions usually invoke agency law.[20]

The third main area of corporate lawyers' concern is, for reasons I hope are obvious even at this point in the course, contracts. You've already had that.[21] The fourth area is tax, because many of the actions that business entities take have tax consequences. Your client will probably have an accountant or tax lawyer to do the heavy lifting on tax matters. Nonetheless, you must understand enough tax to be able to converse intelligently with the accountants and tax lawyers who, after all, are working for the same client, and on the same matter, as you. For many law students, the introductory course in tax will suffice. Many students find it profitable, though, to take at least one additional tax course, usually called Corporate Tax.

Finally, every corporate lawyer needs to have a fairly high degree of comfort with securities regulation. As you'll see, business entities spend a fair bit of time scrounging dough from investors in exchange for various claims on the entity's future earnings.[22] From a legal standpoint, these exchanges frequently trigger the elaborate registration and compliance obligations of the federal securities acts and, to a lesser extent, state securities laws. However, nearly all these exchanges can be exempt from these obligations with basic planning. Corporate lawyers also need to be conscious of the federal securities laws' antifraud provisions. If you're contemplating a career in corporate law, you should strongly consider taking a course in securities regulation.

2. Secondary Areas of Knowledge

Corporate lawyers encounter other substantive areas with some frequency and so need to be cognizant of the basic principles of those areas even if they're not well versed in them.

A second ancillary area is employment and labor law. Business entities frequently take actions that affect employees, and you should be aware of at least the general outlines of the legal principles that shape the employee-employer relationship. Further, the workforce at many business entities is represented by unions, so you may wish to have a basic knowledge of collective bargaining law.

Third, you should take at least one course that covers secured transactions[23] under the Uniform Commercial Code (UCC). Corporate lawyers need to know how to obtain and perfect security interests regardless of whether their client is a

---

20. See Chapter 4 for a detailed explanation of how agency law is suffused throughout the remainder of this course.

21. Yes you did. It was the one about "more than a peppercorn," "what is a chicken," and "two ships called the Peerless."

22. See in particular Chapter 6.

23. Make sure to keep separate the ideas of "security interests," which are liens on property, and "securities," which are property interests in a business entity. Security interests are covered in UCC and bankruptcy courses (and perhaps a bit in contracts); securities are covered in this casebook and in much more detail in the securities regulation courses.

borrower or a lender. Fourth, you should have some exposure to the law governing intellectual property. Nearly every business entity owns something under this rubric, and you need to know how to protect your client's rights. Indeed, for some business entities, their primary asset consists of intellectual property.

Finally, you need a smattering (and I mean a smattering) of three nonlegal areas: business, economics, and accounting. The next two chapters will give you pretty much everything you need to know in all three of these areas to get you through this course.

Notes and Questions

1. Notes

a. Another corporate lawyer requisite is a skill rather than knowledge of a particular subject matter. Every corporate lawyer must be highly skilled at working with statutory language. As you know by this stage in your legal career, the first-year curriculum is mostly (though not entirely) focused on case-reading skills. For many of you, this course is your first sustained experience in a "statutory course." You'll need to be able to find the applicable statutory section, hone in on the words (often, one word) upon which the legal problem turns, understand the range of possible meanings of those words, and understand the process of selecting one of those meanings over others. This selection will frequently turn on (a) one meaning being seen as the most typical or natural; (b) one meaning being more consonant with the functioning of the remainder of the section and other sections of the statute; (c) the section's and statute's purpose (as expressed by the drafters or legislature); and (d) prior cases interpreting the words, section, or statute.

D. FEDERAL SECURITIES REGULATION

In 2002 Congress passed the Sarbanes-Oxley Act in response to the Enron and WorldCom corporate governance scandals. Among the most controversial provisions was §307, which required the SEC to include "a rule — (1) requiring an attorney to report evidence of a material violation of securities law or breach of fiduciary duty or similar violation by the company or any agent thereof, to the chief legal counsel or the chief executive officer of the company; and (2) if the counsel or officer does not [adopt], as necessary, appropriate remedial measures or sanctions with respect to the violation, requiring the attorney to report the evidence to the audit committee of the board of directors of the issuer or to another committee of the board of directors comprised solely of directors not employed directly or indirectly by the issuer, or to the board of directors." In corporate lawyer parlance, Sarbanes-Oxley implemented "up-the-ladder reporting." The SEC rules implementing §307 flesh out these requirements in often problematic ways. The intricacies of these rules are beyond an introductory course in business entities. You should be aware that neither the statute nor the SEC rules requires a lawyer to report misdeeds outside the corporation nor to withdraw from representing the client.

E. TERMS OF ART IN THIS CHAPTER

Barristers

Corporate lawyer as
   conciliator

Corporate lawyer as
   counselor

Corporate lawyer as
   facilitator

Corporate lawyer as
   guardian

In-house lawyer

Solicitors

2
Business and Businesses

In this chapter we look at commerce, which we'll call *business*.[1] You can't really understand the rest of the course, and you certainly can't have an informed judgment on the propriety of business entities laws, unless you know something about business as it's conducted by business entities.

We start with the idea of *a business*. That is, how do you define a business enterprise, and why are some large and others small? Then we will look at the rise of big business in America and the management patterns of large American corporations. Third, we take up the question of how a business may be owned by more than one human. This is where we first discover the "entities" part of business entities. Within this examination we'll also see why Delaware has become so important to American corporate law and take a look at the question of corporate law in a global setting.

A. WHAT IS A "BUSINESS"?

For our purposes, a *business* or *firm* engages in sustained profit-seeking efforts. Profit seeking means that the intent is to undertake activities that generate more wealth than they use. For a manufacturer, it means selling products for more than it costs to make them. For a trader, it means selling things for more than it costs to buy them. For an investor, it means allowing others to use the investor's assets, often money, in return for more than the cost of those assets. Examples are rent, interest, or dividends. For a worker, that means working for wages greater than the worker's job-related costs such as the costs of clothes, tools, or transportation.

1. Why Businesses Vary in Size

Every business must obtain the ingredients necessary to operate, which means labor; raw materials, which may be natural resources or manufactured component parts; and capital goods, like machines used to produce the goods the business sells.[2] The

---

1. We could continue to call it *commerce*, but a law school course called Commerce Entities sounds odd and Commercial Entities is probably too easily confused with Commercial Law (i.e., UCC).
2. Economists would say each business must obtain inputs, which are the factors of production.

business then has to perform the operations necessary to prepare the goods for sale. A restaurant must cook the food, for example; a sports card business must keep the cards safe and create an inventory. Finally, the business has to sell the goods to customers, who may, themselves, be businesses. That is, a business may manufacture components for sale to other manufacturers.

Conceptually, each business firm might perform only one kind of operation at only one location. Take the potato chip business as an example. Potatoes are grown, processed, and sold to customers. Each of those three activities could be undertaken by a separate business. Each of these firms would be replicated by other firms in other locations, ultimately providing the whole economy with potato chips.

We can change this example along two dimensions. We could imagine that each of these three firms were national in scope, with multiple business locations. We'll call this the *horizontal dimension*. Or, we could imagine that a single business undertook all three activities in a single locale. This is the *vertical dimension*. If we combined these dimensions, we'd have a single firm performing every potato chip-related function from growing potatoes to retailing bags of chips throughout the country.

The potato chip example is more than a little artificial, but if we substitute coffee for potato chips, these two models become surprisingly realistic. On the one hand, many business firms specialize in doing only one of the following operations: growing coffee, importing raw beans, roasting beans, distributing beans to retailers, retailing beans, or retailing coffee drinks latte by latte. Each of these firms tends to be relatively localized in its operations. On the other hand, Starbucks undertakes every one of these operations except growing the beans and it certainly could purchase coffee-growing firms if it chose to do so. Further, Starbucks has retail operations throughout the United States and much of the world.

What determines the boundary between a business, its suppliers, and its customers? Relatedly, what determines how large a business is? In economics language, why are some businesses very *integrated*, vertically, horizontally, or both, while others are not? This may seem a tad esoteric, but the answer has important implications. The answer to the integration question suggests whether your business client is likely to increase in size, either horizontally or vertically, or whether your client itself may be acquired. In any case, your understanding of these business dynamics will help you to understand the kinds of transactions in which your client is involved (e.g., negotiating a contract with a supplier versus negotiating to buy the supplier's firm) and the business choices the client is likely to face.

The economists' answer to the question of horizontal integration has to do, at the core, with the idea of economies of scale. Take the fully integrated potato chip firm we imagined above. If that firm produced just one bag of chips per day, its costs would quickly overrun its revenues and bankruptcy would ensue. Intuitively, the more bags of chips the firm produces, the lower its costs per bag will be. Assuming that the retail price of potato chips is relatively fixed, the lower the per-bag cost, the higher the firm's profits.

These cost reductions have limits, for reasons we won't explore, so there is a theoretical optimum size for every production process. The optimum size for some operations is large, which tends to produce an industry in which most of the firms are large. Conversely, the optimum size for other operations is small, so that each operating unit in the industry is small. Note, though, that in the latter setting one firm might own a great number of these small units. The coffee beverage industry is one example. The optimum size of an espresso machine is small; some coffee drink retailers are single-unit businesses, and others are like Starbucks.

Turning to vertical integration, the most accepted answer to the question of how integrated a business should be has to do with the transaction costs of obtaining raw materials and selling goods. These transaction costs include finding sources of raw materials, finding customers, and negotiating price and terms of supply contracts. When, overall, the transaction costs of contracting between businesses is less than the transaction costs of administering the allocation of assets within a business, the business will not integrate. Thus firms will tend not to integrate with their suppliers (upstream integration) if supplying firms are plentiful, if the products they supply are plentiful, and if the supplied products are relatively fungible. There seems little economic need for a firm that owns a chain of stationery stores to integrate upstream with its supplier of envelopes or printer paper.

a. Background and Context—An Example

We will see more concrete examples of the drive to integrate vertically or horizontally in the next section when we see the rise of big business in America. For now, though, in case you think that the consequences of horizontal or vertical integration are only of theoretical or historical interest, consider the following news story.

Fitting In: In Bow to Retailers' New Clout, Levi Strauss Makes Alterations

Wall St. J. (June 17, 2004) A1

When Levi Strauss & Co. was preparing for its biggest new jeans launch in decades, it hired as a sales executive someone it considered the perfect choice: a vice president from motor-oil maker Pennzoil Co. The main reason he won the job last year, executives say, was that he knew how to sell to Wal-Mart.

The unorthodox bet reflects a fundamental power shift. For much of Levi's 151-year history, it was a powerful supplier. It produced an iconic brand that millions wore, or aspired to wear. It could choose its own styles and sell them where it pleased. Shoppers wanted Levi's and didn't care where they got them.

But in today's world, Levi finds itself the supplicant, and it's retailers who call the shots. Not just in apparel but in a broad swath of product categories, power is swinging to the companies that deliver goods: retailers and other distributors who literally get products into the hands of the consumer. The suppliers are being forced to adapt.

With the tables turned, once-mighty brands such as Levi must undergo transformations to put retailers' wishes ahead of their own. When Levi began to sell to Wal-Mart Stores Inc. last year, it overhauled its entire operation, from design to production, pricing to distribution. The process was wrenching and full of setbacks, and it is only now showing signs of paying off. "We had to change people and practices," [Levi Chief Executive Officer Philip Marineau] says.

Many forces underpin the power shift. Retailers have consolidated. Wal-Mart's vast growth gives it a hugely dominant role, accounting for 9% of all non-auto-related consumer sales in the U.S.

In addition, computer systems now let retailers track sales in real time. While grocers used to rely on a Procter & Gamble Co. to tell them how many tubes of Crest toothpaste to stock, today big retailers know what is selling at each of their stores every day by the hour. So they don't have to rely on suppliers to tell them how much to stock.

As stores have improved inventory controls, they have also been better able to cut costs and lower prices. The lower prices, in turn, helped spur Americans to keep shopping through the recent recession. And to the extent they shop on price, brand clout is weakened and more power flows to the company that comes in direct contact with the consumer.

Retailers' increasing strength has led some to upgrade stores and introduce private-label and exclusive products, such as those bearing famous names like Isaac Mizrahi and Martha Stewart, sold at Target and Kmart respectively. Some of these marketing changes have enticed consumers to buy across traditional demographic lines, so that a shopper who frequents a high-end store like Neiman Marcus may now be willing to shop Target as well, maybe even for part of the same outfit.

The story of Levi Strauss's capitulation to the new power of retail began in 1999. The company was struggling to boost declining sales and to reduce debt, which had ballooned in a buyout that had consolidated ownership in the hands of a few descendants of the founder. To turn itself around, the company hired as chief executive Mr. Marineau, then running PepsiCo Inc.'s North American beverage business.

Mr. Marineau had no apparel or fashion experience and appealed to Levi for marketing reasons. He had been schooled in PepsiCo's direct-to-store delivery system of bringing soda and snacks to stores in its own trucks — bypassing the warehouses and outside trucking companies used by most packaged-goods makers.

Within days of his appointment, Wal-Mart called him to broach the idea of selling Levi's at its stores. It believed the famous Levi brand would add star power to its burgeoning apparel offerings and attract even more shoppers.

The new CEO initially rejected the overture. He says he felt Levi couldn't meet Wal-Mart's strict production demands. Levi had a history of making late and incomplete deliveries. Wal-Mart needed it to be fast and accurate.

In addition, some senior-level executives were dubious about selling a Levi brand to mass retailers. Some managers worried that doing so would damage the brand's cachet and further undermine Levi's shrinking business of selling jeans at regular prices. For a brand that cherishes a classy image, there is always concern that selling at a discounter or mass merchant could downgrade it.

Indeed, Levi already had a retail problem. It had alienated some of its traditional department-store customers by expanding to lower-end chains like J.C. Penney Co. and Sears, Roebuck & Co. over the years. The company also was losing ground to Gap Inc., which stopped selling Levi in 1991 when it went exclusively with its own brand.

But Mr. Marineau believed that Wal-Mart offered an opportunity too great to ignore. Mass merchants such as Wal-Mart were selling a third of all jeans in the U.S., and their share of apparel sales was growing. Selling to Wal-Mart would be the fastest way to boost sales of Levi jeans, which had suffered from declining sales in department stores and specialty chains for years.

Wal-Mart agreed to wait while Mr. Marineau prepared the jeans company to meet its demands. Levi opened an office in Wal-Mart's hometown of Bentonville,

Ark., and, between October 2002 and July 2003, built an entirely new distribution system for Wal-Mart.

Historically, Levi jeans arrived from factories at company-owned distribution centers, where they were labeled with store tags. After a short wait, they were packed back up and sent to retailers' distribution centers or stores. Under the new system, Levi goods would arrive from independent factories with store tags already attached. After a short stay at one of two "pool points," Wal-Mart's own trucks would pick them up and deliver them to Wal-Mart's distribution centers, from where they would be sent to individual stores.

The speed, combined with feedback from Wal-Mart, would let Levi reduce guesswork about the number of pairs needed. The goal was to greatly reduce excess stock and markdowns.

Some big Levi customers such as J.C. Penney and Kohl's worried they might lose shoppers who could buy Levi jeans at Wal-Mart or Target for as much as 25% less. Mr. Marineau contended they would actually benefit from the decision to sell to Wal-Mart. "By learning to do business with Wal-Mart, you improve your supply chain and logistics in general," he says. He recalls telling skeptical department-store retailers, "Our service to you will only get better as we service Wal-Mart."

To persuade the different types of retailers — department stores, specialty chains, upscale boutiques and mass merchants — to all carry Levi-brand products, Mr. Marineau proposed a segmentation strategy: He would sell different versions of jeans for different prices, from Levi Strauss Signature jeans to $150 upscale vintage designs.

The idea included positioning Levi Strauss Signature as a "premium" mass brand. To differentiate Levi Strauss Signature, the company developed new labeling and styles. They'd have no distinctive "red tab" peeking out from the back pocket, no trademark Levi pocket stitching and no famous two-horse logo. Instead, they would bear the Levi name in a cursive scrawl. They also got less-expensive fabric. Levi Strauss Signature jeans were expected to sell at about $23 — higher than other mass brands of jeans but below Levi's regular brand, which often sold for about $29.

Last July 15, Levi Strauss Signature jeans went on sale at all 2,800 Wal-Mart stores in the U.S. The launch didn't go as well as planned. After a few weeks, Wal-Mart complained that some styles were selling more slowly than its other denim brands, which were priced at $15 to $18. "Inventory turns," the rate at which a product sells out and has to be replenished, were slower than planned. Three months later, Wal-Mart slashed the cost of a basic pair of men's Levi Strauss Signature jeans to $19 from $23, hurting Levi's profit margins.

Meanwhile, important parts of Levi's core business began to deteriorate as executives focused on Wal-Mart. Some department stores reduced orders. Sales of regular Levi's, which had begun to show signs of stabilizing before the launch of Levi Strauss Signature, resumed their decline. Fashion experiments, such as a new high-fashion line called Type 1 jeans, flopped. An explosion of new varieties flowing from Mr. Marineau's segmentation strategy didn't do enough to boost volume.

In a sign of how poorly its jeans were doing, last year Levi began selling its regular-price Levi styles to Costco Wholesale Corp., the big warehouse-club chain. Previously, Levi had refused to sell its traditional jeans line in Costco, thinking the warehouse retailer, with its steep discounts, would tarnish its brand image. Levi sold Costco more than $150 million of jeans in 2003, according to industry sources, and Costco now is among Levi's 10 biggest customers, according to filings with the Securities and Exchange Commission.

But things began getting better early this year. After Wal-Mart had cut prices on Levi Strauss Signature, the line's rate of turnover improved, says Mr. LaPorta, the new brand's president.

Levi began to tweak Signature to inject more style into the line, in a move executives hope will help it command higher prices. Mr. LaPorta says sales are rising for $22.95-to-$23.95 jeans that offer more fashion details, such as embroidered tabs tucked into back pockets, pants with cargo pockets and cropped hems, and women's corduroy pants with wider waistbands and button details. With several months of selling to the mass customer under its belt, Levi has adjusted its pricing and product design strategy so that it is giving discount shoppers more fashion at a good price.

Wal-Mart appears satisfied. It says the introduction of Levi's has attracted a new apparel customer to the chain. Instead of existing customers trading up to the Levi Strauss Signature brand, some customers who normally shopped only for necessities have begun to sample clothes, the company's treasurer said at a March meeting with industry analysts.

In its first quarter this year, Levi narrowed its losses and reported a 10% jump in sales, thanks in large part to Signature, which contributed about $105 million in sales. Levi's revamping of its distribution and production to serve Wal-Mart helped the jeans company improve its overall record of timely deliveries. Producing a season of new jeans styles used to take Levi 12 to 15 months, from conception to store shelves. Today, it's just 10 months for Levi Strauss Signature, and for regular Levi's, the time is now down to 7 ½ months.

Levi's expansion into Wal-Mart is part of a turnaround plan aimed at improving style and fit and at making the brand available to a broader range of consumers. Recently, Levi began selling to some higher-end stores that hadn't carried its brand for years, including Bloomingdale's and Barneys New York. Both retailers report strong sales of Levi's higher-priced "premium" line, which is more cutting-edge and uses better quality fabrics than the Levi's sold at Wal-Mart.

Notes and Questions

1. Notes

a. Levi Strauss & Co. was owned by members of the two founding families from the nineteenth century until 1971, when it became a publicly owned company. In 1985 the descendants of the founding families bought out the public shareholders for $1.45 billion, making the company privately owned. The families borrowed much of that purchase price, using the company's shares as security for repayment. In 1996 the company refinanced that debt but the interest and principal payments remained challenging for the company to meet.

2. Reality Check

a. Why are some businesses large and others small?

b. Why are some industries conducive to large businesses and others are not?

c. What is the difference between integrating horizontally and vertically?

d. What problems was Levi Strauss facing in 1999? How did the company try to solve them?

e. Why did negotiating power shift in the apparel industry between manufacturers and retailers?

3. Suppose

a. Suppose no retail company sold a significant percentage of the jeans sold in the United States. Would Levi Strauss have changed its business?

4. What Do You Think?

a. Do you think Levi Strauss would have benefited from increased integration? If so, how? Why didn't Levi Strauss integrate its business?

b. Do you think Wal-Mart would have benefited from increased integration? If so, how? Why didn't Wal-Mart integrate its business?

c. Do you think consumers of jeans were economically better off in 1999 or 2004?

d. Do you think the United States benefited from the changes in the jeans industry that took place between 1999 and 2004?

e. Do you think the changes in jeans retailing will have an economic effect on the companies that supply manufacturers such as Levi Strauss? If so, what is that effect likely to be?

B. THE DEVELOPMENT OF BIG BUSINESS IN AMERICA

How did big businesses such as Levi Strauss and Wal-Mart develop in America? Much of the character and size of American business can be attributed to the increasing availability of information and the decreasing cost of transportation. These changes affected the optimal firm size in many industries. Alfred D. Chandler, the foremost historian of American business, describes a widely accepted view of how American business came to take its current form. As you read this excerpt, look for the way in which optimal size changed, which affected the degree of firm integration. You should also keep in mind Chandler's distinction between production activity (making things), distribution activity (moving things), and communication.

≡ **Alfred D. Chandler, Jr.,** *The Visible Hand:*
≡ *The Managerial Revolution in American Business*
≡ 50-51, 76-78, 82-86, 195-196, 207, 209, 240-241, 285-289, 485-487 (1977)

Of all the technological constraints [in the 1830s], the lack of coal was probably the most significant in holding back the spread of the factory in the United States. As long as...production remained powered by humans, animals, wind, and water, the volume of output was rarely large enough to require the creation of subunits...or to call for the services of a salaried manager to coordinate and monitor the work. ...The opening of the anthracite coal fields in eastern Pennsylvania lifted this constraint. Anthracite first became available in quantity for industrial purposes in the 1830s.

In the decade and a half before the Civil War, as the availability of coal and the introduction of coal-using technologies brought fundamental changes in the processes of production, the railroad and the telegraph were . . . beginning to transform the processes of distribution. They made it possible for middlemen to receive and distribute goods in a far greater volume than ever before. These basic changes in production and distribution reinforced one another. The factory could only maintain high levels of production if materials flowed steadily in and out of the factory site in volume and on schedule. And the new factories provided the goods that railroads carried in unprecedented volume to be distributed by jobbers and other marketers. The almost simultaneous availability of an abundant new form of energy and revolutionary new means of transportation and communication led to the rise of modern business enterprise in American commerce and industry.

During the 1840s the technology of railroad transportation was rapidly perfected. As technology improved, railroads became the favored means of overland transportation. The reason for the swift commercial success of the railroads over canals and other inland waterways is obvious enough. The railroad provided more direct communication than did the river, lake, or coastal routes. They were, of course, faster. The railroad's fundamental advantage, however, was not in the speed it carried passengers and mail but its ability to provide a shipper with dependable, precisely scheduled, all-weather transportation of goods. Railroads were far less affected by droughts, freshets, and floods than were waterways. Most important of all, they remained open during the winter months.

A communication revolution accompanied the revolution in transportation. The railroad permitted a rapid increase in the speed and decrease in the cost of long-distance, written communication; while the invention of the telegraph created an even greater transformation by making possible almost instantaneous communication at great distances. The railroad and the telegraph marched across the continent in unison. [T]he telegraph companies used the railroad for their rights-of-way, and the railroad used the services of the telegraph to coordinate the flow of trains and traffic. In fact, many of the first telegraph companies were subsidiaries of railroads, formed to carry out this essential operating service. The second basic innovation in communication technology, the telephone, . . . was administered through a national enterprise similar to that operating the telegraph. The initial growth of railroads [also] had a powerful impact on the United States postal system. The drop in rates and the speed and certainty of transportation greatly facilitated long-distance business communication. It also encouraged a much greater use of the mails for personal correspondence as well as business correspondence.

The revolution in . . . distribution and production rested in large part on the new transportation and communication infrastructure. Modern mass production and mass distribution depend on the speed, volume, and regularity in the movement of goods and messages made possible by the coming of the railroad, telegraph, and steamship. As the basic infrastructure came into being between the 1850s and 1880s, modern methods of mass production and distribution and the modern business enterprises that managed them made their appearance.

Transformation in the size and activities of business enterprises came most swiftly in distribution. In the 1840s the traditional mercantile firm, operating much as it had for half a millennium, still marketed and distributed the nation's goods. Within a generation it was replaced . . . by . . . the modern commodity dealer, who purchased directly from the farmer and sold directly to the processor. . . . In the same years the full-line, full-service wholesaler began to market most standardized consumer goods. Then in the 1870s and 1880s the modern mass retailer — the department store, the mail-order house, and the chain store — started to make inroads on the wholesaler's markets.

[T]hese mass marketing enterprises, ... by using the railroads, the telegraph, the steamship, and improved postal services, coordinated the flow of agricultural crops and finished goods from a great number of individual producers to an even larger number of individual consumers. By means of such administrative coordination, the new mass marketers reduced the number of transactions involved in the flow of goods, increased the speed and regularity of that flow, and so lowered cost and improved productivity of the American distribution system.

The revolution in production came more slowly than did the revolution in distribution, for it required further technological as well as organizational innovation. The new methods of transportation and communication, by permitting a large and steady flow of raw materials into and finished products out of a factory, made possible unprecedented levels of production. The realization of this potential required, however, the invention of new machinery and processes. Once these were developed, manufacturers were able to place within a single establishment (that is, to internalize) several processes of production.

Where the underlying technology of production permitted, increased throughput from technological innovations, improved organizational design, and perfected human skills led to a sharp decrease in the number of workers required to produce a specific unit of output. The ratio of capital to labor ... became higher. Such high-volume industries soon became capital-intensive, energy-intensive, and manager-intensive.

The modern industrial enterprise — the archetype of today's giant corporation — resulted from the integration of ... mass production with ... mass distribution within a single business firm. Almost nonexistent at the end of the 1870s, these integrated enterprises came to dominate many of the nation's most vital industries within less than three decades.

By integrating mass production with mass distribution, a single enterprise carried out the many transactions and processes involved in making and selling a line of products. The visible hand of managerial direction had replaced the invisible hand of market forces in coordinating the flow of goods from the suppliers of raw and semifinished materials to the retailer and ultimate consumer. The internalizing of these activities and the transactions between them reduced transaction and information costs. More important, a firm was able to coordinate supply more closely with demand, to use its working force and capital equipment more intensively, and thus to lower its unit costs.

The modern industrial enterprise followed two different paths to size. Some ... firms moved directly into building their own national and global marketing networks and extensive purchasing organizations and obtaining their own sources of raw materials and transportation facilities. For others, mergers came first. By 1917 the integrated industrial enterprise had become the most powerful institution in American business and, indeed, in the entire American economy. By then, too, leading American industries and the economy as a whole had taken on their modern form.

As the twentieth century opened, the new integrated multifunctional, often multinational, enterprise was becoming the most influential institution in the American economy. It surpassed the railroad in size and in complexity and diversity of operations. The decisions of its managers affected more businessmen, workers, consumers, and other Americans than did those of railroad executives. It soon replaced the railroad as the focus for political and ideological controversy. In fact, in the first decade of the twentieth century the control of the new industrial corporations became the central domestic political issue of the day.

In all these new enterprises — the railroads, the telegraph, the mass marketers, and the mass producers — a managerial hierarchy had to be created to supervise several operating units and to coordinate and monitor their activities.

Once such a hierarchy had successfully taken over the function of coordinating flows, the desire of the managers to assure the success of their enterprise as a profit-making institution created strong pressures for its continuing growth. Such growth normally resulted from two quite different strategies of expansion. One was defensive or negative and stemmed from a desire for security. Its purpose was to prevent sources of supplies or outlets for goods and services from being cut off or to limit entry of new competitors into the trade. The other strategy was more positive. Its aim was to add new units, permitting by means of administrative coordination a more intensive use of existing facilities and personnel. Such positive growth might be considered as productive expansion and negative or defensive growth as nonproductive expansion. One increased productivity by lowering unit costs, the other rarely did.

Notes and Questions

1. Reality Check

a. Why was the availability of large amounts of coal so important to the development of big businesses?

b. How did the production of goods change after 1830?

c. How did the transportation of goods change after 1840?

d. How did communication change after 1840?

e. How did changes in communication and in producing and transporting goods result in large business enterprises?

2. What Do You Think?

a. Do you think important changes have occurred in communication or in producing or transporting goods since Chandler wrote in the late 1970s? If so, what are they? If so, what effects have these changes had?

1. Management Patterns in Large Corporations

In the last excerpt, Chandler pointed out that large business enterprises need a hierarchy of managers to run them. This hierarchy was not necessary and did not exist until the growth of large railroad companies in the late nineteenth century. In fact, Chandler sees the rise of big business as important mainly for fostering a new type of worker: the middle manager who supervised managers below and reported to managers above.[3] In its most basic form, the middle manager supervised the

---

3. The importance of middle management is underscored in the very title of Chandler's book: *The Visible Hand: The Managerial Revolution in American Business.*

factory shop floor foreman and reported to the owner. These workers conceived of their career as being managers — neither laborers nor owners. The development of middle managers creates a theoretical and philosophical problem that concerns us as lawyers.

As a matter of property law, the presence of middle managers with increasing knowledge of, and therefore power over, a business means that the owners have correspondingly reduced power. Isn't that a big change in the definition of property when the owner has, as a practical reality, attenuated power to make decisions about the property?

As a matter of corporate law, this change has another effect. When businesses are held by a large number of widely scattered owners, as in a publicly held corporation, power over the business resides entirely with the managers. The problem for corporate law is that traditionally the owners — the shareholders — have been endued with ultimate power over the enterprise. How should corporate law respond to this shift of control from owners to managers?

In the next excerpt, Chandler describes how control of large corporations shifted to corporate managers.

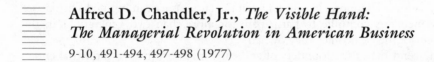

Alfred D. Chandler, Jr., *The Visible Hand: The Managerial Revolution in American Business*
9-10, 491-494, 497-498 (1977)

The rise of modern business enterprise brought a new definition of the relationship between ownership and management and therefore a new type of capitalism to the American economy. Before the appearance of the multiunit firm, owners managed and managers owned. The traditional capitalist firm can, therefore, be properly termed a personal enterprise.

From its very beginning, however, modern business enterprise required more managers than a family or its associates could provide. In some firms the entrepreneur and his close associates (and their families) who built the enterprise continued to hold the majority of stock. They maintained a close personal relationship with their managers, and they retained a major say in top management decisions. [A]n economy or sectors of an economy dominated by such firms may be considered a system of entrepreneurial or family capitalism.

Where the creation and growth of an enterprise required large sums of outside capital, the relationship between ownership and management differed. The financial institutions providing the funds normally placed part-time representatives on the firm's board. In such enterprises, salaried managers had to share top management decisions, particularly those involving the raising and spending of large sums of capital, with representatives of banks and other financial institutions. An economy or sector controlled by such firms has often been termed one of financial capitalism.

In many modern business enterprises neither bankers nor families were in control. Ownership became widely scattered. The stockholders did not have the influence, knowledge, experience, or commitment to take part in the high command. Salaried managers determined long-term policy as well as managing short-term operating activities. They dominated top as well as lower and middle management. Such an enterprise controlled by its managers can properly be identified as managerial, and a system dominated by such firms is called managerial capitalism.

As family- and financier-controlled enterprises grew in size and age they became managerial. Unless the owners or representatives of financial houses became full-time career managers within the enterprise itself, they did not have the information, the time, or the experience to play a dominant role in top-level decisions. Of necessity, they left current operations and future plans to the career administrators. In many industries and sectors of the American economy, managerial capitalism soon replaced family or financial capitalism.

[B]y 1917 representatives of an entrepreneurial family or a banking house almost never took part in middle management decisions on prices, output, deliveries, wages, and employment.... Even in top management decisions concerning the allocation of resources, their power remained essentially negative. They could say no, but unless they themselves were trained managers with long experience in the same industry and even the same company, they had neither the information nor the experience to propose positive alternative courses of action.

[M]embers of the entrepreneurial family rarely became active in top management.... Since the profits of the family enterprise usually assured them of a large personal income, they had little financial incentive to spend years working up the managerial ladder. Therefore, in only a few of the large American business enterprises did family members continue to participate for more than two generations in the management of the companies they owned.

The descendants of the founders of and early investors in such industrial enterprises continued to reap the profits of successful administrative coordination. Indeed, the majority of American fortunes came from the building and operation of modern business enterprises. These families remain the primary beneficiaries of managerial capitalism, but they are no longer involved in the operation of its central institution.

The financiers who provided or arranged to obtain funds... remained on the boards of consolidated industrial enterprises. They rarely, however, had a strong influence on the boards of directors of industrial enterprises.... Their influence was significant only when the enterprise decided to go to the money markets to supplement retained earnings. With a few notable exceptions, such as United States Steel, managers soon came to command those enterprises where financiers were originally influential. Financial capitalism in the United States was a narrowly located, short-lived phenomenon.

As the influence of the families and the financiers grew even weaker in the management of modern business enterprise, that of the workers through representatives of their union increased. Union influence, however, directly affected only one set of management decisions—those made by middle managers relating to wages, hiring, firing, and conditions of work. Such decisions had only an indirect impact on the central ones that coordinated current flows and allocated resources for the future.

The actions of government officials, particularly those of the federal government, have had an increasingly greater impact on managerial decisions than have those of the representatives of workers, owners, or financiers. By and large, however, their impact has been indirect. They have helped to shape the environment in which management makes its decisions, but, except in time of war, these officials have only occasionally participated in the making of the decisions themselves. And since the market has always been the prime factor in management decisions, the government's most significant role has been in shaping markets for the goods and services of modern business enterprise.

In the United States, neither the labor unions nor the government has taken part in carrying out the basic functions of modern business enterprise.... Such decisions remain market-oriented. They continued to reflect the managers' perceptions of how to use technology and capital to meet their estimates of market demand.

The appearance of managerial capitalism has been, therefore, an economic phenomenon. It has had little political support among the American electorate. At least until the 1940s, modern business enterprise grew in spite of public and government opposition. Many Americans — probably a majority — looked on large-scale enterprise with suspicion. The concentrated economic power such enterprises wielded violated basic democratic values. Their existence dampened entrepreneurial opportunity in many sectors of the economy. Their managers were not required to explain or be accountable for their uses of power.

For these reasons the coming of modern business enterprise in its several different forms brought strong political reaction and legislative action. The control and regulation of the railroads, of the three types of mass retailers — department stores, mail-order houses, and the chains — and of the large industrial enterprise became major political issues. In the first decade of the twentieth century, the control of the large corporation was in fact the paramount political question of the day. The protest against the new type of business enterprise was led by merchants, small manufacturers, and other businessmen, including commercial farmers, who felt their economic interests threatened by the new institution. By basing their arguments on traditional ideology and traditional economic beliefs, they won widespread support for their views. Yet in the end, the protests, the political campaigns, and the resulting legislation did little to retard the continuing growth of the new institution and the new class that managed it.

Modern business enterprise has appeared in all technologically advanced market economies. Comparable protests, even stronger ideological and political opposition, has not prevented its emergence and spread in western Europe and Japan. In recent years the same type of multiunit enterprises, using comparable administrative procedures and organizational structures, have come to dominate much the same type of industries as in the United States. In these industries a new managerial class has become responsible for coordinating current flows of goods and services and allocating resources for future production and distribution.

Notes and Questions

1. Notes

a. Managerial capitalism has most famously been described in the 1932 book *The Modern Corporation and Private Property* by law professor Adolf A. Berle[4] and economics professor Gardner C. Means. In corporate law scholarship, the paradigm of the large, publicly held corporation that is run by senior managers, is often called the *Berle and Means type of corporation*. Although many who have not read the book assume that Berle and Means were supportive of the separation of ownership from control, in fact, they were quite critical of it. The premise they started from was the traditional property idea that an owner had (nearly) absolute power

4. Pronounced like "burly."

over the thing owned. Far from being the forward-looking analysis many assume, *The Modern Corporation and Private Property* is a reactionary work that decries the loss of property owners' powers.

Much current corporate law scholarship challenges the normative suggestions of the traditional interpretation of Berle and Means. We will explore the traditional interpretation and its critiques in some detail in Chapter 10.

2. Reality Check

a. What are the three categories of capitalism Chandler describes?

b. Why and how did managerial capitalism become dominant?

c. Why did labor unions not develop more control over the management of large businesses?

d. Why has the federal government not asserted more control over the management of large businesses?

3. What Do You Think?

a. Why did managerial capitalism become so dominant when large businesses were generally looked upon with suspicion by more Americans?

b. Is managerial capitalism a good thing? Is it better than family capitalism or financial capitalism?

c. Should organized labor or the federal government exert more control over the management of large corporations? If so, how would that control be effected?

C. FORM FOLLOWS FUNCTION—ENTITIES FOR BUSINESSES

1. The Current Setting—From Partnerships to Corporations

A concomitant to the growth of businesses was the development of appropriate legal entities, or forms, to own those businesses. Chandler and Margaret Blair sketch the shift from the partnership to the corporation as the dominant legal entity for businesses.

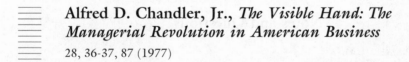

Alfred D. Chandler, Jr., *The Visible Hand: The Managerial Revolution in American Business*

28, 36-37, 87 (1977)

Until well after 1840 the partnership remained the standard legal form of the commercial enterprise. . . . The partnership, normally a family affair, consisted of two or three close associates. It was a contractual arrangement that was changed when a partner retired, died, or decided to go into another business or join another associate. A partnership was often set up for a single voyage or venture. And one man could be involved in several partnerships. The partnership was used by all types of business, from the small country storekeepers to the great merchant bankers who dominated the Anglo-American trade.

The most powerful business enterprises of the day were international interlocking partnerships. Thus, the Brown family was represented by Brown, Shipley & Company in Liverpool; Brown Brothers & Company in New York; Browns and Bowen in Philadelphia; and Alexander Brown & Sons in Baltimore. The name and makeup of all these interlocking partnerships changed constantly over time. Except in forming enterprises...requiring the pooling of [large amounts of] capital (namely banks, insurance, turnpike, and canal companies), American merchants did not yet feel the need for a legal form that could give an enterprise limited liability, the possibility of eternal life, or the ability to issue securities.

Use of the corporate form instead of the partnership was beneficial not only because large amounts of capital needed to be pooled. Margaret Blair details another aspect of the shift from partnerships to corporations.

Margaret M. Blair, *Locking in Capital: What Corporate Law Achieved for Business Organizers in the Nineteenth Century*

51 UCLA L. Rev. 387, 389-394 (2003)

Why did the corporate form become the preferred way to organize large-scale business when it did? And what did the adoption of a corporate form accomplish for the organizers of business that could not have been accomplished through other nineteenth century legal forms? Business historians have hypothesized three possible explanations: the ability to amass large amounts of capital, limited liability, and the centralization of control. While these abilities were important in many situations, it was a fourth factor that turned out to be the critical advantage of the corporate form: the ability to commit capital, once amassed, for extended periods of time — for decades and even centuries. How exactly does organizing a business through a corporation facilitate these things, and why were they important?

The first way was that incorporation gave the enterprise "entity" status under the law, and the second was that incorporation required governance rules that legally separated business decisionmaking from contributions of financial capital.

Entity status for incorporated businesses meant that a chartered corporation was recognized as a distinct legal entity, separate from any of its investors or managers, for purposes of buying, selling, or holding property, of making contracts, and of suing and being sued. [T]he creation of a separate legal entity allows business organizers to partition the assets used in the business. Partitioning has two aspects: Individual participants in the business are not held personally responsible for the debts or liabilities of the business (this aspect is commonly referred to as "limited liability" in the context of business corporations), and participants and third parties are assured that the pool of assets used in the business will be available to meet the needs of the business first (such as, to pay the claims of the business's creditors) before these assets can be distributed to shareholders.

Perhaps as important as protecting the assets of the enterprise from participants' creditors, however, was the role that incorporation played in establishing a pool of assets that was not subject to being liquidated or dissolved by any of the individual participants who might want to recover their investment. This role extends also to the heirs of these participants, who might prefer to see the assets of the business liquidated rather than accept a pro rata claim on potential distributions from the business in the settlement of the estate of the deceased corporate participant. Such a protected pool of assets could therefore be committed more credibly to the enterprise for a substantial amount of time.

Which brings us to the second critical contribution of corporate law, as it evolved in the nineteenth century. Incorporating a firm created a governance mechanism which separated the role of contributing financial capital from the role of operating the business and making regular decisions about the use of assets in the business. [I]nitial investors . . . yield control over the business assets and activities to a board of directors that is legally independent of both shareholders and managers. [S]uch a yielding of legal control rights . . . became increasingly important in bringing together teams of managers who specialized in running the business, as well as in establishing long-term stable relationships with suppliers and customers.

By themselves, entity status and separate governance do not ensure the success of a business. But once the initial capital had been contributed by equity investors, entity status and separate governance helped keep that capital in the enterprise, and thereby helped the firm draw in other valuable resources. If the resources were successfully used, the firm could accumulate both organizational and reputational assets, as well as additional specialized physical assets. These tangible and intangible assets, in turn, further increased the pool of bonding assets in the firm, facilitating the continued use of specialized assets.

Notes and Questions

1. Notes

a. We will look at partnership law in much more detail in Chapter 18.

b. You may have noticed that we have not considered the limited liability company in any detail here. LLCs did not develop into important legal entities until the mid-1990s and so are omitted from this discussion. Chapter 19 explores the legal aspects of LLCs, and their origin and development, in more depth.

2. Reality Check

a. What benefits did incorporation provide that partnerships did not?

3. What Do You Think?

a. Which aspects of incorporation do you think were the most important to the business's owners? Which were most important to the business's creditors?

b. Do you think the United States was best served by permitting the separation of ownership from control and the limited liability of owners found in corporations?

c. Is either of these qualities (separation of ownership from control and limited liability of owners) necessary to facilitate the pooling of large amounts of capital?

2. Background and Context — A Vignette

This discussion of the advantages of incorporation has been quite abstract up until now. Blair provides an example of the consequences of incorporation in the following excerpt, the facts of which are drawn from Ruth Brandon, *A Capitalist Romance: Singer and the Sewing Machine* (1977).

≡ **Margaret M. Blair,** *Locking in Capital: What*
≡ *Corporate Law Achieved for Business Organizers in the*
≡ *Nineteenth Century*
≡ 51 UCLA L. Rev. 387, 442-447 (2003)

[T]he story of the rise of the Singer Sewing Machine Company provides an example in which the corporate form was used . . . to lock in existing capital, to provide a mechanism for settling any subsequent disputes among the leading participants in the firm, and ultimately to support the development of a massive marketing organization. The I.M. Singer & Company began in 1851, when Isaac Merritt Singer got his first patent on a machine that would make a continuous series of stitches.

Singer . . . took on [a] partner, . . . one who was his equal in shrewdness, and who could stand up to his bullying behavior. Edward Clark was a lawyer, and was granted a one-third share in the business in exchange for supplying legal services, especially in the ongoing patent battles. Clark and Singer became the only partners in I.M. Singer & Company.

During the next ten years, the market for sewing machines grew, slowly at first. Building a market for sewing machines was difficult because the machines represented a very substantial investment relative to typical levels of household wealth and income. Moreover the product was at first seen as something that had no purpose other than to save time for women, women were viewed as unlikely to be able to operate such a mechanical device, and in any case, "respectable" women would probably not choose to use a complex mechanical device. Moreover, the legal feuding among holders of various sewing machine patents became increasingly intense, costing I.M. Singer & Company most of their profits, and virtually all of Clark's time and energies during the years from 1851 to 1856. In the fall of that year, . . . [w]ith the patent wars settled, . . . Singer and Clark were rapidly becoming wealthy, and though still organized as a conventional partnership, were beginning to build a substantial manufacturing, distribution, and sales organization. Singer and Clark, though they didn't particularly like or trust each other, had managed to establish a reasonably successful working relationship.

[H]owever, Singer was thoroughly enjoying his new wealth, and was living an unusually flamboyant life. In 1860, a series of incidents brought public attention to the fact that Singer had domestic relationships with, and numerous children by, four different women, only one of whom he was legally married to. To escape the wrath of the woman with whom he had been living the longest and the most openly, who called herself Mrs. Isaac Singer, and with whom he had fathered eight children, Singer fled to England. There he promptly became involved with a fifth woman, whom he eventually did marry once his divorce from his first wife was finalized.

Apart from the unseemliness and notoriety of this lifestyle (which might have had a negative impact on the ability of the firm to market Singer machines to "respectable" households) why did this matter to Clark? The problem, Clark could easily foresee, was that if the firm were still organized as a partnership at the point at which Singer died, the valuable business that the two of them had built over the previous years would be destroyed in the legal battles over claims to Singer's estate. Singer's heirs, however many of them there might be, would all have some legal claim to some share of the business, and it would probably require years of court battles to establish who was to get what. Clark feared that without liquidating much of the firm, he would not be able to come up with enough cash to prevent catastrophe by buying out . . . the heirs.

Clark realized that the solution to this problem was to incorporate the business and to ease Singer out of active management. [O]nce incorporated, the business assets would no longer be the joint property of Clark and Singer, but would belong to the corporation. Equity shares would be issued to Clark and Singer . . . [b]ut any . . . distribution would be at the discretion of a board of directors of the company, and could not be compelled by either former partner, nor by the executor of the estate, nor would it likely be compelled by any court of law handling the proceedings. Heirs could be given equity shares in the business out of Singer's estate without disturbing or breaking up the assets and governance structure of the business.

By this time, the company had no need to raise additional capital, as it was generating cash faster than it could reinvest it. Nor were there any particular concerns about limiting the liability of shareholders: The firm had little or no debt (except perhaps small amounts of trade credit from materials suppliers), and class action lawsuits for fingers injured by sewing machine thread guides and presser feet had not yet been invented. The only function that incorporation served was to ensure that the substantial organizational capital that had been accumulated by the firm could not be torn apart, nor could its reputation be easily destroyed, as a result of the messy personal affairs of one of the partners.

According to Singer's biographer, it took three more years for Clark to get Singer to agree to incorporation of the business, but in August of 1863, I.M. Singer & Company was dissolved, and the business was reorganized as the Singer Manufacturing Company. Within four years after incorporation, it had established manufacturing and sales operations overseas, becoming the first American firm to produce and market extensively in Europe. According to Chandler, Singer was also the first manufacturing company to establish a sales force of its own salaried employees, rather than relying on sales agents. The Singer organization that developed in the 1860s and 1870s included retail branch offices in virtually every community in the United States of at least 5,000 in population (as well as in many communities in Europe and South America).

Notes and Questions

1. Reality Check

a. What benefit of incorporation was most important to Mr. Clark? Why were the other benefits less important?

3. Which State's Law? — The Rise of Delaware

The fact that a business incorporates says nothing about the state in which it incorporates. Chapter 5, on the incorporation process, explains that a business can incorporate in any state, even one in which it has no other connection. By doing so, the business's internal governance matters will be regulated by the law of the state of incorporation, regardless of where the corporation does business. Most small corporations choose to be incorporated in the state in which they will do business, but many businesses choose other states. As the following excerpt shows, there has often been an active competition among the states to attract new incorporations.

William E. Kirk, III, *A Case Study in Legislative Opportunism: How Delaware Used the Federal-State System to Attain Corporate Pre-Eminence*
10 J. Corp. L. 233, 244-259 (1984)

[In the 1870s] New Jersey experienced increasing financial difficulties, due in large part to the tax-exempt status of much property held by her railroads. By 1884, . . . a franchise tax was levied upon all the corporations chartered in the state, a tax which had the sole aim of generating revenue.

Soon after the imposition of the new taxes a young New York corporation lawyer named James B. Dill came to New Jersey with a plan. His plan had been rejected in New York, possibly because that state's financial straits were not as dire as her neighbor's. Dill proposed that the state "liberalize" its general corporation laws (i.e., make them attractive to management), and form a corporation to advertise this fact in the business community. When corporations were attracted by the friendly climate, the resulting increase in franchise tax revenues would alleviate the state's financial difficulties.

Dill's plan received the backing of the Democratic governor and legislature. In 1894, New Jersey elected a Republican governor and legislature for the first time in thirty years. Partisan politics notwithstanding, the new administration gave its blessing to Dill's plan. A commission was appointed to further liberalize the laws, and the resulting corporation act of 1896 (largely Dill's work) was a landmark among corporate statutes.

The success of Dill's plan may . . . be seen by examining the numbers of corporations obtaining charters in New Jersey. In 1889, . . . the year after the first of the revolutionary Dill acts . . . New Jersey passed Ohio as the nation's leading incorporating state. In 1899, New Jersey gave charters to 2,186 corporations, including at least 61 with capitalization in excess of $10 million. These 61 corporations compared with only 60 of equal size in all other states together.

New Jersey had set out quite consciously to attract capital investment, and had done so by permitting management flexibility, coupled with light taxation. By 1894, it had been noted that New Jersey "now runs the state government very largely on revenues derived from New York enterprises."

In 1892, New York granted a special charter to General Electric Company, which included many of the most favorable provisions of the New Jersey general act. According to New York's Governor Flowers, the charter was granted because it "will keep within the state a corporation which, . . . without the concessions allowed by its proposed charter, would be incorporated under the laws of New Jersey."

Still other states joined New York in its belated strategy of imitation. One state, however, was successful in its imitation. [A] group was formed to implement a plan similar to Dill's, under which a liberal incorporation law would be drafted, and a corporation formed to solicit charters for the state [of Delaware]. An act was drafted, and it was piloted through the 1899 session of the General Assembly without a dissenting vote.

Even after the heavy borrowing from New Jersey law, Delaware had little competitive edge over her sister; that edge was supplied by Delaware's tax rates. Delaware's annual franchise taxes were set at half of New Jersey's, up to an authorized capital of $5 million; above that amount, Delaware's franchise taxes were set at sixty per cent of her neighbor's.

The results of Delaware's policy were not as immediate or spectacular as New Jersey's. Delaware's position improved steadily, however. In 1913, Delaware passed New Jersey, with 1,613 charters granted to 1,445. The benefits to Delaware were enormous. In 1899, filing fees and franchise taxes had provided the state with $36,000 of the total state revenues of $511,000. By 1916, $314,000 out of $945,000 had been derived from corporations, and by 1919, the figures were $1.2 million out of $3.5 million.

Part of the explanation for Delaware's early success lies in the willingness of its legislature to adopt new devices as they were thought of by counsel for management. For the rest of the explanation, the historian must look back to New Jersey. In New Jersey's gubernatorial election of 1910, [Woodrow] Wilson had raised the issue of antitrust, but he exercised little leadership in the field. . . . When he revived the issue as a candidate for President in 1912, . . . [President Theodore] Roosevelt pointed out that Wilson had done nothing as governor to reform New Jersey's notorious corporation laws. Wilson was elected, but his bitterness over this rebuke made him determined to pass an antitrust law while still governor; he did not become President until March, 1913.

Accordingly, he had legislation drafted, though he himself was uninterested in the details. The "Seven Sisters," as the bills were called, . . . passed in February 1913 with little serious opposition.

The effects were swift and drastic. Between 1912 and 1914, the number of annual incorporations fell from 1,900 to 1,280. The number of new corporations with over $1 million in authorized capital stock fell from 46 in 1912 to 10 in 1914. The total authorized capital stock of corporations chartered in 1912 was $428 million, and by 1914 the figure had fallen to $95 million.

By 1917, sentiment in the state ran against the acts, and in that year a special commission recommended their repeal. The repeal came too late, however. New Jersey had lost her competitive advantage, and Delaware remained the leader in the field.

Notes and Questions

1. Notes

a. Delaware currently receives about a quarter of its total revenues from incorporation and franchise fees and taxes.

2. Reality Check

a. Why would a state want firms to incorporate under its laws if the firm will conduct little or no actual business there?

b. Why were the states able to compete for business incorporations?

c. How did New Jersey become successful at attracting incorporations? Why did that success end?

d. How did Delaware become the most successful state in attracting incorporations?

3. What Do You Think?

a. Should states be able to compete for incorporations? If not, how should that competition be prevented?

4. Which Nation's Law? — Globalization and Corporation Law

The question of where a business will incorporate, and hence which jurisdiction's laws will govern its management, arises in the international setting as well as within the United States. Will the increasingly global and interconnected qualities of big business affect corporation law among or within countries? Below are two different views of the question.

Ronald J. Gilson, *Globalizing Corporate Governance: Convergence of Form or Function*

49 Am. J. Comp. L. 329, 329-334 (2001)

Globalization has led to a remarkable resurgence in the study of comparative corporate governance. Some corporate governance systems, notably those of the United States and other Anglo-Saxon countries, are built on the foundation of a stock market-centered capital market. Other systems, like those of Germany and Japan, rest on a bank-centered capital market. Some systems are characterized by large groupings of related corporations, like the Japanese *keiretsu*, Korean *chaebol*, or European holding company structures. Still others are notable for concentrated family control of large businesses, including Canada, Italy and, notably, Germany. Management styles also differ across national systems. In the United States and France, managerial power is concentrated, by practice in the U.S. and with statutory support in France, in an imperial-style American chief executive officer or French *présidente directeur générale*.

The explosive decompression of trade barriers that gave rise to global competition also had an impact on academics. [C]omparative scholars began to treat institutional differences as having competitive consequences. Competition was not just between products, but also between governance systems. Michael Porter argued that the bank centered capital markets of Germany and Japan allowed executives to manage in the long run while U.S. managers invested myopically out of fear that, unless catered to by a sharp focus on quarter to quarter earnings growth, the stock market's fickleness would be enforced by the market for corporate control. At the same time, other commentators extolled the American system because its openness to external monitoring through a stock market-centered capital market allowed it to respond quickly to changes in the economic environment. Whichever side of the issue one took, the corporate governance debate came to turn on arguments about the link between particular national governance institutions and competitiveness: Is this institution efficient?

From this point, it was no great leap to predictions of convergence: The force of competition would lead national systems to adopt a single efficient form. To be sure, the form on which systems would converge differed depending on which national system appeared most successful at the time of the prediction. Before the bursting of the Japanese "bubble economy," the main bank system represented the future; this array of complementary governance institutions was necessary to support lean manufacturing, the emerging standard of efficient production. Not long thereafter, the Japanese bubble burst and the American economy boomed...due to its rapid response to global competition, stock market-centered capital market, and the external monitoring to which stock markets are complementary. The American system then became the apparent end point of corporate governance evolution, a consensus that appears clearly from the IMF and the World Bank's response to the 1997-1998 East Asian financial crisis. In addition to these agencies' traditional emphasis on macroeconomic matters..., countries accepting financial assistance also had to commit to fundamental reform of their corporate governance system, in the direction of the American model.

These predictions of governance convergence had a more serious problem than the conflict in their prophecies. National governance systems turned out to be more adaptive..., and therefore more persistent..., than the prophets of convergence expected. For example, it was thought that Japanese lean production, supported both by employees rendered cooperative and inventive by lifetime employment, and by close, long-term ties to suppliers, could not be matched without dramatic changes in U.S. governance institutions. In fact, American manufacturers adopted lean production, but adapted lean production to fit their governance institutions, rather than adapting their institutions to lean production. The American system's functional adaptivity proved to be greater than expected, leaving institutional form largely intact. Thus, the debate over convergence is not quite joined. Are we expecting a formal convergence of legal rules,...or merely functional convergence...?

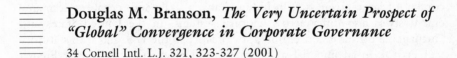

Douglas M. Branson, *The Very Uncertain Prospect of "Global" Convergence in Corporate Governance*
34 Cornell Intl. L.J. 321, 323-327 (2001)

Today the academy has become much enamored with the notion of "global" convergence in corporate governance. That is to say, in the opinion of a number of the élites in the United States corporate law academy, the governance structure and practices of larger corporations all over the world soon will take on a resemblance one to another. The telecommunications revolution, the ease of international jet travel, and pressure from law makers, stock exchanges, pension funds, and others, combine to motivate and enable those who control larger corporations to become conversant with corporate governance structures and practices. Those who control large corporations feel considerable pressure to adopt the best of such practices and structures gleaned from a global inventory.

Assuming that such a convergence is taking place, the further question is toward what point are those global corporate governance vectors converging? According to United States scholars writing on the subject, with little dissent, the agreement is that the convergence will be on a set of governance parameters that will replicate the American model of corporate governance. Increasingly, corporate directors are familiar with governance developments in other nations. But it is a limited phenomenon. There is no massive "global" convergence in corporate governance. At best the evidence is of some incomplete transatlantic convergence with an outlier here and there.

In other cultures and economies great resentment exists toward United States economic imperialism and Americanocentric notions of the United States as the universal nation that, as unstated premises, underlie much of the global convergence scholarship.

Convergence advocates posit convergence based upon their study of capitalism in the United States, the United Kingdom, Germany and perhaps Japan. They ignore most of the world's remaining 6 billion people, the largest nations on earth (the People's Republic of China, India, Indonesia), and the culture beneath law and economic systems that is as or more important than law or capitalism itself. Cultural diversity militates against convergence.

A rich literature, ignored by the global convergence advocates, exists on capitalism in contrasting cultures. While most (but not all) nation states may now be said to have a capitalistic economic system, comparisons to United States and U.K. style capitalism are inapt. Worldwide the prevailing form of capitalism is said to be an "embedded capitalism" that serves and is integrated into the social order rather than the stand alone, highly individualistic Reagan-Thatcher style of capitalism that, for convergence advocates, constitutes the platonic form for capitalism everywhere. There are many cultures and many kinds of capitalism — family capitalism, managed capitalism, bamboo capitalism, crony capitalism, even the gangster capitalism of modern day Russia — and most of them may be ill-suited for United States style corporate governance.

Another worldwide phenomenon is backlash. . . . From France to Indonesia and from South Africa to Sweden there is a backlash against passing off United States culture, including its economic and legal culture, as universal ("one size fits all") culture that presents the obvious solution to national and regional problems. These powerful emerging forces of backlash militate against anything that could be said to be "global" convergence in corporate governance.

Perhaps the best argument against global convergence in corporate governance is its irrelevancy if, indeed, some convergence is taking place. The recent growth of huge multinationals is the most striking worldwide economic development of the late 1990s and the early 21st century. United States style and traditional forms of corporate governance simply are not responsive to the problems the growth of large multinationals portend. Worker exploitation, degradation of the environment, economic imperialism, regulatory arbitrage, and plantation production efforts by the growing stable of gargantuan multinationals, whose power exceeds that of most nation states, is far higher on the global agenda than is convergence in governance.

Notes and Questions

1. Notes

a. Many of the largest corporations in the world are incorporated in the United States. Around 30 to 40 percent of the 500 largest corporations are American. Another 25 to 30 percent are incorporated in European Union nations and 15 to 20 percent are Japanese.

2. Reality Check

a. What is corporate "convergence"?

3. What Do You Think?

a. Do you believe that the law that governs a corporation's management has an effect on the economics of the corporation? In other words, does a corporation's governance structure affect the places where the corporation does business?

b. Do you think corporate governance principles are likely to converge around a common model? If so, what will be the features of that model?

D. TERMS OF ART IN THIS CHAPTER

A business	Family capitalism	Middle manager
Berle and Means type of corporation	Financial capitalism	Vertical integration
Convergence	Horizontal integration	
	Managerial capitalism	

3
Economics

In this chapter you will get an explanation of the economic concepts necessary to be a corporate lawyer. We will treat these concepts under four headings. First, we'll explore the idea of "risk." Then we will look at the question of how one places a value on an economic opportunity. Valuation is probably the most central economic concept in a corporate lawyer's professional life. Third, we will take apart the basic economic assumption that humans, and the business entities they control, make business decisions in an objectively rational way. The final section in this chapter looks at the conventional way in which the financial performance of a business is reported. That is to say, the final section deals with accounting.

A. RISK

Four statements form the core of this discussion:

What you expect to happen might not happen.
There may be many possible alternatives and consequences to what you expect to happen.
The range of consequences among the alternatives may be large or small.
The number of alternatives and the range of their consequences can sometimes be changed by present actions.

Future events are uncertain, but to paraphrase George Orwell, some events are more uncertain than others. This quality of uncertainty is a synonym for *risk*.[1] More specifically, some future events are nearly certain to occur, while others are nearly certain not to occur.

Many people associate the word *risk* with the possibility of a worse-than-expected outcome. But, in most instances uncertainty also includes the possibility of a better-than-expected outcome. If you bet on number 12 at the roulette table, the risk — chance of getting something different — of the ball landing on a different number is

---

1. Some economists distinguish "risk" from "uncertainty." Risk, in this view, means that the likelihood of the possible uncertainties can be quantified while uncertainty means it cannot. This distinction is not universal among economists.

quite high. In that case, of course, you lose your money. But the ball might, indeed, land on number 12, giving you a better than expected result.[2] In reality, risk means the chance that something *different* than expected will happen. **What you expect to happen might not happen.**

Further, some future events have one alternative possibility while others have lots of alternative possibilities. For instance, on the next spin of a roulette wheel the ball could end up in any one of 38 pockets. But the consequence of 37 of those outcomes is the same: you lose. These 38 alternatives really represent only two possible consequences. The consequences of most alternatives, though, are more varied. Suppose your cousin hits you up for a $2,000 loan to buy a new car. The two of you agree on the interest ($100) and repayment date (one year). Your cousin might repay you:

> In full and on time
> In full and late
> In full and early
> Less than agreed upon and on time
> More than agreed upon[3] and on time
> Less than agreed upon and late
> Less than agreed upon and early
> More than agreed upon and late
> More than agreed upon and early.

And, of course, your cousin might not repay you at all, ever. Unlike the roulette table, each of these alternatives has a different economic, and possibly social, consequence. **There may be many possible alternatives and consequences to what you expect to happen.**

Three points are worth exploring here. First and most importantly, measuring how much the outcomes deviate from our *agreement*, may be different from measuring how much the outcomes deviate from our *expectation*. As in the roulette bet, our hope may be different from our realistic expectation. We certainly want to know how much the outcome is likely to vary from our agreement for purposes of ethics and possibly for purposes of litigation. Economically, it is far more important to know how much the outcome is likely to vary from our realistic expectation.

If you were being thoroughly honest, you might assess the loan to your cousin like this: "This cousin is pretty much of a deadbeat, but because the loan is from me, a family member, the likelihood of getting no payment ever is pretty slim. I'll almost certainly get paid late and quite probably less than I'm owed. There's an outside chance I'll get paid in full and on time. The possibility of getting paid early or getting paid more than we agreed is miniscule."

Economists say you should quantify the likelihood of each outcome (i.e., each outcome's probability), which will total 100 percent, then multiply each probability by its economic result and add the products together. This is your *expected return* and

---

2. Note the tension between "hope" and "expectation." When you bet on a particular number in roulette, you *hope* it comes up; you *expect* that it won't.

3. Your relative might pay you more than agreed upon for at least two reasons. First, the extra money might be a way to say thank you, possibly but not necessarily with the idea that you could be induced to make more loans in the future. Also, extra payment might be recompense for paying late; a spontaneous "late fee."

is the point from which you really want to measure the possible alternatives and consequences. The analysis of the loan example might look like this:

Table 3.1

Outcome	Probability	×	Economic Result	=	Value
In full and on time	5%	×	$2,100	=	$105
In full and late	10%	×	$2,100[4]	=	$210
In full and early	1%	×	$2,100	=	$21
Less than agreed upon and on time	15%	×	$1,500	=	$225
More than agreed upon and on time	1%	×	$2,500	=	$25
Less than agreed upon and late	60%	×	$1,500	=	$900
Less than agreed upon and early	5%	×	$1,500	=	$75
More than agreed upon and late	1%	×	$2,500	=	$25
More than agreed upon and early	1%	×	$2,500	=	$25
Nothing ever	1%	×	$0	=	$0
Expected Return					**$1,611**

An economist would say your expected return is $1,611.[5]

A second point is that it isn't clear how much harm each possible outcome causes us. *In full and late* might not be any real harm to you if "late" means one day late or if the loan amount is inconsequential. On the other hand, a day late and a dollar short (to coin a phrase) might be disastrous if you need all the money back on time because, for example, you have a tuition bill due. Third, an alternative's likelihood and its potential harm (i.e., the degree to which the actual result was different from the expected result) are not related. **The range of consequences among the alternatives may be large or small.**

Let's look at the last of the assertions: that it may be possible to affect the number of alternative outcomes or the range of consequences among alternatives. If we reduce the number of possible alternatives or reduce the range of consequences among alternatives (or both), then the outcome we expect is more likely to happen

4. As we will see shortly, the value today of $2,100 to be received later will depend on how much later it is received. Money is more valuable the sooner it is received. For simplicity's sake, however, we'll treat the value today of $2,100 to be received either earlier or later than agreed upon as being $2,100 even though an earlier payment will be worth more and a later payment will be worth less.

5. Notice that you're being asked to shell out $2,000 now and your expected return is $1,611. This isn't a profitable transaction for you economically but, as we all know, it may be a transaction you'll enter into anyway. Don't say I didn't warn you.

or the consequence of something different happening is less likely to be different from the consequence of the expected outcome. That is, there's more certainty and, hence, less risk.

Let's try to detail some of the more common risks involved with investments such as loans or stock. The first, most obvious, risk is that the other side will not perform, either because of unwillingness or inability. This risk is sometimes called a *default* or *counterparty* risk. Another risk is *inflation* (or, less frequently, deflation) in which the buying-power of money received in the future is less.

The *tax laws* may change so the money received in the future may, after taxes, be different from what was anticipated. More generally, a *regulatory risk* may make an investment more uncertain. A government might impose unanticipated regulations, such as environmental regulations.

If the investment involves investing assets in another country, that country might change its rules regarding foreign investment. Thus, a country may change the terms under which foreign investors can withdraw money from the country. This is called a *foreign investment risk*. Further, if the investment involves more than one currency, there is a *currency risk* that exchange rates may change, resulting in more or less home currency than was anticipated.

We can reduce the potential consequences of some risks by contracting for certain minimum returns. An investor might also take a security interest, sometimes called a lien or mortgage, to help ensure repayment. You might take a lien on your cousin's car that permits you to seize the car and sell it if your cousin doesn't repay you on time. We can also reduce risk by contracting for particular actions rather than for specific results. For example, you might require your cousin to deposit money in a savings account each month so that repayment in a year is more certain.

But these contracts are problematic in two ways. First, many investments are simply too complicated to permit meaningful contracting for particular actions. Conversely, they may be too simple to warrant such agreements.

Second, where the contract requires actions, the investor has to monitor whether the actions are, in fact, being performed. Effective monitoring may be difficult or impossible and is always an additional expense.

We can also contractually reduce uncertainty by allocating the consequences of differing outcomes among the parties. A lender, for example, would ordinarily bear the risk that inflation will be greater than anticipated. The parties could agree, however, that the interest will increase if inflation increases more than anticipated. This agreement does not eliminate the possibility that inflation will be greater than expected, but it changes the consequence of that event by moving the disadvantage from one party to the other.

Why would both parties agree to such a clause? First, one party may have deeper pockets, thus the harm may be less for that party, making that party more willing to take on inflation risk. Another reason is that the parties have differing beliefs about the uncertainty. If one party believes that high inflation is very likely while the other believes the possibility of high inflation is quite remote, they may put the risk of high inflation on the party who thinks such occurrence is remote.

Third, a party may take on a particular risk because the other party provides a sufficiently large inducement to do so. Finally, and relatedly, the parties may allocate risk simply because one party has more bargaining power or is a better negotiator. In such cases a party will take on risk in return for little or no compensation simply because the deal hinges upon such an allocation.

One final method to reduce the consequences of risk assumes the possibility of making more than one investment.[6] This method requires no separate contracting, no changing of the terms of any investment. It can also eliminate the consequences of uncertainties that can't be otherwise eliminated. All this method requires is the ability to make multiple investments.

Where an investor makes multiple investments (e.g., buys stock in more than one company) the expected return in toto is simply the proportionate amount of the expected return of each stock. By contrast, the investor's total risk (i.e., the likely range of variation from the expected return) may be significantly reduced (i.e., the range is narrowed) if each investment responds differently to a particular risk. The classic example is a company that makes air conditioners and another that makes room heaters. The economic success of each company is, to a large extent, dependent upon the weather. Hot years are good for the air conditioner company but bad for the room heater company; cold years have the opposite effect. An investor can eliminate the consequence of the uncertainty of hot and cold years by investing in both companies. This method, *diversification*, is the ultimate goal for many investors.

The trick is to make sure the investments truly react differently to the same uncertainty. An investor who invests in both the air conditioner company and a swimsuit company has not reduced the consequences of uncertainty in the weather; in fact, the consequences of that uncertainty have increased. So, the more ways in which investments differ, the more uncertainties become of less consequence.

An investor who invests in a dozen or so companies engaged in completely different businesses has eliminated the consequences of nearly every uncertainty except one: If all the companies are publicly traded in the United States, the investor still bears the consequences of the fact that the prices of publicly traded companies tend to move in the same direction. Thus, the investor still bears the risk of a larger-than-anticipated price movement of the market as a whole. The consequences of that uncertainty can be eliminated by diversifying among different kinds of investments — for example, stock of publicly traded companies, real estate, or collectibles.

To bring this discussion back to the business entities setting, your clients may often focus upon negotiating contract terms that are specifically directed to reducing the consequences of certain risks and to allocating other risks. For example, a contract may require one party or the other to obtain insurance coverage for certain events. Another contract may provide a sinking fund. Yet another may provide for splitting gains. They may also seek to invest in a variety of different businesses so that diversification leaves your client exposed to the consequences of fewer risks. **The number of alternatives and the range of their consequences can sometimes be changed by present actions.**

Notes and Questions

1. Notes

a. At least one other risk concerns investors. Some investments, such as publicly traded stock, can be more easily sold than others, such as a house. Stock in public

---

6. Not all investors are capable of making multiple investments. People who work, for example, are often not able to invest (i.e., work) for a large number of employers. Full-time employees might be able to moonlight one other job while those who work part-time, e.g., cleaning houses, may indeed, be able to make multiple investments (i.e., work for several employers).

companies is usually sold quite easily. By contrast, stock in a privately held company may not be readily transferred at all. This relative ease of transfer, called *liquidity*, is valuable in and of itself. The rise of eBay has increased the value of many objects simply by increasing their liquidity. However, an investment's liquidity may change in an unanticipated way, thus creating a *liquidity risk*.

b. In general, the expected return among investments varies according to their relative riskiness. That is, riskier investments usually have higher expected returns than less risky investments, other things being equal.

2. Reality Check

a. What is risk?
b. Can risk be categorized?
c. How can risk be reduced?

B. VALUATION

We've been talking about making investments but haven't said anything about the price or the value of an investment. Let's start by understanding that *price* means the actual consideration for a particular investment. Price may be determined by active negotiation between the parties or it may be determined by reference to a market. If an asset is sold, then the parties have agreed upon a price. If there's no agreement on price, there's no transaction.

Value, by contrast, is the economic worth of an investment to an owner. Value means, then, the wealth an asset will likely produce for its owner. Further, because value is dependent upon an asset's use, the same asset might have different values to different owners. For example, a small business located on property it owns in the middle of a block might have one value to someone who wants to run that sort of a business. It might, though, have a different, much higher, value to the business that owns the rest of the real estate on the block and that would very much like to redevelop the entire block.

Generally speaking, throughout this book we will encounter four uses, and hence four values, for assets. First is simply running the asset as a discrete business, as the current small business owner does above. This is sometimes called the asset's *going concern value*. Second is operating the asset in conjunction with other assets the investor already owns. As you saw in Chapter 2, this conjoined operation might produce more profits than operating the assets separately. We can value the asset, then, for its *synergy value*.

Third is a business comprising assets that would be worth more if operated separately. The asset's value in that case would be called a *break-up value*. Finally, assets have a value even when they're not operating. Typically this value is derived from the value of the components, which may be simply the value of the metal out of which the asset is made. This value is called the *salvage* or *scrap value*.

Different potential owners may place different values on the same asset depending upon such things as the use to which they intend to put the asset, the information each person has about the asset, and each person's assessment of that information.

1. Value as Discounted Cash Flow

If economic value is the amount of wealth an asset likely will create for its owner, how can we measure that? An asset generates wealth in two ways. It can produce something that can be sold for more than the total costs of production. This *net cash flow* is one form of wealth to the owner. Second, an asset might generate wealth if it appreciates in price.

One dynamic should be clear: We need to value the wealth to be generated over the entire time the owner intends to own the asset. So first we need to determine for each time period (probably year by year, but it could be any period) how much net cash the asset is likely to generate. Note that while revenues are likely to be relatively smooth, costs may be more variable. This variability arises because many assets require periodic large infusions of cash. So there will likely be periods in which the net cash drops significantly and then rebounds. An automotive analogy is apt. A car requires periodic maintenance, much of which is of modest cost. On occasion, however, a car requires quite expensive periodic maintenance.[7]

A second datum will be the length of time the asset will be owned. At the end of the ownership period, the asset will be disposed of for a price. Another datum is the likely sales price[8] of the asset at the end of the holding period.[9] This price is sometimes called the *terminal price*. Again a good example is an automobile. Some owners intend to own their cars for only a couple of years while others intend to own them for ten years or more. Relatedly, at the end of the holding period, we find that some cars actually get more valuable over the years, but most lose value either slowly or quickly.

So up to now we've determined[10] three things: net cash flows throughout the holding period, the holding period, and the terminal price. We're on the verge of calculating the asset's total wealth, and hence its value, but we need to take a detour.

a. "I'll Gladly Pay You Tuesday, For a Hamburger Today" — The Time Value of Money

Why does Wimpy want to pay next Tuesday for a hamburger he receives today? Because he has no intention of paying at all; he's stealing the hamburger. For the hamburger seller, Wimpy is the classic embodiment of counterparty risk. If Wimpy is honorable, though, and economically rational, he still would prefer to pay next Tuesday for a hamburger he receives today. Here's why. He has three options:

1. Pay next Tuesday for a hamburger today;
2. Pay today for a hamburger today; and
3. Pay next Tuesday for a hamburger next Tuesday.

Wimpy will prefer to enjoy the hamburger today instead of next Tuesday because people generally prefer to consume in the present rather than in the future. This preference is in part a reflection of human nature, in part a reflection of the uncertainty as to whether one will be able to enjoy a hamburger next Tuesday, and in part a reflection of the expectation that one will be wealthier in the future so that a unit

---

7. Note that this expense is different from unanticipated major expenses.

8. Note that we're concerned with the price we can get at the end of the holding period, not the asset's economic value. That is, we want to know what someone else is likely to pay us for the asset at the end of the holding period.

9. The highest price might simply be salvage value — indeed, we may have to pay to get rid of the asset — a negative price!

10. That is to say, guessed at.

of consumption (e.g., the hamburger) will have less additional value in the future than it does now. So Wimpy will prefer either 1 or 2 to 3.

This pervasive human preference for current consumption means that those who want to borrow money need to offer an interest rate sufficiently high so that people with money will lend it rather than spend it on their own current consumption. This inducement to postpone consumption means that each unit of money in the present is more valuable to its owner than the same unit of money in the future. Thus each unit of money in the present is worth the same unit *and interest* in the future. This phenomenon is known as the *time value of money*.

Wimpy can lend the hamburger's purchase price today to some third party, collect the loan and interest next Tuesday, pay his hamburger bill next Tuesday, and wallow in the left-over money (i.e., the interest) he has. To make the example concrete, suppose Wimpy buys a $10.00 hamburger today with payment due in one week and loans $10.00 to another person for one week. If interest rates for one-week loans are, say, 0.2 percent (which is around 10% per year), Wimpy will have $10.02 next Tuesday, leaving him $0.02 better off than if he had paid for his hamburger last Tuesday.

While one week's interest on the price of a hamburger is minimal, imagine that Wimpy purchased a house today with payment due in a year. Assume that Wimpy has $200,000. If Wimpy buys a house for $200,000 with payment due in one year and loans $200,000 to a third party for one year at 10 percent interest, he will pay for the house in one year and have an extra $20,000. So, Wimpy would prefer alternative 1 over alternative 2. That is, he'd gladly pay you Tuesday for a hamburger today. Note that one requirement in this setting is that the price of the hamburger or house not increase during the time between sale and payment. If the house seller sells to Wimpy today in return for payment next year at next year's house price, Wimpy may find that he owes more than $200,000 next year.

Wimpy may go even one step further. Wimpy can loan less than $200,000 today and be owed exactly $200,000 in one year. The trick is to figure out exactly how much less than $200,000 he needs to loan today to get $200,000 in one year. This turns out not to be much of a trick at all. Any basic handheld calculator can do the math. To have $200,000 in one year Wimpy must lend only $181,818.18 today at 10 percent. Wimpy will have the $200,000 he needs in one year to pay for his house and he still has $18,181.82 to use today.

Economically, of course, it is to Wimpy's benefit to take this second approach because the extra money can be consumed now or used in a chain of transactions. For instance, if Wimpy buys a house he can also buy a new car for $20,000 due in one year, loan $18,181.82 today at 10 percent for one year, and have a house *and a car*, fully paid for, in one year. Wimpy could get a hamburger *and fries*.

b. Discounting to Present Value

This process of figuring out how much money one needs to loan today to receive a given amount at a certain time in the future is called *discounting to present value*. To return to the question of how to value the wealth likely to be generated by an asset, the answer is that we have to take the likely net cash flows for each period between now and the end of the holding period and the likely sales price of the asset at the end of that period and discount each amount to present value. Then we can add those amounts together to arrive at the total wealth the asset seems likely to generate during the period we intend to own it. If we subtract the cost of the asset from its present value, we get the *net present value*.

If an asset's net present value is negative, it doesn't make economic sense to purchase it. Just because the net present value is positive, though, doesn't mean we should buy it. You and your clients need to make two further assessments. Each of these consumes a large part of client (and often lawyer) time so you should understand that you will discuss these things fairly often with clients. First is the question of whether the price can be lowered through negotiating. If so, the net present value will become greater. Second, an investment decision is actually comparative. Your client needs to compare one investment to others currently available. Using the net present value technique, investments in very different kinds of businesses can be readily compared.

We've seen that determining the net cash flows, holding period, and sales price at the end of the holding period are all subject to significant conjecture. The amounts become more conjectural the further out in time the projections go. Here's one more element of conjecture: the interest rate, which we'll call the *discount rate* because we're computing backward in time. We've talked about one component of the interest rate, the preference for current consumption over future consumption. Here are two more. First, interest is, in part, simply a function of the supply and demand for money. Second, remember that "what you expect to happen might not happen." Another component of interest is compensation for lenders assuming the uncertainty of repayment.

How on earth are you or your client supposed to take these components and come up with a discount rate? Fortunately, this is one case in which the market works relatively well. The worldwide market for money provides a ready-made set of interest rates we can adapt. The Web shows interest rates for a variety of standardized loans. These loans differ from one another in three important ways: amount (larger loans usually incur higher interest because of the difficulty in putting together such a large sum and because the lender is more exposed to the risk of default); maturity (interest rates usually increase with maturity); and type of borrower (government, corporation, individual).

As a first approximation you determine a discount rate by looking at comparable loans. Then you adjust the rate in light of the degree to which the contemplated investment presents, in your view, more or less overall uncertainty than the comparable loan. It's partly a matter of reasoning and largely a matter of judgment.

c. An Example

Let's now use an example of these elements and look at a possible acquisition by your client of an apartment house.[11] We know we need to make assumptions about three aspects of this asset. First, your client has told you that he or she intends to retain the building for ten years. Second, your client, based upon representations by the seller, believes that:

> The building has 100 apartments
> It is nearly always fully rented
> The apartments average $1,000 per month in rent

---

11. This apartment house opportunity will recur throughout this chapter so you might as well pay attention.

The annual maintenance costs are $100,000[12]
Insurance is $75,000 per year
Property taxes are $25,000 per year.

Based on these assumptions, you and your client conclude that the apartment building currently generates $1,000,000 per year in net cash. To simplify this example, let's assume that you and your client believe that these numbers are not likely to change over the course of the next ten years except for inflation, which you expect to be 3 percent per year. The expected net cash flow each year from the present until the end of the anticipated holding period is:

Table 3.2

	Expected Net Cash
This Year	$1,000,000.00
Year 2	$1,030,000.00
Year 3	$1,060,900.00
Year 4	$1,092,727.00
Year 5	$1,125,508.81
Year 6	$1,159,274.07
Year 7	$1,194,052.30
Year 8	$1,229,873.87
Year 9	$1,266,770.08
Year 10	$1,304,773.18

Next, you and your client need to determine a discount rate. You look up the interest rates for ten-year mortgages[13] and see that the rates run around 7 percent. Your client believes that the operation of the apartment house is subject to more risks than a home mortgage to an individual would be. Thus you and your client come to the conclusion that an appropriate discount rate is 12 percent per year.

With expected net cash flows and a discount rate you can now discount each cash flow to its present value. Another way to think about this process is to ask: What amount do I need to invest at 12 percent today to get $1,000,000 this year, $1,030,000 next year, and $1,060,900 the year after that...? The answers are:

---

12. These costs include utilities, a free apartment for the building manager, lost rent while vacant apartments are prepared for new tenants, frequently incurred maintenance such as vacuuming the common areas and minor repairs to the apartments, and infrequently incurred maintenance such as a new roof every ten years and exterior painting every three years. Note that the costs of large but infrequent maintenance items are taken into consideration each year by putting a portion of those expenses aside each year. This makes such funds available when needed and smoothes out the anticipated cash flow.

13. Which seems a more appropriate analogue than an investment in government debt or corporate debt because mortgages on houses involve at least some of the same risks as a loan on an apartment building.

Table 3.3

	Present Value
This Year	$1,000,000.00
Year 2	$919,642.86
Year 3	$845,742.98
Year 4	$777,781.49
Year 5	$715,281.20
Year 6	$657,803.24
Year 7	$604,944.06
Year 8	$556,332.48
Year 9	$495,471.86
Year 10	$470,514.29
Total	**$7,043,514.46**

Adding the discounted cash flows together, we get $7,043,514.46 as the present value of the expected net rental payments for the next ten years.

Now we need to estimate the likely price of the apartment building when we sell it in ten years and discount that price to present value. Guessing that the building will continue to produce the same net cash flows after we sell it, we estimate that the economic value of the building ten years from now will be about $10.8 million.[14] We'll also assume that $10.8 million will be the sales price. Discounting $10.8 million to present value gives $3,477,310.96. Finally, we add the discounted cash flows and the discounted value of the price when we dispose of the building in ten years and get $10,520,825.42 as the present value of the apartment building.

Then you and your client will need to decide what price the seller would likely accept, subtract that price and transaction costs such as your professional fee, from the present value, and arrive at the net present value. Finally, your client will need to decide whether this investment represents the best investment for him or her in light of each other possible alternative investment. Then you two can break for lunch.

Notes and Questions

1. Notes

a. You can use a discounted cash flow analysis to find the present value of anything that will generate cash over time. For example, you could figure out the present value of your legal career.

b. We need to think about value more broadly for just a moment. We've implied that an asset's desirability (i.e., its allure to a potential owner) is a function of its economic value. What we're leaving out is that some assets may be desirable to

---

14. The question to ask is, what amount of money will I need to invest ten years from now at 12 percent interest to generate $1,304,773.18 per year? The answer is $10,873,109.83.

some owners because of additional, noneconomic, qualities. For example, it is not uncommon to see a very rich person purchase a major sports team. Quite often the price distinctly exceeds the value, yet often there is no lack of interested buyers.

The reason is that ownership of such an asset generates more than economic value. The owner benefits (in a subjective if not objective sense) by becoming a local celebrity, from socializing with the players, and in other ways. Economists refer to the complete benefits an asset provides to its owner as the asset's *utility*. The noneconomic aspects of an asset's utility are often central to the decision to buy or sell and to other decisions regarding the asset's operation.

2. Reality Check

a. What are the four kinds of uses to which capital assets can be put?

b. When is market price likely to approximate economic value?

c. Why do people prefer to consume things now? How does this propensity affect the process of valuing assets?

d. What is the time value of money?

e. How do you determine the value today of future money?

f. What is net present value and how is it different from discounted cash flow?

3. Suppose

a. Suppose your school were selling its law school. How would you determine its value?

2. A Practical Illustration

Discounted cash flow (DCF) is the standard approach to valuing a capital asset, but it is not the only approach in frequent use. The Delaware Court of Chancery details other valuation methods.

> The following valuation approaches have been routinely utilized by this court...: (1) the DCF approach; (2) the comparable company approach; and (3) the comparable transactions approach. The DCF approach "involves projecting operating cash flows for a determined period, setting a terminal value at the end of the projected period, and then discounting those values at a set rate to determine the net present value of a company's shares." "The comparable compan[y] method of valuation determines the equity value of the company by: (1) identifying comparable publicly traded companies; (2) deriving appropriate valuation multiples [i.e. ratios] from the comparable companies; (3) adjusting those multiples to account for the differences from the company being valued and the comparables; and (4) applying those multiples to the revenues, earnings, or other values for the company being valued." The comparable transactions approach involves finding similar transactions, quantifying those transactions through financial metrics, and applying those metrics to the company at issue in order to arrive at a value.
>
> Despite the prevalence of the DCF approach..., the Delaware Supreme Court has clearly stated that "the ultimate selection of a valuation framework is within the Court of Chancery's discretion." "As this court has recognized, methods of valuation, including a discounted cash flow analysis, are only as good as the inputs to the model."

Dobler v. Montgomery Cellular Holding Co., Inc., 2004 WL 2271592 (Del. Ch.) (Lamb, V.C.) (citations omitted)

Where the asset is a publicly traded company, much of its value can be measured by its *market cap*, or *float*, which is the price per share multiplied by the number of shares outstanding. That measure does not capture the entire value of the public company, though. An additional component is the value of the right to control the company. A purchaser of an entire public company would pay the market cap and a *control premium* for the right to run the enterprise. Conversely, the market price per share is said to include a *minority discount* from the full value (i.e., float plus control premium) of the corporation.

The following case shows the practical problems that arise in valuing corporations. It also involves a control premium/minority discount aspect. At one point Vice Chancellor Lamb discusses something called EBITDA (pronounced with a long "e" and short "i"). That's an acronym for earnings before interest, taxes, depreciation, and amortization. It is a popular way to measure a company's profitability and is similar, but not identical, to the company's cash flow.

Doft & Co. v. Travelocity.Com Inc.
2004 WL 1152338 (Del. Ch.)

LAMB, V.C.

[Sabre Holdings Corp. ("Sabre") owned 70% of the shares of Travelocity.Com Inc., a Delaware corporation ("Travelocity"). In April 2002 Sabre paid $28 per share in cash for each of the Travelocity shares it did not already own.* In such a forced sale, corporate law gives shareholders the right to have their shares valued by the court and to receive "fair value" *instead of* the buyer's price. The court may find that "fair value" is higher or lower than the buyer's price and shareholders who have elected "fair value" are bound by the court's valuation. Sabre set its price with the assistance of Salomon Smith Barney ("Salomon"), an investment bank that prepared an analysis for Sabre of Travelocity's value. Doft & Co. is a Travelocity shareholder that has sued to obtain "fair value." The only issue is the value of Travelocity at the time Sabre bought out the other shareholders.]

Travelocity is in the business of providing online travel services. When Travelocity went public in 2000, the online travel industry was in nascent form and the future of the online travel industry was uncertain. By early 2001, the online travel industry was beginning to show profitability. By that time, Travelocity was the leading online travel agency.

The events of September 11, 2001, however, created great uncertainty in the online travel business. Even though the industry slowed in the period after September 11, analysts predicted that the negative effect would be temporary. Travelocity, however, also faced strong competition in the market at this time. Expedia, Travelocity's main competitor, surpassed Travelocity as the industry leader in early 2002....

Additionally, airlines began reducing the traditional commissions paid to travel agencies for airline tickets in the mid-1990s. The airlines specifically targeted online travel agents in mid-2000 and began actively cutting commissions for online travel

---

*Sabre was able to purchase those shares, even over the objections of the shareholders who owned them, through a merger. Mergers are explained in more detail in Chapter 17. For now, simply understand that the majority shareholder, Sabre, can force out the minority shareholders, though it must pay "fair value." ED.

agents. In June 2001, in a further effort to reduce the commissions paid to online travel agencies, five major airlines created Orbitz to sell discounted airfares directly to online consumers. Orbitz had exclusive access to the discounted web fares offered by its owners and online travel agents were forced to renegotiate their relationships with major airlines in order to have access to web fares.

Even though Travelocity was facing tough competition from Expedia in the fourth quarter of 2001, analysts expressed the belief that the gap in performance was temporary and that Travelocity would continue to be competitive. In fact, Travelocity's performance in early 2002 was ahead of the management forecast.

The petitioners' trial expert was William H. Purcell. Purcell has a B.A. in Economics from Princeton University and an M.B.A. from New York University. He has been an investment banker for more than 35 years, 24 years of which are with Dillon, Read & Co. Inc. Over the span of his career, Purcell has worked on approximately 100 merger and acquisition related projects. He has performed numerous financial valuations of private and public companies in various industries. He also served as advisor to special committees of boards of directors in connection with corporate transactions. Purcell has testified many times as an expert regarding a wide range of investment banking matters, including a number of valuation issues. He has also testified as an expert before various regulatory agencies, including the Securities and Exchange Commission.

Travelocity's trial expert was Professor Paul A. Gompers of the Harvard Business School. Gompers has an A.B. in Biology from Harvard College, a M.Sc. in Economics from Oxford, and a Ph.D in Business Economics from Harvard University. He was an assistant professor of Finance and Business Policy at the Graduate School of Business at the University of Chicago for two years before joining the Harvard Business School faculty. He is also the Director of Research at the Harvard Business School and his research focuses on financial issues, valuation financing, and the markets related to young, growing technology companies. Although Gompers had never before testified as a trial expert, he had been retained 15 times as an expert in the area of finance and valuation of emerging technology companies in other legal matters.

Both experts used essentially the same methods to value Travelocity's stock; i.e., a discounted cash flow analysis ("DCF") and a comparable company analysis. Despite the similar approaches taken, the results arrived at by Gompers and Purcell vary widely. Gompers opines that, on a DCF basis, Travelocity common stock was worth between $11.38 and $21.29 per share. Using the same methodology, but using different inputs, Purcell opines that a share of Travelocity common stock was worth between $33.70 and $59.95 as of the Merger Date. The two experts' comparable company analyses also yield significantly divergent results because they disagree about the appropriate discount to apply to reflect Travelocity's competitive disadvantages.

DCF involves projecting operating cash flows for a determined period, setting a terminal value at the end of the projected period, and then discounting those values at a set rate to determine the net present value of a company's shares. It is an exercise in appraising the present value at a set date of the expected future cash flows earned by the company. A DCF analysis is a useful tool for valuing shares and is frequently relied on by this court in appraisal actions.

The utility of a DCF analysis, however, depends on the validity and reasonableness of the data relied upon. The problem in this case is that the most fundamental input used by the experts — the projections of future revenues, expenses and cash flows — were not shown to be reasonably reliable.

Delaware law clearly prefers valuations based on contemporaneously prepared management projections because management ordinarily has the best first-hand knowledge of a company's operations. Here, management prepared . . . 5-year projections for the period 2002-2005 and gave them to Sabre for use in its routine planning processes. In this case, however, the court is persuaded from a review of all the evidence that the Travelocity 5-year plan does not provide a reliable basis for forecasting future cash flows.

To begin with, Travelocity's management held the strong view that these projections should not be relied upon because the industry was so new and volatile that reliable projections were impossible. Punwani [Travelocity's CFO] . . . testified that because of the limited financial history of Travelocity, together with a rapidly evolving marketplace, it was difficult "to forecast the next quarter, let alone five years out." He also confirmed that the events of September 11 led to more doubt about the future of the industry and Travelocity's positioning in the market.

Although it was aware of the 5-year forecasts, Salomon did not conduct a DCF analysis of Travelocity as part of its work in connection with the merger. Purcell's DCF relies more or less uncritically on the Travelocity 5-year plan. Despite the normal preference for management projections, the court concludes that the petitioners failed to prove that Purcell's reliance on these projections was justified. Thus, the court must disregard Purcell's DCF analysis.

Gompers takes a different approach, after concluding that the 5-year projections were "merely meant as a rough plan and were considered to be optimistic targets" and not a reliable basis for a DCF analysis. Instead of eschewing a DCF analysis, however, Gompers sets about to create a new set of projections, covering periods of 10 and 15 years into the future, based on his expert analysis of Travelocity and post-merger discussions with certain members of its management. Gompers's exercise is strikingly at odds with the views of Travelocity management and Salomon that no one could reliably predict Travelocity's future cash flows.

The reliability of Gompers's projections is further undermined by the fact that he selectively picks and chooses variables from management's 5-year forecast that conveniently fit into his exercise in creating less "optimistic" projections. Although Gompers's valuation is facially more credible than Purcell's, in that he provides both the numerical calculations and the academic theories for his assumptions, his selective reliance on aspects of management's projections is suspect.

The only reasonable conclusion the court can draw from the record evidence is that no one, including Professor Gompers, is able to produce a reliable set of long-range projections for Travelocity, as of the Merger Date. This conclusion is substantially reinforced by the observation that Gompers's DCF produced values ranging from $11.38 to $21.29 relative to a . . . merger in which Travelocity's 70% parent agreed to pay $28 per share to acquire the minority interest.

For these reasons, the court reluctantly concludes that it cannot properly rely on either party's DCF valuation. The goal of the DCF method of valuation is to value future cash flows. Here, the record clearly shows that, in the absence of reasonably reliable contemporaneous projections, the degree of speculation and uncertainty characterizing the future prospects of Travelocity and the industry in which it operates make a DCF analysis of marginal utility as a valuation technique in this case. If no other method of analysis were available, the court would, reluctantly, undertake a

DCF analysis and subject the outcome to an appropriately high level of skepticism. The court, however, now turns to the other method of valuation offered by the parties.

The comparable company approach entails the review of publicly traded competitors in the same industry, then the generation of relevant multiples* from public pricing data of the comparable companies and finally the application of those multiples to the subject company to arrive at a value. Both experts and Salomon use Expedia as the single comparable company in their analyses, but disagree on the appropriate discount to be applied to the multiples derived from their analyses of Expedia. The court agrees that Expedia is clearly comparable to Travelocity.

Gompers states that the discount to Expedia should be at least 40% and concludes that Travelocity's valuation as of the merger date is $22.08. Purcell states that a 10% discount to Expedia is appropriate and concludes that the value should be no less than $35 a share. Salomon applies a 20%-30% discount range to Expedia and concludes that the appropriate value is between $24 and $32 a share. The independent valuation performed by Salomon provides the court with a neutral framework from which to analyze Purcell and Gompers's divergent values. With all of these factors in mind, the court concludes that it should apply a 35% discount to the valuation multiples derived from the analysis of Expedia, to reflect the competitive obstacles Travelocity confronted as of the Merger Date. This decision reflects the court's view that Gompers is substantially correct, albeit unduly pessimistic, in his critical comparison of Travelocity to Expedia. Instead of relying on Gompers's assessment that a discount of at least 40% is warranted, the court adopts, instead, the mid-point of Gompers's 40% and the high end of Salomon's 20%-30% range.

Gompers and Purcell agree that [the ratio of] firm value to EBITDA is the most important valuation metric. Based on the expert reports . . . , the court isolates the 2002 [firm-value-to-]EBITDA multiple and the price-to-earnings multiple as the most important multiples in calculating Travelocity's firm value.

Discounting Expedia's [firm-value-to-]EBITDA multiple (34.8) by 35% produces an EBITDA multiple of 22.62 [for Travelocity]. Applying this multiple to Travelocity's expected 2002 EBITDA of $47.80 million yields a value of $1,081,236,000. Discounting Expedia's [price-to-earnings] multiple (50.77) by 35% produces [a price-to-earnings] multiple of 33.00 [for Travelocity]. Applying this multiple to Travelocity's expected 2002 net earnings of $39.45 million yields a value of $1,301,850,000. The court gives 2/3 weight to the EBITDA calculation and 1/3 weight to the [price-to-earnings] calculation, yielding an enterprise value of $1,154,774,000. To determine the equity value, Gompers adds back the cash of $114 million and subtracts out the debt of $4.03 million. This leads to an equity valuation of $1,264,744,000, or $25.20 per share.

Delaware law recognizes that there is an inherent minority trading discount in a comparable company analysis because "the [valuation] method depends on . . . trading information for minority blocks of the comparable companies." Therefore, the court, in appraising the fair value of the equity, "must correct this minority trading discount by adding back a premium designed to correct it." Relying on recent precedents, the court will adjust the $25.20 per share value by adding a 30% control premium. This results in a per share value of $32.76.

---

* I.e., ratios. ED.

Notes and Questions

1. Reality Check

a. Which valuation method did the court use? Why did it use that method?

b. How did the court arrive at a price of $32.76 per share?

c. How did Purcell and Gompers differ in their approach to valuing Travelocity? How were their approaches alike?

d. Did Vice Chancellor Lamb find one expert more credible than the other?

e. Which elements of a DCF analysis did Vice Chancellor Lamb find most problematic when applied to Travelocity? Do you agree?

2. What Do You Think?

a. Do you think the different values proposed by Purcell and Gompers were the result of genuinely held views of Travelocity's worth?

b. Which expert did you find more reliable? Why?

c. Do you think the parties could have generated better projections of Travelocity's future? If so, how?

d. Do you think the DCF approach is valid in the real world? If not, what alternative would you propose?

3. Background and Context: Options and How to Value Them

Children learn very early on that parents or caregivers can force them to do very few things. The alternatives to not doing something may be so unattractive that the child, in the end, chooses to comply with the parent's or caregiver's request, but the child almost always has a choice. This knowledge is reflected in young children's delight in saying "no."

So it is in the business world. Business people, especially if they have had formal business education, learn that many business settings can be described as a choice, hence they have the power to say "no." This insight turns out to be quite central to much of the planning that businesses undertake.

A latent example of this power is a business that has taken out a loan. The business has the power to default—to say "no" to repayment. The consequences of doing so may be unacceptably high to the business, but sometimes may not be. Another example is the contract principle of efficient breach. A business might, for economically rational reasons, repudiate or breach a contract. Economists and business people refer to these choices as *options*. Businesses use options in three main ways. First, they can be part of a business's plan to obtain money from investors: the corporation may grant options to invest in the company in the future in return for a current payment. These options are briefly described in Chapter 6.

Second, firms often obtain or grant options with third parties to reduce risk in their business. A prime example is a business that uses a commodity such as chocolate or coffee beans as a raw ingredient. One serious risk such businesses face is fluctuation in the supply and the price of that raw ingredient. To reduce this risk many businesses enter into option agreements with suppliers to provide fixed quantities of the needed commodity at fixed prices in the future. The business pays money to the supplier as consideration for the option, which increases the business's costs. However, that cost is more than offset by the reduction in risk; the business is more certain to be able to obtain the commodities it needs at prices it can predict. Options that are used to reduce business risk in this way are sometimes called *hedges*.

Third, a business might characterize relationships with others as options. These options are sometimes called *real options* to distinguish them from financial options and hedges. Two reasons to characterize relationships as options are to understand more clearly the choices the firm has and to quantify the value of those choices. Options are valuable because it's worth more to have a choice than not to have a choice, and modern finance theory gives methods to quantify and compare that value.

We will focus on real options. Real options can be categorized on several dimensions, but for our purposes it is sufficient to divide them into those that permit the business to do something (a *call option*) and those that permit the business to cease doing something (a *put option*).

Perhaps the most common, and certainly the most readily apprehended, real option is the option to invest now or later. Suppose the decision to purchase the apartment building does not need to be made now. The offeree, your client, has the power to invest now or to wait and see. Intuitively, that power is valuable, but how do you analyze it? This option to decide later is a call option. That is, the option, if exercised, gives your client the power to do something—own and operate the apartment building. Another example of a commonly encountered real option is the option to cease a particular business activity. For example, many large retail companies entered the Internet retail business in the late 1990s, usually to their regret. After they did so, each firm had the option to cease retailing on the Internet.[15] The choice to cease their Internet retailing business is a put option.

Many other business opportunities can be conceived of as options, but the next issue we need to explore is how to value an option. Ah, you may say, we've just finished learning how business folks value things: by looking at the present value of anticipated future cash flows. That must be what happens here.

No, it isn't. The reason why is that an option's value depends upon the value of the thing optioned (in option-talk called the *underlying*). In the apartment house example, our client's call option is the right to invest at a fixed price at any time between now and the option's expiration. But the apartment house's DCF is likely to vary during the option period. As events unfold, the underlying might become more or less valuable. Thus, our option to make the investment at a fixed price might become more or less valuable. Because an option's value is a function of the underlying's constantly changing value we can't use the DCF method to value options.

There are methods to value options, though. These methods are among the most esoteric topics in corporation finance, so we won't even begin to work through the theory. Here's what you need to know about option valuation. First, the further the option price is from the underlying's initial value, the higher the option's value because the chance of getting a good price is increased. So, the more the purchase price is below the apartment house's economic value, the more valuable the option is. Second, the more the underlying's value is likely to change (up or down or both) during the option period, the higher the option's value. This is because the more

---

15. They also, of course, had the option to cease retailing in traditional fashion and continue to retail goods only through the Internet.

volatile the underlying's value, the more likely the option holder is to get a great deal at the time of exercise. Thus an option on the apartment house is less valuable than an option on a new restaurant, for example, because the apartment house is less likely to change in value than a new restaurant is. Third, an option is more valuable the longer its duration.

These considerations are the core of any option valuation technique. Two economists, Fisher Black and Myron Scholes, derived the first successful method of valuing financial options, and several other methods are now in use, as well. Your business-savvy clients will frequently refer to the Black-Scholes formula when talking about options. You should nod knowingly and reply that, while Black-Scholes is great, it can't be used on all real options so the value needs to be approximated by a binomial method. They will then nod knowingly and the two of you can get on with the rest of your day.

C. MAKING ECONOMIC DECISIONS

Understanding risk and valuation techniques are essential to assessing an economic decision. But those insights do not, by themselves, dictate the decision. We now look at how economic decisions get made. This is of quite practical importance to corporate lawyers because they are constantly involved in economic decisions either as participants or as observers. We start with the long-standing paradigm of economic rationality and then look at how that paradigm has changed.

1. Rational Self-Interest: The Classical Paradigm

The same basic assumptions about behavior are used in all applications of economic analysis.... The two key assumptions are rationality and self-interest. People are assumed to want to get as much for themselves as possible, and are assumed to be quite clever in figuring out how best to accomplish this aim.

The most prominent defense of the rational model was offered by Milton Friedman. He uses the analogy of an expert billiards player who doesn't know either physics or geometry, but makes shots as if he could make use of this knowledge. Basically, Friedman's position is that it doesn't matter if the assumptions [that people are self-interested and rational] are wrong if the theory still makes good predictions.

A defense in the same spirit as Friedman's is to admit that of course people . . . [are not always self-interested or rational], but the mistakes are not a problem in explaining aggregate behavior as long as they tend to cancel out. Unfortunately, this line of defense is . . . weak because many of the departures from rational choice that have been observed are systematic — the errors tend to be in the same direction. If most individuals tend to err in the same direction, then a theory which assumes that they are rational also makes mistakes in predicting their behavior.

Richard H. Thaler, *The Winner's Curse: Paradoxes and Anomalies of Economic Life* 2-3 (1992)*

2. The Myth of Rational Self-Interest: How Humans Actually Make Economic Decisions

Obviously, rational self-interest is a model that does not cover every economic decision. We now look at how real humans make real decisions. We look at self-interest first and then the idea of rationality.

a. Self-Interest

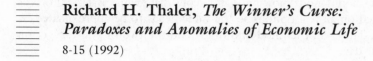

Richard H. Thaler, *The Winner's Curse:*
Paradoxes and Anomalies of Economic Life
8-15 (1992)

A public good is one which has the following two properties: (1) once it is provided to one person, it is costless to provide to everyone else; (2) it is difficult to prevent someone who doesn't pay for the good from using it. The traditional example of a public good is national defense. Another example is public radio and television. [E]conomic theory [of rational self-interest] predicts that when confronted with public goods, people will "free ride." That is, even if they enjoy listening to public radio, they will not make a contribution because there is no (selfish) reason to do so.

The predictions derived from this assumption of rational selfishness are, however, violated in many familiar contexts. Public television in fact successfully raises enough money from viewers to continue to broadcast. The United Way and other charities receive contributions from many if not most citizens. Even when dining at a restaurant away from home in a place never likely to be visited again, most patrons tip the server. And people vote in presidential elections where the chance that a single vote will alter the outcome is vanishingly small.

One currently popular explanation of why we observe so much cooperation...invokes reciprocal altruism as the mechanism. This explanation...is based on the observation that people tend to reciprocate—kindness with kindness, co-operation with cooperation, hostility with hostility, and defection with defection. Thus, being a free rider may actually be a less fruitful strategy when the chooser takes account of the probable future response of others to his or her cooperation or defection. A cooperative act itself—or a reputation for being a cooperative person—may with high probability be reciprocated with cooperation, to the ultimate benefit of the cooperator.

There are other explanations of why people cooperate....One is that people are motivated by "taking pleasure in others' pleasure." Termed pure altruism..., this motive has been eloquently stated by Adam Smith, in the *Theory of Moral Sentiments* (1759): "how selfish soever man may be supposed to be, there are evidently some principles in his nature, which interest him in the fate of others, and render their happiness necessary to him, though he derive nothing from it, except the pleasure of seeing it." While the pleasure involved in seeing it may be considered "selfish" (following the sophomoric argument that altruism is by definition impossible, because people do what they "want" to do), the passage captures the idea that people are motivated by positive payoffs for others as well as for themselves. Consequently, they may be motivated to produce such results through a cooperative act.

Another type of altruism that has been postulated to explain cooperation is that involved in the act of cooperating itself, as opposed to its results. "Doing the right (good, honorable, . . .) thing" is clearly a motive for many people. Sometimes termed impure altruism, it generally is described as satisfaction of conscience, or of noninstrumental ethical mandates.

Notes and Questions

1. Reality Check

a. What are the two assumptions underlying classic economic decision making?
b. Why does it make sense to use those assumptions if they're widely acknowledged to be, at best, artificial?
c. What are the varieties of altruism and how do they differ?

2. Suppose

a. Imagine your client were contemplating purchasing the apartment building, as discussed above. How would classical economics suggest that the actual purchase decision would be made? Would your client make the purchase?

3. What Do You Think?

a. Why are people altruistic?
b. Is altruism incompatible with economic well-being? If so, how should the tension between the two be resolved?

b. The Limits of Rationality

Economic rationality, in its classical understanding, posits that unlimited time is available for gathering information, that all information can be gathered, and that all information can be correctly assessed, which includes correctly calculating the probabilities of future events. These are assumptions that, of course, never obtain in the real world. Nonetheless, for reasons pointed out above, they have been used to define economic rationality and to measure whether a decision is economically rational. Beginning in the 1950s, a coherent theory of rationality emerged that does not require the artificial assumptions of the classic model. That theory is described here:

> [Herbert] Simon's vision of bounded rationality has two interlocking components: the limitations of the human mind, and the structure of the environments in which the mind operates. Because of the mind's limitations, humans "must use approximate methods to handle most tasks." These methods include recognition processes that largely obviate the need for further information . . . , heuristics that guide search and determine when it should end, and simple decision rules that make use of the information found.
>
> One form of bounded rationality is Simon's concept of satisficing — . . . a method for making a choice from . . . alternatives encountered sequentially when one does not know much about the possibilities ahead. . . . In such situations there may be no optimal solution for when to stop searching for further alternatives. . . . Satisficing takes the shortcut of setting an adjustable aspiration level and ending the search for alternatives as soon as one is encountered that exceeds the aspiration level. Satisficing . . . respects the limitations of human time and knowledge: it does not

require finding out or guessing about all the options and consequences the future may hold....

Gerd Gigerenzer, et al., *Simple Heuristics That Make Us Smart* 12-14 (1999)

i. Heuristics. Heuristics are shortcuts, rules of thumb as it were, that people routinely employ in deciding how much information to get, how to analyze information, and how to decide. Heuristics are a fact of life, but whether they are good or bad in economic settings is subject to some debate. Gigerenzer, et al., see heuristics as fundamentally beneficial. Tversky and Kahneman take a different view.

> The term "heuristic" is of Greek origin, meaning "serving to find out or discover." [U]p until about 1970, "heuristic" referred to useful, even indispensable cognitive processes for solving problems that *cannot* be handled by logic and probability theory. After 1970, a second meaning emerged...: overused, mostly dispensable cognitive processes that people often misapply to situations where logic and probability theory *should* be applied instead.
>
> [W]e see heuristics as the way the human mind can take advantage of the structure of information in the environment to arrive at reasonable decisions, and so we focus on the ways and settings in which simple heuristics lead to accurate and useful inferences.

Gerd Gigerenzer, et al., *Simple Heuristics That Make Us Smart* 25-28 (1999)

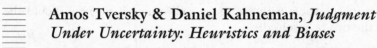

Amos Tversky & Daniel Kahneman, *Judgment Under Uncertainty: Heuristics and Biases*

Reprinted with permission from 185 Science 1124-1131. Copyright 1974 AAAS.

[P]eople rely on a limited number of heuristic principles. In general these heuristics are quite useful, but sometimes they lead to severe and systematic errors. This article describes three heuristics [in bold face all capitals type].... Biases [i.e. systematic errors] to which these heuristics lead are enumerated [in bold face uppercase and lowercase type],....

REPRESENTATIVENESS

Many of the...questions with which people are concerned belong to one of the following types: What is the probability that object A belongs to class B? What is the probability that event A originates from process B? What is the probability that process B will generate event A? In answering such questions, people typically rely on the *representativeness* heuristic,...that is, by the degree to which A resembles B.

[C]onsider an individual who has been described by a former neighbor as follows: "Steve is very shy and withdrawn, invariably helpful, but with little interest in people, or in the world of reality. A meek and tidy soul, he has a need for order and structure, and a passion for detail." How do people assess the probability that Steve is engaged in a particular occupation from a list of possibilities (for example, farmer, salesman, airline pilot, librarian, or physician)? In the representativeness heuristic, the probability that Steve is a librarian, for example, is assessed by the degree to which he is representative of, or similar to, the stereotype of a librarian. This approach...leads to serious errors, because similarity, or representativeness, is not influenced by several factors that should affect judgments of probability.

Insensitivity to Prior Probability of Outcomes

[T]he fact that there are many more farmers than librarians in the population should enter into any reasonable estimate of the probability that Steve is a librarian rather than a farmer. [But if] people evaluate probability by representativeness . . . prior probabilities will be neglected.

Insensitivity to Sample Size

Consider the following question:

For a period of 1 year, each [of two] hospitals recorded the days on which more than 60 percent of the babies born were boys. Which hospital to you think recorded more such days?

The larger hospital
The smaller hospital
About the same

Most of the subjects judged the probability . . . to be the same in the small and in the large hospital. . . . [Statistically,] the expected number of days on which more than 60 percent of the babies are boys is much greater in the small hospital than in the large one, because a large sample is less likely [than a small sample] to stray from 50 percent.

Misconceptions of Chance

After observing a long run of red on the roulette wheel, for example, most people erroneously believe that black is now due, presumably because the occurrence of black will result in a more representative sequence than the occurrence of an additional red. Chance is commonly viewed as a self-correcting process in which a deviation in one direction induces a deviation in the opposite direction to restore the equilibrium. In fact, deviations are not "corrected" as a chance process unfolds, they are merely diluted.

The Illusion of Validity

[P]eople often predict . . . the outcome that is most representative. . . . The confidence they have in their prediction depends primarily on the degree of representativeness (that is, on the quality of the match between [item A and class B]). . . . The unwarranted confidence which is produced by a good fit . . . may be called the *illusion of validity*.

AVAILABILITY

There are situations in which people assess the frequency . . . or the probability of an event by the ease with which instances or occurrences can be brought to mind. For example, one may [predict] the risk of heart attack among middle-aged people by recalling such occurrences among one's acquaintances. This judgmental heuristic is called *availability*. Availability is a useful clue for assessing frequency or probability. . . . However, availability is affected by factors other than frequency and probability. Consequently, the reliance on availability leads to predictable biases. . . .

Biases Due to the Retrievability of Instances

[S]ubjects heard a list of well-known personalities of both sexes and were subsequently asked to judge whether the list contained more names of men than of women.

Different lists were presented to different groups of subjects. In some of the lists the men were relatively more famous than the women, and in others the women were relatively more famous than the men. In each of the lists, the subjects erroneously judged that the class (sex) that had the more famous personalities was the more numerous.

In addition to familiarity, there are other factors, such as salience, which affect the retrievability of instances. For example, the impact of seeing a house burning...is probably greater than the impact of reading about a fire...Furthermore, recent occurrences are likely to be relatively more available than earlier occurrences.

ADJUSTMENT AND ANCHORING

In many situations, people make estimates by starting from an initial value that is adjusted to yield the final answer. The initial value, or starting point, may be suggested by the formulation of the problem, or it may be the result of a partial computation. In either case, adjustments are typically insufficient. That is, different starting points yield different estimates, which are biased toward the initial values. We call this phenomenon *anchoring*.

Biases in the Evaluation of Conjunctive and Disjunctive Events

[P]eople tend to overestimate the probability of conjunctive events and to underestimate the probability of disjunctive events. These biases are readily explained as effects of anchoring. The stated probability of the [first] event...provides a natural starting point.... Since adjustment from the starting point is typically insufficient, the final estimates remain too close to the probabilities of the [first] events....

The successful completion of an undertaking, such as the development of a new product, typically has a conjunctive character: for the undertaking to succeed, each of a series of events must occur. Even when each of these events is very likely, the overall probability of success can be quite low if the number of events is large. The general tendency to overestimate the probability of conjunctive events leads to unwarranted optimism in the evaluation of the likelihood that a plan will succeed or that a project will be completed on time.

Conversely, disjunctive structures are typically encountered in the evaluation of risks. A complex system, such as a nuclear reactor or a human body, will malfunction if any of its essential components fails. Even when the likelihood of failure in each component is slight, the probability of an overall failure can be high if many components are involved. Because of anchoring, people will tend to underestimate the probabilities of failure in complex systems. Thus the direction of the anchoring bias can sometimes be inferred from the structure of the event. The chain-like structure of conjunctions leads to overestimation, the funnel-like structure of disjunctions leads to underestimation.

Notes and Questions

1. Reality Check

a. What is bounded rationality and how is it different from rationality as traditionally understood in economics?

b. What is satisficing?

c. What are heuristics? What are the three principle heuristics?

d. What are the benefits and potential pitfalls of each heuristic?

2. Suppose

a. Suppose your client, who is presented with the opportunity to buy the apartment house, will satisfice. How will he or she make the decision whether to buy the apartment house?

b. Suppose the same client will use heuristics to help in the decision-making process. How might heuristics affect the decision?

3. What Do You Think?

a. Do you think Simon's concept of bounded rationality is consistent with the way people make decisions?

b. Do you believe heuristics are useful decision-making tools that should be explicitly used? Or, do you believe that heuristics are generally unhelpful in making decisions and should be consciously avoided?

c. Are heuristics rational?

c. The Affective Component of Economic Decision Making

Another component of making decisions is affective or emotional. We often think of our emotions as being discrete from, or even antithetical to, the intellectual or rational aspects of our selves. But we can segregate the facets of our personality only so far; at some point emotions combine with our rationality whether we want them to or not. Even further, a rather strong case can be made that we ought to welcome the emotional aspects of our selves when we make decisions.

> [I] wish to stress that avoidance or suppression of one's feelings is likely to impoverish one's ability to cope and solve problems. [M]ost interpersonal situations or chronic social transactions are best dealt with by being aware of our feelings. When we are aware of our emotions, we can seek support . . . or use our feelings as cues to help make a difficult decision vis-à-vis a relationship. Certainly . . . awareness of how we feel generally facilitates effective problem solving. I think intrinsic to acknowledging how we feel and seeing it as part of a complex interaction of ourselves with others means that we are using our feelings as valid cues to a problem to be solved. As a result, we have more complete information for use in generating solutions to problems.

> Carolyn Saarni, *The Development of Emotional Competence* 96 (1999)

The subject of emotions is both broad and deep. For our purposes, the main point is that often economic decision making produces anxiety and stress. By assessing our possible actions in light of the emotions generated we can both shape our emotions and use them to make better decisions. Thus emotion and cognition are inextricably linked. The value of this link is heightened when you reflect that work-related, economic, and business decisions are often stress producing, which frequently means that we are unable to cabin our emotions when resolving these decisions.

People who are good at integrating their emotional and cognitive sides when making decisions are said to be *emotionally competent*. Carolyn Saarni describes emotional competence in the next excerpt.

Emotional competence entails resilience and self-efficacy (and self-efficacy includes acting in accord with one's sense of moral character). When we speak of resilience, we are talking about the capacity to recover after experiencing adversity. . . . Emotional self-efficacy means that . . . we are living in accord with our personal theory of emotion. . . .

Perhaps this is the key issue for emotional self-efficacy: feeling relatively in control of our emotional experience from the standpoint of mastery, positive self-regard, and acknowledgment of our moral commitments. Such individuals do not feel overwhelmed by the enormity, intensity, or complexity of emotional experience nor do they react to emotional experience by inhibiting, distrusting, or "damping down and numbing it out." The capacity for self-efficacy probably entails some understanding of how one's personality interfaces with one's emotional experience.

Carolyn Saarni, *The Development of Emotional Competence* 2, 8, 218-219, 224, 226, 247-248, 278-279 (1999)

Being a business person or being a lawyer who advises business people involves *coping* with a significant amount of stress. Noted psychologist Richard Lazarus describes coping and Carolyn Saarni writes about coping effectively.

Coping . . . consists of . . . efforts to manage specific external or internal demands (and conflicts between then) that are appraised as taxing or exceeding the resources of the person. Coping affects the emotion process in two ways:

1. Some coping processes change the actual relationship, as when an attack or aggressive display wards off or demolishes an enemy.
2. Other coping processes change only the way in which the relationship is *attended to* (e.g. a threat that one avoids perceiving or thinking about) or *interpreted* (e.g. a threat that is dealt with by denial or psychological distancing). Even though they do not change the actual relationship, they change its meaning, and therefore the emotional reaction. For example, if we successfully avoid thinking about a threat, the anxiety associated with it is postponed. And if we successfully deny that anything is wrong, there is no reason to experience the emotion appropriate to the particular threat or harm — say, anxiety, anger, guilt, shame, envy, or whatever.

Richard S. Lazarus, *Emotion and Adaptation* 112-113 (1991)

How do we know when we have coped effectively and adaptively with some upsetting situation that faces us? The answer to this simple question is more complicated than we might at first assume. We have to look at least at three perspectives . . . : (1) whether the resolution that is worked out is mature and functional; (2) whether we can acknowledge our feelings to ourselves, even if they remain unexpressed or otherwise "managed"; and (3) whether we come away with a sense of mastery and resilience, even if the situation itself is not especially under our direct control. [I]t is likely that if our efforts at coping include acting as though our self is not involved, or that our feelings are irrelevant, or that the situation is utterly futile, then our coping attempts will be ineffective. In short, to discount any of these three aspects of coping will probably cause further problems at a later time.

[A] flexible repertoire of coping strategies [includes] . . . active problem solving, . . . recruitment of social support (including gaining social approval), and . . . the capacity to tolerate intensity of aversive emotion. . . . Avoidance, denial, and dissociation appear to be less adaptive coping strategies [because they] short-circuit opportunities for learning or problem solving; they *restrict* one's options rather than expanding them.

Carolyn Saarni, *The Development of Emotional Competence* 2, 8, 218-219, 224, 226, 247-248, 278-279 (1999)

Notes and Questions

1. Reality Check

a. How do we experience and process emotions?

b. What is emotional competence and why is it important?

c. What is coping and what important function does it serve?

2. Suppose

a. If your client had the opportunity to purchase the apartment house, how would the ideas of emotion, emotional competence, and coping affect the decision-making process? How would those ideas affect your participation in the decision?

3. What Do You Think?

a. Are emotions antithetical to rationality?

b. Should decision makers strive to include or exclude emotion in making economic decisions?

d. The Ethical Component of Economic Decision Making

The final component of economic decision making is the ethical one. The following excerpt is from one of the most frequently cited articles on ethics in economic decision. It presents a very concrete explanation of an approach to making ethical economic decisions.

≡≡≡   Joseph L. Badaracco, Jr., *The Discipline of Building*
≡≡≡   *Character*
≡≡   76 Harv. Bus. Rev. 115 (Mar.-Apr. 1998)*

We have all experienced, at one time or another, situations in which our professional responsibilities unexpectedly come into conflict with our deepest values. A budget crisis forces us to dismiss a loyal, hardworking employee. Our daughter has a piano recital on the same afternoon that our biggest client is scheduled to visit our office. At these times, we are caught in a conflict between right and right. And no matter which option we choose, we feel like we've come up short. [T]hese decisions taken cumulatively over many years form the very basis of an individual's character. For that reason, I call them *defining moments*.

Such challenges rarely have a "correct" response. Rather, they are situations created by circumstance that ask us to step forward and, in the words of the American philosopher John Dewey, "form, reveal, and test" ourselves. We form our character in defining moments because we commit to irreversible courses of action that shape our personal and professional identities. We reveal something new about us to ourselves and others because defining moments uncover something that had been hidden or crystallize something that had been only partially known. And we test ourselves because we discover whether we will live up to our personal ideals or only pay them lip service.

As I have interviewed and studied business leaders, I have found that the ones who are most satisfied with the way they resolve their defining moments possess skills that are left off most job descriptions. Specifically, they are able to take time out from the chain of managerial tasks that consumes their time and undertake a process of probing self-inquiry — a process that is more often carried out on the run rather than in quiet seclusion. They are able to dig below the busy surface of their daily lives and refocus on their core values and principles. Once uncovered, those values and principles renew their sense of purpose at work and act as a springboard for shrewd, pragmatic, politically astute action. By repeating this process again and again throughout their work lives, these executives are able to craft an authentic and strong identity based on their own, rather than on someone else's understanding of what is right. And in this way, they begin to make the transition from being a manager to becoming a leader.

DEFINING MOMENTS FOR INDIVIDUALS

The most basic type of defining moment demands that managers resolve an urgent issue of personal identity that has serous implications for their careers. Two "rights" present themselves, each one representing a plausible and usually attractive life choice. When caught in this bind, managers can begin by taking a step back and looking at the conflict not as a problem but as a natural tension between two valid perspectives. To flesh out this tension, we can ask, *What feelings and intuitions are coming into conflict in this situation?* As Aristotle discussed in his classic work *Ethics*, people's feelings can actually help them make sense of an issue, understand its basic dimensions, and indicate what the stakes really are. In other words, our feelings and intuitions are both a form of intelligence and a source of insight.

By framing defining moments in terms of our feelings and intuitions, we can remove the conflict from its business context and bring it to a more personal, and manageable, level. Then we can consider a second question to help resolve the conflict: *Which of the responsibilities and values that are in conflict are most deeply rooted in my life and in the communities I care about?* Tracing the roots of our values means understanding their origins and evolution over time. It involves an effort to understand which values and commitments really mean the most to us.

We have all seen managers who unthinkingly throw themselves into a deeply felt personal cause and suffer serious personal and career setbacks. As the Renaissance philosopher Niccolò Machiavelli and other ethical pragmatists remind us, idealism untempered by realism often does little to improve the world. Hence the next critical question becomes, *What combination of shrewdness and expediency, coupled with imagination and boldness, will help me implement my personal understanding of what is right?* This is, of course, a different question altogether from What should I do? It acknowledges that the business world is a bottom-line, rough-and-tumble arena where introspection alone won't get the job done. The process of looking inward must culminate in concrete action characterized by tenacity, persuasiveness, shrewdness, and self-confidence.

DEFINING MOMENTS FOR WORK GROUPS

As managers move up in an organization, defining moments become more difficult to resolve. [M]anagers must add another dimension: the values of their work group and their responsibilities to the people they manage. How, for example, should a manager respond to an employee who repeatedly shows up for work with the smell of alcohol on his breath? How should a manager respond to one employee who has made sexually suggestive remarks to another? In this type of defining moment, the problem and its resolution unfold not only as a personal drama within one's self but also as a drama among a group of people who work together. The issue becomes public and is important enough to define a group's future and shape its values.

Many managers suffer from a kind of ethical myopia, believing that their entire group views a situation through the same lens that they do. This way of thinking rarely succeeds in bringing people together to accomplish common goals. Differences in upbringing, religion, ethnicity, and education make it difficult for any two people to view a situation similarly — let alone an entire group of people. The ethical challenge for a manager is not to impose his or her understanding of what is right on the group but to understand how other members view the dilemma. The manager must ask, *What are the other strong, persuasive interpretations of the ethics of this situation?*

Identifying competing interpretations, of course, is only part of the battle. Managers also need to take a hard look at the organization in which they work and make a realistic assessment of whose interpretation will win out in the end. A number of factors can determine which interpretation will prevail: corporate goals and company policy, and the inevitable political jockeying and battling inside organizations. Therefore, managers need to ask themselves, *What point of view is most likely to win the contest of interpretations and influence the thinking and behavior of other people?*

Planning ahead is at the heart of managerial work. One needs to learn to spot problems before they blow up into crises. The same is true for defining moments in groups. They should be seen as part of a larger process that, like any other, needs to be managed. Effective managers put into place the conditions for the successful resolution of defining moments long before those moments actually present themselves. For in the words of William James, "The truth of an idea is not a stagnant property inherent in it. Truth happens to an idea. It becomes true, is made true by events. Its verity is in fact an event, a process." Managers can start creating the conditions for a particular interpretation to prevail by asking, *Have I orchestrated a process that can make my interpretation win in my group?*

One of the hallmarks of a defining moment is that there is a lot at stake for all the players in the drama. In this type of business setting, neither the most well-meaning intentions nor the best-designed process will get the job done. Managers must be ready to roll up their sleeves and dive into the organizational fray, putting to use appropriate and effective tactics that will make their vision a reality. They need to reflect on the question, *Am I just playing along or am I playing to win?*

DEFINING MOMENTS FOR EXECUTIVES

[T]he men and women charged with running entire companies sometimes face an even more complex type of defining moment. They are asked to make manifest their understanding of what is right on a large stage — one that can include labor unions, the media, shareholders, and many other company stakeholders. Consider the complexity of the dilemma faced by a CEO who has just received a report of package tampering in one of the company's over-the-counter medications. Or consider the position of an executive who needs to formulate a response to reports in the media that women and children are being treated unfairly in the company's foreign plant. These types of decisions force top-level managers to commit not just themselves or their work groups but their entire company to an irreversible course of action.

From a position of strength, leaders can bring forth their vision of what is right in a situation; from a position of weakness, leaders' actions are hollow and desperate. Also, before CEOs can step forth onto society's broad stage with a personal vision, they must make sure that their actions will not jeopardize the well-being of their companies, the jobs of employees, and the net income of shareholders. That means asking, *Have I done all I can to secure my position and the strength and stability of my organization?*

What makes this third type of defining moment so difficult is that executives are asked to form, reveal, and test not only themselves and their work groups but also their entire company and its role in society. That requires forging a plan of action that functions at three levels: the individual, the work group, and society at large. In which areas do we want to lead? In which areas do we want to follow? How should we interact with the government? With shareholders? Leaders must ask themselves, *Have I thought creatively, boldly, and imaginatively about my organization's role in society and its relationship to its stakeholders?*

To make their ethical visions a reality, top-level executives must assess their opponents and allies very carefully. What allies do I have inside and outside my company? Which parties will resist or fight my efforts? Have I underestimated their power and tactical skill or overestimated their ethical commitment? Whom will I alienate with my decision? Which parties will retaliate and how? These tactical concerns can be summed up in the question, *What combination of shrewdness, creativity, and tenacity will make my vision a reality?* Machiavelli put it more succinctly: "Should I play the lion or the fox?"

Notes and Questions

1. Reality Check

a. What are the three settings in which Badaracco sets his discussion?

b. How are the ethical considerations different in each of the three settings? How are they the same?

2. Suppose

a. Suppose you and your client were presented with the opportunity to purchase the apartment house. Would Badaracco's ethical approach affect the process or result of your decision making?

3. What Do You Think?

a. Do you think the ethical norms Badaracco describes are rooted in the ordinary notion of ethics? If not, where are they rooted? If so, are there competing notions of ethics that Badaracco does not consider?

b. Do you agree with William James that, "The truth of an idea is not a stagnant property inherent in it. Truth happens to an idea. It becomes true, is made true by events. Its verity is in fact an event, a process"?

c. Is ethics the same as morals? If not, how are they different? If morals are different from ethics, is there a place for morality in economic decision making?

D. ACCOUNTING

Accounting is intellectually engaging because it requires both meticulous attention to detail and frequent exercise of judgment on theoretical matters. It can also be quite difficult. The practice of accountancy can be rewarding but also frustrating because the profession typically does not have the social standing, influence, and cachet of other professions. We are going to ignore everything that is difficult about accounting and focus on accounting in a functional way almost exclusively.

The point of accounting is to provide information about the financial performance of a firm (or individual) over a period of time. Every firm needs to know how it has performed and many firms have accountants as full-time employees to provide that information. Many others outside the business, such as investors, potential investors, taxing authorities, and other regulatory agencies, use the recent financial performance of a firm to make important judgments, such as deciding to invest in or loan money to the firm, determining how much tax is owed, and determining whether the public is sufficiently protected from the possibility of the firm's bankruptcy. Because of the importance of accurate financial statements, many accountants work in accounting firms that provide accounting services to other businesses. Because they are independent and because they have demonstrated the requisite degree of skill (i.e., they are certified public accountants), these outside accountants are important actors in the business world. Their certification of a firm's financial position is relied upon both by the firm itself and by other constituencies with which the firm deals.

Independent accountants review the accounting records of their clients and prepare standardized reports, *accounting statements*, based on that review. The accounting firm certifies that the accounting statements fairly represent the financial position of the client business as of the date of the statements. We will not concern ourselves with the methods of reviewing a business's accounting records. Those methods are contained in the *Generally Accepted Auditing Standards* (GAAS).[16] Nor will we concern ourselves with the rules that tell accountants how to present the results of an audit. These are contained in *Generally Accepted Accounting Practices* (GAAP). Our focus is on interpreting those accounting statements. That is, assuming that the accounting statements have been competently and honestly prepared,[17] what can they tell us about a firm that might aid us professionally?

Incidentally, many law students assume that being able to interpret accounting statements is a skill only big firm lawyers need. In fact, this skill is actually one that new lawyers in a large law firm probably don't need. This is because clients of a big law firm will have staff accountants and so won't be relying on the law firm to provide any interpretation of its accounting statements. Further, to the extent the client needs to discuss accounting matters with the law firm, the client is unlikely to consult junior

---

16. Yes, it's pronounced "gas."

17. As you will see in Chapter 14, negligently or fraudulently prepared accounting statements can induce actions that can cause large-scale financial harm. There are sometimes ways to identify such accounting statements, but you can't learn them easily so we won't even begin to discuss them here. You should be aware that some accountants, called *forensic accountants*, make a living investigating such accounting problems.

lawyers. So, new lawyers in big law firms probably do not need to understand accounting statements at the time they first enter practice.

Other lawyers, by contrast, will be called upon to interpret accounting statements with considerable frequency. Obviously, if you're a corporate lawyer, and not working in a big law firm, you will continually encounter financial statements. Clients and other lawyers in the firm will want you to interpret the statements to plan tax and investment strategies and to assess potential litigation. Even if you're not going to be a corporate lawyer, you'll need to know how to read financial statements. For example, in litigation involving a business, the financial statements can disclose much about past actions and about the business's likely ability to respond in damages. Estate-planning lawyers need to know how to interpret accounting statements so they can understand what their clients own. Lawyers engaged in family law frequently interpret financial statements to understand the financial position of a marital community.

Because we're looking at how accounting can tell us something about the economics of a firm, let's start by asking how one might describe the economic state of an economic entity—you, for example. You might describe your financial position in at least three different ways. These ways aren't meant to be mutually exclusive; after all they're describing the same underlying economic being. Rather, there are different ways of describing the economic state of an entity because the descriptions are useful for different purposes. Let's be more concrete.

One very palpable way to describe the financial you is to show someone around your home. You could point to *all the things you own* and point to papers representing the intangibles, such as a checking account or mutual fund. In fairness, of course, you'd have to point to all the things you *owe*, like a mortgage, car loan, and student loan. You'd also point to the pile of bills waiting to be paid for things like cable TV and utilities. If you were extra scrupulous, you'd point out that similar bills for other things haven't come in yet this month, and so aren't in the pile of bills you're pointing to, but will certainly arrive soon. This is certainly an accurate way to describe your financial state. But it isn't the only way.

Another, perhaps more common, way to describe your financial state is to look at your checking account. More precisely, look not only at the balance today, which is something you pointed to when you were showing everything you owned, but at the balance over time, say the last year. This information is in your *check register*. If you looked only at the balance to see how it moved up and down,[18] you could certainly draw some conclusions about how much cash you got and how much you spent over the last year. But you could get more information by looking at what the checks were written for. How much of what you spent went for ordinary living expenses like rent and utilities? How much went to pay obligations (both interest and principal) you incurred earlier, like the car payment and student loan payment? How much went for discretionary things like movies, TiVo, and trips to Vegas? Honestly, would your parents be proud?

Your expenses probably aren't all paid by checks. You doubtless withdraw cash from your checking account via an ATM to pay for many small things in cash. These withdrawals show up on your check register as simply a cash withdrawal. You might

18. Ok, mostly down.

also buy things by credit card, which is reflected in your check register by the monthly check to the credit card company.[19] If we want to know how you're spending your money, rather than simply how much you're spending, we'll keep track of what you buy for cash and look at those credit card purchases, as well as what you write checks for.

Just as we might care about what you spend your cash on, in addition to how much you spend, we might care about where you get your cash from in addition to how much you get. You may get cash from working. If you own a business, you may get cash as profit. You might get cash as a dividend from stock you own. If you're not economically independent, you get periodic cash from someone else such as parents, spouses, or other family members. You might get cash as a gift or as a lottery prize, an ad hoc windfall. You might also get cash by selling something you owned either because you no longer wanted the thing or because you were short on cash. Maybe you've borrowed cash from a bank or a credit card company (i.e., gotten a "cash advance" from the ATM).[20]

If you've borrowed something but that something isn't cash, we're not counting it because it doesn't show up as a deposit on your check register. So, the car loan that sends money right from the bank to the car dealer doesn't get reflected in this method of describing the financial you. We're concerned here simply with the dough-ray-mi.

This checkbook method of describing the financial position of you is probably one you use quite frequently, even though you may intuit the information it provides rather than explicitly examine your check register and credit card statements. Although it doesn't describe your financial state entirely, it has the virtue (vice?) of being pretty explicit. When you were showing people around your home, you could borrow a neighbor's Renoir for the evening or shove some bills in a drawer to make your position look better.[21] By contrast, although it's not impossible to falsify or obscure the cash you get and spend, it's harder and, moreover, it's easier to find out if you've been truthful simply by comparing your check register against the monthly bank and credit card statements to see whether your register is on the up and up.

There's yet one more typical way to describe the financial position of you, one you probably use once a year. You could figure out how much your wealth increased over the last year. In fact, you have to figure out your "income" every year because you have to pay tax on it. By this point in your life, you certainly know how this is done. If you've repressed the memory, just go online to *www.irs.gov* and look at **Form 1040**.

Think for a moment about how this description is different from the other two we've seen. It is unlike the things you own method because it isn't concerned with the value of what you have but with how much the value of what you have has changed.

---

19. If you pay interest on your credit card balance, though, that's a separate expense by itself.

20. We could, of course, analyze your position by percentages as well as absolute dollar amounts. That is, we could describe how you spent your cash, and where you got your cash, in terms of the percent spent on necessities versus the percent spent on discretionary things.

21. In effect, this is what Enron did. It undertook a significant amount of potential liability but was able to omit that debt on its own balance sheet because the debts were incurred by legally separate entities. Under GAAP, those entities' financial performance could not properly be combined, *consolidated*, with Enron's as long as Enron owned no more than 97 percent of the company and did not exert control. While Enron followed these rules for some of these separate entities, it did not do so for all of them. For a while the company simply lied on its financial statements with the complicity of its independent auditor, Arthur Andersen. When the facts came to light, Enron's trading partners refused to do business with the company and it quickly declared bankruptcy.

The "income" method also differs from the checkbook method in a couple of ways. Not all the cash you receive counts as "income." Gifts, for example, or loan proceeds you receive don't count as "income." On the other hand, many things that aren't cash do count in describing yourself by the "income" method. You might be entitled to the Education Credit, which is certainly not cash you received but certainly is a good thing and certainly figures into the calculation of your "income."

So what, more exactly, is this "income" method trying to describe? It's meant to tally some, but not all, wealth changes and to adjust that tally by rewarding you for some actions you took and penalizing you for others. For example, if you are furthering your education according to certain criteria, you're rewarded by being able to claim the Education Credit. If you give to charity, you're rewarded by being able to deduct that donated wealth from the increase in wealth you'd otherwise report. If the value of an investment (like stock) appreciates but you don't sell, you're rewarded by not having to include the increase in your wealth-change calculation. Because of the selective way in which this method calculates the change in your wealth, we're using the ironic quotation marks and calling it the "income" method.[22]

Each of these three ways of describing an economic entity has an analogous financial statement. Now that you have a sense of what these methods entail, let's go through each statement. As we do this, be aware that GAAP makes two principal changes from the way in which we've been thinking about economic description. First, when it measures "income," it typically records money moving in and out according to the date when the obligation to pay or be paid was made, not when the moola actually changed hands.[23]

Second, GAAP distinguishes between *operating* expenses and *capital* expenses. Most of the things you buy will be used up soon, say within the next year. These are operating expenses. But some things, like a new refrigerator, will last longer than that. These are capital expenses. To capture the notion that capital expenses buy things that will be used over several time periods, GAAP requires the buyer to spread out capital expenses over the life of the purchase. For example, the cost of the refrigerator would be spread out over the refrigerator's life, say ten years, with only one-tenth of the cost listed as an expense each year. This reflects a smaller decrease in wealth, and hence in "income," over those years than if the whole expense were lumped only in the first year. By contrast, all operating expenses are considered in calculating each year's "income."[24]

22. A separable aspect of this "income" method of description is that a tax (i.e., a percentage of your wealth change, as defined by the method) is levied on you. Both the selection of which wealth changes to count and the selection of which actions to reward and penalize reflect Congress's value judgments as to how individuals should be taxed. This taxation aspect explains why rewards for actions you took are reflected by a decrease in your wealth change so that you pay less in tax. Ultimately that reward leaves you with more wealth left over because the tax you paid is less than it would be without the reward.

23. This is because, in the normal course of commerce, there ought to be one date per transaction rather than two. So, the date one business agreed to sell something to another entity is the date that counts. If we looked to when money changed hands, we'd probably find that the buying party wrote a check on one day but the selling party didn't receive it for several days.

24. In effect, this is how WorldCom got in trouble. The company paid significant amounts each year to other telecommunications companies in exchange for the right to use those other companies' infrastructure. Under GAAP these expenses were operating expenses, which should have been listed in full on each year's income statement. Instead, WorldCom reported most of those expenses as capital expenses, which means that only a portion of those expenses was reported on each income statement. This had the effect of overstating the firm's operating profit and hence its net profit (ironically, it also increased WorldCom's income taxes). When the facts were made public WorldCom declared bankruptcy.

With this introduction let's (finally!) look at some financial statements. The things you own method is analogous to the ***balance sheet***. This statement divides things you own into assets and liabilities. It further divides both assets and liabilities into those that are liquid and those that are illiquid. It might well make a difference to someone considering loaning you money, for example, whether the things you own are cash or cashlike, and hence easily transferable to pay the debt, or whether they are not very liquid, possibly leaving you wealthy but strapped for cash. Within each of these categories, assets and liabilities are further grouped. On a business's balance sheet you'll see, for example, inventory — i.e., raw materials, partly finished goods, and goods ready for sale — as a separate entry.

GAAP requires that assets on a balance sheet be listed at their cost when they were acquired. This requirement is primarily a recognition that historic cost is a relatively certain number, while an asset's current fair value may be quite subjective. Be aware, then, that when you look at a business's balance sheet, the assets may be worth considerably more (or less) than the value listed. As we noted above, GAAP distinguishes between operating and capital expenses. The goods purchased with capital expenses are, by definition, long-lived. GAAP requires that a long-lived good's historic price on the balance sheet be reduced by a certain amount each year to reflect the fact that a portion of the good's value has been used up. This reduction is called *depreciation* and is broken out separately and subtracted from the cost of long-lived goods.

You'll also see entries for things that seem both unintuitive and frankly rather hair-splitting. Back to the balance sheet for you as a person for a moment. If you subscribe to a magazine, you probably paid the subscription price up front and will receive the magazine for some time in the future. GAAP says that the right to receive something in the future for which you've already paid is an "asset," so you'll see a line item labeled *prepaid expenses*. This concept seems odd for individuals but it may make quite a bit of sense for a business that may have paid for things like insurance or rent in advance. The right to enjoy those things without paying more is an asset. Likewise, suppose TiVo sends you a bill at the end of each month. It really isn't accurate to say that, on the 27th of the month, you have no liability to TiVo; really, you owe nearly all the month's charge. To reflect this impending liability, GAAP includes a line item labeled *accrued liabilities*. A second line item, embodying the same concept, is *accrued income taxes*.

You could, of course, subtract the value of all the things you owe from the value of all the things you own. The resulting number, your net worth, wouldn't be terribly significant in the normal course of things. For example, you might have a high net worth, but if your wealth is not very liquid you might have trouble even getting enough cash from the ATM to buy lattes for the next week.

In the business setting, a firm's net worth goes by a variety of other names such as *partners'* or *shareholders' equity*. Because a business is often owned by several people, GAAP requires that a firm's net worth be described in more detail to show what kind of ownership interests there are. Part of the line item shows how the ownership is divided, for example, the number of shares outstanding is listed. Shareholders' equity also shows how much money was originally paid into the firm by stockholders and how much is earnings from the firm's business (*retained earnings*). Below is an example of the way a business's balance sheet might be presented.

Assets	Liabilities and Shareholders' Equity
Current Assets:	*Current Liabilities:*
Cash and cash equivalents	Accounts payable
Receivables	Accrued liabilities
Inventories	Accrued income taxes
Prepaid expenses	Long-term debt due within
Total Current Assets	one year
	Total Current Liabilities
Property, Plant and Equipment, at Cost:	
Land	Long-term debt
Buildings and	Deferred income taxes and other
improvements	
Fixtures and equipment	*Shareholders' Equity:*
Transportation equipment	Common stock
Less accumulated	(100,000 shares
depreciation	outstanding)
Property, plant and	Retained earnings
equipment, net	**Total Shareholders' Equity**
Other Assets and Deferred Charges:	
Goodwill	**Total Liabilities and Shareholders'**
Other assets and deferred	**Equity**
charges	
Total Assets	

The financial statement analogous to the checkbook register is the ***statement of cash flows***. If we were to analyze your checkbook register we might want to triage by source the cash you received. For example, if $100,000 were deposited in your checking account it might make a big difference whether the source of that cash was:

Wages from your day job, suggesting you're well paid

The sale of your My Little Pony collection, suggesting either that you're changing one form of wealth into a more useful one or that you're so desperate for cash that you're selling important, possibly vital, things

A loan from a bank, suggesting that you need a lot more cash than you have, which might be good, if you have a great idea, or bad if you've simply spent more than you can afford.

Judging a business requires making the same sort of distinctions. GAAP divides all business cash flows into three kinds. First is *cash flow from operations*, a business's "day job." As a convention to tie the financial statements to one another, the cash flow from operations begins with the net "income" figure. It's as though the first entry in your check register were the "taxable income" figure from your tax return. Because that number does not represent cash, the next entries in the statement of cash flows undo all the noncash adjustments to "income." For example, the deduction for depreciation isn't a real expenditure of cash, so depreciation is added back. After these adjustments are made we can see the net cash; that is, the sum of all the checking-account deposits and withdrawals from the business's operations.

The second category of cash flows is, somewhat misleadingly, called *cash flows from investing activities*. Investing in this sense means buying new land and equipment and selling off old equipment. The personal analogue would be a category in which you listed purchases of long-term assets like a refrigerator or car and sales of the old ones. This number is nearly always negative, because businesses usually spend more cash buying new equipment than they receive selling off the old equipment. The third category of cash flows is *cash from financing activities*. The personal analogue would be cash from loans you obtained and principal and interest you repaid. Businesses also undertake these activities but, in addition, they might sell or repurchase shares of their own stock. Cash from those activities is reflected in this category as well.

At the end of the statement of cash flows is both a net number (i.e., all cash received minus all cash spent) and a comparison of the year-end cash on hand to the cash on hand one year ago (i.e., your bank balance on December 31st compared to your bank balance a year ago). A typical statement of cash flows looks like this:

Cash flows from operations
  Income from continuing operations
  Adjustments to reconcile net income to net cash provided by operating
      activities:
          Depreciation and amortization
          Decrease/(increase) in accounts receivable
          Increase in inventories
          Increase in accounts payable
          Increase in accrued liabilities
          Deferred income taxes
Net cash provided by operating activities

Cash flows from investing activities
          Payments for property, plant, and equipment
          Proceeds from the disposal of fixed assets
Net cash used in investing activities

Cash flows from financing activities
          Increase/(decrease) in commercial paper
          Proceeds from issuance of long-term debt
          Purchase of Company stock
          Dividends paid
          Payment of long-term debt
Net cash used in financing activities

Net increase in cash and cash equivalents

Cash and cash equivalents at beginning of year
Cash and cash equivalents at end of year

The final financial statement is the ***statement of income***. Just like a Form 1040 the statement begins with *revenues*—money the business received. The line item *net sales* or *net revenues* is probably a bit deceptive because it does not mean sales revenues minus costs. Rather, it means sales that are net of returned goods; it means sales that are final. It also means sales net of the depreciation charge that GAAP says must be allocated to the current period. Then, all of the business's *costs* during the period are listed. GAAP requires the business to separate costs that are directly attributable to the goods produced (costs of sales) from indirect costs, often called *overhead* (operating, selling, general and administrative expenses). GAAP also requires that a business set out separately expenses that are not intended to yield immediate economic benefit but that are intended to yield profit in the future. These expenses are known as *research and development* (R&D). The costs are subtracted from revenues to yield *operating profit*. This is the business's core profit.

Many businesses earn money from activities other than their core businesses. If these revenues or losses are substantial, GAAP requires that they be separately stated below the company's operating profit. The rubric is *other revenues and expenses*. The firm's operating profit is added to these other profits and the sum is *income before income taxes*.

Income taxes are both important in themselves and analytically separate from the actual business costs, so GAAP requires them to be set out separately after the company's profit is computed. Another reason to set out income taxes separately is that,

Operating Revenues:
    Net sales

Operating Costs and Expenses:
    Cost of sales
    Operating, selling, general and administrative expenses
    Research and development

Operating Profit

Other Revenues and Expenses:
    Interest:
          Paid
          Received
    Investments, net

Income Before Income Taxes

Provision for Income Taxes

Net Income

given the vagaries of the tax code, a firm's income taxes are often only loosely related to its actual performance. Finally, taxes are subtracted to yield *net income*. Here is a typical layout for a business's statement of income:

If you are somewhat keen eyed you will have noticed that the examples of financial statements above have no dollar amounts connected with them. The reason for this is that if you can understand the ideas behind the statements and the categories within each statement, then the numbers on any particular set of financial statements are simply detail. Nonetheless, you will probably want to look at the real financial statements for a real business. Those are easy to come by. Every public corporation has to file financial statements with the SEC and these are online at *www.sec.gov* under the link for EDGAR, the SEC's database.

How can you use financial statements to help advise your client? Well, there are three paradigm settings for corporate lawyers. First, your client might be contemplating extending unsecured credit to another firm. If your client will be exposed to a small amount of credit risk, it may well not be worthwhile to analyze the borrower's financial statements. That's the situation where, for example, a cable company is contemplating installing a cable outlet in a small business such as a bar. The total amount of money the cable company could lose in such a transaction is relatively small.[25]

But suppose your client is a seafood supplier and is contemplating extending credit to a restaurant. Then it may well be worthwhile for your client to obtain and analyze the restaurant's financial statements. What can those statements tell you and your client about the restaurant? The statements can suggest to you whether the restaurant will be able to pay the estimated monthly bill. They won't tell you whether

---

25. E.g., a month or so of unpaid cable charges — until the company cuts off the cable — and possibly some or all of the installation charges.

the restaurant mangers will be motivated to do so, nor will they show whether the restaurant has a good or a bad track record of paying its bills.[26] But in terms of simple ability to pay, the statements will help.

The question to ask is, "if this debtor were motivated to pay my client's bill every month, would it be able to find the money to do so?" Because this kind of debt is recurring, we probably wouldn't expect the restaurant to sell off assets to pay the bill. So, the balance sheet's listing of assets is of little value to us, although the "current assets" might give some clue of how liquid the restaurant's finances are. Because our client is looking to get a check every month, the statement to focus on is the statement of cash flows. We might look at the monthly statements going back a couple of years or so to see whether the restaurant's operations are generating sufficient cash that the restaurant will be able to pay your client's bill, too. If your client is replacing a prior seafood supplier, you'll need to adjust the statement of cash flow to subtract cash paid to the old supplier.

Suppose your client is contemplating lending a large amount of money to another firm with repayment stretched out over ten years. Say your client is a prosperous local businessperson who has been approached about a loan to a business located on the same block. You would want to know the same information as you did before, whether the borrower is likely to be able and willing to make timely repayment, so a similar examination of the borrower's statement of cash flow would be helpful. But, because this loan is large and for a long term, your client will want to know whether the business has assets that can secure the loan. Now the balance sheet will disclose the amount of other long-term debt (at least as of the balance sheet date) and the statement of cash flows will show how much cash the borrower pays in interest on other loans. Also, because this is serious money, our client might indeed expect the borrower to sell off at least some assets if it were having difficulty paying this loan. So, the balance sheet will disclose something about the assets that might be sold if necessary.

Let's return one more time to the possible purchase of the apartment house. What information relevant to the purchase of the apartment house can the financial statements provide? The balance sheet will show, for example, whether the land is owned by someone else. Other assets, such as lobby furniture or tools, will also show up on the balance sheet. The balance sheet will also, of course, show whether the apartment house is mortgaged or otherwise obligated to pay money over time. The apartment house may, for instance, have a contract with a maintenance company and any accrued obligation will show up on the balance sheet.

The statement of cash flows will show not only whether the apartment house is generating more cash than it consumes but whether that cash comes from rent or other sources such as loans. The income statement will show whether the apartment house is profitable, at least in an accounting sense.

To tie the chapter together, you and your client should list the various kinds of risk to which the apartment house may be subject and compare them to the financial statements to see whether, for example, the counterparty to a transaction has defaulted. The financial statements will also show, if you look at past years, whether

---

26. There are other ways to assess these risks. A credit report or check of court filings can reveal whether the restaurant has been in trouble in the past with prior creditors. Also, an analysis of the local business environment for restaurants will help assess the restaurant's motivation to pay. If there are many seafood suppliers and if seafood represents a small proportion of the restaurant's food, then the restaurant may be less attentive to your client's bills. On the other hand, if there are few seafood suppliers and if the restaurant specializes in seafood, then paying your client's monthly bills might be of critical importance to the restaurant.

the apartment building's economics have been relatively stable or relatively volatile. As you'll remember, the more volatile the results, the more likely it is that any particular year's results will be far from the expected return. This possibility may or may not be significant for your client.

Next, the financial statements can be used to see how much cash the apartment building has generated over time. This data can then be used to project the likely future cash flows. Obviously this is central to a DCF analysis and determining a net present value. The net present value, in turn, leads to you and your client formulating a purchase price offer.

Finally, the financial statements can be used to focus the decision-making process. Rational self-interest and the other considerations in decision making will come into play here. In the end, the financial statements are quite useful tools. They really are not mysterious but are functional instead. Once you understand their function, actual financial statements with real numbers shouldn't disturb you.

Notes and Questions

1. Reality Check

a. How can we measure an economic entity's past financial performance?
b. Why would we want to do so?
c. What are the three kinds of financial statements and what does each disclose?

2. Suppose

a. Suppose you and your client were considering purchasing the apartment house. How would the apartment house's financial statements affect the decision whether to purchase?

E. TERMS OF ART IN THIS CHAPTER

Accounting statements	Diversification	Regulatory risk
Adjustment and anchoring	Expected return	Representativeness
Availability	Foreign investment risk	Risk
Balance sheet	GAAP	Salvage value
Break-up value	Going concern value	Scrap value
Call option	Heuristics	Statement of cash flows
Capital expenses	Inflation risk	Statement of income
Coping	Liquidity	Synergy value
Counterparty risk	Net cash flow	Terminal price
Currency risk	Net present value	Time value of money
DCF	Operating expenses	Utility
Default	Options	Value
Discount rate	Price	
Discounted cash flow	Put option	
Discounting to present	Rational self-interest	
value	Real options	

Part II.

AGENCY

4 *Agency*

A. BACKGROUND AND CONTEXT

1. The Economic Concept of "Agency" and the Problem of Agency Costs

Economists usually define an agency relationship as one in which an agent and principal agree that the agent will use some degree of judgment to perform a service for the principal's benefit. This relationship is often reciprocal, such as when two people undertake a project as a team. In that setting, each team member is both a principal and an agent. As we will see, this definition of *agency* is broader than the legal definition. The idea of agency and the economic problems that agency relationships generate have spawned a rich literature in economics. In the taxonomy of economics, agency is a concern of microeconomics and is a particular form of the problems raised by information asymmetries between parties. Reduced to the core, the problem is predicting the future: the principal wants to ensure that the agent will perform well. Although neither the principal nor the agent can predict the future with perfect accuracy, the agent tends to know much more than the principal about two central matters: whether the agent is *capable* of performing well (i.e., has the necessary skills) and whether the agent is *motivated* to perform well.

Before the agency agreement is made, potential principals are looking for suitable agents, and potential agents are looking for suitable principals. Almost certainly one or more of these potential parties are objectively less suitable than others. Principals may mistakenly choose agents (and agents may mistakenly choose principals) who are less than optimal. This is called the problem of *adverse selection* and is said by economists to be a problem *ex ante*. As you may intuit, the problem is one of information; potential principals and potential agents can never be entirely sure that they are entering into an agency relationship with the most suitable person. Although the problem of adverse selection is an important economic one, it is not one that concerns the law of agency, because no agency relationship exists until the parties agree.

Principals and agents may use *signaling* to help convince others that they will perform well. Both principals and agents may provide references from others with whom they have worked. They may also provide evidence from third parties such as degrees from universities or law schools that attest to the skills and training they possess. The parties may locate one another through a clearinghouse that acts as a signal to each side. For example, parents (principals) may use a nanny agency (a clearinghouse) to locate an appropriate nanny (agent). The reputation of the nanny agency may be a signal to each side that both the nanny and the parents have been screened and found suitable for one another. Finally, of course, noneconomic qualities may play an important role. A person's general reputation (apart from specific references) may suggest that he or she will act appropriately. As well, the parties may frequently look for evidence of another's general sense of ethics when deciding whether to form an agency relationship.

After the agency agreement is made (*ex post*) the parties face the problem of *moral hazard*, a concept you may remember from your contracts course. In general, a moral hazard is the risk that a party with discretion to act will choose an action that decreases the expected value of the transaction to the other party in a way that the other party cannot effectively prohibit. On occasion, human nature being what it is, agents and principals may take exactly such actions out of malevolence toward the other party, or even out of an initial intent to deceive the other party, but economics treats these settings as aberrational. Economically, every agency relationship contains the seeds of moral hazard because the goals of the principal and agent are always different. The principal wants the task performed at the lowest cost; the agent wants the highest remuneration with the least effort. It is important to understand that this tension runs through every agency relationship and can never be completely eliminated.

From the agent's point of view, the main moral hazard is sometimes known as *ratcheting*. Although some tasks that are to be performed by an agent are well defined and self-contained, most are at least somewhat open-ended. This is especially the case where the task is really a continuing series of tasks, as in the case of employment. The danger for the agent is that the principal will increase the task without increasing the agent's recompense. The agent, of course, always has the ability to quit, but may as a practical matter be unable to do so. The agent who agrees to be the principal's secretary may be subject to ratcheting. It is not unusual in such settings for principals to add such tasks as serving as the office receptionist during the lunch hour or performing administrative duties like ordering office supplies without any additional reward. Even where the agency agreement includes (as it often does) "other duties as assigned," the addition of such tasks as a routine part of the agent's job is ratcheting. Measured strictly from the principal's economic best interest, principals have an incentive to ratchet because they get the desired task performed at a lower cost.

Principals face two forms of moral hazards from agents. First is *shirking*, in which the agent chooses to perform less well than the parties anticipated. Shirking may take the form of using suboptimal skill (a shoddy repair job, for example) or using optimal skills on fewer than optimal projects (such as an assembly-line worker who makes each item skillfully, but who makes fewer items per shift than he or she could). Ratcheting and shirking can sometimes be two sides of the same coin. Where a homeowner (principal) and housepainter (agent) disagree about the quality of the job done by the housepainter, is the homeowner trying to ratchet or is the housepainter trying to shirk?

The second moral hazard that principals face is the risk that the agent will use his or her discretion opportunistically to obtain *private benefits* for which the agent will bear only part (or even none) of the cost. Imagine that Mary owns a business in which she is the only worker and that has revenues in excess of costs of $100,000 per year.[1] If the business requires her to travel by air, Mary can choose to travel in first class rather than coach. If she chooses to travel first class, the additional cost (say $10,000 per year) is simply a reduction in her overall remuneration (i.e., the business would have revenues in excess of costs of only $90,000).

Now assume that Mary owns just 50 percent of the business, and that Michael, who does not work in the business, owns the other 50 percent. Mary is now the agent for Michael. They agree that Mary should receive a fair market wage (say $50,000) for her work in the business and that Mary and Michael should split equally any profits. If Mary flies in coach, she will receive $50,000 in salary and she and Michael will each receive $25,000 in profit.

But Mary now has an economic incentive to choose to fly first class. She will receive the same fair salary ($50,000) but the first-class air travel that cost her $10,000 when she was the sole owner would now cost her only $5,000. The business will have $90,000 of revenues in excess of its costs (before paying Mary). Mary will receive $50,000 in salary and she and Michael will each receive only $20,000 in profit. This situation gives Mary private benefits of $5,000. That is, she gets $80,000 in economic benefit ($70,000 in money and $10,000 in first-class air travel), which is $5,000 more than she would get if she did not choose to fly first class. Michael receives $20,000 in benefit, which is $5,000 less than he would if Mary flew coach. Michael is thus a victim of Mary's opportunistic behavior. The economic incentive to obtain private benefits is exacerbated if Michael owns the entire business and Mary is simply an employee at $50,000 per year. In that setting, her choice to fly first class rather than coach is costless to her (i.e., she has $10,000 in private benefits); Michael bears the full $10,000 cost.

Note that private benefits can take nonmonetary forms, as well. In the business setting, managers may make decisions that result in private benefits that may make their job more secure. This will happen when the manager has specialized skills and has the discretion to choose between a project in which such skills are essential and one in which they are not. Obviously the manager has an incentive to choose the project in which his or her skills are absolutely necessary in order to obtain an increased measure of job security. Another private benefit that is not explicitly monetary is the manager who uses discretion to increase the size of the business unit he or she manages. This form of empire building may satisfy the manager's professional ego and may also have the economic consequence of making the manager more highly sought after by other firms or becoming entitled to a higher salary within his or her current firm.

In addition to the moral hazard, there usually exists another economic impetus for agents to choose actions that are not in their principal's best economic interest. An agent who chooses an alternative that turns out well does not receive the gain from that choice but simply receives the agreed-upon remuneration. Even if the principal and agent share the gains, the agent never receives the entire gain from the venture's success. On the other hand, an agent who chooses an alternative that turns out extraordinarily badly does not share in that loss but also may find that the principal is now unable to pay the agreed-upon remuneration. This disparity in consequence tends to make agents more *risk averse* than their principals and hence more likely to

---

1. It does not matter (ignoring tax consequences) whether Mary calls the $100,000 "profit" or "salary" or some combination of both.

take different actions than their principals would like them to take. This tendency is frequently compounded by the fact that riskier actions are often harder to undertake successfully than less risky ones. Thus agents who make less risky choices also typically need to expend less effort to be successful, which increases the ratio of reward-to-effort and makes the agency more profitable for the agent.

These risks to both the principal and the agent make an agency relationship more costly than if the principal undertook to perform the task alone. There are techniques that can ameliorate, but never entirely eliminate, these costs. The parties can agree that the agent's compensation will depend in whole or in part on the degree to which the agent acts in the principal's best interest. Profit sharing or *incentive compensation* plans are common examples. These plans obviously reduce the principal's gain from the transaction because they must be shared with the agent. Another technique is for the principal to *monitor* the agent. Monitoring activities can take many forms, such as simply watching the agent work or measuring the agent's efforts where they are amenable to quantification. Other monitoring techniques include contractual limitations on the agent's discretion such as budget or other operational limitations.

Agents may also expend resources to assure principals they will not shirk or behave opportunistically. This assurance may come in the form of *bonding* actions such as obtaining an insurance policy or agreeing to a financial penalty clause in the agency agreement. Principals, too, may take bonding actions to assure agents that they will not ratchet, but most bonding is done by agents.

Basic economics rules suggest that principals and agents will undertake monitoring and bonding activities and agree on incentive compensation arrangements to reduce the costs of the agency relationship only up to the point at which the cost of further amelioration equals the likely loss from moral hazards. Economists use the term *agency costs* to mean the total of the expenditures made in ameliorating the moral hazard plus the residual loss resulting from moral hazard and risk differences between agent and principal.

2. Where Do Agency Questions Arise?

Questions of agency arise in a wide range of commercial settings. In its starkest, most salient, setting an agency relationship exists between the sole shareholder of a corporation and the corporation's sole employee. In the example of Mary and Michael, Michael was a principal because he co-owned the business. Mary was both a principal and an agent, a not infrequent occurrence. Employees with supervisory powers are both agents (of the managers to whom they report) and principals (to the employees who report to them). In a general partnership (or, more generally, in any economic endeavor in which multiple actors are required and in which the results are not easily attributable to the efforts of particular actors — called a *team production* model) each partner is both an owner and an agent.

Looking at the business entity itself as a unit, agency relationships exist between the entity and its suppliers and the entity and its customers. In the entity-supplier setting, the entity is more like the principal because the supplier usually has more power to act opportunistically; the entity primarily pays money, making it more like the principal. The reverse characterizes the entity-customer relationship because the customer mostly pays money, while the entity provides the good or service.

The dealings between an entity and its lenders present particularly sharp agency problems. Ex ante, lenders (principals) face a distinct adverse selection problem. Once the principal lends money, the agent (entity) has several typical incentives to act in a way that conflicts with the lender's best interest. Most pervasively, the entity, which is required to be managed in the best economic interest of its equity owners, has an incentive to undertake riskier projects than it would if the entity were financed strictly with equity. This is so because any gain from the project is allocated entirely to the equity, while the loss is shared between the lender and equity owners. As the entity approaches insolvency that incentive increases. Businesses on the verge of bankruptcy have a great incentive to undertake hugely risky projects, because the success of such projects is often seen as the only realistic way to remain viable, while the failure of such projects does not place the entity in any worse position than it already is in.

A final word about a paradigmatic relationship: that between a corporation and its board of directors. To the extent that directors are also managers, they fit into the principal-agent matrix we have seen; they are people given discretion to act in another's best interest and so agency problems and agency costs exist. The question arises whether the board is an agent of the corporation or its shareholders under legal concepts, such as those embodied in the *Restatement (Third) of Agency*. As we will see, the consequences of labeling someone an "agent" are considerable. The definition of a legal agent is someone who has agreed to act on someone else's behalf and subject to that person's control (*Restatement (Third) of Agency*, §1.01). Note that this is narrower than the economic definition, which simply requires only that the agent have discretion to act in the principal's interest. Because all corporate power is vested in the board of directors (under corporation law), the board is not subject to the corporation's control. Thus it does not meet the legal definition of agent and is not generally held to be subject to the rights and obligations of agents under common law. Individual directors are also not generally considered to be legal agents for an additional reason. Under corporate law, the board's power is collective, such that no individual director has the power to act alone and therefore is not an agent. See *Restatement (Third) of Agency*, §1.01 cmt. f(2).

The common law of agency predates the economic definition and understanding of agency problems. One consequence is that the law of agency has not been influenced to any great extent by economic thought. Further, much of the law of agency has been informed by fiduciary notions, which are antithetical to the classic economic assumption that people act in their own economic best interest. As you read about agency relationships in the rest of this chapter, ask yourself how each agency relation would be analyzed by an economist, whether a tension exists between the economic and legal understanding of agency in a particular setting, and what the appropriate resolution of such a tension should be as a matter of social policy.

Notes and Questions

1. Note

a. This description of the economic analysis of agency relationships is based on traditional notions of economically rational behavior. See Chapter 3 for the suggestion that economic rationality need not be assumed.

2. What Do You Think?

a. Should the social value of agency law be measured by whether it reflects economists' understanding of agency relationships? What if economic thinking about agency changes radically?

B. THE CURRENT SETTING

1. Definition of the Agency Relationship

Agency rules are among the most important sets of rules that concern business entities. This importance stems from the simple fact that corporations, partnerships, and LLCs cannot take actions except through humans who act for them. The common law has long had rules, most of which can be varied by agreement, covering the settings in which one person or entity, the *agent,* acts on behalf of another, the *principal.* These rules became relatively standard across the country. Although a few states such as California enacted these rules in statutes, agency law is, in most states, common law. The American Law Institute adopted a *Restatement (Third) of Agency* (hereinafter the *Restatement (Third)*)) in 2006.

One quality of agency law is worth emphasizing at the beginning. Because agency relationships are formed consensually but not necessarily contractually, they arise in a wide variety of settings. The person who, as a favor, agrees to drive a friend to the airport may be an agent. Further, because a valid contract is not necessary to create an agency relationship, children can sometimes be principals or agents. The focus of this casebook is on business entities rather than on agency relationships generally. For that reason, the remainder of this chapter will deal primarily with agency relationships in which the principal or agent is a business entity.

The *Restatement (Third)* defines an agency relationship:

§1.01 Agency Defined
  Agency is the fiduciary relationship that arises when one person (a "principal") manifests assent to another person (an "agent") that the agent shall act on the principal's behalf and subject to the principal's control, and the agent manifests assent or otherwise consents so to act.

The definition does not require that the parties intend to form an agency relationship and courts will find that an agency relationship exists even though the parties specifically disclaim any intention to create such a relationship as long as the parties meet the definition in *Restatement (Third)* §1.02. The agent is a fiduciary as to the principal, which means that the agent has higher duties than the implied duties of good faith and fair dealing ordinarily found in a contractual setting. See *Restatement (Third)* §8.01.

Employees of a business entity are agents, but the entity may have agents who are not employees such as accountants who are retained to audit the entity. Corporate officers such as the president or assistant secretary are agents (and probably employees). Directors of a corporation are not agents, partly because they cannot act alone but can only act as a board and partly because the directors govern the corporation and thus are not subject to the corporation's control. By analogy, it is unlikely that managers of a manager-managed LLC would be found to be agents. In both the director and the manager setting, though, the business entity could enter into an agency relationship with a director or manager who would then be an agent *in addition to* being a director or manager.

General partners in a general or limited partnership are agents even though, like corporate directors, they must act as a body and are not subject to the partnership's control. This result is determined by partnership law rather than agency rules. See Uniform Partnership Act §301 and Uniform Limited Partnership Act §403.

2. Creation of the Agency Relationship

≡≡≡ **Basile v. H & R Block, Inc.**
≡≡≡ 761 A.2d 1115 (Pa. 2000)

CASTILLE, J.

H & R Block, Inc., provides tax preparation services nationwide through a network of retail offices. . . . As part of its service, Block offers a program known as "Rapid Refund," which involves electronic filing of tax returns with the Internal Revenue Service (IRS), resulting in quicker refunds than a taxpayer filing a paper return would receive. Block also arranged for Mellon Bank . . . to provide a refund anticipation loan (RAL) program to Block's qualified Rapid Refund customers. Under the RAL program, Mellon Bank advanced to the customer the amount of the customer's anticipated tax refund, less a financing charge, within days of Block's filing of the return. Appellee Sandra Basile applied for, and received, such a loan in 1993.

Basile and Laura Clavin filed this class action against Block and Mellon Bank . . . alleging that Mellon Bank . . . participated with Block in practices designed to deceive consumers as to the true nature of the loans. The trial judge . . . granted Block's motion for summary judgment finding that Block was not appellees' agent. . . .

The parties do not dispute the facts material to the issue of whether an agency relationship existed. In 1990, Block began offering its Rapid Refund program whereby its taxpayer customers could receive speedier refunds using one of three services: (1) electronic filing of the tax return for a fee; (2) electronic filing for a fee with direct deposit of the taxpayer's refund by the IRS to the taxpayer's bank account; or (3) electronic filing for a fee with a RAL arranged by Block with a lender such as Mellon Bank. The third option involving the RALs is the service at issue.

Block offered its RAL program through Mellon Bank to Block's Pennsylvania customers. Between 1990 and 1993, more than 600,000 Pennsylvania residents participated in the RAL program. Specifically, Block customers who filed their returns electronically and met the lender's eligibility requirements were informed of the availability of loans in the amount of their anticipated refunds from Mellon Bank. If the customer was interested in the loan, Block would simultaneously transmit the taxpayer's income tax return information to the IRS and Mellon Bank. Within a few days of the transmittal, the taxpayer, if approved, would receive a check in the amount of the loan minus a bank transaction fee. The taxpayer could also elect to have Block's tax preparation and electronic filing fees withheld by the lender from the RAL check so that the taxpayer would not have to advance any money. When the taxpayer's actual tax refund was ready, usually within a matter of weeks, the IRS would deposit the refund check into an account with Mellon Bank to repay the loan. In exchange for the

RAL, the taxpayer paid to Mellon Bank a flat rate finance charge of $29.00 or $35.00, which Block employees presented to the taxpayer as a flat dollar amount rather than as a percentage interest rate on the short term loan.[8] Since the RAL is secured by the tax refund, and the tax refund is paid directly into a proprietary account at Mellon Bank, the lender bank takes on few risks with the program. Block did not disclose to its RAL customers that it received a payment from Mellon Bank for each loan, shared in the profits of the RALs in other ways, or that the taxpayer's endorsement on the back of the loan proceeds check constituted a signature on a loan agreement printed on the reverse of the check.

The law is clear in Pennsylvania that the three basic elements of agency are: "'the manifestation by the principal that the agent shall act for him, the agent's acceptance of the undertaking and the understanding of the parties that the principal is to be in control of the undertaking.'" *Scott v. Purcell*, 415 A.2d 56, 60 (Pa. 1980).... "[A]gency results only if there is an agreement for the creation of a fiduciary relationship with control by the beneficiary." *Smalich v. Westfall*, 269 A.2d 476, 480 (Pa. 1971). The burden of establishing an agency relationship rests with the party asserting the relationship. "An agency relationship is a fiduciary one, and the agent is subject to a duty of loyalty to act only for the principal's benefit." *Sutliff v. Sutliff*, 528 A.2d 1318, 1323 (1987). Thus, in all matters affecting the subject of the agency, the agent must act with the utmost good faith in furthering and advancing the principal's interests, including a duty to disclose to the principal all relevant information.

The pleadings here do not establish an agency relationship. With specific respect to the RALs, there is no showing that appellees intended Block to act on their behalf in securing the RALs. To the contrary, Block offered appellees the opportunity to file their tax returns electronically with the *three* options set forth above, only one of which involved RALs. Appellees were not required to apply for an RAL in order to have their returns prepared by Block or filed electronically through Block. It was appellees alone who decided to take advantage of that particular option. Block was neither authorized to, nor did it in fact, act on its customers' behalf in this regard. If a customer elected to apply for an RAL, Block simply facilitated the loan process by presenting appellees to Mellon Bank as viable loan candidates. Block neither applied for the loan on behalf of appellees nor determined that appellees should apply; appellees undertook that procedure themselves. The RAL program was merely another distinct and separate service offered by Block to its customers. Furthermore, it was a distinct service that Block's customers were fully aware came at a higher price, just as one would expect for an advance of money. Simply introducing appellees to a lender willing to provide a loan is not sufficient to create an agency relationship. Therefore, we hold that, as a matter of law, Block was not acting as appellees' agent in the RAL transactions, such that they were subject to a heightened, fiduciary duty.

We are aware that here Block could be said to have played an "integral part" in arranging the RALs. In our view, however, "integral" or not, Block's mere facilitation of its customers' desire to pursue the loans, as one of the multiple services offered by Block, is not sufficient to establish an agency relationship under Pennsylvania law. The special relationship arising from an agency agreement, with its concomitant heightened duty, cannot arise from any and all actions, no matter how trivial, arguably

8. Due to the short-term nature of these loans (approximately two weeks), the finance charges translate to interest rates as high as 151 percent, depending on the amount of the loan. Appellee Basile's actual interest rate was 77.3 percent.

undertaken on another's behalf. Rather, the action must be a matter of consequence or trust, such as the ability to actually **bind** the principal or alter the principal's legal relations. Indeed, implicit in the long-standing Pennsylvania requirement that the principal manifest an intention that the agent act on the principal's behalf is the notion that the agent has authority to alter the principal's relationships with third parties, such as binding the principal to a contract.

Such power decidedly did not exist here with regard to facilitating the RALs, nor even to preparing and filing the tax returns. Block had no more authority to alter the legal relationship between its customers and the IRS than it had to bind those customers to a loan agreement with Mellon Bank. Block could not file a tax return without the customer's authorization and signature, nor could Block obligate the customer to pay any amount of income tax to the IRS without authorization and consent in the form of the customer's signature on the return. Therefore, no agency relationship existed between Block and its customers.

Our conclusion that there is no agency relationship here carries no judgment regarding Block's business practices. If Block's method of doing business is worthy of the condemnation that appellees suggest, presumably the marketplace will react to correct it. It is not our place to imbue the relationship between Block and appellees with heightened legal qualities that the parties did not agree upon.

NIGRO, J., dissenting:

I respectfully dissent, as I believe that an agency relationship existed between H & R Block and Appellees. [D]irect evidence of specific authority is unnecessary. Rather, the relationship can be inferred from the circumstances of the case by looking at factors such as the relation of the parties and their conduct.

I believe that Appellees met their burden of establishing that an agency relationship existed. Here, the Superior Court found that Appellees "established that they visited the Block offices in response to media promotions of the Rapid Refund Program to engage Block to achieve two results: (1) to complete and file their tax returns, and (2) to obtain a refund of any overpayment of taxes they had made to the Internal Revenue Service ["IRS"]." Appellees remained at the office while H & R Block employees completed the tax forms. After completion, the H & R Block employees requested that Appellees sign the tax returns before H & R Block sent the returns to the IRS and the state Department of Revenue. These facts indicate that: (1) Appellees manifested that H & R Block, through its employees, compute their taxes and complete and send their tax forms, thereby "rendering service but retaining control of the manner of doing it"; (2) H & R Block, through its employees, accepted the undertaking of completing and sending Appellees' tax forms; and (3) Appellees remained in control, that is, they had to sign their own forms and the H & R Block employees completed the forms pursuant to information given to them by Appellees. For these reasons, I believe that an agency relationship existed between Appellees and H & R Block with respect to the computation of their taxes and the completion and submission of their tax returns to the taxing authority. What remains is to determine whether agency extended to the Rapid Refund portion of the transaction. I believe it does.

H & R Block essentially contends that its relationship with the taxpayer is concluded once the tax return is filed, and that once the tax preparer offers her the application for the Rapid Refund, the taxpayer's relationship is a creditor/debtor one with Mellon Bank. I disagree as I believe that H & R Block's role in facilitating the Rapid Refund for the taxpayer is as the taxpayer's agent as all three elements of agency exist. Here, (1) the taxpayer manifested her consent to the tax preparer that she wished to participate or take advantage of H & R Block's Rapid Refund program when it was offered; (2) the preparer facilitated the process of obtaining a Rapid Refund by offering an application; and (3) the preparer consented to act on the taxpayer's need by matching the taxpayer to a source for the early refund, here, Mellon Bank. Accordingly, I also believe an agency relationship existed between Appellees and H & R Block for purposes of the Rapid Refund Program.

As H & R Block was the agent through which the Rapid Refund was facilitated, it had a duty to disclose the nature of its relationship with Mellon Bank in respect to the Rapid Refund Program. As the majority noted, "Block did not disclose to its [refund application loan] customers that it received a payment from Mellon Bank for each loan, shared in the profits of the [refund application loans] in other ways, or that the taxpayer's endorsement on the back of the loan proceeds check constituted a signature on a loan agreement printed on the reverse of the check." I believe that this is a gross violation of H & R Block's fiduciary duty to Appellees. Since I believe that the evidence creates the inference that an agency relationship existed between H & R Block and Appellees for the entire tax return "package" offered and further, that H & R Block violated the fiduciary duty it owed to Appellees, I respectfully dissent.

SAYLOR, J., dissenting:

I agree with the majority that, to the extent that refund anticipated loans ("RALs") are viewed as discrete transactions, no agency relationship between Block and its customers would be discernible. Like the majority, I would not be inclined to conclude, extrinsic of an existing, underlying agency relationship, that a separate agency role is necessarily undertaken by one who merely facilitates a lending transaction. Nevertheless, I join that portion of Mr. Justice Nigro's analysis which concludes . . . that an agency relationship existed between Block and Appellees for the purposes of preparing Appellees' tax returns, filing them with the IRS, and obtaining refunds. Indeed, I note that H & R Block conceded as much, at least for purposes of Maryland law, in *Green v. H & R Block, Inc.*, 735 A.2d 1039, 1049 (Md. 1999). I also believe that the fiduciary duties associated with such relationship may be viewed as sufficiently broad to compel disclosure of aspects of self-interest in a related loan transaction. Thus, I would [remand] "for disposition of questions of fact concerning the extent to which Block's failure to disclose the nature of the Rapid Refund program and its participation in the profits generated by the RALs constituted a violation of Block's duty as an agent." *Basile v. H & R Block, Inc.*, 729 A.2d 574, 582 (Pa. Super. 1999).

Notes and Questions

1. Note

a. H & R Block operated the refund anticipation loan program nationwide and customers in several other states brought suits similar to *Basile*. Courts have reached different results on the question whether an agency relationship existed between Block and its customers. Compare, *Green v. H & R Block, Inc.*, 735 A.2d 1039 (Md. 1999) (agency relationship found) with *Beckett v. H & R Block, Inc.*, 714 N.E.2d 1033 (Ill. 1999), and *Peterson v. H & R Block Tax Services, Inc.*, 971 F. Supp. 1204 (N.D. Ill. 1997) (no agency relationship found).

2. Reality Check

a. What element or elements of the *Restatement (Third)* §1.01 definition of agency are missing from the relationship between Block and Ms. Basile, according to Justice Castille?

b. Does Justice Nigro disagree with the rules Justice Castille uses or with the application of the rules? Or do the two judges disagree about both the rules and their application?

c. How does Justice Saylor differ from Justices Nigro and Castille?

d. Why does it matter whether Block is the plaintiffs' agent?

3. Suppose

a. What if the RAL had not been a separate optional service but instead were included along with Block's tax preparation? Would these facts make a difference to Justice Castille or Justice Nigro?

b. Suppose a CPA had a sole practice in which he or she prepared tax returns for individuals. If one tax client asked the CPA to contact a bank to arrange a loan to the client secured by the client's anticipated tax refund, and if the CPA agreed to do so, would an agency relationship exist between the CPA and client? If so, how is that setting different from *Basile*?

c. If Block rather than Mellon Bank had made the RALs, would an agency relationship exist between Block and its customers as to the RALs?

4. What Do You Think?

a. If an agency relationship exists, the agent's actions may bind the principal. Does an agency relationship exist between Block and Mellon Bank? If so, which is the principal and which the agent? If so, do you think that Block or Mellon Bank or both should be liable to plaintiffs?

b. Is one implication of *Basile* that professionals can seldom if ever be agents for their clients because the nature of professional services is such that clients will retain insufficient control over the professional's work?

c. If plaintiffs were misled about the RALs, should their recovery be based upon agency law or upon other sources such as commercial law or consumer protection?

3. Relation of the Principal to Third Parties

A principal can become liable to a third party (i.e., to a natural person or an entity that is not the agent) for the actions of the agent under five theories, which are not mutually exclusive. In most instances liability is predicated on *actual authority* or *apparent authority*. When neither of those two theories results in liability courts turn to the remaining three theories.

a. Actual Authority

The simplest theory of liability is actual authority. A principal is bound to third parties by anything the agent does that is in accordance with the principal's "manifestation" to the agent. The principal's manifestation is determined by the agent's reasonable interpretation in light of all the circumstances. *Restatement (Third)* §2.02.

This manifestation can be express, for example, "You are authorized to sell my car for any price in excess of $2000." The manifestation might also be implied rather than express. The agent has actual authority to do collateral acts that are incidental, that usually accompany or are usually done in the business, or that are reasonably necessary to accomplish the acts that the principal has expressly authorized. In the example just given, the agent would doubtless have actual authority to advertise the car. See *Restatement (Third)* §2.02(1).

b. Apparent Authority

Actual authority arises from the manifestations of the principal to the agent. Apparent authority stems from a third party's belief, traceable to the principal's manifestation, that the agent is authorized to act for the principal. *Restatement (Third)* §2.03. As we have seen, a principal is bound by an agent's actions within the scope of the agent's actual authority. But a principal is also bound by an agent's actions within the scope of the agent's apparent authority. Where the manifestations the principal makes to the agent are identical to those the principal makes to a third party, the agent's actual authority and apparent authority are coextensive. What happens when the manifestations made to the agent and to the third party are different?

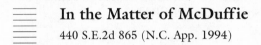

In the Matter of McDuffie

440 S.E.2d 865 (N.C. App. 1994)

[The McDuffies owned the "Woodbriar property" and the "Lowdermilk property," both of which were covered by a single deed of trust that secured a loan from Mutual Savings and Loan Association (Mutual). They sold the Woodbriar property to the Halls and the Lowdermilk property to Summit Enterprises, Incorporated (Summit) and both the Halls and Summit assumed the deed of trust.]

On 2 July 1992, petitioner, J. Rufus Farrior, the . . . trustee of the . . . deed of trust, filed a petition to commence foreclosure proceedings on the Woodbriar and Lowdermilk properties. On 11 September 1992, Judge Cornelius entered a consent order . . . requiring that the Lowdermilk property be sold before the Woodbriar property. Petitioner conducted a foreclosure sale of the Lowdermilk property on 14 September 1992, and placed, on behalf of Mutual, a bid in the amount of $43,361.17 which was the only bid at the foreclosure sale. On 16 September 1992, petitioner filed a motion to withdraw the bid. On 11 December 1992, Judge Martin entered final judgment affirming the assistant clerk's order, denying petitioner's motion to withdraw the bid, and granting the Halls' motion. Mutual appeals.

WELLS, J.

Mutual contends that the trial court erred in finding and concluding that the bid made by petitioner was an authorized bid and in denying petitioner's motion to withdraw the bid. We disagree.

When petitioner placed the bid on behalf of Mutual, petitioner was acting as the agent of Mutual. When Mutual's bid was accepted as the last and highest, a contract was formed. "The principal is liable upon a contract duly made by his agent with a third person . . . when the agent acts within the scope of his apparent authority, unless the third person has notice that the agent is exceeding his actual authority." *Morpul*

Research Corp. v. Westover Hardware Co., 140 S.E.2d 416 (N.C. 1965). A principal cannot restrict his liability for acts of his agent within the scope of his apparent authority by limitations which persons dealing with the agent have no notice. The determination of a principal's liability must be based on what authority the third person, in the exercise of reasonable care, was justified in believing that the principal had conferred upon his agent.

In determining what is equitable, we examine the following facts. Before the 11 September 1992 consent order, Mutual provided petitioner with a bid to be placed on its behalf on the Lowdermilk and Woodbriar properties in an amount sufficient to extinguish the debt secured by the 1983 deed of trust. After the consent order requiring Mutual to proceed first against the Lowdermilk property was entered, petitioner was instructed by Mutual to place a nominal bid on the Lowdermilk property. Petitioner then left for vacation and did not return until the night before the sale. On 14 September 1992, the day of the foreclosure sale, Mutual delivered to petitioner's office manager a letter requesting that petitioner enter a bid on behalf of Mutual on the Lowdermilk property in the amount of $1,000.00. This letter never came to the attention of petitioner. Consequently, petitioner entered a bid on behalf of Mutual in the amount of $43,361.17. Mutual makes no contention that the foreclosure sale was not in accordance with the law. The record fails to disclose that the fair market value of the Lowdermilk property is significantly less than the bid entered by petitioner. Other than petitioner, only the attorneys for the Halls and Summit were present at the foreclosure sale. These individuals were unaware of the limitation sought to be imposed on the power of petitioner by the letter delivered to petitioner's office on the day of the sale.

Under these circumstances, we are of the opinion that the Halls were justified in believing that Mutual had conferred upon petitioner the power to bind it by a bid of $43,361.17 on the Lowdermilk property. Petitioner acted within the scope of his apparent authority, and Mutual is bound on the resulting contract despite the alleged mistaken bid. . . .
Affirmed.

JOHN and MCCRODDEN, JJ., concur.

Notes and Questions

1. Notes

a. A deed of trust is a device that serves the same function as a mortgage: to make repayment of a loan more certain by allowing the lender to sell the borrower's real property if the borrower defaults on the loan. A mortgage is a two-party agreement in which the borrower grants the lender an interest in the real property. With a deed of trust, the borrower transfers title to a third-party trustee (often a bank or title insurance company), which holds the property for the benefit of the lender and reconveys title to the borrower when the loan is repaid.

If the borrower defaults, the trustee sells the real estate at auction and pays the proceeds to the lender. Any proceeds in excess of the indebtedness are paid to the borrower. The lender can bid on the property at the auction and that bid, in effect, is simply an offer to reduce the indebtedness by the amount of the bid. [T]he lender often bids the entire loan amount.

In *McDuffie*, the deed of trust was without recourse if both properties were to be sold together. The deed of trust was effectively with recourse if one property were to be sold first because Mutual retained the right to seek repayment of the loan by having the trustee sell the Woodbriar property later if the proceeds from the Lowdermilk property did not satisfy the entire loan.

2. Reality Check

a. What was Farrior's actual authority? What was his apparent authority?

b. How and to whom did Mutual manifest Farrior's apparent authority?

c. Why did Mutual change the amount it authorized Farrior to bid?

d. How is Mutual harmed by Farrior's action?

e. Do the Halls or Summit (or both) get a windfall by Farrior's action?

3. Suppose

a. Suppose Farrior had bid $433,611.70 instead? $4,336,117.00?

b. How would the court decide this case if Mutual's letter of September 14 had come to Farrior's attention and he still had bid $43,361.17?

c. How would the court decide this case if Mutual's letter had come to the attention of the attorneys for the Halls and Summit but not to Farrior's attention? Would your answer depend upon whether the attorneys remained silent?

4. What Do You Think?

a. If agency is a consensual relationship, how can the principal be held to an action by its agent to which it did not consent? More starkly, as in this case, how can the principal (Mutual) be held to an action by its agent (Farrior) that it specifically directed the agent not to take?

b. Do you think the Halls and Summit could argue that, because Farrior never saw the September 14th letter from Mutual, he still had actual authority to bid the entire $43,361.17?

c. Should the Halls and Summit have to show some reliance on Farrior's action or some potential harm from allowing Mutual to withdraw its bid in order to prevail? Did they or could they have made such a showing?

The scope of apparent authority is determined in analogous fashion to the scope of actual authority. The test is the third party's reasonable interpretation of the principal's manifestations in light of all the circumstances. As with actual authority, an agent has apparent authority to do collateral acts that are incidental, that usually accompany or are usually done in the business, or that are reasonably necessary to accomplish the acts that the agent is apparently authorized to do. See *Restatement (Third)* §2.03 cmt. b & d.

In the business entities context, a concept sometimes called the "power of position" is frequently important. When a principal that is an entity appoints an individual to a particular position, such as Vice President of Purchasing, that appointment may carry with it a great deal of implied actual authority even where the corporation is vague about the actual authority expressly given to that person. Remember that the scope of actual authority is measured by what the agent reasonably believes. So, the question becomes what a reasonable person would believe when the corporation appointed him or her to be Vice President of Purchasing. See *Restatement (Third)* §1.03 cmt c.

More importantly, such an appointment may carry much implied apparent authority as well. Even if the Vice President of Purchasing has been expressly limited in the actions he or she can take, and therefore has a very narrow scope of actual authority, the corporation, as principal, is bound by the agent's actions if they are within the scope of what a third party reasonably believed a Vice President of Purchasing was authorized to do. The extent of this implied apparent authority varies not only within the context of any particular transaction, but also with the title of the position. The Vice President of Purchasing presumably has a great deal of discretion to act for the corporation within the realm of purchasing items for corporate use. The corporation's president obviously has a wide range of powers to act on behalf of the corporation. Ironically, a more generic title such as "vice president" may well carry with it almost no implied powers because the title is so amorphous.

One particular setting is worth noting as a trap for the unwary corporate planner. Virtually every state's corporation statute requires the corporation to have one person whose duties include keeping corporate records and certifying the actions of the corporation's board and its shareholders. See, e.g., Del. §142(a) and MBCA §§1.40(20) and 8.40(c). That person is often called the "Secretary" in the statutes and case law binds the corporation to any representations about corporation board or shareholder actions given by that person (and to a lesser extent any "Assistant Secretary" or "Vice Secretary"). The upshot is that a negligent or, worse, malfeasing corporate secretary can expose the corporation to significant liability by falsely certifying that an action has been approved or that a particular person has actual authority to act for the entity. See *Restatement (Third)* §3.03 cmt. e(5) & rptr's notes e(5).

c. Principal's Liability to Third Parties for Actions Actually or Apparently Authorized

Under the *Restatement (Third)*, a principal is liable in contract if the agent acted either with actual authority or apparent authority. See *Restatement (Third)* §6.01(1). This is true even where the third party knows only that the agent is acting on behalf of a principal but does not know the principal's identity (called an *unidentified principal*). See *Restatement (Third)* §6.02(1). Further, the principal is liable for an agent's actually authorized actions even where the third party had no knowledge that the agent was acting on behalf of any principal (called an *undisclosed principal*). See *Restatement (Third)* §6.03(1). The rationale is that the principal initiated the agent's actions and has a right to control them and so should in fairness be bound under the contract made by the agent. This rule typically gives a windfall to third parties who, as we will see below, can either hold the agent, with whom they believed they were contracting, and therefore receive their expectation interest, or hold the principal of whom they had no knowledge. As you think about these settings, be aware that in the undisclosed principal setting the agent cannot be acting with apparent authority because the principal has manifested nothing to the third party. You should be aware that the *Restatement (Second) of Agency*, and hence nearly all courts and commentators, used the term *partially disclosed principal* rather than *undisclosed principal*.

d. Estoppel

A principal who has neither authorized nor apparently authorized an agent's action is nevertheless liable to third parties who have changed their position in reliance upon their belief that the action was authorized if the principal caused (intentionally or carelessly) the belief or, if the principal, knowing of the belief, did nothing to notify the third parties of the facts. See *Restatement (Third)* §2.05. Although estoppel has wide application elsewhere in the law, it has a very narrow place in agency law. First, remember that estoppel comes into play only where the agent's action was not actually authorized. Second, apparent authority covers many settings in which estoppel might otherwise apply. In those situations, the plaintiff can prevail against the principal simply by showing that the principal manifested to the plaintiff that the agent had the authority to act.

e. Ratification

The fourth theory of liability (in addition to actual and apparent authority and estoppel) is *ratification*. If *A* took action purportedly on behalf of or for the benefit of *B* (regardless of whether *A* was *B*'s agent) but such action did not bind *B*, *B* may nonetheless *ratify* that action. If *B* ratifies the action, *B* is treated as though *A* originally had actual authority to take the action. See *Restatement (Third)* §§4.02 and 4.03. *B* ratifies by manifesting assent, which is a manifestation of *B*'s election to treat the action as authorized. The manifestation can be express but need not be communicated to *A* or any third party to be effective. See *Restatement (Third)* §4.01 cmt. d. Ratification can also be manifested through conduct that is only explicable on the ground that the partner intends to ratify the agent's action. See *Restatement (Third)* §4.01(2)(b).

f. Restitution

The final theory is *restitution*. The principal is liable to make restitution to third parties where the principal is unjustly enriched by the agent's actions that are not within the agent's actual or apparent authority. See *Restatement (Third)* §2.07.

g. Principal's Liability for Agent's Torts

The previous theories have essentially involved liability for the agent's agreements made on the principal's behalf. The *Restatement (Third)* also holds a principal liable for an agent's torts in certain instances. Where the principal authorizes the agent to engage in conduct that is tortious, the principal is liable even though the principal may not have intended the conduct to be tortious. The typical setting would be where the agent is authorized to commit intentional torts that do not involve physical injury to people or property. See *Restatement (Third)* §7.04. The principal is also liable for torts committed by an agent acting with apparent authority where ability to commit the tort is sufficiently related to the agency relationship. Examples are misrepresentation, defamation, or conversion. See *Restatement (Third)* §7.08.

What about torts that cause physical injury to persons or to property? The agent rarely has actual authority to commit such actions and the *Restatement (Third)* makes it clear that such injuries are usually too remote from the agent's apparent authority to render the principal liable. See *Restatement (Third)* §7.08 cmt. b. Nonetheless, principals may be liable for their agents' torts that result in physical injury in certain circumstances. The next case explores this theory of *vicarious liability*.

Fisher v. Townsends, Inc.

695 A.2d 53 (Del. 1997)

HOLLAND, J.

This appeal arises out of a motor vehicle accident in which the plaintiff-appellant, John Fisher ("Fisher"), was seriously injured. At the time of the accident, Fisher was a passenger in a pickup truck being driven by Percy Reid ("Reid"). Fisher's complaint alleged that the defendant-appellee, Townsends, Inc. ("Townsends"), was vicariously liable for Reid's negligent conduct while driving the truck.[1] The jury awarded Fisher damages against Reid in the amount of seven million dollars.

Townsends operates a chicken processing business. Townsends hired seven weighmasters to assemble chicken catching crews. Townsends hired Reid as a weighmaster. Reid performed his services as a weighmaster for Townsends exclusively, for at least five years prior to the time of Reid's accident involving Fisher. The relationship between Townsends and Reid continued pursuant to oral understandings until the summer of 1992.

In July 1992, Townsends presented Reid with a written Catching Crew Agreement. The parties disagree about whether the Catching Crew Agreement was executed prior to Reid's accident.[3] There is a consensus, however, that the written agreement was not intended to change or alter the nature of the longstanding relationship between Reid and Townsends.

Each chicken catching crew consisted of seven members and a foreman. Each crew was transported to and from work sites in vehicles that Reid owned. [On the day of the accident] Reid arrived in a 1979 Chevrolet pickup truck between 4:30 and 5:00 P.M. The bed of the 1979 truck . . . was covered with a pick-up top and contained bus seats that did not have seatbelts. Reid drove and . . . Fisher and six other employees sat in the back bed of the pickup truck.

As part of his weighmaster's job, Reid was required to go to Townsends' processing plant in Millsboro at the end of each day to receive a Flock Movement Sheet for the next day's work. Reid was on his way to obtain such a work order when the accident occurred that injured Fisher.

Reid approached the back of a vehicle driven by Cheryl Tucker ("Tucker"). Tucker testified that she saw Reid's truck through her rearview mirror. According to Tucker, Reid's vehicle appeared to be traveling extremely fast and she believed the Reid truck was going to strike her. Tucker moved to the shoulder of the road. Tucker observed Reid's truck swerve into the northbound lane and strike a telephone pole. As

---

1. Fisher's complaint also alleged that Reid was directly liable for his own negligence. Reid is not a party in this appeal.

3. According to Townsends, Reid entered into a Catching Crew Agreement ("Agreement") dated July 23, 1992 to provide chicken catching services. Pursuant to the Agreement, Reid agreed to assemble a chicken catching crew who would remove chickens from farms Townsends' growers operated for shipment to Townsends' processing plant in Millsboro, Delaware. The Agreement recited that Reid was an independent contractor and that the chicken catchers whom he employed were not employees or agents of Townsends. The Agreement further stated that Reid was solely responsible for hiring, compensating, directing and, if necessary, terminating the chicken catchers. It further made Reid responsible for the transportation of the chicken catching crews and required him to pay all state and federal taxes "and all applicable charges or taxes for Worker's Compensation Insurance, Unemployment Compensation Insurance, FICA or other statutory obligations." The Agreement provided that Reid was to be paid "$27.08 for each 1,000 birds properly caught." According to Fisher, there is a factual dispute about whether the written agreement was signed by Reid prior to the accident.

a result of the accident, Fisher suffered serious injuries. He was hospitalized for more than four months. He is now a "C-5 quadriplegic."

PRINCIPAL AND AGENT VICARIOUS LIABILITY DOCTRINE

Fisher alleges that he was personally injured by the tortious physical conduct of Reid. Fisher further asserts that Reid is an agent of Townsends. Accordingly, Fisher seeks redress against Townsends, as the alleged principal of Reid, on the basis of vicarious liability–respondeat superior. Townsends' defense is that Reid was not its agent.

When a third-party plaintiff's legal theory is based upon vicarious liability, several types of relationships must be identified and distinguished: principal/agent; [and] employer/employee. These distinctions are important in evaluating a defendant's liability to third parties who are harmed by the tortious physical act of another. In fact, the distinctions are often outcome determinative.

One type of principal/agent relationship is characterized by the term "[employer/employee]." There are some agents, however, who are not [employees]. [I]f the principal is the [employer] of an agent who is [an employee], the fault of the agent, if acting within the scope of employment, will be imputed to the principal by the doctrine of respondeat superior. . . .

If the principal assumes the right to control the time, manner and method of executing the work, as distinguished from the right merely to require certain definite results in conformity to the contract, [an employer/employee] type of agency relationship has been created.

In determining whether one who acts for another is a servant or an independent contractor, this Court has recognized Section 220 of the *Restatement (Second) of Agency* [(1958)] as an authoritative source for guidance. The *Restatement (Second) of Agency* states that the following non-exclusive "matters of fact" are to be considered in deciding whether the actual tortfeasor is a servant or an independent contractor:

(a) the extent of control, which, by the agreement, the master may exercise over the details of the work;

(b) whether or not the one employed is engaged in a distinct occupation or business;

(c) the kind of occupation, with reference to whether, in the locality, the work is usually done under the direction of the employer or by a specialist without supervision;

(d) the skill required in the particular occupation;

(e) whether the employer or the workman supplies the instrumentalities, tools, and the place of work for the person doing the work;

(f) the length of time for which the person is employed;

(g) the method of payment, whether by the time or by the job;

(h) whether or not the work is a part of the regular business of the employer;

(i) whether or not the parties believe they are creating the relation of master and servant; and

(j) whether the principal is or is not in business.

Restatement (Second) of Agency §220.

Townsends argues that Reid was not its [employee]. First, Townsends submits that Reid executed a written Catching Crew Agreement prior to the accident that injured Fisher. That agreement recited that Reid was an independent contractor.

Second, Townsends asserts that it did not have or exercise the right to control the precise manner in which Reid carried out his duties as a weighmaster. According to Townsends, Reid was in business for himself. Thus, Townsends submits that it is not answerable to Fisher for Reid's negligence.

It is the actions taken by the parties, not the terms used in the contract, that are dispositive in determining whether they were principal and agent respectively. The record reflects that Townsends supplied Reid with Daily Movement Sheets that identified the farm where the day's work was to be done; the total number of birds to be removed; the number of birds to be placed in each cage hold; which crew was assigned to the job; and the time that the crew was to report. Townsends owned and supplied the trucks, forklifts, cages, and stools that were used when the chickens were caught, as well as the paper masks and disposable gloves worn by the catchers. Townsends' Live Haul Manager visited the farms periodically to see if the weighmasters, Townsends' truck drivers, or forklift operators were experiencing problems. Townsends required its weighmasters to keep two way radios in the vehicles they used to transport their crews. Townsends supplied Reid with radios for both of his transport vehicles. These radios permitted Townsends to keep its weighmasters advised of changes in work sites and work orders. The radios also enabled the weighmasters to communicate with Townsends' processing plant, truck drivers, and forklift operators regarding any work-related problems.

The foregoing evidence, when taken into consideration with the exclusive and long-standing nature of Reid's relationship with Townsends, created a material dispute of fact about whether Reid was Townsends' [employee]. That determination must be made by the jury. Upon remand, the Superior Court should instruct the jury to decide the question of whether Reid was Townsends' [employee], by specifically considering the non-exclusive "matters of fact" set forth in Section 220 of the *Restatement (Second) of Agency*.

The summary judgment entered in Townsends' favor, on the issue of its vicarious liability to Fisher for Reid's negligent conduct, is reversed.

Notes and Questions

1. Note

a. The *Restatement (Second) of Agency* and many courts and commentators use the terms *master* and *servant* in place of *employer* and *employee*. *Fisher* also used master and servant.

b. The factors Justice Holland lists from the *Restatement (Second) of Agency* to determine whether an agent is an employee are approved in the *Restatement (Third)* but are now found in the comments rather than in the text itself. See *Restatement (Third) of Agency* §7.07 cmt. f.

2. Reality Check

a. Why is it important to determine whether Reid was an agent or an employee?
b. Are "agent" and "employee" mutually exclusive?

3. Suppose

a. Suppose Reid and his crews had identical relationships with Townsends and another chicken processor and worked for each company half the time?

4. What Do You Think?

a. Why should Townsends' liability for Reid's negligent driving depend upon such facts as whether Townsends told Reid which farms to travel to, and whether Townsends supplied equipment?

b. Recall that Reid did not appeal from the $7 million summary judgment that was entered against him. Why shouldn't Fisher be limited to that judgment? After all, Reid was the negligent driver and Fisher worked for Reid on his catching crew.

c. More generally, do you think a principal should ever be liable for an agent's unauthorized tort? If so, in what situations should liability attach to the principal? Do you think a principal should always be liable for an agent's unauthorized tort? Remember that in all these situations the agent is personally liable to the plaintiff. Does your answer depend on your view of the purposes of agency law or does it depend on your view of the purposes of torts?

The great majority of personal injury actions brought against principals are based on *respondeat superior*. Justice Holland, in *Fisher*, states the general rule that an employer will be liable for the torts of an *employee* acting within the *scope of employment*. See *Restatement (Third)* §§2.04 and 7.07. Thus defining whether an agent is an "employee" and defining an agent's scope of employment are often of great consequence. The *Restatement (Third)* defines an employee as "an agent whose principal controls or has the right to control the manner and means of the agent's performance of work. . . ." *Restatement (Third)* §7.07(3)(a).

When considering whether the employee's actions were within the scope of employment, some fact settings are obvious and intuitive. An employee who negligently causes a traffic accident on the employee's day off when the employee was driving his or her own car for the purpose of grocery shopping will not subject the employer to liability. Other settings are more difficult to resolve. Suppose the employee were commuting to work rather than driving on a day off? Suppose the employee were driving on a day off but was driving an employer's vehicle (employees are not infrequently allowed to use an employer's vehicle for personal use)? Suppose the employee were making a delivery for the employer in the middle of a work day and stopped off at a near-by mall to run a personal errand? Would an accident in the mall's parking lot be in the scope of employment? An accident on a public street while driving to the mall? An accident on a public street while driving from the mall to make the delivery?

The *Restatement (Third)* states when an agent is acting within the scope and also when an agent is not acting within the scope of employment:

§7.07 EMPLOYEE ACTING WITHIN SCOPE OF EMPLOYMENT

> . . .
>
> (2) An employee acts within the scope of employment when performing work assigned by the employer or engaging in a course of conduct subject to the employer's control. An employee's act is not within the scope of employment when it occurs within an independent course of conduct not intended by the employee to serve any purpose of the employer.

The two definitions are meant to be reciprocal so that "work assigned by the employer" and "course of conduct subject to the employer's control" are the opposite of "independent course of conduct not intended by the employee to serve any purpose of the employer." Courts often use the phrase "frolic and detour" to describe the conclusion that the agent's action was not within the scope of employment.[2]

b. Liability of the Third Party to the Principal

The contract liability of a third party and a principal is essentially reciprocal. If a principal is liable on a contract to a third party under agency law, the principal can likewise enforce the contract against the third party as though the contract had been made directly by the principal. *Restatement (Third)* §§6.01, 6.02, and 6.03. An exception is where the agent has falsely represented that he or she is not acting for the specific principal and the agent or principal knows that the third party would not have dealt with the principal. Where the agent knows the third party will not deal with the principal, the agent's failure to disclose the principal (without any misrepresentation) may be sufficient to make the contract voidable by the third party. Note that unless the agent or principal knows that the third party will not deal with the principal, the misrepresentation of, or failure to disclose, the principal will not affect the validity of the transaction. For example, an agent for a wealthy principal negotiates to purchase land. The agent knows that the landowner is likely to raise the purchase price if the principal's identity were known to the landowner. The agent may misrepresent the principal's identity or may deny that the agent is acting for a principal without jeopardizing the principal's ability to enforce the contract. A misrepresentation in this regard allows the third party to rescind only where the agent or principal knows the third party will not deal with the principal. See *Restatement (Third)* §6.11(4).

4. Relation of the Agent to Third Parties

a. Agent's Liability on Contract

An agent who contracts on behalf of a disclosed principal is not thereby liable to the third person with whom the contract was made. See *Restatement (Third)* §6.01(2). Conversely, an agent who contracts on behalf of an undisclosed principal ordinarily is liable to the third person with whom the contract was made. See *Restatement (Third)* §6.03(2). In between disclosed and undisclosed principals is the unidentified principal. The distinction between these three is important for determining whether the agent is liable to the third party. Under the *Restatement (Third)* §6.02(2), the agent is liable to third parties when acting for an unidentified principal. A principal is unidentified when, "the third party has notice that the agent is acting for a principal but does not have notice of the principal's identity." See *Restatement (Third)* §1.04(2)(c).

Where the principal is an entity rather than an individual, a further issue is presented. That question is the quantum of information about the principal that the third party must have to constitute the principal's "identity." The next case explores this question. The "Barnes" in the caption was another individual who was dismissed early in the action.

---

2. Originally, the two terms had different meanings. If the employee's actions were not within the scope of employment, the agent was said to be on a "frolic." If the actions were within the scope of employment, the agent was said to be on a "detour."

Benjamin Plumbing, Inc. v. Barnes

470 N.W.2d 888 (Wis. 1991)

HEFFERNAN, CJ.

In 1987 [William K.] Whitcomb contacted Benjamin Plumbing, Inc., an incorporated family plumbing business located in Madison, about the possibility of doing some plumbing work on a canning project for the "Response to Hunger Network" on the Mendota State Hospital grounds.

In a letter dated May 5, 1987, to Donald Knapp, the general manager of Benjamin Plumbing, Whitcomb requested a "rock bottom" price for the plumbing work. The letter stated that a minimum subsistence rate would be appreciated because "we have to search for donations to pay for this work and in the end we do not even have a product that will bring us any income." Under Whitcomb's signature were the typed words, "William K. Whitcomb, For Response to Hunger Network." In the letterhead, however, were the words, "National Council of the Churches of Christ in the United States of America, CHURCH WORLD SERVICE," with Whitcomb listed as its regional director.

In a letter dated June 20, 1987, and addressed to "Response to Hunger, To Whom It May Concern," Knapp set forth Benjamin Plumbing's price quotations for work on the cannery project. The letterhead used by Knapp set forth the words, "Benjamin Plumbing, Inc."

In a letter to Knapp dated July 9, 1987, Whitcomb accepted Benjamin Plumbing's rates and authorized Knapp to start the work. Whitcomb advised Knapp that he could be reached at his Church World Service address and phone number. Under Whitcomb's signature were the typed words, "William K. Whitcomb, Canning Committee — RHN." The letterhead was captioned, "RESPONSE TO HUNGER NETWORK."

Benjamin Plumbing completed the work but was subsequently paid only $5,000 of the final bill, which amounted to $10,603.66. The appropriateness of the total bill is not disputed. On December 6, 1988, Benjamin Plumbing, not having received payment, filed an action against Whitcomb and two other members of RHN individually and RHN as an unincorporated association. The complaint alleged that all the defendants were jointly and severally liable for the unpaid balance of the plumbing contract. In their answer, the defendants denied contractual liability and affirmatively asserted that "Response to Hunger Network, Inc., is a Wisconsin corporation...."

We granted Whitcomb's petition for review to determine whether an agent is personally liable on a contract where the other party did not have notice of the corporate status of the principal at the time of contracting, ...

Where the principal is a business entity and not a natural person, a unique set of problems arises. Varying legal rights and liabilities attach to different types of business organizations, e.g., sole proprietor, partnership, voluntary association, and corporation. Under well-accepted legal principles, for example, all partners, as owners of the partnership, are jointly and severally liable for the contractual debts incurred by the partnership.

Similarly, when an entity is considered a voluntary association, all members of the association are jointly and severally liable for the association's contractual obligations. "A voluntary association is defined as individuals who join together for a certain object and are called for convenience by a common name." *Hafenbraedl v. LeTendre for*

Congress Committee, 213 N.W.2d 353 (Wis. 1974) (quoting *Herman v. United Automobile Aircraft & Agricultural Implement Workers*, 59 N.W.2d 475 (Wis. 1953)). It is generally recognized, furthermore, that numerous charitable and religious organizations are unincorporated associations consisting of a large and changing membership.

Where a business entity is a corporation, however, the shareholders, as owners of the corporation, are generally not personally liable for the contractual obligations of the corporation. A corporation, be it for profit or not for profit, enters into contracts and incurs liability as a separate legal entity. The limited liability attribute of corporations is in fact what makes this business organization so significant.

Where a party is contracting with a business entity, therefore, it makes a considerable difference whether or not it is a corporation on the other side of the bargaining table. If the agent with whom the party contracts is a partner, sole proprietor, or member of a voluntary association, the party may expect that agent to be personally liable on the contract. If the party knows the agent is contracting for a corporation, however, the agent would not be liable on the contract unless he or she expressly assumed such liability. The fact that the agent might also be a director or officer of the corporation is generally irrelevant under agency principles.

It is the agent who seeks to escape liability who has the burden of proving that the principal's corporate status was disclosed. Such a duty of disclosure creates no hardship on agents, for it is within their power to relieve themselves of liability. Conversely, the contracting party does not have any duty to inquire into the corporate status of the principal even when it is within that party's capability of doing so. As a matter of fairness, the contracting party should not be saddled with the burden of "ferret[ing] out the record ownership" of the principal's business. See *Van D. Costas, Inc. v. Rosenberg*, 432 So. 2d 656, 659 (Fl. App. 1983).

Because the contracting party needs notice of the principal's corporate status, the use of a trade name is normally not sufficient disclosure. The failure to use the "Inc." notation in correspondence between the agent and third party or in the contract itself is often critical in the determination of whether there was adequate disclosure of corporate status.

Based on the record before us, we conclude that the only reasonable inference that can be drawn from the undisputed facts is that Benjamin Plumbing had neither actual nor constructive notice of the corporate identity of the principal, RHN, at the time of contracting with Whitcomb.

First, the trial court found, and Whitcomb concedes, that there was no express disclosure of RHN's corporate status in the contract or correspondence between the parties. The first time Benjamin Plumbing had actual notice that RHN was a Wisconsin corporation was upon receipt of the defendants' answer to its complaint.

Second, the fact that Benjamin Plumbing was aware that Whitcomb was acting on behalf of an entity called RHN reveals nothing of Benjamin's awareness of the type of business organization it was dealing with. All business entities are not corporations. In fact, being an incorporated business itself, Benjamin Plumbing could have reasonably concluded that RHN would have used its corporate name in its firm letterhead, as did Benjamin, if it were in fact a corporation. As previously noted, Benjamin had no affirmative duty to investigate the business ownership record of the principal, RHN. Whitcomb, as an agent, had the obligation to disclose RHN's corporate status in order to prevent incurring liability on the contract. RHN was essentially using a tradename.

Third, the fact that RHN was manifestly a charitable, nonprofit organization does not lead to the inference that it was a corporation. As noted above, RHN might just as well have been an unincorporated association. While there are admittedly only a limited number of types of business organizations, identifying RHN as a corporation as opposed to an unincorporated association without some evidence of that fact would be mere conjecture. The fact that Benjamin Plumbing actually did bring suit against RHN as an unincorporated association and against Whitcomb and the others as its members was certainly reasonable given the lack of corporate identification.

Finally, the fact that Whitcomb did not in so many words expressly assume contractual liability is not dispositive. Clearly, the opposite is also true. Whitcomb did not expressly disavow personal liability on the contract as he so easily could have. It is exactly because there is a lack of express intentions to the contrary that courts have found an implied intention to hold the agent personally liable where the corporate identity of the principal is not disclosed. Whitcomb is liable because he is the contracting party. Had Benjamin Plumbing known RHN was a corporation with limited liability, it might well have taken precautionary measures to protect its interests.

[Whitcomb] states that it is well accepted that corporations need not contract in their legal corporate name. Whitcomb reasons, therefore, as did the circuit court on summary judgment, that an agent should not incur personal liability for the principal's failure to contract in its corporate name.

The legal principles presented by Whitcomb are inapposite. These general rules only relate to the corporate principal's liability on a contract, not the agent's. Clearly, it has long been the rule in Wisconsin that a corporation can be contractually bound even where the corporate name was not used in the contract. Where the principal's corporate status has not been disclosed, however, the courts have uniformly held the agent liable on the contract as well.

In conclusion, Whitcomb's liability stems from the lack of notice to Benjamin Plumbing that the principal, RHN, was in fact a corporation. The burden of giving such notice was upon Whitcomb. The undisputed facts do not support any reasonable inference that Benjamin had actual or constructive notice of RHN's corporate identity.

Decision affirmed.

Notes and Questions

1. Notes

a. Whitcomb was a director of Response to Hunger Network according to the Court of Appeals. See *Benjamin Plumbing, Inc. v. Barnes*, 456 N.W.2d 628, 630 (Wis. Ct. App. 1990).

2. Reality Check

a. What was Whitcomb's argument against his liability?

3. Suppose

a. Suppose Response to Hunger Network were characterized as a disclosed principal?

b. Suppose Response to Hunger Network were characterized as an undisclosed principal?

c. What if Whitcomb had told the plaintiff that Response to Hunger Network was a corporation? What if the plaintiff had discovered that information through other means?

4. What Do You Think?

a. *Benjamin Plumbing* illustrates the general rule that an agent for an unidentified principal is ordinarily liable on a contract made by the agent for the principal. See *Restatement (Third)* §6.02(2). Do you think this rule makes sense given that the third party knows a principal is involved and has agreed to deal with the principal? Would a better rule be that such an agent is personally liable only if the agent and third party explicitly agree to such liability?

b. Couldn't the plaintiff have checked on the principal's creditworthiness before agreeing to work, and couldn't it have required partial payments as the work progressed? Do you think these possibilities should affect plaintiff's recovery?

5. You Draft It

a. Redraft the signature blocks of Mr. Whitcomb's two letters to make it clear that he is not personally liable. The signature blocks read as follows:

> Under Whitcomb's signature were the typed words, "William K. Whitcomb, For Response to Hunger Network." In the letterhead, however, were the words, "National Council of the Churches of Christ in the United States of America, CHURCH WORLD SERVICE," with Whitcomb listed as its regional director.

> Under Whitcomb's signature were the typed words, "William K. Whitcomb, Canning Committee—RHN." The letterhead was captioned, "RESPONSE TO HUNGER NETWORK."

b. Other Sources of Agent's Liability to Third Party

Two other theories can render an agent liable to a third party with whom the agent deals. First, every agent who purports to contract on behalf of a principal impliedly warrants that he or she is authorized to do so. If the agent is not so authorized, the agent may be liable on the contract and, if the agent has affirmatively misrepresented his or her authority, the agent may be liable to the third party in tort as well. See *Restatement (Third)* §6.10. Second, simply acting as an agent does not, by itself, confer any immunity from tort liability. So, an agent acting on behalf of a principal may be liable in tort to a third party. See *Restatement (Third)* §§7.01 and 7.02.

5. Relation of the Principal to the Agent

a. Duties of the Agent

One of the core elements of the agency relationship is that the agent owes fiduciary duties to the principal, but the principal does not owe such duties to the agent. Because the agent typically has many more actions to perform than the principal does, the *Restatement (Third)* focuses much more on the agent's obligations than on the principal's.

An agent has a fiduciary duty to act loyally for the principal's benefit and several sections of the *Restatement (Third)* flesh out that duty. The agent may not gain any material benefit from the agency relationship, such as receiving a tip or other gratuity from a third party. The agent may not compete with, nor act adversely to, the principal. Finally, the agent must use the principal's property only for agency purposes and cannot communicate confidential information to others. See *Restatement (Third)* §§8.01–8.05, and 8.12.

The agent also owes other, nonfiduciary, obligations to the principal. The agent has a duty to act only within the scope of actual authority, to comply with all reasonable instructions from the principal, and to comply with any contractual obligations between the agent and principal. See *Restatement (Third)* §§8.07 and 8.09. The agent must use reasonable care and act reasonably so as not to damage the principal's enterprise. See *Restatement (Third)* §§8.08 and 8.10. Finally, the agent must render information to the principal that the agent believes the principal would want to know. See *Restatement (Third)* §8.11.

b. Duties of the Principal

Because the agent undertakes actions for the principal, and not the other way around, the principal has fewer duties toward the agent. Most importantly, the principal is not a fiduciary and so is generally free to act in his or her own best interest rather than in the agent's best interest. The principal must deal fairly and in good faith with the agent and must honor any contract duties between the two of them. Further, the principal must indemnify the agent for out-of-pocket costs in performing agency duties and whenever else indemnification would be fair.

6. Termination of the Agency Relationship

a. Termination of Actual and Apparent Authority

The termination of an agent's apparent authority is straightforward and intuitive. Because apparent authority is rooted in the third party's belief, apparent authority ends when it is no longer reasonable for the third party to believe that the agent has actual authority. Note that simply because an agent's actual authority has ended does not mean that the agent's apparent authority has ended. See *Restatement (Third)* §3.11.

Terminating actual authority is trickier. The parties may, of course, agree to end their agency relationship. Further, because agency is based in personal relationships, either party may, with a small exception, unilaterally end the agency relationship. In this setting the agent is said to *renounce* and the principal is said to *revoke* the agency. Renunciation or revocation is effective only when the other party has notice of it. While renunciation is always possible and effective, revocation is not effective if the power given to the agent has been made irrevocable in certain ways. Historically, because the agency relationship was a personal one, either party could unilaterally end the relationship at any time and a promise not to revoke or renounce was unenforceable, even when supported by consideration. Over time, though, some agents had a heightened interest in the continuation of the agency relationship and such agencies were deemed to be irrevocable so long as the agent retained the additional interest. These were agency powers *coupled with an interest*. That phrase has generated innumerable cases and commentaries. The *Restatement (Third)* uses the phrase *power given as security* to embrace a somewhat broader concept. For business entities purposes, an agency that can be made irrevocable is a proxy. A proxy is simply an agency relationship in which the agent has actual authority to vote the principal's shares of stock either as directed by the principal, a limited proxy, or as the agent thinks best in the principal's interest, a general proxy. See *Restatement (Third)* §§3.09, 3.10, 3.12, and 3.13.

Another consequence of the personal nature of an agency relationship is that death or incapacity may terminate the agency. The agent's death, without more, terminates actual authority. A principal's death terminates an agent's actual authority when the agent receives notice of it. Where a principal loses capacity to act, the agent is likewise prohibited from performing that act. See *Restatement (Third)* §§3.07 and 3.08.

C. TERMS OF ART IN THIS CHAPTER

Actual authority	Estoppel	Restitution
Adverse selection	Monitor	Revoke
Agency costs	Moral hazard	Scope of employment
Agent	Principal	Shirking
Apparent authority	Private benefits	Signaling
Bonding	Ratcheting	Team production
Coupled with an interest	Ratification	Undisclosed principal
Disclosed principal	Renounce	Unidentified principal
Employee	Respondeat superior	Vicarious liability

Part III.

CORPORATIONS

A. Creation

5

The Incorporation Process

This chapter focuses on issues that arise during the process of creating a corporation. It begins with a consideration of the circumstances in which the persons who are organizing the corporation (called the *promoters*) will be personally liable for actions they take to begin doing business in the corporate form. A related question is whether the creation of the corporation affects the promoters' liability. This chapter next looks at the consequences of selecting a state in which the corporation is to be incorporated. As we will see, corporate planners have a large degree of control over the law that will be applied to the corporation's internal governance. A third focus of this chapter is on the steps that must be followed to draft the corporation's basic documents, to ensure the filing of the requisite documents with the state, and to complete the initial organization of the corporation. Although that process is not a difficult one conceptually or legally, in a surprising number of instances a problem develops that delays the formation of the corporation beyond the anticipated incorporation date. A fourth topic for this chapter is the consequences of a defect in the incorporation process. More specifically, we look at the circumstances in which the promoters may be shielded from individual liability even though the corporation is not properly formed. Finally, this chapter considers the ethical considerations that become especially prominent when a lawyer represents multiple individuals engaged in a common enterprise (as often occurs when promoters form a corporation) and when a lawyer represents an entity.

A. PROMOTER LIABILITY

Moneywatch Companies v. Wilbers
665 N.E.2d 689 (Ohio Ct. App. 1995)

POWELL, J.

Defendant-appellant, Jeffrey Wilbers, appeals a decision of the Butler County Court of Common Pleas in favor of plaintiff-appellee, Moneywatch Companies, in a breach of contract action.

In December 1992, appellant entered into negotiations with appellee, through its property manager, Rebecca Reed, for the lease of commercial property space in the

Kitty Hawk Center located in Middletown, Ohio. During the negotiations, appellant indicated that he intended to create a corporation and needed the space for a golfing business he wanted to open. Reed testified that although appellant told her that he would be forming a corporation, she advised appellant that he would have to remain personally liable on the lease even if a corporation was subsequently created. Appellant testified that he never intended to assume personal liability on the lease and that appellee never advised him that he would have to be personally liable under the lease. At appellee's request, appellant submitted a personal financial statement and business plan.

On December 23, 1992, a lease agreement was signed naming appellee as land-lord and "Jeff Wilbers, dba Golfing Adventures" as tenant. The lease agreement provided that rent would not be due until March 1, 1993. On January 11, 1993, articles of incorporation for "J & J Adventures, Inc." were signed by "Jeff Wilbers, Incorporator." On February 8, 1993, the Ohio Secretary of State certified the corporation . . . .

Appellant notified appellee of the incorporation of J & J Adventures, Inc. and asked that the name of the tenant on the lease be changed from "Jeff Wilbers, dba Golfing Adventures" to "J & J Adventures, Inc., dba Golfing Adventures." In a letter dated March 1, 1993, from appellee to appellant, appellee informed appellant that the name of the tenant on the lease would be so changed and that "[t]his name change shall be deemed a part of the entire Lease Agreement." Reed testified that appellant did not request a release of personal liability under the lease at this time. Appellant testified that he did not seek release of personal liability because he never thought he was personally liable under the lease.

Throughout the lease period, rent was paid with checks bearing the corporation's name and address. The address listed on the checks was the address of the leased property. The rent checks for March and April 1993 were signed by "Judy G. Wilbers — Secretary/Treasurer" and rent checks signed in July and August, 1993, were signed by "J & J Adventures, Inc. By Jeffrey Wilbers — president." However, all correspondence from appellee to appellant was addressed to "Jeff Wilbers" and mailed to his home address.

At some time during 1993, the corporation defaulted and vacated the premises. Appellee brought a breach of contract action against appellant in his personal capacity. After a bench trial, the trial court entered judgment in favor of appellee and ordered appellant to pay appellee the sum of $13,922.67 plus interest and costs. It is from this decision that appellant now appeals.

In his sole assignment of error, appellant contends that he is not personally liable under the lease agreement because a novation was accomplished by the substitution of "J & J Adventures, Inc., dba Golfing Adventures," a corporate party, for "Jeff Wilbers, dba Golfing Adventures," an individual party. A novation occurs "where a previous valid obligation is extinguished by a new valid contract, accomplished by substitution of parties or of the undertaking, with the consent of all the parties, and based on valid consideration." . . . In order to effect a valid novation, all parties to the original contract must clearly and definitely intend the second agreement to be a novation and intend to completely disregard the original contract obligation. . . . In addition, to be enforceable a novation requires consideration. . . . A novation can never be presumed.

In this case, it is undisputed that both parties agreed to the substitution of the corporation in place of appellant as tenant on the lease. However, there is no clear and definite intent on appellee's part to create a new contract through novation. The record indicates that appellee made statements during the negotiation and execution of the lease to the effect that appellant would have to be personally liable on the lease even if a corporation were formed, that all correspondence from appellee to appellant was mailed to appellant, individually, at his home address, that there was no release of appellant from personal liability under the lease at the time of the name change, and that the lease was not re-executed at the time of the name change and appellant's personal signature, rather than a signature on behalf of the corporation, remained on the lease. Thus, we find insufficient evidence in the record which would indicate an intent on appellee's part to release appellant from individual liability and look solely to the corporation in the event of a breach.

Where the parties to a contract and a third party are all in agreement that one party will be released from the contract obligations and the third party substituted in its place, a novation has occurred and additional consideration, over and above the release and substitution, is not required. As this court stated in *McGlothin* [*v. Huffman*], 640 N.E.2d at 601 (Oh. App. 1994), "[t]he discharge of the existing obligation of a party to a contract is sufficient consideration for a contract of novation."

In this case, the substitution of tenant names on the lease does not constitute a novation because there was no discharge of appellant from his original obligations under the lease. . . . Likewise, the record does not indicate a benefit flowing to appellee by accepting the substitution of tenants. In the absence of a release and benefit to the respective parties, there is insufficient consideration to support a novation. Under the circumstances, we find that the substitution of tenant names on the lease agreement does not constitute a novation.

Appellant also contends that he is not personally liable under the lease agreement because he executed the lease as a corporate promoter on behalf of a future corporation.

Corporate promoters are "those who participate in bringing about the organization of an incorporated company, and in getting it in condition for transacting the business for which it is organized." *Yeiser v. United States Bd. & Paper Co.*, 107 F. 340, 344 (6th Cir., 1901); . . . A promoter is not personally liable on a contract made prior to incorporation which is made "in the name and solely on the credit of the future corporation." *Stewart Realty Co., Inc. v. Keller* 193 N.E.2d 179, 181 (1962). Further, a corporation does not assume a contract made on its behalf by the mere act of incorporation. . . .

In addressing the issue of promoter liability on contracts executed on behalf of a corporation to be formed in the future, the Ohio Supreme Court recently stated:

> "It is axiomatic that the promoters of a corporation are at least initially liable on any contracts they execute in furtherance of the corporate entity prior to its formation. The promoters are released from liability only where the contract provides that performance is to be the obligation of the corporation, the corporation is ultimately formed, and the corporation then formally adopts the contract.
>
> . . .
>
> "Moreover, mere adoption of the contract by the corporation will not relieve promoters from liability in the absence of a subsequent novation. * * * Consequently, the promoters of a corporation who execute a contract on its behalf are personally liable for the breach thereof irrespective of the later adoption of the contract by the corporation unless the contract provides that performance thereunder is solely the responsibility of the corporation." (Citations omitted.) *Illinois Controls, Inc. v. Langham*, 639 N.E.2d 771, 781 (Oh. 1994).

In this case, appellant can be deemed a promoter because he participated in bringing about the organization of the corporation and in getting it ready for business. However, the original lease was not made "in the name and solely on the credit of the future corporation." *Stewart Realty Co., supra.* To the contrary, the lease was executed by appellant, individually, on his own credit, as evidenced by the submission of appellant's personal financial statement during the negotiation and execution of the lease.

In this case, the lease agreement does not provide that the corporation will be exclusively liable under its terms even though the corporation is now listed as tenant. In fact, appellant's individual signature remains on the lease agreement. . . . In addition, there is no evidence that the corporation, once formed, formally adopted the lease agreement as executed by appellant. In the absence of the necessary steps which must be taken to ensure that appellant is not personally liable and the corporation is solely liable under the lease, appellant is liable under the lease.

Judgment affirmed.

WILLIAM W. YOUNG, P.J., and KOEHLER, J., concur.

Notes and Questions

1. Reality Check

a. What is a "promoter"? What is the consequence of deeming someone a promoter?

b. What were Mr. Wilbers's two arguments for avoiding personal liability?

c. What was the purpose of changing the lessee's name on the lease if it was not intended to work a novation?

d. What was Moneywatch's intention in obtaining personal financial information from Mr. Wilbers?

2. Suppose

a. Suppose Mr. Wilbers had no assets but the corporation had sufficient assets to pay the lease obligations. Could Moneywatch recover against the corporation?

b. What if the lease had been executed only in the name of the corporation and both Mr. Wilbers and Moneywatch knew that the corporation had not yet been incorporated?

c. Imagine that the lease had been executed, "Jeff Wilbers, as agent for Golfing Adventures, Inc., a corporation to be formed." Would this have made it more clear or less clear that Mr. Wilbers was to be personally liable?

3. What Do You Think?

a. Cases such as this arise with considerable frequency. What do you think the root cause of such cases is?

b. Do you think careful drafting would eliminate these cases? How would you have advised Mr. Wilbers in this case? Moneywatch?

4. You Draft It

a. Redraft the original lease agreement to make it clear that Mr. Wilbers is not personally liable. Redraft the agreement to make it clear that he is personally liable.

b. Assume that Mr. Wilbers was clearly personally liable on the original lease agreement. Draft language that makes it clear that J & J Adventures, Inc., is replacing Mr. Wilbers as the sole lessee.

B. CHOICE OF JURISDICTION

1. Why the Corporation's Jurisdiction Matters — The Internal Affairs Doctrine

a. The Current Setting

Usually a business that will operate in only one state will choose to incorporate in that state. Nonetheless, a corporation may be incorporated in any state even though it will have no other connection to that state. If the corporation is to be incorporated in another jurisdiction, the attorney often retains a so-called service corporation to handle the mechanics. These service corporations assist lawyers by preparing the appropriate incorporation papers and shepherding them through the administrative process. For an additional fee, these service corporations will provide the new corporation's registered office and act as its agent for service of process within the state of incorporation.

Now that you understand that you can form a corporation in any state, even one with which it will have no connection, the obvious question is, "why would you want to?" The choice of the state of incorporation has no effect on the corporation in many settings. For example, XYZ, Inc., a corporation that does business only in California, is certainly subject to personal jurisdiction in California even if it is incorporated in New York. California can also impose taxes on XYZ, Inc., and can enforce its consumer protection, employee safety, and environmental laws provided it does not discriminate between corporations incorporated in California (called *domestic* corporations) and those incorporated in other U.S. states (called, somewhat misleadingly, *foreign* corporations).

New York (the state of incorporation) could also exercise personal jurisdiction over XYZ, Inc. Can New York apply its own contract law to XYZ, Inc., even though the corporation operates only in California? What about applying New York's consumer protection, employee safety, and environmental laws to XYZ, Inc.? What happens if the law of the state of incorporation conflicts with the law of a state in which the corporation operates? The American Law Institute's *Restatement (Second) of Conflict of Laws* describes the doctrines that resolve these questions, at least in some instances.

> [C]orporations and individuals alike make contracts, commit torts and receive and transfer assets. Issues involving acts such as these when done by a corporation are determined by the same choice-of-law principles as are applicable to non-corporate parties.
>
> *Restatement (Second) of Conflict of Laws* §301, cmt. b

The *Restatement (Second) of Conflict of Laws* provides that corporate actions that could *not* be done by an individual will (with a possible exception noted in the Back-

ground and Context section below) be governed by the law of the state of incorporation. *Restatement (Second) of Conflict of Laws* §302. That section's comment explains
further.

Comment:
  Scope of section. Many of the matters that fall within the scope of the rule of this
Section involve the "*internal affairs*" of a corporation — that is the relations inter se of
the corporation, its shareholders, directors, officers or agents. . . . Other such matters
affect the interests of the corporation's creditors.

  Matters falling within the scope of the rule of this Section and which involve
primarily a corporation's relationship to its shareholders include steps taken in the
course of the original incorporation, the election or appointment of directors and
officers, the adoption of bylaws, the issuance of corporate shares, preemptive rights,
the holding of directors' and shareholders' meetings, methods of voting including
any requirement for cumulative voting, shareholders' rights to examine corporate
records, charter and bylaw amendments, mergers, consolidations and reorganizations and the reclassification of shares. Matters which may also affect the interests of
the corporation's creditors include the issuance of bonds, the declaration and payment of dividends, loans by the corporation to directors, officers and shareholders,
and the purchase and redemption by the corporation of outstanding shares of its
own stock.

  Rationale. Uniform treatment of directors, officers and shareholders is an important objective which can only be attained by having the rights and liabilities of those
persons with respect to the corporation governed by a single law. To the extent that
they think about the matter, these persons would usually expect that their rights and
duties with respect to the corporation would be determined by the [law] of the state of
incorporation. This state is also easy to identify, and thus the value of ease of application is attained when the [law] of this state is applied.

  [I]t would be impractical to have matters . . . which involve a corporation's organic
structure or internal administration, governed by different laws. It would be impractical, for example, if an election of directors, an issuance of shares, a payment of
dividends, a charter amendment, or a consolidation or reorganization were to be
held valid in one state and invalid in another.

Which legal issues are governed by the state of incorporation and which issues
are not is not always clear. The Comment to §302 above lists several legal questions
within the internal affairs doctrine. Other sections list these additional issues as
being within the internal affairs of a corporation: who the shareholders are
(§303); shareholder voting and dividend rights (although not shareholder inspection rights, see Comment d and *Sadler v. NCR Corp.*, 928 F.2d 48 (2d Cir. 1991))
(§304); the voting rights of a trustee of a voting trust (but not the rights of the
trust's beneficiaries, see Comment b) (§305); the fiduciary duty (if any) of a majority shareholder (§306); and director and officer liability (§309). Section 307
includes shareholder liability for the purchase price of shares, but not shareholder
liability under piercing the veil principles. The few state courts that have considered
the question of choice of law in the piercing the veil context have tended to assume,
without significant discussion, that the law of the state of incorporation should
apply. See *Kalb, Voorhis & Co. v. American Financial Corp.*, 8 F.3d 130 (2d
Cir. 1993) (erroneously interpreting *Restatement (Second) of Conflict of Laws*
§307 as applying to piercing issues).

b. Background and Context

The *Restatement (Second) of Conflict of Laws* §302 provides that the internal affairs doctrine will not be applied "in the unusual case where . . . some other state has a more significant relationship to the occurrence and the parties. . . ." The comment and reporter's note to §302 elaborate on this exception:

> **When [law] of state of incorporation will not be applied.** [I]t is in situations where the corporation has little contact with the state of its incorporation that the [law] of some other state is most likely to be applied when (1) the relevant rules of the other state embody an important policy of that state and (2) the matter involved does not affect the corporation's organic structure or internal administration and therefore does not fall within the category of issues which . . . cannot practicably be determined differently in different states.
>
> **Reporter's Note**
>
> The great majority of cases have applied the [law] of the state of incorporation to determine issues involving matters peculiar to corporations. [However], [i]n *Western Airlines, Inc. v. Sobieski*, 12 Cal. Rptr. 719 (Cal. App. 1961), a California statute was applied to prevent a Delaware corporation from eliminating cumulative voting. The corporation did no business in Delaware. On the other hand, it had been originally incorporated in California, did substantial business in that state and a substantial number of its shareholders were domiciled there. The opinion of the court does not indicate whether cumulative voting was required by the [law] of the other States where the corporation did business and where some of its shareholders were domiciled.

The *Restatement (Second) of Conflict of Laws* was adopted before the U.S. Supreme Court decided *CTS Corp. v. Dynamics Corp. of America*, 481 U.S. 69 (1987). That case may, as a practical matter, require the internal affairs doctrine to be applied under the Commerce Clause of the U.S. Constitution. If so, then states no longer have the option to apply their own law to the internal affairs of foreign corporations. Thus the validity of §302(2)'s "more significant relationship" test and the validity of the *Western Airlines* case are in substantial doubt. On the other hand, a few states have statutes that purport to impose their corporations code (or parts of it) on certain foreign corporations. See, e.g., Cal. Corp. Code §2115 and Washington RCW 23B.19.020(19)(b) (purporting to apply Washington's antitakeover act to foreign corporations with specified significant contacts in Washington State).

> [A]pplication of the internal affairs doctrine is not merely a principle of conflicts law. It is also one of serious constitutional proportions — under due process, the commerce clause and the full faith and credit clause — so that the law of one state governs the relationships of a corporation to its stockholders, directors and officers in matters of internal corporate governance. The alternatives present almost intolerable consequences to the corporate enterprise and its managers. With the existence of multistate and multinational organizations, directors and officers have a significant right, under the fourteenth amendment's due process clause, to know what law will be applied to their actions. Stockholders also have a right to know by what standards of accountability they may hold those managing the corporation's business and affairs.
>
> > This Court's [i.e. U.S. Supreme Court] recent Commerce Clause cases also have invalidated statutes that adversely may affect interstate commerce by subjecting activities to inconsistent regulations . . . So long as each State regulates voting rights only in the corporations it has created, each corporation will be subject to the law of only one state. No principle of corporation law and practice is more firmly established than a State's authority to regulate domestic

corporations, including the authority to define the voting rights of shareholders.... This beneficial free market system depends at its core upon the fact that a corporation — except in the rarest situations — is organized under, and governed by, the law of a single jurisdiction, traditionally the corporate law of the state of its incorporation.

CTS Corp. v. Dynamics Corp. of America, 481 U.S. 69 (1987) (citations omitted).

Thus, we conclude that application of the internal affairs doctrine is mandated by constitutional principles, except in "the rarest situations."

In the early part of the twentieth century, the internal affairs doctrine was deemed to have constitutional support under the full faith and credit clause.[13] ... However, in 1935 the Supreme Court developed a balancing test to be used when evaluating whether full faith and credit was applicable. *Alaska Packers Assoc. v. Industrial Accident Commn.*, 294 U.S. 532 (1935). A party bringing a full faith and credit claim thereafter bore the burden of establishing that conflicting interests of a foreign state were superior to those of the forum state. *Id.* at 547.

[W]e believe that full faith and credit commands application of the internal affairs doctrine except in the rare circumstance where national policy is outweighed by a significant interest of the forum state in the corporation and its shareholders.

McDermott Inc. v. Lewis, 531 A.2d 206 (Del. 1987) (Moore, J.)

Notes and Questions

1. Reality Check

a. When a foreign corporation is sued, what choice of law rule will the court adopt?

b. What are the possible sources of the choice of law rules a court will follow?

2. What Do You Think?

a. Do you think corporations and their advisors should, in effect, be able to choose the internal governance rules that will apply? Are those rules any different from tort rules or employee rules such as maximum hours rules that are imposed by the state in which the business operates, regardless of where it is incorporated?

b. If only one state's law is to be applied to internal governance matters, why should that state be the state of incorporation rather than, for example, the state in which the corporation has its headquarters or has the majority of its assets? Would such a rule be constitutional? If it is constitutional, is it workable?

2. The Special Role of Delaware

By choosing the state of incorporation one chooses the corporate governance rules that will apply to a new corporation. At first blush this may seem to open up a wide variety of choices for the lawyer and client because there are fifty states and the District of Columbia. But this choice is deceptive for two reasons. First, the substantive rule on

---

13. This clause directs that "Full Faith and Credit shall be given in each State to the Public Acts, Records, and judicial Proceedings of every other State ..." U.S. Const. art. IV, §1.

many issues is identical in many states. Thus there are not fifty-one completely different sets of rules. Second, the vast majority of provisions in every statute can be varied in the articles or bylaws. No matter in which state a corporation is incorporated, its governance rules can be tailored considerably. Only rarely will a state's statute contain an unmodifiable provision that is important to the planners.

So why should the choice ever be any state other than the one in which the corporation intends to do business? More specifically, why Delaware? Delaware is certainly the most popular choice for publicly traded companies. About 300 of the 500 largest companies, and roughly half of the 1,500 companies on the New York Stock Exchange are incorporated in Delaware. Delaware is also the most popular choice for nonpublic companies that are not incorporated in their home states. Delaware has over 6 percent of the nation's 4.7 million corporations, about 20 times more than its share of the total population (Delaware has 0.3% of the country's population).

What explains this popularity? Delaware's general corporation act is both advantageous to management and quite flexible, so that planners can vary almost any provision. But those qualities do not distinguish Delaware from most other states. The answer is threefold. First, and least importantly, Delaware corporate law is familiar to most corporate lawyers in the United States. It is their natural suggestion for an alternative to the home state. Second, a large body of case law interpreting the statute provides a measure of predictability, and hence comfort, for corporations. Third, Delaware has a specialized court, the Court of Chancery, that handles corporate matters. The chancellor and four vice chancellors handle cases with the speed often required in important business matters. Appeals go directly to the Delaware Supreme Court (Delaware has no intermediate court of appeals), which can also act with dispatch when necessary.

C. INCORPORATION MECHANICS

Incorporating a new corporation is a quintessential lawyer task. The lawyer must be familiar with the minutiae of the requirements in the state in which he or she practices and, usually, Delaware as well. The process entails assembling the requisite information from the client; reserving the new corporation's name; preparing the incorporation documents; arranging for payment of the filing fees (for example, states vary considerably as to whether they will accept credit cards, personal checks, or certified checks); transmitting the documents and fees to the appropriate government office (states also vary as to whether they will accept transmittals via private overnight services, whether papers will be accepted at more than one location, or whether incorporation can be effected electronically); ensuring that the incorporation papers are filed and that the corporation has come into existence; organizing the corporation (i.e., electing directors, appointing officers, adopting bylaws, issuing stock, and beginning to engage in business); and filing any postincorporation forms that may be required.

A misstep in any of these undertakings is often professionally embarrassing, at the least. Sometimes a lawyer's mistake will have more important consequences. For example, suppose the lawyer neglects to determine whether the desired name of the proposed corporation is available. The client may have purchased stationery and signage featuring the desired name and may have to incur additional expenses to reorder such items with a new name if the original name cannot be secured. Even more deleterious is the setting in which a lawyer's mistake delays the formation of a corporation that is to undertake a particular venture. In such instances a valuable business opportunity may be jeopardized because the new corporation cannot enter into agreements because it has not yet been formed. The alternatives are to wait until incorporation is accomplished or to have the promoters bind themselves personally. Neither of these options is particularly appealing to clients, and each has its perils. Business opportunities have an evanescent nature and delay in accepting a proposal may result in the opportunity being lost. On the other hand, if the promoters accept the proposal personally, they are (as you know from the material above) exposed to expanded liability. Hardly the result anticipated when retaining a lawyer!

The next sections outline the tasks a lawyer must undertake to incorporate a new venture.

1. Reserving the Name

State statutes typically provide that a corporate name may be reserved, usually for 90 to 180 days, with the payment of a small fee. See MBCA §4.02. Reserving the name allows clients to prepare to do business immediately following incorporation and ensures that the incorporation will not be delayed because an unavailable name has been selected. Under both Delaware and the MBCA the name must be distinguishable from the name of every other corporation on file with the secretary of state. See DGCL §102(a)(1), MBCA §4.01. In some states this requirement is a narrow one; a corporate name is acceptable if it is different in any way. In other states, including most MBCA states, a name is not distinguishable if it is different in such minor ways as punctuation, capitalization, or use of a definite article or a plural in the name.

Under the law of most states a corporate name must contain some evidence that the entity is a corporation and must not contain words falsely suggesting that the new corporation will engage in certain businesses, usually those involving banking or other financial services. In Delaware, for example, the corporate name must contain the word or abbreviation for *association, company, corporation, club, foundation, fund, incorporated, institute, society, union, syndicate,* or *limited,* or similar words or abbreviations in other languages, and cannot include the word *bank* unless the corporation is licensed to engage in banking. See DGCL §102(a)(1).[1] The MBCA requires the word or abbreviation for *corporation, incorporated, company,* or *limited* and prohibits the use of the words *bank, banking, banker, trust, cooperative,* or any combination of the words *industrial* and *loan,* or any combination of any two or more of the words *building, savings, loan, home, association,* and *society.* See MBCA §4.01.

2. The Incorporation Documents

The document that creates and governs the corporation is called the Certificate of Incorporation in Delaware and the Articles of Incorporation under the MBCA. This book will usually use the term *Articles of Incorporation* or *Articles* unless referring to Delaware alone. In many if not most states the statute authorizes a government

---

1. These restrictions do not apply to corporations with more than $10 million in total assets, presumably because nearly all entities of such size are corporations.

official, usually the secretary of state, to promulgate a standard form that may or must be used to incorporate. In virtually every state the information required in the Articles is relatively minimal. See Del. §102(a), MBCA §2.02(a). The Articles must contain the corporation's name and the name and address of each person who is incorporating the new entity. Often the lawyer or a member of his or her staff acts as the incorporator. The Articles must also name a person, or other corporation, who will act as the corporation's agent upon whom service of process may be made and must identify an address within the state where the registered agent may be served. These requirements exist so that personal jurisdiction may be properly asserted over the corporation. The registered office need not be a place where the corporation does business, nor does the registered agent need to have any other connection to the corporation. Typically, when a corporation has incorporated in a foreign jurisdiction, it will engage a corporation service company to act as its registered agent and to provide the registered office.

The Articles must also state the maximum number of shares the corporation may issue (the actual number issued may be far fewer than the maximum stated in the Articles) and, if the shares are to have different management or economic rights, a statement as to how the shares will differ from one another. Finally, many states require the Articles to state the purpose for which the corporation is being formed. This requirement has become largely a dead letter, because in every state the Articles may simply state that the corporation may engage in any lawful business. See DGCL §102(a)(3). Indeed, at least one state *requires* the Articles to contain such a provision! See Cal. Corp. Code §202(b). The MBCA does not require the Articles to state the corporation's purpose. The MBCA, although not Delaware, also requires that the number of directors or a process for determining the number of directors, be stated in the Articles or bylaws. See MBCA §8.03(a).

States also permit the Articles to contain certain optional provisions. Perhaps the most practically important of these is the ability to name the initial directors in the Articles. See Del. Code §102(a)(6), MBCA §2.02(b)(1). Many persons who agree to act as incorporator intend to have no further power over the new corporation once it is formed. They are often simply the attorney or service corporation employee who is in charge of making sure the new entity is created. By naming the initial directors in the Articles, the incorporator will be automatically relieved of any authority over, and also relieved of any liability for, the new corporation once it is created. Delaware Code §102(b) provides a list of optional provisions for the Certificate of Incorporation. Official Comments 4 and 5 to the Model Act have extremely useful checklists of the governance provisions that may be modified in the Articles or bylaws.

3. Filing

Filing is the action by which the state accepts the Articles. Filing is of great importance because it is through filing that the corporation comes into existence. See DGCL §106, MBCA §2.03(a). The statutes contain surprisingly detailed requirements for filing. The secretary of state (the official usually in charge of corporations) may promulgate additional requirements. A lawyer who fails to follow both the statutory and administrative requirements for incorporating a new venture will find that the Articles are rejected for filing, which will, at best, cause a delay and, at worst, present a large obstacle to the success of the new business venture.

Delaware provides that anyone may form a corporation by delivering a Certificate of Incorporation to the secretary of state. See DGCL §§101(a), 103(c)(1). The Certificate must be executed by an incorporator whose signature is "acknowledged" either by the signature alone or by being notarized. See DGCL §§103(a)(1), 103(b). When the executed and acknowledged Certificate, along with any required taxes and fees, are delivered to the secretary of state, the Certificate is stamped "filed" and becomes effective at that moment. See DGCL §§103(c), 103(d).

The MBCA has a similar process. Anyone may form a corporation by delivering the Articles of Incorporation to the secretary of state. See MBCA §2.01. Among other requirements, the Articles must be executed by an incorporator. The Articles, one copy of them (if the incorporator is filing paper documents rather than filing electronically), and the required fees and taxes must be delivered to the secretary of state, who will file them if they are in order by stamping them and returning the copy of the Articles to the corporation. See MBCA §§1.20, 1.25. The corporation comes into existence as of the close of business on the day the Articles are filed. See MBCA §1.23.

4. Organizing the New Corporation

Once the corporation has been formed, the lawyer must ensure that it is properly organized. Even if the initial directors were named in the Articles, the corporation has no officers or bylaws, nor has it taken any action. It does not, as yet, even have any owners. The organizational meeting is designed to complete these tasks. In most states, the minimum actions to be accomplished are electing directors (if they are not named in the Articles), adopting bylaws, and appointing officers. Under most statutes, an actual meeting is unnecessary if the incorporators (or initial directors) act by unanimous consent. Acting by consent is the typical method of effecting these tasks because it is usually easier than convening an actual meeting. See DGCL §108, MBCA §2.05. Note that the statutes do *not* require the corporation to issue stock at the organizational meeting. Nevertheless, case law in most jurisdictions provides that a corporation cannot engage in business until it has received valid consideration in exchange for shares.

D. DEFECTIVE INCORPORATION

None of the prerequisites for forming a corporation is particularly challenging. Still, promoters frequently enter into obligations before the corporation is actually formed. In *Moneywatch*, the plaintiff claimed to have intended to contract with Jeff Wilbers, the promoter, in his personal capacity. But where the intention of the parties is definitely to contract solely with the promoter's corporation, yet the corporation does not exist when the contract is made, may the third party nonetheless hold the promoter personally liable? This issue and its resolution are known as the problem of *defective incorporation*. The background and context section shows that the problem was more acute in an earlier day and also shows the origins of the modern approaches to defective incorporation.

1. Background and Context

Until after the Second World War, states varied in defining the point in the incorporation process when a corporation actually came into existence. Many states also imposed requirements after incorporation, such as filing the Articles in the county where the corporation's headquarters were to be located, or having received a certain amount of money (often $1,000). These requirements were sometimes conditions subsequent, meaning that the corporation would cease to exist if those subsequent actions were not taken. These variations and uncertainties resulted in many lawsuits in which a promoter was sued personally for obligations ostensibly made in the name of a nascent corporation. The widespread adoption of the original Model Business Corporations Act of 1950 brought a fair degree of clarity to these issues. But by then the common law had developed a number of equitable doctrines that relieved promoters from personal liability in defective incorporation settings. The excerpt from a distinguished pre-War treatise describes how these doctrines operated in the days in which defective incorporation was a frequent occurrence.

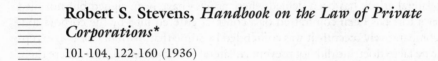 **Robert S. Stevens,** *Handbook on the Law of Private Corporations**

101-104, 122-160 (1936)

[W]hen, in the effort to incorporate, there has been an irregular or incomplete compliance with the statutory requirements, questions arise as to the effect to be attributed to the neglect or noncompliance. Are all of the requirements of equal importance so that full compliance with each of them is a necessary condition precedent to incorporation? The statutes are not always specific. The medley of requirements is too frequently jumbled without distinction. A search has to be made for the legislative intention. [I]s it not probable that the Legislature intended some of its requirements to be complied with before incorporation and some of them after incorporation? May it not have attached different degrees of importance to the several requirements? These are the considerations which lead the courts to the discovery of a legislative intention to distinguish between conditions precedent and conditions subsequent and between mandatory and directory provisions.

As a result of this discriminating whittling by the courts, the conclusion is reached that there will be a corporation *de jure*, that is, one unassailable by the state in a direct proceeding, if there has been a substantial compliance with all mandatory provisions which are intended to be conditions precedent to incorporation. [A] failure to comply with directory provisions will not be fatal to valid incorporation. Whether a particular provision is mandatory or merely directory must be determined by ascertaining the intention of the Legislature. As statutory schemes differ somewhat, legislative intentions may differ, and accordingly, courts of one state reach the conclusion that a certain requirement is only directory, whereas the courts of another state find that its Legislature intended the same type of requirement to be mandatory.

When incorporation is defective to the extent that it is subject to successful attack by the state and yet not open to collateral attack in private litigation, . . . then it is said that there is a *de facto* corporation. The de facto doctrine effects a compromise between conflicting public interests — the one opposed to an unauthorized assumption of corporateness; the other in favor of doing justice to the parties and of establishing a general assurance of security in business dealings with corporations. Is there a statute under which a corporation of this type might have been validly formed? Has there been a real, though insufficient, attempt to comply with the provisions of this statute? Has there been a user or exercise of corporate privileges? If these questions are answered in the affirmative, it is said that the "elements" of the de facto doctrine are present. Then, granting that these mitigating circumstances are present, a second inquiry is pursued as to the nature of the cause of action and whether the facts out of which it grew are such as to warrant the permission or denial of collateral attack.

While the formula of the de facto doctrine embraces the requirement of a bona fide or colorable attempt to comply with the statute, there is no agreement as to what constitutes a bona fide or colorable compliance. Collateral attack has been permitted where the articles of incorporation were not signed until four months after contracting with the plaintiffs, where a contract was entered into after the articles had been signed but before they had been filed in the county clerk's office and published as required, and where they have been executed and recorded but not filed. On the other hand, collateral attack has been denied where articles have been signed but not filed until after a tort has been committed or a contract entered into by the corporation. [U]ntil comparatively recently it was contended by some that, with one or two exceptions, the de facto doctrine did not prevent collateral attack except in cases where there had been a mutual assumption of corporateness.

The expression "estoppel" has . . . been applied in those cases where the third party, who has contracted with the supposed corporation, is prevented from collaterally attacking the validity of the incorporation. This principle that parties who deal with each other upon a mutual assumption of the existence of a certain fact are prevented from disputing that fact is frequently referred to as "estoppel." The associates have reason to believe that they were validly incorporated, and therefore protected against unlimited liability. The third party contracted for corporate liability and to permit him to hold the associates individually would be to impose upon them an unexpected liability and to confer upon him a more extensive right than was contracted for. According to the decisions in some jurisdictions, there can be no estoppel against an attack on the validity of the corporation unless the elements of the de facto doctrine are present; but, according to what seems to be the majority view, an estoppel will be permitted even when the elements of the de facto doctrine are lacking.

The establishment of the de facto doctrine has not been without protest. The objection has been advanced that, since incorporation is a prerogative of the Legislature, it is not for the courts to create corporations. When the Legislature has prescribed the method of incorporating, it is assumed that the Legislature intended that the associates should not, under any circumstances, be treated as incorporated unless the attempt to incorporate was in all respects complete and regular. If, in the face of this intention, the courts find corporateness, it is said that they are proclaiming themselves de facto legislatures in order to create de facto corporations.

When there is no de jure corporation, and when collateral attack may not be denied upon the basis either of the de facto doctrine or the principles of estoppel, should it follow that all the associates have incurred individual and unlimited responsibility because transactions have been entered into on behalf of the company? It seems surprising that the authorities should be conflicting upon so plain a proposition. Two reasons are advanced for relieving the associates from liability as partners: First, it is emphasized that they have not agreed among themselves to be partners. They have entered the association upon the understanding that liability was to be limited, and they have not conferred upon the board of managers authority to bind them individually as partners. Secondly, it is pointed out that the associates have held themselves out as a corporation and not as a partnership, and the party who has contracted with them has assumed that they were incorporated and contracted for limited liability only.

A rule which would impose partnership liability upon associates who are not entitled to the benefits of the de facto doctrine, ... would frequently impose great injustice and hardship on innocent shareholders. When, however, the associates cannot claim the benefits of innocence, when they have fraudulently represented that they were incorporated, knowing full well that they had not complied with the statutory provisions, a reason for shielding them from partnership liability vanishes. Similarly, another reason for insulating them from partnership liability is eliminated when it is found that the creditor did not contract with them as a corporation, but, on the contrary, understood that they were a partnership. Justice would be accomplished if all the associates were held at least to the full extent of the liability which they contemplated; that is, the liability that would have been theirs if incorporation had been perfect.

> Over time, the doctrine of de facto corporations has been "roundly criticized." *Robertson v. Levy*, 197 A.2d 443, 445 (D.C. App. 1964). [T]he [Old] Model Business Corporation Act ("MBCA (1950)") ... strove to ... provide some clarity and bright-line tests to previously clouded areas. MBCA (1950) sections 56 and 146 contain an express intent to abolish the concept of de facto corporations. * The comment to section 56 states:
>
>> Under the [MBCA (1950)], de jure incorporation is complete upon the issuance of the certificate of incorporation. ... [A]ny steps short of securing a certificate of incorporation would not constitute apparent compliance. Therefore a de facto corporation cannot exist under the [MBCA (1950)].
>
> Model Business Corporation Act (1950) Ann., §56 cmt., at 205. Similarly, the comment to section 146 states:
>
>> [S]ection [146] is designed to prohibit the application of any theory of de facto incorporation. The only authority to act as a corporation under the [MBCA (1950)] arises from completion of the [statutory] procedures. ... The consequences of those procedures are specified in section 56 as being the creation of a corporation. No other means being authorized, the effect of section 146 is to negate the possibility of a de facto corporation.
>>
>> Abolition of the concept of de facto incorporation, which at best was fuzzy, is a sound result. No reason exists for its continuance under general corporate

---

* Section 56 provided: Upon the issuance of the certificate of incorporation, the corporate existence shall begin, and such certificate of incorporation shall be conclusive evidence that all conditions precedent required to be performed by the incorporators have been complied with and that the corporation has been incorporated under this Act, except as against the State in a proceeding to cancel or revoke the certificate of incorporation or for involuntary dissolution of the corporation.

Section 146 provided: All persons who assume to act as a corporation without authority so to do shall be jointly and severally liable for all debts and liabilities incurred or arising as a result thereof. ED.

laws, where the process of acquiring de jure incorporation is both simple and clear. The vestigial appendage should be removed.

Id. §146 cmt., at 908-09.

American Vending Services, Inc. v. Morse, 881 P.2d 917 (Ut. App. 1994) (Greenwood, J.)

2. The Current Setting

Even though complying with the statutory requirements for incorporation is easy, promoters regularly contract on behalf of as-yet unincorporated corporations. This section explores whether promoters can be held personally liable in such settings.

a. De Facto Corporations

≡ Hill v. County Concrete Company, Inc.
≡ 672 A.2d 667 (Md. App. 1996)

EYLER, J.

The suit sought payment due on an open account. County Concrete filed an amended complaint and motion for summary judgment against "C & M Builders, Inc.," [Cecil] Hill, and Michael Newman. A judgment by default was entered against Newman..., and summary judgment was granted against "C & M Builders, Inc."...The case was tried without a jury before Judge Stephen M. Waldron on May 10, 1995. County Concrete asserts that Hill never validly incorporated "C & M Builders, Inc." and, thus, is liable in contract to County Concrete. Hill asserts that County Concrete knew it was dealing with a corporation and the corporation existed de facto....The trial judge declined to apply Hill's theories, based on a finding that Hill had not acted in good faith.

In 1988, Hill and Newman decided to start their own construction business, specializing in the pouring of concrete walls and foundations. In the latter part of that year, Hill and Newman sought the assistance of an attorney to form a corporation to be known as "C & M Builders, Inc." They were told by the attorney that the corporate name was available and that they could proceed with their business preparations. Hill and Newman ordered checks, painted trucks, and ordered letterhead, all imprinted or painted with the name "C & M Builders, Inc." A bank account was opened...in the name of "C & M Builders, Inc." on November 10, 1988. For reasons not reflected in the record, the attorney for Hill and Newman did not attempt to file the Articles of Incorporation until the end of February, 1989. At that time, Hill and Newman were informed by the attorney that the name, "C & M Builders, Inc.," had been previously registered with the State Department of Assessments & Taxation and was already being used; thus, it was no longer available to them. Hill and Newman decided to incorporate under another name, "H & N Construction, Inc."

The Articles of Incorporation of "H & N Construction, Inc." were dated May 3, 1989, and were filed...on May 4, 1989. [A bank] account was opened...in the name of "H & N Construction, Inc." on July 31, 1989. H & N Construction, Inc. filed an application for a construction license and indicated in the application that it was trading as "C & M Builders." An organizational meeting occurred, shares of stock were issued, and tax returns were filed. In short, "H & N Construction, Inc." complied with all the prerequisites and was a de jure corporation.

In February, 1989, County Concrete received an order in the name of "C & M Builders, Inc." for a specified amount of concrete. A principal of County Concrete testified that he had no knowledge of that entity and went to the job site identified in the order. He learned that Hill and Newman were involved with that corporation, and because he knew Hill by reputation, he agreed to establish an account in the name of "C & M Builders, Inc." The first payment was made to County Concrete by check dated February 10, 1989, bearing the name, "C & M Builders, Inc." Subsequently, payments were made by various checks bearing the same name. There were letters directed to County Concrete on stationery bearing the letterhead, "C & M Builders, Inc." The first delivery of concrete occurred on February 11, 1989. There were several deliveries thereafter, the last occurring on May 8, 1991. It is uncontroverted that County Concrete thought it was dealing with a corporate entity. It did not request a credit application from anyone, nor did it request a personal guaranty from either Hill or Newman. It extended credit based on the reputation of Hill, having been told that he was involved in the corporation.

Between February, 1989, and May, 1991, over $200,000 worth of product was purchased and paid for by "C & M Builders, Inc." The suit by County Concrete, which is the subject of this litigation, was for the balance due, in the amount of $55,231.77. It is uncontroverted that County Concrete was never advised of Hill and Newman's inability to incorporate as "C & M Builders, Inc.," nor was it advised of the incorporation of "H & N Construction, Inc." Hill explained that he and Newman continued to use the name, "C & M Builders, Inc." subsequent to February, 1989, because of "economic considerations," referring to the cost of obtaining new paper supplies and the repainting of vehicles.

IV

Hill argues that he should not be personally liable because "C & M Builders, Inc." was a "de facto corporation." He bases this assertion on the fact that County Concrete knew it was dealing with a corporate entity and not with an individual or individuals.... Hill relies heavily on *Cranson v. International Business Machines Corp.*, 200 A.2d 33 (Md. 1974), to support his argument. County Concrete asserts that the holding in *Cranson* is inapplicable to the facts of this case because of the absence of good faith by Hill. The trial judge explained the basis for rejecting Hill's defenses as follows:

> [Appellant] starts out okay, . . . lawyer says, okay, now you are a corporation, go off, they go order their different signs and letterheads and checks, et cetera, and at that point in time the actions that they took were certainly understandable and in good faith, and I have no problem.
>
> [Appellant] finds out that not only is he not incorporated as C & M Builders, Inc., but he finds that he can't be incorporated as that company, and yet he continues to operate under that name . . . for years when it could have and should have easily been corrected, and so we have an issue here, and one of the keys to the case is the issue of good faith.

Now he then goes out and properly incorporates under a new name, but he does not let on to this particular creditor . . . who the actual corporation is.

[The] initial good faith is lost to the continued action of [appellant] and his partner misleading the [appellee] by using a corporate name that he knows he could not use.

In *Cranson*, the Court set forth the elements necessary to find a de facto corporation: (1) a law authorizing corporations; (2) a good faith effort to incorporate; and (3) the use or exercise of corporate powers. [W]e believe there is a serious question as to whether it could or should be recognized in a situation other than when the individuals in good faith believe they have done everything necessary validly to incorporate without having realized that there was some omission that prevented valid incorporation. This was the situation in *Cranson* and distinguishes it from the facts before us.

The trial judge below found that County Concrete was, in fact, misled as to the identity of the entity with whom it contracted. The trial judge found that Hill acted in good faith until he was advised by his attorney that he and Newman could not operate as "C & M Builders, Inc." and that there was already in existence an unrelated entity with that name. Despite the fact that this knowledge was obtained in February, 1989, at or about the same time that the relationship began with County Concrete, Hill and Newman continued to use the name, "C & M Builders, Inc." or "C & M Builders," instead of disclosing the proper name.

Judgment affirmed; appellant to pay the costs.

Notes and Questions

1. Reality Check

a. What are the elements for finding a de facto corporation?

b. What element or elements for de facto corporation did the court hold were missing here? Do you agree?

c. Was the plaintiff misled in any way? Why does that fact make a difference?

2. Suppose

a. Suppose the defendants had been able to incorporate as "C and M Builders, Inc." or "C & M Builders Company." Would the analysis and result be the same?

b. Would the analysis and result be the same if the real C & M Builders, Inc., had been defunct?

c. Assume the defendants had initially intended to incorporate under the name H & N Construction, Inc. If they had chosen to do business under the trade name C & M Builders, Inc., and were unaware that an actual corporation already had that name, how would the court analyze the plaintiff's claim?

3. What Do You Think?

a. Is the plaintiff receiving a windfall? If so, on what ground is the windfall defensible?

b. Do you think the defendants have a malpractice claim against their attorney?

c. How could the attorney or the clients have prevented the result in this case? Who is more responsible for the situation that developed?

Harris v. Looney

862 S.W.2d 282 (Ark. Ct. App. 1993)

PITTMAN, J.

This appeal is from an order of the Dallas County Circuit Court which awarded appellant judgment against defendant Joe Alexander but not against appellees, Avanell Looney and Rita Alexander. Appellant contends that, under the terms of [MBCA §2.04], appellees were strictly liable for J & R Construction, Inc.'s debt to him.... We affirm.

On February 1, 1988, appellant, Robert L. Harris, sold his business and its assets to J & R Construction. The articles of incorporation for J & R Construction were signed by the incorporators on February 1, 1988, but were not filed with the Secretary of State's office until February 3, 1988. In 1991, J & R Construction defaulted on its contract and promissory note, and appellant sued the incorporators of J & R Construction, Joe Alexander and appellees, Avanell Looney and Rita Alexander, for judgment jointly and severally on the corporation's debt of $49,696.21. In his amended complaint, appellant alleged that the incorporators were jointly and severally liable for the debt of J & R Construction because its articles of incorporation had not been filed with the Secretary of State's Office at the time Joe Alexander, on behalf of the corporation, entered into the contract with appellant. After a bench trial, the circuit court held that Joe Alexander was personally liable for the debts of J & R Construction because he was the contracting party who dealt on behalf of the corporation. The court refused, however, to hold appellees, Avanell Looney and Rita Alexander, liable, because neither of them had acted for or on behalf of the corporation pursuant to [MBCA §2.04].

On appeal, appellant contends that the trial court erred in not holding appellees jointly and severally liable, along with Joe Alexander. It was undisputed that the contract and promissory note were signed by Joe Alexander on behalf of J & R Construction and that J & R Construction had not yet been incorporated when the contract was executed. Appellant concludes that, because Arkansas law imposes joint and several liability on those purporting to act as or on behalf of a corporation knowing there is no incorporation, the trial court erred in not also awarding him judgment against appellees.

The official comment to §2.04 of the ... Model Business Corporation Act explains:

> Earlier versions of the Model Act, and the statutes of many states, have long provided that corporate existence begins only with the acceptance of articles of incorporation by the secretary of state. Many states also have statutes that provide expressly that those who prematurely act as or on behalf of a corporation are personally liable on all transactions entered into or liabilities incurred before incorporation. A review of recent case law indicates, however, that even in states with such statutes courts have continued to rely on common law concepts of de facto corporations, de jure corporations, and corporations by estoppel that provide uncertain protection against liability for preincorporation transactions. These cases caused a review of the underlying policies represented in earlier versions of the Model Act and the adoption of a slightly more flexible or relaxed standard.
>
> Incorporation under modern statutes is so simple and inexpensive that a strong argument may be made that nothing short of filing articles of incorporation should

create the privilege of limited liability. A number of situations have arisen, however, in which the protection of limited liability arguably should be recognized even though the simple incorporation process established by modern statutes has not been completed.

[I]t seemed appropriate to impose liability only on persons who act as or on behalf of corporations "knowing" that no corporation exists. Analogous protection has long been accorded under the uniform limited partnership acts to limited partners who contribute capital to a partnership in the erroneous belief that a limited partnership certificate has been filed. Uniform Limited Partnership Act §12 (1916); Revised Uniform Limited Partnership Act §3.04 (1976). Persons protected under §3.04 of the latter are persons who "erroneously but in good faith" believe that a limited partnership certificate has been filed. The language of section 2.04 has essentially the same meaning.

While no special provision is made in section 2.04, the section does not foreclose the possibility that persons who urge defendants to execute contracts in the corporate name knowing that no steps to incorporate have been taken may be estopped to impose personal liability on individual defendants. This estoppel may be based on the inequity perceived when persons, unwilling or reluctant to enter into a commitment under their own name, are persuaded to use the name of a nonexistent corporation, and then are sought to be held personally liable under section 2.04 by the party advocating that form of execution. By contrast, persons who knowingly participate in a business under a corporate name are jointly and severally liable on "corporate" obligations under section 2.04 and may not argue that plaintiffs are "estopped" from holding them personally liable because all transactions were conducted on a corporate basis.

Model Business Corporation Act Ann. §2.04 official cmt. at 130.2-33 (3d ed. 1992).

In passing this Act, the Arkansas General Assembly adopted a heightened standard for imposing personal liability for transactions entered into before incorporation. The Act requires that, in order to find liability under [MBCA §2.04], there must be a finding that the persons sought to be charged acted as or on behalf of the corporation and knew there was no incorporation under the Act.

The evidence showed that the contract to purchase appellant's business and the promissory note were signed only by Joe Alexander on behalf of the corporation. The only evidence introduced to support appellant's allegation that appellees were acting on behalf of the corporation was Joe Alexander's and Avanell Looney's statements that they were present when the contract with appellant was signed; however, these statements were disputed by appellant and his wife. Appellant testified that he, his wife, Kathryn Harris, and Joe Alexander were present when the documents were signed to purchase his business and he did not remember appellee Avanell Looney being present. Kathryn Harris testified that appellees were not present when the contract was signed.

The trial court denied appellant judgment against appellees because he found that appellees had not acted for or on behalf of J & R Construction as required by [MBCA §2.04]. The findings of fact of a trial judge sitting as the factfinder will not be disturbed on appeal unless the findings are clearly erroneous or clearly against the preponderance of the evidence, giving due regard to the opportunity of the trial court to assess the credibility of the witnesses. . . . From our review of the record, we cannot say that the trial court's finding in this case is clearly against the preponderance of the evidence, and we find no error in the court's refusal to award appellant judgment against appellees.

Affirmed.

Jennings, C.J., and Rogers, J., agree.

Notes and Questions

1. Reality Check

a. How does one act "on behalf of" a corporation? In the corporate setting, a signature such as

> Acme, Inc.
> by [signature],
> President

should be sufficient to demonstrate that the agent (i.e., the corporation's president) is causing the principal (the corporation) to act. This distinction is important because under agency rules an agent for a fully disclosed principal is not liable on a contract. Consider whether the following signatures bind the corporation, the signer, both, or neither:

> Acme, Inc.
> by [signature]

> Acme, Inc.
> [signature]

> [signature],
> President of Acme, Inc.

> Acme, Inc.
> by [signature],
> Vice President

> Acme, Inc.
> by [signature],
> Vice President of Advertising

2. Suppose

a. What if the Articles of Incorporation had been executed but never filed at all? Would the analysis or result be the same?

b. Suppose Mr. Alexander had misled Ms. Alexander and Mr. Looney into believing that the corporation had been formed on February 1?

c. Would the analysis or result be different if all parties to the transaction had honestly believed that the corporation had been formed on February 1?

d. Would the analysis or result be different if all parties to the transaction knew on February 1 that no corporation had been formed?

e. Would the analysis or result be different if the purchasers had executed the Articles but had no knowledge or belief about whether the Articles had been filed on February 1?

3. What Do You Think?

a. Do you think either the language of MBCA §2.04 or the official comments compels the result in this case? Do you think "passive promoters" such as Mr. Looney and Ms. Alexander should be insulated from liability?

b. Weren't Mr. Alexander, Mr. Looney, and Ms. Alexander carrying on as co-owners a business for profit before the corporation was incorporated? If so, why are not all three liable as general partners for Mr. Alexander's actions?

c. Do you think Mr. Alexander could be considered an agent for Mr. Looney and Ms. Alexander?

b. Corporations by Estoppel

We now turn to a final equitable defense to individual liability in defective incorporation settings. As you read the following case, try to distinguish the corporation by estoppel doctrine from the promoter liability and de facto corporation doctrines.

American Vending Services, Inc. v. Morse
881 P.2d 917 (Utah Ct. App. 1994)

GREENWOOD, J.

The plethora of issues in this case arise from the relatively straightforward transaction of a car wash sale. Wayne L. and Dianne L. Morse built the car wash in 1984 and operated it for approximately eleven months. Thereafter, they entered into a contract with Douglas M. Durbano and Kevin S. Garn, both licensed attorneys acting as officers of American Vending Services, Inc. (AVSI), to purchase the car wash [for a $20,000 down payment and a $45,000 promissory note from AVSI to the Morses]. Mr. Durbano and Mr. Garn claim that they represented to the Morses that the corporate entity, AVSI, would purchase and operate the car wash. At the time the parties executed the contract on July 10, 1985, Mr. Durbano had not filed the Articles of Incorporation for AVSI. . . . Mr. Durbano claims that he had twice tried to file Articles of Incorporation for this corporate entity before the contract was executed. In both cases, however, the Articles of Incorporation were returned because of a name conflict. The Articles of Incorporation for AVSI were finally executed on August 1, 1985 and subsequently filed on August 19, 1985. Mr. Durbano's explanation for not filing the Articles of Incorporation before the parties executed the contract on July 10, 1985 was that he was "moving offices and was too busy and distracted to file the articles." The Morses asserted personal liability of Mr. Durbano and Mr. Garn based on the fact that the corporation did not legally exist when the parties executed the contract.

AVSI operated the car wash for approximately three years. It experienced financial difficulty, however, almost from the beginning and failed to make any payments to the Morses on the balance owing under the sales contract. Unable to profitably operate the car wash, AVSI eventually allowed the bank to foreclose on it. [AVSI filed this action seeking rescission. The Morses filed a counterclaim against AVSI and asserted claims against Mr. Durbano and Mr. Garn seeking damages for breach of contract.]

At the conclusion of trial, the court entered its Findings of Fact. Those relevant to the issues on appeal are summarized as follows: (1) The Morses knew throughout the negotiations that Mr. Durbano and Mr. Garn intended to form a corporation to purchase the car wash; . . . [and] (4) the Morses intended to contract with AVSI rather than with Mr. Durbano and Mr. Garn individually. . . .

Based on these Findings of Fact, the trial court entered the following relevant Conclusions of Law: ... (2) AVSI was a corporation by estoppel when it purchased the car wash; [and] (3) the Morses are estopped from denying the corporate existence of AVSI. ...

The trial court awarded damages to the Morses against AVSI in the amount of $76,832.30, plus costs, interest, and reasonable attorney fees. The Morses now appeal the trial court's ruling because, although favorable to them in most respects, it was apparently a hollow victory; AVSI has no assets or income from which it can satisfy the judgment. Thus, the Morses appeal the trial court's ruling that Mr. Durbano and Mr. Garn are not personally liable on the contract.

ANALYSIS

Corporation by Estoppel in Utah

The doctrine developed in the courts of equity to prevent unfairness. As one court has stated, "Corporation by estoppel is a difficult concept to grasp and courts and writers have 'gone all over the lot' in attempting to define and apply the doctrine." *Timberline Equipment Co. v. Davenport*, 514 P.2d 1109, 1111 (Or. 1973). A treatise on corporations defines the doctrine as follows:

> The so-called estoppel that arises to deny corporate capacity does not depend on the presence of the technical elements of equitable estoppel, viz., misrepresentations and change of position in reliance thereon, but on the nature of the relations contemplated, that one who has recognized the organization as a corporation in business dealings should not be allowed to quibble or raise immaterial issues on matters which do not concern him in the slightest degree or affect his substantial rights.

Id. **514 P.2d at 1111-12 (quoting Ballantine, Manual of Corporation Law and Practice §§28-30 (1930)).** ...

A review of jurisdictions that have addressed this issue reveals a divergence of views. For example, Oklahoma, and apparently Georgia, have adopted the position that the doctrine of corporation by estoppel cannot be invoked to deny corporate existence unless the corporation has at least a de facto existence. The District of Columbia and Tennessee have taken the position that the [old] MBCA [MBCA (1950)] eliminated estoppel corporations altogether.[14] Another view, taken by Alaska, allows corporations by estoppel even when the corporation has not achieved de facto existence. Still another jurisdiction, Arkansas, has stated that corporation by estoppel rests "wholly upon equitable principles ... and should be applied only where there are equitable grounds for doing so." Finally, Florida has adopted the position that the doctrine of corporation by estoppel cannot be invoked where the individual seeking to avoid liability had constructive or actual knowledge that the corporation did not exist.

The fact that directors, officers, and shareholders in Utah generally enjoy limited liability is a benefit conferred by the Legislature and is the result of a public policy

---

14. In addition, the holding in [*Robertson v.*] *Levy* [, 197 A.2d 443, 446 (D.C. App. 1964)] that the [MBCA (1950)] eliminated both de facto and estoppel corporations is unsupported by the comments to the [MBCA (1950)]. The comments to §§56 and 146 specifically address de facto corporations, but except for several annotations to cases discussing estoppel corporations, are silent as to whether the [MBCA (1950)] eliminated corporations by estoppel. [The text of MBCA (1950) §§56 and 146 are set out on p. 129, n.*, *supra*. ED.]

decision aimed at encouraging Utah's citizens to engage in private enterprise with all its attendant risks. To make this limited liability available with relative ease, the [MBCA (1950)], and its successor, the [MBCA], make the act of incorporation fairly painless — both in terms of the financial cost and effort required to incorporate. Given the ease of incorporating, I am hesitant to carve out exceptions to the general rule found in [the statutes] that individuals who assume to act as a corporation before that corporation exists are jointly and severally liable.

Notwithstanding my reluctance to make an exception, I am persuaded by the reasoning of the Florida Court of Appeals that the doctrine of corporation by estoppel should be viable in the narrow situation . . . only where both parties reasonably believe they are dealing with a corporation and neither party has actual or constructive knowledge that the corporation does not exist.

In the present case, the parties dispute whether both sides knew that a corporation was involved. Mr. Garn and Mr. Durbano claim that the Morses knew from the beginning that AVSI was to purchase the car wash. Conversely, the Morses claim that they only discovered the involvement of AVSI when they signed the papers at closing. Despite the parties' conflicting accounts, it is undisputed that at the time the Morses signed the contract, Mr. Durbano and Mr. Garn had actual or constructive knowledge that AVSI did not legally exist under the laws of Utah. Accordingly, neither Mr. Durbano nor Mr. Garn can invoke the doctrine of corporation by estoppel to shield them from personal liability for the debts that they incurred while assuming to act on behalf of the nonexistent corporation.

We reverse the trial court's conclusion[ ] that AVSI was a . . . corporation by estoppel at the time the car wash sale was consummated and hold that Mr. Durbano and Mr. Garn are personally liable . . . for the judgment entered by the trial court against AVSI. . . .

Notes and Questions

1. Reality Check

a. If the Morses prevailed against AVSI, why are they appealing?

b. Are there really five different versions of the corporation by estoppel doctrine, as the court suggests?

c. What are the core requirements for finding a corporation by estoppel?

d. What are the similarities between the de facto corporation doctrine and the corporation by estoppel doctrine? What are the differences between the two?

e. If the Morses both intended to deal only with a corporation and believed they were actually doing so, what justification is there for holding the buyers liable? Did the buyers attempt to defraud the Morses?

f. The parties dispute whether the Morses knew from the beginning that no corporation had been formed or only discovered that fact at the closing. How would the resolution of that fact question make any difference in the analysis or result of this case?

2. Suppose

a. What if Mr. Durbano knew that no corporation had been formed, but Mr. Garn believed that the corporation had been formed. Would the result or analysis be different?

b. What if Mr. Durbano knew that no corporation had been formed, but Mr. Garn had no knowledge whether or not the corporation had been formed? Would the result or analysis be different?

3. What Do You Think?

a. One major question about the corporation by estoppel doctrine is whether the legislature in any given state intended to abrogate the doctrine. Virtually no state has a statute explicitly directed to this question. How do you think this legislative silence should be interpreted? Is your answer for a MBCA state, which has §2.04, different from a state such as Delaware, which has no statutory equivalent to §2.04?

b. Assuming a state's legislature has not forbidden the corporation by estoppel doctrine, and assuming that the plaintiff has intended to deal only with a corporation, why should the defense not apply regardless of whether the promoter knew the corporation did not exist? If something further should be required to establish the defense, should it be the absence of the promoter's intent to defraud? Should it be the absence of the promoter's bad faith generally? Should it be an affirmative showing of the promoter's good faith? If the promoter's good faith should be required, could it be shown by something other than the promoter's belief that the corporation existed?

c. The facts of this case illustrate a typical setting, in which the promoters execute a contract on behalf of a corporation that they know does not exist but that they are in the process of creating. Where the corporation does come into existence shortly after an obligation in its name is incurred, how would third parties such as the Morses be hurt by limiting recovery to the corporate entity to which they intended to look?

d. If you were the attorney representing either the sellers or the buyers at the closing of the car wash sale in this case, how would you advise your clients to alter the written contract to avoid the problem presented here?

e. If a defense of de facto corporation or corporation by estoppel is unsuccessful, what should the remedy be? Should the promoter have unlimited personal liability or should the remedy be limited, for example, to the amount the promoter intended to invest in the corporation? If there are multiple individual defendants, should they be automatically liable as general partners? Should a distinction be drawn between active and passive investors?

f. Do you think the doctrines of corporation by estoppel and de facto corporation should be permitted at all?

4. You Draft It

a. Draft language for the sale contract to make clear that Mr. Durbano and Mr. Garn are not personally liable and that only AVSI will be liable.

E. LAWYER'S PROFESSIONAL RESPONSIBILITY TO MULTIPLE CLIENTS AND ENTITY CLIENTS

The final section of this chapter explores some ethical problems facing lawyers who create corporations on behalf of individual clients. Perhaps the most salient ethical problem is whether the lawyer can represent more than one participant. As you read the next case, think about how many possible "clients" are involved.

≡ **Detter v. Schreiber**
≡ 610 N.W.2d 13 (Neb. 2000)

WRIGHT, J.

In 1991, Schreiber and Detter commenced a business known as Miracle Hills Animal Hospital, P.C. (the corporation). In connection with the formation of the corporation, on February 27, 1992, Schreiber executed two promissory notes in the total principal sum of $19,000 which was payable to Detter. The articles of incorporation provided that Schreiber and Detter would each own 50 percent of the shares of the corporation and would be the only members of the board of directors. In 1996, Schreiber retained the services of Thomas J. Young to draft a shareholder agreement. These services were paid for by the corporation.

Detter commenced an action against Schreiber on the two promissory notes. Detter alleged that... Schreiber had paid $11,000... and that there was then due and owing the sum of $10,430.45 plus interest.

Schreiber's answer and counterclaim denied that there was any balance due on the notes. Schreiber's counterclaim alleged that since the inception and commencement of the business, he had performed all the management duties of the corporation and that pursuant to an oral contract made in March 1998, Schreiber was entitled to ongoing management fees in the amount of $773.33 per month commencing April 1998.

Prior to trial, Detter moved the trial court for an order directing that Young remove himself as attorney of record for Schreiber. The motion alleged that the law firm of Young & LaPuzza had acted as attorneys for the corporation and that Young had acted as the attorney for the corporation with respect to the negotiation of the corporation's lease with Dial Enterprises and a shareholder agreement between Detter and Schreiber.

Detter's affidavit alleged that he was a 50-percent owner of the corporation and was currently serving as its president. Detter claimed that he and Schreiber were the only shareholders of the corporation and that beginning in 1995, the corporation used the services of the law firm of Young & LaPuzza. Detter stated that in 1996, the corporation used the services of Young & LaPuzza to draft a shareholder agreement. Detter claimed that during his discussions with Schreiber and Young, it was his understanding that Young represented the corporation, Detter, and Schreiber with respect to the proposed shareholder agreement. Detter also stated that during his discussions with Young regarding the shareholder agreement, he discussed his thoughts and feelings with respect to the shareholder agreement and that as a result, Young had a great deal of information regarding facts and circumstances surrounding the present litigation and had information regarding Detter's financial plans and needs. The affidavit further claimed that Schreiber had specifically advised Detter that Young was representing Detter's interests, that Detter could ask Young any questions he might have, and that Young & LaPuzza's bill would be paid from the corporate account. Detter also claimed that Young never advised him that Young was not representing his interests.

Schreiber and Young also submitted affidavits which denied that Young was Detter's attorney or that Young had received any confidential information from Detter. Schreiber's affidavit specifically alleged that James T. Blazek was the registered agent of the corporation and its corporate attorney and that Blazek, who had always acted as the attorney for the corporation, continued to do so to date. Schreiber claimed that Detter had specifically refused to allow Young or the Young & LaPuzza law firm to act as the corporate attorneys for the corporation. Schreiber further stated that he had initiated efforts to have a proposed shareholder agreement, which was never executed, signed by Detter and himself and that he had contacted Young to prepare the initial draft of the agreement. Schreiber claimed that Young met with both Detter and Schreiber regarding the proposed shareholder agreement but that at no time during the conversations or discussions was any information relative to Detter's personal financial situation discussed or revealed. Schreiber asserted that he was not privy to Detter's personal financial situation except with regard to the operation, income, and expenses of the corporation.

In addition, Schreiber acknowledged that Detter was free to contact Young or any other attorney regarding the shareholder agreement. Schreiber stated that Young had been his personal attorney since 1990 but that he did not consult Young with regard to the corporation or the various agreements or promissory notes which were executed at the time the corporation was formed.

On November 23, 1998, the trial court found that Young had a conflict of interest and sustained Detter's motion to remove him. Schreiber appeals from the order which sustained Detter's motion to remove Young.

ANALYSIS

An attorney-client relationship is created when a person seeks advice or assistance from an attorney, the advice or assistance sought pertains to matters within the attorney's professional competence, and the attorney expressly or impliedly agrees to give or actually gives the desired advice or assistance.

We have never specifically examined an attorney-client relationship in a closely held corporation setting such as the one presented in the case at bar. There is no dispute that Young was called upon to do some legal work for the corporation regarding a lease and a shareholder agreement. The only evidence of contact between Young and Detter was a conference on June 27, 1996, which concerned the proposed shareholder agreement and which lasted 1½ hours. The remaining contact between Young and the corporation was through Schreiber.

[I]t is Schreiber's position that an attorney-client relationship was never formed between Young and Detter and that all correspondence between Young and the corporation was directed to Schreiber and the corporation only. Schreiber claims that the corporation was billed and paid for Young's legal services and that even though Young may have met with Detter in June 1996 regarding a proposed shareholder agreement, there is no competent evidence that would establish what information, if any, was provided by Detter to Young or what advice or opinions Young allegedly provided Detter.

Schreiber contends that Young's affidavit is sufficient to support his position that the trial court erred in sustaining Detter's motion to remove Young. In his affidavit, Young stated:

> I am aware of absolutely no confidential or privileged information which relates to Dr. Detter that would affect or impact the issues involved in this litigation. Dr. Detter has never revealed to me any financial plans or needs except a discussion with regard to the amount of life insurance and disability insurance which he and Dr. Schreiber carry.
> I know of no matters of which I have personal knowledge which would cause me to be a witness at any trial of this matter.

Schreiber argues that there is no evidence that Detter personally sought advice from Young or that Young gave any advice to Detter and that, therefore, no attorney-client relationship exists between Young and Detter. Schreiber claims that it was error for the trial court to conclude that Young had a conflict of interest with Detter. Schreiber asserts that even assuming Young provided legal services to Detter or that an attorney-client relationship existed relative to the office lease or the proposed shareholder agreement, those two instances did not provide a sufficient factual basis to remove Young as Schreiber's counsel.

It is Detter's position that when Young was requested to assist the corporation with the commercial lease and to draft a shareholder agreement, Young was acting on behalf of the corporation and both of the shareholders.

The shareholder agreement appears to be an agreement to govern and restrict the disposition of the shares of the corporation. It sets forth procedures for the annual evaluation of the corporation, restrictions on buying and selling shares, and the manner in which the stock would be purchased upon the death or disability of a shareholder. Preparation of this type of agreement would require Young to work with both Detter and Schreiber and to ascertain their financial and personal interests in order to determine what each wanted in the agreement. Thus, it could reasonably be inferred that Young had knowledge of the two promissory notes executed by the parties and of the management duties which are the subject of the counterclaim. Furthermore, although the evidence establishes that Young and Detter may have met only one time, Detter believed that Young was representing him at that time. Based on the facts of this case, the trial court found that Young had a conflict of interest and should be removed as Schreiber's attorney.

In disqualifying Young as counsel for Schreiber, the trial court had to factually determine that his representation constituted a conflict of interest. We find no clear error in this determination, and we conclude that the trial court correctly determined that Young should be disqualified as Schreiber's attorney.

AFFIRMED.

Notes and Questions

1. Note

a. The Model Rules of Professional Conduct, promulgated by the ABA, do not deal with the question of when the attorney-client relationship is created. The *Restatement (Third) of the Law Governing Lawyers* does deal with the issue.

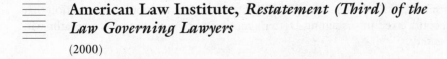 **American Law Institute, *Restatement (Third) of the Law Governing Lawyers***

(2000)

§14. FORMATION OF A CLIENT-LAWYER RELATIONSHIP

A relationship of client and lawyer arises when:

(1) a person manifests to a lawyer the person's intent that the lawyer provide legal services for the person; and either

(a) the lawyer manifests to the person consent to do so; or

(b) the lawyer fails to manifest lack of consent to do so, and the lawyer knows or reasonably should know that the person reasonably relies on the lawyer to provide the services; . . . .

COMMENT

f. Organizational, fiduciary, and class-action clients. Whether the lawyer is to represent the organization, a person or entity associated with it, or more than one such persons and entities is a question of fact to be determined based on reasonable expectations in the circumstances. Where appropriate, due consideration should be given to the unreasonableness of a claimed expectation of entering into a co-client status when a significant and readily apparent conflict of interest exists between the organization or other client and the associated person or entity claimed to be a co-client.

Under Subsection (1)(b), a lawyer's failure to clarify whom the lawyer represents in circumstances calling for such a result might lead a lawyer to have entered into client-lawyer representations not intended by the lawyer. Hence, the lawyer must clarify whom the lawyer intends to represent when the lawyer knows or reasonably should know that, contrary to the lawyer's own intention, a person, individually, or agents of an entity, on behalf of the entity, reasonably rely on the lawyer to provide legal services to that person or entity. Such clarification may be required, for example, with respect to an officer of an entity client such as a corporation. . . . An implication that such a relationship exists is more likely to be found when the lawyer performs personal legal services for an individual as well or where the organization is small and characterized by extensive common ownership and management. But the lawyer does not enter into a client-lawyer relationship with a person associated with an organizational client solely because the person communicates with the lawyer on matters relevant to the organization that are also relevant to the personal situation of the person. In all events, the question is one of fact based on the reasonable and apparent expectations of the person or entity whose status as client is in question.

2. Reality Check

a. What was the basis for the court's finding? What provisions of the Model Rules of Professional Conduct seem applicable?

b. Should Dr. Detter's understanding be given so much weight? Why does the court accept Dr. Detter's understanding over that of Mr. Young?

3. Suppose

a. What if Mr. Young's services had been paid for entirely by Dr. Schreiber rather than by the corporation? Would the analysis or result differ?

b. Would the analysis or result differ if Mr. Young had been engaged to review the shareholder agreement on behalf of Dr. Schreiber, rather than draft it?

c. What if Dr. Detter had retained Mr. Young's services in the suit against Dr. Schreiber? Would Dr. Schreiber have a better or worse case for disqualifying Mr. Young?

4. What Do You Think?

a. Situations frequently arise in the close corporation setting in which the attorney who represented the promoters also represents the corporation. Do you think the Rules of Professional Conduct or the *Restatement (Third) of the Law Governing Lawyers* give sufficient guidance to lawyers and promoters? What changes in the Rules would you make?

Even though the RPC explicitly do not cover the creation of the attorney-client relationship, several Rules deal specifically with the obligations of lawyers to organizational clients.

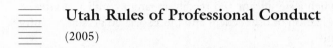

Utah Rules of Professional Conduct
(2005)

RULE 1.13 ORGANIZATION AS CLIENT

(a) A lawyer employed or retained by an organization represents the organization acting through its duly authorized constituents.

(b) If a lawyer for an organization knows that an officer, employee or other person associated with the organization is engaged in action, intends to act or refuses to act in a matter related to the representation that is a violation of a legal obligation to the organization, or a violation of law that reasonably might be imputed to the organization, and that is likely to result in substantial injury to the organization, then the lawyer shall proceed as is reasonably necessary in the best interest of the organization. Unless the lawyer reasonably believes that it is not necessary in the best interest of the organization to do so, the lawyer shall refer the matter to higher authority in the organization, including, if warranted by the circumstances, to the highest authority that can act on behalf of the organization as determined by applicable law.

(c) Except as provided in paragraph (d), if

(1) despite the lawyer's efforts in accordance with paragraph (b) the highest authority that can act on behalf of the organization insists upon or fails to address in a timely and appropriate manner an action or a refusal to act, that is clearly a violation of law, and

(2) the lawyer reasonably believes that the violation is reasonably certain to result in substantial injury to the organization,

then the lawyer may reveal information relating to the representation whether or not Rule 1.6 permits such disclosure, but only if and to the extent the lawyer reasonably believes necessary to prevent substantial injury to the organization.

(d) Paragraph (c) shall not apply with respect to information relating to a lawyer's representation of an organization to investigate an alleged violation of law, or to defend the organization or an officer, employee or other constituent associated with the organization against a claim arising out of an alleged violation of law.

(e) A lawyer who reasonably believes that he or she has been discharged because of the lawyer's actions taken pursuant to paragraphs (b) or (c), or who withdraws under circumstances that require or permit the lawyer to take action under either of those paragraphs, shall proceed as the lawyer reasonably believes necessary to assure that the organization's highest authority is informed of the lawyer's discharge or withdrawal.

(f) In dealing with an organization's directors, officers, employees, members, shareholders or other constituents, a lawyer shall explain the identity of the client when the lawyer knows or reasonably should know that the organization's interests are adverse to those of the constituents with whom the lawyer is dealing.

(g) A lawyer representing an organization may also represent any of its directors, officers, employees, members, shareholders or other constituents, subject to the provisions of Rule 1.7. If the organization's consent to the dual representation is required by Rule 1.7, the consent shall be given by an appropriate official of the organization other than the individual who is to be represented, or by the shareholders.

COMMENT

[1] An organizational client is a legal entity, but it cannot act except through its officers, directors, employees, shareholders and other constituents. Officers, directors, employees and shareholders are the constituents of the corporate organizational client. The duties defined in this Comment apply equally to unincorporated associations. "Other constituents" as used in this Comment means the positions equivalent to officers, directors, employees and shareholders held by persons acting for organizational clients that are not corporations.

[2] When one of the constituents of an organizational client communicates with the organization's lawyer in that person's organizational capacity, the communication is protected by Rule 1.6. Thus, by way of example, if an organizational client requests its lawyer to investigate allegations of wrongdoing, interviews made in the course of that investigation between the lawyer and the client's employees or other constituents are covered by Rule 1.6. This does not mean, however, that constituents of an organizational client are the clients of the lawyer. The lawyer may not disclose to such constituents information relating to the representation except for disclosures explicitly or impliedly authorized by the organizational client in order to carry out the representation or as otherwise permitted by Rule 1.6.

[3] When constituents of the organization make decisions for it, the decisions ordinarily must be accepted by the lawyer even if their utility or prudence is doubtful. Decisions concerning policy and operations, including ones entailing serious risk, are not as such in the lawyer's province. Paragraph (b) makes clear, however, that when the lawyer knows that the organization is likely to be substantially injured by action of an officer or other constituent that violates a legal obligation to the organization or is in violation of law that might be imputed to the organization, the lawyer must proceed as is reasonably necessary in the best interest of the organization.

[10] There are times when the organization's interest may be or become adverse to those of one or more of its constituents. In such circumstances the lawyer should advise any constituent, whose interest the lawyer finds adverse to that of the organization of the conflict or potential conflict of interest, that the lawyer cannot represent such constituent, and that such person may wish to obtain independent representation. Care must be taken to assure that the individual understands that, when there is such adversity of interest, the lawyer for the

organization cannot provide legal representation for that constituent individual, and that discussions between the lawyer for the organization and the individual may not be privileged.

[11] Whether such a warning should be given by the lawyer for the organization to any constituent individual may turn on the facts of each case.

[12] Paragraph (g) recognizes that a lawyer for an organization may also represent a principal officer or major shareholder.

RULE 1.6 CONFIDENTIALITY OF INFORMATION

(a) A lawyer shall not reveal information relating to the representation of a client unless the client gives informed consent, the disclosure is impliedly authorized in order to carry out the representation or the disclosure is permitted by paragraph (b).

(b) A lawyer may reveal information relating to the representation of a client to the extent the lawyer reasonably believes necessary:

(1) to prevent reasonably certain death or substantial bodily harm;

(2) to prevent the client from committing a crime or fraud that is reasonably certain to result in substantial injury to the financial interests or property of another and in furtherance of which the client has used or is using the lawyer's services;

(3) to prevent, mitigate or rectify substantial injury to the financial interests or property of another that is reasonably certain to result or has resulted from the client's commission of a crime or fraud in furtherance of which the client has used the lawyer's services;

(4) to secure legal advice about the lawyer's compliance with these Rules;

(5) to establish a claim or defense on behalf of the lawyer in a controversy between the lawyer and the client, to establish a defense to a criminal charge or civil claim against the lawyer based upon conduct in which the client was involved, or to respond to allegations in any proceeding concerning the lawyer's representation of the client; or

(6) to comply with other law or a court order.

RULE 1.7 CONFLICT OF INTEREST: CURRENT CLIENTS

(a) Except as provided in paragraph (b), a lawyer shall not represent a client if the representation involves a concurrent conflict of interest. A concurrent conflict of interest exists if:

(1) the representation of one client will be directly adverse to another client; or

(2) there is a significant risk that the representation of one or more clients will be materially limited by the lawyer's responsibilities to another client, a former client or a third person or by a personal interest of the lawyer.

(b) Notwithstanding the existence of a concurrent conflict of interest under paragraph (a), a lawyer may represent a client if:

(1) the lawyer reasonably believes that the lawyer will be able to provide competent and diligent representation to each affected client;

(2) the representation is not prohibited by law;

(3) the representation does not involve the assertion of a claim by one client against another client represented by the lawyer in the same litigation or other proceeding before a tribunal; and

(4) each affected client gives informed consent, confirmed in writing.

COMMENT

[6] Loyalty to a current client prohibits undertaking representation directly adverse to that client without that client's informed consent. Thus, absent consent, a lawyer may not act as an advocate in one matter against a person the lawyer represents in some other matter, even when the matters are wholly unrelated. The client as to whom the representation is directly adverse is likely to feel betrayed, and the resulting damage to the client-lawyer relationship is likely to impair the lawyer's ability to represent the client effectively. In addition, the client on whose behalf the adverse representation is undertaken reasonably may fear that the lawyer will pursue that client's case less effectively out of deference to the other client, i.e., that the representation may be materially limited by the lawyer's interest in retaining the current client. Similarly, a directly adverse conflict may arise when a lawyer is required to cross-examine a client who appears as a witness in a lawsuit involving another client, as when the testimony will be damaging to the client who is represented in the lawsuit. On the other hand, simultaneous representation in unrelated matters of clients whose interests are only economically adverse, such as representation of competing economic enterprises in unrelated litigation, does not ordinarily constitute a conflict of interest and thus may not require consent of the respective clients.

[7] Directly adverse conflicts can also arise in transactional matters. For example, if a lawyer is asked to represent the seller of a business in negotiations with a buyer represented by the lawyer, not in the same transaction but in another, unrelated matter, the lawyer could not undertake the representation without the informed consent of each client.

[8] Even where there is no direct adverseness, a conflict of interest exists if there is a significant risk that a lawyer's ability to consider, recommend or carry out an appropriate course of action for the client will be materially limited as a result of the lawyer's other responsibilities or interests. For example, a lawyer asked to represent several individuals seeking to form a joint venture is likely to be materially limited in the lawyer's ability to recommend or advocate all possible positions that each might take because of the lawyer's duty of loyalty to the others. The conflict in effect forecloses alternatives that would otherwise be available to the client. The mere possibility of subsequent harm does not itself require disclosure and consent. The critical questions are the likelihood that a difference in interests will eventuate and, if it does, whether it will materially interfere with the lawyer's independent professional judgment in considering alternatives or foreclose courses of action that reasonably should be pursued on behalf of the client.

[13] A lawyer may be paid from a source other than the client, including a co-client, if the client is informed of that fact and consents and the arrangement does not compromise the lawyer's duty of loyalty or independent judgment to the client. If acceptance of the payment from any other source presents a significant risk that the lawyer's representation of the client will be materially limited by the

lawyer's own interest in accommodating the person paying the lawyer's fee or by the lawyer's responsibilities to a payer who is also a co-client, then the lawyer must comply with the requirements of paragraph (b) before accepting the representation, including determining whether the conflict is consentable and, if so, that the client has adequate information about the material risks of the representation.

[28] Whether a conflict is consentable depends on the circumstances. For example, a lawyer may not represent multiple parties to a negotiation whose interests are fundamentally antagonistic to each other, but common representation is permissible where the clients are generally aligned in interest even though there is some difference in interest among them. Thus, a lawyer may seek to establish or adjust a relationship between clients on an amicable and mutually advantageous basis; for example, in helping to organize a business in which two or more clients are entrepreneurs, working out the financial reorganization of an enterprise in which two or more clients have an interest or arranging a property distribution in settlement of an estate. The lawyer seeks to resolve potentially adverse interests by developing the parties' mutual interests. Otherwise, each party might have to obtain separate representation, with the possibility of incurring additional cost, complication or even litigation. Given these and other relevant factors, the clients may prefer that the lawyer act for all of them.

[31] As to the duty of confidentiality, continued common representation will almost certainly be inadequate if one client asks the lawyer not to disclose to the other client information relevant to the common representation. This is so because the lawyer has an equal duty of loyalty to each client, and each client has the right to be informed of anything bearing on the representation that might affect that client's interests and the right to expect that the lawyer will use that information to that client's benefit. See Rule 1.4. The lawyer should, at the outset of the common representation and as part of the process of obtaining each client's informed consent, advise each client that information will be shared and that the lawyer will have to withdraw if one client decides that some matter material to the representation should be kept from the other. In limited circumstances, it may be appropriate for the lawyer to proceed with the representation when the clients have agreed, after being properly informed, that the lawyer will keep certain information confidential. For example, the lawyer may reasonably conclude that failure to disclose one client's trade secrets to another client will not adversely affect representation involving a joint venture between the clients and agree to keep that information confidential with the informed consent of both clients.

[32] When seeking to establish or adjust a relationship between clients, the lawyer should make clear that the lawyer's role is not that of partisanship normally expected in other circumstances and, thus, that the clients may be required to assume greater responsibility for decisions than when each client is separately represented. Any limitations on the scope of the representation made necessary as a result of the common representation should be fully explained to the clients at the outset of the representation. See Rule 1.2(c).

[33] Subject to the above limitations, each client in the common representation has the right to loyal and diligent representation and the protection of Rule 1.9 concerning the obligations to a former client. The client also has the right to discharge the lawyer as stated in Rule 1.16.

[34] A lawyer who represents a corporation or other organization does not, by virtue of that representation, necessarily represent any constituent or affiliated

organization, such as a parent or subsidiary. See Rule 1.13(a). Thus, the lawyer for an organization is not barred from accepting representation adverse to an affiliate in an unrelated matter, unless the circumstances are such that the affiliate should also be considered a client of the lawyer, there is an understanding between the lawyer and the organizational client that the lawyer will avoid representation adverse to the client's affiliates, or the lawyer's obligations to either the organizational client or the new client are likely to limit materially the lawyer's representation of the other client.

[35] A lawyer for a corporation or other organization who is also a member of its board of directors should determine whether the responsibilities of the two roles may conflict. The lawyer may be called on to advise the corporation in matters involving actions of the directors. Consideration should be given to the frequency with which such situations may arise, the potential intensity of the conflict, the effect of the lawyer's resignation from the board and the possibility of the corporation's obtaining legal advice from another lawyer in such situations. If there is material risk that the dual role will compromise the lawyer's independence of professional judgment, the lawyer should not serve as a director or should cease to act as the corporation's lawyer when conflicts of interest arise. The lawyer should advise the other members of the board that in some circumstances matters discussed at board meetings while the lawyer is present in the capacity of director might not be protected by the attorney-client privilege and that conflict of interest considerations might require the lawyer's recusal as a director or might require the lawyer and the lawyer's firm to decline representation of the corporation in a matter.

F. TERMS OF ART IN THIS CHAPTER

Corporation by estoppel	Defective incorporation	Internal affairs
De facto	Domestic corporation	Promoters
De jure	Foreign corporation	

6

Capital Formation

This chapter explores a central concern for any corporation or other business entity: how does the corporation get money in? More formally, this topic is known as *capital formation*. The answer is that the corporation gets money in exchange for contractual (and, as we'll see in Chapters 11 and 12, fiduciary) rights. The chapter starts by placing the capital formation question in its economic context. Then, we describe the kinds of rights that a corporation can grant in exchange for money. These rights have become relatively standardized and the standard bundles of these rights are known as *securities*. "Common stock" and "debentures" are well-known examples of securities. After a description of the standard corporate securities, we address one of the quintessential tasks for a transaction lawyer: choosing the set of securities that a new corporation will issue. That set of securities is called the corporation's *capital structure*. In selecting a capital structure the monetary needs of the new entity must be balanced with the needs of each of the potential investors. The investors' needs include both economic and managerial components. In this connection we also take a brief look at the venture capital and going public processes.

Our attention then shifts to the corporate law mechanics involved in the actual creation of corporate securities and the process by which those securities are issued by the corporation in exchange for consideration. Finally, we glimpse the federal securities regulations that affect the issuance of corporate securities.

A. FINANCING: GETTING MONEY INTO THE BUSINESS

1. Background and Context

Any business has to decide three things. First, what goods and services will it provide? Second, what assets does it need to provide those goods and services? The assets can be tangible, such as factories, machines, or office furniture; and intangible, such as proprietary knowledge, patents, trademarks, and copyrights. Assets also include the services of employees and cash needed to run the business on a day-to-day basis (frequently called *working capital*).

151

Our concern here is with the third question any business faces, which is how will the needed assets be paid for? When the business is just being formed, its owners have two sources of money. They can contribute the money themselves, or they can borrow it. After the business starts selling goods and services, the business's owners have a third source for money: extra cash generated by the business itself. We'll look at each source separately.

Perhaps the most intuitive source of money for a new business is the owners themselves. They contribute money, and may contribute assets in-kind, in return for their ownership interest. Usually, the owners' interest will be proportional to the value of each owner's contribution. What happens if the business needs more money later on? If the owners agree to contribute in proportion to their past contributions, they can preserve their relative ownership interests. But suppose that the owners are unable or unwilling to contribute proportionately? Will the owners who contribute more money receive a greater proportion of the ownership or will the original division of interests be preserved? A variation of this question, which may arise when the business is first being formed as well as later in the business's existence, is whether the owners will seek additional owners. One of the most classic tensions in the operation of any business is the possibility that the people who had the original Big Idea may see their ownership interest reduced (*diluted*, in the terminology of finance) by later investors.

If the owners do not want to share their ownership with others, they can borrow needed money. In fact, borrowing may be a solution to the problem of the business that needs additional money. Rather than making proportionate additional contributions or facing the prospect of a shift in the owners' relative interests, the owners can borrow the needed money, thus preserving their relative power. The owners do not necessarily need to find a willing lender if they themselves are willing to lend money to the business. Thus an owner might also be a creditor.

Raising money by borrowing poses different questions for a business than does raising money through the sale of ownership interests. An ownership interest is a permanent investment, in contrast to a loan, which must at some point be repaid. One question for a business, then, is how long a term should its loan be? Another question is the rate of interest the business is willing to pay. The interest is, in effect, the price of the money and in that sense is cognate to the question of how much an owner will pay for his or her ownership. Deciding upon an interest rate, though, is more complex because the rate will depend on several factors such as the length of the loan and whether the lender's rights are secured.

The final source of new money for a business is the business itself. Many businesses generate more cash than they need to meet their operating expenses. These operating expenses include buying needed assets, maintaining the business's physical assets, paying employees, paying taxes and interest on loans, and perhaps keeping some assets available for ready use. New businesses and businesses that are growing in size rarely have extra money, but many mature businesses do generate extra money. If the owners of the business decide that the business requires additional money, they may decide to use the business's extra cash rather than to borrow or sell more ownership interests. The primary alternatives to reinvesting this money in the business are to pay it to the owners in the form of dividends or to reduce the business's debts. Which of these choices is best for the business is a subject about which much has been written and about which your clients will spend much time debating.

2. The Current Setting

Corporations get money in three basic ways. They can sell ownership interests (sometimes called *equity*), they can borrow, or they can use money generated by the business itself. When the corporation sells equity or borrows, the person supplying the money receives certain rights in exchange. Those rights delineate whether the supplier is entitled to a return of the money supplied and whether the supplier is entitled to a portion of the business's earnings in addition to or instead of the return of the money supplied. The supplier of money may also receive the right to have some say in the corporation's management. At one level these rights could be infinitely variable depending only upon the inventiveness of the parties and their counsel and the minuteness with which they wish to contract. At a practical level, though, the answers to these basic questions (i.e., "Is my investment permanent or temporary?" "Will my claim on the business's earnings be a fixed *amount* or a fixed *percentage* and will it be paid before, after, or at the same time as other claimants?" and "How much power, if any, over the corporation's management will I have?") have fallen into categories so that corporations and their advisors do not have to start from scratch in devising solutions to these questions.

a. Corporate Securities

One of the great advantages of the corporate form is that the categories of financing solutions have been embodied in traditional forms called *securities*. In this sense, a security is simply a set of rights that, over the years, has proven useful to corporations and those who supply money. Think of the contrast as between couture and ready-to-wear. Sometimes the parties have the resources and the motivation to bargain over, and document, a set of relationships that is unique to the parties and the business. Sometimes they do not have the resources or the motivation and they simply pull something off the rack that, in the end, is serviceable enough and frequently quite good. Often, though, they start with ready-to-wear (i.e., the standard securities terms) and work around the margins to produce a solution that is targeted to the particular parties and setting but not completely built from scratch.

The next four sections describe these standard solutions — these securities — after which we will examine some of the more exotic securities. Throughout the remainder of this section on financing you should pay close attention to the nomenclature. The terms not only have relatively precise meanings that you, as a lawyer, will be expected to use correctly (even though clients have a maddening tendency to misuse the names), but they are a handy shorthand to describe complex bundles of rights.

i. (Common) Stock. Without question, the paradigm corporate security is *stock*. It is a kind of *equity* meaning that it represents an ownership interest in the business rather than a loan to the business. Originally, the term *stock* referred to a business's assets, as in the phrase "stock in trade." Where the business had more than one owner, each was said to own an undivided percentage, or *share*, of the stock. With the development of the modern corporate form in the nineteenth century, the term *stock* came to mean the collective ownership interests in the corporation rather than the corporation's assets. Shareholder and stockholder both referred to someone who owned shares of stock. In common corporate parlance today, *shares*, *shares of stock*, and *stock* are essentially interchangeable. As a matter of precision, the

MBCA uses the term *shares* and refers to owners as *shareholders*. It does not use the term *stock* at all. The Delaware General Corporation Law does not use the term *shares* alone. Rather, it uses the terms *shares of stock* or *stock*. The DGCL refers to owners as *stockholders*.

The early case-law rule, embodied in MBCA §6.01(a) and DGCL §151(f), is that all shares are identical in the absence of an explicit differentiation in the Articles of Incorporation. If no such differentiation is made, each share of stock has: (1) one vote on every matter submitted to the shareholders (MBCA §7.21(a), DGCL §212(a)); (2) the right to its proportionate amount of any dividend (MBCA §6.40, DGCL §170(a)); and (3) the right to its proportionate amount of the corporation's assets, if any, upon dissolution (MBCA §14.05(a)(4), DGCL §281(a)(4)).

Shares that have all three of these characteristics are sometimes called *common stock* although neither the MBCA nor the DGCL uses that term.[1] Where only one kind of stock exists, which is the norm in most corporations, the term *common stock* is simply a synonym for *stock* or *shares*. The term *preferred stock*, as you will see, has a precise meaning and implies that a corporation has at least two kinds of stock. The term *common stock* is often used to distinguish preferred stock from other stock. It can happen, though, that stock is not preferred AND does not possess all three of the attributes typically ascribed to common stock. In that setting, it may be misleading to refer to it as common stock. Nonetheless, the term is frequently used.

ii. Preferred Stock.   Sometimes the various suppliers of money to a corporation will not want to be rewarded proportionately to their investment. Some investors may be more equal than others. Typically this occurs when a particular investor or group of investors is supplying so much money that the success or failure of the business depends upon their investment. For whatever reasons, the investor and the corporation's managers agree that the investor should receive a different reward, which means, economically, either a greater-than-proportionate return, a priority in receiving a return, or both. The investor may also be able to negotiate for heightened management power, as well. Again, standard solutions to these problems have been embodied in securities known as *preferred stock*. Precisely, preferred stock is stock that has a priority or preference over other stock (common stock) in either the payment of dividends or the distribution of assets on dissolution or both.[2]

Again, speaking precisely and categorically, preferred stock, is a *class* of stock, as is common, or non-preferred, stock. It sometimes happens that different investors negotiate for different preferences such that the corporation issues more than one kind of preferred stock. Such a corporation has two classes of stock (common and preferred) and has two *series* of preferred stock. A series is simply a subset of a class of shares. As noted above, a corporation could have stock that does not have all three characteristics of common stock, for example, stock that has no voting power but is not preferred as to dividends or assets on dissolution. In that case the corporation would have two series of stock. While the distinction between class and series was

---

1. The DGCL uses the term *common stock* once, in §251(f).

2. The only thing one can say for certain about preferred stock is that it is in some measure entitled to something more than other stock in either dividends or assets on dissolution. Clients often seem to have the notion that preferred stock must have other characteristics, such as no voting power. While such attributes may be frequent, they are not required. You should be wary of making assumptions about the attributes of preferred stock without reading for yourself the statement in the Articles of Incorporation that sets out the differences between the preferred stock and the other stock.

once of some import, as a practical matter today the terms are essentially interchange-able. You may wish to keep the distinction in mind, however, because many cases and texts you will use in your practice will refer to both series and classes.

The most frequent and most important preference is in the payment of dividends. A typical preference is to grant the preferred stock a fixed amount of money per year as a dividend to be paid before the other stock receives any dividend. This is nearly identical to the payment of interest on debt. The only difference is that interest on a debt is contractually required to be paid. Dividends are always subject to certain statutory restrictions and on the discretion of the board.

Several other concepts apply to preferred stock. First, suppose the preferred stock is entitled to $1 per share per year, but the corporation's board of directors does not declare a dividend in a particular year. If the corporation is prepared to declare dividends in the next year, does the preferred stock receive $1 before the common shares or $2? The answer depends upon whether the preferred stock dividends are *cumulative*. If so, the preferred stock gets $2 per share before the common stock gets any dividend. If the preferred stock is non-cumulative, it only gets $1 per share even though it received no dividends the year before. While cumulative dividends protect the preferred stock to some extent, they can have a perverse effect on the corporation as a whole. During any protracted economic downturn (such as the Great Depression) many companies may be unable to pay dividends, and in companies with cumulative preferred stock the accrued but unpaid dividends may grow quite large. The corporation may need additional infusions of capital to continue its business either to weather the bad times or to revamp as the economy turns around. Unfortunately, the corporation will be hampered in its ability to raise new money because of the continuing, and continually increasing, obligation created by the cumulative dividends.

Now suppose a slightly different scenario. A corporation has declared and paid dividends to its preferred stock and finds it has additional money that may safely be paid out in dividends. Does the common stock receive all of the additional dividend or does the preferred stock receive a portion as well? If the preferred stock is *parti-cipating* it receives dividends along with the common stock even though it has already received its preferential dividend. If the preferred stock is nonparticipating it does not. If the preferred stock is participating, it can do so either *pari pasu* (i.e., equal dividends per share) with the common stock or at a multiple or fraction of the amount paid to each share of common stock.

Preferred stock is typically given preferences on dissolution that are similar to those granted for dividends. That is, preferred stock typically gets a fixed amount at dissolution before the common stock gets any money. Because dissolution only occurs once, preferred stock cannot be cumulative as to assets at dissolution. The preferred stock may or may not participate in dissolution after payment of its preference. In the real world these rights are of little consequence because most businesses, if solvent, continue as going concerns and do not liquidate. If the business is insolvent, there is little or no money left after paying creditors, so any preferences are really illusory.

A final word on preferred stock: Remember that the long-standing rule is that "stock is stock." Therefore, preferred stock has all the attributes of common shares unless stated otherwise. In other words, each share of preferred stock is treated identically to every share of common stock, has one vote per share, and is entitled to equal dividends as declared by the board. In other words, preferred stock is noncumulative and participating unless stated otherwise. On preferred stock generally, see MBCA §6.01(c), DGCL §151(a),(c), and (d).

iii. Other Relative Rights.

Two other aspects of stock need to be discussed. These provisions can attach to stock regardless of whether the stock is preferred. One area is voting rights. The other is the right to have the corporation repurchase shares or convert shares into different securities.

First, a word about voting. A frequent trade-off for granting certain shareholders economic preferences is that they do not receive the right to vote. Sometimes the right to vote is contingent upon the corporation's failure to pay dividends on the preferred stock for a particular period, often one year. In such cases, the preferred stock sometimes gains enough votes to control the management of the corporation either because more shares of preferred stock are outstanding than shares of common stock, or because the preferred stock is entitled to multiple votes per share. Remember that stock could have differing voting rights and yet not be preferred stock. See MBCA §6.01(c)(1), DGCL §151(a).

Next we consider the situation in which the corporation has the right to purchase shares, some shareholders have the right to sell shares to the corporation, or some shareholders have the right to change their shares into other securities. Sometimes shareholders bargain for the right to require the corporation to repurchase their shares. In the absence of a public market for the corporation's shares, this right can be quite valuable because otherwise shareholders would have no ready market for their shares. Hence, repurchase by the corporation may be the only realistic method of ending the investment. This right is called *redemption*.

A variation of redeemable stock is stock that is *convertible*. When stock is convertible, the holder has the option of exchanging the shares for a fixed amount of another security of the corporation. Most typically conversion is available from more senior shares to junior shares (i.e., from preferred stock to common stock or from debt to preferred or common stock) but the statutes permit any sort of conversion agreed to by the corporation and shareholders. The privilege of conversion may have benefits for both the corporation and the investors. The corporation may prefer a conversion provision to a redemption provision because it will not have to return money to its investor; it simply changes the rights among its shareholders. Shareholders may also prefer conversion because it provides a ready-made power to get a different security. In effect, the shareholder has an option to exchange one set of rights for another. Unlike the corporation, however, the shareholder would prefer stock to be both convertible and redeemable, while the corporation would usually prefer convertibility to redemption. Note that shareholders of different classes or series may have different reactions to convertibility. Shareholders of a class or series *into* which another class or series is convertible may be unhappy because they perceive the convertibility ratio to be unfavorable to them. In rare instances, conversion may be at the option of the corporation rather than the shareholder. See MBCA §6.01(c)(2), DGCL §151(e).

Conversely, a corporation may negotiate for the power to require the shareholder to return the shares to the corporation in return for a predetermined price. This protects the corporation from having stock outstanding in perpetuity that has provisions such as heightened voting power or large dividends that may become particularly onerous over time. Stock with this kind of provision is *callable* although both the MBCA and the DGCL use the term *redeemable* to mean stock that must be repurchased at the option of either the shareholder or the corporation. See MBCA §6.01(c)(2), DGCL §151(b).

Any variation from the default version of stock must be carefully documented. The following case shows some problems that can arise when sophisticated counsel try to anticipate future events.

Kaiser Aluminum Corporation v. Matheson
681 A.2d 392 (Del. 1996)

VEASEY, C.J.

Kaiser Aluminum Corporation ("Kaiser"), its directors and its controlling stockholder, MAXXAM, Inc., appeal from the grant of a preliminary injunction preventing Kaiser from implementing a recapitalization plan (the "Recapitalization"). The Recapitalization would create two classes of common stock...from the existing single class of common stock ("Existing Common Stock"). This result would be achieved by an amendment to the certificate of incorporation reclassifying the...authorized shares of Existing Common Stock as...Class A Common shares ("New Class A Common") with full voting rights. The Recapitalization would also authorize the issuance of...new, low-voting common stock ("New Common Stock") possessing voting rights of 1/10 vote per share. Current holders of Existing Common Stock will receive .33 shares of New Class A Common and .67 shares of New Common for each share of Existing Common Stock.

The Plaintiffs own shares of Preferred Redeemable Increased Dividend Equity Securities ("PRIDES") issued by Kaiser in February of 1994. The PRIDES are convertible into .8333 shares of Common Stock at the option of the holder prior to December 31, 1997. On December 31, 1997, each share of PRIDES converts automatically into one share of Common Stock. The PRIDES have 4/5 vote per share and vote with the common shares.

Kaiser intends to adjust the conversion ratio for the PRIDES so that each share of PRIDES will convert on December 31, 1997 into .33 shares of New Class A Common and .67 shares of New Common. The Plaintiffs asserted...that the Certificate of Designations (the "Certificate") for the PRIDES does not permit Kaiser to change ...the security into which the PRIDES are convertible....

The PRIDES are a convertible security. Accordingly, the Certificate sets forth detailed language broadly referred to as anti-dilution adjustments.[5] Such provisions protect the value of the conversion feature in the case of certain events which could otherwise reduce the value of that into which the PRIDES convert, namely the Common Stock of Kaiser.

The provision at issue is section 3(d)(i) of the Certificate, which states:

> (i) If the Corporation shall...
>
>   (4) *issue by reclassification of its shares of* **Common Stock**[6] *any shares of* ***common stock*** *of the Corporation*

---

5. The issues presented by this case are not of recent origin. *See* Parkinson v. West End St. Ry. Co., 53 N.E. 891 (Mass. 1899) (Holmes, J.) (considering rights of convertible security holders); George S. Hills, *Convertible Securities: Legal Aspects and Draftsmanship*, 19 Cal. L. Rev. 1 (1930); Richard M. Buxbaum, *Preferred Stock: Law and Draftsmanship*, 42 Cal. L. Rev. 243 (1954).

6. Common Stock is defined as "fully paid and non-assessable shares of common stock of the Corporation." Certificate §3(a)(i).

> then, ... [the conversion rate] ... shall ... be adjusted so that the *holder of a share of PRIDES shall be entitled to receive, on the conversion of such share of PRIDES, the number of shares of Common Stock of the Corporation which such holder would have owned or been entitled to receive* after the happening of any of the events described above had such share of PRIDES been converted ... *immediately prior to the happening of such event* ...

(Emphasis supplied.) Kaiser contends that the provision contemplates that the PRIDES holders will receive on conversion "whatever new securities the holders of the underlying security received in the corporate transactions covered by those adjustment provisions."

The Plaintiffs contend that ... [s]ection 3(d)(i)(4) clearly differentiates between two kinds of stock: (1) the "Common Stock" that is being reclassified and (2) the "common stock" that is newly issued as a result of the reclassification. The operative language of the "then" clause of the anti-dilution provision states that after such a reclassification the PRIDES still converts into the "Common Stock" that was reclassified ... rather than the new "common stock."

When a contract is ambiguous, a court normally relies upon extrinsic evidence of the parties' intent. Such a course is not appropriate in this case for two reasons. First, such an investigation would reveal information about the thoughts and positions of, at most, the issuer and the underwriter. Whether these parties can legitimately be viewed as "negotiating" indenture provisions is a subject of some dispute. Since these sorts of provisions "are ... not the consequence of the relationship of particular borrowers and lenders and do not depend upon particularized intentions of the parties to an indenture," evidence of the course of negotiations would not be helpful. *Sharon Steel Corp. v. Chase Manhattan Bank, N.A.,* 691 F.2d 1039, 1048 (2d Cir. 1982); *see also* Dale B. Tauke, *Should Bonds Have More Fun? A Reexamination of the Debate Over Corporate Bondholder Rights,* Colum. Bus. L. Rev., 1, 82 (1989) ("the search for expectations is complicated by the fact that investors constitute a diverse group").

Second, we are reluctant to risk disuniformity by adverting to evidence of the course of negotiation in a setting in which the same language can be found in many different contracts. A leading case in the interpretation of indenture provisions remarks:

> [T]he creation of enduring uncertainties as to the meaning of boilerplate provisions would decrease the value of all debenture issues and greatly impair the efficient working of capital markets. Such uncertainties would vastly increase the risks and, therefore, the costs of borrowing with no offsetting benefits either in the capital market or in the administration of justice. Just such uncertainties would be created if interpretation of boilerplate provisions were submitted to juries sitting in every judicial district in the nation.

Sharon Steel Corp., 691 F.2d at 1048. ...

We are left then with a hopelessly ambiguous contract and a reluctance to rely upon extrinsic evidence.

It is a well-accepted principle that ambiguities in a contract should be construed against the drafter. Courts have disagreed, however, whether the principle should apply in the case of detailed indentures or similar documents.

We agree that "[w]hile debtor corporations are not the actual drafters of bond contracts, they are in a much better position to clarify the meaning of...contract terms in advance of disputes than are investors generally." Tauke, 1989 Colum. Bus. L. Rev. at 87. The issuer is "better able to clarify unclear bond contract terms in advance so as to avoid future disputes and therefore should bear the drafting burden that the *contra proferentem* principle would impose upon it." *Id*. at 89....Moreover, when faced with an ambiguous provision in a document such as the Certificate, the Court must construe the document to adhere to the reasonable expectations of the investors who purchased the security and thereby subjected themselves to the terms of the contract.

We caution against this principle becoming "a short-cut for avoiding the sometimes difficult tasks of determining expectations...." Tauke, 1989 Colum. Bus. L. Rev. at 88. Certificates of Designation and indentures are necessarily complex documents prepared by sophisticated drafters. They require some effort and careful thought to understand. In the normal course of events, the four corners of the document will yield a result which is consistent with reasonable expectations. We apply the *contra proferentem* principle here only as a last resort because the language of the Certificate presents a hopeless ambiguity, particularly when alternative formulations indicate that these provisions could easily have been made clear.

Accordingly, the interlocutory order of the Court of Chancery granting the preliminary injunction is **AFFIRMED** and the matter is **REMANDED** to the Court of Chancery for further proceedings consistent with this Opinion.

Notes and Questions

1. Notes

a. Captions in opinions of the Delaware Supreme Court are styled, "appellant v. appellee." Where, as here, the defendant is appealing, its name appears first, which may mislead you into believing it is the plaintiff. In this case, Matheson, et al., are the plaintiffs who own PRIDES; Kaiser Aluminum Corporation and MAXXAM, Inc., are the defendants.

b. The purpose of the recapitalization was to allow Kaiser to sell low-vote common stock that would bring needed funds into the corporation, while allowing MAXXAM to retain voting control. The plan was abandoned after this decision, and eventually Kaiser Aluminum declared bankruptcy.

c. The PRIDES were sold in a public offering rather than to specific purchasers identified by Kaiser. The terms of the PRIDES were negotiated between Kaiser and the investment banks that acted as underwriters—intermediaries who bought the PRIDES from Kaiser and immediately resold them to the public.

2. Reality Check

a. Why did the plaintiffs oppose the actions Kaiser took?

b. If the court found that the language was "hopelessly ambiguous," why did it not look to extrinsic evidence of the parties' intent?

3. Suppose

a. Suppose the language at issue had been specifically negotiated between Kaiser and plaintiffs. Would the result or the court's analysis have been different?

b. What if the evidence showed that the underwriters had had significantly greater bargaining power over the terms of the PRIDES than Kaiser? Would that have changed the court's approach?

4. What Do You Think?

a. Why does the "boilerplate" nature of the language affect the court's views?

b. What caused the Certificate language to be "hopelessly ambiguous"?

c. Do you think that language that is found in lots of documents in use by corporate practitioners should be subject to special rules of interpretation? If so, what rules should apply?

d. Was one side acting particularly opportunistically? If so, which side?

5. You Draft It

a. The key language in dispute is from Kaiser's Certificate, which reads as follows:

> (i) If the Corporation shall . . .
> (4) issue by reclassification of its shares of Common Stock any shares of common stock of the Corporation
> Then . . . [the conversion rate] . . . shall . . . be adjusted so that the holder of a share of PRIDES shall be entitled to receive, on the conversion of such share of PRIDES, the number of shares of Common Stock of the Corporation which such holder would have owned or been entitled to receive after the happening of any of the events described above had such share of PRIDES been converted . . . immediately prior to the happening of such event . . .

Redraft this language so that it clearly effects plaintiffs' best interests. Then redraft the language so that it clearly effects defendants' best interests.

iv. Debt. The difference between *debt* and traditional common stock is clear. A loan is temporary; investment in common stock is permanent. A lender is entitled to periodic interest payments, determined at the time the loan is made. A holder of common stock is entitled to dividends only when and if declared by the board of directors (and subject to other statutory restrictions). If the corporation dissolves, a loan is entitled to be paid in full, but the common stockholders are entitled to all the remaining assets. A lender has no right to participate in the corporation's management; common stock has full voting rights.

But once debt is compared to other stock, the differences nearly disappear. Stock can be made redeemable or callable, making an investment temporary just like a loan. Both debt and stock can be made convertible into other securities. Preferred stock can have a right to periodic dividends, determined at the time the investment is made, which is similar to the right to receive interest.[3] If the corporation dissolves,

---

3. One difference remains, though. If the corporation fails to make an interest payment the lender may sue to compel the payment. If the corporation fails to pay a preferred dividend, the shareholder cannot bring suit to compel the dividend. Nonetheless, the agreement to issue preferred stock may contain other *in terrorem* provisions that give the corporation added incentive to declare the dividend and give the shareholder additional remedies such as voting rights.

preferred stock may have a fixed preference to some of the assets, just as a loan does. Finally, debt can be given voting rights just like typical stock, and stock may have no voting rights just like typical debt.

What difference does it make whether we characterize a security as debt or equity? It matters in two contexts. First, and most importantly, a corporation receives a tax benefit by issuing debt rather than equity. Speaking broadly, the Internal Revenue Code provides that corporations may deduct interest payments from their income; dividend payments are not deductible. Also, shareholders that are themselves corporations (i.e., Corporation A owns stock in Corporation B, a frequent occurrence) can, subject to restrictions, exclude 70 percent of the dividends paid to them from their own income. By contrast, a corporation that lends money to another corporation must include all the interest it receives in its own income. Thus corporations seeking additional investors may find that the most suitable investors are corporations that desire preferred stock instead of debt.

Second, when a corporation enters bankruptcy, or voluntarily dissolves, the debt holders have priority over the equity holders. So, an investor whose investment is characterized as debt may have a more senior, thus more secure, claim on the corporation's assets than an investor whose investment is characterized as stock. Now let's discuss the ways in which corporations and other business entities use debt.

(A) Short-Term Debt. Imagine a small corporation, Fashion Forward! that owns a trendy, retail clothing boutique. After several years of trying, Fashion Forward! has finally gotten a very popular high-end designer of mohair coats, Coats From Goats, to sell to it. Fashion Forward! will be the only store in the area allowed to sell Coats From Goats coats. This sounds like a golden opportunity for Fashion Forward!, and it is, but, as ever in the business world, there are complications.

Because Coats From Goats coats are in such high demand, Fashion Forward! has next to no bargaining power; Coats From Goats will set the terms of the transaction. Coats From Goats will ship a minimum of 100 coats per order because shipping fewer is not efficient. Also, Coats From Goats will not extend credit to Fashion Forward!, because there are plenty of other shops willing to pay cash. Each Coats From Goats coat will cost Fashion Forward! $300, or $30,000 for a minimum order. Coats From Goats coats retail for $750 and Fashion Forward! is certain it can sell the coats quickly and reap a profit of $45,000 on the first order (i.e., $450 profit per coat times 100 coats). Coats From Goats will ship the coats as soon as it receives payment and Fashion Forward! believes the coats will sell out within six weeks.

But, Fashion Forward! is a small establishment and does not have $30,000 in ready cash. Fashion Forward! could sell more equity, but its current owners do not want to share their ownership with others. More importantly, it doesn't make sense to seek a permanent infusion of money (and permanently give up some management rights) when Fashion Forward!'s need for cash is a brief one. Nonetheless, it must find a source for $30,000 for approximately six weeks at reasonable terms.

Fashion Forward!'s solution is to seek a loan from a bank payable in six weeks. This is a relatively safe loan because the amount is small (for a bank, anyway), and the maturity is short (the longer a loan is outstanding, the more things can go wrong and the greater the risk of nonpayment) so the interest rate (which compensates the bank for risking its money) should be low. The bank will probably make its loan even more safe by taking a security interest in the coats. This means that if Fashion

Forward! does not repay the loan, the bank can seize the remaining coats and sell them off itself to recoup its loan.

So far, we have been describing this problem and solution in business rather than legal terms. What do business lawyers have to do with this? Several things. First, they may negotiate some or all of the terms between Fashion Forward! and the bank. Second, they will document the transaction to ensure that the parties' intentions are accurately reflected in legally binding agreements. As a matter of corporate law, the statutes explicitly grant corporations the power to borrow money. See MBCA §3.02(7), DGCL §122(13). The loan will probably be documented in a loan agreement, a promissory note, and possibly a UCC-1.[4]

Lots of businesses face the same kind of problem on a recurring basis. That is, in the normal course of business they face a gap between the time they must spend money and the time they receive the revenues associated with that expense. A vivid example is a toy manufacturer. The vast majority of toys are sold, and hence the vast majority of revenue is received, between November 15th and January 15th. But nearly all of those toys have to be manufactured and shipped during the preceding summer and fall. That means toy manufacturers need large amounts of cash for only a few months each year for raw materials, expanded payrolls, and large shipping costs. Such companies may have standing credit arrangements with a bank that will provide a revolving line of credit. This means that the bank is committed to lend money up to a certain amount and, if the toy company has met the repayment requirements, the company has the right to reborrow that money. This works much like the consumer credit card you may carry. Some corporations are such good credit risks and need to borrow such large amounts of money on a regular cycle that their debt is eagerly sought after by investors looking to loan their money for short periods. These loans make up what is called the *commercial paper market* and is an important source of short-term money.

(B) Long-Term Debt.   Now imagine a corporation, Printing Pros, that operates a local commercial print shop. Advances in printing technology have meant that Printing Pros's current press is rapidly becoming obsolete. Newer presses can do more kinds of printing and do them more cheaply than Printing Pros's press. If Printing Pros wants to remain in business it must purchase a new press, which will last as long as 20 years. Such presses cost $1 million, far more money than Printing Pros has on hand. Because the money will be needed for a long time, it may make sense for Printing Pros to consider selling $1 million in equity to purchase the new press. However, it may not be able to find enough investors willing to put up a total of $1 million, and Printing Pros's current owners will certainly not be happy to see their ownership interests diluted by new equity owners. If Printing Pros decides not to sell more equity, it, like Fashion Forward! may seek a bank loan. Here, though, Printing Pros will want a loan for years rather than weeks. This increases the bank's risk and so it will charge a higher interest rate. Also, a $1 million loan is a much larger percentage of the bank's assets, and so a default will cause more harm than if Fashion Forward! defaults on its $30,000 loan. The bank will also certainly seek to reduce its risk by taking a security interest in the new press. The documentation for this transaction will be similar to the Fashion Forward! loan: a loan agreement, promissory note, and a UCC-1.

---

4. A UCC-1 is a form that lists the collateral for a loan. Filing the form perfects the creditor's security interest in the collateral.

As the amount of money a corporation needs increases and as the length of time it needs that money increases, a number of changes in the typical Printing Pros scenario take place. The loan principal (i.e., the amount borrowed) may grow too large for one bank to supply. Several banks, possibly located in several different countries, may get together in a *syndicate* to make the loan. Alternatively, the loan may be divided into very small pieces (usually $1,000) and sold to the public. These loan pieces are usually called *bonds* or *debentures*. Bonds are typically secured by the corporation's assets, while debentures are typically unsecured. This may sound odd, but it is a typical way for large corporations to borrow large amounts of money. In this setting an investment bank serves as an intermediary between the borrowing corporation and the many ultimate lenders. The intermediary will find the investors and may facilitate an active market for lenders who want to sell their bonds or debentures. These bonds and debentures are as readily transferable as stock. In fact, the market for corporate bonds dwarfs the market for corporate stock. The terms of the loan are set out in a document executed by the borrowing company and the investment bank, acting as trustee for the ultimate lenders, called an *indenture*. Indentures are much more detailed and standardized than typical loan agreements between commercial borrowers and lenders.

As the amount and maturity of the loan increase, the loan agreements contain additional, elaborate, provisions that decrease the lenders' risk. Many large corporations have a complex capital structure with common stock, several series of preferred stock, and short-term and long-term debt. When such a corporation issues new debt, the existing lenders may agree that some debt has priority (i.e., is senior) to other debt. The new debt may, then, by its terms be *subordinated* to some or all of the corporation's other debt. The parties may also agree that the interest rate will vary, or *float*, over the life of the loan, possibly with a minimum or maximum rate (or both, called a *collar*) so that changing conditions will not render the loan unfair for either the borrower or lenders. The debt may also be *convertible*, which gives the lenders the option to change the debt into certain other securities.

Often the borrowing corporation agrees to do or refrain from doing certain things that would make the loan more risky. *Affirmative covenants* include such things as maintaining certain financial ratios (e.g., agreeing to keep the ratio of current assets to current liabilities at a particular level) or agreeing to make all scheduled payments of *other* loans in timely fashion. *Negative covenants* prohibit the corporation from increasing its debt beyond an agreed-upon level or prohibit the corporation from paying more dividends that it currently does. A significant or sustained violation of these covenants will constitute an *event of default* and will permit the indenture trustee, on behalf of the ultimate lenders, to declare the entire loan due and payable. In other words, the loan becomes redeemable at the trustee's option.

The borrowing corporation may be required to put aside a certain amount of money each calendar quarter (or even each month) to ensure that it can make its loan payments when due. This money is called a *sinking fund* and can be used to pay the principal as well as the interest. Finally, if it is economically advantageous to the borrower to terminate the loan (e.g., if interest rates have declined so that the corporation could borrow the same amount of money more cheaply) but the loan is not callable, the corporation may put sufficient assets in a trust so that each time an interest or principal payment is due the money comes from the trust. Although the corporation is still legally obligated to repay the loan, as an economic matter the loan has already been prepaid. In this instance, the debt is said to have been *defeased*.

v. More Exotic Securities. Stock, preferred stock, and the varieties of debt discussed above represent the most frequently used corporate securities. Nonetheless, you should at least be aware of other, slightly more exotic or esoteric, securities available to corporations and their planners. Sometimes a corporation will sell (or give) an option to purchase its securities. Holders of these options are not shareholders and so are not entitled to dividends or a share of the assets upon dissolution, and they do not vote. The nomenclature for these options is more connotative than denotative so it is important to understand exactly which sort of option is being considered when discussing this question with clients, bankers, accountants, and other lawyers.

A *right* usually means an option granted to an existing security holder. Rights are usually short term (because the corporation needs money soon) and are often used when the corporation believes its current security holders are a likely source of new capital. For example, when the corporation's prospects are relatively bleak, existing shareholders may be more likely than new investors to put up more money because they hope to salvage their existing investment. Another setting in which rights are used is when the current shareholders care enough about their voting power that they will be likely to invest more money rather than see their interest diluted. Rights are usually, although not always, transferable so that shareholders who do not choose to exercise their rights can realize some gain by selling them.

A *warrant* is usually a long-term (i.e., over one year) option to purchase securities. Warrants are usually sold to the general public rather than only to existing security holders. Frequently a corporation will sell both stock and warrants as a package (sometimes called *units*) and purchasers then become security holders and have an option to purchase other securities in the future. Warrants are nearly always transferable and, because of their long life, an active market frequently develops.

In corporate law and finance parlance an *option* can have one of three meanings. At the broadest level, it has its ordinary meaning: the power but not the obligation to do something. In this sense, rights and warrants are both options. Second, an option can connote a power granted by the corporation to a particular person (often a key employee) to purchase securities. Options in this sense are usually granted for services rendered or to be rendered by the employee and are not transferable. Because this sort of option is typically intended to be an incentive to the employee to work diligently, the option may not be exercisable (i.e., may not *vest*) until several years have passed. Finally, *option* may connote a standardized right sold by someone (the option *writer*) *other than* the corporation to *purchase* securities of the corporation *from* the writer (a *call option*) or *sell* securities of the corporation *to* the writer (a *put option*). These options are a form of speculation and can be used by sophisticated traders to modify their financial risks. There is a very active market in these kinds of financial options. It is important to understand that the corporation is not a party to these kinds of options; they are strictly agreements between other parties.[5] For the

---

5. Options in this last sense are a kind of *derivative*, so called because their value is a function of — derives from — the value of the security on which the option is granted. Another kind of derivative is a *future* that, like put and call options, is usually created by and traded among persons other than the corporation. A future is a standardized contract for delivery of stock at a certain future date at a fixed price. You may remember such agreements from your contracts class when they were called forward contracts. The difference between a forward contract and a future is that a future has standard terms to facilitate active trading, while a forward contract connotes a particular agreement that is probably not transferable. A future is different from an option because it *requires* (rather than permits) the purchase or sale of the securities at expiration.

statutory grants of power to issue rights, warrants, and options, see MBCA §6.24, DGCL §157.

b. Planning the Corporate Capital Structure

When a new business corporation is being launched, deciding which securities to issue and in what proportions is a quintessential lawyer task. It is, of course, undertaken at the same time that the planners choose and create the legal form the business will take. See Chapters 5 and 20. Even if another form is deemed more suitable than a corporation, the owners and their lawyers must still decide the appropriate securities that will be issued. It is simply that the documentation of those interests is a bit more convoluted in other forms than it is in corporations. You should also understand that deciding upon a capital structure may be a continuing process. Many established businesses need additional capital and some have a rather constant need for new investment. Thus you may be called upon to render legal (and business) advice in the context of trying to assimilate new interests into an on-going business.

One challenge, which many lawyers see as simply a complication, is that clients often have ideas about the appropriate capital structure that may differ substantially from your own professional judgment. Where the clients are sophisticated business people, your task is, pretty clearly, to embody their desires in documents that will be legally effective. Where the clients are not as sophisticated as they believe they are, their desires can be frustrating at best and clearly deleterious to the new business at worst. Although you have a professional obligation to explain your conclusions to your clients, in the end you can, and should, effect their desires — provided, of course, that their preference for one capital structure over another is not illegal (a remote possibility) and that you have explained (typically by letter to the clients) exactly why you disagree and the potential problems you foresee with the structure insisted upon by your clients. In any setting, you must be sensitive to the ethical considerations triggered by entity formation (see Chapter 5).

When deciding upon a corporate capital structure, what is your ultimate goal, in addition to satisfying your clients' wishes? One goal is to select a structure that maximizes the value of the entire business. Maximization in this setting means choosing the structure that has the best chance of yielding the most value over time. Is the social value of a new enterprise maximized when the economic value is highest? Nearly all economists recognize that markets fail from time to time and therefore they do not believe that maximizing a business's profits necessarily maximizes social welfare. For example, a business's profits may decline because compliance with environmental regulations has increased its costs. Economists understand that the social benefits from those regulations outweigh the costs of compliance *if* businesses strive to maximize profits while complying with the regulations and *if* those regulations correct for the market failure caused by pollution in a way that is neither too lax nor too strict.

A more nuanced statement of the question is whether businesses should seek to maximize profits even when they believe that government regulations are too lax. Some economists would say that businesses should take actions that those businesses believe increase the overall social welfare even though the business's costs are increased and its profits reduced. This position can be supported by at least two arguments. First, businesses that must comply with regulations are often in the best position to evaluate whether those regulations are socially optimal. Second, businesses are moral actors in society, just as individuals are, and so have the same ethical obligations to act in the manner they perceive will be best for society.

Other economists would say that private businesses should strive to maximize their profits despite their belief that current regulations are inadequate. This view may be supported by the argument that businesses and their managers cannot accurately judge whether regulations are socially optimal. Further, even if they could make such accurate judgments they may be seen as arrogating to private organizations judgments that should only be made by public bodies.[6]

If one measures the success of a corporate capital structure largely by its macro- and microeconomic effects, then the goal of a capital structure is to maximize the entire business and effect a division of management and economic rights among the investors that optimizes their relative preferences.

i. The Consequences of Debt—Leverage. We discussed the tax implications of debt and equity briefly above. Now we will expand our examination and look at the tax differences to understand how they affect the choice of a new corporation's capital structure. As you recall, interest payments are deductible by the corporation but dividends are not. A profitable corporation may increase the value of the enterprise by taking on debt.

An example may make this clear. Assume a corporation owns an apartment house and that it had net revenues before interest and income tax of $1,000,000. The corporation wants to distribute as much of its earnings as possible to its investors. In one scenario, the corporation has no debt; its investors own only equity. In the other scenario, the investors own both equity and debt and the interest payments on the debt total $800,000.

Table 6-1

	Equity Only	Equity and Debt
Net Revenue:	$1,000,000	$1,000,000
Interest Payments:	$0	$800,000
Taxable Income:	$1,000,000	$200,000
Tax (35%):	$350,000	$70,000
Dividends (Taxable Income−Tax):	$650,000	$130,000
Total Paid to Investors (i.e., Dividends + Interest Payments):	$650,000	$930,000

Remember, the only difference is that in one setting the corporation obtained its money by selling equity, while in the other the corporation obtained its money by selling equity and incurring debt. Yet by taking on debt, the corporation was able to return over 40 percent ($280,000) more to its investors. As we saw in Chapter 3, the value (and hence the major determinant of price) of an economic asset is a function of the expected return and the uncertainty (riskiness) of that return. Applying that insight here, the expected return is much greater where the corporation is financed

6. This discussion of the goals of a corporate capital structure was largely informed by my colleague John B. Kirkwood. Thanks, Jack!

in part with debt if the riskiness of the corporation is identical in both settings. The consequence is that economically rational investors should be willing to pay more to invest in the corporation with debt. The corporation is, as an economic matter, more valuable when its capital structure includes debt.[7]

Assume a few more facts about the apartment building. It has 100 apartments that rent for an average of $1,000 per month for a theoretical maximum gross revenue (i.e., assuming every apartment were rented every day of the year) of $1.2 million per year. The costs of the building total $200,000 per year and consist of things such as property taxes, insurance, and maintenance costs.[8] So, the net revenue from the apartment building is $1 million per year.

Using the discounted cash flow analysis from Chapter 3, the assumptions above suggest a present value of about $10 million. The table below assumes that the owners purchased the building for $10 million and financed that purchase in one of three possible ways. First, the owners put 20 percent down (i.e., $2 million) and borrowed 80 percent (i.e., $8 million). Second, the owners put only 10 percent down and borrowed 90 percent; third, the owners put a mere 5 percent down and borrowed 95 percent. For simplicity's sake, assume the loans were at 10 percent interest and that no principal was due for 20 years.

Table 6-2

	20/80	10/90	5/95
Net Revenue:	$1,000,000	$1,000,000	$1,000,000
Interest Payments:	$800,000	$900,000	$950,000
Dividends[9]:	$130,000	$65,000	$32,500

Consider, as well, another aspect. If the corporation flourishes, the debt holder does not share in that good news beyond the decreased risk of default implied by the borrower's financial success.[10] Equity holders receive the entire gain. For example, what if the neighborhood in which the apartment house is located suddenly becomes the trendiest part of town in which to live? Or, suppose the owners refurbish the

7. This example assumes that the investors in both scenarios are identical. That is, that the investors are choosing whether to invest their money in return for equity only or for a mix of equity and debt. While this is frequently accurate, you should understand that the dynamics of the investment decision will change if the lenders will not own equity at all. An example is the typical situation in which the apartment house's equity owners will have gotten a loan from a bank for the bulk of the purchase price. While the total returns will be as set out in Table 6-1, the investors' choice will be between paying the full purchase price and receiving $650,000 in return (the equity only choice) or paying only a portion of the purchase price (a down payment), getting a bank loan for the rest, and receiving $130,000 in return (with the bank receiving all the $800,000 in interest).

8. Maintenance costs include such things as periodic repainting and recarpeting of the apartments. The building's manager lives rent free in one of the apartments so the maintenance cost includes $12,000 of rent that the owners don't receive. Further, when tenants move, it often takes the better part of a month before the apartment can be readied for the next tenant, meaning that the owners receive nothing for those months.

9. The "Dividend" number represents the after-tax money available: 65 percent of (Net Revenue −Interest Payments). That is, it takes the tax benefits of debt into account.

10. That increased assurance of repayment may, to the debt holder, be very valuable indeed, especially if repayment were problematic when the borrower lent. The increased certainty of repayment should mean that the value (though not the principal) of the debt has increased. Still, the debt holder does not share in the increase in the corporation's value.

entire building, thus making the apartments more desirable and, hence, more expensive? As a result, the net income rises 30 percent, from $1 million per year to $1.3 million. Regardless of the level of debt, all that additional income goes to the equity owners. Compare Table 6-2 to the next table:

Table 6-3

	20/80	10/90	5/95
Net Revenue:	$1,300,000	$1,300,000	$1,300,000
Interest Payments:	$800,000	$900,000	$950,000
Dividends:	$325,000	$260,000	$227,500
Percent Increase in Dividends:	150%	300%	600%

But equally importantly, this increase in net revenue, if sustainable in the long run, should mean that the apartment house itself is more valuable. Again, using the discounted cash flow analysis from Chapter 3, the net revenue of $1.3 million suggests a present value of about $13.4 million, an increase of $3.4 million over the $10 million purchase price. If the owners sold the building for $13.4 million, here's how the proceeds would be divided:

Table 6-4

	20/80	10/90	5/95
Sale Proceeds:	$13,400,000	$13,400,000	$13,400,000
Loan Repayment:	$8,000,000	$9,000,000	$9,500,000
Net Proceeds to Equity Owners:	$5,400,000	$4,400,000	$3,900,000
Down Payment:	$2,000,000	$1,000,000	$500,000
Net Gain (Loss):	$3,400,000	$3,400,000	$3,400,000
Net Gain as a Percentage of Down Payment:	170%	340%	680%

In other words, *all* of the increase in value goes to the equity holders. As you see in both Table 6-3 and Table 6-4, the more highly leveraged an investment is, the greater the percentage gains.

ii. The Economic Risks of Excessive Debt   The discussion so far is a tad deceptive because it suggests that planners should choose a capital structure with a very high proportion of debt to equity. But implementing a capital structure that has too much debt in relation to the equity poses both economic and legal risks. This section enlarges upon this idea and its consequences for planning a capital structure.

As the amount of debt increases, the margin for error in predicting future cash falls, which increases the enterprise's risk. The increase in risk should result in a lower value of the enterprise if all other facts remain the same. When the debt level is small or moderate, this increased risk is outweighed by the tax benefits. But when the debt becomes a large percentage of the enterprise's capital, the increased risk makes the enterprise less valuable as a whole.

Lenders are as keenly aware of the deleterious effects of leverage as equity owners are aware of leverage's benefits. As the percentage of debt increases, lenders will seek a higher price (i.e., charge a higher interest rate) for lending their money. Of course, as the interest rate increases the debt service increases, thus increasing a venture's risk even more. To make the apartment house example a bit more realistic, assume that the buyers' financing choices are: (1) 20 percent down (i.e., $2 million) and borrow 80 percent at 10 percent per year; (2) 10 percent down and borrow 90 percent at 11 percent per year; or (3) 5 percent down and borrow 95 percent at 13 percent per year.

Table 6-5

	20/80 (10%)	10/90 (11%)	5/95 (13%)
Net Revenue:	$1,000,000	$1,000,000	$1,000,000
Interest Payments:	$800,000	$990,000	$1,235,000
Dividends:	$130,000	$6,500	($235,000)

In the last example, the interest exceeds the net revenues, and therefore the borrowers must either have another source of income to make up anticipated short-fall or must have a plan for increasing the apartment house's net revenues, and quickly! As a practical matter, the last option is not likely to be available to any but the most sophisticated borrowers and then only if the lender is convinced that the borrowers' plan for meeting the interest payments is economically sound.

Let's return to the apartment house example. Perhaps the primary risk is that the owner will be unable to rent the apartments at sufficient rent to cover the costs of running the building *including the interest on the debt.* If the amount of debt is low, the risk that the rents will not cover the debt service is low. But, if the buyer financed the purchase with a high percentage of debt, even one empty apartment may mean insufficient revenue to cover the debt service.

Think about what happens if the net revenue drops. This could happen in a number of ways, such as an increase in property taxes or insurance premiums. Most likely, though, the net revenue would drop when fewer apartments are occupied. Perhaps the neighborhood has become unfashionable. Perhaps it has become more crime ridden. Perhaps the apartment house's owners or managers cut back on maintenance and the apartment house itself is now a less desirable place to live. Whatever the cause(s), look at the consequences of having only one apartment unrented for a year.[11] The net revenue will decline by $12,000 ($1,000 × 12) only 1.2 percent.[12] Again, assume the more realistic scenario in which the interest rate rises with the proportion of debt.

11. Of course, this needn't mean the same apartment. It simply means some combination of vacancies that totals one fewer apartment over the course of the year.

12. In reality, the maintenance costs will also have gone down a bit, which will offset the loss of revenue, but probably those costs will not have decreased very much as many of the largest costs, such as property taxes and insurance, are the same regardless of how many apartments are rented.

Table 6-6

	20/80 (10%)	10/90 (11%)	5/95 (13%)
Net Revenue:	$988,000	$988,000	$988,000
Interest Payments:	$800,000	$990,000	$1,235,000
Dividends:	$122,200	($2,000)	($247,000)

In the first setting, where the debt is only 80 percent, the owners' gain fell by 6 percent ($7,800) compared to the dividends in Table 6-2. In the second setting, the gain turned into a small loss. Where the owners put up only 5 percent of the purchase price, they must now find $247,000 somewhere to pay the interest. If they don't, the lender presumably will foreclose on the mortgage and sell the building.

If the dip in net revenue is temporary, the owners may be able to survive, but if the decline is long term, the value of the apartment house should decline as well. A discounted cash flow approach suggests that if the net revenue falls by 10 percent ($100,000) per year to $900,000 the present value is about $9.25 million. If the owners foresee no likelihood that they can increase that revenue, and they sell the building, the next table shows the consequences. Compare this to Table 6-4.

Table 6-7

	20/80	10/90	5/95
Sale Proceeds:	$9,250,000	$9,250,000	$9,250,000
Loan Repayment:	$8,000,000	$9,000,000	$9,500,000
Net Proceeds to Equity Owners:	$1,250,000	$250,000	$0 or ($250,000)[13]
Down Payment:	$2,000,000	$1,000,000	$500,000
Net Gain (Loss):	($750,000)	($750,000)	($500,000) or ($750,000)

iii. Other Costs of Debt. Consider these additional facts. First, payment of interest is mandatory, while payment of dividends is in the discretion of the board. This means that a corporation that is in financial difficulty can cut back on, or eliminate entirely, any dividends so that those funds can be used to alleviate the financial problems. By contrast, a corporation's managers have no such discretion as to interest payments. They must be paid even though the corporation's financial state will worsen.

Second, debt, no matter how long term, must be paid back. When this happens, the investor who held debt is no longer an investor in the corporation. By contrast, the investor who owns stock remains an investor, assuming he or she has not sold the stock. Depending upon the corporation's prospects at the time the debt is repaid, the investor who held debt may regret that he or she is no longer an investor.

---

13. In this scenario, the borrowers' entire interest has been wiped out. If the loan was "with recourse" the borrowers remain liable to the bank for the $250,000 shortfall. If the loan was "without recourse," the borrowers are not liable and the bank must absorb the loss. As you may intuit, loans with recourse are typically at lower interest rates than those made without recourse. Likewise, when calculating the borrowers' Net Gain (Loss) the two possibilities represent the setting in which the loan was without recourse ($500,000 loss) or with recourse ($750,000 loss).

Obviously the investor and corporation can agree to continue the investment, but such an agreement cannot be assured and, the greater the corporation's prospects the harder the bargain it may drive with the investor. Economists call this danger a *reinvestment risk*. Thus one incentive for equity financing is the assurance to investors (and to the corporation) that the investment is permanent.

Adding debt also has agency costs. Remember from Chapter 4 that from an economic perspective, equity owners are agents of the lenders. This creates the potential for opportunistic behavior, a form of moral hazard that increases the agency costs of the venture. See Chapter 4 for a description of those hazards. Devices designed to ameliorate those costs have, themselves, costs that are irreducible.

Finally, there are costs associated when a venture prepares for, and enters, bankruptcy. These costs include lost management time spent trying to stave off the bankruptcy and the management time involved with the proceedings. Obviously there are transaction costs such as lawyer fees and administrative fees, as well.

iv. The Legal Dangers of Excessive Debt.

You should be aware of three particular legal risks associated with the choice of a capital structure that relies too heavily on debt. The first risk has to do with the deductibility of interest on debt. Remember that this deductibility increases the value of the enterprise more than the increase in risk caused by modest levels of debt. However, conceptually, an enterprise cannot be 100 percent debt; someone must have an ownership stake. Because the deduction for interest paid is money that would otherwise be taxed, the Internal Revenue Service is rather suspicious of corporations that deduct large amounts of interest from their income. The consequence of a recharacterization of interest as dividends is that the entity is denied the deduction it took, may have to amend prior tax returns, and must pay tax on the amounts paid out and possibly additional sums as penalties and interest on delayed taxes, as well.

The Service and the courts have two kinds of inquiries to determine whether the "debt" upon which interest is paid (and hence deductible) is genuine debt or is really equity disguised so that payments are characterized as interest rather than dividends. The first inquiry looks to whether the obligation has the traditional indicia of debt: for example, an unconditional obligation to pay a sum certain, a fixed maturity date, and interest payable regardless of the debtor's income. Where the debt is owed to equity holders, the Service and courts give greater scrutiny than where the debt is owed to outsiders. For example, where the debt is owed to equity holders, the absence of a written agreement might lead a court to conclude that the debt is not genuine and, hence, to disallow an interest deduction.

The other inquiry for recharacterizing debt is sometimes called the *economic realities* test. This is essentially an objective inquiry to ask whether an unrelated third party would have been willing to make a loan of similar size on similar terms to the corporation. If not, the Service or court may conclude that the debt is really a contribution to equity. Although it is clear that the loan need not be on terms as stringent as a completely disinterested third party would offer, the further away from such terms (i.e., the more favorable the terms to the borrowing corporation) the more likely it is to be found to be a contribution to equity rather than a loan.

One important element in this inquiry is a comparison of the corporation's debt to its equity. It is quite common for corporations to have debt several times the size of their equity. Whether a particular debt/equity ratio is "excessive," sometimes described as a "top heavy" capital structure or a "thin" capitalization, is really a question of comparing the particular corporation's capital structure to that of similar companies in the same industry. Industries vary widely in their reliance on debt, and it is impossible in the absence of such comparison to opine whether a particular corporation has excessive debt. Another important consideration in this inquiry is to compare the percentage of total equity held by each shareholder to the percentage of total debt that shareholder owns. If each shareholder's percentage of the debt is identical to his or her percentage of the equity, the debt is said to be held proportionally, and this may suggest that at least some of the debt is actually equity in disguise. By contrast, where the percentage of debt is different from the percentage of equity, this militates toward a finding that the debt is genuine.

The second kind of legal risk for a corporation with significant debt is *equitable subordination* in bankruptcy. When an entity declares bankruptcy, the bankruptcy code provides that the entity's assets shall be applied to satisfy the claimants in a fixed order. Debt holders are paid before equity holders. As we have seen, it is frequently the case that equity holders also, and legitimately, hold debt as well. If a bankruptcy judge believes that the equity holder's intention in taking debt was to raise up a portion of his or her investment in the bankruptcy priority system, the judge may reduce the priority of (i.e., subordinate) some or all of that debt. In effect, the judge declares that, for reasons of equity, repayment of debt owned by equity holders should be delayed until debt to nonequity holders, such as trade creditors or bank lenders, has been paid first. This result is particularly likely when equity holders advance new money, in the form of loans, on the eve of bankruptcy or when their investment, which was all equity, is recast as part equity and part debt close to bankruptcy. Equitable subordination is also called the Deep Rock doctrine, after the bankrupt subsidiary in *Taylor v. Standard Gas & Electric Co.*, 306 U.S. 307 (1939).

The third danger of a capital structure with a large proportion of debt is piercing the corporate veil. If the corporation incurs a liability that it cannot satisfy, especially if that liability is incurred near the corporation's formation, a court may disregard the corporate entity and hold its owners personally liable. This doctrine is explored in more detail in Chapter 8, but you should be aware that one factor that may weigh heavily on a court's decision is whether the entity had a significant part of its capital in the form of debt held by the equity holders. If so, the possibility of piercing is heightened.

v. Other Factors That Make Equity Attractive.   For our purposes, an even greater insight into crafting a capital structure comes from understanding that the owner does not have to sell or declare a dividend when the asset appreciates in value. In an economic sense, when the value of the apartment house increases from $10 million to $13.4 million, the owners of the apartment are $3.4 million richer even though they do not convert that wealth to cash by selling. Similarly, if the corporation generated an extra $300,000 in net income in one year, the equity holders do not have to distribute that money as dividends. If that money simply sits in the corporation's bank account, the value of the corporation has, presumably, increased by $300,000 and the owners are thus $300,000 richer even though they have no additional cash in their own hands. As a more general description, an equity holder's total return from his or her investment must be measured by the dividends *and* the increase in the value of the corporation.

Under the Internal Revenue Code, an equity holder receives two advantages from this increase in wealth that is unaccompanied by a sale or dividend. First, the gain is not taxed at all until it is realized. In other words, regardless of how much the value of the equity holder's stock increases, the equity holder will not pay tax on that gain until he or she sells the equity. Only the dividends, if any, will be taxed. This gives the equity holder control over when to realize the gain. The second advantage is that, when gain is recognized, it will result in a lower tax for two reasons. First, as you remember from Chapter 3, a dollar in the future is worth less than a dollar today. So, a tax dollar paid in the future, when the equity holder realizes gain, is less than the same dollar paid today. Second, when the equity holder does sell equity, any gain will be considered a *capital gain* and may be taxed at a lower rate than ordinary income such as wages, dividend, or interest income.

In most start-up companies there is yet another factor that attenuates the value of debt over equity. Some or all of the investors will be providing services to the corporation as employees. Most of these people will desire or need periodic payments to cover their own living expenses. Although in theory the corporation could have debt that requires monthly (or weekly or even daily) interest payments and could declare and pay dividends with equal frequency, such solutions are a bit cumbersome. The usual solution is for the investors to become employees of the corporation they own. In return, they receive salaries. As long as the salaries are reasonable and necessary, they can be deducted from the corporation's income, just as interest payments are deducted. Further, the vast majority of new businesses cannot realistically expect profits in the short term. In light of this, the investor/employees are probably expecting the great bulk of their reward to come via salaries rather than either interest or dividends so at least some of the investors will be fairly neutral as between debt and equity. This reality is yet another attenuation of the need to capitalize the corporation with debt rather than equity.

A further reason why every corporation should not be entirely financed with debt has to do with the nature of the investors. Especially in the start-up corporation the planners will be concerned with a relatively small number of real investors. Assuming our professional obligation runs to each investor equally, which may not necessarily be true, our goal is to maximize the value of the entire business *in the hands of this set of investors.* In the paradigm setting, all investors are individuals. Under the Internal Revenue Code, interest paid to individuals and dividends paid to individuals are treated as *ordinary income* on which the investor will pay income tax. That means that his or her after-tax return from the corporation will be the same, regardless of whether the investor receives a return as interest or dividend. So far, this does not change our conclusion that a corporation is more valuable with debt than without and even that it ought to be financed entirely with debt.

However, the same amount of interest or dividend may have different tax consequences for different investors. Some individual investors may have lower marginal tax rates than others.[14] A typical example is a new corporation that will operate a restaurant. Some investors will be rich individuals with marginal tax rates at the maximum, say 35 percent, while other investors—perhaps the chef or other key, but relatively impecunious, participants—will have marginal tax rates at the mini-

---

14. The *marginal* tax rate is the percent of the next dollar of income that will be taxed. You must be careful to distinguish this from the *effective* tax rate, which is the ratio of all tax paid to all income. Because marginal rates increase as income increases, the effective rate for most taxpayers is lower than their marginal rate.

mum, perhaps 15 percent.[15] Investors with lower marginal rates may prefer to invest in debt because capital gains treatment is less valuable to them and because, with lower income, they may prefer the greater certainly of debt to the increased risk of equity. Further, in some situations a corporation unaffiliated with the new corporation may be an investor. Recall that such corporation/investor can exclude 70 percent of dividends from its income. This is a strong incentive for such investors to take equity rather than debt because each $10 of interest received is only $6.50 after taxes (with a 35% corporate income tax rate) while each $10 of dividends is worth $8.95 (35% of $3.00 = $1.05 paid in tax).

Finally, investors have an incentive to choose equity over debt because equity carries with it management power while debt does not.[16] This is not such a strong incentive as it first appears. If each investor is to have equal voting rights regardless of the size of his or her investment (or if each is making an investment of equal value), each can be issued an equal amount of stock for nominal consideration. If they are to have voting power in proportion to their investments, which are unequal (a common occurrence), the investors could still have differing proportions of debt and equity through using different series or classes of stock that vary from one another only as to voting rights. In a stark example, assume a start-up corporation with two investors who are to have equal voting power, one who wants debt and one who wants equity. One solution is to sell debt to one investor, nonvoting stock to the other, and a small amount of voting stock (i.e., common stock) to each. The investor who wants debt has, essentially, a certain and senior claim on the income and assets of the corporation, while the investor who wants equity has a junior claim but will enjoy all the gain in the corporation's value. The small amount of common stock each owns will be economically inconsequential in comparison to the size of the other securities yet give each investor equal voting power.

vi. Choosing a Capital Structure for the Start-Up Corporation.

How does one actually plan a new corporation's capital structure, at least when the solution is not dictated to you by the investors? One way to approach this is to examine separately the following areas: (1) the investors' relative claims on the business's income (and assets on dissolution); (2) the investors' relative management power; and (3) the dangers that concern capital structures with excessive debt. In considering the relative management power and economic claims of the investors you should bear in mind that much of the ultimate solution will depend upon the bargaining leverage each investor brings. Even in a setting in which your professional obligation runs to each investor equally, some investors' contributions (either knowledge, money, unique assets, or other virtues such as an investor's prestige within the business or other important community) will be more central than others. Those investors have the ability to control the outcome of the management and economic divisions.

In finding the appropriate capital structure as a financial matter, the investors and you, as their advisor, should seek the mix of debt and equity that maximizes the value of the entire enterprise in the hands of the anticipated owners. This means sufficient equity so that the risks of excessive debt are sufficiently dampened while maximizing the tax benefits obtainable from debt. Once an appropriate mix of

15. Congress tinkers with the tax rates rather frequently. In recent decades, however, the minimum individual rate has been around 10 percent -15 percent while the top rates have been in the mid-30 percent. Tax rates for corporations are typically around 35 percent.

16. In Delaware, however, debt with voting power can be created. See DGCL §221.

debt and equity has been decided, the planner can turn his or her attention to the problem of dividing up the management power among the participants.

It is worth emphasizing a point that is probably intuitive. The considerations that are set out here as discrete questions considered in a particular order are, in the real world, compounded, conflated, and simultaneous. Nonetheless, they are dissected here so that you can have a better appreciation of the way in which these aspects need to be approached if a thoughtful and appropriate solution for your clients is to be crafted.

Turning to the division of management power, in the simplest dynamic, each investor will want management control commensurate with his or her economic contribution. In that case, the solution is relatively simple: each investor gets stock in proportion to his or her investment. Often, this means the new corporation will only issue common stock. When this is not the parties' desire, the situation can become more complex very quickly. For our purposes, understand that two frequent arrangements are that certain investors are to have, in essence, veto rights either over every decision or at least over certain important decisions. Also, some investors may have no (or no important) management power unless the business falters, in which instance those investors are to have heightened management powers.

The solution to the first setting is to give the investors with veto power either a separate class of shares that votes on important matters or to have a supermajority requirement as to some issues so that the veto can be exercised in appropriate circumstances. The solution to the second setting is to provide for nonvoting stock that has voting rights in certain settings such as when the corporation's financial position deteriorates. The key to these kinds of problems and solutions is to recognize that there are no predetermined answers but simply time-tested approaches that have proved useful. After studying this chapter you should be able to abstract the concerns of the parties and develop a range of solutions to those concerns.

Notes and Questions

1. Suppose

a. Suppose the IRS or Congress had adopted a bright-line test for determining whether an investment would be considered debt or equity. Would that be better than the current system? What bright-line test would you adopt?

2. What Do You Think?

a. When corporations borrow money, the value of the enterprise increases more than if it had issued equity only because the corporation can deduct the interest it pays on the debt. A corporation that has $1,000 in income can pay only $650 in dividends (because it must pay $350 in income tax) but can pay the entire $1,000 as interest. In other words, investors get $350 more only because the U.S. Treasury gets $350 less. Do you think this is fair? Why did Congress choose to reward investment via debt in a way that does not equally reward investment via equity?

b. Should Congress look at the goods and services produced by an enterprise rather than looking at whether the enterprise is financed by debt or equity? Instead of rewarding lenders over shareholders, should Congress focus on rewarding investment (debt or equity) in corporations that undertake ends or use means that Congress considers particularly valuable to society? Which ends or means should Congress reward?

c. Is it ethical (both as a matter of a lawyer's professional responsibility and more broadly) for lawyers to propose and implement capital structures that minimize their clients' tax liability? Why shouldn't they be required to create structures that maximize that liability?

vii. Background and Context: A Note on Financing by Going Public and by Venture Capital.   The paradigm we have been considering has been the start-up corporation and, primarily, we have been working on an implicit assumption that the equity holders were a small group of individuals or perhaps even a single person. These qualities hold true for the vast majority of corporations. They are generically referred to as *close corporations* or *closely held corporations* because the number of owners is not large. But many corporations do not meet these criteria. They have thousands of shareholders, very few of whom are involved in the corporation's management. Conversely, the managers' total equity investment is a miniscule percentage of the corporation's total equity. How did these large corporations evolve from small ones?

At one level the answer is simply that they were successful in industries that were particularly hospitable, economically speaking, to large firms. For purposes of this chapter, the answer is that those companies typically underwent a fundamental change in their capital structure. That is, at some point in their existence, these corporations obtained significant financing by selling securities (equity, usually, but also debt) to the public. When a corporation sells securities to the general public for the first time, the company is said to *go public* and its sale is called an *initial public offering*, or *IPO*.

One reason to go public is to raise more money than can be raised conveniently from a smaller group of investors, even though those investors might have very deep pockets. An additional reason to go public is that typically the securities sold to the public will thereafter be actively traded among individuals. This is sometimes called the *secondary trading market*. It's the market you and I think of when we think of the stock market. The New York Stock Exchange and NASDAQ[17] are the best-known secondary markets. Shares of IBM or Microsoft may rise or fall every day but none of the money changing hands in those sales goes to the company. Rather, those sales are simply private transactions between sellers who no longer desire to remain security holders and buyers who wish to become security holders.

Still this secondary market indirectly benefits the corporations that issue the securities. Why? Because buyers of securities from corporations will pay more for securities that can be easily disposed of. In a close corporation, shareholders can often find someone willing to buy their shares only with great difficulty. A shareholder of Microsoft, by contrast, can simply contact a stockbroker and the shares can be sold nearly instantly. This characteristic, called *liquidity*, makes initial buyers more confident in their investment because they can more readily end their investment and so they are willing to pay more. So an additional reason for a company to go public is that it can charge a higher price for its securities than if it sold them to a smaller number of investors who would have more difficulty trading them.

---

17. NASDAQ is an acronym for the National Association of Securities Dealers Automated Quotation system of trading.

We should mention, though, that not every large corporation has gone public. Some companies are content to meet their financing needs privately rather than go through the elaborate process of offering securities to the public and the continuing strictures of remaining a public company.[18] Further, the management of some companies believes that it will lose control of the business if significant amounts of stock are sold to the public. Some of the best-known names in corporate America, such as Mars Candy and Hallmark Cards, are not publicly held. The Ford Motor Company was formed in 1903 and remained privately held, primarily by the Ford family, until 1956, even though the corporation was quite large by 1920 and had constant needs for large amounts of capital.

The process of going public consists of the corporation selecting an investment bank to be its lead *underwriter*. That investment bank puts together a syndicate of other such investment banks to share the risks and rewards of the offering. The investment bank also canvasses the market and advises the corporation on the kind of security (debt or equity) it should issue and likely price it should charge. Finally, the underwriting syndicate purchases the securities at a discount, which is, in effect, their fee, from the corporation and immediately resells them to the public at the announced price. Sometimes current shareholders of the corporation sell some of their shares to the underwriters as well, allowing them to cash in on the corporation's success. Usually the underwriters also agree to support a secondary market in the security, offering to buy and sell until the market for that security becomes well established. The process is highly regulated by the Securities and Exchange Commission and a brief outline of the legal implications of going public is found below in Section B.

Most companies that end up going public do so as the culmination of a process of involvement with *venture capital* firms. Venture capital is a description of money supplied to nonpublic corporations by entities unconnected with the corporation. Although some of this venture capital is supplied by rich individuals (sometimes called *angels*) most of it is supplied by venture capital firms usually structured as limited partnerships. Start-up companies seeking venture capital make presentations to venture capital firms. The venture capital firms see hundreds of presentations every year and make very few investments. Ultimately, about one in ten of those investments is a complete loss and eight of the ten will be very modest successes. The one in ten that is a great success provides the venture capital firm with more than enough profits to cover the costs of the other nine investments.

The venture capital firm analyzes the new business's plan and identifies a series of important operational and financial milestones leading to a public offering. The venture capital firm also estimates the amount of money the business will need at each stage of its development. The venture capitalists invest just enough money to carry the business through to the next milestone with no guarantee from the venture capital firm of additional funds. Further, as a condition of the venture capital firm's involvement, the key entrepreneurs in the business will be required to invest essentially all their wealth in the business. This means that any savings or home

---

18. These involve compliance with detailed and pervasive federal regulations, which are summarized below in Section B. The process of going public is subject to considerable federal regulation and, once a company has securities in the hands of the public, it is required to make detailed periodic reports of its financial and operating results. For some companies, these strictures are simply not worth the benefits to be gained from going public.

equity is invested in the business, ensuring that the managers are highly motivated to be successful.

At each stage the venture capital firm provides advice on the business's development and watches that development with keen interest. As the stages progress, other venture capital firms may participate in financing as well. Near the end stages, when the business is ready to go public, the venture capital firm will usually identify and help recruit seasoned executives to replace many of the key employees. This replacement may seem harsh but it adds to the likelihood that the business will succeed. It is not unusual for such key employees as the chief operating officer, the general counsel, the chief financial officer, and even the chief executive officer, who is probably the person who had the initial vision for the business, to be replaced at this point. Sometimes the replaced employees remain in a lesser or advisory capacity. Other times they move on to other pursuits. In either event, they have usually been compensated with stock in the business that, if the public offering is successful, will make them quite rich and that goes far in assuaging any damage to their self esteem.

The nearly universal practice is for venture capital firms to invest only in entities that are Delaware corporations. This does not rule out other forms of businesses, but simply means that they must convert to Delaware corporations, which is a relatively simple task. The venture capital firms tend to receive preferred stock for their investment, which gives them priority over the firm's assets. The preferred stock provisions also typically give the venture capitalists the power to select half the board members. This is accomplished by having only the preferred stock vote for half the board and only the common stock (owned by the entrepreneurs) vote for the other half of the board. The preferred stock usually has veto power over extraordinary actions such as incurring large debt, issuing new stock, dissolving, or merging. Perhaps most importantly, the preferred stock typically gets increased voting power in the event the corporation fails to meet its operational and financial milestones. In such event the venture capitalists essentially take over the corporation and may restructure the enterprise by replacing the founders, renegotiating the terms of their investment, or dissolving the corporation.

Although both the venture capitalists and the business's entrepreneurs want to see the corporation succeed, their interests are not identical. The next case shows the kinds of conflicts that can arise. The lessons from this case are applicable beyond the venture capital-versus-entrepreneur setting. They apply any time both passive and active investors hold different kinds of investments in the same entity.

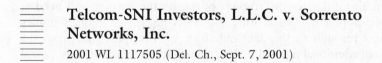

Telcom-SNI Investors, L.L.C. v. Sorrento Networks, Inc.

2001 WL 1117505 (Del. Ch., Sept. 7, 2001)

NOBLE, V.C.

I. FACTUAL BACKGROUND

A. The Parties

Plaintiffs,... who have been characterized by the Defendants as "venture capitalists," hold approximately 7.5 million shares of Sorrento's Series A Preferred Stock which, at one time, constituted approximately 84% of the Series A Preferred Stock issued by Sorrento. The only preferred stock issued by Sorrento is the Series A Preferred.

Sorrento designs, manufactures and markets optical network equipment. [Osicom], . . . owns . . . all of the common stock in Sorrento.

Sorrento Networks, Inc. ("[Sorrento]") was incorporated in California on January 21, 2000. [Sorrento], as a startup corporation with no immediate prospects of profitability, required constant and significant cash infusions to sustain it until an initial public offering ("IPO") could be accomplished. On March 3, 2000, [Sorrento], Osicom, and a group of investors, including Plaintiffs, entered into an agreement for the private placement of 8,880,734 million shares of Sorrento's Series A Preferred Stock at a price of $5.45 per share, thereby generating approximately $48.4 million.

The investors (together with [Sorrento] and Osicom) anticipated that the IPO would occur shortly after the investment. They were wrong, and the collapse of this fundamental premise upon which the investors made their investment decision has resulted, perhaps inevitably, in this litigation.

On August 3, 2000, Sorrento was [re-]incorporated as a Delaware corporation. . . .[6] The provisions in Sorrento's Certificate were identical in all material respects to those of [Sorrento]'s charter.

When Plaintiffs agreed . . . to invest in [Sorrento] . . . , they negotiated several "protective provisions" to secure the integrity of their investment. The protective provisions appear both in the Certificate and in the separate Investors' Rights Agreement.

1. Sorrento's Certificate provides in part at Article V.D(6):

> (a) [S]o long as any shares of Series A Preferred Stock are outstanding, the Corporation shall not without first obtaining the approval . . . of the holders of at least a majority of the then outstanding shares of Series A Preferred Stock:
>
> > (i) alter, change or amend the rights, preferences or privileges of the Series A Preferred Stock;
> > (ii) authorize or issue, or obligate itself to issue, any other equity security, including any other security convertible into or exercisable for any equity security having a preference over, or being on a parity with, the Series A Preferred Stock with respect to voting, dividends or upon liquidation . . . ,

2. The Investors' Rights Agreement conferred upon Plaintiffs significant additional rights. Among those rights are the following:

> b. If the IPO was not completed by March 1, 2001, by the written request of the holders of at least 50% of the outstanding Series A Preferred Stock redemption of their shares could be obtained at a price equal to the original purchase price . . . in cash (§2.4(b));
> d. The Series A Preferred Stock holders were granted a "right of first offer" which assured each investor the opportunity to purchase sufficient shares to maintain its proportionate interest in the equity structure of [Sorrento] each time the company offered equity interests (§2.4).

While Sorrento did not go public and did not become profitable, its capacity to consume cash continued. It borrowed more than $36 million from Osicom. Sorrento's indebtedness in at least that amount has continued to the present.

---

6. Re-incorporation in Delaware appears to have been part of a failed IPO effort.

Between mid-April 2001 and early May 2001, Plaintiffs exercised their rights under the Investors' Rights Agreement to redeem their shares. Sorrento rebuffed these efforts with the explanation that it lacked sufficient legally available funds to meet its redemption obligations.

Less than two weeks after receiving the first redemption request, Sorrento, as authorized by an April 26, 2001 board resolution, filed with Delaware's Secretary of State a certificate of amendment, which purported to authorize an additional 15 million shares of Series A Preferred Stock. No prior approval from the holders of Series A Preferred Stock had been sought or obtained.

Sorrento's board, at the April 26th meeting, approved the sale of 899,437 additional shares of Series A Preferred Stock to Osicom at a price of $5.45 per share. The number of shares issued to Osicom was sufficient, at that time, to reduce the percentage of the Series A shares for which redemption had been sought to slightly below the 50% threshold for redemption. No approval of the Series A holders was sought and no right of first offer was extended until more than two weeks after the sale had closed. No holder of the Series A Preferred Stock exercised its right of first offer.

[P]laintiffs obtained a copy of Osicom's SEC Form 8-K, which indicated that Osicom would acquire more than 6.6 million shares of Sorrento's Series A Preferred Stock to extinguish Sorrento's indebtedness to it. If implemented, that transaction would have reduced Plaintiffs' interests in the Series A Preferred Stock to below 50%.

Plaintiffs promptly, on August 6, 2001, filed this action seeking, *inter alia,* a temporary restraining order prohibiting the issuance of additional Series A Preferred Stock. This Court heard that application on August 7, 2001. However, on August 6, 2001, apparently after it had received notice of the pendency of the temporary restraining order application, Sorrento issued 2.7 million shares of Series A Preferred Stock to Osicom for which Osicom paid $5.45 per share in cash. Sorrento, at the hearing before this Court on August 7, 2001, did not disclose to the Court or to Plaintiffs' counsel that these additional Series A shares had been issued.[13] Evidently, Plaintiffs first learned of the issuance of the additional shares of Series A Preferred Stock on receipt of discovery on or about August 15, 2001.

At the close of the August 7th hearing, the Court issued a temporary restraining order precluding Sorrento from issuing additional shares of Series A Preferred Stock.

II. ANALYSIS

Issuance of additional Series A Preferred Stock has not been supported by the holders of a majority of the outstanding shares of the Series A Preferred Stock. Thus, by the clear language of the Certificate, Sorrento cannot issue additional shares of Series A Preferred Stock if those shares constitute "any other equity security." Plaintiffs and Sorrento part ways, however, on whether additional shares of Series A Preferred Stock are included within the meaning of the phrase "any other equity security."

I start with the plain meaning of the words chosen by sophisticated parties advised by experienced counsel. The phrase "equity security" is defined as "[a]

13. Sorrento had not informed its Delaware counsel that it had issued the 2.7 million shares and, accordingly, the failure to disclose this significant development was not the fault of Delaware counsel. Sorrento's counsel in California attended the temporary restraining order hearing on August 7, 2001, by teleconference, but chose not to be forthcoming.

security representing an ownership interest in a corporation, such as a share of stock."[18] The word "other" means "more, additional."[19] Thus, a fair reading of "any other equity security" equates to "any additional share." Because the additional shares of Series A Preferred Stock that Sorrento has issued and will issue, if not enjoined, constitute "additional shares" of Series A Preferred Stock, issuance of the additional shares is proscribed by the words chosen by the drafters of Article V.D.6(a)(ii) when those words are given their commonly accepted meaning.

The words employed by contract (or certificate of incorporation) drafters must be evaluated in light of the apparent purposes of the drafters. The language at issue is critical to the protective provisions which clearly were designed to benefit the holders of the Series A Preferred Stock by assuring them that their interests would not be diluted without prior majority approval. Many rights of those holders may be waived upon approval by the holders of more than 50% of the Series A Preferred Stock. The apparent intent of the protective provisions is to protect against the issuance of more equity, without the consent of the holders of a majority of the Series A Preferred Stock, that could result in a reduction of their rights through a restructuring of Sorrento's equity. If Sorrento could avoid the protective provisions drafted for the benefit of the holders of the Series A Preferred Stock simply by issuing more Series A Preferred Stock, then the provision would not serve its apparent purpose. Thus, the plain meaning of the phrase at issue as construed above is consistent with the intent of the drafters as manifested in the Certificate's protective provisions.

Sorrento vigorously contests any interpretation of the phrase "any other equity security" that would restrict its ability to issue more Series A Preferred Stock. First, Sorrento argues that the "other equity security" is any equity security that is not subject to approval by the holders of Series A Preferred Stock. Sorrento reads the provision to restrict the issuance of any equity security other than Series A Preferred Stock or, more specifically, as "any other series or class of equity security." Sorrento's "other than" or "different from" logic does not plainly show that the antecedent of "other" for these purposes is Series A Preferred Stock and not those outstanding shares of Series A Preferred Stock.[21] If the antecedent of "other" is the outstanding shares, then all new shares would be "other than" the issued shares. Thus, Sorrento has not demonstrated that the plain and express language supports its proposed construction of the phrase "any other equity security."

Second, Sorrento contends that the phrase "any other equity security" is ambiguous and must be construed against Plaintiffs. Sorrento correctly argues that the rights and preferences of holders of preferred stock must be clearly stated, are strictly construed, and are subject to the interpretative standard that any ambiguity must be resolved against them. Sorrento devotes so much attention to its unavailing plain meaning argument that it has not developed in detail its argument that the critical language in the certificate is ambiguous. Presumably, Sorrento would have the Court

---

18. *Black's Law Dictionary* 1359 (7th ed. 1999).

19. *Webster's Third New International Dictionary* 1598 (3d ed. 1993).

21. The Certificate at Art. V.C. provides that the first series of Preferred Stock will consist of 10,000,000 shares of Series A Preferred Stock. The Plaintiffs would be hard pressed to (and do not seriously) argue that issuance in April and August, 2001 of enough additional shares to reach the 10,000,000 share level was wrongful since they entered into their investment with the understanding that Series A Preferred Stock would eventually consist of 10,000,000 shares.

focus on the question of "other than what" equity security, i.e., what is the antecedent of "other"? The Court, at least at this stage, has accepted Plaintiffs' argument that "equity security" refers to a "share" or "unit of ownership" (as opposed to a series or class of stock). If "equity security" in that context refers to shares (and not to a series) of preferred stock, then it refers back to the "outstanding shares." Thus, while the construction of the phrase is not a simple task and while the language may have been drafted more crisply, it is not ambiguous. That good lawyers can conjure up challenging arguments about multiple meanings of a word or a phrase does not necessarily make the word or phrase ambiguous.

Third, Sorrento asserts that Plaintiffs' suggested construction fails to give meaning to the word "other," thus violating the canon of construction that consideration should be given to every word. In Sorrento's view, Plaintiffs' construction of "any other equity security" is the functional equivalent of "any equity security," since no approval could be required for those shares previously issued. One answer is that "other" when construed to mean "additional" makes apparent that the protective provision applies only to those shares of Series A Preferred Stock that are beyond those already issuable under the Certificate.

Although Sorrento seeks to employ the interpretive guideline to give meaning to all portions of the Certificate, application of that precept actually supports Plaintiffs' reading of the Certificate. For example, under...the Certificate, the dividends for Series A Preferred Stock, the liquidation rights and the conversion rights are all determined with reference to the $5.45 per share price for the initial Series A Preferred Stock private placement. Osicom (or anyone else for that matter) is not required by any of the transactional documents to pay $5.45 per share for additional (newly issued) Series A Preferred Stock. Sorrento would have the Court construe the carefully negotiated Certificate as allowing, without approval by the holders of a majority of the outstanding shares, the sale of additional Series A Preferred Stock (with significant rights based on a per share price of $5.45) at some other, and presumably lower, price. It is unlikely that a reasonable drafter would have intended such a result, but Sorrento's interpretation would permit it.

Moreover, Sorrento's interpretation of Article V.D.6(a)(ii) may be viewed as rendering that provision meaningless. Given the purposes of the protective provisions, apparent from the Certificate itself, Sorrento's interpretation defeats Plaintiffs' ability to safeguard their investment. If Sorrento is indeed free to issue up to 25,000,000 shares of Series A Preferred Stock without the approval of the holders of Series A Preferred Stock, then it would be empowered either to eliminate the efficacy of the protective provisions or, if one considers the right of first offer contained in the Investors' Rights Agreement, to compel the Series A holders to contribute significant additional funds to Sorrento in order to preserve the rights which they had already bargained for, paid for, and, presumably, acquired. Sorrento defends its position by suggesting that "[t]he holders of the Series A Preferred Stock continue to have a series vote on the issuance of any senior or parity equity that does not have the precise terms of the Series A Preferred Stock." [S]orrento's interpretation, even when viewed charitably, requires the Court to divine a wide breach in the protective provisions so carefully negotiated. While the Court cannot find or create rights for a preferred stockholder where the certificate does not grant them, it, nevertheless, is not required to struggle to reduce carefully drafted language into insignificance. In short, the precept that the entire document should be construed harmoniously, if possible, favors Plaintiffs' construction of Sorrento's Certificate.

Fourth, Sorrento contends that anti-dilution concerns and other problems such as the potential for issuing Series A Preferred Stock at a price less than $5.45 per share are resolved by the right of first offer in the Investors' Rights Agreement. Under the right of first offer, the holders of Series A Preferred Stock are entitled to purchase shares, when issued, in proportion to their holdings in order to avoid any consequence that might arise from a diminution of their proportionate holdings.

The right to purchase on a pro rata basis any newly issued shares does provide a rational means for addressing anti-dilution concerns. However, because a holder may have the right to purchase new shares does not necessarily lead to the conclusion that the protective provisions of the Certificate do not also serve an anti-dilution function. If nothing else, the right of first offer provides an option to the holder who opposes the issuance of additional shares of Series A Preferred Stock even if the holders of a majority of the outstanding shares approve the issuance of additional shares.

In short, given the numerous rights of the holders of Series A Preferred Stock that depend upon collective ownership of a certain percentage of the issued shares, the Court is not willing, at least at this stage, to interpret either the Certificate or any of the other transactional documents to require the Plaintiffs (and other holders of Series A Preferred Stock) to confront the choice of contributing additional funds to what was to have been a short-term investment or accepting the risk of dilution of equity ownership and the potentially adverse consequences that might accompany such dilution.

In sum, Plaintiffs were induced to invest in Sorrento through a certificate of incorporation (and related transactional documents) that afforded significant protection to their investment by...imposing restrictions on Sorrento's ability to issue additional equity, including shares of Series A Preferred Stock. [I]n the absence of injunctive relief, Sorrento is likely to continue to issue additional shares of Series A Preferred Stock with the foreseeable (and from Sorrento's perspective, welcomed) consequence of diluting Plaintiffs' equity interests. Plaintiffs have demonstrated a reasonable likelihood of success on the merits....They have also demonstrated the risk of imminent and irreparable harm....The balancing of equities and hardships decidedly tilts in favor of Plaintiffs, who are being denied the benefits of their bargain and the reasonable expectation of effective and continuing protective provisions. Sorrento's ability to raise additional funds without the consent of the holders of a majority of the Series A Preferred Stock may well be limited, but that is the result of the bargain that it made, and, more significantly, the likelihood of exhausting its cash reserves pending final determination seems unlikely, at least on the present record. Accordingly, after balancing all of these considerations, the Court concludes that a preliminary injunction is warranted to preserve the rights of Plaintiffs established by the protective provisions of the Certificate.

III. CONCLUSION

For the foregoing reasons, the Court is entering an Order...preliminarily enjoining Sorrento and those acting in concert with it from...issuing additional shares of

Series A Preferred Stock, without the prior approval of the holders of a majority of the Series A Preferred Stock....

Notes and Questions

1. Notes

a. Osicom was a publicly held corporation that undertook several start-up businesses of which Sorrento's was the most successful.

b. The plaintiffs, who were venture capitalists, also negotiated for restrictions on Sorrento's ability to incur debt without the approval of the Series A stockholders.

2. Reality Check

a. What is the basic business dispute that lead to the legal dispute?

b. Describe each party's definition of the phrase, "any other equity security." Why does it matter which interpretation is correct?

c. How does Vice Chancellor Noble choose between those interpretations?

d. Why does it matter whether the venture capitalists own over 50 percent of the outstanding preferred stock?

e. Could Sorrento have legally issued any more Series A Preferred Stock?

f. Why doesn't the "right of first offer" sufficiently protect the venture capitalists' interests?

3. Suppose

a. Suppose Sorrento's Certificate of Incorporation had originally authorized 25 million of Series A Preferred Stock. Would that have affected the result? See footnote 21.

4. What Do You Think?

a. Do you believe the venture capitalists acted improperly by not agreeing to invest more money in Sorrento or, alternatively, by not, in effect, allowing Osicom to find additional sources of financing?

b. Vice Chancellor Noble implies that Osicom acted improperly on August 6th when it caused Sorrento to issue 2.7 million shares of Series A Preferred Stock for about $14.7 million. Do you agree?

5. You Draft It

a. The most central language at issue was found in Sorrento's Certificate of Incorporation:

> (a) [S]o long as any shares of Series A Preferred Stock are outstanding, the Corporation shall not without first obtaining the approval...of the holders of at least a majority of the then outstanding shares of Series A Preferred Stock:
>
>> (ii) authorize or issue, or obligate itself to issue, any other equity security, including any other security convertible into or exercisable for any equity security having a preference over, or being on a parity with, the Series A Preferred Stock with respect to voting, dividends or upon liquidation...,

Redraft this provision so it clearly effects the plaintiffs' best interests. Then redraft it so it clearly effects the defendant's best interests.

c. The Mechanics of Issuing Stock

In this section we consider the corporate law mechanics involved in the actual issuance of stock. We explore the three principal concepts involved in validly issuing stock: *statutorily authorized*, *issued* (including the kind and amount of valid consideration), and *outstanding*. As you will see, each of these terms has a specialized meaning and lawyers must be aware of those meanings as they advise their corporate clients. We then turn to a further legal implication of issuing stock, preemptive rights.

i. Statutory Authorization. Chapter 5 explained that the Articles of Incorporation must contain a statement of the number and kinds of shares that the corporation may—is *authorized* to—issue. See MBCA §§1.40(2), 2.02(a)(2), and 6.01(a), and DGCL §102(a)(4). The number of shares is essentially arbitrary although, as Chapter 5 detailed, the corporate planner must decide whether more shares are to be authorized than are currently anticipated to be issued to investors. If a corporation desires to issue more shares than its Articles of Incorporation authorize, it must amend the Articles, a process that is time-consuming and somewhat cumbersome because the amendment must usually be approved at a shareholder meeting. See Chapter 15 for a discussion of amending the Articles of Incorporation. A corporation that purports to issue more shares than it has authorized has acted illegally and the newly issued shares, called an *overissue*, are void.

We have seen that a corporation may want to issue stock with different attributes than the default qualities provided in the statute. The attributes of such stock, and the ways in which that stock differs from other stock the company may issue, must be set forth in the Articles of Incorporation so that shareholders are protected by knowing exactly what rights they have as stockholders and how those rights compare to the rights of holders of other kinds of stock. Each separate type of stock must also be given a separate name such as "$1 Cumulative Preferred Shares" or "Class B Common Shares." See MBCA §6.01(a) and DGCL §102(a)(4).

But it frequently happens that the terms of stock to be issued are subject to considerable negotiation between the corporation and the potential investors and that time is of the essence for all. Because it would jeopardize so many potential issuances of noncommon stock for the corporation to have to seek shareholder approval of an amendment to the Articles of Incorporation and would likewise be impossible to predict the precise terms of noncommon stock in advance so that those terms can be included in the Articles from the initial incorporation, the statutes provide that the Articles may include a provision authorizing more than one class (i.e., preferred as well as common) and more than one series of stock with such attributes as the board decides. The maximum number of noncommon shares must still be stated in the Articles but the terms of those shares can be decided later, as the corporation is prepared to sell them to an investor. Once the terms of the new stock have been agreed upon, the corporation's board of directors adopts a resolution setting out the terms and files that resolution with the Secretary of State. That resolution becomes a part of the Articles of Incorporation and thus a public record. A provision allowing this procedure is said to be one that authorizes *blank stock* or *blank check stock*. See MBCA §6.02 and DGCL §§102(a)(4) and 151(g).

ii. Issuance of Stock. Simply because shares of stock have been authorized in the Articles of Incorporation does not mean that anyone owns them. The process of

putting statutorily authorized shares in the hands of investors is called *issuance*.[18]
Issuance comprises two other concepts: the board must approve (authorize) the
issuance of the shares and the corporation must receive appropriate consideration.
When this happens, the shares are said to have been *validly issued* and *fully paid* and
are therefore *nonassessable*.[19]

(A) Board Authorization. The requirement that stock must be authorized
means not only that the appropriate number of shares must be permitted by the
Articles of Incorporation. It also means that the corporation, acting through its
board of directors, has approved a particular transaction in which statutorily authorized shares will be exchanged for consideration. See MBCA §6.21(b) and DGCL
§161. Although the mechanics of board authorization are no different in this setting
than in any other (and therefore are covered in detail in Chapter 9) and are easily
met, the board's failure to observe the statutory requirements can throw significant
doubt on the corporation's and the board's power. The following case shows the
problems that can arise.

Kalageorgi v. Victor Kamkin, Inc.
750 A.2d 531 (Del. Ch. 1999)

JACOBS, V.C.

I. THE FACTS

[Victor Kamkin, Inc., a Delaware corporation ("VKI" or the "Company")] was
founded by Victor and Elena Kamkin in 1953, and is one of the largest importers of
Russian books in the United States. During its entire operating history the Company's
principal supplier of books has been a Soviet (now Russian) trading company called
V/O Mezhdunarodnaya Kniga ("MezhKniga").[1]

From 1953 to 1974, the Company was operated by Victor Kamkin and his wife,
Elena. Until his death in 1974, Mr. Kamkin was VKI's President and sole stockholder.
Thereafter, Mrs. Kamkin succeeded to both positions, and as of 1990, she owned
all of VKI's 49 issued and outstanding common shares. Today, VKI has 100 issued
and outstanding common shares with a par value of $10 per share. Thirty nine (39) of
those shares are owned by the plaintiff, Igor Kalageorgi ("Kalageorgi"), who is

18. You should be careful to note the term *issue* rather than *sale*. When the corporation exchanges
authorized shares for consideration, the corporation issues them. When a shareholder exchanges shares for
consideration, the shareholder sells them. This distinction may seem unimportant, and in the vast majority
of settings it is, but sometimes the statutes and cases use the terms precisely and it is important to understand
that the terms are not always synonymous. We will see this applied in Chapter 7 in connection with treasury
shares.

19. See MBCA §6.21(d) and DGCL §152. Through the early twentieth century it was common for
corporations to issue stock that had not been completely paid for. Such stock was subject to assessment for
the remainder of the purchase price. This requirement became problematic when the original shareholder
had transferred his or her shares. Because stock certificates are negotiable instruments, a transferee for value
who had no notice of the remaining purchase price liability took the shares free from that obligation. So, it
became important for corporations and their creditors to ensure that transferees were on notice that the
shares were subject to assessment by putting a legend on the certificate that the shares had not been fully
paid for. This concern continues today, in the formulaic language on stock certificates that says that the
shares represented by the certificate are "fully paid and nonassessable."

1. "Mezhdunarodnaya Kniga" is the Russian name for "International Books."

Elena Kamkin's great nephew. The remaining 61 shares are held — and are claimed to be owned — by MezhKniga and members of the [Anatoly] Zabavsky family.... The Zabavsky family has been involved in the management of VKI, both as officers and employees, since the 1970s, when they moved from New York City to Washington, D.C. to accept employment with the Company.

For reasons that are not altogether clear from the record, during the spring of 1990, MezhKniga sought to enter into a "partnership" relationship with VKI that would involve MezhKniga owning VKI common stock. Mrs. Kamkin was agreeable, but she and Anatoly Zabavsky, VKI's other director, contemplated that as part of this new relationship the Zabavskys would become stockholders of VKI as well.

On November 30, 1990, [the Company's long-time counsel, Washington, D.C. attorney, Ronald Precup, Esquire ("Precup")] sent Mrs. Kamkin [who was then 76 years old],[3] a letter (with a copy to Mr. Zabavsky), with two enclosures that would accomplish the VKI stock transfer that Mrs. Kamkin wished to achieve. The first enclosure was a Unanimous Written Consent that Mrs. Kamkin, as...a director, and Anatoly Zabavsky as a director, were to sign. The proposed Consent, dated December 3, 1990, was introduced by several preamble ("Whereas") clauses which recited that MezhKniga had offered to buy 20% of VKI's stock, that certain VKI employees had also expressed a desire to own VKI's common stock, that it was in VKI's best interest to provide for the continuity of ownership and management and for the stability of its business operations, and that VKI's board of directors had determined that the fair market value of the Company's stock was $10 per share. There then followed four resolutions which are quoted verbatim:

> RESOLVED, That the president and Vice President be, and they are hereby authorized and directed to enter into a memorandum of understanding with [MezhKniga] with a view to the acquisition of [MezhKniga] of Twenty (20) shares of the Corporation's Common Stock, under terms and conditions to be negotiated for them in consultation with the Corporation's legal counsel; and it is
> FURTHER RESOLVED, That the officers of the corporation be, and they are hereby, authorized to issue 20 shares of the Common Stock of the corporation to [MezhKniga] in accordance with the aforesaid memorandum of understanding, and, in addition, 31 shares of the Common Stock of the Corporation in consideration of the payment to the Corporation of cash in the amount of $10.00 per share, to those persons heretofore designated by the Directors; and it is
> FURTHER RESOLVED, That the Corporation shall require as a condition to the issuance of the aforesaid shares that the transferees enter into a Stockholders Agreement with the Corporation governing the subsequent transfer of such shares;....

The second enclosure accompanying Mr. Precup's November 30th letter was a proposed Memorandum of Agreement between MezhKniga and VKI, which pertinently provided that MezhKniga would purchase 20 shares of VKI at $10 per share, representing 20% of VKI's outstanding shares. That document also provided that as soon as practicable VKI and MezhKniga would enter into a Stockholders Agreement restricting the sale of VKI shares to outside parties; and that if for reasons of state or any other reason it was no longer in MezhKniga's interest to own stock in VKI, the Company would repurchase MezhKniga's shares at $10 per share.

---

3. Mrs. Kamkin, who is now in her mid-eighties, subsequently became disabled and as a result, was unavailable to testify at the trial.

In his November 30, 1990 letter, Mr. Precup also instructed Mrs. Kamkin and Anatoly Zabavsky to sign the Unanimous Written Consent and return it to him for filing in the corporation's minute book. That document was never signed by Mrs. Kamkin or Mr. Zabavsky, and it was never returned to Mr. Precup for filing in the corporate minute book. Nor was the stockholders agreement ever entered into. The record does not disclose why the written Consent was never signed or why no stockholders agreement was entered into. On behalf of VKI, Mrs. Kamkin and Anatoly Zabavsky did, however, execute the Memorandum of Agreement with Mezh-Kniga on December 10, 1990.

On January 14, 1991, Mr. Precup again wrote to Mrs. Kamkin, with a copy to Anatoly Zabavsky, advising her that the annual meeting of shareholders and directors of VKI would occur the following day. In his letter Mr. Precup stated:

> Finally, I enclose the following stock certificates

Cert. No.	No. of Shares	Owner
1	39	Elena Kamkin
2	23	Anatoly Zabavsky and Desanka Zabavsky, as Joint Tenants with Right of Survivorship
3	20	VB/O Mezhdunarodnaya Kniga
4	10	Kira J. Caiafa
5	4	Natalie Zabavsky
6	4	Andrew Zabavsky

> Each of the certificates should be signed by you as President and by [Desanka Zabavsky, Anatoly's wife] as Secretary in all the blanks provided. The records reflect that all of the new shares are issued by the company except certificate no. 4 to Kira [Caiafa, Anatoly Zabavsky's sister]. The ten shares she receives are transferred from you, reducing your holdings from 49 to 39 shares.
>
> According to the company's records, you have the old form stock certificates no. 7 for 45 shares and no. 8 for 4 shares, which the new certificate no. 1 replaces. If you can locate those certificates, you should return them to me for cancellation. Only the new form of certificate will be recognized from now on. Also, the corporate resolution that authorized the issuance of these shares (included in my letter to you of November 30, 1990) should be signed by you as a stockholder and by you and [Anatoly] as directors, then returned to me for filing in the minute book.

Thereafter, Mrs. Kamkin signed those stock certificates and also had them signed by Desanka Zabavsky as corporate secretary. Mrs. Kamkin then personally delivered the certificates to each of the recipients, and Mr. Precup made entries in the VKI stock ledger to reflect these new shareholders' stock ownership.

It is undisputed that at all times from and after 1991, Mrs. Kamkin, the Zabavskys, and MezhKniga acted in a manner that was consistent with their being duly authorized shareholders of VKI. During this entire period no one ever questioned the validity of the 61 shares held and voted by MezhKniga and the Zabavskys.

During the latter part of 1997, Igor Kalageorgi (Mrs. Kamkin's [great] nephew and the plaintiff in this action) became increasingly involved in the affairs of VKI.

On February 17, 1998, Mrs. Kamkin executed a proxy authorizing plaintiff to vote 39 of her VKI shares.

In connection with the 1998 stockholders meeting, the VKI board of directors was reorganized (apparently at the plaintiff's request) by amending the Company's bylaws to provide that the "number of directors shall be...[5] for the ensuing year...." The five directors elected at that meeting were Mr. Kalageorgi, Anatoly and Andrew Zabavsky, Vladimir Gontchar (MezhKniga's representative), and James Beale, a VKI employee. Voting to elect those directors, as VKI's majority stockholders, were Mr. Kalageorgi, who executed the consent on Mrs. Kamkin's behalf, and Anatoly Zabavsky. That same day, the newly elected directors signed a written consent electing Mr. Gontchar and various members of the Zabavsky family as VKI's officers.

By the summer of 1998, Mr. Kalageorgi's and Anatoly Zabavsky's relationship had become strained. Dissatisfied with Zabavsky's management style, Mr. Kalageorgi began making inquiry into the management of the Company, which included a demand to inspect certain of the Company's books and records. On June 10, 1998, in response to one of Mr. Kalageorgi's specific queries, Mr. Precup advised Mr. Kalageorgi that he was unable to find the written Directors' Consent authorizing the issuance of shares to MezhKniga and the Zabavskys, that he had sent to Mrs. Kamkin in 1990. Mr. Precup also was unable to confirm that any consideration had been paid for the shares issued in 1991. Mr. Precup did confirm, however, that no shareholders agreement had been executed by the VKI shareholders.

Despite having been thus put on notice of a potential legal issue concerning whether MezhKniga's and the Zabavskys' shares had been duly authorized, Mr. Kalageorgi nonetheless proceeded to acquire Mrs. Kamkin's 39 shares of VKI on July 2, 1998.[6] Thereafter, he consulted Delaware counsel, and on the basis of counsel's advice took the position that the shares held by the Zabavskys and Mezh-Kniga had never been duly authorized by the VKI Board and, hence, were invalid and could not be voted.

That position ripened into the present dispute at the VKI stockholders meeting held on February 24, 1999. At that meeting each of the individual defendants voted for a slate of [the five incumbent] directors.... Mr. Kalageorgi, however, voted only for himself, but he did not act or otherwise purport to remove any of the four remaining directors who had held office since their election at the 1998 stockholders meeting.

Immediately after voting for the board of directors, the stockholder-defendants then adopted a series of resolutions ratifying, *inter alia,* the issuance of the contested shares to the defendants in 1991. Those same parties then convened a directors meeting and adopted similar ratifying resolutions. At both meetings Mr. Kalageorgi voted against those resolutions.

[T]he plaintiff and the individual defendants both claimed to be the lawful board of directors of VKI. To bring the dispute to a head, on April 7, 1999 the plaintiff executed a written consent purporting (i) to remove all directors other than himself who had been elected at the February 24, 1999 stockholders meeting and (ii) to amend the bylaws to reduce the size of the board to one (1) director.

---

6. Although plaintiff contends that he did not realize the legal significance of what Mr. Precup had told him until after he consulted with Delaware counsel, the record shows that the plaintiff did understand the significance of Mr. Precup's disclosure, as evidenced by his e-mail to Mr. Precup on June 17, 1998.

Then, purporting to act as the sole director of VKI, the plaintiff executed a written consent removing the Zabavskys and Mr. Gontchar as officers and employees of the Company.

The defendants have refused to recognize these April 7, 1999 consent actions taken by Mr. Kalageorgi, contending that they were invalid and without legal force. In response, Mr. Kalageorgi commenced this §225 proceeding for a judicial declaration that his written consent actions are valid.

II. THE CONTENTIONS

The dispute in this case concerns whether the VKI stock issued to the defendants in 1991 was validly authorized under Delaware law by the VKI board of directors. That question is claimed to be outcome-determinative, because if the contested shares were not validly authorized (as plaintiff claims), then the defendants lacked sufficient voting power to elect their slate at the February 24, 1999 VKI stockholders meeting, leaving the plaintiff as the Company's only stockholder and *de jure* director and officer. If, on the other hand, the defendants' VKI stock was validly authorized, then the votes cast by the defendants at that meeting were sufficient to elect their director slate (which included the plaintiff), and the consent actions taken by the plaintiff on April 7, 1999 were a nullity.

These contentions may be reduced to two issues: (1) Was the issuance in 1991 of VKI stock to the Zabavskys and MezhKniga validly authorized? (2) If not, was any defect in authorization cured by director ratification at the February 24, 1999 directors meeting? Those issues are now addressed.

III. ANALYSIS

A. Validity of Authorization of the 1991 Issuance of Stock

Highly problematic for the Court is the question of whether the shares held by the Zabavskys and MezhKniga were validly authorized when they were issued in 1991. In most instances the imperatives of law and the demands of equity pull in the same direction, but regrettably that is not always and invariably true. This case is one counterexample. On the one hand, our statutory scheme envisions a model for the issuance of corporate securities that is premised upon a certain degree of formality, specifically, formal board authorization to issue stock at a duly called meeting of directors, or in lieu thereof, by unanimous written consent. Delaware case law is in accord with, and supportive of, that model.

Several policy reasons that justify the need for such formality readily come to mind. Corporate securities are a species of property right that represent not only a firm's fundamental source for raising capital, but also now a publicly traded commodity that is a critical component for creating both institutional and individual wealth that may affect the economic well-being of entire societies. Given the foundational importance of such securities to our economic system, it is critical that the validity of those securities, especially those that are widely traded, not be easily or capriciously called into question. Otherwise, the resulting economic uncertainty to investors and institutions that relied upon the integrity of those securities would be destabilizing. Accordingly, our statutory scheme, elucidated by case law, has developed a clear and easily followed legal roadmap for creating these valuable instruments that represent claims upon an enterprise's capital. Under that model, if that roadmap is followed, the investment community will be assured that the corporate securities created by that process will not be vulnerable to legal attack. If, on the other hand, it is not followed, then the securities will become subject to possible invalidation.

Viewed in this perspective, the formal requirement that board authorization to issue securities take the form of a resolution adopted at a directors meeting or a unanimous written consent, may be seen as having important functional significance. If either of these "roadmap" procedures is followed, then there can be no dispute over whether a corporate security was validly authorized. If it is not followed, then there will be a dispute that, in the absence of a rigid "bright line" rule, will subject the economic interests that have invested in those securities to the risks (some might say "vagaries") of an evidentiary hearing and of the fact-finding process. So inimical is that uncertainty to the predictability upon which our capital supply system depends, that it justifies a "bright line" set of procedures that guarantees validity if followed, and "invalidity" if not. Those would be the policy arguments for invalidating the Zabavskys' and MezhKniga's stock, even if it were found that the defendants did, in fact, intend for the stock to be issued to these persons.

The defendants do not dispute the need for or importance of the requirement of board authorization. Their claim is that the Delaware law in this area has not become so rigid that a failure to follow this precise formalism must or should automatically and invariably result in invalidating the affected securities. The defendants support their position by distinguishing the cases cited by plaintiff, and then by emphasizing that despite the absence of a formal board meeting or unanimous written consent, the overwhelming weight of the evidence in this case permits only one inference — that VKI's directors and the other parties in interest in fact did intend for the Zabavskys and MezhKniga to be stockholders of VKI.

This position also has much to commend it. I agree, of course, that it would have been preferable had the VKI board approved the issuance of the stock at a directors meeting or by signing the written consent sent to them by Mr. Precup. But, as a factual matter, the defendants' pattern of conduct after the stock was issued also convinces me to a certainty that Mrs. Kamkin and Mr. Zabavsky did intend to authorize the issuance of VKI stock to the Zabavskys and MezhKniga. That being the case, it is hardly frivolous for defendants to argue that to invalidate their stock for purely formalistic reasons would defeat not only the board's clear intent but also the purpose of the formal requirements themselves, which is to create indisputable evidence that the board intended to authorize the issuance of the securities. The case may be rare where such intent can be proved in the absence of a written consent or a resolution adopted at a board meeting, but if that case is established, no purpose would be served by disregarding that clear proof. Here, the defendants argue, the trial record does supply such clear proof, and the legal conclusion that flows from it should be judicially validated.

Moreover, the defendants emphasize, to defeat the board's intention would work a manifest injustice. The Zabavskys accepted employment with VKI and remained in its employ for 25 years in reliance upon their expectation that they would own equity in the enterprise; yet if plaintiff's position is upheld, the Zabavskys will have been ousted from their jobs for no valid equitable reason. Indeed, the defendants point out, the only person who would benefit from the invalidation of their shares would be plaintiff Kalageorgi, who bought his stock from Mrs. Kamkin with full knowledge of the technical deficiency in the documentation evidencing the board's authorization, and who then proceeded to take advantage of that deficiency in an effort to leverage his 39 share minority interest into a position of absolute ownership and control.

In this case the law and the equities have thus come to collide. To rule in favor of the plaintiff would create, in my view, a wholly unjust result. To rule against the plaintiff would create a not insubstantial risk of injecting uncertainty into what has heretofore been thought to be a predictable area of corporate jurisprudence. Fortunately, however, justice can be done in this case without the Court having to decide this issue. For even if it is assumed — without deciding — that the stock issued to the Zabavskys and MezhKniga in 1991 was not validly authorized, the record establishes that any technical defect in authority was cured by the ratifying vote of a majority of the directors in office at the directors meeting held on February 24, 1999. My reasons for so concluding follow.

B. The Board's 1999 Ratification of the 1991 Stock Issuance

No party disputes the proposition that where board authorization of corporate action that falls within the board's *de jure* authority is defective, the defect in authority can be cured retroactively by board ratification. The undisputed facts of record establish that is what occurred here.

At the 1998 annual meeting of stockholders, five directors were elected. The validity of this election — and of these five directors' *de jure* title to office — cannot be contested, because even if the only validly issued shares were those owned by Mrs. Kamkin, those shares were cast by Mr. Kalageorgi, acting on Mrs. Kamkin's behalf, in favor of that five director slate.

Under Delaware law, each director "shall hold office until such director's successor is elected and qualified or until such director's earlier resignation or removal."[12] It is undisputed that [defendant] directors . . . did not resign, and were not removed, from their offices before the February 24, 1999 stockholders meeting. At that meeting, all five incumbents stood for reelection. The individual defendants and MezhKniga voted their stock for all five incumbents; the plaintiff cast his 39 votes for himself. Assuming again that the only validly issued and outstanding shares were the plaintiff's 39 shares, the legal result was that he was reelected, and the remaining four directors remained in office as "holdover" directors. The reason is that at that meeting, the plaintiff did not purport either to remove those four directors or to designate their successors.[13] Not until April 7, 1999 did plaintiff execute a written consent attempting to take those actions. But, by that point plaintiff's written consent was without legal force or effect, because the four holdover directors had already voted, at a directors meeting held on February 24, 1999, to ratify the original issuance of the VKI stock to the Zabavskys and MezhKniga in 1991.

It follows that any defect in the original authorization in 1991 for the issuance of the VKI stock to those parties was cured by the ratifying vote of a majority of the directors in office on February 24, 1999. As a consequence, the lawful directors of VKI are Anatoly Zabavsky, Andrew Zabavsky, Vladimir Gontchar, James Beale, and Igor Kalageorgi; and the lawful officers are those persons elected by

---

12. [DGCL] §141(b).

13. Since the plaintiff took no steps to remove the four holdover directors, he cannot argue that their director positions became vacant. Under [DGCL] §142(e), a "vacancy" is caused by "death, resignation, removal, or otherwise." As of February 24, 1999, there was no death, resignation, or removal, and the plaintiff makes no argument that a vacancy in the four holdover positions "otherwise" occurred.

those VKI directors (other than Mr. Kalageorgi) at the February 24, 1999 directors meeting.[14]

Notes and Questions

1. Notes

a. Chapter 9 deals in more detail with the methods by which boards of directors can take action.

2. Reality Check

a. Why did the parties want to change the capital structure of VKI?

b. What were the documents that were intended to effect Mrs. Kamkin's wishes? What was each document supposed to accomplish?

c. At the February 24, 1999, meetings, what did Mr. Kalageorgi do that was legally effective? What did the defendants do that was legally effective?

d. What social policies are in conflict in this case? How does Vice Chancellor Jacobs choose between them?

3. Suppose

a. Suppose Mr. Kalageorgi had retained you to give him advice before he purchased Mrs. Kamkin's shares. What course of action would you have advised?

b. Would the result or analysis have been different if, at the February 24, 1999, board meeting, the board had not ratified the issuance of shares to defendants?

c. Suppose at the February 24, 1999, shareholders meeting Mr. Kalageorgi had voted for all five of the incumbent directors. Would the analysis or result have been different?

d. What if, on February 23, 1999, Mr. Kalageorgi had voted to remove the other four directors and reduce the board size from five to one? Should the result in this case depend upon Mr. Kalageorgi's approximately six-week delay in acting?

4. What Do You Think?

a. What actions should Mr. Precup have taken to avoid the problems that arose? Do you think he should have foreseen those problems? Do you think others involved with VKI should have foreseen these problems?

b. Would Mr. Kalageorgi have had a valid claim for relief if he had asserted his claims before he purchased Mrs. Kamkin's shares? Would he have had standing to raise those claims?

c. Do you agree with Vice Chancellor Jacobs that Mr. Kalageorgi's knowledge of the possible invalidity of the defendants' shares at the time he purchased Mrs. Kamkin's shares works against his assertions? Doesn't the fact that he knew there might be legal problems with defendants' shares mean that he legitimately could believe that he might own all the valid shares?

d. Do you think Mr. Kalageorgi should be estopped from challenging the board authorization of the stock to defendants?

---

14. Thus (and perhaps ironically) the formalistic rules set forth in [DGCL] §§141(b) and 142(e) work to serve the ends of equity by depriving a litigant whose claim to control itself rests solely upon a formalism, from benefiting from a self-interested effort to leverage an inadvertence into an unfair advantage over long-term VKI stockholders and employees.

e. Why didn't Mr. Kalageorgi, who had retained Delaware corporate law counsel, act sooner than April 1999 to remove the other directors and reduce the board size?

f. Do you think Vice Chancellor Jacobs's resolution is too neat because it lets him sidestep the deeper policy conflict?

(1) Subscription Agreements. *Subscription agreements* are contracts to purchase shares. If the corporation has been formed and is already doing business, a subscription agreement is simply an ordinary contract and thus does not present any legal issues particularly germane to business entities law. See MBCA §6.21(e). Before a new corporation has been formed, investors may contract among themselves and with the new corporation's promoters to purchase shares after incorporation. These preincorporation subscription agreements pose a basic agency problem of seeking to bind a nonexistent entity. Further, because the investors often have agreed to invest only on the assumption that others will do so, there is a heightened concern with enforceability of such preincorporation subscription agreements. Niceties of contract law may suggest that a preincorporation subscription agreement may be only a revocable offer or may only bind certain of the concerned parties. To increase both the certainty of such agreements and to broaden their reach, both the MBCA and the DGCL provide that a preincorporation subscription agreement is enforceable for six months unless another period is expressly agreed to. See MBCA §6.20(a) and DGCL §165.

(B) Consideration. The provisions dealing with consideration under both the MBCA and the DGCL are meant to deal with four basic problems. First, because each share is equivalent to every other share, investors contemporaneously purchasing shares from the corporation must pay the same amount per share. A second concern is that the corporation actually receive the agreed-upon consideration. This problem is acute where the consideration is to be received in the future. A third problem, related to each of the others, is the possibility that a corporation will issue shares to new investors at a price per share that is less than fair. The final problem is the possibility that the corporation's management will overvalue noncash consideration. These problems are addressed by statutory provisions and long-standing common law precepts.

(1) The Problem of Ensuring Equal Payment by Contemporaneous Purchasers (Par Value). The common law solution to this first problem was the idea of *par value*. When a corporation is being organized, the number of shares to be issued and the price per share are completely arbitrary. The only economic constraint is that the corporation receive enough assets to enable it to begin its business. So, in the simplest setting of a new corporation with one shareholder who will contribute, say, $100,000, it does not matter whether the corporation issues one share for $100,000 or 100,000 shares for $1 each, or any other such combination. In that sense the shares cannot be underpriced or overpriced.

This observation remains true, with a caveat, when more than one investor is making the initial investment. It still does not matter whether the corporation issues a few shares at a high price per share or lots of shares at a low price as long as the aggregate consideration is sufficient. But where more than one investor is purchasing from the corporation at the same time, each is concerned that no other contemporaneous purchaser is getting a better deal per share. Par value was a judicial presumption that shareholders had agreed that they would pay an equal amount per share (a par, or equal, value) when purchasing at the same time. This presumed agreement could be enforced by shareholders who purchased for more consideration than others who purchased at the same time. It could also be enforced by a corporation's creditors, if the corporation were insolvent and it were discovered that some shareholders had paid less than other contemporaneous purchasers. Statutes required corporations to state the par value of their shares explicitly in their Articles of Incorporation.

Two developments undercut the effectiveness of the par value system. First, case law determined that, although shares could not be issued for less than par value, they could be issued for more. Second, corporations that fell on hard times found that they could not raise more money because no rational investor would pay par value and the shares could not legally be issued for less. These developments created a strong incentive for corporations to set very low par value, as low at $0.01 per share, and to issue shares for consideration substantially greater than par value. This virtually ensured that the corporation could raise money in the future because it was unlikely that the value of the corporation's shares would drop below par.

But this low par value technique eviscerated any protection investors derived from the knowledge that other investors were paying par value. The only thing they knew was that each other investor was paying *at least* par value but that par value was a very small percentage of the total consideration. From the 1920s states began to make par value optional and no-par value stock became more frequent. Although the common law rule required (and still requires) that contemporaneous purchasers pay the same price per share, par value is no longer a method of ensuring compliance with this rule.

Why should you care about par value if it is not required by statutes and does not really serve to protect either creditors or shareholders? First, a significant percentage of corporations have par value even though it is no longer required. Thus if you are called upon to advise such a corporation or to deal with such a corporation on behalf of a client, you need to understand how par value works. Further, although Delaware permits the use of no-par value stock, its franchise tax rates penalize corporations that make that choice. Instead, it is advantageous in Delaware to issue low par value stock. Par value also is important because it bears upon whether the corporation can pay dividends and, if so, how much it can pay.

The MBCA recognizes that the par value system does not provide protection either for shareholders or corporate creditors and is simply a trap for unwary corporate lawyers and their clients. Accordingly, shares under the MBCA do not have par value, although such shares can be issued if desired by placing a par value on shares in the Articles of Incorporation. See MBCA §2.02(b)(2)(iv). How are contemporaneous shareholders protected from the original danger that others are paying less per share than they? Simply through case law that provides relief (either by making the other shareholders pay more per share or allowing the aggrieved shareholders to recover the excess they paid) upon a showing of disparate share price.

(2) The Problem of Ensuring That the Corporation Receives the Consideration. A second concern is with consideration that is to be received in the future. Such consideration presents the danger that it will not be received. This situation, of course, harms shareholders who have actually paid for their shares and creditors of the corporation. Classically, this danger led to the rule that promissory notes and contracts for future services were invalid consideration for shares even though, as an economic matter, such consideration may well have been of sufficient value. Over time, this

blanket prohibition on future consideration was deemed too harsh. Today, any kind of property is valid consideration. See DGCL §152 and MBCA §6.21(b).

Corporations may take further precautions to ensure they receive the agreed-upon consideration for shares. First, shares that are issued for future consideration may be placed in escrow until all the consideration is received. This prevents their transfer to a bona fide purchaser for value without notice that the shares are not fully paid for. Because stock certificates are negotiable instruments, such a purchaser would own the shares free from the obligation to pay the remaining consideration, although the transferor would remain liable. See MBCA §6.21(e). Second, corporations may issue shares that are explicitly partially paid for. The remainder of the consideration must be paid on the corporation's demand or as provided in the agreement between the corporation and the investor. See MBCA §6.21 and DGCL §156.

(3) *The Problem of Later Issuance at an Inadequate Price.*   Where a corporation is just being organized, the only problems regarding consideration are ensuring that the investors will pay the same price per share, ensuring that the corporation actually receives the consideration, and ensuring that the total consideration will be sufficient for the corporation to begin its business. Once the corporation has commenced doing business, though, further share issuances raise another problem: ensuring that the shares are issued at a price at least equal to the value of the currently outstanding shares.[19]

New shares issued at too low a price dilute the value of the existing shares. This danger theoretically leaves the corporation and the new investors liable to lawsuits by existing shareholders to challenge the consideration at which the new shares were issued. Where the corporation's stock is publicly traded, the market price is, presumably, the price at which new stock should be issued. In privately held corporations, though, there is no reliable objective reference to determine the value of currently outstanding shares. At common law, directors were liable to lawsuits by existing shareholders claiming that a subsequent stock issuance was at too low a price. To cut off this latent liability, modern statutes provide that the board of directors' judgment that the consideration for newly issued shares is adequate is conclusive. See MBCA §6.21(c) and DGCL §152 (directors' judgment conclusive in the absence of actual fraud).

(4) *The Problem of Noncash Consideration.*   When the consideration for shares is something other than cash, there is a danger that the consideration may be overvalued by the board. This danger is heightened when the shares are to be issued to investors connected in some way with the corporation's management, because the management obviously then has a concrete incentive to overvalue the consideration. In the late nineteenth century, this problem was thought to be particularly endemic and acquired the name *watered stock.* This name alludes to the deceptive practice of some cattle drivers who, at the end of the drive, would feed the cattle excessive amounts of salt to increase their thirst. The cattle would then drink copious amounts of water, which increased their weight. This added to the cattle driver's profits because the cattle were sold on the hoof with the price based on the cattle's weight. The problem of

---

19. The new investors themselves are also, of course, concerned that they not pay a price *greater than* fair, but that is not, economically, a concern of the corporation or its existing shareholders.

noncash consideration is a specialized instance of the problem of assuring that shares are issued at an adequate price.

Today, valuing noncash consideration has a renewed importance. This is so because so many of the most vital assets in businesses today are intangible "intellectual property." This property often is unique, which makes valuation comparisons to similar property difficult or impossible. Further, such property frequently had no other, secondary, use, unlike physical property, which usually has some other value even if only for sale as scrap. Therefore, its value is a function of the success of the business's plan; if the plan fails, the property is worthless. For example, a software code (intellectual property) that coordinates online purchases of groceries and facilitates those groceries' delivery to the customer's home is worth billions of dollars *if* customers will shop for groceries online. If they won't, the code may have next to no value.

These characteristics of intangible property make valuation particularly problematic. For our purposes, owners of such property who wish to contribute property in return for securities, other investors in the same enterprise who will contribute cash rather than property, creditors of the enterprise, and the board of directors of the enterprise are all keenly concerned that the property be fairly valued. Each constituency probably has a different view of the value of that property. Where the intellectual property's owner is also represented on the board of directors (a frequent occurrence in a start-up company) the conflict of interest is clear and obviously increases the complexity of fairly valuing the property. At the core, the solution is the same as it always has been: the board's decision is conclusive, at least in the absence of fraud. Whether courts will take a harder look at valuations of intellectual property remains to be seen.

iii. The Meaning of *Outstanding*.   Shares are said to be *outstanding* when they have been statutorily authorized, validly issued, and remain in the hands of someone or some entity other than the corporation itself. The shareholder need not be the original shareholder; shares are still outstanding in the hands of a transferee as long as the transferee is not the issuing corporation. See MBCA §6.03(a). The concept of outstanding shares (sometimes referred to in the somewhat redundant phrase, "authorized, issued, and outstanding shares") has importance in two settings. Only outstanding shares are entitled to vote and only outstanding shares may receive dividends. See MBCA §§7.21(a) and 6.40 and DGCL §§160(c) and 170. Chapter 7 looks at the legal problems of a corporation acquiring its own shares.

iv. Preemptive Rights: The Economic Component.   Even if validly issued, a subsequent issuance of shares can harm current shareholders. First, the price at which the new shares are issued, although legally unassailable by current shareholders, may not, in reality, be the highest price available. Thus the value of the currently outstanding shares will be diluted by the issuance of other shares. Further, current shareholders will have to share all future increases in value and future dividends with the new shareholders and would not have had to do so if the corporation had taken on debt rather than sold equity.

To protect current shareholders from these economic impairments, the courts of equity devised the doctrine of *preemptive rights*. This was the right of each current shareholder to maintain his or her proportionate interest by purchasing the same percentage of to-be-issued shares on the same terms and conditions as proposed

by the board of directors. Preemptive rights were never absolute and were traditionally subject to several categories of exceptions. We will revisit the doctrine of preemptive rights when we discuss shareholder voting because, obviously, shareholders
can be hurt in their management rights as well as in their economic rights by a new
issuance of shares.

Under both the MBCA and the DGCL preemptive rights do not exist unless
granted by the Articles of Incorporation. See MBCA §6.30(a) and DGCL
§102(b)(3). This represents a decision by the drafters of those acts that shareholders'
economic and management rights are better protected by imposing duties on the
board of directors than by granting shareholders preemptive rights. Speaking broadly,
there are three settings in which the issuance of new shares does not trigger preemptive rights. The first is where the consideration for the new shares is something other
than cash. The theory is that such noncash consideration is likely unique (such as
intellectual property or a particular person's services) and therefore an existing shareholder's cash, even though nominally equivalent in value, is not a genuine substitute
for the proposed consideration and so preemptive rights should not apply.

The second setting is where the newly issued shares are issued pursuant to the
corporation's initial plan of financing. A corporation's initial plan probably anticipates
several investors; delay in issuing shares to some of these investors is frequent. Denying preemptive rights to existing shareholders when the shares are to be issued
pursuant to the original financing plan simply prevents opportunistic behavior
among the initial participants. The final scenario in which preemptive rights are
frequently unavailable is where the corporation has, or is to have, more than one
class or series of shares. If the shares proposed to be issued are significantly different
in management or economic rights than the existing shares, courts will frequently
deny preemptive rights on the ground that the existing shareholders' rights are not
being substantially affected by the newly issued shares.

B. FEDERAL SECURITIES REGULATION

Nearly every "corporate" or "transactional" lawyer has some familiarity with federal
securities regulation. The most frequent questions that arise for the corporate lawyer
are whether a client's issuance of stock or debt is exempt from federal registration and
whether a client is the perpetrator or victim of a fraud in which securities changed
hands. Other areas of federal securities regulation that affect a corporate lawyer's
professional life, although less frequent, tend to involve publicly held companies.
These areas include compliance with periodic filing obligations, the regulation of
proxies, and securities transactions by corporate insiders. More esoteric securities
questions focus on the regulation of mutual funds, the regulation of stock brokers
and stock exchanges, and the federal regulation of takeovers. Some lawyers specialize
in securities regulation or in some aspect of that work. Focusing on securities work
has many rewards. It is intellectually challenging, involves many important issues
of national economic importance, and typically involves working with other lawyers
who are equally knowledgeable.

Despite the many advantages, there are frustrations as well. The federal securities
laws and regulations entail a welter of restrictions. Quite often these regulations
provide counterintuitive rules of conduct. Further, it often seems as if every word

in every statute and rule is a term of art defined by significant cases. Although the treatment of securities regulation in this book is no substitute for a basic course in the subject, I hope you will pick up enough substance to identify points at which securities regulation may be germane.

First, a word about the hierarchy of federal securities regulation. The highest authority are acts of Congress, of which two merit our attention here. First is the Securities Act of 1933 (15 USC §77a) which is often called the *Securities Act* or the *'33 Act*. The second main act is the Securities Exchange Act of 1934 (15 USC §78a) which is often called the *Exchange Act* or the *'34 Act*. No one ever uses the official USC section numbers. Instead, the provisions are referred to by their original section numbers in the acts themselves.

Congress established the Securities and Exchange Commission (SEC) to oversee and enforce the securities laws. The SEC is an independent regulatory agency comprising five commissioners appointed by the President and confirmed by the Senate. Each commissioner serves for a five-year term and the President has the power to designate one commissioner as chair. The SEC has the power to promulgate regulations under the acts and it has done so in considerable detail. These are embodied in rules that are officially found in the Code of Federal Regulations but, as with the acts, they are routinely cited by their SEC rule number rather than their CFR designation. Rules under the '33 Act are three digits; rules under the '34 Act are keyed to the '34 Act section under which they are adopted. Thus, perhaps the most famous SEC rule, Rule 10b-5, is a rule adopted under the '34 Act. It is the fifth rule adopted pursuant to Exchange Act Section 10(b). You should be aware that, although Congress seldom amends the acts in significant ways, the SEC is constantly changing its regulations in ways large and small.

With this background, we discuss two aspects of federal securities regulation that affect the financing of corporations. First, we look at the definition of *security* because the federal regulations do not apply at all unless a security is involved. Second, we examine the requirement that issuances of securities be registered with the SEC. In the vast majority of instances, registration is not required, but it is vital for a corporation's attorney to know which transactions are exempt from registration and why, as the penalties for failing to register when required are severe. In this connection, we also look at the process of registering stock so that it may be sold to the public.

1. Definition of a Security

You would think that a fundamental concept such as the definition of a security would be uncontroversial. It isn't. Both the Securities Act and the Exchange Act have nearly identical definitions that consist primarily of a list of investments that are thereby defined as being securities. See '33 Act §2(a)(1) and '34 Act §3(a)(10).[20]

---

20. Section 2(a)(1) of the '33 Act provides: "The term 'security' means any note, stock, treasury stock, security future, bond, debenture, evidence of indebtedness, certificate of interest or participation in any profit-sharing agreement, collateral-trust certificate, preorganization certificate or subscription, transferable share, investment contract, voting-trust certificate, certificate of deposit for a security, fractional undivided interest in oil, gas, or other mineral rights, any put, call, straddle, option, or privilege on any security, certificate of deposit, or group or index of securities (including any interest therein or based on the value

For our purposes, we need to focus on two more subtle notions. One excludes things that intuitively should be included (such as some stock and debt); the other includes things that intuitively should be excluded (such as ownership of a row of orange trees).

First, both acts state that their lists of items are defined as securities "unless the context otherwise requires." The Supreme Court has excluded stock in a nonprofit housing corporation because it did not have the traditional indicia of stock. That is, it did not have the right to receive dividends, could not effectively be borrowed against, could not be sold for a profit, and did not have voting power proportional to the number of shares held. See *United Housing Foundation v. Forman*, 421 U.S. 837 (1975). It seems unlikely that shares issued by a for-profit corporation would lack sufficient indicia of "stock" to be considered outside the definition of security.

More problematic is certain debt, such as a bank certificate of deposit or a promissory note, that might or might not be considered a security. The Supreme Court has, not terribly helpfully, adopted a "family resemblance" test for debt.[21] Some kinds of debt, such as a home mortgage, are excluded from the definition of a security. Other debt, corporate debentures sold to the public, certainly are securities. The task is to determine whether a particular instrument resembles a category that is included or excluded. The factors to be taken into account are (1) whether the motivations of the buyer and seller are akin to those who finance businesses; (2) whether the instrument could be amenable to common trading; (3) whether the investors would reasonably expect the federal securities laws to apply; and (4) whether the investment's risk is significantly reduced (thereby diminishing the need for the securities laws to provide protection) by another regulatory scheme such as federal bank regulation. See *Reves v. Ernst & Young*, 494 U.S. 56 (1990).

On the other hand, a seemingly innocuous instrument listed in the acts is the source for including any number of relationships that would not ordinarily be thought of as securities. In this regard, a lawyer must be careful to consider whether a particular undertaking might fall into this category. The term by which these investments are brought under the aegis of the federal securities laws is *investment contract*. In an early case the Supreme Court defined an investment contract as (1) an *investment of money* (nearly always easy to meet); (2) in a *common enterprise*, which means that the investor's financial success is bound up with that of others; (3) in which the investor has an *expectation of profit* (rather than some other return such as a place to live or fresh orange juice from the trees one has bought); (4) to come *solely from the efforts of others*, which means primarily from the efforts of others. See *SEC v. W.J. Howey Co.*, 328 U.S. 293 (1946). The *Howey* test is the catch-all of the securities laws. It is applied to determine whether partnership interest and LLC interests are securities (they may be or they may not be!) and has brought such things as cosmetics retailing arrangements under the federal securities laws. Any time you are counseling a client involved in an undertaking you should pause, however briefly, and run the *Howey* checklist through your mind.

---

thereof), or any put, call, straddle, option, or privilege entered into on a national securities exchange relating to foreign currency, or, in general, any interest or instrument commonly known as a 'security', or any certificate of interest or participation in, temporary or interim certificate for, receipt for, guarantee of, or warrant or right to subscribe to or purchase, any of the foregoing."

21. Unfortunately, DNA testing does not help in this context.

2. Registration

a. Registration Requirements and Exemptions

The registration requirements are contained in the '33 Act and rules. Under the literal terms of the Securities Act, it is illegal to use a means of interstate commerce (such as a telephone, the mails, or the Internet) to *offer* a security unless a *registration statement* (which is a very elaborate document) has been filed with the SEC, and it is illegal to sell a security unless the registration statement has been reviewed by the SEC and declared effective. To compound the problem, the term *offer* has been quite broadly defined to include any attempt to arouse interest in the issuing company or its securities. Such an attempt might easily be construed to include favorable publicity about a company at a time when it intends to issue shares. On the face of it, this includes issuing stock in a start-up corporation, a situation that occurs hundreds of times each day! The costs of registering stock are considerable, and the process takes months to accomplish. For those reasons, most planners structure transactions to avoid the registration requirements. We'll look at the process of complying with these registration requirements in the next section. Here the focus will be on identifying exemptions from these registration requirements. They fall into three principal categories.

First, the statute excludes certain kinds of securities, such as those issued by governments or by charitable corporations, from the registration requirements. These exemptions are largely unavailable for ordinary, for-profit corporations. Second, §3(a)(11) of the '33 Act excludes securities that are issued only to residents of the state in which the issuing corporation is incorporated and doing business. This is the so-called *intrastate exemption*. Rule 147 elaborates on the requirements for this exemption, which allows a small amount (20%) of the corporation's business to be done out of state. One trap for planners is that they must ensure that the purchasers are bona fide residents of the state and, more problematically, that they do not intend to transfer their shares to someone out of state. A single share issued or transferred to an out-of-state person renders the exemption unavailable. This restriction on transfer applies for (roughly speaking) nine months from the date that the last share was issued by the corporation. Many corporations issue shares in reliance upon the intrastate exemption.

The third principal exemption is the so-called *private placement* exemption, which really subsumes two other approaches to exemption. Section 4(2) exempts securities sold by the corporation in transactions *not involving any public offering*. This is one of the key counterintuitive phrases in all of securities regulation. The Supreme Court has held that a public offering is one in which the offerees (regardless of how few) need the protection of the Securities Act, which is primarily designed to provide corporate information to investors. If all offerees can fend for themselves, there is no public offering and the transaction is exempt from registration. See *SEC v. Ralston Purina Co.*, 346 U.S. 119 (1953). Whether offerees can fend for themselves involves the interplay of two concepts: their investment sophistication and their access to corporate information of the kind that would be contained in a registration statement. Sophisticated investors who are given sufficient information (or realistic access to such information) can clearly fend for themselves. But investors, no matter how sophisticated, cannot fend for themselves if they are not given (or given access to) sufficient information. So, sophisticated offerees alone are not sufficient to make the transaction exempt. Although some courts of appeals would hold that providing sufficient information to an unsophisticated investor is enough to make the transaction exempt (on the theory that this setting replicates the protection provided by a registered public offering) other courts would hold that information alone is insufficient; some showing of sophistication is required.

Section 3(b) of the Securities Act allows the SEC to exempt certain transactions from the registration requirements either because they involve issuing securities for less than $5 million or because of the limited nature of the offering. The SEC has responded by adopting *Regulation D*, which provides three kinds of transactions that will be exempt from registration. Regulation D offerings are the heart and soul of a corporate lawyer's exemption repertoire. The actual provisions of Reg. D are far too meticulous to discuss here. In overview, Rules 504 and 505 (which are included in Reg. D) allow corporations to raise up to $1 million or $5 million, respectively. Under Rule 504, there are few restrictions (except, of course, a prohibition on fraud!) but Rule 505 requires that there be no general advertising and that the purchasers be either rich people (gussied up as *accredited investors*, a term of art) of whom there is no limit, and not more than 35 nonaccredited investors. There are strong regulatory incentives to structure the transaction so that it is offered and sold only to accredited investors, which raises significant public policy questions about the access of ordinary people to potentially remunerative investments. The third Reg. D offering provision, Rule 506, is really a safe harbor (i.e., a nonexclusive method of compliance) for §4(2).

b. The Process of Registration — "Going Public"

While the vast majority of stock issuances are exempt from registration, and designed to be so, sometimes a corporation wants to go through the registration process. The goal in doing so is to allow the corporation to offer and sell its stock to anyone in the United States and, at least as importantly, to allow those persons to resell that stock without restriction on stock exchanges such as the New York Stock Exchange or the NASDAQ. The process of registration begins when the corporation negotiates with an investment banker to serve as the lead *underwriter* for the offering. The lead underwriter will form a syndicate of other investment bankers to buy the securities from the issuer, resell them to a broad cross-section of the investing public, and usually agrees to make a market (i.e., offer to buy and sell) in the security at least until a market for the stock has become established. The underwriters make a profit by purchasing the stock from the corporation at a discount from the public offering price.

As this negotiation proceeds, the company's lawyers, and lawyers for the underwriter, collaborate on drafting a registration statement on *Form S-1*. This is not a fill-in-the-blank kind of form but rather is a long (sometimes 200 pages) document that addresses precise topics prescribed by the SEC. In general, the registration statement details the corporation's business (and includes audited financial statements), the legal characteristics of the securities to be issued, and the issuer's intentions for the money to be raised.

From the time the company begins to negotiate with potential underwriters until the time the registration statement is filed with the SEC, a period of several weeks, the company may not "offer" its securities. Remember, this term has an extremely broad meaning and it is easy to violate this restriction. Once the registration statement is on file, the securities may be offered, but many restrictions on the kinds of written offers that may be made are still in effect. The SEC staff will review the registration statement and respond to the company with comments that, in theory, are supposed to be concerned only with the form of the company's disclosure but that, in fact, often go to the substance of the company's operational or financial performance. This comment period typically takes between three and six weeks. In the interim, the underwriters have lined up potential buyers. When the SEC is satisfied with the registration statement it declares the statement effective and the securities are sold to the underwriters and, in turn, to the public. Afterward, trading in the stock does not involve the corporation at all. Once the shares are sold to the underwriters, the company has received all the consideration it will ever receive for those shares. Subsequent price increases or decreases serve to provide profit or loss for the shareholders, not the company.

C. TERMS OF ART IN THIS CHAPTER

Accredited investors
Affirmative covenants
Angels
Blank (or blank check) stock
Bonds
Call option
Callable
Capital formation
Capital gain
Capital structure
Class of stock
Close (or closely held)
   corporations
Collar
Commercial paper market
Common stock
Convertible
Cumulative
Debentures
Debt
Defeased
Diluted
Economic realities test
Equitable subordination
Equity
Event of default

Exchange Act (or the '34
   Act)
Floating interest rate
Form S-1
Go public
Indenture
Initial public offering
   (IPO)
Intrastate exemption
Investment contract
Issued
Liquidity
Negative covenants
Option
Option writer
Ordinary income
Outstanding
Overissue
Par value
Participating
Preemptive rights
Preferred stock
Private placement
   exemption
Put option
Redemption

Registration statement
Regulation D
Reinvestment risk
Secondary trading market
Securities
Securities Act (or the '33
   Act)
Securities and Exchange
   Commission (SEC)
Series of stock
Share
Shareholder
Sinking fund
Stock
Stock right
Stockholder
Subordinated
Subscription agreements
Syndicate
Underwriter
Units
Venture capital
Vest
Warrant
Working capital

7

Cashing Out: Distributing Money to Shareholders

In the last chapter we covered the basics of capital formation. In other words, we managed to get money into a corporation. Now we turn our attention to a related topic: how to get money out of the business. After all, a primary reason to put money into a firm is the expectation (or at least the hope) of getting something monetary in return. This chapter focuses on getting money from the corporation into the hands of its shareholders. How do shareholders realize a profit on their investment? The next chapter analyzes the ability of creditors to compel payment to them when the corporation has insufficient assets.

In an economic sense, shareholders gain whenever the value of the business increases. Conversely, they lose when the value of the business decreases. But even if the value of their business increases, shareholders are unable to translate that increase into something else. They can't spend that increase unless it is somehow converted into money. Shareholders have two ways to convert the increase in the corporation's value into money.[1] First, the corporation can distribute the increased value (or part of it) to the shareholders. This is called a *dividend*. Second, a shareholder can sell some or all of his or her shares for (one hopes) more than he or she paid for them. Like most other property, shares of stock are presumed to be freely alienable.

Section A explores the corporate law contours of dividends. We look at the discretion placed in the board of directors to decide when dividends will be paid. We also cover the statutory restrictions on dividends. Finally, we examine stock splits and reverse stock splits. Section B deals with restrictions on a shareholder's power to transfer his or her stock. That section also covers the setting in which the shares are sold to the corporation that issued them.

---

1. All right, there's a third way, which is for the shareholder to borrow money using the shares as collateral. Analytically, though, this is really just anticipating a dividend or sale because the loan will have to be repaid either by future dividends or the proceeds of a future sale by the shareholder.

A. MAKING A PROFIT PART I: DIVIDENDS

1. *The Current Setting*

a. *Board Discretion*

Modern corporations statutes are straightforward, on the surface, in permitting corporations to pay dividends. Both the MBCA and the DGCL provide that a corporation's board "may" authorize the corporation to pay dividends, subject to certain restrictions we'll see shortly. See MBCA §6.40 and DGCL §170(a). This means that, under the statutes, a corporation cannot pay dividends unless its board of directors approves. When the board authorizes the dividends they are said to have been *declared*. Because dividends put wealth in the hands of the corporation's owners, why would a board *not* declare dividends when it could legally do so?

One reason would be the board's judgment that the corporation needs to retain the increased wealth to expand the business or to ensure that the corporation can meet future obligations. New businesses almost always need to retain all the wealth they can, so dividends in such corporations are a rarity. Another reason is that the corporation's shareholders may not need dividends to meet their ordinary living expenses. Because shareholders will be taxed on dividends but not on the increased but undistributed value of the corporation, the board may conclude that the shareholders are best served by retaining the increased wealth in the corporation rather than distributing it to the shareholders. This decision is most likely to be made in the closely held corporation where the board knows the economic preferences of its shareholders.

Publicly held corporations will, of course, have shareholders with widely differing economic needs. Typically, established public corporations pay dividends every three months, and an increase in the quarterly dividend is a signal to the investment community that the corporation is continuing to prosper. Conversely, a corporation that cuts or eliminates its dividend sends the opposite message to Wall Street. Thus public companies are usually conservative in their dividend policy because they do not want to increase the dividend unless they are fairly certain it can be maintained in the future for fear of sending the wrong message to investors.

Another reason the board may refuse to declare dividends is strategic. In closely held corporations the board may be controlled by one faction of shareholders that, by virtue of that control, has given its members employment with the corporation. Thus the controlling faction may have no need for dividends because it gets money in the form of corporate salaries. If the controlling group wishes to punish the remaining shareholders, it may refuse to employ them and may refuse to declare dividends. The only recourse for those noncontrolling shareholders to realize gain is to sell their shares. This may be exactly what the control group desires: to eliminate the other shareholders. As you may intuit, there are fiduciary constraints on such actions but they are not entirely effective. Chapter 16 explores those dynamics in more detail.

If the statutes place dividends in the discretion of the board, and valid reasons not to declare dividends often exist, can shareholders ever compel the board to declare dividends?

More than 75 years ago, the Illinois Supreme Court addressed the issue before us, stating: "There is a difference of opinion among the stockholders as to the reason or desirability of maintaining so large a cash surplus, [one side] believing that . . . it is wise business management to keep a large surplus in reserve . . . , and the [other side] believing that good business judgment and wise economy require the distribution of a large part of the surplus. . . . These are questions of business judgment to be determined by the directors of the corporation in their discretion, which will not be controlled by the court so long as it is exercised in good faith and in honesty of purpose. . . . Each party has sought to avail itself of such advantages as the law gave it, but the record does not show *fraud, oppression, or dishonest conduct.*" (*Hall v. Woods* 156 N.E. 258, 268, (Ill. 1927) italics added.)

Less than 10 years later, the Illinois Appellate Court explained that "[c]ourts will not compel [the declaration of a dividend] on the part of a corporation unless the withholding of the dividend is *oppressive and entirely without merit.* Courts of chancery will not concern themselves with the operations of a private corporation except on the ground of *fraud* or an impairment of the capital structure which would result in complete or very substantial loss. . . .

"[W]e can see no reason for compelling a dividend, particularly in view of the present [economic downturn] and the present attitude of all corporations to conserve as far as possible its working capital for future contingencies. The question of a dividend at this time is one which rests wholly in the business judgment of the board of directors and a court of chancery should not substitute its judgment for that of [the directors] actively engaged in business in the community." (*Hofeller v. General Candy Corp.* 275 Ill. App. 89, 96 (1934) italics added, citation omitted.)

"The decision concerning the declaration of a dividend where a legal dividend fund is available rests within the sole discretion of the board of directors. Courts are reluctant to interfere with the exercise of the directors' business judgment unless the withholding is *fraudulent, oppressive or totally without merit.*" (*Romanik v. Lurie Home Supply Center, Inc.* 435 N.E.2d 712, 723 (Ill. App. 1982) italics added.)

Illinois law is in accord with a leading treatise on corporate decision-making: "The business judgment rule protects a board's decision regarding payment of a dividend or the making of a distribution. A court will not compel a distribution unless withholding the distribution is explicable only on the theory of an *oppressive or fraudulent abuse of discretion.*" (3A Fletcher, *Cyclopedia of the Law of Private Corporations* (2002 rev.) §1041.20, 58, italics added, fn. omitted.)

"The fact that a corporation has earned profits out of which directors might lawfully declare a dividend . . . is insufficient alone to justify judicial intervention compelling a declaration and payment. Because the decision of the board of directors to declare and pay dividends is protected by the business judgment rule, the burden of proof on the shareholder seeking to compel the declaration and payment . . . is particularly stringent." (11 Fletcher, *Cyclopedia of the Law of Private Corporations* (2002 rev.) §5325, 584-586, fns. omitted.)

State Farm Mutual Automobile Ins. Co. v. Superior Court, 8 Cal. Rptr. 3d 56, 70-71 (Cal. App. 2003) (Mallano, J.)

It is settled law in this State that the declaration and payment of a dividend rests in the discretion of the corporation's board of directors in the exercise of its business judgment; that, before the courts will interfere with the judgment of the board of directors in such matter, fraud or gross abuse of discretion must be shown, *Moskowitz v. Bantrell*, 190 A.2d 749 (Del. 1963). There, this Court quoted with approval the time-honored statement of Chancellor Wolcott in *Eshleman v. Keenan*, 194 A. 40, 43 (Del. Ch. 1937) that courts act to compel the declaration of a dividend only upon a demonstration "that the withholding of it is explicable only on the theory of an oppressive or fraudulent abuse of discretion." See also *Baron v. Allied Artists Pictures Corp.*, 337 A.2d 653, 659 (Del. Ch. 1975).

Gabelli & Co., Inc., Profit Sharing Plan v. Liggett Group, Inc., 479 A.2d 276 (Del. 1984)
(Herrmann, C.J.)

Although these excerpts, which are representative of the rule in nearly every state,
suggest that stockholders could conceivably compel the payment of dividends, the
cases show a near uniform refusal to compel dividends in the publicly held corporation
setting. In the closely held corporation, courts also generally refuse to compel
dividends. The only setting in which courts seem at all willing to entertain the idea
of forcing the payment of dividends is as a remedy for shareholder oppression. Chapter
16 deals with oppression and its consequences in more detail.

Notes and Questions

1. What Do You Think?

a. A primary way for shareholders to receive a return on their investment is
through dividends. Because dividends are so central to shareholders' investments,
do you believe shareholders should have more say over a corporation's dividend
policy? If so, what rule would you adopt?

b. Do you think that the shareholders of a public company that has paid quarterly
dividends for some length of time should have an enforceable expectation of a quarterly dividend? If so, when should that right accrue? Should the time be measured
by the length of time the company has regularly paid dividends? The length of
time the plaintiff has held stock in the company? Or a combination of both? Once
an enforceable interest attaches, should the corporation have to pay exactly the
same amount of dividends as in the past, or should the board have some discretion
over the amount?

b. Statutory Restrictions

The board's declaration of dividends, while necessary, is not sufficient. Every state's
corporations statutes restrict the ability of a corporation to pay a dividend even
when its board wishes to declare one. The public policy behind these restrictions is
that shareholders are not the only people interested in getting money from the
corporation. That is, creditors, whether employees, suppliers, or lenders, have an
expectation that they will be paid by the corporation. If the corporation is financially
healthy, of course, these expectations will no doubt be satisfied.

If the corporation is in financial difficulty, though, the corporation's directors
(who may also be shareholders) have a distinct incentive to ensure that the shareholders, in whose best interest the directors must act, get as great a return as possible.
This means that the board may be tempted to declare large dividends if the corporation's situation seems hopeless. Conversely, the creditors have an incentive to
prohibit all dividends so that as much as possible remains for their claims. In some
settings creditors have sufficient bargaining power and sophistication to negotiate
in advance for contractual restrictions on the board to limit or prohibit dividends.
Nonetheless, statutes exist to prevent the payment of dividends in circumstances
where creditors may be especially harmed. Unlike nearly every other kind of
provision in modern corporate statutes, these restrictions are not waiveable and

directors are personally liable for knowing breach of these provisions. See MBCA §8.31 and DGCL §174 (directors liable for knowing *or negligent* violation).

Although every state's corporations statute addresses this problem, the MBCA and older statutes such as the DGCL take quite different approaches. Under the MBCA, a corporation may not pay a dividend if, afterward, "the corporation would not be able to pay its debts as they become due in the usual course of business" or "the corporation's total assets would be less than . . . its total liabilities" plus, the amount necessary to pay the preferred shares (if any) their liquidation preference. See MBCA §6.40. While these tests may appear to be mechanical, quantitative, and bright line, the statute specifically permits the directors to make the necessary judgments (i.e., that the corporation will be able to pay its debts as they become due and that the corporation's assets will exceed its liabilities) using any method of valuation that is reasonable under the circumstances. Thus the directors are not bound by the corporation's financial statements or traditional accounting methods if it is reasonable to depart from them. The MBCA approach is sometimes called the *insolvency test* approach.

Delaware and other par value states rely on the so-called *legal capital test* to regulate dividends. Remember that a share's par value is the minimum consideration for which it may be issued (and remember that today par value is typically set very low and that shares are typically issued for many times their par value). The DGCL defines a concept of *capital* that is related to par value. In effect, every corporation, even those that issue only no-par value stock, must have some amount of capital. When the corporation issues shares, the DGCL requires the board to designate how much of the consideration is to be capital. For no-par value stock the board need only designate some portion of the consideration as capital. For par value shares, the minimum amount that can be designated as capital is the par value. If the board does not make the requisite designation, the statute provides that the capital shall be the aggregate par value (for par value shares) and the entire consideration for no-par value shares. See DGCL §154.

The DGCL goes on to provide that a corporation's net assets (its total assets minus its total liabilities) less its capital is its *surplus*. See DGCL §154. Now, at last, comes the payoff. Dividends can ordinarily be paid only out of a corporation's surplus. See DGCL §170(a)(1). Thus in the normal course of a Delaware corporation's existence, you, as the corporation's lawyer, must be able to determine the total assets and total liabilities (for which you may rely on the corporation's financial officers or its outside accountants) and the corporation's capital. Subtract the total liabilities and capital from the total assets and you have the corporation's surplus and, hence, you know the maximum amount that may be paid to shareholders in dividends.

What is the point of requiring "capital"? As you see, this capital does not mean the money that is paid into the company. It is a much more artificial concept than that. For this reason, "capital" in the sense we have been using it in this section, is sometimes called "legal capital" to distinguish it from capital in an economic sense. Although a corporation's capital is a specific dollar amount, related to par value, it is not a separate fund. The capital needn't be kept in cash or kept separate from other corporate assets. It's just a number that has importance in declaring dividends. This fact alone should tell you that the legal capital test does not protect corporate creditors. It is, at bottom, a trap for those lawyers who are insufficiently alert.

Nonetheless, because directors face severe personal liability for paying an unlawful dividend, you must understand this system and be able to conclude with some confidence whether a particular corporation can or cannot legally pay a particular dividend.

The DGCL provides another avenue for paying dividends, if a corporation has no surplus, it may nonetheless pay dividends up to the amount of its net profits for the current and preceeding fiscal year. See DGCL §170(a)(2). Note that this process is available only if the corporation has no surplus. The DGCL does not define "net profits," leaving that concept to the board's good faith judgment.

c. The Mechanics of Paying Dividends

Once the board has passed a resolution declaring a dividend, the shareholders as a group become creditors as to that dividend, assuming the corporation has legally available funds to pay the dividend. Although a corporation could, in theory, issue checks to its shareholders on the date the dividend is declared, there is typically a lag time between declaration and payment. At a minimum, prudence suggests that a corporation wait until the board has officially declared the dividend because unexpected late developments may result in the board failing to make the declaration on the anticipated date. As a result, board resolutions typically fix a future date on which the dividends will be paid.

A further complication is that shares may change hands between the declaration and the payment. In a closely held corporation such a transfer may be unlikely, but in a publicly held corporation shares change hands every day. Who is entitled to the dividend: shareholders on the date the dividend is declared or shareholders on the date the dividend is paid? The default rule is that shareholders on the date of the board's declaration are entitled to the dividend even if they transfer their shares before the payment date. This *record date* is simply a way to fix the list of shareholders entitled to a dividend.

Under every corporations statute, though, the board is given the power to set a different record date between the declaration date and payment date. The reason to provide discretion to set a future record date is to give notice to current (and perhaps to potential) shareholders that an important event — payment of money — will soon occur. Those shareholders who intended to transfer their shares may wish to retain them in light of the dividend to come. Likewise, persons interested in becoming shareholders may have an added incentive to purchase shares before the record date so that they will receive the dividend. A timeline of about six weeks between declaration and payment is typical of a public corporation's dividend process.

The concept of a record date also applies to shareholder meetings — there must be a fixed list of shareholders entitled to notice of a meeting and entitled to vote. Suffice it to say that in the voting context the ability to set a future record date can be used strategically by the board to enhance the possibility of its views prevailing. Shareholder meetings are covered in detail in Chapters 15 and 16. As to record dates for dividends, see MBCA §6.40(b) and DGCL §213(c).

Both the MBCA and DGCL provide that the list of shareholders entitled to a dividend shall be fixed as of "the close of business" on the record date. See MBCA §1.40(19) and DGCL §213. What if a shareholder dies on the record date? Does it matter whether the shareholder dies before or after the close of business? By this point in your legal career you are no doubt thinking this is simply a law professor's stupid hypo.[2] If you were still in your first year of law school no doubt your professor could fill enormous amounts of class time debating this point. We're past all that now, thank goodness. You should be aware, though, that shareholders (and people generally) have a rather tactless inclination to present just such situations with some regularity.

McIlvaine v. AmSouth Bank, N.A.

581 So. 2d 454 (Ala. 1991)

INGRAM, J.

AmSouth Bank, as trustee of an inter vivos trust created in 1943 by Neva E. McIlvaine (settlor),... alleged that the trust agreement provides that the net income ... be paid in equal shares to the settlor's three children during their respective lifetimes, [and], upon the death of a child, to the "lawful issue of the body" of such child for his or her lifetime. The complaint further alleged that Eugene Thomas McIlvaine, Jr. (Tommy), one of the settlor's children, died on April 11, 1989, the record date for the payment of a ... dividend to the trust. The trustee, therefore, sought instructions as to whether, under the terms of the trust, Tommy's estate or the successor beneficiaries were entitled to the dividend.

AmSouth also alleged that Tommy was survived by a ... son named Eugene Thomas McIlvaine III (Gene).... The trial court instructed the trustee to pay the April 11, 1989, dividend to ... Tommy's estate.... Gene appeals.

On appeal, Gene argues that the trial court erred in instructing the trustee to pay the April 11 dividend to Tommy's estate, because, he argues, Tommy died before the close of business on that date.

The trial court found the facts related to this issue to be undisputed. The principal asset of the McIlvaine trust is common stock of the Torchmark Corporation. Torchmark, a Delaware corporation with its principal place of business in Birmingham, Alabama, declared a dividend on February 23, 1989, payable to stockholders of record at the close of business on April 11, 1989. The dividend was to be distributed on May 1, 1989. Tommy, the beneficial owner of one-third of the shares and, thus, of one-third of the dividends, died in New York City on April 11, 1989, at 7:15 A.M., E.S.T.

Initially, we note that as a general rule, a dividend belongs to those who are owners of the shares at the time it is declared and not to those who are owners of the shares at the time the dividend is paid. 3A W. Fratcher, *Scott on Trusts* §236.2 (4th ed. 1988). When a corporation declares a dividend, the dividend is separated from the assets of the corporation, and a debt to those who are shareholders at the time of the declaration is created, although payment of the debt is postponed. *Selly v. Fleming Coal Co.*, 180 A. 326 (Del. 1935); *Scott on Trusts, supra.*

However, where the dividend is payable to shareholders of record on a specified date subsequent to the declaration date, those who are shareholders on the record date are entitled to the dividend, because the debt created by the declaration is a debt to those who are shareholders on that date. *Scott on Trusts, supra.* Likewise,

---

2. Or, even less charitably, a stupid law prof's stupid hypo.

where corporate stock is held in trust, the estate of the income beneficiary is entitled to all regular cash dividends declared for the benefit of stockholders of record on dates prior to the beneficiary's death, despite the fact that the trustee may not actually receive such dividends until after the death of the income beneficiary. *Wilmington Trust Co. v. Wilmington Trust Co.*, 15 A.2d 665 (Del. Ch. 1940).

Thus, where a dividend is declared during the life of the income beneficiary and is payable to shareholders of record on a date prior to the death of the beneficiary, the dividend is included in the estate of the beneficiary, even though it is not payable until after the death of the beneficiary. Conversely, where a dividend is declared during the life of the income beneficiary and is payable to shareholders of record on a date subsequent to the death of the beneficiary, the dividend is not included in the estate of the beneficiary.

In the present case, however, we are confronted with the unusual situation wherein the beneficiary died *on* the date designated by the corporation for the determination of its shareholders of record. Although there is no Delaware case considering the exact issue raised by the facts of this case, the trial court relied on a New York case that is on point. *In re Estate of Donahue*, 357 N.Y.S.2d 777 (N.Y. Sur. Ct. 1974).... The court...reasoned that the shareholder's death on the day the dividend accrued required the court to consider the dividend as if it had been paid...on that date. Therefore, the court held that the dividend belonged to the estate.

In reaching its conclusion, the *Donahue* court expressly refused to consider the fact that the shareholder lived through only a part of the record date and was, in fact, dead at the close of business on the record date. The *Donahue* court opined that to require a fiduciary to take into account the precise time of the shareholder's death and the exact hour and minute at which the corporation's business day ended would be burdensome and complicated. The court also noted that if fractions of a day were considered, fiduciaries would have to take into account time zones and time changes in distributions occurring close to the date of shareholder's death.

Although Gene cites to us cases from various jurisdictions wherein the respective courts have taken into account fractions of a day, we have examined those cases and find none of them to be analogous to the facts in the present case. On the other hand, we find merit in the approach taken by the *Donahue* court, which refused to take into account a fraction of a day under facts similar to those presented here.

Generally, a day is considered to be an indivisible unit or period of time, and, thus, it is frequently stated that the law will not take into account fractions of a day. Under this general rule, any fraction of a day is deemed to be a full day. To apply a "fraction of a day" rule to facts like those in the present case would lead to confusion as courts attempt to ascertain such factors as the exact hour and minute that an event takes place, the applicable time zones, or the hours of business of a particular corporation, to name but a few. We find that the trial court correctly held that Tommy was the beneficial shareholder of the stock on April 11, 1989, the record date, and that, as a result, his estate is entitled to the dividend.

AFFIRMED.

HORNSBY, C.J., and ALMON, ADAMS and STEAGALL, JJ., concur.

Notes and Questions

1. Notes

a. The maxim of jurisprudence that guides the court is *fractionem diei non recipit lex* which is usually translated as, "The law does not regard a fraction of a day."

b. Note that the court looked to Delaware law, the law of the state in which Torchmark was incorporated, to decide this case.

2. Reality Check

a. Who are the two factions that are in disagreement?

b. Why should Tommy be deemed to be alive for the entire day of April 11, 1989? Why shouldn't Tommy be deemed to be dead for the entire day?

3. Suppose

a. Suppose Tommy had died in San Francisco at 9:15 P.M. on April *10*, 1989, which was 11:15 P.M. in Alabama and 12:15 A.M. on April 11, in Delaware?

4. What Do You Think?

a. The court, citing the *Donahue* case, said that, "if fractions of a day were considered, fiduciaries would have to take into account time zones and time changes in distributions occurring close to the date of shareholder's death." Doesn't the court's holding have exactly the same effect?

b. Do you think this holding simply changes the bright-line rule from the instant of death to midnight at the end of the day of death?

c. Do you think this problem could be almost entirely avoided by corporations making their dividends payable to shareholders of record at a particular time (rather than the close of business) in a particular time zone (e.g. Eastern Time or GMT) outside of normal business hours?

d. Stock Splits

There is one further concept to explore when considering dividends. You may have heard of a stock split and gotten the impression that such things are good. That's true in part but, as with many things generally pronounced to be good, a large part is illusory. As you remember, when a corporation is first organized, the number of shares to be authorized and issued initially is, in essence, an arbitrary decision. For example, if the new corporation needs $100,000, it probably doesn't matter whether it issues 100,000 shares at $1 each or one share for $100,000. Issuing more shares makes it easier for shareholders to transfer small proportions of their holdings while issuing fewer shares makes such transfer more difficult. A *stock split* is simply the division of the outstanding shares into more shares. An old analogy is that a stock split simply divides the pie into more slices. Note that the corporation receives nothing in a stock split. Nor do the shareholders change their relative ownership interests. A stock split simply means that those ownership intersts are represented by more shares. Nothing is created; no assets are transferred. In that sense a stock split is simply an illusion, although one that fools a great many people. As Yogi said, when asked whether he wanted his pizza cut into four slices or eight, "Four. I don't think I can eat eight."[3]

---

3. Yogi Berra, *The Yogi Book* 80 (1998).

Why does a board of directors want to split the stock? One reason, in the privately held corporation, is to permit transfer of smaller percentages of each shareholders' ownership. In the public company, the received wisdom of Wall Street is that stocks are most popular when they trade somewhere between $10 and $100 per share. This lets an investor buy a *round lot* (i.e., 100 shares, a typical trading unit) for $1,000 to $10,000. If a corporation has successfully increased its value, the price of its stock may, over time, approach or exceed the $100 per share level. At that point the board of directors may effect a split to reduce the price per share.[4]

Few corporations declare a true stock split. Instead, most "splits" are effected through a *stock dividend* of authorized but unissued shares to the existing shareholders. See DGCL §173 and MBCA §6.23. If the corporation does not have enough authorized but unissued shares, the board can, without shareholder approval, increase the number of authorized but unissued shares, but only to facilitate a stock dividend. See MBCA §10.05(4). Note that Delaware does not have a comparable statute.

If a Delaware corporation is issuing new shares, it must designate at least the aggregate par value of the newly issued shares as capital, which means that the corporation's surplus is reduced by that amount. Because the corporation has already received the capital associated with treasury shares, no capital adjustment is needed when the corporation declares a stock dividend using treasury stock. See DGCL §173.

As a matter of nomenclature, stock splits are expressed as a ratio as in a "2-for-1" split or a "3-for-2" split. It is important to realize that a 2-for-1 split means that, after the split is effected, each shareholder will *own* two shares for each share owned before the split. It does *not* mean that each shareholder will *receive* two more shares (i.e., giving the shareholder three shares in total). In a 3-for-2 split, for example, each shareholder will own three shares after the split for every 2 shares he or she owned before the split. This nomenclature is a frequent source of confusion for investors. By contrast, stock dividends are typically described as a percentage of the outstanding predividend shares. Thus a company that has 100 million shares outstanding and is declaring a 1 million share dividend is said to have declared a "1-percent dividend."

In some sense, the illusory nature of a stock split seems harmless enough. However, investors' misunderstanding of the effect of a stock split can lead to serious problems, as the next case illuminates.

≡ **Lynam v. Gallagher**
≡ 526 A.2d 878 (Del. 1987)

Before HORSEY, MOORE, WALSH, and HOLLAND, constituting the Court En Banc.

HORSEY, J.

Husband appeals Family Court's ancillary rulings, following divorce of the parties, relating to the marital property division.... The main issue on appeal is whether stock dividends that one spouse receives during marriage on shares of stock acquired before marriage are marital property under Del. Code. Ann. tit. 13

---

4. Although in theory a 2-for-1 split should result in a halving of the share price (i.e., each share that was worth $100 is now two shares so each should be worth $50), in practice sophisticated investors believe that a stock split is a signal that the board foresees further increases in the firm's value and so the share price tends to fall by a bit less than half.

§1513(a). Under the facts of this case, all of the stock dividends declared on husband's premarital shares of stock are not marital property subject to division under section 1513(a). We, therefore, affirm in part, reverse in part and remand the case to Family Court for modification of the judgment consistent with our Opinion.

The relevant facts are as follows: the parties were married in 1959, separated in 1983, and divorced in 1984. Prior to their marriage, husband received...960 shares of Wilmington Trust Company ("WTC") stock valued at $20,000. These 960 shares...were held in husband's individual name.

In 1961, husband sold 100 shares of WTC stock to a third party. Husband also transferred an additional 100 shares of the stock to wife and himself as joint tenants with right of survivorship. Husband testified that his motive for transferring the 100 shares into joint names was to take advantage of a federal income tax exemption for dividends received.

In 1966, WTC declared a 100% stock dividend. As a result of the bank's action, husband's holdings increased to 1,720 shares: 1,520 in his individual name and an additional 200 shares in joint title with wife. In accounting for the stock dividend, WTC debited its surplus account and credited its capital stock account in an amount equal to the number of newly-issued shares multiplied by the par value of the shares. WTC's total capital funds were unchanged by the stock dividend and each stock-holder's proportional share of equity in the bank remained the same.

Immediately before the stock dividend, WTC stock was trading on the over-the-counter market at a price of $140 bid and $144 asked. Immediately after the dividend, the price of the stock fell to $70 bid and $73 asked. Thus, as a result of the dividend, husband owned twice as many shares of WTC stock, with each share equal to half the value of a pre-dividend share of WTC stock.

In 1983, WTC declared a second 100% stock dividend. In 1985, eight months after the entry of the parties' final divorce decree, WTC declared a third 100% stock dividend. The accounting for this dividend was the same as for the earlier stock dividends. As with the two previous stock dividends, there was no change in husband's proportional ownership in WTC and the market price of each share immediately after the dividend was equal to half the price of a share immediately before the dividend.

Thus, the number of WTC shares held in husband's individual name increased from 760 to 6,080 shares and the number of shares jointly owned by husband and wife increased from 100 to 800 shares. During this time period husband did not purchase, inherit or receive any other shares of WTC stock except those he acquired through the stock dividends. Nor did husband dispose of any WTC stock, with the exception of the 100 shares he sold in 1961 to a third party.

In the 1985 ancillary hearing following the divorce of the parties, husband and wife disagreed over whether the stock dividends paid during the marriage on the 760 shares of WTC stock, titled in husband's individual name and acquired before marriage, were marital property pursuant to Del. Code. Ann. tit. 13 §1513. The Family Court adopted wife's argument and held...that all of husband's shares of stock acquired from stock dividends during marriage, excluding only the 760 shares which he owned in his individual name prior to marriage, constituted marital property subject to division under section 1513(a).

[W]e start with a statutory presumption that: all property acquired by either spouse during marriage, regardless of how such property be titled, is "presumed" to be marital property, subject to division by the Family Court upon divorce. Del.

Code. Ann. tit. 13 §1513(c). Section 1513(b), however, provides that the marital property presumption is subject to three exceptions. Those exceptions are: "(1) Property acquired in exchange for property acquired before marriage; (2) Property excluded by valid agreement of the parties; and (3) The increase in value of property acquired before marriage." The burden of overcoming this statutory presumption and proving that the property sought to be excluded falls within one of the three statutory exceptions is placed upon the party seeking to exclude the property from division between the parties.

Under the facts of this case, we conclude that all of the shares of WTC stock that husband received during the marriage from three 100% stock dividends upon his premarital shares of WTC stock represent an increase in value of property that is excluded from marital property under Del. Code. Ann. tit. 13 §1513(b)(3).

The record in this case supports the conclusion that husband did not receive any property of value at the time of the stock dividends above what property he owned prior to the parties' marriage. Immediately after each stock dividend, the market price of WTC stock decreased by 50% and each stockholder's proportional ownership in WTC remained the same. Had WTC not declared any stock dividends, the price of husband's premarital shares of WTC stock would have been approximately eight times their present value. Therefore, any increase in value of husband's WTC stock during the twenty-seven-year period was due to the economic appreciation in price of husband's 760 premarital shares and not due to the three stock dividends.

We find that the stock dividends fall within the exception embodied in Del. Code. Ann. tit. 13 §1513(b)(3) and that husband overcame the statutory presumption that the stock dividends are marital property.

We also reject wife's argument that the WTC stock certificates husband received through the stock dividends constitute "new" property acquired during the parties' marriage.[8] Stock certificates are mere evidence of property. Here the record discloses that the new WTC stock certificates represent husband's premarital ownership interest in WTC divided into smaller pieces.

Husband's final contention is that the Family Court erred in holding that the 800 shares of WTC stock held by the parties in joint names were marital property. The only evidence husband offered to rebut the presumption that the jointly-held shares of WTC stock were marital property was his testimony that he transferred the 100 shares to joint title in order to take advantage of a federal income tax exemption for dividends received. Upon this record, we find that husband's testimony failed to establish an agreement between the parties that the jointly-held stock was not marital property. Thus, husband did not rebut the statutory presumption that the 800 shares of jointly-held stock were marital property subject to division under section 1513(a).

AFFIRMED in part; REVERSED in part; and REMANDED.

---

8. *See also* Revised Model Business Corporation Act Annotated §§1.40(6) and 6.23, Official Comment at 394 (1984), which states: "A share dividend is solely a paper transaction: No assets are received by the corporation for the shares and any 'dividend' paid in shares does not involve the distribution of property by the corporation to its shareholders."

Notes and Questions

1. Notes

a. The court notes that in 1961 the husband transferred 100 shares to himself and his wife jointly to obtain a tax benefit. From 1954 until 1986 individuals could exclude a certain amount of dividends from their income. To maximize the deduction, a married couple could file separately and separate ownership of the shares between them.[5]

2. Reality Check

a. How is it that shares can be issued to shareholders yet the shareholders receive nothing?

3. Suppose

a. Suppose WTC had paid only cash dividends instead of stock dividends. Would those payments have been marital property? How did the parties treat the cash dividends that WTC paid?

4. What Do You Think?

a. Do you agree with Justice Horsey that the share dividends "represent an increase in value of property"?

e. Reverse Stock Splits

A board may decide that it is in the best interest of the corporation for fewer, but correspondingly more valuable, shares to be outstanding. This may happen when a public company's stock trades below $10 per share. In fact, stock exchanges may *delist* (refuse to allow trading in) companies whose stock trades below $1 per share. To reduce the number of shares outstanding, the corporation may effect a *reverse stock split*, which is not a split at all but an amalgamation. A 1-for-2 reverse split means that each shareholder will have one share after the split for each two shares he or she owned before. Axiomatically, of course, each remaining share should be twice as valuable as before. Because shares cannot be taken away from shareholders without their consent, a reverse stock split requires an amendment to the articles of incorporation, which must be approved by the board and shareholders. See MBCA §10.03 and DGCL §§242(a)(3), 242(b).

Stock splits and reverse stock splits may have ancillary, and sometimes unintended, effects. For example, suppose a shareholder has borrowed money and put up "100 shares of XYZ Corp." stock as collateral. If the corporation declares a 2-for-1 stock split and the shareholder thereafter defaults on the loan, is the lender entitled to sieze 100 shares or 200? The next case concerns another area in which this same question arises.

---

5. My colleague Lily Kahng provided the explanation for the otherwise baffling 1961 transfer. Thanks, Lily.

Reiss v. Financial Performance Corporation

715 N.Y.S.2d 29 (N.Y. App. Div. 2000)

FRIEDMAN, J.

Where a warrant to purchase stock is silent as to the effect of a reverse stock split on a warrant holder's right to purchase shares of stock, must the warrant be deemed, after such a split, to reflect a proportional change in both the number of shares that may be purchased and the price of each share? We conclude that, in the absence of any evidence that the parties to a warrant contemplated otherwise, the warrant holder, because of the reverse stock split, is limited to purchasing shares proportionally adjusted as to both number and price.

[In 1993,] the Board of Directors of defendant Financial Performance Corporation (Financial), [issued] a warrant to Rebot Corporation, permitting Rebot to purchase 1,198,904 shares of Financial's common stock at a price of 10 cents per share. [F]inancial's Board also gave authorization to issue a warrant to Marvin Reiss (who was, at the time, a member of Financial's Board and apparently Rebot's President), permitting him to purchase 500,000 shares of stock at 10 cents per share. Both the Rebot and Reiss warrants provided that the right to purchase stock would extend for a period of five years. . . .

In . . . 1996, at an annual meeting, Financial's shareholders approved a one-for-five reverse stock split. As a result, each stockholder owned one-fifth the original number of shares, with each share representing that amount of ownership previously represented by five shares of stock.

Thereafter, [in] 1998, plaintiffs sought to partially exercise their warrants. In seeking to do so, plaintiffs asserted that they were entitled to purchase shares of Financial in accordance with the literal language of the warrants without adjustment for the reverse stock split. Financial, on the other hand, asserted that any right to purchase stock under the warrants had to be proportionally adjusted to reflect the reverse stock split.

The line in the sand having been drawn, plaintiffs commenced the instant action seeking a judgment . . . declaring that Rebot and Reiss remained entitled to purchase 1,198,904 and 500,000 shares of stock respectively at 10 cents per share.

Analysis of the issue presented must begin with a detailed examination of *Cofman v. Acton Corp.,* 958 F.2d 494 (1st Cir. 1992), a case bearing striking similarities to the instant case.

[D]efendant corporation executed a reverse stock split that resulted in each stockholder owning one-fifth the original number of shares, with a concomitant increase in value for the new shares. A letter was then sent to the plaintiffs advising them of the reverse stock split and indicating that their [interest] would be deemed modified to reflect the split. The plaintiffs disagreed, contending that their agreement did not provide for any adjustment based upon changes in the structure of the stock.

The court . . . observed that, if plaintiffs' construction of the agreement were accepted, an absurd result would follow. In this regard, if the agreement were read literally, as the plaintiffs urged, the corporation could have eviscerated any possibility of the plaintiffs benefitting from the agreement by simply declaring a stock split, as opposed to a reverse stock split. Stated otherwise, the corporation would be able to dilute the value of its stock to such an extent that the plaintiffs' [interest] was valueless. This being so:

"It defies common sense" that [plaintiffs] would have agreed that [the corporation]
could effectively escape the specified consequences of a rising market price by increasing the number of shares. And if [plaintiffs] would not suffer from any increas[e in
the number of shares], it would follow, since a contract must be construed consistently . . . [the corporation] should not suffer from any decreas[e in the number of
shares] *id.*, at 497.

We find *Cofman* to be dispositive of the issue presented here by force of its
logic. . . . In this connection, to accept plaintiffs' interpretation of the contract,
namely, that the warrants did not allow for a proportional adjustment to reflect a
reverse stock split, would necessarily mean that the warrants also did not allow for a
proportional adjustment if there were a stock split. Flowing from that reasoning is
the observation that Financial, like the corporation in *Cofman,* could have eviscerated
the value of plaintiffs' warrants and escaped its contractual obligations by simply
declaring a massive stock split instead of a reverse stock split. Here, as in *Cofman,*
it defies all bounds of common sense to believe that plaintiffs could have ever intended
such an outcome. We therefore conclude that, just as plaintiffs should not suffer
from the possibility of dilution of their warrants resulting from a stock split, so too
Financial should not suffer from the consolidation of its shares resulting from a
declaration of a reverse stock split (*Cofman v. Acton Corp., supra; cf., Restatement
(Second) of Contracts* §204 (1981), comment c [a term can be supplied by logical
deduction from the agreed terms and the circumstances of the making of the
contract]). Any other conclusion would ignore the plain intent of the parties in issuing
and receiving the subject warrants.

Notwithstanding *Cofman,* plaintiffs and the dissent assert that a literalistic
approach to the interpretation of the warrants is compelled as a matter of law. We
cannot agree. Surely a court is not required to disregard common sense and slavishly
bow to the written word where to do so would plainly ignore the true intentions of
the parties in the making of a contract. Such formalistic literalism serves no function
but to contravene the essence of proper contract interpretation, which, of course, is to
enforce a contract in accordance with the true expectations of the parties in light of the
circumstances existing at the time of the formation of the contract. We point out that
no one makes the claim that there is any other evidence to be offered on the issue of
the parties' expectations, other than what has been presented on this appeal. Nor does
anyone claim that a trial is necessary to resolve any ambiguity.[4]

In any event, to the extent that the warrants may be viewed as not containing an
implicit requirement for the proportional adjustment of Financial's stock upon a
split or reverse-split, it means that the parties omitted what is undeniably an essential
term of the agreement. Contrary to the dissent's contention, a provision dealing
with this eventuality is essential since it fundamentally affects both the number of
shares that may be purchased and the price to be paid. In a circumstance where an
essential term is omitted, section 204 of the *Restatement (Second) of Contracts* is
instructive. That section provides:

---

4. Although certainly not dispositive, plaintiffs themselves seemingly recognized the lack of logic
inherent in their position. Thus, at oral argument plaintiffs were forced to concede that, had there been
a stock split as opposed to a reverse stock split, they would have asserted a contrary position to that which
they presently advocate and would have argued that the parties did not intend that Financial be able to dilute
its stock to the point of rendering the warrants valueless.

When the parties to a bargain sufficiently defined to be a contract have not agreed with respect to a term which is essential to a determination of their rights and duties, a term which is reasonable in the circumstances is supplied by the court.

Here, following the *Restatement* approach, the only reasonable term would be the one consistent with the self-evident expectations of the parties when the warrants were executed, namely, a term requiring a proportional adjustment of both the number of shares that may be purchased and their price.

SULLIVAN, P.J., and WALLACH and RUBIN, JJ., concur with FRIEDMAN, J.

SAXE, J. (dissenting in part):

The law of contracts offers relief from a hard bargain only upon a showing of fraud, duress, mistake, misrepresentation, illegality, impossibility of performance or unconscionability. But, when none of those grounds has been established, and the terms of the agreement under consideration are clearly set forth within the four corners of the document, courts should not alter those terms, even where the alteration achieves a more equitable result. As Judge Cardozo noted:

> A contract is made. Performance is burdensome and perhaps oppressive. If we were to consider only the individual instance, we might be ready to release the promisor. We look beyond the particular to the universal, and shape our judgment in obedience to the fundamental interest of society that contracts shall be fulfilled.

> Benjamin N. Cardozo, *The Nature of the Judicial Process*, at 139-140 (1921).

The warrants, by their clear terms, gave plaintiffs an absolute, unconditioned right to purchase the specified number of shares for the price set forth in the warrants, and nothing in the warrants permits their terms to be altered by a reverse stock split.

Defendant believes it to be "axiomatic" that a stock warrant necessarily converts in exactly the same manner as existing common stock converts upon any sort of adjustment to the form of the stock. However, this is an unfounded assumption. If stock warrants were deemed automatically adjusted upon consolidations or reclassifications of corporate stock, so that they maintained their proportionate value, there would be no need for the use of warrant agreements to establish the concept of proportional adjustment of stock warrants.

The majority, employing an analysis grounded in "common sense," reasons that the parties "must have" intended for the stock warrants issued to plaintiffs to be altered in the same proportions as actual shares of stock would be by any stock split occurring during their effective period. However, resort by a court to its subjective view of common sense is not a proper basis for a legal conclusion, particularly when it ignores both plaintiff's assertion of what the parties negotiated and intended, as well as "[t]he cardinal rule of contract interpretation . . . that, where the language of the contract is clear and unambiguous, the parties' intent is to be gleaned from the language of the agreement and whatever may be reasonably implied therefrom" (*see, H.K.S. Hunt Club v. Town of Claverack*, 634 N.Y.S.2d 816 (N.Y. App. Div. 1995)).

There is nothing ambiguous about the terms of these stock warrants; they clearly provide that plaintiffs have an absolute right to purchase the named number of shares at the stated price within the defined time frame.

Furthermore, while a new contract provision may be added by a court if the additional term is "essential to a determination" (*see, Restatement (Second) of Contracts*, §204), the majority's assertion that "the parties omitted what is undeniably an essential term of the agreement" is simply incorrect, since clearly the agreement can be enforced by reference solely to the terms contained in the document. These terms — amount, price, and time frame — constitute all the essential elements of the agreement. The term the majority believes to have been accidentally omitted amounts to merely a possible condition or limitation.

The majority's insertion of a limitation cannot be accurately characterized as a simple construction of the document's terms. Rather, the majority is actually altering a basic, definite term of the contract, as to the price at which plaintiffs were entitled to purchase stock of the corporation. However, the rules of contract construction do not permit an alteration of a clear contract term, based upon a change in circumstances not provided for by the parties at the time of the contract.

In view of the definitive language of the contract, grafting limitations or conditions onto those warrants amounts to rewriting the contracts, and may not be justified as the application of logic or common sense.

In modifying the parties' rights based upon their presumed intention in the event of future stock splits, the majority adopts the reasoning of the First Circuit Court of Appeals in *Cofman v. Acton Corp.* The crux of *Cofman* is that when the parties gave no thought to the eventuality of a reverse stock split, which thereafter occurred, the omission constituted an ambiguity, and the court could infer the parties' presumed intention on that issue by "reference to all of its language and to its general structure and purpose and in the light of the circumstances under which it was executed" (*id.* at 498 . . .).

Nothing in the language of the stock warrants or their general structure and purpose gives rise to an inference that the parties intended plaintiffs' rights to be automatically altered in the event of a stock split. Moreover, assuming that the purported omission creates an ambiguity, determination of the parties' intent is an issue of fact requiring consideration of the extrinsic evidence submitted by the parties.

Accordingly, at the very least, the finding of an ambiguity by omission creates a disputed issue of fact regarding the parties' intent, which must be resolved at trial. In concluding that the parties "could not have" intended an outcome in which a reverse stock split would have no effect on plaintiffs' rights, the majority weighs the evidence and rejects a factual assertion, neither of which is appropriate in the context of a dismissal or summary judgment motion.

In order to justify inclusion in the agreement of a new term that limits rights set forth in the document, the majority also offers the novel proposition that the court must consider not only the situation at hand, but what the parties' legal positions would be if the reverse situation had occurred. In other words, the majority is making a factual finding that plaintiffs necessarily would not have advanced the same argument had a forward stock split occurred instead,[9] in order to reject the plaintiffs' position in the context of a reverse stock split.

Interesting and, perhaps, commonsensical as this proposition at first appears, it has no foundation in the law of contract construction. The question of what plaintiffs

---

9. The majority buttresses its factual conclusion regarding the plaintiffs' intent by referring to counsel's response to a question at oral argument. Of course, counsel's statements cannot properly be the basis for a finding as to the clients' intent.

intended when entering into the stock warrant arrangement must be answered based upon what the parties did and said, not upon what the court assumes they would be inclined to argue in a hypothetical situation.

Moreover, had a forward stock split taken place, plaintiffs need not have taken a position contrary to that they take here. Initially, they would have had the option they had all along: to decline to purchase shares whose value was lower than the option price. Additionally, in the event the corporation effectively reduced the value of warrants by arranging for a forward stock split, the warrantholders would be entitled to challenge the corporation's conduct as violative of its obligation of good faith and fair dealing; they would not necessarily have to seek an alteration of the terms of the contract.

The concern expressed by defendant, namely, that plaintiffs will unfairly reap a "windfall" if their warrants are not deemed to have been automatically altered by operation of the Corporation's reverse stock split, should not affect the court's analysis of the situation. While an aversion to applying the precise terms of the contract under consideration here is at least facially understandable, the law of contracts offers no relief simply because the contract, as applied, may be unfair. This windfall could have been avoided by inclusion of standard terms and conditions referable to the stock warrants, a precaution which, for whatever reason, the corporation did not take in this instance.

Finally, as a practical matter, it should be recognized that the majority's ruling amounts to a reformation of the contract, in the absence of proper grounds. "Reformation is...solely for the purpose of stating correctly a mutual mistake shared by both parties to the contract...when it clearly and convincingly appears that the contract, as written, does not embody the true agreement as mutually intended" (*Nash v. Kornblum*, 186 N.E.2d 551 (N.Y. 1962)). Here, there was no mutual mistake in that there was no agreement to any terms other than those in the warrants, the provisions of the warrants were all intended, and no intended provision was accidentally omitted. Nor was there any fraud which resulted in a unilateral mistake on the part of the plaintiffs which would have induced the contract. What the present circumstances amount to is, at best, merely a unilateral mistake, namely, a mistake on the part of the corporation to make provision in the terms of the document for the possibility of an alteration in the character of the stock.

Accordingly, I would reverse....

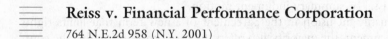

Reiss v. Financial Performance Corporation
764 N.E.2d 958 (N.Y. 2001)

SMITH, J.

Duly executed stock warrants are contracts entitling the holder to purchase a specified number of shares of stock for a specific price during a designated time period. Here, the warrants are enforceable according to their terms. They have all the material provisions necessary to make them enforceable contracts, including number of shares, price, and expiration date, and were drafted by sophisticated and counseled business persons.

That the warrants do not address the contingency of a reverse stock split does not, of itself, create an ambiguity. Even where a contingency has been omitted, we will not necessarily imply a term since "'courts may not by construction add or excise terms, nor distort the meaning of those used and thereby "make a new contract for the parties under the guise of interpreting the writing"'" (*Schmidt, supra,* quoting *Morlee Sales Corp. v. Manufacturers Trust Co.,* 172 N.E.2d 280 (N.Y. 1961)).

Further, *Cofman v. Acton Corp.,* the decision relied upon by the Appellate Division majority, is inapposite here. The Appellate Division, applying the *Cofman* analysis, reasoned that, in the event of a forward stock split, supplying a term providing for the proportionate adjustment of the number of shares that could be purchased, and the exercise price, would be necessary to save the warrant holders from having the value of their warrants "eviscerated." The Appellate Division then followed *Cofman* in taking a second step, reasoning that "just as plaintiffs should not suffer from the possibility of dilution of their warrants resulting from a stock split, so too Financial should not suffer from the consolidation of its shares resulting from a declaration of a reverse stock split." The second step, however, does not necessarily follow from the first. . . .

It may be that Reiss would be entitled to a remedy if Financial performed a forward stock split, on the theory that he "did not intend to acquire nothing" (*Cofman, supra,* 958 F.2d, at 497). We should not assume that one party intended to be placed at the mercy of the other (*Wood v. Duff-Gordon,* 118 N.E. 214 (N.Y. 1917)). It does not follow, however, that Financial should be given a comparable remedy to save it from the consequences of its own agreements and its own decision to perform a reverse stock split.

Chief Judge KAYE and Judges LEVINE, CIPARICK, WESLEY, ROSENBLATT and GRAFFEO concur.

Notes and Questions

1. Notes

a. A provision that adjusts an option to purchase stock in the event of an increase or decrease in outstanding shares is known as an *antidilution provision.*

b. Amelia Bedelia, the housekeeper with the literal mind, is the protagonist of a series of books by Peggy Parish. In one book, she is told to "dust the furniture" so she sprinkles the furniture with talcum powder. In another story she is hired as a file clerk and told to "file these papers." She takes a nail file and shreds them. Consider whether some of the judges involved in this case have read too many Amelia Bedelia books.

2. Reality Check

a. The question of antidilution adjustments is obviously an old one. How can the Appellate Division rule 4-1 in favor of defendant while the Court of Appeals was 7-0 in favor of plaintiffs?

3. Suppose

a. Suppose Financial Performance Corporation, for reasons unconnected with plaintiffs, effected a 5-for-1 stock split. If plaintiffs sued to adjust the warrants so that it could purchase five times as many shares at one-fifth the price per share, how would the court rule and why?

4. What Do You Think?

a. Do you think Justice Saxe's view that, "If stock warrants were deemed automatically adjusted upon consolidations or reclassifications of corporate stock, so that they maintained their proportionate value, there would be no need for the use of warrant agreements to establish the concept of proportional adjustment of stock warrants" is a bit circular?

b. Why is the default rule that no antidilution provision will be assumed? In what setting would parties ever explicitly agree to such a rule? Was it reasonable for Financial Performance Corporation to believe the warrants automatically adjusted for the reverse stock split?

c. If the court should impose an antidilution term, should such a term be symmetrical? In other words, should the warrants adjust when the outstanding shares are either increased or decreased? Or is justice best served by an asymmetrical antidilution provision?

d. Is the court impermissibly interfering with the parties' agreement?

e. How did this problem arise? Which side do you believe was more responsible for the problem? Should the court consider the answers to those questions in deciding who has the better claim?

5. You Draft It

a. Draft a clause for the warrant that clearly adjusts the number of shares and the purchase price in the event of a stock split or reverse stock split. Draft a clause for the warrant that makes clear that no such adjustments will be made.

2. *Background and Context: The Difference Between "Stock Splits" and "Stock Dividends"*

A stock split is different from a stock dividend. Suppose a corporation desires to have twice as many shares outstanding as it currently does, the shareholders are to retain their proportionate interests, and the corporation is to receive no new assets. At the most basic level, it makes no difference whether that doubling of outstanding shares is thought of as an issuance of shares (share dividend) or a division of currently outstanding shares in two (share split). But those two approaches do make a difference in at least three ways. First, where the shares have par value, the first approach — share dividend — means the corporation must increase its capital by at least the aggregate par value of the newly issued shares. By contrast, a share split should mean that the corporation's capital remains constant, but that each share of stock has half the par value it did before.

A second way in which it matters whether a Delaware corporation effects a stock split or a stock dividend is in the mechanics of bringing such an increase about. A share dividend requires only a board of directors resolution if sufficient authorized but unissued shares (or sufficient treasury shares) remain and if the corporation has sufficient surplus to transfer to capital to cover the aggregate par value of the newly issued shares. To split shares in Delaware requires that the Certificate of Incorporation be amended to halve the par value of each currently existing share (and, of course, possibly to increase the number of authorized shares if there are not enough to split the stock). This is a much more cumbersome process and in Delaware, unlike under the MBCA, the board alone does not have the power to amend the Certificate. A review of *Lynam v. Gallagher, supra,* will show that the WTC transactions were clearly stock dividends rather than stock splits. Given the distinction in Delaware do you think the Delaware Supreme Court made the right decision in *Lynam?*

Finally, in trusts and estates the difference between a split and a dividend is important. Documents frequently provide that dividends are to be allocated to the income and splits to the principal. This distinction may make a very large difference to the recipients of the income and the principal, who may well be different, and antagonistic, groups.

The New York Stock Exchange uses another way to distinguish a stock split from a stock dividend. Under this conception, the difference depends upon how many new shares, expressed as a percentage of the currently outstanding shares, are to be outstanding after the increase. If the number of shares is to increase by 25 percent or less (equivalent to a 5-for-4 split) the transaction is considered a stock dividend. If the increase is greater than 25 percent the transaction is considered a stock split. This method of distinguishing splits from dividends is, obviously, completely unrelated to the traditional corporate law method.

The following case highlights the continuing importance of distinguishing between stock splits and stock dividends, whether defined by corporate law niceties or by the New York Stock Exchange approach.

In the Matter of the Estate of Dudley B. Dawson
641 A.2d 1026 (N.J. 1994)

CLIFFORD, J.

This appeal poses the issue of the correct interpretation and application of the term "stock dividend" as used in the testator's will. The narrow question is whether trustees...should allocate eight different stock distributions to income or to principal. The will provided that...the trustees should allocate stock dividends to income and allocate stock splits to principal. The will did not define those terms, however.

Adopting the New York Stock Exchange rule, the trial court characterized stock distributions as dividends if they constituted less than twenty-five percent of the outstanding shares of stock and as splits if they equaled twenty-five percent or more of the outstanding shares. In an unpublished opinion, the Appellate Division reversed the trial court's judgment, rejecting that court's twenty-five-percent rule and relying instead on the traditional approach. We granted certification to determine the correct rule.

The question presented is how to determine whether a distribution is a stock dividend or a stock split when the distribution has characteristics of both types of transactions. In this case, all eight distributions had...transfers from a surplus account to a capital account (indicating stock dividend), but all eight also involved distributions of a large number of shares that affected the market price (indicating stock split).

The traditional approach . . . will find a stock dividend when a corporation transfers assets from surplus . . . , from which a corporation may pay cash dividends, to a capital account, from which a corporation may not pay cash dividends.

Our cases have accepted the traditional approach to stock dividends. Courts from other jurisdictions as well have identified stock dividends by determining whether the issuing corporations transferred funds from a surplus account to stated capital. See, *e.g., Keller Industries, Inc. v. Fineberg,* 203 So. 2d 644, 646 (Fla. Dist. Ct. App. 1967); *Anacomp, Inc. v. Wright,* 449 N.E.2d 610, 617 (Ind. Ct. App. 1983); *In re Estate of Mellott,* 574 P.2d 960, 969 (Kans. App. 1977); *Geier v. Mercantile-Safe Deposit and Trust Co.,* 328 A.2d 311, 321 (Md. 1974); *In re Fosdick's Trust,* 152 N.E.2d 228, 232 (N.Y. 1958); *Millar v. Mountcastle,* 119 N.E.2d 626, 632 (Oh. 1954); *In re Estate of Rees,* 311 P.2d 438, 441 (Or. 1957); *In re Trust Estate of Pew,* 158 A.2d 552, 555 (Pa. 1960).

The [remainder beneficiaries] argue, however, that the traditional approach produces absurd results, that it is outdated, and accordingly that the trial court . . . correctly replaced it with a different rule. We agree.

We are convinced that the better approach is a functional one. We need a rule that more accurately reflects the issuing corporation's intention: whether to reduce the market price of its shares to attract more investors, or to reorganize its capital structure, or to distribute earnings.

The rule that we adopt today is similar to the trial court's bright-line rule that a stock dividend is a distribution of less than twenty-five percent of the sharehold. We modify that rule only to temper its arbitrariness, by treating the twenty-five percent as a rebuttable presumption. Although twenty-five percent is *usually* the maximum share increase for a stock dividend, see New York Stock Exchange, *Listed Company Manual* §703.02 (1983), a twenty-five-percent cut-off may not work well in every case. So complex are stock distributions that we cannot safely discern their character by falling back on generalizations. Accordingly, although twenty-five percent is the presumptive benchmark, courts may look behind a transaction to determine what the issuing corporation intended to accomplish through the transaction.

We therefore adopt a rebuttable presumption that a distribution of less than twenty-five percent is a stock dividend and a distribution of twenty-five percent or more is a stock split. In looking behind the transaction, courts should inquire into all the facts and circumstances surrounding the distribution, including (1) the effect of the distribution on the market price of the stock and (2) the issuing corporation's description of the transaction. We caution that of course a corporation's mere use of the word "dividend" should not be controlling.

The foregoing presumptive rule provides at least two benefits: (1) it better reflects the true nature of stock distributions than does the traditional rule, and (2) it is easy to follow.

Applying that rule to this case, we conclude that all eight distributions are stock splits; accordingly, we direct that the trustees allocate them to principal. All eight transactions involved distributions of more than twenty-five percent of the issuing corporations' respective shareholds (the distributions ranged from fifty percent to 200 percent). Moreover, accompanying all eight distributions was a significant decrease in the market price of the shares (the decreases in stock price ranged from approximately thirty-three percent to sixty-six percent). Further, in most cases the transfers from surplus accounts to capital accounts were quite small. Finally, in seven out of the eight disputed transactions, the issuing corporations themselves characterized the transactions as stock splits. In the remaining case, the issuing corporation put no label on the transaction. Thus, all eight transactions represent stock splits rather than efforts to capitalize assets or to distribute earnings.

For reversal and reinstatement — Justices CLIFFORD, HANDLER, O'HERN, GARIBALDI, and STEIN — 5.

Opposed — None.

Notes and Questions

1. Reality Check

a. Who are the two sides in this dispute? How does the characterization of the transactions as "splits" or "dividends" resolve the dispute?

b. Why does the corporation's intention matter?

2. What Do You Think?

a. The New York Stock Exchange requires corporations to use the term *split* if possible or, if necessary, the phrase, "stock split effected by a stock dividend." See *NYSE Listed Company Manual* §703.02. Do you think the court was aware of this requirement?

b. In this setting, is it meaningful to try to resolve the issue by reference to the testator's intent?

3. You Draft It

a. Draft a clause for the will that clearly effects Dawson's intent. Draft a clause for the will that effects the court's holding.

B. MAKING A PROFIT PART II: SALE OF STOCK BY SHAREHOLDERS

Paying dividends is one way shareholders make a profit on their investment. The other way is by selling their stock for more than they paid for it. The norm in the corporate form is that ownership — that is, stock — may be transferred by its owner without any restrictions. While this may seem unremarkable, it actually is one of the key advantages of the corporate form over the partnership model. In a partnership, only a portion of a partner's ownership interest may be transferred. The partner remains connected to the partnership and, equally importantly, the transferee does not become a partner by virtue of the transfer. He or she simply accedes to some of the transferring partner's rights.

Free alienability of shares is bound up with shareholders' limited liability, although the link is not immediately obvious. Because shareholders are (with notable exceptions described in Chapter 8) liable only for paying in full for their shares, it does not matter to creditors who the shareholders are as long as the shares have been fully paid for. Likewise, as an economic matter it does not matter to the shareholders who the other shareholders are. Because of this indifference to the identity of the shareholder, there is no economic reason to prohibit the transfer of shares. Once a shareholder has sold a share, he or she has no further interest and the buyer becomes a shareholder, exactly as the seller was. Given these economic virtues and the distinction between the corporate and partnership attitudes toward owners' interests, courts have long approached restrictions on transfer with suspicion. The classic judicial incantation is that courts will construe such restrictions narrowly.

In light of this preference for free alienation, why do shareholders want to restrict transfer? There are two main reasons. One is that even though shareholders are indifferent economically about the identity of other shareholders, they may care very much as a matter of management. Particularly where the corporation is closely held, it may be a central expectation of all investors that their coinvestors will remain shareholders for the long term. Second, there may be regulatory reasons to ensure that a corporation's shareholders meet certain criteria. For example, to maintain its status as a Subchapter S corporation, all of the shareholders must (with limited exceptions) be individuals. Similarly, to be exempt from federal securities regulations regarding registration, the number of shareholders may be limited or their residence may be restricted to only one state.

It is intuitive to think of *restrictions on transfer* as meaning limitations on a shareholder's power to sell, give, or bequeath shares. This is true, but restrictions on transfer can also mean an obligation to transfer. In other words, sometimes a shareholder may be required to transfer his or her shares even though the shares are not callable and the shareholder does not desire to part with them. Concomitantly, the corporation or other shareholders may be required to purchase a shareholder's shares even though they do not wish to do so.

Shareholders may be compelled to transfer their shares in certain circumstances so that the other shareholders can, in effect, have influence over the management or so that the existing shareholders will have a kind of right of survivorship. Conversely, the corporation or the other shareholders may be compelled to purchase shares to provide the shareholder with cash in some settings. The most frequent triggering of this power is the shareholder's death. Requiring the corporation or other shareholders to buy a deceased shareholder's shares ensures that suffient money will be available to pay estate taxes and ensures that the shareholder's heirs have a means of exit because they may well not wish to be shareholders of a closely held corporation and would otherwise have little realistic hope of finding a buyer for their shares. Corporate planners typically have the corporation buy life insurance policies on the lives of the shareholders whose shares are subject to repurchase to ensure that the corporation will have sufficient money to pay for that shareholder's shares.

Because restrictions on share transfers are disfavored by courts, every corporations statute explicitly provides that certain restrictions are enforceable. Both the MBCA and the DGCL provide that restrictions are enforceable for any reasonable purpose, including maintaining the corporation's status under tax or securities laws. See MBCA §6.27(c); DGCL §202(c), (d). Both statutes also permit a prohibition on transfer that either limits transfer to certain classes of transferees (provided those classes are reasonable) or requires prior consent of the corporation or other shareholders. See MBCA §6.27(d)(3), (4); DGCL §202(c)(3), (5).

Restrictions on transfer may require transfer or may grant an option to purchase to either the corporation, the other shareholders, or both seriatim. See MBCA §6.27(d)(1), (2); DGCL §202(c)(1), (2), (4). Note also that a restriction that requires a transfer is sometimes called a *buy-sell agreement* meaning that both sides are required to effect a transaction. Often lay people, and sometimes even lawyers and courts, loosely refer to any agreement restricting transfer as a buy-sell agreement. Note also that frequently courts and lawyers mistakenly refer to such an option as a "preemptive right." As you remember, a preemptive right is the right of existing shareholders to purchase (preempt the issuance of) additional shares the *corporation* intends to issue. Here, this option is a right of first refusal to purchase shares from a *shareholder*.

Although restrictions on transfer are sometimes placed in the Articles of Incorporation, they are more frequently found in bylaws or in shareholder contracts that may also be entered into by the corporation itself. Sometimes the restriction is triggered when a shareholder wishes to transfer shares inter vivos such as when he or she wishes to sell to a third party or give shares to his or her children or other relatives. Other times the restriction is triggered even though the shareholder has no desire to transfer to anyone, such as when the shareholder dies or is divorced. The following cases show common settings and common problems involved in drafting and enforcing restrictions on alienation of shares.

Harrison v. NetCentric Corp.

744 N.E.2d 622 (Mass. 2001)

COWIN, J.

The plaintiff filed a complaint against his former employer, NetCentric Corporation (NetCentric); its chief executive officer, Sean O'Sullivan (O'Sullivan); four of its directors; and two venture capital firms that invested in NetCentric (collectively, the defendants). The plaintiff alleged that the defendants breached their fiduciary duty of utmost good faith and loyalty; breached the implied covenant of good faith and fair dealing; [and] wrongfully terminated his employment....All of the plaintiff's claims stem from his termination as an officer of NetCentric and the company's attempt to repurchase from him certain shares of his stock pursuant to a stock restriction agreement (stock agreement). The defendants asserted a counterclaim for specific enforcement of the purchase option provision of the stock agreement. A Superior Court judge allowed the defendants' motion for summary judgment on all the plaintiff's claims and...on their counterclaim. The plaintiff appealed from the grant of summary judgment,[3] and we transferred the case to this court on our own motion. We affirm the judgment of the Superior Court.

Background. In 1994, the plaintiff, O'Sullivan, and his brother, Donal O'Sullivan (Donal) (collectively, the founders) discussed forming a business entity to develop a medium for delivering facsimile transmissions across the world by way of the internet. The founders agreed to a stock ownership arrangement whereby O'Sullivan would receive approximately 4.5 million shares, the plaintiff 2.9 million shares, and Donal 1.5 million shares. They incorporated NetCentric the following year under Delaware law and established offices in Massachusetts.

O'Sullivan was named the chief executive officer and a director. At some point, he became the chairman of the board as well. The plaintiff served initially as the company's president, later as its vice-president of sales and marketing, and as a director.

---

3. The plaintiff did not appeal from the judgment with respect to his wrongful termination claim.

The plaintiff executed a stock agreement and an employee noncompetition, non-disclosure, and developments agreement (noncompetition agreement). His stock agreement, executed May 16, 1995, provided that he would purchase 2,944,842 shares of stock in NetCentric at $0.001 a share. Forty per cent of the shares (1,177,938) would vest* on May 1, 1996, and an additional five per cent (147,242) would vest each succeeding quarter, until all the shares were vested. According to the agreement, if the plaintiff ceased to be employed by NetCentric "for any reason . . . with or without cause," the company had the right to buy back his unvested shares at the original purchase price.

Both the plaintiff's stock agreement and his noncompetition agreement contained clauses providing that the agreements did not give the plaintiff any right to be retained as an employee of NetCentric and that each agreement represented the entire agreement between the parties and superseded all prior agreements and understandings relating to the same subject matter. In addition, the agreements contained a choice of law provision, providing that they "shall be construed, interpreted and enforced in accordance with the laws of the Commonwealth of Massachusetts."

In June, 1996, Donal's employment was terminated, and the company exercised its right pursuant to Donal's stock agreement to buy back his unvested shares. In September, 1996, the plaintiff's employment was terminated. At that time, forty-five per cent of the plaintiff's shares (1,325,180) had vested; the remaining fifty-five per cent (1,619,662) had not vested. A month later, NetCentric notified the plaintiff in writing that it was exercising its right pursuant to the stock agreement to buy back the plaintiff's unvested shares. The plaintiff has refused to tender the shares to the company.

During and after the time that Donal and the plaintiff were fired, NetCentric was in the process of hiring additional staff. New employees often were offered stock options in the company, issued from the employee stock option pool (pool), as part of their compensation packages. Some employee-shareholders expressed concern that this practice of authorizing new shares from the corporate treasury for issuance to new hires would dilute the value of their shares. Existing shares would not be diluted, however, if NetCentric acquired outstanding shares and offered those to new employees.

After Donal was fired, the number of shares in the pool was increased by the same number that NetCentric had repurchased from him. Within one month after the plaintiff's employment was terminated, NetCentric hired a president and two vice-presidents, one of whom replaced the plaintiff as vice-president of sales. All three new employees were granted stock options, totaling 1,812,500 shares.

Breach of fiduciary duty. Initially, we must resolve a choice of law question. As a minority shareholder in a close corporation, the plaintiff maintains that the defendants owed him a duty of good faith and loyalty and that they breached this duty by terminating his employment in order to repurchase his unvested shares. This claim is based on Massachusetts law, which provides that shareholders in a close corporation owe each other the duty of "utmost good faith and loyalty." *Wilkes v. Springside Nursing Home, Inc.,* 353 N.E.2d 657 (Mass. 1976) . . . ; *Donahue v. Rodd Electrotype Co. of New England, Inc.,* 328 N.E.2d 505 (Mass. 1975). . . .

The defendants claim, however, that Massachusetts law is of no avail to the plaintiff, as Massachusetts law is inapplicable to his fiduciary duty claim; NetCentric

---

* "Vest" in this context means the shares were not subject to a contractual obligation to sell. ED.

is a Delaware corporation, Delaware law applies and Delaware law does not impose the heightened fiduciary duty of utmost good faith and loyalty on shareholders in a close corporation. See *Riblet Prods. Corp. v. Nagy*, 683 A.2d 37, 39 (Del. 1996) (noting that Delaware has not adopted duty of utmost good faith and loyalty established in *Wilkes v. Springside Nursing Home, Inc., supra*); *Nixon v. Blackwell*, 626 A.2d 1366, 1380-1381 (Del. 1993) (declining "to fashion a special judicially-created rule for minority investors"). Instead, under Delaware law, minority shareholders can protect themselves by contract (i.e., negotiate for protection in stock agreements or employment contracts) before investing in the corporation. Additionally, founding shareholders can elect to incorporate the company as a statutory close corporation under Delaware law, which provides special relief to shareholders of such corporations.[7]

Traditionally, we have applied the law of the State of incorporation in matters relating to the internal affairs of a corporation (including both closely and widely held corporations), such as the fiduciary duty owed to shareholders.

Today, we adhere to and reaffirm our policy that the State of incorporation dictates the choice of law regarding the internal affairs of a corporation. Our decision accords with that of a majority of the jurisdictions that have addressed this issue. Similarly, our policy is consistent with the *Restatement (Second) of Conflict of Laws* §302 (1971)....All three founders, including the plaintiff, deliberately chose to incorporate in Delaware. By so doing, they "determine[d] the body of law that [would] govern the internal affairs of the corporation and the conduct of their directors....The corporation and its shareholders rightfully expect that the laws under which they have chosen to do business will be applied." *Hart v. General Motors Corp.*, 517 N.Y.S.2d 490 (N.Y. App. Div. 1987).

As NetCentric is, and always has been, a Delaware corporation, Delaware law applies to the plaintiff's claim that the defendants breached their fiduciary duty.[10] Because Delaware law does not impose a heightened fiduciary duty on shareholders in a close corporation,... summary judgment was properly granted to the defendants on this claim.

Breach of implied covenant of good faith and fair dealing. The plaintiff next claims that the defendants violated the implied covenant of good faith and fair dealing implicit in all Massachusetts contracts, including contracts for employment at will. See *Fortune v. National Cash Register Co.*, 364 N.E.2d 1251 (Mass. 1977). The *Fortune* case and its progeny provide that an employer is accountable to a discharged employee for unpaid compensation if the employee were terminated in bad faith and the compensation is clearly connected to work already performed. The plaintiff argues that the defendants terminated his employment in bad faith because they were trying to prevent his remaining shares from vesting; that his unvested shares

---

7. The special protections apply only to a corporation "designated as a 'close corporation' in its certificate of incorporation, and which fulfills other requirements, including a limitation to 30 on the number of stockholders, that all classes of stock have to have at least one restriction on transfer, and that there be no 'public offering.'" *Nixon v. Blackwell*, 626 A.2d 1366, 1380 (Del. 1993), citing [DGCL] 8, §342. There is no claim that NetCentric is a statutory close corporation under Delaware law.

10. That the plaintiff's stock and noncompetition agreements provide that they are governed by Massachusetts law does not mean that the plaintiff's breach of fiduciary duty claim must also be governed by the law of this State. The Restatement distinguishes between the law that governs corporate acts with respect to third persons and the law that governs the corporation's relationship to its shareholders. See *Restatement (Second) of Conflicts of Laws, supra* §302 comment e, at 309 ("There is no reason why corporate acts [such as the making of contracts] should not be governed by the local law of different states").

represent compensation previously earned; and that he was unlawfully deprived of this compensation by the defendants' attempt to repurchase his unvested shares.

In support of his contention, the plaintiff relies on the fact that he accepted a salary substantially lower than he had received in recent years because of the equity he received in NetCentric and because he expected he would be retained at least until his stock had fully vested. He also cites the fact that other employees received only stock options, while the founders received shares up front. . . .

The defendants did not deprive the plaintiff of any income that he reasonably earned or to which he was entitled. His shares vested over time only if he continued to be employed; thus, the unvested shares are not earned compensation for past services, but compensation contingent on his continued employment. The plaintiff's argument to the contrary is belied by the terms of his stock agreement. At the time the plaintiff's employment was terminated, forty-five percent of his shares had vested. He had not yet earned the remaining fifty-five percent. These unvested shares were contingent on the plaintiff providing future services for NetCentric. . . .

The defendants' counterclaim. The defendants filed a counterclaim seeking the return of the plaintiff's unvested shares. Pursuant to the plaintiff's stock agreement, NetCentric has the right to repurchase these shares if the plaintiff ceases working for the company for any reason and the company exercises its right in writing within sixty days after the plaintiff's termination. The plaintiff is then required to tender his unvested shares to NetCentric within ten days. It is undisputed that the plaintiff was fired, that fifty-five percent of his shares were unvested, and that he received a letter from NetCentric exercising its repurchase rights within sixty days of his discharge. The plaintiff has refused to tender his unvested shares to the company. Accordingly, the defendants were entitled to summary judgment on their counterclaim.

We affirm the Superior Court's order allowing the defendants' motion for summary judgment on the plaintiff's claims and the defendants' counterclaim.

So ordered.

Notes and Questions

1. Notes

a. The provisions of the stock agreement and noncompetition agreement are typical for start-up corporations financed with venture capital.

b. Note that NetCentric is defunct. Where a corporation's assets consist primarily of assets that cannot easily be used in other contexts (such as intellectual property that has been shown to be not commercially viable) the corporation may not bother declaring bankruptcy. There simply is no purpose in going through bankruptcy because there are so few assets available for creditors.

2. Reality Check

a. What are the theories of Harrison's claim that the court discusses?

b. According to Harrison, why did NetCentric terminate his employment?

c. What are the two legal standards for finding a breach of fiduciary duty? How does the court choose between the two?

3. Suppose

a. Suppose the court had applied Massachusetts law of fiduciary duty? Would the analysis or result have been different?

4. What Do You Think?

a. NetCentric, like nearly all venture capital financed entities, is a Delaware corporation. Given the analysis and result in this case, do you think corporate planners should have the power to choose rules of fiduciary duties?

b. Do you think it is fair that Harrison was required to sell his stock back at exactly the same price as he purchased it for?

Man o' War Restaurants, Inc. v. Martin
932 S.W.2d 366 (Ky. 1996)

LAMBERT, J.

When John Martin, Jr., was hired as manager of appellant's Sizzler Restaurant, he was permitted to purchase 25% of the stock in the corporation for the sum of $1,000. However, according to the terms of his five-year employment contract, Martin was required to return the stock in exchange for the amount he paid if his employment was terminated during the five-year term. Otherwise Martin's ownership of the stock was unrestricted. As a member of the board of directors, Martin participated in stock dividends, and was at liberty to sell his stock for whatever sum the market would have produced. Less than three years after the contract was entered into, Martin's employment was terminated and demand was made for return of the stock. This litigation followed.

A number of subsidiary issues and arguments have been raised which tend to distract from our analysis. Variously, contentions are made that the purchase price was a nominal price; that other shareholders, by virtue of their wealth, incurred greater financial risk than Martin; that Martin lacked the financial capability to obtain a franchise on his own; and that the stock was "given" for the purpose of performance motivation. It had also been suggested that appellant had a powerful incentive to terminate Martin's employment and thereby acquire stock of a substantial value for a modest sum; or that the stock was sold at a reduced price in lieu of greater compensation. While some or all of these factors may have been present, they are not reflected in the parties' contract or in the trial court's relevant findings of fact.

Under the contract, the Board of Directors was authorized to terminate appellee's employment for any reasonable cause. Martin sued challenging the termination of his employment and contended that appellant was without sufficient cause to terminate. From the evidence the trial court held otherwise. As its findings of fact were not clearly erroneous, we are bound thereby. For purposes of this analysis, we fully accept that sufficient cause was shown for Martin's termination and that it was not in bad faith or for the purpose of improperly obtaining his stock. While fully accepting that appellee was rightfully terminated...we must nevertheless determine whether the stock repurchase provision...is enforceable. In our view, the fact of appellee's "for cause" termination is not decisive.

In support of its decision to enforce the stock return provision, the trial court found that appellant's executive officer, Robert Langley, had a policy to have franchise managers acquire an ownership interest. In this vein the trial court also found facts such as appellee's having earned more from this employment than from previous employment. Frankly, we fail to see how Langley's business policy or appellee's greater earnings with this employer has anything to do with the enforceability of the stock surrender provision. It could be argued that Langley's policy should be construed in appellee's favor as Langley was serving his own purpose by vesting appellee with stock ownership.

Rather than risk being led astray by the subtleties and nuances urged by the parties, we feel greater confidence if our focus is limited to the certain facts without gloss or adornment. The facts are that for valuable consideration, appellee purchased stock in the appellant corporation. A provision of the contract provided that upon termination of appellee's employment by appellant, appellee would be required to return the stock which he had purchased in exchange for the sum originally paid. Whether a contract provision which compels the transfer of property without regard to its value or without resort to a formula for equitable compensation is enforceable under Kentucky law is the question we must answer.

Meticulously we have examined the view expressed on this issue by the Court of Appeals. [T]he court said:

> [T]he stock return provision of the Agreement operated as a forfeiture or penalty for breach of a contract and, therefore, is unenforceable. Martin is both a minority stock-holder and he was also an employee. Terms of the Agreement which require a return of the stock at the price paid, without interest or appreciation, is to us a form of unreasonably excessive liquidated damages. In our view, the only way the stock return provision in the employment contract can be upheld is if Martin is paid book value or fair market value for the stock. To hold otherwise would require Martin to forfeit the enhanced value of his stock. Equity detests forfeiture provisions and frequently will find them unenforceable.

We fully agree with this view and adopt it hereby. We hasten to add, however, that book value or fair market value may not be the exclusive point of reference for ascertainment of equitable compensation in "buy-back" circumstances, if the contract so provides. Courts have approved various formulae for price determination and in general have given considerable deference to the parties' agreements. We are reluctant to invalidate contracts which have been negotiated by parties but feel compelled by principles of equity and fair-dealing to take such a step here. The stock return provision made no reference to any concept of value. It was utterly arbitrary and inimical to the concept of property ownership. One who may be compelled to surrender property to another for a sum which bears no relationship to the value of the property can hardly be said to be an owner.

A corporation and its shareholders are allowed to contract for a re-purchase or "buy-back" right. This right enables the corporation to reacquire shares on the occurrence of certain events whether or not the holder wants to sell. Such an event may be retirement, or as in this case, termination of employment. The exercise of such a right requires that a valuation be placed on the stock. All accepted valuation methods take into consideration the corporation's fiscal performance as well as its current financial condition. We note that if Martin had died before termination, his estate would have realized the appreciated value rather than the original issue price.

The flaw in this contract is its failure to recognize that upon transfer of the stock to Martin, he held it independently of his status as an employee. At that moment the stock became his property and strong public policy against forfeiture protects property from being taken without appropriate compensation.

If appellant had wished to avoid vesting Martin with an ownership interest, it would have been an easy matter to have created stock options exercisable upon the occurrence of definite events, after a certain date, or with regard to some other objective measures. By the terms of the contract, it would not have been in appellant's best financial interest to have kept Martin. Such a circumstance is so totally against sound public policy that we cannot sustain it.

STEPHENS, C.J., and BAKER, GRAVES, KING, LAMBERT, STUMBO and WINTERSHEIMER, JJ., concur.

Notes and Questions

1. Notes

a. The corporation was owned equally by Martin and three other shareholders, each of whom paid $1,000 for 100 shares. The corporation apparently declared and paid dividends monthly. Martin's employment agreement provided for a $27,000 per year salary in addition to any dividends. See Jonathan M. Skeeters, Man O War Restaurants, Inc. v. Martin: *Law Altering Economic Performance*, 88 Ky. L.J. 135, 143 (2000).

b. Martin was the plaintiff in this action.

c. As you see from this case and *Harrison*, employees are often shareholders, as well.

2. Reality Check

a. Why did Man o' War Restaurants give Martin the shares?

b. How did Man o' War Restaurants and Martin benefit from the agreement as written?

c. Why do you think the shares were subject to repurchase upon Martin's termination but not otherwise?

d. What aspect(s) of the repurchase agreement were invalid? Which were valid?

3. Suppose

a. What if the repurchase agreement had provided that the shares must be resold for the purchase price increased by 10 percent per year? Would that agreement have been enforced? Suppose the contract increased the purchase price by 1 percent per year. Enforced?

b. Suppose Martin suspected he was about to be terminated and sold his shares to a friend just before termination. Would the transferee have been bound by the transfer restriction? If not, could Martin repurchase the shares from the friend after his termination and keep them?

4. What Do You Think?

a. Do *Man o' War Restaurants* and *Harrison* deal with the same issue? If not, how and why are the issues different?

b. Do you think Harrison could have made the same argument Martin did?

c. Do you agree with Justice Lambert that "upon transfer of the stock to Martin, he held it independently of his status as an employee"? If so, why did Man o' War Restaurants give Martin his shares? If not, how should his employee status affect the interpretation of the repurchase agreement?

d. Harrison alleged the purpose of his termination was to get his stock so it could be given to other employees. The court held that that purpose was valid. In *Man o' War Restaurants*, the court specifically held that the purpose of Martin's termination was not to get his stock, yet the court refused to enforce the repurchase agreement as written. Can these holdings be reconciled?

5. You Draft It

a. Redraft the restriction on transfer that effects Man o' War Restaurant's intentions and would be enforced by the Supreme Court of Kentucky. The relevant language of Martin's employment contract reads,

> If Employee owns stock in Employer and this Agreement is terminated under paragraph 9 hereof [permitting termination for, *inter alia*, any reasonable cause] or by the voluntary action of Employee, then Employee shall tender to Employer for purchase by it all of his stock in Employer, the purchase price of which stock shall be a return of the consideration paid by Employee for such stock, without interest.

Jonathan M. Skeeters, Man O War Restaurants, Inc. v. Martin: *Law Altering Economic Performance*, 88 Ky. L.J. 135, 144 (2000)

When drafting a restriction on transfer, the parties must decide upon the price and terms for any required transfers or options. Where the restriction is in the form of a right of first refusal triggered by a shareholder's desire to transfer shares to an outsider, the parties often provide that the option may be exercised only at the price and on the terms agreed to by the shareholder and outside party. In other settings, the most difficult planning and drafting aspect typically is deciding on the price at which the shares will be transferred. There are three basic approaches to this problem. First, the parties may establish a formula for determining the price. This is usually based upon an accounting concept such as book value, earnings, or cash flow at some date near to the restriction's triggering event.

Second, the parties may establish a price in the agreement and may agree that, in the future, they will review or revise the price. In the majority of cases, the parties never review the price once the agreement has been reached. This leaves them, and the courts, with the choice of either transferring the shares at a price the parties may not have intended or guessing what the parties would have agreed to had they revised the price. Third, the parties may provide that one or more neutral appraisers or arbitrators will determine the price based on a standard such as "fair value," "fair market value," or "value as a going concern." This approach may have considerable uncertainty, especially if the corporation's business is unique or difficult to value. It is also expensive and may require significant outlays of money at a time (for example the death of a key shareholder) when prudence would suggest that the corporation conserve its resources.

Note that the parties may not be seeking to find a way to set a price that is "fair" in the sense of representing the price a willing buyer and willing seller would likely agree to. Instead, the parties may deliberately provide a mechanism that undervalues the shares. This may be intended to act as an *in terrorem* inducement to the shareholders to avoid triggering the restrictions or may be to provide as low a value as realistically possible to minimize the value of the shares in the hands of a deceased shareholder's estate and hence minimize estate taxes.

In addition to the question of providing a price, the parties need to consider whether every possible divestment of shares should be subject to the restrictions. A frequent exemption from restriction is a provision allowing a shareholder to leave shares by will to a surviving spouse or direct descendants. Another exemption may be for shares transferred between spouses. Another possible exemption is all or certain gratuitous transfers, which allows shareholders to give shares to direct descendants inter vivos, which may be useful for estate planning purposes. All of these issues present questions of ascertaining your client's best interests, ensuring that all parties are in agreement on the solutions, and providing written documents that effect those solutions. This is an area in which many practicing lawyers make serious mistakes, often because they rely on forms for language they simply adopt in their own agreements without ensuring that the language is suitable.

Because restrictions on transfer are strictly construed in favor of alienation, lawyers and their clients must be careful to be explicit in describing the transfers that are prohibited and to understand that those transfers that are not definitely prohibited are likely to be permitted by a court. A relatively frequent issue is involuntary transfers and transfers by operation of law. Shares that are transferred by a court order in a marital dissolution case or shares that pass by intestacy are common examples.

The following case deals with several problematic areas regarding restrictions on transfer.

F.B.I. Farms, Inc. v. Moore
798 N.E.2d 440 (Ind. 2003)

BOEHM, J.

F.B.I. Farms, Inc., was formed in 1976 by Ivan and Thelma Burger, their children, Linda and Freddy, and the children's spouses. Each of the three couples transferred a farm and related machinery to the corporation in exchange for common stock in the corporation. At the time, Birchell Moore ["Birchell"] was married to Linda.

In 1977, the Board of Directors of F.B.I. consisted of [Birchell], Ivan, Freddy and Linda. The minutes of a 1977 meeting of the Board recite that the following restrictions on the transfer of shares were "adopted":

1) No stock of said corporation shall be transferred, assigned and/or exchanged or divided, unless or until approved by the Directors thereof;

2) That if any stock be offered for sale, assigned and/or transferred, the corporation should have the first opportunity of purchasing the same at no more than the book value thereof;

3) Should said corporation be not interested, and could not economically offer to purchase said stock, any stockholder of record should be given the next opportunity to purchase said stock, at a price not to exceed the book value thereof;

4) That if the corporation was not interested in the stock, and any stockholders were not interested therein, then the same could be sold to any blood mem-

ber of the family. Should they be desirous of purchasing the same, then at not more than the book value thereof.

Linda's marriage to [Birchell] was dissolved in 1982. As part of the dissolution proceedings, Linda was awarded all of the F.B.I. shares and [Birchell] was awarded a monetary judgment in the amount of $155,889.80, secured by a lien on Linda's shares.

[Birchell]'s judgment against Linda remained unsatisfied, and in April 1998 he sought a writ of execution of his lien. A sheriff's sale went forward and in February 2000 [Birchell] purchased all 2,924 shares owned by Linda at the time for $290,450.67. In December 2000 [Birchell] instituted this suit against F.B.I., its shareholders, and Linda seeking a declaratory judgment that . . . [Birchell] properly retained ownership of the shares, and that the shares were unencumbered by restrictions and were freely transferable.

TRANSFER RESTRICTIONS

A. General Principles

Most of the issues in this case are resolved by the Indiana statute governing share transfer restrictions. Corporate shares are personal property. At common law, any restriction on the power to alienate personal property was impermissible. Despite this doctrine, Indiana, like virtually all jurisdictions, allows corporations and their shareholders to impose restrictions on transfers of shares. The basic theory of these statutes is to permit owners of a corporation to control its ownership and management and prevent outsiders from inserting themselves into the operations of the corporation. Chief Justice Holmes stated the matter succinctly a century ago: "Stock in a corporation is not merely property. It also creates a personal relation analogous otherwise than technically to a partnership. . . . [T]here seems to be no greater objection to retaining the right of choosing one's associates in a corporation than in a firm." *Barrett v. King*, 63 N.E. 934, 935 (Mass. 1902). As applied to a family-owned corporation, this remains valid today.

Transfer restrictions are treated as contracts either between shareholders or between shareholders and the corporation.[1] Apart from any statutory requirements, restrictions on transfer are to be read, like any other contract, to further the manifest intention of the parties. Because they are restrictions on alienation and therefore disfavored, the terms in the restrictions are not to be expanded beyond their plain and ordinary meaning.

For a party to be bound by share transfer restrictions, that party must have notice of the restrictions. [MBCA §6.27](b). Here, the restrictions on transfer of F.B.I. shares were neither "noted conspicuously" on the certificates nor contained in the information statement referred to in [MBCA §6.27](b), but there is no doubt that [Birchell], the buyer at the sheriff's sale, had notice of the restrictions. He was therefore bound by them.

---

1. The Indiana statute provides that restrictions are valid if included in the articles, the bylaws, an agreement among shareholders or an agreement between the corporation and shareholders. [MBCA §6.27](a). None of these was done here. However, no one challenges the restrictions as defective in their initial adoption. At least as to [Birchell], who approved them as a director and had actual knowledge of them, under these circumstances, the restrictions constitute a contract as to all of those shareholders who approved the adoption of the restrictions.

Finally, a closely held corporation is a "corporation in which all of the outstanding stock is held by just a few individuals, or by a small group of persons belonging to a single family." J.R. Kemper, *Validity of "Consent Restraint" on Transfer of Shares of Close Corporation*, 69 A.L.R.3d 1327, 1328 (1976). In 1977, F.B.I. plainly fell within that description; it was owned by six individuals, all members of a single family. Closely held corporations have a viable interest in remaining the organization they envision at incorporation and transfer restrictions are an appropriate means of maintaining the status quo.

B. Rights of First Refusal

Paragraphs (2) and (3) of the restrictions created rights of first refusal in F.B.I. and its shareholders. A transfer in violation of restrictions is voidable at the insistence of the corporation. F.B.I. and its shareholders argue that [Birchell] should have been obliged to offer the shares to the corporation or a shareholder pursuant to those provisions. [Birchell] responds, and the Court of Appeals agreed, that he was not a shareholder until he purchased the shares at the sheriff's sale. He contends he therefore had no power to offer the shares. This misses the point that before Linda could transfer her shares, she was obliged to offer them to F.B.I. and the other shareholders. [Birchell] was on notice of that requirement. [Birchell], as the buyer, had the right to demand that Linda initiate the process to exercise or waive the right to first refusal.

Thus, if the corporation had insisted on its right of first refusal, Linda would have been obliged to sell to F.B.I. (or its shareholders). And [Birchell], as a buyer on notice of the restrictions, had the right to insist that that process go forward. But the corporation and its shareholders were aware of the sheriff's sale and did nothing to assert the right of first refusal. They cannot sit back and let the sale go forward, await future events, then claim a right to purchase on the same terms as [Birchell]. In sum, F.B.I. and its shareholders had rights of first refusal, but failed to exercise them. As a result, the sale to [Birchell] proceeded as if the shares had been offered and the corporation refused the opportunity. To hold otherwise would be to give F.B.I. and its shareholders a perpetual option to purchase but no obligation to do so. Having failed to demand their right to buy at the time of the sale, the rights of first refusal gave them no ability to upset the sale conducted by the sheriff.

C. Restrictions on Transfer with Board Approval

The restrictions "adopted" in paragraphs (1) and (4) are more problematic. Indiana's statute, reflecting the common law, requires that restrictions on share transfers be reasonable. [MBCA §6.27](c)(3), (d)(3), and (d)(4). The general common law doctrine surrounding evaluation of the reasonableness of restrictions is well established. A restriction is reasonable if it is designed to serve a legitimate purpose of the party imposing the restraint and the restraint is not an absolute restriction on the recipient's right of alienability. The Indiana statute is somewhat more generous in allowing restrictions on classes of buyers unless "manifestly unreasonable." [MBCA §6.27](d)(4). Several factors are relevant in determining the reasonableness of any transfer restriction, including the size of the corporation, the degree of restraint upon alienation; the time the restriction was to continue in effect, the method to be used in determining the transfer price of shares, the likelihood of the restriction's contributing to the attainment of corporate objectives, the possibility that a hostile stockholder might injure the corporation, and the probability of the restriction's promoting the best interests of the corporation. At one extreme, a restriction that merely prescribes procedures that must be observed before stock may be transferred is not unreasonable. At the other end of the spectrum, restrictions that are fraudulent, oppressive, unconscionable, ... or the result of a breach of the fiduciary duty that shareholders in a close corporation owe to one another, will not be upheld. The restrictions on F.B.I.'s shares, like most, are somewhere in the middle. They impose substantive limitations on transfer, but are not alleged to be the result of fraud or breach of fiduciary duty.

The trial court, in its order granting partial summary judgment, concluded that the restriction precluding transfer without Board approval was reasonable at the time that it was adopted, but the lengthy and difficult history between the parties had rendered the restriction unreasonable. Under basic contract law principles, the reasonableness of a term of a contract is evaluated at the time of its adoption. The same is true of share transfer restrictions. As a result, evaluating the reasonableness of the restrictions in light of subsequent developments is inappropriate. For that reason, we do not agree that the restriction requiring director approval became unreasonable based upon events and disputes within the family that occurred after the restrictions had been adopted. To be sure, the parties find themselves in a difficult dispute as is sometimes the case in a family business following a dissolution. But when F.B.I. was formed and the family farms were effectively pooled, the shareholders agreed that the Board would be permitted to restrict access to the shares. To the extent that restriction devalues the shares in the hands of any individual shareholder by reason of lack of transferability, it is the result of the bargain they struck. The policy behind enforcement of these restrictions is to encourage entering into formal partnerships by permitting all parties to have confidence they will not involuntarily end up with an undesired co-venturer. Presumably for that reason, the statute permits a restriction that requires a transferee to be approved by the Board of Directors, and to that extent may severely limit transferability.

A "consent restriction" such as this has been considered unreasonable by some courts. However, the General Assembly has allowed precisely this type of restriction in [MBCA §6.27](d)(3). That section provides that transfer restrictions may require the approval of "the corporation, the holders of any class of its shares, or another person" before the shares may be transferred. Board approval is one permissible way of implementing approval by "the Corporation" under this section.

D. Restrictions on Transfer Except to "Blood Members of the Family"

We also find the "blood-member" restriction to be enforceable as protecting a viable interest. These are family farmers in corporate form. It is apparent from the nature of the corporation that the Burger family had an interest in maintaining ownership and operation of F.B.I. in the hands of family members. Although one may quibble with the terminology, and there may be some individuals where status as blood members is debatable, we think it plain enough that all parties to this dispute either are or are not blood members of the Burger family. All are either direct descendants of Ivan or spouses of Ivan or of one of his children.

RESTRICTIONS AS APPLIED TO INVOLUNTARY TRANSFERS

The Court of Appeals held that the restrictions on Linda's shares did not apply by their terms to the sheriff's sale and, as a result, did not bar the sheriff's sale to [Birchell]. We agree that [Birchell] acquired the shares at the sheriff's sale, but not because the restrictions were inapplicable by their terms.

The Court of Appeals relied on cases stating that involuntary transfers fall within the terms of a restriction only if the language of the restrictions specifically identifies them. This doctrine has been developed largely in cases involving intestate transfers by a decedent,... and in marriage dissolution proceedings where a transfer is made to a spouse.

The sheriff's sale where [Birchell] purchased Linda's shares was an involuntary transfer. Transfers ordered incident to marriage dissolutions and transfers under intestate law may also be deemed involuntary. We think the governing principle is not the same for all forms of "involuntary" transfers. The language of the restrictions in this case does not specifically refer to involuntary transfers of any kind. Rather, it seems to contemplate restricting all transfers, voluntary and involuntary, by providing that no stock of the corporation should be "transferred, assigned, exchanged, divided, or sold" without complying with the restrictions. The intent of the parties is thus rather plain: to restrict ownership to the designated group, and to preclude transfer by any means. The question is whether that intent should be permitted to prevail in the face of countervailing policies.

Transfer by intestacy is in some sense involuntary, but it may also be viewed as a voluntary act of the decedent who had the option to leave a will. If a transfer could not be made by gift during lifetime, for example, to an offspring regarded by other shareholders as an undesirable partner, we see no reason to permit it at death by the decedent's choice to die intestate. There are, however, forms of involuntary transfers that a private agreement may not prevent because the agreement would unreasonably interfere with the rights of third parties. In a dissolution, the interests of the spouse require permitting transfer over the stated intent of the parties. Similarly, creditors of the shareholder cannot be stymied by a private agreement that renders foreclosure of a lien impossible. For that reason, we agree with the trial court that the sheriff's sale transferred the shares to [Birchell] despite the restrictions. Transfer restrictions cannot preclude transfer in a foreclosure sale and thereby leave creditors without recourse. This does not turn on a doctrine of construction. Rather we hold that requiring an explicit bar specifically naming transfer by intestacy or by testamentary disposition should not be necessary. If the language purports to bar all transfers, and by its terms would apply to intestacy, devise or any other means of transfer, it should be given effect unless the restriction violates some policy.

Although we agree with [Birchell] that he could purchase the shares at the sale, it is also the case that he purchased the shares with knowledge of the restrictions. We conclude that he could not acquire more property rights than were possessed by Linda as his seller. The shares in Linda's hands were valued with restrictions in place, and therefore it is not unfair to her creditors that a purchaser at a foreclosure sale acquire the disputed shares subject to the same restrictions, and with whatever lessened value that produces. To be sure, the effect of such a restriction may be to make the shares unmarketable to any buyer. But the creditor retains the option to bid at the sale and, if successful, succeed to the shareholders' interest. The creditor then gets the assets the debtor used to secure the underlying obligation. If the creditor wants collateral free of restrictions, the creditor must negotiate for that at the outset of the arrangement.

CONCLUSION

We affirm the trial court's ruling that... the transfer restrictions did not prevent the sheriff's sale, and that the transfer restrictions remain applicable to the shares in

[Birchell]'s hands. We reverse the trial court's ruling that the two disputed transfer restrictions are unreasonable and therefore unenforceable, and find that the director-approval and blood-member restrictions are reasonable and enforceable. The case is remanded for further proceedings consistent with this opinion.

SHEPARD, C.J., and DICKSON and SULLIVAN, JJ., concur.

RUCKER, J., concurs in result without opinion.

Notes and Questions

1. Notes

a. Indiana's statute governing restrictions on transfer is identical to the MBCA.

b. "Chief Justice Holmes" referred to by Justice Boehm is Oliver Wendell Holmes, Jr. (1841-1935) who left the Harvard Law School faculty in 1882 to become a Justice of Massachusetts's highest court. He became Chief Justice of that court in 1899, and, in 1902, President Theodore Roosevelt appointed him to the Supreme Court of the United States. He retired from the Court in 1932.

2. Reality Check

a. How did Linda acquire the shares?

b. How did Birchell get a lien on the shares?

c. Why did the parties want to restrict transfer?

d. Describe the mechanics of the restrictions.

e. Who contests Birchell's ownership of the shares? Why?

f. Why are some of the restrictions more problematic than others?

g. What should Linda or the company have done when Birchell sought to foreclose?

h. What additional steps should Birchell have taken to ensure that his purchase at the sheriff's sale would be effective?

i. Is Birchell now bound by the restrictions on transfer? Why?

j. If Birchell transfers the shares, is the transferee bound by the restrictions on transfer? In this regard, the Indiana Court of Appeals noted, "We express no opinion as to whether a purchaser of stock at a sheriff's sale without knowledge of the transfer restrictions would be subject to such restrictions in future transfers of the shares." *F.B.I. Farms, Inc. v. Moore*, 769 N.E.2d 688, 693 n.2 (Ind. App. 2002). See also MBCA §6.27(b).

3. Suppose

a. Suppose F.B.I. Farms had been incorporated in Delaware. Would the analysis or result have been different? See DGCL §202(a).

b. Suppose F.B.I. Farms had prevailed. How would the result and analysis have been different?

c. If the restrictions on transfer had been clearly applicable to the sheriff's sale, would that affect the price a purchaser would be willing to pay for those shares? Why?

d. Imagine that the restrictions on transfer purported to prohibit transfers made voluntarily, involuntarily, or by operation of law. Would the court's analysis or the result have been different?

4. What Do You Think?

a. Do you think each of the restrictions on transfer is equally valid? If not, which restrictions have more claim to legitimacy and why?

b. Do you think courts should be bound by restrictions on transfer that, by their terms, apply to transfers ordered by a court?

c. Is one of the parties especially culpable? If so, who and why?

d. In general, what steps should each of the parties and their lawyers have taken to ensure that this conflict did not arise in the first place?

5. You Draft It

a. Redraft the restrictions on transfer so that they are clearly permissible under the MBCA.

b. Redraft the restrictions on transfer so that they clearly apply to transfers ordered to satisfy judgment creditors of the stockholder, to transfers by will or intestacy, and to transfers pursuant to a marital dissolution. Then redraft the restrictions so that they clearly do not apply to such transfers.

1) No stock of said corporation shall be transferred, assigned and/or exchanged or divided, unless or until approved by the Directors thereof;

2) That if any stock be offered for sale, assigned and/or transferred, the corporation should have the first opportunity of purchasing the same at no more than the book value thereof;

3) Should said corporation be not interested, and could not economically offer to purchase said stock, any stockholder of record should be given the next opportunity to purchase said stock, at a price not to exceed the book value thereof;

4) That if the corporation was not interested in the stock, and any stockholders were not interested therein, then the same could be sold to any blood member of the family. Should they be desirous of purchasing the same, then at not more than the book value thereof.

1. When the Purchaser Is the Corporation That Issued the Shares

a. Limitations on a Corporation's Power to Purchase Its Shares

Through the late nineteenth century there was considerable doubt whether a corporation had the power to repurchase its own shares. This doubt centered not only on the propriety of the potential shift in the balance of economic and management power among its shareholders but on the rather metaphysical question of what would happen to such shares. That is, in what meaningful sense could a corporation be a stockholder of itself? Conceptually, this problem is different from the question whether stock can be made redeemable or callable. In those settings, all shares in a particular class or series have the same quality and that quality is embedded in the corporation's Articles of Incorporation. A corporation's purchase of its own shares that it can neither compel to be sold to it nor is under an obligation to purchase is a different matter. This question was of sufficient importance that legislatures specifically provided corporations with the power to purchase their own shares. See MBCA §6.31 and DGCL §160(a).

Corporations statutes place two primary limitations on the power of a corporation to repurchase its shares. First, such purchases are subject to the same economic test as dividends. See MBCA §6.03(b) and DGCL §160(a). Economically, a repurchase has the same effect as a dividend on a corporation's creditors: fewer corporate assets are available to satisfy the creditors' claims. The second limitation is meant to ensure that at least some shareholder has the power to vote and, in some states, at least some shareholder has the right to the corporate assets on dissolution. Accordingly, the statutes require that at least one such share remain outstanding at all times. See MBCA §6.03(d) (at least one outstanding share must have unlimited voting rights and at least one outstanding share must be entitled to the assets on dissolution) and DGCL §151(b) (at least one outstanding share must have full voting powers).

b. Motivations to Repurchase Shares

Given that a corporation *can* buy its own shares, why would it *want* to? One answer is that, as we've seen in the closely held setting, a corporation's managers might wish the corporation to purchase its shares to provide liquidity for a deceased shareholder's estate. The managers might also approve a repurchase where the managers believe it to be in the best interest of a corporation's shareholders to purchase the shares of a living shareholder to terminate that person's interest in the corporation. This is a common solution to the problem of the shareholder who has become chronically at odds with the other shareholders or the corporation's managers. Note that having the corporation purchase those shares allows the economic and voting rights of each remaining shareholder to increase proportionately, which is frequently the desired outcome. Managers and controlling shareholders can use this technique to increase their control at the expense of the minority shareholders, although (as we will see in later chapters) fiduciary duties impose limits on this power. Finally, because repurchasing shares is the functional equivalent of a dividend, a corporation may repurchase shares to provide shareholders a tax advantage because the consideration for the shares purchased is treated as a return of the shareholder's investment (on which no tax is imposed) and then as a capital gain (which may be taxed at a lower rate than ordinary income).[6]

Publicly held corporations, of course, need not repurchase a particular shareholder's shares to provide liquidity because, by definition, shareholders can readily dispose of them on the open market. On occasion, a public corporation will buy back the shares of a large shareholder as a way to ensure that that shareholder's management power is eliminated. The shareholder might prefer to sell to the corporation rather than on the open market in part because of low transaction costs (selling on the open market involves brokerage commissions and may also result in a lower total sale price because the availability of a large number of shares for sale may drive the price down) and in part because the corporation's managers may be willing to pay a premium price (known as *greenmail*) to be rid of the obstreperous shareholder.

Public corporations might also repurchase their shares as part of a change in their capital structure. If the corporation believes it needs a higher ratio of debt to equity, it may borrow money, often by selling debt securities, and use the money to

---

6. If the corporation repurchases shares from all shareholders pro rata, though, the Internal Revenue Service treats that transaction as a dividend and no tax advantages exist.

repurchase shares. Not only is the interest on the debt tax deductible to the corporation, unlike dividend payments on the stock, but the mandatory nature of interest payments means that the corporation's senior managers have less discretion over excess cash. For many public corporations, the investment community perceives this reduction of managerial discretion as a sign that the corporation's excess cash is less likely to be mismanaged (!) and hence the stock price will rise.

Finally, corporate managers may cause the corporation to repurchase its shares as a signal to the investment community that the managers believe the corporation's prospects are good. This seems a bit obtuse at first, somewhat like understanding the signals sent by various bidding conventions in bridge. At its starkest, the idea is that a corporation must decide what to do with cash that it does not need for its current operations. If the corporation wants neither to expand its own business nor purchase other businesses, a dividend would seem to be a likely use for the money. However, by buying back shares instead, the corporation's stock price should rise. This is so because the corporation's value is exactly the same before as after the stock repurchase — remember, the corporation's managers have decided not to use the money in the business — yet there are fewer shares outstanding so the value, hence the price, of each should rise. Sometimes this works. This is especially true where the investment community shares management's belief that the best use for a particular corporation's excess cash is to give it to the shareholders; the only question then is whether to do so via dividends or repurchases. In many settings, though, a decision to repurchase large amounts of shares suggests to investors that corporate managers are bereft of ideas for expanding the current business or for identifying new investment opportunities. In that case, this decline in investors' confidence in management may offset any price increase that should result from fewer outstanding shares. In fact, often a corporation that announces a large buyback sees its stock fall rather precipitously.

c. The Metaphysics of Repurchased Shares

In every state, repurchased shares are not "outstanding" so they cannot be voted nor do they count as being present for quorum purposes nor, obviously, may they receive dividends. Repurchased shares also do not count in calculating the proportion (i.e., the denominator) of shares that must be present for a quorum or the shares needed to take action. See DGCL §160(c), 216 (which limits those calculations to "shares entitled to vote"). The MBCA provides that shares that have been authorized and issued are outstanding "until they are reacquired, redeemed, converted, or canceled."[7] See MBCA §6.03(a). We have already talked about redeemable and convertible stock. The MBCA provides a default rule that reacquired shares become authorized but unissued. The Articles may provide, though, that reacquired shares may not be reissued. In that case, they simply evaporate and the number of authorized shares is reduced by the number of shares reacquired. See MBCA §6.31. In traditional corporate nomenclature, shares treated in either fashion are said to have been *retired*.

---

7. "*Canceled*" shares are not reacquired by the corporation but are simply voided. This may happen if the board purported to "issue" shares to third parties but such shares were in excess of number of authorized shares. Cancellation may also happen when two corporations merge and, as frequently happens, the surviving corporation owns some shares of the disappearing corporation. The remaining shareholders of the disappearing corporation receive some consideration for their shares while the shares owned by the surviving corporation are cancelled.

Although the difference may seem a bit attenuated, the difference between the two approaches makes an immense practical difference. If reacquired shares become authorized but unissued, the board has the power to reissue those shares as it sees fit, which provides the board with the discretion to seek more capital and more shareholders (subject to existing shareholders' preemptive rights) and the board may exercise that power strategically. If the shares evanesce, the shareholders have more control because, if the corporation has exhausted its supply of authorized but unissued shares, the shareholders must approve any amendment to the Articles increasing the number of authorized shares.

In Delaware and many other states, especially those with par value, reacquired shares are not automatically retired. Instead, they remain authorized, issued, but not outstanding. Such shares are traditionally called *treasury stock*. The board of directors clearly has the power to sell (note that the corporation does not reissue them; they remain issued as treasury stock) treasury stock and, because the corporation already received at least the par value of such shares when they were issued, the board is free to sell them for any price it considers adequate. See DGCL §§153(c), 160(b). This is sometimes an important power if the stock's par value is higher than an arm's length buyer would reasonably pay. Because stock cannot be issued for less than par value, a corporation could obtain an infusion of cash by selling treasury stock in a setting in which it is, as a practical matter, unable to issue new stock because the price per share will be below par value. Selling treasury shares does not trigger preemptive rights, which may provide the board with another advantage over issuing new shares. See DGCL §102(b)(3) (providing that preemptive rights attach to "additional issues of stock"). Treasury stock may be retired by board action and, as under the MBCA, the default rule is that retired stock becomes authorized but unissued, although the Certificate of Incorporation may provide that retired stock cannot be reissued. See DGCL §243.

C. FEDERAL SECURITIES REGULATION

You may remember from Chapter 6 that federal securities regulations affect the professional lives of corporate lawyers in two main settings. In this section we consider one of those settings: resales of stock. The '34 Act provides extensive regulation of the stock exchanges and of the stock brokerage companies and their employees. These regulations are highly esoteric but are, in general, designed to protect the investing public by requiring that transactions be public and that the brokerage houses and employees maintain adequate supervision over trading and customer accounts. Our concern here is with federal restrictions on the sale of stock by stockholders — in other words, with restrictions on resale.

1. Restrictions on Resale

a. Section 16(b)

Some restrictions apply only to stockholders in publicly held corporations. Section 16(a) of the '34 Act requires all directors, officers, and holders of 10 percent or more of a public company's stock to file reports that describe their stock holdings in the company. The purpose is to allow the public to know how much stock is held by such key people. Most changes in stockholding must be reported in two business days. The original purpose of §16(a) was to discourage insider trading by making insiders' trades public. A byproduct, however, is the existence of an active group of investors who closely monitor changes in insider holdings. Those investors believe, for obvious reasons, that trends in purchases or sales are good early indicators of near-term stock price changes.

Section 16(b) was originally designed to prevent these insiders from trading on private information. It provides a seemingly bright-line rule that allows the corporation to recover from such insiders any gain made from a purchase and sale (or sale and purchase) of company stock within six months. The statute imposes strict liability on the shareholder without regard to the actor's state of mind.

Because §16(a) covers ownership of *more than* 10 percent of a public company's stock, the Supreme Court has held that the transaction that puts a shareholder above the 10 percent level does not count for §16(b) purposes. On the other hand, the sale that takes a shareholder below 10 percent does count. The Securities and Exchange Commission (SEC) takes the view that all shares are fungible. For example, suppose a shareholder had owned 11 percent of a public company for years. On February 1st the shareholder bought an additional 1 percent and on March 1st the shareholder sold 1 percent. The shareholder has violated §16(b) even though the actual shares sold might have been held for longer than six months. To effect the statute's purpose in deterring insiders from making quick profits, where a shareholder makes multiple sales or purchases within a six-month period, the courts will award the highest damages. That is, the courts will match the shares sold at the highest price with the shares sold at the lowest. Under a strict reading of the statute, a shareholder who loses money on some trades may not offset that loss against gains for §16(b) purposes.

b. Rule 144

You will remember that the vast majority of shares are issued in transactions that are exempt from federal registration. Perfecting such an exemption is only half the battle, because such shares cannot be resold without registration unless the shareholder can use an exemption. Under the intrastate exemption, resale is easy if made to another in-state resident. Shares purchased in reliance on Reg. D are more difficult to resell. At bottom are two dangers. One is that a sale made a short time after the shares were initially issued might suggest that the original purchaser was just a conduit for purposes of claiming an exemption. Hence, there is a danger that a quick resale could be recharacterized as, in effect, the corporation's sale to the new purchaser whose purchase may or may not be in accord with the exemption upon which the issuer is relying.

Second, an unbelievably convoluted series of defined terms in the Securities Act has the effect of rendering unregistered resales by persons who control or are controlled by the issuing corporation illegal when that resale is accomplished with the aid of another person (such as a stockbroker). To avoid the uncertainties of these settings, the SEC has adopted Rule 144, which provides a very detailed safe harbor for such resales. The basic solution is that, with regard to the first danger, a shareholder may resell shares after holding them for one year. As to the second danger, a control person may resell shares if he or she complies with regulations that ensure that the public has sufficient information about the corporation and the resales are done in small enough amounts so as not to disrupt the trading market.

2. Rule 10b-5

This rule, under the '34 Act, is a wide-ranging prohibition against fraud in the purchase or sale of securities. Note that it applies to purchases or sales made through some instrumentality of interstate commerce, such as the telephone, but need not involve stock of publicly traded companies. It also applies to stock that was sold in transactions exempt from the registration requirements. Thus the vast majority of securities transactions, from start-up company financing to IPOs to sales of stock in well-established public companies, come within the 10b-5 ambit. The rule prohibits fraudulent trading practices and, most germanely, prohibits misstatements of material fact or half-truths about such facts. The rule provides that,

> It shall be unlawful for any person, directly or indirectly, by the use of any means or instrumentality of interstate commerce, or of the mails or of any facility of any national securities exchange,
>
> (a) To employ any device, scheme, or artifice to defraud,
>
> (b) To make any untrue statement of a material fact or to omit to state a material fact necessary in order to make the statements made, in the light of the circumstances under which they were made, not misleading, or
>
> (c) To engage in any act, practice, or course of business which operates or would operate as a fraud or deceit upon any person, in connection with the purchase or sale of any security.
>
> **Rule 10b-5**

The next case shows a typical 10b-5 case and describes the elements of a cause of action.

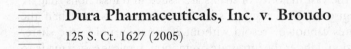

Dura Pharmaceuticals, Inc. v. Broudo
125 S. Ct. 1627 (2005)

Justice BREYER delivered the opinion of the Court.

I

Respondents are individuals who bought stock in Dura Pharmaceuticals, Inc., on the public securities market between April 15, 1997, and February 24, 1998. They have brought this securities fraud class action against Dura and some of its managers and directors (hereinafter Dura) in federal court. In respect to the question before us, their detailed amended (181 paragraph) complaint makes substantially the following allegations:

(1) Before and during the purchase period, Dura (or its officials) made false statements concerning both Dura's drug profits and future Food and Drug Administration (FDA) approval of a new asthmatic spray device.

([2]) In respect to the asthmatic spray device, Dura falsely claimed that it expected the FDA would soon grant its approval.

([3]) [I]n November 1998, Dura announced that the FDA would not approve Dura's new asthmatic spray device.

([4]) The next day Dura's share price temporarily fell but almost fully recovered within one week.

Most importantly, the complaint says the following (and nothing significantly more than the following) about economic losses attributable to the spray device misstatement: *"In reliance on the integrity of the market, [the plaintiffs]... paid artificially inflated prices for Dura securities"* and the plaintiffs suffered *"damage[s]" thereby* (emphasis added).

In the portion of the court's decision now before us — the portion that concerns the spray device claim — the [Ninth] Circuit held that the complaint adequately alleged "loss causation." The Circuit wrote that "plaintiffs establish loss causation if they have shown that the price *on the date of purchase* was inflated because of the misrepresentation." 339 F.3d, at 938 (emphasis in original; internal quotation marks omitted). It added that "the injury occurs at the time of the transaction." *Ibid.* Since the complaint pleaded "that the price at the time of purchase was overstated," and it sufficiently identified the cause, its allegations were legally sufficient. *Ibid.*

Because the Ninth Circuit's views about loss causation differ from those of other Circuits that have considered this issue, we granted Dura's petition for certiorari. We now reverse.

II

The courts have implied... a private damages action [under §10(b) of the 1934 Act and Rule 10b-5], which resembles, but is not identical to, common-law tort actions for deceit and misrepresentation. In cases involving publicly traded securities and purchases or sales in public securities markets, the action's basic elements include:

(1) *a material misrepresentation (or omission)*;
(2) *scienter, i.e.,* a wrongful state of mind;
(3) *a connection with the purchase or sale of a security*;
(4) *reliance,* often referred to in cases involving public securities markets... as "transaction causation," ... ;
(5) *economic loss*; and
(6) *"loss causation," i.e.,* a causal connection between the material misrepresentation and the loss.

Dura argues that the complaint's allegations are inadequate in respect to these last two elements.

A

We begin with the Ninth Circuit's basic reason for finding the complaint adequate, namely, that at the end of the day plaintiffs need only "establish," *i.e.,* prove, that "the price *on the date of purchase* was inflated because of the misrepresentation." 339 F.3d, at 938 (internal quotation marks omitted). In our view, this statement of the law is wrong. Normally, in cases such as this one..., an inflated purchase price will not itself constitute or proximately cause the relevant economic loss.

For one thing, as a matter of pure logic, at the moment the transaction takes place, the plaintiff has suffered no loss; the inflated purchase payment is offset by ownership of a share that *at that instant* possesses equivalent value. Moreover, the logical link between the inflated share purchase price and any later economic loss is not invariably strong. Shares are normally purchased with an eye toward a later sale. But if, say, the purchaser sells the shares quickly before the relevant truth begins to leak out, the misrepresentation will not have led to any loss. If the purchaser sells later after the truth makes its way into the market place, an initially inflated purchase price *might* mean a later loss. But that is far from inevitably so. When the purchaser subsequently resells such shares, even at a lower price, that lower price may reflect, not the earlier misrepresentation, but changed economic circumstances, changed investor expectations, new industry-specific or firm-specific facts, conditions, or other events, which taken separately or together account for some or all of that lower price. (The same is true in respect to a claim that a share's higher price is lower than it would otherwise have been—a claim we do not consider here.) Other things being equal, the longer the time between purchase and sale, the more likely that this is so, *i.e.,* the more likely that other factors caused the loss.

Given the tangle of factors affecting price, the most logic alone permits us to say is that the higher purchase price will *sometimes* play a role in bringing about a future loss. It may prove to be a necessary condition of any such loss, and in that sense one might say that the inflated purchase price suggests that the misrepresentation (using language the Ninth Circuit used) "touches upon" a later economic loss. But, even if that is so, it is insufficient. To "touch upon" a loss is not to *cause* a loss, and it is the latter that the law requires.

For another thing, the Ninth Circuit's holding lacks support in precedent. Judicially implied private securities fraud actions resemble in many (but not all) respects common-law deceit and misrepresentation actions. The common law of deceit subjects a person who "fraudulently" makes a "misrepresentation" to liability "for pecuniary loss caused" to one who justifiably relies upon that misrepresentation. *Restatement (Second) of Torts* §525, p. 55 (1977) (hereinafter *Restatement of Torts*);.... And the common law has long insisted that a plaintiff in such a case show not only that had he known the truth he would not have acted but also that he suffered actual economic loss.

Given the common-law roots of the securities fraud action (and the common-law requirement that a plaintiff show actual damages), it is not surprising that other courts of appeals have rejected the Ninth Circuit's "inflated purchase price" approach to proving causation and loss. Indeed, the *Restatement of Torts*, in setting forth the judicial consensus, says that a person who "misrepresents the financial condition of a corporation in order to sell its stock" becomes liable to a relying purchaser "for the loss" the purchaser sustains "when the facts . . . become generally known" and "as a result" share value "depreciate[s]." §548A, Comment *b*, at 107. Treatise writers, too, have emphasized the need to prove proximate causation. W. Keeton, et al., *Prosser and Keeton on Law of Torts* §110, at 767 (5th ed. 1984) (losses do "not afford any basis for recovery" if "brought about by business conditions or other factors"). We cannot reconcile the Ninth Circuit's "inflated purchase price" approach with these views of other courts. And the uniqueness of its perspective argues against the validity of its approach in a case like this one where we consider the contours of a judicially implied cause of action with roots in the common law.

Finally, the Ninth Circuit's approach overlooks an important securities law objective. The securities statutes seek to maintain public confidence in the marketplace. They do so by deterring fraud, in part, through the availability of private securities fraud actions. But the statutes make these latter actions available, not to provide investors with broad insurance against market losses, but to protect them against those economic losses that misrepresentations actually cause.

The [Private Securities Litigation Reform Act of 1995] insists that securities fraud complaints "specify" each misleading statement; that they set forth the facts "on which [a] belief" that a statement is misleading was "formed"; and that they "state with particularity facts giving rise to a strong inference that the defendant acted with the required state of mind." 15 U.S.C. §§78u-4(b)(1), (2). And the statute expressly imposes on plaintiffs "the burden of proving" that the defendant's misrepresentations "caused the loss for which the plaintiff seeks to recover." §78u-4(b)(4).

The statute thereby makes clear Congress' intent to permit private securities fraud actions for recovery where, but only where, plaintiffs adequately allege and prove the traditional elements of causation and loss. By way of contrast, the Ninth Circuit's approach would allow recovery where a misrepresentation leads to an inflated purchase price but nonetheless does not proximately cause any economic loss. That is to say, it would permit recovery where these two traditional elements in fact are missing.

In sum, we find the Ninth Circuit's approach inconsistent with the law's requirement that a plaintiff prove that the defendant's misrepresentation (or other fraudulent conduct) proximately caused the plaintiff's economic loss.

We reverse the judgment of the Ninth Circuit, and we remand the case for further proceedings consistent with this opinion.

It is so ordered.

Notes and Questions

1. Notes

a. The complaint also included the following allegations:

(1) In respect to drug profits, Dura falsely claimed that it expected that its drug sales would prove profitable.

(2) On the last day of the purchase period, February 24, 1998, Dura announced that its earnings would be lower than expected, principally due to slow drug sales.

(3) The next day Dura's shares lost almost half their value (falling from about $39 per share to about $21).

These allegations are surely sufficient to show that plaintiffs suffered actual loss. Do you think that they sufficiently show loss causation?

2. Reality Check

a. Which elements of a 10b-5 claim did the Supreme Court find missing from the complaint?

b. In what way did the Ninth Circuit approach differ from that of the Supreme Court?

3. Suppose

a. Suppose the price of Dura stayed lower after the company announced that the FDA would not approve Dura's new asthmatic spray device. Would the complaint have stated a claim for relief under Rule 10b-5?

4. What Do You Think?

a. When it is clear that the defendant has made a misstatement of a material fact, why should a shareholder have to show damages and loss causation? Should the burden be on the defendant to show lack of damage or causation?

Dura Pharmaceuticals ticked off six elements for a claim under Rule 10b-5 and discussed two of them. Two of the other elements, the requirement that the fraud be "in connection with" a securities transaction and scienter, are explored in much more detail in the course in securities regulation. Nonetheless, a word or two about each of these requirements is appropriate here. The "in connection with" requirement was broadly defined by the Supreme Court in 1971. It is enough that a fraud touch or concern a securities transaction. The requirement is a frustrating one in that courts, in the end, find the requisite connection whenever the purposes of the securities act (i.e., protecting investors in securities) are met. This open standard generates a fair bit of litigation.

Since the mid-1970s the Supreme Court has held that the words of Section 10(b) proscribe actions that have deception at their core. The Court then held that 10b-5 liability requires that the defendant intend to deceive because deception implies intentional wrongdoing. That is, defendants must have scienter to be liable. Other courts have elaborated on this requirement of scienter. It is clear that the requisite intent to deceive is met where the defendant is aware that the misstatement could mislead. The defendant does not have to intend to bilk the plaintiff. For example, a mining company puts out a press release that falsely states that the company has not had a major ore discovery in a particular area. It does so not to deceive investors but to give the company's employees time to obtain the mineral rights from other property owners adjacent to the ore discovery. Most courts would hold that the company nonetheless has the requisite scienter to render it liable under 10b-5 because it would have been aware that it was misstating an important fact. Virtually all courts hold that recklessness (that is, an extreme departure from the standards of ordinary care) as to whether a statement is true or false is sufficient to meet the scienter requirement. The Private Securities Litigation Reform Act of 1995 requires plaintiffs in class actions involving publicly traded securities to allege with particularity facts that create a "strong inference" that the defendant acted with scienter. Compare this to FRCP 9(b), which requires only that fraud be stated "with particularity."

The remaining two elements of a 10b-5 claim are that the defendant made a misstatement of a material fact, and that the plaintiff relied on that misstatement in deciding to enter into the transaction. This reliance is sometimes called *transaction causation*. As we will see in the next case, what makes a statement *material* is a subject of intense scrutiny. The next case, *Basic*, also discusses the reliance requirement in one particularly problematic setting. In face-to-face transactions, the reliance requirement is relatively straightforward. But when the trade occurs in a publicly traded stock, the defendant, usually the corporation or a director or officer, seldom has any direct contact with the plaintiff. Can the plaintiff rely in any meaningful sense?

Basic, Inc. v. Levinson
485 U.S. 224 (1988)

Justice BLACKMUN delivered the opinion of the Court.

Prior to December 20, 1978, Basic Incorporated was a publicly traded company primarily engaged in the business of manufacturing chemical refractories for the steel industry.

Beginning in September 1976, Combustion representatives had meetings and telephone conversations with Basic officers and directors . . . concerning the possibility of a merger. During 1977 and 1978, Basic made three public statements denying that it was engaged in merger negotiations. On December 18, 1978, Basic asked the New York Stock Exchange to suspend trading in its shares and issued a release stating that it had been "approached" by another company concerning a merger. On December 19, Basic's board endorsed Combustion's offer of $46 per share for its common stock, and on the following day publicly announced its approval of Combustion's tender offer for all outstanding shares.

Respondents are former Basic shareholders who sold their stock after Basic's first public statement of October 21, 1977, and before the suspension of trading in December 1978. Respondents brought a class action against Basic and its directors, asserting that the defendants issued three false or misleading public statements and thereby were in violation of §10(b) of the 1934 Act and of Rule 10b-5. Respondents alleged that they were injured by selling Basic shares at artificially depressed prices in a market affected by petitioners' misleading statements and in reliance thereon.

We granted certiorari . . . to resolve the split . . . among the Courts of Appeals as to the standard of materiality applicable to preliminary merger discussions, and to determine whether the courts below properly applied a presumption of reliance in certifying the class, rather than requiring each class member to show direct reliance on Basic's statements.

The Court previously has addressed various positive and common-law requirements for a violation of §10(b) or of Rule 10b-5. The Court also explicitly has defined a standard of materiality under the securities laws, see *TSC Industries, Inc. v. Northway, Inc.,* 426 U.S. 438, (1976), concluding in the proxy-solicitation context that "[a]n omitted fact is material if there is a substantial likelihood that a reasonable shareholder would consider it important in deciding how to vote." *Id.,* at 449. Acknowledging that certain information concerning corporate developments could well be of "dubious significance," *id.,* at 448 the Court was careful not to set too low a standard of materiality; it was concerned that a minimal standard might bring an overabundance of information within its reach, and lead management "simply to bury the shareholders in an avalanche of trivial information — a result that is hardly conducive to informed decisionmaking." *Id.,* at 448-449. It further explained that to fulfill the materiality requirement "there must be a substantial likelihood that the disclosure of the omitted fact would have been viewed by the reasonable investor as having significantly altered the 'total mix' of information made available." *Id.,* at 449. We now expressly adopt the *TSC Industries* standard of materiality for the §10(b) and Rule 10b-5 context.

The application of this materiality standard to preliminary merger discussions is not self-evident. Where the impact of the corporate development on the target's fortune is certain and clear, the *TSC Industries* materiality definition admits straightforward application. Where, on the other hand, the event is contingent or speculative in nature, it is difficult to ascertain whether the "reasonable investor" would have considered the omitted information significant at the time. Merger negotiations, because of the ever-present possibility that the contemplated transaction will not be effectuated, fall into the latter category.

Even before this Court's decision in *TSC Industries,* the Second Circuit had explained the role of the materiality requirement of Rule 10b-5, with respect to contingent or speculative information or events, in a manner that gave that term meaning that is independent of the other provisions of the Rule. Under such circumstances, materiality "will depend at any given time upon a balancing of both the indicated probability that the event will occur and the anticipated magnitude of the event in light of the totality of the company activity." *SEC v. Texas Gulf Sulphur Co.,* 401 F.2d 833, 849 (2d Cir. 1968).

In a subsequent decision, the late Judge Friendly, writing for a Second Circuit panel, applied the *Texas Gulf Sulphur* probability/magnitude approach in the specific context of preliminary merger negotiations. After acknowledging that materiality is something to be determined on the basis of the particular facts of each case, he stated:

> Since a merger in which it is bought out is the most important event that can occur in a small corporation's life, to wit, its death, we think that inside information, as regards a merger of this sort, can become material at an earlier stage than would be the case as regards lesser transactions — and this even though the mortality rate of mergers in such formative stages is doubtless high.

SEC v. Geon Industries, Inc., 531 F.2d 39, 47-48 (2d Cir. 1976).

We agree with that analysis.

Whether merger discussions in any particular case are material therefore depends on the facts. Generally, in order to assess the probability that the event will occur, a factfinder will need to look to indicia of interest in the transaction at the highest corporate levels. Without attempting to catalog all such possible factors, we note by way of example that board resolutions, instructions to investment bankers, and actual negotiations between principals or their intermediaries may serve as indicia of interest. To assess the magnitude of the transaction to the issuer of the securities allegedly manipulated, a factfinder will need to consider such facts as the size of the two corporate entities and of the potential premiums over market value. No particular event or factor short of closing the transaction need be either necessary or sufficient by itself to render merger discussions material.[17]

---

17. To be actionable, of course, a statement must also be misleading. Silence, absent a duty to disclose, is not misleading under Rule 10b-5. "No comment" statements are generally the functional equivalent of silence. See *In re Carnation Co.,* Exchange Act Release No. 22214, 33 S.E.C. Docket 1025 (1985). See also New York Stock Exchange Listed Company Manual §202.01, reprinted in 3 CCH Fed. Sec. L. Rep. ¶23,515 (1987) (premature public announcement may properly be delayed for valid business purpose and where adequate security can be maintained); American Stock Exchange Company Guide §§401-405, reprinted in 3 CCH Fed. Sec. L. Rep. ¶¶23,124A-23, 124E (1985) (similar provisions).

It has been suggested that given current market practices, a "no comment" statement is tantamount to an admission that merger discussions are underway. That may well hold true to the extent that issuers adopt a policy of truthfully denying merger rumors when no discussions are underway, and of issuing "no comment" statements when they are in the midst of negotiations. There are, of course, other statement policies firms could adopt; we need not now advise issuers as to what kind of practice to follow, within the range permitted by law. Perhaps more importantly, we think that creating an exception to a regulatory scheme founded on a prodisclosure legislative philosophy, because complying with the regulation might be "bad for business," is a role for Congress, not this Court.

As we clarify today, materiality depends on the significance the reasonable investor would place on the withheld or misrepresented information. The fact-specific inquiry we endorse here is consistent with the approach a number of courts have taken in assessing the materiality of merger negotiations. Because the standard of materiality we have adopted differs from that used by both courts below, we remand the case for reconsideration of the question whether a grant of summary judgment is appropriate on this record.

We turn to the question of reliance and the fraud-on-the-market theory. Succinctly put:

> The fraud on the market theory is based on the hypothesis that, in an open and developed securities market, the price of a company's stock is determined by the available material information regarding the company and its business. . . . Misleading statements will therefore defraud purchasers of stock even if the purchasers do not directly rely on the misstatements. . . . The causal connection between the defendants' fraud and the plaintiffs' purchase of stock in such a case is no less significant than in a case of direct reliance on misrepresentations.

> *Peil v. Speiser*, 806 F.2d 1154, 1160-1161 (3rd Cir. 1986).

Petitioners and their *amici* complain that the fraud-on-the-market theory effectively eliminates the requirement that a plaintiff asserting a claim under Rule 10b-5 prove reliance. We agree that reliance is an element of a Rule 10b-5 cause of action. Reliance provides the requisite causal connection between a defendant's misrepresentation and a plaintiff's injury. There is, however, more than one way to demonstrate the causal connection. Indeed, we previously have dispensed with a requirement of positive proof of reliance, where a duty to disclose material information had been breached, concluding that the necessary nexus between the plaintiffs' injury and the defendant's wrongful conduct had been established. See *Affiliated Ute Citizens v. United States*, 406 U.S. 128, 153-154 (1972).

The modern securities markets, literally involving millions of shares changing hands daily, differ from the face-to-face transactions contemplated by early fraud cases, and our understanding of Rule 10b-5's reliance requirement must encompass these differences.

> In face-to-face transactions, the inquiry into an investor's reliance upon information is into the subjective pricing of that information by that investor. With the presence of a market, the market is interposed between seller and buyer and, ideally, transmits information to the investor in the processed form of a market price. Thus the market is performing a substantial part of the valuation process performed by the investor in a face-to-face transaction. The market is acting as the unpaid agent of the investor, informing him that given all the information available to it, the value of the stock is worth the market price.

> *In re LTV Securities Litigation*, 88 F.R.D. 134, 143 (ND Tex. 1980).

Accord, *e.g.*, *Peil v. Speiser*, 806 F.2d 1154, 1161 (3d Cir. 1986) ("In an open and developed market, the dissemination of material misrepresentations or withholding of material information typically affects the price of the stock, and purchasers generally rely on the price of the stock as a reflection of its value"); *Blackie v. Barrack*, 524 F.2d 891, 908 (9th Cir. 1975) ("[T]he same causal nexus can be adequately established indirectly, by proof of materiality coupled with the common sense that a stock purchaser does not ordinarily seek to purchase a loss in the form of artificially inflated stock").

Presumptions typically serve to assist courts in managing circumstances in which direct proof, for one reason or another, is rendered difficult. The courts below accepted a presumption, created by the fraud-on-the-market theory and subject to rebuttal by petitioners, that persons who had traded Basic shares had done so in reliance on the integrity of the price set by the market, but because of petitioners' material misrepresentations that price had been fraudulently depressed. Requiring a plaintiff to show a speculative state of facts, *i.e.*, how he would have acted if omitted material information had been disclosed, . . . or if the misrepresentation had not been made, . . . would place an unnecessarily unrealistic evidentiary burden on the Rule 10b-5 plaintiff who has traded on an impersonal market.

Arising out of considerations of fairness, public policy, and probability, as well as judicial economy, presumptions are also useful devices for allocating the burdens of proof between parties. The presumption of reliance employed in this case is consistent with, and, by facilitating Rule 10b-5 litigation, supports, the congressional policy embodied in the 1934 Act. In drafting that Act, Congress expressly relied on the premise that securities markets are affected by information, and enacted legislation to facilitate an investor's reliance on the integrity of those markets:

> The idea of a free and open public market is built upon the theory that competing judgments of buyers and sellers as to the fair price of a security brings *[sic]* about a situation where the market price reflects as nearly as possible a just price. Just as artificial manipulation tends to upset the true function of an open market, so the hiding and secreting of important information obstructs the operation of the markets as indices of real value.

H.R. Rep. No. 1383, at 11.

The presumption is also supported by common sense and probability. Recent empirical studies have tended to confirm Congress' premise that the market price of shares traded on well-developed markets reflects all publicly available information, and, hence, any material misrepresentations. It has been noted that "it is hard to imagine that there ever is a buyer or seller who does not rely on market integrity. Who would knowingly roll the dice in a crooked crap game?" *Schlanger v. Four-Phase Systems, Inc.*, 555 F. Supp. 535, 538 (S.D.N.Y. 1982). Indeed, nearly every court that has considered the proposition has concluded that where materially misleading statements have been disseminated into an impersonal, well-developed market for securities, the reliance of individual plaintiffs on the integrity of the market price may be presumed. Commentators generally have applauded the adoption of one variation or another of the fraud-on-the-market theory. An investor who buys or sells stock at the price set by the market does so in reliance on the integrity of that price. Because most publicly available information is reflected in market price, an investor's reliance on any public material misrepresentations, therefore, may be presumed for purposes of a Rule 10b-5 action.

The Court of Appeals . . . acknowledged that petitioners may rebut proof of the elements giving rise to the presumption, or show that the misrepresentation in fact did not lead to a distortion of price or that an individual plaintiff traded or would have traded despite his knowing the statement was false.

Any showing that severs the link between the alleged misrepresentation and either the price received (or paid) by the plaintiff, or his decision to trade at a fair market price, will be sufficient to rebut the presumption of reliance. For example, if petitioners could show that the "market makers" were privy to the truth about the merger discussions here with Combustion, and thus that the market price would not have been affected by their misrepresentations, the causal connection could be broken: the basis for finding that the fraud had been transmitted through market price would be gone. Similarly, if, despite petitioners' allegedly fraudulent attempt to manipulate market price, news of the merger discussions credibly entered the market and dissipated the effects of the misstatements, those who traded Basic shares after the corrective statements would have no direct or indirect connection with the fraud. Petitioners also could rebut the presumption of reliance as to plaintiffs who would have divested themselves of their Basic shares without relying on the integrity of the market. For example, a plaintiff who believed that Basic's statements were false and that Basic was indeed engaged in merger discussions, and who consequently believed that Basic stock was artificially underpriced, but sold his shares nevertheless because of other unrelated concerns, *e.g.*, potential antitrust problems, or political pressures to divest from shares of certain businesses, could not be said to have relied on the integrity of a price he knew had been manipulated.

The judgment of the Court of Appeals is vacated, and the case is remanded to that court for further proceedings consistent with this opinion.

It is so ordered.

THE CHIEF JUSTICE, Justice SCALIA, and Justice KENNEDY took no part in the consideration or decision of this case.

Justice WHITE, with whom Justice O'CONNOR joins, concurring in part and dissenting in part.

At the bottom of the Court's conclusion that the fraud-on-the-market theory sustains a presumption of reliance is the assumption that individuals rely "on the integrity of the market price" when buying or selling stock in "impersonal, well-developed market[s] for securities." Even if I was prepared to accept (as a matter of common sense or general understanding) the assumption that most persons buying or selling stock do so in response to the market price, the fraud-on-the-market theory goes further. For in adopting a "presumption of reliance," the Court *also* assumes that buyers and sellers rely — not just on the market price — but on the "*integrity*" of that price. It is this aspect of the fraud-on-the-market hypothesis which most mystifies me.

To define the term "integrity of the market price," the majority quotes approvingly from cases which suggest that investors are entitled to "'rely on the price of a stock as a reflection of its value.'" But the meaning of this phrase eludes me, for it implicitly suggests that stocks have some "true value" that is measurable by a standard other than their market price. While the scholastics of medieval times professed a means to make such a valuation of a commodity's "worth," I doubt that the federal courts of our day are similarly equipped.

Even if securities had some "value" — knowable and distinct from the market price of a stock — investors do not always share the Court's presumption that a stock's price is a "reflection of [this] value." Indeed, "many investors purchase or sell stock because they believe the price *inaccurately* reflects the corporation's worth." See Black, *Fraud on the Market: A Criticism of Dispensing with Reliance Requirements in Certain Open Market Transactions*, 62 N.C. L. Rev. 435, 455 (1984) (emphasis added). If investors really believed that stock prices reflected a stock's "value," many sellers would never sell, and many buyers never buy (given the time and cost associated with executing a stock transaction). As we recognized just a few years ago: "[I]nvestors act on inevitably incomplete or inaccurate information, [consequently] there are always winners and losers; but those who have 'lost' have not necessarily been defrauded." *Dirks v. SEC,* 463 U.S. 646, 667, n.27 (1983). Yet today, the Court allows investors to recover who can show little more than that they sold stock at a lower price than what might have been.[7]

I do not propose that the law retreat from the many protections that §10(b) and Rule 10b-5, as interpreted in our prior cases, provide to investors. But any extension of these laws, to approach something closer to an investor insurance scheme, should come from Congress, and not from the courts.

Notes and Questions

1. Notes

a. Securities lawyers and their clients spend endless hours debating whether a particular fact is material. They spend countless more hours massaging language to be released publicly to ensure that any statement is not misleading.

2. Reality Check

a. Why is the concept of materiality important?

b. What definition of materiality does the Court use? Where does it get that definition?

c. Is reliance an element of a 10b-5 claim? Why?

d. What is the fraud-on-the-market theory? Why is it necessary?

e. Why can't the plaintiffs include more precise allegations of reliance in their complaint?

3. Suppose

a. Suppose Basic had replied "no comment" whenever it was asked whether it was in merger discussions. Would the company have made a misstatement of a material fact?

b. Suppose Basic had not replied at all—that is, was silent—whenever it was asked whether it was in merger discussions. Would the company be liable under 10b-5?

4. What Do You Think?

a. Does the Court define materiality properly? Is it a standard that lawyers and their clients can apply easily?

---

7. This is what the Court's rule boils down to in practical terms. For while, in theory, the Court allows for rebuttal of its "presumption of reliance"—a proviso with which I agree, in practice the Court must realize, as other courts applying the fraud-on-the-market theory have, that such rebuttal is virtually impossible in all but the most extraordinary case.

Consequently, while the Court considers it significant that the fraud-on-the-market presumption it endorses is a rebuttable one, the majority's implicit rejection of the "pure causation" fraud-on-the-market theory rings hollow. In most cases, the Court's theory will operate just as the causation theory would, creating a nonrebuttable presumption of "reliance" in future Rule 10b-5 actions.

b. Should reliance be a necessary element of a 10b-5 action? What language in the Rule requires reliance?

A close reading of 10b-5(b) shows that two things are prohibited. One is a misstatement of a material fact. The other is omitting to state a material fact necessary in order to make the statements made, in the light of the circumstances under which they were made, not misleading. That's a long-winded way of saying that half-truths are prohibited. The corollary of these prohibitions is that corporations (and other potential defendants) have a duty to correct misstatements of material facts and half-truths they have made. A related concept is a duty to update. A statement may be true when made (and not a half-truth), but subsequent events may render the statement untrue. Case law supports an obligation to update the statement if the statement is still likely to be relied upon by the investment community. Seen in this way, the duty to update is really a duty to correct, because the theory is that statements are in some sense continuously "made" until investors stop relying on them. The reality of the securities markets is that publicly made statements have a relatively short half-life. This aspect of the securities markets means that the duty to update is of relatively short duration as to any particular statement.

Notice that 10b-5 does not impose liability for omissions except when a defendant has stated a half-truth. Nonetheless, courts have held that a defendant may be liable for an omission when under a duty to speak, even when no half-truth has been made. A duty to speak can arise in several ways. First, a publicly held company is under a duty to file reports every three months with the SEC. Those reports call for specific disclosure, and surely omitting such disclosure is actionable under 10b-5. Second, state corporate law may impose a fiduciary duty to disclose certain information to shareholders. For example, corporations must disclose all material information to shareholders whenever shareholders are voting. Third, the stock markets, such as the New York Stock Exchange, impose an obligation on listed corporations to release material information quickly, though that standard is applied rather flexibly to permit corporations a fair bit of leeway in deciding when to make disclosures.

a. Insider Trading

A special application of the antifraud provisions of Rule 10b-5 is the prohibition against insider trading. Insider trading is a shorthand phrase meaning a trade made while in possession of material nonpublic information. We have covered the concept of materiality above. You can intuit the contours of issues surrounding whether information has become public. These involve temporal questions — how long must information be available before it's public — and spatial questions — where must the information appear to be considered public? These are developed in the securities regulation course. For our purposes, we'll look at the development of insider trading liability under Rule 10b-5.

We start with the most basic question. Assuming that a high corporate official (e.g., an officer or director, to pick the easy cases) or even the corporation itself buys or sells stock while in possession of material nonpublic information, how does 10b-5 liability attach? Remember, by definition there is no misstatement of a material fact, because there's no statement at all. Likewise, there is no half-truth that must be corrected. In other words, insider trading is a subset of the cases imposing liability for omissions. The first case, which was an SEC administrative proceeding, sets out what is sometimes called the classic theory of insider trading liability.

In the Matter of Cady, Roberts & Co.

40 S.E.C. 907 (1961)

By CARY, Chairman:

On the morning of November 25, the Curtiss-Wright [Corporation] directors...approved a dividend for the fourth quarter at the reduced rate of $.375
per share. At approximately 11:00 A.M., the board authorized transmission of information of this action by telegram to the New York Stock Exchange. There was a short
delay in the transmission of the telegram because of a typing problem and the
telegram,...was not delivered to the Exchange until 12:29 P.M. [T]he announcement
did not appear on the Dow Jones ticker tape until 11:48 A.M.

Sometime after the dividend decision, there was a recess of the Curtiss-Wright
directors' meeting, during which Cowdin [a Board member and a broker at Cady,
Roberts & Co.] telephoned...and left a message for Gintel [also a Cady, Roberts
broker] that the dividend had been cut. Upon receiving this information, Gintel
entered two sell orders for execution on the Exchange.... These orders were
executed at 11:15 and 11:18 A.M. at 40 $\frac{1}{4}$ and 40 $\frac{3}{8}$, respectively.

When the dividend announcement appeared on the Dow Jones tape at 11:48 A.M.,
the Exchange was compelled to suspend trading in Curtiss-Wright because of the
large number of sell orders. Trading in Curtiss-Wright stock was resumed at 1:59
P.M. at 36 $\frac{1}{2}$, ranged during the balance of the day between 34 $\frac{1}{8}$ and 37, and closed at
34 $\frac{7}{8}$.

So many times that citation is unnecessary, we have indicated that the purchase
and sale of securities is a field in special need of regulation for the protection of
investors. To this end one of the major purposes of the securities acts is the prevention
of fraud, manipulation or deception in connection with securities transactions.
Consistent with this objective,...Section 10(b) of the Exchange Act and Rule
10b-5, issued under that Section, are broad remedial provisions aimed at reaching
misleading or deceptive activities, whether or not they are precisely and technically
sufficient to sustain a common law action for fraud and deceit.

[They] apply to securities transactions by "any person." Misrepresentations will
lie within their ambit, no matter who the speaker may be. An affirmative duty to
disclose material information has been traditionally imposed on corporate "insiders,"
particularly officers, directors, or controlling stockholders. We, and the courts
have consistently held that insiders must disclose material facts which are known to
them by virtue of their position but which are not known to persons with whom
they deal and which, if known, would affect their investment judgment. Failure
to make disclosure in these circumstances constitutes a violation of the antifraud
provisions. If, on the other hand, disclosure prior to effecting a purchase or sale
would be improper or unrealistic under the circumstances, we believe the alternative
is to forego the transaction.

These three groups, however, do not exhaust the classes of persons upon whom
there is such an obligation. Analytically, the obligation rests on two principal
elements; first, the existence of a relationship giving access, directly or indirectly, to
information intended to be available only for a corporate purpose and not for the
personal benefit of anyone, and second, the inherent unfairness involved where a
party takes advantage of such information knowing it is unavailable to those with
whom he is dealing. Thus our task here is to identify those persons who are in a

special relationship with a company and privy to its internal affairs, and thereby suffer correlative duties in trading in its securities.

Respondents further assert that they made no express representations and did not in any way manipulate the market, and urge that in a transaction on an exchange there is no further duty such as may be required in a "face-to-face" transaction. We reject this suggestion. It would be anomalous indeed if the protection afforded by the antifraud provisions were withdrawn from transactions effected on exchanges, primary markets for securities transactions. If purchasers on an exchange had available material information known by a selling insider, we may assume that their investment judgment would be affected and their decision whether to buy might accordingly be modified. Consequently, any sales by the insider must await disclosure of the information.

Notes and Questions

1. Notes

a. William L. Cary was a longtime corporate and securities law professor at Columbia Law School. He was tapped by President Kennedy to serve as chair of the SEC.

b. The SEC has adopted Rule 10b5-1, which provides a safe harbor for sale of stock by insiders. In brief, the rule provides that insiders may sell shares without violating Rule 10b-5 if they do so pursuant to a preexisting plan of trading. Most top executives of public companies sell their shares pursuant to a plan of this kind.

2. Reality Check

a. Who violated 10b-5? How did they violate the rule?
b. What material fact was omitted?

3. What Do You Think?

a. Should 10b-5 liability for omissions turn on whether a duty runs from the defendant to the plaintiff?

Cady, Roberts predicates its holding on two assertions. "[F]irst, the existence of a relationship giving access, directly or indirectly, to information intended to be available only for a corporate purpose and not for the personal benefit of anyone, and second, the inherent unfairness involved where a party takes advantage of such information knowing it is unavailable to those with whom he is dealing." May liability be imposed when only one of these is met? The next case explores that question.

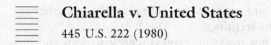

Chiarella v. United States

445 U.S. 222 (1980)

Mr. Justice POWELL delivered the opinion of the Court.

I

Petitioner is a printer by trade. In 1975 and 1976, he worked as a "markup man" in the New York composing room of Pandick Press, a financial printer. Among documents that petitioner handled were five announcements of corporate take-over bids. When these documents were delivered to the printer, the identities of the acquiring and target corporations were concealed by blank spaces or false names. The true names were sent to the printer on the night of the final printing.

The petitioner, however, was able to deduce the names of the target companies before the final printing from other information contained in the documents. Without disclosing his knowledge, petitioner purchased stock in the target companies and sold the shares immediately after the takeover attempts were made public. By this method, petitioner realized a gain of slightly more than $30,000 in the course of 14 months.

In January 1978, petitioner was indicted on 17 counts of violating §10(b) of the Securities Exchange Act of 1934 (1934 Act) and SEC Rule 10b-5. After petitioner unsuccessfully moved to dismiss the indictment, he was brought to trial and convicted on all counts.

The Court of Appeals for the Second Circuit affirmed petitioner's conviction. We granted certiorari and we now reverse.

II

This case concerns the legal effect of the petitioner's silence. The District Court's charge permitted the jury to convict the petitioner if it found that he willfully failed to inform sellers of target company securities that he knew of a forthcoming take-over bid that would make their shares more valuable.

Although the starting point of our inquiry is the language of the statute, §10(b) does not state whether silence may constitute a manipulative or deceptive device. Section 10(b) was designed as a catchall clause to prevent fraudulent practices. But neither the legislative history nor the statute itself affords specific guidance for the resolution of this case. When Rule 10b-5 was promulgated in 1942, the SEC did not discuss the possibility that failure to provide information might run afoul of §10(b).

That the relationship between a corporate insider and the stockholders of his corporation gives rise to a disclosure obligation is not a novel twist of the law. At common law, misrepresentation made for the purpose of inducing reliance upon the false statement is fraudulent. But one who fails to disclose material information prior to the consummation of a transaction commits fraud only when he is under a duty to do so. And the duty to disclose arises when one party has information "that the other [party] is entitled to know because of a fiduciary or other similar relation of trust and confidence between them."[9] In its *Cady, Roberts* decision, the Commission recognized a relationship of trust and confidence between the shareholders of a

---

9. *Restatement (Second) of Torts* §551(a)(2) (1976).

corporation and those insiders who have obtained confidential information by reason of their position with that corporation. This relationship gives rise to a duty to disclose because of the "necessity of preventing a corporate insider from . . . tak[ing] unfair advantage of the uninformed minority stockholders." *Speed v. Transamerica Corp.*, 99 F. Supp. 808, 829 (D. Del. 1951).

The federal courts have found violations of §10(b) where corporate insiders used undisclosed information for their own benefit. The cases also have emphasized, in accordance with the common-law rule, that "[t]he party charged with failing to disclose market information must be under a duty to disclose it." *Frigitemp Corp. v. Financial Dynamics Fund, Inc.*, 524 F.2d 275, 282 (2d Cir. 1975). Accordingly, a purchaser of stock who has no duty to a prospective seller because he is neither an insider nor a fiduciary has been held to have no obligation to reveal material facts.

Thus, administrative and judicial interpretations have established that silence in connection with the purchase or sale of securities may operate as a fraud actionable under §10(b) despite the absence of statutory language or legislative history specifically addressing the legality of nondisclosure. But such liability is premised upon a duty to disclose arising from a relationship of trust and confidence between parties to a transaction. Application of a duty to disclose prior to trading guarantees that corporate insiders, who have an obligation to place the shareholder's welfare before their own, will not benefit personally through fraudulent use of material, nonpublic information.

III

In this case, the petitioner was convicted of violating §10(b) although he was not a corporate insider and he received no confidential information from the target company. Moreover, the "market information" upon which he relied did not concern the earning power or operations of the target company, but only the plans of the acquiring company. Petitioner's use of that information was not a fraud under §10(b) unless he was subject to an affirmative duty to disclose it before trading. In this case, the jury instructions failed to specify any such duty. In effect, the trial court instructed the jury that petitioner owed a duty to everyone; to all sellers, indeed, to the market as a whole. The jury simply was told to decide whether petitioner used material, nonpublic information at a time when "he knew other people trading in the securities market did not have access to the same information."

The Court of Appeals affirmed the conviction by holding that "*[a]nyone* — corporate insider or not — who regularly receives material nonpublic information may not use that information to trade in securities without incurring an affirmative duty to disclose." 588 F.2d, at 1365 (emphasis in original). Its decision thus rested solely upon its belief that the federal securities laws have "created a system providing equal access to information necessary for reasoned and intelligent investment decisions." *Id.*, at 1362. The use by anyone of material information not generally available is fraudulent, this theory suggests, because such information gives certain buyers or sellers an unfair advantage over less informed buyers and sellers.

This reasoning suffers from two defects. First not every instance of financial unfairness constitutes fraudulent activity under §10(b). Second, the element required to make silence fraudulent — a duty to disclose — is absent in this case. No duty could arise from petitioner's relationship with the sellers of the target company's securities, for petitioner had no prior dealings with them. He was not their agent, he was not a fiduciary, he was not a person in whom the sellers had placed their trust and confidence. He was, in fact, a complete stranger who dealt with the sellers only through impersonal market transactions.

We cannot affirm petitioner's conviction without recognizing a general duty between all participants in market transactions to forgo actions based on material, nonpublic information. Formulation of such a broad duty, which departs radically from the established doctrine that duty arises from a specific relationship between two parties, . . . should not be undertaken absent some explicit evidence of congressional intent.

As we have seen, no such evidence emerges from the language or legislative history of §10(b). Moreover, neither the Congress nor the Commission ever has adopted a parity-of-information rule.

We see no basis for applying such a new and different theory of liability in this case. As we have emphasized before, the 1934 Act cannot be read "'more broadly than its language and the statutory scheme reasonably permit.'" *Touche Ross & Co. v. Redington,* 442 U.S. 560, 578 (1979), quoting *SEC v. Sloan,* 436 U.S. 103 (1978). Section 10(b) is aptly described as a catchall provision, but what it catches must be fraud. When an allegation of fraud is based upon nondisclosure, there can be no fraud absent a duty to speak. We hold that a duty to disclose under §10(b) does not arise from the mere possession of nonpublic market information. The contrary result is without support in the legislative history of §10(b) and would be inconsistent with the careful plan that Congress has enacted for regulation of the securities markets.

The judgment of the Court of Appeals is *reversed.*

Notes and Questions

1. Reality Check

a. Why was Mr. Chiarella's conviction reversed?

2. Suppose

a. Suppose Mr. Chiarella traded in the stock of a company that had hired his employer to print its annual report to stockholders. Would he be liable under 10b-5? How is that setting different from the facts of *Chiarella?*

3. What Do You Think?

a. Do you agree that a relationship of trust and confidence should be a requirement of insider trading? What about *Cady, Roberts*'s predicate of the unfairness of insider trading? Isn't what Mr. Chiarella did fundamentally unfair?

Cady, Roberts provides a theoretical structure for traditionally conceived insider trading. What about the situation in which the insider does not trade but transmits material, nonpublic information to someone else who does trade? Is the trader, called the tippee, automatically liable? The next case describes the legal theory for tippee liability.

≡≡≡   **Dirks v. SEC**
≡≡≡   **463 U.S. 646 (1983)**

Justice POWELL delivered the opinion of the Court.

Petitioner Raymond Dirks received material nonpublic information from "insiders" of a corporation with which he had no connection. He disclosed this information to investors who relied on it in trading in the shares of the corporation. The question is whether Dirks violated the antifraud provisions of the federal securities laws by this disclosure.

In 1973, Dirks was an officer of a New York broker-dealer firm who specialized in providing investment analysis of insurance company securities to institutional investors. On March 6, Dirks received information from Ronald Secrist, a former officer of Equity Funding of America. Secrist alleged that the assets of Equity Funding, a diversified corporation primarily engaged in selling life insurance and mutual funds, were vastly overstated as the result of fraudulent corporate practices. Secrist also stated that various regulatory agencies had failed to act on similar charges made by Equity Funding employees. He urged Dirks to verify the fraud and disclose it publicly.

Dirks decided to investigate the allegations. He visited Equity Funding's head-quarters in Los Angeles and interviewed several officers and employees of the corporation. The senior management denied any wrongdoing, but certain corporation employees corroborated the charges of fraud. Neither Dirks nor his firm owned or traded any Equity Funding stock, but throughout his investigation he openly discussed the information he had obtained with a number of clients and investors. Some of these persons sold their holdings of Equity Funding securities, including five investment advisers who liquidated holdings of more than $16 million.

While Dirks was in Los Angeles, he was in touch regularly with William Blundell, the *Wall Street Journal*'s Los Angeles bureau chief. Dirks urged Blundell to write a story on the fraud allegations. Blundell did not believe, however, that such a massive fraud could go undetected and declined to write the story. He feared that publishing such damaging hearsay might be libelous.

During the two-week period in which Dirks pursued his investigation and spread word of Secrist's charges, the price of Equity Funding stock fell from $26 per share to less than $15 per share. This led the New York Stock Exchange to halt trading on March 27. Shortly thereafter California insurance authorities impounded Equity Funding's records and uncovered evidence of the fraud. Only then did the Securities and Exchange Commission (SEC) file a complaint against Equity Funding and only then, on April 2, did the *Wall Street Journal* publish a front-page story based largely on information assembled by Dirks. Equity Funding immediately went into receivership.

The SEC began an investigation into Dirks' role in the exposure of the fraud. After a hearing by an administrative law judge, the SEC found that Dirks had aided and abetted violations of . . . §10(b) of the Securities Exchange Act of 1934, and SEC Rule 10b-5 by repeating the allegations of fraud to members of the investment community who later sold their Equity Funding stock. Recognizing, however, that Dirks "played an important role in bringing [Equity Funding's] massive fraud to light," 21 S.E.C. Docket, at 1412, the SEC only censured him. Dirks sought review in the Court of Appeals for the District of Columbia Circuit. The court entered judgment against Dirks "for the reasons stated by the Commission in its opinion."

In view of the importance to the SEC and to the securities industry of the question presented by this case, we granted a writ of certiorari. We now reverse.

We were explicit in *Chiarella* [*v. United States*, 445 U.S. 222 (1980)] in saying that there can be no duty to disclose where the person who has traded on inside information "was not [the corporation's] agent,...was not a fiduciary, [or] was not a person in whom the sellers [of the securities] had placed their trust and confidence." 445 U.S., at 232. Not to require such a fiduciary relationship, we recognized, would "depar[t] radically from the established doctrine that duty arises from a specific relationship between two parties" and would amount to "recognizing a general duty between all participants in market transactions to forgo actions based on material, nonpublic information." *Id.*, at 232, 233. This requirement of a specific relationship between the shareholders and the individual trading on inside information has created analytical difficulties for the SEC and courts in policing tippees who trade on inside information. Unlike insiders who have independent fiduciary duties to both the corporation and its shareholders, the typical tippee has no such relationships.[14] In view of this absence, it has been unclear how a tippee acquires the *Cady, Roberts* duty to refrain from trading on inside information.

The SEC's position, as stated in its opinion in this case, is that a tippee "inherits" the *Cady, Roberts* obligation to shareholders whenever he receives inside information from an insider.

This view differs little from the view that we rejected as inconsistent with congressional intent in *Chiarella*. Here, the SEC maintains that anyone who knowingly receives nonpublic material information from an insider has a fiduciary duty to disclose before trading.

In effect, the SEC's theory of tippee liability in both cases appears rooted in the idea that the antifraud provisions require equal information among all traders. This conflicts with the principle set forth in *Chiarella* that only some persons, under some circumstances, will be barred from trading while in possession of material nonpublic information. We reaffirm today that "[a] duty [to disclose] arises from the relationship between parties...and not merely from one's ability to acquire information because of his position in the market." 445 U.S., at 232-233, n.14.

Imposing a duty to disclose or abstain solely because a person knowingly receives material nonpublic information from an insider and trades on it could have an inhibiting influence on the role of market analysts, which the SEC itself recognizes is necessary to the preservation of a healthy market. It is commonplace for analysts to "ferret out and analyze information," 21 S.E.C., at 1406, and this often is done by meeting with and questioning corporate officers and others who are insiders. And information that the analysts obtain normally may be the basis for judgments as to the market worth of a corporation's securities. The analyst's judgment in this respect is made available in market letters or otherwise to clients of the firm. It is the nature of this type of information, and indeed of the markets themselves, that such information

---

14. Under certain circumstances, such as where corporate information is revealed legitimately to an underwriter, accountant, lawyer, or consultant working for the corporation, these outsiders may become fiduciaries of the shareholders. The basis for recognizing this fiduciary duty is not simply that such persons acquired nonpublic corporate information, but rather that they have entered into a special confidential relationship in the conduct of the business of the enterprise and are given access to information solely for corporate purposes. When such a person breaches his fiduciary relationship, he may be treated more properly as a tipper than a tippee. For such a duty to be imposed, however, the corporation must expect the outsider to keep the disclosed nonpublic information confidential, and the relationship at least must imply such a duty.

cannot be made simultaneously available to all of the corporation's stockholders or the public generally.

The conclusion that recipients of inside information do not invariably acquire a duty to disclose or abstain does not mean that such tippees always are free to trade on the information. The need for a ban on some tippee trading is clear. Not only are insiders forbidden by their fiduciary relationship from personally using undisclosed corporate information to their advantage, but they may not give such information to an outsider for the same improper purpose of exploiting the information for their personal gain. Thus, the tippee's duty to disclose or abstain is derivative from that of the insider's duty. As we noted in *Chiarella,* "[t]he tippee's obligation has been viewed as arising from his role as a participant after the fact in the insider's breach of a fiduciary duty." 445 U.S., at 230, n.12.

Thus, some tippees must assume an insider's duty to the shareholders not because they receive inside information, but rather because it has been made available to them *improperly.* And for Rule 10b-5 purposes, the insider's disclosure is improper only where it would violate his *Cady, Roberts* duty. Thus, a tippee assumes a fiduciary duty to the shareholders of a corporation not to trade on material nonpublic information only when the insider has breached his fiduciary duty to the shareholders by disclosing the information to the tippee and the tippee knows or should know that there has been a breach. Tipping thus properly is viewed only as a means of indirectly violating the *Cady, Roberts* disclose-or-abstain rule.

In determining whether a tippee is under an obligation to disclose or abstain, it thus is necessary to determine whether the insider's "tip" constituted a breach of the insider's fiduciary duty. All disclosures of confidential corporate information are not inconsistent with the duty insiders owe to shareholders. In contrast to the extraordinary facts of this case, the more typical situation in which there will be a question whether disclosure violates the insider's *Cady, Roberts* duty is when insiders disclose information to analysts. In some situations, the insider will act consistently with his fiduciary duty to shareholders, and yet release of the information may affect the market. For example, it may not be clear — either to the corporate insider or to the recipient analyst — whether the information will be viewed as material nonpublic information. Corporate officials may mistakenly think the information already has been disclosed or that it is not material enough to affect the market. Whether disclosure is a breach of duty therefore depends in large part on the purpose of the disclosure. This standard was identified by the SEC itself in *Cady, Roberts:* a purpose of the securities laws was to eliminate "use of inside information for personal advantage." 40 S.E.C., at 912, n.15. Thus, the test is whether the insider personally will benefit, directly or indirectly, from his disclosure. Absent some personal gain, there has been no breach of duty to stockholders. And absent a breach by the insider, there is no derivative breach.

Under the inside-trading and tipping rules set forth above, we find that there was no actionable violation by Dirks. It is undisputed that Dirks himself was a stranger to Equity Funding, with no pre-existing fiduciary duty to its shareholders. He took no action, directly or indirectly, that induced the shareholders or officers of Equity Funding to repose trust or confidence in him. There was no expectation by Dirk's sources that he would keep their information in confidence. Nor did Dirks misappropriate or illegally obtain the information about Equity Funding. Unless the insiders breached their *Cady, Roberts* duty to shareholders in disclosing the nonpublic information to Dirks, he breached no duty when he passed it on to investors as well as to the *Wall Street Journal*.

It is clear that neither Secrist nor the other Equity Funding employees violated their *Cady, Roberts* duty to the corporation's shareholders by providing information to Dirks. The tippers received no monetary or personal benefit for revealing Equity Funding's secrets, nor was their purpose to make a gift of valuable information to Dirks. As the facts of this case clearly indicate, the tippers were motivated by a desire to expose the fraud. In the absence of a breach of duty to shareholders by the insiders, there was no derivative breach by Dirks. Dirks therefore could not have been "a participant after the fact in [an] insider's breach of a fiduciary duty." *Chiarella*, 445 U.S., at 230, n.12.

We conclude that Dirks, in the circumstances of this case, had no duty to abstain from use of the inside information that he obtained. The judgment of the Court of Appeals therefore is *reversed*.

Notes and Questions

1. Notes

a. Equity Funding was one of the largest corporate frauds up to that time. It was the 1970s equivalent of Enron or WorldCom. Chapter 14 has more detail on the Enron and WorldCom scandals. It also has a fuller examination of the role that security analysts such as Mr. Dirks play in corporate governance.

2. Reality Check

a. Mr. Dirks clearly traded (indirectly, by giving information to his clients) on material nonpublic information. Why did he not violate Rule 10b-5?

3. Suppose

a. Suppose a corporate insider gave information to a stock analyst to curry favor with the analyst. Would the analyst be liable as a tippee?

b. Suppose the conductor of the local symphony orchestra attends a ballet as the guest of the symphony's board chair. During intermission, the conductor overhears the board chair disclosing material nonpublic information to another of the chair's guests. If the conductor trades before that information becomes public is he or she liable as a tippee?

4. What Do You Think?

a. Did the Supreme Court draw the right line in defining tippee liability? Why shouldn't every tippee be liable, regardless of whether the tip violated a duty or whether the tippee knew the tip was a violation?

The result in *Chiarella* turned on the notion that insider trading, in the air, so to speak, will not do. If the defendant breached a duty to someone, but not the plaintiff, is that sufficient to impose liability under 10b-5? The final case resolves that question.

United States v. O'Hagan
521 U.S. 642 (1997)

Justice GINSBURG delivered the opinion of the Court.

Respondent James Herman O'Hagan was a partner in the law firm of Dorsey & Whitney in Minneapolis, Minnesota. In July 1988, Grand Metropolitan PLC (Grand Met), a company based in London, England, retained Dorsey & Whitney as local counsel to represent Grand Met regarding a potential tender offer for the common stock of the Pillsbury Company, headquartered in Minneapolis. Both Grand Met and Dorsey & Whitney took precautions to protect the confidentiality of Grand Met's tender offer plans. O'Hagan did no work on the Grand Met representation. Dorsey & Whitney withdrew from representing Grand Met on September 9, 1988. Less than a month later, on October 4, 1988, Grand Met publicly announced its tender offer for Pillsbury stock.

On August 18, 1988, while Dorsey & Whitney was still representing Grand Met, O'Hagan began purchasing call options for Pillsbury stock. Each option gave him the right to purchase 100 shares of Pillsbury stock by a specified date in September 1988. Later in August and in September, O'Hagan made additional purchases of Pillsbury call options. By the end of September, he owned 2,500 unexpired Pillsbury options, apparently more than any other individual investor. O'Hagan also purchased, in September 1988, some 5,000 shares of Pillsbury common stock, at a price just under $39 per share. When Grand Met announced its tender offer in October, the price of Pillsbury stock rose to nearly $60 per share. O'Hagan then sold his Pillsbury call options and common stock, making a profit of more than $4.3 million.

The Securities and Exchange Commission (SEC or Commission) initiated an investigation into O'Hagan's transactions, culminating in a 57-count indictment. The indictment alleged that O'Hagan defrauded his law firm and its client, Grand Met, by using for his own trading purposes material, nonpublic information regarding Grand Met's planned tender offer. According to the indictment, O'Hagan used the profits he gained through this trading to conceal his previous embezzlement and conversion of unrelated client trust funds. O'Hagan was charged with 20 counts of mail fraud, in violation of 18 U.S.C. §1341; 17 counts of securities fraud, in violation of §10(b) of the Securities Exchange Act of 1934 (Exchange Act) and SEC Rule 10b-5; 17 counts of fraudulent trading in connection with a tender offer, in violation of §14(e) of the Exchange Act and SEC Rule 14e-3(a); and 3 counts of violating federal money laundering statutes, 18 U.S.C. §§1956(a)(1)(B)(i), 1957. A jury convicted O'Hagan on all 57 counts, and he was sentenced to a 41-month term of imprisonment. A divided panel of the Court of Appeals for the Eighth Circuit reversed all of O'Hagan's convictions. Liability under §10(b) and Rule 10b-5, the Eighth Circuit held, may not be grounded on the "misappropriation theory" of securities fraud on which the prosecution relied.

Decisions of the Courts of Appeals are in conflict on the propriety of the misappropriation theory under §10(b) and Rule 10b-5.... We granted certiorari and now reverse the Eighth Circuit's judgment.[4]

---

4. Twice before we have been presented with the question whether criminal liability for violation of §10(b) may be based on a misappropriation theory. In *Chiarella v. United States*, 445 U.S. 222, 235-237 (1980), the jury had received no misappropriation theory instructions, so we declined to address the question. In *Carpenter v. United States*, 484 U.S. 19, 24 (1987), the Court divided evenly on whether, under the circumstances of that case, convictions resting on the misappropriation theory should be affirmed.

The "misappropriation theory" holds that a person commits fraud "in connection with" a securities transaction, and thereby violates §10(b) and Rule 10b-5, when he misappropriates confidential information for securities trading purposes, in breach of a duty owed to the source of the information. Under this theory, a fiduciary's undisclosed, self-serving use of a principal's information to purchase or sell securities, in breach of a duty of loyalty and confidentiality, defrauds the principal of the exclusive use of that information. In lieu of premising liability on a fiduciary relationship between company insider and purchaser or seller of the company's stock, the misappropriation theory premises liability on a fiduciary-turned-trader's deception of those who entrusted him with access to confidential information.

The [classical and misappropriation] theories are complementary, each addressing efforts to capitalize on nonpublic information through the purchase or sale of securities. The classical theory targets a corporate insider's breach of duty to shareholders with whom the insider transacts; the misappropriation theory outlaws trading on the basis of nonpublic information by a corporate "outsider" in breach of a duty owed not to a trading party, but to the source of the information. The misappropriation theory is thus designed to "protec[t] the integrity of the securities markets against abuses by 'outsiders' to a corporation who have access to confidential information that will affect th[e] corporation's security price when revealed, but who owe no fiduciary or other duty to that corporation's shareholders." Brief for United States 14.

In this case, the indictment alleged that O'Hagan, in breach of a duty of trust and confidence he owed to his law firm, Dorsey & Whitney, and to its client, Grand Met, traded on the basis of nonpublic information regarding Grand Met's planned tender offer for Pillsbury common stock. This conduct, the Government charged, constituted a fraudulent device in connection with the purchase and sale of securities.[5]

We agree with the Government that misappropriation, as just defined, satisfies §10(b)'s requirement that chargeable conduct involve a "deceptive device or contrivance" used "in connection with" the purchase or sale of securities. We observe, first, that misappropriators, as the Government describes them, deal in deception. A fiduciary who "[pretends] loyalty to the principal while secretly converting the principal's information for personal gain," Brief for United States 17, "dupes" or defrauds the principal.

Deception through nondisclosure is central to the theory of liability for which the Government seeks recognition. As counsel for the Government stated in explanation of the theory at oral argument: "To satisfy the common law rule that a trustee may not use the property that [has] been entrusted [to] him, there would have to be consent. To satisfy the requirement of the Securities Act that there be no deception, there would only have to be disclosure."

We turn next to the §10(b) requirement that the misappropriator's deceptive use of information be "in connection with the purchase or sale of [a] security." This element is satisfied because the fiduciary's fraud is consummated, not when the fiduciary gains the confidential information, but when, without disclosure to his

---

5. The Government could not have prosecuted O'Hagan under the classical theory, for O'Hagan was not an "insider" of Pillsbury, the corporation in whose stock he traded. Although an "outsider" with respect to Pillsbury, O'Hagan had an intimate association with, and was found to have traded on confidential information from, Dorsey & Whitney, counsel to tender offeror Grand Met. Under the misappropriation theory, O'Hagan's securities trading does not escape Exchange Act sanction . . . simply because he was associated with, and gained nonpublic information from, the bidder, rather than the target.

principal, he uses the information to purchase or sell securities. The securities transaction and the breach of duty thus coincide. This is so even though the person or entity defrauded is not the other party to the trade, but is, instead, the source of the nonpublic information. A misappropriator who trades on the basis of material, nonpublic information, in short, gains his advantageous market position through deception; he deceives the source of the information and simultaneously harms members of the investing public.

The misappropriation theory targets information of a sort that misappropriators ordinarily capitalize upon to gain no-risk profits through the purchase or sale of securities. Should a misappropriator put such information to other use, the statute's prohibition would not be implicated. The theory does not catch all conceivable forms of fraud involving confidential information; rather, it catches fraudulent means of capitalizing on such information through securities transactions.

The Government notes another limitation on the forms of fraud §10(b) reaches: "The misappropriation theory would not . . . apply to a case in which a person defrauded a bank into giving him a loan or embezzled cash from another, and then used the proceeds of the misdeed to purchase securities." Brief for United States 24, n.13. In such a case, the Government states, "the proceeds would have value to the malefactor apart from their use in a securities transaction, and the fraud would be complete as soon as the money was obtained." *Ibid.* In other words, money can buy, if not anything, then at least many things; its misappropriation may thus be viewed as sufficiently detached from a subsequent securities transaction that §10(b)'s "in connection with" requirement would not be met. *Ibid.*

The misappropriation theory comports with §10(b)'s language, which requires deception "in connection with the purchase or sale of any security," not deception of an identifiable purchaser or seller. The theory is also well tuned to an animating purpose of the Exchange Act: to insure honest securities markets and thereby promote investor confidence. Although informational disparity is inevitable in the securities markets, investors likely would hesitate to venture their capital in a market where trading based on misappropriated nonpublic information is unchecked by law. An investor's informational disadvantage vis-à-vis a misappropriator with material, nonpublic information stems from contrivance, not luck; it is a disadvantage that cannot be overcome with research or skill.

[C]onsidering the inhibiting impact on market participation of trading on misappropriated information, and the congressional purposes underlying §10(b), it makes scant sense to hold a lawyer like O'Hagan a §10(b) violator if he works for a law firm representing the target of a tender offer, but not if he works for a law firm representing the bidder. The text of the statute requires no such result. The misappropriation at issue here was properly made the subject of a §10(b) charge because it meets the statutory requirement that there be "deceptive" conduct "in connection with" securities transactions.

In sum, the misappropriation theory, as we have examined and explained it in this opinion, is both consistent with the statute and with our precedent. Vital to our decision that criminal liability may be sustained under the misappropriation theory, we emphasize, are two sturdy safeguards Congress has provided regarding scienter. To establish a criminal violation of Rule 10b-5, the Government must prove that a person "willfully" violated the provision. Furthermore, a defendant may not be imprisoned for violating Rule 10b-5 if he proves that he had no knowledge of the Rule. O'Hagan's charge that the misappropriation theory is too indefinite to permit the imposition of criminal liability thus fails not only because the theory is limited to those who breach a recognized duty.

The Eighth Circuit erred in holding that the misappropriation theory is inconsistent with §10(b). The Court of Appeals may address on remand O'Hagan's other challenges to his convictions under §10(b) and Rule 10b-5.

The judgment of the Court of Appeals for the Eighth Circuit is reversed, and the case is remanded for further proceedings consistent with this opinion.

It is so ordered.

Notes and Questions

1. Notes

a. After *O'Hagan*, it is clear that many people who breach a confidence may be liable under 10b-5. A psychiatrist, for example, who uses information gleaned from an executive/patient to trade in company stock may be liable under the misappropriation theory. Similarly, a family member may breach a confidence with another family member. To give some certainty to this area, the SEC adopted Rule 10b5-2. The rule provides that a "duty of trust or confidence" exists

> (1) Whenever a person agrees to maintain information in confidence;
> (2) Whenever the person communicating the material nonpublic information and the person to whom it is communicated have a history, pattern, or practice of sharing confidences, such that the recipient of the information knows or reasonably should know that the person communicating the material nonpublic information expects that the recipient will maintain its confidentiality; or
> (3) Whenever a person receives or obtains material nonpublic information from his or her spouse, parent, child, or sibling; provided, however, that the person receiving or obtaining the information may demonstrate that no duty of trust or confidence existed with respect to the information, by establishing that he or she neither knew nor reasonably should have known that the person who was the source of the information expected that the person would keep the information confidential, because of the parties' history, pattern, or practice of sharing and maintaining confidences, and because there was no agreement or understanding to maintain the confidentiality of the information.

Rule 10b5-2

2. Reality Check

a. What is the misappropriation theory? How is it different from the classical theory of insider trading?

b. Where is the deception under the misappropriation theory?

c. Is the defendant's misappropriation "in connection with" the purchase or sale of a security?

3. Suppose

a. Suppose the facts of *Chiarella* arose today? Would Mr. Chiarella be held to have violated 10b-5?

b. Suppose Dorsey & Whitney had a policy of permitting its lawyers to trade on nonpublic information, as a way of providing additional compensation. Would Mr. O'Hagan be liable under 10b-5?

c. Suppose Mr. O'Hagan had told Dorsey & Whitney he intended to trade in Pillsbury stock and options. Would Mr. O'Hagan be liable under 10b-5?

4. What Do You Think?

a. Is the misappropriation theory consonant with the classic theory? If not, which should prevail?

b. Does the O'Hagan holding essentially impose liability for insider trading on the ground that such trading is fundamentally and inherently unfair?

D. TERMS OF ART IN THIS CHAPTER

Antidilution provision	Greenmail	Reverse stock split
Buy-sell agreement	Insolvency test	Round lot
Capital	Legal capital test	Scienter
Declared	Record date	Stock split
Delist	Restrictions on transfer	Surplus
Dividend	Retired	Treasury stock

8

Getting Money to Creditors When the Corporation Can't Pay

Corporations ordinarily pay their creditors in full as their liabilities become due. This is true for suppliers, lenders, and employees and for other claimants on the corporation's funds such as taxing authorities. By and large, it is also true for tort creditors, although much of a corporation's payment may come from insurance that the corporation has purchased, rather than from assets the corporation has on hand. Where the corporation's managers are recalcitrant in paying, which is different from the setting where those managers believe, in good faith, the corporation is not liable, creditors have an array of devices to ensure satisfaction. Litigation is the most obvious of these devices, as well as other dispute resolution mechanisms such as arbitration and mediation. Where a judgment is entered against the corporation, the creditor can seize and sell corporate assets to obtain satisfaction.

Contract creditors frequently bargain in advance for a security interest or mortgage, which permits them to seize specific corporate property in lieu of payment. Ultimately, a corporation's creditors can force an insolvent corporation into bankruptcy, which, although almost guaranteeing that the creditors will not be paid in full, at least assures an orderly and relatively consistent treatment of creditors' claims.

This chapter deals with situations in which the corporate debtor may have insufficient assets to satisfy its creditors. It explores five areas in which creditors can look to others connected with the corporation for payment. Because the others to whom creditors look are often key people in the planning and management of a corporation, they, and you as their attorney, need to consider these possible avenues of liability. Conversely, because your clients may be owed money by an insolvent corporation, you need to be conversant with these avenues of obtaining redress for your client. Finally, as a matter of social policy, the availability or absence of these avenues of payment directly affects the willingness of third parties to deal with corporations. Where third parties believe that they must look only to the corporation for payment, they will be more likely to demand higher compensation. If they believe they may be able to look beyond the corporation for repayment, at least in some settings, they will be more willing to accept lesser compensation.

The five areas we will consider are: first, liability of individual shareholders by piercing the corporate veil; second, holding related corporations liable through enterprise liability; third, preserving corporate assets for creditors through commercial law and bankruptcy concepts, in particular the doctrine of equitable subordination; fourth, holding successor corporations liable for a predecessor corporation's debts; and finally, holding corporate officers personally liable as direct participants in corporate torts.

A. THE CURRENT SETTING

1. Individual Shareholder Liability by Piercing the Corporate Veil

Corporations statutes typically provide that shareholders are only liable to pay the agreed-upon issuance price for their shares. The statutes also typically go further to make clear that shareholders are not liable for corporate debts. Delaware, for example, provides that, unless a provision for personal liability is placed in the Certificate of Incorporation, stockholders "shall not be personally liable for the payment of the corporation's debts except as they may be liable by reason of their own conduct or acts." DGCL §102(b)(6). The MBCA has a similar provision in §6.22(b). The language "by reason of their own conduct or acts" means that a shareholder is not immune from primary liability simply by virtue of being a stockholder. Despite these statutory provisions, courts assume they have the power to hold shareholders liable for corporate debts in appropriate instances. When this power is exercised, the corporation is said to have been disregarded; the corporate veil has been pierced.

The doctrine of *piercing the corporate veil* is a mystery. It is one of the most frequently litigated issues in corporate law but, although the doctrine is quite old, courts are vague and inconsistent in their statement of the legal principles involved. When courts apply the doctrine, their opinions are nearly always simply gestalt results rather than genuinely articulated decisions. Yet, like Daniel Webster's Dartmouth College, there are those who love it. Judge Cardozo called piercing the corporate veil a doctrine "enveloped in the mists of metaphor" while reminding us that "metaphors in the law are to be narrowly watched." *Berkey v. Third Ave. Ry. Co.*, 155 N.E. 58, 61 (N.Y. 1926). Most business entities casebooks devote lots of pages to piercing and law professors seem to devote a fair bit of class time to the subject. Law students, despite forgetting everything else in the course, can always remember "the taxicab case[1]," in which a New York City taxicab ran down a pedestrian. The pedestrian, Walkovszky, tried to sue the sole shareholder of the corporation that owned the cab. The plaintiff lost.[2]

Piercing the corporate veil is an equitable doctrine that holds a corporation's shareholders liable for the corporation's debts if the corporation is unable to pay. Although it could, in theory, apply in publicly held corporations, in practice it is only germane to the closely held corporation. In fact, once the number of shareholders increases above two or three, there is little likelihood that a court will pierce. It is important to know what piercing the corporate veil does *not* do. It does *not* dissolve the corporation and it does *not* make the shareholders liable for all the

---

1. The taxicab case is *Walkovszky v. Carlton*, 223 N.E.2d 6 (N.Y. 1966).
2. Walkovszky's problem was in the drafting of his complaint. It named Carlton, the individual shareholder, as a defendant, but the facts, as alleged, showed, at most, grounds for holding several other cab companies also owned by Carlton liable. With very broad hints from Judge Fuld, Walkovszky's attorney managed to get the complaint right enough on remand to avoid dismissal and the case ultimately settled before trial.

corporation's debts. If applied, the doctrine renders the shareholders liable only for the plaintiff's claims against the corporation.

What are the elements for piercing the corporate veil? The following excerpt is from a well-written, thoughtful discussion of the standard in one state:

> The principal exception to the limited liability rule is the doctrine of "piercing the corporate veil." This doctrine is equitable in nature and is used by the courts to disregard the distinction between a corporation and its shareholders to prevent fraud or injustice. The general rule which has emerged is that a corporation will be looked upon as a legal entity separate and distinct from its shareholders, officers and directors unless and until sufficient reason to the contrary appears, but when the notion of a legal entity is used to defeat public convenience, justify wrong, protect fraud, or defend crime, then sufficient reason will exist to pierce the corporate veil.
>
> "In deciding whether the corporate veil will be pierced, we recognize that 'each case is *sui generis* and must be decided in accordance with its own underlying facts.'" *Mobridge* [*Community Ind. v. Toure*], 273 N.W.2d [128,] 132 [(S.D. 1978)] (quoting *Brown Brothers Equipment Co. v. State*, 215 N.W.2d 591, 593 (Mich. App. 1974)).
>
> In our past decisions, we have discussed a number of factors[6] that might justify "piercing the corporate veil." After review of those decisions and the factors discussed therein, it is apparent that in making this determination, we have applied a two-part test: (1) was there such unity of interest and ownership that the separate personalities of the corporation and its shareholders, officers or directors are indistinct or non-existent; and (2) would adherence to the fiction of separate corporate existence sanction fraud, promote injustice or inequitable consequences or lead to an evasion of legal obligations?
>
> As to the first part of the test, the "separate corporate identity" prong, we note:

> The "separate corporate identity" prong is meant to determine whether the stockholder and the corporation have maintained separate identities. There are strong public policy reasons for upholding the corporate fiction. Where stock-holders follow the technical rules that govern the corporate structure, they are entitled to rely on the protections of limited liability that the corporation affords. In determining whether the personalities and assets of the corporation and the stockholders have been blurred we consider (i) the degree to which the corporate legal formalities have been maintained, and (ii) the degree to which individual and corporate assets and affairs have been commingled.

> [*NLRB v.*] *Greater Kansas City Roofing*, 2 F.3d [1047,] 1052 [(10th Cir. 1993)]

> Of the six specific factors which we have considered in the past, four are used in determining whether the first prong is met: (1) undercapitalization; (2) failure to observe corporate formalities; (3) absence of corporate records; and (4) payment by the corporation of individual obligations. If these factors are present in sufficient number and/or degree, the first prong is met and the court will then consider the second prong.[9]

---

6. These factors include:

(1) fraudulent misrepresentation by corporation directors;
(2) undercapitalization;
(3) failure to observe corporate formalities;
(4) absence of corporate records;
(5) payment by the corporation of individual obligations; and
(6) use of the corporation to promote fraud, injustice or illegality.

9. We have held that a court should pierce the corporate veil only upon the strongest evidence of these factors.

As to the second part of the test, the "fraud or inequitable consequences" prong, we note:

> Under the fraud, injustice, or evasion of obligations prong of the test we ask whether there is adequate justification to invoke the equitable power of the court. We require an element of unfairness, injustice, fraud, or other inequitable conduct as a prerequisite to piercing the corporate veil.
>
> [T]he showing of inequity necessary to satisfy the second prong must flow from the misuse of the corporate form. The mere fact that a corporation ... breaches a contract ... does not mean that the individual shareholders of the corporation should personally be liable. To the contrary, the corporate form of doing business is typically selected precisely so that the individual shareholders will not be liable. It is only when the shareholders disregard the separateness of the corporate identity *and when that act of disregard causes the injustice or inequity or constitutes the fraud* that the corporate veil may be pierced.... In most cases the mere fact that a corporation is incapable of paying all of its debts is insufficient for a finding of injustice.... That condition will exist in virtually all cases in which there is an attempt to pierce the corporate veil.

Greater Kansas City Roofing, 2 F.3d at 1052-53 (citations omitted) (emphasis original).

The two factors which we have considered in the past to satisfy the second prong include: (1) fraudulent misrepresentation by corporation directors; and (2) use of the corporation to promote fraud, injustice, or illegalities.

If both the "separate corporate identity" prong and the "fraud or inequitable consequence" prong of the test are met and "the court deems it appropriate to pierce the corporate veil, the corporation and its stockholders will be treated identically."

Kansas Gas & Electric Co. v. Ross, 521 N.W.2d 107, 111-113 (S.D. 1994).

This is a comparatively clear statement of the doctrine. Note that the court has used six factors. These turn out to be, on inspection, a two-pronged test. The court will pierce the corporate veil if the three parts of the two-pronged test are met "by the strongest evidence." The first prong is the "no separate corporate identity" prong; the second is the "fraud or inequitable consequence" test and the third is the "court deems it appropriate to pierce" test. Got it?

Professor Stephen M. Bainbridge, in his typically pungent and accurate way, suggests that a necessary but not sufficient predicate for piercing is that the individual shareholder defendant(s) must have control of the corporation, either by owning more than 50 percent of the voting stock or by exercising actual control. Sometimes control is described by courts as using the corporation as the "alter ego" of its shareholders, in which the corporation acts to bring about its shareholders' desires instead of its own. This conception of control is stupid for two reasons. First, anyone with control and ownership of a corporation uses it to effect his or her business ends. Second, at what level of reification (or anthropomorphism) does it make any logical sense at all to say that a corporation has a "personality" or "identity" or "will" of its own?

Control is not enough to pierce the corporate veil. According to Professor Bainbridge, different courts require different additional showings, such as that control was used to bring about some sort of inequity or fraud. Different states vary considerably in both the phrasing of their tests and in the kind and degree of injustice that will suffice to pierce. See generally, Stephen M. Bainbridge, *Abolishing Veil Piercing*, 26 J. Corp. L. 479 (2001).

Three commonly cited factors are worth focusing on because they are emblematic of the generally unsatisfactory nature of piercing the corporate veil analyses. First, many courts say they look to see whether the corporation has observed the requisite corporate formalities such as holding shareholder and director meetings, appointing officers, and filing annual reports with the secretary of state. Lacking in these discussions is any justification for using this criterion as a reason to hold an individual shareholder personally liable for the corporation's debts. Certainly any causation between the corporate formalities and plaintiff's debt is missing. To the extent courts justify this criterion, they tend to fall back on the argument that, because doing business in corporate form is a "privilege," the concomitant limited liability should attach only where the owner of the corporation has had the decency to observe the corporate formalities. Weak at best.

A second criterion, which is sometimes also called observing the corporate formalities, really means evaluating whether the owner has commingled property with the corporation. Where the owner and corporation have a single bank account or where the owner moves funds from corporate to individual accounts or vice versa or, in general, where there is a blurring of the distinction between the individual owner and the corporation, the courts are more likely to pierce. This criterion has at least two valid purposes in a piercing the corporate veil analysis. Often this commingling will be evidence of fraud; the owner is shuffling assets at least in part to create the illusion that the corporation has more assets than it really does. In many instances, as well, the court uses evidence of commingling as a surrogate for a finding that the owner controlled the corporation. But sometimes the commingling has in no way defrauded the plaintiff, and the individual's control is undisputed. In these instances, commingling seems to be simply a makeweight argument.

Finally, many courts use "undercapitalization" as a criterion. Usually this means the court will look to the time when the corporation was first incorporated, which might be some considerable time before the debt in dispute was incurred, to see whether the owner provided enough equity, and insurance, to cover reasonably foreseeable obligations that the corporation might incur. Deliberate undercapitalization can be seen as, in effect, an attempt to defraud (externalize risk might be a better description) others by having the corporation engage in activities as to which there is a likelihood (increasing in probability to a near certainty) of situations in which the corporation will be unable to satisfy its obligations in full. As with the other tests, where this criterion is directly related to the plaintiff's inability to be compensated by the corporation, piercing seems intuitively to be appropriate. However, many courts use these criteria in settings in which they seem to have only the most tenuous connection to the plaintiff's claim.

Although I am tempted to end the discussion of piercing the corporate veil at this point, I'm required, as a business entities law professor, to include at least one full case dealing with the doctrine. Here it is. It is very typical of piercing the corporate veil opinions.

Brevet International, Inc. v. Great Plains Luggage Company

604 N.W.2d 268 (S.D. 2000)

MILLER, C.J.

During 1994 and 1995, Great Plains Luggage Company was engaged in the business of manufacturing and selling golf bags and golf bag travel covers from its plant located at Tyndall, South Dakota. Its principal officers, directors and share-holders were Christopher D. Crosby, W. Greg Coward, and Alan Krutsch. During that time, Brevet International, Inc., provided management consulting services to businesses, universities, government entities and labor unions.

In early March 1995 Crosby contacted Brevet president Donald MacKintosh about installing a management system in its plant. Great Plains was having difficulty manufacturing its products in a cost-efficient and timely manner so as to ensure prompt delivery to its customers. Because of these difficulties, Great Plains had resolved to close unless a solution could be found for its manufacturing problems. There is no dispute that Crosby informed MacKintosh of Great Plains' precarious financial position in their initial phone conversation.

After speaking with Crosby and visiting the plant, MacKintosh orally agreed to provide management consulting services on behalf of Brevet. This agreement was never reduced to writing. The agreed-upon price for Brevet's services was $35,000. [H]owever, out-of-pocket expenses incurred by Brevet were to be reimbursed by Great Plains as invoiced. In reliance on Brevet's assurances of success, Crosby injected $100,000 of his personal funds into the business, in addition to money he had previously invested.

Over the next three months, Brevet's consultants worked with Great Plains' plant manager installing a management system. Brevet submitted weekly invoices addressed to "Chris Crosby, The Great Plains Luggage Company," for professional fees and expenses incurred. Great Plains reimbursed Brevet for its expenses, but did not pay any of the $35,000 professional fee. Brevet sent Great Plains a final demand letter on November 28, 1995, asking for payment. Great Plains did not respond to the letter.

There is much dispute about the specific terms of the consulting arrangement. First, there is disagreement about the identity of the entity that contracted with Brevet. Brevet maintains that it contracted with the individual defendants, not the corporation. Crosby and the other individual defendants argue, however, that the contract was between Great Plains (the corporation) and Brevet.

Brevet initiated this suit against Great Plains and the individual defendants alleging breach of contract and fraud, for failure to pay the management consulting fee.

On appeal, Brevet raises the following issues:

. . .

2) Whether the trial court properly refused to pierce the corporate veil and hold the individual defendants personally liable.

[I]n discussing whether Brevet had satisfied the test for piercing the corporate veil, the trial judge summarily stated: "The plaintiff has been unable to point to anything arising to the level of fraud, injustice or inequitable consequences."

In granting the defendants' motion for partial summary judgment, the trial court found that although there were some irregularities in the record keeping of the company, Great Plains was a lawfully formed corporation under the laws of the State of South Dakota. Notwithstanding some undisputed problems in formalities, the trial court held the failure to observe corporate rules did not reach the level of the first prong of the test for piercing the corporate veil as found in *Kansas Gas & Electric Co. v. Ross*, 521 N.W.2d 107 (S.D. 1994).

Brevet first contends that the management consulting contract was entered into with the individual defendants, not the corporation. Alternatively, it argues that if Great Plains was a valid corporation, then the corporate veil should be pierced and the individual defendants should be held personally liable.

We only briefly address Brevet's first argument that the contract was entered into with Crosby, Coward and Krutsch individually, rather than with Great Plains as a corporation. This claim is totally contradictory to the evidence in the record. In particular, invoices sent by Brevet were addressed to "Chris Crosby, The Great Plains Luggage Company." Moreover, the invoices were paid by corporate check, not personal checks, without objection by Brevet. An experienced businessman like MacKintosh would surely know that contracting with "Great Plains Luggage Company" is not the same as contracting with Crosby, Coward and Krutsch on an individual basis. Finally, the name "Great Plains Luggage Company" meets the statutory requirements for identification of a corporate entity. If Brevet had any doubt as to the form of the business organization with which he was dealing, he need only have contacted the secretary of state's office for verification of corporate status.

We have long recognized that, as a general rule, a corporation is to be considered a legal entity separate and distinct from its shareholders, officers and directors unless and until there is sufficient reason to the contrary. The concept of limited liability is considered one of the central purposes for choosing the corporate form, because it permits shareholders to limit their personal liability to the extent of their investment. A corporation is looked upon as a distinct entity, but when the notion of a separate legal existence is used to "defeat public convenience, justify wrong, protect fraud, or defend crime, then sufficient reason will exist to pierce the corporate veil." [*Kansas Gas*, 521 N.W.2d at] 112 (citations omitted). Decisions about whether to pierce the corporate veil must be decided in accordance with the unique, underlying facts of each case.

In *Kansas Gas*, we enumerated six factors to consider when determining whether equity demands piercing the corporate veil. Those factors include: (1) undercapitalization; (2) failure to observe corporate formalities; (3) absence of corporate records; (4) payment by the corporation of individual obligations; (5) fraudulent misrepresentation by corporate directors; and (6) use of the corporation to promote fraud, injustice or illegality. The six factors can be grouped into two separate prongs: the "separate corporate identity" prong and the "fraud or inequitable consequences" prong. If the four factors under the "separate corporate identity" prong are present in sufficient number and/or degree, then this Court will consider the two factors under the "fraud or inequitable consequences" prong. "[A] court should pierce the corporate veil only upon the strongest evidence of these factors." *Id.* at 113 n.9.

Kansas Gas controls. Applying those factors to these facts, we conclude the trial court did not err. Brevet has not met its burden of showing why the corporate veil should be pierced.

For all the reasons stated above, we . . . affirm as . . . to the personal liability of the individual defendants.

Notes and Questions

1. Notes

a. This case is from the same jurisdiction, South Dakota, as the excerpt from *Kansas Gas & Electric* above and makes reference to the standard articulated in that case.

2. Reality Check

a. Why did Great Plains hire Brevet?
b. What is the underlying dispute between the parties?

3. What Do You Think?

a. Do you think the court should have pierced the corporate veil here?
b. If you were counsel for Great Plains, what advice would you have given your client to minimize the possibility that Brevet could successfully pierce?

All of this is fodder for some amusement, but the potential for piercing raises real problems for corporate planners and their clients. Predictability is a virtue in prospective activities like business planning and the lack of certainty in this area means that you can never assure your clients that they will not be held liable under a piercing the corporate veil theory, at least where there are fewer than half a dozen or so shareholders. Conversely, if you are representing clients who have been harmed by a corporation that seems unlikely to have sufficient assets, the lack of precision for piercing's application may also be undesirable because you and your clients will have to make litigation decisions, often expensive ones, in deciding whether to pursue a piercing claim or not. Greater certainty would help everyone.

One question is whether the piercing doctrine is part of the internal affairs of a corporation. If so, as you'll remember from Chapter 5, then the law of the state of incorporation applies regardless of the state in which the litigation is brought. While there is no definitive answer, and the *Restatement (Second) of Conflict of Laws* is silent, most courts that have addressed the issue have decided that piercing should be subject to the internal affairs doctrine. But while this means that the test that will be applied will probably be that of the state of incorporation (and hence not only predictable but within the planners' choice when they decide on the state in which to incorporate) you should be aware that the actual court applying the test to the facts may be in another state. In practice, such a court may be inclined to use its own sense of equity to decide whether to pierce regardless of the test it believes it is applying.

Treating piercing as part of the internal affairs doctrine makes Delaware law of special importance. Delaware courts are extremely reluctant to pierce, although they do not hesitate to hold individual shareholders of closely held corporations liable for their own actions and, in that regard, are probably a bit more accurate in assigning liability on the ground of direct action than other states are when they impose liability on the same individual actors under a piercing theory. The issue is seldom litigated in the Delaware courts, presumably because the theory simply doesn't succeed. Nonetheless, in recent years the Delaware Court of Chancery has at least left open the possibility of piercing, and a few cases have denied summary judgment on the ground that the possibility of piercing exists. One of the few modern statements of the Delaware rule is:

> "Persuading a Delaware court to disregard the corporate entity is a difficult task." In order to state a cognizable claim to pierce the corporate veil . . . plaintiffs must allege facts that, if taken as true, demonstrate . . . complete domination and control . . . . The degree of control required to pierce the veil is "exclusive domination and control . . . to the point that [the corporation] no longer ha[s] legal or independent significance of [its] own."
>
> Piercing the corporate veil under the alter ego theory "requires that the corporate structure cause fraud or similar injustice." Effectively, the corporation must be a sham and exist for no other purpose than as a vehicle for fraud.

Wallace v. Wood, 752 A.2d 1175, 1183-1184 (Del. Ch. 1999) (Steele, V.C. (citations omitted)

One way to decrease the likelihood of piercing when planning a corporation is to use a checklist of things to do and things to avoid. It may be good practice to review this checklist when forming a new entity and counsel your client to avoid as many of them as possible. Recall in *Kansas Gas & Electric* the court ticked off six factors, divided into two prongs, which it used to decide whether to pierce. Many states have such lists in their case law and the lists keep growing. Doubtless lists are passed from law clerk to law clerk at state supreme courts around the country. If you thought South Dakota's list of 6 was impressive, you should be aware that Kansas has 10 factors, Oklahoma has 11, Maine and Massachusetts have 12, and California and West Virginia have 19. A Hawaii case listed the California factors and added others not on the California list. Herewith the factors:

> In *Associated Vendors, Inc. v. Oakland Meat Co., Inc.*, 26 Cal. Rptr. 806, 813 (Cal. App. 1962) the California Court of Appeal catalogued factors that many courts have weighed in determining whether a corporate entity is the alter ego of another. These include:

> [1] Commingling of funds and other assets, failure to segregate funds of the separate entities, and the unauthorized diversion of corporate funds or assets to other than corporate uses; [2] the treatment by an individual of the assets of the corporation as his own; [3] the failure to obtain authority to issue stock or to subscribe to or issue the same; [4] the holding out by an individual that he is personally liable for the debts of the corporation; [5] the identical equitable ownership in the two entities; [6] the identification of the equitable owners thereof with the domination and control of the two entities; [7] identi[ty] of . . . directors and officers of the two entities in the responsible supervision and management; [8] sole ownership of all of the stock in a corporation by one individual or the members of a family; [9] the use of the same office or business location; [10] the employment of the same employees and/or attorney; [11] the failure to adequately capitalize a corporation; [12] the total absence of corporate assets, and undercapitalization; [13] the use of a corporation as a mere shell, instrumentality or conduit for a single venture or the business of an individual or another corporation; [14] the concealment and misrepresentation of the identity of the responsible ownership, management and financial interest, or concealment of personal business activities; [15] the disregard of legal formalities and the failure to maintain arm's length relationships among related entities; [16] the use of the corporate entity to procure labor, services or merchandise for another person or entity; [17] the diversion

stockholder [sic] or other person or entity, to the detriment of creditors, or the manipulation of assets and liabilities between entities so as to concentrate the assets in one and the liabilities in another; [18] the contracting with another with intent to avoid performance by use of a corporate entity as a shield against personal liability, or the use of a corporation as a subterfuge of illegal transactions; and [19] the formation and use of a corporation to transfer to it the existing liability of another person or entity.

This list, however, is not exhaustive. For example, other courts have looked at: (1) incorporation for the purpose of circumventing public policy or statutes; (2) whether the parent finances the subsidiary; (3) whether the subsidiary has no business or assets except those conveyed to it by the parent; (4) whether the parent uses the subsidiary's property as its own; (5) whether the directors of the subsidiary do not act independently in the interest of the corporation but take their orders from and serve the parent; and (6) whether the "fiction of corporate entity...has been adopted or used to evade the provisions of a statute." *Kavanaugh v. Ford Motor Co.*, 353 F.2d 710, 717 (7th Cir. 1965). Ultimately, no one factor is dispositive.

Robert's Hawaii School Bus, Inc. v. Laupahoehoe Transportation Company, Inc., 982 P.2d 853, 871 (Haw. 1999)

2. Enterprise Liability

Analytically, the piercing the corporate veil theory should be equally applicable regardless of whether the defendant shareholder is an individual or another corporation. But holding a corporate parent liable for its subsidiary's debt is best considered a kind of *enterprise liability*. The difference is that enterprise liability seeks to aggregate corporations into a single enterprise and hold the entire enterprise liable. This aggregation can be *vertical*, where the creditor seeks to hold the debtor corporation's corporate parent, or *horizontal*, where the creditor seeks to aggregate one or more corporations that are under common control.

Conceptually, enterprise liability should be easier to accomplish than piercing the veil to hold individual shareholders liable, because under enterprise liability the ultimate individuals who own the enterprise retain their limited liability. All that happens is that the individuals' attempt to apportion risk among separate corporations is disallowed. As you might imagine, courts have not been any better at articulating a consistent view of enterprise liability than they have in approaching piercing the corporate veil. Because enterprise liability has not been as thoroughly critiqued as other corporate law concepts, you should think particularly carefully about whether the courts are using appropriate standards.

Having said that, though, there seem to be four ways courts think about enterprise liability. Perhaps the most common is simply to treat enterprise liability identically to piercing the corporate veil. The difference between the two being that, as applied, courts are somewhat less reticent to aggregate *affiliated corporations* (that is, corporations under common control whether parent-subsidiary or sibling corporations) than they are to pierce the corporate veil to hold an individual shareholder liable.

The second approach is to impose enterprise liability where, in essence, the court finds that the distinctions between the corporations are sufficiently indistinct that equity is best served by aggregating the corporations. This blurring might be to bring about some sort of fraud, but it might also stem only from sloppiness and inattention to corporate niceties.

Smith v. McLeod Distributing, Inc.

744 N.E.2d 459 (Ind. Ct. App. 2000)

BARNES, J.

CASE SUMMARY

Defendants, Colonial Mat Company, Inc. ("Colonial Mat") and Michael B. Smith, appeal the judgment entered against them for a commercial debt owed to Plaintiff, McLeod Distributing, Inc. ("McLeod"). We affirm in all respects.

FACTS

McLeod was a corporation involved in the wholesale distribution of floor coverings, including carpets. It appears from the evidence that Colonial Mat installed carpets and other floor products in residences and other locations; it was incorporated in 1987. Colonial Industrial Products Company, Inc., ("Colonial Industrial") was incorporated in 1981. At the time Colonial Mat was incorporated, Colonial Industrial was distributing a certain brand of industrial rubber products. A few months after Colonial Mat was incorporated, it applied for a line of credit with McLeod. McLeod initially refused to ship goods to Colonial Mat on credit, but eventually approved a line of credit for Colonial Mat after Smith, the president of both Colonial Mat and Colonial Industrial, signed a personal guarantee for any debt Colonial Mat might incur.

After McLeod and Colonial Mat had been doing business for nearly one-and-a-half years, Smith sent the following letter to McLeod, which we reprint in its entirety:

> March 17, 1989
> To: Carpet Suppliers
> Re: Colonial Carpets
>
> Dear Supplier,
>   In the near future we will be selling our matting products under the name of "Logomatts of America." We are obtaining licensing for custom logo mats from several universities and companies. For marketing reasons we feel a need for a name change.
>   However, we will be registering "Colonial Carpets" to the corporation that we sell floor products under. We presently use "Colonial Carpets" as the name we invoice our carpet jobs.
>   So, as soon as our printing is completed we will be ordering, as well as selling, all floor products except Mats & Matting as "Colonial Carpets" a corporate division of Colonial Industrial Products Co., Inc.
>   If you have any questions, feel free to call me at any time.
>
> Very truly yours,
> Michael B. Smith
> President

On March 27, 1989, Colonial Industrial filed a certificate of assumed name with the Secretary of State, indicating that it would be doing business as Colonial Carpets. After receiving this letter, McLeod changed Colonial Mat's name on its computer billing system to "Colonial Carpets, Inc." It never closed the account originally opened by Colonial Mat, however, and neither Smith nor anyone associated with his businesses did so.

McLeod continued doing business with Colonial Industrial d/b/a Colonial Carpets until February and March of 1990, when several invoices for goods delivered went unpaid. The total unpaid balance accrued to $6,132.65 as of May 11, 1990, when demand for payment was made, and McLeod filed a complaint against Colonial Mat and Smith on September 20, 1990. After this case remained pending for nearly ten years, the trial court conducted a bench trial and entered judgment in favor of McLeod . . . .

ANALYSIS

Colonial Mat argues that it was not a proper party to this suit because it is undisputed that all of the invoices at issue were addressed to "Colonial Carpets, Inc.," which Colonial Mat claims was a distinct corporate entity. It also claims that McLeod had notice before these invoices were issued, via the March 17, 1989, letter, that Colonial Mat and Colonial Industrial d/b/a Colonial Carpets were separate companies. McLeod essentially responds that it would be inequitable not to hold Colonial Mat liable for this debt because Colonial Mat and Colonial Carpets were indistinguishable entities.

Although Indiana courts are reluctant to disregard a corporate entity, they may do so to prevent fraud or unfairness to third parties. That fiction may be disregarded where one corporation is so organized and controlled and its affairs so conducted that it is a mere instrumentality or adjunct of another corporation. "Indiana courts refuse to recognize corporations as separate entities where the facts establish several corporations are acting as the same entity." *General Finance Corp. v. Skinner,* 426 N.E.2d 77, 84 (Ind. Ct. App. 1981).

> an Indiana court considers whether the plaintiff has presented evidence showing: (1) undercapitalization; (2) absence of corporate records; (3) fraudulent representation by corporation shareholders or directors; (4) use of the corporation to promote fraud, injustice or illegal activities; (5) payment by the corporation of individual obligations; (6) commingling of assets and affairs; (7) failure to observe required corporate formalities; or (8) other shareholder acts or conduct ignoring, controlling, or manipulating the corporate form.

Aronson v. Price, 644 N.E.2d 864, 867 (Ind. 1994).

However, *Aronson* specifically concerned piercing the corporate veil in order to hold a shareholder personally liable for a corporate debt; our supreme court was not asked in that case to hold one corporation liable for another closely related corporation's debt. We do not believe the eight *Aronson* factors were intended to be exclusive, particularly when a court is asked to decide whether two or more affiliated corporations should be treated as a single entity. In fact, Indiana courts (in cases cited by *Aronson*) have often evaluated additional factors in such a situation, factors that would not be applicable where one was attempting to pierce the corporate veil to hold a corporation's directors, officers, or shareholders personally liable for a corporate debt.

Some of these factors have included whether similar corporate names were used, . . . ; whether there were common principal corporate officers, directors, and employees, . . . ; whether the business purposes of the corporations were similar, . . . ; and whether the corporations were located in the same offices and used the same telephone numbers and business cards, ... Additionally, we have previously noted that other jurisdictions have disregarded the separateness of affiliated corporations when the corporations are not operated as separate entities but are manipulated or controlled as one enterprise through their interrelationship to cause illegality, fraud, or injustice or to permit one economic entity to escape liability arising out of an operation conducted by one corporation for the benefit of the whole enterprise. Indicia of common "identity," "excessive fragmentation," or "single business enterprise" corporations may include, among other factors, the intermingling of business transactions, functions, property, employees, funds, records, and corporate names in dealing with the public.

McLeod failed to present much evidence relevant to the *Aronson* factors in support of its claim; it presented no evidence of undercapitalization, fraud, absence of corporate records, failure to observe formalities, or shareholder misconduct, for example. Nonetheless, we believe there was sufficient evidence presented from which the trial court might have concluded that Colonial Mat and Colonial Industrial were effectively one and the same corporation, thus justifying a holding that Colonial Industrial was merely an adjunct to or alter ego of Colonial Mat, which is liable for this debt.

First, we note the obvious similarity between the names of the two companies. "Colonial" was apparently used by Smith at the time to identify his businesses generally; the business card that McLeod introduced into evidence had in one corner "Colonial Mat Co., Inc.," and in the opposite corner was simply "Colonial." Second, Colonial Mat and Colonial Industrial d/b/a Colonial Carpets were engaged in virtually identical lines of business. Colonial Industrial's Articles of Incorporation indicated its purpose was "to engage in the sales and distribution of industrial products," while Colonial Mat's purpose was "to engage in the sale, distribution and services related to industrial products including, but not limited to, floor covering products . . . ." The only apparent difference between Colonial Mat and Colonial Industrial d/b/a Colonial Carpets was that Colonial Mat dealt in all floor coverings, while Colonial Industrial dealt in all floor coverings except mats. Third, Smith was president of both Colonial Mat and Colonial Industrial; the only other director for both corporations was the same individual, the treasurer Joe Eller. The two companies also shared the same office manager, Lois Jean Bennett, who testified that she was the only office personnel Smith had at the time. Fourth, the two companies operated at the same address and used an identical phone number. Fifth, while not of major importance, we find it interesting that Colonial Mat's credit application states that it had been in business since 1970. Given that Colonial Mat was incorporated in 1987, it would appear to be reasonable to infer that Smith was referring to 1970 as the date when he, personally, went into business.

Sixth, there is evidence from which a fact finder could have reasonably inferred that Colonial Mat and Colonial Industrial intermingled their assets, or that Colonial Mat paid for obligations of Colonial Industrial, which would satisfy two of the *Aronson* factors. McLeod introduced certain invoices directed to Colonial Mat that were paid by Colonial Mat checks following the March 17, 1989, letter that Colonial

Mat and Smith claims gave notice of a change in corporate structure. We understand that a corporation that is going out of business will have a period of "winding up," where it will pay debts incurred before it went out of business. However, included among those invoices, for example, was an order for 500 business cards placed on March 23, 1989, paid for with a Colonial Mat check. It would seem unusual for a company going out of business to order 500 business cards; a reasonable inference would be that this represented some of the "printing" referred to in the March 17, 1989, letter, and that it was paid for out of Colonial Mat's checking account. The record also contains several payroll checks to Smith and Bennett written on Colonial Mat checks in April of 1989, as well as a Colonial Mat check written to McLeod itself in May of 1989. Finally, we address Smith's and Colonial Mat's claim that "[i]t is undisputed that by letter dated March 17, 1989, Michael B. Smith served notice upon McLeod that its carpet business would be affected by a corporate change." Appellant's Brief p. 7. We find this to be far from undisputed; rather, the letter is ambiguous in this regard. First, the letter at no point states that Colonial Mat is going out of business, and in fact makes no mention of Colonial Mat at all. It can be argued that it refers to Colonial Mat inferentially by stating, "we will be registering 'Colonial Carpets' to the corporation that we sell floor products under." That corporation was Colonial Mat, and thus this sentence may have indicated "Colonial Carpets" was going to be "registered" to Colonial Mat, thus lending support to the idea that Colonial Carpets and Colonial Mat were one and the same. The letter also states that the change to Colonial Carpets was a name change made for marketing reasons. Ron McLeod, McLeod's president, testified that this indicated to him that the name change "was a marketing thing that had no bearing on anything else. . . . It didn't change the company, it just had another name. . . . It was just all the same stuff." McLeod also testified that the meaning of the letter to him was "they are adding a name to their Colonial Industrial Products Company, Inc. a company called Colonial Carpets." Thus, far from providing clear and unambiguous notice of a change in corporate structure, the letter appears to have only added to the confusion about the purported corporate separateness of Colonial Mat and Colonial Industrial d/b/a Colonial Carpets.

There is ample indication that, in dealing with the public, Smith treated Colonial Mat and Colonial Industrial d/b/a Colonial Carpets as if they were adjunct corporations, or mere alter egos or instrumentalities of each other that shared a common identity. Therefore, equity requires that Colonial Mat be held liable for the debt at issue here in order to protect an innocent third party, McLeod, from unfairness.

Notes and Questions

1. Notes

a. Smith was the shareholder of both Colonial Mat and Colonial Industrial but plaintiff did not include a cause of action against Smith under a traditional piercing the corporate veil theory.

b. Colonial Mat could not obtain credit from McLeod unless Smith personally guaranteed the indebtedness. This is a typical situation. In this case, although Smith challenged his liability on the guarantee the court had little difficulty holding him liable.

c. Smith described Colonial Carpets as a "corporate division" of Colonial Industrial. The term "division" indicates an aspect of a business that is run relatively separately from other aspects but that is not conducted in a separate corporation.

2. Reality Check

a. Which corporation was the debtor corporation?

b. How does McLeod benefit if Colonial Mat is liable for Colonial Industrial's debt?

3. Suppose

a. What if it were clear that McLeod had not confused the two corporations. Would the analysis or result have been different?

b. Suppose Colonial Mat and Colonial Industrial had had very distinct names. Would the court have imposed enterprise liability?

4. What Do You Think?

a. Why would Smith want to form two different corporations?

b. Which of the enterprise liability factors do you think were most important to the court? Do you think the court focused on the right factors?

5. You Draft It

a. Redraft Smith's March 17, 1989 letter to minimize the possibility of piercing the corporate veil and the possibility of aggregating the corporations under the doctrine of enterprise liability. The text read

To: Carpet Suppliers
Re: Colonial Carpets

Dear Supplier,
   In the near future we will be selling our matting products under the name of "Logomatts of America." We are obtaining licensing for custom logo mats from several universities and companies. For marketing reasons we feel a need for a name change.
   However, we will be registering "Colonial Carpets" to the corporation that we sell floor products under. We presently use "Colonial Carpets" as the name we invoice our carpet jobs.
   So, as soon as our printing is completed we will be ordering, as well as selling, all floor products except Mats & Matting as "Colonial Carpets" a corporate division of Colonial Industrial Products Co., Inc.
   If you have any questions, feel free to call me at any time.

Very truly yours,
Michael B. Smith
President

A third way courts approach the idea of enterprise liability is to aggregate affiliated corporations that perform complementary aspects of a single business.

In re U-Haul International, Inc.

87 S.W.3d 653 (Tex. App.-San Antonio 2002)

Sitting: SARAH B. DUNCAN, Justice, PAUL W. GREEN, Justice, SANDEE BRYAN MARION, Justice.

PER CURIAM.

The plaintiffs sued [U-Haul International, Inc. ("UHI")] and three others for injuries arising from an accident involving a tow dolly, which the plaintiffs alleged was designed and manufactured by UHI. A second defendant was towing a car with the tow dolly when the accident occurred. Plaintiffs contended a third defendant owned the tow dolly. The plaintiffs alleged (1) the tow dolly had not been materially altered by the second defendant, (2) the tow dolly was defective and unreasonably dangerous when it left UHI's possession and entered the stream of commerce, and (3) UHI knew that using a loaded tow dolly behind a 1988 Ford LTD would result in an accident that could produce serious death and injury.

After a series of discovery disputes, the trial court issued an order directing UHI to produce any documents, accident reports, and petitions that relate to "tow dollies involved in incidents where the tow dolly was said to fishtail, swerve, weave, whip, sway, jackknife, or any other means of describing the tow dolly or tow dolly/tow vehicle combination becoming unstable or uncontrollable" for years 1996 through 2001. The trial court ordered UHI to obtain the documents "from any and all corporations, companies, affiliates, subsidiaries, or other entities within the U-Haul system or U-Haul chain of companies." The order set a deadline of February 27, 2002 at 5:00 P.M., and stated that failure to comply would result in a sanctions hearing set for February 28, 2002. UHI and UHI's insurer, Republic Western Insurance Company ("Republic"), are wholly-owned subsidiaries of Amerco, and are, therefore, companies "within the U-Haul system." UHI filed a motion to reconsider in which it contended that it could not produce records not within its control. Specifically, UHI asserted that Republic had custody and control of accident claims files and other documents, and that it (UHI) could not force Republic to respond to plaintiffs' discovery request. Plaintiffs did not request documents directly from Republic... until February 27th.

On February 28th, the trial court heard evidence on plaintiffs' motion for sanctions. Plaintiffs argued that UHI and Republic are not independent companies, and UHI could obtain the requested documents from Republic. Plaintiffs asserted that UHI had "defied" the court's order; thus, sanctions...were appropriate. UHI presented evidence that it had produced all the documents in its possession; that it had asked Republic for the responsive documents, but Republic refused the request; and it could not force Republic to produce documents because Republic was an independent company. Following the hearing, the court sanctioned UHI, ordering that the following matters were "established": (1) the design of the tow dolly in question was defective, (2) the tow dolly was unreasonably dangerous, and (3) UHI had notice of the defect. On May 7th, UHI filed a petition for writ of mandamus, complaining of the sanctions order.

One of UHI's defenses is that the tow dolly was not purchased or rented from U-Haul, was probably stolen, and had been altered after it left UHI's possession.

We agree with UHI that the trial court's "findings" prevent it from litigating these defenses at trial; therefore, UHI is entitled to seek mandamus relief.

UHI asserts the trial court abused its discretion by sanctioning it for not fully responding to a document request that UHI contends should have been addressed to Republic. A party is required to produce only those documents within its "possession, custody, or control." Tex. R. Civ. P. 192.3(b). Plaintiffs rely on *Home Indemnity Company v. Giles,* 392 S.W.2d 568, 569 (Tex. Civ. App. — Austin 1965, no writ) for the proposition that an insured has the right to obtain its claims file information. However, UHI presented evidence that it had requested the information from Republic, but Republic refused to honor the request. Thus, even if UHI has the right to the files, plaintiffs were still required to prove UHI had the ability to compel Republic to turn over its claims files. Plaintiffs contend UHI and Republic are sibling-companies, and share similar officers and directors; therefore, UHI has the ability to compel Republic to provide the responsive documents.

For the purposes of legal proceedings, subsidiary corporations and parent corporations are separate and distinct "persons" as a matter of law and the separate entity of corporations will be observed by the courts even where one company may dominate or control, or even treat another company as a mere department, instrumentality, or agency. Courts are willing to disregard the corporate form when it is used as part of an unfair device to achieve an inequitable result, such as when a corporation is organized and operated as a mere tool or business conduit of another corporation, or when the corporate fiction is resorted to as a means of evading an existing legal obligation. Under the "single business enterprise" doctrine, when corporations are not operated as separate entities, but rather integrate their resources to achieve a common business purpose, each constituent corporation may be held liable for the debts incurred in pursuit of that business purpose. Even if UHI and Republic are closely related, the plaintiffs have not met their burden of proving that UHI and Republic form a single business enterprise. There is no evidence that UHI treats Republic like "a mere department" or that the two companies "integrate their resources to achieve a common business purpose."

We hold that because the plaintiffs did not meet their burden of establishing that UHI has "possession, custody, or control" of the responsive documents, the trial court abused its discretion in sanctioning UHI as it did.

Notes and Questions

1. Notes

a. The principal reason why a single business might be conducted by separate but affiliated corporations is because different aspects of the business may have very different risks. By establishing a separate corporation to engage in each separate aspect of the business, only those assets directly connected with a particular risk are liable to be used for liabilities related to that risk. For example, owning and operating a shopping mall might be divided among several corporations. The real estate might be owned by corporation *A*. A second corporation, corporation *B*, might develop the mall (i.e., hire architects and contractors, obtain building permits, etc.). A third corporation, corporation *C*, might own the buildings after the mall is built. This results in the risks of development and operation being contained within corporations *B* and *C*, respectively, without the land, which is owned by corporation *A*, being at risk. Modern finance theory suggests that a corollary to separating the risks is that financing, whether equity or debt, is less expensive to obtain than if the business were operated by a single corporation.

b. U-Haul International, Inc., is owned by AMERCO, a publicly traded corporation controlled by the founding Shoen family. AMERCO's 2002 Annual Report contains the following information about the corporation's business and its corporate structure:

> AMERCO, a Nevada corporation (AMERCO), is the holding company for U-Haul International, Inc. (U-Haul), Amerco Real Estate Company (Real Estate), Republic Western Insurance Company (RepWest) and Oxford Life Insurance Company (Oxford). AMERCO has four industry segments represented by Moving and Storage Operations (U-Haul), Real Estate, Property and Casualty Insurance (RepWest) and Life Insurance (Oxford).

> **HISTORY**
> U-Haul was founded in 1945 under the name "U-Haul Trailer Rental Company." From 1945 to 1974, U-Haul rented trailers...through independent dealers. Since 1974, U-Haul has developed a network of Company managed rental centers (U-Haul Centers) through which U-Haul rents its trucks and trailers and provides related products and services (e.g., the sale and installation of hitches, as well as the sale of boxes and moving supplies). At March 31, 2002, U-Haul's distribution network included 1,345 Company operated centers and 14,905 independent dealers.

> **MOVING AND STORAGE OPERATIONS**
> Moving and self-storage operations consist of the rental of trucks and trailers, the sale of moving aids such as boxes and the rental of self-storage spaces to the do-it-yourself mover.

> **MOVING OPERATIONS**
> As of March 31, 2002, the U-Haul rental equipment fleet consisted of 97,000 trucks, 87,000 trailers and 21,000 tow dollies. Additionally, U-Haul provides support rental items such as furniture pads, utility dollies and handtrucks. Approximately 90% of U-Haul's rental revenue is from do-it-yourself movers.

> U-Haul sells a wide selection of moving supplies that include boxes, tape and packaging materials. U-Haul Centers also sell and install hitches and towing systems, and sell propane.

> U-Haul designs and manufactures its truck van boxes, trailers and various other support rental equipment items. Truck chassis are manufactured by both foreign and domestic truck manufacturers. These chassis receive certain post-delivery modifications and are joined with van boxes at strategically located Company-owned manufacturing and assembly facilities in the United States.

> U-Haul services and maintains its trucks and trailers through an extensive preventive-maintenance program, generally performed at Company-owned facilities located at or near U-Haul Centers. Major repairs are performed either by the chassis manufacturers' dealers or by Company-owned repair shops.

> **SELF-STORAGE BUSINESS**
> Through 1,023 owned, managed or participating self-storage locations in the United States and Canada, U-Haul offers for rent more than 361,600 self-storage spaces at March 31, 2002.

> **REAL ESTATE OPERATIONS**
> Real Estate owns approximately 90% of AMERCO's real estate assets.... The remainder of the real estate assets are owned by various U-Haul entities. Real Estate is responsible for managing all of the properties including the environmental risks

of the properties. Real Estate is responsible for the purchase of all properties used by AMERCO or any of its subsidiaries. Real Estate also handles all the dispositions (sale or lease) of unused real estate.

PROPERTY AND CASUALTY INSURANCE

RepWest originates and reinsures property and casualty-type insurance products for various market participants, including independent third parties, U-Haul's customers, independent dealers and AMERCO. For the year ended December 31, 2001, approximately 19.6% of RepWest's written premiums resulted from U-Haul underwriting activities.

LIFE INSURANCE

Oxford originates and reinsures annuities,...life and disability coverage, and Medicare supplement insurance. Oxford also administers the self-insured employee health and dental plans for AMERCO.

2. Reality Check

a. Who are the defendants and how (if at all) are they related to one another?

3. Suppose

a. If Republic were named as a defendant, would the result or analysis be different? Do plaintiffs have a claim against Republic?

4. What Do You Think?

a. Do you think AMERCO, the parent corporation, separated the operations of U-Haul specifically to reduce its overall risks? If so, should that separation be considered a form of "fraud" and therefore used to justify enterprise liability? If not, what further evidence would you require before aggregating the corporations?

b. Do you think plaintiffs have met their burden as to UHI's constructive possession once they showed AMERCO's corporate structure? If not, what more should they show and how should they show it?

The final setting in which enterprise liability may be applied is where a single business is separated into separate corporations, each of which performs the same (or nearly the same) functions. In other words, one business is fragmented into several.

≣ Goldberg v. Lee Express Cab Corporation

634 N.Y.S.2d 337 (Sup. Ct. 1995)

BARBARA R. KAPNICK, J.

While plaintiff Marina Bosi Goldberg, a resident of California, was a pedestrian on the sidewalk in front of the New York Hilton on Sixth Avenue between 53rd and 54th Streets in Manhattan on October 10, 1993, she was hit and severely injured by a taxicab which jumped the curb while attempting to exit the New York Hilton's driveway.

Plaintiffs then commenced this personal injury action against the following defendants: (a) The Hilton Hotels Corporation ("Hilton"); (b) Azad Kabir a/k/a Kabir Azad, the driver of the subject taxicab; (c) Lee Express Cab Corporation ("Lee Express"), the corporate owner of the taxicab; (d) Natan More a/k/a Nathan

More, the sole owner and shareholder of Lee Express Cab Corporation; and (e) sixteen other corporations (the "Taxi Corporations") owned and operated solely by Natan More.

Defendants More and the Taxi Corporations now move ... to dismiss plaintiffs' complaint on the grounds that it fails to state a cause of action against them as they have no connection to the accident. While defendant More does not dispute that he is the sole shareholder of the sixteen Taxi Corporations as well as of Lee Express, he argues that each of the Taxi Corporations is maintained as a separate corporate entity, and thus neither he as an individual nor the separate Taxi Corporations may be held liable for plaintiff's accident.

The issues raised by the instant motion were addressed by the Court of Appeals almost thirty years ago in the landmark case of *Walkovszky v. Carlton*, 223 N.E.2d 6 (N.Y. 1966). The plaintiff in that case was allegedly injured when he was run down by a taxicab owned by the Seon Cab Corporation. The action was commenced not only against the Seon Cab Corporation, but also against its stockholder, William Carlton, who was allegedly also a stockholder of ten additional corporations. Plaintiff sought to pierce the corporate veil on the grounds that the corporations were allegedly "'operated ... as a single entity, unit and enterprise' with regard to financing, supplies, repairs, employees and garaging ..." *Walkovszky v. Carlton, supra*. Defendant Carlton moved to dismiss the complaint as to him on the ground that it failed to state a cause of action.

The Court of Appeals ... state[d] that

> [h]ad the taxicab fleet been owned by a single corporation, it would be readily apparent that the plaintiff would face formidable barriers in attempting to establish personal liability on the part of the corporation's stockholders. The fact that the fleet ownership has been deliberately split among many corporations does not ease the plaintiff's burden in that respect. The corporate form may not be disregarded merely because the assets of the corporation, together with the mandatory insurance coverage of the vehicle which struck the plaintiff, are insufficient to assure him the recovery sought.

> *Walkovszky v. Carlton, supra.*

Finding the complaint to be "barren of any 'sufficiently particular[ized] statements' ... that the defendant Carlton and his associates are actually doing business in their individual capacities, shuttling their personal funds in and out of the corporations 'without regard to formality and to suit their immediate convenience,'" the Court of Appeals dismissed the complaint against the individual defendant. *Walkovszky v. Carlton, supra* (citations omitted).

In contrast to the complaint in *Walkovszky*, however, plaintiffs' complaint in this action sets forth, upon information and belief, the following specific allegations:

> ... the defendant More individually operated all of the CORPORATIONS; interchanged and commingled the receipts, disbursements, assets and properties of the said corporations as their own; purchased centrally all supplies, automobile parts, oil, gas and tires for all of the said corporations; acted as dispatchers to assign drivers to all of the taxicabs; the said taxicabs are registered in the names of the individual corporations; were garaged centrally; and all other operations and properties of all of the said corporations were operated, controlled, managed and maintained as a single entity, unit and enterprise by the defendant MORE.

Plaintiffs' complaint further alleges that

"the CORPORATIONS were mere shams and fictions; the instruments and agents of the defendant MORE, and each of them, in that none of the CORPORATIONS had a separate existence of their own, and their existence served no other purpose than to enable the defendant MORE to defraud the public, including the plaintiff."

[T]his Court finds that plaintiffs have set forth "a cognizable action for piercing the corporate veil[s] and assigning personal liability" to defendant More in this action. *29/35 Realty Associates v. 35th Street New York Yarn Center,* [581 N.Y.S.2d 43 (1st Dept. 1992)]. Of course, whether or not plaintiffs are ultimately able to set forth sufficient proof to sustain these claims is another question, which is not before this Court for determination at this time.

Accordingly, this Court finds that the motion by defendants More and the Taxi Corporations to dismiss plaintiffs' complaint . . . must be denied.

Notes and Questions

1. Notes

a. One reason to fragment a business into several nearly identical corporations is to limit creditors, especially tort creditors, to only those assets most directly responsible for their claims. As *Goldberg* illustrates, the taxicab industry is a classic business for such fragmentation. In general, any business that anticipates frequent tort claims might seek to fragment the entire enterprise.

b. Note that many industries, such as taxicabs, are required to maintain minimum amounts of insurance to fully compensate tort claimants.

c. Another reason why a business might be fragmented is simply historical. A business that acquires a competing business might well do so by purchasing all the competing business's stock with the result that the larger business is fragmented into two corporations, each engaging in the same business.

2. Reality Check

a. Is the key to this decision that one business was fragmented into several corporations? Or is the key that the distinctions between the separate corporations were blurred, as in *Smith v. McLeod Distributing, Inc.?* Consider the Appellate Division's opinion affirming the trial court:

Plaintiffs' claim that all of the corporate defendants are part of a larger corporate combine is particularized and includes, for example, specific allegations that all of the corporations' cabs are centrally maintained and garaged; that borrowed funds are commingled to finance medallions and vehicles for all the entities; and that all the corporate books are under the control of the same persons. We also find the allegations supporting the claim that the corporations are the alter ego of defendant More to be sufficient to withstand this motion to dismiss addressed to the pleading. We have considered defendants' remaining contentions and find them to be without merit.

Goldberg v. Lee Express Cab Corp., 642 N.Y.S.2d 292 (App. Div. 1996)

3. Suppose

a. Suppose all More's taxicabs were owned by Lee Express Cab Corporation and the ancillary services, such as maintenance and garaging, were owned by another corporation wholly owned by More. Would the court be more or less likely to hold More liable or to use enterprise liability?

4. What Do You Think?

a. Do you think proof that Lee Express Cab Company maintained the legislatively mandated minimum tort insurance should, by itself, defeat a claim for enterprise liability? Should proof that the corporation maintained insurance at a level that it reasonably, and in good faith, believed would fully compensate nearly all tort plaintiffs defeat enterprise liability?

b. What will plaintiffs need to show at trial to prevail against More and the sixteen other corporations?

c. Do you believe fragmentation, without more, should be sufficient to aggregate affiliated corporations? If not, what more would you require?

3. Commercial and Bankruptcy Doctrines

Another line of approach in trying to satisfy a corporate debt from noncorporate sources lies in the areas of commercial and bankruptcy law, both of which are beyond the scope of this book. Commercial law provides the doctrine of *fraudulent conveyances* to protect creditors. Briefly, if a corporate debtor transfers assets for less than fair value at a time when it was insolvent and for the purpose of harming its other creditors, those other creditors can trace the transferred assets into the hands of the transferees.

Similarly, bankruptcy law provides protection through *voidable preferences* and *equitable subordination*. A bankrupt corporation's creditors can recover corporate property transferred to certain corporate insiders within one year of the bankruptcy if the transfer was for an antecedent debt, had the effect of giving the insiders more than they would have received in the bankruptcy, and was made while the corporation was insolvent. Such transfers are considered to be impermissible preferences for insiders.

The concept of *equitable subordination* was discussed in Chapter 6 in connection with planning the corporation's capital structure. The next case is a classic example of equitable subordination in action.

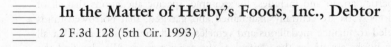

In the Matter of Herby's Foods, Inc., Debtor
2 F.3d 128 (5th Cir. 1993)

POLITZ, C.J.

BACKGROUND

Herby's Foods, Inc. produced and distributed fast foods to convenience stores. [The Insiders] are interrelated companies that advanced funds to Herby's and possess claims as unsecured creditors in the Herby's bankruptcy.

[The Insiders] purchased Herby's on October 26, 1987 pursuant to a Stock Purchase Agreement. The purchase price was $5,500,000, $2,800,000 of which was actually a loan to Herby's to pay off an intercompany debt to its previous owner. Herby's executed a note and security agreement in favor of [the Insiders] for $2,800,000. [T]he security interest, however, was not perfected at that time.

In addition, [the Insiders] provided a working capital line of credit to Herby's in the amount of $4,000,000. The parties have stipulated that no third-party lender would make a working capital loan to Herby's on any terms. The line of credit was evidenced by Herby's promissory note and security agreement.... Once again, the security interest was not timely perfected. [H]erby's eventually borrowed the maximum amount available under this line of credit.

[The Insiders] did not file a UCC-1 to perfect [their] security interest under the purchase money loan until...13 months after the note and security agreement had been executed. Similarly, [the Insiders] did not file a UCC-1 to perfect [their] security interest under the working capital loan until June 9, 1989, 20 months after the date of the underlying note and security agreement. [The Insiders]...admitted that, "[w]e delayed putting in the UCC's because we were hoping to get a secured lender."

Between [the Insiders]'s acquisition of Herby's and the filing of its petition in bankruptcy on September 7, 1989, the amount that Herby's owed to its unsecured creditors (other than the Insiders) increased fivefold, from $929,550.23 to $4,635,675. Further, between January 6, 1989 and September 1, 1989, [the Insiders] made unsecured advances to Herby's exceeding $579,000, advances which were not evidenced by loan agreements or any other documentation and which apparently bore no interest.

After Herby's filed its voluntary Chapter 11 bankruptcy petition, the Insiders, as unsecured creditors, submitted proofs of claims [totaling $7,720,367.11].

The Official Unsecured Creditors Committee (the Committee) responded with a Complaint to Subordinate Claims.... In its complaint the Committee sought to subordinate...the claims of the Insiders.... The Insiders opposed the avoidance of their claims and, alternatively their subordination to a level below that of general unsecured creditors.

The bankruptcy court applied the test for equitable subordination which we detailed in *In re Mobile Steel Co.*[3] Under that test, equitable subordination is justified only if: (1) the claimant engaged in inequitable conduct; (2) the misconduct resulted in injury to the creditors or conferred an unfair advantage on the claimant; and (3) equitable subordination of the claim would not be inconsistent with the provisions of the Bankruptcy Act (now Bankruptcy Code). The bankruptcy court found in the affirmative on each of the three *Mobile Steel* inquiries and subordinated the claims of the Insiders to the level of equity holders, finding that this ranking was necessary to offset the harm that the debtor and its non-insider creditors had suffered as a result of the inequitable conduct of the Insiders.

Timely appealing the affirmance by the district court, the Insiders assert five points of error: (1) the finding that Herby's was undercapitalized on the date of [the Insiders]'s acquisition; (2) the finding that the late perfection by [the Insiders] of their security interests constituted inequitable conduct;...(4) the finding that the Insiders' actions harmed the other creditors sufficiently to warrant subordination; and (5) the affirmance of the extent of the equitable subordination ordered by the bankruptcy court.

---

3. *Benjamin v. Diamond (In re Mobile Steel Co.)*, 563 F.2d 692 (5th Cir. 1977).

ANALYSIS

Principles of Equitable Subordination

In *Mobile Steel* we established the test to determine when equitable subordination is appropriate. In addition to the tripartite test noted above, we further held in *Mobile Steel* that three additional principles must be considered in determining whether the three prongs of the subordination test have been satisfied. First, the inequitable conduct by the claimant may be sufficient to warrant subordination whether or not the misconduct related to the acquisition or assertion of the claim. Second, a claim should be subordinated only to the extent necessary to offset the harm that the bankrupt and its creditors suffered as a result of the inequitable conduct. Third, the claims arising from the dealings between the debtor and its fiduciaries must be subjected to rigorous scrutiny, and, if sufficiently challenged, the burden shifts to the fiduciary to prove both the good faith of the transaction and its inherent fairness.

Although the exact parameters of inequitable conduct have not been comprehensively or precisely delineated, such conduct does encompass: (1) fraud, illegality, breach of fiduciary duties; (2) undercapitalization; and (3) the claimant's use of the debtor corporation as a mere instrumentality or alter ego.

Undercapitalization generally refers to the insufficiency of capital contributions made to the debtor corporation. Inadequate capitalization may be established by the testimony of a skilled financial analyst that the capitalization "would definitely be insufficient to support a business of the size and nature of the bankrupt in light of the circumstances existing at the time the bankrupt was capitalized."[16] Capitalization is also inadequate "if, at the time when the advances were made, the bankrupt could not have borrowed a similar amount of money from an informed outside source."[17]

Even though undercapitalization alone generally does not justify equitable subordination, evidence of additional inequitable conduct may do so. For example, if an insider makes a loan to an undercapitalized corporation, the combination of undercapitalization and the insider loan may allow the bankruptcy court to recharacterize the loan as a capital contribution, or to equitably subordinate the loan to the claims of other creditors.

C. Equitable Subordination of Appellants' Claims
UNDERCAPITALIZATION

The record contains evidence to support the finding that Herby's was undercapitalized on the date of [the Insiders]'s purchase. An expert financial witness tendered by the Committee testified that as of the date of its acquisition by [the Insiders], Herby's capital was not sufficient to support its operations. The testimony of a former financial officer of Herby's corroborated the fact that on the date of its acquisition, Herby's was incapable of paying its debts as they became due and therefore was insolvent.

We need not rely solely on the first prong of the *Mobile Steel* test for inadequate capitalization, however. The Insiders stipulated before trial that . . . Herby's could not have borrowed a similar amount from an informed outside source on acceptable

---

16. *Mobile Steel*, 563 F.2d at 703.
17. *Id.*

terms, either to complete the acquisition or to obtain working capital. We find no error in the bankruptcy court's determination that Herby's was undercapitalized on the date of acquisition.

DELAYED PERFECTION AS INEQUITABLE CONDUCT

As stated, undercapitalization alone generally is insufficient to justify equitable subordination. The Insiders contend that the bankruptcy court erroneously treated the untimely perfection of their security interests as sufficient additional inequitable conduct to warrant subordination. We need not decide, however, whether the combination of undercapitalization plus merely the late perfection of security for the avowed purpose of "hoping to get a secured lender" constitutes sufficient inequitable conduct to support subordination; the Insiders herein did more.

The Insiders never injected any equity capital into Herby's, electing instead to advance funds through tardily perfected secured loans made at times when no bona fide third-party lender would have done so. With full knowledge that Herby's was undercapitalized and insolvent, the Insiders persisted with their practice of advancing funds only in the form of loans.

Further, the loan from [the Insiders] was not initially reflected on Herby's books. When finally booked, it was listed as an unsecured loan. Similarly, the [the Insiders] debt was never definitively identified on Herby's books. Finally, the purported working capital loans from [the Insiders], totaling over one-half million dollars, were never evidenced by any form of loan agreement.

[The Insiders] received only minimal interest payments and no principal payments on its note. It perfected its security position only after Herby's stopped making the interest payments. Likewise, [the Insiders] received only five interest payments and did not perfect its security interest until seven months after Herby's stopped payments. The working capital advances from [the Insiders] apparently never purported to bear any interest. We find more than adequate evidence of inequitable conduct on the part of the Insiders to support the court's equitable subordination of their claims.

HARM TO OTHER CREDITORS

The Insiders next maintain that their conduct did not harm the creditors of Herby's sufficiently to warrant subordination. They acknowledge, however, that the aggregate size of Herby's unsecured debt to its trade creditors increased from approximately $900,000 to over $4,600,000, and that the average number of days outstanding for trade payables increased almost elevenfold, from approximately seven to approximately seventy-five, between the date of [the Insiders]'s acquisition of Herby's and its filing for relief in bankruptcy. Nevertheless, they insist that no evidence was presented to the bankruptcy court that any specific creditor was deceived or lured into extending additional unsecured credit by the actions.... The Insiders' reliance on this argument is misplaced.

The bankruptcy court found that the Insiders' conduct harmed Herby's outside creditors by significantly increasing their trade credit exposure and by reducing their ultimate dividend in the liquidation. Most importantly, the court found that the Insiders had secured an unfair advantage by structuring their cash contributions to Herby's as loans, rather than as equity capital. If the Insiders were allowed to retain their ranking as unsecured creditors, they would have gained an advantage in the priority scheme by encouraging outside creditors to increase their credit exposure to Herby's. Their efforts were successful; those trade creditors substantially increased their credit to Herby's during the period in question. We are persuaded that the inequitable conduct of the Insiders produced sufficient injury to the unsecured trade creditors and secured a sufficiently unfair advantage for the Insiders to warrant equitable subordination.

DEGREE OF SUBORDINATION

The Insiders finally contend that their claims should have been subordinated only to the level of general unsecured creditors. "The prerogative to relegate claims to inferior status on equitable grounds, though broad, is not unlimited."[25] As noted earlier, a claim should be subordinated only to the extent necessary to correct the harm or unfair advantage caused by the inequitable conduct.

The harm or unfair advantage that resulted from the Insiders' inequitable conduct is not limited to whatever may have resulted from their late perfection of [the Insiders]'s security interests. Both the harm and the unfair advantage are much more pervasive. Herby's was undercapitalized from the date of [the Insiders]'s acquisition, and the Insiders did nothing to rectify that situation. Further, the advances from [the Insiders] were neither accurately nor timely reflected on Herby's financial records and the purported loans from [the Insiders] were never evidenced on the records or by any form of a loan agreement.

While these deceptive practices were being perpetrated, the aggregate sums owed by Herby's to its trade creditors increased by 3.7 million dollars. According to the record before us, the total amount distributable from Herby's estate will approximate 2.1 million dollars. If the claims of the Insiders are allowed a ranking equal to that of the unsecured trade creditors, the Insiders would receive approximately 75% of Herby's estate. This cannot be permitted. Even with subordination, the harm to the trade creditors will not be completely rectified. Anything less than full subordination would lend judicial approval to the unfair advantage secured by the Insiders. This we will not do.

Notes and Questions

1. Notes

a. The Insiders purchased all of Herby's Foods' stock from a subsidiary of Anheuser-Busch. Anheuser-Busch later sued the Insiders for failing to make a subsequent purchase payment. The Insiders counterclaimed, asserting that plaintiff had made false representations that significantly understated Herby's Foods' liabilities at the time they purchased the stock. A verdict for the Insiders was later overturned on appeal. See *Anheuser-Busch Companies, Inc. v. Summit Coffee Co.*, 858 S.W.2d 928 (Tex. App.-Dallas 1993).

2. Reality Check

a. How much in assets does Herby's have? What are its liabilities?

b. How are Herby's outside creditors hurt by what the Insiders did?

c. How are Herby's outside creditors protected by the court's holdings?

---

25. *Mobile Steel*, 563 F.2d at 699 (internal citation omitted).

3. Suppose

a. Suppose the Insiders had perfected their security interests in timely fashion. Would Herby's other creditors have acted differently? Would the court's analysis or the result have been different?

4. What Do You Think?

a. Why did the Insiders make their postacquisition infusions of money in the form of loans rather than in the form of equity?

b. Which factors do you think were the most important to the court in affirming the equitable subordination?

4. Successor Liability

The next method by which corporate creditors can seek satisfaction comes into play when control of the corporation has changed in certain ways. Because a corporation is separate from its owners, a change of ownership does not affect a creditor's claim against the corporation. In other words, a corporation does not shed any of its liabilities simply because all its stock has changed hands. Further, as we will see in Chapter 17, when two corporations merge, which is a common way to effect a change of control of one of the corporations, the resulting corporation has the assets *and liabilities* of each of the two merging corporations. See MBCA §11.06 and DGCL §259(a).

But what about the liabilities of a corporation that sells its assets?[3] In the clearest setting, a corporation that sells a small amount of its assets does not thereby eliminate any liabilities. Conversely, the purchaser does not acquire any of the selling corporation's liabilities. The purchaser is simply obligated to pay for the assets as it agreed to do. As noted above, where the selling corporation is approaching bankruptcy, an asset sale for less than fair value may render the buyer liable to the seller's creditors. But leaving aside the bankruptcy possibility, and assuming that the sale is to an unrelated third party acting at arm's length, sales of corporate assets should have no effect on the selling corporation's liabilities.

In theory, this rule should apply even where the selling corporation sells a large percentage of its assets; even where it sells all its assets. In fact, where one corporation wants to acquire another, the transaction may be structured as a sale of assets, rather than as a purchase of 100 percent of the seller's stock or as a merger, so that the purchaser does not become liable for the seller's liabilities. Again, assuming no fraud, the selling corporation's creditors are not harmed. Instead of looking to a corporation that has $X in assets, the creditors are now looking to a corporation that has $X in cash. In some settings, this may make their claims more likely to be satisfied than if the corporation had assets but not much cash. Nonetheless, in some instances creditors of the selling corporation can hold the buying corporation liable for the seller's debts under doctrines that are collectively known as *successor liability*. The following case shows a typical scenario.

---

3. Of course, corporations sell goods and services all the time. That's how they engage in business and make money (one hopes). The situation posed in this paragraph is meant to focus on the corporation that sells assets in settings that are not in the normal course of its business.

Pancratz v. Monsanto Company

547 N.W.2d 198 (Iowa 1996)

NEUMAN, J.

Plaintiffs Gary and Cindy Pancratz (hereinafter "Pancratz") sued Monsanto for personal injuries sustained by Gary when he fell from a ladder attached to an exterior wall of the Monsanto building where he was working. The fall was caused by separation of the ladder's hand rails at welds as he reached for the extended hand rails above the roof line. Pancratz also sued Knutson Construction Company, the corporate successor to the general contractor for the Monsanto building, and various subcontractors involved in fabricating and installing the ladder. Pancratz sued these defendants on theories of negligence, strict products liability, and breach of warranty.

Monsanto cross-claimed against Knutson Construction Company and the subcontractors for indemnification in the event Monsanto was found liable for any of Pancratz's damages. At the close of all the evidence, the district court granted Knutson Construction Company's motion for directed verdict, ruling the record contained no proof that any of the exceptions to the general rule of successor non-liability applied. On appeal, Monsanto renews its challenge to the directed verdict, theorizing that the application of the "mere continuation" exception raises a factual question that should have been submitted to the jury.

To understand the parties' contentions, we must review the transaction between Knutson Construction Company and its predecessor. The facts are undisputed. The original Knutson Construction Company was a wholly owned subsidiary of Knutson Companies, Inc. (hereinafter "KCI"). The Knutson family owned all the stock of KCI.... John Curry was president and chief executive officer of KCI for several years until he resigned in 1983 to work part-time as a consultant for the company. Curry never owned any stock in either Knutson Construction Company or KCI, nor is he in any way related to the Knutson family.

In 1985, KCI sought a buyer for Knutson Construction Company. Curry and his friend, James Michael (who had no prior association with the Knutson companies), formed Michael-Curry Companies, Inc. (hereinafter "MCCI"). MCCI in turn formed a wholly owned subsidiary, Michael-Curry Construction Company, for the purchase of Knutson Construction Company. Curry and Michael were the sole directors and shareholders of MCCI. No one from the Knutson family has ever owned stock in MCCI or participated in its management.

Upon Michael-Curry Construction Company's acquisition of Knutson Construction Company's assets, the transferring corporation changed its name to "Knut Co." Because Michael-Curry succeeded to the name of Knutson Construction Company, we shall hereinafter refer to the new (or successor) corporation as "Knutson," and the predecessor corporation as "Knut Co."

Knutson paid approximately $1.3 million for Knut Co.'s assets. The sale included prime construction contracts, a construction yard, and various equipment and supplies, as well as the company's name, logo, and good will. Certain other assets were specifically excluded; Knut Co. also retained some contracts. The parties agree that the transaction was intentionally structured as an asset purchase, rather than a stock purchase, to insulate Knutson from the debts and liabilities of Knut Co.

Knutson hired most of Knut Co.'s employees. Curry served as president and CEO of Knutson from its creation until 1993, when he became chairman of its board of directors. Knutson had four vice presidents. One of them, Larry Trom, had worked for Knut Co. at the time of sale. No evidence was presented, however, that Trom held any management role at Knut Co.

For a few months after the sale, Knutson operated at the same location as Knut Co. had for many years. By the end of 1985, however, the business had moved and changed its registered address, stationery, and other records. Knut Co. continued to exist for a short time, but eventually declared bankruptcy.

DISCUSSION

Monsanto contends substantial evidence in the record shows that Knutson was a mere continuation of Knut Co. It notes that the two corporations shared common assets, employees, business location, and trade name. They also provided the same services. Without contesting these factual findings, Knutson counters that the two corporations were at all times separate entities, sharing no common ownership or management. Thus the controversy on appeal centers on what factors are relevant to application of the "mere continuation" exception, and whether the district court appropriately decided the question as a matter of law.

As a general rule, a corporation that purchases the assets of another corporation assumes no liability for the transferring corporation's debts and liabilities. Exceptions arise only in four circumstances: (1) the buyer agrees to be held liable; (2) the two corporations consolidate or merge; (3) the buyer is a "mere continuation" of the seller; or (4) the transaction amounts to fraud. Here Knutson argues that the general rule of nonliability applies, while Monsanto contends the third, or "mere continuation," exception applies.

The mere continuation exception, as traditionally applied, focuses on continuation of the *corporate entity*. *Grand Lab., Inc. v. Midcon Lab.*, 32 F.3d 1277, 1283 (8th Cir. 1994) (applying Iowa law). The exception has no application without proof of continuity of management and ownership between the predecessor and successor corporations. Thus, "'[t]he key element of a "continuation" is a common identity of the officers, directors and stockholders in the selling and purchasing corporations.'" *Id.* (quoting *Leannais v. Cincinnati, Inc.*, 565 F.2d 437, 440 (7th Cir. 1977))....

It is generally recognized that the general rule of corporate successor nonliability developed "as a response to the need to protect bonafide purchasers from unassumed liability." *Tucker* [*v. Paxson Mach. Co.*, 645 F.2d 620 (8th Cir. 1981)] at 623. To mitigate the potentially harsh results of the general rule, legal devices (such as corporate survival statutes) have developed to protect the rights of creditors after corporate dissolution. Such methods, however, would not ordinarily protect the person injured by a defective product manufactured by a company whose assets have long since been sold. Thus concern has arisen that the general rule may be inconsistent with the policies of strict liability. This concern has prompted a few courts to expand the basis for successor liability in products liability cases, either by creating new exceptions or broadening the old ones. Under the expanded approach to the mere continuation exception,

> the focus is on the continuity of the seller's *business operation* and not the continuity of
> its management and ownership. Thus, using a kind of "totality of the circumstances"

approach, courts look at factors such as whether the successor corporation used the same employees, business location, assets, and trade name and produced the same products as the predecessor to determine if there was a continuity of the predecessor's enterprise.

Grand Lab., 32 F.3d at 1283 (citing *Cyr v. B. Offen & Co.*, 501 F.2d 1145, 1151-53 (1st Cir. 1974) (emphasis added)).

Monsanto argues on appeal that Iowa decisions tend to follow the expanded or "totality of the circumstances" approach when considering successor liability. We, however, find no departure in our cases from the traditional formulation of the rule. Nor do we believe public policy would be served by such an expansion of the "mere continuation" exception.

In determining whether a successor corporation is liable under the mere continuation exception, this court has consistently looked for a continuity of management and ownership. We have never applied the mere continuation exception where the buying and selling corporations had different owners.

Moreover, we made plain in *DeLapp* [*v. Xtraman, Inc.*, 417 N.W.2d 219 (Iowa 1987)] that we did not believe strict liability policies would be furthered by imposing liability on a successor corporation that was without fault in creating the defective product. Such a radical departure from traditional corporate principles, we observed, should be left to the legislature.

Monsanto nevertheless argues that this court's decision in *C. Mac Chambers Co. v. Iowa Tae Kwon Do Academy, Inc.*, 412 N.W.2d 593 (Iowa 1987), essentially focused on continuity of the business operation, not identity of ownership, in imposing liability on a successor corporation. The case, however, is factually distinguishable. In *C. Mac Chambers*, a father owned and controlled the original corporation. Facing insolvency, he formed a successor corporation whose sole director and shareholder was his son. The son paid no consideration for his shares in the new corporation, and the father remained in charge. The business continued in the same location, providing the same services to the same clientele.

Although we held in *C. Mac Chambers* that the successor corporation was liable for the obligations of its predecessor despite the change in ownership, we did not thereby reject the traditional approach to the "mere continuation" exception to nonliability. To the contrary, we relied on authority expressly adopting the traditional view. But in retrospect the holding perhaps better exemplifies the fraud exception, not the mere continuation exception, to the general rule of nonliability. As recently observed by the Eighth Circuit Court of Appeals, the case "stands for the unremarkable proposition that parties cannot circumvent the mere continuation exception by inserting relatives as sham owners and directors of a new company that is in substance the predecessor." *Grand Lab.*, 32 F.3d at 1284.

As demonstrated by *C. Mac Chambers*, we need not expand the mere continuation exception in order to protect creditors and others from sham transfers. Thus we reject Monsanto's invitation to abandon the majority rule in favor of one adopted in a distinct minority of jurisdictions.

Applying Iowa's longstanding rule to the record before us, we find beyond dispute that Knutson is not a mere continuation of Knut Co. Monsanto tendered no evidence of continuity of ownership. The two corporations shared no common stockholders. While it is true that Knutson's president and CEO, John Curry, had at one time served in a similar capacity with KCI, Curry resigned his management position with KCI two years before the sale. Thus the record contains no proof of identity in management. Other common factors urged by Monsanto (same employees, same location, same trade name) are irrelevant when evaluating the mere continuation exception under the traditional standard.

Furthermore, the evidence establishes that Knut Co. survived, at least for some time, after the sale. While it is true that Knutson continued Knut Co.'s general corporate activities, it carried out such operations as a distinct and separate corporate entity. Unlike *C. Mac Chambers,* the record reveals no hint of a sham transfer. The substantial purchase price evidences an arm's-length transaction.

We are convinced the district court did not err in its refusal to submit the question of whether Knutson was a "mere continuation" of Knut Co. to the jury. The commonly accepted indicia point unmistakably to nonliability. Knutson was entitled to judgment as a matter of law. Accordingly, we affirm the judgment of the district court.

Notes and Questions

1. Notes

a. The expanded successor liability rule Monsanto was arguing for is usually known as the *continuity of enterprise* exception and was first adopted by the Michigan Supreme Court in *Turner v. Bituminous Casualty Co.,* 244 N.W.2d 873 (Mich. 1976). As the *Pancratz* court points out, the focus of the continuity of enterprise test is on whether the business itself has continued as a going concern and would hold a successor corporation liable when there is *no* continuation of ownership between the transferor and transferee corporations.

A very few states have gone further and adopted the *product line* exception. California introduced this test in *Ray v. Alad Corp.,* 560 P.2d 3 (Cal. 1977). Under this exception, the court looks to see only whether the successor acquired substantially all the transferor's assets and whether it produces essentially the same products. In other words, the product line exception would hold a successor corporation liable even where there is no continuity of ownership, or management, or employees between the transferor and transferee corporations.

Both the continuity of enterprise exception and the product line exception have been rejected by the great majority of courts that have considered them and the *Restatement (Third) of Torts* has rejected both tests. Nonetheless, because the states in which they have been accepted are quite populous (Michigan has adopted the continuity of enterprise exception; New Jersey, California, and Pennsylvania have adopted the product line exception), the tests remain important. As a matter of choice of law, the few courts that have considered the matter have used the law of the state with the most important contacts to the injury or contract rather than the law of the state of incorporation. Thus, planners usually cannot predict with certainty whether expanded notions of successor liability will attach or not.

b. Justice Newman adverted to *"corporate survival statutes."* These are designed to protect both shareholders and a corporation's creditors when a solvent corporation dissolves. Without such statutes two undesirable results may come about. First, creditors might not be paid because they did not assert their claims prior to dissolution. Second, shareholders would remain liable to the corporation's creditors, at least to the extent of the corporate assets they received in the dissolution. Corporate survival statutes solve these problems essentially by permitting a soon-to-be-dissolved corporation to notify its known creditors and also to give notice to the public (i.e., to unknown creditors) of the impending dissolution. Those who wish to assert claims against the corporation then must do so within a relatively short period of time. If the corporation complies with the corporate survival statutes, its shareholders are shielded from later liability for corporate debts. See DGCL §280 and MBCA §§14.06 and 14.07.

2. Reality Check

a. What are the four well-recognized exceptions to the rule that a corporation that obtains all the assets of another corporation is not liable for that corporation's liabilities?

b. What are the elements for the mere continuation exception?

c. How are the continuity of enterprise exception and the product line exception different from the mere continuation exception?

3. Suppose

a. Suppose Knut Co. had been purchased by a corporation formed by the youngest generation of the Knutson family, who had no ownership interest in KCI. If all the other facts remained the same, would the court hold the successor corporation liable? If so, under which exception?

4. What Do You Think?

a. As the court notes, the corporate law approach (mere continuation exception) is in tension with the products liability law approach. How do you think the law should resolve this tension?

b. Do you think that application of successor liability doctrine (regardless of the particular rules adopted) should be made by the court or by a jury? If you think a jury is the appropriate body to apply the law in this setting, do you believe plaintiffs showed sufficient evidence to get to a jury?

B. BACKGROUND AND CONTEXT: DIRECT LIABILITY OF CORPORATE OFFICERS

When a corporation enters into a contract, which it can do only through its agent (who may or may not be an officer), the agent is not bound on the contract, assuming the third party knows the identity of the corporation and that the agent is acting on its behalf. See *Restatement (Third) of Agency* §6.01. Of course the parties may agree that the agent will be liable on the contract as well as the corporation. This frequently occurs when a corporation is just beginning business. Creditors are reluctant to contract only with a corporation with few assets and no operating history. The corporation's promoters, who will likely be its officers and directors and possibly its shareholders, too, are required to become personally liable as a condition to entering into the contract at all. None of this is controversial.

But, a creditor may also look to a corporate officer (or director or shareholder) who has, subsequent to the contract's formation, guaranteed performance. This is a frequent allegation when a corporation is experiencing financial difficulty and needs help from creditors either in the form of more funds or in forbearing from enforcing contract terms. Corporate insiders may well find themselves personally liable for corporate debts if a court finds that they represented to creditors that they, personally, would in some way guarantee a corporate obligation and the creditor relies to its detriment on that guarantee. You should note that courts will often enforce these representations even when made orally rather than in writing.

A corporation's agent, such as an officer, is liable for his or her own tort that causes personal injury to a third person and the corporation is liable, as well, if the agent is an employee acting within the scope of employment. A corporation's agent is also liable to a third party where his or her actions constitute fraud or conversion on behalf of the corporation, even though the corporation alone benefits and not the agent. See *Restatement (Third) of Agency* §§7.01 and 7.02.

Apart from these settings, the agent is not liable to a third party if the agent's actions constitute only a failure to perform duties owed to the corporation. This is true even where the agent's failure to perform his or her duties is intentional. See *Restatement (Second) of Agency* §357.

An officer, who is probably responsible for supervising other agents, may have greater tort exposure than an employee who does not supervise others.

Although courts frequently analyze the liability of corporate officers to third persons under the *Restatement (Third) of Agency*, they also approach the issue through the corporation law doctrine known as the *participation theory of liability*. The following case describes the contours of that doctrine.

Saltiel v. GSI Consultants, Inc.

788 A.2d 268 (N.J. 2002)

STEIN, J.

I

In December 1997, plaintiff Jan Saltiel, doing business as Edgewater Design Associates, filed suit against GSI Consultants, Inc. (GSI), a Pennsylvania corporation, Dr. Henry Indyk, a GSI corporate officer, and Richard Caton, a former GSI corporate officer. The complaint sought damages arising from allegedly defective turfgrass specifications prepared by defendants and used by plaintiff in the reconstruction of a softball field and soccer field located at William Paterson University (WPU) in Wayne, New Jersey. Plaintiff is a landscape architect and GSI is a turfgrass consulting company doing business under the name Turfcon. Plaintiff has since voluntarily dismissed her claims against GSI.

The underlying transaction involved WPU's award to plaintiff in March 1995 of a contract to provide landscaping architectural services for the reconstruction of its athletic fields. Plaintiff in turn requested a proposal from GSI outlining turfgrass specifications for the reconstruction. In February 1995, GSI submitted a proposal, signed by Caton, listing the services that it would perform in connection with the WPU contract. Plaintiff accepted the proposal and engaged GSI to prepare the specifications for the WPU athletic fields.

The soccer field was completed in September 1996. Indyk did not visit the soccer field on a regular basis as had been his practice with respect to the softball field. Almost immediately after its completion, the soccer field developed problems of standing water and inadequate drainage. In response to the problems, WPU installed additional drainage facilities and began core aerification of the soccer field's turf. However, the drainage did not improve and the turfgrass was consistently damp or soggy. The soccer field remained unfit for athletic use.

Plaintiff hired Turf Diagnostics and Design, Inc. (TDD) to determine the cause of the drainage failure. After an investigation, TDD informed plaintiff that, although the soccer field had been constructed in accordance with GSI's field specifications, the field specifications had been negligently prepared because the rootzone designed by GSI formed a nearly impermeable barrier that did not allow for proper water drainage. As required under plaintiff's contract with WPU, she prepared new specifications for the field and hired a contractor to reconstruct it at a cost of $351,000. Plaintiff's contract with GSI did not require GSI to provide a bond or demonstrate evidence of professional liability insurance.

Plaintiff's complaint alleges claims against all defendants for negligent design, negligent misrepresentation, breach of contract, breach of warranty, promissory estoppel, and agency liability. In an unreported opinion the Appellate Division . . . concluded that both Indyk and Caton could be personally liable for negligence under the so-called "participation theory of personal liability."

II

[This case] requires us to consider: (1) the proper application of the participation theory of personal liability for tortious conduct by corporate officers under New Jersey law; and (2) whether the plaintiff's claim against Indyk and Caton sounds in tort or contract.

A

The Appellate Division's opinion correctly determined that our caselaw has recognized the applicability of the participation theory of personal liability for the tortious conduct of corporate officers. [T]he essence of the participation theory is that a corporate officer can be held personally liable for a tort committed by the corporation when he or she is sufficiently involved in the commission of the tort. A predicate to liability is a finding that the corporation owed a duty of care to the victim, the duty was delegated to the officer and the officer breached the duty of care by his own conduct.

New Jersey cases that have applied the participation theory to hold corporate officers personally responsible for their tortious conduct generally have involved intentional torts. More specifically, the majority of the cases have involved fraud and conversion.

The conduct at issue in this appeal does not implicate intentional tortious conduct, but rather the individual defendants' allegedly negligent conduct in designing the specifications for the soccer field. Indyk and Caton assert that the participation theory is limited to intentional torts by corporate officers. The Appellate Division . . . was unwilling to limit the doctrine to intentionally tortious acts. That court relied on three New Jersey decisions to support its broader application of the participation theory.

[Those decisions] arguably support plaintiff's contention that the participation theory is not limited to intentional torts, and that the theory's application turns only on the question of whether there was actual participation in allegedly tortious conduct rather than on the nature of the tortious conduct. Although the theory may encompass conduct other than intentional torts, that issue has not been settled. Based on the application of the participation theory in other state courts, it may be argued that the theory should be limited to cases involving intentional wrongful conduct by corporate officers, or negligent conduct by such officers that results in personal injuries.... Application of the participation theory to negligent conduct by corporate officers in other jurisdictions also has involved personal injury claims.

B

Whatever may be the appropriate standard for limiting corporate officers' liability under the participation theory, the essential predicate for application of the theory is the commission by the corporation of tortious conduct, participation in that tortious conduct by the corporate officer and resultant injury to the plaintiff. If, however, the breach of the corporation's duty to the plaintiff is determined to be governed by contract rather than tort principles, the participation theory of tort liability is inapplicable. Accordingly, because the plaintiff's relationship with GSI initially was defined by the contract between them, we consider the principles that reliably serve to distinguish contract and tort claims.

III

[B]ecause we are convinced that plaintiff has not pled and supported a cause of action sounding in tort, and has failed to establish that either GSI or defendants Indyk and Caton owed an independent duty to plaintiff outside the scope of the contract, the theory cannot be applied to the facts in this record.

In rejecting the Appellate Division's reliance on the participation theory of liability, we rely on the principles set forth in state and federal cases on whether a cause of action sounds in tort or contract. Plaintiff's complaint alleged causes of action based on negligent design and negligent misrepresentation. Irrespective of the terminology used in the complaint, however, we are persuaded that this case is essentially a basic breach of contract case, and that plaintiff, through her tort allegations, simply is seeking to enhance the benefit of the bargain she contracted for with defendant GSI.

In this case the scope of the parties' obligations was defined by the contract, and the contract imposed responsibilities on defendant GSI only, and not on defendants Indyk and Caton. The expectation was that defendant corporation would design and prepare the requisite specifications for the athletic fields and that plaintiff would compensate the corporation for the work. There appears to have been no expectation that the individual defendants would be personally liable under the contract. Plaintiff's original request for a proposal was directed toward defendant GSI, and the responses received by plaintiff were on a letterhead that specifically included the corporate names "Turfcon" and "GSI, Inc." Clearly, plaintiff was aware throughout the transaction that she was dealing with a corporate entity and that defendants Indyk and Caton were acting on GSI's behalf.

We acknowledge that a different analysis and result could be implicated if a soccer player sustained personal injuries proximately caused by the allegedly deficient design work provided by GSI. In that context, because no contract defined the obligations of the parties, a critical issue would be whether GSI owed an independent duty of care to prospective users of the field and, if so, whether the participation theory would apply. We need not resolve those issues. Here, however, plaintiff alleges damages that do not arise from any duty imposed by law but rather result from

GSI's alleged breach of contract, and include the cost of preparing new specifications and of hiring a new contractor to reconstruct the soccer field.

None of the parties dispute the existence of a valid contract between plaintiff and defendant GSI, and GSI's alleged breach of that contract clearly can give rise to contractual liability. However, plaintiff has since voluntarily dismissed her claims against defendant GSI. As noted, that contract did not require GSI to provide a bond or demonstrate evidence of professional liability insurance. Nonetheless, irrespective of the allegations in the complaint that sound in tort, plaintiff cannot convert basic contract claims into negligence claims in order to create a basis for the imposition of personal liability on corporate officers.

IV

Because this appeal essentially involves a breach of contract claim, making the participation theory of individual liability inapplicable, we reverse the Appellate Division's judgment and reinstate summary judgment for defendants Indyk and Caton.

Notes and Questions

1. Notes

a. See also Chapter 10 for a discussion of the potential civil and criminal liability of corporate officers under certain statutes such as CERCLA.

2. Reality Check

a. What element(s) of the direct participation theory did the court find was lacking? Do you agree?

3. Suppose

a. Suppose a soccer player were injured on the field and sued Caton and Indyk individually. How would the court analyze the cause of action?

b. Suppose Saltiel had been injured on the soccer field while inspecting it. If she brought suit against Caton and Indyk individually, would the court's analysis or the result be different?

4. What Do You Think?

a. Why do you think plaintiff voluntarily dismissed her claims against the corporation?

b. Do you think the courts should use agency doctrines or corporate law doctrines to decide the liability of corporate officers to third parties? Why?

You should be aware of two other approaches to finding corporate insiders personally liable. First, think about whether the insider could be considered the *principal* of a principal-agent relationship. If so, you may find liability under the *Restatement (Third) of Agency*. See generally Chapter 4. Second, analyze whether the corporate insider and any other person or entity are carrying on as co-owners a business for profit. If so, they may be liable as partners in a general partnership. See generally Chapter 18.

C. TERMS OF ART IN THIS CHAPTER

Affiliated corporations
Continuity of enterprise
  exception
Corporate survival statute
Enterprise liability
Equitable subordination

Fraudulent conveyances
Mere continuation
  exception
Participation theory of
  liability
Piercing the corporate veil

Product line exception
Successor liability
Voidable preferences

9

How Corporations Take Actions

In this chapter we begin to focus on the ways in which corporations are governed and take actions. We start by considering the board of directors. First we examine the conceptual purposes of the board. Next we will explore the way in which directors are selected for the board. Finally we will detail the mechanical aspects of board action — for example, the requirements for meetings. The last part of this chapter deals with the way in which corporate actions are actually performed—that is, the role of officers and other agents. If you have covered Chapter 4 on agency, some of this material may be a review.

A. THE BOARD OF DIRECTORS

1. The Role of the Board of Directors

a. The Current Setting

As you may have realized by now, corporations are fictional entities that can only act through humans. You surely know that employees provide the needed labor, that suppliers provide raw materials to, and that customers purchase finished goods or services from, the corporation. Managers supervise the employees (and other managers) and coordinate the corporation's activities. You may also be aware that shareholders (owners) and lenders contribute the money to pay employees and managers and to purchase raw materials.

Conspicuously absent from this list of humans is a group that is nonetheless central to the theory of corporate law and is often central as a practical matter to the functioning of corporations. This group is the *board of directors*. The theoretical place of the board is so vital to corporate law that it warrants highlighting the statutory provisions:

> The business and affairs of every corporation organized under this chapter shall be managed by or under the direction of a board of directors....
>
> **DGCL §141(a)**

All corporate powers shall be exercised by or under the authority of, and the business and affairs of the corporation managed under the direction of, its board of directors....

MBCA §8.01(b)

The statutes provide that corporations may engage in any lawful business and that they have the same powers an individual has to effect that business. Those provisions mean that the board, in which all those powers reside, is really the center of corporate activity. One concomitant of placing all power in the board is that the shareholders, who are the corporation's owners, do not possess the ultimate management power. In fact, a literal reading of the statutes suggests that the shareholders have absolutely no power. As we will see in Chapters 15 and 16, shareholders do have some powers, notably the power to elect the directors. We will also see that the corporate scheme of power allocation is very different from the partnership paradigm and perhaps from the limited liability company (LLC) paradigm as well. See Chapter 18 and Chapter 19.

To be strictly accurate, both the DGCL and the MBCA allow a corporate structure that does not have a board of directors. But both statutes anticipate that the person or persons exercising traditional board power will be treated analogously to the board. See DGCL §§141(a), 351, and MBCA §§7.32(a)(1), 8.01(c). Analytically, this suggests that the alternative to a board is to place corporate power in the hands of the owners, because if power is placed with nonowners then the corporation is, in effect, governed by a "board of directors" that simply has a different name. In practice, very few corporations are organized without a board, although many corporations provide limitations on the board's power. Where the parties desire to place the entity's management power in the owners, a limited liability company or limited liability partnership would typically be preferable to a corporation without a board. This is because those other forms accommodate such allocations of power better than the corporate form does. See Chapters 18, 19, and 20.

As you read the rest of the material on corporate governance, ask yourself how the power allocations are different from other business forms, the reasons for those differences, and whether those differences can be justified.

In the world of corporations, every act must have its genesis in the board of directors. Notice that the statutory words "under the direction of" means that the board itself need not perform, or even approve the performance of, every corporate act. When you buy a latte at Starbucks, the barista is (probably) not a member of the board. Neither does the Starbucks board authorize each latte sale. Nonetheless it should be possible to trace each sale to some action of the board. In the latte example, the board may have authorized the opening of the particular store at which the transaction took place. If not, the board certainly authorized certain senior employees to decide where and when to open new stores. The board doubtless also authorized certain senior employees to decide the menu of drinks the stores will offer and authorized certain senior employees to hire, probably indirectly, baristas. In other words, the senior employees charged with hiring hired other, less senior, employees who, with authorization from those senior employees, hired even less senior employees, so that, eventually, someone with actual authority hired the barista. By contrast, in a small coffee bar the barista might well be a board member, an officer, and a shareholder, too.

Are there limitations on the power of the board to delegate? If so, what is the source of those limits? Our first case discusses this question.

☰ Grimes v. Donald
1995 WL 54441 (Del. Ch.), 20 Del. J. Corp. L. 757

ALLEN, CH.

This suit, brought by a shareholder of DSC Communications Corporation ("DSC"), seeks a judicial declaration of the invalidity of certain compensation agreements between DSC and James L. Donald, its CEO and chairman on the ground, *inter alia* that they . . . result in an abdication of board authority and responsibility in violation of Section 141(a) of the [DGCL].

Mr. Donald's employment contract is on its face unusual and troubling in that it contains a provision to the effect that should he unilaterally determine in good faith that the company's board of directors has unreasonably interfered with his management of the corporation, then he may declare his employment terminated and, in doing so qualify for what are alleged to be large payments. It is the ill-conceived concept of the board of directors interfering with the CEO's management that has attracted the most attention from plaintiff.

Under Section 141 of the [DGCL], as under analogous provisions of the incorporation statutes of other states, it is the elected board of directors that bears the ultimate duty to manage or supervise the management of the business and affairs of the corporation. Ordinarily, this responsibility entails the duty to establish or approve the long-term strategic, financial and organizational goals of the corporation; to approve formal or informal plans for the achievement of these goals; to monitor corporate performance; and to act, when in the good faith, informed judgment of the board it is appropriate to act. While these responsibilities may be satisfied in various ways and with varying degrees of formality, it is essential that the members of the board understand that it is with the board and not with the officers of the corporation that ultimate responsibility lies. It is in the light of this fact that I refer to the contractual concept of board interference with the CEO as ill-conceived.

Pending is a motion of all defendants to dismiss . . . all claims arising from Mr. Donald's various employment agreements for a failure to state a claim upon which relief may be granted; . . . .

ALLEGATIONS

A. The Parties

DSC is a publicly held telecommunications manufacturer, marketer, and servicer incorporated in the State of Delaware. According to the complaint, in 1990 the Compensation Committee of the DSC board approved the three contracts in contention: an employment agreement (the "Employment Agreement"); the Executive Income Continuation Plan (the "Income Continuation Plan"); and a benefits plan . . . (the "Long-Term Plan") (collectively, the "Donald Agreements"). They did this at a July 23, 1990 meeting, and immediately thereafter the Committee recommended the contracts to the full board. The full board heard from an outside compensation consultant and then approved the Donald Agreements . . . .

B. The Donald Agreements

The three contracts delegate to Donald extensive, and allegedly exclusive, managing authority over DSC and provide for his compensation. It is the combination of the comprehensive power delegated, the unilateral power to declare a termination, and the benefits payable in the event of termination that plaintiff claims together constitute an abandonment by the board of its obligation to manage the enterprise.

The Employment Agreement . . . designates Donald as chief executive officer of the Company. In his capacity as CEO, Donald is "responsible for the general management of the affairs of the [c]ompany," and "in carrying out his duties . . . [he] shall report to the [b]oard" of directors.

Under the Employment Agreement, Donald may declare that he has been "constructively terminated without cause," in a number of identified circumstances. Among these are events that would be expected to constitute substantial concerns of an officer or employee. . . . More problematically, under §1(f)(vii) Mr. Donald may declare a constructive termination of his Employment Agreement, without cause, if DSC's board of directors "unreasonabl[y] interfere[s] . . . in [Donald's] carrying out his duties and responsibilities" under the Employment Agreement.

In the event that Donald does in good faith declare himself constructively terminated without cause, or DSC terminates him without cause, Donald is entitled to [money and benefits that exceed $1 million per year for six ½ years]. [D]onald will also receive monetary benefits under the other two agreements, the Income Continuation Plan and the Long-Term Plan. The wisdom of these contracts as a business matter is not a question upon which this court is required or qualified to express an opinion.

THE ALLEGED ABDICATION OF MANAGERIAL DUTIES

Plaintiff's central claim is that the DSC board has, through the Donald Agreements, unlawfully *abdicated its power to manage the corporation*. He alleges that the delegation of power to Donald and the contract obligation to pay Donald substantial sums of money if the board, in Donald's unilateral good faith judgment, "unreasonably interferes" with his management, *effectively prohibits any management by the board* in violation of Section 141 of the DGCL.

A fundamental precept of Delaware corporation law is that it is the board of directors, and neither shareholders nor managers, that has ultimate responsibility for the management of the enterprise. Of course, given the large, complex organizations through which modern, multi-function business corporations often operate, the law recognizes that corporate boards, comprised as they traditionally have been of persons dedicating less than all of their attention to that role, cannot themselves manage the operations of the firm, but may satisfy their obligations by thoughtfully appointing officers, establishing or approving goals and plans and monitoring performance. Thus Section 141(a) of DGCL expressly permits a board of directors to delegate managerial duties to officers of the corporation, except to the extent that the corporation's certificate of incorporation or bylaws may limit or prohibit such a delegation.

Absent specific restriction in the certificate of incorporation, the board of directors certainly has very broad discretion in fashioning a managerial structure appropriate, in its judgment, to moving the corporation towards the achievement of corporate goals and purposes. In designing and implementing such a structure, the board of course may delegate such powers to the officers of the company as in the board's good faith, informed judgment are appropriate. But this power is not without limit. The board may not either formally or effectively abdicate its statutory power and its fiduciary duty to manage or direct the management of the business and affairs of this corporation. Thus in *Abercrombie v. Davis*, 123 A.2d 893 (Del. Ch. 1956) *rev'd on other grounds*, 130 A.2d 338 (Del. 1957), this court voided a shareholders' agreement that purported to bind signatories in their director capacity:

> [b]ecause [the agreement] *tends to limit in a substantial way* the freedom of director decisions on matters of management policy, it violates the duty of each director to exercise his own best judgment on matters coming before the board.

> *Id.* at 899 (emphasis added). *See also Chapin v. Benwood Foundation Inc.*, 402 A.2d 1205 (Del. Ch. 1979).

Thus it is well established that while a board may delegate powers subject to possible review, it may not abdicate them.

Unlike the agreements or arrangements at issue in *Abercrombie* and *Chapin*..., the Donald Agreements do not, under any circumstances, formally foreclose DSC's directors from exercising their business judgment. The Donald Agreements do not covenant that DSC directors will not "interfere" with Donald's management; rather they trigger rights to be paid if the board does "unreasonably interfere" with Donald's management. In *Abercrombie* the directors were formally bound to vote as seven out of eight of them agreed. The directors in *Chapin* were formally bound to elect the person earlier designated as a successor trustee. Under the Donald Agreements, the DSC directors' actions could only be illegally hindered or effectively bound if the amount of money that DSC could owe to Donald in the event that he declared a termination were so great in relation to the wealth of DSC as to preclude reasonable directors from freely exercising their business judgment. Thus, unlike the agreements considered in *Abercrombie* and *Chapin*, the Donald Agreements do not formally preclude the DSC board from exercising its statutory powers and fulfilling its fiduciary duty. It is the alleged *practical effect* of these contracts that is said to constitute the abdication of directorial responsibility.

I assume for purposes of resolving this dispute that, at least under some circumstances, that such an effect of an employment contract would render it voidable in equity. On that assumption,... the issue on this motion, with respect to the abdication claim, is whether the financial consequences of a possible termination determination by Mr. Donald might be such to DSC as substantially to deter defendants from exercising their statutory powers and fulfilling their fiduciary duties. The complaint however alleges very little about factual context of the Donald Agreements.

[I]n 1993 DSC had revenues of $730.8 million and earnings of $81.7 million.... The corporation had...a market capitalization of approximately $2.8 billion at that time. These facts are dramatic in light of the conclusory contentions made by plaintiff. They corroborate the conclusion that plaintiff has failed to allege a claim upon which relief could be granted. In the light that they throw, one can see that the amended complaint charges that directors of a large public corporation with $81 million in earnings last year will, as a practical matter, face "an overwhelming disincentive" to monitor Mr. Donald's performance because such monitoring might cause Mr. Donald to decide to claim board "interference" and possibly allow a termination of his contract obligations. This, in turn, would occasion an obligation to continue to make annual payments to Donald of something more than a million dollars, for six

and one-half years. Assuming the facts alleged were proven (indeed drawing all inferences in plaintiff's favor, one could assume multiples of these numbers without changing the analysis) and assuming that the principle of *Abercrombie, Chapin,* and other
such cases extend to agreements that, as a practical matter rather than formally, have
the effect of preventing the board from exercising its power to continue to govern the
corporate enterprise, nevertheless, in this instance not enough has been pleaded to
possibly permit a fact finder to infer that the financial consequences flowing from the
Donald Agreements would be such to DSC as to render the Donald Agreements a
de facto abdication of directorial obligation. In these circumstances I conclude that it is
appropriate to dismiss this claim.

In concluding, I note, however, that the plaintiff's abdication case is given substantial superficial appeal by the foolish use in Section 1(f)(vii) of the Employment
Agreement of the concept of "unreasonable interference, in the good faith judgment
of the Executive, by the Board . . . in the Executive's carrying out of his duties and
responsibilities." This ill-conceived provision does give rise to the inference that the
outside corporate directors of DSC, and Mr. Donald, or the professional advisors of
both, have fundamentally misunderstood the basic structure and requirements of the
law governing corporate organization and governance. Ultimately, it is the responsibility and duty of the elected board to determine corporate goals, to approve of
strategies and plans to achieve those goals and to monitor progress towards achieving
them. The insertion of the concept of board "interference" into the employment
contract of a senior officer clouds that responsibility; it addresses what may be a
valid negotiating point — a senior officer's understandable desire that he be accorded
substantial freedom in achieving goals set by persons to whom he is accountable — in
an unskillful way that raises problems. In this instance the financial consequences (as
alleged in the amended complaint) of a contract termination under this language
would be such, that, in light of the size, scope and substantial profitability of the
enterprise, one could not possibly conclude that the board of directors would be
substantially impeded in exercising its statutory authority by the prospects of possibly
triggering those consequences. Yet the concept itself is badly flawed and could lead to
problems in other settings.

Thus, for the foregoing reasons, I conclude that . . . the amended complaint fails
to allege facts which if true would entitle plaintiff to any judicial relief.

Notes and Questions

1. Notes

a. Corporations statutes expressly allow the board to appoint committees of
directors. Where these committees simply investigate or recommend action to the
full board, their existence presents no real issue of corporate law. The statutes permit
the full board to rely on such committees in the ordinary course. See DGCL §141(e)
and MBCA §8.30(c). To the extent that a committee is delegated power to act for
the full board, however, the issues raised in *Grimes* come to the fore. The statutes
allow boards to delegate all board powers to committees with certain exceptions. Both
statutes prohibit a board committee from changing the corporation's bylaws and
both prohibit a committee from approving fundamental actions (such as mergers,
dissolution, or sale of all the corporation's assets) that also require shareholder
approval. The MBCA further prohibits a board committee from declaring dividends

except pursuant to a formula approved by the full board, and also prohibits a committee from filling board vacancies. See DGCL §141(c), MBCA §8.25(d), (e).

Perhaps the most typical committee is an executive committee that is usually given the power to take any action (subject, of course, to the statutory restrictions) necessary between full board meetings. In publicly held corporations, other committees include an audit committee, which evaluates the corporation's financial situation and monitors the independent accountants; a compensation committee, which approves the annual compensation for the corporation's most senior executives; and a nominating committee, which identifies suitable candidates for any board openings that may arise. In the public company setting, the SEC heavily regulates the board committees. See Section C, *infra*.

2. Reality Check

a. What standard did Chancellor Allen use to evaluate the Donald Agreements?

b. What did plaintiff fail to demonstrate to become entitled to relief?

c. Describe the board's duties vis-à-vis the shareholders. Vis-à-vis the corporation's officers and managers.

3. Suppose

a. Suppose the DSC board delegated power to Mr. Donald but, in fact, never reviewed any decision Mr. Donald ever made. Would Chancellor Allen uphold such an arrangement? Should he?

b. What if Mr. Donald's consideration for constructive termination without cause were $10 million per year for 6½ years. Suppose it were $1 million for Mr. Donald's life. Finally, suppose it were one lump sum payment of $100 million. Would any of these make a difference to Chancellor Allen's analysis or the result?

4. What Do You Think?

a. Do you agree with Chancellor Allen's decision?

b. Do you think the corporation and its shareholders are harmed by the Donald Agreements? If so, how?

c. Chancellor Allen said, "The wisdom of these contracts as a business matter is not a question upon which this court is required or qualified to express an opinion." Do you agree with this statement as a matter of policy? Do you agree with it as a description of Chancellor Allen's actions?

d. Given the language of DGCL §141(a), why are there any limits on the board's power to delegate power? Do you agree with those limits?

e. Given that the shareholders are the owners of the corporation and have contributed the permanent capital to establish the corporation, why should they not have the complete power to limit the board's actions in any way the shareholders see fit?

5. You Draft It

a. Revise the following language, which is footnote 3 of the opinion, in the form of a contract clause to make it clear that the DSC board has appropriate control over Mr. Donald's termination.

The instances in which DSC may terminate Donald for "Cause" are narrowly defined. Only if Donald has been convicted of a felony "involving moral turpitude" or if his "serious, willful gross misconduct or willful gross neglect of duties . . . has resulted, or in all probability is likely to result, in material economic damage to [DSC]" does the corporation have cause to terminate his contract, "provided that no action or failure to act by [Donald] will constitute "Cause" if [Donald] believed in good faith that such action or failure to act was in [DSC's] best interest . . . ." Am. Cplt. Ex. 1 §1(d)(i) and (ii).

b. Redraft the following language from the Donald Agreements to make it clear that the DSC board has not impermissibly delegated its obligations.

Mr. Donald may declare a constructive termination of his Employment Agreement, without cause, if DSC's board of directors "unreasonabl[y] interfere[s] . . . in [Donald's] carrying out his duties and responsibilities" under the Employment Agreement.

b. Background and Context

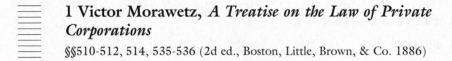

1 Victor Morawetz, *A Treatise on the Law of Private Corporations*

§§510-512, 514, 535-536 (2d ed., Boston, Little, Brown, & Co. 1886)

The active management and direction of the affairs of a business corporation are ordinarily vested in a board of directors or trustees. The board of directors of a corporation have implied authority to do all acts in the management of the company's *regular* business, which the company itself can do without a departure from its chartered powers.

Although the appointment of the directors rests with the majority [of shareholders], it does not follow that the majority can control them or interfere with their management of the business of the company. The authority of the board of directors is derived from the unanimous agreement of the shareholders, expressed in their charter or articles of association; and hence those powers which it is intended shall belong to the directors exclusively cannot be impaired by the majority, or any other agent.

The rule limiting the powers of the majority [of shareholders] to the general supervision of the affairs of the corporation, and the appointment of the regular managing agents, is established for the protection of the individual shareholders, as well as for reasons of practical convenience. It is obvious that a board of directors, selected by the shareholders of a corporation on account of their known business experience and capacity, are far better adapted to carry on the business of the company successfully, than the shareholders themselves assembled at a general meeting.

However, the exclusive powers of the board of directors extend only to the management of the regular business of the corporation. Even an express provision that the powers of the corporation shall be exercised by its board of directors does not deprive the majority [of shareholders] of the power of directing the general policy of the corporation, and of deciding upon the propriety of important changes in the company's business.

A board of directors has no implied authority to make a material and permanent alteration of the business or constitution of a corporation, even though the alteration be within the company's chartered powers. Such an alteration can be effected only by authority of the shareholders at a general meeting.

The board of directors are impliedly authorized to do all acts which are proper to carry out the company's chartered purposes, but they cannot depart from these purposes under any circumstances.

However, the authority of the directors of a corporation to appoint inferior agents with power to represent the company can be implied only where such appointment would be a reasonable measure in carrying on the company's business in the ordinary manner. Those powers of the directors of a corporation which it is intended they should exercise personally, can in no case be delegated.

The general supervision and direction of the affairs of a corporation are especially intrusted by the shareholders to the board of directors; it is upon the personal care and attention of the directors that the shareholders depend for the success of their enterprise. It follows that authority to delegate these general powers of management cannot be implied.

Notes and Questions

1. Notes

a. Victor Morawetz (1859-1938) was graduated from the Harvard Law School in 1878. He moved to Chicago to practice corporate law but was unsuccessful, primarily because he was unknown and, due to the prevailing constraints on lawyer advertising, could not ethically make his talents known to potential clients. At 23 he published the first edition of *A Treatise on the Law of Private Corporations*. He revised that book four years later into the two-volume work, which is quoted throughout this chapter. The first edition was immediately recognized as a classic and, even more, the second edition was *the* standard reference work on classical corporation law as late as the 1930s. The success of this book allowed Morawetz to move to New York, where he became a partner in the city's most prominent corporate law firm. He left that position in 1896 (at the age of 37) and served as general counsel for a major railroad corporation for 13 years. In 1909, at the age of 50, he retired. See 15 Am. Nat. Bio. 805 (1999).

2. Reality Check

a. How does Morawetz view the power of the board?

b. What control over the board do the shareholders possess, according to Morawetz?

3. Suppose

a. If Morawetz were deciding *Grimes*, would the analysis or result be the same?

4. What Do You Think?

a. Between the time Morawetz wrote and the time *Grimes* was decided, do you think there was a shift in the allocation of corporate power between the board and shareholders? If so, why do you think such a shift occurred? If so, was the shift beneficial?

b. Between the time Morawetz wrote and the time *Grimes* was decided, do you think there was a shift in the power of the board of directors to delegate? If so, why do you think such a shift occurred? If so, was the shift beneficial?

c. Given the great increase in the ability of widely dispersed shareholders to communicate via the Internet, do you believe the allocation of power between the shareholders and the board should be reconsidered? If so, what allocation would you suggest?

2. Number, Selection, Election, Term, and Removal of Directors

a. Number and Selection of Initial Directors

A board must consist of one or more individuals See MBCA §8.03(a) and DGCL §141(b). One corporation may own shares in another and may be able to elect directors to the other's board, but it cannot itself serve as a director of the other corporation. How is the number of directors determined? As you may remember from Chapter 5, the number must be stated in either the Articles of Incorporation or the bylaws. Frequently the Articles or bylaws set a minimum and maximum number of directors and grant the board itself the power to determine the exact number of directors. This technique is frequently used in public corporations. This approach allows the board to expand or contract to take advantage of *ad hominem* situations, but it also allows the board to act opportunistically to add friendly members or repel the appointment of hostile members.

Statutes permit the initial directors to be named in the articles of incorporation. See DGCL §102(a)(6), MBCA §2.02(b)(1). If the initial directors are not named in the articles, the incorporator must name the initial directors as part of the organizational meeting process. See DGCL §108(a), MBCA §2.05(a)(2), and Chapter 5. The first method is by far preferable to the second because it is immediately certain who the first directors are. This also means that the initial directors are invested with all corporate power at the time of incorporation. Where the directors are instead chosen as part of the organizational meeting process, there is always a time lag during which the incorporator has corporate power. See DGCL §107. Of course, where the incorporator will be the sole director, no harm is done, but that is not always the case.

b. Election and Term of Directors

Thereafter, at least one director must be elected at every annual shareholder meeting and the default rule is that all directors are elected annually by all the shareholders. See DGCL §211(b), MBCA §8.03(c). This default rule can be varied in two ways. The first way is to create a *classified board*. Under this model, the power to elect at least one director is vested in, or denied to, at least one class or series of stock. The corporation's planners may choose this approach when the shareholders anticipate that they may have strong disagreements in the future. This approach is also useful when the planners desire to give one set of shareholders power disproportionate to their capital contribution. As you doubtless recall, investors purchasing shares contemporaneously must pay the same price per share. By creating a classified board, the different factions of shareholders can receive securities that are identical in all respects except that one faction has the power to select more directors than another faction. When implementing a classified board structure, the practical variations are nearly endless. See DGCL §141(d), MBCA §8.04.

The second way to vary the default rule is to divide the directors into two or three classes with each class holding *staggered terms* of two or three years. When this approach is taken, the nearly universal approach is to divide the board into thirds so that each director has a three-year term. See DGCL §141(d), MBCA §8.06. Most public Delaware corporations have staggered boards. Note that some courts and commentators use the term *classified board* to refer to a board with staggered terms as well as one that is truly classified.

A close reading of the statutes reveals that the expiration of a director's term does not, by itself, oust the director from office. Rather, a director remains in office until he or she is reelected, another person is elected to fill his or her slot, the board is reduced in number at the end of the director's term, or the slot become vacant. See DGCL §141(b), MBCA §8.05. Although every corporation statute requires an annual meeting of the shareholders to elect directors (DGCL §211(b), MBCA §8.03(c)), that requirement does not translate into fact.[1] Directors who continue in office after the expiration of their term because no election has been held are called *holdover* directors. Holdovers are a surprisingly frequent occurrence. Remember that the directors of Victor Kamkin, Inc., were holdovers during critical events. See *Kalageorgi v. Victor Kamkin, Inc.*, in Chapter 6.

Sometimes a vacancy occurs either through resignation, death, or removal of an incumbent. Although no statute requires that a vacancy be filled, all corporation statutes provide methods for selecting replacement directors. In Delaware, the default rule is that vacancies can only be filled by the remaining board members. See DGCL §223(a)(1). Under the Model Act, the default rule is that vacancies may be filled by either the remaining board members or by the shareholders, whichever constituency acts first. See MBCA §8.10(a)(1), (2). As a practical matter, this ordinarily means that the board can fill the vacancy if it chooses to do so because it is usually able to act more quickly than the shareholders.

c. *Removal of Directors*

Shareholders have the power, called *amotion*, to remove directors during their term. The default rule under both the DGCL and the MBCA is that directors may be removed with or without cause. See DGCL §141(k), MBCA §8.08(a). However, under both statutes directors elected to a classified board may only be removed by the same set of shareholders that elected them. See DGCL §141(k)(2), MBCA §8.08(b). Further, if the corporation permits cumulative voting (see Chapter 16), under which a minority of shareholders have the power to elect at least some directors, the quantum of votes required to amote must be greater than the quantum required to elect a director. See DGCL §141(k)(2), MBCA §8.08(c). Note that the board itself has *no* power to remove a director or to limit the right of a director to obtain corporate information.

Finally, under the DGCL default rule, directors on a staggered or classified board may be removed only for cause. See DGCL §141(k)(1). This provision has become an important element by which incumbent directors of public corporations protect

---

1. Glendower
   I can call spirits from the vasty deep.
   Hotspur
   Why, so can I, or so can any man,
   But will they come when you do call for them?

William Shakespeare, *Henry IV* act 3, sc. 1, ll. 55-57 (Barbara A. Mowat & Paul Werstine, eds., Pocket Books 1994)

themselves against unwanted takeovers. A common takeover technique for hostile acquiring corporations is to wage a proxy fight seeking to remove the incumbent directors of the target corporation and replace them with more "enlightened" directors. If the target has a staggered board and has not waived the default rule, the raider can amote the target directors only for cause.

This, of course, raises the question of what constitutes "cause." Surprisingly, there is nearly no case law on the question and the statutes are silent. What case law there is deals primarily with the question of process—how corporations must proceed with determining whether cause for removal exists.

Superwire.com, Inc. (Superwire) was a large shareholder of Entrata Communications Corporation (Entrata), a Delaware corporation. Dean Hampton was the chair of Entrata's board, its chief executive officer, its president, and its secretary. Superwire had a falling out with Hampton and, on November 8, 2001,

> Superwire joined with other Entrata shareholders to execute an action by written consent of the holders of a majority of Entrata's voting stock purporting to remove Hampton from the board of directors "for cause." The complaint alleges that Superwire delivered the consents to Entrata and that "Hampton's removal was, therefore, effective on that date." The complaint further alleges that Hampton claims to have received revocations of consents from those stockholders other than Superwire who executed the November 8, 2001 consent and that Hampton and others claim to "have executed a consent of the holders of a majority of Entrata stock to maintain Mr. Hampton as a director."
>
> Defendants move to dismiss because the complaint does not allege facts showing that Hampton was afforded notice of specific charges and an opportunity to be heard. Superwire responds that (a) the consent is valid even if no notice or opportunity to be heard was afforded to Hampton because the certificate of incorporation permitted his removal without cause and, (b) in any case, it is not obligated to allege those facts in order to survive a motion to dismiss.
>
> Superwire misstates the law in contending that the fact that it might have proceeded "without cause" can serve to validate an otherwise invalid attempt to remove Hampton "for cause." Directors of Delaware corporations can be removed "for cause" or, where permitted by the governing documents and the law, "without cause." But there are additional requirements that must be observed when doing so "for cause." A "for cause" removal of a director requires that the individual be given (i) specific charges for his removal, (ii) adequate notice, and (iii) a full opportunity to meet the accusation.[28] The same is true whether the action is taken at a meeting of stockholders or by written consent.[29]
>
> These procedural safeguards are of some importance. In many cases, there are substantial collateral affects of being removed "for cause" that do not attend a removal "without cause." These can include differences in the treatment of rights flowing from contracts or other terms of employment. There are also likely to be significant reputational affects flowing from a "for cause" removal. These consequences alone might justify the conclusion that one choosing to act "for cause" must follow the prescribed procedures.
>
> Moreover, it is a fallacy to suppose that a stockholder who succeeds in obtaining enough consents to remove a director "for cause" without affording the director notice and an opportunity to be heard would necessarily obtain the requisite number of consents if it complies with the law, or even if it seeks to remove the director "without cause." In this case, for example, the complaint reflects a contention that

28. *Campbell v. Loew's, Inc.*, 134 A.2d 852, 859 (Del. Ch. 1957).
29. *Bossier v. Connell*, 1986 Del. Ch. Lexis 511, at *15 (Del. Ch.).

the stockholders who joined with Superwire in executing the November 8 consent promptly executed revocations of those consents, claiming that Superwire misled them into agreeing to remove Hampton. Those revocations may not have been legally effective, since they were expressed after the November 8 consent was delivered to Entrata. But they do serve to illustrate the point that compliance with established legal standards can affect the outcome.

Thus, the validity of the November 8 consent will depend on whether it was solicited in compliance with the procedural safeguards articulated in *Campbell v. Loew's* and specifically applied to actions taken by written consent in *Bossier v. Connell*.

For the purposes of the motion to dismiss, however, the question is whether Superwire was obliged to include in its complaint factual allegations that would support a finding that it gave Hampton notice of the charges against him and an opportunity to be heard. The answer to this question must be "no" because it is sufficient under the general notice pleading standard found in Court of Chancery Rule 8(a) that the complaint "contain . . . a short and plain statement of the claim showing that the pleader is entitled to relief." The allegations found in paragraph 22 of the complaint are sufficient for this purpose because they identify the consent, allege that it was executed by holders of the requisite number of shares, that it was delivered to the corporation and that it was effective on the date of its delivery. These are the elements described in Section 228 of the DGCL. The defense is free to show that the November 8 consent was invalid for whatever reason or reasons may exist. However, there is no requirement that the complaint allege facts sufficient to disprove any of those matters.

Superwire.com, Inc. v. Hampton, 805 A.2d 904 (Del. Ch. 2002) (Lamb, V.C.)

Notes and Questions

1. What Do You Think?

a. Should directors be allowed to hold over? What would be wrong with a rule that provided that a director ceased to be a director at the expiration of his or her term?

b. Should the shareholders have the power to amote without cause? Why shouldn't directors be entitled to hold office during the term for which they were elected?

c. How would you define "cause" for removal of a director?

d. What process should be used to remove a director for cause? Should there be a presumption that the director has acted properly? Who should decide whether cause is shown? Should an appeal from such a finding be allowed? If so, to whom?

What happens if a corporation fails to hold an annual meeting? See DGCL §211(c), MBCA §7.03(a)(1). The following case discusses some aspects of the problem of electing directors and also deals with the power of shareholders to act by consent in lieu of holding an actual meeting.

Hoschett v. TSI International Software, Ltd.

683 A.2d 43 (Del. Ch. 1996)

ALLEN, CH.

The material facts are few and apparently not controverted. Plaintiff Fred G. Hoschett is the registered owner of 1,200 shares of common stock of the defendant

TSI International Software, Ltd., a Delaware corporation having its principal place of business in Wilton, Connecticut. Formed in 1993, TSI is a privately-held corporation having...less than 40 stockholders of record. TSI has never held an annual meeting for the election of directors.

On October 5, 1995, plaintiff filed this action against TSI seeking, among other things...an order compelling an annual meeting of stockholders for the election of directors. On February 2, 1996, after some discovery, plaintiff moved for summary judgment.... TSI responded with a cross motion for summary judgment supported by an affidavit establishing that on November 16, 1995, the company received a written consent representing a majority of the voting power of the corporation that "elected" five individuals each "to serve as a director of [TSI] until his or her successor is duly elected and qualified." On the basis of the validity of that action defendant asserts that it has satisfied the need to hold an annual meeting for the election of directors.

Most fundamentally the current motion requires the court to interpret the legal meaning of [DGCL §§211(b) and 228(a)] in a way that, to the maximum extent feasible, gives full effect to the literal terms of the language of each. For the reasons that follow I conclude that the mandatory requirement that an annual meeting of shareholders be held is not satisfied by shareholder action pursuant to Section 228 purporting to elect a new board or to re-elect an old one.

The obligation to hold an annual meeting at which directors are to be elected, either for one year or for staggered terms, as the charter may provide, is one of the very few mandatory features of Delaware corporation law. Delaware courts have long recognized the central role of annual meetings in the scheme of corporate governance. Even the shareholders' power to approve amendments to the charter does not extend so far as to permit a Delaware corporation legitimately to dispense with the annual meeting. The critical importance of shareholder voting both to the theory and to the reality of corporate governance...may be thought to justify the mandatory nature of the obligation to call and hold an annual meeting. The annual election of directors is a structured occasion that necessarily focuses attention on corporate performance. Knowing that such an occasion is necessarily to be faced annually may itself have a marginally beneficial effect on managerial attention and performance. Certainly, the annual meeting may in some instances be a bother to management, or even, though rarely, a strain, but in all events it provides a certain discipline and an occasion for interaction and participation of a kind. Whether it is welcome or resented by management, however, is in the end, irrelevant under Section 211(b) and (c) of the DGCL and similar statutes in other jurisdictions.

The question this case presents is whether a controlling shareholder or a majority group may effectively avoid the annual meeting requirement, despite the command of Section 211, by the latter-day expedient of exercising consent to designate directors under Section 228. The Delaware courts apparently have not previously addressed this precise issue. There is of course a rather strong practical argument that it is efficient to recognize such a power or effect. The argument, as I see it, would run as follows: Only a relatively small and more or less tightly bound group of shareholders comprising a voting majority could effectively exercise a Section 228 consent action.... Where such a small and coherent group seeks to exercise control it is especially unlikely that the formality of notice to all shareholders and a meeting will have any practical effect whatsoever. Therefore, if the law requires an annual meeting where a small, controlling group of shareholders is willing to act by consent to designate directors, it is highly likely that the law will simply be commanding expenditure of funds in a pointless exercise.

The flaws in this position appear to be at least three. First, the principle for which this practicality argument must contend is not limited to small coherent groups of shareholders who together can exercise control. If the principle is correct, management of public companies without a small controlling group, could solicit consents (albeit in conformity with SEC proxy rules) to "re-elect" or "elect" some or all of the board without ever having an annual meeting. Second, the purposes served by the annual meeting include affording to shareholders an opportunity to bring matters before the shareholder body, as provided by the corporations charter and bylaws, such as bylaw changes. These other matters of possible business are not necessarily made irrelevant by a consent designation of directors, even if such designation is effective. Finally, while the model of democratic forms should not too strictly be applied to the economic institution of a business corporation (where for instance votes are weighted by the size of the voter's investment), it is nevertheless a not unimportant feature of corporate governance that at a noticed annual meeting a form of discourse (i.e., oral reports, questions and answers and in rare instances proxy contests) among investors and between shareholders and managers is possible. The theory of the annual meeting includes the idea that a deliberative component of the meeting may occur. Shareholders' meetings are mandated and shareholders authorized by statute to transact proper business because we assume that at such meetings something said may matter. Obviously these meetings are very far from deliberative convocations, but a keen realization of the reality of the degree of deliberation that is possible, should make the preservation of residual mechanisms of corporate democracy more, not less, important.

Thus, on balance I find an argument predicated on alleged efficiency and practicality, unpersuasive. I conclude absent unanimous consent that the mandatory language of Section 211(b) places on TSI the legal obligation to convene a meeting of shareholders to elect directors . . . .

What then is the legal meaning of the clause in Section 228 that authorizes "any action required by this chapter to be taken at an annual or special meeting" to be taken by written consent of shareholders? The established preference of our law is of course to give to such statutory language a literal reading, if that is possible. Thus "any action" must include shareholder action to remove directors from office and to designate persons as directors when there is a vacancy and the constitutional documents of the firm contemplate filling such vacancies by shareholders. See DGCL §141(k) (removal), §211(b)(e) (election). Since the term of office of each of the directors of the company had expired, they acted as holdovers even though they continued to hold office. Thus the action to reelect them or to elect their successors logically entailed removal and filling of the resulting vacancy.

The pertinent question is, when directors are designated through a consent process that removes holdovers and designates replacements, as here, for what term do they hold office? It is this question that is raised by the intersection of Section 211 and Section 228 and whose resolution can accommodate the command of each statute. That resolution is based on an interpretation that such directors hold office only until the next annual meeting of the shareholders, at which meeting the whole body of the company's shareholders may participate, to the extent the charter and bylaws define, in the election of the board. That is shareholders may (if the certificate of incorporation and bylaws so provide) remove holdovers and fill vacancies on the board through exercise of the consent power, but doing so does not affect the obligation under Section 211 to hold an annual meeting.

This accommodation is suggested by the fact that appointment of directors to fill vacancies is for such a limited term. See [DGCL] §223(b) Logically, directors appointed to replace ousted holdover directors by the exercise of stockholder consent serve for that same limited term. The interpretation that directors appointed by stockholder consent to replace holdover directors only hold office until the next annual meeting of shareholders respects both the corporation's need to have its directorships filled and the right of all shareholders to attend an annual meeting of shareholders at which the directors of the company will be chosen for the succeeding year, pursuant to the charter and bylaws of the firm.

Thus, in my opinion, the effort of a group constituting a majority of the voting power of the corporation to preclude an annual meeting by acting pursuant to Section 228 is of limited effect. Specifically, while it did remove directors and may well have filled vacancies, it did so only until the next annual meeting of shareholders, which continues to be a mandatory obligation of the corporation. The Court of Chancery, in all events, maintains its traditional discretionary role when administering the equitable remedies of injunction and specific performance. See DGCL §211(c) (court "may" order holding of meeting). In this instance I apprehend no reason why equity should not specifically enforce the legal obligation imposed by Section 211(b). TSI will therefore be ordered to hold an annual meeting and make available a complete list of stockholders as required by those statutory sections.

Notes and Questions

1. Notes

a. In reaction to *Hoschett*, the Delaware General Assembly amended DGCL §211(b). Additional text is shown in **bold face** type and a deletion in ~~strikethrough~~.

> **Unless directors are elected by written consent in lieu of an annual meeting as permitted by this subsection, an** ~~An~~ annual meeting of stockholders shall be held for the election of directors on a date and at a time designated by or in a manner provided in the bylaws. **Stockholders may, unless the certificate of incorporation otherwise provides, act by written consent to elect directors; provided, however, that, if such consent is less than unanimous, such action by written consent may be in lieu of holding an annual meeting only if all of the directorships to which directors could be elected at an annual meeting held at the effective time of such action are vacant and are filled by such action.** Any other proper business may be transacted at the annual meeting.

The legislative Synopsis to the amendment stated,

> Thus, the replacement of sitting directors by less than unanimous stockholder action will require their removal or resignation prior to the effectiveness of the consent action that substitutes for the election of directors at the annual meeting. Unanimous written consent . . . may be taken in lieu of an annual meeting whether or not the directorships to be filled are then vacant (i.e. without the prior removal or resignation of sitting directors).

In practice, this amendment allows for nonunanimous shareholder election of directors by consent in lieu of an annual meeting only when approved by the current board, because that setting is the only one in which it is likely that the directors whose terms are expiring will resign before the written consent is begun.

2. Reality Check

a. What is the tension between DGCL §211 and §228? How does Chancellor Allen resolve that tension?

b. Why do the parties care whether electing directors by written consent obviates the need for an annual meeting?

3. What Do You Think?

a. Do you agree with Chancellor Allen's assessment of the importance of an annual meeting?

b. Do you agree with the Delaware legislature's amendment of Section 211(b)?

4. You Draft It

a. Redraft DGCL §211(b), as it stood when *Hoschett* was decided, to provide that stockholder action by consent can never substitute for an annual meeting. Then redraft the statute to provide that stockholder action by consent can always substitute for an annual meeting. Third, redraft the statute to effect the intent of the Delaware legislature when it amended the section. Finally, redraft the statute to effect what you believe is the optimal solution to the tension between action by consent and the requirement of an annual meeting.

> An annual meeting of stockholders shall be held for the election of directors on a date and at a time designated by or in a manner provided in the bylaws. Any other proper business may be transacted at the annual meeting.

d. Background and Context

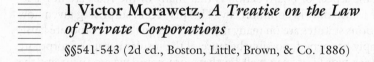

1 Victor Morawetz, *A Treatise on the Law of Private Corporations*

§§541-543 (2d ed., Boston, Little, Brown, & Co. 1886)

The majority of the board clearly have no power to expel an individual director, or to exclude him from inspecting the company's books and participating in its management, although they may believe him to be hostile to the interests of the association.

Nor have the majority at a shareholders' meeting implied authority to revoke the powers of the directors or managing agents, if their term of office is prescribed by the charter or the articles of association or by-laws of the company. The power of removing the directors of a corporation is sometimes conferred by express provision. If the charter or articles of a company provide that the shareholders at a general meeting may remove any director "for negligence, misconduct in office, or other reasonable cause," the expression "reasonable cause" does not refer to such a cause as would be deemed reasonable in a court of justice, but only to such a cause as is deemed reasonable by the shareholders, and the discretion of the shareholders in determining what is reasonable cannot be interfered with, in the absence of direct fraud.

Hence, if the removal of the directors is absolutely essential to the protection of the corporation, and the corporation has no means of removing them or of revoking their powers, individual shareholders may apply to the court on behalf of the company, and the courts will grant such redress as justice requires.

It should be observed, that the courts will not remove the directors from office, or restrain them generally from representing the corporation, except in a case of absolute necessity.

Notes and Questions

1. Reality Check

a. How is Morawetz's conception of "cause" different from the modern day conception?

2. What Do You Think?

a. Is Morawetz's idea of "cause" functionally equivalent to removal without cause?

3. The Mechanics of Board Action

a. The Current Setting

Now that you understand the reasons why corporations are governed by boards of directors and how directors are selected by the shareholders, we can turn our attention to the more practical question of how the board takes valid action. One key is to remember that the board is a collective body. A consequence is that each director, individually, has no power and next to no rights. He or she has a right to information about the corporation but cannot act on behalf of the corporation, absent, of course, the creation of an agency relationship between the corporation as principal and the director as agent. See DGCL §220(d).

Another important aspect of board action is that many of the rules are not statutory but instead are found only in common law. This may seem surprising given how detailed the corporations statutes are on many matters. This quality of corporate law is not deliberate; it simply happened, possibly because of the insular nature of corporate legal practice. In other words, it may well be that corporate lawyers (who are the primary drafters of corporations statutes) saw no need to write statutes covering many of the most basic workings of boards because such rules were axiomatic among corporate practitioners.

Among the rules governing directors that are not usually found in the statutes are:

The board has no power to remove a director.
The default term of office is one year.
Nonunanimous board action without a meeting is invalid.
Board meetings may be called in any manner approved in advance by the board.
Each director has one vote on all matters.[2]
Directors may not vote by proxy; each must vote in person.

2. But note that in late 2005 the DGCL was amended to permit a certificate of incorporation to endue one or more directors with greater or lesser voting power than other directors, regardless of whether the directors are elected by a particular class of stock. See DGCL §141(d).

Boards take action in two ways. First, if they are unanimous in their intention, they may act without a meeting. This action is effected by having each director execute a consent, which, in Delaware and many states, may be electronic. See DGCL §§141(f), 232(c) and MBCA §8.21(a). Lawyers who are "inattentive to detail" frequently describe board actions taken by unanimous consent as having been taken at a meeting. These descriptions are likely to appear in correspondence, in certificates prepared for the corporate secretary's certification that certain actions have been authorized, and in other documents. Often such lawyers will even prepare "minutes" purporting to describe a meeting that never occurred and at which a board action was described as having been approved by a vote.

Although the MBCA explicitly permits action by consent to be described as action taken at a meeting, you should avoid doing so. See MBCA §8.21(c). In the first place, it is simply inaccurate to describe a board action as having been approved at a meeting when, in fact, it was approved by unanimous consent. Second, the question whether all the directors really had a meeting at a particular place and time may become important, regardless of whether a particular action was approved at such meeting or by consent. Inaccurate minutes will, at best, impede the resolution of the question and, at worst, may cast strong doubts upon your competence and honesty.

The second way in which boards of directors act is at a meeting. Four elements must be met for a board action taken at a meeting to be valid. The meeting must be properly *called*, the corporation must give each director proper *notice*, a *quorum* of directors must be present at the meeting, and the action must be approved by a *sufficient vote*. If any of these elements is lacking, the board's action is subject to attack as being ultra vires. Chapter 10 discusses the ultra vires doctrine in more detail.

i. Call. The *call* of the meeting is simply the decision to hold a meeting at a particular time and place and, often, for a particular reason. *Regular meetings*, which is to say periodic (e.g., monthly, quarterly, or even weekly or annually), may be provided for in the corporation's bylaws. No separate call is necessary for regular meetings, as they are automatically called. In every corporation *special meetings* (i.e., not periodically scheduled) will no doubt be necessary from time to time in addition to the regularly scheduled meetings. Some corporations may not feel the need to provide for periodic board meetings at all. In such instances, the board may call each meeting as the last order of business at the prior meeting or they may act by consent to call a meeting when they feel the need to do so. The bylaws (or, less frequently, the Articles of Incorporation) may also give the power to call board meetings to the chair or to other key participants in the corporation's governance. In the absence of such provision, however, the call is a board action that must be made, as every board action is, by unanimous consent or at a meeting. Doubtless in many informally governed corporations key participants convene board meetings even without the explicit power to do so in shocking ignorance or reckless disregard of corporate law niceties. Neither the DGCL nor the MBCA addresses the question of the call of board meetings.

ii. Notice. The directors must obviously become aware that a meeting has been called. Because the directors are presumed to be knowledgeable about the corporation's business, the notice requirements for board meetings are minimal. The DGCL does not contain explicit provisions for giving notice of board meetings. It relies on common law notions and, thus, gives the board great discretion in establishing procedures for notifying the members so long as each director is given "due notice." The MBCA is more prescriptive. It provides a default rule that no notice need be given for regularly scheduled board meetings. In effect, the fact that the board has a schedule of meetings is notice enough. See MBCA §8.22(a). The default rule for special board meetings is that the directors must be given two days notice of the location and time of the meeting but need not be given notice of the meeting's purpose. See MBCA §8.22(b). The Model Act further provides that a director who does not receive proper notice waives any objection by attending the meeting unless the director immediately protests the insufficient notice and does not vote in favor of any measure at that meeting. See MBCA §8.23(b).

iii. Quorum.   The third element for a valid board of directors meeting is the presence of a quorum. A *quorum* is simply the minimum amount of voting power that must be present at a meeting for actions to be valid. Because each director has one vote, the quorum for board meetings is defined by the number of directors present. The idea behind a quorum requirement is to prevent a collective body, such as the board or the shareholders, from taking action when so few members are present that the action may be thought to be unrepresentative of the whole body's intent. Under both the Delaware statute and the Model Act, the default rule is that a quorum is half the total number of directors. That number may be raised but may not be lowered below one-third of the total number of directors. See DGCL §141(b), MBCA §8.24(a).

Note that the number that constitutes a quorum is measured by the number of authorized director positions, not the number of directors currently in office. For example, suppose a corporation has a board of five directors. The default quorum is three, even when there are fewer than five directors in office. That is, if two vacancies exist (through resignation, removal, or death), *all three* remaining directors must be present to transact business. The presence of two of those three (even though a majority of the directors in office) is not a quorum under the statutory default rule.

What does it mean for a director to be present at a meeting? You yourself may have been physically present in many law school classes yet not "present" in any meaningful sense.[3] Both statutes provide that board meetings may be held by conference call. See DGCL §141(i), MBCA §8.20(b). Note that neither statute specifically permits directors to be considered present when they participate by Internet communication, even though such communication may be in real time, unless the connection is oral rather than written.

iv. Sufficient Vote.   Finally, a board action must be approved by a sufficient vote. Remember that if the board is acting by consent, it must do so unanimously. If the board is acting at a meeting, an action is approved if it receives the assent of a majority of directors present at the meeting. See DGCL §141(b), MBCA §8.24(c). Delaware and the Model Act take different views as to a strategic tactic: leaving the meeting before a vote. The idea is to prevent approval of a faction's proposal where that faction has sufficient board votes to approve it. If the directors favoring the proposal are insufficient to constitute a quorum of the board, may the opposing directors thwart the proposal's approval by leaving the meeting? This tactic is called *breaking a quorum.* Under the Model Act, a quorum of directors must be present

---

3. For example, during your Business Entities class, you may be physically located in a classroom yet "present" at *www.craigslist.com* or, even better, *www.BusinessEntitiesOnline.com.*

every time a vote is taken. Hence, if the opposing directors' absence would leave too few directors remaining, those opposed to an action can simply leave the meeting, breaking the quorum, and preventing the remaining directors from taking valid action. See MBCA §8.24(c). The wording of the DGCL, by contrast, is a tad ambiguous on the efficacy of breaking a quorum, but case law supports the view that directors *cannot* break a quorum. See *Henry v. Delaware Law School of Widener University, Inc.*, 1998 WL 15897 (Del. Ch., Lamb, V.C.).

Suppose the number of directors in office has fallen below a quorum. Is there no remedy except to wait until the next shareholder meeting at which more directors will, one hopes, be elected? Nearly every statute provides that the remaining directors, even though fewer than a quorum, can fill board vacancies. Thus, such directors can add members to bring the number of directors over the number required for a quorum. Indeed, the remaining directors could fill all vacancies at once, if they desire, and the corporation can then continue to function. See DGCL §223(a)(1), MBCA §8.10(a)(3).

Notes and Questions

1. Reality Check

a. May a director be considered "present" if he or she is connected to a board meeting by instant messenger?

2. What Do You Think?

a. Would you allow boards to act by majority consent without a meeting?

b. Should directors be able to act unanimously without a meeting?

c. On a nine-person board, a quorum is present if five directors attend a meeting. In such a situation, action is valid if taken by a vote of three to two. Do you think it is fair to allow such a result? If not, what rule would you prefer?

d. Both the DGCL and the MBCA allow for director quorum to be lowered to one-third of the number of director slots. If three directors of a nine-person board attend a meeting, a quorum is present under that rule. In such a setting action would be approved by the affirmative vote of only two directors. Fair?

When the board has divided into factions, each faction may try to impose its views on the corporation by strategically using the governance mechanics. As you read the next case, make sure you understand exactly how the requirements for board meetings were observed. Then ask yourself how you would have advised each side to act had you been retained to represent them. Suffusing your consideration of these issues should be your assessment of when strategic action to effect your (or your client's) ends crosses over to behavior that is impermissible because it is unethical, in either the professional responsibility sense or the more pervasive "real life" sense.

Adlerstein v. Wertheimer

2002 WL 205684 (Del. Ch.)

LAMB, V.C.

This is an action pursuant to Section 225 of the DGCL brought by Joseph Adlerstein, the former Chairman and CEO of SpectruMedix Corporation

("SpectruMedix" or "the Company"), a Delaware corporation. SpectruMedix is in the business of manufacturing and selling instruments to the genetics and pharmaceutical industries and is headquartered in State College, Pennsylvania. Adlerstein's complaint is against the Company and three individuals who claim to be the current directors of the Company: Steven N. Wertheimer, Judy K. Mencher, and Ilan Reich.

At issue in the Complaint are a series of actions taken on July 9, 2001, at or in conjunction with a purported meeting of the SpectruMedix board of directors held at the New York City offices of McDermott, Will & Emery ("MW&E").[1] First, a board majority (consisting of Wertheimer and Mencher) voted to issue to the I. Reich Family Limited Partnership ("Reich Partnership"), an entity affiliated with Reich, a sufficient number of shares of a new class of supervoting preferred stock to convey to the Reich Partnership a majority of the voting power of the Company's stock. Second, the same majority voted to remove Adlerstein for cause as Chief Executive Officer of the Company, to strip him of his title as Chairman of the Board, and to appoint Reich to serve as Chief Executive Officer and as Chairman of the Board. Third, immediately after the board meeting, the Reich Partnership executed and delivered to SpectruMedix a written consent in lieu of stockholders meeting purporting to remove Adlerstein as a director. When the dust settled, the board consisted of Wertheimer, Mencher, and Reich; the Reich Partnership had replaced Adlerstein as holder of majority voting control; and Reich had replaced Adlerstein as Chairman and CEO.

Adlerstein seeks a determination that the July 9 meeting was not properly convened and, therefore, all actions taken at or in conjunction with that meeting are null and void. Adlerstein also contends that, even if the meeting was duly noticed and convened, the actions taken at the meeting by Wertheimer and Mencher were the product of a breach of the fiduciary duties they owed to him in his capacity as a director and the controlling stockholder.

Adlerstein is a scientist and entrepreneur. He has a Ph.D. in physics and was involved with the funding and management of a number of start-up technology companies before founding SpectruMedix . . . in 1992.

Wertheimer, an investment banker, was introduced to Adlerstein by Selbst and was elected to the board by Adlerstein on January 1, 2000. Mencher is a money manager with an expertise in high yield and distressed investments. On Wertheimer's recommendation, Adlerstein elected Mencher to the board on March 22, 2000.

In 1999, to avoid a liquidity crisis, Adlerstein loaned SpectruMedix $500,000. In exchange, SpectruMedix gave Adlerstein a note that was convertible (at Adlerstein's option) into shares of a new Series B Preferred Stock of SpectruMedix that voted with the common and carried 80,000 votes per share. In January 2000, Adlerstein converted approximately $103,000 outstanding under this loan agreement into shares of Series B Preferred Stock. As a result, although Adlerstein owned only 21.41% of the equity of SpectruMedix, he controlled 73.27% of the voting power of the Company.

As reflected in the board's minutes for [an April 30, 2001] meeting Adlerstein on the one hand and Wertheimer and Mencher on the other had very different reactions to the Company's financial state:

> [Adlerstein] did not regard the situation as quite as desperate as the other directors.
> He said that the Company had previously faced similar cash crises and had weathered

1. Over the years Adlerstein was represented in various personal capacities by Stephen Selbst, a partner in MW&E's New York City office. Eventually Selbst also began to serve as counsel to SpectruMedix. Selbst was present at the July 9 meeting and, as counsel to SpectruMedix, schemed with Wertheimer, Mencher, and Reich to engineer Adlerstein's ouster.

them. He said that he had found money to keep the Company alive in the past, and if required to do so again, he would find the resources. Mr. Wertheimer and Ms. Mencher lauded him for his past efforts to save the Company, but said that the[y] were seeking to bring the Company to a cash neutral or profitable position as promptly as possible. The point, Ms. Mencher said, was to put the Company in a position where Dr. Adlerstein wouldn't be required to keep the Company afloat personally in the future.

This divergence in perspective continued through the July 9 meeting.

The board met again on May 25, 2001. Adlerstein reported that the Company was "low on cash" but delivered an upbeat report on the status of discussions he was having with several potential strategic partners. Wertheimer and Mencher remained concerned about the Company's deteriorating financial condition and began to question seriously the information Adlerstein was providing to them. As Mencher testified:

> [I]t became clear that we were not getting the entire picture of what was going on with the company and that the company was quickly heading . . . toward a major liquidity crisis — if it wasn't already in one — and that the company needed a crisis manager, just for somebody to get in and tell the board what was really going on and how long the company had to survive.

In June 2001, Wertheimer contacted Reich to discuss involving him as both an investor and manager of SpectruMedix. Wertheimer knew that Reich had the personal wealth and managerial experience to take on a restructuring of SpectruMedix.[7] As he testified at trial: "Ilan was the only guy I knew that had money and had the skills to go in and . . . pull this out of the fire . . . . No institutional investor would go anywhere near a company like this. It had to be somebody that liked to get his hands dirty, who liked to go into a company and basically try and make something out of something that was in a lot of trouble."

On June 27, 2001, Reich met with Selbst and O'Donnell to discuss the business of SpectruMedix. Adlerstein was unaware of this meeting. The next day, Reich and Adlerstein met in New York. Reich testified that he then determined that he would only be willing to invest in SpectruMedix if he, and not Adlerstein, were in charge of the Company.

On July 2, 2001, Reich participated in a conference call with Wertheimer and Mencher and later that day met with Wertheimer to discuss his potential investment. At that meeting, the option of firing Adlerstein for cause from his position as CEO due to his sexual harassment of a Company employee was discussed, as was Adlerstein's voting control over the Company. Adlerstein had no idea this meeting was taking place. But by this time Reich knew he would have an opportunity to take over SpectruMedix.

By the beginning of July 2001, if not earlier, SpectruMedix was either insolvent or operating on the brink of insolvency. The Company had very little cash (or cash equivalents) and no material accounts receivable due. At the same time, the Company had substantial and increasing accounts payable, Adlerstein was not communicating with creditors, and key parts vendors were refusing to make deliveries unless paid in cash. Indisputably, SpectruMedix did not have sufficient cash on hand to meet its next

---

7. Wertheimer was aware that in the mid-1980s Reich had pleaded guilty to federal charges of trading on inside information while he was a partner in a prominent New York City law firm and served a one-year prison sentence. Nevertheless, he also knew that, from 1998 to 2000, Reich was employed as the President and CEO of Inamed Corporation, a publicly traded company, and had accomplished a significant turnaround of that company. Wertheimer knew that Reich had left Inamed in 2001 and might be interested in a new challenge.

employee payroll on July 13, 2001, and had no realistic expectation of receiving sufficient funds to do so from its operations.

Wertheimer testified that, on or about July 5, 2001, he and Adlerstein spoke on the telephone about the deteriorating financial condition of the Company and matters relating to a significant arbitration involving SpectruMedix.[11] In that proceeding, MW&E had moved to withdraw as counsel to SpectruMedix, as a result, among other things, of disputes over non-payment of fees and expenses. Wertheimer and Adlerstein may have discussed the fact that the arbitrator planned to hold a conference on the motion to withdraw on Monday, July 9, and wished to be able to speak to Adlerstein by telephone. Wertheimer testified that, during this conversation, Adlerstein agreed to convene a meeting of the board of directors at 11 A.M. on July 9, 2001, at MW&E's New York City offices. Adlerstein maintains that, while he agreed to meet with Wertheimer on July 9 in MW&E's offices, the only purpose of that meeting was to be available to speak to the arbitrator about the motion to withdraw. He denies that he ever agreed to call a board meeting for that time or knew that one was to be held.

Mencher's notes show that Reich first proposed terms for an acquisition of SpectruMedix no later than July 5. On that date, she had a teleconference with Wertheimer and Reich in which they discussed the outline of the transaction and the need to terminate Adlerstein. Her notes contain the entry "fire Joe + negotiate a settlement," followed by a summary of terms for his separation.

The documents necessary for a transaction with Reich were in draft form by July 6, 2001. Selbst sent these documents by e-mail to Wertheimer, Mencher, and Reich. He did not send them to Adlerstein, who was deliberately kept unaware that Reich had made a proposal until the July 9 meeting. At trial, Wertheimer was asked whether "[b]etween the time you got the proposal from Mr. Reich — until the time you walked in to the board meeting on July 9th, did you tell Doctor Adlerstein that you were negotiating a proposal with Ilan Reich . . . ." He responded that he had not:

> A. Because I wanted to save the company at that point . . . . So, no, I didn't tell him that this was going on, because I had no faith that he would — that he would, first of all, you know, go along with the deal; but secondly, I was also worried that he would do something to scare off the investor.

Although Adlerstein argues that the Reich proposal was finalized on Friday, July 6, the record supports the conclusion that Reich and Wertheimer were still negotiating some terms of the deal on the morning of July 9 and that final documents were not ready until that time. The deal finally negotiated provided, subject to board approval, that the Reich Partnership would invest $1 million in SpectruMedix, Reich would assume the active management of SpectruMedix, and SpectruMedix would issue shares of its Series C Preferred Stock to the Reich Partnership carrying with them voting control of the Company.

Adlerstein arrived late at MW&E's New York City offices to find Selbst and Wertheimer waiting for him. He inquired about the conference with the arbitrator and was told that the matter had been postponed. Mencher was hooked in by phone and, according to Wertheimer, Adlerstein called the meeting to order and "wanted to talk about lawyers and the arbitration." Wertheimer then interrupted and said that they needed to talk about finances. He then told Adlerstein that there was a proposal from Reich and handed him a term sheet showing the material elements of the deal.

---

11. The arbitration posed a substantial risk to the future viability of SpectruMedix.

After reviewing it, Adlerstein told Wertheimer and Mencher that he was not interested in the Reich proposal because it would dilute his shares in the Company and result in him losing voting control. He has since testified that his lack of interest was also because he believed the price of $1 million to be insufficient for control of SpectruMedix. He did not, however, voice this concern at the time.

In response to the objection that he did voice, Wertheimer and Mencher explained that in their judgment the Company was in immediate need of funds and the investment by Reich was needed to avoid liquidation. Wertheimer asked Adlerstein directly if he was personally in a position to provide the needed funds. Adlerstein responded that he was not.

Wertheimer and Mencher tried to engage Adlerstein in further discussion about the Reich proposal, but Adlerstein sat silent. He testified that the reason for his silence was advice given to him by Selbst in the past: "when in doubt about what to do in a situation like this, keep your mouth shut." Because he and Mencher could not get Adlerstein to engage in any dialogue regarding the proposed transaction, Wertheimer moved the transaction for a vote. Wertheimer testified:

> There was no use in talking about it, because [Adlerstein] wouldn't talk.... So the fact that the discussion didn't go any longer, the finger should not be pointed at us, it should be pointed at the person that cut off the discussion. That is Doctor Adlerstein.

Adlerstein has testified that when the vote on the transaction was called he did not participate. The minutes of the meeting reflect that he voted "no." Each of the others present at the meeting — Wertheimer, Mencher, and Selbst — confirms the statement in the minutes.[19]

The board then took up the question of removing Adlerstein "for cause" from his office as CEO and Chairman of SpectruMedix. The elements of "cause" assigned were mismanagement of the Company, misrepresentations to his fellow board members as to its financial situation, and sexual harassment in contravention of his employment contract. After the meeting, the Reich Partnership executed and delivered a stockholder's written consent removing Adlerstein as a director of SpectruMedix. Reich was chosen to replace him.

Some months after July 9, Adlerstein executed a written consent purporting to vote his Series B Preferred shares to remove Wertheimer and Mencher from the board. Adlerstein initiated this Section 225 action on September 11, 2001.

Here, the question is whether the meeting held on July 9 was a meeting of the board of directors or not. If it was not, Adlerstein continues to exercise a majority of the voting power and is now the sole lawful director. If it was, I must then address a welter of arguments advanced by Adlerstein to prove that the actions taken at the July 9 meeting ought to be invalidated because Wertheimer and Mencher (and Selbst) all operated in secret to negotiate terms with Reich while keeping Adlerstein deliberately uninformed about their plan to present the Reich proposal at the July 9 meeting.

---

19. Adlerstein also testified that, when he realized Wertheimer and Mencher were prepared to act against his interests, he asked Selbst about using his voting power to prevent this from happening. According to Adlerstein, Selbst told him that he could not, due to a 10-day notice requirement for convening a meeting of shareholders. The others deny that this exchange took place. According to the minutes of the July 9 meeting, the second item of business was an amendment to the Company's bylaws, approved by a vote of 2 to 1, with Adlerstein opposed. Prior to its amendment, the bylaw purported to proscribe shareholder action by written consent. Of course, this bylaw was very likely unenforceable as a matter of Delaware law. The importance of this bylaw and its effect on Adlerstein's right to remove Wertheimer and Mencher was not explored by the parties at trial.

For the reasons next discussed, I conclude that, although the meeting of July 9 was called as a board meeting, the actions taken at it must be invalidated.

There are several factors that weigh against a finding of invalidity. The first is the absence from SpectruMedix's bylaws of any requirement of prior notice of agenda items for meetings of the board of directors, coupled with the absence of any hard and fast legal rule that directors be given advance notice of all matters to be considered at a meeting. Second, is the good faith belief of Wertheimer and Mencher that Adlerstein should be removed from management and that, if they had told him about the Reich proposal ahead of time, he would have done something to kill the deal. Third, is the fact of SpectruMedix's insolvency and the argument that the exigencies created by that insolvency gave Wertheimer and Mencher legal warrant to "spring" the Reich proposal on Adlerstein without warning.

Ultimately, I am unable to agree that these factors, either singly or in the aggregate, provide legal justification for the conduct of the July 9 meeting. Instead, I conclude that in the context of the set of legal rights that existed within SpectruMedix at the time of the July 9 meeting, Adlerstein was entitled to know ahead of time of the plan to issue new Series C Preferred Stock with the purposeful effect of destroying his voting control over the Company. This right to advance notice derives from a basic requirement of our corporation law that boards of directors conduct their affairs in a manner that satisfies minimum standards of fairness.

Here, the decision to keep Adlerstein in the dark about the plan to introduce the Reich proposal was significant because Adlerstein possessed the contractual power to prevent the issuance of the Series C Preferred Stock by executing a written consent removing one or both of Wertheimer and Mencher from the board. He may or may not have exercised this power had he been told about the plan in advance. But he was fully entitled to the opportunity to do so and the machinations of those individuals who deprived him of this opportunity were unfair and cannot be countenanced by this court.[28]

Had [Adlerstein] known beforehand that Wertheimer and Mencher intended to approve the Reich proposal and to remove him from office at the July 9 meeting, he could have exercised his legal right to remove one or both of them and, thus, prevented the completion of those plans.

Wertheimer and Mencher argue that SpectruMedix's dire financial circumstances and actual or impending insolvency justify their actions because, they believe, it was necessary to keep Adlerstein uninformed in order for them to "save the Company." From the record at trial, it is fair to conclude that SpectruMedix was insolvent as of July 9, 2001, in the sense that it was unable to meet its obligations as they came due. This was already true of ordinary supply contracts and fees for its attorneys and consultants. It was also about to be true for a payroll due a few days after the July 9 meeting. Nevertheless, I conclude that these facts do not alter the outcome of the

---

28. The outcome in this case flows from the fact the Adlerstein was both a director and a controlling stockholder, not from either status individually. In the absence of some special contractual right, there is no authority to support the argument that Adlerstein's stockholder status entitled him to advance notice of actions proposed to be taken at a meeting of the board of directors. The actions may be voidable if improperly motivated. But the absence (or presence) of notice is not a critical factor. Similarly, in the absence of a bylaw or other custom or regulation requiring that directors be given advance notice of items proposed for action at board meetings, there is no reason to believe that the failure to give such notice alone would ordinarily give rise to a claim of invalidity. Nevertheless, when a director either is the controlling stockholder or represents the controlling stockholder, our law takes a different view of the matter where the decision to withhold advance notice is done for the purpose of preventing the controlling stockholder/director from exercising his or her contractual right to put a halt to the other directors' schemes.

case. Quite the opposite, it is in such times of dire consequence that the well established rules of good board conduct are most important.

There is authority in this court suggesting the possibility that a board of directors could, "consistent with its fiduciary duties, issue a dilutive option in order to protect the corporation or its minority shareholders from exploitation by a controlling shareholder who was in the process of threatening to violate his fiduciary duties to the corporation."[34] Nevertheless, neither this nor any other authority suggests that directors could accomplish such action through trickery or deceit, and I am not prepared to hold otherwise.

For all the foregoing reasons, I have concluded that the actions taken at the July 9, 2001 meeting must be undone. Nevertheless, I recognize that the financial and business condition of SpectruMedix has changed materially since July 9, 2001. I also note plaintiff's proposal, during the trial, that I should appoint a custodian for SpectruMedix rather than reinstate Adlerstein's control. Under these circumstances, before entering a final order, the court will solicit the parties' views as to the appropriate form of relief. To this end, I direct that the parties confer, through counsel or otherwise, in an effort to agree upon the form of an order implementing this decision.

Notes and Questions

1. Notes

a. Section 225 is the typical procedural way to test election procedures. It provides for a summary proceeding in the Court of Chancery.

2. Reality Check

a. Which elements of a valid board meeting were problematic here according to Vice Chancellor Lamb? Do you agree?

3. Suppose

a. What would have happened if Dr. Adlerstein had simply left the July 9th meeting?

b. Suppose SpectruMedix were incorporated under the MBCA. Would the analysis or result have been different? What would have happened under the MBCA if Dr. Adlerstein had left the July 9th meeting?

c. Suppose Dr. Adlerstein had been a director but not the controlling shareholder. Suppose he were only the controlling shareholder and not a director. In either instance, would Vice Chancellor Lamb's analysis or result have been different? See footnote 28.

d. Would the defendants have fared better had they simply waited for a regularly scheduled board meeting? Suppose they had asked Dr. Adlerstein to call a special board meeting but said nothing about its purpose. Would that have helped their case?

4. What Do You Think?

a. Should the parties have anticipated the sort of disagreement that arose? If so, what corporate law precautions should they have taken? Would the precautions that would be best for Dr. Adlerstein be the same as those that would be best for Mr. Wertheimer and Ms. Mencher?

34. *Mendel v. Carroll*, 651 A.2d 297, 306 (Del. Ch. 1994).

b. Do you think that the dire financial and operational position of SpectruMedix justifies Mr. Wertheimer, Ms. Mencher, and Mr. Reich's actions?

c. Did Mr. Selbst act appropriately at the July 9th meeting? Did he do so before? After?

d. Would Dr. Adlerstein, SpectruMedix, Mr. Wertheimer, or Ms. Mencher have a potential malpractice claim against Mr. Selbst? If so, which?

b. Background and Context

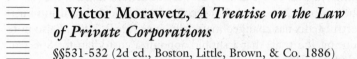

1 Victor Morawetz, *A Treatise on the Law of Private Corporations*

§§531-532 (2d ed., Boston, Little, Brown, & Co. 1886)

The general rule is, that the directors of a corporation have no implied authority to act singly; they can act only as a board, unless there be a different custom, or an express delegation of authority to act individually. Either all must be present at a meeting, or the meeting must be called in a regular manner, and all the directors given notice; and in the latter case, if a majority assemble, they may act by a major[ity] vote. A majority of the directors form a quorum, in the absence of a different regulation, and a majority of the quorum determine the action of the board.

It has been held, that, if a quorum of the directors of a corporation meet and unite in any determination, the company is bound thereby, whether the other directors were notified or not. But this view is certainly not correct. The shareholders in a corporation are entitled not only to the votes of the directors, but also to their influence and argument in the discussion which leads to the passage of their resolutions. While it may not be the duty of every director to be present at every meeting of the board, yet it is certainly the intention of the shareholders that every director shall have a right to be present at every meeting, in order to acquire full information concerning the affairs of the corporation, and to give the other directors the benefit of his judgment and advice. If meetings could be held by a bare quorum, without notifying the other directors, the majority might virtually exclude the minority from all participation in the management of the company. If it appears that a meeting of the directors was attended by a quorum, it will be presumed, in the absence of the contrary, that due notice of the meeting was given to all the directors, and that all necessary formalities have been complied with.

B. OFFICERS

1. Officers and Agents

a. Background and Context. Review of Chapter 4 on Agency

H-D Irrigating, Inc. v. Kimble Properties, Inc.

8 P.3d 95 (Mont. 2000)

Justice TERRY N. TRIEWEILER delivered the Opinion of the Court.

The Plaintiffs, H-D Irrigating, Inc. and William H. Lane, Jr., (Buyers), filed this action . . . to recover damages from the Defendants, Kimble Properties, Inc., Hobble

Diamond Cattle Co., and Lloyd L. Kimble (Sellers), for misrepresentation and breach of a duty to disclose. The Defendants filed a counterclaim to recover payments due from the Plaintiffs for the property purchased. Following a nonjury trial, the District Court found the Defendants were liable for constructive fraud and that the Plaintiffs were liable for payment pursuant to the promissory note. The Defendants appeal and the Plaintiffs cross-appeal. We affirm in part and reverse in part . . . .

On February 13, 1991, [Buyers] agreed with Hobble Diamond Cattle Co. and Kimble Properties, Inc. to purchase land from Hobble Diamond Cattle Co. for $1,650,000 and irrigation equipment from Kimble Properties, Inc. for $350,000. Lloyd L. Kimble was the president of both companies. Lane was the president of H-D Irrigating, Inc.

On June 16, 1992, the Buyers filed a complaint, in which, among other claims, they alleged misrepresentation and breach of a duty to disclose. The Buyers alleged that Lloyd Kimble falsely represented that the irrigation equipment was in working order; that all pivots could be operated at the same time; that the irrigation system provided sufficient water for the acreage; and that he knew of no irrigation system deficiencies.

Following the trial, the District Court entered findings of fact and conclusions of law. The District Court found:

> 21. Mr. Kimble's failure to disclose the extent and cause of the erosion on pivot three could not be reasonably discovered by Mr. Lane prior to closing and constitutes a material misrepresentation upon which Mr. Lane reasonably relied to his detriment.

The Sellers contend that if anyone, "the entity responsible for constructive fraud . . . was Hobble Diamond Cattle Co., not Kimble Properties or Lloyd 'Monty' Kimble." The Sellers argue "Hobble Diamond Cattle Co. owned and sold the real property to Lane, and Kimble Properties owned and sold only the irrigation equipment." The Buyers respond that Kimble is individually liable for his own conduct regardless of who his principal was at the time. The Buyers argue that a principal and its agent are jointly and severally liable for the agent's wrongful acts.

A principal is liable for wrongs committed by an agent while the agent acts within the scope of his employment. Further, a director or officer is individually liable for his false representations. *Poulsen v. Treasure State Indus., Inc.*, 626 P.2d 822, 829 (Mont. 1981). In *Poulsen,* we said:

> It is clearly established that a director or officer of a corporation is individually liable for fraudulent acts or false representations of his own or in which he participates even though his action in such respect may be in furtherance of the corporation's business. This personal liability attaches regardless of whether liability also attaches to the corporation.

626 P.2d at 829 (citations omitted).

In this case, Lloyd Kimble was the president of Hobble Diamond Cattle Co. and Kimble Properties, Inc., which made him an agent of both companies. Hobble Diamond Cattle Co. sold land to the Buyers and Kimble Properties, Inc. sold irrigation equipment to the Buyers. In assessing liability, neither the District Court's findings of fact and conclusions of law, nor its judgment, make a distinction between Hobble Diamond Cattle Co. and Kimble Properties, Inc.; rather, both documents simply refer to the "Defendants." However, when Lloyd Kimble represented to the Buyers that the irrigation equipment was in working order; that all pivots could be operated at the same time; that the irrigation system provided sufficient water for the acreage; and that he knew of no problems or deficiencies with the irrigation equipment or the irrigation system, he was acting within the scope of his employment as the president of Kimble Properties, Inc., which owned the irrigation equipment. Lloyd Kimble's representations concerned the irrigation equipment, not the land. [A]t the time of the representation Lloyd Kimble was referring to the irrigation equipment and acting as an agent of its owner Kimble Properties, Inc. Hobble Diamond Cattle Co., however, is not liable for Lloyd Kimble's misrepresentations because he was not acting on its behalf when he made representations regarding the irrigation system. Kimble Properties, Inc. and Lloyd Kimble are jointly and severally liable for the Buyers' damages resulting from Lloyd Kimble's constructive fraud, but Hobble Diamond Cattle Co. has no liability. Accordingly we hold the District Court did not err when it assessed damages against Kimble Properties, Inc. and Lloyd Kimble, but the District Court did err when it assessed damages against Hobble Diamond Cattle Co.

Notes and Questions

1. Reality Check

a. For whom was Mr. Kimble acting?
b. Why did plaintiffs not prevail on their claims against all the entities?

2. Suppose

a. Suppose Mr. Kimble had misrepresented the size of the parcel being conveyed. Would that have made a difference in the analysis or result? Should it?
b. Assume that Mr. Kimble and Kimble Properties, Inc. are impecunious and that Hobble Diamond Cattle Co. has large assets. Would that scenario make a difference in the result?
c. Assume that only Mr. Kimble has large assets and that the two corporations have negligible assets. Would that scenario make a difference in the result?

3. What Do You Think?

a. Do you think it is fair to hold only one of the two corporations for which Mr. Kimble was acting liable to plaintiffs? Why?

The rules of agency law are largely common law rules that have been systematized by the American Law Institute in its *Restatement (Third) of Agency* (2006). Nearly every state uses these concepts. This discussion will provide a brief overview of the most important agency concepts as they relate to business entities but is not meant to be a complete synopsis. See Chapter 4 for more details.

An agency relationship is a consensual, though not necessarily contractual, relationship in which one person (the agent) agrees to act on behalf of the other person (the principal) and subject to the principal's control. The principal need not have the right to control the physical performance of the agent's task; it is enough that the principal controls the general performance and outcome. An agency relationship, once established, may be ended unilaterally by either the agent or the principal, even if doing so constitutes a breach of contract.

Once an agency relationship is established, the agent may bind the principal in several ways. First, the principal is bound by any acts of the agent within the scope of the agent's actual authority. Actual authority is the agent's reasonable interpretation of the principal's manifestation to the agent. Second, and importantly for corporate purposes, an agent binds the principal for any act done in accordance with apparent authority. Apparent authority is a third party's reasonable interpretation of the principal's manifestation to that third party that the agent is authorized. In many settings actual authority and apparent authority are coterminous. Nonetheless, either is sufficient to bind the principal, and therefore a principal is bound by an agent's actions made in accordance with apparent authority even if done in contravention of actual authority. The principal may also be bound to a third party through estoppel and through ratification of the agent's (originally) unauthorized actions. The agent is not bound to the third party as long as the third party knows that the agent is acting for the principal.

A principal is ordinarily bound by the agent's tortious actions that cause personal injury if (a) the agent is an "employee," a term of art meaning that the principal has the right to control the physical performance of the agent's tasks, and (b) the agent was acting "within the scope of employment," meaning the act giving rise to liability was close in time, space, and manner to those the agent was employed to perform and undertaken at least in part for the principal's benefit. The classic example of such a setting is the delivery person who hits a pedestrian by accident while working. Certainly the agent didn't have actual authority to hit the pedestrian nor did the agent have apparent authority to do so. Liability in this setting is through the concept of "inherent power" a sort of catch-all for unauthorized actions of agents that nonetheless render principals liable essentially on foreseeability and public policy grounds.

b. The Current Setting

Once a corporation's board of directors has authorized an act, someone must actually effect the act for the corporation. That person is the corporation's agent. Of course, all the corporation's employees are agents but the corporation may have other agents who are not employees. For example, the outside accountants and outside lawyers retained by the corporation are agents. Further, the corporation may make use of people to perform services for it but who are not agents; they are non-agent independent contractors. People who supply component parts, for example, are likely to be nonagent independent contractors. Finally, the corporation's directors are *not* agents. This is so because the board must act collectively rather than individually and also because the board is not under the control of the corporation (an agent must be subject to the principal's control). See *Restatement (Third) of Agency* §1.01 cmt. f(2).

Unlike directors, who have their power defined and granted by statute, officers inhabit a much more nebulous world. Strictly speaking, an *officer* is a person who holds an office, which, in turn, is a position to which particular kinds of duties or powers are attached. Thus, by contrast, an agent who is not an officer would have powers and duties defined in a more explicit and ad hoc manner: by board resolution or grant from another agent. The statutes simply provide that a corporation has whatever officers its bylaws or board determines and that those officers have whatever powers are specifically granted to them. See DGCL §142(a), MBCA §8.40(a).

Perhaps the best practical definitions of officer are provided by the Securities and Exchange Commission:

> The term *officer* means a president, vice president, secretary, treasurer or principal financial officer, comptroller or principal accounting officer, and any person routinely performing corresponding functions....
>
> The term *executive officer*,...means...president, any vice president...in charge of a principal business unit, division, or function (such as sales, administration or finance), or an officer who performs a policy making function or any other person who performs similar policy making functions....

Rule 405, 17 C.F.R. §230.405

Notice how the definition of *officer* is narrower than the definition of an *agent*. What difference does it make whether a person who acts on behalf of a corporation does so as an agent or as an officer? It makes a difference in a number of settings. First, officers are explicitly held to fiduciary duties comparable to those of corporate directors, while other agents are held to a less explicit and less stringent standard. Similarly, officers may be statutorily entitled to indemnity and the corporation may be able to purchase insurance (so-called directors and officers insurance) for officer malfeasance. Agents are sometimes entitled to indemnity, but such protection is more amorphous. Third, officers are sometimes expressly exposed to liability under certain statutes (such as environmental protection laws), whereas ordinary agents are not. Statutes often provide that service of process on a corporation may be effected by service on any (or certain named) officers; service on an ordinary agent is typically insufficient to bring about personal jurisdiction over the corporation. Fifth, officers (or at least some of them) are usually required to be named in the corporation's annual report filed with the secretary of state, which means that the names and titles held are a matter of public record. Finally, an officer may have certain powers to bind the corporation (called the power of position) that comprise both actual authority and apparent authority. This aspect of being an officer is explored in more depth below.

Given that the corporations statutes seem to be rather unconcerned with what officers the corporation has, and given that being an officer brings with it some heightened obligations, can a corporation protect the people who act on its behalf by having only agents and no officers? A closer reading of the statutes reveals that the corporation must have at least one office (at least two in Delaware). Under MBCA §8.40(c), at least one office is required and its incumbent has "responsibility for preparing minutes of the directors' and shareholders' meetings and for authenticating records of the corporation." That officer could have any title the corporate planners desire but the statute refers to that person as the "secretary" of the corporation. See MBCA §1.40(20) [defining *secretary*].

In Delaware, the question of officers gets a bit more complicated. Section 142(a) provides that "[o]ne of the officers shall have the duty to record the proceedings of the meetings of the stockholders and directors in a book to be kept for that purpose." As with the MBCA, that person is typically referred to as the corporate secretary, although the DGCL, unlike the MBCA, does not explicitly define the office "secretary" and under the DGCL those duties could be assigned to any officer. But §142(a) also requires that a corporation must have such officers "as may be necessary to enable it to sign instruments and stock certificates which comply with §§103(a)(2) and 158 of this title." Section 103(a)(2) is disappointing in that it simply requires that all documents filed after the corporation's initial organization must be signed by "any authorized officer." Section 158, however, has some actual requirements. It provides that every shareholder has the right to receive a certificate, which ordinarily would be a stock certificate, signed:

> by the chairperson or vice-chairperson of the board of directors, or the president or vice-president, and by the treasurer or an assistant treasurer, or the secretary or an assistant secretary of such corporation . . . .

Thus a Delaware corporation must have at least two officers, one of which must be designated "chairperson of the board of directors," "vice-chairperson of the board of directors," "president," or "vice-president," and the other of which must be designated "treasurer," "assistant treasurer," "secretary," or "assistant secretary." The DGCL goes on to provide, as a default rule, that "[a]ny number of offices may be held by the same person," and further provides that the corporation's failure to elect officers shall have no effect on the corporation(!). See DGCL §142(a), (d). The MBCA also allows all offices to be held by the same person. See MBCA §8.40(d). Within these constraints, however, you and your clients are free to have as many or as few officers as you desire and with whatever titles seem best. For example, the head of one major corporation holds the titles of chairman of the board and chief software architect. At another such corporation, the head is styled chairman of the board of directors and chief global strategist.[3]

Peter Bart, *The Studios' Plethora of Presidents*
Variety (Mar. 2, 2003)

If you believe the titles, just about everyone is the boss.

In the opening days of my first studio job at Paramount some years ago, I remember telling a writer-producer, "you've got a deal." He seemed delighted, even though at the time I wasn't a president of the studio or even a lowly vice president, but I was still closing deals like crazy. In that era, the head of a studio held a mere vice president's title while the president was a "suit" headquartered in New York.

At Paramount today the executive roadmap is more complex. At last count there were eight presidents of something or other spread around the Paramount landscape. There were two co-presidents of production. All these, to be sure, functioned under the overall tutelage of Sherry Lansing and Jonathan Dolgen, who were sort of presidents of presidents.

Something tells me that if I were at Paramount today, I wouldn't be able to close deals unless I could levitate myself into the hierarchy, which is already too crowded.

At Sony Pictures Entertainment as well, there are no less than four vice-chairmen under [John] Calley. There's a president of Columbia Pictures, two co-presidents of production and also a president of production administration, not to mention 11 other presidents (Sony even has a president of releasing, but it's not clear what he's releasing that the others don't want to).

I can't figure out what triggered this proliferation, but the thicket of fancy titles surely adds to the level of bureaucratic confusion.

---

3. The chief software architect is William H. Gates, III, of Microsoft Corporation. Starbucks Corp.'s Howard Schultz is its chief global strategist.

Over at Twentieth Century-Fox, there's no confusion about the identity of the uber-boss, but while Rupert [Murdoch] reigns supreme, a look at the executive register makes you wonder about everyone else. At last count there were 17 presidents roaming the lot, all of them serving under Peter Chernin, the boss chairman, Tom Rothman and Jim Gianopulos, co-chairmen, and Robert Harper, vice chairman.

I think it's great that everyone is president of something, but, since this is supposedly a creative business, couldn't anyone come up with another designation? Does the marketing head of little Fox Searchlight have to be a president of marketing? Does there have to be a president of post-production? Will there soon be a president of parking?

Not that things are any better elsewhere.

There are 13 presidents serving under Stacey Snider over at Universal, along with 11 executive vice presidents waiting their turn to become presidents — and that doesn't even count Focus Features. There are also scores of vice presidents with fascinating titles — there's even a vice president of guest entertainment at Universal Studios. I'd like being entertained by someone while I'm visiting the lot.

At Disney there's a senior vice president in charge of Corporate Alliances and yet another senior VP for Worldwide Outreach. I suppose this means Outreach can go just so far, short of forming an alliance. There's also a VP for synergy, but synergy is a dirty word so his title is now being changed.

Even independent production companies have become title-heavy.

Jersey Films recently announced a new CEO and a president of production. The CEO was doing fine, until the three people who call themselves "partners" last month decided to break up the company.

Then, of course, there's DreamWorks, which also has three partners but absolutely no titles, and has no intention either of breaking up or of making anyone president of anything.

In the interest of full disclosure, I should confess that I was once president of something. It was a middle-sized independent company and I was the only — that's right, only — president. It was very lonely.

As a matter of fact, I hated the job. But I was very young at the time.

Peter Bart is vice president and editor-in-chief of Variety.

The officers themselves are appointed by the board. The DGCL says that the officers are "elected" but in truth they are decided upon in the same fashion that the board makes any other decision. See DGCL §142(a), MBCA §8.40(a). Does being an officer give one a heightened expectation or right to remain in office? Or can an officer be dismissed at will, as an ordinary agent can be dismissed by the principal?

Andrews v. Southwest Wyoming Rehabilitation Center
974 P.2d 948 (Wyo. 1999)

LEHMAN, C.J.

[Southwest Wyoming Rehabilitation Center (SWRC)] hired [Phil] Andrews on January 2, 1990, for the position of employee relations coordinator. In May 1991, he was promoted to vice president of SWRC, the position he held when his employment was terminated on June 21, 1995. Andrews' supervisor was Kathy Horn-Dalton, the president of SWRC. According to Andrews, Horn-Dalton fired him because he tried to inform SWRC's board of directors that she was mishandling corporate assets and causing employee morale problems.

On February 5, 1996, Andrews filed suit against SWRC. Andrews alleged that he had a special fiduciary relationship with SWRC and that his termination was wrongfully motivated, and, thus, SWRC breached the duty of good faith and fair dealing.

Wyoming recognizes a limited tort claim for breach of the implied covenant of good faith and fair dealing in employment contracts. Only in those rare and exceptional cases where a special relationship of trust and reliance exists between the employer and employee is a duty created which can give rise to tort liability. A special relationship sufficient to support a cause of action can be found by the existence of separate consideration, rights created by common law or statute, or rights accruing with longevity of service.

Andrews contends that a special relationship existed between him and SWRC by virtue of [MBCA §8.42] He argues that, as a corporate officer with a fiduciary duty to the corporation and its members, he was not an "ordinary employee," but occupied a position of trust and reliance. In essence, Andrews' argument is that the "fiduciary relationship" created by the statute amounts to the "special relationship" necessary to support a cause of action for breach of the implied covenant.

We do not agree with Andrews' position. The implied good faith covenant involves a "special element of reliance" by the aggrieved party, the type of trust and dependency that is found, for example, in insurance relationships. Section [8.42] establishes the standard of conduct for corporate officers, imposing on officers a duty of care to their corporations. While an officer may be able to rely on the statute to protect him from personal liability if he has acted in accordance therewith, see [8.42(c)], it goes too far to say that an officer exercising his duty of care under the statute has a right not to be terminated. On the contrary, the Act provides that a board may remove an officer at any time with or without cause. [MBCA §8.43(b)]. Section [8.43(b)] clearly vitiates Andrews' contention that he should be allowed to rely on his employer to maintain his employment until it is determined that he has not acted, or can no longer act, in the corporation's best interest.

In sum, [§8.42] simply does not establish rights on which Andrews was entitled to rely and which would create a special relationship upon which tort liability can rest. Because Andrews did not establish the existence of a special relationship of trust and reliance, the court properly entered summary judgment on Andrews' claim for breach of the implied covenant of good faith and fair dealing.

SWRC was entitled to summary judgment as a matter of law, and the district court's order hereby is affirmed.

Notes and Questions

1. Notes

a. The DGCL is silent on the point raised by this opinion but case law clearly has adopted the same rule. See also MBCA §8.44.

b. Morawetz wrote,

The directors and managing agents of a corporation have undoubted authority to revoke the powers of the inferior agents whom they have appointed. The power is a discretionary one, and the rightfulness of its exercise cannot be investigated by the courts.

But the directors of a corporation have no implied authority to revoke the powers of those agents who are appointed by vote of the shareholders, or whose office is fixed and regulated by the charter. So it would be difficult to imply authority in the board of directors to revoke the powers of any agent, like a president or treasurer, whose term of office is fixed by the charter or articles of association of the company. It does not follow that the directors have authority to remove an agent of this character merely because they appointed him pursuant to the provisions of the charter. There should be an express provision granting the power of removal.

The majority at a shareholders' meeting have no power to revoke the powers of the inferior agents of a corporation because the power of appointing and controlling these agents is delegated to the board of directors exclusively.

1 Victor Morawetz, *A Treatise on the Law of Private Corporations* §§541-542 (2d ed., Boston, Little, Brown, & Co. 1886)

2. Reality Check

a. Mr. Andrews claimed that his status as an officer provided him certain benefits. What were they? Why did the court disagree?

3. Suppose

a. Suppose Mr. Andrews had had a contract for employment to be SWRC's vice president?

4. What Do You Think?

a. Should officers' employment be terminable at will in the absence of an explicit employment contract? Shouldn't corporate officers have some security against capricious board action?

2. Power of Officers

a. The Current Setting

When an outside party deals with a corporation, how does the outsider know whether the humans' acts supposedly on behalf of the corporation actually bind it? As you'll remember, if an agent, including an officer, for a corporation has actual authority, the corporation is bound even if the outsider has no knowledge of the agent's authority. The principal's manifestation to the outsider that the agent has authority creates apparent authority, which also binds the principal, regardless of the agent's actual authority. What if the manifestation to the outsider is simply, "This is our president" (or vice president, or chief global strategist)? Does this create apparent authority? If so, what are the contours of such power? The following case deals with this question. In a larger context, the next case addresses the chronic problem of how a third party may be certain that a corporation is bound by a human's actions where the human purports to be acting for the corporation. Note that the court uses the term *ostensible authority*, which is simply a synonym for *apparent authority*. See *Restatement (Third) of Agency* §2.03, cmt. b.

Snukal v. Flightways Manufacturing, Inc.

3 P.3d 286 (Cal. 2000)

GEORGE, C.J.

I

In October 1992, plaintiff Robert Snukal leased a residence he owned in Malibu, California, to defendant Flightways Manufacturing, Inc. (hereafter, Flightways) for a two-year term commencing in November 1992. The residence was to be occupied by Kirt Lyle, who at that time was president, chief financial officer, and secretary of Flightways. On behalf of Flightways, Lyle alone executed the lease agreement, designating his title as president, without indicating that he also was chief financial officer and secretary of the corporation.

Within several months of the commencement of the lease term, Flightways was in arrears in its monthly rent payments, and in September 1993, plaintiff sent Flightways a notice to pay rent or quit. Lyle vacated the premises approximately one year after the inception of the lease term. Plaintiff commenced the present action, seeking recovery of past due rents, payment of future rents according to the terms of the lease, and other relief. In its answer to the complaint, Flightways denied that Lyle was authorized to enter into the lease agreement on its behalf. Flightways filed a cross-complaint alleging that it had not authorized Lyle to enter into the lease agreement on its behalf, and seeking relief in the amount of the monthly rent payments previously made.

The parties stipulated to trial by the court. Plaintiff testified that he personally did not meet with Lyle or Flightways and that the lease transaction was conducted through real estate brokers. Plaintiff was unaware of Lyle's actual interest in Flightways. Plaintiff's secretary received and deposited certain rent checks bearing the name "Lyle Kirtisine" rather than Flightways, but most of the rent checks received were issued on an account bearing the name "Flightways Manufacturing, Inc."

A member of its board of directors testified that Flightways did not authorize Lyle to enter into the lease agreement, and in fact was attempting to reduce its expenses during the period in which Lyle executed the agreement on its behalf. Although Flightway's monthly bank statements clearly reflected the checks (numbered in a sequence distinct from that of most of the checks written on the corporate bank account) written by Lyle on Flightway's bank account to pay the monthly rent for the residence, Lyle's duties also included the preparation (based upon those records) of the monthly corporate financial statements that were examined by the board of directors. At one point, in order to determine the reliability of the financial records, the board of directors employed an accounting firm to review the company's financial statements, but that firm did not detect anything unusual. Lyle told the board members that he was house-sitting for a girlfriend who lived in Malibu.

The municipal court determined that Flightways was bound by the lease agreement, noting that although Flightways had been the apparent victim of fraud on the part of Lyle, in view of the circumstance that a corporation reasonably might lease a residence on behalf of a corporate officer, Flightways was in a better position than plaintiff to detect and prevent the fraud. The municipal court entered a judgment in favor of plaintiff in the amount of $22,300 for past due rent and attorney fees. The parties stipulated to the entry of judgment in favor of plaintiff on Flightway's cross-complaint.

The appellate department [of the superior court] affirmed the judgment of the municipal court, concluding that Corporations Code section 313 was dispositive.

The Court of Appeal reversed the judgment, holding that this statute applies only when the signatures of two corporate officers appear on the document, and therefore was inapplicable in the present case.

II

We now determine whether Corporations Code section 313 is applicable in view of the circumstances that Lyle, holding the corporate offices of president, chief financial officer, and secretary, executed the lease agreement purportedly on behalf of Flightways, but expressly identified himself in the agreement solely as its president.

Corporations Code section 313 provides: "[A]ny . . . instrument in writing . . . executed or entered into between any corporation and any other person, *when signed by the chairman of the board, the president or any vice president and the secretary, any assistant secretary, the chief financial officer or any assistant treasurer of such corporation,* is not invalidated as to the corporation by any lack of authority of the signing officers in the absence of actual knowledge on the part of the other person that the signing officers had no authority to execute the same." (Italics added.)[7]

Corporations Code section 313 . . . may be construed to apply when a single individual who holds a corporate office listed in the first series — the chairman of the board, president, or any vice-president — *as well as* an office listed in the second series — the secretary, assistant secretary, chief financial officer, or assistant treasurer — executes the instrument on behalf of the corporation, regardless whether the individual specifies on the instrument itself all of the designated corporate offices he or she holds.

In the alternative, the provision may be interpreted to apply only when *both* an officer listed in the first series *and* an officer listed in the second series execute the agreement *and* name the corporate offices held on the instrument itself, whether the same individual holds both designated corporate offices or different individuals hold the designated corporate offices.

At common law, a corporate officer may have express authority to enter into an agreement on behalf of the corporation, granted by the board of directors or the corporate bylaws. (*Black v. Harrison Home Co.* 99 P. 494 (Cal. 1909)). In the alternative, a corporate officer may have ostensible authority to enter into an agreement on behalf of the corporation if he or she "assumed and exercised the power in the past" with the apparent consent and acquiescence of the corporation. (*Black v. Harrison Home Co., supra,* 99 P. 494). In this setting, as is the case generally, ostensible authority requires justifiable reliance by a third party. It must be shown that "the business done by the supposed agent, so far as open to the observation of third parties, is consistent with the existence of an agency, and, as to the transaction in question, the third party was justified in believing that an agency existed. [Citation.]" (*County etc. Bk. v. Coast D. & L. Co.,* 115 P.2d 988 (Cal. App. 1941)).

---

7. The use of the plural . . . "signing officers" in the body of the statute, is not controlling. The General Provisions of the Corporations Code include the following . . . : "The singular number includes the plural, and the plural number includes the singular." (*Id.,* §13.)

At common law, the party seeking to enforce a contract with a corporation generally has the burden of establishing the contracting officer's authority to bind the corporation.[8]

For the party seeking to establish the validity of a contract at common law, formerly a corporate seal affixed to an agreement, although "not essential to the validity of such contract," provided presumptive evidence that the officer executing the agreement had the requisite authority to bind the corporation. (*City Street Improvement Co. v. Laird,* 70 P. 916 (Cal. 1902)).

That rule eventually was codified. [H]owever, effective January 1, 1977 . . . former section 833, providing that the corporate seal is prima facie evidence of corporate authority, was repealed. The Legislative Committee comment to Corporations Code section 313 states that the purpose of the statute is "to allow third parties to rely upon the assertive authority of various senior executive officers of the corporation concerning the execution of any instrument on behalf of the corporation." (Legis. Com. com., 23E West's Ann. Corp. Code, *supra,* foll. §313, p. 192.) "Such extra protection for third parties who deal with corporations is warranted since corporations necessarily act through agents." (*Taormina Theosophical Community, Inc. v. Silver,* 140 Cal. App. 3d 964, 971 (1983)).

It is apparent that, if its criteria are met, Corporations Code section 313 precludes the invalidation of an instrument entered into by a corporation, *despite* the presentation of evidence demonstrating that the signing officers lacked authority to execute the instrument on its behalf. Thus, the statute provides a conclusive, rather than a merely rebuttable, evidentiary presumption of authority to enter into the agreement on the part of the specified corporate officers.[10]

In addition, Corporations Code section 313 applies so long as the other party does not have *actual knowledge* that the executing officers lack authority. Because the statute applies even when the other party should have, but does not have, actual knowledge of the officers' lack of authority, that party is relieved of the burden of establishing *justifiable* reliance upon the authority of the executing officers.

At the same time, Corporations Code section 313 leaves intact the other party's ability to assert the validity of an instrument under existing common law doctrines when the signatory or signatories do not hold the corporate offices specified in that statute.

Corporations Code section 313 appears designed to establish a level of formality that, if attained because the requisite number and type of officers have executed the subject instrument, affords the third party protection from subsequent efforts by the corporation to disavow its agents' authority in order to avoid its obligations pursuant to the agreement. The Legislature apparently considered that execution of an instrument on behalf of the corporation by two officers — one officer having general, operational responsibilities (i.e., the chairman of the board, president, or any vice-president) and one officer having recordkeeping or financial responsibilities (i.e., the secretary, assistant secretary, chief financial officer, or treasurer) — sufficed for that

---

8. At common law, when the corporate officer's actual authority to execute the agreement has been established or is not in doubt, the circumstance that he or she does not specify the office held does not invalidate the agreement as to the corporation.

10. We stress that when Corporations Code section 313 is applicable and the corporation is prevented from seeking to invalidate the agreement by asserting a lack of authority to enter into it on the part of its signing officers, the corporation is not prevented thereby from asserting the invalidity of the agreement on an alternative theory other than lack of authority (e.g., fraud, mistake, failure of consideration).

purpose. Corporations Code section 313 thus creates a "safe harbor" for persons entering into an agreement with a corporation: pursuant to that section, a corporation may not disclaim its authorization of those persons entering into an agreement on its behalf.

The circumstances of the present case compel us to examine next whether that prerequisite is satisfied when an individual who in fact holds at least one of the designated corporate offices from each category executes an instrument but merely lists thereon *one* of his or her offices.

In determining the legislative intent underlying this enactment, "we consider the statute read as a whole, harmonizing the various elements by considering each clause and section in the context of the overall statutory framework." (*People v. Jenkins*, 893 P.2d 1224 (Cal. 1995)). Corporations Code section 312, also enacted during the 1975 revision of the Corporations Code, provides in part: "(a) A corporation shall have a chairman of the board or a president or both, a secretary, a chief financial officer and such other officers with such titles and duties as shall be stated in the bylaws or determined by the board and as may be necessary to enable it to sign instruments and share certificates. The president, or if there is no president the chairman of the board, is the general manager and chief executive officer of the corporation, unless otherwise provided in the articles or bylaws. Any number of offices may be held by the same person unless the articles or bylaws provide otherwise."

Corporations Code section 313 does not contain any language directing that the signing officers be separate individuals, or that the signing officers specify the office or offices they hold. Accordingly, although Corporations Code section 313 applies only where corporate officers in each of the two designated series or categories execute the instrument, that statute, considered in light of Corporations Code section 312, is satisfied when one individual who in fact holds two of the specified corporate offices executes the instrument.[13]

In view of the statutory purpose, context, and derivation of Corporations Code section 313, we believe that the Legislature did not intend to limit the statute's application only to instances in which two corporate offices are set forth on the face of the instrument. Rather, the signature of one person alone is sufficient to bind a corporation, as long as he or she holds corporate offices in each of the two series or categories described in that statute. In the present case, therefore, because Lyle served both as Flightways' president and as its chief financial officer (and secretary), and because plaintiff did not have actual knowledge of any lack of authority on Lyle's part, the lease agreement was not invalidated by Lyle's lack of authority to enter into such an agreement on behalf of Flightways.

The judgment of the Court of Appeal is reversed, and the matter is remanded to the Court of Appeal with directions to affirm the judgment of the municipal court in favor of plaintiff.

13. Our conclusion that Corporations Code section 313 applies when a corporate officer holding at least one of the designated corporate offices in each series or category of offices executes an instrument on behalf of the corporation, even if he or she omits to record thereon both designated offices, also finds support in Corporations Code section 1502. Subdivision (a) of that statute makes a matter of public record the names and addresses of a corporation's chief executive officer, secretary, and chief financial officer, as part of the information required to be filed biennially with the Secretary of State. Although subdivision (g) of section 1502 expressly forbids construction of that statute "to place any person dealing with the corporation on notice of, or under any duty to inquire about, the existence or content of a statement filed pursuant to this section," nonetheless the statute effectively produces public information as to the actual identities of three primary officeholders of a given corporation, and this information may be relied upon by a third party even if a particular agreement does not list all of the offices held by those signing the agreement.

Notes and Questions

1. Notes

a. Neither the DGCL nor the MBCA has a provision analogous to Cal. Corp. Code §313 but many other states do.

b. Every corporation statute requires a corporation to have one officer whose function is to keep the corporate records and, often, to certify that corporate actions (i.e., shareholder actions and board actions) have been taken. That officer is usually referred to as the secretary. A moment's reflection will reveal that a consequence of these provisions is to imbue the secretary with important powers of position. Even the most careful outsider is entitled to rely on a corporate secretary's certificate that a particular transaction has been validly authorized or that particular people are authorized to bind the corporation (at least in the absence of information that makes such reliance unwarranted). An extremely careful (or paranoid) outsider can easily ascertain the corporate secretary's identity by checking with the secretary of state; the secretary is typically one of the officers who must be identified each year in the corporation's annual report. Thus a careless or perfidious corporate secretary can render the corporation liable for large unintended obligations. Hence the selection of the corporate secretary is one that should be made carefully.

2. Reality Check

a. What is the current function of the corporate seal? Has that function changed over time?

b. Did Flightways authorize Mr. Lyle to rent the Malibu residence? If not, why is it liable for the rent?

3. Suppose

a. What if Mr. Lyle had signed the lease but indicated no title at all. Would the analysis or result be different? Would it matter whether Mr. Snukal (or his agent) knew of Mr. Lyle's positions with Flightways?

b. Suppose Mr. Lyle had signed the lease but indicated the wrong offices. Would Flightways be liable?

c. Assume Flightways had a corporate seal and that that seal had been affixed to the lease. What additional signatures, if any, would be necessary to bind Flightways to the lease?

4. What Do You Think?

a. Do you think corporation statutes should be prescriptive about the ways in which agreements must be executed to bind a corporation? If so, should those statutes provide a safe harbor or should they be the exclusive method of binding the corporation in writing?

b. Do you believe that principals (including corporations) should ever be liable for their agents' actions unless those actions were authorized by the principal?

5. You Draft It

a. Redraft Cal. Corp. Code §313 so that it clearly supports plaintiff's claim. Then redraft it so it clearly supports Flightways' claim.

> [A]ny . . . instrument in writing . . . executed or entered into between any corporation and any other person, when signed by the chairman of the board, the president or any

vice president and the secretary, any assistant secretary, the chief financial officer or any assistant treasurer of such corporation, is not invalidated as to the corporation by any lack of authority of the signing officers in the absence of actual knowledge on the part of the other person that the signing officers had no authority to execute the same.

b. Background and Context

The extent of the powers of agents of a well-defined class, such as presidents, directors, or cashiers, is determined largely by general custom, of which the courts will take judicial notice; and parties dealing with such agents are entitled to assume that they possess all the powers which are usually accorded to agents of the class to which they belong.

1 Victor Morawetz, *A Treatise on the Law of Private Corporations* §509 (2d ed., Boston, Little, Brown, & Co. 1886)

Normally, the president is merely the presiding officer of the board of directors; the secretary is a ministerial officer charged with the duty of preparing and keeping the corporate records and with the custody of the corporate seal, if there be one; the treasurer is a fiscal agent whose duties are to receive, disburse, and account for the corporate moneys. It is not unusual to-day to find that the function of presiding over the board of directors is conferred upon a chairman of the board, while the functions of an executive business manager are conferred upon a president.

Robert S. Stevens, *Handbook on the Law of Private Corporations* §§159-160 (1936)

Notes and Questions

1. Reality Check

a. Have officers been given greater or lesser powers since Morawetz wrote?

2. Suppose

a. Suppose the *Snukal* case had been heard by Morawetz. Would his analysis and result have been the same as Chief Justice George's?

C. FEDERAL SECURITIES REGULATION

Speaking broadly, federal securities laws are designed to protect public company investors primarily by requiring disclosure, rather than by mandating substantive governance rules. Those laws are not intended to displace the traditional role of state corporate law in regulating the internal governance of corporations. Nonetheless, as early as 1934 the SEC was given rather broad powers to regulate the process of obtaining proxies in connection with corporate elections. In the 1970s, and again at the turn of the century, federal regulation of corporate governance, specifically, regulation of boards, increased.

This increase has been effected in two main ways. First, the SEC has used its power to compel disclosure to coerce corporations to adopt desired board structures. For example, the SEC requires public corporations to disclose "whether" the members of the nominating committee are independent of corporate management. Public companies do not wish to say that they do not have structures the SEC deems salutary so, as a practical matter, public companies have only independent directors on their nominating committee. The second device used to impose federal governance ideas on corporations is through the stock exchanges. Although the exchanges, such as the New York Stock Exchange and the National Association of Securities Dealers are private organizations, Congress has placed the SEC in a supervisory role over them. Not only must the SEC approve any rule change, but the SEC can require the exchanges to adopt any rule the SEC believes appropriate. Thus the SEC has used its powers to persuade the stock exchanges to amend their *listing requirements* (i.e., the standards corporations must follow if they want their shares traded on the exchange) to require various corporate governance features. The Sarbanes-Oxley Act of 2002, which was enacted in response to the Enron and WorldCom scandals, gave added impetus to the SEC to impose substantive governance requirements on public companies.

The stock exchanges require that boards have a majority of members who are independent of the company's management and that regular meetings of the non-management directors are held. They also require companies to have audit, compensation, and nominating/corporate governance committees, each of which must be composed only of directors independent of management. The reforms in Sarbanes-Oxley and its aftermath have affected corporate board membership and power principally as they relate to the audit committee.

D. TERMS OF ART IN THIS CHAPTER

Amotion	Holdover	Regular meetings
Board of directors	Notice	Special meetings
Call	Officer	Staggered terms
Classified board	Quorum	

10

Restrictions on the Board's Power

We saw in the last chapter that all corporate power is ultimately in the hands of the board of directors. See DGCL §141(a), MBCA §8.01(b). This chapter and the four that follow it now take up the question of the limits of that power. Chapters 11, 12, and 13 together focus on what are usually called *director fiduciary duties*. As you may intuit from the number of pages devoted to that subject, fiduciary duties comprise and compose a rather elaborate system that restrains directors' actions. That system is largely immediate and inward looking. It prescribes and evaluates director action primarily by reference to standards that link the director to the corporation and its shareholders. By contrast, the restrictions in this chapter are more mediated and outward looking. They derive from the relationship between the corporation and the state. The restrictions here are most directly ones that limit *corporate* rather than *board* action. The board is indirectly restrained because it cannot legally cause the corporation to take certain actions. The final chapter in this unit, Chapter 14, asks you to assess the efficacy of the restrictions in this chapter and in the fiduciary duties chapters.

This chapter begins by considering legislation that cabins corporate, and by extension, board, actions. We next look briefly at a common law restriction, ultra vires, that has some theoretical but not much practical interest. Finally, we examine restrictions that flow from perhaps the most conceptual aspect of corporate law: Why do corporations exist?

A. LEGISLATION THAT RESTRICTS BOARD POWER

Legal rules typically apply to natural persons as well as artificial entities. The law of contracts, torts, and property, for example, do not typically distinguish between humans and corporations. In some cases, such as taxation, somewhat different rules apply to business entities than apply to natural persons, but on the whole such systems regulate both people and entities alike.

In many instances entities will be more likely to be affected because the regulated activities are undertaken by businesses, most of which are owned by entities rather than by a single individual. Environmental regulations, occupational health and safety (OSHA) requirements, the antitrust laws, and the securities laws are instances of regulatory schemes that primarily restrict business entities rather than individuals. Since business entities can act only via humans, the principles of agency law (Chapter 4) loom large here. Some regulatory schemes, most notably federal environmental regulations (CERCLA) explicitly impose duties and liabilities upon individuals acting on behalf of entities.

All of these restrictions on corporate actions have the obvious effect of restraining board power. We could explore all of them here but that would subsume the entire law school curriculum in this one course; we've got to leave something for you to do in your other courses. We will, though, explore one regulatory area that explicitly, though indirectly, regulates business entities. That area is the Federal Sentencing Guidelines.

When a business entity has committed a federal crime, the Federal Sentencing Guidelines provide a matrix for determining the punishment. Important practical constraints on the entity's response to its discovery that it may have committed a federal crime are imbedded in the Guidelines' matrix. The Guidelines provide that an entity's punishment be, in large part, a function of its "culpability score." That score is adjusted upward or downward by various factors, some of which are entity actions. We will examine the Guideline factors that affect corporate action before a crime is committed in Chapter 12 when we take up the duty of care. Here we are concerned with the entity's actions vis-à-vis the government.

The Guidelines include a strong incentive to report possible criminal activity and to cooperate with the government, including providing information about the roles of corporate employees and other agents. The Guidelines provide a reduction in the culpability score,

> If the organization (A) prior to an imminent threat of disclosure or government investigation; and (B) within a reasonably prompt time after becoming aware of the offense, reported the offense to appropriate governmental authorities, fully cooperated in the investigation, and clearly demonstrated recognition and affirmative acceptance of responsibility for its criminal conduct....

U.S. Sentencing Guidelines Manual §8C2.5(g)(1)

The Application Notes to the Guidelines flesh out the requirements for an entity to obtain a reduction in its culpability score:

> [C]ooperation must be both timely and thorough. To be timely, the cooperation must begin essentially at the same time as the organization is officially notified of a criminal investigation. To be thorough, the cooperation should include the disclosure of all pertinent information known by the organization. A prime test of whether the organization has disclosed all pertinent information is whether the information is sufficient for law enforcement personnel to identify the nature and extent of the offense and the individual(s) responsible for the criminal conduct.

U.S. Sentencing Guidelines Manual §8C2.5(g)(1) (Application Note 12)

The Department of Justice is even more aggressive in ascertaining whether the corporation has "fully cooperated" with the authorities. The department's prosecution guidelines state, "In gauging the extent of the corporation's cooperation, the prosecutor may consider the corporation's willingness . . . to disclose the complete results of its internal investigation; and to waive attorney-client and work product protection . . . both with respect to its internal investigation and with respect to communications between specific officers, directors and employees and counsel." If the individuals within the entity refuse to cooperate with the entity's lawyers they may face discipline, including termination, by the entity. Further, the department frowns on an entity paying the legal costs of an individual involved in the criminal investigation.

In sum, the Federal Sentencing Guidelines constrain, as a practical matter, the power of a corporation's board to act in response to the discovery of information that it may have violated federal law.

B. ULTRA VIRES

The second restriction on board power is of interest to us primarily because of what it might have been and, perhaps, may be. From the late nineteenth century, corporation statutes required the articles to state the purpose for which the corporation was formed and a common law rule quickly arose that a corporation could be formed for a single purpose only.

Over time, of course, corporate drafters pushed the limits of these restrictions and Articles of Incorporation with purpose clauses running to many pages were quite common. Finally, in the late 1960s, state legislatures realized that the point of the specific purpose clause had been defeated and amended their corporation statutes to permit all purpose clauses. See DGCL §102(a)(3), MBCA §3.01(a).

During the time when specific purpose clauses were required, the doctrine of *ultra vires* arose and had some potency. The intention of the ultra vires doctrine was to create an avenue to enforce the specific purposes clauses by granting relief when a corporation took actions that were not related to its purposes (i.e., which were beyond — *ultra* — its powers — *vires*). In this way the ultra vires doctrine was a real constraint on board power.

The doctrine was never clear or unified throughout the United States. Its uncertainty was captured by one corporate law commentator,

> In a sense, "ultra vires" was to corporate law what "res gestae" was to the law of hearsay — a concept of uncertain meaning and scope, deplored by academicians and a *bête noire* of law students. Its application was riddled with exceptions and exceptions to exceptions to such an extent that its proper use and impact, if any, was difficult to predict. Nonetheless, during the formative years of corporation law in the 19th and early 20th centuries, the ultra vires doctrine was an oft-recurring theme in litigation seeking to enforce or avoid corporate contractual obligations, leading to much confusion and patently inequitable results.
>
> **David A. Drexler, Lewis S. Black, Jr., & A. Gilchrist Sparks,** *Delaware Corporation Law and Practice* §11.05 (2000)

The main reason for the decline of ultra vires was the demise of the limited purpose clause. Once corporations could be incorporated for any lawful business, nearly nothing could be ultra vires in the precise sense. About the only act that is beyond the power of a corporation (excluding illegal acts, of course) is waste. That is,

> [A]n exchange of corporate assets for consideration so disproportionately small as to lie beyond the range at which any reasonable person might be willing to trade. Most often the claim is associated with a transfer of corporate assets that serves no corporate purpose; or for which no consideration at all is received. Such a transfer is in effect a

gift. If, however, there is *any substantial* consideration received by the corporation, and if there is a *good faith judgment* that in the circumstances the transaction is worthwhile, there should be no finding of waste, even if the fact finder would conclude *ex post* that the transaction was unreasonably risky.

Lewis v. Vogelstein, **699 A.2d 327, 336 (Del. Ch. 1997) (Allen, Ch.)**

Today, ultra vires is sometimes used to describe corporate actions that are permissible but that have not been properly authorized by the board. This distinction between actions that the corporation cannot take (i.e., pure ultra vires) and those that it could take were they to have been properly approved retains some currency in corporate law. Vice Chancellor Strine describes this situation.

Harbor Finance Partners v. Huizenga
751 A.2d 879 (Del. Ch. 1999)

STRINE, V.C.

This matter involves a challenge to the acquisition of AutoNation, Incorporated by Republic Industries, Inc. A shareholder plaintiff contends that this acquisition (the "Merger") was a self-interested transaction effected for the benefit of Republic directors who owned a substantial block of AutoNation shares, [and] that the terms of the transaction were unfair to Republic and its public stockholders, ... [The Merger was approved by both corporations' boards and both corporations' shareholders, as required by the DGCL.] The defendant directors of Republic seek to dismiss the complaint because . . . the complaint fails to state a claim . . . .

The affirmative stockholder vote on the Merger was informed and uncoerced, and disinterested shares constituted the overwhelming proportion of the Republic electorate. As a result, . . . the Merger may only be attacked as wasteful. [U]nder an unbroken line of authority dating from early in this century, a non-unanimous . . . vote of disinterested stockholders does not extinguish a claim for waste.

The origin of this rule is rooted in the distinction between voidable and void acts, a distinction that appears to have grown out of the now largely abolished *ultra vires* doctrine. Voidable acts are traditionally held to be ratifiable because the corporation can lawfully accomplish them if it does so in the appropriate manner.

In contrast, void acts are said to be non-ratifiable because the corporation cannot, in any case, lawfully accomplish them. Such void acts are often described in conclusory terms such as *"ultra vires"* or "fraudulent" or as "gifts or waste of corporate assets." [I]t is unsurprising that it has been held that stockholders cannot validate such action by the directors, even on an informed basis.

One of the many practical problems with this seemingly sensible doctrine is that its actual application has no apparent modern day utility . . . . There are several reasons I believe this to be so.

First, the types of "void" acts susceptible to being styled as waste claims have little of the flavor of patent illegality about them, nor are they categorically *ultra vires*. [I]n the real world stockholders are not asked to ratify obviously wasteful transactions. Rather than lacking any plausible business rationale or being clearly prohibited by statutory or common law, the transactions attacked as waste in Delaware courts are ones that are quite ordinary in the modern business world.

Second, the waste vestige is not necessary to protect stockholders and it has no other apparent purpose. While I would hesitate to permit stockholders to ratify a blatantly illegal act — such as a board's decision to indemnify itself against personal liability for intentionally violating applicable environmental laws or bribing government officials to benefit the corporation — the vestigial exception for waste has little to do with corporate integrity in the sense of the corporation's responsibility to society as a whole. [I]t is difficult to imagine how elimination of the waste vestige will permit the accomplishment of unconscionable corporate transactions, unless one presumes that stockholders are, as a class, irrational and that they will rubber stamp outrageous transactions contrary to their own economic interests.

Third, I find it logically difficult to conceptualize how a plaintiff can ultimately prove a waste or gift claim in the face of a decision by fully informed, uncoerced, independent stockholders to ratify the transaction. Finally, it is unclear why it is in the best interests of disinterested stockholders to subject their corporation to the substantial costs of litigation in a situation where they have approved the transaction under attack. The costs to corporations of litigating waste claims are not trifling.

For all these reasons, a reexamination of the waste vestige would seem to be in order. Otherwise, inertia alone may perpetuate an outdated rule fashioned in a very different time.

For the foregoing reasons, defendants' motion to dismiss . . . is GRANTED. It is so ordered.

Beginning in the 1930s, state legislatures passed statutes to limit the reach of ultra vires both to curb the perceived abuses and in recognition that the doctrine's ambit was effectively reduced by all purpose clauses. Today, such statutes limit ultra vires to three settings. First, the statutes retain the rule that a shareholder may sue to enjoin executory ultra vires actions. Second, a director, officer, employee, or agent can be held personally liable for causing the corporation to engage in an ultra vires action. This was the plaintiff's theory in *Harbor Finance Partners*. Third, and doubtless the most rare setting, permits the state attorney general to sue to enjoin corporations from acting ultra vires. See DGCL §124, MBCA §3.04.

Notes and Questions

1. Notes

a. One of the most chronic ultra vires and waste problems was whether a corporation could make a charitable donation. The theory was that a donation was waste because the corporation received no benefit. Because the donation was waste, it was ultra vires. To the extent the donation could be linked to any long-term corporate benefit, however mild or indirect, courts tended to uphold the action. This linkage was almost always possible for corporations that dealt in any way with the public. Corporations that dealt only with other businesses or that were holding companies (i.e., corporations engaged in the business of owning stock in other companies) had a more difficult conceptual time. Beginning in the 1940s, Delaware and other states passed statutes specifically empowering corporations to make charitable donations. See DGCL §122(9), MBCA §3.02(13).

b. Many corporations statutes, including the DGCL and MBCA, grant specific powers to corporations in addition to a general grant of power. These specific grants are nearly always artifacts of distant case law that prohibited or at least called into question a corporation's power to take certain actions. Look at DGCL §122 and MBCA §3.02 and imagine why a corporation would be denied the powers explicitly granted.

2. Reality Check

a. What are the various ways in which the phrase *ultra vires* is used in corporate law?

b. How is the ultra vires doctrine related to the doctrine of waste?

c. Why did the ultra vires doctrine cease to have practical importance?

3. What Do You Think?

a. Do you think the revival of ultra vires would, as a practical matter, constrain boards? If so, is that a good thing?

b. Do you think corporations should be required to state express, limited purposes in their articles of incorporation?

c. Should a corporation's board of directors be able to change the corporation's line of business without shareholder approval? Does your answer depend upon whether the corporation is closely held or public?

d. Should corporations be able to take any action an individual can lawfully take?

4. You Draft It

a. Draft a statute that does not permit every corporation to engage in any lawful business but does not unduly inhibit any corporation from engaging in an appropriate variety of businesses.

DGCL §102. CONTENTS OF CERTIFICATE OF INCORPORATION

(a) The certificate of incorporation shall set forth:
. . .

(3) The nature of the business or purposes to be conducted or promoted. It shall be sufficient to state, either alone or with other businesses or purposes, that the purpose of the corporation is to engage in any lawful act or activity for which corporations may be organized under the General Corporation Law of Delaware, and by such statement all lawful acts and activities shall be within the purposes of the corporation, except for express limitations, if any;

MBCA §3.01. PURPOSES

(a) Every corporation incorporated under this Act has the purpose of engaging in any lawful business unless a more limited purpose is set forth in the articles of incorporation.

b. Draft a statute that appropriately constrains the common law ultra vires doctrine.

DGCL §124. EFFECT OF LACK OF CORPORATE CAPACITY OR POWER; ULTRA VIRES

No act of a corporation and no conveyance or transfer of real or personal property to or by a corporation shall be invalid by reason of the fact that the corporation was without capacity or power to do such act or to make or receive such conveyance or transfer, but such lack of capacity or power may be asserted:

(1) In a proceeding by a stockholder against the corporation to enjoin the doing of any act or acts or the transfer of real or personal property by or to the corporation. If the unauthorized acts or transfer sought to be enjoined are being, or are to be, performed or made pursuant to any contract to which the corporation is a party, the court may, if all of the parties to the contract are parties to the proceeding and if it deems the same to be equitable, set aside and enjoin the performance of such contract, and in so doing may allow to the corporation or to the other parties to the contract, as the case may be, such compensation as may be equitable for the loss or damage sustained by any of them which may result from the action of the court in setting aside and enjoining the performance of such contract, but anticipated profits to be derived from the performance of the contract shall not be awarded by the court as a loss or damage sustained;

(2) In a proceeding by the corporation, whether acting directly or through a receiver, trustee or other legal representative, or through stockholders in a representative suit, against an incumbent or former officer or director of the corporation, for loss or damage due to such incumbent or former officer's or director's unauthorized act;

(3) In a proceeding by the Attorney General to dissolve the corporation, or to enjoin the corporation from the transaction of unauthorized business.

MBCA §3.04. ULTRA VIRES

(a) Except as provided in subsection (b), the validity of corporate action may not be challenged on the ground that the corporation lacks or lacked power to act.

(b) A corporation's power to act may be challenged:

(1) in a proceeding by a shareholder against the corporation to enjoin the act;

(2) in a proceeding by the corporation, directly, derivatively, or through a receiver, trustee, or other legal representative, against an incumbent or former director, officer, employee, or agent of the corporation; or

(3) in a proceeding by the Attorney General under section 14.30.

(c) In a shareholder's proceeding under subsection (b)(1) to enjoin an unauthorized corporate act, the court may enjoin or set aside the act, if equitable and if all affected persons are parties to the proceeding, and may award damages for loss (other than anticipated profits) suffered by the corporation or another party because of enjoining the unauthorized act.

C. ULTIMATE BENEFICIARIES

Our final constraint on board power is a highly conceptual and philosophical one yet one that is of immense practical importance. Simply put, corporations must be operated for the benefit of some group. Boards of directors and other corporate managers should be prevented from taking actions that deviate from that end. Potentially, identifying the ultimate beneficiaries is a powerful constraint on board actions.

Chancellor Allen describes the philosophical contours of this question.

1. The Current Setting

William T. Allen, *Our Schizophrenic Conception of the Business Corporation*

14 Cardozo L. Rev. 261, 262-277, 279-281 (1992)

I want to discuss this most basic question: What is a corporation? — Two inconsistent conceptions have dominated our thinking about corporations since the evolution of the large integrated business corporation in the late nineteenth century. Each conception could claim dominance for a particular period, or among one group or another, but neither has so commanded agreement as to exclude the other from the discourses of law or the thinking of business people.

At least by the mid-nineteenth century, when the movement to enact general laws of incorporation had become firmly planted, the corporation was seen in this country as an artificial creation of the state designed to enable individuals to associate together for state approved purposes. The emphasis was on the individuals — the shareholders who had been constituted a corporation.

The dominant perception was that the corporation, while an artificial entity, was essentially the stockholders in a special form. This perception colored the way in which the role and power of the board of directors was seen. Directors were seen as agents of stockholders.

Thus, if towards the close of the [nineteenth] century one would have asked to whom directors owe a duty of loyalty, a confident answer could have been expected: The corporation . . . is . . . the property of the shareholders. The directors are elected by shareholders and it is unquestionably on their behalf that the directors are bound to act. This view, with its genesis in the mid-nineteenth century, was plainly expressed in the law and, I suppose, was the view held beyond the legal community as well.

In this conception, [t]he rights of creditors, employees and others are strictly limited to statutory, contractual, and common law rights. Once the directors have satisfied those legal obligations, they have fully satisfied all claims of these "constituencies." This property view of the nature of corporations, and of the duties owed by directors, equates the duty of directors with the duty to maximize profits of the firm for the benefit of shareholders.

This model of the public corporation is highly coherent and offers several alternative arguments to support the legitimacy of corporate power in our democracy. The first argument in favor of the property concept is political and normative. It is premised on the conclusionary notion that shareholders "own" the corporation, and asserts that to admit the propriety of non-profit maximizing behavior is to approve agents spending other people's money in pursuit of their own, perhaps eccentric, views of the public good. This can be seen as morally wrong without more. On a broader level, proponents of this view assert that it is repugnant to our democratic ideals to have corporate oligarchies determining which of many competing claimants for financial support should be awarded that support.

The second rationale for the property model is that the model, and action consistent with it, maximize wealth creation. This rationale asserts that the purpose of business corporations is the creation of wealth, nothing else. It asserts that business corporations are not formed to assist in self-realization through social interaction; they are not formed to create jobs or to provide tax revenues; they are not formed to endow university departments or to pursue knowledge. All of these other things — job creation, tax payments, research, and social interaction — desirable as they may be, are said to be side effects of the pursuit of profit for the residual owners of the firm.

This argument asserts that the creation of more wealth should always be the corporation's objective, regardless of who benefits. The sovereign's taxing and regulatory power can then address questions of social costs and re-distribution of wealth. Thus, profit maximizing behavior is seen as affording the best opportunity to satisfy human wants and is the most appropriate aim of corporation law policy. This second argument for the legitimacy of the corporation as shareholder property is not premised on the conclusion that shareholders do "own" the corporation in any ultimate sense, only on the premise that it can be better for all of us if we act as if they do.

The property conception of the corporation was the conception generally held during the nineteenth century and . . . in the early part of this century as well. But, the last quarter of the nineteenth century saw the emergence of social forces that would oppose the conception of business corporations as simply the property of contracting stockholders. The scale and scope of modern integrated business enterprise that emerged in the late nineteenth century required distinctive professional management skills and huge capital investments that often necessitated risk sharing through dispersed stock ownership. National securities markets emerged and stockholders gradually came to look less like flesh and blood owners and more like investors who could slip in or out of a particular stock almost costlessly. These new giant business corporations came to seem to some people like independent entities, with purposes, duties, and loyalties of their own; purposes that might diverge in some respect from shareholder wealth maximization.

This social entity conception sees the purpose of the corporation as not individual but social. Surely contributors of capital (stockholders and bondholders) must be assured a rate of return sufficient to induce them to contribute their capital to the enterprise. But the corporation has other purposes of perhaps equal dignity: the satisfaction of consumer wants, the provision of meaningful employment opportunities, and the making of a contribution to the public life of its communities. Resolving the often conflicting claims of these various corporate constituencies calls for judgment, indeed calls for wisdom, by the board of directors of the corporation. But in this view no single constituency's interest may significantly exclude others from fair consideration by the board. This view appears to have been the dominant view among business leaders for at least the last fifty years.

One would think that whether the corporation law endorses the property conception or the social entity conception would have important consequences. Our experience in the 1980s demonstrated that it could. But equally as interesting as that 1980s conflict is the fact that for the fifty years preceding that contentious decade, we did not share agreement on the legal nature of the public business corporation and that failure did not seem especially problematic.

The law "papered over" the conflict in our conception of the corporation by invoking a murky distinction between long-term profit maximization and short-term profit maximization. Corporate expenditures which at first blush did not seem to be profit maximizing, could be squared with the property conception of the corporation by recognizing that they might redound to the long-term benefit of the corporation and its shareholders. Thus, without purporting to abandon the idea that directors ultimately owe loyalty only to stockholders and their financial interests, the law was able to approve reasonable corporate expenditures for charitable or social welfare purposes or other actions that did not maximize current profit.

There is a utility in this long-term/short-term device. But corporate directors are also afforded very considerable latitude to deal with all groups or institutions having an interest in, or who are affected by, the corporation.

Thus, while early on much ink was spilled on the question to whom should directors be responsible, in practice the question of the nature of the corporation seemed essentially unproblematic until the emergence of the cash tender offer of the 1980s. The long-term/short-term distinction proved a serviceable, if an intellectually problematic way, for the corporation law to avoid choosing between the alpha of property and the omega of relationships.

[T]he takeover movement [of the 1980s] put so much at stake. The issue was frequently whether all of the shareholders would be permitted to sell their shares; whether a change in corporate control would occur; and often whether a radical restructuring of the enterprise would go forward, with dramatic effects on creditors, employees, management, suppliers, and communities.

The effects of a takeover were seen by those affected as a form of shareholder exploitation of others who had made contributions of various sorts to the corporation. In the financial setting of the 1980s, dramatically higher stock prices could often be achieved by sharply increasing the debt of the corporation and reducing or eliminating certain operations. But increasing debt substantially made the enterprise riskier and thus reduced the value of the corporation's existing bonds; and restricting operations injured workers and management, who were thrown out of work. The bondholders and employees felt that radical corporate changes made in order to increase share value breached implicit understandings that had been the basis of their participation in the organization, or so one argument went. Thus, the scale of the problems raised by the takeover movement made evasion of the fundamental question of corporate definition difficult.

Courts were not anxious to grapple with this question. To resolve the matter seemed plainly to call for the making of policy in an environment that was warmly contested by powerful interests and in which no widely accepted doctrine offered a clear guide. Nevertheless, ultimately both our courts and, more importantly, our legislatures have, in effect, endorsed the entity view.

The entity conception was . . . clearly endorsed by the law in a remarkable series of legislative acts adopted in some twenty-eight jurisdictions over the course of the last few years of the 1980s. These so-called constituency statutes differ from each other in a number of particulars but they share the same soul. In one way or another each of them authorizes a board of directors to consider the interest of all corporate "stakeholders" when the board exercises corporate power. These statutes seem plainly to be animated by a social entity conception of the corporation.

Thus, under them, a central notion of corporation law as it has developed over the last 150 years—that the law ought to try to align directors' action with shareholder interests by imposition of fiduciary duties—is arguably eviscerated. Surely, stealing is still proscribed and self-dealing transactions still have to be justified as fair to the corporation, but what arguably is eradicated is the command—which while equivocal in practice under the prior regime still demanded respect—that maximizing the financial interests of shareholders through lawful means over some time period is the core duty of a corporate director.

The enactment of the stakeholder statutes...came just at the end of the "deal decade," and with those developments the schizophrenia that had long existed in our thinking about corporations was arguably resolved. But was it?

The law, like ourselves, is always in flux, always "becoming." The concept of the corporation is such a structure. [T]he ever-emergent quality of law suggests that the resolution of the conceptual conflict that was reached in the late 1980s by the endorsement of the entity concept, will not be a final answer to the question, what is a corporation.

We cannot of course know the future, but we can see the future stresses that the entity conception of the public corporation will generate. The entity conception inevitably will give rise to claims of inefficiency and illegitimacy; and those are claims that the blunt instruments of stakeholder statutes can neither answer nor suppress.

I suppose that there will be no final move in defining the nature or the purpose of the business corporation. It is perhaps asking too much to expect us, as a people — or our law — to have a single view of the purpose of an institution so large, pervasive, and important as our public corporations. These entities are too important to generate that sort of agreement. Within them exists the tension that a dynamic market system creates between the desire to achieve increases in total wealth and the desire to avoid the losses and injuries — the redistribution — that a dynamic system inevitably engenders.

Thus I conclude that we have been schizophrenic on the nature of the corporation, but as a society we will probably always be so to some extent. The questions "What is a corporation?" and "For whose benefit do directors hold power?" are legal questions only in the sense that legal institutions will be required at certain points to formulate or assume answers to them. But they are not simply technical questions of law capable of resolution through analytical rule manipulation. Even less are they technical questions of finance or economics. Rather in defining what we suppose a public corporation to be, we implicitly express our view of the nature and purpose of our social life. Since we do disagree on that, our law of corporate entities is bound itself to be contentious and controversial. It will be worked out, not deduced. In this process, efficiency concerns, ideology, and interest group politics will commingle with history (including our semi-autonomous corporation law) to produce an answer that will hold for here and now, only to be torn by some future stress and to be reformulated once more. And so on, and so on, evermore.

Notes and Questions

1. Reality Check

a. Why is our conception of the corporation schizophrenic?
b. What are the different conceptions of the corporation?
c. What are the arguments for and against each conception?
d. Why are those conceptions inconsistent?
e. Why does our conception of a corporation matter?

2. What Do You Think?

a. Chancellor Allen says, "It is perhaps asking too much to expect us, as a people — or our law — to have a single view of the purpose of an institution so large, pervasive, and important as our public corporations. These entities are too important to generate that sort of agreement." Do you agree?

b. Is Chancellor Allen's "second rationale for the property model" really a rationale for managing in the shareholders' interest?

c. Which conception of the corporation is more accurate?

2. Background and Context

The shareholder primacy model was first strongly articulated in the early 1930s. What follows is the classic statement of the classic rationale behind the shareholder primacy rule. *The Modern Corporation and Private Property* is an iconic book in corporation law circles. But as the next excerpt makes clear, it makes a much more complex argument than simply a description of shareholder primacy. In fact, the book describes two other models of ultimate beneficiaries. As you identify them, consider how the selection of one set of beneficiaries over others dictates the operational goals of the corporation's managers.

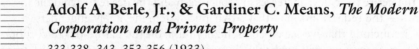

Adolf A. Berle, Jr., & Gardiner C. Means, *The Modern Corporation and Private Property*
333-338, 343, 353-356 (1933)

[C]ertain legal, economic, and social questions . . . must now be squarely faced. Of these the greatest is the question in whose interests should the great quasi-public corporations . . . be operated. This problem really asks in a different form the question, who should receive the profits of industry?

The lawyer answers this question in no uncertain terms by applying . . . the traditional logic of property. The common law . . . logically demands the award of the entire profit to the . . . stockholders. According to this logic a corporation should be operated primarily in their interests.

The legal argument is largely historical; but it has been built up through a series of phases which make this conclusion inevitable. From earliest times the owner of property has been entitled to the full use or disposal of his property . . . . Since the use of industrial property consists primarily of an effort to increase its value — to make a profit — the owner of such property, in being entitled to its full use, has been entitled to all accretions to its value — to all the profits which it could be made to earn. The state and the law have sought to protect him in this right.

Yet, . . . are we justified in applying this logic? In the past, the ownership of business enterprise, has always, at least in theory, involved two attributes, first the risking of previously collected wealth . . . ; and, second, the ultimate management of and responsibility for that enterprise. But in the modern corporation [t]he stockholder has surrendered control over his wealth. He has become a supplier of capital, a risk-taker pure and simple, while ultimate responsibility and authority are exercised by directors . . . . Must we not, therefore, recognize that we are no longer dealing with property in the old sense? Does the traditional logic of property still apply? May not this surrender have so essentially changed his relation to his wealth as to have changed the logic applicable to his interest in that wealth? An answer to this question cannot be found in the law itself. It must be sought in the economic and social background of law.

Where is the social advantage in setting aside for the security holder, profits in an amount greater than is sufficient to insure the continued supplying of capital and taking of risk? The prospect of additional profits cannot act as a spur on the security holder to make him *operate* the enterprise with more vigor . . . , since he is no longer in control. Such extra profits if given to the security holders would seem to perform no useful economic function.

Observable throughout the world, and in varying degrees of intensity, is this insistence that power in economic organization shall be subjected to the same tests of public benefit which have been applied in their turn to power otherwise located. In the strictly capitalist countries, and particularly in time of depression, demands are constantly put forward that the men controlling the great economic organisms be made to accept responsibility for the well-being of those who are subject to the organization, whether workers, investors, or consumers. In a sense the difference in all of these demands lies only in degree. [A]s an economic organism grows . . . and its power is concentrated in a few hands, the possessor of power is more easily located, and the demand for responsible power becomes increasingly direct.

In direct opposition to the above doctrine of strict property rights is the view, apparently held by the great corporation lawyers and by certain students of the field, that corporate development has created a new set of relationships, giving to the groups in control powers which are absolute and not limited by any implied obligation with respect to their use. This logic leads to drastic conclusions. For instance, if . . . the men in control of a corporation can operate it in their own interests, and can divert a portion of the . . . income stream to their own uses, such is their privilege. Under this view, since the new powers have been acquired on a quasi-contractual basis, the security holders have agreed in advance to any losses which they may suffer by reason of such use. The result is, briefly, that the existence of the legal and economic relationships giving rise to these powers must be frankly recognized as a modification of the principle of private property.

On the one hand, the owners of passive property, by surrendering control and responsibility over the active property, have surrendered the right that the corporation should be operated in their sole interest . . . . At the same time, the controlling groups, by means of the extension of corporate powers, have in their own interest broken the bars of tradition which require that the corporation be operated solely for the benefit of the owners of passive property. Eliminating the sole interest of the passive owner, however, does not necessarily lay a basis for the alternative claim that the new powers should be used in the interest of the controlling groups. The latter have not presented, in acts or words any acceptable defense of the proposition that these powers should be so used. No tradition supports that proposition. The control groups have, rather, cleared the way for the claims of a group far wider than either the owners or the control. They have placed the community in a position to demand that the modern corporation serve not alone the owners or the control but all society.

This . . . alternative offers a wholly new concept of corporate activity. Neither the claims of ownership nor those of control can stand against the paramount interests of the community. It remains only for the claims of the community to be put forward with clarity and force. When a convincing system of community obligations is worked out and is generally accepted, in that moment the passive property right of today must yield before the larger interests of society. Should the corporate leaders, for example, set forth a program comprising fair wages, security to employees, reasonable service to their public, and stabilization of business, all of which would divert a portion of the profits from the owners of passive property, and should the community generally accept such a scheme as a logical and human solution of industrial difficulties, the interests of passive property owners would have to give way. Courts would almost of necessity be forced to recognize the result, justifying it by whatever of the many legal theories they might choose. It is conceivable, — indeed it seems almost essential if the corporate system is to survive that the "control" of the great corporations should develop into a purely neutral technocracy, balancing a variety of claims by various groups in the community and assigning to each a portion of the income stream on the basis of public policy rather than private cupidity.

Notes and Questions

1. Reality Check

a. What *is* the "traditional logic of property"?
b. What are the two attributes of ownership of a business?
c. How would the traditional logic apply to the modern corporation?
d. Do Berle and Means believe that the traditional logic applies to the modern corporation? If not, for what ultimate beneficiaries *do* corporate managers manage?
e. For what ultimate beneficiaries *should* corporate managers manage?
f. Why shouldn't the traditional logic be applied to the modern corporation?
g. What is Berle's and Means's alternative to the traditional logic of property?

2. What Do You Think?

a. Do you agree that the traditional logic of property should not be applied to large public corporations?
b. Is the alternative suggested by Berle and Means workable? Do you agree with it?
c. Do Berle and Means see the demise of the traditional logic of property as a good development or a bad one? Do you agree with their view?

In the next article Professor Bainbridge sets out a contemporary argument for shareholder primacy.

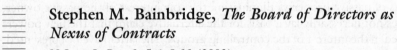

Stephen M. Bainbridge, *The Board of Directors as Nexus of Contracts*
88 Iowa L. Rev. 1, 5-6, 9-11 (2002)

Traditional variants of shareholder primacy claim that shareholders own the corporation and, accordingly, directors and officers are mere stewards of the shareholders' interests. A more recent variation . . . blends two economic theories — the nexus of contracts theory of the firm and agency cost economics. In contractarian theory, shareholders are merely one of many factors of production bound together in a complex web of explicit and implicit contracts. Influenced by agency cost economics, however, most law and economics scholars continue to treat directors and officers as agents of the shareholders, with fiduciary obligations to maximize shareholder wealth. Shareholders therefore retain a privileged position among the corporation's various constituencies, because their contract with the firm has ownership-like features, including the right to vote and the fiduciary obligations of directors and officers.

The dominant model of the corporation in legal scholarship is the so-called nexus of contracts theory. [M]odern law and economics scholars view the corporation not as an entity but as an aggregate of various inputs acting together to produce goods or services. Employees provide labor. Creditors provide debt capital. Shareholders initially provide equity capital and subsequently bear the risk of losses and monitor the performance of management. Management monitors the performance of employees and coordinates the activities of all the firm's inputs. The firm is the nexus of explicit and implicit contracts establishing rights and obligations among the various inputs making up the firm.

The name "nexus of contracts" is somewhat unfortunate. For lawyers, the term "contracts" carries with it all of the baggage learned in Contracts class during the first year of law school. Among that baggage are two particularly problematic features. First, the word "contract" focuses attention on legal notions such as consideration and mutuality. Second, the word "contract" mainly seems to invoke transactions on spot markets that are thick and relatively untroubled by asymmetric information. Neither has much to do with the internal governance of corporations.

As used by contractarians, however, the term is not limited to relationships constituting legal contracts. Instead, contractarians use the word "contract" to refer generally to long-term relationships characterized by asymmetric information, bilateral monopoly, and opportunism.

Notes and Questions

1. Notes

a. Professor Bainbridge proposes a variation of the nexus of contract model, which he calls the director primacy model:

> In the director primacy model, the corporation is a vehicle by which the board of directors hires various factors of production. Hence, the board of directors is not a mere agent of the shareholders, as standard contractarian theory claims, but rather is a *sui generis* body — a sort of Platonic guardian — serving as the nexus for the various contracts making up the corporation. The board's powers flow from that set of contracts in its totality and not just from shareholders.

Stephen M. Bainbridge, *The Board of Directors as Nexus of Contracts*, 88 Iowa L. Rev. 1, 8 (2002)

2. Reality Check

a. What is the nexus of contracts theory?

b. Where did the nexus of contracts theory come from?

c. Does the nexus of contracts theory depend on shareholder primacy?

3. What Do You Think?

a. Do you think the nexus of contract vision essentially differs from Berle's and Means's vision or is it essentially the same?

b. Is Berle's and Means's approach more accurate than the nexus of contracts approach?

c. Is Professor Bainbridge's variation of the nexus of contracts analysis an improvement?

Chancellor Allen calls the alternative to shareholder primacy the "social entity" or "entity" theory. As you have seen, even Berle and Means did not contend that shareholder primacy was, or should be, the norm. The nexus of contract model does not require shareholder primacy, although many proponents of the nexus of contract model advocate such a position. The more nuanced question is how shall the shareholders' interest in the corporation be balanced against that of other constituencies or of society generally. The final reading places this question in its historical context while emphasizing, as Chancellor Allen does, the timeless nature of this question.

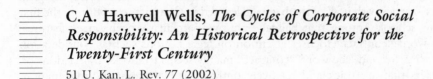

C.A. Harwell Wells, *The Cycles of Corporate Social Responsibility: An Historical Retrospective for the Twenty-First Century*
51 U. Kan. L. Rev. 77 (2002)

Legal debates over corporate social responsibility stretch from the 1930s to the twenty-first century. They have engaged some of the leading legal minds of the century, and advocates and enemies of corporate social responsibility still win publication in the country's most prestigious legal journals. But there is a problem with these debates: they rarely seem to go anywhere. Viewed in historical perspective, it is clear that each new round of debate on corporate social responsibility largely recapitulates the earlier debate in a slightly altered form.

Though separate in time, all these debates shared conceptual foundations. They all were premised on the idea that the American economy was dominated by a relatively small number of enormous, powerful, and stable business corporations that were qualitatively different from their smaller competitors, and the debates all assumed that the solution to pressing social ills was neither to eliminate corporations nor let them alone, but rather to implement legal mechanisms that would lead corporate managers and directors to take into account the needs not only of shareholders but of workers, consumers, and communities when making business decisions.

[From the 1930s], the debate over corporate social responsibility lay dormant for nearly twenty years. Several factors likely contributed to its quiescence. [C]ertainly by 1933 the deepening Depression had thrown into doubt not only the beneficence but even the survival of large corporations. In the New Deal, many of the abuses ... were solved by legislation such as the Securities Act and the Exchange Act, while the New Deal also offered new vistas for legal reform through new government programs and administrative law, drawing scholars' attention away from issues of corporate social responsibility. World War II and postwar reconstruction provided their own challenges.

Beginning in the mid-1950s, however, attention again turned to corporations' social responsibility. The 1950s legal debate over corporate social responsibility was part of that decade's wider discussion of the corporation's role in American society and politics .... Despite its reputation as strait-laced, the 1950s witnessed an outpouring of critical writings on the large corporation. Taken together, ... these authors agreed that large corporations had been fantastically successful in economic terms, that they had come to wield significant economic, political, and social power, and that their power posed a dilemma for America's democratic society. The implications of such new concentrations of power were unclear; most writers preferred to voice concerns over "corporate power" rather than make specific proposals for reform.

One area where radical proposals did appear was in legal scholarship. Leading the new analysis of corporate social responsibility was a familiar figure: Adolf A. Berle. The skepticism he displayed about managers in the 1930s was largely gone, replaced by a faith in managers' ability to use their newfound power to benefit all groups involved in the corporation. The legal changes Berle advocated were intended to free managers from their singular duties to shareholders and allow them to direct the corporation's resources for the general welfare.

In [Berle's] *The 20th Century Capitalist Revolution* [1954],... the unfettered corporation would produce a kind of utopia, its managers successfully balancing all of society's competing interests. Although Berle was not forthcoming on the details of just how corporate managers would bring about social harmony, he made clear his hopes in the title of the last lecture in his book: Corporate Capitalism and the City of God.

The author he had closest affinity with,... and one who would have greater influence on the developing legal debate over corporate social responsibility, was Peter Drucker. Known today chiefly as a pioneering management consultant, in the 1950s Drucker was viewed as a serious analyst of corporate power, having already written two classic works on corporate power.... The ideal corporation, Drucker implied, would be run by enlightened managers for the benefit of its shareholders, workers, and the wider community.

Thus Drucker's most dramatic proposal: that managers be freed from their legal subservience to both shareholders and directors. He would transform the board from a governing body to a "maker of policy," with representatives not only of share-holder/investors but from management, labor, and the communities where the enterprise operated. He did not reject the profit motive as a primary guide for this new-model corporation, but he believed it should be sought even as the corporation fulfilled its larger social mission.

Berle and Drucker's chief failing was their inability to clearly address the problems raised by their proposals. How management would reconcile constituents' conflicting demands, or why it would not simply line its own pockets, was left largely unad-dressed. They were also not able to articulate precisely what problem they were trying to solve. "Corporate power" was a generalized concern, not a specific issue readily fixed by restructuring the legal duties of director and managers. The vagueness of concerns with the corporation prevented the articulation of a clear reform program. Berle and Drucker's ideas met a chilly reception. For all the popular criticism of corporations, there was little public sentiment to reform them.

The debate over corporate social responsibility was transformed by the events of the 1960s. Genteel discussions over how business statesmen could use their positions to improve society became — under pressure from social unrest, perceptions of envi-ronmental degradation, and protests over the Vietnam War — populist campaigns to redirect corporate power to solve looming social and political problems. In the pro-cess, the debate over corporate social responsibility underwent a reversal. In the 1950s, advocates of the socially responsible corporation demanded that managers be freed from the shackles of shareholder primacy. By the 1970s, however, reformers were no longer enamored of the "business statesman," and sought to make the corporation more responsible to other constituencies by taking away the manager's autonomy and instituting greater oversight by directors or shareholders.

While in retrospect the Vietnam War appears to be the central event of the 1960s, it was actually domestic concerns that first prodded corporations to be "socially responsible." The riots that broke out in major American cities beginning in 1965 pushed business leaders to implement new programs to help resolve, as they put it, "the urban problem." Large corporations launched a series of programs intended to solve urban ills, as they redirected charitable donations, started new employee training programs, targeted disadvantaged populations, and promised to support a nascent movement for "black capitalism." In part, corporate social activism was a response to public pressure. Whether their programs actually meant the corporation had assumed new legal responsibilities, however, was less clear. Even the most ambitious social investments could be justified as directed to a firm's long-run profits. In short, the majority of corporations that adopted "socially responsible" policies did not thereby acknowledge new legal duties to nonshareholder constituents.

During the late 1960s and early 1970s, [w]hile many on the left simply disdained business, others with a more reformist bent sought to use existing legal mechanisms, or to invent new ones, to force corporations to take into account constituencies beyond their shareholders when making business decisions.

[T]here was at least one legal mechanism already available: the shareholder proposal. Under S.E.C. Rule 14a-8, a shareholder of a public corporation, who meets certain conditions, can demand that a proposal he or she has prepared be included in the proxy mailed to shareholders before an annual meeting, to be voted on by all shareholders. In the late 1960s, activists seized on the shareholder proposal as a lever to push corporations towards socially responsible actions. [I]n the hands of social activists, shareholder proposals became a way to voice social disapproval of a corporation's actions. Through their proposals, social activists hoped to mobilize shareholders into insisting there were more important things than profits. Despite their opposition to the "corporate system," the activists were surprisingly optimistic, believing that, if asked, shareholders would demand that directors and managers act in a socially responsible manner.

That shareholders ultimately refused to adopt even the most melioristic proposals highlights the problems that likely limited the success of public-interest shareholder proposals: most shareholders did not want their firms governed in the interests of the wider community. The few public-interest proposals that reached shareholders' hands were overwhelmingly defeated. Yet this immediate record of failure should not obscure the longer-range impact of this movement. [T]hey pioneered a means of bringing shareholder concerns before corporate boards that is still used today.

In the early 1960s, several legal scholars argued that corporate social responsibility made little economic sense, promising as it did to distort the price function and so make corporations less efficient, while saddling them with an ill-suited social role. In 1970, this view received its most forceful statement, not in a law review, but in a *New York Times Magazine* article, written by the era's best-known free-market economist, Milton Friedman.

In part, he noted, advocates of corporate social responsibility ultimately believed in replacing market mechanisms with political mechanisms when determining how resources should be used, a process guaranteed to produce economic inefficiency. The funds spent on social projects were . . . in effect "taxed" from the shareholder and then used by the corporate executive as he judged best, "all this guided only by general exhortations from on high . . . ." In Friedman's view, corporate social responsibility was not only inefficient, it was theft.

Although Friedman's was a lonely voice in 1970, over the rest of the decade legal scholars would join the attack on corporate social responsibility, also using economic theory.... In 1979 David Engel launched a wide-ranging attack on the decade's social responsibility proposals, arguing that they were not only wrongheaded but incoherent, skipping over major procedural issues, assuming away perhaps intractable problems, and presuming that corporate management would somehow prove better than elected officials at deciding which social goals a firm should pursue.

Public enthusiasm for corporate social responsibility flagged after the mid-1970s. Academic criticism certainly had a role to play in this. At least as important,... however, was the changing climate of public opinion concerning government and business. The public trust evinced in business leaders in the early 1960s never returned, but it was not replaced by renewed faith in government. Increasingly, the free market and private ordering were preferred to any legislative or court-ordered economic planning.

From the late 1970s to the mid-1980s, the academic debate over corporate social responsibility dwindled and splintered. As in earlier cycles of scholarly effort, it would take economic and legal developments outside the legal academy to give impetus and form to the next iteration of the debate. This time, the external impetus was the 1980s' boom in corporate takeovers.... Producing huge profits for the takeover artists, and significant gains for shareholders of firms bought, the takeovers also resulted in unemployed managers and — at least in public perceptions — shuttered factories and downsized workers. In response, corporations developed anti-takeover defenses and states that feared takeovers and decimation of locally based firms adopted laws aimed at preventing such takeovers. Particularly popular were so-called "corporate constituency statutes."

Corporate constituency statutes explicitly broadened the kinds of constituencies directors could consider when evaluating a takeover bid.... Within a decade twenty-nine states had passed similar measures. Even in states where such laws were not passed, notably the corporate-charter capital Delaware, court decisions gave directors greater leeway to weigh a bid's "impact on 'constituencies' other than shareholders." [T]he statutes offered a more capacious view of directors' fiduciary duties, and promised that the needs of a range of "constituencies" could (or must) be taken into account in corporate decision-making. Almost inadvertently, the legal mechanism for corporate social responsibility seemed at last to have been put in place.

Out of the takeover movement, resulting downsizing, and the consequent passage of corporate-constituency statutes came a new round of scholarly work on corporate social responsibility, or as its proponents would rename it, "progressive corporate law." Two other developments also shaped the debate. One was...: new concern over the United States' economic competitiveness. Overseas competitors appeared to exceed the productivity of the United States' firms, while also maintaining workplace harmony alien to the American experience. The apparent failure of the giant American corporation opened up new possibilities for legal reform of corporate governance.

A final development... was the appearance... of the contractarian theory of the firm. This approach conceptualized a corporation as a "nexus of contracts" between the corporation's various constituencies. If... the corporation were only a web of contracts,... then the corporation as a distinct entity apart from these constituencies was attenuated if not erased. Progressive corporate-law scholars never accepted this vision of the corporation, but the dominance of the nexus-of-contracts approach in the 1990s would force them to spend considerable time grappling with it.

[M]any progressive scholars eagerly seized on corporate-constituency statutes passed in the 1980s. In part, they hoped that the new statutes signaled the end of shareholder primacy. Some scholars simply took the statutes as a sign that shareholder primacy was gone. The statutes encouraged a few scholars to envision further legal steps to insert nonshareholder concerns into board decisions. Ultimately, the enthusiasm for such corporate-constituency statutes faded, as their effects did not meet the expectations of either their supporters or their enemies.

In [1995], a coherent group of scholars...set forth a program for their work in the collection *Progressive Corporate Law*. The scholars represented in this volume advanced a new agenda for corporate law, based on their argument that the corporation itself should be viewed as a community (hence the other label, "communitarian") comprised of shareholders, creditors, directors, managers, employees, and maybe even customers. The "social responsibility" they sought to impose on the corporation was, then, responsibility not to society in general, but to those groups that made up the corporation-as-society.

On the surface, the essays proposed several distinct programs for reforming the corporation. Despite their differences, the articles all fit squarely in the line of work on corporate social responsibility stretching back to Berle.... First,... the articles shared the assumption that there was something distinctive about large corporations that set them qualitatively apart from small firms and made it appropriate to assign them greater responsibilities. Second, the authors all aimed to reform corporate law; none were radical in the sense of believing in either nationalizing or eliminating large corporations. Third, most authors shared the belief that the best way to reform corporate law (and thus corporations) was to make corporate directors and managers legally responsible to a wider range of constituents, including employees, communities, and even the environment, thus abandoning the shareholder primacy norm.

[T]he cycles of legal debates over corporate social responsibility have, since the 1930s, shared deep similarities despite superficial differences. All the separate debates have (1) presupposed that the problems created by business are really problems created by this nation's large publicly held corporations, (2) aimed to reform those corporations, rather than to eliminate them, and (3) seen the imposition of new duties towards nonshareholder constituents on directors and officers as the best way to make corporations answerable not just to shareholders, but to the wider society. To be sure, each debate has also differed from its predecessors and successors, but chiefly in the problems they profess to tackle. [T]he problems change; the solutions remain the same. The result has been an often-stale scholarly critique of corporations as each new cycle of debate recapitulates debates in the past, and as ideas are unwittingly recycled with little awareness of their predecessors, much less why they were rejected thirty (or even seventy years) before.

This is a shame, for the history of corporate social responsibility is of more than historical interest. Corporations remain today, as they were in the 1920s, the most powerful nongovernmental institutions in America. In innumerable ways they shape the nation's politics and culture, and the lives of their employees and consumers. They create great wealth and opportunities, but often deliver them unevenly; they frequently use their power in ways that benefit shareholders and managers, but harm the rest of us. From time to time we are reminded of this, when investors discover their money has disappeared in the collapse of a stock-market bubble, employees wake to find their 401(k) plans are worth nothing, or shareholders discover their firms have been looted by self-serving executives. The task of ameliorating the influence of corporations, and of channeling and limiting their power, should be of concern to all of us.

Notes and Questions

1. Reality Check

a. How has the problem for which social responsibility is the solution changed?

b. What is social responsibility?

c. Why are corporations obligated to be socially responsible?

d. How are the cycles of debate over social responsibility alike? How are they different?

e. What objections to the social responsibility model have been posed?

2. What Do You Think?

a. Has any major commentator seriously argued in favor of the shareholder primacy model?

b. Do you think the debates have pitted shareholder primacy against social responsibility? If not, what have they entailed?

c. Corporate managers were among the most vocal proponents of corporate constituent statutes. Why?

d. Do you agree that, "Corporate social responsibility is not a novel solution to an unchanging problem; quite the contrary, it is an unchanging solution to an ever-new problem"?

e. What will the next debate over the nature of the corporation look like?

f. In whose interest should corporations be managed?

D. FEDERAL SECURITIES REGULATION

1. Foreign Corrupt Practices Act

In the mid-1970s an SEC investigation discovered that over 400 public corporations, including almost a quarter of the 500 largest, had made "questionable or illegal payments," that is to say bribes, to foreign governments, political parties, and politicians. While the SEC investigation focused on whether those corporations had made misleading filings with the SEC about those payments, Congress decided that broader remedial action was necessary. It quickly enacted the Foreign Corrupt Practices Act (FCPA) of 1977, which is most pertinently found as section 30A of the Securities Exchange Act of 1934. Violation is a criminal offense.

The FCPA constrains American corporations that do business in other countries. No public company may pay anything of value to any foreign official or foreign political party for the purpose of influencing a decision, inducing an action, or inducing an official to use his or her influence to obtain or retain business. Corrupt intent is required. Although the basic statement of the FCPA's workings is straightforward, application can be problematic. In brief, two kinds of issues are most frequently faced by public companies. First, it is not unusual for companies doing business in other countries to have relationships with many individuals who act as conduits, finders, or consultants. If those people make payments that would be illegal under the FCPA, when is the corporation liable? Essentially, this becomes an agency problem but the facts of any particular case can often be murky. Second, companies frequently provide gifts of various sorts to suppliers, customers, and others who interact with the business. When such payments are made to a recipient covered under the FCPA, a recurring question is whether such payment is intended to achieve ends the FCPA prohibits.

E. TERMS OF ART IN THIS CHAPTER

All purpose clause
Corporate social responsi-
   bility
Nexus of contract

Progressive corporate
   law
Shareholder primacy
Special purpose clause

Traditional logic of prop-
   erty
Ultra vires
Waste

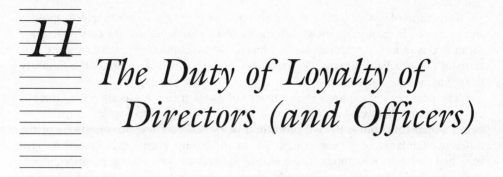

The Duty of Loyalty of Directors (and Officers)

Many corporate law experts would suggest that the topic of the next three chapters is the most important one of all. Even more controversially, some argue that the question of director fiduciary duties is the only corporate law topic worth studying. The basis for these assertions is the recognition that corporation statutes are largely enabling; they provide a set of default rules, nearly all of which are waivable in the Articles of Incorporation, in the bylaws, or by contract. Even more flexibility is provided by the internal affairs doctrine, which allows corporate planners to select the corporation statute of the state they find most beneficial to their legal needs. In this view of corporation law the one legal constraint on a corporation's governance is the fiduciary duties of officers and directors. Hence public policy regarding corporations is, effectively, exclusively concerned with fiduciary duties.

What are these fiduciary duties and where do they come from? One obvious consequence of a person's agreement to serve as a director is the understanding that he or she will strive for the corporation's financial success. Chapter 9 discusses the fact that, broadly speaking, all corporate power is located in the board of directors. Chapter 10 focuses on some of the constraints on the board's exercise of its power arising from the definition of the corporation's ultimate beneficiaries. Further, although directors are not "agents" of the corporation in a legal sense, they are certainly "agents" in an economic sense. Chapter 4, on agency, sets out some of the incentives that keep economic agents from acting solely in their own best economic interest rather than that of their principal.

This chapter, and the next two, are concerned with similar issues. "Fiduciary duties" is a shorthand way of describing the legal restrictions on board discretion that are imposed as a consequence of having agreed to act on behalf of a corporation's ultimate beneficiaries. The chapter begins by considering the standard of director allegiance — in what way do directors have to act to meet what is called their *duty of loyalty*? You may remember from Contracts that parties are typically under an obligation of good faith and fair dealing. If you have taken a course involving trust law you know that trustees are under a much more strict obligation to act in the utmost best interest of the trust's beneficiaries. Partners and agents are under a fiduciary duty that includes "not honesty alone, but the punctilio of an honor the most sensitive...." *Meinhard v. Salmon*, 164 N.E. 545, 546 (N.Y. 1928) (Cardozo, C.J.). What these differing standards and formulations may, in reality, come down to is an obligation to act in accordance with minimal standards of honesty (contracts), maximum other-directed intentions (trusts), or something in between.

Paradigms of problematic director actions have given rise to predictable responses by the courts. In examining these patterns we will understand how the courts' abstract incantations of fiduciary duties are incarnated. More importantly, by seeing the patterns of director behavior we will have a basis upon which to evaluate the fiduciary duty standards of conduct.

The next chapter explores the same sort of issues arising under directors' duty of care. After that chapter, Chapter 13 will turn to issues that may strike you as being better suited to a course in civil procedure or evidence. These are questions of the different standards of review courts use in evaluating claims that directors have breached their fiduciary duties. These standards of review, and their application, inhere in the standards of conduct; one simply cannot understand one without understanding the other. If it is any comfort (and it probably isn't) we will deal with other procedural questions, more discrete from fiduciary duty questions, in Chapter 15 when we take up shareholder litigation. When judges apply a particular standard of review they are, in effect, asking "how do I know whether the plaintiff has proved the requisite elements of his or her claim?" From your first year you are familiar with the standards of "preponderance," "clear and convincing," and "reasonable doubt." If you have taken Evidence you are also comfortable with various evidentiary presumptions. In the procedural courses one policy danger is making the standards too complex for juries to understand and apply. In Delaware, though, that danger does not exist because the Court of Chancery, in which all corporate law cases are heard, is a true court of equity, which means that juries are not used.

Directors' fiduciary duties are traditionally divided into the duty of loyalty and the duty of care. Although those labels are a bit problematic, the case law generally adheres to the traditional division and so it may be useful to continue the separation in the materials below. We begin in this chapter with the duty of loyalty.

A. THE CURRENT SETTING

The MBCA has codified the duty of loyalty in §8.30. Delaware has not codified the duty of loyalty but has adopted a similar statement in its case law. The Delaware Supreme Court has explained,

> This Court has traditionally and consistently defined the duty of loyalty of officers and directors to their corporation and its shareholders in broad and unyielding terms:
>
> > Corporate officers and directors are not permitted to use their position of trust and confidence to further their private interests. . . . A public policy, existing through the years, and derived from a profound knowledge of human characteristics and motives, has established a rule that demands of a corporate officer or director, peremptorily and inexorably, the most scrupulous observance of his [or her] duty, not only affirmatively to protect the interests of the corporation committed to his charge, but also to refrain from doing anything that would work injury to the corporation, or to deprive it of profit or advantage which his [or her] skill and ability might properly bring to it, or to enable it to make in the reasonable and lawful exercise of its powers. The rule that requires an undivided and unselfish loyalty to the corporation demands that there be no conflict between duty and self-interest.

> *Guth* [*v. Loft, Inc.*], 5 A.2d [503] at 510 [(Del. 1939)] .... Essentially, the duty of loyalty mandates that the best interest of the corporation and its shareholders takes precedence over any interest possessed by a director, officer or controlling shareholder and not shared by the stockholders generally.

Cede & Co. v. Technicolor, Inc., 634 A.2d 345, 361 (Del. 1993) (Horsey, J.)

What sort of actions constitute acting in bad faith or in a manner the director knows is not in the best interest of the corporation? Surely stealing comes within this rubric, and it is clear that directors may not, consistently with their fiduciary duties, steal from the companies they serve. Put less pejoratively and more broadly than the criminal law's definition of "theft," directors may not take things that belong to the corporation. That restriction comfortably covers the easy cases in which a director or officer takes a Van Gogh or Renoir that belongs to the corporate art collection. It also covers situations in which the director or officer takes home a ream of paper for the family computer or a package of sticky notes. Further, this restriction on director or officer action prohibits using corporate assets for noncorporate purposes. For example, a director may not use the corporate telephone to make personal calls and may not use the nearest company photocopier to make copies of his or her child's progress report from school.[1] Incidentally, you should note that the same restrictions apply to agents, which includes all employees, even those who are not directors or officers.

1. The Corporate Opportunity Doctrine

None of this should really be controversial, but there is a chronic uncertainty in corporate law about a particular kind of "thing" a corporation may "have" that a director may not take. The buzz phrase for this thing is a *corporate opportunity*. We start with corporate opportunity because it is a form of taking and the notion that taking is impermissible is easily apprehended. Here is a description of what a corporate opportunity is and a more formal elaboration of why it is not allowed.

> The classic corporate opportunity cases involve instances in which officers or directors use for personal advantage information that comes to them in their corporate capacity, by diverting a profitable transaction from the corporation. Such cases are simply a form of misappropriation, not conceptually dissimilar from general torts of that description. See *Restatement (Second) of Torts* §§222A, 223 (1965).
>
> Since business men and women are not infrequently involved in a number of enterprises (this is especially true of corporate directors and principals in close corporations) the law of misappropriation of corporate opportunities has generated a number of tests to determine whether an opportunity that comes to the attention of such an individual was in equity one that should be regarded as "belonging to" a particular corporation. One question . . . is whether the directors' obligation of loyalty under the corporate opportunity doctrine goes further than the tort of misappropriation would go to restrict business activity. That question is presented because it seems clear from the evidence that Mr. Broz [the defendant] did not misuse proprietary information that came to him in a corporate capacity nor did he otherwise use any

---

1. Most people reading the foregoing paragraph are shocked in one of two ways. One set of people finds it incredible that employees, especially those more senior than they or making more money than they, would take things from the company. The other set of people, intuiting that trying to wrangle the Remington bronze from the corporate headquarters lobby to one's car is wrong, nonetheless is shocked that taking sticky notes or a box of pens or photocopying services is wrong.

power he might have over the governance of the corporation to advance his own interests. Thus if Mr. Broz is guilty of violating the duty of loyalty it must be by reason of a restriction assumed by a corporate director that is greater than the restriction that prevents persons generally from misusing the property or information of another. The corporate law teaches that there is such an obligation voluntarily assumed by every man and woman who agrees to serve as a corporate director. That duty for example prevents a director from personally engaging in material business competition with his corporation without the approval of the corporation.

Cellular Information Systems, Inc. v. Broz, 663 A.2d 1180, 1184-85 (Del. Ch. 1995) (Allen, Ch.)

If a "corporate opportunity" is not coterminous with "property or information of" the corporation, what is it? The question of the definition of corporate opportunity is an important one because corporations, as well as the people who serve them, need a fair degree of predictability in this area. This is especially so, as Chancellor Allen points out, in the close corporation setting because the officers and directors of such enterprises are less likely to be engaged full-time in the corporation's affairs and may be undertaking more than one project at a time. The following case is typical of the factual settings that arise in the corporate opportunity arena but the legal analysis is much more thorough than courts generally accord.

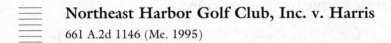

Northeast Harbor Golf Club, Inc. v. Harris

661 A.2d 1146 (Me. 1995)

ROBERTS, J.

Northeast Harbor Golf Club, Inc., appeals from a judgment entered in the Superior Court . . . following a nonjury trial. The Club maintains that the trial court erred in finding that Nancy Harris did not breach her fiduciary duty as president of the Club by purchasing and developing property abutting the golf course. Because we today adopt principles different from those applied by the trial court in determining that Harris's activities did not constitute a breach of the corporate opportunity doctrine, we vacate the judgment.

I. THE FACTS

Nancy Harris was the president of the Northeast Harbor Golf Club, a Maine corporation, from 1971 until she was asked to resign in 1990. The Club also had a board of directors that was responsible for making or approving significant policy decisions. The Club's only major asset was a golf course in Mount Desert. During Harris's tenure as president, the board occasionally discussed the possibility of developing some of the Club's real estate in order to raise money. Although Harris was generally in favor of tasteful development, the board always "shied away" from that type of activity.

In 1979, Robert Suminsby informed Harris that he was the listing broker for the Gilpin property, which comprised three noncontiguous parcels located among the fairways of the golf course. The property included an unused right-of-way on which the Club's parking lot and clubhouse were located. It was also encumbered by an easement in favor of the Club allowing foot traffic from the green of one hole to the next tee. Suminsby testified that he contacted Harris because she was the president of the Club and he believed that the Club would be interested in buying the property in order to prevent development.

Harris immediately agreed to purchase the Gilpin property in her own name for the asking price of $45,000. She did not disclose her plans to purchase the property to the Club's board prior to the purchase. She informed the board at its annual August meeting that she had purchased the property, that she intended to hold it in her own name, and that the Club would be "protected." The board took no action in response to the Harris purchase. She testified that at the time of the purchase she had no plans to develop the property and that no such plans took shape until 1988.

In 1984, while playing golf with the postmaster of Northeast Harbor, Harris learned that a parcel of land owned by the heirs of the Smallidge family might be available for purchase. The Smallidge parcel was surrounded on three sides by the golf course and on the fourth side by a house lot. It had no access to the road. With the ultimate goal of acquiring the property, Harris instructed her lawyer to locate the Smallidge heirs. Harris testified that she told a number of individual board members about her attempt to acquire the Smallidge parcel. At a board meeting in August 1985, Harris formally disclosed to the board that she had purchased the Smallidge property. The minutes of that meeting show that she told the board she had no present plans to develop the Smallidge parcel. Harris testified that at the time of the purchase of the Smallidge property she nonetheless thought it might be nice to have some houses there. Again, the board took no formal action as a result of Harris's purchase. Harris acquired the Smallidge property . . . , paying a total of $60,000. In 1990, Harris paid $275,000 for the lot and building separating the Smallidge parcel from the road in order to gain access to the otherwise landlocked parcel.

The trial court expressly found that the Club would have been unable to purchase either the Gilpin or Smallidge properties for itself, relying on testimony that the Club continually experienced financial difficulties, operated annually at a deficit, and depended on contributions from the directors to pay its bills. On the other hand, there was evidence that the Club had occasionally engaged in successful fund-raising, including a two-year period shortly after the Gilpin purchase during which the Club raised $115,000. The Club had $90,000 in a capital investment fund at the time of the Smallidge purchase.

In 1988, Harris, who was still president of the Club, . . . began the process of obtaining approval for a five-lot subdivision known as Bushwood on the lower Gilpin property. Even when the board learned of the proposed subdivision, a majority failed to take any action. A group of directors formed a separate organization in order to oppose the subdivision on the basis that it violated the local zoning ordinance. After Harris's resignation as president, the Club also sought unsuccessfully to challenge the subdivision. After Harris's plans to develop Bushwood became apparent, the board grew increasingly divided concerning the propriety of development near the golf course.

In particular, John Schafer, a Washington, D.C., lawyer and long-time member of the board, took issue with Harris's conduct. He testified that he had relied on Harris's representations at the time she acquired the properties that she would not develop them. According to Schafer, matters came to a head in August 1990 when a number of directors concluded that Harris's development plans irreconcilably conflicted with the Club's interests. As a result, Schafer and two other directors asked Harris to resign as president. In April 1991, after a substantial change in the board's membership, the board authorized the instant lawsuit against Harris for the breach of her fiduciary duty to act in the best interests of the corporation. The board simultaneously resolved that the proposed housing development was contrary to the best interests of the corporation.

[T]he complaint alleged that during her term as president Harris breached her fiduciary duty by purchasing the lots without providing notice and an opportunity for the Club to purchase the property and by subdividing the lots for future development. The Club sought an injunction to prevent development and also sought to impose a constructive trust on the property in question for the benefit of the Club.

II. THE CORPORATE OPPORTUNITY DOCTRINE

Despite the general acceptance of the proposition that corporate fiduciaries owe a duty of loyalty to their corporations, there has been much confusion about the specific extent of that duty when, as here, it is contended that a fiduciary takes for herself a corporate opportunity. This case requires us for the first time to define the scope of the corporate opportunity doctrine in Maine.

Various courts have embraced different versions of the corporate opportunity doctrine. The test applied by the trial court and embraced by Harris is generally known as the "line of business" test. The seminal case applying the line of business test is *Guth v. Loft, Inc.*, 5 A.2d 503 (Del. 1939). In *Guth*, the Delaware Supreme Court adopted an intensely factual test stated in general terms as follows:

> [I]f there is presented to a corporate officer or director a business opportunity which the corporation is financially able to undertake, is, from its nature, in the line of the corporation's business and is of practical advantage to it, is one in which the corporation has an interest or a reasonable expectancy, and, by embracing the opportunity, the self-interest of the officer or director will be brought into conflict with that of his corporation, the law will not permit him to seize the opportunity for himself.

Id. at 511. The "real issue" under this test is whether the opportunity "was so closely associated with the existing business activities...as to bring the transaction within that class of cases where the acquisition of the property would throw the corporate officer purchasing it into competition with his company." *Id.* at 513. The Delaware court described that inquiry as "a factual question to be decided by reasonable inferences from objective facts." *Id.*

The line of business test suffers from some significant weaknesses. First, the question whether a particular activity is within a corporation's line of business is conceptually difficult to answer. The facts of the instant case demonstrate that difficulty. The Club is in the business of running a golf course. It is not in the business of developing real estate. In the traditional sense, therefore, the trial court correctly observed that the opportunity in this case was not a corporate opportunity within the meaning of the *Guth* test. Nevertheless, the record would support a finding that the Club had made the policy judgment that development of surrounding real estate was detrimental to the best interests of the Club. The acquisition of land adjacent to the golf course for the purpose of preventing future development would have enhanced the ability of the Club to implement that policy. The record also shows that the Club had occasionally considered reversing that policy and expanding its operations to include the development of surrounding real estate. Harris's activities effectively foreclosed the Club from pursuing that option with respect to prime locations adjacent to the golf course.

Second, the *Guth* test includes as an element the financial ability of the corporation to take advantage of the opportunity. The court in this case relied on the Club's supposed financial incapacity as a basis for excusing Harris's conduct. Often, the injection of financial ability into the equation will unduly favor the inside director or executive who has command of the facts relating to the finances of the corporation. Reliance on financial ability will also act as a disincentive to corporate executives to solve corporate financing and other problems. In addition, the Club could have prevented development without spending $275,000 to acquire the property Harris needed to obtain access to the road.

The Massachusetts Supreme Judicial Court adopted a different test in *Durfee v. Durfee & Canning, Inc.*, 80 N.E.2d 522 (Mass. 1948). The *Durfee* test has since come to be known as the "fairness test." According to *Durfee,* the

> true basis of governing doctrine rests on the unfairness in the particular circumstances of a director, whose relation to the corporation is fiduciary, taking advantage of an opportunity [for her personal profit] when the interest of the corporation justly call[s] for protection. This calls for application of ethical standards of what is fair and equitable . . . in particular sets of facts.

Id. at 529 (quoting *Ballantine on Corporations* 204-05 (rev. ed. 1946)). As with the *Guth* test, the *Durfee* test calls for a broad-ranging, intensely factual inquiry. The *Durfee* test suffers even more than the *Guth* test from a lack of principled content. It provides little or no practical guidance to the corporate officer or director seeking to measure her obligations.

The Minnesota Supreme Court elected "to combine the 'line of business' test with the 'fairness' test." *Miller v. Miller,* 222 N.W.2d 71, 81 (Minn. 1974). It engaged in a two-step analysis, first determining whether a particular opportunity was within the corporation's line of business, then scrutinizing "the equitable considerations existing prior to, at the time of, and following the officer's acquisition." *Id.* The *Miller* court hoped by adopting this approach "to ameliorate the often-expressed criticism that the [corporate opportunity] doctrine is vague and subjects today's corporate management to the danger of unpredictable liability." *Id.* In fact, the test adopted in *Miller* merely piles the uncertainty and vagueness of the fairness test on top of the weaknesses in the line of business test.

Despite the weaknesses of each of these approaches to the corporate opportunity doctrine, they nonetheless rest on a single fundamental policy. At bottom, the corporate opportunity doctrine recognizes that a corporate fiduciary should not serve both corporate and personal interests at the same time. As we observed in *Camden Land Co. v. Lewis,* 63 A. 523, 531 (Me. 1905), corporate fiduciaries "owe their whole duty to the corporation, and they are not to be permitted to act when duty conflicts with interest. They cannot serve themselves and the corporation at the same time." The various formulations of the test are merely attempts to moderate the potentially harsh consequences of strict adherence to that policy. It is important to preserve some ability for corporate fiduciaries to pursue personal business interests that present no real threat to their duty of loyalty.

III. THE AMERICAN LAW INSTITUTE APPROACH

In an attempt to protect the duty of loyalty while at the same time providing long-needed clarity and guidance for corporate decision-makers, the American Law Institute has offered the most recently developed version of the corporate opportunity doctrine. *Principles of Corporate Governance* §5.05 (May 13, 1992), provides as follows:

§5.05 TAKING OF CORPORATE OPPORTUNITIES BY DIRECTORS OR SENIOR EXECUTIVES

(a) *General Rule.* A director or senior executive may not take advantage of a corporate opportunity unless:

(1) The director or senior executive first offers the corporate opportunity to the corporation and makes disclosure concerning the conflict of interest and the corporate opportunity;

(2) The corporate opportunity is rejected by the corporation; and

(3) Either:

(A) The rejection of the opportunity is fair to the corporation;

(B) The opportunity is rejected in advance, following such disclosure, by disinterested directors, or, in the case of a senior executive who is not a director, by a disinterested superior, in a manner that satisfies the standards of the business judgment rule; or

(C) The rejection is authorized in advance or ratified, following such disclosure, by disinterested shareholders, and the rejection is not equivalent to a waste of corporate assets.

(b) *Definition of a Corporate Opportunity.* For purposes of this Section, a corporate opportunity means:

(1) Any opportunity to engage in a business activity of which a director or senior executive becomes aware, either:

(A) In connection with the performance of functions as a director or senior executive, or under circumstances that should reasonably lead the director or senior executive to believe that the person offering the opportunity expects it to be offered to the corporation; or

(B) Through the use of corporate information or property, if the resulting opportunity is one that the director or senior executive should reasonably be expected to believe would be of interest to the corporation; or

(2) Any opportunity to engage in a business activity of which a senior executive becomes aware and knows is closely related to a business in which the corporation is engaged or expects to engage.

(c) *Burden of Proof.* A party who challenges the taking of a corporate opportunity has the burden of proof, except that if such party establishes that the requirements of Subsection (a)(3)(B) or (C) are not met, the director or the senior executive has the burden of proving that the rejection and the taking of the opportunity were fair to the corporation.

. . .

(e) *Special Rule Concerning Delayed Offering of Corporate Opportunities.* Relief based solely on failure to first offer an opportunity to the corporation under Subsection (a)(1) is not available if: (1) such failure resulted from a good faith belief that the business activity did not constitute a corporate opportunity, and (2) not later than a reasonable time after suit is filed challenging the taking of the corporate opportunity, the corporate opportunity is to the extent possible offered to the corporation and rejected in a manner that satisfies the standards of Subsection (a).

The central feature of the ALI test is the strict requirement of full disclosure prior to taking advantage of any corporate opportunity. *Id.,* §5.05(a)(1). "If the opportunity is not offered to the corporation, the director or senior executive will not have satisfied §5.05(a)." *Id.*, cmt. to §5.05(a). The corporation must then formally reject the opportunity. *Id.*, §5.05(a)(2). A "good faith but defective disclosure" by the corporate officer may be ratified after the fact only by an affirmative vote of the disinterested directors or shareholders. *Principles of Corporate Governance* §5.05(d).

The ALI test defines "corporate opportunity" broadly. It includes opportunities "closely related to a business in which the corporation is engaged." *Id.*, §5.05(b). It also encompasses any opportunities that accrue to the fiduciary as a result of her position within the corporation. *Id.* This concept is most clearly illustrated by the testimony of Suminsby, the listing broker for the Gilpin property, which, if believed by the factfinder, would support a finding that the Gilpin property was offered to Harris specifically in her capacity as president of the Club. If the factfinder reached that conclusion, then at least the opportunity to acquire the Gilpin property would be a corporate opportunity. The state of the record concerning the Smallidge purchase precludes us from intimating any opinion whether that too would be a corporate opportunity.

Under the ALI standard, once the Club shows that the opportunity is a corporate opportunity, it must show either that Harris did not offer the opportunity to the Club or that the Club did not reject it properly. If the Club shows that the board did not reject the opportunity by a vote of the disinterested directors after full disclosure, then Harris may defend her actions on the basis that the taking of the opportunity was fair to the corporation. *Id.*, §5.05(c). If Harris failed to offer the opportunity at all, however, then she may not defend on the basis that the failure to offer the opportunity was fair. *Id.*, cmt. to §5.05(c).

[T]oday we follow the ALI test. The disclosure-oriented approach provides a clear procedure whereby a corporate officer may insulate herself through prompt and complete disclosure from the possibility of a legal challenge. The requirement of disclosure recognizes the paramount importance of the corporate fiduciary's duty of loyalty. At the same time it protects the fiduciary's ability pursuant to the proper procedure to pursue her own business ventures free from the possibility of a lawsuit.

IV. CONCLUSION

The trial court made a number of factual findings based on an extensive record.[3] The court made those findings, however, in the light of legal principles that are different from the principles that we today announce. Similarly, the parties did not have the opportunity to develop the record in this case with knowledge of the applicable legal standard. In these circumstances, fairness requires that we remand the case for further proceedings. Those further proceedings may include, at the trial court's discretion, the taking of further evidence.

All concurring.

---

3. Harris raised the defense of laches and the statute of limitations but the court made no findings on those issues. We do not intimate what result the application of either doctrine would produce in this case. Similarly, it was not necessary for the court to address the issue of remedy in the first trial. The court has broad discretion to fashion an equitable remedy based on the facts and circumstances of the case. We decline to invade its province by commenting prematurely on what remedy, if any, may be appropriate.

Notes and Questions

1. Notes

a. After remand, the trial court entered judgment for the Club, but on appeal the Supreme Judicial Court entered judgment for Harris on the grounds of laches and the running of the statute of limitations. See *Northeast Harbor Golf Club, Inc. v. Harris*, 725 A.2d 1018 (Me. 1998).

b. In that second appeal, the Maine Supreme Judicial Court adds the following facts:

> From 1972 until 1984, the board, at Harris's insistence, discussed either purchasing and developing land surrounding the Club or developing some of the Club's real estate in order to raise money. At the 1976 annual meeting, the Club was informed that a consultant, after investigating the matter, had concluded that the Club's land, surrounding the golf course, was suitable for development. In 1977, the board authorized Harris to form a committee to study in more detail developing some of the Club's land. The purpose of development was to improve the financial condition of the Club.
>
> At the 1982 meeting, Harris made it clear that she strongly advocated housing development on Club property and volunteered to finance construction of the first house. Although some directors opposed development, the board eventually approved building houses on Club property by a 14 to 4 vote. At the 1984 annual meeting, Harris presented an "Outline of Proposal for Sale and Management of Excess Land" and the board approved her proposal to sell two lots of Club land to raise revenue. No lots were ever sold.

Northeast Harbor Golf Club, Inc. v. Harris, 725 A.2d 1018, 1020 (Me. 1998) (Clifford, J.)

c. The Delaware Supreme Court has summarized the corporate opportunity doctrine it uses:

> The corporate opportunity doctrine, as delineated by *Guth* [*v. Loft, Inc.*, 5 A.2d 503 (Del. 1939)] and its progeny, holds that a corporate officer or director may not take a business opportunity for his own if: (1) the corporation is financially able to exploit the opportunity; (2) the opportunity is within the corporation's line of business; (3) the corporation has an interest or expectancy in the opportunity; and (4) by taking the opportunity for his own, the corporate fiduciary will thereby be placed in a position inimicable to his duties to the corporation. The Court in *Guth* also derived a corollary which states that a director or officer *may* take a corporate opportunity if: (1) the opportunity is presented to the director or officer in his individual and not his corporate capacity; (2) the opportunity is not essential to the corporation; (3) the corporation holds no interest or expectancy in the opportunity; and (4) the director or officer has not wrongfully employed the resources of the corporation in pursuing or exploiting the opportunity. *Guth*, 5 A.2d at 509.

Broz v. Cellular Information Systems, Inc., 673 A.2d 148, 154-155 (Del. 1996) (Veasey, C.J.)

d. The DGCL permits corporations to decline corporate opportunities in advance. See DGCL §122(17). Is this a good idea?

e. By contrast, the MBCA is completely silent on the question of corporate opportunities. Is this silence a good idea? Does that silence mean that a corporation may not decline corporate opportunities in advance? Does it mean that a corporation may do so?

2. Reality Check

a. If taking a corporate opportunity is a duty of loyalty problem, why does the court say that it may be permissible?

b. According to the Club, how did Ms. Harris harm the Club? How did she "take" a "thing" that "belonged" to the Club?

c. How much financial gain did Ms. Harris get from the real estate transactions?

d. What is the line of business test and why does the court reject it? Do you agree with the court's action?

e. What is the fairness test and why does the court reject it? Do you agree with the court's action? If so, are you and the court in favor of unfairness?

f. What is the Minnesota test? Don't even bother explaining why the court rejects that test.

g. Why does the court accept the ALI test?

h. Describe the ALI test.

3. Suppose

a. If the court had found Ms. Harris had usurped a corporate opportunity, how should it measure the damages?

b. Suppose Ms. Harris had only purchased the land and not developed it. Would the court have found her to have usurped a corporate opportunity? Should it find for her or for the Club?

c. Suppose Ms. Harris had purchased the land and later sold it to an unrelated third party at its fair value ($1,550,000). Would the court have found her to have usurped a corporate opportunity? Should it find for her or for the Club?

d. Now imagine that Ms. Harris purchased the land and later sold it to the Club for its fair value. Would the court have found her to have usurped a corporate opportunity? Should it find for her or for the Club?

e. If Ms. Harris had simply declined the chances to purchase the real estate but the parcels had all been purchased and developed by a single unrelated third party, wouldn't the Club have been harmed in exactly the same way it claims it was injured by Ms. Harris? Would the Club have any claim for relief against that third party? Would the Club have any claim for relief against Ms. Harris?

4. What Do You Think?

a. Justice Roberts noted that the question of the corporation's financial ability to accept a particular opportunity is the subject of much debate, with some arguing that financial ability should be part of the plaintiff's claim for relief, while others argue that it should be an affirmative defense and still others argue that it should be wholly irrelevant because, if the opportunity is economically viable, the corporation can find financing. What role do you think the corporation's financial ability should play (if any)?

b. Do you think the ALI test does a better job of defining "corporate opportunity" than the tests that the court rejects? In this regard, the Delaware Supreme Court has candidly acknowledged:

> The language in the *Guth* [*v. Loft, Inc.*, 5 A.2d 503 (Del. 1939)] opinion relating to "line of business" is less than clear:

> Where a corporation is engaged in a certain business, and an opportunity is presented to it embracing an activity as to which it has fundamental knowledge, practical experience and *ability to pursue,* which, logically and naturally, is adaptable to its business *having regard for its financial position,* and *is consonant with its reasonable needs and aspirations for expansion,* it may properly be said that the opportunity is within the corporation's line of business.

Guth, 5 A.2d at 514 (emphasis supplied). This formulation of the definition of the term "line of business" suggests that the business strategy and financial well-being of the corporation are also relevant to a determination of whether the opportunity is within the corporation's line of business.

Broz v. Cellular Information Systems, Inc., 673 A.2d 148, 156 n.7 (Del. 1996) (Veasey, C.J.)

c. If offering a corporate opportunity to the corporation is of such paramount importance, why do the ALI and DGCL allow a corporation to reject such opportunities in advance? The Delaware Supreme Court has noted,

> [T]he director or officer must analyze the situation *ex ante* to determine whether the opportunity is one rightfully belonging to the corporation. If the director or officer believes . . . that the corporation is not entitled to the opportunity, then he may take it for himself. Of course, presenting the opportunity to the board creates a kind of "safe harbor" for the director, which removes the specter of a *post hoc* judicial determination that the director or officer has improperly usurped a corporate opportunity. Thus, presentation avoids the possibility that an error in the fiduciary's assessment of the situation will create future liability for breach of fiduciary duty. It is not the law of Delaware that presentation to the board is a necessary prerequisite to a finding that a corporate opportunity has not been usurped.

Broz v. Cellular Information Systems, Inc., 673 A.2d 148, 157 (Del. 1996) (Veasey, C.J.)

d. How would you advise a corporation that has a senior officer or director who is frequently engaged in business ventures apart from the corporation?

2. Self-Dealing

Taking a corporate opportunity is one of the paradigms of duty of loyalty problems. Another paradigm is *self-dealing.* Indeed, self-dealing is such a frequent example of duty of loyalty concerns that courts and commentators occasionally use the term *self-dealing* to mean any duty of loyalty question. As the name implies, self-dealing occurs when a director or officer enters into a contract with the corporation, usually to buy something from, or sell something to, the corporation.

A moment's reflection (don't worry, I'm not actually asking you to reflect) will reveal that simply because a director has sold something to the corporation does not mean that he or she has necessarily violated the duty of loyalty. The director might well honestly believe that the contract is in the best interest of the corporation. Viewed entirely objectively, such contracts might indeed be in the corporation's best interest. Certainly such situations frequently arise during the start-up phase of a corporation's existence. One of the promoters will contribute the Big Idea or the unique piece of real estate without which the corporation cannot flourish, in return for stock. Such a transaction is surely in the corporation's best economic interest.

The rub, of course, is whether the corporation is exchanging too much for what it is receiving. This question, which is central to whether a self-dealing transaction violates the duty of loyalty, sometimes raises delicate and difficult questions of valuation. If the asset that is changing hands is untested, it may be difficult to ascertain its value using a discounted cash flow analysis. If the asset is genuinely unique, it may be difficult to find appropriately comparable assets to which to compare its value. Further, the asset's uniqueness may mean that its value to the corporation far outstrips its value in its next-most remunerative use. For example, a delivery truck painted with the company logo might be worth $X to a bakery company but also worth $X (or very nearly so) to another company, which would simply have to repaint the logo. On the other hand, a huge, specially designed machine that only makes My Little Ponies, could be enormously valuable to the company that makes My Little Pony and much less valuable (i.e., scrap value only) to any other company.

As you think about the question of self-dealing, think about the problem of valuation and also think about whether the director's subjective views about the fairness of the transaction to the corporation should be determinative, irrelevant, or somewhere in between. The next case presents an ironic situation regarding whether the corporation received value from the self-dealing transaction.

Tomaino v. Concord Oil of Newport, Inc.
709 A.2d 1016 (R.I. 1998)

WEISBERGER, C.J.

In 1976 [Joseph M.] Tomaino became a 25-percent owner of Concord Oil Company (Concord), a closely held Massachusetts corporation.... Tomaino, who brought with him seventeen years of experience from his previous employment with Texaco, Inc., became a member of the board of directors and vice president of Concord. His primary area of responsibility with Concord was the development, maintenance, and enhancement of Concord's retail-gasoline business. The president of Concord was Arthur R. Bethke (Bethke), who...owned the rest of the Concord stock [and] ran the company.

Between 1976 and 1978 Concord developed several gasoline retail outlets. Concord would as a general rule either lease its service-station locations [to others] and/or negotiate a supply contract with an existing operator. Regardless of the form of the business, it was routine for Concord to acquire ownership of the underground tanks at each location where it was supplying gasoline. Three witnesses in the business of gasoline retailing...testified that during the 1970s it was very common for gasoline distributors to own the underground tanks and related petroleum-marketing equipment (that is, underground fuel lines, underground pump systems, gas pump islands, and the like) at retail locations with which the distributor had a supply or a commission contract. [B]y securing ownership of the gasoline storage tanks, the supplier could "put a lock on [the] business through [the] contractual relationship." In addition, by owning the tanks, the supplier had the power to remove the equipment from the property in the event the onsite vendor was unable or unwilling to meet the supplier's business expectations. According to two of the witnesses this practice did not change until the mid-1980s, upon the advent of greater environmental-testing procedures and the consequent environmental liability, which was never an issue in the 1970s.

Prior to joining Concord, Tomaino had investigated the possibility of purchasing/leasing several retail gasoline businesses...owned by Newport Oil Corporation (Newport Oil). In 1978, after joining Concord, Tomaino and Bethke agreed that Tomaino would renew negotiations with Newport Oil in order to pursue jointly these opportunities on behalf of [Tomaino and] Concord. Tomaino negotiated an agreement [to lease from] Newport Oil...three properties upon which retail-gasoline businesses were in operation. Specifically the locations were...Newport...; One Mile Corner...; and...Portsmouth.

Tomaino and Bethke formed a separate corporation, Concord Oil of Newport, Inc. (Concord/Newport)...to supply and/or operate the retail-gasoline businesses at each location. Concord owned 68 percent of the stock and Tomaino owned 32 percent. Tomaino served as president of the new entity.... Tomaino...purchased [the real estate and] all the buildings and improvements constituting the gasoline service stations, including all petroleum-marketing equipment, underground tanks, and ancillary facilities [from Newport Oil] at the price of one dollar.[7]

[Three months later, on] June 12, 1978, [Tomaino] transferred ownership...of the underground tanks, pump islands, pump systems, and related lighting at each location to Concord/Newport for $5,000. Tomaino testified that this figure was below market value for the tanks and other improvements. There was additional testimony that this amount was substantially less than Concord/Newport had paid on previous occasions for similar acquisitions.

Tomaino left Concord's employ in February 1993. In May 1993 Concord/Newport notified Tomaino of its intention to quit its tenancy at the One Mile Corner location. Tomaino requested that Concord/Newport remove its underground tanks at that site. After Concord/Newport failed to do so, Tomaino, after notifying Concord/Newport of his intention, removed the tanks at a cost of $18,600.

Frank M. Oliveira..., a commercial real estate broker engaged by [Tomaino] to rent the property testified that the presence of the tanks frustrated his efforts because suitable tenants were unwilling to assume the potential liability that the presence of the tanks created. Domino's Pizza...eventually agreed to rent the premises on the condition that the tanks be removed. Thereafter Tomaino paid for the removal of the tanks at the One Mile Corner location. When Domino's finally assumed tenancy, the property had been unoccupied for eleven and one-half months. Oliveira's undisputed testimony was that the fair rental value of the One Mile Corner property at that time was $3,000 per month....

On February 3, 1994, plaintiff filed a complaint seeking declaratory relief, injunctive relief, and money damages. In August 1994 Tomaino received further notice from Concord/Newport of its intention to terminate its tenancy at both the Portsmouth and the Newport locations. Concord/Newport removed a portion of the petroleum marketing equipment from each location, but did not remove the underground tanks or the related piping. Tomaino did not, however, remove at his own expense the tanks at either the Newport or the Portsmouth locations. Tomaino was unsuccessful in renting either of these two properties from that time until the time of trial.

A trial was held in Superior Court in June 1995. The jury determined that the tanks were the property of defendant Concord/Newport and awarded plaintiff

---

7. Tomaino testified that such an apparent bargain was justified owing to the value Newport received on the lease itself.

$88,950 in damages, representing costs incurred in removing two tanks from one location and for lost rental revenue at each additional location. The trial justice denied defendant's motion for a new trial and directed defendant to remove the remaining underground tanks and related equipment. The trial justice conditioned the denial of defendant's motion upon plaintiff's acceptance of a remittitur of $37,650 . . . because . . . Tomaino had failed to mitigate damages by not removing the remaining tanks located at the Newport and the Portsmouth locations and thus render those properties eligible for lease or sale.

The duty of loyalty requires, inter alia, that a director or an officer act in good faith toward the corporation and that transactions or contracts into which he or she enters with the corporation be fair to the corporation. Good faith in this context means full and honest disclosure by the fiduciary of all material facts to allow for a disinterested decision maker to exercise its informed judgment. Fairness to the corporation requires that a transaction or contract benefit the corporation and the stockholders thereof and not confer undue or unjust advantage on the fiduciary.

An interested transaction occurs when a corporate fiduciary (officer, director, or in the case of a close corporation, a shareholder) enters into a contract or transaction with that corporate entity that he or she serves as a fiduciary. Such a transaction is not per se voidable but may be challenged if it was not entered into in good faith and/or was unfair to the corporation.

To be valid, the transaction must have been assented to by the disinterested officers and/or stockholders of the corporation with full knowledge of all the facts. The burden of proving that the challenged transaction both was fair to the corporation and was authorized, approved, or ratified lies with the interested party. Ratification need not, however, be by formal vote but may be implied from a corporation's course of conduct in instances in which the corporation derives a benefit from the challenged contract or transaction and in which the directors had "knowledge of such facts or circumstances as would put a reasonable person on inquiry and [which] would lead to full discovery." *Puritan Medical Center, Inc. v. Cashman*, 596 N.E.2d 1004, 1008 (Mass. 1992). . . .

It is important to appreciate that what lies at the heart of the instant dispute is . . . a significant change in perception, between the time the transaction was effected and the time plaintiff filed suit, about whether an underground gasoline storage tank constitutes an asset or a liability. A reasonable jury could have determined that the sale of the tanks conferred a benefit to the corporation, was not uncommon in the industry or in the usual course of Concord's business, was arguably fair to Concord/Newport at the time of sale, and had the sale been effected by a third party, its validity could not have been doubted.

The defendant argues that even had the sale of the tanks been ratified by Concord/Newport, the deal was not mutually beneficial or fair to the corporation. In support of this assertion it points to the discrepancy between the price [Tomaino] paid for the tanks and equipment and the price Concord/Newport paid for just a portion thereof. Further, defendant insists that the testimony adduced by plaintiff that it was standard practice within the industry for gasoline suppliers to purchase the underground tanks of retail vendors to whom they supplied gasoline is not persuasive on the facts of this case. Concord/Newport, the argument went, had no need to "lock in" Tomaino because Tomaino was in effect Concord/Newport, owning 32 percent of that company's stock. Concord/Newport maintains that it would be ludicrous to conclude that it would seek to lock Tomaino into a gasoline-supply contract.

We find these arguments interesting but ultimately unavailing. The markup on the price of the improvements from [Tomaino] to Concord/Newport is not so shocking in context as the seemingly stark inequity of the increase considered in the abstract. After all, trial testimony established that this amount was below market value and substantially less than what Concord or Concord/Newport had paid for similar acquisitions on previous occasions. Examining the dynamics of all the transactions involved, the jury could reasonably conclude that the difference in price was attributable to business judgment, arm's-length negotiation, or some other justification and did not represent a hidden windfall to Tomaino. Moreover, this $5,000 transaction placed in the context of Concord's and Concord/Newport's financial landscape was slight: testimony at trial revealed that in retail-gasoline business alone, the corporations together supplied gasoline to over thirty service stations throughout New England.

Viewing the evidence and all reasonable inferences therefrom in a light most beneficial to plaintiff, the trial justice properly determined that a jury question existed concerning whether (1) full disclosure of the material facts concerning the tank transaction had been made by plaintiff to Concord/Newport, (2) the sale had been approved, authorized, or ratified by Concord/Newport, and (3) the transaction was fair to Concord/Newport at the time of authorization, approval, or ratification. Accordingly we discern no error in the trial justice's denial of defendant's motion for judgment as a matter of law.

BOURCIER, J., did not participate.

Notes and Questions

1. Reality Check

a. Where is the self-dealing transaction?
b. Which party is trying to nullify the self-dealing transaction? Why?
c. What test does the court use to evaluate self-dealing transactions?
d. Why does the court allow the self-dealing transaction to stand?

2. Suppose

a. Suppose environmental concerns had made underground storage tanks disadvantageous at the time of the sales from Tomaino to Concord/Newport. Would the transaction still be "fair" to Concord/Newport?

3. What Do You Think?

a. Should self-dealing transactions be void per se?
b. Should self-dealing transactions be subjected to any different tests than other board actions?
c. Did Tomaino usurp a corporate opportunity?

3. Trying to Generalize

Can we move from these examples of duty of loyalty problems to a more generalized understanding? The basic statement of the duty of loyalty requires each director to act in good faith, of which, more below, and with the genuine belief that his or her actions are in the best interest of the corporation. In other words, the test for whether a director has met his or her duty of loyalty should turn, *entirely*, on whether the director actually believes that the action will be in the corporation's best interest. One way to demonstrate that a director has breached the duty of loyalty is a statement by the director that he or she did not have the requisite belief. This is obviously seldom a reality.

Short of a confession, then, are there objective indications that the director did not act, or may not have acted, with the requisite belief? At bottom, there are two objective indicators, one of which clearly shows the director breached the duty of loyalty. That indicator is where the director takes something from the corporation because the director surely could not believe that the corporation's best interest is served by losing something it had for no recompense. The corporate opportunity doctrine is simply a chronically recurring setting.

The second objective indication that a director may have violated the duty of loyalty is self-dealing. But, the consequence of self-dealing is different from that of taking a corporate opportunity in two ways. First, unlike taking a corporate opportunity, a transaction between a corporation and one of its directors is quite possibly a transaction that the director could reasonably believe is in the corporation's best interest. Finding that a director has engaged in self-dealing does not, then, definitely establish that the director violated his or her fiduciary duty of loyalty.

Second, self-dealing has more shades than does taking a corporate opportunity. Without exploring psychological, epistemological, or literary theories of "self," it is fair to say that the reason a self-dealing transaction may mean a duty of loyalty violation is that directors (like other humans) have an incentive to prefer their own welfare to that of others. Hence a self-dealing transaction raises the possibility that the director believes that the transaction is not in the corporation's best interest, but in the best interest of the director. It is possible, of course, for the director to believe, honestly, that a proposed self-dealing transaction is in the best interest of both the corporation and the director. But in terms of identifying objective suggestions that a director may not have the appropriate belief, the idea of "self" may be larger than simply the director.

Directors care about themselves, of course, but also their families, friends, co-workers, and other businesses with which they may have a relation (e.g., as an employee, director, or owner). A more generalized label for this objective suggestion is *conflict of interest*. It is helpful to remember that *self-dealing* and *conflict of interest* are not synonymous, although many use the terms interchangeably. Self-dealing is a subset of conflict of interest and probably the easiest to grasp. The presence of a director's conflict of interest is in the nature of a warning, a red flag, that the proposed transaction may represent one that the director does not actually believe is in the best interest of the corporation.

In terms of identifying possible breaches of the duty of loyalty, the varieties of conflict of interest are not of equal usefulness. In true self-dealing, as in *Tomaino*, the potential for a directorial breach is clear and strong. But as the connection between the director and benefit becomes more attenuated, the less likely it is that the director violated the duty of loyalty. A good analogy is red nail polish. Really Really Ruby and Code Red are paradigms, but Tickled Pink, Tutu Pink, and Pinkini are included under the rubric of red even though their shades are not close to a pure, deep, red. And we haven't even begun to think about the amalgamations like Champagne, and Limitless Lilac, which could also be considered red nail polish.

Consider *A* Corporation's proposed transaction, to be voted upon by the board of directors, and ask whether a director's conflict of interest should raise a strong presumption, weak presumption, or no presumption at all as to whether a director who votes in favor of the transaction is violating his or her duty of loyalty.

The transaction is between *A* Corporation and the director.

The transaction is between *A* Corporation and *B* Corporation, which is
  Wholly owned by the director.
  Half-owned by the director.
  1 percent owned by the director.

The transaction is between *A* Corporation and *B* Corporation. The director has no ownership interest in *B* Corporation but serves on the *B* Corporation board of directors.

The transaction is between *A* Corporation and the director's
  Spouse.
  Adult child.
  First cousin.
  Live-in nanny.

The transaction is between *A* Corporation and *B* Corporation. The director has no prior connection to *B* Corporation but,
  The director will be paid a "finder's fee" by *B* Corporation if the transaction is approved.
  The director will be paid a "finder's fee" by *A* Corporation if the transaction is approved.
  The director will be paid a "finder's fee" by *B* Corporation regardless of whether the transaction is approved.
  The director will be paid a "finder's fee" by *A* Corporation regardless of whether the transaction is approved.
  The director anticipates being asked to become a member of *B* Corporation's board, a prestigious directorship, if the transaction is approved.
  The director anticipates that a close friend of many years' standing who works for *B* Corporation will get a major promotion if the transaction is approved.

At bottom, the proper inquiry should be whether objective facts suggest (or show) that the director may not (or does not) believe a corporate action is in the best interest of the corporation. As you read the next case, ask which kind or kinds of conflict of interest are present here and ask how strong is the concomitant suggestion that Mr. Geller violated his duty of loyalty.

Geller v. Allied-Lyons plc

674 N.E.2d 1334 (Mass. App. 1997)

FLANNERY, J.

Leonard Geller, a former senior vice president of Dunkin Donuts Incorporated (Dunkin), appeals from summary judgment entered in the defendants' favor in his action to recover a finder's fee which Allied-Lyons PLC (Allied), through a subsidiary, allegedly promised the plaintiff in the event that Allied acquired Dunkin. The Superior Court judge determined that the oral finder's fee agreement was unenforceable for reasons of public policy and the Statute of Frauds.... We affirm on the ground of public policy.

The summary judgment record reveals the following facts, which we view in the plaintiff's favor. In 1985, the plaintiff, as Dunkin's senior vice president for international development, was contacted by David H. Lipka, the president and chief executive officer of DCA Food Industries, Inc. (DCA), a Dunkin supplier and a subsidiary of Allied. In the course of their conversation, Lipka asked Geller whether Dunkin would be interested in being acquired by Allied and also stated that Allied would pay Geller a one percent finder's fee if he would help Allied to acquire Dunkin. Geller communicated Lipka's inquiry to Robert Rosenberg, Dunkin's chief executive officer and chairman of Dunkin's board of directors, who bristled at the mention of acquisition and rejected the overture. When Geller informed Lipka of Rosenberg's response, Lipka reiterated Allied's interest and the promised finder's fee. In the course of their subsequent dealings with one another, Lipka periodically reaffirmed the fee agreement with Geller.[2]

In April, 1989, Dunkin learned that an entity called Kingsbridge had acquired a significant percentage of Dunkin stock and was attempting a takeover. This was not viewed favorably by Dunkin management, which then hired Goldman Sachs to find other buyers. Upon request, Geller provided Goldman Sachs with the names of Allied and another company as possible purchasers. In September, 1989, Rosenberg met with Dunkin's senior executives, including Geller, and announced that none of the potential purchasers contacted by Goldman Sachs was interested. At some point during this meeting, Geller expressed his surprise that Allied was not interested, adding that Allied had previously contacted him about an acquisition and had offered him a one percent finder's fee. Geller claims that those present, including Rosenberg; Dunkin's president...; and Dunkin's general counsel..."could have heard" or "would have been exposed to" Geller's statement about the one percent finder's fee. Geller then requested Rosenberg's permission to contact Lipka personally regarding the acquisition; Rosenberg, at first reluctant, acquiesced, and Geller flew to New York to meet with Lipka. Following this and other meetings between Allied representatives and Dunkin management, Allied's interest in acquiring Dunkin was renewed.

Allied eventually purchased Dunkin in November, 1989, and Rosenberg gave Geller a $20,000 bonus for his efforts. Geller told Rosenberg, however, that he expected to receive a finder's fee from Allied. Rosenberg responded that that was between Geller and Allied. Neither Allied nor Dunkin paid Geller the anticipated fee which, at one percent of the purchase price, amounted to $3.23 million, and the plaintiff brought this action to recover on the contract.

On appeal, the plaintiff challenges the two grounds upon which summary judgment was entered. We address the plaintiff's arguments in turn.

1. *Public policy considerations.* Under Massachusetts law, officers and directors owe a fiduciary duty to protect the interests of the corporation they serve. Senior executives are considered to be corporate fiduciaries and to owe their company a duty of loyalty. Corporate fiduciaries are required to be loyal to the corporation and to refrain from promoting their own interests in a manner injurious to the corporation.

---

2. In his deposition testimony, Geller stated that the finder's fee agreement required him to represent Allied in helping it to acquire Dunkin and to do whatever he could on Allied's behalf to effect the acquisition; he also testified that he did not know whether he would be representing Dunkin or Allied in the acquisition process.

The prohibition against self-dealing on the part of corporate fiduciaries requires that the corporation receive the full benefit of transactions in which an officer engages on the corporation's behalf, without thought to personal gain; this is part of the bargain upon which investors rely when they purchase a corporation's stock. For that reason, a contract for personal gain which could cause a corporate fiduciary to breach his or her fiduciary duty of loyalty to the corporation is generally held to be unenforceable as against public policy. Accordingly, Massachusetts courts vigorously scrutinize self-interested transactions involving corporate fiduciaries.

As a senior vice president of Dunkin, Geller was prohibited from using his strategic position within the corporation to enter into an agreement for personal gain that could compromise his duty of loyalty to Dunkin and its shareholders. By pledging his assistance to Allied in return for a multimillion dollar finder's fee, the plaintiff placed himself in a position in which his contractual obligation to Allied and his own pecuniary interests could have prevented him from acting in Dunkin's best interest.

Geller counters that his finder's fee agreement with Allied did not cause financial harm to Dunkin and therefore did not cause a breach of his duty of loyalty. The fact that Allied's acquisition of Dunkin may have ultimately benefited Dunkin shareholders does not eliminate the danger that was inherent in the finder's fee agreement. The plaintiff's impropriety, as we see it, was in accepting an opportunity for personal gain when the paramount interests of the corporation called for protection; this is particularly true in the sensitive area of acquisition.[5] In creating a temptation for the plaintiff to favor Allied, the finder's fee agreement could have induced the plaintiff to facilitate an acquisition that was not in Dunkin's best interest, had the events of 1989 unfolded differently.

2. *Full disclosure of self-dealing.* Despite the foregoing, the plaintiff maintains that the finder's fee agreement did not violate his duty of loyalty because he disclosed it in the presence of Rosenberg and others prior to the acquisition and they failed to object.[7] Because of this disclosure, the plaintiff argues, the finder's fee agreement should be enforced. At best, the plaintiff asserts that he made a statement regarding Allied's previous promise of a one percent finder's fee at a meeting which Rosenberg...and other senior Dunkin executives attended, that Rosenberg could have heard him or would have been exposed to the statement, and that Rosenberg made no response.

As matter of law, sotto voce indications do not fulfill a fiduciary's duty of full disclosure of self-dealing. The plaintiff's actions here to inform Dunkin of the finder's fee agreement did not rise to the level of full and fair disclosure that has long been required before a fiduciary may procure personal profit in the conduct of corporate affairs.

5. The rule forbidding a corporate fiduciary from reaping private profit through his position with the corporation "does not rest upon the narrow ground of injury or damage to the corporation resulting from a betrayal of confidence, but upon a broader foundation of wise public policy that, for the purpose of removing all temptation, extinguishes all possibility of profit flowing from a breach of the confidence imposed by the fiduciary relation." *Durfee v. Durfee & Canning, Inc.,* 80 N.E.2d 522 (Mass. 1948).

7. In addition to informing Rosenberg, the plaintiff claims to have told various other senior Dunkin executives about the finder's fee agreement, including...Dunkin's general counsel, and...a vice president. As the cases cited in our discussion, *supra,* make clear, full disclosure must be made to a disinterested decision-maker, typically the board of directors or the shareholders. The plaintiff points out that the Dunkin code of ethics required disclosure of potential conflicts of interest to the general counsel, the controller, and the director of financial reporting. Lacking complete information in the record as to which Dunkin officers served in those posts, we will presume that, at minimum, full disclosure to Rosenberg, as chief executive officer and chairman of the board of Dunkin directors, was required of the plaintiff.

The plaintiff's disclosure here was at best half-hearted. There is no evidence, nor could it be reasonably inferred, that Geller informed Rosenberg that the one percent finder's fee agreement previously offered to Geller was still in effect, that Geller had agreed to its terms, or that he was required by the agreement to do whatever he could on Allied's behalf to effect the acquisition. It also appears from the plaintiff's deposition testimony, as well as from the context in which the plaintiff's disclosure took place, that he alluded to the earlier promise of a finder's fee as an indication of Allied's previous interest in acquiring Dunkin and as a sign that Allied's interest might be rekindled. There is nothing in the record to suggest that the plaintiff raised the subject of the finder's fee in such a manner as to apprise Dunkin that he wished to take advantage of Allied's offer and that he was seeking Dunkin's consent. Nor is there any indication that Rosenberg even heard the disclosure; we are unwilling, therefore, to allow the inference that Rosenberg's lack of response constituted acquiescence.

Accordingly, we believe that evidence of the kind of direct and informed communication that would be necessary to satisfy a fiduciary's obligation of full, fair, and contemporaneous disclosure is lacking here.

3. *The Statute of Frauds.* In light of our affirmance of the Superior Court judge's holding that the claimed agreement is unenforceable on account of public policy, we need not and do not decide the Statute of Frauds issue.

Judgments affirmed.

Notes and Questions

1. Notes

a. Goldman Sachs is a well-known investment banking firm. One of the services such firms provide to corporations is to seek out (discreetly or not) potential acquirers.

2. Reality Check

a. Why would any company want to buy Dunkin Donuts?
b. Why did the court invalidate the finder's fee agreement?
c. Did the court find that Dunkin Donuts had been damaged by Mr. Geller's actions?
d. How did Mr. Geller violate his fiduciary duties to Dunkin Donuts?

3. Suppose

a. Suppose Allied had simply paid Mr. Geller 1 percent of the acquisition price, as Mr. Rosenberg paid him $20,000, without an agreement to do so. Would Mr. Geller have been able to keep that money?
b. Suppose Dunkin Donuts had paid Mr. Geller 1 percent of the acquisition price (rather than $20,000). Would the court's analysis or result be different?
c. Suppose Dunkin Donuts had agreed in advance with Mr. Geller that it would pay him 1 percent of the acquisition price if he helped the transaction go through. Would that agreement be subject to legal attack?
d. What if the court had found that Mr. Geller had fully disclosed to Dunkin Donuts his agreement with Allied? Would the court still have invalidated the agreement?
e. If the court had found not only full disclosure by Mr. Geller but explicit approval of the finder's fee agreement by the Dunkin Donuts board, would the court's analysis or result have been different?

4. What Do You Think?

a. Do you think Allied suspected its promise to Mr. Geller would be unenforceable? If so, should that make a difference in the analysis or result of this case?

b. Are there legal, factual, or ethical differences between Dunkin Donuts' payment of $20,000 and Allied's promise of a finder's fee? If so, how should the court evaluate those differences?

c. Did Dunkin Donuts' payment to Mr. Geller create a conflict of interest for him?

d. Do you think the party challenging a conflict of interest should be required to show actual breach of the duty of loyalty?

e. Do you think the party challenging a conflict of interest should be required to show actual damage?

4. Compensation of Directors and Senior Officers

Perhaps the starkest example of director self-dealing is compensation. At common law directors could not award themselves compensation for performing their duties as directors. The theory (often backed up by legal requirements) was that directors were to be shareholders as well and thus would receive their compensation in the form of increased share value or dividends. Once the requirement of share ownership by directors fell away, the statutes were amended to permit boards of directors to provide compensation to themselves. See DGCL §141(h) and MBCA §3.02(11). While it is not uncommon for directors of closely held corporations to receive no compensation (they may be compensated either as officers, employees, or shareholders instead), directors of publicly held companies receive remuneration some would consider munificent. Six-figure compensation is not unheard of, and keep in mind that many directors of public companies are not senior executives of that company (such "inside directors" typically do not take additional compensation for serving as directors) and so spend a few hours a month, at most, in return for their compensation.

Compensation of a corporation's senior officers may also be problematic in a duty of loyalty sense. Some senior executives typically serve on the board of directors of public companies. In closely held companies, all the directors may be officers. In theory, of course, a board's approval of executive compensation should not raise a conflict of interest problem directly because directors and officers are separate people. When there is an overlap between the two groups, though, a conflict is presented. Typically a direct conflict is avoided because the inside directors abstain from voting on (and often abstain from participating in the discussion of) their own compensation. Do you think this is a sufficient solution to the conflict of interest problem? If not, what would you propose?

B. BACKGROUND AND CONTEXT

1. Is There a Duty of Good Faith?

What about the MBCA's statement in §8.30(a)(1) that directors must act "in good faith" in addition to §8.30's duty of loyalty and the requirement to use appropriate care? You will see in the shibbolethic statements of the Delaware courts that they, too, view good faith as a separate duty. That this is not unintentional is gleaned from the emphasis a few Supreme Court opinions place on the separate requirement of good faith.

If good faith is a distinct duty, what does it consist of? If it subsumes or is subsumed by the duty of loyalty or the duty of care, why is it called out separately? The drafters of the MBCA danced around this question in the Official Comment to §8.31, saying, "If a director's conduct can be successfully challenged pursuant to other clauses of subsection (a)(2) [which sets out the MBCA's standards of liability for breaching the duties of loyalty or care], there is a substantial likelihood that the conduct in question will also present an issue of good faith. . . ." After an example or two, the drafters then say, "If subsection (a)(2) included only [liability for breach of the duty of good faith], much of the conduct with which the other clauses are concerned could still be considered pursuant to the subsection, on the basis that such conduct evidenced the actor's lack of good faith." MBCA, §8.30, Official Comment.

As noted, the Delaware Supreme Court has insisted that directors are under a duty of good faith separate from the duties of loyalty and care. However, the members of the Court of Chancery are less convinced:

> Within [the] traditional duty [of loyalty] would logically rest the subsidiary requirement to act in good, rather than bad, faith toward the company and its stockholders. E.g., Eric A. Chiappinelli, *The Life and Adventures of Unocal — Part I: Moore the Marrier*, 23 Del. J. Corp. L. 85, 86 (1998) . . . (defining duty of loyalty as "the duty to act in good faith and in the company's best interest").
>
> Indeed, the very Supreme Court opinion that refers to a board's "triads [sic] of fiduciary duty [sic] — good faith, loyalty [and] due care," *Cede II*, [*Cede & Co. v. Technicolor, Inc.*, 634 A.2d 345 (Del. 1993)] equates good faith with loyalty. *Cede II*, 634 A.2d at 361: *see also* B. Ellen Taylor, *New and Unjustified Restrictions On Delaware Directors' Authority*, 21 Del J. Corp. L. 837, 881 n.234 (1996) . . . (remarking on the close relationship between good faith and loyalty in *Cede II*). In the following sentence from *Cede II*, the Supreme Court quotes its earlier opinion in *Barkan v. Amsted Industries, Inc.*, 567 A.2d 1279, 1286 (Del. 1989), but adds bracketed text to clarify meaning. The sentence, with the bracketed text emphasized, reads as follows:
>
>> [A] board's actions must be evaluated in light of relevant circumstances to determine if they were undertaken with due diligence [*care*] and good faith [*loyalty*]. If no breach of duty is found, the board's actions are entitled to the protections of the business judgment rule.
>
> *Cede II*, 634 A.2d at 368 n.36 (*quoting Barkan*, 567 A.2d at 1286) (emphases added); *see also* Taylor, *New and Unjustified Restrictions*, at 881 n.234). In *Barkan* itself, it is clear that the Supreme Court used the terms "due diligence" and "good faith" as a fresh way of referring to the "fundamental duties of care and loyalty" it discussed three sentences earlier in the same paragraph. *Barkan*, 567 A.2d at 1286. Moreover, *Cede II* contains two lengthy sections focusing on the duties of loyalty and care but has no comparable section on good faith, despite its putative equality in the triad. 634 A.2d at 361-66 (loyalty), 366-71 (due care); *see also id.* at 359 (breaking down key issues on appeal into questions of loyalty and due care).

In re Gaylord Container Corp., 753 A.2d 462, 475 n.41 (Del. Ch. 2000) (Strine, V.C.)

Does it make any earthly difference whether good faith is a separate requirement? It may, because a separate standard gives lawyers another opportunity to argue around unfavorable (for their clients) interpretations of the traditional duties of loyalty and care. Further, as we'll see below, legal doctrines that ameliorate potential director liability may ameliorate only liability for violation of the duty of care or loyalty and may not address a duty of good faith.

C. TERMS OF ART IN THIS CHAPTER

Conflict of interest   Duty of loyalty   Self-dealing
Corporate opportunity

12

The Duty of Care of Directors (and Officers)

We have seen that corporate directors and officers have an obligation to be single-minded in their actions. They must put the best interest of the corporation ahead of all other considerations. What about a director who genuinely intends to act in the best interest of the corporation but who makes absolutely no effort to find out anything about the corporation? Or, who makes no effort to find out anything about a proposed corporate action? If such directors exist (and are not simply phantasms, apparitions, spectres, wraiths, figments of a law professor's underactive imagination) have they met their duty of loyalty? If not, is it meaningful to describe the duty of loyalty's tenor as being solely concerned with directors' intention to benefit the corporation? How else would you describe the duty's requirements? On the other hand, if the duty of loyalty is met by well-intentioned but uninformed directors, is the corporation sufficiently protected from director-inflicted harm? Do we need to impose an additional duty on directors to become informed about the corporation and proposed corporate actions? As you may have guessed from the new chapter title, directors and officers are under a duty to be informed and this duty, the *duty of care*, is usually considered to be distinct from the duty of loyalty.

A. THE CURRENT SETTING

We start with the MBCA's formulation of the duty of care in §8.30, which was revised in 1998. The case that follows was decided under the prior formulation, which is substantially identical to the Idaho statute quoted in the opinion.

Crown v. Hawkins Co., Ltd.
910 P.2d 786 (Idaho App. 1996)

WALTERS, C.J.

Wayne Crown, Clark Bean and Steve Bean (the "Growers") appeal from a district court judgment which held that William Nungester did not breach any duties he owed as a director of the warehouse where the Growers deposited their beans, and that Nungester's actions were not the proximate cause of the Growers' injury. For the reasons stated below, we affirm.

FACTUAL BACKGROUND

Hawkins Co., Ltd. (the "warehouse") began business as a corporation in 1978. A warehouse that had existed prior to incorporation was purchased by Robert Blass, Jerry Hawkins and William Nungester, each of whom . . . were issued one-third of the shares of stock in the corporation. The board of directors was composed of Blass, Hawkins and Nungester. Hawkins was president and general manager, and was in charge of operating the warehouse from the corporation's inception until the warehouse's closure. Blass and Nungester were not active in the day-to-day management of the warehouse.

During the operation of the warehouse, Nungester was an attorney practicing with the law firm of Hepworth, Nungester and Lezamiz. Other than occasionally preparing the annual statement for filing with the Secretary of State, Nungester provided no legal services or legal representation for the warehouse.

In addition to operating under the Bonded Warehouse Law, . . . the warehouse acted as a broker in selling beans to third party wholesalers. Deposited beans remained in the ownership of the depositors until the beans were sold to the warehouse, at which point they became company-owned beans. The purchase of beans from the depositors throughout the period at issue was generally conducted by Hawkins. Hawkins had no authority to sell the beans without the depositors' approval.

By April 1987, the warehouse began experiencing a cash flow shortage. In August or September of the same year, First Security Bank discovered that Blass and Hawkins had established a check kiting scheme in an attempt to cover the warehouse's insufficient cash flow. Nungester first learned of these activities from First Security Bank who had discovered that approximately 2.2 million dollars in check kiting had occurred. Once informed, Nungester instructed both Blass and Hawkins to discontinue the practice, which they did. Nungester made no further inquiries, and he did not inform any authorities of the scheme.

From 1986 through 1988, Nungester made several checks payable to the warehouse for the purchase of beans, although he never actually took possession. [Certified Public Accountant Tom] Schabot noted this activity during his 1987 certified audit and recharacterized the purchases as loans by Nungester to the warehouse. Subsequent to these activities, additional loans were also made to the warehouse by various individuals including Nungester. These activities provided temporary cash flow to the warehouse.

Near the end of the summer in 1987, Jerre Hills was employed by the warehouse to replace, in part, Hawkins as a broker. Hills reviewed the Grower Lot Sheets. Every grower who had deposited beans with the warehouse had a sheet prepared for each variety of beans for the year that the beans were deposited. After reviewing the Grower Lot Sheets, Hills discovered that several of the sheets had printed on them negative balances which indicated that more beans were sold on that specific account than were on deposit at the warehouse. To cover these negative balances, Hawkins had altered the warehouse's copies of the Grower Lot Sheets so the books would balance. Upon seeing these balances, Hills went to Nungester's home and informed him of the situation. Nungester confronted Hawkins with this information and the explanations provided by Hawkins regarding the negative balances were to Nungester's satisfaction. Nungester did not investigate the matter further.

In 1988, several irregularities at the warehouse were discovered. Interim financial statements prepared by Schabot in January of 1988 revealed that the accounts receivable were large and were increasing. Hawkins had neither billed the accounts, nor had he charged any interest on them. In his audit letter, Schabot recommended to the board that these accounts be billed. In response, the board directed Hawkins to bill and collect the accounts receivable. The board was not aware, however, that Hawkins purposely failed to undertake collection of some of the accounts.

In May of 1988, Hawkins requested that the DOA [Idaho Department of Agriculture] inspect the warehouse. Prior to the inspection, Hawkins had several bean boxes filled with culls and dirt moved into the warehouse. David Sparrow, an inspector with the DOA, reviewed the warehouse records and counted the physical inventory. The inspection found a shortage of at least 6,475 sacks of pinto beans, which was explained by Hawkins to the DOA's satisfaction. The fact that many of the boxes contained culls and dirt was not discovered.

By September 18, 1988, Schabot had begun reviewing the warehouse's records again. He first contacted Nungester on September 29, 1988, to inform him that problems existed with the audit. Schabot told Nungester that he could not reconcile the physical inventory count with the warehouse's books. Schabot and Nungester met with Hawkins. Hawkins informed them that he could provide documentation to reconcile the shortage. While waiting for the documentation from Hawkins, neither Schabot nor Nungester investigated the matter further, and the warehouse continued to receive the 1988 bean crops. On or about November 14, 1988, Hawkins collapsed at the warehouse and was hospitalized at a mental health facility in Boise. The documentation to reconcile the shortages was never obtained.

On November 22, 1988, Nungester called the DOA because of the unreconcilable shortage. On the same day, the warehouse was placed under the supervision of the Idaho Bureau of Warehouse Control. It was determined that a shortage of 110,000 hundred weight of beans existed. The 1988 crop of 204,000 hundred weight remained at the warehouse upon its closure. The shortage was written off, and on January 6, 1989, Hawkins Co., Ltd., filed a Chapter 11 business reorganization plan. . . .

During this time, Nungester relied on the information provided to him from the DOA, Schabot and Hawkins regarding the accounts receivable, books and records, and cash shortages. He did not inspect the records himself nor did he personally go to the warehouse to review matters with the employees. Unbeknownst to Nungester, Hawkins had informed the employees not to discuss any business with Nungester and that, if Nungester made any inquiries, to direct him to speak to Hawkins.

PROCEDURAL BACKGROUND

The plaintiffs, representing approximately 180 bean growers [the "Growers"], brought the action against the defendants for the bean shortage. The original action in this case was brought against Hawkins Co., Ltd.; the Idaho Department of Agriculture; . . . and against the directors of the warehouse: Blass, Hawkins and Nungester.

All of the defendants but Nungester were dismissed. Hawkins Co., Ltd., filed a petition in bankruptcy and, pursuant to a stipulation, was dismissed from this suit. . . . [T]he DOA was dismissed from the action because the Growers had failed to comply with the Idaho Torts Claims Act's requirement that they first present their claim to the governmental defendant. Blass filed a Chapter 11 bankruptcy and was discharged by the bankruptcy court. [T]he action against Blass in this case was dismissed. Hawkins also filed bankruptcy and was discharged.

The claim against the remaining defendant, Nungester, is based on the theory of negligence, brought by the Growers pursuant to the Bonded Warehouse Law. The complaint centered on the duty, if any, that Nungester, as a director of the warehouse, owed to the Growers; whether Nungester breached that duty; and whether the breach was the proximate cause of the Growers' injury. Upon stipulation of the parties, the liability and damage issues were bifurcated. The issue of damage was to be tried at a later date.

With regard to the liability issue, the district court held, after a bench trial, that Nungester was not negligent in his duties as a director. The Growers have appealed from the judgment and the court's dismissal of the Growers' pretrial motion requesting disqualification of Nungester's counsel.

DISCUSSION

B. Director's Duties Pursuant to I.C. §30-1-35

Decisions of the Idaho Supreme Court establish that the directors of a warehouse corporation may be personally liable to depositors for losses caused by the directors' negligence. A director's fiduciary duties are provided, in pertinent part, by Idaho Code §30-1-35 as follows:

> A director shall perform his duties as a director, . . . in good faith, in a manner he reasonably believes to be in the best interests of the corporation, and with such care as an ordinarily prudent person in a like position would use under similar circumstances. In performing his duties, a director shall be entitled to rely on information, opinions, reports or statements, including financial statements and other financial data, in each case prepared or presented by:
>   (a) One (1) or more officers or employees of the corporation whom the director reasonably believes to be reliable and competent in the matters presented,
>   (b) Counsel, public accountants or other persons as to matters which the director reasonably believes to be within such person's professional or expert competence. . . .

The question whether Nungester's actions constituted proper performance of his duties as a director pursuant to I.C. §30-1-35 is a question of fact, which must be determined in each case in view of all of the circumstances.

The Growers assert that pursuant to Section 30-1-35, the term "duties" includes independent duties, which means that once a director has been placed on inquiry notice, he or she must investigate the issues, and cannot rely solely on reports, inspections and information provided by certain experts once such notice has arisen. The Growers submit that if Nungester had adequately investigated the problems which arose, Hawkins' acts would have been stopped and the Growers' losses would have been significantly less if not altogether eliminated. The Growers maintain that Nungester's failure to perform these duties was the proximate cause of their injury.

The Growers argue that Nungester received notice that the warehouse was experiencing problems on several occasions. These occasions included the following points in time: (1) from September 1986 through September 1987, when Nungester infused over $300,000 dollars in the warehouse to provide additional cash flow; (2) during the summer of 1987, when Blass and Hawkins were caught kiting checks for over 2.2

million dollars to improve the warehouse's liquidity; and (3) during September 1987, when Hills discovered negative balances on the Grower Lot Sheets and informed Nungester of the problem. The Growers contend that Nungester's actions in response to these notices were insufficient. Rather than relying on Hawkins' explanations and assurances, the Growers submit that Nungester should have reviewed documents other than those prepared by Schabot and the DOA, that he should have discussed the issues with warehouse employees and that he should have followed up to ensure that the auditor's recommendations were being implemented.

Nungester responds that, as a director, he had the right to rely on the audits and inspection reports as allowed by I.C. §30-1-35 because each were prepared by qualified experts. He states that from 1978 through July 31, 1987, none of the reports or inspections revealed any commodity shortages nor did they uncover any irregularities in the warehouse's bookkeeping methods. Nungester argues that if the accountants could not uncover any shortages, he surely would not have been able to discover them given his lack of expertise in accounting. Nungester further claims that once problems were brought to his attention, he addressed them. For example, when Hills discovered the negative balances, Nungester and the DOA inspector discussed the issue with Hawkins. Hawkins provided an explanation which the auditors found reasonable. Furthermore, Nungester testified that once he became aware of the check kiting scheme, he requested a meeting between Hawkins, a bank officer with First Security Bank and himself, during which he instructed Hawkins to stop all check kiting activities. Hawkins agreed, and no additional problems were experienced by the warehouse with regard to that activity.

As a director, Nungester attended directors' meetings, reviewed financial statements and assisted in the formation of the warehouse's policies. He did not possess any specific skills in the day-to-day operation of the warehouse or in the brokeraging of commodities. Hawkins, who did have experience in the bean business, was retained by the directors to be president and manager in charge of the warehouse's day-to-day operations. As a director with no specific skills in this industry, Nungester relied upon the information provided to him by Hawkins and the opinions, reports, and inspections of Schabot and the DOA.

Based upon this evidence, the district court found that Nungester performed his duties as a director in good faith and in a manner he reasonably believed was in the best interest of the warehouse. The court concluded that Nungester used such care as an ordinary prudent person in a like position would use under similar circumstances. Further, having found that Nungester was not negligent and did not breach any duty owed to the Growers, the district court concluded that none of Nungester's actions proximately caused or contributed to any damage suffered by the Growers. The district court's findings are based upon substantial evidence and are not clearly erroneous. Because we uphold the district court's findings and conclusions on the question of the lack of negligence, we need not address the Growers' arguments on the issue of proximate cause.

Next, the Growers argue that as a lawyer, Nungester should be held to a higher standard of care as a director than I.C. §30-1-35 requires. Nungester's actions, they submit, should be compared to that of an "ordinary prudent person in a like position." The Growers contend that the phrase "like position" means that if a director is a lawyer, that director is obligated to use his or her lawyering skills in the performance of the directorship.

We disagree. The fact that Nungester was a lawyer during his directorship does not increase, change or otherwise modify the duty he owed to the warehouse.

CONCLUSION

For the reasons stated, we affirm the district court's judgment....

LANSING and PERRY, JJ., concur.

Notes and Questions

1. Notes

a. A *check kiting* scheme is one in which the perpetrator has control over checking accounts at different banks. The key to the scheme's success is the time lag (or *float*) between the time one bank credits an account for a deposited check and the time the paying bank debits the account on which the check is drawn. The perpetrator deposits a check drawn on account *A* in account *B*, both of which he or she controls. The amount of the check is greater than the balance in account *A* so the check would ordinarily be dishonored by the paying bank. But, the perpetrator deposits in account *A* a check drawn on account *B* to cover the first check before it is dishonored. This second check, though, is also greater than the balance in account *B*. The perpetrator continues to deposit checks to the accounts in this fashion, which increases the ostensible balance in each account. While this kiting is taking place, the perpetrator can withdraw cash from each of the accounts, which will be covered by later illicit checks. Eventually, of course, the scheme collapses when one bank or another discovers the false deposits.

b. It appears that the warehouse corporation was the victim of a classic *skimming* scheme. The essence of a skim is that the perpetrator is able to divert money that should go to the business before that money is ever recorded within the business. Because the money is never recorded by the business, a skim is difficult to detect. Skims can occur in two fundamental ways. First, in a *sales skim*, the perpetrator can sell company products and divert the proceeds. In that instance the company's inventory will decrease without a corresponding increase in revenue. Second, in a *receivables skim*, the perpetrator can divert money customers are paying to the business. In that setting the company's accounts receivable (i.e., the list of customers and the amounts they owe) will increase. In either type of skim one of the perpetrator's primary difficulties is concealing the skim for any length of time. To hide a sales skim, the perpetrator can falsify the inventory records to show that inventory that has really been sold by the perpetrator is still in the company's possession. To hide a receivable skim, the perpetrator can, among other things, credit other company revenue to the accounts of the customers whose payments have been skimmed, or indicate that those accounts are uncollectible, causing the company to eliminate (i.e., write off) the balance owed as "bad debts." In either kind of skim, the perpetrator can run a check kiting scheme with the company bank account to create the illusion that the company has received the appropriate amount of cash.

c. The DGCL does not contain a statutory statement of directors' duty of care. However, Delaware case law describes the duty of care as,

> The duty of the directors of a company to act on an informed basis, as that term has been defined by this Court numerous times, forms the duty of care....

[W]e have defined a board's duty of care in a variety of settings. For example, we have stated that a director's duty of care requires a director to take an active and direct role in the context of a sale of a company from beginning to end. In a merger or sale, we have stated that the director's duty of care requires a director, before voting on a proposed plan of merger or sale, to inform himself [or herself] and his [or her] fellow directors of all material information that is reasonably available to them.

Cede & Co. v. Technicolor, Inc., 634 A.2d 345, 367 (Del. 1993) (Horsey, J.)

2. Reality Check

a. How did Mr. Hawkins's actions result in the warehouse's insolvency?

b. What part of the statute was most at issue?

c. Why did the court hold that Mr. Nungester's actions were appropriate? Do you agree?

d. How large a role did Mr. Nungester's reliance on others play in his vindication?

e. Why doesn't the fact that Mr. Nungester is a lawyer heighten his potential liability?

3. Suppose

a. Suppose this case were decided under the current version of §8.30. Would the court's analysis or the result be different?

b. Suppose Mr. Nungester had been an accountant rather than a lawyer. Would the court's analysis or the result have been different?

c. Imagine that Mr. Nungester had been actively involved in the warehouse's day-to-day management. Would the court's analysis or the result have been different?

4. What Do You Think?

a. Is the current version of MBCA §8.30 better than the prior version?

b. Notice that one change between the MBCA versions is that the requirement to act as an *ordinarily prudent person* would act has been deleted. Chancellor Allen discussed the policy reason behind this kind of change:

> It is doubtful that we want business men and women to be encouraged to make decisions as hypothetical persons of *ordinary* judgment and prudence might. The corporate form gets its utility in large part from its ability to allow diversified investors to accept greater investment risk. If those in charge of the corporation are to be adjudged personally liable for losses on the basis of a substantive judgment based upon what an persons of ordinary or average judgment and average risk assessment talent regard as "prudent," "sensible" or even "rational," such persons will have a strong incentive at the margin to authorize less risky investment projects.

In re Caremark International Inc. Derivative Litigation, 698 A.2d, 959, 967 n.16 (Del. Ch. 1996) (Allen, Ch.)

Do you think that prudence ought to be an element of the duty of care?

c. Most courts that have considered the question have held that the duty of care, whether embodied in a statute or in common law, imposes what is called a "unitary standard" of conduct. That is, the standard is a minimum to which all directors will be held, even when a particular director is incapable of meeting that standard. The Official Comment to the MBCA describes these attributes as "common sense, practical wisdom, and informed judgment." See MBCA §8.30 Official Comment. But on the other hand, directors who have specialized skills germane to the corporation and its business, will be held to a higher standard of care that reflects what a reasonable director *with those skills* would do. Do you think that this asymmetry makes sense?

d. Should the duty of care for a particular director depend upon whether that director is actively involved in the corporation's business?

5. You Draft It

a. Draft a statute that appropriately describes a director's duty of care. The MBCA versions (current and pre-1998) are set out below:

CURRENT §8.30

The members of the board of directors..., when becoming informed in connection with their decision-making function or devoting attention to their oversight function, shall discharge their duties with the care that a person in a like position would reasonably believe appropriate under similar circumstances.

PRE-1998 §8.30

A director shall perform his duties as a director,... with such care as an ordinarily prudent person in a like position would use under similar circumstances.

b. Accountants are sometimes referred to (usually derisively) as bean counters. Note also that the surname of two of the plaintiffs is Bean. Draft a humorous, yet tasteful, joke that includes as many of the facts of *Crown* as possible.

The most intuitive settings for the duty of care are when the board of directors is contemplating a particular action or course of action. Keep in mind that these settings are analytically identical regardless of whether the board's actions are *initiated by* the board or are *in reaction to* developments from inside or outside the corporation. Remember, as well, that a board "acts" for purposes of its fiduciary duties when it decides to take no action.

Can directors violate their duty of care when they do not "act" at all? That is, are there instances when the board's failure to consider any action may constitute failing to act "on an informed basis" while possessing "all material information reasonably available"? The following case discusses this question.

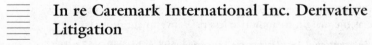

In re Caremark International Inc. Derivative Litigation

698 A.2d 959 (Del. Ch. 1996)

ALLEN, CH.

Pending is a motion pursuant to Chancery Rule 23.1 to approve as fair and reasonable a proposed settlement of a consolidated derivative action on behalf of Caremark International, Inc. ("Caremark"). The suit involves claims that the members of Caremark's board of directors (the "Board") breached their fiduciary duty of care to Caremark in connection with alleged violations by Caremark employees of federal and state laws and regulations applicable to health care providers. As a result of the alleged violations, Caremark was subject to an extensive four year investigation by the United States Department of Health and Human Services and the Department of Justice. In 1994 Caremark was charged in an indictment with multiple felonies. It thereafter entered into a number of agreements with the Department of Justice and others. Those agreements included a plea agreement in which Caremark pleaded guilty to a single felony of mail fraud and agreed to pay civil and criminal fines. Subsequently, Caremark agreed to make reimbursements to various private and public parties. In all, the payments that Caremark has been required to make total approximately $250 million.

This suit was filed in 1994, purporting to seek on behalf of the company recovery of these losses from the individual defendants who constitute the board of directors of Caremark. The parties now propose that it be settled and, after notice to Caremark shareholders, a hearing on the fairness of the proposal was held on August 16, 1996.

A motion of this type requires the court to assess the strengths and weaknesses of the claims asserted in light of the discovery record and to evaluate the fairness and adequacy of the consideration offered to the corporation in exchange for the release of all claims made or arising from the facts alleged. The ultimate issue then is whether the proposed settlement appears to be fair to the corporation and its absent shareholders.

Legally, evaluation of the central claim made entails consideration of the legal standard governing a board of directors' obligation to supervise or monitor corporate performance. For the reasons set forth below I conclude, in light of the discovery record, that there is a very low probability that it would be determined that the directors of Caremark breached any duty to appropriately monitor and supervise the enterprise. Indeed the record tends to show an active consideration by Caremark management and its Board of the Caremark structures and programs that ultimately led to the company's indictment and to the large financial losses incurred in the settlement of those claims. It does not tend to show knowing or intentional violation of law. Neither the fact that the Board, although advised by lawyers and accountants, did not accurately predict the severe consequences to the company that would ultimately follow from the deployment by the company of the strategies and practices that ultimately led to this liability, nor the scale of the liability, gives rise to an inference of breach of any duty imposed by corporation law upon the directors of Caremark.

I. BACKGROUND

During the relevant period Caremark was involved in two main health care business segments, providing patient care and managed care services. As part of its patient care business, which accounted for the majority of Caremark's revenues, Caremark provided alternative site health care services, including infusion therapy, growth hormone therapy, HIV/AIDS-related treatments and hemophilia therapy. Caremark's managed care services included prescription drug programs and the operation of multi-specialty group practices.

A. Events Prior to the Government Investigation

A substantial part of the revenues generated by Caremark's businesses is derived from third party payments, insurers, and Medicare and Medicaid reimbursement programs. The latter source of payments are subject to the terms of the Anti-Referral Payments Law ("ARPL") which prohibits health care providers from paying any form of remuneration to induce the referral of Medicare or Medicaid patients. Caremark entered into a variety of agreements with hospitals, physicians, and health care providers for advice and services, as well as distribution agreements with drug manufacturers.... Specifically, Caremark did have a practice of entering into contracts for services (e.g., consultation agreements and research grants) with physicians at least some of whom prescribed or recommended services or products that Caremark provided to Medicare recipients and other patients. Such contracts were not prohibited by the ARPL but they obviously raised a possibility of unlawful "kickbacks."

As early as 1989, Caremark... issued an internal "Guide to Contractual Relationships" ("Guide") to govern its employees in entering into contracts with physicians and hospitals. The Guide tended to be reviewed annually by lawyers and updated. Each version of the Guide stated as Caremark's and its predecessor's policy that no payments would be made in exchange for or to induce patient referrals. But what one might deem a prohibited *quid pro quo* was not always clear. Due to a scarcity of court decisions interpreting the ARPL, however, Caremark repeatedly publicly stated that there was uncertainty concerning Caremark's interpretation of the law.

To clarify the scope of the ARPL, the United States Department of Health and Human Services ("HHS") issued "safe harbor" regulations in July 1991 stating conditions under which financial relationships between health care service providers and patient referral sources, such as physicians, would *not* violate the ARPL. Caremark contends that the narrowly drawn regulations gave limited guidance as to the legality of many of the agreements used by Caremark that did not fall within the safe-harbor. Caremark's predecessor, however, amended many of its standard forms of agreement with health care providers and revised the Guide in an apparent attempt to comply with the new regulations.

B. Government Investigation and Related Litigation

In August 1991, the HHS Office of the Inspector General ("OIG") initiated an investigation of Caremark.... In March 1992, the Department of Justice ("DOJ") joined the OIG investigation and separate investigations were commenced by several additional federal and state agencies.

C. Caremark's Response to the Investigation

During the relevant period, Caremark had approximately 7,000 employees and ninety branch operations. It had a decentralized management structure. By May 1991, however, Caremark asserts that it had begun making attempts to centralize its management structure in order to increase supervision over its branch operations.

The first action taken by management, as a result of the initiation of the OIG investigation, was an announcement that as of October 1, 1991, Caremark... would no longer pay management fees to physicians for services to Medicare and Medicaid patients. Despite this decision, Caremark asserts that its management, pursuant to advice, did not believe that such payments were illegal under the existing laws and regulations.

During this period, Caremark's Board took several additional steps consistent with an effort to assure compliance with company policies concerning the ARPL and the contractual forms in the Guide. In April 1992, Caremark published a fourth revised version of its Guide apparently designed to assure that its agreements either complied with the ARPL and regulations or excluded Medicare and Medicaid patients altogether. Although there is evidence that inside and outside counsel had advised Caremark's directors that their contracts were in accord with the law, Caremark recognized that some uncertainty respecting the correct interpretation of the law existed.

Throughout the period of the government investigations, Caremark had an internal audit plan designed to assure compliance with business and ethics policies. In addition, Caremark employed Price Waterhouse as its outside auditor. On February 8, 1993, the Ethics Committee of Caremark's Board received and reviewed an outside auditors report by Price Waterhouse which concluded that there were no material weaknesses in Caremark's control structure. Despite the positive findings of Price Waterhouse, however, on April 20, 1993, the Audit & Ethics Committee adopted a new internal audit charter requiring a comprehensive review of compliance policies and the compilation of an employee ethics handbook concerning such policies. The Board appears to have been informed about this project and other efforts to assure compliance with the law.

During 1993, Caremark took several additional steps which appear to have been aimed at increasing management supervision. These steps included new policies requiring local branch managers to secure home office approval for all disbursements under agreements with health care providers and to certify compliance with the ethics program. In addition, the chief financial officer was appointed to serve as Caremark's compliance officer. In 1994, a fifth revised Guide was published.

D. Federal Indictments Against Caremark and Officers

On August 4, 1994, a federal grand jury in Minnesota issued a 47 page indictment charging Caremark, two of its officers (not the firm's chief officer), an individual who had been a sales employee of Genentech, Inc., and David R. Brown, a physician practicing in Minneapolis, with violating the ARPL over a lengthy period. According to the indictment, over $1.1 million had been paid to Brown to induce him to distribute Protropin, a human growth hormone drug marketed by Caremark.[6] The substantial payments involved started, according to the allegations of the indictment, in 1986 and continued through 1993. Some payments were "in the guise of research grants," and others were "consulting agreements." The indictment charged, for example, that Dr. Brown performed virtually none of the consulting functions described in his 1991 agreement with Caremark, but was nevertheless neither required to return the money he had received nor precluded from receiving future funding from Caremark. In addition the indictment charged that Brown received from Caremark payments of staff and office expenses, including telephone answering services and fax rental expenses.

Caremark denied any wrongdoing relating to the indictment and believed that the OIG investigation would have a favorable outcome. Management reiterated the grounds for its view that the contracts were in compliance with law.

Subsequently, five stockholder derivative actions were filed in this court and consolidated into this action. The original complaint, dated August 5, 1994, alleged, in relevant part, that Caremark's directors breached their duty of care by failing adequately to supervise the conduct of Caremark employees, or institute corrective measures, thereby exposing Caremark to fines and liability.

E. Settlement Negotiations

Caremark began settlement negotiations with federal and state government entities in May 1995. In return for a guilty plea to a single count of mail fraud by the

---

6. In addition to prescribing Protropin, Dr. Brown had been receiving research grants from Caremark as well as payments for services under a consulting agreement for several years before and after the investigation. According to an undated document from an unknown source, Dr. Brown and six other researchers had been providing patient referrals to Caremark valued at $6.55 for each $1 of research money they received.

corporation, the payment of a criminal fine, the payment of substantial civil damages, and cooperation with further federal investigations on matters relating to the OIG investigation, the government entities agreed to negotiate a settlement that would permit Caremark to continue participating in Medicare and Medicaid programs. On June 15, 1995, the Board approved a settlement ("Government Settlement Agreement") with the DOJ, OIG, U.S. Veterans Administration, U.S. Federal Employee Health Benefits Program, federal Civilian Health and Medical Program of the Uniformed Services, and related state agencies in all fifty states and the District of Columbia. No senior officers or directors were charged with wrongdoing in the Government Settlement Agreement or in any of the prior indictments. In fact, . . . the United States stipulated that *no senior executive of Caremark participated in, condoned, or was willfully ignorant of wrongdoing in connection with the home infusion business practices.*

Settlement negotiations between the parties in this action . . . resulted in . . . the execution of the Stipulation and Agreement of Compromise and Settlement on June 28, 1995, which is the subject of this action.[13] The MOU, approved by the Board on June 15, 1995, required the Board to adopt several resolutions, discussed below, and to create a new compliance committee. The Compliance and Ethics Committee has been reporting to the Board in accord with its newly specified duties.

II. LEGAL PRINCIPLES . . .

B. Directors' Duties to Monitor Corporate Operations

The complaint charges the director defendants with breach of their duty of attention or care in connection with the on-going operation of the corporation's business. The claim is that the directors allowed a situation to develop and continue which exposed the corporation to enormous legal liability and that in so doing they violated a duty to be active monitors of corporate performance. The complaint thus does not charge either director self-dealing or the more difficult loyalty-type problems arising from cases of suspect director motivation, such as entrenchment or sale of control contexts. The theory here advanced is possibly the most difficult theory in corporation law upon which a plaintiff might hope to win a judgment.

1. POTENTIAL LIABILITY FOR DIRECTORIAL DECISIONS

Director liability for a breach of the duty to exercise appropriate attention may, in theory, arise in two distinct contexts. First, such liability may be said to follow *from a board decision* that results in a loss because that decision was ill advised or "negligent." Second, liability to the corporation for a loss may be said to arise from an *unconsidered failure of the board to act* in circumstances in which due attention would, arguably, have prevented the loss. What should be understood, . . . is that compliance with a director's duty of care can never appropriately be judicially determined by reference to *the content of the board decision* that leads to a corporate loss, apart from consideration of the good faith *or* rationality of the process employed. That is, whether a judge or jury considering the matter after the fact, believes a decision substantively wrong, or degrees of wrong extending through "stupid" to "egregious" or "irrational," provides no ground for director liability, so long as the court determines that the process

---

13. Plaintiffs' initial proposal had both a monetary component, requiring Caremark's director-officers to relinquish stock options, and a remedial component, requiring management to adopt and implement several compliance related measures. The monetary component was subsequently eliminated.

employed was either rational or employed in *a good faith* effort to advance corporate interests.

Indeed, one wonders on what moral basis might shareholders attack a *good faith* business decision of a director as "unreasonable" or "irrational." Where a director *in fact exercises a good faith effort to be informed and to exercise appropriate judgment,* he or she should be deemed to satisfy fully the duty of attention. If the shareholders thought themselves entitled to some other quality of judgment than such a director produces in the good faith exercise of the powers of office, then the shareholders should have elected other directors.

2. LIABILITY FOR FAILURE TO MONITOR

The second class of cases . . . entail circumstances in which a loss eventuates not from a decision but from unconsidered inaction. Most of the decisions that a corporation, acting through its human agents, makes are, of course, not the subject of director attention. Legally, the board itself will be required only to authorize the most significant corporate acts or transactions: mergers, changes in capital structure, fundamental changes in business, appointment and compensation of the CEO, etc. As the facts of this case graphically demonstrate, ordinary business decisions that are made by officers and employees deeper in the interior of the organization can, however, vitally affect the welfare of the corporation and its ability to achieve its various strategic and financial goals. [W]hat is the board's responsibility with respect to the organization and monitoring of the enterprise to assure that the corporation functions within the law to achieve its purposes?

Modernly this question has been given special importance by an increasing tendency, especially under federal law, to employ the criminal law to assure corporate compliance with external legal requirements, including environmental, financial, employee and product safety as well as assorted other health and safety regulations. The [Federal Sentencing] Guidelines offer powerful incentives for corporations today to have in place compliance programs to detect violations of law, promptly to report violations to appropriate public officials when discovered, and to take prompt, voluntary remedial efforts.

I start with the recognition that in recent years the Delaware Supreme Court has made it clear . . . the seriousness with which the corporation law views the role of the corporate board. Secondly, I note the elementary fact that relevant and timely *information* is an essential predicate for satisfaction of the board's supervisory and monitoring role under Section 141 of the Delaware General Corporation Law. Thirdly, I note the potential impact of the federal organizational sentencing guidelines on any business organization. Any rational person attempting in good faith to meet an organizational governance responsibility would be bound to take into account this development and the enhanced penalties and the opportunities for reduced sanctions that it offers.

In light of these developments, it would, in my opinion, be a mistake to conclude that . . . corporate boards may satisfy their obligation to be reasonably informed concerning the corporation, without assuring themselves that information and reporting systems exist in the organization that are reasonably designed to provide to senior management and to the board itself timely, accurate information sufficient to allow management and the board, each within its scope, to reach informed judgments concerning both the corporation's compliance with law and its business performance.

Obviously the level of detail that is appropriate for such an information system is a question of business judgment. And obviously too, no rationally designed information and reporting system will remove the possibility that the corporation will violate laws or regulations, or that senior officers or directors may nevertheless sometimes be misled or otherwise fail reasonably to detect acts material to the corporation's compliance with the law. But it is important that the board exercise a good faith judgment that the corporation's information and reporting system is in concept and design adequate to assure the board that appropriate information will come to its attention in a timely manner as a matter of ordinary operations, so that it may satisfy its responsibility.

Thus, I am of the view that a director's obligation includes a duty to attempt in good faith to assure that a corporate information and reporting system, which the board concludes is adequate, exists, and that failure to do so under some circumstances may, in theory at least, render a director liable for losses caused by non-compliance with applicable legal standards. I now turn to an analysis of the claims asserted with this concept of the directors' duty of care, as a duty satisfied in part by assurance of adequate information flows to the board, in mind.

III. ANALYSIS OF THIRD AMENDED COMPLAINT AND SETTLEMENT

A. The Claims
1. KNOWING VIOLATION OF STATUTE

Concerning the possibility that the Caremark directors knew of violations of law, none of the documents submitted for review, nor any of the deposition transcripts appear to provide evidence of it. Certainly the Board understood that the company had entered into a variety of contracts with physicians, researchers, and health care providers and it was understood that some of these contracts were with persons who had prescribed treatments that Caremark participated in providing. The board was informed that the company's reimbursement for patient care was frequently from government funded sources and that such services were subject to the ARPL. But the Board appears to have been informed by experts that the company's practices while contestable, were lawful. There is no evidence that reliance on such reports was not reasonable. Thus, this case presents no occasion to apply a principle to the effect that knowingly causing the corporation to violate a criminal statute constitutes a breach of a director's fiduciary duty. It is not clear that the Board knew the detail found, for example, in the indictments arising from the Company's payments. But, of course, the duty to act in good faith to be informed cannot be thought to require directors to possess detailed information about all aspects of the operation of the enterprise. Such a requirement would simply be inconsistent with the scale and scope of efficient organization size in this technological age.

2. FAILURE TO MONITOR

Since it does appear that the Board was to some extent unaware of the activities that led to liability, I turn to a consideration of the other potential avenue to director liability that the pleadings take: director inattention or "negligence."

[I]nsofar as I am able to tell on this record, the corporation's information systems appear to have represented a good faith attempt to be informed of relevant facts. If the directors did not know the specifics of the activities that lead to the indictments, they cannot be faulted.

The liability that eventuated in this instance was huge. But the fact that it resulted from a violation of criminal law alone does not create a breach of fiduciary duty by directors. The record at this stage does not support the conclusion that the defendants either lacked good faith in the exercise of their monitoring responsibilities or conscientiously permitted a known violation of law by the corporation to occur. The claims asserted against them must be viewed at this stage as extremely weak.

B. The Consideration for Release of Claim

The proposed settlement provides very modest benefits. Under the settlement agreement, plaintiffs have been given express assurances that Caremark will have a more centralized, active supervisory system in the future. Specifically, the settlement mandates duties to be performed by the newly named Compliance and Ethics Committee on an ongoing basis and increases the responsibility for monitoring compliance with the law at the lower levels of management. In adopting the resolutions required under the settlement, Caremark has further clarified its policies concerning the prohibition of providing remuneration for referrals. These appear to be positive consequences of the settlement of the claims brought by the plaintiffs, even if they are not highly significant. Nonetheless, given the weakness of the plaintiffs' claims the proposed settlement appears to be an adequate, reasonable, and beneficial outcome for all of the parties. Thus, the proposed settlement will be approved.

Notes and Questions

1. Notes

a. Note the distinction between an obligation to follow up on information that comes to a director's attention that suggests the possibility of wrongdoing by the corporation or its agents and an obligation to establish, and monitor the efficacy of, a system of ensuring that sufficient information about the corporation is brought to the directors' attention. *Crown* deals with the first setting; *Caremark* the second.

b. The Federal Sentencing Guidelines were amended in November 2004, in part to be consonant with the requirements imposed by the Sarbanes-Oxley Act of 2002 and SEC rules. A corporation that is convicted of a federal crime may receive more favorable sentencing treatment "[i]f the offense occurred despite an effective program to prevent and detect violations of law." U.S. Sentencing Guidelines Manual §8C2.5(f). This program is further elaborated in the Guidelines:

> To have an effective compliance and ethics program, . . . an organization shall—
> (1) Exercise due diligence to prevent and detect criminal conduct; and
> (2) Otherwise promote an organizational culture that encourages ethical conduct and a commitment to compliance with the law.
> Such compliance and ethics program shall be reasonably designed, implemented, and enforced so that the program is generally effective in preventing and detecting criminal conduct. The failure to prevent or detect the instant offense does not necessarily mean that the program is not generally effective in preventing and detecting criminal conduct.
>
> **U.S. Sentencing Guidelines Manual §8B2.1**

c. The MBCA conceives of the duty of care as encompassing an obligation to oversee the corporation's actions, which is functionally similar to the obligation imposed in *Caremark*. Compare MBCA §§8.30 and 8.31(a), Official Comments.

2. Reality Check

a. What was the procedural setting for this opinion? Do you think that setting made a difference in Chancellor Allen's approach to the facts or legal theories?

b. How does Chancellor Allen describe the board's obligations to obtain information?

c. From what source or sources does the court derive the obligations to set up information systems?

d. Given the board's understanding of the potential for corporate liability through the policies the board put in place, how can Chancellor Allen find that the plaintiffs' claims were weak?

3. Suppose

a. Suppose Caremark had not been indicted but instead had been sued by the government in civil court. Would the court's analysis or the result have been different?

4. What Do You Think?

a. The conduct that resulted in Caremark's liability was criminal. Obviously corporations and their directors are under the same obligations as everyone else is to obey the law. Should a violation of the criminal law be considered an automatic violation of a director's duty of care? Should the fact that an act violates the law have any bearing on whether a director has met his or her fiduciary duties?

b. The complaint in this case was filed one day after Caremark's indictment was announced. How do you think the plaintiffs' lawyers could file such a complaint in accordance with Rule 11?

c. Do you think directors should be able to deflect liability by demonstrating that they relied on others within the corporation? More specifically, should directors be able to avoid liability by demonstrating that they relied on information prepared at their specific request? That they relied on information prepared in the ordinary course of business? That they relied on those corporate officers and other corporate agents to whom the board has delegated authority? In this connection, the MBCA and DGCL provisions on directorial reliance are set out below.

5. You Draft It

a. Draft a statute that appropriately describes a director's ability to rely on the actions of others (including the ability to rely on information provided by others). The MBCA versions (current and pre-1998) and the DGCL are set out below:

MBCA CURRENT §8.30

(c) In discharging board or committee duties a director, who does not have knowledge that makes reliance unwarranted, is entitled to rely on the performance by any of the persons specified in subsection (e)(1) or subsection (e)(3) to whom the board may have delegated, formally or informally by course of conduct, the authority or duty to perform one or more of the board's functions that are delegable under applicable law.

(d) In discharging board or committee duties a director, who does not have knowledge that makes reliance unwarranted, is entitled to rely on information, opinions, reports or statements, including financial statements and other financial data, prepared or presented by any of the persons specified in subsection (e).

(e) A director is entitled to rely, in accordance with subsection (c) or (d), on:

(1) one or more officers or employees of the corporation whom the director reasonably believes to be reliable and competent in the functions performed or the information, opinions, reports or statements provided;

(2) legal counsel, public accountants, or other persons retained by the corporation as to matters involving skills or expertise the director reasonably believes are matters (i) within the particular person's professional or expert competence or (ii) as to which the particular person merits confidence; or

(3) a committee of the board of directors of which the director is not a member if the director reasonably believes the committee merits confidence.

MBCA PRE-1998 §8.30

In performing his duties, a director shall be entitled to rely on information, opinions, reports or statements, including financial statements and other financial data, in each case prepared or presented by:

(a) One (1) or more officers or employees of the corporation whom the director reasonably believes to be reliable and competent in the matters presented,

(b) Counsel, public accountants or other persons as to matters which the director reasonably believes to be within such person's professional or expert competence. . . .

DGCL §141(e)

A member of the board of directors, or a member of any committee designated by the board of directors, shall, in the performance of such member's duties, be fully protected in relying in good faith upon the records of the corporation and upon such information, opinions, reports or statements presented to the corporation by any of the corporation's officers or employees, or committees of the board of directors, or by any other person as to matters the member reasonably believes are within such other person's professional or expert competence and who has been selected with reasonable care by or on behalf of the corporation.

B. BACKGROUND AND CONTEXT

Before we leave the duty of care, there are two further aspects we ought to consider. As you have seen, the basic standard of conduct looks very much like the standard of care each of us is under not to be negligent. There is a temptation, then, to graft other tort concepts onto the duty of care. The first aspect of the duty of care we will examine is whether the analogy to tort law is valid and valuable or, instead, is unwarranted and harmful.

Finally, we ask the question we posed at the beginning of this chapter. That is, whether it really makes sense to describe a duty of care that is separate from the duty of loyalty.

1. The Propriety of Analogy to Tort

In *Crown*, the court ticked off the traditional common law elements of negligence when it analyzed Mr. Nungester's behavior:

> The court concluded that Nungester used such care as an ordinary prudent person in a like position would use under similar circumstances. Further, having found that Nungester was not negligent and did not breach any duty owed to the Growers, the district court concluded that none of Nungester's actions proximately caused or contributed to any damage suffered by the Growers. The district court's findings are based upon substantial evidence and are not clearly erroneous. Because we uphold the district court's findings and conclusions on the question of the lack of negligence, we need not address the Grower's arguments on the issue of proximate cause.

> *Crown v. Hawkins Co., Ltd.*, 910 P.2d 786 (Idaho App. 1996) (Walters, C.J.)

In Delaware, the plaintiff, at least initially, need not show damage to the corporation or proximate cause. See *Cede & Co. v. Technicolor, Inc.*, 634 A.2d 345, 370-371 (Del. 1994). The rationale of the Delaware rule is that the plaintiff's initial task is simply to overcome a presumption that the board acted properly. Given the difficulty of overcoming that presumption, the Delaware courts believe that adding an additional initial burden would be unfair to plaintiffs. The presumption and other aspects of the standards by which courts evaluate director actions are the subject of the next chapter.

Under the MBCA, by contrast, a shareholder/plaintiff seeking monetary damages from directors has the burden of proving both monetary harm to the corporation and proximate cause between the directors' (in)action and the harm. See MBCA §8.31(b)(1). Yet the drafters of the MBCA share a concern with other commentators, many of whom are distinguished Delaware practitioners.

The concern with analogizing the duty of care to negligence begins with the observation that in the negligence setting it is frequently fair to infer negligence from the fact of harm. For example, a traffic accident seldom occurs unless someone has been negligent. In the business world, however, harm in the sense of a bad outcome is always a possibility. If the duty of care is linked too closely to the idea of negligence, finders of fact may be too prone to impose liability for what is, at bottom, simply a suboptimal business result. Given that the damage to the corporation may easily be quite large and given that the directors are often not the only actors who contributed to the damage, it seems disproportionate to impose liability too quickly.

Notes and Questions

1. What Do You Think?

a. Are there other common situations in which the potential damage is large and the defendants may not be wholly responsible for the loss? If so, how does the law treat those settings? What is the purpose in treating those settings in particular ways? Is it to deter certain conduct? To promote certain conduct? To make plaintiffs whole? To penalize defendants? Do those settings inform your view of the way in which corporate law ought to treat violations of the duty of care?

2. Is there a Duty of Care?

Now that you've read about the duty of care in more detail, think again about the observation at the beginning of this chapter regarding whether the duty of care even exists, or whether it is better to conceive of extreme cases of lapse of care as really involving the duty of loyalty. The following excerpts may help elaborate on the puzzle:

> I start with what I take to be an elementary precept of corporation law: in the absence of facts showing self-dealing or improper motive, a corporate officer or director is not legally responsible to the corporation for losses that may be suffered as a result of a decision that an officer made or that directors authorized in good faith. Thus, to allege that a corporation has suffered a loss as a result of a lawful transaction, within the corporation's powers, authorized by a corporate fiduciary *acting in a good faith pursuit of corporate purposes,* does not state a claim for relief against that fiduciary no matter how foolish the investment may appear in retrospect.
>
> The rule could rationally be no different. Shareholders can diversify the risks of their corporate investments. Shareholders don't want (or shouldn't rationally want) directors to be risk averse. Shareholders' investment interests, across the full range of their diversifiable equity investments, will be maximized if corporate directors and managers honestly assess risk and reward....
>
> But directors will tend to deviate from this rational acceptance of corporate risk *if* in authorizing the corporation to undertake a risky investment, the directors must assume some degree of personal risk relating to *ex post facto* claims of derivative liability for any resulting corporate loss.
>
> Corporate directors of public companies typically have a very small proportionate ownership interest in their corporations and little or no incentive compensation. Thus, they enjoy (as residual owners) only a very small proportion of any "upside" gains earned by the corporation on risky investment projects. If, however, corporate directors were to be found liable for a corporate loss from a risky project on the ground that the investment was too risky (foolishly risky! stupidly risky! egregiously risky!—you supply the adverb), their liability would be joint and several for the whole loss (with I suppose a right of contribution). Given the scale of operation of modern public corporations, this stupefying disjunction between risk and reward for corporate directors threatens undesirable effects. Given this disjunction, only a very small probability of director liability based on "negligence," "inattention," "waste," etc., could induce a board to avoid authorizing risky investment projects to any extent! Obviously, it is in the shareholders' economic interest to offer sufficient protection to directors from liability for negligence, etc., to allow directors to conclude that, as a practical matter, there is no risk that, if they act in good faith and meet minimal proceduralist standards of attention, they can face liability as a result of a business loss.

Gagliardi v. TriFoods International, Inc., 683 A.2d 1049, 1051-1052 (Del. Ch. 1996) (Allen, Ch.)

> Where a director *in fact exercises a good faith effort to be informed and to exercise appropriate judgment,* he or she should be deemed to satisfy fully the duty of attention. If the shareholders thought themselves entitled to some other quality of judgment than such a director produces in the good faith exercise of the powers of office, then the shareholders should have elected other directors.

In re Caremark International Inc. Derivative Litigation, 698 A.2d 959, 969 (Del. Ch. 1996) (Allen, Ch.)

Notes and Questions

1. Reality Check

a. Chancellor Allen wrote both of the squibbed opinions in the same year. Do they represent the same basis for critiquing a separate duty of care?

b. Chancellor Allen's argument envisions investors as being economically rational. How accurate is that vision?

2. What Do You Think?

a. Is there a logical link between the argument that the duty of care should be different from negligence and the argument that a separate duty of care should not exist?

b. In settings in which the directors were *completely* uninformed about a proposed action, their failure to become informed can be seen as evidence (possibly quite strong evidence) that the directors did not believe the proposed action was in the corporation's best interest. That is, they might have *hoped* the action would be beneficial but they had no information upon which to rest that hope. In the more typical setting, the directors will have *some* information about a proposed corporate action but did not (arguably, at least) have all material information reasonably available. Do you think that more typical setting can or should be treated as a duty of loyalty problem?

C. FEDERAL SECURITIES REGULATION

Although the federal securities acts operate largely by requiring disclosure of important corporate information, in some respects the laws impose substantive obligations on public companies. In the wake of the Enron and WorldCom scandals (see Chapter 14), Congress enacted the Sarbanes-Oxley Act. The SEC implemented Sarbanes-Oxley in part by requiring that public companies "must maintain disclosure controls and procedures and internal control over financial reporting." See SEC Rule 13a-15(a). Further, these controls must be evaluated by the CEO and chief financial officer every calendar quarter.

The disclosure controls and procedures are further defined as those "that are designed to ensure that information required to be disclosed by the issuer in the reports that it files or submits under the [Exchange] Act is recorded, processed, summarized and reported, within the time periods specified in the Commission's rules and forms. Disclosure controls and procedures include, without limitation, controls and procedures designed to ensure that information . . . is accumulated and communicated to the issuer's management, including its principal executive and principal financial officers, . . . as appropriate to allow timely decisions regarding required disclosure." See SEC Rule 13a-15(e).

The internal controls over financial reporting, which were the primary focus of Sarbanes-Oxley, are "a process designed . . . to provide reasonable assurance regarding the reliability of financial reporting and the preparation of financial statements . . . and includes those policies and procedures that: 1. Pertain to the maintenance of records that in reasonable detail accurately and fairly reflect the transactions and dispositions of the assets of the issuer; 2. Provide reasonable assurance that transactions are recorded as necessary to permit preparation of financial statements in accordance with generally accepted accounting principles, and that receipts and expenditures of the issuer are being made only in accordance with authorizations of management and directors of the issuer; and 3. Provide reasonable assurance regarding prevention or timely detection of unauthorized acquisition, use or disposition of the issuer's assets that could have a material effect on the financial statements." See SEC Rule 13a-15(f).

As you see, these reforms, and the incentives of the Federal Sentencing Guidelines, are entirely consonant with Chancellor Allen's views in *Caremark*.

D. TERMS OF ART IN THIS CHAPTER

Check kiting	Receivables skim	Sales skim
Duty of care		

13

Standards of Review of Board Actions

In this chapter we turn to the judicial review of board actions that are challenged on the ground that the directors breached their fiduciary duty of loyalty or care. Why do we need this chapter? In the last two chapters we covered the directors' (and officers') fiduciary duties of loyalty and care. Doesn't the trial judge (or jury), in this kind of lawsuit, as in ordinary civil litigation, determine whether the plaintiff has shown, by a preponderance of the evidence, each element in the claim for relief?

No. This is different.

The Delaware Supreme Court explains why litigation raising fiduciary duties claims is different from ordinary litigation and describes what the plaintiff must show to prevail:

> Our starting point is the fundamental principle of Delaware law that the business and affairs of a corporation are managed by or under the direction of its board of directors. [DGCL] §141(a). In exercising these powers, directors are charged with an unyielding fiduciary duty to protect the interests of the corporation and to act in the best interests of its shareholders.
>
> The business judgment rule is an extension of these basic principles. The rule operates to preclude a court from imposing itself unreasonably on the business and affairs of a corporation. The rule, though formulated many years ago, was ... restated by this Court as follows:
>
>> As a rule of evidence, it creates a "presumption that in making a business decision, the directors of a corporation acted on an informed basis [i.e., with due care], in good faith and in the honest belief that the action taken was in the best interest of the company." *Aronson v. Lewis,* 473 A.2d 805, 812 (Del. 1984). The presumption initially attaches to a director-approved transaction within a board's conferred or apparent authority in the absence of any evidence of "fraud, bad faith, or self-dealing in the usual sense of personal profit or betterment." *Grobow v. Perot,* 539 A.2d 180, 187 (Del. 1988).
>
> *Citron v. Fairchild Camera & Instr. Corp.,* 569 A.2d 53, 64 (Del. 1989)
>
> The rule posits a powerful presumption in favor of actions taken by the directors in that a decision made by a loyal and informed board will not be overturned by the courts unless it cannot be "attributed to any rational business purpose." *Sinclair Oil Corp. v. Levien,* 280 A.2d 717, 720 (Del. 1971) .... Thus, a shareholder plaintiff challenging a board decision has the burden at the outset to rebut the rule's presumption. To rebut the rule, a shareholder plaintiff assumes the burden of providing evidence that directors, in reaching their challenged decision, breached any one of

425

the *triads* of their fiduciary duty—good faith, loyalty or due care. If a shareholder plaintiff fails to meet this evidentiary burden, the business judgment rule attaches to protect corporate officers and directors and the decisions they make, and our courts will not second-guess these business judgments. If the rule is rebutted, the burden shifts to the defendant directors, the proponents of the challenged transaction, to prove to the trier of fact the "entire fairness" of the transaction to the shareholder plaintiff.

Cede & Co. v. Technicolor, Inc., 634 A.2d 345, 360-361 (Del. 1993) (Horsey, J.)

Thus the famous *business judgment rule* is a procedural device that places the initial burden on the plaintiff to show something different than that the director-defendants have breached their fiduciary duties. The nearly universal incantation by the Delaware courts is that the business judgment rule "is a presumption that in making a business decision, the directors of a corporation acted on an informed basis, in good faith and in the honest belief that the action taken was in the best interests of the company" and that the obligation to act on an informed basis means that the directors have "all material information reasonably available to them." *Aronson v. Lewis*, 473 A.2d 805, 812 (Del. 1984).

It is probably more accurate to think of the business judgment rule as an acknowledgment that corporate law recognizes a disconnect between the *stated* fiduciary duties of directors, which we covered in the last two chapters, and the *actual conduct* that will result in sanctions. One consequence of this disconnect is that there is a zone of director conduct that does not satisfy the directors' fiduciary duties but that nonetheless will not result in sanctions.

Well, if the plaintiff must show something other than that the directors breached their fiduciary duties, what is it? The Delaware Supreme Court has described the plaintiff's burden this way:

> [D]irectors' decisions will be respected by courts unless the directors are interested or lack independence relative to the decision, do not act in good faith, act in a manner that cannot be attributed to a rational business purpose[,] or reach their decision by a grossly negligent process that includes the failure to consider all material facts reasonably available.

Brehm v. Eisner, 746 A.2d 244, 264 n.66 (Del. 2000) (Veasey, C.J.)

The revisers of the Model Act sidestepped some of this intricacy by expressly stating that they did not intend to codify the business judgment rule. Nonetheless, they admit that their formulation of the standards for director liability "embeds" the business judgment rule's "principal elements." See MBCA §8.31, Official Comment. As in Delaware, the MBCA's standards for *liability* (MBCA §8.30) diverge from the standards of director *conduct* (MBCA §8.31). As the Official Comment to MBCA §8.31 puts it, "And while a director whose performance meets the standards of section 8.30 [duties of loyalty and care] should have no liability, the fact that a director's performance fails to reach that level does not automatically establish personal liability for damages that the corporation may have suffered as a consequence."

Notes and Questions

1. Notes

a. When the plaintiff alleges a failure to establish and monitor information systems within the corporation (which has come to be called a *Caremark* claim), a plaintiff can prevail only by showing "... a sustained or systematic failure of the board to exercise oversight — such as an utter failure to attempt to assure a reasonable information and reporting system exists — will establish the lack of good faith that is a necessary condition to liability." *In re Caremark International Derivative Litigation*, 698 A.2d 959, 971 (Del. Ch. 1996) (Allen, Ch.)

2. Reality Check

a. Parse the Delaware and MBCA requirements into those that apply to duty of loyalty claims and those that apply to duty of care claims. Why are the requirements so jumbled together?

3. What Do You Think?

a. Why is there a divergence between directors' aspirational conduct and their conduct that will render them liable to the corporation? Do you think this divergence is a good idea?

Let us move to a more detailed look at those requirements. Ask yourself two questions: What does the plaintiff need to show to stave off an adverse judgment? And what happens when the plaintiff makes that showing? I suspect you're intuiting that simply because the plaintiff has satisfied the initial showing does not mean he or she is entitled to judgment. You're right. Let's start with the duty of loyalty.

A. THE DUTY OF LOYALTY

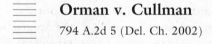

Orman v. Cullman

794 A.2d 5 (Del. Ch. 2002)

CHANDLER, CH.

Joseph Orman ("Orman") is and was the owner of General Cigar Class A common stock at all times relevant to this litigation. Orman brings this suit on behalf of himself and the Public Shareholders of General Cigar Class A common stock against General Cigar and its eleven-member board of directors (collectively the "Board").[1]

The defendants moved pursuant to Court of Chancery Rule 12(b)(6) to dismiss the complaint on the grounds that: 1) Orman failed to plead facts sufficient to overcome the presumption of the business judgment rule with respect to the Board's approval of the merger transaction....

II. FACTUAL HISTORY

General Cigar, a Delaware Corporation with its principal executive offices located in New York, New York, is a leading manufacturer and marketer of premium cigars.

---

1. The individual defendant Board members are: Edgar M. Cullman, Sr. ("Cullman Sr."), Edgar M. Cullman, Jr. ("Cullman Jr."), Susan R. Cullman ("Susan Cullman"), John L. Ernst ("Ernst"), Peter J. Solomon ("Solomon"), Bruce A. Barnet ("Barnet"), John L. Bernbach ("Bernbach"), Thomas C. Israel ("Israel"), Dan W. Lufkin ("Lufkin"), Graham V. Sherren ("Sherren"), and Frances T. Vincent, Jr. ("Vincent"). The first four directors listed are related to one another ... and are collectively referred to as the "Cullman Group."

The Company has exclusive trademark rights to many well-known brands of cigars, including seven of the top ten brands that were previously manufactured in Cuba.

The Company went public in an initial public offering ("IPO")... Class A stock at $18.00 per share on February 28, 1997. Class A stock was publicly traded and Class B stock was not publicly traded. Class A stock had one vote per share and Class B had ten votes per share. At the time of the proposed merger, the Cullman Group owned approximately... 37% of the Company's total outstanding stock.... The Cullman Group's equity interest... gave it approximately 67% of the voting power in the corporation.

In the early fall of 1999, Swedish Match AB ("Swedish Match") approached certain members of the Cullman Group (the "Cullmans") about purchasing the interest in General Cigar owned by its Public Shareholders. This was seen to be a logical business combination because General Cigar had a strong presence in the United States premium cigar market and Swedish Match had strength in the international cigar and smokeless tobacco markets through its established network of international contacts and resources. At a November 4, 1999 General Cigar board meeting, the Cullmans informed the Board of Swedish Match's interest. The Board then authorized the Cullmans to pursue discussions with Swedish Match assisted by defendant director Solomon's financial advising firm, Peter J. Solomon & Company ("PJSC"). By the end of December 1999 the structure for a proposed transaction had been determined.

Once the negotiations reached agreement..., the Board created a special committee (the "Special Committee"), consisting of outside defendant directors Lufkin, Israel, and Vincent, to determine the advisability of entering into the proposed transaction. [T]he Special Committee received copies of the proposed agreements previously reached between the Cullmans and Swedish Match. After a review of these proposals by the Special Committee and its legal and financial advisors, the Special Committee directly negotiated with Swedish Match over the terms of the agreement. On January 19, 2000 the Special Committee unanimously recommended approval of the transaction as modified as a result of their negotiations. That same day, the General Cigar Board unanimously approved the transaction.

Following the merger, [the Cullman Group's] remaining interest would aggregate to approximately 36% of the total outstanding equity interest in the Company. [A]ll publicly owned Class A and Class B shares (those not owned by the Cullman Group) would be purchased for $15.25 per share.

[T]he transaction was structured in such a way that the Cullman Group could not dictate its approval. Despite the fact that the Cullman Group possessed voting control over the Company both before and after the proposed transaction, approval of the merger required that a majority of the Unaffiliated Shareholders of Class A stock, voting separately as a class, vote in favor of the transaction.[28]

III. ANALYSIS

A. Fiduciary Duty Claims

Because a board is presumed to have acted properly, "[t]he burden is on the party challenging the decision to establish facts rebutting the [business judgment rule]

---

28. In order to assure the Unaffiliated Shareholders had the unobstructed right to determine whether or not the merger would close, the Cullman Group "agreed to vote any Class A shares held by them pro rata in accordance with the vote of the Unaffiliated Shareholders."

presumption."[33] Specifically, Orman must allege facts that raise a reasonable doubt as to whether the Board breached either its duty of care or its duty of loyalty to the corporation. In his complaint, Orman alleges that the Board breached its duty of loyalty.

As a general matter, the business judgment rule presumption that a board acted loyally can be rebutted by alleging facts which, if accepted as true, establish that the *board* was either interested in the outcome of the transaction or lacked the independence to consider objectively whether the transaction was in the best interest of its company and all of its shareholders. To establish that a *board* was interested or lacked independence, a plaintiff must allege facts as to the interest and lack of independence of the *individual members* of that board. To rebut successfully business judgment presumptions in this manner, thereby leading to the application of the entire fairness standard, a plaintiff must normally plead facts demonstrating "that a *majority* of the director defendants have a financial interest in the transaction or were dominated or controlled by a materially interested director."[38]

If a plaintiff alleging a duty of loyalty breach is unable to plead facts demonstrating that a majority of a board that approved the transaction in dispute was interested and/ or lacked independence, the entire fairness standard of review is not applied and the Court respects the business judgment of the board.

General Cigar had an eleven-member board. In order to rebut the presumptions of the business judgment rule, Orman must allege facts that would support a finding of interest or lack of independence for a majority, or at least six, of the Board members. Orman asserts, and defendants appear to concede, that the four members of the Cullman Group were interested because they received benefits from the transaction that were not shared with the rest of the shareholders. Orman, therefore, would have to plead facts making it reasonable to question the interest or independence of two of the remaining seven Board members to avoid dismissal based on the business judgment rule presumption. With varying levels of confidence, Orman's complaint alleges that each of the seven remaining Board members — Israel, Vincent, Lufkin, Barnet, Sherren, Bernbach, and Solomon — were interested and/or lacked independence.[50]

___

33. *Aronson v. Lewis,* 473 A.2d 805, 812 (Del. 1984).

38. *Crescent/Mach I Partners, L.P. v. Turner,* 2000 WL 1481002 (Del. Ch.) (Steele, V.C., by designation) (emphasis added); ....

50. Although interest and independence are two separate and distinct issues, these two attributes are sometimes confused by parties. Many plaintiffs allege facts which they assert establish that the defendant "lacked the disinterest and/or independence" necessary to consider the challenged transaction objectively. The plaintiff then asks the Court to select whichever type of disabling attribute is consistent with the facts alleged and that will support the plaintiff's claim. But it is not for the Court to divine the claims being made. A plaintiff must make clear to the Court the bases upon which his claims rest.

As described above, a disabling "interest," as defined by Delaware common law, exists in two instances. The first is when (1) a director personally receives a benefit (or suffers a detriment), (2) as a result of, or from, the challenged transaction, (3) which is not generally shared with (or suffered by) the other shareholders of his corporation, and (4) that benefit (or detriment) is of such subjective material significance to that particular director that it is reasonable to question whether that director objectively considered the advisability of the challenged transaction to the corporation and its shareholders. The second instance is when a director stands on both sides of the challenged transaction. *See* DGCL §144. This latter situation frequently involves the first three elements listed above. As for the fourth element, whenever a director stands on both sides of the challenged transaction he is deemed interested and allegations of materiality have not been required.

"Independence" does not involve a question of whether the challenged director derives a benefit *from the transaction* that is not generally shared with the other shareholders. Rather, it involves an inquiry into whether the director's decision resulted from that director being *controlled* by another. A director can be controlled by another if in fact he is *dominated* by that other party, whether through close personal or familial relationship or through force of will. A director can also be controlled by another if the challenged

1. Directors Israel and Vincent

Perhaps the weakest allegations of interest and/or lack of independence are aimed at directors Israel and Vincent, who were both members of the Special Committee that investigated the advisability of the merger and negotiated with Swedish Match. The complaint states that these two defendants "had longstanding business relations with members of the Cullman Group which impeded and impaired their ability to function independently and outside the influence of the Cullman Group." The only fact pled in support of this assertion is the mere recitation that Israel and Vincent had served as directors of General Cigar since 1989 and 1992, respectively.

To make clear my opinion as to the independence of directors Israel and Vincent, therefore, I conclude that the allegations in the complaint with regard to the lack of independence of these two directors fail as a matter of law. The naked assertion of a previous business relationship is not enough to overcome the presumption of a director's independence. The law in Delaware is well settled on this point. For instance, in *Crescent/Mach I Partners, L.P.* this Court held that allegations of a "long-standing 15-year professional and personal relationship" between a director and the CEO and Chairman of the Board of his company were insufficient to support a finding of control.[54] The Court stated that such allegations, without more, "fail[ed] to raise a reasonable doubt that [the director] could not exercise his independent business judgment in approving the transaction. Therefore, these allegations lack the specific factual predicate" necessary to survive a motion to dismiss. Here too, allegations concerning longstanding business relations fail as a matter of law to place in issue the independence of directors Israel and Vincent.

2. Director Lufkin

Orman asserts that director Lufkin, who was the third member of the Special Committee, lacked independence and was also interested in the merger transaction. With regard to Lufkin's purported lack of independence, Orman makes the same allegations as were directed at Israel and Vincent, namely, Lufkin "had longstanding business relations with members of the Cullman Group which impeded and impaired [his] ability to function independently and outside the influence of the Cullman Group. For the reasons stated above . . . , such bare allegation fails as a matter of law to assert a lack of independence on the part of director Lufkin.

Lufkin's supposedly disabling interest results from the fact that he was "a founder of Donaldson, Lufkin & Jenrette ("DLJ") [and that] DLJ, or a successor or affiliate thereof, was one of two lead underwriters in the Company's IPO and obtained a substantial fee as a result thereof." This bare statement of fact does not suggest, or even lead to a reasonable inference of, a disabling interest on the part of Lufkin as that statement does not show that he "'will receive a personal financial benefit from [the] transaction that is not equally shared by the stockholders.'"[59] Inadequate pleadings in

---

director is *beholden* to the allegedly controlling entity. A director may be considered beholden to (and thus controlled by) another when the allegedly controlling entity has the unilateral power (whether direct or indirect through control over other decision makers), to decide whether the challenged director continues to receive a benefit, financial or otherwise, upon which the challenged director is so dependent or is of such subjective material importance to him that the threatened loss of that benefit might create a reason to question whether the controlled director is able to consider the corporate merits of the challenged transaction objectively.

54. 2000 WL 1481002 (Del. Ch. Steele, V.C., by designation).

59. *In re the Walt Disney Co. Derivative Litig.*, 731 A.2d 342, 354 (Del. Ch. 1998) (quoting *Rales v. Blasband*, 634 A.2d 927, 936 (Del. 1993)). It is of no help to Orman that he improperly attempts to expand

support of separate allegations of interest and lack of independence cannot be combined to create an inference that a director's conduct was improper. Here, the complaint fails, as a matter of law, to set forth facts that would lead this Court to question the presumed objectivity of director Lufkin in making his decision to vote in favor of the merger with Swedish Match.

3. Director Barnet

The *only* fact alleged in support of Orman's allegation of director Barnet's interest is that he "has an interest in the transaction since he will become a director of the surviving company." No case has been cited to me, and I have found none, in which a director was found to have a financial interest *solely* because he will be a director in the surviving corporation. To the contrary, our case law has held that such an interest is not a disqualifying interest. Even if I were to infer that Orman was alleging that the fees Barnet was to receive as a director with the surviving company created a disabling interest, without more, that assertion would also fail. Because Orman alleges no facts in addition to the assertion of continued board membership on the part of Barnett, his assertion of interest fails as a matter of law.

4. Director Bernbach

Orman alleges that director Bernbach was both interested in the merger and lacked the independence to make an impartial decision regarding that transaction because he has "a written agreement with the Company to provide consulting services [and that] [i]n 1998 . . . Bernbach was paid $75,000 for such services . . . and additional funds since that date."

Orman . . . further alleges that the surviving company will be obligated to uphold the contracts of the existing company. Such well-pleaded facts, accepted as true on a motion to dismiss, plainly allege a continuing obligation. Unfortunately for Orman, however, this clearly stated allegation is fatal to his assertion that Bernbach was interested in the transaction. As this Court has stated previously, "a director is considered interested when he will receive a personal financial benefit *from a transaction* that is not equally shared by the stockholders."[66] Accepting Orman's allegations as true reveals that Bernbach does not meet this definition of "interest." Bernbach had a contract with General Cigar. If the merger were consummated, he would have a contract that the surviving company would be obligated to honor. If the merger were not consummated he would still have his contract with the existing General Cigar that it would be obligated to honor. Therefore, director Bernbach would have received no benefit *from the transaction* being challenged that was not shared by the other General Cigar shareholders. As a result of the merger, shareholder

---

the scope of his complaint in his brief opposing the motion to dismiss by adding the new allegation that "his [Lufkin's] company could not reasonably hope to attract the future business of General Cigar . . . if he were to vote against the merger." As stated above, at this stage of litigation, the Court is only permitted to consider the well pleaded facts contained in the complaint and any documents incorporated by reference into that complaint. Should a plaintiff become aware that the allegations set forth in his complaint are inadequate to support his claim, he should request leave of the Court to amend his complaint rather than attempt to expand its scope through briefing. Briefs relating to a motion to dismiss are not part of the record and any attempt contained within such documents to plead new facts or expand those contained in the complaint will not be considered. Even if Orman's new allegation were to be considered by the Court, which it is not, it would still be unconvincing as the Proxy Statement, which is incorporated by reference into the complaint and *is* a proper document for consideration, reveals that Lufkin is no longer a part of DLJ, thus rendering null Orman's already inadequate pleading with regard to this defendant.

66. *In re Western Nat'l Corp. Shareholders Litig.*, 2000 WL 710192 (Del. Ch. Chandler, Ch.) (citing *Aronson v. Lewis*, 473 A.2d 805, 812 (Del. 1984)) (emphasis added).

Bernbach would be cashed out and receive the same consideration for his General Cigar stock as the rest of the Unaffiliated Shareholders. Since he was to receive the same benefit as the Company's other shareholders, his interest in getting as high a price as possible for the Company's stock from the merger transaction was aligned with the Unaffiliated Shareholders. Orman's complaint, therefore, fails to plead adequately that director Bernbach was interested in the merger.

Orman also argues that Bernbach's consulting agreement suggests a lack of independence. At this stage of the litigation, the facts supporting this allegation are sufficient to raise a reasonable inference that director Bernbach was controlled by the Cullman Group because he was beholden to the controlling shareholders for future renewals of his consulting contract. [A]t the time of the challenged transaction, Bernbach's principal occupation was "Chairman and Chief Executive officer of the Bernbach Group, Inc." I believe it is reasonable to question the objectivity of a director who has a consulting contract with his company and will continue to have a consulting contract with the surviving company. This is particularly true when, regardless of whether the merger is approved or not, the challenged director is beholden to the identical group of controlling shareholders favoring the challenged transaction. The Cullman Group would continue to be in a position to determine whether particular contracts are to be renewed as well as the extent to which the company will make use of the consulting services already under contract. Even though there is no bright-line dollar amount at which consulting fees received by a director become material, at the motion to dismiss stage and on the facts before me, I think it is reasonable to infer that $75,000 would be material to director Bernbach and that he is beholden to the Cullman Group for continued receipt of such fees. Although not determinative, the inference of materiality is strengthened when the allegedly disabling fee is paid for the precise services that comprise the principal occupation of the challenged director.

5. Director Solomon

Orman alleges that "Defendant Solomon has an interest in the transaction since his company, PJSC, stands to reap fees of $3.3 million if the transaction is effectuated." The reasonable inference that can be drawn from this contention is that if the merger is consummated PJSC will receive $3.3 million. If the merger is not consummated PJSC will not receive $3.3 million. PJSC, therefore, has an interest in the transaction. Because director Solomon's principal occupation is that of "Chairman of Peter J. Solomon Company Limited and Peter J. Solomon Securities Company Limited," it is reasonable to assume that director Solomon would personally benefit from the $3.3 million *his* company would receive if the challenged transaction closed. I think it would be naïve to say, as a matter of law, that $3.3 million is immaterial. In my opinion, therefore, it is reasonable to infer that director Solomon suffered a disabling interest when considering how to cast his vote in connection with the challenged merger when the Board's decision on that matter could determine whether or not his firm would receive $3.3 million.

Directors Bernbach and Solomon, at this stage, cannot be considered independent and disinterested. Orman has thus pled facts that make it reasonable to question the independence and/or disinterest of a majority of the General Cigar Board — the four Cullman Group directors, plus Bernbach and Solomon, or six out of the eleven directors. Accordingly, I cannot say, as a matter of law, that the General Cigar Board's actions are protected by the business judgment rule presumption. Defendants' motion to dismiss the fiduciary duty claims — based as it is on a conclusion that the challenged transaction was approved by a disinterested and independent board — must be denied.[70]

Notes and Questions

1. Notes

a. The capital structure of General Cigar includes a frequently used psychological technique. When a corporation is to have one class of stock with clear advantages (either economic or voting benefits, or both) over another class, corporate planners often name the more advantageous class "Class B" and the less advantageous class "Class A." This is done, of course, to suggest to potential purchasers of Class A shares that they are getting stock that is somehow "better" than Class B. As long as the differences between the classes of stock are fully disclosed (and remember that the differences must be stated in the Articles), the corporate planners have not committed fraud. Do you think planners should be allowed to engage in this practice?

b. General Cigar appointed a Special Committee of independent and disinterested directors to analyze the proposed transaction. Note also that the transaction was contingent upon approval of a majority of the shares not controlled by the Cullman Group. This technique is called a "majority of the minority" provision. Both Special Committees and majority of the minority provisions are frequently used when a transaction involves a corporation and its controlling interests and are intended to heighten the integrity of the negotiation and approval process.

2. Reality Check

a. Why did Swedish Match want to control General Cigar?

b. Why are the General Cigar shareholders upset at the proposed transaction?

c. What does Mr. Orman have to demonstrate to prevail in his claim? How is that different from the conduct required of directors by their duty of loyalty?

d. Are the terms *independent* and *disinterested* synonymous? Are they mutually exclusive of one another?

e. Why are Messrs. Israel, Vincent, Lufkin, and Barnet differently situated from Messrs. Bernbach and Solomon?

f. Why is Mr. Bernbach disinterested but not independent? Do you agree with Chancellor Chandler's analysis of Mr. Bernbach's situation?

3. Suppose

a. Assume that Mr. Bernbach had not had a consulting contract with General Cigar. What difference would that fact make in analyzing Mr. Orman's claims for relief?

b. Suppose that this case had arisen in an MBCA jurisdiction. What portions of the MBCA would be germane? Would the analysis or result have been different?

4. What Do You Think?

a. Chancellor Chandler cites case law for the proposition that a director's previous business relationship with a controlling shareholder is not enough to defeat the presumption that the director is independent. Do you think that rule makes sense? If a different rule applied, which directors in this case would be analyzed differently?

---

70. Since Orman has pled facts from which it is reasonable to question the independence of two of the seven disputed directors, it is unnecessary for me to consider his allegations with regard to director Sherren.

b. Outside directors (i.e., those without full-time jobs with the corporation on whose board they serve) of public companies nearly always have personal, social, or business relationships with someone who has significant input into the selection of candidates for the board. Frequently such directors have multiple relationships with several such influential insiders. Do you think this *structural bias*, as it is called, should render every such director "beholden"?

1. The Entire Fairness Standard

A consequence of Chancellor Chandler's ruling in *Orman* is that the parties now engage in full discovery. If Mr. Orman is successful in establishing his assertions about the General Cigar board of directors' lack of disinterest and independence, he has rebutted the business judgment rule and the court will apply the *entire fairness* standard. What does that standard entail? The next case shows what is involved. Note that Vice Chancellor Strine has held a trial on the merits.

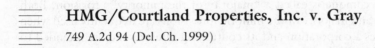 ### HMG/Courtland Properties, Inc. v. Gray
749 A.2d 94 (Del. Ch. 1999)

STRINE, V.C.

This case involves thirteen year old real estate sales transactions [the Wallingford and NAF transactions ("Transactions") and the Grossman's Portfolio transactions ("Portfolio")] between HMG/Courtland Properties, Inc. as seller and two of HMG's directors, Lee Gray and Norman Fieber as buyers. While Fieber's self-interest in the transactions was properly disclosed, neither he nor Gray informed their fellow directors that Gray—who took the lead in negotiating the sales for HMG—had a buy-side interest. Gray's interest was concealed from HMG for a decade and was only discovered inadvertently by the company in 1996.

A. BREACH OF FIDUCIARY DUTY

Gray and Fieber must demonstrate the fairness of the Wallingford and NAF Transactions.

2. The Entire Fairness Standard

In a recent case, Vice Chancellor Lamb well-summarized the entire fairness standard of review as follows:

> It is a well-settled principle of Delaware law that where directors stand on both sides of a transaction, they have "the burden of establishing its entire fairness, sufficient to pass the test of careful scrutiny by the courts." *Weinberger v. UOP, Inc.,* 457 A.2d 701, 710 (Del. 1983) ("There is no 'safe harbor' for such divided loyalties in Delaware."). Directors will be found to have acted with entire fairness where they "demonstrate their utmost good faith *and* the most scrupulous inherent fairness of the bargain." *Id.*

* * * * * *

The concept of entire fairness has two components: fair dealing and fair price. See *Weinberger,* 457 A.2d at 711. Fair dealing "embraces questions of when the transaction was timed, how it was initiated, structured, negotiated, disclosed to the directors, and how the approvals of the directors and the stockholders were obtained." *Id.* Fair price "relates to the economic and financial considerations of the proposed merger, including all relevant factors: assets, market value, earnings, future prospects, and any other elements that affect the intrinsic or inherent value of a company's stock." *Id. In making a determination as to the entire fairness of a transaction, the Court does not focus on one component over the other, but examines all aspects of the issue as a whole. Id.*

Boyer v. Wilmington Materials, Inc., 1999 WL 39549 (Del. Ch.) (Lamb, V.C.) (emphasis added).

i. FAIR DEALING

The defendants have failed to convince me that the Wallingford and NAF Transactions were fairly negotiated or ratified. From the beginning of the negotiations, Gray, the primary negotiator for the seller in the Transactions, was interested in taking a position on the buyer's side. As such, Gray lacked the pure seller-side incentive that should have been applied on behalf of HMG—particularly in Transactions in which one director was already on the other side.

Given the intrinsically unique nature of real estate, the bargaining skills and incentives of HMG's negotiator were likely to be more important than if the negotiator was arranging for the sale of a financial asset. As the defendants' own expert conceded, in the context of a real estate sales transaction negotiation skills are "exceedingly important."

Gray took the lead in discussing these Transactions with the Fiebers. His colleagues Wiener and Rothstein relied on his depiction of the bargaining in determining whether to agree to the Fiebers' proposed terms. They did so in ignorance of Gray's conflict. Similarly, HMG's Executive Committee and Board were deprived of information about Gray's conflict.

The process was thus anything but fair. Because neither Gray nor Fieber disclosed Gray's interest, the HMG Board unwittingly ratified Transactions in which a conflicted negotiator was relied upon by the Adviser to negotiate already conflicted Transactions.

ii. FAIR PRICE

The defendants attempt to meet their burden of demonstrating fair price by trying to convince me that the prices used in the Transactions were in a range of fairness, as proven by [independent] 1984 Appraisals.

Once again, I believe the defendants misconceive their burden. On the record before me, I obviously cannot conclude that HMG received a shockingly low price in the Transactions or that the prices paid were not within the low end of the range of possible prices that might have been paid in negotiated arms-length deals. In that narrow sense, the defendants have proven that the price was "fair." But that proof does not necessarily satisfy their burden under the entire fairness standard. As the American Law Institute corporate governance principles point out:

> A contract price might be fair in the sense that it corresponds to market price, and yet the corporation might have refused to make the contract if a given material fact had been disclosed .... Furthermore, fairness is often a range, rather than a point, so that a transaction involving a payment by the corporation may be fair even though it is consummated at the high end of the range. *If an undisclosed material fact had*

been disclosed, however, the corporation might have declined to transact at that high price, or might have bargained the price down lower in the range.

1 *Principles of Corporate Governance, Analysis and Recommendations,* Part V at 202 (1994) (emphasis added); . . . .

The defendants have failed to persuade me that HMG would not have gotten a materially higher value for Wallingford and the Grossman's Portfolio had Gray and Fieber come clean about Gray's interest. That is, they have not convinced me that their misconduct did not taint the price to HMG's disadvantage. I base this conclusion on several factors.

First, the defendants' own expert on value, James Nolan, testified that his opinion that the prices paid in the Transactions were fair was premised on his assumption that Gray was not the leading negotiator from HMG's side. To the extent that Gray was a principal player in discussing terms with Fieber, Nolan said that his conclusion about the fairness of the price might well be different.

Second, the 1984 Appraisals understated the values of the Wallingford Property and the Portfolio as of early 1986. The Leased Fee Values [$391,000] in the 1984 Appraisals were generated through a discounted cash flow analysis utilizing 1983 actual rents and projected rents for 1984-1986. By 1986, it was clear that the Grossman's stores operating at Portfolio sites were performing better, and thereby generating higher lease payments (because a portion of the lease payments was tied to store sales) than estimated by the appraisers who conducted the 1984 Appraisals. If an update had been done in 1986, it would have produced values well in excess of the 1984 Appraisals.

Third, a skilled and properly motivated negotiator could have done better than Leased Fee Value in price negotiations. As the defendants' expert Nolan testified, the skills of a negotiator are "exceedingly important" in a real estate transaction. Even without an updated appraisal, a properly motivated negotiator could have argued from the actual rents in 1984 and 1985 that the Leased Fee Value understated the value of the Portfolio. Furthermore, a properly motivated negotiator would have focused on the Fee Simple Value [$711,800*] because of the likelihood that many of the Portfolio properties would come off lease from Grossman's. That eventuality — which came true — justified a higher price than the Leased Fee Value. I have no confidence that Gray negotiated with the Fiebers in any vigorous or skillful way. Since he wanted to participate on the buy-side, he had less than a satisfactory incentive to do so. Since the outcome of a real estate negotiation is often heavily influenced by the skills of the negotiators, this factor undercuts the claim that the price was fair to HMG. *See* 1 *Principles of Corporate Governance: Analysis and Recommendations* §5.02 at 220 (1994) (in evaluating the fairness of a transaction, the court should consider the fact that the corporation was not represented by an unconflicted negotiator).

Finally, had Gray disclosed his interest, I believe that HMG would have terminated his involvement in the negotiations and have taken a much more traditional approach to selling the affected properties. To the extent that HMG continued to consider a sales transaction, I believe it would have commissioned new appraisals and would have sought purchasers other than Fieber. This would have been in keeping with the recommendations of Lavin's January 1986 memorandum suggesting

---

* The Fee Simple Value is the value of the land without the leases. The land was encumbered by leases that generated below-market rents. Thus, the value of the unencumbered land was higher than the value with tenants in place. ED.

rejection of the $300,000 third-party offer for Wallingford. Such an approach would have led to a sales transaction at a level more akin to the Fee Simple Value in the 1984 Appraisals than the Leased Fee Value.

Taken together, these factors lead me to conclude that the defendants have not demonstrated that they paid a fair price in the sense inherent in the entire fairness standard. Therefore, Gray and Fieber have failed to establish to my "satisfaction that the [T]ransaction[s] [were] the product of both fair dealing *and* fair price." *Cinerama,* [*Inc. v. Technicolor, Inc.,*] 663 A.2d 1156, 1179 (Del. 1995) (quotations & citations omitted) (emphasis added).

Notes and Questions

1. Notes

a. The *entire fairness* test is also called the *intrinsic fairness* test.

b. The entire fairness test under the MBCA is substantially the same as under Delaware law. See the Official Comments to MBCA §8.31 and §8.61.

2. Reality Check

a. What are the elements of the entire fairness test?

b. Wasn't Mr. Fieber's disclosure sufficient to insulate the Transactions from legal attack?

3. What Do You Think?

a. Conceptually, at some point the consideration for a transaction may be so favorable to the plaintiff that the process by which that consideration was reached becomes irrelevant to the question whether the transaction is entirely fair. Should the courts examine the fair dealing aspect nonetheless? If so, why? If not, doesn't that mean that in the end the courts are indeed concerned only with the substance of a transaction and not the process?

b. Vice Chancellor Strine finds that the prices for the Transactions were, "within the low end of the range of possible prices that might have been paid in negotiated arms-length deals." He goes on to find that defendants failed to meet their burden because they, "have failed to persuade me that HMG would not have gotten a materially higher value for Wallingford and the Grossman's Portfolio had Gray and Fieber come clean about Gray's interest. That is, they have not convinced me that their misconduct did not taint the price to HMG's disadvantage." How could defendants make the showing Vice Chancellor Strine requires? How could they have proven, by a preponderance of the evidence, that the company "would not have" gotten a much better price if facts had been different? What sort of evidence would be relevant to this question? Is any such evidence anything other than speculation?

B. THE DUTY OF CARE

We saw in Chapter 12 that the duty of care is, in Delaware, a duty to be informed, which includes a duty to ensure that a system is in place designed to bring important information to the attention of the board. Under the MBCA, becoming informed is certainly an important component of the duty of care. Before you read the next case you should reread the Delaware and MBCA formulations for the standard of conduct in duty of care settings. The next case discusses the standard of review in cases in which the plaintiff asserts that the board violated its duty of care.

In re NCS Healthcare, Inc., Shareholders Litigation
825 A.2d 240 (Del. Ch. 2002)

[The facts are largely drawn from the Delaware Supreme Court's decision in this case.

NCS is a leading independent provider of pharmacy services to long-term care institutions including skilled nursing facilities, assisted living facilities and other institutional healthcare facilities. Jon H. Outcalt is Chairman of the NCS board of directors. Kevin B. Shaw is President, CEO and a director of NCS. Messrs. Outcalt and Shaw collectively owned over 65% of the voting power.

The NCS board has two other members, defendants Boake A. Sells and Richard L. Osborne. Sells is a graduate of the Harvard Business School. He currently sits on the boards of both public and private companies. Osborne is a full-time professor at the Weatherhead School of Management at Case Western Reserve University. He has been at the university for over thirty years. Osborne currently sits on at least seven corporate boards other than NCS.

Genesis is a leading provider of healthcare and support services to the elderly. Omnicare, Inc. is in the institutional pharmacy business.

Beginning in late 1999, NCS began to experience a precipitous decline in the market value of its stock. In the summer of 2001, NCS invited Omnicare to begin discussions regarding a possible transaction. Omnicare responded that it was not interested in any transaction other than purchasing NCS's assets at a sale in bankruptcy. There was no further contact between Omnicare and NCS between November 2001 and January 2002.

In January 2002, Genesis was contacted concerning a possible transaction with NCS. Genesis previously lost a bidding war to Omnicare in a different transaction. This led to bitter feelings between the principals of both companies.

In March 2002, NCS decided to form an independent committee of board members who were neither NCS employees nor major NCS stockholders (the "Independent Committee"). Sells and Osborne were selected as the members of the committee, and given authority to consider and negotiate possible transactions for NCS. The entire four member NCS board, however, retained authority to approve any transaction.

The Independent Committee met for the first time on May 14, 2002. Two days later, Boake Sells met with George Hager, CFO of Genesis, and Michael Walker, who was Genesis's CEO. In June 2002, Genesis proposed a transaction .... At the June 26 meeting, Genesis's representatives demanded that, before any further negotiations take place, NCS agree to enter into an exclusivity agreement with it. Genesis wanted the Exclusivity Agreement to be the first step towards a completely locked up transaction that would preclude a higher bid from Omnicare.

By late July 2002, Omnicare came to believe that NCS was negotiating a transaction, possibly with Genesis or another of Omnicare's competitors, that would potentially present a competitive threat to Omnicare. Thus, Omnicare faxed to NCS a letter outlining a proposed acquisition. Late in the afternoon of July 26, 2002, NCS representatives received voicemail messages from Omnicare asking to discuss the letter. The exclusivity agreement prevented NCS from returning those calls.

Despite the exclusivity agreement, the Independent Committee met to consider a response to Omnicare. It concluded that discussions with Omnicare about its July 26 letter presented an unacceptable risk that Genesis would abandon merger discussions. The Independent Committee believed that, given Omnicare's past bankruptcy proposals and unwillingness to consider a merger, the risk of losing the Genesis proposal was too substantial. Nevertheless, the Independent Committee used Omnicare's letter to negotiate for a more favorable transaction with Genesis. On July 27, Genesis proposed substantially improved terms. In return for these concessions, Genesis stipulated that the transaction had to be approved by midnight the next day, July 28, or else Genesis would terminate discussions and withdraw its offer.

The Independent Committee and the NCS board both scheduled meetings for July 28. After concluding that Genesis was sincere in establishing the midnight deadline, the committee voted unanimously to recommend the transaction to the full board. The full board concluded that "balancing the potential loss of the Genesis deal against the uncertainty of Omnicare's letter, results in the conclusion that the only reasonable alternative for the Board of Directors is to approve the Genesis transaction." Under the terms of the merger agreement, NCS would be prohibited from canceling its shareholders' meeting and, because Messrs. Shaw and Outcalt, representing in excess of 50% of the outstanding voting power, would be required by Genesis to enter into stockholder voting agreements, shareholder approval of the merger would be assured even if the NCS Board were to withdraw or change its recommendation. DGCL §251 requires both board and shareholder approval to authorize a merger. These facts would prevent NCS from engaging in any alternative or superior transaction in the future. The board then resolved that the merger agreement and the transactions contemplated thereby were advisable and fair and in the best interests of all the NCS stakeholders. The NCS board further resolved to recommend the transactions to the stockholders for their approval and adoption. A definitive merger agreement between NCS and Genesis and the stockholder voting agreements were executed later that day.

On July 29, 2002, hours after the NCS/Genesis transaction (including the agreement with Messrs. Shaw and Outcalt) was executed, Omnicare faxed a letter to NCS restating its proposal, which offered significantly higher consideration than the Genesis transaction and which Omnicare made irrevocable, and attaching a draft merger agreement. On August 1, 2002, Omnicare expressed a desire to discuss the terms of the offer with NCS. On August 8, 2002, and again on August 19, 2002, the NCS Independent Committee and full board of directors met separately to consider the Omnicare tender offer in light of the Genesis merger agreement. As a result of this offer, on October 21, 2002, the NCS board withdrew its recommendation that the stockholders vote in favor of the NCS/Genesis merger agreement.

The NCS independent committee and the NCS board of directors recognize that (1) the existing contractual obligations to Genesis currently prevent NCS from accepting the Omnicare merger proposal; and (2) the existence of the voting agreements entered into by Messrs. Outcalt and Shaw, whereby Messrs. Outcalt and Shaw agreed to vote their shares of NCS stock in favor of the Genesis merger, ensure NCS stockholder approval of the Genesis merger. This litigation was commenced by minority shareholders of NCS, to prevent the consummation of the inferior Genesis transaction.]

LAMB, V.C.

In fulfilling their responsibilities to manage the Company's "business and affairs," the Director Defendants certainly owe fiduciary duties to NCS and its stockholders.

The duty of care relates to the process by which a board of directors makes a decision. The applicable standard of conduct when deciding whether directors have properly exercised their duty of care is whether they acted with "gross negligence," and whether they were adequately informed at the time they made their decision.[35] This is the business judgment standard of review. Under the business judgment rule, "[c]ourts do not measure, weigh or quantify directors' judgments," rather they merely look to see if the process employed by the board was reasonable, with "irrationality" functioning as "the outer limit of the business judgment rule."[37] "Where judgment is inescapably required, all that the law may sensibly ask of corporate directors is that they exercise independent, good faith and attentive judgment, both with respect to the quantum of information necessary or appropriate in the circumstances and with respect to the substantive decision to be made."[38]

With this legal backdrop in mind, the plaintiffs make essentially two arguments in attacking the NCS directors' exercise of due care. First, they argue that there was an actionable failure to include Omnicare in negotiations over a possible transaction from as early as May 14, when the Independent Committee first met to consider its options. Second, the NCS stockholders allege it was a breach of the directors' duty of care to fail to contact Omnicare after its July 26 conditional proposal arrived.

With respect to the first argument, the history of relations between Omnicare and NCS demonstrate that NCS made a significant effort to solicit Omnicare's interest in a suitable transaction for more than a year. These attempts failed because Omnicare was only interested in pursuing an asset sale in bankruptcy. In fact, all offers Omnicare made before July 26, 2002, involved a . . . sale in bankruptcy. Such a transaction would have resulted in . . . NCS stockholders receiving nothing for their shares, and NCS's trade and other creditors being left to fight over the remains of the corporation. Such an offer was unacceptable to the NCS directors who felt, at a minimum, they should strive to [obtain] at least . . . some recovery for the NCS stockholders.

In sum, the record does not support an inference that the Independent Committee or the NCS board of directors breached their duty of care by pursuing a transaction with Genesis by a process that did not include additional contact with Omnicare. On the contrary, the record fully supports a conclusion that Omnicare would have continued to press for a bankruptcy transaction in which . . . the NCS stockholders recovered nothing.

The post-May discussions focused on Genesis because (unlike earlier discussions with Omnicare) they quickly moved in a very positive direction. By June 2002, Genesis proposed a transaction outside of bankruptcy . . . and, for the first time since NCS began its search for restructuring alternatives, provided a recovery for NCS stockholders. By July 3, when the exclusivity agreement was signed, Genesis had improved its offer significantly. NCS's stockholders would receive $24 million in

---

35. *Smith v. Van Gorkom,* 488 A.2d 858, 873 (Del. 1985).
37. *Brehm v. Eisner,* 746 A.2d 244, 264 (Del. 2000).
38. *Equity-Linked Investors, L.P. v. Adams,* 705 A.2d 1040, 1058 (Del. Ch. 1997).

Genesis stock. Also, the proposal was structured as a merger and was expected to include a full recovery for NCS trade creditors and other accounts payable. Genesis, however, refused to go any further in negotiations without an exclusive dealing arrangement. It was because this last proposal was so superior to the ones Omnicare had made, . . . that the Independent Committee agreed to a short period of exclusive dealing with Genesis.

At oral argument, the plaintiffs' counsel contended that, by entering into the exclusivity agreement with Genesis, the NCS board breached its duty of care. This argument is unpersuasive. The Independent Committee purposely understood that entering into an exclusivity agreement was the only way to see if a firm deal could be negotiated between NCS and Genesis. And, there was very little reason to believe that, without a competing deal from Genesis, Omnicare would have ever offered a deal other than [an] . . . asset sale in bankruptcy. The record shows that the directors considered these factors and made a rational (and, indeed, reasonable) decision to pursue a transaction with Genesis. Certainly, the record does not reveal any important information that they overlooked in reaching the conclusion they did.

Viewing the actions of the NCS directors during the period of July 26 (when Omnicare's conditional proposal was received) through July 28 (when NCS executed the merger agreement with Genesis) under the business judgment rule, the court easily concludes that the NCS directors acted with adequate knowledge of all material facts and made a rational judgment as to the risks and rewards of agreeing to the Genesis offer.

The NCS directors realized that the various conditions to the Omnicare proposal, . . . would create real risk if the directors tried to explore that proposal. To begin with, the exclusivity agreement did not permit the NCS directors to discuss or negotiate the July 26 letter with Omnicare. Moreover, Independent Committee member Osborne testified that, even apart from the exclusivity agreement, he would not have considered it wise to risk losing a definitive deal with Genesis for the sake of pursuing Omnicare's "highly conditional expression of interest."[46] According to Osborne, this was a very clear decision. Similarly, in discussing the risk of losing the Genesis bid, director and Independent Committee member Sells noted that, given NCS's past negotiations with Omnicare that had led only to . . . bankruptcy proposals, NCS simply could not assume that Omnicare's conditional proposal would be likely to result in an agreement superior to the Genesis offer.

Although hesitant to approach Omnicare, the Independent Committee members put Omnicare's conditional proposal to good use by [negotiating] with Genesis for better terms. This gambit succeeded in extracting a substantial increase in the consideration offered . . . . This increased offer from Genesis, however, did not come without a cost. Genesis made clear that its new offer was a "take it or leave it" proposition. If the revised proposal was not accepted and the requisite agreements executed by the end of the day on July 28, Genesis would withdraw its offer and terminate negotiations. It is true that in some cases courts have expressed skepticism over threats of this nature. But, the record here is convincing that Genesis would have withdrawn its offer and walked away from the deal if NCS violated the exclusivity agreement or allowed Genesis's deadline to pass.

---

46. The overall quality of testimony given by the NCS directors is among the strongest this court has ever seen. All four NCS directors were deposed, and each deposition makes manifest the care and attention given to this project by every member of the board.

Given the dynamic existing on July 28, the record before the court does not support even a preliminary finding that the NCS directors failed to fulfill their fiduciary duties when they "shopped" Omnicare's proposal to Genesis, obtained a substantial improvement in the terms of that offer and then approved the transaction without contacting Omnicare. The process they followed was certainly a rational one, given the circumstances they then confronted. After looking for more than two years for a transaction that offered fair value to all NCS stakeholders, the board acted appropriately in approving the Genesis merger proposal, including the "deal protection" devices demanded by Genesis.

Notes and Questions

1. Notes

a. The Delaware Supreme Court, in a deeply divided and highly controversial decision, reversed on the ground that the NCS directors had violated their duty of loyalty by agreeing to provisions that prevented NCS from abandoning the Genesis agreement if a superior transaction presented itself. The court assumed, without deciding, that the NCS board had met its duty of care. *Omnicare, Inc. v. NCS Healthcare, Inc.*, 818 A2d 914, 929 (Del. 2003).

b. *Smith v. Van Gorkom*, 488 A.2d 858, 873 (Del. 1985), cited by the court, was just as divided and even more controversial than the supreme court's decision in *NCS*. In *Smith*, the directors were held personally liable for violating their duty of care in approving the sale of the entire company. There was no allegation of any duty of loyalty breach. The *Smith* decision presented the first realistic possibility that unquestionably loyal directors could nonetheless be held personally liable for acting with insufficient information. Where the plaintiff can, at some point, show causation between the directors' lack of care and damage to the corporation, a remedy is compensatory. However, where a duty of care violation leads to rescission, then no damage link has been shown; the award is simply to punish the directors. Chancellor Allen describes the case law setting and explores a bit of the theoretical underpinnings:

> Cases holding directors liable for a breach of the duty of attention or care, uncomplicated by self-dealing or conflict of interest are rare. *See, e.g.,* Joseph W. Bishop, Jr., *Sitting Ducks and Decoy Ducks: New Trends in the Indemnification of Corporate Directors and Officers,* 77 Yale L.J. 1078 (1968). One authority identifies only ten modern cases as finding actionable director negligence without a concurrent breach of loyalty or conflict of interest. *See Dennis J. Block, Nancy E. Barton & Stephen A. Radin, The Business Judgment Rule: Fiduciary Duties of Corporate Directors* 72-75 (4th ed. 1993). Of those cases in which liability has been imposed upon directors for failure to act on an informed basis, none has employed a rescissory damage measure of remedy. Date of transaction or out-of-pocket damages have been the sole remedy afforded.[17]

---

17. The remaining cases identified by Block, Barton and Radin involved direct losses to the corporation due to negligence, not loss of appreciation which could have accrued to the benefit of the shareholders but for the directors' negligence. In these cases as well, courts did not calculate damages to include the appreciated value of a lost opportunity. *See, e.g., Hoye v. Meek,* 795 F.2d 893 (10th Cir. 1986) (directors liable for the actual losses incurred due to their negligent investing); *Brane v. Roth,* 590 N.E.2d 587 (Ind. Ct. App. 1992) (awarding damages equal to the loss suffered by the corporation attributable to the directors' negligent failure to hedge grain futures); *Francis v. United Jersey Bank,* 432 A.2d 814 (N.J. 1981) (holding a director liable for corporate funds misappropriated by corporate officers).

The lack of authority actually imposing rescissory damages on a corporate director in a negligence case, should not itself be fatal to plaintiff's claim. It does require us to move to the level of principle and policy. That deeper analysis must begin with trust law, which provides a fertile, if sometimes risky, analogy for corporate law.

But before undertaking that analysis, it is important to note the ways in which trust law differs from corporate law. In general, the duties of a trustee to trust beneficiaries (those of loyalty, good faith, and due care), while broadly similar to those of a corporate director to his corporation, are different in significant respects. Corporate directors are responsible for often complex and demanding decisions relating to the operations of business institutions. The nature of business competition insures that these directors will often be required to take risks with the assets they manage. Indeed, an unwillingness to take risks prudently is inconsistent with the role of a diligent director. The trustees role is, classically, quite different. The role of the trustee is prudently to manage assets placed in trust, within the parameters set down in the trust instrument. The classic trusteeship is not essentially a risk taking enterprise, but a caretaking one. Hence, while trustees may be surcharged for negligence, a corporate director is only considered to have breached his duty of care in instances of gross negligence.

The duty of loyalty of a trustee also developed differently than that of a corporate director. Traditionally a trustee could not enter self-dealing transactions, even if the transaction was in all other respects, fair. Modernly at least, corporate directors may negotiate transactions with respect to which they "stand on both sides" if the terms of the deal, and the process by which it was negotiated are entirely fair. This reflects a significant difference in the expectations of the parties to these two relationships. A trusteeship from its inception has been imbued with a moral element; it is considered fundamental that trustees avoid even the appearance of dishonesty or disloyalty to maintain the integrity of this institution. The essence of the director-shareholder relationship while not devoid of moral overtones is more firmly grounded in economics: shareholders expect, and directors are required to avoid only those self-interested actions which come at the expense of the corporation or its shareholders.

The differing nature of the duty of loyalty in these relationships is also reflected in the idea that a trustee's failure to adhere to the requirements set down in the trust instrument is itself a breach of loyalty. A trustee's obligation flows to both the beneficiary, the person for whose benefits the assets are held, as well as the settlor, who often gives specific instructions which constitute an essential aspect of the "trust" placed in the trustee. When a trustee fails to fulfill the dictates of the trust instrument, he has failed in his obligation to the settlor to loyally carry out the settlor's wishes. In corporation law, by contract, such a concept is alien. Typically the certificate of incorporation confers broad minimally constrained authority upon the board to engage the corporation in business in all lawful ways.

These distinctions between trust law and corporate law, while of tone and tenor, are important. They do suggest that, insofar as negligence uncomplicated by a breach of loyalty is concerned, important policies having to do with the nature of the legal institutions of trust and of corporation require that the corporate liability rule should certainly remain less stringent than that of the trust law. To the extent that corporate directors are exposed to liability for negligence under a rescissory damages formula, their ability to fulfill their basic function as prudent risk-takers may be hindered.

Cinerama, Inc. v. Technicolor, Inc., 663 A.2d 1134, 1147-1148 (Del. Ch. 1994) (Allen, Ch.)

c. Chancellor Allen, in *Caremark*, set out his understanding of the standard of review in failure to monitor settings:

Generally where a claim of directorial liability for corporate loss is predicated upon ignorance of liability creating activities within the corporation, . . . in my opinion only a sustained or systematic failure of the board to exercise oversight — such as an utter failure to attempt to assure a reasonable information and reporting system exists — will establish the lack of good faith that is a necessary condition to liability. Such a test of liability — lack of good faith as evidenced by sustained or systematic failure of a director to exercise reasonable oversight — is quite high. But, a demanding test of liability in the oversight context is probably beneficial to corporate shareholders as a class, as it is in the board decision context, since it makes board service by qualified persons more likely, while continuing to act as a stimulus to *good faith performance of duty* by such directors.

In re Caremark International Derivative Litigation, 698 A.2d 959, 971 (Del. Ch. 1996) (Allen, Ch.).

2. Reality Check

a. Why do plaintiffs claim that the NCS board breached the duty of care?
b. What standard of review does Vice Chancellor Lamb use?
c. How is the standard of review different from the board's standard of conduct?

3. Suppose

a. Suppose this case had arisen in an MBCA jurisdiction. What portions of the MBCA would be relevant? Would the analysis or result have been different?

4. What Do You Think?

a. Do you think the board was grossly negligent in entering into the Genesis transaction?
b. How much did Omnicare's prior actions influence the NCS board? Do you think that influence was warranted?
c. Do you think the standard of review in duty of care cases should be gross negligence? If not, what standard would you propose?
d. Should typical duty of care cases and *Caremark*-type claims have different standards of review?

C. PREVAILING DESPITE THE APPLICATION OF THE BUSINESS JUDGMENT RULE

The Delaware Supreme Court has frequently suggested that a plaintiff who has not overcome the business judgment rule might still succeed if he or she can show that the corporation's action cannot be attributed to any "rational business purpose." See *Sinclair Oil Corp. v. Levien,* 280 A.2d 717, 720 (Del. 1971) (Wolcott, C.J.).

If the Delaware courts mean what they say, is a board decision that has no rational business purpose a violation of the duty of care, the duty of loyalty, a duty of good faith, or a duty to be sane? Chancellor Allen had this to say about this possibility:

There is a theoretical exception . . . that holds that some decisions may be so "egregious" that liability for losses they cause may follow even in the absence of proof of conflict of interest or improper motivation. The exception, however, has resulted in no awards of money judgments against corporate officers or directors in this jurisdiction and, to my knowledge only the dubious holding in this Court of *Gimbel v. Signal*

Companies, Inc., 316 A.2d 599 (Del. Ch.) *aff'd* 316 A.2d 619 (Del. 1974), seems to grant equitable relief in the absence of a claimed conflict or improper motivation. Thus, to allege that a corporation has suffered a loss as a result of a lawful transaction, within the corporation's powers, authorized by a corporate fiduciary *acting in a good faith pursuit of corporate purposes,* does not state a claim for relief against that fiduciary no matter how foolish the investment may appear in retrospect.

Gagliardi v. TriFoods International, Inc., 683 A.2d 1049, 1051-1052 (Del. Ch. 1996) (Allen, Ch.)

As a practical matter, how likely is it that a plaintiff who can neither show a duty of loyalty issue nor show that the directors acted without all material information reasonably available can nonetheless show that the board's decision has no rational business purpose? If such a setting seems impossible to you, why do you think the Delaware courts have reiterated this possibility?

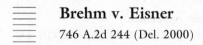

Brehm v. Eisner
746 A.2d 244 (Del. 2000)

Before VEASEY, C.J., WALSH, HOLLAND, HARTNETT and BERGER, JJ., constituting the Court en Banc.

VEASEY, C.J.

The claims before us are that: (a) the board of directors of The Walt Disney Company ("Disney") as it was constituted in 1995 (the "Old Board") breached its fiduciary duty in approving an extravagant and wasteful Employment Agreement of Michael S. Ovitz as president of Disney; [and] (b) the Disney board of directors as it was constituted in 1996 (the "New Board") breached its fiduciary duty in agreeing to a "non-fault" termination of the Ovitz Employment Agreement, a decision that was extravagant and wasteful; . . .

The Complaint, consisting of 88 pages and 285 paragraphs, is a pastiche of prolix invective. It is permeated with conclusory allegations of the pleader and quotations from the media, mostly of an editorial nature (even including a cartoon). A pleader may rely on factual statements in the media as some of the "tools at hand" from which the pleader intends to derive the particularized facts necessary to comply with Chancery Rule 11(b)(3) and Chancery Rule 23.1. But many of the quotations from the media in the Complaint simply echo plaintiffs' conclusory allegations. Accordingly, they serve no purpose other than to complicate the work of reviewing courts.

This is potentially a very troubling case on the merits. On the one hand, it appears from the Complaint that: (a) the compensation and termination payout for Ovitz were exceedingly lucrative, if not luxurious, compared to Ovitz' value to the Company; and (b) the processes of the boards of directors in dealing with the approval and termination of the Ovitz Employment Agreement were casual, if not sloppy and perfunctory. On the other hand, the Complaint is so inartfully drafted that it was properly dismissed under our pleading standards for derivative suits. From what we can ferret out of this deficient pleading, the processes of the Old Board and the New Board were hardly paradigms of good corporate governance practices. Moreover, the sheer size of the payout to Ovitz, as alleged, pushes the envelope of judicial respect for the business judgment of directors in making compensation decisions. Therefore, both as to the processes of the two Boards and the waste test, this is a close case.

But our concerns about lavish executive compensation and our institutional aspirations that boards of directors of Delaware corporations live up to the highest standards of good corporate practices do not translate into a holding that these plaintiffs have set forth particularized facts excusing a pre-suit demand under our law and our pleading requirements.

This appeal presents several important issues, including: . . . the scope of the business judgment rule as it interacts with the relevant pleading requirements. To some extent, the principles enunciated in this opinion restate and clarify our prior jurisprudence.

FACTS

This statement of facts is taken from the Complaint. We have attempted to summarize here the essence of Plaintiffs' factual allegations on the key issues before us, disregarding the many conclusions that are not supported by factual allegations.

A. The 1995 Ovitz Employment Agreement

By an agreement dated October 1, 1995, Disney hired Ovitz as its president. He was a long-time friend of Disney Chairman and CEO Michael Eisner. At the time, Ovitz was an important talent broker in Hollywood. Although he lacked experience managing a diversified public company, other companies with entertainment operations had been interested in hiring him for high-level executive positions. The Employment Agreement was unilaterally negotiated by Eisner and approved by the Old Board. Their judgment was that Ovitz was a valuable person to hire as president of Disney, and they agreed ultimately with Eisner's recommendation in awarding him an extraordinarily lucrative contract.

Ovitz' Employment Agreement had an initial term of five years and required that Ovitz "devote his full time and best efforts exclusively to the Company," with exceptions for volunteer work, service on the board of another company, and managing his passive investments.[5] In return, Disney agreed to give Ovitz a base salary of $1 million per year, a discretionary bonus, and two sets of stock options (the "A" options and the "B" options) that collectively would enable Ovitz to purchase 5 million shares of Disney common stock.

The "A" options were scheduled to vest . . . beginning on September 30, 1998 (i.e., at the end of the third full year of employment) and continuing for the following two years . . . . The agreement specifically provided that the "A" options would vest immediately if Disney granted Ovitz a non-fault termination of the Employment Agreement. Although scheduled to vest annually starting in September 2001 (i.e., the year *after* the last "A" option would vest), the "B" options were conditioned on Ovitz and Disney first having agreed to extend his employment beyond the five-year term of the Employment Agreement. Furthermore, Ovitz would forfeit the right to qualify for the "B" options if his initial employment term of five years ended prematurely for any reason, even if from a non-fault termination.

The Employment Agreement provided for three ways by which Ovitz' employment might end. He might serve his five years and Disney might decide against offering him a new contract. If so, Disney would owe Ovitz a $10 million termination

---

5. The agreement implicitly emphasized the importance of having Disney receive Ovitz' full attention by mentioning, in a section stating the unique nature of Ovitz' services, that the Company would specifically be entitled to equitable relief if Ovitz failed to provide it with "the exclusivity of his services."

payment.[6] Before the end of the initial term, Disney could terminate Ovitz for "good cause" only if Ovitz committed gross negligence or malfeasance, or if Ovitz resigned voluntarily. Disney would owe Ovitz no additional compensation if it terminated him for "good cause." Termination without cause (non-fault termination) would entitle Ovitz to the present value of his remaining salary payments through September 30, 2000, a $10 million severance payment, an additional $7.5 million for each fiscal year remaining under the agreement, and the immediate vesting of the . . . "A" Options.

Plaintiffs allege that the Old Board knew that Disney needed a strong second-in-command. Disney had recently made several acquisitions, and questions lingered about Eisner's health due to major heart surgery. The Complaint further alleges that "Eisner had demonstrated little or no capacity to work with important or well-known subordinate executives who wanted to position themselves to succeed him," citing the departures of Disney executives Jeffrey Katzenberg, Richard Frank, and Stephen Bollenbach as examples. Thus, the Board knew that, to increase the chance for long-term success, it had to take extra care in reviewing a decision to hire Disney's new president.

But Eisner's decision that Disney should hire Ovitz as its president was not entirely well-received. When Eisner told three members of the Old Board in mid-August 1995 that he had decided to hire Ovitz, all three "denounced the decision." Although not entirely clear from the Complaint, the vote of the Old Board approving the Ovitz Employment Agreement two months later appears to have been unanimous. Aside from a conclusory attack that the Old Board followed Eisner's bidding, the Complaint fails to allege any particularized facts that the three directors changed their initial reactions through anything other than the typical process of further discussion and individual contemplation.

The Complaint then alleges that the Old Board failed properly to inform itself about the total costs and incentives of the Ovitz Employment Agreement, especially the severance package. This is the key allegation related to this issue on appeal. Specifically, plaintiffs allege that the Board failed to realize that the contract gave Ovitz an incentive to find a way to exit the Company via a non-fault termination as soon as possible because doing so would permit him to earn more than he could by fulfilling his contract. The Complaint alleges, however, that the Old Board had been advised by a corporate compensation expert, Graef Crystal, in connection with its decision to approve the Ovitz Employment Agreement. Two public statements by Crystal form the basis of the allegation that the Old Board failed to consider the incentives and the total cost of the severance provisions, but these statements by Crystal were not made until after Ovitz left Disney in December 1996, approximately 14½ months after being hired.

The first statement, published in a December 23, 1996 article in the web-based magazine *Slate,* quoted Crystal as saying, in part, "Of course, the overall costs of the package would go up sharply in the event of Ovitz's termination (*and I wish now that I'd made a spreadsheet showing just what the deal would total if Ovitz had been fired at any time*)." The second published statement appeared in an article about three weeks later in the January 13, 1997 edition of *California Law Business*. The article appears first to paraphrase Crystal: "With no one expecting failure, the sleeper clauses in Ovitz's contract seemed innocuous, Crystal says, explaining that no one added up the total cost of the severance package." The article then quotes Crystal as saying that the amount of Ovitz' severance was "shocking" and that "*[n]obody quantified this and I wish we had.*" One of the charging paragraphs of the Complaint concludes:

6. All the "A" options would have vested, but he would not receive the "B" options.

57. As has been conceded by Graef Crystal, the executive compensation consultant who advised the Old Board with respect to the Ovitz Employment Agreement, the Old Board *never* considered the costs that would be incurred by Disney in the event Ovitz was terminated from the Company for a reason other than cause prior to the natural expiration of the Ovitz Employment Agreement.

Although repeated in various forms in the Complaint, these quoted admissions by Crystal constitute the extent of the factual support for the allegation that the Old Board failed properly to consider the severance elements of the agreement. This Court, however, must juxtapose these allegations with the legal presumption that the Old Board's conduct was a proper exercise of business judgment. That presumption includes the statutory protection for a board that relies in good faith on an expert advising the Board.[9] We must decide whether plaintiffs' factual allegations, if proven, would rebut that presumption.

B. The New Board's Actions in Approving the Non-Fault Termination

Soon after Ovitz began work, problems surfaced and the situation continued to deteriorate during the first year of his employment. To support this allegation, the plaintiffs cite various media reports detailing internal complaints and providing external examples of alleged business mistakes. The Complaint uses these reports to suggest that the New Board had reason to believe that Ovitz' performance and lack of commitment met the gross negligence or malfeasance standards of the termination-for-cause provisions of the contract.

The deteriorating situation, according to the Complaint, led Ovitz to begin seeking alternative employment and to send Eisner a letter in September 1996 that the Complaint paraphrases as stating his dissatisfaction with his role and expressing his desire to leave the Company. The Complaint also admits that Ovitz would not actually resign before negotiating a non-fault severance agreement because he did not want to jeopardize his rights to a lucrative severance in the form of a "non-fault termination" under the terms of the 1995 Employment Agreement.

On December 11, 1996, Eisner and Ovitz agreed to arrange for Ovitz to leave Disney on the non-fault basis provided for in the 1995 Employment Agreement. Eisner then "caused" the New Board[11] "to rubber-stamp his decision (by 'mutual consent')." This decision was implemented by a December 27, 1996 letter to Ovitz from defendant Sanford M. Litvack, an officer and director of Disney.

Although the non-fault termination left Ovitz with what essentially was a very lucrative severance agreement, it is important to note that Ovitz and Disney had negotiated for that severance payment at the time they initially contracted in 1995, and in the end the payout to Ovitz did not exceed the 1995 contractual benefits. Consequently, Ovitz received the $10 million termination payment, $7.5 million for part of the fiscal year remaining under the agreement and the immediate vesting of . . . the "A" options. As a result of his termination Ovitz would not receive the . . . "B" options that he would have been entitled to if he had completed the full term of the Employment Agreement and if his contract were renewed.

The Complaint charges the New Board with waste, computing the value of the severance package agreed to by the Board at over $140 million, consisting of cash payments of about $39 million and the value of the immediately vesting "A" options

---

9. *See* [DGCL] §141(e) . . . .
11. The composition of the New Board differed slightly from the composition of the Old Board.

of over $101 million. The Complaint quotes Crystal, the Old Board's expert, as saying in January 1997 that Ovitz' severance package was a "shocking amount of severance."

The allegation of waste is based on the inference most favorable to plaintiffs that Disney owed Ovitz nothing, either because he had resigned (*de facto*) or because he was unarguably subject to firing for cause. These allegations must be juxtaposed with the presumption that the New Board exercised its business judgment in deciding how to resolve the potentially litigable issues of whether Ovitz had actually resigned or had definitely breached his contract. We must decide whether plaintiffs' factual allegations, if proven, would rebut that presumption.

PRINCIPLES OF CORPORATION LAW COMPARED WITH GOOD CORPORATE GOVERNANCE PRACTICES

This is a case about whether there should be personal liability of the directors of a Delaware corporation to the corporation for lack of due care in the decisionmaking process and for waste of corporate assets. This case is not about the failure of the directors to establish and carry out ideal corporate governance practices.

All good corporate governance practices include compliance with statutory law and case law establishing fiduciary duties. But the law of corporate fiduciary duties and remedies for violation of those duties are distinct from the aspirational goals of ideal corporate governance practices. Aspirational ideals of good corporate governance practices for boards of directors that go beyond the minimal legal requirements of the corporation law are highly desirable, often tend to benefit stockholders, sometimes reduce litigation and can usually help directors avoid liability. But they are not required by the corporation law and do not define standards of liability.

The inquiry here is not whether we would disdain the composition, behavior and decisions of Disney's Old Board or New Board as alleged in the Complaint if we were Disney stockholders. In the absence of a legislative mandate, that determination is not for the courts. That decision is for the stockholders to make in voting for directors, urging other stockholders to reform or oust the board, or in making individual buy-sell decisions involving Disney securities. The sole issue that this Court must determine is whether the particularized facts alleged in this Complaint provide a reason to believe that the conduct of the Old Board in 1995 and the New Board in 1996 constituted a violation of their fiduciary duties.

PLAINTIFFS' CONTENTION THAT THE OLD BOARD VIOLATED THE PROCESS DUTY OF CARE IN APPROVING THE OVITZ EMPLOYMENT AGREEMENT

Certainly in this case the economic exposure of the corporation to the payout scenarios of the Ovitz contract was material, particularly given its large size, for purposes of the directors' decisionmaking process.[49] And those dollar exposure numbers were reasonably available because the logical inference from plaintiffs' allegations is that Crystal or the New Board could have calculated the numbers. Thus, the objective

---

49. The term "material" is used in this context to mean relevant and of a magnitude to be important to directors in carrying out their fiduciary duty of care in decisionmaking. One must also keep in mind that the size of executive compensation for a large public company in the current environment often involves huge numbers. This is particularly true in the entertainment industry where the enormous revenues from one "hit" movie or enormous losses from a "flop" place in perspective the compensation of executives whose genius or misjudgment, as the case may be, may have contributed substantially to the "hit" or "flop."

tests of reasonable availability and materiality were satisfied by this Complaint. But that is not the end of the inquiry for liability purposes.

Although the Court of Chancery did not expressly predicate its decision on Section 141(e), Crystal is presumed to be an expert on whom the Board was entitled to rely in good faith under Section 141(e) in order to be "fully protected." Plaintiffs must rebut the presumption that the directors properly exercised their business judgment, including their good faith reliance on Crystal's expertise. What Crystal *now* believes *in hindsight* that he and the Board *should have done* in 1995 does not provide that rebuttal. That is not to say, however, that a rebuttal of the presumption of proper reliance on the expert under Section 141(e) cannot be pleaded consistent with Rule 23.1 in a properly framed complaint setting forth particularized facts creating reason to believe that the Old Board's conduct was grossly negligent.

To survive a Rule 23.1 motion to dismiss in a due care case where an expert has advised the board in its decisionmaking process, the complaint must allege particularized facts (not conclusions) that, if proved, would show, for example, that: (a) the directors did not in fact rely on the expert; (b) their reliance was not in good faith; (c) they did not reasonably believe that the expert's advice was within the expert's professional competence; (d) the expert was not selected with reasonable care by or on behalf of the corporation, and the faulty selection process was attributable to the directors; (e) the subject matter (in this case the cost calculation) that was material and reasonably available was so obvious that the board's failure to consider it was grossly negligent regardless of the expert's advice or lack of advice; or (f) that the decision of the Board was so unconscionable as to constitute waste or fraud.[56] This Complaint includes no particular allegations of this nature, and therefore it was subject to dismissal as drafted.

Plaintiffs also contend that Crystal's latter-day admission is "valid and binding" on the Old Board. This argument is without merit. Crystal was the Board's expert *ex ante* for purposes of advising the directors on the Ovitz Employment Agreement. He was not their agent *ex post* to make binding admissions.

We conclude that, although the language of the Court of Chancery was flawed in formulating the proper legal test to be used and in its reading of the Complaint, that pleading, as drafted, fails to create a reasonable doubt that the Old Board's decision in approving the Ovitz Employment Agreement was protected by the business judgment rule. Plaintiffs will be provided an opportunity to replead on this issue.

PLAINTIFFS' CONTENTION THAT THE OLD BOARD...COMMITTED WASTE AB INITIO WITH OVITZ' EMPLOYMENT AGREEMENT

Plaintiffs' principal theory is that the 1995 Ovitz Employment Agreement was a "wasteful transaction for Disney *ab initio*" because it was structured to "incentivize" Ovitz to seek an early non-fault termination. The Court of Chancery correctly dismissed this theory as failing to meet the stringent requirements of the waste test, i.e., "'an exchange that is so one sided that no business person of ordinary, sound

---

56. To be sure, directors have the power, authority and wide discretion to make decisions on executive compensation. *See* [DGCL] §122(5). As the often-cited Court of Chancery decision by Chancellor Seitz in *Saxe v. Brady* warns, there is an outer limit to that discretion, at which point a decision of the directors on executive compensation is so disproportionately large as to be unconscionable and constitute waste. 184 A.2d 602, 610 (Del. Ch. 1962); *see Grimes* [*v. Donald*], 673 A.2d [1207] at 1215 (Del. 1996) (noting that compensation decisions by an independent board are protected by the business judgment rule "unless the facts show that such amounts, compared with the services to be received in exchange, constitute waste or could not otherwise be the product of a valid exercise of business judgment") (citing *Saxe*, 184 A.2d at 610); ....

judgment could conclude that the corporation has received adequate considera-tion.'"[58] Moreover, the Court concluded that a board's decision on executive com-pensation is entitled to great deference. It is the essence of business judgment for a board to determine if "a 'particular individual warrant[s] large amounts of money, whether in the form of current salary or severance provisions.'"[59]

Specifically, the Court of Chancery inferred from a reading of the Complaint that the Board determined it had to offer an expensive compensation package to attract Ovitz and that they determined he would be valuable to the Company. The Court also concluded that the vesting schedule of the options actually was a disincentive for Ovitz to leave Disney. When he did leave pursuant to the non-fault termination, the Court noted that he left 2 million options (the "B" options) "on the table." Although we agree with the conclusion of the Court of Chancery that this particular Complaint is deficient, we do not foreclose the possibility that a properly framed complaint could pass muster.

Plaintiffs' disagreement on appeal with the decision of the Court of Chancery is basically a quarrel with the Old Board's judgment in evaluating Ovitz' worth *vis-à-vis* the lavish payout to him. We agree with the analysis of the Court of Chancery that the size and structure of executive compensation are inherently matters of judgment. As former Chancellor Allen stated in *Vogelstein*:

> The judicial standard for determination of corporate waste is well developed. Roughly, a waste entails an exchange of corporate assets for consideration so disproportionately small as to lie beyond the range at which any reasonable person might be willing to trade. Most often the claim is associated with a transfer of corporate assets that serves no corporate purpose; or for which no consideration at all is received. Such a transfer is in effect a gift. If, however, there is *any substantial* consideration received by the corporation, and if there is a *good faith judgment* that in the circumstances the transac-tion is worthwhile, there should be no finding of waste, even if the fact finder would conclude *ex post* that the transaction was unreasonably risky. Any other rule would deter corporate boards from the optimal rational acceptance of risk, for reasons explained elsewhere. Courts are ill-fitted to attempt to weigh the "adequacy" of consideration under the waste standard or, *ex post*, to judge appropriate degrees of business risk.[63]

To be sure, there are outer limits, but they are confined to unconscionable cases where directors irrationally squander or give away corporate assets. Here, however, we find no error in the decision of the Court of Chancery on the waste test.

Courts do not measure, weigh or quantify directors' judgments. We do not even decide if they are reasonable in this context. Due care in the decisionmaking context is *process* due care only. Irrationality[65] is the outer limit of the business judgment rule. Irrationality may be the functional equivalent of the waste test or it may tend to show that the decision is not made in good faith, which is a key ingredient of the business judgment rule.[66]

---

58. *In re The Walt Disney Co. Derivative Litig.*, 731 A.2d at 362 (quoting *Glazer v. Zapata Corp.*, 658 A.2d 176, 183 (Del. Ch. 1993)).

59. *Id.* (quoting *Grimes*, 673 A.2d at 1215).

63. [*Lewis v.*] *Vogelstein*, 699 A.2d 327 at 336 (Del. Ch. 1997) (emphasis in original) (citations omitted) . . . .

65. Directors' business "decisions will not be disturbed if they can be attributed to any rational business purpose." *Sinclair Oil Corp. v. Levien*, 280 A.2d 717, 720 (Del. 1971).

66. The business judgment rule has been well formulated by *Aronson* and other cases. *See, e.g., Aronson*, 473 A.2d at 812 ("It is a presumption that in making a business decision the directors . . . acted

PLAINTIFFS' CONTENTION THAT THE NEW BOARD COMMITTED WASTE IN ITS DECISION THAT OVITZ' CONTRACT SHOULD BE TERMINATED ON A "NON-FAULT" BASIS

The plaintiffs contend in this Court that Ovitz resigned or committed acts of gross negligence or malfeasance that constituted grounds to terminate him for cause. In either event, they argue that the Company had no obligation to Ovitz and that the directors wasted the Company's assets by causing it to make an unnecessary and enormous payout of cash and stock options when it permitted Ovitz to terminate his employment on a "non-fault" basis. We have concluded, however, that the Complaint currently before us does not set forth particularized facts that he resigned or unarguably breached his Employment Agreement.

The Complaint does not allege facts that would show that Ovitz had, in fact, resigned before the Board acted on his non-fault termination. Plaintiffs contend, in effect, that the sum total of Ovitz' actions constituted a *de facto* resignation. But the Complaint does not allege that Ovitz had *actually* resigned. It alleges merely that he: (a) was dissatisfied with his role; (b) was underperforming; (c) was seeking and entertaining other job offers; and (d) had written to Eisner on September 5, 1996, "express[ing] his desire to quit." These are not particularized allegations that he resigned, either actually or constructively.

Additionally, the Complaint is internally inconsistent with plaintiffs' argument that Ovitz had resigned. The Complaint alleges that Ovitz would not actually resign before he could achieve a lucrative payout under the generous terms of his 1995 Employment Agreement. The clear inference from the Complaint is that he would lose all leverage by resigning.

The Complaint alleges that it was waste for the Board to pay Ovitz essentially the full amount he was due on the non-fault termination basis because he should have been fired for cause. Ovitz' contract provided that he could be fired for cause only if he was grossly negligent or committed acts of malfeasance. Plaintiffs contend that ample grounds existed to fire Ovitz for cause under these terms.

Construed most favorably to plaintiffs, the facts in the Complaint (disregarding conclusory allegations) show that Ovitz' performance as president was disappointing at best, that Eisner admitted it had been a mistake to hire him, that Ovitz lacked commitment to the Company, that he performed services for his old company, and that he negotiated for other jobs (some very lucrative) while being required under the contract to devote his full time and energy to Disney.

All this shows is that the Board had *arguable* grounds to fire Ovitz for cause. But what is alleged is only an *argument*—perhaps a good one—that Ovitz' conduct constituted gross negligence or malfeasance. First, given the facts as alleged, Disney would have had to persuade a trier of fact and law of this argument in any litigated dispute with Ovitz. Second, that process of persuasion could involve expensive litigation, distraction of executive time and company resources, lost opportunity costs, more bad publicity and an outcome that was uncertain at best and, at worst, could have resulted in damages against the Company.

---

on an informed basis, in good faith and in the honest belief that the action taken was in the best interests of the corporation."). Thus, directors' decisions will be respected by courts unless the directors are interested or lack independence relative to the decision, do not act in good faith, act in a manner that cannot be attributed to a rational business purpose or reach their decision by a grossly negligent process that includes the failure to consider all material facts reasonably available.

The Complaint, in sum, contends that the Board committed waste by agreeing to the very lucrative payout to Ovitz under the non-fault termination provision because it had no obligation to him, thus taking the Board's decision outside the protection of the business judgment rule. Construed most favorably to plaintiffs, the Complaint contends that, by reason of the New Board's available arguments of resignation and good cause, it had the leverage to negotiate Ovitz down to a more reasonable payout than that guaranteed by his Employment Agreement. But the Complaint fails on its face to meet the waste test because it does not allege with particularity facts tending to show that no reasonable business person would have made the decision that the New Board made under these circumstances.

To rule otherwise would invite courts to become super-directors, measuring matters of degree in business decisionmaking and executive compensation. Such a rule would run counter to the foundation of our jurisprudence.

Nevertheless, plaintiffs will have another opportunity — if they are able to do so consistent with Chancery Rule 11 — to file a short and plain statement alleging particularized facts creating a reasonable doubt that the New Board's decision regarding the Ovitz non-fault termination was protected by the business judgment rule.

CONCLUSION

One can understand why Disney stockholders would be upset with such an extraordinarily lucrative compensation agreement and termination payout awarded a company president who served for only a little over a year and who underperformed to the extent alleged. That said, there is a very large — though not insurmountable — burden on stockholders who believe they should pursue the remedy of a derivative suit instead of selling their stock or seeking to reform or oust these directors from office.

Delaware has pleading rules and an extensive judicial gloss on those rules that must be met in order for a stockholder to pursue the derivative remedy. Sound policy supports these rules, as we have noted. This Complaint, which is a blunderbuss of a mostly conclusory pleading, does not meet that burden, and it was properly dismissed.

Notes and Questions

1. Notes

a. An omitted portion of the opinion affirmed the Chancellor's finding that the boards were disinterested and independent, essentially equivalent to a finding that the boards had met their duty of loyalty. The issue was presented in an odd posture because the plaintiffs did not challenge the Chancellor's findings on appeal; only amici curiae did so. Nonetheless, the Supreme Court affirmed the Chancellor's findings and precluded relitigation of the issue.

b. A subsequent opinion in this litigation is found on pages 476 and 482.

c. The Old Board comprised the following individuals:

Inside or retired inside directors
   Mr. Eisner, chairman of the board and chief executive officer
   Stephen F. Bollenbach, chief financial officer
   Roy E. Disney, vice chair of the board and head of the Animation Department
   Sanford M. Litvak, senior executive vice president and chief of corporate operations

Richard A. Nunis, chair of Walt Disney Attractions (theme parks and resorts)

E. Cardon Walker, retired chair of the board, chief executive officer, and president

Gary L. Wilson, former executive vice president and chief financial officer

Advisors to certain directors

Irwin E. Russell, Mr. Eisner's personal attorney

Stanley P. Gold, Mr. Disney's personal attorney

Outside directors

Reveta F. Bowers, head of school for the Center for Early Education, a private school in Los Angeles that some of Mr. Eisner's children attended

Ignacio E. Lozano, Jr., owner and publisher of *La Opinion*, the largest Spanish-language newspaper in Los Angeles and former U.S. ambassador to El Salvador

George J. Mitchell, former U.S. Senator

Sidney Poitier, actor, director, and writer

Robert A.M. Stern, internationally prominent architect

Raymond L. Watson, head of a major Southern California land company.

The New Board was the same as the Old Board except that Mr. Bollenbach resigned and three new members were added:

Thomas S. Murphy, retired head of the American Broadcasting Corporation (ABC), a Walt Disney Company subsidiary

Fr. Leo J. O'Donovan, S.J., President of Georgetown University, which one of Mr. Eisner's children attended

Mr. Ovitz, President.

d. The MBCA has possibly avoided the problem presented by *Brehm* by not expressly stating that directors can be liable for a transaction that violates neither their duty of loyalty nor their duty of care. The Official Comments to MBCA §§8.30 and 8.31 suggest that the rare "irrational" decision by an unconflicted, informed board is nonetheless actionable either on the ground that the director could not have "reasonably believed" the action to be appropriate, thus violating the duty of care under §8.30 or on the grounds that the director is acting in bad faith or does not reasonably believe the action to be in the corporation's best interest under §8.31(a)(2)(i) or (a)(2)(ii)(A). Does it make any practical difference whether such actions are treated as a violation of the fiduciary duties, the standards of review, or are simply, substantively, impermissible?

2. Reality Check

a. Chief Justice Veasey wrote, "[I]t appears from the Complaint that: (a) the compensation and termination payout for Ovitz were exceedingly lucrative, if not luxurious, compared to Ovitz' value to the Company; and (b) the processes of the boards of directors in dealing with the approval and termination of the Ovitz Employment Agreement were casual, if not sloppy and perfunctory." How can the plaintiffs lose?

b. What were the elements of Mr. Ovitz's compensation?

c. How did the Old Board meet its duty of care?

d. How did the New Board meet its duty of care?

e. What is the standard for waste? When does it apply?

f. Why did the plaintiffs fail to meet their burden as to waste?

g. What is the relation between the duty of care, waste, rational business purpose, and good faith?

3. Suppose

a. Imagine that Mr. Ovitz's compensation upon termination were $1.4 million. Would that affect the court's reasoning or the result? Imagine Mr. Ovitz's compensation upon termination were $1.4 billion. Would that affect the court's reasoning or the result?

4. What Do You Think?

a. Why did Mr. Ovitz's compensation consist of so many different elements? Did these elements serve different functions? If so, what were they? Were they effective?

b. Do you think some of the directors could have their loyalty to the company questioned? If so, which ones?

c. Chief Justice Veasey said that courts do not evaluate the substance of board decisions but only the process by which those decisions were approved. Is he correct? Why does he make this assertion?

5. You Draft It

a. Assume that the New Board decided to terminate Mr. Ovitz for good cause. Draft a letter to Mr. Ovitz that effects that termination, that articulates the board's reasons for termination, and that states the compensation consequences of that termination.

D. AMELIORATION OF LIABILITY FOR VIOLATIONS OF FIDUCIARY DUTIES

This and the two previous chapters have set out, in a rather elaborate way, the potential liabilities for officers and directors. Now we turn to several methods by which that liability can be ameliorated. These methods, of course, raise the question whether amelioration should even be permitted. After all, what sense does it make to set up a careful and nuanced system of conduct and liability and then permit directors to circumvent that system?

Before we work through these techniques, though, three other approaches to limiting liability are discussed elsewhere and are simply noted here. First, as we've seen in Chapter 12, boards are permitted to rely on reports made to them by board committees and others inside the corporation, (and certain advisors not within the corporation) at least in the absence of indications that reliance is unwarranted. See DGCL §141(e) and MBCA §8.30(d). In Delaware, to overcome the presumption that reliance is warranted a plaintiff must show that

> (a) the directors did not in fact rely on the expert; (b) their reliance was not in good faith; (c) they did not reasonably believe that the expert's advice was within the expert's professional competence; (d) the expert was not selected with reasonable care by or on behalf of the corporation, and the faulty selection process was attributable to the directors; (e) the subject matter . . . that was material and reasonably available was so obvious that the board's failure to consider it was grossly negligent

regardless of the expert's advice or lack of advice; or (f) that the decision of the Board was so unconscionable as to constitute waste or fraud.

Brehm v. Eisner, 746 A.2d 244, 262 (Del. 2000) (Veasey, C.J.)

A second approach, related to the first, is the ability of the board to delegate its powers either to a board committee or, more generally, to others within the corporation. Again, in the absence of an indication that those to whom powers have been delegated are not exercising those powers appropriately, the board is entitled to rely on the assumption that their delegates are acting in the corporation's best interest. See DGCL §§141(c) (delegation to board committees) and 142(a) (delegation to corporate officers) and MBCA §8.30(c). Further, DGCL §141(a) has been interpreted to give the board great discretion to delegate by virtue of the requirement that "The business and affairs of every corporation . . . shall be managed by *or under the direction of* a board of directors . . . ."

The third approach is a special case of the power to delegate. When some, but fewer than all, directors are sued for breaching their fiduciary duties, the board frequently constitutes the nondefendant directors as a committee (usually called a *special litigation committee*) to investigate the allegations and recommend whether pursuing those allegations is in the best interest of the corporation. Similar special committees are also frequently appointed when the corporation intends to enter into a transaction that, for some directors, presents a conflict of interest transaction. In that setting the committee is charged with determining whether the transaction is in the best interest of the corporation. Because these transactions are particularly sensitive, the amount of deference, if any, the court should give to these special committees is frequently a hotly contested issue. The use of special committees in these settings is treated separately in Chapter 15 dealing with shareholder litigation and Chapter 17 dealing with change of control situations.

1. Duty of Loyalty: Statutory Safe Harbor for Conflict of Interest Transactions

In Chapter 11 we defined "conflict of interest" as any objective suggestion that a director might not believe that the corporation's action was in the best interest of the corporation. We also saw that conflicts of interest can be laid out on a rough continuum from transactions between the director and the corporation (classic self-dealing) through transactions in which the "conflict" seems quite attenuated. We now revisit that issue in the context of ameliorating the potential for director liability in approving such transactions.

Most states have adopted statutes that affect at least some transactions that raise duty of loyalty problems. The DGCL section is 144(a) and the MBCA provisions are in Subchapter F, §§8.60-8.63. These statutes, which in this chapter we will call *CoI Safe Harbor* statutes, are nonexclusive, which means that parties and courts need not rely upon them. These statutes typically raise three principal issues, which we will examine separately:

1. Which *transactions* are eligible to be affected by the CoI Safe Harbors?
2. What are the procedural or substantive *prerequisites* that eligible transactions must meet to be affected by the CoI Safe Harbors?
3. What is the CoI Safe Harbor's *effect* on transactions that meet those prerequisites?

a. The Current Setting

i. Transactions Eligible to Be Affected.   The following case provides a nice canvass of the kinds of CoI Safe Harbors that have been adopted. Although the focus is on analyzing whether the statute extends to the transactions at issue, you should pay attention to the other two issues listed above, as well.

Shapiro v. Greenfield
764 A.2d 270 (Md. App. 2000)

KENNEY, J.

Charles Shapiro was the operating officer for [College Park Woods, Inc. ("College Park")] during the relevant time period. Other officers and directors included Joan Smith, Charles' sister, and Michael Shapiro, Charles' son. Appellee Marvin Greenfield is Charles Shapiro's cousin [and, along with his wife, Betty, is a minority shareholder of College Park].

In 1961, College Park acquired ... land in Prince George's County, on which it constructed the ... Clinton Plaza shopping center. By 1991, Clinton Plaza was only 50% leased and generating insufficient cash flow. It was decided that the best use of the land was not the continuation of Clinton Plaza, but redevelopment of the property into a substantially larger shopping center. Having determined that College Park was not capable of redeveloping Clinton Plaza on its own, the directors explored suitable partnerships or joint ventures, but for some time did not find any.

Charles Shapiro, the operating officer of College Park, subsequently developed a joint venture with ... an occasional business partner of his with experience developing retail space. The joint venture required the creation of ... Clinton Crossings Limited Partnership ("Clinton Crossings Partnership"), which was to own the redeveloped Clinton Plaza shopping center ... [Charles and Michael Shapiro were to own 50% of Clinton Crossings Partnership through certain other entities Charles controlled]. College Park was to transfer its fee simple interest in Clinton Plaza to Clinton Crossings Partnership in exchange for a fifty percent limited partnership interest in Clinton Crossings Partnership, the owner of the redeveloped center. Clinton Associates was to contribute everything necessary for the shopping center's redevelopment with the exception of the land.

As a limited partner, College Park would have no rights to manage, direct or control the affairs of Clinton Crossings Partnership. Clinton Crossings Partnership and [the Shapiro entities], on the other hand, would assume the risk associated with the redevelopment, while College Park would assume none.

On October 26, 1991, a special meeting of College Park's shareholders was called for the purpose of "considering and approving a resolution authorizing the corporation to enter into a limited partnership agreement with [the Shapiro Entities]" Advance notice of the meeting included documents that described the joint venture in detail [and disclosed the Shapiros' interest].

Appellees, Marvin and Betty Greenfield did not attend this special meeting. At the meeting, the shareholders present unanimously voted for the proposal. Appellees contend that following the October 26, 1991 meeting, they protested that the votes taken at the meeting were not valid as none of the directors could be considered disinterested directors and thus their votes as shareholders could not be counted.

On April 2, 1992, College Park directors met to ratify actions taken by the corporation at the special meeting and other occasions. Appellees filed this suit on July 15, 1992, against College Park and its directors, Charles S. Shapiro, Michael Shapiro, and Joan Smith, requesting "damages, an accounting, the appointment of a receiver, the imposition of a constructive trust, the dissolution of the corporation, attorneys' fees, costs and other legal and equitable relief."

The matter was tried before the Circuit Court for Montgomery County from May 1 to May 4, 1995. On June 29, 1995, the trial court entered an interlocutory order granting appellees' request for an accounting, and appointed a special master to determine specific factual issues. The special master filed his Report of Factual Findings, Conclusions, and Recommendations ("Report") on October 17, 1997.

On December 2, 1997, appellees filed a motion to appoint a receiver for College Park. On February 23, 1998, the trial court granted appellees' motion, appointing a single receiver for College Park .... Appellants filed a notice of appeal.

Concepts related to corporate opportunities and interested director transactions find their genesis in a director's duty of loyalty to the corporation. The longstanding common law rule in Maryland was "that any contract between a corporation and one of its officers or directors as to a matter in which the officer or director had a substantial personal interest was void or voidable." *Sullivan v. Easco Corp.,* 656 F. Supp. 531, 533 (D. Md. 1987) (quoting *Chesapeake Const. Corp. v. Rodman,* 536, 261 A.2d 156 (Md. 1970)). In 1976, Maryland adopted Md. Code §2-419 of the Corporations and Associations Article and rejected the common law rule. Such action recognized that "an interest conflict is not in itself a crime or a tort or necessarily injurious to others" and "in many situations, the corporation and the shareholders may secure major benefits from a transaction despite the presence of a director's conflicting interest." Dennis Block, et al., 1 *The Business Judgment Rule: Fiduciary Duties of Corporate Directors,* 266 (5th ed. 1998) (citing 2 Model Bus. Corp. Act Ann. §§8.60 to .63 Introductory Comment at 8-397 (3d ed. 1996)).

Corporations and Associations §2-419 provides that an interested director transaction is not void or voidable solely because of the conflict of interest and creates a "safe harbor" for certain transactions which satisfy the statute. Under the statute, an interested director could inform the shareholders or directors of his conflicting interests and give the board of directors or shareholders an opportunity to approve or ratify the transaction. Moreover, a nondisclosed interested director transaction may be valid, if it is found to be fair and reasonable to the corporation.

Essentially, appellees complain about the propriety of the transaction, with emphasis on College Park's relinquishment of College Park's fee simple interest in its property, College Park's reduced management role in the redevelopment project, and appellants' personal use of corporate assets. Although Charles Shapiro's involvement in the redevelopment project clearly demonstrates a conflict of interest, this is not a situation where appellants capitalized on an opportunity that should have been presented to the corporation, but was not. Rather, the corporation entered into a business arrangement with other entities in which certain directors had, or potentially had, a direct financial interest. Therefore, we hold that the transaction did not constitute a usurpation of corporate opportunity.

We turn now to the issue of whether the trial court properly conducted the analysis required under CA §2-419 for interested director transactions. In reviewing the Order of February 23, 1998, we note that the order refers to previous rulings on the various transactions, the "Report of the Special Master," .... Although there is reference to the Report of the Special Master, to which no exceptions were taken, ... the trial court does not direct the findings of that Report to an interested director analysis and to the determination of whether the Clinton Crossings transaction was fair and reasonable. Thus, we are unable to review the factual underpinnings of the trial court's conclusion that the Clinton Crossings transaction was not fair and reasonable. Under the circumstances, we will remand for reconsideration based on the analysis of an interested director transaction.

Part of that analysis will involve a determination of who are the interested directors. The trial court found that there were no disinterested directors. At oral argument, the parties disputed whether appellant Joan Smith was properly considered an interested director. Because the case is to be remanded to the trial court for reconsideration under CA §2-419, we will discuss Joan Smith's classification as an interested director, based on her family and financial relationship with Charles Shapiro and his financial interest in the transaction.

[T]he Model Business Corporations Act ("MBCA") ... expressly define[s] interested director.

The MBCA defines "conflicting interest" as

> (1) "Conflicting interest" with respect to a corporation means the interest a director of the corporation has respecting a transaction effected or proposed to be effected by the corporation ... if:
>
>   (i) whether or not the transaction is brought before the board of directors of the corporation for action, the director knows at the time of commitment that he or a related person[10] is a party to the transaction or has a beneficial financial interest in or so closely linked to the transaction and of such financial significance to the director or a related person that the interest would be reasonably expected to exert an influence on the director's judgment if he were called upon to vote on the transaction. [or
>
>   (ii) the transaction is brought (or is of such character and significance to the corporation that it would in the normal course be brought) before the board of directors of the corporation for action, and the director knows at the time of commitment that any of the following persons is either a party to the transaction or has a beneficial financial interest in or so closely linked to the transaction and of such financial significance to the person that the interest would reasonably be expected to exert an influence on the director's judgment if he were called upon to vote on the transaction: (A) an entity (other than the corporation) of which the director is a director, general partner, agent, or employee; (B) a person that controls one or more of the entities specified in subclause (A) or an entity that is controlled by, or is under common control with, one or more of the entities specified in subclause (A); or (C) an individual who is a general partner, principal, or employer of the director.]

Model Bus. Corp. Act. §8.60 (1999).

---

10. Related person is defined as "(i) the spouse (or a parent or sibling thereof) of the director, or a child, grandchild, sibling, parent (or spouse thereof) of the director, or an individual having the same home as the director, or a trust or estate of which an individual specified in this clause (i) is a substantial beneficiary; or (ii) a trust, estate, incompetent, conservatee, or minor of which the director is a fiduciary."

Appellants assert that Maryland rejected the MBCA...of "interested director" and thereby rejected the concept that a director who may be related to a party with a material financial interest in the transaction would also be classified as an interested party. The history of CA §2-419 suggests that that conclusion is too broad.

The Official Comment to the section provided:

> Prior to 1976, the Maryland General Corporation Law, unlike most state business corporation laws, contained no provision relating to so called "interested director transactions": that is, transactions between a corporation and any corporation, firm, or other entity in which any of its directors is a director or has a material financial interest.
>
> Chapter 567, Acts of 1976, adds a new §2-419 to the Corporation Law to apply to those transactions. This section — which was modeled after similar provisions in Delaware, New York, California, and other jurisdictions — was added to ensure uniformity of treatment of those transactions in Maryland, as well as to provide clear standards to corporations and directors who engage in such transactions.

Section 2-419 (1977 Cum. Supp.). The Delaware, New York, and California statutes are all quite alike in the treatment of interested director transactions. Similar to Maryland's statute, none define the term "interested director." In New York, case law has defined a director's interest as "either self-interest in the transaction at issue or a loss of independence because a director with no direct interest in a transaction is controlled by a self-interested director." *Park River Owners Corp. v. Bangser Klein Rocca & Blum, LLP,* 703 N.Y.S.2d 465, 466 (App. Div. 2000). All of the cited approaches ultimately focus on a director's ability to exercise independent judgment and the expected influence of a particular relationship on the director. That is the appropriate subject of inquiry in determining whether a director is to be considered an interested director in a particular transaction.

The underlying purpose of the interested director statute is clear. "Directors are required to avoid only those self-interested actions which come at the expense of the [corporation] or its shareholders." *Cinerama, Inc. v. Technicolor, Inc.,* 663 A.2d 1134, 1148 (Del. Ch. 1994), *aff'd,* 663 A.2d 1156 (Del. 1995). An interested director transaction may still be approved by a neutral decision making body. In other words, when a director's loyalty is questioned, courts must seek to ascertain whether the conflict "has deprived stockholders of a 'neutral decision-making body.'" *Technicolor,* 663 A.2d at 1170.

The definitions of the MBCA...related to interested directors and conflicting interests reflect this same consideration. When the director is actually involved in the transaction, determination is easy. When the director has no direct interests in the conflicting transaction, neither model creates a per se rule based on a familial or business relationship because a relationship between the parties does not necessarily destroy an individual's independent judgment. The pivotal provision is the second prong of the analysis, whether the relationship "would reasonably be expected to exert an influence on the director's judgment." MBCA.... The adoption of a per se rule would effectively undermine the purpose of the statute. If an otherwise uninterested director were to be adjudged an interested director based solely on his relationship, familial or otherwise, to another director interested in the transaction, directors who may well retain independence and their own business judgment will be precluded from considering the transaction. On the other hand, to conclude that directors are automatically disinterested because they are not directly involved in the transaction would also undermine the goal of a neutral decision making body, as some directors, because of their familial, personal, or financial relationship, may well be influenced by those relationships to the detriment of the corporation.

Therefore, when a director does not personally benefit from the transaction but, because of that director's relationship to a party interested in the transaction, it would reasonably be expected that the director's exercise of independent judgment would be compromised, that director will be deemed an interested director within the meaning of the statute.

We are unsure whether the trial court determined Joan Smith to be an interested director simply by virtue of her status as Charles Shapiro's sister. On remand, the trial court should evaluate whether the relationship between Joan Smith and Charles Shapiro, together with their direct or indirect interests in the transaction, would reasonably be expected to influence her decision and compromise her impartiality. If it is then determined that there were no disinterested directors, the trial court should evaluate the Clinton Crossings transaction from the "fair and reasonable" perspective with findings that support the determination.

Notes and Questions

1. Notes

a. Greenfield is the plaintiff and Shapiro is the defendant.

2. Reality Check

a. Which directors have potential conflicts of interest? Will all such directors be treated in the same way?

b. How was the company alleged to have been hurt by the transactions? Who was alleged to gain from those transactions and how did that gain come about?

c. Why was there no usurpation of a corporate opportunity?

3. Suppose

a. Suppose that this transaction arose in a corporation incorporated in a state that has adopted Subchapter F of the MBCA. How should the court analyze the conflicts of interest?

b. Suppose that this transaction arose in a Delaware corporation? How should the court analyze the conflicts of interest?

c. Suppose that this transaction arose in a corporation incorporated in a state that had no CoI Safe Harbor at all? How should the court analyze the conflicts of interest?

4. What Do You Think?

a. Do you think conflict of interest transactions that are not within the statutory definitions are affected at all by the CoI Safe Harbors? Should courts draw any implication about those transactions from the fact that they are not included in the statutory definition?

b. Should CoI Safe Harbors provide a narrow or a broad definition of the kinds of transactions that may be protected?

c. Are CoI Safe Harbors more trouble than they are worth? Why do you think state legislatures adopted them in the first place?

ii. Prerequisites to Being Affected by the CoI Safe Harbors. The CoI Safe Harbor statutes typically function as affirmative defenses. That is, the burden is on the defendants to establish both that the challenged transaction comes within the CoI Safe Harbor and that the requirements for being affected by the CoI Safe Harbor are met.

The CoI Safe Harbor statutes provide three avenues for affecting covered transactions. First, the transaction can be approved by certain directors. Second, the transaction can be approved by certain shareholders. Finally, the transaction can be found to be "fair" to the corporation. These are disjunctive; only one need be met. Further, attempted, but failed, compliance with one avenue does not preclude compliance with another avenue. As a practical matter, corporate managers rely on approval by certain directors rather than approval by certain shareholders, especially in publicly held corporations where a shareholder vote can be particularly expensive. Reliance on a shareholder vote is typically only in situations where the corporation law would require a shareholder vote to effect the particular transaction, even if that transaction did not present a conflict of interest.

Compliance with DGCL §144(a)(1) requires full disclosure to the board and approval by a majority of the *disinterested directors*, a term not defined in the statute, but that, as you might imagine, is defined consistently with the Delaware courts' definition of *disinterested* for duty of loyalty purposes. The MBCA also requires disclosure and approval by a majority (but at least two) of the "qualified directors," which is defined in §1.43.

In similar, but not identical, fashion, compliance with DGCL §144(a)(2) requires full disclosure to the shareholders and approval "in good faith by vote of the shareholders." Compare the MBCA, which, of course, requires disclosure to the shareholders but requires approval of a majority of the "qualified shares" — those shares not controlled by a director with a conflicting interest. See MBCA §8.63. Notice that the DGCL does not explicitly disenfranchise shares controlled by conflicted directors. Are such shares implicitly disenfranchised by the requirement that shareholder approval must be "in good faith"?

Finally, and conceptually most troublesome, is the alternative of establishing "fairness." Almost certainly this statutory concept is functionally identical to the entire fairness test we studied above. Theoretically, though, why is fairness a separate *statutory* test? If it were omitted from the statutes, transaction proponents could presumably still fall back on establishing fairness as a justification for the transaction. Further, in at least some states, case law holds that obtaining the requisite director or shareholder approval does not relieve the court of its obligation to do equity, which entails assessing the fairness of the transaction. In those states, a fairness alternative is not really an alternative at all.

iii. The Effect of Compliance with the CoI Safe Harbor. DGCL §144(a) is written in a rather passive fashion. It provides that no covered transaction that has met (1), (2), or (3) "shall be void or voidable solely [because of the conflict of interest], or solely because the director or officer is present at or participates in the meeting of the board or committee which authorizes the contract or transaction, or solely because any such director's or officer's votes are counted for such purpose ...." Case law suggests that compliance with §144(a) shifts the burden to the plaintiff to show that the transaction was not entirely fair.

By contrast, the MBCA is much more explicit about the effect of compliance. Section 8.61(b) provides that a complying transaction "may not be enjoined, set aside, or give rise to an award of damages or other sanctions, in a proceeding by a share-holder or by or in the right of the corporation, because the director, or any person with whom or which he has a personal, economic, or other association, has an interest in the transaction...."

Both statutes leave a few questions, though. What other reasons may render the transaction vulnerable to shareholder attack, particularly if compliance is achieved through a finding of fairness rather than director or shareholder approval? May or must a court draw any inference from compliance (or noncompliance) with the direc-tor or shareholder approval provisions?

Perhaps the most intriguing part of MBCA's Subchapter F is the provision that protects certain transactions that are *not* covered by the CoI Safe Harbor. The *Shapiro* case focused on the policy question of deciding upon which conflict of interest trans-actions should be eligible for protection. All the CoI Safe Harbor statutes include the core self-dealing situation as the paradigm and then include some other more atten-uated transactions. The MBCA goes further and immunizes every transaction not included in the definition of "conflict of interest" from attack on the ground of conflict of interest! See MBCA §8.61(a).

Notes and Questions

1. You Draft It

a. Compare DGCL §144(a) and MBCA. Then draft an optimal CoI Safe Harbor statute.

b. Background and Context

i. A Note on Shareholder Ratification.   One of the methods for protecting a conflict of interest transaction is to have the transaction ratified by a fully informed vote of shareholders unaffiliated with the conflicted directors. Shareholder ratification becomes important in several corporate law contexts and Chancellor Chandler explains those contexts and the nuances of shareholder ratification under Delaware law.

SHAREHOLDER RATIFICATION

For some time Delaware law has recognized that the shareholder franchise can be employed as a powerful tool in fashioning a fair process. The power of fully informed shareholder ratification to cloak transactions in the business judgment rule, or to extinguish a breach of fiduciary duty claim entirely, is by no means absolute. Unfor-tunately for boards of directors, shareholders, litigants, and their attorneys, Delaware's law concerning the effect of shareholder ratification in the face of an alleged breach is not a model of clarity.

THE DUTY OF LOYALTY AND RATIFICATION

The legal effect of shareholder ratification, as it relates to alleged breaches of the duty of loyalty, may be one of the most tortured areas of Delaware law. A different rule exists for every permutation of facts that fall under the broad umbrella of "duty of loyalty" claims.

The first type of loyalty claim is self-interest or, as it is more aptly put, self-dealing transactions. In Delaware, those transactions are specifically covered by statute, [DGCL] §144, the interested directors provision.

Recently, in *In re Walt Disney Company* this Court had the opportunity to revisit the subject of shareholder ratification and full disclosure in the context of a §144(a)(2) interested transaction claim.[50] In that context, the Court reaffirmed the settled proposition that shareholder ratification by a majority of the disinterested shareholders acts as a safe harbor .... Thus, in a classic self-dealing transaction the effect of a fully informed shareholder vote in favor of that particular transaction is to maintain the business judgment rule's presumptions. To rebut those presumptions at the motion to dismiss stage the plaintiff must "allege facts showing that no person of ordinary sound business judgment could view the benefits received as a fair exchange for the consideration paid by the corporation," i.e., that the transaction was irrational or amounted to waste.[52]

The second scenario which often gives rise to duty of loyalty allegations that can be affected by shareholder ratification involves transactions between a corporation and its controlling stockholder (e.g., a parent-subsidiary merger) or fundamental changes of corporate policy sponsored by a controlling shareholder (e.g., charter amendments). Generally, in a parent-subsidiary merger where the parent controls the subsidiary, and can thereby "force" the merger, the standard of review is entire fairness and the burden of proof is on the sponsoring directors.

The Delaware Supreme Court, in *Kahn v. Lynch*,[56] explicitly recognized that an informed ratification by a majority of minority shareholders of a transaction between a controlling shareholder and a corporation has the effect of shifting the burden of proof on the issue of entire fairness from the controlling shareholder to the challenging shareholder.

A third fact pattern exists where breach of duty of loyalty allegations are made (but not often successfully) and where shareholder ratification can have a penetrating legal effect. These are situations where shareholder approval is sought (e.g., approval of a merger) and where there is no controlling shareholder, control group, or dominating force that can compel a particular result. Absent any other allegations that might cast doubt on the board's disinterest vis-à-vis the merits of the transaction, an informed and uncoerced shareholder vote on the matter provides an independent reason to maintain business judgment protection for the board's acts.

Solomon v. Armstrong, 747 A.2d 1098, 1113-17 (Del. Ch. 1998) (Chandler, Ch.)

Although many other jurisdictions choose to follow Delaware jurisprudence, other jurisdictions take a simpler approach to shareholder ratification. Generally speaking, because the shareholders are the ultimate owners and beneficiaries of the directors' actions, shareholder ratification cuts off all judicial power to redress a finding of breach of fiduciary duty. In virtually every state (including Delaware) the defendant/directors, as proponents of the ratification, have the burden of showing that full disclosure was made to the shareholders, that the shareholders were not

50. *In re The Walt Disney Co. Derivative Litig.*, 731 A.2d 342, 368 (Del. Ch. 1998).
52. *Disney,* at 362-64.
56. 638 A.2d 1110, 1117 (Del. 1994).

coerced, and that approval was given by a majority of shares not controlled by the board.

2. Duty of Care: Limitations Contained in the Articles of Incorporation

In 1985 the Delaware General Assembly added DGCL §102(b)(7). This section permits a corporation to add a provision to its certificate of incorporation capping or eliminating monetary liability of directors for breach of their fiduciary duties. The MBCA and nearly every state have adopted similar statutes, which are sometimes called *charter limitations*. See MBCA §2.02(b)(4). As a matter of corporate law theory these charter limitations are like an advance shareholder ratification because existing corporations must amend their articles, which requires shareholder approval, and new corporations make their articles available to the original shareholders who, in some sense, approve the charter limitation by their purchase. Public companies have commonly taken advantage of these statutes and have adopted limitations in their articles, usually choosing to eliminate, rather than cap, monetary liability.

Does a charter limitation make a great deal of practical difference? The following case shows how Delaware thinking about such provisions has evolved.

Emerald Partners v. Berlin
787 A.2d 85 (Del. 2001)

HOLLAND, J.

This matter is before us for the third time. The present appeal is from a posttrial final judgment entered by the Court of Chancery.

FACTS

The appellant, Emerald Partners, a [May Petroleum, Inc. ("May") shareholder], filed this action on March 1, 1988, to enjoin the consummation of a merger between May Petroleum, Inc. ("May"), a Delaware corporation and thirteen corporations owned by Craig Hall ("Hall"), the Chairman and Chief Executive Officer of May. Also joined as defendants were May's directors, Ronald P. Berlin, David L. Florence, Rex A. Sebastian, and Theodore H. Strauss (collectively the "director defendants").

In October 1987, Hall, at that time a holder of 52.4% of May's common stock, proposed a merger of May and thirteen...corporations owned by Hall .... The board of directors of May consisted of Hall and Berlin, the inside directors, and Florence, Sebastian and Strauss, the outside directors.

May and the Hall corporations entered into a proposed merger agreement on November 30, 1987. The May shareholders approved the merger on March 11, 1988, despite the pendency of Emerald Partners' request for injunctive relief.

[F]ollowing the consummation of the merger, Emerald Partners continued its class and derivative actions. Those efforts are reflected in numerous subsequent rulings by the Court of Chancery. Several of those decisions by the Court of Chancery resulted in a second appeal to this Court.

In the second appeal to this Court, we ... reversed the grant of summary judgment in favor of the director defendants. We remanded the matter to the Court of Chancery for a trial pursuant to the entire fairness standard of review.

SECTION 102(b)(7)

In 1986, Section 102(b)(7) was enacted by the Delaware General Assembly, following a "directors and officers insurance liability crisis and the 1985 ... decision [of this Court] in *Smith v. Van Gorkom*."[23] In *Van Gorkom*, we held that directors were personally liable in monetary damages for gross negligence in the process of decisionmaking. The purpose of Section 102(b)(7) was to *permit shareholders*— who are entitled to rely upon directors to discharge their fiduciary duties at all times — to adopt a provision in the certificate of incorporation to exculpate directors from any personal liability for the payment of monetary damages for breaches of their duty of care, but not for duty of loyalty violations, good faith violations and certain other conduct.[25] Following the enactment of Section 102(b)(7), the shareholders of many Delaware corporations [including May] approved charter amendments containing these exculpatory provisions with full knowledge of their import.

[I]n *Malpiede,* this Court held that if a shareholder complaint unambiguously asserts *only* a due care claim, the complaint is dismissible once the corporation's Section 102(b)(7) provision is properly invoked.[35] [W]e stated that the exculpation afforded by a Section 102(b)(7) charter provision must be *affirmatively* raised by the director defendants. Recognizing that it is appropriate for the Court of Chancery to consider a properly raised Section 102(b)(7) charter provision in a pretrial context illustrates why this Court characterized such provisions in *Emerald Partners v. Berlin* as in the "*nature* of an affirmative defense."[38]

The rationale of *Malpiede* constitutes judicial cognizance of a practical reality: unless there is a violation of the duty of loyalty or the duty of good faith, a trial on the issue of entire fairness is unnecessary because a Section 102(b)(7) provision will exculpate director defendants from paying monetary damages that are exclusively attributable to a violation of the duty of care. The effect of our holding in *Malpiede* is that, in actions against the directors of Delaware corporations with a Section 102(b)(7) charter provision, a shareholder's complaint must allege well-pled facts that, if true, implicate breaches of loyalty or good faith. Otherwise, in those cases that begin with the presumption of the business judgment rule, ... our holding in *Malpiede* establishes that the proper invocation of a Section 102(b)(7) provision can obviate a trial pursuant to the entire fairness standard, even if the presumption of the

---

23. *Malpiede v. Townson,* 780 A.2d 1075, 1095 (2001) (citing *Smith v. Van Gorkom,* 488 A.2d 858 (Del. 1985)).

25. *Malpiede v. Townson,* 780 A.2d at 1095. Such a charter provision does not affect injunctive proceedings based on gross negligence. *Id.; see also* E. Norman Veasey et al., *Delaware Supports Directors with a Three-Legged Stool of Limited Liability, Indemnification and Insurance,* 42 Bus. Law. 399, 401-04 (1987).

35. *Malpiede v. Townson,* 780 A.2d 1075, 1093 (Del. 2001). In *Malpiede,* as guidance for future cases, we described several methods that are available to the director defendants to raise and argue the applicability of the bar of a Section 102(b)(7) charter provision to a due care claim. *Id.* at 1092. "The Section 102(b)(7) bar may be raised on a Rule 12(b)(6) motion to dismiss (with or without the filing of an answer), a motion for judgment on the pleadings (after filing an answer), or a motion for summary judgment (or partial summary judgment) under Rule 56 after an answer, with or without supporting affidavits." *Id.*

38. *Emerald Partners v. Berlin,* 726 A.2d at 1223.

business judgment rule is successfully rebutted by a duty of care violation, since liability for duty of loyalty violations or violations of good faith are not at issue.

A determination that a transaction must be subjected to an entire fairness analysis is not an implication of liability. Therefore, when entire fairness is the applicable standard of judicial review, this Court has held that injury or damages becomes a proper focus only *after* a transaction is determined *not* to be entirely fair. *A fortiori*, the exculpatory effect of a Section 102(b)(7) provision only becomes a proper focus of judicial scrutiny after the directors' potential personal liability for the payment of monetary damages has been established. Accordingly, although a Section 102(b)(7) charter provision may provide exculpation for directors against the payment of monetary damages that is attributed exclusively to violating the duty of care, even in a transaction that requires the entire fairness review standard ... it cannot eliminate an entire fairness analysis by the Court of Chancery.

ENTIRE FAIRNESS ANALYSIS REQUIRED

When the General Assembly enacted Section 102(b)(7), three years after this Court's landmark decision in *Weinberger v. UOP, Inc.*,[70] it not only recognized but reinforced *Weinberger's* restatement of a venerable and fundamental principle of our common law corporate fiduciary jurisprudence: "there is no 'safe harbor' for ...divided loyalties in Delaware."[71] The fact that Section 102(b)(7) does not permit shareholders to exculpate directors for violations of loyalty or good faith reflects that the provision was a thoughtfully crafted legislative response to our holding in *Van Gorkom* and, simultaneously, reflected the General Assembly's own expression of support for our assertion in *Weinberger* that when the standard of review is entire fairness "the requirement of fairness is unflinching in its demand ... ."[72]

Upon remand, the Court of Chancery must analyze the factual circumstances, apply a disciplined balancing test to its findings on the issue of fair dealing and fair price, and articulate the basis upon which it decides the ultimate question of entire fairness. If the Court of Chancery determines that the transaction was entirely fair, the director defendants have no liability for monetary damages. The Court of Chancery should address the Section 102(b)(7) charter provision only if it makes a determination that the challenged transaction was not entirely fair. The director defendants can avoid personal liability for paying monetary damages only if they have established that their failure to withstand an entire fairness analysis is exclusively attributable to a violation of the duty of care.

Notes and Questions

1. Notes

a. This litigation has been among the longest in corporate law history. The complaint was filed in March 1988 and generated almost a dozen opinions in the Court of Chancery (by three different vice chancellors) and four Delaware Supreme Court opinions. Following the opinion above, the Court of Chancery found that the director defendants demonstrated the entire fairness of the transaction.

70. *Weinberger v. UOP, Inc.*, 457 A.2d 701 (Del. 1983).
71. *Id.* at 710.
72. *Id.*

The court went on to hold that, should the supreme court disagree as to entire fairness, any unfairness could only have been caused by the directors' violation of their duty of care and that the company's Certificate of Incorporation contained a valid charter limitation that eliminated all monetary liability. See *Emerald Partners v. Berlin*, 2003 WL 21003437 (Del. Ch.) (Jacobs, V.C.).

2. Reality Check

a. What claims are not eliminated by DGCL §102(b)(7)?

b. Why can't directors of Delaware corporations always raise an available charter limitation defense immediately?

3. Suppose

a. Suppose *Emerald Partners* had been decided under the MBCA. Would the court's analysis or the result have been different?

4. What Do You Think?

a. Do you think the practical effect of charter limitations has been undercut by *Malpiede* and *Emerald Partners*? If so, it that a good thing?

b. Earlier we asked whether it made much difference whether a director's action was analyzed under the duty of loyalty, the duty of care, good faith, or waste/no rational business purpose. Now that you've considered the role of charter limitations, would your answer or reasoning change?

5. You Draft It

a. Review DGCL §102(b)(7) and MBCA §2.02(b)(4) and then draft an ideal charter limitation statute.

3. Indemnification by the Corporation

a. The Current Setting

It seems counterintuitive to suggest that the corporation might indemnify a director or officer when such persons are sued by virtue of their service to the corporation but indemnification is a frequent occurrence. The statutory provisions are quite complex and an exhaustive look at indemnification is out of the question. See DGCL §145 and MBCA Subchapter E, §§8.50-8.59. Nonetheless, indemnification is one of the most often litigated areas in corporate law and it raises questions of statutory construction and public policy that are worth exploring and, more importantly, can be presented with (relative) concision.

We'll divide indemnification into three facets. First we'll look at the most important practical issue, advancement of expenses. Then we'll look at when indemnity is required, rather than simply permitted. Third we briefly limn the procedural and substantive predicates to indemnification.

i. Advancement of Expenses. For corporate officers and directors, and only slightly less so for corporations, the question of advancement of expenses looms large. Imagine you are a director who is being sued for some official action you've taken. To make this as pleasant as it can be, imagine further that you are certain to be indemnified should you prevail, and are nearly certain that you will prevail. Even in that setting you face months or years of litigation expenses, especially attorneys' fees, before you are indemnified by the corporation. Where will you get the money to pay those expenses until you are indemnified? Before you read the next case you may find it helpful to read DGCL §145(e) and MBCA §8.53.

Reddy v. Electronic Data Systems Corp.

2002 WL 1358761 (Del. Ch.)

STRINE, V.C.

The origins of this dispute can be traced to the purchase of FACS Incorporated ("FCI") by [Electronic Data Systems Corporation ("EDS")] in 1995. At the time of purchase, FCI was headed by [Michael T.] Reddy.

EDS bought FCI under the terms of a stock purchase agreement calling for an initial payment of $9 million to FCI stockholders, the largest of whom was Reddy. An additional $3 million was escrowed and placed in an account held by FCI's attorney. Two million dollars of these funds could be earned by the former FCI stockholders, subject to FCI's performance during the remainder of 1995. The other $1 million could be earned if certain performance targets were achieved and certain outstanding receivables of FCI were collected.

FCI's post-purchase performance was to occur under the rubric of Global Financial Markets Group ("GFMG"), the new EDS business division created to operate the purchased FCI operations. After the sale, Reddy became division vice-president of the larger EDS strategic business unit of which GFMG was a part. Despite his title, Reddy was not an officer of EDS under its bylaws, but simply an employee. In connection with his new position, Reddy entered into both an employment agreement and an incentive compensation agreement with EDS. Under the incentive compensation agreement, Reddy and other former FCI stockholders could receive up to $14 million in incentive compensation payments over a three-year period beginning in 1996. These payments were tied to the earnings of GFMG.

In 2001, two actions were filed against Reddy arising out of his conduct as an employee of EDS. The first action ... is a criminal action brought by the United States Attorney for the Southern District of New York (the "Criminal Action"). The Criminal Action involves charges of conspiracy, mail fraud, and wire fraud ... .

In sum, the Criminal Action alleges that Reddy purposely manipulated the financial records of EDS to increase the payments he would receive from the escrowed funds and the incentive compensation agreement. In accomplishing his ends, Reddy is alleged to have conspired with the attorney holding the escrowed funds, who helped by falsifying and mislabeling financial entries and payments in order to create the false impression that the pre-requisites for release of those funds to the former FCI stockholders had been met.

The second action was filed against Reddy by EDS itself (the "EDS Action") and is based on the same conduct alleged in the Criminal Action. That is, the EDS Action contends that Reddy manipulated and falsified the financial records of GFMG to inflate improperly the incentive compensation and escrowed funds payments to him and other former FCI stockholders, and to conceal his wrongdoing.

The complaint in the EDS Action avers that this misconduct is actionable as: i) negligence; ii) gross negligence; iii) common law fraud; and iv) breaches of Reddy's employment agreement and the incentive compensation agreement. Among other relief, the complaint seeks tens of millions of dollars in damages to remedy the over-payments supposedly harvested by Reddy and former FCI stockholders, and liabilities incurred by EDS to clients...because of Reddy's conduct ....

Reddy demanded advancement for both the Criminal and the EDS Action. EDS refused to provide it. Reddy then brought this lawsuit, alleging that he was due advancement under the EDS bylaws.

The only factual dispute raised in the briefs is whether Reddy engaged in the wrongdoing that is alleged in the two actions for which he seeks advancement. That dispute of fact is not a material one, however, in this action for advancement, and does not preclude the entry of a dispositive order.

Reddy contends that he is due advancement under the advancement provision in the EDS bylaws, which he asserts imposes a mandatory obligation on EDS to advance funds to former employees facing charges of official misconduct in their capacities as employees of EDS. By contrast, EDS argues that its bylaws simply give its board the discretion to advance funds to Reddy if they choose to do so, which they do not.

The bylaw provision in question reads:

> *Each person who at any time shall serve or shall have served as a* Director, officer, *employee* or agent *of the Corporation...shall be entitled to* (a) indemnification and (b) *the advancement of expenses* incurred by such person *from the Corporation as, and to the fullest extent, permitted by Section 145 of the DGCL* or any successor stat-utory provision, as from time to time amended.[4]

Although EDS contends otherwise, the plain import of this provision is to require EDS to advance funds to former employees like Reddy if §145 of the DGCL would permit it to do so. By its own scrivening hand, EDS has bound itself to advance funds to Reddy so long as the DGCL allows it to do so.

The pertinent parts of §145 of the DGCL state:

> (e) Expenses (including attorneys' fees) incurred by an officer or director in defending any civil, criminal, administrative or investigative action, suit or proceeding may be paid by the corporation in advance of the final disposition of such action, suit or proceeding upon receipt of an undertaking by or on behalf of such director or officer to repay such amount if it shall ultimately be determined that such person is not entitled to be indemnified by the corporation as authorized in this section. Such expenses (including attorneys' fees) incurred by former directors and officers or other employees and agents may be so paid upon such terms and conditions, if any, as the corporation deems appropriate.
>
> (f) The indemnification and advancement of expenses provided by, or granted pursuant to, the other subsections of this section shall not be deemed exclusive of any other rights to which those seeking indemnification or advancement of expenses may be entitled under any bylaw, agreement...or otherwise, both as to action in such person's official capacity and as to action in another capacity while holding such office.[5]

These capacious provisions of our law clearly provide corporations with the flex-ibility to advance litigation expenses to former employees like Reddy.

4. EDS Bylaws, Art. 6.1 (emphasis added).
5. [DGCL] §145(e), (f).

EDS...seeks to shift the burden of the company's drafting decisions to Reddy. That argument rests on the absence of any language in the EDS bylaws dealing with the conditions the company may impose on former employees who invoke their right to advancement — in particular, the failure of the bylaws to require former employees to execute an undertaking to repay the advanced funds.

Because directors and officers who seek advancement must — by statute — execute an undertaking,[6] EDS argues that its bylaws cannot reasonably be read as providing mandatory advancement to former employees. Otherwise, former employees would have greater rights than current directors and officers, a result that EDS considers anomalous.

The anomaly to which EDS points, however, is one authorized by §145(e) itself. The General Assembly specifically amended that statutory subsection to give corporations the flexibility to advance funds to employees and agents without an undertaking.[7] In lieu of this required undertaking, corporations may specify by bylaw or contract the terms and conditions upon which employees and agents may receive advancement, which could include an undertaking and more onerous pre-requisites to advancement. Having been accorded the freedom to craft its bylaws as it wished, EDS cannot point to its own drafting failures as a defense to Reddy's advancement claim, however. If it chose, EDS could have conditioned former employees' advancement rights on an undertaking, proof of an ability to repay, or even the posting of a secured bond. But it did not do so.

As a practical matter, moreover, I fail to see the great danger to the corporate republic posed by the lack of a formal undertaking. As the Supreme Court has noted, all contracts for advancement and indemnification are subject to an implied reasonableness term. When that implied term is utilized in concert with the actual language of the EDS bylaw in question, no horrific scenario arises. Rather, by accepting payments expressly termed an "advancement," Reddy necessarily acknowledges that his ultimate right to keep those payments depends on whether his underlying conduct is indemnifiable. If his conduct is not the proper subject of indemnification by EDS, Reddy must repay the funds advanced to him by the corporation.

EDS's next argument is that Reddy is not entitled to any advancement payments because he is a party to neither the Criminal Action nor the EDS Action "by reason of the fact that" he was an "employee" of EDS.[9] The foundation for this argument rests in the proposition that Reddy's motivation for the allegedly wrongful actions he took as an EDS employee was personal — i.e., the desire to increase the amount of escrowed funds and incentive compensation payments he and other former FCI stockholders would receive. As a result of this personal motivation, EDS claims that the conduct for which Reddy is being prosecuted civilly and criminally does not implicate the policy concerns addressed by §145, which broadly empowers corporations to provide advancement and indemnification to corporate employees.

The problem with EDS's argument is that it has no logical stopping point. It is not uncommon for corporate directors, officers, and employees to be sued for breach

---

6. See [DGCL] §145(e).

7. The evolution of §145(e) suggests that the General Assembly intended to mandate that an undertaking be received only from directors and officers, and not from other possible indemnitees, such as former employees. In 1983, the requirement that employees or agents execute an undertaking was dropped from the statute, leaving corporations free to set the conditions on which advancement to them would take place. See 64 Del. Laws. Ch. 112, §7 & commentary (1983).

9. [DGCL] §145(a), (b).

of the fiduciary duty of loyalty, and to have to defend claims that they took official action for the primary purpose of diverting corporate resources to their own pocketbooks — in the form of contractual compensation benefits (*e.g.*, severance payments or stock options) or an unfair return on a self-dealing transaction. Therefore, it is highly problematic to make the advancement right of such officials dependent on the motivation ascribed to their conduct by the suing parties. To do so would be to largely vitiate the protections afforded by §145 and contractual advancement rights.

Corporate advancement practice has an admittedly maddening aspect. At the time that an advancement dispute ripens, it is often the case that the corporate board has drawn harsh conclusions about the integrity and fidelity of the corporate official seeking advancement. The board may well have a firm basis to believe that the official intentionally injured the corporation. It therefore is reluctant to advance funds for his defense, fearing that the funds will never be paid back and resisting the idea of seeing further depletion of corporate resources at the instance of someone perceived to be a faithless fiduciary.

But, to give effect to this natural human reaction as public policy would be unwise. Imagine what EDS believes to be unthinkable: that the United States government and EDS are in fact wrong about Reddy. What if he in fact did not falsify records? What if he in fact did not do anything that was even grossly negligent? In that circumstance, it would be difficult to conceive of an argument that would properly leave him holding the bag for all of his legal fees and expenses resulting from two cases centering on his conduct as an employee of EDS. That result would make the promise made to Reddy in the EDS bylaws an illusory one.

For these reasons, this court has often been required to uphold the indemnification and advancement rights of corporate officials accused of serious misconduct, because to do otherwise would undermine the salutary public policies served by §145.

EDS's next argument to defeat Reddy's advancement claim involves a bold proposition. Because Reddy seeks advancement to defend accusations that he engaged in serious financial fraud intended to benefit himself at the expense of EDS, EDS contends that the equitable doctrine of unclean hands is implicated. If Reddy in fact purposely harmed EDS, he should be estopped from demanding advancement under EDS's bylaws. To do so would, EDS argues, be to permit a thief to steal twice.

If adopted, EDS's rule would turn every advancement case into a trial on the merits of the underlying claims of official misconduct. Section 145 of the DGCL is an explicit rejection of this approach, because the clear authorization of advancement rights presupposes that the corporation will front expenses before any determination is made of the corporate official's ultimate right to indemnification.

For the foregoing reasons, EDS's motion to dismiss is denied. Reddy's motion for summary judgment is granted and EDS shall advance him his reasonable expenses in the Criminal Action and the EDS Action promptly.

Notes and Questions

1. Notes

a. The provision in the EDS-FCI stock purchase agreement calling for a higher purchase price if FCI met certain financial benchmarks in the near future is a common one. Where the selling company's owners will continue to run the business after the sale, as Reddy did here, they have an economic motivation to shirk because they no longer receive the full benefit of their efforts. The function of an *earn-out* provision is to place the economic consequence of shirking on those best able to avoid shirking: the former owners who now manage.

b. The attorney with whom Mr. Reddy is alleged to have conspired is named John Fasciana. He also filed an action against EDS involving his right to be indemnified. See *Fasciana v. Electronic Data Systems Corp.*, 2003 WL 21538108 (Del. Ch.) (Strine, V.C.)

2. Reality Check

a. What was Mr. Reddy alleged to have done wrong?

b. Why is the issue of whether Mr. Reddy acted wrongfully (or even criminally) irrelevant to this case?

c. Where does the court look to find whether Mr. Reddy is entitled to advancement of his litigation expenses?

d. What are the predicates to EDS's obligation to advance Mr. Reddy's litigation expenses? Do you agree with Vice Chancellor Strine that they are met?

e. What were EDS's arguments against advancing Mr. Reddy's litigation expenses? Why was each rejected?

3. Suppose

a. If EDS were incorporated in a state that had adopted the MBCA (and if EDS's bylaws referenced that statute rather than the DGCL), would the court's analysis or the result be any different?

4. What Do You Think?

a. Do you think that EDS acted wisely in adopting a bylaw that provides for maximum indemnification and advancement?

b. Do you think that EDS acted wisely in adopting a bylaw that explicitly references the DGCL rather than tracking the statute's language? What are the differences between those two approaches?

c. Is DGCL §145(e) wise?

d. Is DGCL §145(k) wise?

e. If you represented EDS would you have made each argument EDS did? If not, how would you select the arguments to present? Which arguments would you press and which would you abandon?

5. You Draft It

a. Redraft EDS's bylaws to make it clear that EDS may, but need not, advance Mr. Reddy's litigation expenses. Then redraft the bylaws to make it clear that EDS must advance those expenses. The bylaw reads,

> Each person who at any time shall serve or shall have served as a Director, officer, employee or agent of the Corporation ... shall be entitled to (a) indemnification and (b) the advancement of expenses incurred by such person from the Corporation as, and to the fullest extent, permitted by Section 145 of the DGCL or any successor statutory provision, as from time to time amended.

ii. When Must the Corporation Indemnify?   As the court in *Reddy* pointed out, indemnity questions often arise when the corporation and the potential indemnitee have had a falling out. In such settings the natural tendency is for both sides to take a hard line — the corporation taking the narrowest view of its obligation and the indemnitee taking the broadest. Much litigation is generated between corporations and their former officers or directors about the scope of the indemnity provision.

At the other end of the process, both DGCL §145(c) and MBCA §8.52 require a corporation to indemnify an officer or director who is exonerated "on the merits or otherwise." The courts take these words literally so that an officer or director who successfully raises a statute of limitations defense, for example, or who escapes criminal prosecution after a trial ends in a hung jury and the government elects to dismiss the charges is entitled to full indemnification. Note that this entitlement is statutorily required so that the provisions of any indemnification agreement with the corporation are irrelevant. Courts also read the statutes to require partial indemnification if the defendant is successful as to discrete claims or as to some but not all lawsuits.

Notes and Questions

1. What Do You Think?

a. Should the statutes require indemnification for a defendant who is successful for reasons other than the merits?

b. Should the statutes limit mandatory indemnification to those who were wholly successful? Predominately successful?

iii. Procedural and Substantive Prerequisites to Indemnification. If indemnification is permissive rather than mandatory (or ordered by a court), certain constituencies within the corporation must make certain findings before indemnification may be paid. Under the DGCL, the unconflicted directors or, in the absence of any such directors, the shareholders must make the requisite findings. Under the MBCA authorization may be made by disinterested directors, or disinterested shareholders, or by special legal counsel appointed by the corporation. See DGCL §145(d) and MBCA §8.55.

In essence, the appropriate constituency must make a finding that indemnification is permitted by the statute and then a further finding that indemnity is in the best interest of the corporation. In both derivative and nonderivative litigation, there must be an explicit finding by the corporation that the indemnitee has the requisite status to be indemnified (i.e., was a director, officer, or agent who is being sued "by reason of" such status) and had the appropriate state of mind when acting. This state of mind is, at bottom, an intention to aid rather than harm the corporation. The actual statutory requirements are more nuanced than this description so you ought to read the statutes carefully. See DGCL §145(a) and (b) and MBCA §8.51. As to the second finding, that indemnity is in the best interest of the corporation, in Delaware and under the MBCA, the corporation may bind itself in advance. That is, the corporation may make a valid decision that it is in the best interest of the corporation to promise to indemnify if possible under the statute. The practical effect of such provisions, which are quite common, is to provide assurance to potential indemnitees that they will be indemnified even if they have a falling out with the corporation. See MBCA §8.58(a).

The indemnification statutes draw a distinction between shareholder derivative actions and other litigation. For derivative actions, the corporation may only indemnify for expenses (including attorney's fees) involved in settling the matter. Conceptually this makes sense because otherwise the indemnitee may be held liable to the corporation and then immediately receive indemnification. For nonderivative litigation, the defendant may be indemnified not only for expenses but for settlement amounts and judgments and fines. See DGCL §145(a) and (b) and MBCA §8.51.

Despite all these elaborate procedural and substantive requirements, two further methods of indemnification may be available. Under both the DGCL and MBCA a court may determine that indemnification is appropriate even when the statutory provisions are not met. This seems an extraordinary grant of power to the courts, especially in the face of such carefully crafted statutory systems. Undoubtedly this power is not exercised much. See DGCL §145(b) and MBCA §8.54.

Second, both statutes permit corporations to provide for indemnification beyond that permitted by the statutes. In Delaware, section 145(f) essentially provides that section 145 is not exclusive. Clearly, however, this section cannot give corporations carte blanche to adopt any indemnification plan they wish because otherwise the rest of section 145 would become superfluous. Some case law suggests that any provision adopted under section 145(f) must at least require a finding that the indemnitee acted in good faith.

The MBCA is a bit murkier in this regard because section 8.59 provides that Subchapter E is exclusive as to indemnity provision but 8.51(a)(2), part of Subchapter E, permits corporations to provide broader indemnity than the remainder of Subchapter E would permit. Specifically, §8.51(a)(2) permits corporations to include a provision in their articles (pursuant to MBCA §2.02(b)(5)) that allows or requires indemnification without regard to the limitations or procedures of Subchapter E so long as (speaking broadly) the director does not receive improper benefits or knowingly breaks the law. This certainly allows corporations incorporated in MBCA states greater power to craft indemnity provisions than Delaware corporations enjoy, but, as with Delaware, it is unclear exactly how far a corporation may stray from Subchapter E before a court would find that the indemnification provisions violate a public policy.

4. Insurance

The final technique to ameliorate director and officer liability is tied to indemnification. Virtually every corporations statute permits corporations to purchase insurance covering liability incurred by directors and officers. See DGCL §145(g) and MBCA §8.57. The standard *D&O insurance policy* provides two kinds of coverage. First, it reimburses directors and officers for their unindemnified losses in connection with litigation against them by reason of their service as directors or officers. Second, the D&O insurance policy reimburses the corporation itself for indemnity paid to the directors and officers. Note that this policy does not pay the corporation for any loss it suffers by reason of a judgment, fine, or settlement paid to third parties. It only reimburses the company for money it pays to indemnify its own directors and officers.

Nearly every publicly held corporation and many privately held companies have D&O insurance. Statistics suggest that the greater a corporation's assets, the more likely it is to be involved in an indemnification setting and thus to make a D&O insurance claim. Public corporations that report a loss for the first time or those engaged in mergers and acquisitions activity are the most likely to become embroiled in litigation that triggers indemnification and D&O insurance.

E. AN EXERCISE IN SYNTHESIS

The final section is a summation of many of the issues that have arisen in this chapter and the prior two chapters. You should reread *Brehm*, p.445, *supra* because the next case is Chancellor Chandler's opinion on remand. I have divided the case into two parts; the first presents the facts and the second is the court's legal analysis. After reading the facts you should pause to think about the duties the directors had to meet, the possible claims for relief, and the possible techniques to ameliorate the directors' liability. Then read the second part of the opinion.

≡ **In re The Walt Disney Co. Deriv. Litig.**
≡ 825 A.2d 275 (Del. Ch. 2003)

CHANDLER, CH.

I. PROCEDURAL AND FACTUAL BACKGROUND

[T]his case involves an attack on decisions of the Walt Disney Company's board of directors, approving an executive compensation contract for Michael Ovitz, as well as impliedly approving a non-fault termination that resulted in an award to Ovitz (allegedly exceeding $140,000,000) after barely one year of employment. After the Supreme Court's remand regarding plaintiffs' first amended complaint,[4] plaintiffs used the "tools at hand," a request for books and records as authorized under [DGCL] §220, to obtain information about the nature of the Disney Board's involvement in the decision to hire and, eventually, to terminate Ovitz. Using the information gained from that request, plaintiffs drafted and filed the new complaint, which is the subject of the pending motions. The facts, as alleged in the new complaint, portray a markedly different picture of the corporate processes that resulted in the Ovitz employment agreement than that portrayed in the first amended complaint. For that reason, it is necessary to set forth the repleaded facts in some detail. The facts set forth hereafter are taken directly from the new complaint and, for purposes of the present motions, are accepted as true. Of course, I hold no opinion as to the actual truth of any of the allegations set forth in the new complaint; nor do I hold any view as to the likely ultimate outcome on the merits of claims based on these asserted facts.

A. The Decision to Hire Ovitz

Michael Eisner is the chief executive officer ("CEO") of the Walt Disney Company. In 1994, Eisner's second-in-command, Frank Wells, died in a helicopter crash. Two other key executives — Jeffrey Katzenberg and Richard Frank — left Disney shortly thereafter, allegedly because of Eisner's management style. Eisner began looking for a new president for Disney and chose Michael Ovitz. Ovitz was founder and head of CAA, a talent agency; he had never been an executive for a publicly owned entertainment company. He had, however, been Eisner's close friend for over twenty-five years.

Eisner decided unilaterally to hire Ovitz. On August 13, 1995, he informed three Old Board members — Stephen Bollenbach, Sanford Litvack, and Irwin Russell

---

4. *Brehm v. Eisner*, 746 A.2d 244, 249 (Del. 2000).

(Eisner's personal attorney) — of that fact. All three protested Eisner's decision to hire Ovitz. Nevertheless, Eisner persisted, sending Ovitz a letter on August 14, 1995, that set forth certain material terms of his prospective employment. Before this, neither the Old Board nor the compensation committee had ever discussed hiring Ovitz as president of Disney. No discussions or presentations were made to the compensation committee or to the Old Board regarding Ovitz's hiring as president of Walt Disney until September 26, 1995.

Before informing Bollenbach, Litvack, and Russell on August 13, 1995, Eisner collected information on his own, through his position as the Disney CEO, on the potential hiring of Ovitz. In an internal document created around July 7, 1995, concerns were raised about the number of stock options to be granted to Ovitz. The document warned that the number was far beyond the normal standards of both Disney and corporate America and would receive significant public criticism. Additionally, Graef Crystal, an executive compensation expert, informed board member Russell, via a letter dated August 12, 1995, that, generally speaking, a large signing bonus is hazardous because the full cost is borne immediately and completely even if the executive fails to serve the full term of employment. [6] Neither of these documents, however, were submitted to either the compensation committee or the Old Board before hiring Ovitz. Disney prepared a draft employment agreement on September 23, 1995. A copy of the draft was sent to Ovitz's lawyers, but was not provided to members of the compensation committee.

The compensation committee, consisting of defendants Ignacio Lozano, Jr., Sidney Poitier, Russell, and Raymond Watson, met on September 26, 1995, for just under an hour. Three subjects were discussed at the meeting, one of which was Ovitz's employment. According to the minutes, the committee spent the least amount of time during the meeting discussing Ovitz's hiring. In fact, it appears that more time was spent on discussions of paying $250,000 to Russell for his role in securing Ovitz's employment than was actually spent on discussions of Ovitz's employment. The minutes show that several issues were raised and discussed by the committee members concerning Russell's fee. All that occurred during the meeting regarding Ovitz's employment was that Russell reviewed the employment terms with the committee and answered a few questions. Immediately thereafter, the committee adopted a resolution of approval.

No copy of the September 23, 1995 draft employment agreement was actually given to the committee. Instead, the committee members received, at the meeting itself, a rough summary of the agreement. The summary, however, was incomplete. It stated that Ovitz was to receive options to purchase five million shares of stock, but did not state the exercise price. The committee also did not receive any of the materials already produced by Disney regarding Ovitz's possible employment. No spreadsheet or similar type of analytical document showing the potential payout to Ovitz throughout the contract, or the possible cost of his severance package upon a non-fault termination, was created or presented. Nor did the committee request or receive any information as to how the draft agreement compared with similar agreements throughout the entertainment industry, or information regarding other similarly situated executives in the same industry.

6. Graef Crystal had been retained to advise Disney on Eisner's employment contract. Although not absolutely clear in the new complaint, it was apparently in this context that Crystal advised Russell of the dangers of a large signing bonus.

The committee also lacked the benefit of an expert to guide them through the process. Graef Crystal, an executive compensation expert, had been hired to provide advice to Disney on Eisner's new employment contract. Even though he had earlier told Russell that large signing bonuses, generally speaking, can be hazardous, neither he nor any other expert had been retained to assist Disney regarding Ovitz's hiring. Thus, no presentations, spreadsheets, written analyses, or opinions were given by any expert for the compensation committee to rely upon in reaching its decision. Although Crystal was not retained as a compensation consultant on the Ovitz contract, he later lamented his failure to intervene and produce a spreadsheet showing the potential costs of the employment agreement.

The compensation committee was informed that further negotiations would occur and that the stock option grant would be delayed until the final contract was worked out. The committee approved the general terms and conditions of the employment agreement, but did not condition their approval on being able to review the final agreement. Instead, the committee granted Eisner the authority to approve the final terms and conditions of the contract as long as they were within the framework of the draft agreement.

Immediately after the compensation committee met on September 26, the Old Board met. Again, no expert was present to advise the board. Nor were any documents produced to the board for it to review before the meeting regarding the Ovitz contract. The board did not ask for additional information to be collected or presented regarding Ovitz's hiring. According to the minutes, the compensation committee did not make any recommendation or report to the board concerning its resolution to hire Ovitz. Nor did Russell, who allegedly secured Ovitz's employment, make a presentation to the board. The minutes of the meeting were fifteen pages long, but only a page and a half covered Ovitz's possible employment. A portion of that page and a half was spent discussing the $250,000 fee paid to Russell for obtaining Ovitz. According to the minutes, the Old Board did not ask any questions about the details of Ovitz's salary, stock options, or possible termination. The Old Board also did not consider the consequences of a termination, or the various payout scenarios that existed. Nevertheless, at that same meeting, the Old Board decided to appoint Ovitz president of Disney. Final negotiation of the employment agreement was left to Eisner, Ovitz's close friend for over twenty-five years.

B. Negotiation of the Employment Agreement

Ovitz was officially hired on October 1, 1995, and began serving as Disney's president, although he did not yet have an executed employment agreement with Disney. On October 16, 1995, the compensation committee was informed, via a brief oral report, that negotiations were ongoing with Ovitz. The committee was not given a draft of the employment agreement either before or during the meeting. A summary similar to the one given on September 26, 1995, was presented. The committee did not seek any further information about the negotiations or about the terms and conditions of Ovitz's agreement, nor was any information proffered regarding the scope of the non-fault termination provision. And, as before, no expert was available to advise the committee as to the employment agreement.

Negotiations continued among Ovitz, Eisner, and their attorneys. The lawyers circulated drafts on October 3, October 10, October 16, October 20, October 23, and December 12, 1995. The employment agreement was physically executed between Michael Ovitz and the Walt Disney Company on December 12, 1995.

The employment agreement, however, was backdated to October 1, 1995, the day Ovitz began working as Disney's president. Additionally, the stock option agreement associated with the employment agreement was executed by Eisner (for Disney) on April 2, 1996. Ovitz did not countersign the stock option agreement until November 15, 1996, when he was already discussing his plans to leave Disney's employ. Neither the Old Board nor the compensation committee reviewed or approved the final employment agreement before it was executed and made binding upon Disney.

C. The Final Version of Ovitz's Employment Agreement

The final version of Ovitz's employment agreement differed significantly from the drafts summarized to the compensation committee on September 26, 1995, and October 16, 1995. First, the final version caused Ovitz's stock options to be "in the money"* when granted. The September 23rd draft agreement set the exercise price at the stock price on October 2, 1995, the day after Ovitz began as president. On October 16, 1995, the compensation committee agreed to change the exercise price to the price on that date (October 16, 1995), a price similar to that on October 2nd. The agreement was not signed until December 12, 1995, however, at which point the value of Disney stock had increased by eight percent — from $56.875 per share on October 16th to $61.50 per share on December 12th. The overall stock market, according to the Dow Jones Industrial Average, had also increased by about eight percent at the same time. By waiting to sign the agreement until December, but not changing the date of the exercise price, Ovitz had stock options that instantly were "in the money." This allowed Ovitz to play a "win-win" game at Disney's expense — if the market price of Disney stock had fallen between October 16 and December 12, Ovitz could have demanded a downward adjustment to the option exercise price; if the price had risen (as in fact it had) Ovitz would receive "in the money" options.

Another difference in the final version of Ovitz's employment agreement concerned the circumstances surrounding a non-fault termination. The September 23rd draft agreement stated that non-fault termination benefits would only be provided if Disney wrongfully terminated Ovitz, or Ovitz died or became disabled. The October 16th draft contained a very similar definition. These were the only two drafts of which the compensation committee was made aware. The final version of the agreement, however, offered Ovitz a non-fault termination as long as Ovitz did not act with gross negligence or malfeasance. Therefore, instead of protecting Ovitz from a wrongful termination by Disney, Ovitz was able to receive the full benefits of a non-fault termination, even if he acted negligently or was unable to perform his duties, as long as his behavior did not reach the level of gross negligence or malfeasance. Additionally, a non-compete clause was not included within the agreement should Ovitz leave Disney's employ.

---

* [Stock options such as those granted to Mr. Ovitz in this case are the right (but not the obligation) to purchase a fixed number of shares at a fixed price (called the *exercise price*, usually the market price at the time the options are given to the employee) at any time between the exercise date and the date they expire. If the stock price rises above the exercise price by the time the option is exercisable, the employee benefits because he or she can exercise the option and immediately sell the stock for a profit. Stock options are an incentive to the employee to improve the corporation so that the stock price rises. Employee stock options are said to be *at the money* if the exercise price and the market price are the same. These options are said to be *in the money* if the market price exceeds the exercise price and are said to be *out of the money*, or *under water*, if the market price is below the exercise price. Obviously, an employee will not exercise options that are out of the money. A grant of stock options that are immediately in the money would be unusual because it lessens the employee's incentive as the market price is already above the exercise price. ED.]

The employment agreement had a term of five years. Ovitz was to receive a salary of $1 million per year, a potential bonus each year from $0 to $10 million, and a series of stock options (the "A" options) that enabled Ovitz to purchase three million shares of Disney stock at the October 16, 1995 exercise price. The options were to vest at one million per year for three years beginning September 30, 1998. At the end of the contract term, if Disney entered into a new contract with Ovitz, he was entitled to the "B" options, an additional two million shares. There was no requirement, however, that Disney enter into a new contract with Ovitz.

Should a non-fault termination occur, however, the terms of the final version of the employment agreement appeared to be even more generous. Under a non-fault termination, Ovitz was to receive his salary for the remainder of the contract, discounted at a risk-free rate keyed to Disney's borrowing costs. He was also to receive a $7.5 million bonus for each year remaining on his contract, discounted at the same risk-free rate, even though no set bonus amount was guaranteed in the contract. Additionally, all of his "A" stock options were to vest immediately, instead of waiting for the final three years of his contract for them to vest. The final benefit of the non-fault termination was a lump sum "termination payment" of $10 million. The termination payment was equal to the payment Ovitz would receive should he complete his full five-year term with Disney, but not receive an offer for a new contract. Graef Crystal opined in the January 13, 1997, edition of *California Law/Business* that "the contract was most valuable to Ovitz the sooner he left Disney."

D. Ovitz's Performance as Disney's President

Ovitz began serving as president of Disney on October 1, 1995, and became a Disney director in January 1996. Ovitz's tenure as Disney's president proved unsuccessful. Ovitz was not a good second-in-command, and he and Eisner were both aware of that fact. Eisner told defendant Watson, via memorandum, that he (Eisner) "had made an error in judgment in who I brought into the company." Other company executives were reported in the December 14, 1996 edition of the *New York Times* as saying that Ovitz had an excessively lavish office, an imperious management style, and had started a feud with NBC during his tenure. Even Ovitz admitted, during a September 30, 1996 interview on "Larry King Live," that he knew "about 1% of what I need to know."

Even though admitting that he did not know his job, Ovitz studiously avoided attempts to be educated. Eisner instructed Ovitz to meet weekly with Disney's chief financial officer, defendant Bollenbach. The meetings were scheduled to occur each Monday at 2 P.M., but every week Ovitz cancelled at the last minute. Bollenbach was quoted in a December 1996 issue of *Vanity Fair* as saying that Ovitz failed to meet with him at all, "didn't understand the duties of an executive at a public company[,] and he didn't want to learn."

Instead of working to learn his duties as Disney's president, Ovitz began seeking alternative employment. He consulted Eisner to ensure that no action would be taken against him by Disney if he sought employment elsewhere. Eisner agreed that the best thing for Disney, Eisner, and Ovitz was for Ovitz to gain employment elsewhere. Eisner wrote to the chairman of Sony Japan that Ovitz could negotiate with Sony without any repercussions from Disney. Ovitz and Sony began negotiations for Ovitz to become head of Sony's entertainment business, but the negotiations ultimately failed. With the possibility of having another company absorb the cost of Ovitz's departure now gone, Eisner and Ovitz began in earnest to discuss a non-fault termination.

E. The Non-Fault Termination

Ovitz wanted to leave Disney, but could only terminate his employment if one of three events occurred: (1) he was not elected or retained as president and a director of Disney; (2) he was assigned duties materially inconsistent with his role as president; or (3) Disney reduced his annual salary or failed to grant his stock options, pay him discretionary bonuses, or make any required compensation payment. None of these three events occurred. If Ovitz resigned outright, he might have been liable to Disney for damages and would not have received the benefits of the non-fault termination. He also desired to protect his reputation when exiting from his position with Disney. Eisner agreed to help Ovitz depart Disney without sacrificing any of his benefits. Eisner and Ovitz worked together as close personal friends to have Ovitz receive a non-fault termination. Eisner stated in a letter to Ovitz that: "I agree with you that we must work together to assure a smooth transition and deal with the public relations brilliantly. I am committed to make this a win-win situation, to keep our friendship intact, to be positive, to say and write only glowing things . . . . Nobody ever needs to know anything other than positive things from either of us. This can all work out!"

Eisner, Litvack, and Ovitz met at Eisner's apartment on December 11, 1996, to finalize Ovitz's non-fault termination. The new complaint alleges that the New Board was aware that Eisner was negotiating with Ovitz the terms of his separation. Litvack sent a letter to Ovitz on December 12, 1996, stating that, by "mutual agreement," (1) Ovitz's term of employment would end on January 31, 1997; and (2) "this letter will for all purposes of the Employment Agreement be given the same effect as though there had been a 'Non-Fault Termination,' and the Company will pay you, on or before February 5, 1997, all amounts due you under the Employment Agreement, including those under Section 11(c) thereof. In addition, the stock options granted pursuant to Option A, will vest as of January 31, 1997 and will expire in accordance with their terms on September 30, 2002." On December 12, 1996, Ovitz's departure from Disney became public. Neither the New Board of Directors nor the compensation committee had been consulted or given their approval for a non-fault termination. In addition, no record exists of any action by the New Board once the non-fault termination became public on December 12, 1996.

On December 27, 1996, Litvack sent Ovitz a new letter superseding the December 12th letter. The December 27th letter stated that Ovitz's termination would "be treated as a 'Non-Fault Termination.'" This differed from the December 12th letter, which treated Ovitz's termination "as though there had been a 'Non-Fault Termination.'" It also made the termination of Ovitz's employment and his resignation as a Disney director effective as of the close of business on December 27th, instead of on January 31, 1997, as in the December 12th letter. Additionally, it listed the amount payable to Ovitz as $38,888,230.77, and stated that the "A" options to purchase three million shares of Disney vested on December 27th, instead of January 31, 1997, as in the December 12th letter. Both Eisner and Litvack signed the letter. Again, however, neither the New Board nor the compensation committee reviewed or approved the December 27th letter. No record exists of any New Board action after the December 27th letter became public, nor had any board member raised any questions or concerns since the original December 12th letter became public.

According to the new complaint, Disney's bylaws required board approval for Ovitz's non-fault termination. Eisner and Litvack allegedly did not have the authority to provide for a non-fault termination without board consent. No documents or board minutes currently exist showing an affirmative decision by the New Board or any of its committees to grant Ovitz a non-fault termination. The New Board was already aware that Eisner was granting the non-fault termination as of December 12, 1996, the day it became public. No record of any action by the New Board affirming or questioning that decision by Eisner either before or after that date has been produced. There are also no records showing that alternatives to a non-fault termination were ever evaluated by the New Board or by any of its committees.

Notes and Questions

1. Notes

a. You may wish to review the table of contents for this chapter and the prior two chapters as an aide-mémoire.

2. Reality Check

a. How are the facts as alleged in this opinion different from the facts as alleged in *Brehm*? Which set of facts do you find more believable?

3. Suppose

a. Imagine that you are the law clerk to Chancellor Chandler. Make an outline of the possible claims for relief presented by the facts set out above.

b. Suppose the company were incorporated in a state that has adopted the MBCA. Would your outline be different?

4. What Do You Think?

a. Do you believe plaintiffs' counsel violated Rule 11 by filing the complaint in issue here? Did they violate Rule 11 by filing the complaint in *Brehm*? Did they violate Rule 11 by filing both complaints?

b. Did any of the directors violate any of their fiduciary duties?

c. Is any of the directors' conduct actionable under Delaware law? If so, what amelioration of that possible liability may be available?

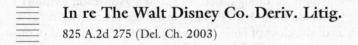

In re The Walt Disney Co. Deriv. Litig.

825 A.2d 275 (Del. Ch. 2003)

CHANDLER, CH.

In this derivative action filed on behalf of nominal defendant Walt Disney Company, plaintiffs allege that the defendant directors breached their fiduciary duties when they blindly approved an employment agreement with defendant Michael Ovitz and then, again without any review or deliberation, ignored defendant Michael Eisner's dealings with Ovitz regarding his non-fault termination. Plaintiffs seek rescission and/or money damages from defendants and Ovitz, or compensation for damages allegedly sustained by Disney and disgorgement of Ovitz's unjust enrichment.

As will be explained in greater detail below, I conclude that plaintiffs' new complaint sufficiently pleads a breach of fiduciary duty by the Old and the New Disney

Board of Directors[2] so as to withstand a motion to dismiss under Chancery Rules 23.1 and 12(b)(6). Stated briefly, plaintiffs' new allegations give rise to a cognizable question whether the defendant directors of the Walt Disney Company should be held personally liable to the corporation for a knowing or intentional lack of due care in the directors' decision-making process regarding Ovitz's employment and termination. It is rare when a court imposes liability on directors of a corporation for breach of the duty of care, and this Court is hesitant to second-guess the business judgment of a disinterested and independent board of directors. But the facts alleged in the new complaint do not implicate merely negligent or grossly negligent decision making by corporate directors. Quite the contrary; plaintiffs' new complaint suggests that the Disney directors failed to exercise *any* business judgment and failed to make *any* good faith attempt to fulfill their fiduciary duties to Disney and its stockholders. Allegations that Disney's directors abdicated all responsibility to consider appropriately an action of material importance to the corporation puts directly in question whether the board's decision-making processes were employed in a good faith effort to advance corporate interests. In short, the new complaint alleges facts implying that the Disney directors failed to "act in good faith and meet minimal proceduralist standards of attention."[3] Based on the facts asserted in the new complaint, therefore, I believe plaintiffs have stated cognizable claims for which demand is excused and on which a more complete factual record is necessary.

[The facts are set out above]

III. ANALYSIS

The primary issue before the Court is whether plaintiffs' new complaint survives the Rule 23.1 motion to dismiss under the second prong of *Aronson v. Lewis.*[25] In order for demand to be excused under the second prong of *Aronson,* plaintiffs must allege particularized facts that raise doubt about whether the challenged transaction is entitled to the protection of the business judgment rule. Plaintiffs may rebut the presumption that the board's decision is entitled to deference by raising a reason to doubt whether the board's action was taken on an informed basis or whether the directors honestly and in good faith believed that the action was in the best interests of the corporation. Thus, plaintiffs must plead particularized facts sufficient to raise (1) a reason to doubt that the action was taken honestly and in good faith or (2) a reason to doubt that the board was adequately informed in making the decision.

Defendants contend that the new complaint cannot be read reasonably to allege any fiduciary duty violation other than, at most, a breach of the directors' duty of due care. They further assert that even if the complaint states a breach of the directors' duty of care, Disney's charter provision, based on [DGCL] §102(b)(7), would apply and the individual directors would be protected from personal damages liability for

2. The Disney Board of Directors changed from the time Ovitz was hired to the time of his non-fault termination. Therefore, the board at the time Ovitz was hired is referred to as the "Old Board," and the board at the time of the non-fault termination is the "New Board."

3. *Gagliardi v. TriFoods Int'l, Inc.,* 683 A.2d 1049, 1052 (Del. Ch. 1996).

25. 473 A.2d 805, 814 (Del. 1984). The Supreme Court affirmed the dismissal of plaintiffs' previous complaint under the first prong of *Aronson* and prohibited that issue from being relitigated. *Brehm,* 746 A.2d at 258 & n.42. As discussed earlier, the new complaint must survive a Rule 23.1 motion to dismiss because it is a derivative action. The facts alleged here are the same for both the 23.1 motions and the 12(b)(6) motions. Thus, since the standard for a Rule 23.1 dismissal is more stringent than that under Rule 12(b)(6), should the new complaint survive under the second prong of *Aronson,* it will survive under Rule 12(b)(6) if its facts otherwise state a cognizable claim.

any breach of their duty of care. A §102(b)(7) provision in a corporation's charter does not "eliminate or limit the liability of a director: (i) [f]or any breach of the director's duty of loyalty to the corporation or its stockholders; (ii) for acts or omissions not in good faith or which involve intentional misconduct or a knowing violation of the law; (iii) under §174 of this title; or (iv) for any transaction from which the director derived an improper personal benefit." A fair reading of the new complaint, in my opinion, gives rise to a reason to doubt whether the board's actions were taken honestly and in good faith, as required under the second prong of *Aronson*. Since acts or omissions not undertaken honestly and in good faith, or which involve intentional misconduct, do not fall within the protective ambit of §102(b)(7), I cannot dismiss the complaint based on the exculpatory Disney charter provision.

Defendants also argue that Ovitz's employment agreement was a reasonable exercise of business judgment. They argue that Ovitz's previous position as head of CAA required a large compensation package to entice him to become Disney's president. As to the non-fault termination, defendants contend that that decision was reasonable in that the board wished to avoid protracted litigation with Ovitz. The Court is appropriately hesitant to second-guess the business judgment of a disinterested and independent board of directors. As alleged in the new complaint, however, the facts belie any assertion that the New or Old Boards exercised *any* business judgment or made *any* good faith attempt to fulfill the fiduciary duties they owed to Disney and its shareholders.

A. The Old and New Boards

According to the new complaint, Eisner unilaterally made the decision to hire Ovitz, even in the face of internal documents warning of potential adverse publicity and with three members of the board of directors initially objecting to the hiring when Eisner first broached the idea in August 1995. No draft employment agreements were presented to the compensation committee or to the Disney board for review before the September 26, 1995 meetings. The compensation committee met for less than an hour on September 26, 1995, and spent most of its time on two other topics, including the compensation of director Russell for helping secure Ovitz's employment. With respect to the employment agreement itself, the committee received only a summary of its terms and conditions. No questions were asked about the employment agreement. No time was taken to review the documents for approval. Instead, the committee approved the hiring of Ovitz and directed Eisner, Ovitz's close friend, to carry out the negotiations with regard to certain still unresolved and significant details.[30]

The Old Board met immediately after the committee did. Less than one and one-half pages of the fifteen pages of Old Board minutes were devoted to discussions of Ovitz's hiring as Disney's new president. Actually, most of that time appears to have been spent discussing compensation for director Russell. No presentations were made to the Old Board regarding the terms of the draft agreement. No questions were raised, at least so far as the minutes reflect. At the end of the meeting, the Old Board authorized Ovitz's hiring as Disney's president. No further review or approval of the employment agreement occurred. Throughout both meetings, no expert consultant was present to advise the compensation committee or the Old Board. Notably, the

---

30. The allegation that Eisner and Ovitz had been close friends for over twenty-five years is not mentioned to show self-interest or domination. Instead, the allegation is mentioned because it casts doubt on the good faith and judgment behind the Old and New Boards' decisions to allow two close personal friends to control the payment of shareholders' money to Ovitz.

Old Board approved Ovitz's hiring even though the employment agreement was still a "work in progress." The Old Board simply passed off the details to Ovitz and his good friend, Eisner.

Negotiation over the remaining terms took place solely between Eisner, Ovitz, and attorneys representing Disney and Ovitz. The compensation committee met briefly in October to review the negotiations, but failed again to actually consider a draft of the agreement or to establish any guidelines to be used in the negotiations. The committee was apparently not otherwise involved in the negotiations. Negotiations with Eisner continued until mid-December, but Ovitz had already started serving as Disney's president as of October 1, 1995.

Eisner and Ovitz reached a final agreement on December 12, 1995. They agreed to backdate the agreement, however, to October 1, 1995. The final employment agreement also differed substantially from the original draft, but evidently no further committee or board review of it ever occurred. The final version of Ovitz's employment agreement was signed (according to the new complaint) without *any* board input beyond the limited discussion on September 26, 1995.

From the outset, Ovitz performed poorly as Disney's president. In short order, Ovitz wanted out, and, once again, his good friend Eisner came to the rescue, agreeing to Ovitz's request for a non-fault termination. Disney's board, however, was allegedly never consulted in this process. No board committee was ever consulted, nor were any experts consulted. Eisner and Litvack alone granted Ovitz's non-fault termination, which became public on December 12, 1996. Again, Disney's board did not appear to question this action, although affirmative board action seemed to be required. On December 27, 1996, Eisner and Litvack, without explanation, accelerated the effective date of the non-fault termination, from January 31, 1997, to December 27, 1996. Again, the board apparently took no action; no questions were asked as to why this was done.

Disney had lost several key executives in the months before Ovitz was hired. Moreover, the position of president is obviously important in a publicly owned corporation. But the Old Board and the compensation committee (it is alleged) each spent less than an hour reviewing Ovitz's possible hiring. According to the new complaint, neither the Old Board nor the compensation committee reviewed the actual draft employment agreement. Nor did they evaluate the details of Ovitz's salary or his severance provisions. No expert presented the board with details of the agreement, outlined the pros and cons of either the salary or non-fault termination provisions, or analyzed comparable industry standards for such agreements.[31] Notwithstanding this alleged information vacuum, the Old Board and the compensation committee approved Ovitz's hiring, appointed Eisner to negotiate with Ovitz directly in drafting the unresolved terms of his employment, never asked to review the final terms, and were never voluntarily provided those terms.

During the negotiation over the unresolved terms, the compensation committee was involved only once, at the very early stages in October 1995. The final agreement varied significantly from the draft agreement in the areas of both stock options and the

---

31. In the earlier proceedings in this case, defendants represented that Graef Crystal served as the expert with regard to Ovitz's employment, arguably providing the board with the statutory safe harbor under [DGCL] §141(e). The new complaint, however, alleges that Graef Crystal was hired as the expert with regard to *Eisner's* new employment agreement, *not* Ovitz's agreement. Accepting this change in facts as true for purposes of this motion, Disney's board is not entitled to invoke §141(e)'s protection based on a board's reliance upon a qualified expert selected with reasonable care.

terms of the non-fault termination. Neither the compensation committee nor the Old Board sought to review, nor did they review, the final agreement. In addition, both the Old Board and the committee failed to meet in order to evaluate the final agreement before it became binding on Disney. To repeat, no expert was retained to advise the Old Board, the committee, or Eisner during the negotiation process.

The new complaint, fairly read, also charges the New Board with a similar ostrich-like approach regarding Ovitz's non-fault termination. Eisner and Litvack granted Ovitz a non-fault termination on December 12, 1996, and the news became public that day. Although formal board approval appeared necessary for a non-fault termination, the new complaint alleges that no New Board member even asked for a meeting to discuss Eisner's and Litvack's decision. On December 27, 1996, when Eisner and Litvack accelerated Ovitz's non-fault termination by over a month, with a payout of more than $38 million in cash, together with the three million "A" stock options, the board again failed to do anything. Instead, it appears from the new complaint that the New Board played no role in Eisner's agreement to award Ovitz more than $38 million in cash and the three million "A" stock options, all for leaving a job that Ovitz had allegedly proven incapable of performing.

The New Board apparently never sought to negotiate with Ovitz regarding his departure. Nor, apparently, did it consider whether to seek a termination based on fault. During the fifteen-day period between announcement of Ovitz's termination and its effective date, the New Board allegedly chose to remain invisible in the process. The new complaint alleges that the New Board: (1) failed to ask why it had not been informed; (2) failed to inquire about the conditions and terms of the agreement; and (3) failed even to attempt to stop or delay the termination until more information could be collected. If the board had taken the time or effort to review these or other options, perhaps with the assistance of expert legal advisors, the business judgment rule might well protect its decision. In this case, however, the new complaint asserts that the New Board directors refused to explore any alternatives, and refused to even attempt to evaluate the implications of the non-fault termination — blindly allowing Eisner to hand over to his personal friend, Ovitz, more than $38 million in cash and the three million "A" stock options.[32]

These facts, if true, do more than portray directors who, in a negligent or grossly negligent manner, merely failed to inform themselves or to deliberate adequately about an issue of material importance to their corporation. Instead, the facts alleged in the new complaint suggest that the defendant directors *consciously and intentionally disregarded their responsibilities,* adopting a "we don't care about the risks" attitude concerning a material corporate decision. Knowing or deliberate indifference by a director to his or her duty to act faithfully and with appropriate care is conduct, in my opinion, that may not have been taken honestly and in good faith to advance the best interests of the company. Put differently, all of the alleged facts, if true, imply that the defendant directors *knew* that they were making material decisions without adequate information and without adequate deliberation, and that they simply did not care if the decisions caused the corporation and its stockholders to suffer injury or loss. Viewed in this light, plaintiffs' new complaint sufficiently alleges a breach of the directors' obligation to act honestly and in good faith in the corporation's best

---

32. Plaintiffs allege that the present value of the cash and the value of the stock options totaled over $140 million to Ovitz as severance. At this time I need not determine whether plaintiffs' allegations as to the value of the payout are correct or incorrect.

interests for a Court to conclude, if the facts are true, that the defendant directors' conduct fell outside the protection of the business judgment rule.

Of course, the alleged facts need only give rise to a reason to doubt business judgment protection, not "a judicial finding that the directors' actions are not protected by the business judgment rule."[34] For this reason, I conclude that plaintiffs have satisfied the second prong of *Aronson,* and that demand is excused.

I also conclude that plaintiffs' pleading is sufficient to withstand a motion to dismiss under Rule 12(b)(6). Specifically, plaintiffs' claims are based on an alleged knowing and deliberate indifference to a potential risk of harm to the corporation. Where a director consciously ignores his or her duties to the corporation, thereby causing economic injury to its stockholders, the director's actions are either "not in good faith" or "involve intentional misconduct." Thus, plaintiffs' allegations support claims that fall *outside* the liability waiver provided under Disney's certificate of incorporation.

B. Ovitz

Defendant Ovitz contends that the action against him should be dismissed because he owed no fiduciary duty not to seek the best possible employment agreement for himself. Ovitz did have the right to seek the best employment agreement possible for himself. Nevertheless, once Ovitz became a fiduciary of Disney on October 1, 1995, according to the new complaint, he also had a duty to negotiate honestly and in good faith so as not to advantage himself at the expense of the Disney shareholders. He arguably failed to fulfill that duty, according to the facts alleged in the new complaint.

Ovitz and Eisner had been close friends for over twenty-five years. Ovitz knew when he became president of Disney on October 1, 1995, that his unexecuted contract was still under negotiation. Instead of negotiating with an impartial entity, such as the compensation committee, Ovitz and his attorneys negotiated directly with Eisner, his close personal friend. Perhaps not surprisingly, the final version of the employment agreement differed significantly from the draft version summarized to the board and to the compensation committee on September 26, 1995. Had those changes been the result of arms-length bargaining, Ovitz's motion to dismiss might have merit. At this stage, however, the alleged facts (which I must accept as true) suggest that Ovitz and Eisner had almost absolute control over the terms of Ovitz's contract.

The new complaint arguably charges that Ovitz engaged in a carefully orchestrated, self-serving process controlled directly by his close friend Eisner, all designed to provide Ovitz with enormous financial benefits. The case law cited by Ovitz in support of his position suggests that an officer may negotiate his or her own employment agreement *as long as the process involves negotiations performed in an adversarial and arms-length manner.* The facts, as alleged in the new complaint, belie an adversarial, arms-length negotiation process between Ovitz and the Walt Disney Company. Instead, the alleged facts, if true, would support an inference that Ovitz may have breached his fiduciary duties by engaging in a self-interested transaction in negotiating his employment agreement directly with his personal friend Eisner.

The same is true regarding the non-fault termination. In that instance, Ovitz was also serving as a member of the Disney board of directors. The Supreme Court

---

34. *Grobow [v. Perot],* 539 A.2d [180], 186 [(Del. 1988)].

recently held in *Telxon Corp. v. Meyerson* that "directoral self-compensation decisions lie outside the business judgment rule's presumptive protection, so that, where properly challenged, the receipt of self-determined benefits is subject to an affirmative showing that the compensation arrangements are fair to the corporation."[37] According to the facts alleged in the new complaint, Ovitz did not advise the Disney board of his decision to seek a departure that would be fair and equitable to all parties. Instead, he went to his close friend, Eisner, and, working together, they developed a secret strategy that would enable Ovitz to extract the maximum benefit from his contract, all without board approval.

Although the strategy was economically injurious and a public relations disaster for Disney, the Ovitz/Eisner exit strategy allegedly was designed principally to protect their personal reputations, while assuring Ovitz a huge personal payoff after barely a year of mediocre to poor job performance. These allegations, if ultimately found to be true, would suggest a faithless fiduciary who obtained extraordinary personal financial benefits at the expense of the constituency for whom he was obliged to act honestly and in good faith. Because Ovitz was a fiduciary during both the negotiation of his employment agreement and the non-fault termination, he had an obligation to ensure the process of his contract negotiation and termination was both impartial and fair. The facts, as plead, give rise to a reasonable inference that, assisted by Eisner, he ignored that obligation.

IV. CONCLUSION

It is of course true that after-the-fact litigation is a most imperfect device to evaluate corporate business decisions, as the limits of human competence necessarily impede judicial review. But our corporation law's theoretical justification for disregarding honest errors simply does not apply to intentional misconduct or to egregious process failures that implicate the foundational directoral obligation to act honestly and in good faith to advance corporate interests. Because the facts alleged here, if true, portray directors consciously indifferent to a material issue facing the corporation, the law must be strong enough to intervene against abuse of trust. Accordingly, all three of plaintiffs' claims for relief concerning fiduciary duty breaches and waste survive defendants' motions to dismiss.

The practical effect of this ruling is that defendants must answer the new complaint and plaintiffs may proceed to take appropriate discovery on the merits of their claims. To that end, a case scheduling order has been entered that will promptly bring this matter before the Court on a fully developed factual record.

Notes and Questions

1. Reality Check

a. What claims are plaintiffs asserting? Which ones does Chancellor Chandler find are valid? Do you agree?

b. What defenses do the directors assert? Do you agree with the court's analysis of those defenses?

---

37. 802 A.2d 257, 265 (Del. 2002).

c. Which amelioration devices does the court discuss? Do you agree with Chancellor Chandler's analysis?

d. After a thirty-seven day trial, Chancellor Chandler found for the defendants on all claims. As for Mr. Ovitz's hiring, the Chancellor found that the Compensation Committee had the power to hire without full board approval. Two of the Committee members (Messrs. Russell and Watson) were fully informed and they informed the other two members (Messrs. Lozano and Poitier). The Chancellor found that retaining and relying on Mr. Crystal was appropriate. Thus the full board's action, or inaction, was not at issue.

Under the corporation's certificate of incorporation and bylaws, either the board or the CEO, Mr. Eisner, had the power to terminate senior officers. Mr. Eisner met his fiduciary duties in terminating Mr. Ovitz. The board, then, could not have been liable for terminating Mr. Ovitz regardless of their knowledge, or lack thereof. Finally, the Chancellor found that Mr. Ovitz did not violate his duty of loyalty regarding his termination because he played no part in making the termination decision and did not "improperly inject himself into" nor "manipulate" the process. See *In Re The Walt Disney Company Derivative Litigation*, 2005 WL 2056651 (Del. Ch. Aug. 9, 2005).

2. Suppose

a. Suppose the company had been incorporated in a state that has adopted the MBCA. Would the court's analysis or the result have been different?

b. Suppose you had been retained by the plaintiffs, or the directors, or Mr. Ovitz before any negotiations took place regarding Mr. Ovitz's possible employment at Disney. What advice would you give your client?

c. Suppose you had been retained by the plaintiffs, or the directors, or Mr. Ovitz after Mr. Ovitz had been hired at Disney but before he ceased to be employed there. What advice would you give your client?

d. Suppose you had been retained by the plaintiffs, or the directors, or Mr. Ovitz after Mr. Ovitz left Disney. What advice would you give your client?

3. What Do You Think?

a. Do you believe plaintiffs asserted every viable claim? If not, what else could they have asserted? Are some defendants more culpable than others?

b. Do you believe the defendants asserted every viable defense? If not, what else could they have asserted? Do some defendants have better defenses than others?

F. TERMS OF ART IN THIS CHAPTER

Business judgment rule	Entire fairness	Special litigation committee
Caremark claim	Indemnification	Waste
Charter limitations		

14

Do the Restrictions Work?

We come to the end of our five-chapter consideration of the exercise of, and restriction on, board power over the corporation. Chapter 10 discussed restrictions imposed on the corporation itself. Restrictions on the board are simply a consequence of restrictions on corporate actions. Chapters 11 and 12 explored directors' fiduciary duties of loyalty and care. Chapter 13 looked at the standards of review courts use to assess whether liability will be imposed for breach of those fiduciary duties. Now we reflect on whether all these limitations work. That is, are corporate boards genuinely constrained from exercising corporate power in ways deleterious to others? This chapter is divided into three sections. First we will explore the facts surrounding two of the major corporate accounting scandals of the early twenty-first century. Second, and most centrally, we will look at structural constraints that might have been expected to constrain corporations and their boards. Finally, we will take a step back and ask you to decide whether the costs of reforming the current system of constraints are worth the benefits and whether these corporate scandals are exceptions to the norm or represent proof that the system of restraints is fundamentally broken.

Between late 2001 and the end of 2003 a series of corporate financial scandals became public. In response, Congress enacted reforms, the SEC became revivified, and accounting firms, investment bankers, and stock brokerages all reformed their business practices. This section looks at two of the most emblematic of these scandals. We start by describing what happened and what the motivations were. Then we will take a structural approach and ask what institutions were designed to check board power. Third, we will see the responses to these scandals. Finally we will ask whether these scandals were spectacular anomalies or exemplars of systemic problems.

A. TWO TWENTY-FIRST CENTURY EXAMPLES

1. Enron[1]

Enron was one of the largest companies in the world and was considered to be one of the most innovative and successful. *Fortune* magazine ranked Enron as the seventh

---

1. The facts in this discussion are taken, largely verbatim and without further indication, from *In re Enron Corp.*, Second Interim Report of Neal Batson, Court-Appointed Examiner (Jan. 21, 2003).

largest corporation in the world based on its $100 billion in annual revenues. Starting out as a company that had a concentration in natural gas pipelines, it became, by the mid-1990s, a company that depended less on pipelines and transportation and more on energy trading (which was successful) and investing in new technologies and businesses (which was largely unsuccessful).

Enron's expansion during this time made Enron a voracious consumer of cash. Enron's management made it clear to the investment community that it was aware of the issues posed by its expansion and gave assurances that Enron could manage its way through these risks without upsetting investor expectations.

Enron's energy trading segment was by far the most significant of Enron's business segments, accounting for 66 percent of its 1999 income. Enron acted as a principal, buying and selling energy from producers and wholesale users (such as utility companies) and also as a broker between other parties. When it brokered transactions, it also guaranteed performance to each party by the other. In effect, Enron was committed to every trade. To continue the growth of this business, Enron needed to trade with other market participants without being required to post collateral. To do so, Enron needed to keep its credit rating for its unsecured long-term debt at the "investment grade" level. Enron considered its credit ratings critical to its success. Enron's need to maintain its credit rating was known throughout the institution, from its board of directors to its mid-level management.

The continued success of Enron's entire business was dependent upon the continued success of its energy trading segment, which in turn was dependent upon Enron's credit ratings, which depended on achieving certain financial ratios. These ratios were calculated, in large part, by comparing various financial factors to Enron's total debt.

Enron so engineered its reported financial position and results of operations that its financial statements bore little resemblance to its actual financial condition or performance. This financial engineering in many cases violated GAAP and applicable disclosure laws, and resulted in financial statements that did not fairly present Enron's financial condition.

Two key factors drove Enron's management of its financial statements: its need for cash and its need to maintain its investment grade credit rating. Enron was reluctant to issue equity to raise money for fear of an adverse effect on its stock price because the new shares would dilute the existing shares' value .... In addition, Enron was reluctant to incur debt to raise money because of the adverse affect on its credit ratings.

In the fall of 2001, Enron made a series of financial disclosures that triggered a chain of events culminating in its bankruptcy. In outline, Enron raised the cash it needed by borrowing. To keep that debt from showing up on its financial statements, Enron created many separate legal entities, called *special purpose entities* (SPEs). The SPEs borrowed money that was then used in Enron ventures. Under GAAP, Enron did not have to report the SPEs' debt as its own if Enron owned no more than 97 percent of the SPE and did not manage the SPE. Enron violated both these requirements and thus had to restate its financial statements to reflect that it had significantly more debt than it had disclosed and to reflect that it was losing money on the nonenergy trading segments of its business.

As a result of these disclosures, its trading partners reduced the volume of business they did with Enron, which cut its revenues. Further, Enron's credit rating was reduced severely, which resulted in the acceleration of much of Enron's long-term debt. Unable to service its debt with the assets in hand, Enron declared bankruptcy. Enron stockholders lost $66 billion.

2. WorldCom

WorldCom was a telecom corporation engaged in local, long-distance, and cellular telephone services, as well as Internet services. Through a series of aggressive acquisitions, WorldCom was a leader in all these areas.

Report of Investigation by the Special Investigative Committee of the Board of Directors of WorldCom, Inc.

(2003)

From 1999 until 2002, WorldCom suffered one of the largest public company accounting frauds in history. As enormous as the fraud was, it was accomplished in a relatively mundane way: more than $9 billion in false or unsupported accounting entries were made in WorldCom's financial systems in order to achieve desired reported financial results. The fraud did not involve WorldCom's network, its technology, or its engineering. Most of WorldCom's people did not know it was occurring. Rather, the fraud occurred as a result of knowing misconduct directed by a few senior executives centered in its Clinton, Mississippi, headquarters, and implemented by personnel in its financial and accounting departments in several locations. The fraud was the consequence of the way WorldCom's Chief Executive Officer, Bernard J. Ebbers, ran the Company. Though much of this Report details the implementation of the fraud by others, he was the source of the culture, as well as much of the pressure, that gave birth to this fraud. That the fraud continued as long as it did was due to a lack of courage to blow the whistle on the part of others in WorldCom's financial and accounting departments; inadequate audits by [independent accounting firm] Arthur Andersen; and a financial system whose controls were sorely deficient. The setting in which it occurred was marked by a serious corporate governance failure.

Line costs are the costs of carrying a voice call or data transmission from its starting point to its ending point. They are WorldCom's largest single expense: from 1999 to 2001, line costs accounted for approximately half of the Company's total expenses. As a result, WorldCom management and outside analysts paid particular attention to line cost levels and trends. One key measure of performance both within WorldCom and in communications with the public was the ratio of line cost expense to revenue (the "line cost E/R ratio").

In 1999 and 2000, WorldCom reduced its reported line costs by approximately $3.3 billion. This was accomplished by improperly releasing "accruals," or amounts set aside on WorldCom's financial statements to pay anticipated bills. These accruals were supposed to reflect estimates of the costs . . . , which WorldCom had not yet paid. "Releasing" an accrual is proper when it turns out that less is needed to pay the bills than had been anticipated. It has the effect of providing an offset against reported line costs in the period when the accrual is released. Thus, it reduces reported expenses and increases reported pre-tax income.

By the end of 2000, WorldCom had essentially exhausted available accruals, at least on the scale needed to continue this manipulation of reported line costs. Thereafter, from the first quarter of 2001 through the first quarter of 2002, WorldCom improperly reduced its reported line costs by $3.8 billion, principally by capitalizing $3.5 billion of line costs—at [CFO Scott] Sullivan's direction—in violation of WorldCom's capitalization policy and well-established accounting standards. The line costs that WorldCom capitalized were ongoing, operating expenses that accounting rules required WorldCom to recognize immediately. Sullivan made comments indicating that he intended ultimately to reduce these inflated asset accounts by including them in a large restructuring charge later in 2002.

By capitalizing operating expenses, WorldCom . . . increased its reported pre-tax income and earnings per share. Had WorldCom not capitalized these expenses, it would have reported a pre-tax loss in three of the five quarters in which the improper capitalization entries occurred. By reducing reported line costs, the capitalization entries also significantly improved WorldCom's line cost E/R ratio. In its public filings, WorldCom consistently emphasized throughout 2001 that its line cost E/R ratio stayed the same—about 42%—quarter after quarter. That representation was false. Had it not capitalized line costs, WorldCom's reported line cost E/R ratio would have been much higher, typically exceeding 50%. This device also made it appear that softening markets were not reducing the Company's profitability, when the opposite was the case. To implement the capitalization strategy, Sullivan needed the acquiescence of a significant number of people within the financial and accounting departments at the Company.

WorldCom marketed itself as a high-growth company, and revenue growth was clearly a critical component of WorldCom's early success. As market conditions throughout the telecommunications industry deteriorated in 2000 and 2001, World-Com . . . nevertheless continued to post impressive revenue growth numbers, and Ebbers and Sullivan continued to assure Wall Street that WorldCom could sustain that level of growth. In essence, WorldCom claimed it was successfully managing industry trends that were hurting all of its competitors. These promises of double-digit growth translated into pressure within WorldCom to achieve those results. As one officer told us, the emphasis on revenue was "in every brick in every building." Ebbers was intensely focused on revenue performance, receiving and closely examining Monthly Revenue . . . reports from the Revenue Reporting and Accounting group ("Revenue Accounting group").

Beginning in 1999, WorldCom personnel made large revenue accounting entries after the close of many quarters in order to report that it had achieved the high revenue growth targets that Ebbers and Sullivan had established. The questionable revenue entries included in Corporate Unallocated [revenue accounts] often involved large, round-dollar revenue items (in millions or tens of millions of dollars). They generally appeared only in the quarter-ending month, and they were not recorded during the quarter, but instead in the weeks after the quarter had ended. As a result, the total amounts reported in the Corporate Unallocated revenue accounts spiked upward during quarter-ending months, and the largest spikes (ranging from $136 million to $257 million) occurred in those quarters in which WorldCom's operational revenue lagged furthest behind its quarterly revenue targets—the second and third quarters of 2000 and second, third and fourth quarters of 2001.

In the period under investigation, the amounts booked in the Corporate Unallocated revenue accounts were critical to WorldCom's perceived success. Without the revenue booked in those accounts, WorldCom would have failed, in six out of the twelve quarters between the beginning of 1999 and the end of 2001, to achieve the double-digit growth it reported. Our investigation has identified over $958 million in revenue that was improperly recorded by WorldCom between the first quarter of 1999 and the first quarter of 2002. Our accounting advisors have identified $1.107 billion of additional revenue items recorded during this period that they consider questionable, based on the circumstances in which they were recorded and the lack of available or adequate support.

Ebbers, in addition to his full-time job as Chief Executive Officer of WorldCom, was actively involved in buying, building, and running several businesses unrelated to WorldCom. Between 1998 and 2000, Ebbers and the companies he controlled significantly expanded their holdings by purchasing, among other things, the largest working cattle ranch in Canada (approximately 500,000 acres), and approximately 540,000 acres of timberland in four Southern U.S. states. The total scope of Ebbers' non–WorldCom businesses . . . included a Louisiana rice farm, a luxury yacht building company, a lumber mill, a country club, a trucking company, a minor league hockey team, an operating marina, and a building in downtown Chicago.

Nothing we have reviewed indicates that the Compensation Committee [of the Board] or the Board imposed any limits on Ebbers' conduct of non–WorldCom businesses. It does not appear that any Board members seriously pursued, prior to 2002, the question whether Ebbers could devote sufficient attention to managing WorldCom amid his outside business obligations . . . .

The method Ebbers chose to finance many of his acquisitions involved substantial financial risk. Ebbers and companies he controlled took out loans from commercial banks. Many of these commercial loans were margin loans secured by shares of Ebbers' WorldCom stock. Although the terms varied among the various margin loans, each required that the value of Ebbers' stock remain greater than or equal to some multiple of the amount of the loan.

These margin loans totaled hundreds of millions of dollars — perhaps more at various times. This massive indebtedness left Ebbers exposed to declines in the price of WorldCom stock, which began to occur in late 1999. The stock price went from a high of $62.00 a share on June 21, 1999, to $36.52 on Friday, April 14, 2000. The following Monday, Bank of America made a margin call to Ebbers, noting that he was in default and calling for him either to pledge additional collateral or to reduce his outstanding loan amount.

The price of WorldCom stock continued to decline during 2000, and Ebbers continued to face margin calls from his lenders. By September 6, 2000, the day of a scheduled meeting of the Compensation Committee, the stock price was down to $30.27 a share. Shortly before the meeting, Ebbers told . . . the Committee's chairman, about the margin calls he was facing and they discussed the possibility that the Company would give him a loan. There is conflicting evidence whether it was Ebbers who first suggested the loan.

From . . . late September 2000 until Ebbers' forced resignation in April 2002, the Compensation Committee took various steps — including extending . . . loans and guaranties — to enable Ebbers to avoid selling . . . WorldCom stock. Ebbers' personal financial situation became a focus of Compensation Committee attention, particularly in early 2002. From October 18, 2000, until April 1, 2002, the Compensation Committee met and discussed the Company's financial arrangements with Ebbers 26 times, and for 13 of these meetings, Ebbers' financial situation is the only topic specifically identified in the minutes. Unable to persuade Ebbers' lenders to relax their demands or accept other collateral from Ebbers, the Committee proceeded to approve numerous additional loans and guaranties for Ebbers, eventually totaling (including interest) $408 million.

The most serious risk the Committee and the Board overlooked was the risk that Ebbers' personal financial stress posed to his corporate decision making. As a substantial long-term stockholder, Ebbers' interests had been aligned with those of the Company. Beginning in 2000, however, once he was subject to the daily pressure of margin calls and thus in financial jeopardy based on any short-term decline in the price of WorldCom stock, Ebbers' interests were no longer fully aligned with those of the Company. He had strong incentives to pursue whatever short-term action might be necessary to push up the stock price. [T]he fact that Ebbers was so far overextended financially should have prompted much closer Board attention to the way he was running the Company, and he should not have been allowed to use the Company as his personal bank.

Late in the Spring of 2002, the enormous capitalization entries — approximately $3.5 billion — were finally detected and disclosed to the public. They had, of course, been well known for some time in the General Accounting, Property Accounting and Capital Reporting groups. Internal Audit had come across references to the corporate adjustments while doing an audit of Capital Expenditures in late 2001, and first made inquiries at that time. In the Spring of 2002, Internal Audit focused on the adjustments and brought the fraud to the attention of the Board. Simultaneously, others within the Company became aware of these improper adjustments, and some took steps to raise questions about them.

On June 25, 2002, WorldCom announced that it intended to restate its financial statements for 2001 and the first quarter of 2002. It stated that it had determined that certain transfers totaling $3.852 billion during that period from "line cost" expenses (costs of transmitting calls) to asset accounts were not made in accordance with generally accepted accounting principles ("GAAP"). Less than one month later, WorldCom and substantially all of its active U.S. subsidiaries filed voluntary petitions for reorganization under Chapter 11 of the Bankruptcy Code. WorldCom subsequently announced that it had discovered an additional $3.831 billion in improperly reported earnings before taxes for 1999, 2000, 2001, and first quarter 2002. It has also written off approximately $80 billion of the stated book value of the assets on the Company's balance sheet at the time the fraud was announced.

Notes and Questions

1. Notes

a. As a result of these disclosures, its lenders accelerated much of WorldCom's debt. Unable to service its debt with the assets in hand, WorldCom declared bankruptcy. WorldCom stockholders lost $156 billion.

b. Although the stock of Enron and WorldCom lost nearly all value, you should be aware that the value of all stock in NYSE listed companies was approximately $10 trillion in 2001 and 2002. The stock losses for all companies that experienced accounting fraud in the early twenty-first century aggregated about 3 percent of the value of all companies.

c. Both Enron and WorldCom sponsored retirement plans for their employees. About 60 percent of Enron's retirement plan was invested in Enron stock. That plan lost about $1.3 billion in value when Enron declared bankruptcy. WorldCom's retirement plan has about one-third of its assets invested in company stock; the plan lost about $280 million.

d. WorldCom's $408 million in loans to Mr. Ebbers constituted about 1 percent of WorldCom's annual revenue.

e. Later in the chapter we will look at the workings of credit-rating agencies.

f. Senior managers have several incentives to commit accounting fraud. First, much of their compensation depends upon the company's economic performance. Second, their desire for professional success may motivate them to conceal the company's true economic performance. As you see from the above descriptions, among the immediate pressures to commit accounting fraud are the desire to keep the company's credit rating high, which, in turn, permits the company to borrow more money and to avoid having payment of existing debt accelerated. The executives may also desire to tailor the company's performance to the expectations of securities analysts so that the company's stock price remains high. See Joseph T. Wells, *Principles of Fraud Examination* (2005).

g. Accounting frauds fall into a few categories. First, executives may fraudulently increase revenues, either by improperly characterizing certain transactions, by engaging in sham transactions with others, or, as WorldCom did, by simply making up numbers to be included in the company's revenues. Second, executives may fraudulently overstate the value of assets or, more commonly, understate the value of liabilities so that the company appears to have a higher ratio of assets to liabilities than is really the case. This essentially increases the company's borrowing ability. Enron engaged in this activity by concealing the scope of its debt. Third, managers may fraudulently understate costs, which increases profit. This can be accomplished by ignoring contingent liabilities (like the possibility of customer returns or customer warranty claims), or, as WorldCom did, by improperly designating expenses for current goods and services (which should be reported in full) as expenses for long-term goods and services (which should be reported over time). See Joseph T. Wells, *Principles of Fraud Examination* (2005).

2. Reality Check

a. What kinds of accounting fraud did WorldCom commit?

b. Why did WorldCom's managers commit fraud?

B. STRUCTURAL CONSTRAINTS

Statistics strongly suggest that the kinds of financial scandals that most concern us here nearly always involve the top corporate officers. In over 70 percent of financial fraud cases the CEO is complicit and the CFO is involved in over 40 percent of such cases. Either the CEO, the CFO, or both, is a participant in more than 80 percent of reported financial fraud cases. It seems clear, then, that constraining these two senior officers, at the least, is required to stem financial frauds. Four principal institutional constraints work to keep financial frauds from taking place. And yet, financial frauds are perpetrated with some regularity anyway. Because our primary focus in this chapter is on the board of directors, we start with assessments of the Enron and WorldCom boards.

1. Board of Directors

a. Enron

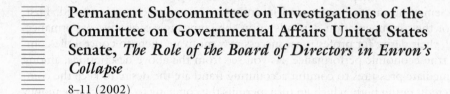

Permanent Subcommittee on Investigations of the Committee on Governmental Affairs United States Senate, *The Role of the Board of Directors in Enron's Collapse*
8–11 (2002)

In 2001, Enron's Board of Directors had 15 members, several of whom had 20 years or more experience on the Board of Enron or its predecessor companies. Many of Enron's Directors served on the boards of other companies as well. At the hearing, John Duncan, former Chairman of the Executive Committee, described his fellow Board members as well educated, "experienced, successful businessmen and women," and "experts in areas of finance and accounting." The Subcommittee interviews found the Directors to have a wealth of sophisticated business and investment experience and considerable expertise in accounting, derivatives, and structured finance.

Enron Board members uniformly described internal Board relations as harmonious. They said that Board votes were generally unanimous and could recall only two instances over the course of many years involving dissenting votes. The Directors also described a good working relationship with Enron management. Several had close personal relationships with Board Chairman and Chief Executive Officer (CEO) Kenneth L. Lay. All indicated they had possessed great respect for senior Enron officers, trusting the integrity and competence of Mr. Lay; President and Chief Operating Officer (and later CEO) Jeffrey K. Skilling; Chief Financial Officer Andrew S. Fastow; Chief Accounting Officer Richard A. Causey; Chief Risk Officer Richard Buy; and the Treasurer Jeffrey McMahon and later Ben Glisan. Mr. Lay served as Chairman of the Board from 1986 until he resigned in 2002. Mr. Skilling was a Board member from 1997 until August 2001, when he resigned from Enron.

The Enron Board was organized into five committees. (1) The **Executive Committee** met on an as needed basis to handle urgent business matters between scheduled Board meetings. (2) The **Finance Committee** was responsible for approving major transactions which, in 2001, met or exceeded $75 million in value. It also reviewed transactions valued between $25 million and $75 million; oversaw Enron's risk management efforts; and provided guidance on the company's financial decisions and policies. (3) The **Audit and Compliance Committee** reviewed Enron's accounting and compliance programs, approved Enron's financial statements and reports, and was the primary liaison with Andersen. (4) The **Compensation Committee** established and monitored Enron's compensation policies and plans for directors, officers and employees. (5) The **Nominating Committee** nominated individuals to serve as Directors.

The Board normally held five regular meetings during the year, with additional special meetings as needed. Board meetings usually lasted two days, with the first day devoted to Committee meetings and a Board dinner and the second day devoted to a meeting of the full Board. Committee meetings generally lasted between one and two hours and were arranged to allow Board members, who typically sat on three Committees, to attend all assigned Committee meetings. Full Board meetings also generally lasted between one and two hours. Special Board meetings, as well as meetings of the Executive Committee, were typically conducted by telephone conference.

Committee chairmen typically spoke with Enron management by telephone prior to Committee meetings to develop the proposed Committee meeting agenda. Board members said that Enron management provided them with these agendas as well as extensive background and briefing materials prior to Board meetings including, in the case of Finance Committee members, numerous deal approval sheets ("DASHs") for approval of major transactions. Board members varied in how much time they spent reading the materials and preparing for Board meetings, with the reported preparation time for each meeting varying between two hours and two days. On some occasions, Enron provided a private plane to transport Board members from various locations to a Board meeting, and Board members discussed company issues during the flight. Enron also organized occasional trips abroad which some Board members attended to view company assets and operations.

During the Committee meetings, Enron management generally provided presentations on company performance, internal controls, new business ventures, specific transactions, or other topics of interest. The Finance Committee generally heard from Mr. Fastow, Mr. Causey, Mr. Buy, Mr. McMahon and, occasionally, Mr. Glisan. The Audit Committee generally heard from Mr. Causey, Mr. Buy, and [Enron's outside auditor, Arthur] Andersen personnel. The Compensation Committee generally heard from the company's top compensation official, Mary Joyce, and from the company's compensation consultant, Towers Perrin. On occasion, the Committees heard from other senior Enron officers as well. At the full Board meetings, Board members typically received presentations from each Committee Chairman summarizing the Committee's work and recommendations, as well as from Enron management and, occasionally, Andersen or the company's chief outside legal counsel, Vinson & Elkins. Mr. Lay and Mr. Skilling usually attended Executive, Finance, and Audit Committee meetings, as well as the full Board meetings. Mr. Lay attended many Compensation Committee meetings as well. The Subcommittee interviews indicated that, altogether, Board members appeared to have routine contact with less than a dozen senior officers at Enron. The Board did not have a practice of meeting without Enron management present.

Regular presentations on Enron's financial statements, accounting practices, and audit results were provided by Andersen to the Audit Committee. The Audit Committee Chairman would then report on the presentation to the full Board. On most occasions, three Andersen senior partners from Andersen's Houston office attended Audit Committee meetings. The Audit Committee offered Andersen personnel an opportunity to present information to them without management present.

Minutes summarizing Committee and Board meetings were kept by the Corporate Secretary, who often took handwritten notes on Committee and Board presentations during the Board's deliberations and afterward developed and circulated draft minutes to Enron management, Board members, and legal counsel. The draft minutes were formally presented to and approved by Committee and Board members at subsequent meetings.

Outside of the formal Committee and Board meetings, the Enron Directors described very little interaction or communication either among Board members or between Board members and Enron or Andersen personnel, until the company began experiencing severe problems in October 2001. From October until the company's bankruptcy on December 2, 2001, the Board held numerous special meetings, at times on almost a daily basis.

Enron Board members were compensated with cash, restricted stock, phantom stock units, and stock options. The total cash and equity compensation of Enron Board members in 2000 was valued by Enron at about $350,000 or more than twice the national average for Board compensation at a U.S. publicly traded corporation.

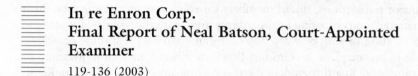

In re Enron Corp.
Final Report of Neal Batson, Court-Appointed Examiner

119-136 (2003)

The Enron Board could have been the ultimate check in preventing or minimizing the impact of the officers' misconduct. The Board had the authority to stop the misconduct by, for example, terminating the employment of these officers, refusing to approve Enron's financial statements, and other disclosures in its . . . public filings or notifying the SEC of wrongdoing. In practice, however, particularly in circumstances involving complex matters and obfuscation by officers of a company, there are limitations to a board serving as an effective check in the area of oversight. This may help to explain why director liability for breach of the duty of oversight is rare absent egregious facts.

The Enron Board did not serve as an effective check on the officers' misuse of Enron's SPE transactions. There are several factors that might explain this failure. Some of these factors were not within the control of the Enron Board. Other factors, however, were within the control of the Enron Board and, if handled differently, might have resulted in the Board limiting the harm caused to Enron.

The Enron Board generally was not asked to, and did not, approve Enron's SPE transactions . . . . As a result, the Board's role for most of these transactions consisted primarily of providing oversight and being alert for signals or red flags of wrongdoing. The following discusses Enron's policies relating to its transaction approval process and the conduct of the two committees most responsible for monitoring the SPEs: the Finance Committee and the Audit Committee.

ENRON BOARD'S TRANSACTION APPROVAL POLICIES

The Enron Board did not approve most of the SPE transactions. There were several policies established by the Enron Board that were relevant to determining whether a transaction could be consummated without Board approval. These included: (i) Enron's Risk Management Policy; (ii) Enron's Guaranty Policy; and (iii) Enron's asset divestiture policy. Because of the way in which many of the SPE transactions were structured, these policies effectively permitted Enron's officers to incur a virtually unlimited amount of debt through the SPE transactions, without prior approval of the Enron Board.

The Enron Board apparently devoted significant attention to these policies, as evidenced by seven amendments to the Risk Management Policy from December 1998 through May 2000. [T]he Enron Board apparently put significant emphasis on its ability to manage risk under the Risk Management Policy. While these controls may work well in managing true trading activities involving assets that have publicly quoted prices and substantial market liquidity, they did not allow the Board the opportunity to prevent the incurrence of debt through SPE transactions (structured as trading activities).

FINANCE AND AUDIT COMMITTEES

Finance Committee

In the area of SPE transactions and off-balance sheet finance transactions, the Finance Committee failed to serve as an effective check. It should be noted that in the area in which its members had an interest and concern, e.g., the . . . status reports about the trading activities . . . , the Finance Committee appears to have performed well in its oversight function. Perhaps because of this interest and attention on the part of the Finance Committee, this process worked effectively to prevent trading losses at Enron.

The Finance Committee did not do as well in the SPE transactions and the structured finance areas. From at least 1997 until August 2001, the Finance Committee apparently neither requested nor received a schedule of the total amount and maturities of Enron's on- and off-balance sheet obligations.

The Finance Committee Charter required that this committee: review and monitor [the Company's] liquidity, including debt maturities, and its contingent liabilities, including its counter-party and currency risk, exposure under outstanding letters of indemnity, letters of credit and corporate guarantees, and review and approve for recommendation to the Board of Directors, if appropriate, the Company's policies with regard thereto.

Instead of monitoring the amounts and maturities of Enron's obligations, however, the Finance Committee focused on the ratios that guided the credit agency ratings. The problems with relying solely on this system of monitoring Enron's obligations were twofold. First, Enron's use of many of its SPE transactions was designed to have no adverse impact on the ratios. Second, the maturities of these SPE off-balance sheet transactions were not apparent from those ratios. Therefore, the $11 billion of obligations coming due from October 2001 through December 2002 were not disclosed in the ratios.

Management failed to present clearly Enron's SPE transactions and the total amount and maturities of its off-balance sheet debt to the Finance Committee. Similarly, management failed to disclose these transactions adequately in its financial statements. The Finance Committee, however, is subject to criticism for failing to recognize that they were not getting adequate information from management on this increasingly important part of Enron's financial structure. This criticism is not meant to imply that there was not any information being supplied to the Board. In fact, in some circumstances it appears that there was so much information presented that it inhibited any meaningful discussion.

It is not the use of SPE off-balance sheet transactions *per se* that should have concerned the Finance Committee. As the Examiner has observed, their use is acceptable if accounted for and disclosed properly. The question is whether these presentations to the Finance Committee should have caused its members to ask additional questions. A full discussion of questions as simple as the following may have elicited some useful information:

How many transactions?

How much cash was raised?

What are Enron's obligations under these transactions?

When are these obligations due?

How is Enron reporting them?

Why don't these transactions adversely affect Enron's investment grade credit rating ratios?

Audit Committee

The Audit Committee also did not serve as an effective check. It had many items to watch and devoted too little time to watching them. The Audit Committee meetings in February 2000 and 2001 illustrated the shortcomings. In each of these meetings, the committee had three major items to consider. In addition to these three items, it was to consider any other matters brought before it. In February 2000, these other matters included: (i) a report on final New York Stock Exchange and SEC rules regarding audit committees; (ii) a report on the 2000 Internal Audit Plan; (iii) a report on the significant reserves in the financial statements; (iv) a report on market risk including the 1999 profit and loss and value-at risk by commodity group; (v) an executive session to consider the appointment of independent auditors for 2000; and (vi) an executive session with Andersen to discuss any problems or disagreements with management. The February 2000 Audit Committee meeting lasted one hour and ten minutes. That amount of time does not appear to be sufficient for meaningful reports, much less full and complete questions and discussion of those matters presented.

Andersen reported that "the Company's sophisticated business practices introduced a high number of accounting models and applications requiring complex interpretations and judgments and that the broadness of the SEC business-related disclosure requirements added to the complexity of the Company's financial reporting." Again, a full discussion of questions as simple as the following may have elicited some helpful information:

What were some of the disclosure issues in the financial statements that are before us and that we are being asked to approve at this meeting?

What are some of the areas on the financial statements that required complex interpretations and accounting judgments so that I can see how much is at stake if others were to reach different judgments than you?

Is there anything we should be doing to make those accounting judgments easier or the disclosures more transparent and complete?

What is the likelihood that these judgments could be incorrect? If so, what are the consequences?

What alternative accounting treatments exist and why did management select and you concur in the treatments used in these financial statements?

There is no record of whether or to what extent any meaningful discussion took place in which Andersen was asked to explain the accounting and disclosure judgments or the magnitude of their impact on Enron's financial statements. In the Audit Committee's defense, however, it did not have the benefit of the concerns that Andersen had expressed internally and it was told that a "clean" opinion would be delivered.

Nonetheless, asking questions like those described above may have provoked meaningful discussion of some of these issues.

In February 2001, the Audit Committee meeting lasted one hour and thirty-five minutes plus an additional ten minutes the following morning when the Audit Committee went into executive session to recommend the approval of Andersen as the company's independent accountants for the following year. In addition to . . . three major items the Audit Committee was to consider and discuss . . . there were six other items: (i) a presentation by Enron's General Counsel, Derrick, on the legal matters in the footnotes to the financial statements; (ii) the required report of the committee to be included in the proxy statement; (iii) the revised Audit and Compliance Committee Charter; (iv) the annual report on executive and director use of company aircraft; (v) a report on the 2001 Internal Control Audit Plan; and (vi) a report on the company's polices and practices for management's communications with analysts.

The minutes of the meeting do not indicate the time spent on individual issues. The length of the meeting, however, raises a question as to whether there could have been meaningful consideration and discussion on any of them. Andersen reminded the Audit Committee, although somewhat obliquely, that "the Company continued to utilize highly structured transactions, such as securitizations and syndications, in which there was significant judgement required in the application of GAAP." Yet again, a full discussion of questions as simple as the following may have elicited some helpful information:

What transactions?

How much money is involved?

Should we consider other products and transactions?

Should we consider alternative accounting treatments or models?

What happens if these judgments are wrong?

Which transactions or judgments are the most risky and what are the primary issues?

POSSIBLE EXPLANATIONS FOR THE ENRON BOARD'S FAILURE

Many of Enron's Outside Directors had skills and talents that likely were beneficial to Enron in the operation of its business, and these contributions should not be underestimated. It appears from the evidence, however, that the Outside Directors did not understand important aspects about Enron's use of SPE transactions.

There may be several possible explanations for the Board's failure to understand these transactions. As discussed above, Enron officers often used misleading terms and confusing jargon, and they presented information to the Enron Board and its committees in a manner that obfuscated the substance of the SPE transactions. In addition, the length of Board and committee meetings, given the complexity and the number of agenda items covered, raises questions of whether sufficient time was devoted to allowing the Outside Directors to understand the transactions. Finally, Enron's Board was unusually large, which may have increased the tendency for individual directors not to feel personally responsible for understanding complex matters. Despite the large number of directors, however, the Board did not appear to have sufficient expertise in the kinds of complicated structured financings in which Enron engaged.

Time

In addition to being large and complex, Enron changed its business strategy dramatically during the late 1990s, requiring the Outside Directors to learn and adjust to the company's transition from a "pipeline company" to a "trading company." Board meetings typically lasted a total of about four to five hours, and committee meetings were generally not more than ninety minutes each. With the large number of significant agenda topics presented at each meeting, these circumstances raise questions of whether the Outside Directors had sufficient time to discuss and understand the matters fully. Although none of the Outside Directors admitted in testimony that they felt the Board or committee meetings were too short, several directors provided such criticism in a Board self-assessment they completed in 2001 . . . :

Reliance on Other Board Members

The Enron Board was unusually large. A recent survey of public companies reported an average board size of 9.4 total directors, with an average of 6.9 "independent" or outside directors, less than Enron's 15 to 19 directors. A consequence of the large size can be a tendency for the individual directors not to feel personal responsibility for understanding complex matters. Several of the Outside Directors testified that they might not have understood an area of the company's operations or a particular matter, but they were not concerned because they expected that someone else on the Board did. For example, Chan, who served on both the Audit and Finance Committees, testified that he relied on other Audit Committee members Jaedicke, Gramm and John Duncan to understand whether it was appropriate for Andersen to provide both external and internal audit functions at Enron: "For something like that, I do rely on my colleagues at the audit committee — such as Bob Jaedicke was much more qualified in this regard, and certainly he has, you know, mentioned about — these concepts, and that's how I learned about it."

Lack of Structured Finance Expertise

The Board did not include a large number of Outside Directors who had hands-on experience in the types of sophisticated financings employed by Enron. In the 2001 Board Assessment, the directors acknowledged this lack of depth on the Board.

CONCLUSIONS

For several reasons, the Enron Board did not function as an effective check and balance. This failure may have resulted from (i) a carefully orchestrated strategy of Enron's senior officers, (ii) the failure of Lay and Skilling, in their capacities as executive officers, to assist the Outside Directors, (iii) inadequate assistance from Enron's professionals, (iv) inattention by the Enron Board to its oversight function, or (v) insufficient understanding of how the SPE transactions were being used by Enron's officers.

b. WorldCom

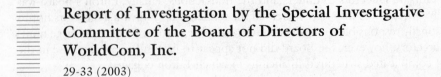

Report of Investigation by the Special Investigative Committee of the Board of Directors of WorldCom, Inc.

29-33 (2003)

WorldCom's collapse reflected not only a financial fraud but also a major failure of corporate governance. The Board of Directors, though apparently unaware of the fraud, played far too small a role in the life, direction and culture of the Company. Although the Board, at least in form, appeared to satisfy many checklists of the time, it did not exhibit the energy, judgment, leadership or courage that WorldCom needed.

We found no evidence that members of the Board of Directors, other than Ebbers and Sullivan, were aware of the improper accounting practices at the time they occurred. We have reviewed materials (including slide presentations) the Board received and have not found information that should reasonably have led it to detect the practices or to believe that further specific inquiry into the accounting practices at issue was necessary.

The Board received regular financial and operational presentations that included a level of detail consistent with what we believe most properly run Boards received during that period. The reduced levels of line costs that resulted from release of accruals and improper capitalization did not appear unusual, in part because the entire purpose of the improper accounting exercise was to hold line costs at a level consistent with earlier periods. It is possible, however, that a Board more closely familiar with what was happening operationally in the Company might have questioned financial trends and comparisons with competitors, including the level of reported capital expenditures: the Board received reports that capital expenditures were declining — as the Board had directed — but in fact capital spending was being slashed much more heavily. There was a disparity between the large cuts that were actually taking place and the reported numbers, which were being pushed back up by the improperly added capitalized line costs.

The Board and its Committees did not function in a way that made it likely that they would notice red flags. The outside Directors had little or no involvement in the Company's business other than through attendance at Board meetings. Nearly all of the Directors were legacies of companies that WorldCom, under Ebbers' leadership, had acquired. They had ceded leadership to Ebbers when their companies were acquired, and in some cases viewed their role as diminished. Ebbers controlled the Board's agenda, its discussions, and its decisions. He created, and the Board permitted, a corporate environment in which the pressure to meet the numbers was high, the departments that served as controls were weak, and the word of senior management was final and not to be challenged.

The Audit Committee in particular needed an understanding of the Company it oversaw in order to be effective. However, the Audit Committee members do not appear to have had a sufficient understanding of the Company's internal financial workings or its culture, and they devoted strikingly little time to their role, meeting as little as three to five hours per year. WorldCom was a complicated Company in a fast-evolving industry. It had expanded quickly, through a series of large acquisitions, and there had been virtually no integration of the acquisitions. WorldCom had accounting-related operations scattered in a variety of locations around the country. These facts raised significant accounting, internal control and systems concerns that required Audit Committee knowledge and attention, and that should also have elicited direct warnings from Andersen. However, the Audit Committee members apparently did not even understand — though the evidence indicates that Andersen disclosed — the nontraditional audit approach Andersen employed. To gain the knowledge necessary to function effectively as an Audit Committee would have required a very substantial amount of energy, expertise by at least some of its members, and a greater commitment of time.

The outside Directors had virtually no interaction with Company operational or financial employees other than during the presentations they heard at meetings. While in this respect the Directors were far from unique among directors of large corporations, this lack of contact meant that they had little sense of the culture within the Company, or awareness of issues other than those brought to them by a few senior managers. They were not themselves visible to employees, and there were no systems in place that could have encouraged employees to contact them with concerns about either the accounting entries or operational matters. In short, the Board was removed and detached from the operations of WorldCom to the extent that its members had little sense of what was really going on within the Company.

Ebbers was autocratic in his dealings with the Board, and the Board permitted it. With limited exceptions, the members of the Board were reluctant to challenge Ebbers even when they disagreed with him. They, like most observers, were impressed with the Company's growth and Ebbers' reputation, although they were in some cases mystified or perplexed by his style. This was Ebbers' company. Several members of the Board were sophisticated, yet the members of the Board were deferential to Ebbers and passive in their oversight until April 2002.

The deference of the Compensation Committee and the Board to Ebbers is illustrated by their decisions beginning in September 2000 to authorize corporate loans and guaranties that grew to over $400 million, so that Ebbers could avoid selling WorldCom stock to meet his personal financial obligations. This was not the first occasion on which Ebbers had overextended himself financially and borrowed from the Company: he had done so in 1994 as well. On neither occasion did anyone on the Board challenge Ebbers with respect to his use of WorldCom stock to extend his personal financial empire to the point that it threatened to cause involuntary liquidation of his stock. The approach of the Board, as one member characterized his own view, was to say nothing to Ebbers because they thought Ebbers was a grownup and could manage his own affairs — even though Ebbers' management of his own affairs involved the use of Company funds, eventually to the tune of hundreds of millions of dollars.

We believe that the extension of these loans and guaranties was a 19-month sequence of terrible decisions — badly conceived, and antithetical to shareholder interests — and a major failure of corporate governance. Indeed, we do not understand how the Compensation Committee or the Board could have concluded that these loans were an acceptable use of more than $400 million of the shareholders' money. These decisions reflected an uncritical solicitude for Ebbers' financial interests, a disregard of the incentives the situation created for Ebbers' management of the Company, and a willingness to subordinate shareholders' interests to Ebbers' financial well-being.

A second example of the Board's deference is its failure to challenge Ebbers on the extent of his substantial outside business interests (and the resulting claim on his time and energies). Those interests included a Louisiana rice farm, a luxury yacht building company, a lumber mill, a country club, a trucking company, a minor league hockey team, an operating marina, and a building in downtown Chicago. We do not believe most properly run Boards of Directors would permit a Chief Executive Officer to pursue an array of interests such as these, certainly not without careful examination of the time and energy commitments they would require. Yet we have seen no evidence of any such challenge.

Notes and Questions

1. Notes

a. Enron is incorporated in Oregon and WorldCom in Georgia. Both are MBCA states.

b. In the wake of Enron, WorldCom, and other corporate scandals, Congress passed the Sarbanes-Oxley Act of 2002 (SOx). Among the requirements applicable to boards of directors, are that audit committees must be directly responsible for retaining the independent accountants and must establish internal corporate procedures for receiving whistle-blowing information. Further, every audit committee must contain at least one "financial expert."[2]

2. Reality Check

a. What sort of activities should the Enron and WorldCom boards have engaged in?

b. How did the directors' conduct fall short?

c. Are there significant differences in the conduct or dynamics of the Enron and WorldCom boards?

In terms of corporate law, it seems clear that the wrongdoers in Enron and WorldCom are liable to the corporation for breach of their fiduciary duties. Even those wrongdoers who were not officers or directors doubtless owe fiduciary duties under agency law. But what about the board members who were not actively involved in the frauds? Presumably they have met their duty of loyalty. Thus, if they are to be liable to the corporation it must be because they have violated the duty of good faith (if one exists) or the duty of care, including *Caremark* duties. You may be thinking that Enron and WorldCom shareholders brought actions against those loyal directors, but in fact derivative actions were not pressed. The reason is probably due to the nature of derivative actions, which we will see in more detail in Chapter 15. A breach of fiduciary duty is a harm to the corporation, not a harm to the shareholders directly. Any recovery goes to the corporation. In the normal course of things, a corporate recovery benefits the shareholders, but when the corporation is bankrupt, as both Enron and WorldCom were, the recovery would benefit the creditors rather than the shareholders. Thus shareholders have little incentive to bring breach of fiduciary duty actions against the loyal directors. Further, given the business judgment rule presumption, how likely is it that a complaint against the loyal directors would survive past the 12(b)(6) stage? As we will see at the end of this chapter, the loyal directors entered into settlements involving significant payments from their personal assets. The theory of that litigation was not state corporate law but federal securities law.

2. Internal Actors Below the Board

All corporate power is located in the board of directors. Obviously, though, the board does not approve every corporate act nor can the board have knowledge of everything that occurs within the corporation. Thus, when we consider whether the constraints explored in Chapters 10-13 are effective, we must also look at the behavior of

---

2. Actually, SOx only requires companies to state whether the audit committee has at least one financial expert and, if not, why not. As a practical matter, this imposes a requirement that every audit committee have at least one financial expert.

individuals within the corporation who are not directors. As noted above, nearly every financial accounting fraud, and every such fraud of large size, involves senior officers. These officers report to, and the CEO is typically a member of, the board of directors. The initial descriptions of the Enron and WorldCom scandals detailed the involvement of the senior officers. The following extract speaks to the possible rationalization of Enron and WorldCom officers' conduct. Before you read these excerpts you may wish to review the material on decision making in Chapter 3.

a. *Officers*

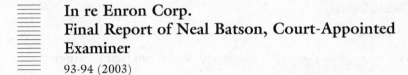

In re Enron Corp.
Final Report of Neal Batson, Court-Appointed Examiner
93-94 (2003)

The Examiner now focuses on several methods used by these officers to facilitate their use of the [fraudulent] accounting techniques. These methods include:

Justification of Desired Results. In many cases, Enron officers were less concerned about making the correct or best decision, and more concerned with justifying a desired result. Evidence suggests that Enron officers: (i) used accounting rules that did not directly address the accounting question at issue but provided an argument to justify an aggressive position; (ii) searched for reasons to avoid public disclosure; and (iii) obtained professional opinions or advice merely as a necessary procedural step.

Use of Economic Leverage on Third Parties. Evidence suggests that by using Enron's economic power, Enron officers were able to pressure third parties, such as financial institutions and Enron's professionals, to accommodate Enron's financial statement objectives. In many instances, this economic pressure appears responsible for overcoming concerns about reputational risk or other reservations by these third parties.

Lack of Candor. There are many examples of incomplete disclosure by these officers to the Enron Board and the public. In some cases, it appears that officers provided hints or glimpses of facts suggesting possible misuse of SPEs to the Enron Board. In other cases, Enron officers' frequent use of misleading terms and jargon in connection with Enron's SPE transactions appears to have obscured their economic substance. Finally, evidence indicates that when information was presented by the officers to the Enron Board, the information was delivered in a manner not conducive to a full understanding of the SPEs.

Notes and Questions

1. Notes

a. SOx imposed many new obligations on senior officers of public companies. The CEO and CFO must now certify the accuracy of the financial information in each quarterly and annual SEC filing and that they have told the independent auditors of any significant deficiencies in internal controls and any fraud of which they are aware. They must also certify that they are responsible for establishing and maintaining internal controls that, in effect, conform to *Caremark* requirements. Further, the corporation's annual report must describe and assess the corporation's internal controls. Corporations must also adopt a code of ethics for their CFOs. Corporations are now prohibited from making loans to senior executives, such as those made to Mr. Ebbers.

2. What Do You Think?

a. Do you think individuals who have careers as senior officers at large public corporations have a greater propensity to commit fraud than other people do? Do you think individuals who have careers as corporate managers have a greater propensity to commit fraud than other people do?

b. In-House Attorneys and Internal Auditors

Within every large corporation (and many small ones, too) are in-house lawyers and other people employed to conduct audits of the corporation's activities. These actors are different from most other employees because their tasks do not lead directly to the production and sale of goods or services. Rather, they are ancillary to the principal activities of the corporation. Nonetheless, they may have important roles to play in constraining corporate actions. You may wish to review the material in Chapter 1 on practicing corporate law.

In re Enron Corp.
Final Report of Neal Batson, Court-Appointed Examiner
114-116 (2003)

By analyzing the structure of the SPE transactions and documenting them, and by providing opinions in various transactions, Enron's attorneys also played a vital role in Enron's access to the capital markets. These attorneys could have provided a check and balance against the Enron officers' wrongdoing. Among other things, these attorneys could have apprised [Enron's general counsel] or the Enron Board when they knew of conduct that could result in Enron disseminating materially misleading financial information, or they could have refused to render legal services in connection with SPE transactions when they had concerns about their propriety.

One explanation for the attorneys' failure may be that they lost sight of the fact that the corporation was their client. It appears that some of these attorneys considered the officers to be their clients when, in fact, the attorneys owed duties to Enron. Another explanation may be that some of these attorneys saw their role in very narrow terms, as an implementer, not a counselor. That is, rather than conscientiously raising known issues for further analysis by a more senior officer or the Enron Board or refusing to participate in transactions that raised such issues, these lawyers seemed to focus only on how to address a narrow question or simply to implement a decision (or document a transaction). In other cases, Enron's in-house attorneys knew that the Enron Board did not have all relevant facts before it, but took no action to correct that problem.

Report of Investigation by the Special Investigative Committee of the Board of Directors of WorldCom, Inc.
31 (2003)

Neither WorldCom's legal department nor Internal Audit was structured to maximize its effectiveness as a control structure upon which the Board could depend. At

Ebbers' direction, the Company's lawyers were in fragmented groups, several of which had General Counsels who did not report to WorldCom's General Counsel for portions of the relevant period; they were not located geographically near senior management or involved in its inner workings; and they had inadequate support from senior management. Internal Audit — though eventually successful in revealing the fraud — had been structured in ways that made this accomplishment more difficult: it reported in most respects to Sullivan, and until 2002 its duties generally did not include financial reporting matters.

Notes and Questions

1. Notes

a. The SEC rules adopted in light of SOx impose a duty on lawyers to report misconduct up the corporate hierarchy to the board of directors, if necessary. See Chapter 1 for a discussion of this newer attorney role.

2. What Do You Think?

a. How could these professionals have become so marginalized within the corporations?

b. How can this kind of marginalization be prevented? What do you think are the early warning signs of this kind of dynamic?

3. Reputational Intermediaries

A third, and vital, check on board action comprises independent institutions that vouch for the corporation's actions. You might recall from Chapter 4 that agents and principals often use third parties to signal their quality to one another. Third parties who themselves have a high reputation are able, in effect, to endow others with that reputation. Of course, third parties who vouch for those who turn out to be of low quality will lose their own reputations. Hence they have an incentive to seek out only those for whom they can safely vouch. These third parties are sometimes called *reputational intermediaries*. In the business world, there may be many such reputational intermediaries, but three are of particular importance.

a. Outside Law Firms

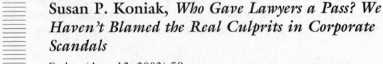

Susan P. Koniak, *Who Gave Lawyers a Pass? We Haven't Blamed the Real Culprits in Corporate Scandals*

Forbes (Aug. 12, 2002) 58

We're pointing the finger at everyone but the real culprits in corporate scandals.

We know the usual suspects in the current wave of corporate scandals: accountants, greedy bosses, lackadaisical directors, the projections-for-hire analysts and institutional investors asleep at the switch. But a group's missing: lawyers. The dirty secret of the mess is that without lawyers few scandals would exist, and fewer still would last long enough to cause any real harm. Lawyers need to be regulated. No other legal reform enacted will do any good as long as there are no consequences to lawyers who bless anything a manager wants to do.

Take the Enron case. When Vinson & Elkins, a Texas-based law firm, wasn't approving one of Enron's shady related transactions, another firm was. Chicago's Kirkland & Ellis represented Andrew Fastow's Enron-related partnerships, which engaged in transactions of such doubtful legality that it is difficult to imagine a lawyer not noticing.

Some set of lawyers wrote Arthur Andersen's "document retention" policy, which encourages the destruction of documents even when doing so might be a crime. A lawyer, Nancy Temple, instructed former Andersen partner David Duncan to heed that policy, and he did. A month later, when she told Duncan to preserve everything, he again complied. The testimony given under oath leads me to this conclusion: Had a lawyer explained the law and advised Duncan to follow it from the beginning, Andersen would not have faced obstruction charges.

Is it good that a profession so prone to harming clients and shareholders remain virtually unpoliced? Three avenues of regulation exist: state disciplinary authorities, the Securities & Exchange Commission and private lawsuits against lawyers. None of them now works.

Disciplinary authorities are charged with enforcing state ethics rules, which are law. In all my research, I have come across no state disciplinary authority that has initiated charges against a big law firm for aiding securities fraud. The disciplinary authority would be absurdly outgunned.

Every state's ethics rules prohibit assisting client fraud and demand that a lawyer resign when he "knows" his services are being used for fraud. Lawyers never "know," and thus never have to resign. Other ethics rules allow lawyers to do certain things, like alert the chief executive or board to corporate fraud; some allow lawyers to tell the SEC. But none of that is required.

The law that prohibits aiding and abetting fraud applies to everyone, including lawyers. But prosecutors rarely enforce it against lawyers. Private suits for aiding were allowed until the Supreme Court eliminated those in 1994. Congress worsened matters by limiting the SEC's ability to bring aiding-and-abetting cases.

The SEC scarcely needed any curbing. Twice in its history it had gotten serious about regulating the bar. Both times the bar beat the agency back. In 1981 the SEC in effect conceded defeat, ending efforts to rein in lawyers. And [the] SEC, even post-Enron, has said that policing lawyers is not on its agenda.

Because lawyers are necessary to commit almost any fraud of more than a moment's duration, their firms' survival should be on the line. What's needed is to restore aiding-and-abetting liability, joint-and-several liability and the recklessness standard, at least for lawyers. The Senate passed Senator John Edwards' amendment requiring lawyers to report evidence of fraud up the corporate ladder . . . .

The lawyer problem is systemic: no "few bad apples" here. Neither moral outrage nor proposals for reform have come from the President, our financial wise men like Warren Buffett and Alan Greenspan, or the press. Even companies that suffered greatly from outsize management fraud, all of which should be suing their lawyers for malpractice, aren't and won't — too many skeletons. This is a disgrace.

Susan Koniak is Professor of Law, Boston University; coauthor, *The Law & Ethics of Lawyering*.

Notes and Questions

1. Notes

a. SEC rules adopted under SOx requiring lawyers to report misconduct up the ladder to the board, if necessary, also apply to outside counsel.

b. Until the late 1980s virtually every state's laws prohibited lawyers from practicing in entities that provide limited liability. In other words, law firms were general partnerships in which every partner was individually liable for the professional actions of every other partner. Now, virtually every large law firm is either a professional corporation, an LLC, or an LLP. Consider whether there is a link between the rise of limited liability entities for lawyers and the conduct described by Professor Koniak.

b. Independent Accountants

The outside accountants are the quintessential reputational intermediaries. Every public company must be audited each year by an independent accounting firm. Nearly every major public corporation retains one of the Big Four accounting firms. The following excerpts describe the accounting firm's auditing duties and assess the performance of Arthur Andersen, the auditor for both Enron and WorldCom.

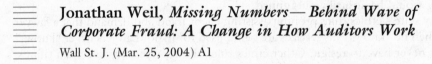

Jonathan Weil, *Missing Numbers— Behind Wave of Corporate Fraud: A Change in How Auditors Work*

Wall St. J. (Mar. 25, 2004) A1

The recent wave of corporate fraud is raising a harsh question about the auditors who review and bless companies' financial results: How could they have missed all the wrongdoing? One little-discussed answer: a big change in the way audits are performed. Consider what happened when James Lamphron and his team of Ernst & Young LLP accountants sat down early last year to plan their audit of HealthSouth Corp.'s 2002 financial statements. When they asked executives of the Birmingham, Ala., hospital chain if they were aware of any significant instances of fraud, the executives replied no. In their planning papers, the auditors wrote that HealthSouth's system for generating financial data was reliable, the company's executives were ethical, and that HealthSouth's management had "designed an environment for success."

As a result, the auditors performed far fewer tests of the numbers on the company's books than they would have at an audit client where they perceived the risk of accounting fraud to be higher. That's standard practice under the "risk-based audit" approach now used widely throughout the accounting profession. Among the items the Ernst & Young auditors didn't examine at all: additions of less than $5,000 to individual assets on the company's ledger.

Those numbers are where HealthSouth executives hid a big part of a giant fraud. This blind spot in the firm's auditing procedures is a key reason why former HealthSouth executives, 15 of whom have pleaded guilty to fraud charges, were able to overstate profits by $3 billion without anyone from Ernst & Young noticing until March 2003, when federal agents began making arrests.

A look at the risk-based approach also helps explain why investors continue to be socked by accounting scandals, from WorldCom Inc. and Tyco International Ltd. to

Parmalat SpA, the Italian dairy company that admitted faking $4.8 billion in cash. Just because an accounting firm says it has audited a company's numbers doesn't mean it actually has checked them.

In a September 2003 speech, Daniel Goelzer, a member of the auditing profession's new regulator, the Public Company Accounting Oversight Board, called the risk-based approach one of the key factors "that seem to have contributed to the erosion of trust in auditing." Faced with difficulty in raising audit fees, Mr. Goelzer said, the major accounting firms during the 1990s began to stress cost controls. And they began to place greater emphasis on planning the scope of their work based on auditors' judgments about which clients are risky and which areas of a company's financial reports are most prone to error or fraud.

Auditors still plow through "high risk" items, such as derivative financial instruments or "related party" business dealings between a company and its executives. But ostensibly "low risk" items — such as cash on the balance sheet or accounts that fluctuate little from year to year — often get no more than a cursory review, for years at a stretch. Instead, auditors rely more heavily on what management tells them and the auditors' assessments of a company's "internal controls."

A 2001 brochure by KPMG LLP, which claims to have pioneered the risk-based audit during the early 1990s, explained the difference between the old and new ways. Under a traditional "bottom up" audit, "the auditor gains assurance by examining all of the component parts of the financial statements, ensuring that the transactions recorded are complete and accurate." By comparison, under the "top down" risk-based audit methodology, auditors focus "less on the details of individual transactions" and use their knowledge of a company's business and organization "to identify risks that could affect the financial statements and to target audit effort in those areas."

In theory, the risk-based approach should work fine, if an auditor is good at identifying the areas where misstatements are most likely to occur. Proponents advocate the shift as a cost-efficient improvement. They also say it forces auditors to pay needed attention to areas that are more subjective or complex.

"The problem is that there's not a lot of evidence that auditors are very good at assessing risk," says Charles Cullinan, an accounting professor at Bryant College in Smithfield, R.I., and co-author of a 2002 study that criticized the re-engineered audit process as ineffective at detecting fraud.

Auditors can't check all of a company's numbers, since that would make audits too expensive, particularly in an age of sprawling multinationals. The tools at auditors' disposal can't ensure the reliability of a company's numbers with absolute certainty. And in many ways, they haven't changed much over the modern industry's 160-year history.

Auditors scan the accounting records for inconsistencies. They ask people questions. That can mean independently contacting a client's customers to make sure they haven't struck undocumented side deals — such as agreeing to buy more products today in exchange for a salesperson's oral promises of future discounts. They search for unrecorded liabilities by tracing cash disbursements to make sure the obligations are recorded properly. They examine invoices and the terms of sales contracts to check if a company is recording revenue prematurely.

Auditors are supposed to avoid becoming predictable. Otherwise, a client's management might figure out how to sneak things by them. It's also important to sample-test tiny accounting entries, even as low as a couple of hundred dollars. An old accounting trick is to fudge lots of tiny entries that appear insignificant individually but materially distort a company's financial statements when taken together.

Facing a crush of shareholder lawsuits over the accounting scandals of the past four years, the Big Four accounting firms say they are pouring tens of millions of dollars into improving their auditing techniques. KPMG's investigative division has doubled to 280 its force of forensic specialists, some hailing from the Federal Bureau of Investigation. PricewaterhouseCoopers LLP auditors attend seminars run by former Central Intelligence Agency operatives on how to spot deceitful managers by scrutinizing body language and verbal cues. Role-playing exercises teach how to stand up to a company's management.

But the firms aren't backing away from the concept of the risk-based audit itself. "It would really be negligent" not to take a risk-based approach, says Greg Weaver, head of Deloitte & Touche LLP's U.S. audit practice. Auditors need to "understand the areas that are likely to be more subject to error," he says. "Some might believe that if you cover those high-risk areas, you could do less work in other areas." But, he adds, "I don't think that's been a problem at Deloitte."

Mr. Lamphron, the Ernst & Young partner, and his firm blame HealthSouth's former executives for deceiving them. Mr. Lamphron declined to comment for this article. Testifying before a congressional subcommittee in November, he said he had looked through his audit papers and "tried to find that one string that, had we yanked it, would have unraveled this fraud. I know we planned and conducted a solid audit. We asked the right questions. We sought out the right documentation. Had we asked for additional documentation here or asked another question there, I think that it would have generated another false document and another lie."

[I]n the U.S., the notion of the auditor as detective never quite took off. The Securities and Exchange Commission in the 1930s made audits mandatory for public companies. The auditing profession faced its first real public test in 1937, when an accounting scandal broke open at McKesson & Robbins: More than 20% of the assets reported by the drug company were fictitious inventory and customer IOUs. The auditors had been fooled by forged documents.

The case triggered some reforms. Auditing standards began requiring that auditors perform more substantive tests, such as contacting third parties to confirm customer IOUs and physically inspecting clients' warehouses to check inventories.

By the 1970s, a new force emerged to erode audit quality: price competition. Bidding wars ensued. The pressures to hold down hours on a job "inadvertently discouraged auditors to look for" fraud, says Toby Bishop, president of the Association of Certified Fraud Examiners, a professional association.

Increasingly, audits became a commodity product. Economic pressures also brought a wave of mergers, winnowing down the number of accounting firms just as the number of publicly traded companies was exploding and corporate financial statements were becoming more complex.

Looking back, the risk-based approach's flaws are on display at a variety of accounting scandals, from WorldCom to Tyco to HealthSouth.

In re WorldCom, Inc.
First Interim Report of Dick Thornburgh,
Bankruptcy Court Examiner
49-50 (2002)

The objective of an audit of a company's financial statements by an independent auditor is the expression of an opinion on the fairness with which the financial statements present, in all material respects, the financial position, results of operations, and cash flows of the company in conformity with GAAP. An independent auditor is required under GAAS to state whether, in its opinion, the financial statements are presented in conformity with GAAP.

[A]n auditor has a responsibility to plan and perform the audit to obtain reasonable, but not absolute, assurance about whether the financial statements are free of material misstatement, whether caused by error or fraud. A proper audit includes examining, on a test basis, evidence supporting the amounts and disclosures in the financial statements, assessing the accounting principles used and significant estimates made by management, and evaluating the overall financial statements presentation. An audit is not intended to provide a guarantee regarding the accuracy of the financial statements. Accordingly, a material misstatement may remain undetected.

Ultimately, a company's financial statements are the responsibility of management. Management is responsible for adopting sound accounting policies and for establishing and maintaining internal controls that will, among other things, record, process, summarize, and report transactions consistently and accurately.

Report of Investigation by the Special Investigative Committee of the Board of Directors of WorldCom, Inc.
25-28 (2003)

WHY WORLDCOM'S AUDITORS DID NOT DISCOVER THE FRAUD

We have found no evidence that WorldCom's independent, external auditors, Arthur Andersen, were aware of the capitalization of line costs or determined that WorldCom's revenues were improperly reported. We had access to only a portion of Andersen's documents, and Andersen personnel refused to speak with us. Therefore, we cannot answer with certainty the question why Andersen failed to detect such a large fraud.

Based on the materials available to us, the blame for Andersen's failure to detect the fraud appears to lie with personnel both at Andersen and at WorldCom. There were apparent flaws in Andersen's audit approach, which limited the likelihood it would detect the accounting irregularities. Moreover, Andersen appears to have missed several opportunities that might have led to the discovery of management's misuse of accruals, the capitalization of line costs, and the improper recognition of revenue items. For their part, certain WorldCom personnel maintained inappropriately tight control over information that Andersen needed, altered documents with the apparent purpose of concealing from Andersen items that might have raised questions, and were not forthcoming in other respects. Andersen, knowing in some instances that it was receiving less than full cooperation on critical aspects of its work, failed to bring this to the attention of WorldCom's Audit Committee.

Andersen employed an approach to its audit that it itself characterized as different from the "traditional audit approach." It focused heavily on identifying risks and assessing whether the Company had adequate controls in place to mitigate those risks, rather than emphasizing the traditional substantive testing of information maintained in accounting records and financial statements. This approach is not unique to

Andersen, and it was disclosed to the Audit Committee. But a consequence of this approach was that if Andersen failed to identify a significant risk, or relied on Company controls without adequately determining that they were worthy of reliance, there would be insufficient testing to make detection of fraud likely.

Andersen does not appear to have performed adequate testing to justify reliance on WorldCom's controls. We found hundreds of huge, round-dollar journal entries made by the staff of the General Accounting group without proper support.... And where we did find documentary support it was frequently disorganized and maintained haphazardly. These deficiencies made reliance on controls impossible. We do not understand how they escaped Andersen's notice.

Andersen concluded year after year that the risk of fraud was no greater than a moderate risk, and thus it never devised sufficient auditing procedures to address this risk. It did so despite rating WorldCom a "maximum risk" client — an assessment Andersen never disclosed to the Audit Committee — and having given management less than favorable ratings in a few areas (such as accounting and disclosure practices, behavior toward Andersen's work, and policies to prevent or detect fraud) in Andersen internal documents. Andersen relied heavily on senior management and did not conduct tests to corroborate the information it received in many areas. It assumed incorrectly that the absence of variances in the financial statements and schedules — in a highly volatile business environment — indicated there was no cause for heightened scrutiny. As a result, Andersen conducted only very limited audit procedures in many areas where we found accounting irregularities.

WorldCom, for its part, exerted excessive control over Andersen's access to information, and was not candid in at least some of its dealings with Andersen. The WorldCom personnel who dealt most often with Andersen controlled Andersen's access to information in several respects. They denied Andersen's requests to speak with some employees. They "struck" Andersen's requests for detailed information, supporting documentation, or material that they felt was overly burdensome. WorldCom personnel also repeatedly rejected Andersen's requests for access to the computerized General Ledger through which Internal Audit and others discovered the capitalization of line costs. And they fostered an attitude in which questions from Andersen were to be parried, rather than answered openly. Of course, it was Andersen's responsibility to overcome those obstacles to perform an appropriate audit, and to inform the Audit Committee of the difficulties it faced, but it did not do so. Moreover, certain members of WorldCom's management altered significant documents before providing them to Andersen, with the apparent purpose of hampering Andersen's ability to identify problems at the Company.

Notes and Questions

1. Notes

a. Arthur Andersen's involvement with Enron resulted in its indictment and conviction for obstruction of justice. As a consequence, it could no longer act as an accountant for public companies. Arthur Andersen effectively went out of business, reducing the number of major accounting firms to four.

b. Many SOx provisions affect public accounting firms. First, it severely restricts the additional services a company's auditing firm can provide. This is to reduce the accounting firm's incentive to go lightly on the audit in hopes of currying favor with corporate management, who will purchase nonaudit services from the firm. Second, the accounting firm partner (but not the firm itself) in charge of a particular corporation's account must rotate off such assignment every five years. Third, the auditors must report directly to the corporation's audit committee.

2. Reality Check

a. What is the difference between traditional auditing and risk-based auditing?

b. Why has risk-based auditing become so popular?

3. What Do You Think?

a. How do you think Arthur Andersen should have acted differently?

b. If the accountants simply failed to catch fraud that was actively being concealed from them, is it fair to fault them?

c. Credit-Rating Agencies

Both Enron and WorldCom were greatly concerned with the credit rating on their corporate debt. Much of the purpose of the financial fraud at both corporations was to preserve high credit ratings. The following article puts the role of credit-rating agencies in perspective.

Alec Klein, *Borrowers Find System Open to Conflicts, Manipulation*

Wash. Post (Nov. 22, 2004) A01

In the months leading to the collapse of WorldCom Inc., its shares were in a nose-dive, traders were selling its bonds at junk levels and its chief executive was forced out. But not until investors lost several billion dollars did Congress and others begin to rivet attention to a little-known player in this unfolding drama: the credit raters. WorldCom rose to prominence through voracious acquisitions, including the bold 1998 purchase of MCI, the District-based long-distance telephone company. And it couldn't have done it without the rating companies. WorldCom borrowed money through the sale of bonds, which the rating firms approved by giving them good grades, a signal that they were relatively safe investments.

As it turned out, nothing could have been further from the truth. But the rating firms were among the last to recognize it. It wasn't until weeks before WorldCom disclosed massive fraud and filed the biggest bankruptcy in U.S. history in 2002 that the credit raters finally cut the firm's debt to junk status.

The rating companies say they are not in the business of detecting fraud; rather, they say they give an opinion of the creditworthiness of a company, municipality or nation. But some critics say the WorldCom case highlights a broader problem: that the world's big three credit raters — Moody's Investors Service, Standard & Poor's and Fitch Ratings — have become some of the most important gatekeepers in capitalism without the commensurate oversight or accountability.

From their Manhattan offices, they can, with the stroke of a pen, effectively add or subtract millions from a company's bottom line, rattle a city budget, shock the stock and bond markets and reroute international investment. Without their ratings, in many cases, factories can't expand, schools can't get built, highways can't be paved. Yet there is no formal structure for overseeing the credit raters, no one designated to take complaints about them, and no regulations about employee qualifications.

The big three ostensibly function as a disinterested priesthood. When a company, town or entire nation wants to borrow money by selling bonds, the market almost always requires that the rating companies bless the move by running a kind of credit check. Bonds they deem safe get a good rating. The higher the rating, the lower the interest rate the borrower must pay.

But at the heart of the increasingly profitable business is a conflict: The rating companies get the bulk of their revenue from the fees they charge to the very entities they are rating. Industry insiders say the desire of a rater to hold on to a paying client — or recruit a new one — at times has interfered with the objectivity of a rating.

Those who disagree with a rating have little recourse. Lawsuits generally have been unsuccessful because courts have upheld the rating companies' argument that they are publishers of opinions, like newspapers, and that their views are protected by the First Amendment.

With little public debate about the industry, the rating business has eluded a series of reforms that have been imposed on other parts of the U.S. financial system. For example, while hundreds of companies and institutions, such as the New York Stock Exchange, have eliminated potential conflicts on their boards, Moody's directors continue to serve on the boards of companies that also are Moody's clients. (Moody's officials say that their directors play no role in ratings decisions.)

And even as accounting firms have curtailed offering consulting services to their clients to avoid conflicts, some credit raters have begun to sell their own consulting services, raising concerns that clients may feel pressured to buy them.

For their part, the credit raters say they ably manage potential conflicts. They say they adhere to strict codes of conduct, such as prohibiting any link between the pay and bonuses of their rating analysts and the fees that come in from the companies those analysts rate. The rating companies also say they perform a public service by allowing investors to compare the relative risk of buying bonds from almost any seller.

And the credit raters say their success over time shows the ratings process works, and that their ratings bring stability to the markets, giving companies and countries access to capital.

The rating companies say they do their job without regard to the impact, basing their ratings largely on statistical calculations of a borrower's likelihood of default. Subjective factors sometimes come into play, rating officials say, given that there are some two dozen categories ranging from the best, "AAA," to a low of "C" or "D." That subjectivity can be costly. For a borrower, the difference of a single rating notch could mean millions of extra dollars in interest payments.

The rating companies officially fall under the purview of the Securities and Exchange Commission. But even as the SEC has clamped down on accountants, stock analysts and investment bankers, the regulator has not imposed rules on the rating companies. The SEC, which declined to comment for this article, said it continues to study the issue.

Despite their complaints, the industry has received little public attention largely because its workings are complex and its clients are institutions rather than people.

(The creditworthiness of consumers is rated by a different set of companies, which operate under extensive federal and state regulation.) But after the collapse of such companies as WorldCom and Enron Corp., Congress ordered the SEC to consider whether new rules were needed.

The big three credit-rating firms wield power through letter grades they hand out. They explain their ratings approach in pamphlets and on their Web sites. But the process itself has remained a mystery of finance.

Committees of rating analysts, headed by one lead analyst, meet privately to weigh the financial strengths and weaknesses of those who want to sell bonds. Then, they emerge to give the bond a rating, announcing it to the world. The companies don't say who voted or how the vote broke down.

The rating companies say they get their ratings right most of the time, pointing to their own studies showing that the higher the rating, the lower the rate of default. Out of 98 defaults in 2003, S&P said, only three were companies that had in the past 12 months held investment-grade ratings, which are considered relatively safe for investors. Still, since only a tiny fraction of all bond issuers ever default, the odds of being right are very high, some critics point out.

[Vickie A. Tillman, executive vice president of S&P's credit market services] said that because it takes a majority of the committee to approve a rating, no one person can skew the process. Those familiar with the process, however, say the committee usually follows the lead analyst because the others often don't have the time to review the work as closely.

The lead analyst's recommendation is "the basis on which everything is turning" and is upheld about 80 percent of the time, said Hans van den Houten, a former Fitch and Moody's executive who also served as an outside recruiter for S&P until earlier this year.

That can sometimes tempt the lead analyst to let personal feelings influence the review of a client's finances. This happened to a former Moody's analyst rating a company at which one executive was a close friend from a previous job.

"I bent over backward to come up with the best result because I care for this person," said the analyst, who spoke on the condition that neither he nor the company he was rating be identified. Later, after the company's performance sagged, the analyst came to see that he had rated it too high.

If an analyst's feelings go the other way, it can cost a company money. Computer Associates International Inc., which has had recent run-ins with U.S. authorities about its accounting, earned a tough reputation for the way it deals with rating analysts. "They were definitely aggressive and abrasive and engendered a combative response from the rating agency," a former rating analyst said.

Computer Associates, which declined to comment, held a rating last year barely at investment-grade. Based on financials alone, it would likely have been higher, but its combative executives alienated some analysts. The company's rating ended up lower than expected, costing it potentially millions in extra interest payments. "Maybe a full notch is [due to] their personality," the former analyst said.

Analysts say it's reasonable to use their judgment to assess how well a company's executives make business decisions. But reservations about management will not necessarily show up in the rating firm's public report.

"You don't want to say you don't like these guys," another former rating official said. "You have nothing to point to, but it was discussed in the committee."

Moody's president, Raymond W. McDaniel Jr., declined to discuss specific cases. "The ratings process is produced by human beings, and human beings have views and emotions about certain things," he said, adding that Moody's tracks the quality of its ratings.

"We do not deny there are latent or inherent conflicts of interest in our business," McDaniel said. "The important thing is, how do we manage those conflicts?"

Credit raters say that other industries, including newspapers, have to cope with similar conflicts. "Our practice is no different from the *Washington Post* who will run ads from Ford, AT&T, Merrill Lynch or dozens of other companies while at the same time reporting on them every day," Fitch said in a written response to questions.

Some rating companies cited a 2003 study by two economists who work for the Federal Reserve who found "no evidence" that ratings are affected by conflicts of interest, but rather that credit raters "appear to be relatively responsive to reputation concerns and so protect the interests of investors."

Because the major rating companies juggle tens of thousands of debt issues at any given time, many are given cursory attention, according to current and former rating analysts and those they rate. An analyst will cover as many as 55 borrowers at once. And in recent years, the credit raters say analyzing debt has become more complicated, involving more financial provisions.

"You can't monitor all those companies," one former rating analyst said.

So why don't raters hire more analysts? "It would cut into their profitability," he said.

The credit raters say they have a sufficient number of analysts to cover companies throughout the world. Still, at Moody's at least, according to some current officials and former analysts, committee meetings on occasion are hastily arranged, include only two analysts and last minutes, or seconds.

"We had a colloquial term for that," said W. Bruce Jones, a former Moody's official who works for a small competitor, Egan-Jones Ratings Co. "We called it a 'water cooler rating.'"

One meeting that took only minutes involved Omnicare Inc., a supplier of pharmaceutical services to nursing homes, when it announced plans to acquire competitor NCS HealthCare Inc. in 2002, according to another former Moody's analyst.

As soon as the deal, worth more than $400 million, looked imminent, the analyst said he dropped into a supervisor's office and quickly explained that he assumed Omnicare would sell bonds to make the acquisition. As a result, he was going to put its rating on review for a potential downgrade.

He didn't need to explain why: By carrying more debt, the company would become a bigger credit risk. The supervisor promptly gave the analyst approval to proceed.

That was the committee meeting.

Within about a half-hour, the decision flashed to some 5,000 news services around the globe. About six months later, however, Moody's took Omnicare's credit off review. The company planned to use stock, not just loans, to buy its competitor. That meant Omnicare's debt wouldn't be as large as the Moody's analyst had anticipated.

McDaniel of Moody's said his company works diligently to provide well-researched ratings. "We treat the ratings committee process very seriously," he said, but added, "We don't want to waste people's time."

The rating companies said they already have strong internal controls designed to minimize mistakes or conflicts, including codes of conduct at S&P and Moody's.

Moody's, for instance, instructs employees to do nothing that "might, or might appear to, compromise the integrity" of the rating process. The credit raters say they also conduct ethics training in-house.

Still, some lawmakers — Republicans and Democrats — say the system is flawed. In a House hearing last year, Rep. Paul E. Kanjorski (D-Pa.) said the credit raters' failure to identify problems at WorldCom and other major companies "ultimately resulted in the loss of billions of dollars for American investors who little understood the true credit risks."

Notes and Questions

1. Notes

a. SOx required the SEC to investigate whether more stringent regulation of the credit-rating agencies is called for.

2. Reality Check

a. Why are credit rating agencies so important?
b. How can credit rating agencies help to constrain corporate boards?

d. Securities Analysts

The final reputational intermediary is somewhat different from the other three because the relationship between the intermediary and the corporation is not contractual. Rather, it is more symbiotic. Securities analysts work for brokerage houses, many of which are also investment bankers. Securities analysts, much like journalists, are assigned to cover a particular industry, sometimes even a single corporation. They are expected to investigate the industry and its businesses and to write analytical assessments of both the industry and the businesses that compete. These analyses are used by brokerage houses to recommend stock to their clients. They are also used by the investment banks themselves to decide whether to invest for their own account.

Even though there is no direct contractual relationship between securities analysts and the companies they cover there are mutual advantages to be had or withheld. Analysts have an incentive to ferret out important information and so have an incentive to stay within the good graces of corporations so that their informal access to information will not be cut off. Even better, analysts hope that companies will steer important information to them before giving it to others. Securities analysts have another incentive to please the corporations they cover. That is, that the investment banking side of their employer is always looking for new clients and new work. The investment bank whose analyst writes positive reports on a company believes it has a better chance of landing that company's investment banking business.

Corporations, in contrast, have a great incentive to curry favor with the securities analysts, as well. Some analysts are quite well known in the investment community and thus their views are quite influential. A change in a recommendation from such an analyst is likely to have an immediate and often strong effect on the corporation's stock price.

In re WorldCom, Inc.
First Interim Report of Dick Thornburgh,
Bankruptcy Court Examiner
81-99 (2002)

In theory, at least, analysts promote market efficiency by providing investors with a distillation and interpretation of all relevant information about the companies they follow, including public filings, press releases, presentations and conference calls.

In recent months there has been a great deal of discussion and debate about the potential conflicts that arise when securities firms provide analytic, banking and brokerage services. It is generally accepted that, while investment banking generates substantial profits, research, standing alone, is at best a loss leader. Some believe that an analyst can only contribute to a firm's profits if he or she enhances its investment banking business. Some also believe that analysts may be encouraged by their transactional colleagues to publish favorable reports to ingratiate their firms with existing or potential investment banking clients. Indeed, this encouragement may include financial incentives, if an analyst's compensation is tied to the brokerage firm's investment banking revenues. In the view of some regulators, the objectivity of the analyst's research and conclusions may be compromised by these incentives.

In the months following WorldCom's bankruptcy, a great deal of attention has been focused on the Company's relationships with Salomon Smith Barney ("SSB"). Public officials and members of the financial media have strongly suggested that an unhealthy relationship developed between WorldCom and SSB. They have alleged that SSB used the promise of lucrative IPO allocations and flattering analyst reports to entice corporate executives, like Mr. Ebbers, to reward them with highly profitable investment banking assignments. In addition, they have suggested that SSB's chief telecommunications analyst, Jack Grubman, combined forces with corporate executives, like Mr. Sullivan, to project inflated prospects for WorldCom's fortunes, resulting in bloated stock valuations.

Although it would be premature to reach any conclusions on these subjects, the following facts have begun to emerge:

1. In the transactions we have reviewed to date, SSB and its predecessors, Salomon Brothers and Smith Barney, collectively received more engagements from WorldCom than any other investment banking firm during the past five years.

2. SSB and its predecessors also allocated millions of dollars of valuable IPOs to a number of WorldCom directors, including Mr. Ebbers. These directors, in turn, sold their IPO shares for an aggregate profit of more than $18 million.

3. Until April 2002, Mr. Grubman and SSB repeatedly gave WorldCom's stock its highest ratings, enthusiastically urging investors to purchase WorldCom shares, even at times when Mr. Grubman was privately advising WorldCom management on business strategy, acquisitions and investor relations.

4. Until the third quarter of 2000, WorldCom's reported earnings per share consistently met or came close to analyst expectations. In subsequent quarters, WorldCom management publicly attributed its faltering financial performance to a series of allegedly non-recurring causes.

At a minimum, the generous IPO allocations given by SSB to Mr. Ebbers and others created the appearance that valuable corporate business opportunities were being traded for personal gain. Mr. Grubman's behavior also created at least an appearance of impropriety.

WORLDCOM'S GENERAL INTERACTIONS WITH SECURITIES ANALYSTS

As a large and rapidly growing public company, WorldCom had frequent interaction with the many securities analysts who covered its stock. WorldCom executives generally held teleconferences with securities analysts on a quarterly basis. Each call would normally begin with prepared statements from Company executives regarding WorldCom's financial position, financial outlook, and issues of particular importance to the Company. The executives would then answer analysts' questions regarding their prepared statements and other subjects.

WorldCom's management and directors paid very close attention to the views expressed by Wall Street's securities analysts and carefully tracked their stated expectations of the Company. The Company's Investor Relations Department regularly sent memoranda and charts to senior management describing analysts' expectations regarding the Company's quarterly and annual financial performance. Even the materials prepared for Board meetings regularly included transcripts of the most recent teleconference with analysts, a memorandum regarding analysts' expectations, and a summary of their reactions to WorldCom's quarterly financial announcements. Clearly, senior management and the Board recognized the significance of maintaining Wall Street's confidence.

MR. GRUBMAN'S EXTREMELY FAVORABLE ANALYST REPORTS

Prior to their merger in late 1997, Salomon Brothers and Smith Barney expressed substantially different views concerning the future performance of and risks associated with WorldCom stock. In 1997, Smith Barney issued four World-Com reports.... These reports reflected a relatively restrained assessment of the stock's prospects.

At the same time, Mr. Grubman, who worked for Salomon, issued a report in which he rated WorldCom a strong buy and declared that "no telecom company of WorldCom's market cap can come close to matching WorldCom's top-line growth, margin expansion potential or strategic position, much less having all of these attributes which is why WorldCom remains our favorite stock." Mr. Grubman's strong buy rating represented an emphatically higher recommendation than Smith Barney's neutral and outperform ratings. Notably, Mr. Grubman said little about the stock's risk factors in his report.

In the wake of the Salomon Smith Barney merger [in 1998], Mr. Grubman emerged as SSB's chief telecommunications analyst and the author of all its World-Com reports from the time of the merger until March 2002. Consistent with Mr. Grubman's pre-merger view, each and every SSB report during this period included a "buy" recommendation (SSB's highest rating) and a "medium" assessment of risk. Mr. Grubman's reports during this period consistently proclaimed ringing endorsements of WorldCom and its stock.

As WorldCom's stock price steadily rose in 1998 and 1999, Mr. Grubman gave and maintained his highest ratings on WorldCom stock and set target prices that were 17% to 60% (and 100% over a 2 year time frame) higher than the current value of the stock.

Mr. Grubman urged investors to "load up the truck" with WorldCom stock. In fact, he declared that any investor who did not take advantage of current prices to buy every share of WorldCom should seriously think about another vocation.

Mr. Grubman attributed WorldCom's declining stock price during the early part of the year 2000 to the market's ignorance in assessing the realities of the Company's compelling story and to the fact that the market instead was acting on sentiment. Mr. Grubman stated that "investors who are selling WorldCom in the $40s will be buying WorldCom in the $60s in six months."

From the beginning of 2000 through August 2001, when WorldCom's stock fell from $50.06 to $12.44 per share, SSB consistently set target prices that were 90% to 244% higher than the current stock quote.

In June 2000, Mr. Grubman stated categorically that WorldCom was by far the cheapest stock in the world of global telecom and that analysts who continued to worry about WorldCom's failure to excel in the wireless area would be sorely disappointed that they downgraded the stock. As the stock continued to decline, from a high of $49 per share in July to $14 per share in December, Mr. Grubman continued to project a tripling of WorldCom's stock price and labeled the stock "dirt cheap." In November 2000, Mr. Grubman lowered his price target from $87 to $45 a share, but held steadfast to his buy-medium risk ratings.

In 2001, WorldCom revised its earnings estimates downward on several occasions. At the same time, the stock price fell below $20.00 and ultimately to the $12.00 range in September and October 2001. Yet Mr. Grubman maintained his highest rating on WorldCom and announced that WorldCom stock continued to be undervalued. He even claimed that if the Company made its numbers, the stock price could double or triple over the next 12-18 months. In his January 9, 2001 report, Mr. Grubman conceded that WorldCom's line costs would likely be higher, but depreciation would be lower due to intercompany classifications. Mr. Grubman continually advocated that investors take advantage of misguided analysis by aggressively buying WorldCom's shares, noting that there were very few sponsors on "the Street" for the stock.

Mr. Grubman lowered his price target to $35 in July 2001, and subsequently lowered it again in October 2001 to $22 and again in January 2002 to $20. While these downward revisions appear significant on a relative basis, the revised targets still reflected price targets that were 50% to 174% more than contemporaneous stock prices. Moreover, Mr. Grubman maintained his buy-medium risk ratings on the Company.

By the first quarter of 2002, even Mr. Grubman acknowledged that widespread rumors were circulating that: (1) WorldCom was going to be dropped from the S&P 500; (2) the Company's debt rating was being lowered to junk status; (3) the Company's stock was going to be downgraded by a competitor; (4) UUNET's business from AOL was going elsewhere; (5) the Company's accounting and balance sheets were under scrutiny; and (6) Mr. Ebbers was having significant financial problems. Despite all of these significant concerns, Mr. Grubman maintained his buy-medium risk ratings on WorldCom's stock and set a stock price target that was almost 150% of the current price at that time. In fact, Mr. Grubman maintained his buy-medium risk ratings even after the SEC initiated its inquiry into WorldCom's financial reporting, and did not change his risk rating to a buy-*high* risk rating until a week later.

SSB's first downgrade of WorldCom stock came in April 2002. In this report, Mr. Grubman admitted that his previous evaluations of WorldCom were clearly wrong.

Mr. Grubman stated that he decided to downgrade the stock even though it "would obviously be easier not to downgrade the stock, and therefore not to suffer the inevitable and justified slings from various parties."

In May 2002, Mr. Grubman further downgraded his risk rating to speculative in response to the deterioration of WorldCom's debt ratings. A final downgrade, to "underperform—speculative," followed on June 21, 2002, a little over a month before WorldCom's filing for bankruptcy.

By then, WorldCom shareholders had lost more than $180 billion in market capitalization since 1999. Conversely, from 1998 until 2001, when he consistently encouraged investors to buy WorldCom's stock, it is alleged that Mr. Grubman reportedly averaged approximately $20 million per year in compensation. When Mr. Grubman resigned from SSB on August 15, 2002, he stated in his resignation letter that "the current climate of criticism has made it impossible to perform my work to the standards I believe the clients of SSB deserve." SSB reportedly agreed to buy out the rest of Grubman's 1998 $32.2 million contract, which included $12 million in stock and options and forgiveness of a $15 million loan, plus about $4 million in interest. Grubman further maintained publicly that he and other analysts were simply "wrong" about the future of telecom.

MR. GRUBMAN'S DEPARTURES FROM THE ROLE OF AN INDEPENDENT SECURITIES ANALYST

Although we are not currently in a position to reach any conclusion on this point, Mr. Grubman's behavior seems to have departed from the role of an independent securities analyst as described above.

Our review of internal WorldCom and SSB documents has revealed a large number of meetings, conferences, e-mail messages and other contacts between Mr. Grubman and WorldCom executives. These include at least four instances in which Mr. Grubman attended WorldCom Board meetings to discuss major transactions, such as the proposed merger between WorldCom and MCI in late 1997 and the proposed merger between WorldCom and Sprint in October 1999. Minutes from these meetings indicate that Mr. Grubman and other SSB representatives were invited to make extensive presentations to the Board analyzing the financial impacts of these mergers on WorldCom's operations as well as other transactions involving the merger parties. These minutes indicate that Mr. Grubman attended the Board's meetings as a "financial advisor" to the Company and performed roles that seem inconsistent with that of an independent securities analyst.

WorldCom employees also consulted with Mr. Grubman from time to time to obtain information about the Company's investors, the opinions and actions of other Wall Street analysts and Mr. Grubman's reactions to negative press reports regarding WorldCom. Moreover, there is evidence that Mr. Grubman consulted with World-Com's management in advance of analyst conference calls to suggest how they should handle certain topics during those calls. Further, we have seen evidence that Mr. Grubman even suggested a question he might ask during an analyst conference call that might elicit a favorable response.

There is also some evidence to suggest that Mr. Grubman may have played a role in the allocation of valuable IPOs to Mr. Ebbers, since he was copied on internal SSB e-mails regarding those allocations. In March and May 1999, Mr. Grubman received copies of internal SSB e-mails indicating that Mr. Ebbers was on a list of "private wealth clients" who had requested shares....

 Randall Smith, et al., *Wall Street Firms to Pay $1.4 Billion to End Inquiry — Record Payment Settles Conflict-of-Interest Charges*
Wall St. J. (Apr. 29, 2003) A1

In a pact that could change the face of Wall Street, 10 of the nation's largest securities firms agreed to pay a record $1.4 billion to settle government charges involving abuse of investors during the stock-market bubble of the late 1990s.

The long-awaited settlement, which followed an intense investigation that brought together three national regulatory bodies and a dozen state securities authorities, centers on civil charges that the Wall Street firms routinely issued overly optimistic stock research to investors in order to curry favor with corporate clients and win their lucrative investment-banking business. The pact also settles charges that at least two big firms, Citigroup Inc.'s Citigroup Global Markets unit, formerly Salomon Smith Barney, and Credit Suisse Group's Credit Suisse First Boston, improperly doled out coveted shares in initial public offerings to corporate executives in a bid to win banking business from their companies.

Regulators unveiled dozens of previously undisclosed examples of financial analysts tailoring their research reports and stock ratings to win investment-banking business. They added up to a scathing critique that scorched all the firms involved.

The penalties included lifetime bans from the securities business for two former star analysts, Jack Grubman of Salomon and Henry Blodget of Merrill Lynch & Co., who were charged with issuing fraudulent research reports and agreed to pay penalties of $15 million and $4 million, respectively. Both the firms and the individuals consented to the charges without admitting or denying wrongdoing. But the regulators vowed to pursue cases against analysts and their supervisors as far up the chain of command as possible.

Bowing to political pressure from Congress, the regulators, which also included the National Association of Securities Dealers, the New York Stock Exchange and state regulators led by New York's Eliot Spitzer, also won a promise by the firms not to seek insurance repayment or tax deductions for $487.5 million of the settlement payments.

The agreement sets new rules that will force brokerage companies to make structural changes in the way they handle research. Analysts, for instance, will no longer be allowed to accompany investment bankers during sales pitches to clients. The pact also requires securities firms to have separate reporting and supervisory structures for their research and banking operations, and to tie analysts' compensation to the quality and accuracy of their research, rather than how much investment-banking fees they help generate.

Moreover, stock research will be required to carry the equivalent of a "buyer beware" notice. Securities firms, regulators said, must include on the first page of research reports a note making clear that the reports are produced by firms that do investment-banking business with the companies they cover. This, the firms must acknowledge, may affect the objectivity of the firms' research.

Notes and Questions

1. Notes

a. SOx requires the SEC to adopt rules that effectively separate the analysts from the investment bankers within the same firm and requires disclosure of conflicts of interest.

2. Reality Check

a. What do securities analysts do?
b. How can securities analysts constrain corporate behavior?

3. What Do You Think?

a. Who was more culpable, in your view? WorldCom, Mr. Grubman, or SSB?
b. Do you think the reforms are realistic?

4. Intentionality

In the Notes that followed the selections above we adverted to various reforms, chiefly those required by SOx. Here we look at a different approach: reform through people being intentional about reforming themselves, the businesses in which they work, and the system of business. The catalyst for this kind of reform is education.

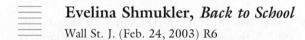

Evelina Shmukler, *Back to School*

Wall St. J. (Feb. 24, 2003) R6

When Institutional Shareholder Services Inc. put together a formula for rating corporate governance three years ago, the proxy-adviser firm weighed a host of factors — everything from executive compensation to the structure of the board to the level of stock ownership among a company's leaders.

But ISS's special counsel, Patrick McGurn, got an underwhelming reaction when he pressed for another criterion: training for members of the board. Directors, he reasoned, bring diverse business experience to the table, but few have special education in sitting on a corporate board. "People started laughing, saying, 'Oh, you've got to be kidding,'" Mr. McGurn recalls. "'Directors are busy people. They're never going to get continuing education.'"

Then came the scandals at Enron Corp., WorldCom Inc. and a host of other companies. Suddenly, director training is hot on both sides of the Atlantic. Organizations that provide training courses report massive increases in interest and enrollment in their classes, where board members learn everything from how to read a company's books to how to set ethics guidelines for executives.

In the U.K., the Institute of Directors, a business-lobby group, has seen membership triple in its accreditation program for board members. The New York Stock Exchange, meanwhile, is starting its own director-training courses, and its chairman and CEO, Richard Grasso, plans to write the chairmen of all companies listed on the exchange encouraging them to send their directors through one of the courses.

The premise behind training both executive directors — that is, those who work at a company and serve on its board — and nonexecutive, or outside, directors is simple. "Everybody gets trained at companies but directors," says Alexander Keyserlingk, a 30-year veteran of International Finance Corp., the private-sector arm of the World Bank Group, who qualified for the Institute of Directors' "chartered director" accreditation two years ago. "They train the lowest bookkeeper and the lowest truck driver, but they don't spend any time training directors."

"All of the executives have an opinion now on everything we discuss," says [Mike Hall, chief executive of Standard Life Healthcare in the U.K., who qualified as a chartered director last year]. Two years ago, he says, board members would focus on their particular specialty, be it finance, marketing, legal and so on. "Now I see them participating because they know what they're talking about, and they can ask proper, informed questions."

Indeed, the point of many director-training courses is to bring a board member up to speed in an area that isn't his or her specialty. For example, one Institute of Directors program explains complicated finance-director and accountant terminology, and teaches techniques for evaluating and monitoring the financial health of a company — as well as spotting warning signs of financial trouble.

Other courses are broader, teaching directors the ins and outs of sitting on a board. A course from the Washington-based National Association of Corporate Directors, "Role of the Board in Risk Oversight," offers advice on guidelines that a board can adopt to ensure the integrity of company officers — and what to do if the company finds itself melting down. Another course looks at the duties, roles and legal responsibilities of directors as well as ways to improve board effectiveness.

This education doesn't come cheap. The Institute of Directors' full chartered-director program costs about $12,000. A three-day program at the French business school Insead costs about $8,000. In the U.S., one-day courses at the National Association of Corporate Directors cost almost $800. Who picks up the tab, the corporation or the individual director? Many executives, including Mr. Hall, say the company should foot the bill — he says he looks on the expense as staff development.

In the U.S., ISS has made training for directors part of its "corporate governance quotient," a measure used by ISS's 750 institutional-investor clients. If directors want to boost their companies' governance rating, they can take a training course at one of about 20 programs ISS has accredited. Mr. McGurn says ISS is now "inundated" with calls from education providers, 10 to 20 a week, looking to receive accreditation.

Because of this demand, ISS says it's careful to screen providers for the kind of training it's looking for. "There are a lot of people out there providing education on directors' liability and things like that," Mr. McGurn says. "That's not what we consider to be director education related to governance. We want it to be substantive training — how to look over a financial statement or be a member of an audit committee — or more general programs about improving your governance behavior or how the market views your company."

One group that offers ISS-accredited director education, the National Association of Corporate Directors, has seen demand for programs rise dramatically. Classes are now often sold out, and Mr. McGurn says other programs report similar enrollment gains.

Notes and Questions

1. What Do You Think?

a. Director education programs such as those described above have sometimes been described as "home schooling" for business people. Do you agree?

b. Is there a danger that director education programs will produce director dilettantes rather than directors who are genuinely better educated?

c. What should the components of a director education program be?

Ronald Alsop, *Right and Wrong*
Wall St. J. (Sept. 17, 2003) R9

Harvard Business School boasts that it offered its first course on business ethics — "Social Factors in Business Enterprise" — nearly a century ago, in 1915. But this is no time for Harvard — or any business school, for that matter — to rest on its laurels. Harvard plans to launch a more in-depth, required ethics course called "Leadership, Governance and Accountability" in January. "The new course will expose students to more of the kinds of pressures they are inevitably going to face in business," says Lynn Paine, professor of business administration.

In the post-Enron era, M.B.A. programs — Harvard in particular — have come in for some caustic criticism for producing graduates obsessed with making money regardless of the ethical consequences. To some people, M.B.A. graduates are at the root of all the corporate greed and dishonesty. After all, two infamous Enron executives — former Chief Executive Jeffrey Skilling and former Chief Financial Officer Andrew Fastow — hold M.B.A. degrees from Harvard and Northwestern University's Kellogg School of Management, respectively.

Business schools have gotten the message. They are busy infusing more ethics training than ever before into their curricula, as well as trying to screen applicants for integrity before admitting them. Recently, AACSB International, the major business-school accrediting organization, increased the emphasis on ethics in the standards that business schools must meet to receive accreditation.

Notre Dame, a Roman Catholic university, has a long tradition of ethics research and education, including its Institute for Ethical Business Worldwide and Center for Ethics and Religious Values. Indeed, some recruiters say they are drawn more these days to religious schools like Notre Dame and Brigham Young University.

There's no foolproof method for measuring virtue in M.B.A. students, but many recruiters feel confident they can easily weed out the potential sinners by conducting rigorous interviews, observing students' body language and conversation in social settings, consulting character references, and checking the accuracy of resumes.

Sometimes, though, it just boils down to a gut reaction. More than half of the respondents to [a *Wall St. Journal*] survey said they rely on "a gut feeling or hunch" when interviewing students. But three-quarters said they also depend on responses to interview questions about ethical dilemmas, and about half find students' previous work experience a revealing clue to their character.

M.B.A. students with ties to any of the scandal-tarred companies will encounter resistance from some recruiters. Several respondents to the *Wall Street Journal* survey said they are loath to interview a former employee of Enron or Arthur Andersen, especially with so many other talented graduates to choose from.

The Enron and Andersen cases bring up the issue of whether a student can be taught to behave ethically. When Harvard administrators wondered about the effectiveness of ethics courses, they retained a developmental psychologist for advice. "The psychologist concluded that M.B.A. students in their mid- to late 20s are particularly ripe for discussions about such issues as conflicting responsibilities," says Prof. Paine of Harvard.

Some corporate recruiters are more skeptical. In the *Wall Street Journal/ Harris Interactive* survey, nearly a quarter of the respondents said that integrity is inherent in an individual's character and that business schools can't teach ethics. About 60%, however, said they believe schools can provide guidance on making ethical choices.

"I'm not sure you can teach ethics, but you certainly can teach the severe ramifications that come from doing something unethical in business," says Timothy Schuetze, a recruiter for a consumer-products company and graduate of the Yale School of Management.

Academics disagree on the ideal approach to embedding ethics in the curriculum. Should schools require students to take courses focused primarily on ethical responsibilities? Or is it better to sprinkle ethics lessons throughout all of the major courses, including finance, accounting, international business and marketing?

The best answer is probably some of both. That's the strategy at the Columbia University Business School. Its Center for Leadership and Ethics, created with funding from Sanford C. Bernstein & Co., offers elective courses with an ethics theme, and has adopted an ambitious new ethics curriculum that all students must take. It's a unique year-long hybrid of stand-alone lectures plus lessons woven into all of the M.B.A. program's required core courses.

Some corporate recruiters believe schools should go well beyond simply presenting case studies about ethical dilemmas. They favor a community-service requirement, as well. "A one-semester practicum with a nonprofit organization could provide a student with a life-transforming experience," says Marvin Pannell, a project manager at Wells Fargo & Co. "Many students today aren't growing up with religion and aren't replacing religion with their own brand of spirituality."

Besides creating ethics programs, some business schools are working harder to foster a culture of integrity and collegiality on their own campuses. At Ohio State University, the Fisher College of Business created a new honor code that the class of 2003 M.B.A.s were the first to sign. "Honesty and integrity are the foundation from which I will measure my actions," the code states. "I will hold myself accountable to adhere to these standards."

This year, Indiana University's Kelley School of Business has developed a 20-page code of conduct that is modeled closely after the corporate codes that graduates will ultimately have to abide by. Among the areas covered: cheating, fabrication, plagiarism, professional behavior with recruiters, and proper classroom manners ("do not surf on the Internet, avoid eating noisy or odiferous foods, and always close computers during any guest speaker's presentation"). "We especially have to emphasize the code with our international students who may have different ethical standards in their countries," says Idalene Kesner, M.B.A. program chairwoman. "Some cultures don't view plagiarism, for example, in the same serious way that we do."

Colleen DeBaise, *Corporate-Governance Law Is the Rage*

Wall St. J. (Sept. 1, 2004) B7

When Tulane University Law School in New Orleans offered a course this spring on "Corporate Governance in a Post-Enron World," the professors expected 20 students to sign up. Instead, 75 students clamored to get in. At Seattle University School of Law, nearly 90 students enrolled in the spring term's corporate-governance course, more than quadruple the 20 students who took it a year earlier.

"Students' interest in the word 'governance' has peaked," said James Cox, a law professor at Duke University, of Durham, N.C., who is teaching a course this fall on "Governance, Responsibility and Crime in the Public Corporation." The class size is limited to 16; more than 30 students are on the waiting list. "It's off the scale this year."

Many law schools say they are adding units to address legal issues raised by corporate misconduct and new regulations encompassed by the Sarbanes-Oxley Act. At Ave Maria School of Law in Ann Arbor, Mich., the new casebooks for the fall term discuss the Enron, Tyco International Ltd., WorldCom Inc. and Martha Stewart cases. Rutgers University School of Law at Camden added a new course, "The Law of Organizational Fraud," to its fall curriculum. Last year, the New Jersey school launched the course "Problems in Corporate Disclosure and Securities Fraud."

At Seattle University School of Law, the response to the newly created Center on Corporations, Law & Society, which hosts debates and conferences on corporate accountability, has been "phenomenally enthusiastic," said Dana Gold, director. Students who might not be interested in traditional "corporate" issues—those studying environmental law, for instance—now understand "that how corporations work is really important," Ms. Gold said. "People are moving a step back and not just dealing with the symptom of whatever the problem is but trying to deal with root causes."

Alexandra Filutowski, a second-year law student at Seattle University, said she decided to study law partly because one of her college classes focused on Enron and other corporate scandals. "Corporations cannot get away with everything that they have in the past," said Ms. Filutowski, a fellow at the center. "Nowadays, we're becoming more and more open to breaking the tradition, and hearing other ideas."

Notes and Questions

1. Reality Check

a. How is MBA ethics education different from business ethics education for JDs?

b. What are the elements common to both programs?

c. Why do some employers and business schools eschew former employees of companies such as Enron or Arthur Andersen?

2. What Do You Think?

a. Is it possible to provide business ethics education to MBA and JD students or are their "moral compasses" already set?

b. Should MBA ethics education be modeled after law school professional responsibility courses?

c. Do law school professional responsibility courses have much relevance for JD business ethics courses?

d. Is the attraction some employers have to religiously affiliated MBA or JD programs justified with regard to ethics programs?

e. Perhaps most importantly, do you agree with the assertion that surfing the Internet during class violates accepted norms of business conduct?

Intentionality can have its motivation in something other than education. In the excerpt below Professor Stout looks at a vision of internally generated intentionality.

Lynn A. Stout, *On the Proper Motives of Corporate Directors (Or, Why You Don't Want to Invite Homo Economicus to Join Your Board)*
28 Del. J. Corp. L. 1 (2003)

Given directors' apparent lack of external incentives to do a good job—the absence both of good carrots, and of effective sticks—why do we trust directors to manage tens of trillions of dollars of corporate assets? And, why do they seem to mostly live up to our trust? Or at least, live up to it well enough that the U.S. system of corporate governance often is held up as a model for the rest of the world, and board failures of the sort recently observed at Enron and WorldCom can still, one hopes, be viewed as the highly publicized exceptions rather than the rule.

The discussion below...explores the hypothesis that the institution of the corporate board works because we do not, in fact, rely on external incentives and pressures, alone, to motivate directors to do a good job. We also rely on internal pressures—including such internal pressures as a director's sense of honor; her feelings of responsibility; her sense of obligation to the firm and its shareholders; and, her desire to "do the right thing."

[I]f we want to understand how boards of directors work, we need to develop a better understanding of the sorts of internal pressures encompassed by terms like "honor," "integrity," "trustworthiness," and "responsibility." Yet how can we gain a firm grasp on such soft and slippery concepts? The neoclassical economic literature offers little guidance. Guidance is available, however, if we expand the search to include the broader social sciences, including psychology, sociology, biology, and anthropology.

There is a large body of literature in the broader social sciences on the phenomenon that will be described below, in general terms, as "other-regarding" behavior. As this label suggests, this literature examines instances in which people behave as if they care about something other than their own payoffs. This "other" might be the welfare of another person, or the fate of an institution like "the firm," or even an abstract principle such as "do the right thing." The point is that the evidence demonstrates that people sometimes behave altruistically—as if they care about others, and not only about themselves.

As an example, let us consider the lessons that can be drawn from studies of human behavior in a kind of experimental game called a social dilemma. In brief, these games are designed to place players in a position where their self-interest conflicts with the interests of other players. This is done by presenting subjects with a choice of strategies: either "cooperate" in a way that benefits the other members of the group, or "defect" and maximize your own personal payoffs. The experiment is structured, however, so that if all the subjects behave self-interestedly and defect, they end up worse off than if all had cooperated. Social dilemma studies . . . do not prove psychological altruism (that people truly care about others' welfare). They do, however, offer compelling evidence of behavioral altruism (people often act as if they care about others).

[P]erhaps we can harness the phenomenon of other-regarding behavior, and encourage directors of public corporations to behave even more altruistically than they already do in looking after the firm's interests.

Let us begin by considering the variable that, perhaps more than any other, seems to influence individuals' decisions about whether or not to cooperate in a social dilemma. This critical variable is something that might be called "social context." Social context can be defined as an amalgam of signals we receive about such matters as what other people expect, what other people need, and what other people are likely to do.

There is a second variable that has proven significant in predicting cooperation rates in social dilemma games that is far more "economic" in flavor. This second variable is the personal cost of altruistic behavior to the actor. It is a common finding in the social dilemma literature that, as the cost of cooperation to the individual player rises, the incidence of cooperative behavior tends to fall. In other words, people are more inclined to behave "nicely" when it does not cost them too much.

What does this result tell us about the behavior of corporate directors? Most important, it tells us that if we want directors to do a good job of looking out for the interests of the firm and its shareholders, it is essential to make sure that "doing a good job" is not too personally costly to the directors. Put differently, if we want directors to do a good job, we do not want to ask them to take on too many tasks. This observation is consistent with the way corporate governance is actually practiced in most large firms. Directors generally do not run the business on a day-to-day basis (this job is delegated to executives and employees), but instead serve an oversight or monitoring role. In effect, directors select senior managers and then step aside, intervening only in times of crisis, or on very large issues such as a merger or major refinancing.

This pattern of relative uninvolvement is sometimes offered as proof of director malfeasance, evidence that directors are not working as hard as they should. Such critiques misunderstand the director's role. Because directors' rewards and punishments are only very loosely tied to their performance, we must inevitably rely on directors' internalized sense of responsibility as their primary if not their sole motive for exercising judgment and care. The empirical evidence suggests that if we place too heavy a burden on such altruistic motivations, they will crumble under the weight. It thus makes sense for large corporations to rely on professional managers for most decisions, and to limit directors' responsibilities primarily to monitoring. Monitoring is not nearly as demanding or as time-consuming as managing. Nevertheless, it can be every bit as important.

A related and very important lesson that can be drawn from the social dilemma evidence on the inverse relationship between cooperation and personal cost is that it is essential that we do not rely too heavily on director altruism in situations where a director has a substantial personal interest adverse to the firm. [I]f we want to rely on outside directors to curb the predictably self-interested behavior of inside directors whose prospects for substantial personal loss or gain may undermine their altruistic motivations, outside directors must be truly independent.

No analysis of the role of other-regarding behavior in promoting good corporate governance would be complete, however, without mentioning a third factor that has proven important in determining cooperation rates in experimental games. This third factor is something a psychologist might call "personality type." Laypersons might call it "character."

Let us return to the general finding that cooperation rates among U.S. subjects playing social dilemma games average 50%. This average cooperation rate, it turns out, reflects a blend of two strategies people tend to adopt in social dilemma games: either they donate all the money they have been given to the common pool, or they donate none of it. Social scientists have investigated whether these patterns of behavior somehow reflect basic personality characteristics. They have concluded that the answer, to some extent, is yes. Although cooperation rates in social dilemmas are highly dependent on social context and considerations of personal cost, people also seem to bring to the experiments a predisposition to either cooperate or defect.

[R]esearchers also found a strong correlation between cooperation rates and the frequency of cooperation and market exchange in the culture studied. This finding suggests that habits of cooperation may be learned: the more frequently members of a particular society cooperate with others in their daily economic lives, the more likely they are to cooperate with strangers in a social dilemma experiment as well.

[T]he evidence also suggests that some people, whether by nature or nurture, are more inclined toward other-regarding behavior than others. These "cooperators" behave altruistically even in situations where the social signals they receive are somewhat mixed, and altruism requires more than a nominal personal sacrifice. In everyday business life, directors often face such situations. Thus, if we want corporate directors to serve an other-regarding role, we should select as directors those individuals who are more inclined toward other-regarding behavior in the first place.

How can we find these directors? There are a number of possibilities, but one of the most obvious is to look at a person's history as evidence of her character. Has she lived up to her commitments, even in situations where she did not have to? Has she undertaken activities that demonstrate that she can care about something other than her own payoffs? Has she given evidence, in the past, of a desire and an ability to do the right thing, even when doing the right thing was not personally advantageous, or particularly popular? If the answers to these questions are "yes," then it is this type of person ... whom you want to invite to join your board.

Of course, these are lessons that most experienced business people, including most experienced business lawyers, have already learned. Most of us are sophisticated, if not always conscious, observers of human nature. The point here is simply that we should pay attention to what we already know. Personal payoffs count. But so do social context and the quality we call "character."

Notes and Questions

1. What Do You Think?

a. Is intentionality something that can be fostered by education or is it primarily internally generated?

C. BACKGROUND AND CONTEXT

We close this chapter with a look at two broader questions related to whether the current restraints on corporations and boards are effective. First, are the reforms imposed in the wake of Enron and WorldCom effective and worth the costs of compliance? Second, are scandals such as these (1) proof that the current system of constraints is fundamentally ineffective or (2) particularly egregious exceptions in a system that constrains boards and companies appropriately?

1. Are Reforms Working?

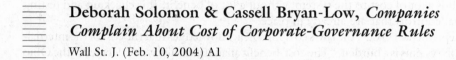

Deborah Solomon & Cassell Bryan-Low, *Companies Complain About Cost of Corporate-Governance Rules*
Wall St. J. (Feb. 10, 2004) A1

Some U.S. companies are complaining that new rules aimed at improving corporate accountability will cost them in dollars and in time this year. Most of the rules stem from the 2002 Sarbanes-Oxley Act, which Congress enacted to beef up corporate governance in the aftermath of accounting fraud uncovered at Enron Corp., WorldCom Inc. and elsewhere. Written by the Securities and Exchange Commission, the regulations are aimed at toughening corporate accountability to restore investor confidence and are just now starting to hit bottom lines. Advocates say they will help companies avoid costly problems down the road.

"We can't lose sight of the fact that we came close to an all-out breakdown of investor trust in financial statements and the integrity of the financial-reporting process," says Charles Mulford, an accounting professor at the Georgia Institute of Technology.

While there is agreement that governance rules are needed, some companies cited the increased cost of complying. "The real cost isn't the incremental dollars, it is having people that should be focused on the business focused instead on complying with the details of the rules," said Peter Bible, chief accounting officer at General Motors Corp. "Everybody feels they have to do something to react to the corporate scandals, [but] you really have to scratch your head and say, 'How is this really benefiting our shareholders?'"

The rules are coming into effect at a time when corporations already are battling other increasing costs, including health-care expenses. Even before the most expensive Sarbanes-Oxley rules take effect, companies say their audit costs are increasing by as much as 30% or more this year due to tougher audit and accounting standards, including complex rules to bring more off-balance-sheet items onto the books.

[M]ost companies say they understand the need for tougher standards but complain that some of the rules are duplicative while others force them to devote thousands of staff hours to formalize procedures already in place. The most pointed criticism is aimed at a rule — Section 404 of the act — to improve internal controls over financial reporting. [M]anagement at most large companies must have in place tight internal controls, assess the effectiveness of those controls and then pay for an independent assessment by outside auditors.

A survey of 321 companies to be released today shows that businesses with more than $5 billion in revenue expect to spend an average of $4.7 million each implementing the new 404 rule this year, according to Financial Executives International, which represents top corporate officials. Much of the money is being spent on consultants, lawyers, auditors and new software.

Many costs, such as installing software and designing systems, will decrease after the first year. But other costs are expected to stay constant, including paying an outside auditor to assess the controls every year. Companies with more than $5 billion in revenue expect those fees to be $1.5 million annually, according to the survey.

At World Wrestling Entertainment Inc., management began ramping up internal controls three months ago and is still considering whether to pay $250,000 to hire an outside consultant to oversee the project. The company, which reported revenue of $374 million during fiscal 2003, which ended April 30, already plans to spend about $50,000 on software to help document and track internal-control tests.

It is "a big headache," says Philip Livingston, the company's chief financial officer. "It is a lot of cost to the system without a lot of benefit. It is checking and testing internal controls that are already in place."

Rep. Michael Oxley, the law's co-sponsor, acknowledges that the cost of the internal-controls systems is a burden. "The cost-benefit analysis will always be debated," the Ohio Republican says. But it is "encouraging" that companies already are starting to make disclosures about potential weaknesses, he adds. In the past several months Adecco SA and BearingPoint Inc. disclosed "material weaknesses" in their internal controls.

Douglas Carmichael, the Public Company Accounting Oversight Board's chief auditor, says most companies need to make significant improvements to comply with the rules. "People in the past had a very exaggerated idea of how much time the auditor spent on internal controls," Mr. Carmichael says. "It was viewed by the auditor as strictly an efficiency matter" and auditors "paid little or no attention to internal controls."

One encouraging result of the Financial Executives International survey, according to Mr. Carmichael, is that small companies don't appear to be bearing a disproportionate amount of the cost. Some market observers were worried that increasing costs will dissuade smaller companies from going public. But Mr. Carmichael says small companies may actually benefit from the new requirements, because fraud tends to be more prevalent among small companies, making access to the capital markets harder. The new requirements should reduce uncertainty and therefore improve access, he says.

Notes and Questions

1. What Do You Think?

a. Are the legislative and regulatory reforms enacted in the wake of Enron and WorldCom effective? If not, what reforms would you suggest?

b. Is the value of the reforms worth their costs? What are the elements of those costs?

2. Systemic Problem or Cyclical Anomalies?

Joseph Nocera, et al., *System Failure*
Fortune (June 24, 2002) 62

Goldman Sachs CEO Hank Paulson is not a touchy-feely guy. Even by Wall Street standards, he's fairly buttoned down. But the daily drumbeat of news about horrifying corporate behavior would get to anyone — and it's clearly getting to Paulson. "In my lifetime, American business has never been under such scrutiny, and to be blunt, much of it deserved," he said in a recent speech. To *Fortune* he added, "You pick up the paper, and you want to cry."

Phony earnings, inflated revenues, conflicted Wall Street analysts, directors asleep at the switch — this isn't just a few bad apples we're talking about here. This, my friends, is a systemic breakdown. Nearly every known check on corporate behavior — moral, regulatory, you name it — fell by the wayside, replaced by the stupendous greed that marked the end of the bubble. And that has created a crisis of investor confidence the likes of which hasn't been seen since — well, since the Great Depression.

Even Harvey Pitt and Bill Lerach, who are poles apart on most issues, agree on this point. "I'm really afraid that investor psychology in this country has suffered a very serious blow," says the controversial Lerach, the plaintiffs attorney best known as the lead counsel representing Enron's beleaguered shareholders. SEC Chairman Pitt, who made his name defending big corporations, concurs: "It would be hard to overstate the need to remedy the loss of confidence," he said at a recent conference at Stanford Law School. "Restoring public confidence is the No. 1 goal on our agenda."

Despite the constant reports of misconduct, investors can't cast all the blame for the market's troubles on the actions of CEOs and Wall Street analysts — much as they might like to. There was a time not too long ago when everyone, it seemed, was day trading during lunch breaks. As Gail Dudack, chief strategist for SunGard Institutional Brokerage, puts it, "A stock market bubble requires the cooperation of everyone."

Still, the unending revelations — and the high likelihood that there are more to come — have underscored the extent to which the system has gone awry. That has taken a toll on investors' psyches. According to a Pew Forum survey conducted in late March, Americans now think more highly of Washington politicians than they do of business executives. (Yes, it's that bad.) A monthly survey of "investor optimism" conducted by UBS and Gallup shows that the mood among investors today is almost as grim as it was after Sept. 11 — and has sunk by nearly half since the giddy days of late 1999 and early 2000. Similarly, the average daily trading volume at Charles Schwab & Co. — another good barometer of investor confidence — is down 54% from the height of the bull market. "People deeply believed, as an article of faith, in the integrity of the system and the markets," Morgan Stanley strategist Barton Biggs wrote recently. "Sure, it may at times have seemed like a casino, but at least it was an honest casino. Now many people are questioning that basic assumption. Are they players in a loser's game?" Investing, notes Vanguard founder John C. Bogle, "is an act of faith." Without that faith — that reported numbers reflect reality, that companies are being run honestly, that Wall Street is playing it straight, and that investors aren't being hoodwinked — our capital markets simply can't function.

Is the situation today as dire as it was in 1929? Of course not. But it is serious — serious enough that real reform is once again needed to restore confidence in the system. Already there has been a flood of proposals, which range from the good to the not-so-good.

In the end, though, all the rules in the world won't change a thing until directors realize that ultimately they've got to reform themselves. They have to go beyond the rules: They have to ask better, tougher questions, be more skeptical and critical of management, and never forget that their No. 1 job is to watch out for us, the shareholders, not their buddy, the CEO.

E.S. Browning, *Burst Bubbles Often Expose Cooked Books and Trigger SEC Probes, Bankruptcy Filings*

Wall St. J. (Feb. 11, 2002) C1

History confirms what a lot of stock analysts and investors have been discovering to their chagrin lately—that burst bubbles and accounting controversies tend to go hand in hand.

Accounting scandals and bankruptcies, in fact, are one important reason that it can take the stock market years to recover fully from a bubble.

"This is not an isolated event," says Ray Dalio, president of Bridgewater Associates, a money-management firm in Westport, Conn., that oversees $35 billion. "This is something that will spread" as many companies' accounting practices are examined. "Many more stories will come out. The examination will inevitably turn up more cases of aggressive accounting and there will be a penalty for that aggressive accounting."

Consider past experience. Corporate bankruptcies and unraveling frauds were among the hallmarks of the 1930s, following the crash of 1929. One accounting trick of that era was to create elaborate webs of holding companies, each helping hide the others' financial weaknesses, an artifice strangely similar to what Enron did with its partnerships. One of the biggest shocks of the '30s was the collapse of a vast, once-highflying utilities empire called Middle West Utilities, run by an energy magnate and financier named Samuel Insull.

"Our view would be that bubbles create greed on the part of investors but they also create greed on the part of management," says Jeremy Grantham, a co-founder of Boston money-management firm Grantham, Mayo, Van Otterloo. "That was very much the case in 1929 when holding companies put on leverage and bought other holding companies' stock."

As the fallout from the 1929 crash spread, former New York Stock Exchange President Richard Whitney was sucked in and eventually was arrested and jailed for fraud.

A less extensive bubble was inflated in the late 1960s and burst in the early 1970s, when the "Nifty 50" stocks fell apart. Accounting scandals multiplied again. The Securities and Exchange Commission in 1975 censured Peat, Marwick, Mitchell, one of the largest accounting firms of the day, for failing to perform proper audits of five companies that collapsed soon after getting clean opinions.

More trouble followed the crash of 1987, although it was shorter-lived than the problems of the '30s or the '70s. The once-hot junk-bond market unraveled, insider-trading scandals proliferated, the savings-and-loan crisis grabbed the front pages and real-estate investments went bust.

Some market analysts worry that these problems aren't going to go away soon. "It is absolutely what almost invariably happens after every bubble," says investment strategist Barton Biggs at Morgan Stanley, referring to the scandals, bankruptcies and accounting disclosures. "You should expect them, but that doesn't mean that people who haven't been through it before aren't going to be surprised. The bigger the binge, the longer and more severe the hangover."

The root of the accounting problem, say Mr. Dalio and others who have studied the phenomenon, is that stock-market bubbles reward aggressive accounting, since it inflates earnings and helps push up companies' stock prices. As bubbles develop and the continued inflation of stock prices becomes paramount, conservative accountants and executives become discredited, and bending the rules becomes standard.

≡ **Phyllis Plitch,** *When Market Scandals Erupt,*
≡ *Regulation Can Come in a Flood*
≡ Wall St. J. (Jan. 15, 2003)

NEW YORK—When two professors exposed trading anomalies in the mid-1990s that raised the specter of collusion among NASDAQ dealers, a top exchange official denounced their work as "unseemly" and sought to have the "unsubstantiated allegations" scrubbed from their paper.

One in-depth investigation later, market regulators were chastened. To settle Securities and Exchange Commission allegations that it failed to investigate signs of possible trading violations, the National Association of Securities Dealers—NASDAQ's parent—pledged $100 million to beef up enforcement and surveillance and restructured itself to strengthen market oversight.

While it may seem like ancient history, NASDAQ's upheaval is reminiscent of what transpired following the fall of Enron Corp.—albeit on a smaller scale.

In the months and years to come, U.S. companies will be operating under new rules. In just about every corner of the capital markets, the perceived evils of once-accepted business practices have become fodder for regulatory changes, many of which will become reality in 2003.

It is what social scientists call a "frame shift," said Dalton Conley, director of New York University's Center for Advanced Social Science Research. "Once something is perceived as wrong, all past history is put through a new lens," he said. "Once it shifts, it's like a flood."

William Christie, one of the two finance professors on the NASDAQ study and now dean of the Owens School of Management at Vanderbilt University, Nashville, Tenn., sees parallels between the events of the 1990s and the past year.

NASDAQ traders' behavior—however suspect in retrospect—had become the norm. Those charged with oversight either failed to see what was going on or looked the other way. Similarly, the scandals of 2002 showed that management and directors failed in their oversight duties to shareholders and employees, he said.

"Human nature sometimes dictates that if you can get away with something on the margins, you have the temptation to do so," said Mr. Christie, who keeps in his scrap book the letter from NASDAQ's then president, Joseph Hardiman, the official who criticized the study. "Someone had to stand up and say the emperor has no clothes."

Regulatory and congressional changes—most notably the sweeping Sarbanes-Oxley Act . . . —contain prescriptive measures that take aim at a wide range of corporate and Wall Street activities, from compensation, accounting and disclosure practices to the way securities analysts recommend stocks and how lawyers do their jobs.

Such frame shifts don't happen often, given the fragmentation of the American political system and anti-big-government feeling, said Rogan Kersh, a professor at Syracuse University's Maxwell School of Citizenship & Public Affairs.

A period of as long as half a century can go by before a cataclysmic event, or series of events, propels significant change, he said.

But it is hard to connect the dots between the recent rush for change to a single root cause, NYU's Mr. Conley said. The change in landscape can't be entirely laid at Enron Corp.'s door, for instance. Several months after the energy company's fall, the drive toward change had actually been losing steam, only to regain momentum after new scandals surfaced, most notably WorldCom Inc.'s outright acknowledgment of accounting fraud in June. The centerpiece of recent accounting measures — Sarbanes-Oxley — might not have become a reality if not for WorldCom.

This shift in thinking can also be seen at the stock exchanges, at times accused by institutional investors of being in "a race to the bottom" to make the regulatory landscape looser to entice new corporate listings. As members of a special New York Stock Exchange corporate governance committee — formed in February — debated what changes to make, scandals continued erupting around them. Concern for restoring market confidence eventually outweighed worries about being at a competitive disadvantage with rival markets, said Leon Panetta, the former White House chief of staff who was co-chairman of the NYSE committee.

"There was no way we could simply tiptoe around, with the scandals taking place," Mr. Panetta said. "We had to deal with them directly."

Academics also invoke "the great man theory," when an influential person suddenly spearheads a new agenda, as in New York Attorney General Eliot Spitzer's relentless effort against Wall Street research and banking conflicts of interest. Mr. Spitzer's crusade culminated in the recent agreement with Wall Street firms.

In terms of the changes of 2002, experts say that without the collapse of the stock market, the stars probably wouldn't have aligned for change. During the frothy bull market days of the late 1990s, before companies like Enron and WorldCom sank under the weight of accounting scandals, naysayers didn't stand much of a chance, anyway.

D. FEDERAL SECURITIES REGULATION

The federal securities laws provide both indirect and direct methods of controlling board power. The indirect methods are of long standing. The direct methods are primarily from the Sarbanes-Oxley Act of 2002 (SOx).

When we looked at a corporation's power to raise capital we adverted to the federal regulations on selling securities to the public. In the next chapter we will see that publicly held companies are required to make public important information concerning their financial and operational aspects. These regulations are couched in the form of mandatory disclosure of facts rather than as substantive restrictions on corporate action. Nonetheless, even the disclosure regulations affect board power in two ways. First, as we've seen, to the extent that the federal regulations require corporations to disclose whether a corporation has certain qualities, such as an independent compensation committee, the regulations effectively require such qualities because companies are loathe to have to disclose that they do not have such beneficial qualities.

Second, the regulations provide for severe penalties, both civil and criminal, for filings that contain false or misleading information. These penalties can be levied both on the corporation and on those officers and directors who sign the filings. Every director signs the most important of such filings and so is exposed to potential liability. One of the most potent penalties is levied on corporations and directors under Section 11 of the Securities Act of 1933. This provision covers filings in connection with selling securities to the public. If a prospectus that is filed with the SEC contains misleading or false information, the corporation is strictly liable and the directors (among other potential defendants) are liable unless they can demonstrate that they exercised due diligence in ascertaining whether the information was true or false. This demonstration is, as a practical matter, quite difficult.

The outside directors of both Enron and WorldCom were sued on the theory that they executed prospectuses that contained false or misleading information. Both sets of directors settled those suits and paid significant amounts of money from their own pockets. Ten of 18 former outside Enron directors settled for $13 million. Twelve former directors of WorldCom settled for over $25 million, each director paying at least 20 percent of his or her net worth.

The more direct methods of controlling board power are contained in SOx, which contains two principal kinds of constraints. First, every public company must have an audit committee of independent directors at least one of whom is a "financial expert." The audit committee must be responsible for retaining and overseeing the corporation's independent accounting firm. Second, the act requires senior officers to certify the corporation's financial statements and to certify that, in effect, the corporation has a *Caremark* system of effective internal controls.

E. TERMS OF ART IN THIS CHAPTER

Credit rating agencies	Sarbanes-Oxley Act of 2002	Securities analyst
Reputational intermediaries		

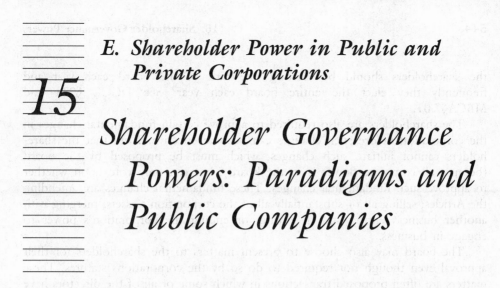

E. Shareholder Power in Public and Private Corporations

15

Shareholder Governance Powers: Paradigms and Public Companies

This chapter begins a shift in emphasis from the board's power to govern the corporation (and the restrictions on that power) to the shareholders' power to govern. You may remember that one of the central distinguishing marks of the corporate form is that the ultimate owners, the shareholders, have very little power over the entity. While it is common in closely held corporations for the shareholders to be members of the board and officers or employees, as well, and in those capacities to exercise great control over the business, *as shareholders* their powers are quite limited.

We will begin with an examination of the shareholders' power to take actions that affect the corporation. First, we'll look at the areas in which the shareholders can act. These areas are rather limited. Second, we'll describe the mechanics of shareholder meetings, voting of shares (including the use of proxies), and the mechanics of acting without a meeting. If you have already covered Chapter 9, much of the mechanics of this chapter will be familiar. Third, we'll explore the somewhat arcane, yet often vitally important, facets of tabulating votes. This is harder than it sounds.

After looking at the shareholders' power to take action we'll move to another, related, area of shareholder governance, the right to be informed about the corporation. When we've finished that topic, we'll move to a (mercifully) brief overview of shareholder power to redress harms to the corporation. This power is exerted through the shareholder derivative lawsuit. Although many important aspects of derivative suits are, in essence, advanced civil procedure, and thus elided over in this book, some are genuinely corporate law-based and so will be the subject of our examination here.

This chapter contains topics that apply to both privately held corporations and those that are publicly traded. The emphasis, though, is on the public corporation. The next chapter focuses on shareholder governance questions that are mostly encountered in the closely held corporation rather than the public company.

A. SHAREHOLDERS' POWER TO TAKE ACTION

1. Actions That the Shareholders May Take as a Group

In the normal course of a corporation's existence, its shareholders vote on one matter, and one matter only: the people who are to serve as directors. At a minimum,

543

the shareholders should be electing one-third of the board each year and frequently they elect the entire board each year. See DGCL §211 and MBCA§7.01.

The shareholders are also required to approve certain fundamental changes in the corporation before such changes can become effective. Note that the shareholders cannot initiate such changes, which must be proposed by the board (because all corporate power is in the board), but can only vote upon whether to approve such fundamental changes. These fundamental changes are amending the Articles; selling all or substantially all of the corporation's assets; merging with another business entity; and dissolving, or ending the corporation's power to engage in business.

The board may also choose to present matters to the shareholders for their approval even though not required to do so by the corporations statutes. These matters are often proposed transactions in which some or all of the directors have a conflict of interest. Although shareholder approval is not required for such transactions, a fully informed vote of shareholders unaffiliated with the conflicted directors may either render the transaction immune from attack on the ground of conflict of interest or may provide the corporate planners with greater comfort that the transaction will be found by a court to be fair if challenged. Relatedly, shareholders may be asked to approve indemnification payments to officers or directors.

Shareholders have the power to act in two settings without board concurrence and without the possibility of the board overriding the decision. First, the shareholders have the power, in certain settings, to remove, or *amote*, some or all of the directors and to replace those directors by others. Aside from amoting directors, corporations statutes permit shareholders, as a group and without board interference, to amend the corporation's bylaws, though that power is frequently eliminated in the corporation's Articles. See DGCL §§141(k), 109 and MBCA §§8.08, 10. 20.

If the corporation is publicly held, and therefore subject to federal securities regulations, the shareholders vote on additional matters, which are discussed more fully at the end of the chapter.

Under state corporate law, the question of so-called *precatory* motions is murkier. Statutes usually permit a certain quantum of the shareholders to force the board to call a special shareholders meeting, but those statutes, by themselves, do not expand the power of shareholders to take action beyond what has been described so far. All those statutes do is provide an avenue for obtaining the opportunity for the shareholders to take permitted actions. Note, though, that the DGCL default rule does not permit the shareholders to call a special meeting. See DGCL §211(d) and MBCA §7.02(b). Similarly, the fact that the board may call a special shareholder meeting does not give the shareholders the power to effect action. It occasionally happens that a group, sometimes a large group, of shareholders has validly called a special shareholders meeting to vote upon a matter outside of the shareholders' power, which the board opposes. As push comes to shove, the shareholders or the board may go to court to seek a declaratory judgment or equitable relief permitting or prohibiting the meeting and vote. The results of such lawsuits have been mixed. Some courts, especially in an earlier time, have refused to allow shareholder votes on purely precatory matters. Other courts, often in more recent times, have permitted such votes.

Notes and Questions

1. What Do You Think?

a. Shareholders are the ultimate owners of the corporation. Do you think they should be able to vote on any matter that a sufficient percentage of them (say 10 percent, 25 percent, or 33 percent) desires to vote on and to have the result of that vote be binding on the corporation? If, in your view, they shouldn't be allowed to vote on every such matter, are there particular issues on which the shareholders should have this power? If so, which ones?

b. What is the harm in permitting shareholder votes on precatory matters? Should shareholders be permitted to vote on any precatory issue? Every precatory issue? Some precatory issues?

2. How Shareholders Take Action in a Meeting

a. The Current Setting

The paradigm vehicle by which the shareholders act is the shareholder meeting. As with board of director meetings, four elements are required for shareholder action taken at a meeting to be valid. The meeting must be properly *called*, the corporation must give proper *notice*, a *quorum of shares* (*not* shareholders) must be present at the meeting, and the action must be approved by a *sufficient vote*. If any of these elements is lacking, the action is subject to attack as being ultra vires. Chapter 8 discusses the ultra vires doctrine in more detail.

i. Call. The *call* of the meeting is simply the decision to hold a meeting at a particular time and place[1] and, often, for a particular reason. *Annual meetings*, at which the directors are to be elected and at which other valid shareholder actions may be taken, are required by the corporations statutes. See DGCL §§211(b) and MBCA §§7.01. The bylaws, or less typically the Articles, provide the call for the annual shareholder meeting. Where the board has failed, through oversight or intention, to hold the annual shareholder meeting for a certain length of time, any shareholder may bring suit to compel such a meeting. See DGCL §211(c) (earlier of 30 days after scheduled annual meeting or 13 months after the last annual meeting) and MBCA §7.03 (earlier of 6 months after the end of the corporation's fiscal year or 15 months after the last annual meeting).

You may remember that directors hold office until their successors are elected, so that even though their term has expired they remain directors and may collectively take valid board actions. As mentioned above, the owners of a certain quantum of shares can usually compel a special meeting of shareholders. A *special meeting* is simply any shareholder meeting other than the annual meeting. Special shareholder meetings can also be called by the board or by a person or persons designated in the bylaws or Articles, such as the president. See DGCL §§211(d) and MBCA §§7.02.

ii. Notice. Unlike notice to the board, notice to the shareholders is regulated by the statutes. The statutes require between 10 and 60 days notice of the date, time,

---

1. Under the DGCL a meeting can be held no place. That is, a real-time virtual meeting of shareholders may validly transact shareholder business. See DGCL §211(a).

and place of the annual meeting and require notice of a special meeting's purpose. See DGCL §222(a) and MBCA §§7.05(a), (c). In Delaware, for fundamental changes, the DGCL requires that notice be given between 20 and 60 days in advance of the meeting See, e.g., DGCL §§251(c), 271(a).

In closely held corporations the shareholders might not change between the call of the meeting and the meeting itself. But suppose a shareholder has the temerity to sell his or her shares between the call and the meeting. Intuitively, the new shareholder should be able to vote the shares at the meeting. Suppose the sale occurs minutes before the meeting begins. In a closely held corporation such events might be easy enough to deal with. In a publicly held corporation, though, shares change hands every day and it would be impractical to keep track of transfers occurring close to the meeting.

Perhaps more importantly, if a transfer of shares takes place between the call and the meeting should notice to the transferring shareholder be imputed to the transferee shareholder? Should the transferring shareholder be under an obligation to inform the new shareholder of the impending meeting? If you have read Chapter 7, you remember the concept of a record date. The record date is an arbitrary date between the board's decision to undertake some action that requires a fixed list of shareholders (such as paying a dividend or holding a shareholder meeting) and the action itself. All shareholders of record on the record date, usually meaning shareholders at the close of business on the record date, are entitled to notice of the meeting and to vote the shares they hold on the record date at the meeting. See DGCL §213(a) and MBCA §§1.40(19), 7.07.

When the corporation's shareholders have divided into factions, management may want to aid one side or the other in the struggle. If a shareholder vote is looming, the board may be tempted to establish an early or late record date depending upon the board's assessment of whether the shareholder profile is shifting against or in favor of its desired outcome. The corporations statutes prevent the board from acting too opportunistically in this regard by providing that the record date cannot be a past date.

All of this may seem both hypertechnical and hypointeresting. Nonetheless, complying with the requirements of the statutes articles, bylaws, and board resolutions is undeniably the lawyer's task, and failure to observe all requirements can lead to trouble as the next case shows. If your attention to this case starts to flag, imagine you were McKesson's corporate counsel.

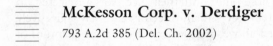

McKesson Corp. v. Derdiger

793 A.2d 385 (Del. Ch. 2002)

CHANDLER, CH.

BACKGROUND FACTS

McKesson [Corporation] is a Delaware corporation with its principal corporate office in San Francisco, California. Defendant [Howard] Derdiger is a stockholder of McKesson. On June 13, 2001, McKesson mailed copies of its proxy statement ("Proxy Statement") to its stockholders informing them of its Annual Meeting, scheduled for July 25, 2001. McKesson set the record date for stockholders eligible to vote at the Annual Meeting to be the close of business Friday, May 25, 2001, the day before the Memorial Day weekend. Due to the holiday, both exchanges trading McKesson stock, the New York Stock Exchange and the Pacific Stock Exchange, were closed from May 26 to May 28. Consequently, the parties agree that the identity of McKesson's record stockholders on May 25 remained identical until the Exchanges reopened on May 29.

On July 17, 2001, Derdiger's counsel delivered a letter to McKesson asserting that the record date failed to comply with the sixty-day requirement of §213(a). In addition, this letter requested that McKesson's Board reschedule the Annual Meeting and redistribute proxy materials to the stockholders who would be eligible to vote under the new record date. In response . . . , McKesson's counsel delivered a letter, dated July 23, 2001, to Derdiger's counsel, insisting that the May 25 record date complied with §213(a) and notifying Derdiger of the Company's intention to go forward with the Annual Meeting as scheduled. On July 24, 2001, the day before the Annual Meeting, Derdiger's counsel faxed a reply to McKesson's July 23 letter explaining his concern that the meeting, if held as scheduled, would be void for statutory non-compliance. As a result, any actions taken at the meeting would also be void, thereby exposing McKesson to potential "significant harm" in the future.[3] No response to defendant's July 24 letter was made and on July 25, 2001 McKesson held its Annual Meeting. Although McKesson's counsel asserts in his brief that the three management proposals were approved overwhelmingly and the three stockholder proposals were disapproved by wide margins, the parties have stipulated only that the inspector of elections certified "certain voting" results following the meeting.

In order to remove any uncertainty as to the legal validity of actions taken at the Annual Meeting on July 25, 2001, McKesson brought this action against Derdiger.[6] The Company seeks a declaratory judgment affirming both its compliance with §213(a) and the validity of all actions taken during the Annual Meeting. McKesson moved for summary judgment pursuant to Chancery Rule 56.

Derdiger, in turn, moved to dismiss McKesson's complaint for failure to state a claim upon which relief can be granted pursuant to Chancery Rule 12(b)(6). He also moved for summary judgment on his cross-claim, asking the Court to declare that the record date for McKesson's July 25, 2001 annual meeting did not comply with §213(a) and, accordingly, that the actions taken at the meeting are void and invalid.

ANALYSIS

A. Compliance with §213(a)

McKesson contends that it complied with §213(a) as there are precisely sixty days between May 25 and July 25. The Company cites *Aprahamian v. HBO & Co.*[8] in support of its contention that its choice of dates was consistent with the sixty-day

---

3. Compl., Ex. C (July 24, 2001 Letter from Derdiger's counsel to McKesson's counsel) (warning that . . . "someone could assert that seven board seats will need to be filled at next year's annual meeting. Also, the stockholders whose proposals are being submitted could assert claims in connection with the failure to legally submit their proposals").

6. Derdiger and his counsel are no strangers to litigation in this Court involving McKesson.

8. 531 A.2d 1204 (Del. Ch. 1987).

maximum permitted under §213(a). In *Aprahamian,* the shareholder meeting at issue was scheduled for May 15, 1987 and the record date, as reported in the Opinion of the Court, was March 15, 1987. Consistent with the McKesson record and meeting dates, there were exactly sixty days *between* the record and meeting dates in *Aprahamian.*

Derdiger's counsel, however, points out that the clear language of §213(a) states that a record date "shall not be more than 60 . . . days *before*" the meeting date, not that there "shall not be more than 60 . . . days *between*" the record date and the meeting date. The defendant correctly sets forth the only way to determine whether the statutory imperative of §213(a) has been met. The statute looks at the number of days *before* the meeting date to determine a valid period of time within which a record date may be set. In this case, the meeting date was July 25, 2001. One day before July 25 is July 24. Two days before July 25 is July 23. Three days before July 25 is July 22. Continuing counting the number of days *before* the meeting date in this manner ends with May 26, 2001 as the sixtieth day *before* July 25, 2001. The statute commands that a record date "*shall not* be more than 60" days before the meeting date. McKesson's May 25, 2001 record date was sixty-one days before the Annual Meeting.

Derdiger also attacks McKesson's reliance on *Aprahamian* as support for the Company's method of calculating when a valid record date may be set under §213(a). The defendant asserts that McKesson's reading of *Aprahamian* is flawed due to a "typographical error" in the published version of the *Aprahamian* Court's decision. Derdiger's counsel found record evidence in the *Aprahamian* case indicating that the record date in HBO's notice of its annual shareholder meeting was actually *March 16, 1987* (not March 15 as the Court's published opinion erroneously recites), *i.e.*, exactly sixty days before HBO's May 15, 1987 annual meeting.[10] As a result, Derdiger argues that *Aprahamian* actually contradicts McKesson's position and supports his position that the May 25, 2001 record date did not correspond to the directive of §213(a). Alternatively, Derdiger contends that, even if the Court does not accept his argument regarding a typographical error in *Aprahamian,* that case cannot serve as binding precedent on an issue in which it is in apparent conflict with a statutory command.

McKesson insists that *Aprahamian* authorizes a new and expansive way of calculating the statutory sixty-day maximum allowed by the statute. In *Aprahamian,* on the eve of HBO's scheduled shareholder meeting, the management of HBO decided to postpone the meeting upon receiving information from their proxy solicitor that a group of insurgent shareholders might defeat the management's proposals. The plaintiff challenged that delay and this Court held that the postponement served no significant stockholder interest and directed that the annual meeting be convened as scheduled on May 15, 1987. The Court also directed the Company to immediately adjourn the May 15 meeting and shortly thereafter reconvene the meeting after giving notice to all the shareholders of the Court's decision. The explicit purpose of the Court's directives was to preserve HBO's established March 16, 1987 record date so that the identity of the shareholders originally entitled to vote, including those whose

---

10. *See, e.g.,* Def.'s Opening Br. at 6 ("The record date here fixed by the board for this annual meeting was *March 16.* . . . If that meeting is not convened . . . then under Section 213 arguably the record date of *March 16* will no longer be any good.") (emphasis added) (quoting *Aprahamian v. HBO & Co.,* Del. Ch., C.A. No. 8989, Hartnett, V.C. (May 11, 1987) (Tr. of Inj. Hr'g at 41)).

proxies had been garnered by the insurgents, would not change. The directives were necessary to preserve that record date because if HBO's "annual meeting does not convene by May 15, 1987, the proxies submitted by the stockholders may expire because of... §213 which provide[s] that a record date shall not be fixed for a date more than 60 days before the date of the annual meeting."[14] Although McKesson is correct that the *Aprahamian* Court apparently calculated the permissible sixty-day window of §213(a) in the manner the Company advocates, McKesson's erroneous belief resulted from that decision mistakenly referring to the record date as *March 15, 1987* (*i.e., sixty-one* days before May 15, 1987).

Unlike McKesson, however, I am convinced that the *Aprahamian* Court calculated the sixty-day window in the same way as I explained above. That Court was neither employing a new method of counting the permissible sixty-day time period nor accepting sixty-one days as "close enough." The actual Order to adjourn and reconvene, as well as the notice of annual meeting of HBO stockholders, substantiates the *Aprahamian* Court's intention to calculate §213(a)'s sixty-day window as described herein. The *Aprahamian* Court's stated objective "to protect the record date" makes it clear that it intended to observe the sixty-day mandate of §213(a). Thus, the Order's only purpose for directing that the meeting be convened on May 15, albeit only long enough to adjourn, was to remain within the sixty-day statutory window, thereby preserving the *March 16* record date. Nothing in *Aprahamian* can be read, in my view, to support McKesson's position that either sixty days *between* the meeting and record date is statutorily acceptable or that sixty-one days is "close enough" to comply with §213(a).

The Legislature includes immutable time limits in statutes to serve particular purposes and such time limits are usually strictly enforced. An example of this can be seen in this Court's recent *Nelson v. Frank E. Best Inc.*[23] decision concerning the "Sunday rule." In that case, the Court held that even when the last day of the limitations period for making an appraisal demand pursuant to [DGCL] §262 falls on a Sunday, the statute calls for strict compliance. Recognizing the General Assembly's appreciation of the issue whether or not to exclude weekend days from limitation periods, the Court noted that the clear language of the statute is the most important factor upon which its interpretation hinges.[24]

No reason appears for treating the timing requirements of §213 less strictly than the timing requirements of §262. The Legislature's command in each instance is clear and unequivocal. Section 213(a) prescribes a maximum period of exactly sixty days that may separate the record date from a stockholder meeting date. Had the Legislature intended a more flexible interpretation of §213(a), it would have so provided with enabling language. The Court, therefore, is obliged to respect the statute's literal terms.

Sixty-one days separated the May 25, 2001 record date from McKesson's July 25, 2001 Annual Meeting. I conclude, therefore, that under §213(a) May 25, 2001 was not a valid record date for McKesson's Annual Meeting.

14. [*Aprahamian*, 531 A.2d] at 1206.
23. 768 A.2d 473 (Del. Ch. 2001).
24. *Id.* at 475 (noting that in contrast to a provision excepting Sundays from the period of time permitted for sending a demand for appraisal under §262, there are many other instances where "the General Assembly has explicitly excluded final Sundays from the calculation of statutory deadlines").

B. Consequences of Non-Compliance

McKesson contends that . . . equitable considerations should lead me nonetheless to declare that the actions taken at the July 25 Annual Meeting are valid. To this end, McKesson offers two related arguments.

First, according to McKesson, an order invalidating the actions taken at the Annual Meeting and requiring another meeting will impose a substantial and unnecessary burden on the Company. Because the group of shareholders on the May 25 record date was the same on May 28 (as a result of the legal holiday), McKesson posits that the results of the votes taken on July 25 would have been the same anyway. To convene another meeting, it contends, would thus be a costly, and useless, exercise.[25]

Second, McKesson insists that its conduct in these circumstances is not inconsistent with the policy reasons underlying the statute. The statute's purpose is to "permit and facilitate reasonable methods of notification" to stockholders eligible to vote in an upcoming shareholder meeting.[26] By establishing that a record date may not be set less than ten days before a shareholder meeting, the Legislature prevents a board from suddenly calling a shareholder meeting with a time horizon that would not permit proper notification of the company's shareholders. On the other hand, the ten-day minimum also "recogniz[es] the 'practical necessity of dispensing with notice to persons who attempt to become registered shareholders shortly before a meeting.'"[27] The sixty-day maximum time period helps to assure that the list of stockholders eligible to vote at a shareholder meeting is not "stale" and represents those who still have a stake in the company. Therefore, by establishing a time period from ten to sixty days prior to a scheduled shareholder meeting during which §213(a) permits a board to set a corresponding record date, "the Legislature has balanced the interest of the corporation and its shareholders — that is, to allow the corporation sufficient time to determine the shareholders in order to give effective notice of corporate action and to assure that the shareholders who vote have an interest in the corporation."[28]

McKesson argues that since its May 25, 2001, record date was followed by non-trading holidays . . . , the composition of the Company's shareholder list did not change before May 26, the last day within the sixty-day time span. The shareholder list existing on May 25, therefore, did not become "stale" and McKesson's shareholders did not suffer harm as a result. Moreover, McKesson asserts that the

---

25. McKesson also seems to suggest that this is not a stew of its own making in which it finds itself. It accuses Derdiger's counsel of delaying notification of the problem until eleven days before the date of the Annual Meeting. If McKesson had had more notice, it could have avoided this dispute by sending a notice to stockholders scheduling the meeting for July 24. The July 24 meeting, which would have been held solely to preserve the May 25 record date, would have been immediately adjourned and reconvened on July 25. *See* [DGCL] §222(c). . . . By waiting until July 17 to make his position known, Derdiger made it too late to send out a notice for a July 24 meeting. *See* [DGCL] §222(b) (written notice of any meeting shall be not less than 10 . . . days before the date of the meeting to each stockholder entitled to vote at such meeting).

Derdiger does not directly address this point, perhaps because McKesson did not formally advance it as an argument. Nevertheless, I need not address it, because it is based on speculation about what McKesson should or might have done in circumstances different from those that the parties have stipulated to in this proceeding, because the parties have not properly advanced it for decision by this Court, and because consideration of that argument would involve a balancing of equities that is not necessary to my final conclusion as to the consequences of McKesson's improperly set record date.

26. *Bryan v. Western Pac. R.R. Corp.*, 35 A.2d 909, 914 (Del. Ch. 1944); *Pabst Brewing Co. v. Jacobs*, 549 F. Supp. 1068, 1072 (D. Del. 1982) (same).

27. *Pabst Brewing*, 549 F. Supp. at 1072 (quoting *Bryan v. Western Pac. R.R. Corp.*, 35 A.2d 909, 914 (Del. Ch. 1944)).

28. *Id.*

"overwhelming" majorities that adopted the uncontroversial actions in question during the July 25 Annual Meeting still exist and would presumably cast the same votes.
McKesson thus urges a "substantial compliance" or "no harm, no foul" approach to
statutory interpretation when a corporate act does no violence to the fundamental
statutory purpose. The most "equitable" outcome, McKesson concludes, is for the
Court to recognize the underlying validity of the actions taken at the July 25 meeting,
even if I find that the record date for the Annual Meeting was not in strict compliance
with §213(a)'s sixty-day maximum.

It is tempting to accept McKesson's invitation to apply a "no harm, no foul" rule in
the unusual circumstances of this case. That is particularly true when McKesson's Board
acted in apparent good faith and in light of assertions by the Company of the uncontroversial nature of the issues voted on at the Annual Meeting, the overwhelming approval of
management's proposals, and the likelihood of a similar result if those actions were
declared void and another vote was required. Relying on equitable principles so as to
modify an explicit statutory requirement, however, is a dangerous path for this Court to
tread because of its "slippery slope" characteristics. It is true that our courts have, on
occasion, invoked principles of equity and fairness to strike down corporate actions even
when those actions technically satisfied every legal requirement. But McKesson has cited
no authority for the reverse of that proposition — that equity properly may be invoked to
rescue a corporate act or decision that violates a statutory command. In fact, this Court
has been cautioned about the over use of its equitable powers.

The drafters of §213 sought to institute an unambiguous guideline for the scheduling of shareholder meetings. Thus, the Legislature adopted a bright-line rule,
requiring that a board, in advance of a shareholder meeting, fix a record date
which "shall not be more than 60 nor less than 10 days before the date of such
meeting."[32] The language is clear and admits of no discretion to depart from its
evident command.

If the Court were to accommodate McKesson's request to rewrite the statute "in
this particular circumstance," it would expose the Court to accusations that it was
engaged in judicial legislation. It would also open the door to similar claims, in which
companies could attempt to rely on exceptional or "equitable" circumstances in order
to cure an action that violates a clear statutory command. Injecting such legal uncertainty into an otherwise unambiguous statutory regime would neither advance the
Legislature's intent nor the stability of the Delaware General Corporation Law. I
cannot, therefore, hold that the actions taken at the Annual Meeting are valid
based on the Company's "equitable" arguments.

There is one aspect of this case, however, that does permit me to hold that the
actions taken at the Annual Meeting are valid. This is the fact that McKesson could,
conceivably, have relied on a decision of this Court for the Company's stated belief
that, by selecting a record date that had sixty days *between* it and the meeting date, it
had complied with the requirements of §213(a). Although the extraordinary diligence
of defendant's counsel has demonstrated that a typographical error could have been

32. The statute does contain a default provision, see [DGCL] §213(a), which applies in those instances
in which "no record date has been fixed." If the board has fixed no record date, the default record date is at
the close of business on the day next preceding the day on which notice of the meeting was given. In this
case, since McKesson mailed notices of the meeting on June 13, Derdiger has argued (in the alternative) that
if McKesson's flawed May 25 record date is treated as "no record date having been fixed," then under
§213(a)'s default provision, the record date was actually June 12 (i.e., the day next preceding the day on
which notice was given). In light of the conclusion I reach in this case, however, I do not need to reach the
defendant's alternative argument on this issue.

responsible for McKesson's erroneous belief, it is not reasonable to require that counsel seek out the trial transcript or other record material to determine whether the Court really meant what was contained in its published opinion. This is even the case when, as the defendant suggests, there was an obvious mistake in a judicial opinion.

If the defendant had been able to cite even one case pertaining to this issue directly contradicting *Aprahamian* that would have placed the plaintiff on notice (either constructively or actually) of the error in that case, then perhaps I would reach the contrary conclusion. In this Opinion, I clarify that the correct method for counting the maximum allowed sixty-day period for setting a record date for a shareholder meeting pursuant to §213(a) is to be conducted as described above. No company should ever be led astray in the future based on any misconception caused by this Court's *Aprahamian* Opinion. Due to the circumstances presented here (which by definition cannot occur again), and in light of the fact that there were no allegations as to any impropriety in connection with the Annual Meeting other than an improper record date, I hold that the actions taken at McKesson's July 25, 2001 Annual Meeting are valid.

Notes and Questions

1. Notes

a. McKesson Corporation's 2001 annual meeting was held on July 25, 2001. Chancellor Chandler's opinion was issued on January 10, 2002.

b. Mr. Derdiger was a shareholder of Access Health, Inc., which, in late September 1998, announced that it had negotiated to be acquired by HBO & Company in a transaction in which Access shareholders would receive HBO stock. Less than one month later, HBO & Company announced that it had negotiated to be acquired by McKesson Corporation in a transaction in which HBO shareholders would receive McKesson stock. These transactions were effected by January 12, 1999.

As Chancellor Chandler described it,

> Between April 28, 1999, and June 21, 1999, [McKesson] made a series of stunning announcements to the financial markets. These announcements indicated that its information technology subsidiary, formerly HBOC, had significantly overstated revenues, net income, earnings per share and other financial information for the three preceding financial years. [McKesson]'s stock price fell precipitously in reaction to this announcement. [McKesson] shareholders experienced paper losses of almost $34 per share, or just over fifty percent, on the day of the first announcement.

Derdiger v. Tallman, 773 A.2d 1005, 1008 (Del. Ch. 2000)

Many shareholders, including Mr. Derdiger, sued, seeking damages for fraud and breach of fiduciary duties.

c. The HBO & Company that was the defendant in *Aprahamian* is the same company that acquired Access Health and that, in turn, was acquired by McKesson. It is possible that the parties in this litigation had access to *Aprahamian* litigation documents that brought to light the typographical error.

d. Four management-sponsored items were on the annual meeting agenda. Electing three directors to three-year terms; approving an amendment to the certificate of incorporation to change the company's name from McKesson HBOC, Inc., to McKesson Corporation; ratifying the appointment of the independent auditors; and amending the compensation plan for the outside directors.

The voting was closest on the proposal to amend the compensation plan for outside directors. That proposal passed by a vote of 192,692,929 votes in favor; 63,888,328 votes against; and 2,414,293 votes abstaining. In percentages, the proposal passed with slightly over 74 percent of the votes.

The three shareholder-proposed items were also on the agenda. One dealt with performance-based options, another with severance payments, and the third with the sale of the company. The voting was closest on a proposal regarding stock options. The proposal was defeated by a vote of 55,711,172 in favor; 139,667,310 against; and 13,224,895 abstaining. That is, the proposal received less than 27 percent of the votes cast.

2. Reality Check

a. Why was the record date impermissible?

b. If the record date was impermissible, why doesn't Chancellor Chandler order a new meeting?

c. Could McKesson have remedied the problem at some point between June 13 (the date it mailed notice to its shareholders) and the meeting? If so, how?

d. What equitable arguments did McKesson make and why did Chancellor Chandler reject them?

3. Suppose

a. Suppose the stock markets had been open on Memorial Day. Would the court's analysis or the result have been different?

b. For the McKesson Corporation 2002 annual meeting, the board set a record date of June 3, 2002; sent notice to shareholders on June 14, 2002; and held the meeting on July 31, 2002. Given the July 31 meeting, what are the earliest and latest possible record dates and notice dates under the DGCL?

c. If Chancellor Chandler had chosen to use the default rule in the DGCL for instances in which the board does not set a record date, what date would have been used? See footnote 32.

4. What Do You Think?

a. Is there any evidence that McKesson actually relied on the legal interpretation of *Aprahamian* that it asserts as precedent? If so, what is it? If not, should the court predicate its decision on such reliance?

b. Why might McKesson have set the record date as it did? How could this problem have happened? How could the problem have been avoided?

c. Why do you think Mr. Derdiger brought this lawsuit? What do you think he intended to accomplish?

iii. Quorum. The third element for a valid meeting is the presence of a quorum. A *quorum* is simply the minimum amount of voting power that must be present at a meeting for actions to be valid. The requirement of a quorum is to prevent a collective body from acting when so few members are present that the action may be thought to be unrepresentative of the whole body's intent. A quorum for shareholder meetings is defined by the percentage of *voting power* represented at the meeting, not by the percentage of *shareholders* present.

Under both the Delaware statute and the Model Act, the default rule is that a quorum for shareholder meetings is a majority of the voting power. That number may be raised under either statute. In Delaware, the quorum may not be lowered below one-third of the total voting power. See DGCL §216 and MBCA §7.25.

One strategic difference between a quorum for board meetings and a quorum for shareholder meetings is that a shareholder quorum once established is valid for the remainder of the meeting. This means that dissident shareholders cannot prevent unfavorable action by leaving the meeting and breaking the quorum. Strategically, they must decide in advance of the meeting whether adverse action is likely to be taken and decide whether to stay away in hopes that a quorum will not be present. It is typical practice for the chair of a shareholder meeting to declare the presence of a quorum as the very first item of business because, until such a declaration is made, shareholders can leave and possibly stymie any further action. See MBCA §7.25(b) (Delaware has a similar rule via case law).

iv. Sufficient Vote. The final requirement for valid shareholder action is a sufficient vote. The default rule in Delaware is that a matter is approved if it receives a majority of the votes present at the meeting. See DGCL §216(2). The MBCA default rule is slightly different: a matter is approved if it receives a *simple majority*. That is, if the "yes" votes are greater than the "no" votes regardless of how few votes are cast. See MBCA §7.25(c). Under the Delaware approach, an abstention has the effect of a "no" vote, while under the MBCA an abstention is a true abstention (i.e., a refraining from participation in the particular vote).

Here is an example of the two approaches. Assume a corporation has 1,000 shares outstanding, each of which has one vote per share. A shareholder meeting is properly called and noticed. The holders of 800 shares attend the meeting, meaning that a quorum (more than 500 shares) is present. A particular matter is put to a shareholder vote and the result is 375 yes, 370 no, and 55 abstain or not voted. Does the matter pass? It passes under the MBCA (because there were more "yes" votes than "no" votes) but fails under the DGCL (because fewer than half the 800 shares present voted yes). Indeed, under the MBCA the matter would have been adopted had the vote been 1 yes, 0 no, 799 abstain or not voted!

The DGCL, and the laws of most states (but not the MBCA), require a higher quantum of shareholder voting power for approval of fundamental changes such as amending the articles, mergers, dissolution, and selling all or substantially all of the corporation's assets, because such changes are, well, fundamental. See, e.g., DGCL §§251, 271. The DGCL requires approval of such actions by an *absolute majority*, which means a majority of all the voting power, regardless of whether that power is present at the meeting. Thus, shares that are not present at the meeting are effectively "no" votes.

Finally, under both the DGCL and the MBCA, yet another definition of sufficient vote applies to electing and removing directors, because electing directors is seen as so central to healthy corporate operations. Directors are elected by a *plurality* of votes, meaning the candidates with the most votes are elected, regardless of how few votes are cast, as long as a quorum is present. See DGCL §216(3) and MBCA §7.28(a). The reason for this rule is to ensure that directors can be elected if a quorum exists. Directors do not run for particular slots but instead are elected at large.[2] The combination of the plurality rule and at-large qualities of director elections means that ties

---

2. Remember, though, that some boards are classified and in those circumstances directors run for election as representing a particular class or classes of stock.

among candidates are not necessarily a hindrance to selecting a board. For example, assume a board of five directors and assume that the following candidates receive the following votes:

Candidate	Votes
A	350
B	350
C	300
D	200
E	200
F	150
G	150

In this instance A, B, C, D, and E are all elected, because they are the five candidates with the most votes. Sometimes, however, ties become important. Suppose the same board and candidates but a vote distribution like this:

Candidate	Votes
A	350
B	350
C	300
D	250
E	200
F	200
G	50

Now, A, B, C, and D are elected but E and F are tied for the final slot. Case law supports the view that no one has been elected to the fifth slot, which means that the current incumbent remains in office because the statutes provide that a director remains in office until his or her successor has been elected. See DGCL §141(b) and MBCA §8.05(e). Such a director is called a *holdover*. If no incumbent is in the fifth slot then a vacancy exists, which can be filled by the newly elected board, in Delaware, and by either the newly elected board or the shareholders under the MBCA. See DGCL §223(a)(1) and MBCA §8.10(a).

In some corporations, both public and private, directors are elected by cumulative voting. This method is designed to allow a minority of shareholders to be certain of electing at least one director on a board. Although cumulative voting exists in some public corporations, it is primarily useful in the close corporation setting. For that reason, a more detailed discussion of cumulative voting is set out in the next chapter.

v. The Importance of Being Present. Presence is an important concept in quorum and sufficient vote contexts. A certain percentage of the shareholder voting power must be present to constitute a quorum and the validity of many shareholder votes is measured, in Delaware and other states, by the amount of shareholder voting power present. Under both the DGCL and the MBCA the refreshingly intuitive rule is that shares are present when their owner is physically in attendance at the meeting. See DGCL §216(2), MBCA §§7.21(a), 7.22(1).

Shares can be present in two other ways. The first is through a proxy. See DGCL §212(b), MBCA §7.22(a). A *proxy* is an agency relationship in which a shareholder appoints another person to attend a shareholders meeting on the shareholder's behalf and to vote the shareholder's shares. The word *proxy* itself is used to describe the relationship, the agent (who may also be called the *proxyholder*), or the writing (if any) in which the agency relationship is created and defined. The context should make clear which of these uses is intended. A proxy may be *limited*, in which the shareholder authorizes the agent to vote in a particular way, or *general*, in which the agent is authorized to use his or her discretion in voting. The common law, embodied in nearly every state in the principles expressed in the *Restatement (Third) of Agency*, governs proxies as a typical agency relationship.

The corporations statutes, especially the MBCA, make a few changes to the common law rules. A proxy relationship may be created only by a writing or electronic transmission. See MBCA §7.22(b) The DGCL explicitly leaves the common law rules in place, although it gives safe harbors of the ways in which a proxy can be created. See DGCL §212(c). Both the MBCA and DGCL provide that a proxy is irrevocable if it explicitly states that intention and if it is coupled with an interest. See DGCL §212(e), MBCA §7.22(d). You may recall from Chapter 4 that the term "coupled with an interest" is a rather murky term of art in agency law. The MBCA gives some examples of an interest sufficient to support irrevocability, but the DGCL simply references the common law. See DGCL §212(e), and MBCA §7.22(d). The MBCA provides that the principal's (i.e., shareholder's) death does not invalidate the proxy in the absence of actual knowledge by the corporation. See MBCA §7.22(e); the DGCL is silent in this regard. Both statutes provide a default period for a proxy's validity. The MBCA provides 11 months and the DGCL provides 3 years. See DGCL §212(b), MBCA §7.22(c). Why did the drafters choose these rather odd time periods?

The second way shares can be present without their owner being physically at the meeting is through a virtual presence. In Delaware and many other states (though not, as yet, under the MBCA), shares are present if their owner (or a proxyholder) may participate in the shareholder meeting through an electronic medium in which they may read or hear the proceedings in real-time and in which they have the opportunity to participate themselves. See DGCL §211(a)(2)(b). Certainly a conference telephone call meets the requirements and many kinds of computer linkages may, as well.

b. Background and Context — The Annual Meeting of the Public Corporation

As you might imagine, the logistics of holding a meeting of shareholders in a public company are frequently quite intricate and planning for such a meeting is very elaborate. This section describes a typical public company meeting.

Planning for the meeting usually begins a year or more in advance. Many public companies like to hold their annual meeting in a different location every year, sometimes to provide the opportunity for shareholders who live in disparate parts of the country to attend more easily, and sometimes to make attendance more difficult. The planners, who may be corporate employees or may be an independent firm retained to plan the meeting, must find and rent a venue that will accommodate the anticipated number of shareholders, which may range from a few dozen to several hundred. Because most public companies use a calendar fiscal year, that is, one that ends on

December 31st, they schedule their annual meeting in the following spring. Probably 80 percent or more of public company annual meetings are held between February 15th and May 15th.

Once the date and place have been established, counsel can work backward to determine the range of dates within which notice must be sent and the range of consequently permissible record dates. Note that the corporation's bylaws (and, less frequently, the Articles) may contain provisions about the setting of the annual meeting or notice or record dates that, obviously, must be adhered to. The New York Stock Exchange suggests that corporations select a record date that is at least 30 days before the meeting date to ensure enough time for shareholders to receive and return their voting materials. Corporations usually plan to send notices to shareholders within a few days of the record date to minimize the number of notice recipients who have sold their shares.

Although the corporate statutes require only that directors be elected, at public company annual meetings at least one other item is typically included on the agenda: approval of the accounting firm that will serve as the company's independent auditor. The board of directors may have other items to bring before the shareholders, frequently approval of stock option plans for senior executives. See, e.g., *NYSE Listed Company Manual* §§303A.08, 312.03.

Further, shareholders may propose items for shareholder action. Many public corporations have an *advance notice bylaw* that requires a shareholder to give the board notice of his or her intention to move a proposal or nominate directors at the meeting. Such advance notice bylaws may require notice to the corporation's management months in advance of the meeting. Clearly the intent of such a bylaw is to thwart precipitous shareholder unrest and to provide management with information about shareholder dissent so that management can react. As a practical matter, a shareholder proposal first presented on the floor of the meeting would have little chance of passage because the vast majority of shares are present by proxy and the proxyholders either do not have the power to vote on unscheduled matters or, if they do have the power, tend to vote against such proposals.

The meeting itself may be a festive, welcoming celebration of the corporation and its achievements or a barebones, no nonsense, formality lasting fifteen minutes. Corporations that are financially successful tend to have the more elaborate meetings, while those corporations with dismal recent performance or callous management may prefer to sponsor more austere meetings. If the corporation manufactures consumer goods they may provide samples to shareholders who attend the meeting. Sometimes light refreshments, or even a real breakfast or lunch, is provided.

Only those who were record or beneficial shareholders on the record date and their proxyholders have a right to attend the annual meeting but in practice members of the press may be invited and others are usually permitted to attend. Often the chair of the board of directors or the company's chief executive officer will preside over the meeting. In any event, it is typical for such people to make presentations even if someone else presides. Usually all board members attend if possible, and at least some (frequently all) senior managers attend, as well. These people are seated on the stage and are available to answer questions from the audience, although in practice the presiding officer answers all questions. A lawyer is always seated next to the presiding officer to give immediate advice on the conduct of the meeting if necessary. That lawyer may be an employee of the corporation or someone from an independent law firm.

It may surprise you to learn that very few companies have explicit rules governing the conduct of the annual meeting. As you know, the DGCL simply requires a meeting and does not provide any conduct rules or guidelines. Likewise the articles are usually silent on the question. The bylaws sometimes name the person who is to preside over the meeting but, again, they do not usually contain any detailed provisions for running the meeting.

By now you may be assuming that *Roberts' Rules of Order* is typically used as a guide. Nope. *Roberts'* is designed for collective bodies that deliberate as well as approve actions. Because such a large proportion of shares are represented by limited proxies, no deliberation is possible. Further, as you recall, corporate law permits the shareholders to vote on only a few matters, and the consequences of those questions are often relatively circumscribed such that deliberation would be unproductive. Case law simply requires that annual meetings satisfy basic notions of "fairness." The MBCA provides that the bylaws or board shall appoint a chair of the meeting and that the chair may adopt "fair" rules for the conduct of the meeting. See MBCA §7.08.

Meetings usually begin with a declaration that a quorum is present. Often the next order of business is the opening and closing of the polls. Ushers hand out ballots to those record shareholders who wish to vote in person, though a miniscule percentage of shares is voted in this fashion. After those ballots are collected, the polls are closed and no more votes can be accepted. Then the presiding officer may introduce other senior people who may make presentations, or there may simply be a video presentation on the state of the company.

At some point, generally after the polls have been closed, the shareholders are given an opportunity to question management. The meeting may take anywhere from half an hour to two hours or so, at the end of which the presiding officer declares the meeting adjourned.

3. How Shareholders Take Action by Consent in Lieu of a Meeting

Just as directors may act without holding an actual meeting, so shareholders may act. The DGCL, but not the MBCA, permits consents to be obtained and submitted to the corporation electronically. See DGCL §§228(d), 232(c). Under the MBCA, shareholder action without a meeting must be unanimous, which obviously limits such provisions to closely held corporations where the shareholders are of a single mind. See MBCA §7.04. Where the shareholders and the board are at odds, this shareholder power can become important because it permits the shareholders to amote the recalcitrant directors even where the board refuses to call a shareholder meeting.

Under the DGCL, shareholders may take action even if they are not unanimous. See DGCL §228. Thus this power, which can only be abridged by a provision in the Certificate of Incorporation, can be a useful tool in both the public and private company settings. If the consent action is proposed by the corporation's board, their resolution to seek consents is, in effect, the call. Where shareholders intend to act without board approval (most often attempting to act without the board's knowledge), the call is just the leaders of the shareholder group beginning to solicit consent.

If the board is soliciting consents it may send a request to every shareholder, which serves as notice that a consent solicitation is taking place. Insurgent shareholders, by contrast, usually do not solicit every shareholder but only those whom the leaders believe will be sympathetic to their cause. Under DGCL §228(e), however, if the consent solicitation is successful, the corporation must give "prompt" notice to all shareholders who would be entitled to vote that the shareholder action has been taken by consent.

Because no actual meeting takes place, the concepts of quorum and sufficient vote collapse into one. The proponents must obtain consents from shareholders holding an absolute majority of voting shares. For shareholder actions requiring a supermajority vote, the consents required are increased accordingly. See DGCL §228(a). Many Delaware public corporations have bylaws that require shareholders to notify the board if they intend to take action by consent and to permit the board to set a record date if it chooses. Obviously, the intent of such a bylaw is to defeat the element of surprise. In corporations without such a bylaw, the record date for consent solicitations is the date the first consent is delivered to the corporation. See DGCL §213(b).

Conceptually, a consent is unlike a proxy in that a consent is the equivalent of a vote, while a proxy is an authorization to someone else to vote in the future. In Delaware, it is unclear whether a consent can be revoked once it is delivered to the corporation and it may be unclear whether a consent can be revoked before delivery. The MBCA provides that a consent is revocable until such time as consents from all shareholders are delivered. See MBCA §7.04(b). To prevent consent solicitations from taking an inordinate amount of time, and thus presenting the danger that some consenting shareholders have changed their minds, both statutes provide that all valid consents must be delivered no later than 60 days after the date of the earliest dated delivered consent. See DGCL §228(c), MBCA §7.04(b).

4. Tabulating the Votes

The process of counting votes is purely mechanical in many senses but also presents situations when a lawyer's skills are vital. The outline of the basic process is the same regardless of whether the corporation is closely held or publicly held, but in the public corporation the process becomes more elaborate. This section is divided into two complementary questions. First, we look at who may vote. That is, which humans may cast votes in corporate elections. Second, we will look at the process of counting the votes with special emphasis on the process in the public corporation.

a. Whose Vote Counts?

One guiding principle of shareholder voting has been that elections must be concluded rapidly because uncertainty in determining the directors or whether a question put to the shareholders has been approved are extraordinarily detrimental to corporate welfare. Accordingly, the statutory requirements and presumptions have been adopted with the goal of swift resolution of corporate elections. In a similar policy choice, judicial review for corporate elections is available in summary form. See DGCL §225.

The key statutory provision that effects this bright-line ethos for elections provides that only shareholders of record may cast votes.[3] See DGCL §219(c) and MBCA §§7.07[4] and 7.21. This provision heightens the importance of the record date shareholder list, which must be prepared rapidly after the record date and must be made available to shareholders until the meeting is adjourned. See DGCL §219 and MBCA §7.20.

The upshot is that the corporation must be able to trace a ballot or proxy to the record holder. If the shareholder of record is a single individual, his or her signed ballot or proxy is sufficient. The corporation need not verify that the person signing is actually the shareholder of record, unless the corporation has some information suggesting that the person is not the shareholder of record. The voting process can, however, quickly get more complicated when the name signed on the ballot or proxy is not that of the sole individual shareholder of record.

First, the shares might be held of record by more than one individual, such as a married couple, domestic partners, siblings, or simply joint owners. Second, the shares might be held of record by an entity such as another corporation, a partnership, or an LLC. In this setting the question becomes who can act for the record holder? Third, someone might assert the power to vote or give a proxy because the record holder is legally unable to do so. Examples are the trustee of a record shareholder (individual or entity) in bankruptcy, the executor or administrator of a deceased record shareholder, or the guardian of a minor or incompetent record shareholder. Note that this setting might be compounded where the record shareholder has co-executors or co-guardians. The DGCL has bright-line provisions covering these situations. See DGCL §217. The MBCA has adopted a similar provision but gives the corporation the power to accept or reject such votes or proxies in good faith. See MBCA §7.24.

These issues arise and may be quite important in closely held corporations, but the nature of shareholdings in public companies makes these problems chronic. First, the vast majority of public company shares are voted by proxy rather than in person. This is because public company shareholders are widely dispersed, because most have diversified investments and so have a small percentage of their wealth invested in one company, and their ownership percentage of a public company is ordinarily miniscule. Usually 98 or 99 percent of the shares voted at a public company's shareholder meeting are voted by proxy.[5]

Second, in public companies very few shareholders of record are also beneficial holders. This is the result of the way in which shares are traded in the public securities markets. Hundreds of millions of shares are traded every day and the great proportion of trades are *settled* (i.e., the seller gets the money and the buyer gets the shares) three business days after the day on which the trade was made. Most transactions involve a

---

3. The MBCA contains a provision allowing the corporation to adopt, in advance, a policy of recognizing beneficial holders, but few companies take advantage of this method. See MBCA §7.23.

4. The MBCA contains one of the most curiously formalistic provisions in modern corporation law. It provides that, "Only shares are entitled to vote." See MBCA §7.21(a). Fortunately, we do not have to dwell on this provision in any detail as section 7.07 obliquely obviates the import of section 7.21 by providing that "The bylaws may fix or provide the manner of fixing the record date . . . in order to determine the shareholders entitled to . . . vote. . . . If the bylaws do not fix or provide for fixing a record date, the board of directors of the corporation may fix a future date as the record date." MBCA §7.07(a).

5. Be careful to understand that this statement does not mean that 98 or 99 percent of the shares entitled to vote are represented at the meeting. In fact, unless a battle for control or some other controversial matter is being voted upon, upwards of 30 percent of the outstanding voting shares may not be represented. On occasion, the turnout is so low that corporate employees solicit large shareholders to ensure their presence to avoid the embarrassment of a lack of a quorum.

broker for the buyer and a broker for the seller and the official transaction is recorded as being between the two brokers rather than between the ultimate buyer and ultimate seller. Although in theory every trade could be settled separately, it would be impractical to do so. Instead, at the end of each trading day a central clearinghouse nets every brokerage firm's trades made with every other brokerage firm.

Transferring money between brokerage firms is easy, but transferring shares of stock is more difficult. If all shares were held of record by the beneficial holder, the selling shareholder would have to endorse the stock certificate (much as one endorses a check) deliver it to his or her brokerage firm, which would have to forward it to the corporation's *transfer agent* (i.e., the agent in charge of reissuing shares from sellers to buyers and noting such transfers on the shareholder list[6]), which would have to cancel the seller's certificate, reissue the shares in the name of the ultimate purchaser, and deliver that new certificate to the buyer's brokerage house so that it could be given to the new owner.

At the same time, the buyer's brokerage house would collect the purchase price from its customer and forward those funds to the seller's brokerage house to be delivered to the seller when the new share certificate was ready to be delivered to the buyer. All this would have to be completed by the third day after the trade. Even if this process could realistically be accomplished, it would be more than a tad Sisyphean because the next day more trades would take place, often involving the same ultimate buyers and sellers and stock in the same companies.

One way to simplify the system would be to have shareholders agree to allow their brokerage firms to be the record owner while the ultimate shareholder became a beneficial owner only. Then, the number of share transfers would be greatly reduced because the brokerage firm would aggregate the shares in each company its customers owned into one certificate per company. Each customer would simply receive a statement each month showing how many shares of each company he or she owned, the shares of which were being held of record by the brokerage house. In fact, this is partially a solution. Most individual beneficial shareholders do not receive stock certificates when they purchase shares. They simply become beneficial holders who have left their shares in *street name*, as this practice is called.[7] This solution would still be too cumbersome because nearly every stock certificate held by nearly every brokerage house would have to be reregistered every day to reflect the changes in the brokerage house's customers' accounts.

The real solution involved the creation of an entity, the Depository Trust Company (*DTC*), that acts simply as a custodian of shares. Each brokerage house has an account at DTC in which it deposits all the shares of all the corporations it holds for its customers. Thenceforth DTC simply debits and credits the account of each of its participating brokerage house customers (note that DTC does *not* have accounts for the brokerage houses' customers) with the net number of shares of each corporation owed or owing to other brokerage houses at the end of each trading day. The actual shares do not need to be transferred except when an ultimate beneficiary wishes to become a holder of record and so must obtain a share certificate. This *book entry system*, as it is known, has greatly reduced the administrative problems with trading in the public securities markets.

6. Most public companies retain a specialized subsidiary of a bank or trust company to act as transfer agent.

7. The "street" in question meaning Wall Street.

Now for the *coup de grâce*. It turns out that DTC is not the shareholder of record, either. To facilitate transfers when share certificates do need to be surrendered and reissued, DTC has established a partnership, *Cede & Co.*, to hold the shares. To sum up, most investors have accounts with brokerage houses, which in turn have accounts with DTC, which controls Cede & Co., which is the shareholder of record.

Now let's look at the consequence of this elaborate yet largely invisible system of share ownership for shareholder voting. If the beneficial owner is also the shareholder of record, he or she either can attend the shareholder meeting and vote in person (few public companies have made provision for their shareholders to vote in real time either online or by conference call) or the shareholder can vote by proxy.

As you remember, the vast majority of shares voted are voted by proxy. Public companies usually provide three methods for shareholders of record to grant a proxy. First is the traditional written proxy, which is usually a card sent by the management to each shareholder of record along with a letter asking the shareholder to fill out the card and date, sign, and return it to management (typically a committee of three trusted company employees acts as the proxyholders). Second, nearly all public companies provide a toll-free telephone number that the shareholder can call and, by using a menu of options and a unique PIN sent along with the proxy request, authorize a proxy. Finally, nearly all public companies provide a Web site at which the shareholder may also authorize a proxy, again using a unique PIN. As the proxies are received by the committee, they are submitted to the corporation and the committee of proxy holders thus votes the shares.

If the shares are held in street name the process is different. Because Cede & Co. is the record holder, the corporation holding the meeting (let's call it XYZ Corp.) must be able to trace all proxies to Cede & Co. After the record date for the XYZ Corp. shareholder meeting, Cede & Co. sends a general proxy to each brokerage house covering the number of XYZ Corp. shares that brokerage house owned on the record date. Each brokerage house then sends a request for instructions to each customer account that beneficially owns XYZ Corp. shares on the record date.[8] The customers' responses to that request are tallied and the brokerage house executes a limited proxy (usually written or via the Internet) instructing the XYZ Corp. proxy committee to vote.

Note that the brokerage house's proxy will doubtless instruct the XYZ Corp. proxy committee to vote some shares in favor and some shares against every matter presented at the meeting because its customers (the ultimate beneficial holders) will vote in different ways. On occasion, the beneficial holder wants to vote in person at the shareholder meeting. In such instances the beneficial holder must request the brokerage firm to execute a general proxy to the beneficial holder.

b. Who Counts the Votes?

In privately held corporations the votes are probably counted by senior managers or perhaps by the shareholder meeting's chair in front of the assembled shareholders. Proxies are not usually a serious problem because most shares are probably cast in person, and those that are cast by proxy typically involve only a simple written proxy

---

8. These requests for instruction look very much like the request for proxies that XYZ Corp. sends to its shareholders of record. Many ultimate beneficial holders assume that they are casting votes or giving a proxy when they return these requests for instructions but, as you now see, they are actually directing their brokerage firm to instruct the XYZ Corp. proxy committee to vote in a particular way.

from the shareholder of record to an agent. Even where the shareholders are bitterly divided, the process of counting the votes is still straightforward.

By contrast, counting the votes for a public company shareholder meeting is much more complicated, even where none of the matters to be voted upon is contested. Fortunately, both statutory provisions and accepted practice in public corporations makes this process at least somewhat more orderly than it might otherwise be. First off, the DGCL and MBCA require public companies to appoint inspectors of election. These inspectors are charged with performing four tasks:

1. Determining the number of shares outstanding and the voting power each share possesses;
2. Determining how many shares are "present" at the meeting;
3. Determining the validity of all proxies and ballots; and
4. Counting the vote.

See DGCL §231(b) and MBCA §7.29(a).

Under the MBCA the inspectors also determine the result of each matter submitted to the shareholders. Under the DGCL the inspectors do not take this step, presumably leaving the task of actually declaring the result to the chair of the meeting. Compare DGCL §231(b)(5) with MBCA §7.29(a)(5).

Complicating the inspectors' job are the following:

1. Public companies have thousands of record holders and five to ten times as many beneficial holders.[9] For example, H-P Corporation, a large U.S. company, had 121,000 shareholders of record and about 900,000 beneficial owners. Wal-Mart Stores, Inc., among the largest U.S. companies, has over 300,000 shareholders of record.
2. Probably 98 percent or more of the shares present will be present by proxy. The validity of a proxy is usually harder to ascertain than is the presence of a record shareholder.
3. Perhaps 80 percent of the outstanding shares are held in street name, which means that proxies for those shares are submitted through the multilevel system of Cede & Co., brokerage house, beneficial holder, which further complicates the job of ascertaining a proxy's validity.
4. Many brokerage houses submit multiple proxies, often on a daily basis, as the meeting date approaches, to reflect instructions from their customers. These multiple proxies may be cumulative (i.e., restating the votes from the prior proxy) or partial (i.e., simply reflecting the newly received instructions). Inspectors of elections must ascertain which type of proxy each brokerage house is submitting and must guard against the brokerage house inadvertently executing proxies for more shares than it is entitled to vote (a situation called a *broker overvote*). The DGCL, but not the MBCA, specifically permits the inspectors to go beyond the material submitted to them to resolve broker overvotes. See DGCL §231(d).

---

9. Note that the number of outstanding *shares* doesn't really complicate the public company voting process, but the number of share*holders* certainly does. To see this more clearly, imagine a privately held company with only two stockholders. Each of them might own millions of shares, but the voting and counting process is simple because in the end there will only be two ballots and, at most, two proxies.

Where a matter is contested, as in a takeover or other proxy fight setting, the pressures increase. Small wonder that the great majority of public companies retain a single independent firm to act as inspector of elections. That firm has experienced inspectors who not only know the process but, equally importantly, know the habits and practices of the various brokerage houses that will be submitting proxies.

In outline, the counting process is the same regardless of whether the election is routine or contested. Because of the paper-intensive nature of shareholder voting, much of the tabulation is done by hand. First the ballots and proxies are put in alphabetical order to match the shareholder list as of the record date. Ballots and proxies submitted by those whose name does not appear on the shareholder list are removed and the votes are not counted. Ballots and proxies that, on their face, are submitted by or on behalf of shareholders of record are counted if they are not overvotes. Ballots and proxies that represent overvotes or other problems are culled out and separately investigated in a process known as the "snake pit." Common problems in addition to overvotes are illegible signatures, variations between the signature and the record name, and multiple proxies or ballots purporting to vote the same shares.

In the last setting, where shares are "voted" by more than one proxy or ballot, the law of agency provides that the last act of the principal (i.e., the ultimate owner of the shares) controls over earlier acts. So, only the last-dated ballot or proxy is counted. Where multiple proxies are of even date, the last transmitted (determined by postmark or electronic transmission) controls. In the end, some of these problems cannot be resolved. In those settings the shares are effectively disenfranchised and the votes not counted because the inspectors cannot determine with sufficient certainty the intention of the ultimate owner.

B. SHAREHOLDERS' RIGHTS TO INFORMATION

1. Periodic and Transaction Reporting

Shareholders are provided information by their corporation, without the shareholders having to take any action, in two settings. *Transaction reporting* means information sent by the corporation with respect to a contemplated transaction, usually one the shareholders will vote upon. *Periodic reporting* is information provided at specific intervals, such as annually or quarterly, regardless of whether the corporation is anticipating a transaction. In Delaware, shareholders need not be provided with any periodic reporting. However, each Delaware corporation must file an annual franchise tax report by March 1st which contains very basic information about the company but does not contain any report of the corporation's finances or operations. These reports are available online from the Delaware secretary of state's Web site. See DGCL §502. Delaware corporations need not provide shareholders with any transaction reporting but Delaware case law requires that the corporation provide shareholders with all material information before a shareholder vote. Corporate management must provide this information to all shareholders if the management is requesting that shareholders vote by proxy. However, if the management is not soliciting proxies, the information can be presented orally at the meeting prior to the shareholder vote and need not be sent to absent shareholders. See *Malone v. Brincat*, 722 A.2d 5 (Del. 1998).

The MBCA requires periodic but not transaction reporting. Under the MBCA, every corporation must send annual financial statements to each shareholder. See MBCA §16.20. Nonetheless, many states add additional reporting requirements either by statute or through case law.

Shareholders in public companies must receive *periodic reports* on the financial and operational condition of the company at least four times each year under the federal securities laws. Public corporations also make detailed public reports when they seek to raise more money from the public. This kind of *transaction reporting* is not required to be sent to existing shareholders but detailed information about the company and the securities to be sold is given to prospective purchasers. Both periodic and transaction reports are filed with the SEC and are available to the public on the commission's Web site. Many public companies also make such reports available on their own Web sites.

2. Inspection Right

a. Background and Context

Shareholders have another avenue for obtaining information about their corporation. They may examine certain corporate documents in certain circumstances. The following excerpt describes the origin and development of the shareholder inspection right in Delaware.

> It is well established that, as a matter of common law, a stockholder of a Delaware corporation possessed a qualified right to inspect or examine the stock ledger, as well as the books and records of the corporation. The stockholder's common law right of inspection may not be divested except by statutory enactment. At common law, the right of inspection was enforceable only through the issuance of a writ of mandamus from the Superior Court compelling the corporation to permit inspection by the stockholder. *State ex rel. Richardson v. Swift*, 30 A. 781, 781-82 (Del. Super. 1885) ("*Swift I*"), aff'd, *Swift v. State ex rel Richardson*, 6 A. 856 (Del. Ct. Err. & App. 1886) ("*Swift II*").
>
> For a writ of mandamus to issue, "[t]he right which it is sought to protect must [ ] be clearly established." *Swift II*, 6 A. at 861. The stockholder was therefore required to make specific factual averments in the petition to show clearly that he or she was entitled to the relief (inspection) sought.
>
> [T]he stockholder demanding inspection had to show that the inspection was for "proper purposes." Although hardly self-defining, a proper purpose was viewed under the common law as a purpose relating to the *interest* that the stockholder sought to protect by seeking inspection.
>
> In other words, the propriety of a demanding stockholder's purpose was measured by whether it related to the stockholder's interest *qua* stockholder, that is, a proper purpose in seeking inspection was viewed as a purpose germane to the petitioner's interest or status as a stockholder.
>
> In short, a stockholder's right to inspection is status-related. In this regard, inspection rights have been viewed as an incident to the stockholder's ownership of corporate property. As an equitable owner of the corporation's assets, a stockholder possessed a right to reasonable information concerning the conduct of corporate management, as well as the condition of the corporation's business and affairs. As a matter of self-protection, the stockholder was entitled to know how his agents were conducting the affairs of the corporation of which he or she was a part owner.

In addition to the common law right of inspection, the right has been codified in some form in Delaware since the turn of the [twentieth] century. The original statutory enactment eliminated the formalistic pleading requirements of the extraordinary writ of mandamus by giving the stockholder a "positive right" to inspection of corporate books and records. Nevertheless, if the corporation could show that the petitioner sought inspection for an improper purpose, the court had the discretion to deny the stockholder access to the corporation's books and records.

With its enactment of Section 220 in 1967, the General Assembly sought to replace the formalized and burdensome mandamus procedure in the Superior Court with a summary procedure in the Court of Chancery by which a stockholder who has demonstrated a purpose reasonably related to his or her interest as such may gain swift access to the corporate books and records.

Shaw v. Agri-Mark, Inc., 663 A.2d 464, 466-468 (Del. 1995) (Walsh, J.)

b. The Current Setting

Under both the DGCL and the MBCA, shareholders have the right to examine some corporate documents. This right is called the shareholder *inspection right*. The shareholder bears nearly the entire cost of obtaining corporate information, while the corporation bears the cost of periodic and transaction reporting. For many shareholders inspection rights are largely of theoretic value for one of two reasons. First, the shareholder's stock might not be of sufficient value to justify spending the time and money to exercise the right of inspection. Second, even if the shareholder's stake is large enough to justify inspecting corporate records the shareholder's overall wealth might be diversified (spread over a number of unrelated stocks or other assets) so that any gain from inspecting a particular corporation's documents would not contribute a meaningful amount to the shareholder's total investment return. For some shareholders, whether economically rational actors or not, the inspection right may be a realistic avenue to obtain information the shareholder considers valuable.

The legal questions surrounding shareholder inspection rights fall into two categories. First, what information does a shareholder have a right to inspect simply by virtue of being a shareholder? Second, what information does a shareholder have a right to inspect if the shareholder makes an additional showing of some sort? The first category of questions is answered principally by reference to the statutes. The second category generates considerable litigation. Suffusing both categories is the question of whether a shareholder who may inspect a record may also copy it.

Both the DGCL and the MBCA provide shareholders at least some information simply by virtue of shareholder status. Any shareholder may inspect the list of record date shareholders before the shareholder meeting. This allows a shareholder to determine who else may vote and how many shares each other shareholder owns. Under the DGCL, any shareholder also has the right to inspect any voting trust agreements. The MBCA allows any shareholder to inspect (and copy) the basic constitutive documents (articles and bylaws), list of current officers and directors, the current annual report filed with the secretary of state, and other similar basic information simply by virtue of being a shareholder. See DGCL §§218(a), 219(a); MBCA §§7.20, 16.01(e), 16.02(a).

Other corporate information may be inspected or copied (and the record shareholder list and, in Delaware, a voting trust agreement, may be copied) only if the shareholder makes additional showings. Under both statutes the test is whether the shareholder has a "*proper purpose.*" Delaware puts the burden of showing a proper purpose on the corporation for demands to inspect a shareholder list and on the shareholder for other demands. See DGCL §220(b) and MBCA §16.02(c)(1). The DGCL defines a proper purpose as "a purpose reasonably related to such person's interest as a stockholder"; the MBCA does not define "proper purpose." DGCL §220(b).

The New Mexico Supreme Court has described the contours of "proper purpose":

> Shareholder access to corporate information should be limited to information reasonably related to the legitimate interests of the shareholder. A proper purpose is not harmful to the corporation or its shareholders. A proper purpose can be surmised where the shareholder's purpose in requesting the information bears some reasonable relationship to the interest that the shareholder wants to protect by seeking inspection. Generally, shareholders are entitled to full information as to the management of the corporation and the manner of expenditure of its funds, and to inspection in order to obtain information. A proper purpose can include a desire to place a monetary value on stock interests and to evaluate the conduct of officers and directors. Suitable subject matter for proper shareholder oversight also extends to efforts by the shareholder to determine the value of his stock and to determine the financial condition of the corporation. The propriety of such access is premised primarily on the rationale that a stockholder has the right to know corporate information that might affect his losses or gains, affecting the shareholder's ability to protect himself. In addition, such access allows for discovery and deterrence of abuses by corporate directors and officers.

Schein v. Northern Rio Arriba Electric Cooperative, Inc., 932 P.2d 490, 493-494 (N.M. 1997) (Baca, J.)

Suppose a shareholder believes that corporate managers have caused the corporation to take actions that will harm the corporation. If the shareholder seeks to inspect and copy information to solicit other shareholders to sue the corporation and its managers, has the shareholder stated a "proper purpose"? Justice Moore considered that question in the next case.

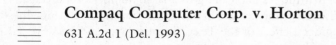

Compaq Computer Corp. v. Horton

631 A.2d 1 (Del. 1993)

MOORE, J.

I.

Compaq Computer Corporation ("Compaq") refused to permit Charles E. Horton ("Horton"), a Compaq stockholder, to inspect its stock ledger and other related materials. Horton has beneficially owned 112 shares of Compaq common stock continuously since December 6, 1990.

On July 22, 1991, Horton and seventy eight other parties sued Compaq, fifteen of its advisors and certain management personnel (the "Texas litigation"). Horton and the other plaintiffs allege that Compaq and its co-defendants violated the Texas Security Act and the Texas Deceptive Trade Practices Consumer Protection Act. Plaintiffs also charge defendants with a continuing pattern of misconduct involving common law fraud, conspiracy, aiding and abetting, fraudulent concealment and breach of fiduciary duty. All these claims arise from the contention that Compaq misled the public as to the true value of its stock at a time when members of management were selling their own shares. The plaintiffs seek individual damages.

On September 22, 1992, Horton, through counsel, delivered a letter demanding to inspect Compaq's stock ledger and related information for the period from October 1, 1990 to June 30, 1991, ... The demand letter stated that the purpose of the request was:

> [T]o enable Mr. Horton to communicate with other Compaq shareholders to inform them of the pending shareholders' suit . . . and to ascertain whether any of them would desire to become associated with that suit or bring similar actions against Compaq, and assume a pro rata share of the litigation expenses.

On September 30, 1992, Compaq refused the demand, stating that the purpose described in the letter was not a "proper purpose" under Section 220(b) of the [DGCL]. After this action was filed in the Court of Chancery, the parties presented cross-motions for summary judgment. Compaq conceded that Horton had met all of the technical requirements for making a demand under [DGCL] §220, and that the only issue remaining for the trial court to resolve was whether Horton stated a proper purpose for inspecting the various documents.

II.

A.

Under Section 220, when a stockholder complies with the statutory requirements as to form and manner of making a demand, then the corporation bears the burden of proving that the demand is for an improper purpose. [DGCL] §220(c). . . . If there is any doubt, it must be resolved in favor of the statutory right of the stockholder to have an inspection.

B.

Essentially, Horton alleges that it is in the interests of Compaq's shareholders to know that acts of mismanagement and fraud are continuing and cannot be overlooked. Thus, it is assumed that the resultant filing of a large number of individual damage claims might well discourage further acts of misconduct by the defendants. In this specific context, the antidotal effect of the Texas litigation may indeed serve a purpose reasonably related to Horton's current interest as a Compaq stockholder.

C.

We recognize that even though a purpose may be reasonably related to one's interest as a stockholder, it cannot be adverse to the interests of the corporation. In this respect, it becomes clear that a stockholder's right to inspect and copy a stockholder list is not absolute. Rather, it is a qualified right depending on the facts presented.

Horton's ultimate objective, to solicit additional parties to the Texas litigation, may impose substantial expenses upon the company. Compaq argues, therefore, that such a purpose is per se improper as adverse to the interests of the corporation. Significantly, however, Compaq conceded at oral argument that it could cite no authority in support of its proposition that the purpose behind a demand must benefit the defendant corporation.

Horton, as a current stockholder of Compaq, has nothing to gain by harming the legitimate interests of the company. Moreover, as he argues, the prospect of the Texas litigation poses no legitimate threat to Compaq's interests. The Texas litigation is already pending with seventy-nine plaintiffs. The inclusion of more plaintiffs will not substantially increase Compaq's costs of defending the action. The real risk to Compaq is that any additional plaintiffs, who may join the suit, potentially increase the damage award against the company. Yet, insofar as law and policy require corporations and their agents to answer for the breaches of their duties to shareholders, Compaq has no legitimate interest in avoiding the payment of compensatory damages which it, its management or advisors may owe to those who own the enterprise. Thus, common sense and public policy dictate that a proper purpose may be stated in these circumstances, notwithstanding the lack of a direct benefit flowing to the corporation.

Equally important is the fact that if damages are assessed against Compaq in the Texas litigation, the company is entitled to seek indemnification from its co-defendant managers and advisors or to pursue its own claims against them. The availability of this diminishes the possibility that Compaq will suffer any harm at all. It is well-settled that the mere prospect of harm to a corporate defendant is insufficient to deny relief under Section 220. Any doubt on the issue must be resolved in favor of the statutory right of the stockholder to an inspection. This is especially true where the burden is on the corporation to show an improper purpose. [DGCL] §220(c).... Accordingly, we are satisfied that the purpose for which Horton seeks to inspect the stock ledger and related materials is not adverse to the legitimate interests of the company.

D.

This conclusion does not suggest that Compaq's burden of showing an improper purpose is impossible to bear. Previous cases provide valuable examples of the degree to which a stated purpose is so indefinite, doubtful, uncertain or vexatious as to warrant denial of the right of inspection. In *State ex rel. Linihan v. United Brokerage Co.*, 101 A. 433, 437 (Del. Super. 1917), the trial court held that instituting annoying or harassing litigation against the corporation was an improper purpose. In *Carpenter v. Texas Air Corp.*, 1985 WL 11548 (Del. Ch. April 18, 1985) (Hartnett, V.C.), the court ruled improper the stockholder's plan to use a stocklist in furtherance of a scheme to bring pressure on a third corporation. In *General Time Corp. v. Talley Indus., Inc.*, 240 A.2d 755, 756 (Del. 1968), it was recognized that obtaining a list for purposes of selling the stockholder's names was also improper. Finally, in *Insuranshares Corp. of Delaware v. Kirchner*, 5 A.2d 519, 521 (Del. 1939), the Court stated that neither conducting a "fishing expedition" nor satisfying idle curiosity were proper purposes to justify inspection. On the whole, a fair reading of these cases leads to the conclusion that where the person making demand is acting in bad faith or for reasons wholly unrelated to his or her role as a stockholder, access to the ledger will be denied. That simply is not the case here.

Horton seeks in good faith to solicit the support of other similarly situated Compaq stockholders, not only to seek monetary redress for their individual economic injuries, but also *to prevent further acts of fraud or mismanagement* from disrupting the fair market value of Compaq's stock. These goals are consistent with at least two different, but analogous purposes that have been previously upheld by our courts, *regardless* of whether the purpose benefitted the corporation or just the claimant alone.

First, in *Weiss v. Anderson, Clayton & Co.*, 1986 WL 5970, (Del. Ch. May 22, 1986) (Allen, Ch.), the Chancellor held that a stockholder's desire to contact other stockholders for the purpose of encouraging them to dissent from a merger and seek their appraisal rights was proper. *Weiss* is analogous to this case insofar as both claimants seek to solicit other stockholders to bring actions against the corporation which may ultimately protect the value of its stock. Second, in *Nodana Petroleum Corp. v. State ex rel. Brennan*, 123 A.2d 243, 246 (Del. 1956), this Court upheld a stockholder's right to inspect the ledger for the purposes of investigating allegedly improper transactions or mismanagement. *Nodana* is similar to this case because Horton also seeks to curb managerial fraud and mismanagement.

III.

We find, therefore, that Compaq's arguments simply fail to meet the burden imposed on it by law to show that Horton acts from an improper purpose. First, Compaq's contention that Horton's demand is not connected to his status as a stockholder is unsubstantiated. Horton's demand is connected to his status as a stockholder because he seeks to bring an end to injuries sustained, past and present, that directly, and adversely, affect his stock ownership. Second, Compaq's complaint that Horton seeks an historical stocklist is inconsequential. Many cases recognize a stockholder's right to investigate past acts of mismanagement. Furthermore, Section 220(b) expressly grants the right to inspect not only a corporation's list of present stockholders, but also the stock ledger. Third, Compaq's accusation that Horton only seeks inspection for his personal gain is immaterial. So long as Horton establishes a single proper purpose *related to his role as a stockholder*, all other purposes are irrelevant.

Finally, Compaq's contention that Horton's purpose is contrary to the best interests of the corporation and its current stockholders is both speculative and specious. Any harm that may accrue to the corporation as a result of releasing the list is too remote and uncertain to warrant denial of the stockholder's statutory right to inspection. If anything, the corporation and its stockholders, as well as public policy, will best be served by exposure of the fraud, if that is the case, and restoration of the stock to a value set by a properly informed market.

Notes and Questions

1. Reality Check

a. How does Mr. Horton stand to benefit from the inspection he seeks?

b. How will Compaq Computer benefit from allowing Mr. Horton the inspection he seeks?

c. Which side has the burden of persuasion?

d. Why does Justice Moore hold that encouraging litigation against the company is a "proper purpose"?

2. Suppose

a. Imagine that Mr. Horton decided to seek the names of shareholders shortly before the Compaq Computer annual meeting. Could he inspect and copy the list of record date shareholders without showing a proper purpose?

b. Suppose that Compaq Computer were incorporated under the MBCA. Would the analysis or result of this case be different?

3. What Do You Think?

a. Do you think that, under the court's analysis, any shareholder who distrusts management can inspect and copy the shareholder list?

Several other issues recur in connection with shareholder inspection rights. One is whether statutory inspection rights supersede common law rights. Another is whether a shareholder has a right to information about share holdings that is not contained on the list of record shareholders. The next case deals with these questions and more!

≡ Parsons v. Jefferson-Pilot Corp.
≡ 426 S.E.2d 685 (N.C. 1993)

MITCHELL, J.

The plaintiff, Louise Price Parsons, is a shareholder of Jefferson-Pilot Corporation and owns 300,000 shares of its stock, which are worth several million dollars. On 14 February 1991, the plaintiff sent a letter to the defendant corporation requesting that it allow her to inspect and copy designated corporate records that would enable her to communicate with its other shareholders. The defendant allowed the plaintiff to inspect and copy certain records. However, the defendant refused to provide the plaintiff with a list of beneficial owners of its stock, stating that it did not possess such information or maintain such a list. [T]he plaintiff also requested that the defendant allow her to inspect and copy certain "accounting records" so that she could determine "any possible mismanagement of the company or any possible misappropriation of the company's assets." In refusing the plaintiff's request, the defendant stated that such records "are not within the scope of [MBCA §16.02(b)]." On 4 March 1991, the plaintiff sent another letter to the defendant narrowing her request for accounting records to those dealing with "compensation paid to, perquisites made available to and relationships with only the executive officers and directors of the company, their family members and companions." The defendant still refused to allow the plaintiff to inspect and copy any "accounting records." As a result, on 6 May 1991, the plaintiff filed a motion for preliminary injunction seeking, among other things, an order directing the defendant to give her access to its accounting records and to give her a list of beneficial owners of its stock.

I.

By her first assignment of error, the plaintiff contends that the Court of Appeals erroneously concluded that [MBCA §16.02(b)] abrogated a shareholder's common law right to inspect the accounting records of a public corporation. The statute provides, in pertinent part, that a qualified shareholder of any corporation is entitled to inspect and copy accounting records of the corporation if she gives the corporation written notice of her demand at least five [business] days before the date on which she wishes to inspect and copy such records. [MBCA §16.02(b)]. This right as guaranteed by the statute is limited, however, by its proviso that a shareholder of a public corporation shall not be entitled to inspect or copy any accounting records of the corporation.*

---

* The North Carolina exception for public companies is a variation from the MBCA. ED.

Under common law, a shareholder of a corporation has a right to make reasonable inspection of its books and records. This Court has expressly recognized that the shareholders of a corporation have a common law right to make a reasonable inspection of its books to assure themselves of efficient management. We have also noted that the rationale behind the common law right of inspection is that those in charge of the corporation are merely agents of the shareholders, and a shareholder's right to inspect a corporation's books and records is only the right to inspect and examine that which is his own.

The issue to be resolved here, then, is whether that common law right to inspect accounting records has been abrogated by [MBCA §16.02(b)] or, to the contrary, has been preserved by [MBCA §16.02(e)(2)], which provides that section 16.02 does not affect "the power of a court, independently of this [Act], to compel the production of corporate records for examination."

The North Carolina Business Corporation Act, *inter alia,* provides shareholders certain rights of inspection of corporate records which did not exist under the common law. There seems to be general agreement, however, that the General Assembly did not intend the granting of such new or expanded rights of inspection under the Act to abrogate shareholders' rights of inspection already existing at common law; instead, it intended that [MBCA §16.02(e)(2)] preserve all existing common law rights of inspection of corporate records.

The Official Comment states that "Section 16.02(e) provides that the right of inspection granted by section 16.02 is an independent right of inspection that is not a substitute for or in derogation of rights of inspection that may exist . . . as a 'common law' right of inspection, if any is found to exist by a court, to examine corporate records. Section 16.02(e) simply preserves whatever independent right of inspection exists. . . ." [MBCA §16.02 official cmt. 4].

We conclude that [MBCA §16.02(e)(2)] preserves a shareholder's common law rights of inspection, including the right to make reasonable inspections of the accounting records of a public corporation for proper purposes. Further, a shareholder who seeks to exercise her common law right — as opposed to a statutory right — to examine corporate records for a proper purpose also has a common law right to utilize the mandamus power of the courts to compel a reluctant corporation to disclose its corporate records pertinent to that purpose. Therefore, we reverse that part of the Court of Appeals' opinion which concluded that the plaintiff in the present case did not retain these common law rights after the adoption of the North Carolina Business Corporation Act.

II.

By her next assignment of error, the plaintiff shareholder contends that the Court of Appeals erred in failing to compel the defendant corporation to provide her with a NOBO list for inspection. A NOBO list is a list of beneficial owners of a corporation's stock who do not object to the disclosure of their names and addresses by the registered owner of the stock (typically, a stock broker or a bank) to the corporation itself for the limited purpose of allowing direct communication on corporate matters. Only recently have NOBO lists been recognized under federal law. When creating the rules requiring banks, stock brokers and dealers to create such lists upon requests by issuing corporations, the Securities Exchange Commission reviewed the question of whether a corporation's shareholders should themselves be granted the right to compel the production of a NOBO list on the same terms as the issuer of the shares. However, the Commission has not promulgated any rule providing shareholders with such a right.

A qualified shareholder has a statutory right to inspect a "record of shareholders." [MBCA §16.02(b)(3)]. The plaintiff contends that the record of shareholders made available by this statute includes a NOBO list. Our Court of Appeals concluded in the present case that the defendant corporation does not have to provide the plaintiff shareholder with a NOBO list, because the defendant corporation does not have the information needed to create such a list and does not use such a list in communicating with shareholders. We agree.

Other courts have held that where a corporation has obtained a NOBO list and is or will be using it to solicit shareholders, a shareholder should be allowed the same channel of communication. However, there is a paucity of cases addressing the issue before us in the present case—whether a corporation must provide a shareholder a NOBO list even though the corporation does not have in its possession the names of its non-objecting beneficial owners and does not use such information to solicit shareholders.

[I]n *Cenergy Corp. v. Bryson Oil & Gas P.L.C.*, 662 F. Supp. 1144 (D. Nev. 1987), the court refused to require the corporate defendant to obtain the names and addresses of beneficial owners of its stock in order to create a NOBO list for a shareholder, because the defendant corporation did not already have such information in its possession. This ruling was based in part upon the view that requiring a corporation to divulge all of the shareholder information *in its possession* would completely effectuate the goal of fairness and equality between a corporation and its shareholders in proxy solicitation. *Id.* at 1147. Therefore, the court refused to order the corporation to "acquire specially any shareholder information which it does not already possess in order to then distribute it to [the shareholder] Bryson." *Id.* at 1148. We find the decision in *Cenergy Corp.* persuasive.

We believe that the legislative intent embodied in [MBCA §16.02(b)(3)] is that shareholders be entitled to the information concerning the identity of shareholders which is *possessed by the corporation* in order that they may have the same opportunity as the corporation to communicate with the other shareholders. In order to effectuate that legislative goal, it is necessary that shareholders have access to NOBO lists or other information which the corporation itself has in its possession; however, a shareholder is not granted a right under the statute to require a corporation to obtain NOBO lists or the information necessary to compile NOBO lists when the corporation does not possess or use such information. Since the defendant corporation does not have in its possession a NOBO list or the information needed to compile a NOBO list, it is not required to obtain that information simply because the plaintiff shareholder has requested that it do so for an otherwise proper purpose. Therefore, we affirm that part of the opinion of the Court of Appeals which affirmed the trial court's holding that the defendant corporation was not required to provide the plaintiff with a NOBO list.

III.

In its sole assignment of error, the defendant contends that the Court of Appeals erred in concluding that the plaintiff had satisfied the "reasonable particularity" requirement of [MBCA §16.02(c)(2)]. In her demand, the plaintiff requested

> for the purpose of determining any possible mismanagement of the Company or any possible misappropriation, misapplication or improper use of any property or asset of

the Company, all records of any final action taken, with or without a meeting, by the Board of Directors of the Company, or by a committee of the Board of Directors of the Company while acting in place of the Board of Directors of the Company on behalf of the Company, minutes of any meeting of the shareholders of the Company and records of action taken by the shareholders of the Company without a meeting.

Since no court has yet construed the "reasonable particularity" requirement of [MBCA §16.02(c)(2)], we find it helpful to consider the interpretation placed upon the "reasonable particularity" requirement contained in Rule 34(b) of the Federal Rules of Civil Procedure. In determining whether the "reasonable particularity" requirement of this federal rule governing document production has been satisfied, it has been recognized that

> the test must be a relative one, turning on the degree of knowledge that a movant in a particular case has about the documents he requests. In some cases he has such exact and definite knowledge that he can designate, identify, and enumerate with precision the documents to be produced. This is the ideal designation, since it permits the party responding to go at once to his files and without difficulty produce the document for inspection. But the ideal is not always attainable and Rule 34 does not require the impossible. Even a generalized designation should be sufficient when the party seeking discovery cannot give a more particular description and the party from whom discovery is sought will have no difficulty in understanding what is wanted. The goal is that the designation be sufficient to apprise a man of ordinary intelligence what documents are required.

8 Charles A. Wright & Arthur R. Miller, *Federal Practice and Procedure* §2211, at 628-31 (1970).

In the present case, the record does not show that the plaintiff had any specific knowledge of corporate mismanagement or of any improper use of corporate assets at the time that she made the demand. The record shows only that the plaintiff was dissatisfied with the return on her investment in the defendant corporation. In light of the plaintiff's actual knowledge at the time of the demand, it would not have been feasible to state her purpose with any greater particularity. In addition, the plaintiff specifically described the desired records in her demand. The plaintiff sought "all records of any final action taken by the Board or by a committee of the Board, the minutes of any meeting of the shareholders, and records of action taken by the shareholders of the Company without a meeting." Although the plaintiff's demand was broad, we agree with the Court of Appeals' determination that there is nothing in this record to show that the plaintiff could have described the desired records with any greater particularity than she did, and the defendant company should not have had any trouble understanding what the plaintiff desired. Assuming *arguendo* that [MBCA §16.02(c)] controls situations in which a shareholder exercises a common law right of inspection, as well as situations in which the statutory right is being exercised, we conclude that the plaintiff described both her purpose and the desired records with the "reasonable particularity" required by that statute. This assignment of error is overruled.

In conclusion, we agree with the holding of the Court of Appeals that the plaintiff was not entitled to require the defendant to obtain the information needed to prepare a NOBO list or to provide such a list to the plaintiff. We also agree with the holding of the Court of Appeals that the plaintiff described her purpose and the desired records with "reasonable particularity." Accordingly, we affirm the results reached in those parts of the opinion of the Court of Appeals. The Court of Appeals erred, however, in holding that the plaintiff does not have a common law right to inspect the accounting records of the defendant, and we reverse that part of the opinion of the Court of Appeals. This case is remanded for further proceedings not inconsistent with this opinion.

Affirmed in part; reversed in part; and remanded.

Notes and Questions

1. Reality Check

a. What information did Ms. Parsons want from Jefferson-Pilot? Why did she want it?

b. On what basis did Justice Mitchell decide that a shareholder's common law inspection rights survived the passage of the MBCA?

c. What is a "*NOBO list*"? Does the court hold that a shareholder has a right to inspect or copy a NOBO list?

d. Why does the court hold that Ms. Parsons stated her claims with sufficient particularity?

2. Suppose

a. Suppose Jefferson-Pilot did not have a NOBO list but did have a list, from Cede & Co., of the brokerage firms whose clients held Jefferson-Pilot stock. Would Ms. Parsons be able to inspect and copy that list?

b. If Jefferson-Pilot were incorporated in Delaware, how would the court resolve each issue?

3. What Do You Think?

a. Why do you suppose Jefferson-Pilot was so resistant to Ms. Parsons's requests that it litigated the matter to the North Carolina Supreme Court?

b. Given that Jefferson-Pilot is publicly held, will the list of shareholders of record help Ms. Parsons?

C. SHAREHOLDERS' POWER TO REDRESS HARM TO THE CORPORATION

1. The Current Setting

We now move to the third, and final, area of shareholder governance powers. It is different from the other areas in several important ways. First, much of the legal questions are actually civil procedure questions rather than business entities questions. The consequence of that difference is that this section will cover only a few of the legal issues. Second, the shareholders participate in the corporation's governance in a rather oblique way: they bring a lawsuit in which any remedy inures to the corporation itself rather than the shareholder. Perhaps the most important thing to take away from this section is the basic conception of this litigation. We start with that conception.

Imagine an ordinary situation in which a corporation has contracted with another party that breaches the contract. The board (or perhaps officers or other agents who have been authorized by the board) would decide how to react. Typically the corporation would make demand on the other party, perhaps engage in negotiations, and decide whether to bring suit against the breaching party. In this situation the shareholders clearly have no power to intervene in the corporation's decision about how to respond to the breach. The bedrock corporate law rule is that all corporate power is vested in the board, not the shareholders. See DGCL §141(a) and MBCA §8.01(b).

Now suppose that the harm to the corporation was caused not by a breaching party to a contract but by the directors themselves. An example would be where the board caused the corporation to violate environmental laws that resulted in the corporation being fined. By now it may seem intuitive to you to conclude that the board might not be able to decide, consistent with their fiduciary duties, how to proceed in the best interest of the corporation. The directors are unlikely, to say the least, to cause the corporation to sue themselves! A similar example is where the senior officers, rather than the directors, caused the corporation to violate environmental laws. The board would be deciding whether to cause the corporation to sue people who are presumably close to the board members. Obviously the directors' judgment as to how to proceed in the corporation's best interest might be clouded.

It is in this situation — where the board's decision-making ability may be compromised — that the law of business entities allows the shareholders to file suit on the corporation's behalf to redress the harm. This type of litigation is called *derivative* because the shareholders' power to sue is derived from the corporation's power (putatively exercised by the board) to redress harm to itself. Thus the shareholder brings suit against the directors, officers, or other agents who are alleged to have harmed the corporation. Depending upon the jurisdiction, the corporation itself may be a nominal plaintiff, a nominal defendant, or neither. By far the most common theory of derivative actions is that the individual defendants have breached their fiduciary duties to the corporation and thus have harmed the corporation.

Because derivative litigation is an exception to the core idea that corporate affairs are strictly in the hands of the board, there are restrictions on shareholders' ability to file and maintain a derivative lawsuit. Potential plaintiffs obviously try to avoid these restrictions and so typically try to characterize their claims as individual rather than derivative. The line between individual and derivative litigation is sometimes murky and the case law is typically less than helpful. The Delaware Supreme Court has framed the test as follows:

> The derivative suit has been generally described as "one of the most interesting and ingenious of accountability mechanisms for large formal organizations."[10] It enables a stockholder to bring suit on behalf of the corporation for harm done to the corporation. Because a derivative suit is being brought on behalf of the corporation, the recovery, if any, must go to the corporation. A stockholder who is directly injured, however, does retain the right to bring an individual action for injuries affecting his or her legal rights as a stockholder. Such a claim is distinct from an injury caused to the corporation alone. In such individual suits, the recovery or other relief flows directly to the stockholders, not to the corporation.
>
> Determining whether an action is derivative or direct is sometimes difficult and has many legal consequences, some of which may have an expensive impact on the parties

---

10. *Kramer v. Western Pacific Industries, Inc.*, 546 A.2d at 351 (quoting R. Clark, *Corporate Law* 639-40 (1986)).

to the action. For example, if an action is derivative, . . . the recovery, if any, flows only to the corporation. The decision whether a suit is direct or derivative may be outcome-determinative. Therefore, it is necessary that a standard to distinguish such actions be clear, simple and consistently articulated and applied by our courts.

[A] court should look to the nature of the wrong and to whom the relief should go. The stockholder's claimed direct injury must be independent of any alleged injury to the corporation. The stockholder must demonstrate that the duty breached was owed to the stockholder and that he or she can prevail without showing an injury to the corporation.

Tooley v. Donaldson, Lufkin, & Jenrette, Inc., 845 A.2d 1031, 1036, 1040 (Del. 2004)
(Veasey, C.J.)

In brief, the distinctive aspects of derivative litigation include these:

1. To have standing, plaintiff must have been a shareholder at the time of the alleged harm to the corporation and at the time he or she files suit.
2. Nearly half the states (although neither Delaware nor the MBCA) permit defendants to require plaintiff to post security bonds if the plaintiff's share-holdings are minimal (typically less than 5% of the outstanding shares).
3. The ordinary statutory presumption that all corporate powers should be in the board means that the board should decide whether the corporation will bring suit. From this presumption comes the procedural rule that a shareholder may not file a derivative action unless one of two procedural settings obtains. In one setting, the plaintiff must have requested (*demanded* is the word universally used) the board to initiate litigation, the board must have refused to do so, and that refusal must have been "wrongful." In the second setting, the plaintiff may file suit without making demand on the board if he or she can demonstrate that prior demand on the board would have been "futile" because the board could not have evaluated the demand fairly. FRCP 23.1 embodies this demand requirement and nearly all states have comparable procedural rules.
4. As with other representative litigation, such as class actions, the named plaintiff litigates on behalf of all shareholders and so cannot settle the litigation without court approval.

Our first case, *Beam v. Stewart,* takes up the question of when prior demand on the board would be futile, and therefore is excused.

Beam v. Stewart
833 A.2d 961 (Del. Ch. 2003)

CHANDLER, CH.

Monica A. Beam, a shareholder of Martha Stewart Living Omnimedia, Inc. ("MSO"), brings this derivative action against the defendants, all current directors and a former director of MSO, and against MSO as a nominal defendant. The defendants seek [ ] . . . to dismiss the amended complaint under Court of Chancery Rule 23.1 for failure to comply with the demand requirement and for failure adequately to plead demand excusal. . . .

Plaintiff Monica A. Beam is a shareholder of MSO and has been since August 2001. Derivative plaintiff and nominal defendant MSO is a Delaware corporation that operates in the publishing, television, merchandising, and internet industries marketing products bearing the "Martha Stewart" brand name.

Defendant Martha Stewart ("Stewart") is a director of the company and its founder, chairman, chief executive officer, and by far its majority shareholder. MSO's common stock is comprised of Class A and Class B shares. Class A shares are traded on the New York Stock Exchange and are entitled to cast one vote per share on matters voted upon by common stockholders. Class B shares are not publicly traded and are entitled to cast ten votes per share on all matters voted upon by common stockholders. Stewart owns or beneficially holds 100% of the B shares in conjunction with a sufficient number of A shares that she controls roughly 94.4% of the shareholder vote. Stewart, a former stockbroker, has in the past twenty years become a household icon, known for her advice and expertise on virtually all aspects of cooking, decorating, entertaining, and household affairs generally.

Defendant Sharon L. Patrick ("Patrick") is a director of MSO and its president and chief operating officer. The amended complaint reports that in 2001, MSO paid Patrick a salary of $700,000, a $280,000 bonus, and granted her options for 130,000 Class A shares. She also serves as the secretary of M. Stewart, Inc., which is described in the complaint as "one of Stewart's personal companies." Prior to Patrick's employment at MSO, she was a consultant to the magazine, *Martha Stewart Living*, and developed extensive experience in the media, entertainment, and consulting businesses. Patrick is also a longtime personal friend of Stewart.

Defendant Arthur C. Martinez ("Martinez") has been a director of MSO since January 2001. Martinez is the former chairman of the board of directors and chief executive officer of Sears Roebuck and Co. Martinez was also the chairman and chief executive officer of that company's retail arm, Sears Merchandise Group. Sears was a high-volume retailer of MSO products during Martinez's tenure there. He has served on the boards of Sears Roebuck and Co., Sears Merchandise Group, and Saks Fifth Avenue. In addition, Martinez now serves as a director of MSO, PepsiCo, Inc., Liz Claiborne, Inc., and International Flavors & Fragrances, Inc., and as the chairman of the Federal Reserve Bank of Chicago. A March 2001 article in *Directors & Boards* reported that Patrick and Stewart both consider Martinez to be "an old friend." Also, Martinez was recruited to serve on MSO's board by then-board member Charlotte Beers ("Beers"), another "longtime friend and confidante" of Stewart.

Defendant Darla D. Moore ("Moore") has been a director of MSO since September 2001, when Beers resigned and Moore replaced her. Moore's professional background includes a partnership at Rainwater, Inc., a private investment firm, a managing directorship with Chase Bank, and service as a trustee of Magellan Health Services, Inc. Moore, too, is reported to be a longtime friend of both Stewart and Beers, as evidenced by a 1996 *Fortune* magazine article highlighting the close friendship among the three women and by the amended complaint's report of Moore's attendance at a wedding reception in 1995, which was attended by both Stewart and Samuel Waksal and hosted by Stewart's lawyer, Allen Grubman.

Defendant Naomi O. Seligman ("Seligman") has been a director of MSO since 1999. She is a co-founder and senior partner of Cassius Advisors and a co-founder and former senior partner of Research Board, Inc. Seligman serves as a director of several public companies, including John Wiley & Sons ("JWS"), a publisher. The amended complaint relates a *Wall Street Journal* report that Seligman contacted the chief executive officer of JWS on behalf of Stewart to express concern over an unflattering biography of Stewart that was scheduled for publication by JWS.

Defendant Jeffery W. Ubben ("Ubben") has been a director of MSO since January 2002. He is the founder and managing partner of ValueAct Capital Partners, L.P. and a director of Insurance Auto Auctions, Inc. Ubben has formerly served as a managing partner and as a portfolio manager, working in the investment industry since at least 1987.

The amended complaint states that compensation paid to MSO's directors includes all of the following:

- $20,000 as an annual retainer;
- $1,000 for each meeting attended in person;
- $500 for each meeting attended telephonically; and
- $5,000 annually for serving as chairman of any committee.

Twenty-five percent of directors' fees are paid in shares of MSO's Class A common stock, with the remaining 75% payable either in Class A shares or cash at the choice of the director. In addition, MSO has a stock option plan for the directors.

The plaintiff seeks relief in relation to . . . the well-publicized matters surrounding Stewart's alleged improper trading of shares of ImClone Systems, Inc. ("ImClone") and her public statements in the wake of those allegations.

The market for MSO products is uniquely tied to the personal image and reputation of its founder, Stewart. MSO retains "an exclusive, worldwide, perpetual royalty-free license to use [Stewart's] name, likeness, image, voice and signature for its products and services." In its initial public offering prospectus, MSO recognized that impairment of Stewart's services to the company, including the tarnishing of her public reputation, would have a material adverse effect on its business. The prospectus distinguished Stewart's importance to MSO's business success from that of other executives of the company noting that, "Martha Stewart remains the personification of our brands as well as our senior executive and primary creative force." In fact, under the terms of her employment agreement, Stewart may be terminated for gross misconduct or felony conviction that results in harm to MSO's business or reputation but is permitted discretion over the management of her personal, financial, and legal affairs to the extent that Stewart's management of her own life does not compromise her ability to serve the company.

Stewart's alleged misadventures with ImClone arise in part out of a longstanding personal friendship with Samuel D. Waksal ("Waksal"). Waksal is the former chief executive officer of ImClone as well as a former suitor of Stewart's daughter. More pertinently, with respect to the allegations of the amended complaint, Waksal and Stewart have provided one another with reciprocal investment advice and assistance, and they share a stockbroker, Peter E. Bacanovic ("Bacanovic") of Merrill Lynch. Bacanovic, coincidentally, is a former employee of ImClone. Although the other investments recommended and facilitated by Waksal have thus far proven to be of no great news value, the ImClone investment — or more particularly Stewart's December 27, 2001, ImClone *divestment* — has been found to be somewhat more noteworthy. The speculative value of ImClone stock was tied quite directly to the likely success of its application for FDA approval to market the cancer treatment drug Erbitux. On December 26, Waksal received information that the FDA was rejecting the application to market Erbitux. The following day, December 27, he tried to sell his own shares and tipped his father and daughter to do the same. Stewart also sold her shares on December 27. That day she was traveling with another friend, Marianna Pasternak ("Pasternak"), when Stewart spoke with Bacanovic's assistant, Douglas

Faneuil, and sold all of her ImClone shares. The next day, December 28, Pasternak's husband, Bart Pasternak, also sold 10,000 shares of ImClone. After the close of trading on December 28, ImClone publicly announced the rejection of its application to market Erbitux. The following day the trading price closed slightly more than 20% lower than the closing price on the date that Stewart had sold her shares. By mid-2002, this convergence of events had attracted the interest of the *New York Times* and other news agencies, federal prosecutors, and a committee of the United States House of Representatives. Stewart's publicized attempts to quell any suspicion were ineffective at best because they were undermined by additional information as it came to light and by the other parties' accounts of the events. Ultimately Stewart's prompt efforts to turn away unwanted media and investigative attention failed. Stewart eventually had to discontinue her regular guest appearances on CBS' *The Early Show* because of questioning during the show about her sale of ImClone shares. After barely two months of such adverse publicity, MSO's stock price had declined by slightly more than 65%. In August 2002, James Follo, MSO's chief financial officer, cited uncertainty stemming from the investigation of Stewart in response to questions about earnings prospects in the future.

Defendants have moved to dismiss the amended complaint under Court of Chancery Rule 23.1 for failure to make demand upon MSO's board of directors or adequately to plead why demand would be futile. Rule 23.1 . . . confers substantive rights that result in derivative complaints being subjected to more stringent pleading requirements. The plaintiff must state with particularity the efforts made to cause the company's board of directors to take action on the matters of concern to the plaintiff—to state how demand was made. If, as in this action, the plaintiff has failed to make a demand on the board, the plaintiff must state with particularity the reasons that demand should be excused.

Plaintiff concedes that demand was not made but asserts that demand would be futile because the board of directors is incapable of acting independently and disinterestedly in evaluating demand with respect to plaintiff's claims. Count I alleges that Stewart breached her fiduciary duties to MSO and its shareholders by selling (perhaps illegally) shares of ImClone in December of 2001 and by public statements she made regarding that sale. Because this claim does not challenge an action of the board of directors of MSO, the appropriate test for demand futility is that articulated in *Rales v. Blasband*. Particularly, the Court's task is to evaluate whether the particularized allegations "create a reasonable doubt that, as of the time the complaint [was] filed, the board of directors could have properly exercised its independent and disinterested business judgment in responding to a demand."[50] *Rales* requires that a majority of the board be able to consider and appropriately to respond to a demand "free of personal financial interest and improper extraneous influences."[51] Demand is excused as futile if the Court finds there is "a reasonable doubt that a majority of the Board would be disinterested or independent in making a decision on demand."[52]

The original complaint was filed on August 15, 2002. At that time the board members were defendants Stewart, Patrick, Martinez, Seligman, Moore, and Ubben. Thus, these six individuals constitute the board for purposes of evaluating demand futility. Demand is required if, in view of all the particularized allegations in the

50. *Rales* [*v. Blasband*], 634 A.2d. [927] at 934 [(Del. 1993)].
51. *Id*. at 935.
52. *Id*. at 930.

complaint and drawing all reasonable inferences in favor of the plaintiff, there is no reasonable doubt of the ability of a majority, here four of the six directors, to respond to [plaintiff's] demand appropriately.

[Chancellor Chandler then applied the tests of independence and disinterestedness we saw in *Orman v. Cullman* in Chapter 13 to the defendant directors. The Chancellor found that Ms. Stewart was not disinterested and that Ms. Patrick was not independent. As to Mr. Martinez, Ms. Moore, and Ms. Seligman, the Chancellor found that the plaintiff had not sustained her burden of proof. The Chancellor did not discuss Mr. Ubben. The Chancellor then commented on the plaintiff's failure of proof:]

In sum, plaintiff offers various theories to suggest reasons that the outside directors might be inappropriately swayed by Stewart's wishes or interests, but fails to plead sufficient facts that could permit the Court reasonably to infer that one or more of the theories could be accurate. Evidence to support (or refute) any of the theories might have been uncovered by an examination of the corporate books and records, to which the plaintiff would have been entitled for this purpose.[64] Board minutes or voting records, for example, could reveal if the outside directors have in the past challenged Stewart's proposals, or not, voted in line with Stewart, or in opposition to her, and shown on which issues the outside directors have been more or less likely to go along with Stewart's wishes. Armed with such information, plaintiff (and this Court) would be in a much better position to evaluate whether there exists a reasonable doubt of the outside directors' resolve to act independently of Stewart. It appears, however, that plaintiff made no such investigation, instead relying largely, if not solely, on information from media reports to support the assertion that demand would be futile.

It is troubling to this Court that, notwithstanding repeated suggestions, encouragement, and downright admonitions over the years both by this Court and by the Delaware Supreme Court, litigants continue to bring derivative complaints pleading demand futility on the basis of precious little investigation beyond perusal of the morning newspapers. This failure properly to investigate whether a majority of directors fairly can evaluate demand may lead to either (or both) of two equally appalling results. If there is no reasonable doubt that the board could respond to demand in the proper fashion, failure to make demand and filing the derivative action results in a waste of the resources of the litigants, including the corporation in question, as well as those of this Court. If the facts to support reasonable doubt could have been ascertained through more careful pre-litigation investigation, the failure to discover and plead those facts still results in a waste of resources of the litigants and the Court and, in addition, ties the hands of this Court to protect the interests of shareholders where the board is unable or unwilling to do so. This results in the dismissal of what otherwise may have been meritorious claims, fails to provide relief to the company's shareholders, and further erodes public confidence in the legal protections afforded to investors.

It would be inappropriate to speculate on the merits of the underlying claims in any case, including this one, on a motion to dismiss under Rule 23.1. Therefore I have and express no opinion regarding the merits of Count I as may have been determined had it survived for trial. I would be remiss, though, if I failed to point out that with a bit more detail about the "relationships," "friendships," and "inter-connections" among Stewart and the other defendants or with some additional arguments as to

---

64. [DGCL] §220; *Rales,* 634 A.2d at 934 n.10.

why there may be a reasonable doubt of the directors' incentives when evaluating demand with respect to Count I, there may have been a reasonable doubt as to one or all of the outside directors disinterest, independence, or ability to consider and respond to demand free from improper extraneous influences. Nevertheless, on this pleading, no such doubt is raised. The defendants' motions to dismiss the amended complaint for failure adequately to plead demand futility are granted with respect to Count I.

Notes and Questions

1. Notes

a. In footnote 58 of the opinion Chancellor Chandler expanded a bit on the theory of the case against the directors other than Ms. Stewart.

> At oral argument, plaintiff's counsel suggested that the MSO board should have fired Stewart before the announcement of the federal indictment and of the SEC civil action. The failure to do so is purported to be a strong indication that the board as a whole is dominated and controlled by Stewart. This argument is unpersuasive for two reasons. First, the sole factual allegation upon which this inference is to be made is merely that Stewart was not removed from her positions as board chairman and chief executive officer before the indictment but has since been replaced. Even at oral argument plaintiff could not make factual allegations that would support an inference (1) that the board failed to consider what if any action might be taken in response to the negative media attention; (2) that the board failed to evaluate the risks and benefits of possible responses including those likely to result from taking no action; or (3) that the board's decision to wait before taking action was made on any basis other than the business judgment that to take action prematurely could unnecessarily worsen any harm to MSO and its shareholders that was already resulting from the negative publicity. The identification of which matters were or were not officially considered by the directors is precisely the sort of information that should be readily ascertainable by a shareholder through a books and records action authorized under [DGCL] §220. Second, the allegation is simply not made in the amended complaint and therefore cannot be considered by this Court for the purpose of demand futility analysis.

b. In the three years since the investigation of Ms. Stewart was made public in early 2002, MSO lost over $66 million. These losses stem primarily from the fact that (1) advertisers significantly reduced the advertising they purchased in MSO magazines; (2) MSO magazine circulation fell significantly; and (3) television stations and cable networks significantly reduced their purchases of the right to show MSO's television programs.

2. Reality Check

a. How have the directors hurt the corporation, according to the complaint?

b. What standard applies when director-defendants challenge a derivative plaintiff's assertion that prior demand would have been futile? Who carries what kind of burden?

3. Suppose

a. Suppose Ms. Beam had made use of DGCL §220. Which corporate records should Ms. Beam have requested?

4. What Do You Think?

a. Why does FRCP 23.1 exist? Do you think such heightened procedural prerequisites should apply to derivative litigation? Do you think such prerequisites should apply to other kinds of litigation? If so, which?

b. Do you think Delaware places the burden appropriately in demand futility cases? If not, what changes would you make?

2. Background and Context

When a board of directors receives a shareholder demand to institute litigation, the directors may be compromised in terms of their ability to evaluate the demand fairly. This is certainly so when the demand indicates that the entire board should be defendants but may also be the case when only some of the board, or even none of the board are the targets of the proposed litigation. To enhance the likelihood of a fair decision on the shareholder demand, the board quite often delegates the task of evaluating the shareholder demand to a *special committee* of nonimplicated directors. Where all directors (or all but a small number) are putative defendants, the board sometimes expands the board and appoints new members for the express purpose of serving on the demand evaluation committee. Boards and special committees rarely find that acceding to the shareholder demand is in the best interest of the corporation. Rather, demand is almost always refused.

A similar dynamic applies where a derivative suit is filed on the theory that demand is excused because it would have been futile. That is, the board appoints directors who are not defendants as a special litigation committee. The committee may consist of, or be supplemented by, newly appointed directors. The litigation committee decides whether the litigation is in the best interest of the corporation. If, as is nearly always the case, the litigation committee finds that the litigation should be dismissed (or settled), a motion to that effect is made in the court in which the litigation is pending.

Where a shareholder's demand has been refused by the board, how should a court evaluate that refusal? This issue may be postured as a suit by the shareholder challenging the refusal or as a response by the board to a derivative suit filed despite demand refusal (on the theory that the board's refusal was wrongful). Likewise, where a derivative action is properly filed with no prior demand and the board or a special litigation committee determines that the derivative action is not in the best interests of the corporation and should be dismissed, the board or committee may file a motion seeking dismissal of the suit. In all these settings the constant question is what standard should the court use to evaluate the assertions? The final case in this chapter details an astonishingly wide range of judicial responses to that question.

In re PSE&G Shareholder Litigation

718 A.2d 254 (N.J. Ch. Div. 1998)

WEISS, A.J.S.C.

In October, 1995, Plaintiff shareholders demanded that [Public Service Group Incorporated (Enterprise) and its wholly owned subsidiary, Public Service Electric and

Gas Company (PSE&G) (collectively referred to as Enterprise)] commence litigation against their officers and directors alleging mismanagement of PSE&G's nuclear plants. Subsequent to the rejection of the demand, plaintiffs brought this suit against certain officers and directors of Enterprise and PSE&G. Defendants moved to dismiss for failure to state a claim upon which relief could be granted. [T]he New Jersey Superior Court, Chancery Division, denied defendants' motion.... One year later defendants filed a motion for summary judgment to dismiss the complaint.

It is well-settled that "directors, rather than shareholders, manage the business and affairs of the corporation." *Matter of Prudential Ins. Co. Litig.*, 659 A.2d 961 (N.J. Ch. Div. 1995).... The law requires that, prior to a shareholder derivative suit, a shareholder must demand that the board institute proceedings on behalf of the corporation,... and that shareholders must first show that the board refused to bring a suit on behalf of the corporation....

It is also settled that a board's decision to reject the demand will not be overturned unless it is wrongful. "A board's refusal is only wrongful if it is not a valid exercise of its business judgment." *Maul v. Kirkman*, 637 A.2d 928 (N.J. App. Div. 1994).... There is a presumption under the business judgment rule that disinterested directors act "on an informed basis, in good faith and in the honest belief that their actions are in the corporation's best interest." *Grobow v. Perot*, 539 A.2d 180, 187 (Del. 1988). If the refusal to proceed with the litigation is protected by the business judgment rule, the shareholder may not continue the derivative proceeding.

The procedure followed by courts in other jurisdictions in shareholder's derivative actions have not been uniform. Under Delaware law, once a demand has been made and refused, the complaint must allege with sufficient specificity facts which, taken as true, create a reasonable doubt that the demand that was made and wrongfully refused was a result of a decision protected by the business judgment rule. Where a shareholder makes a demand on the board to commence litigation, that shareholder "tacitly concedes the independence of a majority of the board to respond. Therefore, when a board refuses a demand, the only issues to be examined are the good faith and reasonableness of its investigation." *Spiegel v. Buntrock*, 571 A.2d 767, 777 (Del. 1990).

Delaware courts have held that plaintiffs must show wrongful refusal in the pleadings without the benefits of discovery. However, the Delaware Supreme Court has determined that "[a] stockholder who makes a serious demand and receives only a peremptory refusal has the right to use the 'tools at hand' to obtain the relevant corporate records, such as reports or minutes, reflecting the corporate action and related information in order to determine whether or not there is a basis to assert the demand was wrongfully refused." *Grimes v. Donald*, 673 A.2d 1207, 1218 (Del. 1996).

When a majority of directors decide that they should not consider the demand either because too many of them are named as defendants or they may be interested parties, they may appoint a special litigation committee to investigate the demand.

Under Delaware law, where demand is *excused*, the corporation has the burden to demonstrate that the special litigation committee was independent, acted in good faith, and had a reasonable basis for its decision. *Zapata Corp. v. Maldonado*, 430 A.2d 779, 789 (Del. 1981). If the corporation meets that burden, then the court, in its discretion, may apply its own business judgment in determining that the dismissal was in the best interests of the corporation or, alternatively, can choose to terminate the suit based on the fairness to the corporation.

New York applies a more conservative approach than Delaware. This approach limits the court's review to the independence and disinterestedness of the committee and the appropriateness of the procedures used in reaching its decision. *See Auerbach v. Bennett,* 393 N.E.2d 994, 1002-03 (N.Y. 1979).

Responding to both *Zapata* and *Auerbach,* other jurisdictions have developed their own standards of review. North Carolina has adopted a "modified *Zapata* rule" for both demand-refused and demand-excused cases. In *Alford v. Shaw,* 358 S.E.2d 323, 326 (N.C. 1987), a case in which a special litigation committee had been formed, the Supreme Court of North Carolina held that

> the court must make a fair assessment of the report of the special committee, along with all the other facts and circumstances in the case, in order to determine whether the defendants will be able to show that the transaction complained of was just and reasonable to the corporation.

[*Id.* 358 S.E.2d at 328.]

The Supreme Judicial Court of Massachusetts has developed yet another approach. *Houle v. Low,* 556 N.E.2d 51 (Mass. 1990). The court, agreeing with both *Zapata* and *Auerbach,* stated that "[a]t a minimum, a special litigation committee must be independent, unbiased, and act in good faith" while conducting a "thorough and careful analysis" of the shareholder's demand. *Id....* The court also held that the corporation has the burden of proving these requirements. *Id.* However, after recognizing the weaknesses in both the *Zapata* and *Auerbach* approaches, the *Houle* court held that in conducting its review the court must determine whether the committee reached "a reasonable and principled decision." *Id....* In addition, the court held that the reviewing court should look to the following factors identified by the American Law Institute (ALI): "(1) the likelihood of a judgment in plaintiff's favor; (2) the expected recovery as compared to out-of-pocket costs; (3) whether the corporation itself took corrective action; (4) whether the balance of corporate interests warrants dismissal; and (5) whether dismissal would allow any defendant who has control of the corporation to retain a significant improper benefit." *Id....*

The American Bar Association in its Model Business Corporation Act (MBCA) has also proposed a standard to review a board or committee's decision to reject shareholder's demand. *See* Model Business Corp. Act §7.44 official cmt. (1991). Pursuant to the MCBA, the court shall dismiss the derivative suit if the board or committee determined in good faith after conducting a reasonable investigation that the derivative proceeding is not in the best interests of the corporation. *Id.* §7.44(a). The section does not permit the court to review the decision but instead limits the court's review to "whether the determination has some support in the findings in the inquiry." *Id.* §7.44 official cmt. at 208. The shareholder must assert that the majority of the decision makers were not independent. *Id.* §7.44(d). If a majority of the board that rejected the demand was independent, then the *plaintiff* must establish the lack of good faith and reasonableness of the decision. *Id.* §7.44(e). Conversely, if the majority is found to be not independent, then the *corporation* must demonstrate management's good faith and reasonableness.

Many commentators have questioned the current approaches to the problem of judicial monitoring of stockholder derivative actions. The continuation of the futility exception to shareholder demand has been criticized. Requiring universal demand would place the burden of responding upon the board of directors, where it belongs, and would remove from the courts the necessity of engaging in a tortured inquiry of whether demand is excused. Courts would then be in a position to properly apply the business judgment rule to the action of the board of directors or any special litigation committee appointed to review and act upon a shareholder's demand.

A concomitant to a universal demand rule would be to require the corporation to justify its refusal of a shareholder's demand, i.e., whether the directors or committee reached "a reasonable and principled decision." *Houle v. Low.* By requiring justification of its refusal of a shareholder's demand, the "structural bias" arising from the perception that directors may be consciously or unconsciously favoring their colleagues will be dissipated. The preparation of a submission setting forth the justification for the determination not to proceed with a claim will enable the court to determine if the action satisfies the business judgment rule. Such a decision by the court would not involve a substitution of the exercise of business judgment by the directors or a committee, but would enable the court to better judge the action taken in light of the charges alleged by the shareholder.

Placing the burden of proof on the corporation is both logical and consistent with the responsibility that courts have in this area. It is the corporate directors and management which have the necessary facts and information upon which the decision to discontinue the derivative litigation is based. It is the corporation which conducts the investigation and assembles the necessary facts upon which it acts. Placing the burden upon the corporation to establish that the group which recommended against derivative litigation acted reasonably, in good faith and in a disinterested manner is not unduly burdensome. The court would be able to consider the evidence put before it in determining whether the corporation met its burden without substituting its business judgment for that of the directors or special litigation committee. So long as the corporation met its burden of proof that the decision makers were disinterested, exercised due care in the decision making process, acted in good faith and that their decision was just and reasonable to the corporation, courts would have to dismiss the derivative litigation.

This court finds that the criticism directed towards the Delaware and New York approaches to derivative actions is well founded. Requiring shareholders to allege facts with specificity without discovery places them in a position bordering on the impossible. The decisions by the Massachusetts and North Carolina courts represent a sounder approach to the problems of shareholder derivative actions. The decisions by those courts that the corporation bears the burden of establishing the decision makers' independence, lack of bias, good faith and thoroughness of its investigation is fair and just. Even if the corporation shows that the committee's process was fair, the court still must determine whether the committee reached a reasonable and principled decision. Thus, the Massachusetts court in *Houle v. Low, supra,* although it does not allow the court to substitute its own business judgment for that of the directors or special litigation committee, the review by the court of the decision not to proceed with any claim against management does involve an evaluation of the substantive merits of plaintiff's allegations. The adoption of a modified business judgment rule, the key feature being that the corporation, not the shareholder, would have to meet an initial burden of proof is more consistent with the realities of shareholder-corporate existence. Courts would have to dismiss a shareholder derivative suit in accordance with management's recommendation so long as the corporation could establish the decision maker acted reasonably, in good faith, and in a disinterested fashion. The suggested standard would not permit the court to substitute its own business judgment for that of management. In determining whether the corporation has met its burden, the court would be able to consider all relevant justifications for management's determination, including the seriousness and weight of the plaintiff's allegations. This rule would protect corporate management by disallowing judicial intrusion into the substantive allegations except to the minimal extent necessary for the corporation to meet its burden.

Placing the burden upon the corporation makes good sense. After all, corporate management possess all the relevant information and facts surrounding the determination to discontinue the derivative litigation. Corporations could more easily show the reasonableness of its decision maker's determination in the face of mere allegations of corporate mismanagement implicating duty of care. The corporation should be able to present the requisite showing in a cost effective manner. In response to a shareholder's demand, the corporation will presumably conduct a reasonable inquiry assembling relevant underlying facts. Moreover, the standards of good faith and reasonableness are quite low and should be readily met. Given the general judicial reluctance to meddle in the corporate sphere, this proposed standard should not overly concern corporate practitioners.

Defendants have filed their motion for summary judgment and presently assert that there are no genuine issues of material fact as to the good faith and reasonableness of the board's decision to refuse to institute litigation and, thus, summary judgment must be granted. Based on the court's decision to adopt a modified business judgment rule in line with the highest courts of Massachusetts and North Carolina, plaintiffs are entitled to discovery on the issues of the board's disinterestedness, . . . good faith, due care in its investigation and the reasonableness of its decision. Under the summary judgment standard . . . , plaintiffs must establish that a material genuine issue of fact exists as to the nature of the investigation, the good faith or reasonableness of the board's decision in order to defeat defendants' motion for summary judgment under the business judgment rule.

The Court finds that discovery should be limited to the narrow issue of what steps the directors took to inform themselves of the shareholder demand and the reasonableness of its decision. Furthermore, the court directs that discovery should be made available from the time the demand was made. Any discovery which relates to actions that occurred prior to the demand would go to the merits of the litigation, and not this narrow issue. Plaintiffs may *not* have discovery on the merits of their claim nor may they require defendants to produce documents which were utilized in making the decisions which resulted in alleged mismanagement. Plaintiffs' discovery is to be limited and focused in order to meet defendants' motion for summary judgment.

The court therefore determines that the relevant discovery to be taken is as follows: (1) plaintiffs should have the opportunity to take the depositions of all the directors and officers who were on the board when the demand was refused; (2) plaintiffs should have access to the minutes of any meetings in which the decision to either proceed with the litigation or reject the demand was discussed; and (3) defendants are required to produce any documents which were generated to inform the directors upon which they based their decision to reject the demand.

Notes and Questions

1. Reality Check

a. What is the procedural posture of this case?

b. What test does Justice Weiss finally adopt?

c. What alternatives to that test are discussed?

2. Suppose

a. Suppose that the court had adopted the Delaware or MBCA test. Would the analysis or result have been different?

3. What Do You Think?

a. Do you think the Delaware rule that, by making a demand a shareholder conceded the board's independence, is a good one?

b. Is a universal demand rule a panacea for the troubles of derivative litigation?

4. You Draft It

a. Draft the ideal statute embodying the best rule for raising and evaluating challenges to a board.

D. FEDERAL SECURITIES REGULATION

The federal securities laws affect shareholder power in public companies in several ways. The dominant thrust of the securities laws is disclosure rather than substantive requirements. Nevertheless, at least one area of shareholder power, the solicitation of proxies by company management, has been heavily regulated under federal law since the 1930s. In this section we will briefly see four aspects of federal securities regulation of shareholder power.

First, we will look at federal rules that require public companies to place certain shareholder-proposed resolutions on the agenda for the annual shareholder meeting. Second, we will look at the federal rules governing proxies. Third, we will see that public companies have periodic disclosure requirements, which puts important information into the hands of shareholders. Finally, federal law requires certain shareholders to disclose information about their shareholdings and intentions.

1. Matters Requiring Shareholder Vote Under Federal Law

SEC Rule 14a-8 requires public companies to include a shareholder's proposal in its proxy materials sent to all shareholders if certain conditions are met. The rule is layperson friendly and is written in "plain English" in question-and-answer form. A person who has owned the lesser of 1 percent or $2,000 worth of voting stock for more than one year may submit one proposal each year. The proposal and any supporting statement may not exceed 500 words and must be submitted prior to the deadline, which must be stated in the prior year's proxy statement. The proponent must appear at the annual meeting to formally move the proposal.

A properly submitted proposal may be excluded by the company, but the company bears the burden of proving that the proposal is excludable. The company may exclude a proposal if it has been substantially included within the last five years and failed to garner 3 percent of the vote (if presented once), 6 percent (if twice), or 10 percent (if three times).

The grounds for excluding a new proposal fall into three broad categories. First are objections based essentially on state corporate law. Thus a company may exclude a proposal on the grounds that the proposal is impermissible under state corporate law (precatory motions are almost always permissible), the proposal relates to the election of directors or other matters already on the meeting agenda, or the proposal relates to specific amounts of dividends.

The second area for exclusion is, essentially, that passage would be a nullity. A corporation may exclude a proposal on the grounds that the corporation could not implement the proposal, the proposal has already been substantially implemented, or the proposal would be a violation of law including the proxy rules.

Third, proposals that are of minimal relevance to the corporation as a whole may be excluded. So, shareholder proposals may be excluded on the grounds that the proposal is to redress a personal grievance or the proposal relates to less than 5 percent of the company business and is not otherwise significantly related to the company's business.

The most contentious area, though, allows a corporation to exclude a shareholder proposal that "deals with a matter relating to the company's ordinary business operations." See Rule 14a-8(i)(7). The reason is that proposals that particularly rankle management are typically not excludable under any of the other categories. The SEC, which is the final arbiter of whether a shareholder proposal may be excluded, has vacillated between proshareholder and promanagement mindsets. Although the ultimate decision is intensely fact specific, in general, matters that concern day-to-day management issues are excludable and those that concern corporate policy may not be excluded. Often the policy proposals are matters of considerable, and controversial, public interest rather than narrowly related to the particular corporation.

2. Regulation of Proxy Solicitations

One criticism of public companies during the Great Depression of the 1930s was that corporate management controlled the outcome of corporate elections. This was because the incumbent board typically proposed a slate of directors (usually the incumbents) for nomination and election. The dispersed nature of public company shares made it unlikely that any significant alternative to the incumbents would be proposed. Congress, in 1934, punted the issue by declaring that no public company may solicit proxies from its shareholders in contravention of SEC rules. This left the SEC to invent the proxy rules, which are contained in Regulation 14A.

The SEC rules take a broad view of the definition of *proxy* and *solicitation*. *Proxy* means any collective shareholder action, and is not limited to shareholder meetings. *Solicitation* means any request to grant or revoke a proxy. Many kinds of communications between management and shareholders and communications among shareholders could thus be "solicitation" of "proxies." The SEC has exempted communications among shareholders that are not directed toward eventually obtaining a written proxy in connection with a shareholder vote.

Proxies must comply with rather precise SEC rules concerning form. The rules also require relatively comprehensive disclosure of material information regarding the corporation and its financial and operational performance and regarding the nominees for board positions. The company must file its proposed proxy statement with the SEC in advance of sending it to shareholders if the meeting agenda contains any contested matters or any nonroutine matters. In addition to the shareholder proposal rules set out above, the SEC has serious antifraud provisions to prevent false or misleading statements in proxy requests. The SEC also requires management to make certain shareholder information available to dissidents who intend to wage a proxy contest.

3. Reporting Requirements

Every public company must make periodic reports to its shareholders. The principal report is the annual report to shareholders, which is filed with the SEC on Form 10-K. This report is a comprehensive discussion of the company and the financial and operational results of the prior year. The 10-K also contains audited financial statements covering the prior year. Similar, but less comprehensive, reports are filed each quarter on Form 10-Q. These reports contain unaudited financial statements.

Finally, and perhaps most interestingly, public companies must file Form 8-K promptly after the occurrence of certain significant events. Many investors pay particular attention to 8-K filings. An 8-K must be filed when a company enters into or terminates a material contract not in the ordinary course of business, such as a merger agreement. Other areas requiring an 8-K filing include material, negative, financial developments; the resignation of a director or principal officer; and the amendment of the Articles or bylaws.

4. Ownership Reporting Requirements

The federal securities laws impose two basic kinds of reporting requirements for certain shareholders. First, any person or group, which is broadly defined, that acquires 5 percent of the voting stock of a public company must file a Schedule 13D. The schedule requires basic information about the stockholder, the source of the funds used to acquire the stock, and the purpose of the stockholding (e.g., investment or to effect a change in control). The purpose of the Schedule 13D requirement is to alert corporate management to potential hostile raiders and to alert other shareholders that a significant amount of stock has been accumulated under common control.

Second, Section 16(a) of the '34 Act requires all officers and directors, regardless of how little stock they hold, and all owners of 10 percent or more of the company's voting stock, to file Form 3. This describes the ownership status of any company stock held by the filer. Changes in ownership, whether purchases or sales, are reported on Form 4. Section 16(b) provides that the corporation may recover from anyone required to file under 16(a), any profit made or loss avoided on sales or purchases made within six months of each other. The provision is one of strict liability and the calculation of the six-month period can be tricky; corporate executives violate the provisions with some regularity.

E. TERMS OF ART IN THIS CHAPTER

Absolute majority
Advance notice bylaw
Amote
Annual meetings
Book entry system
Broker overvote
Call
Cede & Co.
Demand excused
Demand refused
Derivative action

DTC
General proxy
Holdover
Inspection right
Limited proxy
NOBO list
Notice
Periodic reporting
Plurality
Precatory motion
Proper purpose

Proxy
Quorum
Settled
Simple majority
Special committee
Special meeting
Street name
Transaction reporting
Transfer agent

16

Shareholder Governance Questions Most Often Seen in the Privately Held Corporation

In this chapter we continue to explore the role of shareholders in corporate governance. The last chapter introduced you to the general corporate law principles of shareholder powers and used the publicly held corporation as the typical setting. Our focus here is on questions of shareholder participation that are typically encountered in nonpublic corporations. Many of these corporations, as you will see, are owned and operated by members of a single family, raising issues of family dynamics as well as corporate law.

We'll consider two main areas of shareholder governance in this chapter. First, we'll investigate the kinds of restrictions that can be imposed by the corporation, and ultimately, by the shareholders themselves, on corporate governance powers. Second, we'll look at the restrictions on shareholder governance powers that are imposed externally, that is, by courts and legislatures. In that section we'll see yet another aspect of fiduciary duties and look at the potential plight of minority shareholders in closely held corporations.

A. SELF-IMPOSED RESTRICTIONS ON SHAREHOLDER GOVERNANCE RIGHTS

Chapter 15 described the principal shareholder governance powers. These primarily concern the power to vote. In this portion of the chapter we take up five devices that planners may employ that affect shareholder governance powers in important ways.

1. Preemptive Rights: The Management Component

When we considered how money moves into a corporation and the concomitant economic rights given in return, we saw that a later issuance of shares could reduce the economic interests of the current shareholders if the newly issued shares were issued for less than their fair value. See Chapter 6. A similar dilution in management power occurs when voting shares are issued even where the current shareholders' economic interests are protected. Consider this example:

593

> Each of the four shareholders of a corporation owns 250 shares of common stock.
>
> The fair value of the entire corporation is $1 million.
>
> The corporation needs another $1 million in permanent capital.
>
> As a consequence, the board (in reality, quite probably the four shareholders) resolves to issue 1,000 shares of common stock at $1,000 each to people who are not currently shareholders.

Economically, the current shareholders are probably not harmed. Each owned one-fourth of a corporation worth $1 million and thus had $250,000 in wealth. After the issuance of new shares, each of the original shareholders owns one-eighth of a corporation worth about $2 million[1] and thus retains his or her $250,000 of wealth.

But regardless of whether the original shareholders are helped or hurt economically by the new issuance, their voting interests have changed. True, each still has 250 votes (assuming one vote per share) but now, those 250 votes are only one-eighth of the total votes rather than one-fourth. If the newly issued shares will be held by a large number of unaffiliated shareholders, the original shareholders might retain, as a practical matter, their voting control. If the new shares are issued to a single shareholder, though, that shareholder has half the voting power, effectively relegating the original shareholders' voting power to that of minority shareholder status.

The voting power dilution from issuing shares can, obviously, be used strategically. In public companies, this danger is only theoretical because the shares are already so widely held and the newly issued shares are probably going to be equally widely distributed so no real harm to the current shareholders' voting power, which is functionally nonexistent, is done. In closely held corporations considerable harm can be done to existing shareholders.

As we described in Chapter 6, the courts, from an early date, found an equitable right in existing shareholders to purchase shares proposed to be issued so that their aliquot economic and managerial interests would be preserved. This right, called the *preemptive right*, permits each current shareholder to maintain his or her proportionate interest by purchasing the same percentage of to-be-issued shares on the same terms and conditions as proposed by the board of directors. Broadly speaking, preemptive rights were unavailable where

> the newly issued shares were to be issued for noncash consideration (on the theory that the corporation's need for the particular consideration was probably so important that cash was not a viable substitute);
>
> the newly issued shares were to be issued as part of the corporation's initial plan of financing; or
>
> the newly issued shares were to be of a different class than those outstanding.

---

1. This assumes that the additional money from the stock issuance increases the value of the company dollar for dollar. That assumption, although not unreasonable, is not always accurate. If the new money will allow the corporation to compete much more successfully than it did before, the value of the company might increase more than the money contributed. Thus, a company worth $1 million, that obtains an infusion of $1 million, might legitimately be worth $2.5 or $3 million. Conversely, if the additional money will not be sufficient for the company to prosper the corporation may lose value. This might be the case where management will misinvest the proceeds. So, the same company that was worth $1 million may, after the infusion of another $1 million, have a value of only $1.5 million. In fact, paradoxically, it is possible that the corporation might be worth even less than $1 million after the infusion of an additional $1 million!

The corporation statutes in many states (although not Delaware) explicitly embody these exemptions See MBCA §6.30(a). Under the DGCL and MBCA, preemptive rights are opt-in. That is, a corporation's shareholders have no right to preempt subsequent issuances of stock unless the Articles so provide. See DGCL §102(b)(3) and MBCA §6.30(a).

2. Supermajority Provisions

A very common technique for changing the default governing structure in a closely held corporation is to require a *supermajority* vote. A supermajority provision for board meetings may be placed in the Articles or bylaws. A supermajority provision for shareholder meetings must be in the Articles under the MBCA but may be in either the Certificate or the bylaws in Delaware. See DGCL §§102(b)(4), 141(b), 216 and MBCA §§7.24, 8.24.

The first case in this chapter, *Whetstone*, is designed to introduce you to some of the problems that shareholders in closely held corporations face. As you will see, these problems are quite different from those faced by shareholders in publicly held companies. In particular, *Whetstone* is intended to illustrate how supermajority provisions may provide protection to shareholders. You should also pay some attention to the question of remedy. That question becomes quite important in shareholder disputes and this chapter will consider remedies in more detail near the end. Nonetheless, you should be sensitive now to the remedy sought.

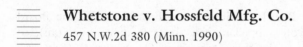

Whetstone v. Hossfeld Mfg. Co.
457 N.W.2d 380 (Minn. 1990)

YETKA, J.

Appellant is a shareholder in a Minnesota closely held corporation. In 1988, the president of the corporation initiated amendments to the corporation's articles of incorporation and bylaws.... Appellant dissented from the corporation's amendment of the articles and bylaws, but the corporation refused to purchase his shares. Shortly thereafter, appellant commenced this action. No claim is made that appellant failed to follow the statutory procedure for asserting his right to dissent. The trial court granted summary judgment in favor of appellant.

The court of appeals reversed, holding that elimination of veto powers is not among the events which entitle dissenting shareholders to receive the fair value of their shares.

Article V of the corporation's articles of incorporation and article II, section 1 of the bylaws reserve the following power in certain shareholders with respect to electing directors:

> No person shall be elected a member of the Board of Directors without the written consent of every stockholder of record who owns 30% or more of the issued and outstanding stock of the corporation, unless such person shall be the owner of record of at least 30% of the outstanding stock of the corporation.

With respect to electing or appointing officers and employees, article VIII of the articles of incorporation provided the following:

> No person shall be elected or appointed an officer, assistant officer, manager, or agent of the corporation without the written consent of every stockholder of record who owns 30% or more of the issued and outstanding stock of the corporation, unless such person shall be the owner of record of at least 30% of the outstanding stock of the corporation.

Article III, section 6 of the bylaws of the corporation provided the following for the appointment of a manager of the corporation:

> The Board of Directors shall by a majority vote appoint a Manager of the corporation, and give such Manager full control and direction of the operations of the business, manufacturing and sales, under the control of the Board of Directors. No person, however, shall be elected or appointed such assistant officer, manager or agent of the corporation without the written consent of every stockholder of record who owns 30% or more of the issued and outstanding stock of the corporation, unless such person shall be the owner of record of at least 30% of the outstanding stock of the corporation.

Finally, article V, section 1 of the bylaws provided as follows: "The By-Laws of the corporation shall be subject to alteration, amendment or repeal by a seventy-five (75%) vote of all shareholders, at any regular meeting, or special meeting called therefor."

At the time this action was commenced, there were 13 shareholders. Appellant owns 36 percent of the corporation's shares. The president of the corporation and his wife, individually and as joint tenants, own 50.93 percent of the corporation's shares.

At a special meeting of the Board of Directors on July 23, 1988, the Board of Directors voted, by a 2-1 vote (appellant cast the sole dissenting vote), to amend the bylaws so as to eliminate the above provisions. On August 6, 1988, at a special meeting of the stockholders, the articles were amended to eliminate the above veto powers.

Minn. Stat. §302A.471, subd. 1 (1988) provides in pertinent part as follows:

> A shareholder of a corporation may dissent from, and obtain payment for the fair value of the shareholder's shares in the event of, any of the following corporate actions:
>> (a) An amendment of the articles that materially and adversely affects the rights or preferences of the shares of the dissenting shareholder in that it:
>>> . . .
>>> (4) excludes or limits the right of a shareholder to vote on a matter, or to cumulate votes . . . .

In *Westland* [*Capital Corp. v. Lucht Engineering Inc.*, 308 N.W.2d 709, 712 (Minn. 1981)], this court observed that minority shareholders in a closely held corporation are vulnerable because the majority can deny them income by refusing to employ them or pay dividends. The *Westland* court also noted that, because legal remedies for majority shareholder abuse were somewhat ineffective, the practice of entering into shareholder agreements in the form of charter provisions, bylaws or contracts *inter se* developed.

As indicated in *Westland,* the use of veto power arrangements and super majority[2] voting requirements have long been recognized as a means of providing a minority shareholder in a closely held corporation protection against prejudicial conduct by the majority shareholder(s). Investors in closely held corporations frequently seek to control the election of directors, officers, and managers because the investors' return on investment often comes only in the form of compensation for serving as directors or officers rather than from dividends on stock. Accordingly, the investors are typically most interested in being able to prevent those in control of the corporation from removing them as directors or officers so as to cut off this return on investment. To achieve further protection against the removal of officers, a provision requiring an affirmative vote of not less than a stated number of directors may be inserted. However, such provision is of practical effect only when coupled with a provision against an increase in the number of directors.[3]

The difficulty of disposing of an investment in a close corporation also increases the desire of minority shareholders for a veto over corporate decisions. Consequently, amendments to the articles of incorporation and bylaws of a closely held corporation which eliminate veto arrangements agreed to by the shareholders when they incorporated the business will invariably cause a fundamental change in the investment contract between shareholders.

Eliminating a minority shareholder's veto power over decisions of the majority shareholder, particularly in cases such as this,[4] unquestionably limits the voting rights of the minority shareholder. Without a veto power, a minority shareholder has no control over numerous crucial corporate actions, including decisions to:

(1) Drain off earnings by paying excessive salaries, bonuses, fringe benefits, or excessive travel and entertainment expenses;
(2) Make loans or advances to officers with or without security;
(3) Not pay dividends;
(4) Sell, transfer or pledge assets of the corporation; and
(5) Refuse to disclose results of operations and withhold books and records.

Before the amendments, appellant had the right to cast the *deciding* vote in these key decisions. Following the amendments, appellant's right to vote on these decisions is little more than a formality. Thus, the amendments in question fundamentally altered the investment contract between appellant and respondent corporation.

The existence of veto power increases the risk of corporate deadlock. Nevertheless, the existence of this risk does not justify allowing a majority shareholder to change the investment contract fundamentally or freeze out a minority shareholder.

2. The term "supermajority" refers to a method of providing veto power by requiring approval of a high percentage of shares entitled to vote and setting that vote requirement at a level which cannot be obtained without the votes of shareholders who desire the veto. A provision requiring an affirmative vote of holders of 75 percent of the voting shares outstanding gives a veto power to any shareholder or group of shareholders holding more than 25 percent of the shares. In the present case, a 75 percent majority shareholder voting requirement was necessary for approval of certain actions before the amendments in question were made.

3. In the present case, the articles did not require the affirmative vote of a stated number of directors for approval of officers and managers. The articles did, however, permit a maximum of five directors. The amendments in question reduced the maximum number of directors and, therefore, as a practical matter, assured that minority shareholders without veto power would not be able to elect additional directors in order to undercut or circumvent the majority shareholder(s)' control of the corporation.

4. In this case, more than 50 percent of the shares are controlled by one shareholder who is also the president.

Although veto power in the hands of a minority shareholder is subject to abuse, so is the voting power held by the majority shareholder(s). Enhanced availability of the "appraisal remedy" under section 302A.471 will deter both forms of oppression. Moreover, the availability of such a legal remedy will relieve courts, in an exercise of their equitable powers, from performing the difficult task of balancing the equities when there has been unfair conduct by both factions. In the context of closely held corporations, the availability of such a remedy will also make the closely held corporation more like a partnership, a result which is consistent with the basic goal of most investors in a closely held corporation as well as Minn. Stat. ch. 302A.

For all of the above reasons, the decision of the court of appeals is reversed and the case is remanded to the trial court for a determination of the fair value of appellant's shares to be awarded to him in accordance with Minn. Stat. ch. 302A.471.

Notes and Questions

1. Notes

a. The Minnesota statute permitting appraisal when an amendment to the articles excludes or limits shareholder voting rights appeared in the old MBCA (1950). Neither the current MBCA nor the DGCL has comparable provisions.

b. Paradoxically, supermajority provisions in public companies serve to protect the incumbent management rather than the shareholders. In public companies the shareholders are typically widely dispersed without any effective control over management. Supermajority provisions, at the shareholder level, serve to increase the difficulty of an insurgent group of shareholders gaining influence over the corporation. Thus the company's directors are more securely in control of the corporation.

c. At common law courts frequently held that a requirement of shareholder unanimity was unenforceable because it was contrary to public policy. The theory behind such results was that a primary difference between a corporation and a partnership was that shareholders' power should be proportional to their investment (i.e., to the shares they held) in contrast to the partnership model of treating partners as having equal management rights regardless of the disparity in their investments. Corporate drafters circumvented this case law by drafting supermajority provisions that, on their face, did not require unanimity but which, as a practical matter, did. For example, in a corporation with four 25 percent shareholders, a supermajority provision would require an 80 percent shareholder vote to effect certain shareholder actions. This provision would pass muster under the older common law rule. This approach to drafting supermajority provisions continues today in part because of uncertainty as to whether modern courts would strike down unanimity requirements.

2. Reality Check

a. What kinds of votes were subject to supermajority provisions?
b. Where were those supermajority provisions contained?
c. How do the supermajority provisions work?
d. How were the supermajority provisions eliminated?
e. According to Justice Yetka, what dangers do minority shareholders in close corporations face?
f. How do supermajority provisions protect minority shareholders?
g. Why did the court grant relief to the plaintiff?

3. What Do You Think?

a. Can the dangers of being a minority shareholder be described in terms of the agency principles we saw in Chapter 4?

b. Do you think appraisal is the appropriate remedy in this case? Why does the court not simply declare the changes to the corporate structure invalid?

c. Were the amendments properly adopted under the corporation statutes? If so, how can the court impose any remedy? If so, how has the plaintiff been hurt? Didn't the plaintiff simply get a result that was possible under the bargain struck with the corporation?

a. *Superquorum Provisions*

A related technique for giving minority shareholders more protection is to raise the quorum required for board meetings or shareholder meetings. See DGCL §§141(b) (director meetings), 216 (shareholder meetings) and MBCA §§7.27 (shareholder meetings), 8.24(a) (director meetings). A superquorum requirement for board meetings may be placed in the Articles or the bylaws. Under the DGCL, shareholder superquorum requirements may also be in either the Certificate or bylaws but the MBCA permits such provisions in the Articles only. See DGCL §216 and MBCA §7.27.

At least three pitfalls exist that may make superquorum provisions undesirable. First, the converse of the requirement that superquorum provisions need only be in the bylaws is that the bylaws may more easily be amended than the Articles and thus the provision more easily done away with. Second, a superquorum provision without supermajority provisions means that, if a quorum exists at a board or shareholder meeting, the minority could more easily be outvoted than if a supermajority provision existed. Thus the "protection" afforded by superquorum provisions may be illusory. Finally, superquorum provisions are rather blunt in their effect. That is, if a group of directors determines to stay away from a meeting to avoid a quorum, the corporation can take no action at all. If this situation becomes chronic, the corporation is in deadlock, which may result in dissolution or other dire remedies being imposed by a court. On the other hand, if the corporation has only a supermajority provision, the board may take action on a potentially wide range of vital but uncontroversial matters. So, as a matter of planning, supermajority voting provisions are usually preferable to superquorum provisions.

3. Cumulative Voting

Ordinarily, shareholders are entitled to cast one vote for every share they own for each matter presented for a shareholder vote. When electing directors, each director slot is considered a separate election, although the candidates run at large, so each shareholder may cast his or her shares for as many different candidates as there are slots. For example, when electing a board of three directors, the holder of 100 shares may cast (up to) 100 votes for three different people. This method is called *straight voting* or *statutory voting*.

The plurality rule combined with the straight voting method means that the shareholder or coalition of shareholders that controls the most shares is able to elect all the directors. Where shares are widely dispersed or where other barriers to collective action exist the quantum of shares necessary to control the board may be no more than 20 percent or perhaps even less. In many settings such hegemony may be short-lived and competing shareholder factions are likely to arise, but in other settings the dominant shareholder group seems likely to remain so indefinitely. In the starkest situation of a corporation with two shareholders, a shareholder with slightly more than 50 percent of the shares can elect every member of the board — leaving the other shareholder, who owns nearly half the corporation, powerless, as in *Whetstone.*

The cumulative voting method was developed to redress this perceived inequity. Under *cumulative voting,* each shareholder may cast votes equal to the product of the number of shares owned multiplied by the number of director slots to be filled. The shareholder may cast those votes for one candidate or distribute the product among several candidates. Assume, again, a board of three directors and a shareholder owning 100 shares. That shareholder has 300 votes and may cast all 300 for one person or divide them as he or she sees fit. For example, the shareholder might cast 150 votes each for two candidates or 200 votes for one candidate and 100 for another. DGCL §214, MBCA §7.28(c).

So what? How does this help shareholders who control fewer shares than others? It means that as long as more than one director slot is being filled, some percentage of otherwise unrepresented shareholders can elect a candidate of its choice. How small or large a percentage is required to elect a candidate depends on how many director slots are to be filled. The more slots, the lower the percentage of shares needed to elect one candidate. The following chart shows the percentage required to elect one director:

Board Slots to Be Filled:	Shares Needed to Elect One Director:
2	>33%
3	>25%
4	>20%
5	>16%

In practice, cumulative voting issues often arise when it is impossible to obtain more shares. This is so because cumulative voting is primarily important in closely held corporations. By the time one set of shareholders is concerned with trying to elect a board candidate, the views of the shareholders have hardened and transfer of shares from one faction to another is unlikely. The question then becomes how many directors can be elected with a given number of shares? The following formula tells the answer:

Formula 1

$$\frac{s(D+1)}{S} = INT(d)$$

s = number of voting shares your faction controls
S = total number of voting shares
D = total number of director slots to be filled
INT(d) = the integer (i.e., drop — *don't round* — any fraction) of the number of director slots your faction can be certain of electing.

For those occasions when controlling more shares is possible, you can determine the number of shares necessary to elect a desired number of directors by using this formula:

Formula 2

$$\frac{(s \times d)}{(D + 1) + 1} = INT(s)$$

$INT(s)$ = the integer of the number of voting shares your faction needs to elect "d" directors.

Finally, and often critically, one must know how many *votes* to give one's candidate(s) to ensure election. The formula is:

Formula 3

$$\frac{(S - s)D}{(D - d) + 1} + 1 = INT(V)$$

$INT(V)$ = the integer of the number of votes that must be cast per candidate to ensure election of "d" directors.

Under the DGCL and the MBCA, cumulative voting is an opt-in provision meaning that straight voting applies unless the Articles provide for cumulative voting. You should be aware, though, that many states provide that cumulative voting is an opt-out provision (i.e., cumulative voting is the default rule) and a few states, such as California, require cumulative voting for electing directors.

The practical application of cumulative voting is often very nerve-wracking for lawyers. First, of course, its importance is greatest when shareholder factions are most at loggerheads, so your client will perceive that he or she has much at stake. Second, although the formulas are not difficult, clients and counsel have a way of miscalculating, which, of course, frequently leads to grief.[2] Third, under the MBCA, where cumulative voting exists, a shareholder must give notice of his or her intention to cumulate; thereafter all shareholders may vote cumulatively without notice. This is to prevent inattentive shareholder factions from being sandbagged by another faction that may garner extra seats by cumulating while the inattentive faction loses because it voted straight. Many states, however, do not include such a provision, thus making it possible to act strategically. Remember that the common law rule is that votes may be changed until the polls are declared closed and that once closed, the polls may not be reopened.

Notes and Questions

1. Notes

a. Remember, your candidate(s) don't need to receive the highest number of votes. You want them to get only the minimum number necessary to be certain that they will be elected.

---

2. In part, these miscalculations are caused by the fact that many corporate resources print only formula 2, which is often not germane to the parties. Compounding this source of confusion is that those other corporate resources also tend to print a misleading (though not actually incorrect) version of the formulas, which often contributes to miscalculations.

b. A related observation: Quite frequently you will have votes left over after casting the minimum necessary to ensure election of your candidate(s). Frequently these extra votes are simply distributed equally among the faction's candidates, which has the effect of wasting those extra votes. Rather, those extra votes should be cast for one additional candidate. It is sometimes possible to win a director slot to which your faction would not be "entitled" under cumulative voting by such an approach.

c. If you are reasonably certain that some shares controlled by opposing factions will not be voted at the meeting, you can reduce S in the formulas by the number of shares likely to be missing. Doing so will change the number of votes per candidate you must cast to ensure election and may suggest that you can win an additional board seat. Remember, though, that if you overestimate the number of shares that are absent, your faction may come to grief because you cast too few votes per candidate to elect all (or even to elect any) of your candidates.

d. Cumulative voting's effects can be blunted in three ways. First, a classified board can reduce (or increase) a particular faction's power to elect board members. Second, a staggered board increases the percentage of shares necessary to elect one more candidate because it reduces the number of slots to be elected at each annual meeting. At the most extreme, a shareholder faction that controls slightly more than 25 percent of the shares, and which can therefore elect one director on a three-person board, will have that power eviscerated if the board is staggered with three-year terms. In that setting only one director will be elected each year and, obviously, the shareholder faction that controls the most shares can elect all three directors, although it may take two years — three annual meetings — to achieve this result completely. Finally, reducing the size of the board has the same functional effect as staggering the board terms.

2. Suppose

a. Assume that a corporation with cumulative voting has 1,000 shares outstanding, seven directors are to be elected, and your faction controls 300 shares. How many candidates can your faction be certain of electing to the board?

b. Using the same assumptions, how many votes should you cast for each of your candidates to ensure all of them are elected? The answers are at the end of this Notes and Questions section.

3. What Do You Think?

a. Is cumulative voting an appropriate way to protect shareholders? Are all shareholders benefited by cumulative voting?

b. If you believe cumulative voting is beneficial, do you believe it should be mandatory for all corporations? If not, should it be mandatory for some corporations? If so, which ones?

c. Should a corporation with cumulative voting be allowed to blunt the consequences by classifying, staggering or reducing the size of its board? How would you enforce such restrictions?

4. Answers to "Suppose" Questions

a. Your faction can elect two directors. The calculation, using Formula 1, is,

$$\frac{s(D+1)}{S} = INT(d)$$

$$\frac{300(7+1)}{1,000} = \text{INT(d)}$$

$$\frac{2,400}{1,000} = \text{INT(d)}$$

$$2.4 = \text{INT(d)}$$

$$2 = d$$

b. You should cast 817 votes for each of your two candidates. That answer is found using Formula 3:

$$\frac{(S-s)D}{(D-d)+1} + 1 = \text{INT(V)}$$

$$\frac{(1,000-300)7}{(7-2)+1} + 1 = \text{INT(V)}$$

$$\frac{4,900}{6} + 1 = \text{INT(V)}$$

$$817.66... = \text{INT(V)}$$

$$817 = V$$

Note that your faction's 300 shares means you have 2,100 votes to cast (i.e., 300 × 7). If you simply give half your votes (1,050) to each candidate, each will certainly be elected. However, by using Formula 3 you know that 817 votes each will be sufficient to guarantee election. If you cast 817 votes per candidate you have 466 votes remaining (2,100 − 1,634), which you should cast for a third candidate. By doing so you might capture a third director slot if your opponents miscalculate or are sufficiently inattentive.

4. Agreements Regarding Shareholder Voting

Shareholders in nonpublic corporations frequently enter into agreements with one another about the way in which their shares will be voted. These agreements, obviously, modify the agreeing shareholders' governance powers and may affect the voting power of shareholders who are not parties to the agreement. Conceptually, these agreements should simply raise contract law, rather than corporate law, issues. Shareholders, as the owners of the corporation, classically have the right to take action solely in their own best interest and surely a voting agreement with other shareholders may be such an action. Nevertheless, the courts have long found certain shareholder voting agreements to be impermissible or subject to court-imposed restrictions. Likewise, the state legislatures have enacted statutes that cabin the power of shareholders to enter into and enforce voting agreements.

This section looks at the contours of shareholder voting agreements. We start with *voting trusts* and then look at *pooling agreements*. You ought to pay close attention to the definitions of these terms but also look behind the definitions to figure out why courts and legislatures have subjected certain kinds of agreements to heightened requirements. As we will see, the labels are largely conclusions applied to agreements that possess certain important characteristics.

a. The Current Setting

i. Voting Trusts. We start with a discussion of a classic corporate law technique affecting shareholder voting power: the voting trust. At common law voting trusts were viewed with great suspicion and usually were held to be unenforceable. In the early twentieth century, state legislatures began to pass statutes that permitted voting trusts, provided the trusts conformed to the requirements of the statutes. Read DGCL §218 and MBCA §7.30. Go ahead, read them.

Voting trusts are used in three basic situations. The intention is to give the economic rights of stock to one person or group and the management rights to another person or group. In close corporations voting trusts are often used as a device to smooth the transfer of wealth from one generation to the next. Take, as an example, a typical family-owned business corporation. The parents, who own all the stock, wish to pass the economic benefits to their children but do not wish to give the children the concomitant power to manage the corporation. By using a voting trust, the parents put the stock (or some of it) into the trust with themselves as the trustees and their child-ren as the beneficiaries. During the life of the trust, the parents vote the shares, while the children are entitled to the dividends and other capital appreciation of the shares.

A second use of voting trusts is when a corporation enters bankruptcy, but the underlying economic business is viable. If the corporation is reorganized (rather than liquidated) the former creditors have often had their debt converted into stock. The attitude of the former creditors may remain hostile to the business. After all, the creditors want their money. They don't want to own a business. In such a setting, these new, involuntary, shareholders may have an incentive to vote in ways that are not economically rational for the business as a whole. A voting trust, with the former creditors receiving the economic benefits, and the corporation's new management as trustees may solve the tension. Finally, a corporation that is in economic difficulty but not yet bankrupt may enter into a voting trust agreement as a condition of receiving a necessary loan.

The Delaware Supreme Court described the purpose of regulating voting trusts:

> First, . . . Section 218, from its original enactment in 1925, was designed to regulate agreements by "(o)ne or more stockholders." Not all trusts of corporate stock which, either expressly or by implication, give voting rights to a trustee are voting trusts. The Court of Chancery defined a voting trust in *Peyton v. William C. Peyton Corp.*, 194 A. 106, 111 (Del. Ch. 1937), *rev'd on other grounds*, 7 A.2d 737 (Del. 1939) in the following manner:
>
>> A voting trust as commonly understood is a device whereby two or more persons owning stock with voting powers, divorce the voting rights thereof from the ownership, retaining to all intents and purposes the latter in themselves and

transferring the former to trustees in whom the voting rights of all the depositors in the trust are pooled.

This definition has been adopted in several cases. Regulation of voting trusts is directed to a class of trusts created to unify voting. Thus, the voting trust statute was not intended to be all inclusive in the sense that it was designed to apply to every set of facts in which voting rights are transferred to trustees incident to or as part of the assignment of other stockholder rights. Rather, a voting trust is a stockholder pooling arrangement with the criteria that voting rights are separated out and irrevocably assigned for a definite period of time to voting trustees for control purposes while other attributes of ownership are retained by the depositing stockholders.

Second, our case law makes it clear that the main purpose of a voting trust statute is "to avoid secret, uncontrolled combinations of stockholders formed to acquire control of the corporation to the possible detriment of non-participating shareholders." *Lehrman* [*v. Cohen*] 222 A.2d [800] at 807 [(Del. 1966)].

Third, it is important to recognize there has been a significant change from the days of our original 1925 statute. Voting trusts were viewed with "disfavor" or "looked upon...with indulgence" by the courts. Other contractual arrangements interfering with stock ownership, such as irrevocable proxies, were viewed with suspicion. The desire for flexibility in modern society has altered such restrictive thinking. E. Folk, *The Delaware General Corporation Law*, Section 218 at 240-42 (1972). The trend of liberalization was markedly apparent in the 1967 changes to our own §218.[7] Voting or other agreements and irrevocable proxies were given favorable treatment and restrictive judicial interpretations as to the absolute voiding of voting trusts for terms beyond the statutory limit were changed by statute. The trend was not to extend the voting trust restrictions beyond the class of trust being regulated and beyond the reasons for statutory regulation. That public policy cannot be ignored here.

Oceanic Exploration Co. v. Grynberg, 428 A.2d 1 (Del. 1981) (Quillen, J.)

Notes and Questions

1. Notes

a. The usual formulation of the common law definition of a voting trust is,

(1) the voting rights of the stock are separated from the other attributes of ownership; (2) the voting rights granted are intended to be irrevocable for a definite period of time; and (3) The principal purpose of the grant of voting rights is to acquire voting control of the corporation.

Lehrman v. Cohen, 222 A.2d 800, 805 (Del. 1966) (quoting *Abercrombie v. Davies*, 130 A.2d 338 (Del. Ch. 1957)

---

7. As Professor Folk's treatise points out, in the voting trust area, even prior to 1967, some cases "show a marked disposition to uphold transactions rather than strike them down for non-conformity with the voting trust statute." Folk, *supra*, Section 218 at 235, particularly n.15 (1972). *See also id.* at 236 n.19. Thus, the Delaware courts have on occasion avoided the harshness of the exclusivity by finding the arrangement not to be a voting trust (*Lehrman v. Cohen, supra*), by specifically enforcing statutory requirements the parties had neglected to implement (*In re Farm Industries, Inc.*, 196 A.2d 582, 592-94 (Del. Ch. 1963)) and by "expressly (disaffirming) the suggested proposition that any illegality in a voting trust renders the entire agreement illegal" (*Tracey v. Franklin*, 67 A.2d 56, 61 (Del. 1949)).

b. Note that a common law voting trust that does not meet the requirements of the statute is void. In other words, the statute is the exclusive method of creating a valid voting trust.

c. The beneficiaries of a voting trust receive voting trust certificates that represent their ownership interest. These voting trust certificates are ordinarily transferable so beneficiaries can transfer their economic interest. When the trust expires, the beneficiary's transferee receives the shares.

2. Reality Check

a. What are the elements of a voting trust?

b. What are the elements of a valid voting trust under DGCL §218 and MBCA §7.30?

3. What Do You Think?

a. Do voting trusts have the potential to cause harm to corporations, shareholders, or third parties? If so, what dangers exist?

b. Do you believe the voting trusts statutes (DGCL §218 and MBCA §7.30) are traps for the unwary?

ii. Pooling Agreements. As you see, if a court finds an agreement to be a "voting trust," the agreement must comport with the statutory requirements or it is unenforceable. What other voting agreements may shareholders enter into? One such agreement is a proxy (see Chapter 15). Where the shareholder grants a general proxy (i.e., giving the proxyholder discretion as to how to vote) and where the proxy is irrevocable, the agreement looks much like a common law voting trust. Yet courts almost always refrain from recharacterizing voting agreements that purport to be proxies as voting trusts. Thus even though irrevocable general proxies and voting trusts can effect similar ends, their validity will be judged under different criteria.

But shareholders may enter into other voting agreements that are neither common law voting trusts nor proxies. These agreements are typically lumped under the rubric *pooling agreements*.

The legislatures adopted provisions explicitly approving such agreements. The MBCA provides that agreements that determine how the shareholders *themselves* will vote *their own* shares are specifically enforceable. Axiomatically, those agreements are removed from the voting trust section. See MBCA §7.31. In a related provision, the MBCA also provides that being a party to a pooling agreement is an interest in shares that supports an irrevocable proxy. See MBCA §7.22(c)(5).

The cognate Delaware provision (DGCL §218(c)) is much more problematic. It validates written agreements that state how shares shall be voted, that state a procedure for determining how shares shall be voted, and that contain "agreements to agree" on how shares shall be voted. The statute is written in the passive voice, thus it is not explicit whether the agreement must require the shareholders to vote their own shares. It would seem, then, to encompass both some voting trusts and some proxies. As if the issue weren't muddled enough, DGCL §218(d) says that section 218 does not prohibit other shareholder agreements and irrevocable proxies, if they are "not otherwise illegal." What on Earth can this include?

Conceptually, if the statutes permit pooling agreements to be specifically enforced, how are those agreements functionally different from irrevocable proxies or voting trusts?

b. Background and Context

i. Vote Buying.   One other category of shareholder voting agreements continues to present sometimes difficult legal issues: agreements that may constitute "vote buying." Certainly a director who sells his or her vote has breached the duty of loyalty and possibly the duty of care, as well. But aren't shareholders entitled to vote their shares as they please? If so, shouldn't that logically include the power to sell their votes? Obviously a general proxy is simply a gratuitous form of transferring the power to vote. If shareholders may not sell their votes, what is the basis of this prohibition? Unless the shareholder owns a majority of the shares (and possibly where the shareholder owns a controlling, though not a majority, amount of the shares) no fiduciary duty runs to other shareholders.

The following excerpt discusses the rule against vote buying and the underlying policies for that rule. In this case, the company, Hewlett-Packard Co., was soliciting shareholder proxies in favor of the acquisition of Compaq Computer Corp. The acquisition was vehemently opposed by the descendents of the founders, Mr. Hewlett and Mr. Packard, who waged a bitter proxy campaign soliciting shareholders to vote against the merger. The final vote was very close and, on the day prior to the shareholder meeting, a shareholder switched its votes from "no" to "yes." That shareholder was an investment bank that had done work for Hewlett-Packard and hoped to do more work for the company.

> This Court has, on several earlier occasions, addressed so-called "vote-buying" allegations. In some instances the claims were successful and in others they were not. There does not, however, appear to be an obvious predisposition on the part of the Court one way or another toward vote-buying claims.[5]
>
> The appropriate standard for evaluating vote-buying claims is articulated in *Schreiber v. Carney. Schreiber* indicates that vote-buying is illegal *per se* if "the object or purpose is to defraud or in some way disenfranchise the other stockholders." *Schreiber* also notes, absent these deleterious purposes, that "because vote-buying is so easily susceptible of abuse it must be viewed as a voidable transaction subject to a test for intrinsic fairness."[8]

5. In the seminal Delaware case on vote-buying, *Schreiber v. Carney*, the Court recounted the history of challenges to vote-buying agreements in Delaware jurisprudence. 447 A.2d 17, 23-26 (Del. Ch. 1982). The *Schreiber* Court noted that earlier cases "had summarily voided the challenged votes as being purchased and thus contrary to public policy and in fraud of the other stockholders." *Id.* at 23. Two principles were apparent from those cases. First, those cases held that vote-buying was illegal *per se* if that agreement was entered into for the purpose of either defrauding or disenfranchising other shareholders. Second, they indicated that vote-buying was illegal *per se* "as a matter of public policy, [because] each stockholder should be entitled to rely upon the independent judgment of his fellow stockholders." *Id.* at 24.

This second principle was based on the notion that there was a duty owed by all shareholders to each other. The rationale for that notion was that "while self-interest motivates a stockholder's vote, theoretically, it is also advancing the interests of other stockholders. Thus, any agreement entered into for personal gain, whereby a stockholder separates his voting right from his property right was considered a fraud upon this community of interests." *Id.* The *Schreiber* Court noted that the notion that vote-buying was illegal *per se* as a matter of public policy was "'obsolete because it is both impractical and impossible of application to modern corporations . . . and [that] the courts have gradually abandoned it.'" *Id.* at 25 (quoting 5 Fletcher, *Cyclopedia Corporation* (Perm. Ed.) §2066). Furthermore, the Legislature has codified, at [DGCL] 218(c), the permissibility of creating voting agreements. As noted below, however, the principle that vote-buying is illegal *per se* if entered into for deleterious purposes survives.

8. [*Schreiber*] at 26; *see also In re IXC Communications, Inc. Shareholders Litig.*, 1999 WL 1009174 at *8 (Del. Ch.) ("Generally speaking, courts closely scrutinize vote-buying because a shareholder who divorces property interest from voting interest, fails to serve the 'community of interest' among all shareholders, since the 'bought' shareholder votes may not reflect rational, economic self-interest arguably common to all shareholders.").

At first blush this proposition seems difficult to reconcile with the General Assembly's explicit validation of shareholder voting agreements in §218(c). Significantly, however, it was the management of the defendant corporation that was buying votes in favor of a corporate reorganization in *Schreiber*. Shareholders are free to do whatever they want with their votes, including selling them to the highest bidder. Management, on the other hand, may not use corporate assets to buy votes in a hotly contested proxy contest about an extraordinary transaction that would significantly transform the corporation, unless it can be demonstrated, as it was in *Schreiber*, that management's vote-buying activity does not have a deleterious effect on the corporate franchise.

I also disagree with HP's assertion that to establish the invalidity of a vote-buying agreement, a plaintiff must show that a majority of all outstanding shares was obligated to vote in favor of the transaction as a result of the vote-buying. Again, the focus of the Court's analysis should be on possible deleterious effects of a challenged vote-buying agreement on shareholders. Less than a majority of votes can be decisive in tipping the results of an election one way or another. If voiding the votes cast in accordance with a fraudulent vote-buying agreement with corporate management is sufficient to change the result of a vote, I am again of the opinion that the defrauded or disenfranchised shareholders should not be prevented from bringing a vote-buying claim.

Schreiber is instructive in demonstrating how a vote-buying agreement in which a board expends corporate assets to purchase votes in support of a board-favored transaction may be validly consummated. There, a vote-buying agreement was being contemplated in which corporate assets were to be loaned to a 35% shareholder on favorable terms as consideration for that shareholder's agreement to vote in favor of a management-endorsed merger. The company formed a special committee to consider the merger and also the advisability of entering into the vote-buying agreement. The special committee hired independent counsel and then determined that both the merger and the shareholder agreement would be in the best interests of the company and its shareholders. After arm's-length bargaining with the 35% shareholder, the parties arrived at agreeable terms for the loan and the special committee recommended the shareholder agreement to the full board. The board of directors unanimously approved the agreement as proposed and submitted the vote-buying proposal to the shareholders for a separate vote—in effect a vote on vote-buying in that particular setting. As a condition for passage of the vote-buying proposal, a majority of outstanding shares, as well as a majority of the shares neither participating in the agreement nor owned by directors and officers of the company, had to be voted in favor of the proposal. After distribution of a proxy statement that fully disclosed the terms of the agreement, the vote-buying proposal was easily approved by the shareholders.

The *Schreiber* Court noted all of these protective measures and ultimately held that "the subsequent ratification of the [shareholder agreement] by a majority of the independent stockholders, after a full disclosure of all germane facts with complete candor precludes any further judicial inquiry." I agree with the well-reasoned opinion by then-Vice Chancellor Hartnett in *Schreiber*. Absent measures protective of the shareholder franchise like those taken in *Schreiber*, this Court should closely scrutinize transactions in which a board uses corporate assets to procure a voting agreement. This is not to say that all of the protective measures taken in *Schreiber* must be present before the Court will validate vote-buying by management using company assets. Each case must be evaluated on its own merits to determine whether or not the legitimacy of the shareholder franchise has been undercut in an unacceptable way. It is certainly possible for management to enter into vote-buying arrangements with salutary purposes.

Hewlett v. Hewlett-Packard Co., 2002 WL 549137 (Del. Ch. April 8, 2002) (Chandler, Ch.)

Notes and Questions

1. Notes

a. The merger was narrowly approved by a majority of Hewlett-Packard Co. shareholders. The number of shares switched by the institutional shareholder would not have made a difference in the outcome.

2. Reality Check

a. What are the elements of vote buying?

b. Is vote buying always impermissible?

3. Suppose

a. Suppose Compaq, the other party to the merger, had paid Hewlett-Packard Co. shareholders to vote "yes" on the merger. Would that have constituted impermissible vote buying?

b. Suppose the younger Mr. Hewlett, the leader of the faction opposing the merger (and himself a board member of Hewlett-Packard Co.—at least, he was a director until the merger was approved) had paid Hewlett-Packard Co. shareholders to vote "no" on the merger? Would that have constituted impermissible vote buying?

4. What Do You Think?

a. Does the distinction between vote buying using the corporation's funds and vote buying using other funds make sense?

b. Do you think vote buying has the potential to harm the corporation, its shareholders or third parties?

c. Should the courts look at these transactions as vote selling rather than as vote buying? If they did, would that shift of emphasis suggest a different analysis of the transactions?

5. Other Shareholder Agreements Affecting Shareholder Governance Power

Two other types of agreements are worthy of some attention here. You should remember that the Articles of Incorporation may provide for explicit variation from the statutory norms we've set out at the beginning of this chapter. Also, you should remember that other kinds of governance provisions may affect shareholder power to govern. For instance, a capital structure with different classes of shares may have the effect, intended or not, of shifting or reducing certain shareholders' governance powers.

The first kind of shareholder agreement meriting examination is one that governs the conduct of the participating shareholders in their capacity as directors. A shareholder/director may find that acting in accordance with such an agreement may conflict with performing his or her fiduciary duties. For example, the shareholder agreement may commit the parties, as directors, to vote for certain individuals to serve as officers. When the board meets to choose officers, however, a director/shareholder may find that voting for the agreed-upon person is not in the corporation's best interest. Courts generally held that a director's fiduciary duties override any agreement that may require action inconsistent with those fiduciary duties. Exceptions to this rule were sometimes made when (1) all shareholders were parties to the agreement (on the rationale that the ultimate beneficiaries of the directors' fiduciary duties had agreed to limit those duties); (2) the shareholder agreement contained (expressly or by implication) a provision requiring adherence only where doing so would be in the best interest of the corporation; and (3) where the infringement on the directors' powers was said to be "slight." Many corporations statutes now address this question directly. Under the MBCA, the board's power, and hence the directors' fiduciary duties, can be curtailed if allowed by the Articles of Incorporation and if certain other restrictions are met (see below). MBCA §7.32(a)(4).

Delaware takes a slightly different approach. The DGCL provides that "close corporations," as defined in the DGCL, may implement shareholder agreements that restrict board power. See DGCL §350. Close corporations under the DGCL are those that have 30 or fewer shareholders, have 1 or more restrictions on share transfer, are not registered with the SEC, and have explicitly elected to be governed under the DGCL's close corporation provision by placing such an election in the Certificate of Incorporation. See DGCL §342.

The second kind of shareholder agreement is more radical, in the literal sense, because it does more than restrict the ability of shareholder/directors to exercise fully their directorial fiduciary duties. The core, hence radical, change is that in such corporations it may no longer be fair to say that the business and affairs of the corporation are managed by or under the direction of the board. We will describe the legitimacy of these agreements only briefly because, for reasons we will see, they are seldom used.

In a Delaware close corporation the shareholders can control the business and affairs entirely and a minority of shareholders (or even a single shareholder) can be given the power to dissolve the corporation. See DGCL §§351, 355. Under the MBCA similar changes to the corporate power paradigm are permitted, and the MBCA is more explicit about the kinds of changes permitted. See MBCA §7.32(a)(1)-(8).

Two theoretical problems arise with such agreements. First, they may result in the shareholders being characterized as co-owners of a business for profit. That, as you will see in Chapter 18, is the definition of a partnership and, under partnership law, all partners are individually liable for the partnership's debts. Certainly shareholders would wish to avoid the possibility that they might lose the limited liability that was doubtless one of the attractions of incorporating in the first place. Second, variation from the corporate paradigm is one element permitting a court to pierce the corporate veil and hold the shareholders personally liable. The MBCA cuts off these possibilities by stating that no partnership-like liability or veil-piercing liability may be imposed on shareholders simply because they have entered into an agreement permitted by the statute. See MBCA §7.32(f). The DGCL is more oblique on these questions but probably has the same effect. See DGCL §354.

These far-reaching shareholder agreements are seldom used in practice for two reasons. First, the statutes permitting them are of relatively recent vintage and so the contours of the permitted and prohibited agreements are not clear. Few lawyers and even fewer clients want to be the test case for a particular kind of agreement. Second, and more importantly, the pervasive validation of the limited liability company (see Chapter 19) since 1996 has given entity planners and their clients a surer power to divide entity power. The LLC statutes expressly anticipate that the default governance provisions can be varied in nearly any way by the operating agreement (which functions like the Articles of Incorporation). Thus there is usually little reason to resort to the kinds of radical shareholder agreements described in this subsection.

Notes and Questions

1. Notes

a. Some states have enacted a separate statute for close corporations. Planners can choose whether to incorporate a new venture under the close corporation statute or the general corporation statute. Other states, such as Delaware, have certain provisions that are applicable only to close corporations that have made an election to be governed under those close corporation provisions. See DGCL §§341-356. These close corporation statutes have not met with success, as discussed below.

6. The Problem of Deadlock

Deadlock, meaning an impasse among directors or among shareholders, is seldom a problem in publicly held corporations. From a shareholder perspective, the large number of shareholders makes the possibility of deadlock remote. At the director level, boards of directors of public companies typically act unanimously or at least with a strong consensus. Seldom do the boards of public companies take action by a bare majority vote. Where an action seems to be so controversial that unanimity is unlikely, boards tend to defer action until something close to a consensus can be reached. If such a consensus is not possible, boards in public companies generally decline to act rather than act by a sharply divided vote.

In closely held corporations, by contrast, the possibility of deadlock is often very real at both the shareholder and the board level. Note that supermajority provisions can produce deadlock even when the factions are of unequal strength. Thus a 25 percent shareholder can stymie corporate action if the Articles require, say, an 80 percent vote on certain actions, even though holders of 75 percent of the shares (which could be one shareholder) favor an action. The supermajority provisions in *Whetstone* were of this character.

Sometimes deadlock is the unintended consequence of bad corporate planning. For example, a corporate planner may include a supermajority provision for all board actions, obviously raising the potential for deadlock. In reality, the clients may only have wanted to ensure that certain important corporate actions, such as issuing more stock, taking on a large debt, or merging with another company were approved by a supermajority. Thus the plan, as implemented, has a latent deadlock possibility. But often the possibility of deadlock is understood clearly and is accepted by the clients as an acceptable risk. One frequent setting for such a decision is where two parties want to form a corporation and each insists on absolutely equal division of managerial control.

Let's take a step back for a minute and ask what we mean by the "problem" of deadlock. One way in which deadlock may not be a serious problem is if the deadlock covers only one matter. For example, if the shareholders are deadlocked in the election of directors, the corporate statutes provide that the incumbent directors retain their offices. Thus unless the directors are deadlocked as well the corporation can continue to function. Another deadlock that may not affect the corporation centrally is the question of declaring dividends. Assuming the corporation could legally pay dividends, a board may be deadlocked in deciding whether (or deciding how much) to pay dividends. Again, the corporation as a going concern is not affected in its day-to-day operations, at least in the short term, by the failure of the board to decide whether to pay dividends.

Even where the deadlock extends to every corporate question, one might legitimately ask whether deadlock is a "problem." Presumably each faction understands the consequences of the corporation's inability to act. Each faction could surely decide the best course of action for itself and either continue the deadlock, capitulate to the other faction's preference, or seek a compromise. None of these three outcomes is inherently better or worse than the others, and so deadlock is only a "problem" to the extent we wish to view it as a suboptimal choice.

Further, every corporation statute provides for voluntary dissolution, which would permit the parties to end the business entity. Thus an additional solution to deadlock is to sell the corporation's assets (usually as a going concern rather than piecemeal) and divide the proceeds (net of creditor claims) among the shareholders in proportion to their shareholdings. Voluntary dissolution requires a board resolution and shareholder vote; if the deadlocked factions believe dissolution is the best solution, it is easily obtained. See DGCL §275 and MBCA §14.02. Thus the parties can create their own exit from deadlock.

Is deadlock a societal problem? That is, does society have an interest in ending corporate deadlocks? One argument is that deadlock often means that assets are not being used as productively as possible, that society is usually worse off in such settings, and that society as a result has an interest in breaking deadlocks. In effect, this means that it is legitimate for the state (acting through the courts) to impose relief that ends deadlocks. Do you find this argument persuasive? Are there other arguments that bear on the question of society's interest in corporate deadlocks?

Corporate planners can provide at least three methods for ameliorating the possibility of deadlock. First, at the shareholder level, cumulative voting avoids deadlock if each faction can elect at least one director. Likewise a capital structure that provides for directors to be elected by different classes or series of stock can ensure that at least some directors can be elected as long as the separate classes or series are held by shareholders that are not at loggerheads. Second, the parties can agree to participate in dispute resolution mechanisms such as mediation or nonbinding arbitration to explore the possibility of resolving the deadlock. Finally, under the MBCA, a shareholder agreement under §7.32 can include a provision that "transfers to one or more shareholders or other persons all or part of the authority to exercise the corporate powers or to manage the business and affairs of the corporation, including the resolution of any issue about which there exists a deadlock among directors or shareholders." MBCA §7.32(6). See also DGCL §355, permitting comparable provisions in Delaware close corporations.

B. EXTERNAL RESTRICTIONS ON SHAREHOLDER GOVERNANCE RIGHTS

Up until now, this chapter has looked at various devices that planners can impose on a corporation that modify the default shareholder governance powers. Now we see similar devices that are imposed regardless of the planners' intentions. That is, these are restrictions on shareholder governance powers that are imposed by law. This area is one of the most curious in any business entities casebook. In this section we deal with yet another instance of fiduciary duties. Then we'll see that the state legislatures have provided additional shareholder rights and remedies. These topics are curious in that one might not think that additional fiduciary duties are necessary (reflect on the robust nature of the fiduciary duties in Chapters 11, 12, and 13). Further, these additional fiduciary duties aren't very well defined by the courts. We'll also see that the way in which the legislatures have provided additional shareholder protections might not be the most logically cogent approach. As you read the rest of this chapter (and I hope you do read it) you might find it particularly helpful to think of the issues as a puzzle rather than as an explication of doctrine. One question that will probably be constant here is: Why does corporate law need the rules that are being imposed?

1. Shareholder Fiduciary Duties

a. The Current Setting

In prior chapters we worked though, in some detail, the fiduciary duties owed by directors to their corporations and shareholders. But in at least some of the cases we've considered in this course the courts have suggested that (some) shareholders are (sometimes) owed fiduciary duties by (some) other shareholders. In contrast to the fiduciary duties of directors, the fiduciary duties of shareholders are much more amorphous. At the most conceptual level, the idea of shareholder fiduciary duties seems nonsensical. The directors' function is to act on behalf of another (the corporation or its shareholders) so it may be natural to impose fiduciary duties on directors. Partners, who are both managers and owners, might also have fiduciary duties imposed on them as an intuitive matter. But shareholders are different because they are the owners, answerable to no one, and one of the purposes of a corporation is to decouple the owners' dependence on one another.

As you read this section, look for the origins of the shareholder fiduciary duties discussed in the cases. Think especially about *who* owes *what kind of duty* and *to whom*. Finally, think about whether imposing these duties makes sense as a matter of public policy.

The first case involves disputes among shareholders in closely held corporations, as did the *Whetstone* case earlier.

≡ **Fought v. Morris**
543 So. 2d 167 (Miss. 1989)

ANDERSON, J.

I.

This is an appeal from an action of the Chancery Court of Warren County dismissing a complaint filed by Billy L. Fought (Fought) and Elza Fought against Brady M. Morris (Morris) and Vicksburg Tool and Manufacturing, Inc.

Finding that Morris breached his fiduciary duty, we reverse and remand the case for further proceedings.

II.

In 1974, Fought and Morris, along with Clayton A. Strong (Strong) and John S. Peyton (Peyton), organized Vicksburg Mold and Die, Inc., for the purpose of designing and manufacturing plastic and metal products, each having twenty-five shares. All four were experienced machinists and employed by the company. Morris was unanimously elected president because of his managerial experience and Fought was elected vice-president.

The shareholders entered into a stock redemption agreement, section two of which provided:

> In the event any stockholder should desire to dispose of any of his stock in the Company during his lifetime, he shall first offer to sell all of his stock to the company. The offer shall be based on a price determined in accordance with the provisions of Paragraph 6 hereof. Any share not purchased by the Company within thirty days of receipt of such offer shall be offered to the other stockholders, each of whom shall have the right to purchase such portion of the stock offered for sale as the number of shares owned by him on such date shall bear to the total number of shares owned by all the other stockholders; provided, however, that if any stockholder does not purchase his full proportionate share of the stock, the unaccepted stock may be purchased by the other stockholders. If the offer is not accepted by the Company or the other stockholders within thirty days of receipt thereof, the stockholder desiring to sell his stock shall have the right to sell it to any other person, but should not sell it without giving the Company and the remaining stockholders the right to purchase such stock at a price and on the terms offered by such other person.

In 1979, Strong sold his stock in accordance with the stock redemption agreement to the corporation. Strong's shares were divided equally among the remaining three stockholders....

At the time of Strong's stock sale, the corporation was profitable, but by late 1981 or early 1982, business declined. The shareholders ceased to receive wages from the Company and were given the freedom to seek other employment while maintaining their shareholder status in the corporation. Peyton chose to work at another company, while Fought and Morris remained with the corporation.

In May 1983, Peyton decided to sell his shares in the corporation. Peyton's sale...is what initiated the conflict and dissention between Fought and Morris and consequently led to the lawsuit filed by the Foughts. Peyton's stock was not sold in accordance with the stock redemption agreement. Peyton sold his stock to Morris for the consideration of $4,000, transfer of an insurance policy and release as guarantor from a bank note for the corporation.

The record is undisputed that Morris bypassed the stock redemption agreement in purchasing Peyton's stock. Fought objected to the sale of Peyton's stock, making a counter-offer to purchase his pro-rata share; however, Peyton rejected the counter-offer because Fought would not release him as a guarantor from the bank note.

The chancellor...concluded that there had been no breach of Morris' fiduciary responsibility and denied all relief prayed for by the Foughts at their cost.

III.

This case involves dissention among shareholders in a close corporation. A close corporation is a business entity with few shareholders, the shares of which are not publicly traded. Management typically operates in an informal manner, more akin to a partnership than a corporation. The traditional view that shareholders have no fiduciary duty to each other, and transactions constituting "freeze outs" or "squeeze outs" generally cannot be attacked as a breach of duty of loyalty or good faith to each other, is outmoded.

In *Ross v. Biggs*, 40 So. 2d 293 (Miss. 1949), this Court held that stockholders in a family corporation do not bear toward each other the same relationship of trust and confidence which prevails in partnerships. The Court stated: "A partnership is based almost wholly on the trust and confidence reposed by each partner in the other and the fact of existence of a partnership is one of the evidences of a confidential relationship between the partners." *Id.* 40 So. 2d at 296. While this statement is generally true, it ignores the practical realities of the organization and function of a close corporation which operates as a small business enterprise where the shareholders, directors, and managers often are the same persons.

While this Court has not spoken on this matter since *Ross,* other jurisdictions have done so. The Supreme Judicial Court of Massachusetts in *Donahue v. Rodd Electrotype,* 328 N.E.2d 505 (Mass. 1975), imposed a "strict good faith standard" upon shareholders in a close corporation because of its resemblance to a partnership. The court stated that standards for the discharge of management and responsibilities of shareholders are substantially the same as standards applicable to partners, and are stricter than standards imposed on shareholders and directors of publicly held corporations. *Id.* at 515.

The Massachusetts Court considered several aspects of the close corporation, such as: (1) the existence of only a small number of shareholders, (2) the lack of an available ready market for the corporate stock, and (3) the substantial majority stockholder participation in the management, direction and operation of the corporation. The Court then stated, "[s]tockholders in close corporations must discharge their management and stockholder responsibility in conformity with this strict good-faith standard. They may not act out of avarice, expediency, or self-interest in derogation of their duty of loyalty to other stockholders and to the corporation." *Id.* at 515.

The case of *Orchard v. Covelli,* 590 F. Supp. 1548 (W.D. Penn. 1984), *aff'd* 802 F.2d 448 (3rd Cir. 1986), dealt with a close corporation where the majority shareholders acted unfairly toward the minority in regard to dissolution. Recognizing that the controlling interest owes a duty of loyalty and fairness to minority shareholders, the court stated that where a majority shareholder stands to benefit as a controlling stockholder, the law requires that the majority's action be "intrinsically fair" to the minority interest. *Id.* at 1556.

The *Orchard* court also stated that adherence by the majority interest to its fiduciary duty is particularly critical in the context of the closely held corporation, and recognized the acute vulnerability of minority shareholders in such a corporation. This vulnerability stems from several factors. The majority is able to dictate the manner in which the corporation is run. Shares are not publicly traded so that a fair market for them is seldom available. Dissention makes the minority interest unattractive to a prospective purchaser. Consequently, the minority shareholder can neither profitably leave, nor safely stay with, the corporation. Thus, the only prospective buyer is usually a majority shareholder. Finally, close corporations frequently originate in the context of relationships personal in nature, often undertaken by family members or friends. Thus, the *Orchard* court went on to hold that

> any attempt to squeeze out a minority shareholder must be viewed as a breach of his fiduciary duty...such conduct is injurious when the result is the exclusion of the minority shareholders without adequate recompense and it is particularly harmful when carried out with malevolence or indifference.... The law recognizes a right to recovery under such circumstances

Id. at 1557.

These decisions evince the evolving awareness by courts of the distinctive characteristics and needs of close corporations. We recognize that often close corporations consist of friends or family members where the directors, officers and shareholders are synonymous. Each contributes his or her capital, skill, experience, and labor to the company. Management and ownership are substantially identical. Each shareholder has an inside view of the company's operations and maintains an element of trust and confidence in each other which is commonly lacking in a large or publicly held corporation. Persons involved in a close corporation should act, therefore, at all times in good faith toward each other and to the corporation in order to maintain this confidence.

We find the *Orchard* court rationale and standard more appropriate and therefore, hold that in a close corporation where a majority stockholder stands to benefit as a controlling stockholder, the majority's action must be "intrinsically fair" to the minority interest. Thus, stockholders in close corporations must bear toward each other the same relationship of trust and confidence which prevails in partnerships, rather than resort to statutory defenses. This holding does not mean that directors, executive officers and stockholders are not required to adhere to the corporate statutes; rather, we mean that blind adherence to corporate statutes may not be used to circumvent the corporation's by-laws, charter or various agreements, such as a stock redemption agreement, because of the "intrinsically fair" standard we here adopt today. To the extent that *Ross, supra,* differs from our holding today, it is overruled.

IV.

The evidence indicates that Morris' intent in offering to purchase all Peyton's shares was to "freeze out" Fought.

As we discussed above, directors and officers of a corporation stand in a fiduciary relationship to the corporation and its stockholders. These duties include exercising the utmost good faith and loyalty in discharge of the corporate office.

The chancellor found that Morris won in the scramble between Fought and Morris for Peyton's stock. However, at the inception of the corporation the four stockholders entered into a Stock Redemption Agreement to prevent such a scramble. This agreement insured that stock in the corporation always would be offered to the corporation, or in the alternative, each shareholder would have a right to purchase a pro-rata share.

A Stock Redemption Agreement is one guide for corporate policy, which may restrain the transferability of stock. Shareholders in a close corporation have an interest in maintaining a balance of power that frequently is protected by such agreements.

Generally, a director violates no duty by dealing in his own stock on his own account. This rule is not applicable, however, when there is a showing that a closely held corporation has a practice of purchasing its own stock, or that it ever contemplated doing so, as evidenced by a stock redemption agreement, in order to maintain proportionate control of the corporation.

In the case *sub judice* the stockholders had entered into an agreement which constituted corporate policy. This policy was adhered to when Strong sold his stock. However, the record reveals that Morris was unhappy with Fought. When Peyton decided to sell his stock, Morris saw a way to take control, as evidenced by his statement that he would undertake to relieve Peyton from liability on the bank note only if he could purchase all of Peyton's stock.

The court below failed to perceive Morris' fiduciary duty, as an officer and director of Vicksburg Mold and Die, Inc., to conduct his office with prudence and all good fidelity. Morris' intended exclusion of Fought from the purchase of Peyton's shares was a breach of the Stock Redemption Agreement and bylaws, and, therefore, a breach of his fiduciary duty as an officer, a director and a stockholder under the good faith standard we adopt today. We hold, therefore, that Morris breached his fiduciary duty in purchasing all of Peyton's stock, contrary to the Stock Redemption Agreement.

CONCLUSION

Upon remand, the lower court should determine the appropriate relief to which the Foughts are entitled. We reverse and remand for further proceedings in the lower court consistent with this opinion.

Notes and Questions

1. Notes

a. One instrumental reason to impose fiduciary duties on shareholders has to do with shareholder litigation. In Chapter 15 we discussed shareholder derivative litigation and saw that it is disadvantageous to shareholder/plaintiffs who would much prefer to bring direct actions. By imposing fiduciary duties on majority shareholders that run directly to other shareholders, plaintiffs can bring direct actions, rather than having to sue derivatively.

b. The Massachusetts Supreme Judicial Court modified the rule it announced in *Donahue* in a later case:

> The *Donahue* decision acknowledged, as a "natural outgrowth" of the case law of this Commonwealth, a strict obligation on the part of majority stockholders in a close corporation to deal with the minority with the utmost good faith and loyalty. On its face, this strict standard is applicable in the instant case. The distinction between the majority action in Donahue and the majority action in this case is more one of form than of substance. Nevertheless, we are concerned that untempered application of the strict good faith standard enunciated in *Donahue*...will result in the imposition of limitations on legitimate action by the controlling group in a close corporation which will unduly hamper its effectiveness in managing the corporation in the best interests of all concerned. The majority, concededly, have certain rights to what has been termed "selfish ownership" in the corporation which should be balanced against the concept of their fiduciary obligation to the minority.
>
> Therefore, when minority stockholders in a close corporation bring suit against the majority alleging a breach of the strict good faith duty owed to them by the majority, we must carefully analyze the action taken by the controlling stockholders in the individual case. It must be asked whether the controlling group can demonstrate a legitimate business purpose for its action. In asking this question, we acknowledge the fact that the controlling group in a close corporation must have some room to maneuver in establishing the business policy of the corporation. It must have a large measure of discretion, for example, in declaring or withholding dividends, deciding whether to merge or consolidate, establishing the salaries of corporate officers, dismissing directors with or without cause, and hiring and firing corporate employees.
>
> When an asserted business purpose for their action is advanced by the majority, however, we think it is open to minority stockholders to demonstrate that the same legitimate objective could have been achieved through an alternative course of action

less harmful to the minority's interest. If called on to settle a dispute, our courts must weigh the legitimate business purpose, if any, against the practicability of a less harmful alternative.

Wilkes v. Springside Nursing Home, Inc., 353 N.E.2d 657, 663 (Mass. 1976) (Hennessey, C.J.)

2. Reality Check

a. Where did the court find the authority to impose fiduciary duties on shareholders?

b. What are the duties that shareholders owe one another?

c. How, precisely, did Mr. Morris breach his fiduciary duties *as a shareholder?*

d. Did the corporation, acting through its board of directors, take any action that harmed the Foughts?

3. Suppose

a. Suppose the court held that shareholders do not owe one another a fiduciary duty. Would the analysis or the result have been different?

b. What if Mr. Morris had caused the corporation to repurchase Mr. Peyton's shares. Would the court's analysis or the result have been different?

c. Suppose this case had been brought as a breach of contract action. Would the court's analysis or the result have been different?

4. What Do You Think?

a. What relief should the trial court grant?

b. Do you think shareholders should be subject to fiduciary duties to one another? If so, should those duties be imposed by courts or legislatures?

c. Should every shareholder owe fiduciary duties to every other shareholder? What about shareholders in publicly traded corporations?

d. Should minority shareholders owe fiduciary duties to majority shareholders? If so, does that constrain other protections that minority shareholders in close corporations frequently resort to?

e. Do you agree that a close corporation is like a partnership and that shareholders should, therefore, be treated like partners? Isn't it just as accurate to say that a partnership is like a close corporation and that partners should, therefore, be treated like shareholders?

f. Should shareholder fiduciary duties be different from director fiduciary duties? If you believe they should be different, should they be more or less strict?

The Delaware courts have been surprisingly (and refreshingly?) brief about the question of shareholder fiduciary duties.

b. Background and Context

In *Allied Chemical & Dye Corp. v. Steel & Tube Co. of America*, 120 A. 486 (Del. Ch. 1923), a syndicate of speculators bought a majority of shares in the Steel & Tube Co. The board of directors, which was controlled by the syndicate, negotiated to sell all the corporation's assets to an unrelated corporation. The plaintiffs, Steel & Tube Co. minority shareholders, filed suit to enjoin the sale on the ground that the transaction was fraudulent because the price was inadequate. Chancellor Wolcott analyzed the claim for relief in this way:

In reading this statute [the predecessor of DGCL §271] it will be observed that two things with respect to a sale are contemplated, viz. (a) an authorization of sale by the stockholders, and (b) a fixing of the terms and conditions by the directors.

The majority [of stockholders] thus have the power in their hands to impose their will upon the minority in a matter of very vital concern to them. That the source of this power is found in a statute, supplies no reason for clothing it with a superior sanctity, or vesting it with the attributes of tyranny. When the power is sought to be used, therefore, it is competent for any one who conceives himself aggrieved thereby to invoke the processes of a court of equity for protection against its oppressive exercise. When examined by such a court, if it should appear that the power is used in such a way that it violates any of those fundamental principles which it is the special province of equity to assert and protect, its restraining processes will unhesitatingly issue.

The requirements of the statute and of the certificate of incorporation all being satisfied, as they are in this case, it will be manifest that the only ground upon which [the complaining stockholder] can base his claim for relief is that of fraud. Notwithstanding that the right of the majority to sell all the assets is given by the statute, yet if the proposed sale is a fraud on the minority, it cannot stand.

[I]t will be in order first to define the relations which equity will regard as subsisting between the controlling majority members of the corporation and the minority. That under certain circumstances these relations are of a fiduciary character is clear. The same considerations of fundamental justice which impose a fiduciary character upon the relationship of the directors to the stockholders will also impose, in a proper case, a like character upon the relationship which the majority of the stockholders bear to the minority. When, in the conduct of the corporate business, a majority of the voting power in the corporation join hands in imposing its policy upon all, it is beyond all reason and contrary, it seems to me, to the plainest dictates of what is just and right, to take any view other than that they are to be regarded as having placed upon themselves the same sort of fiduciary character which the law impresses upon the directors in their relation to all the stockholders. Ordinarily the directors speak for and determine the policy of the corporation. When the majority of stockholders do this, they are, for the moment, the corporation. Unless the majority in such case are to be regarded as owing a duty to the minority such as is owed by the directors to all, then the minority are in a situation that exposes them to the grossest frauds and subjects them to most outrageous wrongs.

Accordingly it has been held that if the majority stockholders so use their power to advantage themselves at the expense of the minority, their conduct in that regard will be denounced as fraudulent and the minority may obtain appropriate relief therefrom upon application to a court of equity. But the general language by which this rule is stated is not to be given its widest possible application. For it is not true that every personal advantage which the majority secures is to be regarded as vitiating in character. An examination of the cases to which special attention is directed by the complainants in this connection will disclose that the personal advantage accruing to the majority is in some way derived from, or intimately associated with, the corporate assets themselves.

After examining all the authorities cited on the briefs of both sides, I find that . . . the personal advantage which the alleged wrongdoers attempt to gather to themselves is in some way directly incident to the very property towards which they stand in the fiduciary relationship and which they seek to appropriate either in whole or in part to themselves, to the exclusion and injury of those whom they have at their mercy.

In the instant case there is no pretense that the personal advantage which the majority may derive from the sale consists in any wise in securing to themselves either the whole or any part of the corporate assets. So far as appears, they and the purchasers are complete strangers in interest. The complainants, however, contend that, though there is nothing in common between the interests of the purchaser and the majority favoring the sale, there is, nevertheless, such a personal advantage to be derived from the sale by the majority as in equity will vitiate the whole transaction.

My conclusion with respect to this branch of the case is, that the evidence before me fails to disclose such a peculiar and personal interest or advantage to be served by the sale as will, on the principles applicable to the conduct of one who acts in a fiduciary capacity, taint the proposed transaction with fraud, either actual or constructive. Whatever advantage is gained is purely incidental and collateral. This prospect of personal gain, though not thus to be condemned as fraudulent in character, may however be very properly regarded when, as will subsequently appear, the fairness and adequacy of the terms of sale are considered in connection with the present application.

The majority who are favoring the sale owe something more to the minority than to merely refrain from appropriating, either directly or indirectly, the corporate assets unto themselves. They owe the further duty of seeing to it that the assets shall be sold for a fair and adequate price. Any other kind of price would fail to meet the requirement of the statute that the terms and conditions of the sale should be such as are expedient and for the best interest of the corporation. Indeed, even if the statute contained no such requirement, equity would impose it. For if a trustee who has the right to sell the assets of his cestui que trust undertakes to do so, the duty is exacted of him that he demand and secure an adequate price. Even though the sale is of no affirmative advantage or profit to himself, yet, taking the negative aspect of the matter, if it injures the beneficiary by letting his equitable assets go for an unfair and inadequate price, the act of the trustee in making the sale will in equity be condemned as wrongful. I take it that authority need not be cited in support of this proposition.

This is the reason which underlies the rule, applicable here, that if the majority sell the assets they are required to obtain a fair and adequate price therefor and thus save from loss the minority who are helpless.

When the question is asked whether in a given case the price is adequate, it is readily seen that room is afforded for honest differences of opinion. When the price proposed to be accepted is so far below what is found to be a fair, one that it can be explained only on the theory of fraud, or a reckless indifference to the rights of others interested, it would seem that it should not be allowed to stand.

On final hearing, . . . it may be true that the view may be honestly entertained that at a fair price the assets would bring no more than the sum named in the contract. I have difficulty, however, in reaching such a conclusion on the present showing.

I now mention a feature of the case that contributes quite materially to that difficulty. The syndicate is in control of this corporation. It owns 57 percent of the common stock. It would not consider the proposition of buying into the corporation, unless it could secure a controlling interest. It got such an interest. I shall not reflect upon the gentlemen whom it elected as directors by characterizing them as mere tools to work the syndicate's will. At the same time, I shall not assume that capable and shrewd business men would deliberately purchase only on condition that their purchase would yield the control, and then, having secured the control, be so neglectful of their purposes as not to make sure of their realization. Until something more convincing appears, common sense demands that the proposed sale be regarded as the act of the syndicate.

Now what was the purpose of the syndicate? The affidavits are to the effect that the purpose and only purpose was to make a profit on the purchase of the [majority of the company] stock. If to make this profit it appeared advisable to put money into the plant and continue operations, that would be done; or if it appeared advisable to sell the stock, that would be done; or, if it appeared advisable to sell out the business, that would be done. "My purpose," says Mr. Williams, "was to follow whichever of these two (three) courses appeared to offer the greatest profit to the syndicate."

Now, while none of these things, either alone or in combination, will, as I have heretofore said, suffice to show such a personal interest as will raise a presumption of fraud, yet when the question of the fairness of price to the minority is under consideration they may be fairly taken into account, at least in disposing of the application for a preliminary injunction. These things will in no wise, in event of liquidation, give to the persons named any disproportionate advantage at the expense of the minority out of the assets of the corporation. But they are of such a nature as very reasonably suggests that in approaching the determination of the question of adequacy of price they might cause the interested persons to view the question not so much from the angle of stockholders interested primarily in securing the best possible price for assets, but from the angle of purchasers of stock interested primarily in securing a fair profit on a speculation. It is difficult to escape from the thought that the prospect of making about $2,000,000 within a year upon a layout of $1,500,000 with interest, is such an alluring one that those who are tempted by it are very apt to pass upon the interests of others who happen to be concerned in the transaction with less regard for their welfare than otherwise would be the case.

The preliminary injunction restraining the sale will issue as prayed . . . .

Allied Chemical & Dye Corp. v. Steel & Tube Co. of America, 120 A. 486 (Del. Ch. 1923) (Wolcott, Ch)

c. The Current Setting

Delaware cases have emphasized that a majority (or controlling) shareholder owes fiduciary duties, equivalent to those owed by directors, to minority shareholders when the majority shareholder causes the corporation to enter into a self-dealing transaction involving the disposition of the corporation's assets. That is, in such a setting the majority shareholder must show the entire fairness of the transaction. See *Sterling v. Mayflower Hotel Corp.*, 93 A.2d 107 (Del. 1952); *Singer v. Magnavox Co.*, 380 A.2d 969 (Del. 1977), *rev'd on other grounds*; *Weinberger v. UOP, Inc.*, 457 A.2d 701 (Del. 1983). The Delaware courts have declined to impose a *Wilkes*-like fiduciary duty outside of the self-dealing context. See *Riblet Products Corp. v. Nagy*, 683 A.2d 37 (Del. 1996).

2. Oppression and Unfairness by Shareholders

Now that you're as comfortable as you're going to be with the concept of shareholder fiduciary duties, we reach a sort of confluence of ideas. This confluence takes us back to the problem of deadlock. It moves to a new cause of action for minority shareholders, "oppression," and ends with the expansion of equitable remedies to be wielded in support of minority shareholder rights. As you read this material, try to keep the concepts of deadlock, dissolution, fiduciary duty, oppression, and expanded remedies separate. It seems easy (because each concept has a separate name) but you'll see that the concepts run together in a way that can be quite maddening.

a. From a New Remedy for Deadlock . . .

We asked above whether courts ought to break deadlocks. Because most deadlocks are the result of planning choices and every deadlock can be broken by compromise or capitulation, a good argument can be made that courts should not intervene when the harm is deadlock alone, without any allegation of statutory or fiduciary duty violation.

If courts do intervene to break deadlocks, what form of relief should the court enter? Presumably money damages will not end a deadlock, though it may compensate a party who has been financially injured by a deadlock. The court will have to enjoin one or both factions to do or refrain from doing something. The court could, in a proper case, order the corporation itself to take (or refrain from taking) some action if the corporation has been named as a party. Although at first blush these remedies seem to be simply examples of a court's classic power to do equity, remember that the claim for relief is deadlock — the factions' inability to agree on a course of action. If a court awards injunctive relief, on what basis will the judge decide who wins? Isn't the court doing nothing but imposing its own view of the corporation's best economic interest?

If the deadlock seems likely to be chronic, the court could appoint a neutral person to oversee the decision-making process to head off future deadlocks or to act as a tie-breaker. This solution, though, simply shifts the location of the decision from the court to a court-appointed person. Again, how will the outsider decide between two factions on any basis other than his or her own view of the corporation's best course of action?

In the mid-twentieth century courts frequently concluded that they could not break deadlocks by dissolving the corporation but that they did have the power to order the corporation's assets liquidated so that the proceeds would be distributable to the owners. As a practical matter, this liquidation brought about the corporation's dissolution. Strictly, courts almost uniformly held that they had no inherent power to dissolve a corporation because dissolution would be undoing something the legislature had affirmatively created.

State legislatures understood that court-ordered liquidation was substantially equivalent to dissolution. Many corporation statutes were then amended to grant courts the explicit power to dissolve a corporation because of deadlock. The MBCA grants courts the power to dissolve for deadlock, while the DGCL permits the Court of Chancery to liquidate, but not dissolve, a corporation. Note that where the *shareholders* are deadlocked, both the MBCA and DGCL permit relief to be awarded upon a showing simply that the shareholders are sufficiently deadlocked. Where the *directors* are deadlocked, both statutes require an additional showing of entitlement to equitable relief before the court may intervene. Does the distinction between shareholder deadlock and director deadlock make any sense? See MBCA §§14.30(2)(i), (iii) and DGCL §§226(b), 291, and 352(a). Thus dissolution became a new remedy for deadlock.

b. ... to a New Cause of Action ...

Once legislatures became comfortable with the idea that courts should break at least some deadlocks by ordering that a corporation be dissolved, they began to think about whether other corporate dysfunctions could also be alleviated by dissolution. The results of that thinking are embedded in MBCA §14.30(2), which you should read now.

Charles W. Murdock, *The Evolution of Effective Remedies for Minority Shareholders and Its Impact Upon Valuation of Minority Shares*
65 Notre Dame L. Rev. 425, 452-470 (1990)

[I]t is worthwhile to examine the traditional four bases for involuntary judicial dissolution to evaluate them for their potential to afford relief. [See MBCA §14.30(2)(i)-(iv).]

The provision that empirically seems to be the most fruitful avenue for minority shareholders to pursue, . . . is one using a finding of oppression as the basis for liquidation. While the provision also speaks of illegal and fraudulent acts, the courts have consistently observed that, not only is oppression a concept separate and distinct from fraud and illegality, but also that it embraces conduct that would not be encompassed within those terms.

The Illinois Business Corporation Act of 1933 (the "1933 Act") is often viewed as the first modern corporation code and was the basis for the Model Business Corporation Act [1950]. Section 86(a)(3) of the 1933 Act was the basis for section 90(a)(2), later section 97(a)(2), and finally section 14.30(2)(ii) of the various versions of the [MBCA], and introduced the concept of oppression as a basis for liquidation.

In interpreting the scope of "oppression" . . . , no clear pattern developed until the 1960s. However, in 1957, the Illinois Supreme Court considered the concept of oppression and took a very broad view. In *Central Standard Life Insurance Co. v. Davis*, the court stated: "[W]e reject defendants' argument that the word [oppression] is substantially synonymous with "illegal and fraudulent." Misapplication of assets or mismanagement of funds are not, as we read the statute, indispensable ingredients of "oppressive" conduct."

The rhetoric providing a broad gloss in defining oppression bore fruit three years later when the court confronted another alleged case of oppression. The following factors combined to indicate oppression within the meaning of the statute: officers were hired and salary increases were given without director approval; loans were made to corporations in which the president had an interest without director approval; a subsidiary was organized without director approval; the matter of payment of dividends had not been presented to the board of directors; and the other family was excluded from all incidents of control and corporate participation. The court pointed out that it was "not necessary that fraud, illegality or even loss be shown to exhibit oppression"[209] and concluded that the cumulative effects of the aforementioned acts, and their indicated continuing nature, established oppression entitling the plaintiffs to liquidation. Although corporate dissolution was deemed to be a drastic remedy, "when oppression is positively shown, the oppressed are entitled to the protection of the law."[210]

[T]here followed a series of appellate court decisions decreeing dissolution based upon a broad reading of what constitutes oppressive conduct. Conduct which excludes a minority shareholder from participation in the enterprise or which can be characterized as heavy-handed or overbearing has sufficed to warrant dissolution.

209. *Gidwitz v. Lanzit Corrugated Box Co*, 170 N.E.2d 131, 138 (Ill. 1960).
210. *Id*. at 138.

Misuse of corporate funds or assets has also led to a conclusion of oppression. Thus, where the defendant has taken excessive salaries or misused corporate assets, the courts have found oppressive conduct justifying dissolution. And, in a case in which an accounting was sought, the court indicated that the failure "to pay dividends to minority stockholders, due to large salaries drawn by officer-majority stockholders" could constitute oppressive conduct.[216]

Following, at least in part, the lead of Illinois, several other jurisdictions have adopted an expansive definition of oppression.

While the abstract formulations of what constitutes oppressive conduct appeared favorable to minority shareholders, such shareholders had difficulty in the 1970s obtaining relief in jurisdictions other than Illinois.

Finally, in 1979, a New Jersey court, in *Exadaktilos v. Cinnaminson Realty Co.*, . . . concluded that, "[w]hile the terminology employed by both the statute and case law certainly provides the court with the latitude necessary to deal with all the circumstances peculiar to any case brought to its attention, it fails to suggest any perspective from which to judge what is oppressive or unfair."[237] The *Exadaktilos* court . . . concluded that "[t]he special circumstances, arrangements and personal relationships that frequently underlie the formation of close corporations generate certain expectations among the shareholders concerning their respective roles in corporate affairs, including management and earnings."[238]

While the New Jersey court in *Exadaktilos* introduced the notion of expectations as a standard by which to measure whether the challenged conduct was oppressive, the reasonable expectations test reached full bloom in New York after the legislature, in 1979, provided for a buy-out of the minority shareholder as an alternative to dissolution when the minority alleged oppressive conduct by those in control.[242] [S]ince 1980 New York has played the dominant role by developing the reasonable expectations test to define oppressive conduct.

This approach stands in marked contrast . . . to the shareholder fiduciary duty rule — at least in those situations in which a court would, in effect, permit a "business purpose" defense to a claim of breach of fiduciary duty. For example, even *Wilkes* [*v. Springside Nursing Home, Inc.*, 353 N.E.2d 657, 663 (Mass. 1976)] recognized that conduct that appears to be a breach of duty can be justified by a business purpose. The difference in result may be rationalized by the difference in focus and the difference in remedy. In determining whether there has been a breach of fiduciary duty, the focus is upon wrongdoing by the person in control and the remedy is to invalidate the transaction, either by enjoining it or by awarding damages. In the reasonable expectations test, the focus is on the minority shareholder and the remedy is not to undo a corporate transaction but to permit or order another transaction — a buy-out of the minority shareholder. Thus, the crux is not identifying a traditional wrong but rather identifying the basis of the bargain — what were the explicit or implicit conditions pursuant to which the parties associated themselves together in the corporate form. This approach has become the touchstone for evaluating oppressive conduct in the 1980s.

216. *Gray v. Hall*, 295 N.E.2d 506, 509 (Ill. App. 1973) (the court also indicated that withholding dividends to freeze-out a minority shareholder could be oppressive).
237. 400 A.2d 554, 560 (N.J. 1979).
238. *Id.* at 154, 400 A.2d at 561.
242. N.Y. Bus. Corp. Law §§1104-a, 1118 (McKinney 1986 & Supp. 1988).

[T]he New York Court of Appeals in *In re Kemp & Beatley, Inc.,*[283] . . . clarified that the concept of oppressive conduct, under the statute, is distinct from illegality or fraud and that the distinction has been resolved "by considering oppressive actions to refer to conduct that substantially defeats the 'reasonable expectations' held by minority shareholders in committing their capital to the particular enterprise."[284] Accordingly, the court held that "utilizing a complaining shareholder's 'reasonable expectations' as a means of identifying and measuring conduct alleged to be oppressive is appropriate."[285] The court cautioned that expectations must be reasonable and objective.[286]

What the New York decisions make clear is that those in control of a corporation may no longer use the business judgment rule to shield from judicial scrutiny actions that are detrimental to minority shareholders. The courts have recognized the reality that compensation paid to those in control has a twofold function: to recompense services and to provide a return on investment. To deny a minority shareholder employment when a job was part of his rationale in investing is oppressive, as is the failure to pay dividends to nonemployee shareholders when employed shareholders are receiving de facto dividends through salaries.

While a reasonable expectations test may appear as elusive to apply as oppression, it does provide a focus from which to evaluate a situation. That people often invest in a closely held corporation to provide a job is almost self-evident; if there is doubt, the proposition can be confirmed empirically by surveying representative businesses.

Notes and Questions

1. Reality Check

a. Why did legislatures create a cause of action for *oppression*?
b. What are the two approaches to defining oppression?

---

283. 473 N.E.2d 1173 (N.Y. 1984).
284. *Id.* 1179. Before determining what reasonable expectations might be, the court stated:

It is widely understood that, in addition to supplying capital to a contemplated or ongoing enterprise and expecting a fair and equal return, parties comprising the ownership of a close corporation may expect to be actively involved in its management and operation.
. . . .
His [the shareholder in the close corporation] participation in that particular corporation is often his principal or sole source of income. As a matter of fact, providing employment for himself may have been the principal reason why he participated in organizing the corporation. He may or may not anticipate an ultimate profit from the sale of his interest, but he normally draws very little from the corporation as dividends. In his capacity as an officer or employee of the corporation, he looks to his salary for the principal return on his capital investment, because earnings of a close corporation, as is well known, are distributed in major part in salaries, bonuses and retirement benefits.

Id. 1178, (*quoting* F. O'Neal, *Close Corporations* 21-22 (2d ed. 1971)).

285. *Id.* at 1179.
286. The court stated:

Majority conduct should not be deemed oppressive simply because the petitioner's subjective hopes and desires in joining the venture are not fulfilled. Disappointment alone should not necessarily be equated with oppression.
      Rather, oppression should be deemed to arise only when the majority conduct substantially defeats expectations that, objectively viewed, were both reasonable under the circumstances and were central to the petitioner's decision to join the venture.

Id.

2. What Do You Think?

a. Should shareholders be able to recover for oppression? Isn't the claim for relief simply a claim for damages on the ground that one has been treated shabbily?

The preceding discussion of a cause of action for oppression and the varying definition of oppression may seem a bit removed from real life. The next case shows rather vividly the consequences of allowing relief for oppression and, even more centrally, the consequences of applying one definition of oppression rather than another.

Kiriakides v. Atlas Food Systems & Services, Inc.
541 S.E.2d 257 (S.C. 2001)

TOAL, C.J.

FACTS

This is a case in which respondents, minority shareholders in a closely held family corporation, claim the majority shareholders have acted in a manner which is fraudulent, oppressive and unfairly prejudicial.[1] They seek a buyout of their shares under South Carolina's judicial dissolution statutes. A rather detailed recitation of the facts is necessary to an understanding of the plaintiffs' claims.

Respondents are 72-year-old John Kiriakides and his 74-year-old sister Louise Kiriakides. John and Louise are the minority shareholders in the family business, Atlas Food Systems & Services, Inc. (Atlas). Petitioners are their older brother, 88-year-old Alex Kiriakides, Jr., and the family business....

Atlas is a food vending service which provides refreshments to factories and other businesses. The business began prior to World War II but slowed down while Alex was away during the war. After the war, Alex, John, and their father Alex, Sr., began working together to build the family business. Alex, Sr. died in 1949. Atlas was incorporated in 1956. Currently, Alex is the majority stockholder, owning 57.68%; John owns 37.7%, and Louise owns 3%.

Throughout Atlas' history, Alex has been in charge of the financial and corporate affairs of the family business; he has had overall control and is Chairman of the Board of Directors. John is also on the three member Board. In 1986, John became President of Atlas, after years of running client relations and field operations. Two of Alex' children are also employed by Atlas, his son Alex III, and his daughter Mary Ann.[5] Alex III is (since John's departure as discussed below) President and is on the Board; Mary Ann is a CPA who performs accounting and financial functions;....[6]

For years, Atlas operated as a prototypical closely held family corporation. Troubles developed, however, in 1995, when a rift began between Alex and John. The initial dispute arose over property owned by John and Alex in Greenville. Alex convinced John

---

1. See S.C. Code Ann. §§33-14-300 & 33-14-310 (1990).

5. Neither John nor Louise have any children; Alex has four children: Alex III, Michael, Mary Ann and Cathryn.

6. Louise worked for several years in the counting room but has not worked for the company since the 1970's. She served as Secretary until 1988.

to transfer his interest in the property to his son Alex III for a price less than it was worth. John signed the deed prepared by Alex believing he was conveying only a small portion of his interest in the property to Alex III. After discovering his entire interest had been transferred to Alex III, John became distrustful of Alex and began requesting documents and records concerning the family business. The relationship between the two became very strained. Several subsequent incidents served to heighten the tension.

In December 1995, the Board and shareholders of Atlas decided to convert Atlas from a subchapter C corporation to a subchapter S corporation. However, in March 1996, Alex, without bringing a vote, unilaterally determined the company would remain a C corporation. Later, in mid-1996, a dispute arose over Atlas' contract to purchase a piece of commercial property. Notwithstanding the contract, John, Alex III and William Freitag (Senior Vice President of Finance and Administration) decided not to go through with the sale. Alex however, without consulting or advising John, elected to go through with the sale. When John learned of Alex' decision, he became extremely upset and allegedly advised Alex III he was quitting his job as President.[8] The next day, Alex III made plans with managers to continue operations in John's absence; John, however, went to the Atlas office in Greenville and visited Atlas offices in Columbia, Orangeburg and Charleston.

The following Monday, John went to work at Atlas doing "business as usual." He was told later that day...that management was planning John would no longer be President of Atlas. John circulated a memo indicating he intended to remain President; Alex III replied in a memo prepared with the aid of his father, refusing to allow John to continue as president of the company. The following day, Alex refused to allow John to stay on as president of Atlas, and designated Alex III as President. John was offered, but refused a position as a consultant.

In September 1996, Atlas offered to purchase John's interest in Atlas...for one million dollars, plus the cancellation of $800,000 obligations owed by John. John refused this offer, believing it too low.[10] John filed this suit in November 1996.... The complaint was subsequently amended, naming Louise as a plaintiff, and adding claims for fraud under the judicial dissolution statute. The complaint sought an accounting, a buyout of John and Louise's shares, and damages for fraud.

After a five day hearing, the referee found Alex had engaged in fraud in numerous respects, and found Atlas had engaged in conduct which was fraudulent, oppressive and unfairly prejudicial toward John and Louise. The Court of Appeals affirmed in result.

LAW/ANALYSIS

a. Oppression Under S.C. Code Ann. §33-14-300

The referee found that, taken together, the majority's actions were "illegal, fraudulent, oppressive or unfairly prejudicial,"...under S.C. Code Ann. §33-14-300(2)(ii) and §33-14-310(d)(4).[16]

---

8. The referee found John subsequently made it clear he had no intentions of quitting.

10. In March, 1998, Atlas offered to buy the interests of John and Louise for four million dollars, less obligations of $825,000. John was advised by a tax attorney in 1995 that his stock in Atlas was worth about ten million dollars.

16. Section 33-14-300(2)(ii) permits a court to order dissolution if it is established by a shareholder that "the directors or those in control of the corporation have acted, are acting, or will act in a manner that is illegal, fraudulent, oppressive, or unfairly prejudicial either to the corporation or to any shareholder (whether in his capacity as a shareholder, director, or officer of the corporation)."

The Court of Appeals affirmed the referee's holdings. In making this ruling, the Court of Appeals defined the statutory terms "oppressive" and "unfairly prejudicial" as follows:

1) A visible departure from the standards of fair dealing and a violation of fair play on which every shareholder who entrusts his money to a company is entitled to rely; or
2) A breach of the fiduciary duty of good faith and fair dealing; or
3) Whether the reasonable expectations of the minority shareholders have been frustrated by the actions of the majority; or
4) A lack of probity and fair dealing in the affairs of a company to the prejudice of some of its members; or
5) A deprivation by majority shareholders of participation in management by minority shareholders.

Atlas contends the Court of Appeals' definitions of oppressive, unfairly prejudicial conduct are beyond the scope of our judicial dissolution statute. We agree. In our view, the Court of Appeals' broad view of oppression is contrary to the legislative intent and is an unwarranted expansion of section 33-14-300.

South Carolina's judicial dissolution statute was amended in 1963 in recognition of the growing trend toward protecting minority shareholders from abuses by those in the majority. Section §33-14-300(2)(ii) now permits a court to order dissolution if it is established by a shareholder that "the directors or those in control of the corporation have acted, are acting, or will act in a manner that is illegal, fraudulent, oppressive, or unfairly prejudicial either to the corporation or to any shareholder (whether in his capacity as a shareholder, director, or officer of the corporation)."[17] The official comment to section 33-14-300 provides:

> The application of these grounds for dissolution to specific circumstances obviously involves judicial discretion in the application of a general standard to concrete circumstances. The court should be cautious in the application of these grounds so as to limit them to genuine abuse rather than instances of acceptable tactics in a power struggle for control of a corporation.

Section 33-14-300 cmt. 2(b).

---

17. Prior to 1963, dissolution could be based only upon illegal, fraudulent or oppressive conduct. In an attempt to afford minority shareholders greater protection, the legislature amended the statute in 1963 to include "unfairly prejudicial" conduct. *See* 1963 S.C. Acts 282 §89; S.C. Code §12-22.15(a)(4) (1970). The statute, as amended, "broadens the scope of actionable conduct by providing the frozen-out minority shareholder a right of action based on conduct by the majority shareholders which might not rise to the level of fraud." Joshua Henderson, *Buyout Remedy for Oppressed Minority Shareholders*, 47 S.C. L. Rev. 195, 199 (Autumn 1995).... This trend arose due to the nationwide epidemic of unfair treatment of minority shareholders. *See* Harry J. Haynsworth, *The Effectiveness of Involuntary Dissolution Suits as a Remedy for Close Corporation Dissension*, 35 Clev. St. L. Rev. 25 (1986-87); F.H. O'Neal, *Oppression of Minority Stockholders: Protecting Minority Rights*, 35 Clev. St. L. Rev. 121 (1986-87). In the latter article, Prof. O'Neal observed:

> Unfair treatment of holders of minority interests in family companies and other closely held corporations by persons in control of those corporations is so widespread that it is a national business scandal.
>
> The amount of litigation growing out of minority shareholder oppression — actual, fancied or fabricated — has grown tremendously in recent years, and the flood of litigation shows no sign of abating.

Id. at 121, 403 S.E.2d 666.

Although the terms "oppressive" and "unfairly prejudicial" are not defined in section 33-14-300, the comment to S.C. Code Ann. §33-18-400 (1990), which allows shareholders in a statutory close corporation to petition for relief on the grounds of oppressive, fraudulent, or unfairly prejudicial conduct provides:

> No attempt has been made to define oppression, fraud, or unfairly prejudicial conduct. These are elastic terms whose meaning varies with the circumstances presented in a particular case, and it is felt that existing case law provides sufficient guidelines for courts and litigants.[18]

Given the Legislature's deliberate exclusion of a set definition of oppressive and unfairly prejudicial conduct, we find the Court of Appeals' enunciation of rigid tests is contrary to the legislative intent.

Under the Court of Appeals' holding, a finding of fraudulent/oppressive conduct may be based upon any **one** of its alternative definitions. We do not believe the Legislature intended such a result. In particular, we do not believe the Legislature intended a court to judicially order a corporate dissolution **solely** upon the basis that a party's "reasonable expectations" have been frustrated by majority shareholders. To examine the "reasonable expectations" of minority shareholders would require the courts of this state to microscopically examine the dealings of closely held family corporations, the intentions of majority and minority stockholders in forming the corporation and thereafter, the history of family dealings, and the like. We do not believe the Legislature, in enacting section 33-14-300, intended such judicial interference in the business philosophies and day to day operating practices of family businesses.

In adopting the "reasonable expectations" approach, the Court of Appeals cited the North Carolina case of *Meiselman v. Meiselman,* 307 S.E.2d 551 (N.C. 1983).[19] In *Meiselman,* a minority shareholder in a family-owned close corporation was "frozen out" of the family corporation in much the same fashion as John and Louise claim they have been frozen out of Atlas. The minority shareholder brought an action requesting a buyout of his interests under N.C.G.S. §55-125.1(a)(4), which permits a North Carolina court to liquidate assets when it is **"reasonably necessary for the protection of the rights or interests of the complaining shareholders."** (Emphasis supplied).

In holding the minority shareholder was entitled to relief, the *Meiselman* court noted that the trial court had focused on the conduct of the majority shareholder,

---

18. The courts of this state have only peripherally addressed the meaning of "oppressive" or "unfairly prejudicial" conduct. In one of the earliest cases, *Towles v. S.C. Produce Assoc.,* 197 S.E. 305 (S.C. 1908), the Court found the failure to pay dividends for three years did not warrant dissolution under the statute since the lack of dividends had been in an attempt to rehabilitate a weak financial corporation. The *Towles* court noted, however, "this statute was intended to afford minority stockholders a method of relief against mismanagement of a corporation by majority stockholders, or the suspension of dividends for the purpose of freezing out minority stockholders, or depressing the market value of the stock of the corporation..." 197 S.E. at 307. In *Segall v. Shore,* 236 S.E.2d 316 (S.C. 1977), the defendants had misappropriated over $1,000,000 of corporate profits in spite of an earlier opinion of this Court directing them to restore profits and account. The master found, and this Court upheld, that the defendants had acted oppressively and unfairly. In *Roper v. Dynamique Concepts, Inc.,* 447 S.E.2d 218 (S.C. App. 1994), the Court of Appeals held the issuance of additional shares of stock as a last ditch effort to raise capital for a financially troubled corporation was sufficient to overcome a claim of oppression, since the shares had been issued in good faith.

19. *Meiselman* has been referred to as a "leading case" in adoption of this approach. See Dean F. Hodge O'Neal, *O'Neal's Close Corporations,* §9.30 at 144 (3d ed. 1991) (hereinafter O'Neal); ....

using standards of "oppression," "overreaching," "unfair advantage," and the like. 307 S.E.2d at 567. The Court found this was error because the North Carolina statute in question required the trial court to focus on the plaintiff's "rights and interests" his "reasonable expectations" in the corporate defendants, and determine whether those rights or interests were in need of protection. *Id.*[20] The focus in *Meiselman,* based upon the language of the North Carolina statute, was upon the **interests** of the minority shareholder, as opposed to the **conduct** of the majority.

Unlike the North Carolina statute in *Meiselman,* section 33-14-300 does not place the focus upon the "rights or interests" of the complaining shareholder but, rather, specifically places the focus upon the **actions** of the majority, i.e., whether they "have acted, are acting, or will act in a manner that is illegal, fraudulent, oppressive, or unfairly prejudicial either to the corporation or to any shareholder." Given the language of our statute, a "reasonable expectations" approach is simply inconsistent with our statute.

We recognize that a number of leading authorities, such as Dean Haynsworth, advocate a "reasonable expectations" approach to oppressive conduct:

> The third definition of oppression, initially derived from English case law and long advocated by close corporation experts like Dean F. Hodge O'Neal, is **conduct which frustrates the reasonable expectations of the investors.** . . . It has gained widespread acceptance in recent years, particularly in cases involving close corporations where all the shareholders expect to be employed by the corporation and to be actively involved in its management and one of the shareholders is fired and then "frozen out" from any compensation or participation in management.

> Harry J. Haynsworth, *Special Problems of Closely Held Corporations,* C688 ALI-ABA 1, 53 (1991) (emphasis supplied; internal citations omitted).

Although several jurisdictions have adopted "reasonable expectations" as a guide to the meaning of "oppression," it has been noted by one commentator that "no court has adopted the reasonable expectations test without the assistance of a statute." Ralph A. Peeples, *The Use and Misuse of the Business Judgment Rule in the Close Corporation,* 60 Notre Dame L. Rev. 456, 505 (1985).[22] One criticism of the "reasonable expectations" approach is that it "ignores the expectations of the parties other than the dissatisfied shareholder." *See Lerner v. Lerner Corp.,* 750 A.2d 709, 722 (Md. 2000). . . . One recent commentator has suggested that a pure "reasonable expectations" approach overprotects the minority's interests. Douglas K. Moll, *Shareholder Oppression in Close Corporations: The Unanswered Question of Perspective,* 53 Vand. L. Rev. 749, 826 (April 2000) (hereinafter Moll). Similarly, it has been suggested that the reasonable expectations approach is "based on false premises, invites fraud, and is an unnecessary invasion of the rights of the majority." J.C. Bruno, *Reasonable Expectations: A Primer on an Oppressive Standard,* 71 Mich. B.J. 434

---

20. As in North Carolina, California also places the emphasis on the interests of the minority, as opposed to the actions of the majority. *See* Cal. Corp. Code §1800 (*cited* in O'Neal, *supra,* §9.29 at 131, n.8). *See also Matter of Kemp & Beatley, Inc.,* 473 N.E.2d 1173 (N.Y. 1984) (interpreting McKinney's Business Corporation Law §1104-a which allows court to liquidate assets if a) it is the only feasible means whereby the petitioners may reasonably expect to obtain a fair return on their investment or b) it is reasonably necessary to protect rights and interests of shareholders).

22. Peeples notes, "[t]he most unique feature of the reasonable expectations analysis is the lack of a bad faith requirement. At most, the plaintiff is required to show that he or she was not at fault, not that the defendant acted in bad faith." 60 Notre Dame L. Rev. at 504.

(May 1992). *See also* Sandra K. Miller, *How Should U.K. and U.S. Minority Shareholder Remedies for Unfairly Prejudicial or Oppressive Conduct Be Reformed?*, 36 Am. Bus. L.J. 579, 632 (Summer 1999) (suggesting the "vague and uncertain reasonable expectation test undermines the institution of stare decisis and fails to foster judicial accountability").

We find adoption of the "reasonable expectations" standard is inconsistent with section 33-14-300, which places an emphasis not upon the minority's expectations but, rather, on the actions of the majority. We decline to adopt such an expansive approach to oppressive conduct in the absence of a legislative mandate. We find, consistent with the Legislature's comment to section 33-18-400, that the terms "oppressive" and "unfairly prejudicial" are elastic terms whose meaning varies with the circumstances presented in a particular case. As noted by one commentator:

> While business corporation statutes may attempt to provide certainty and clarity in the law to enhance the attractiveness of doing business, the definition of oppression has been left to judicial construction on a case-by-case basis. Such an approach has been suggested by the Model Close Corporation Supplement which expressly indicates that no attempt has been made to statutorily define oppression, fraud or prejudicial conduct, leaving these "elastic terms" to judicial interpretation.... The judicial construction of the definition of oppressive conduct is well-suited to the diversified, fact-specific disputes among shareholders of closely held corporations. However, the judicial development of a meaningful standard for defining oppressive conduct, apart from fraud or mismanagement, is a difficult task.
>
> Sandra K. Miller, *Should the Definition of Oppressive Conduct by the Majority Shareholders Exclude a Consideration of Ethical Conduct and Business Purpose,* 97 Dick. L. Rev. 227, 229-230 (Winter 1993).

We find a case-by-case analysis, supplemented by various factors which may be indicative of oppressive behavior, to be the proper inquiry under S.C. Code §33-14-300.[25] Accordingly, the Court of Appeals' opinion is modified to the extent it adopted a "reasonable expectations" approach.

b. Oppression under Circumstances of this Case

The question remains whether the conduct of Atlas toward John and Louise was "oppressive" and "unfairly prejudicial" under the factual circumstances presented. We find this case presents a classic example of a majority "freeze-out," and that the referee properly found Atlas had engaged in conduct which was fraudulent, oppressive and unfairly prejudicial.

The particular problems encountered by those in the close corporation setting was noted in *Meiselman,* 307 S.E.2d at 559 (citing J.A.C. Hetherington,

---

25. We agree with Professor Miller's suggestion that the best approach to the statutory definition of oppressive conduct may well be a case-by-case analysis, augmented by factors or typical patterns of majority conduct which tend to be indicative of oppression, such as exclusion from management, withholding of dividends, paying excessive salaries to majority shareholders, and analogous activities. Sandra K. Miller, *How Should U.K. and U.S. Minority Shareholder Remedies for Unfairly Prejudicial or Oppressive Conduct Be Reformed?*, 36 Am. Bus. L.J. 579, 585-586 (Summer 1999). In this regard, we note that we do not hold that a court may never consider the parties' reasonable expectations, or the other items enumerated by the Court of Appeals, as **factors** in assessing oppressive conduct; such factors, however, are not to be utilized as the sole test of oppression under South Carolina law.

Special Characteristics, Problems, and Needs of the Close Corporation, 1969 U. Ill. L. F. 1, 21):

> The right of the majority to control the enterprise achieves a meaning and has an impact in close corporations that it has in no other major form of business organization under our law. Only in the close corporation does the power to manage carry with it the de facto power to allocate the benefits of ownership arbitrarily among the shareholders and to discriminate against a minority whose investment is imprisoned in the enterprise. The essential basis of this power in the close corporation is the inability of those so excluded from the benefits of proprietorship to withdraw their investment at will.

This unequal balance of power often leads to a "squeeze out" or "freeze out"[26] of the minority by the majority shareholders. *See* F. Hodge O'Neal, *Oppression of Minority Shareholders: Protecting Minority Rights,* 35 Clev. St. L. Rev. 121, 125 (1986/1987); Anthony and Borass, *Betrayed, Belittled . . . But Triumphant: Claims of Shareholders in Closely Held Corporations,* 22 Wm. Mitchell L. Rev. 1173, 1175 (1996). In the close corporation, a shareholder

> [F]aces a potential danger the shareholder of a public corporation generally avoids— the possibility of harm to the fair value of the shareholder's investment. At its extreme, this harm manifests itself as the classic freeze out where the minority shareholder faces a trapped investment and an indefinite exclusion from participation in business returns. The position of the close corporation shareholder, therefore, is uniquely precarious.

Moll, 53 Vand. L. Rev. at 790-91.

Common freeze out techniques include the termination of a minority shareholder's employment, the refusal to declare dividends,[27] the removal of a minority shareholder from a position of management, and the siphoning off of corporate earnings through high compensation to the majority shareholder. Often, these tactics are used in combination.[28] Moll, 53 Vand. L. Rev. at 757-758. In a public corporation, the minority shareholder can escape such abuses by selling his shares; there is no such market,

---

26. "Freeze out" is often used as a synonym for "squeeze out." The term squeeze out means the use by some of the owners or participants in a business enterprise of strategic position, inside information, or powers of control, or the utilization of some legal device or technique, to eliminate from the enterprise one or more of its owners or participants. 2 F. Hodge O'Neal & Robert B. Thompson, *O'Neal's Oppression of Minority Shareholders,* §1.01 at 1 (2d ed. 1999).

27. Majority freeze out schemes which withhold dividends "are designed to compel the minority to relinquish stock at inadequate prices. When the minority stockholder agrees to sell out at less than fair value, the majority has won." *Donahue v. Rodd Electrotype Co.,* 328 N.E.2d 505, 515 (Mass. 1975) (internal citations omitted). *See also* Robert B. Thompson, *The Shareholder's Cause of Action for Oppression,* 48 Bus. Law, 699, 703-4 (1993) (noting that in a classic "freeze out," the majority first denies the minority any return and then proposes to buy the shares at a very low price).

28. A host of factors is identified in 1 F. Hodge O'Neal and Robert B. Thompson, *O'Neal's Oppression of Minority Shareholders,* Chap. 3 (2d ed. 1999), including, but not limited to, dividend withholding, eliminating minority shareholders from directorate and excluding them from employment, siphoning off corporate earnings via high compensation, leases and loans favorable to majority shareholders, failure to enforce contracts for the benefit of the corporation, appropriation of corporate assets, contracts or credit for personal use, usurping corporate opportunities, transactions between a parent corporation and a subsidiary, withholding information from minority shareholders.

however, for the stock of a close corporation. *Id.*[29] "The primary vulnerability of a minority shareholder is the specter of being 'locked in,' that is, having a perpetual investment in an entity without any expectation of ever receiving a return on that investment." Charles Murdock, *The Evolution of Effective Remedies for Minority Shareholders and Its Impact upon Valuation of Minority Shares,* 65 Notre Dame L. Rev. 425, 477 (1990).

The present case presents a classic situation of minority "freeze out." The referee considered the following factors: 1) Alex' unilateral action to deprive Louise of the benefits of ownership in her shares in Atlas, and subsequent reduction in her distributions based upon the reduced number of shares,[30] 2) Alex' conduct in depriving John and Louise of the 21% interest of [a related company's] stock, 3) the fact that there is no prospect of John and Louise receiving any financial benefit from their ownership of Atlas shares,[31] 4) the fact that Alex and his family continue to receive substantial benefit from their ownership in Atlas, 5) the fact that Atlas has substantial cash and liquid assets, very little debt and that, notwithstanding its ability to declare dividends, it has indicated it would not do so in the foreseeable future, 6) the fact that Alex, majority shareholder in total control of Atlas, is totally estranged from John and Louise, 7) Atlas' extremely low buyout offers to John and Louise, and 8) the fact that Atlas is not appropriate for a public stock offering at the present time.

These factors, when coupled with the referee's findings of fraud, present a textbook example of a "freeze out" situation. We find the referee properly concluded the totality of the circumstances demonstrated that the majority had acted "oppressively" and "unfairly prejudicially" to John and Louise.

CONCLUSION

Under South Carolina's judicial dissolution statute, the Court of Appeals erred in attempting to define oppressive and unfairly prejudicial conduct. Further, we reject the "reasonable expectations" approach adopted by the Court of Appeals. Under section 33-14-300, the proper focus is not on the reasonable expectations of the minority but, rather, on the conduct of the majority. Such an inquiry is to be performed on a case-by-case basis, with an inquiry of all the circumstances and an examination of the many factors hereinabove recited. We believe such an inquiry is in keeping with the Legislature's intention in enacting sections 33-14-300 and 33-14-310.

Under the factual circumstances presented here, we find the majority's conduct clearly constitutes oppressive and unfairly prejudicial conduct....

29. Effectively, the minority shareholder's capital investment is "held hostage by those in control of the corporation because there is no marketplace in which the minority may sell their shares." Sandra L. Schlafge, *Comment, Pedro v. Pedro: Consequences for Closely Held Corporations and the At-Will Doctrine in Minnesota,* 76 Minn. L. Rev. 1071, 1076 (1992).

30. As detailed more fully in the Court of Appeals' opinion, Atlas made a 1990 distribution to Louise based upon her ownership of 271 shares of Atlas stock when the referee found Louise, in fact, owns 301 shares of stock.

31. The referee considered a number of factors in determining they would receive no financial benefit including salary, retirement benefits, John's lack of status as President, the fact that John would no longer receive loans from the company since he lost his employment, the loss of fringe benefits, the fact that John and Louise were paying their own attorney's fees, and the fact that a sale of Atlas was not contemplated. The referee then weighed these factors against the benefits still received by Alex and his family.

Notes and Questions

1. Notes

a. The South Carolina statute at issue in this case is substantially identical to MBCA §14.30(2)(iv).

2. Reality Check

a. On what grounds did the statutory provision permit relief?

b. How did the Supreme Court disagree with the Court of Appeals?

c. What definition of "oppression" does the Supreme Court use? Why does it select that definition? How many definitions have we seen now?

3. Suppose

a. If the South Carolina legislature had enacted language similar to that adopted by North Carolina, would the court's analysis have been the same?

b. If the South Carolina statute had been silent as to relief for oppression would the court have granted relief in this case? If so, on what theory?

c. Why was this litigation necessary? Isn't the result in this case simply the court's best judgment on an appellate record that must be very attenuated? Isn't the court just guessing who's been naughty and who's been nice?

4. What Do You Think?

a. I ask you again, should legislatures provide a claim for relief for oppression?

b. Which approach to protecting minority shareholders — that which focuses on the plaintiffs or that which focuses on the defendants — is more efficacious?

5. You Draft It

a. Draft a statute that permits relief for shareholder oppression. The following are reresentative statutes:

MBCA §14.30(2)

§14.30. Grounds for Judicial Dissolution.

The [name or describe court or courts] may dissolve a corporation:

(2) in a proceeding by a shareholder if it is established that:

(ii) the directors or those in control of the corporation have acted, are acting, or will act in a manner that is illegal, oppressive, or fraudulent;

SOUTH CAROLINA, S.C. CODE ANN. §33-14-300

The circuit courts may dissolve a corporation:

(2) in a proceeding by a shareholder if it is established that:

(ii) the directors or those in control of the corporation have acted, are acting, or will act in a manner that is illegal, fraudulent, oppressive, or unfairly prejudicial either to the corporation or to any shareholder (whether in his capacity as a shareholder, director, or officer of the corporation);

NORTH CAROLINA, NGCS §55-14-30

The superior court may dissolve a corporation:

(2) In a proceeding by a shareholder if it is established that . . . (ii) liquidation is reasonably necessary for the protection of the rights or interests of the complaining shareholder.

CALIFORNIA, CAL. CORP. CODE §1800

(b) The grounds for involuntary dissolution are that:

(4) Those in control of the corporation have been guilty of or have knowingly countenanced persistent and pervasive fraud, mismanagement or abuse of authority or persistent unfairness toward any shareholders or its property is being misapplied or wasted by its directors or officers.

NEW YORK, BUS. CORP. LAW §1104-A

(a) The holders of shares representing twenty percent or more of the votes of all outstanding shares of a corporation, . . . entitled to vote in an election of directors may present a petition of dissolution on one or more of the following grounds:

(1) The directors or those in control of the corporation have been guilty of illegal, fraudulent or oppressive actions toward the complaining shareholders;

(b) The court, in determining whether to proceed with involuntary dissolution pursuant to this section, shall take into account:

(1) Whether liquidation of the corporation is the only feasible means whereby the petitioners may reasonably expect to obtain a fair return on their investment; and

(2) Whether liquidation of the corporation is reasonably necessary for the protection of the rights and interests of any substantial number of shareholders or of the petitioners.

The Delaware courts have taken a dim view of minority shareholder oppression as a separate claim for relief. The DGCL does not permit the Court of Chancery to dissolve a solvent corporation. As you remember, Delaware also does not recognize an expansive fiduciary duty owed to minority shareholders. The Delaware Supreme Court spoke to the question of whether Delaware will create rules for the special protection of minority shareholders in close corporations:

> We wish to address one further matter which was raised at oral argument before this Court: Whether there should be any special, judicially-created rules to "protect" minority stockholders of closely-held Delaware corporations.[18]
>
> The case at bar points up the basic dilemma of minority stockholders in receiving fair value for their stock as to which there is no market and no market valuation. It is not difficult to be sympathetic, in the abstract, to a stockholder who finds himself or herself in that position. A stockholder who bargains for stock in a closely-held corporation and who pays for those shares . . . can make a business judgment whether to

---

18. *Compare* Robert B. Thompson, *The Shareholder's Cause of Action for Oppression*, 48 Bus. Law. 699 (1993) and F. Hodge *O'Neal and Robert B. Thompson, O'Neal's Close Corporations: Law and Practice*, §§8.07-8.09 (3d ed. 1987) (favoring court formulation of a special rule protecting the minority from oppression) with Frank H. Easterbrook and Daniel R. Fischel, *The Economic Structure of Corporate Law* 228-52 (1991) (noting that "courts have found the equal opportunity rule . . . impossible to administer," *id.* at 247).

buy into such a minority position, and if so on what terms. One could bargain for definitive provisions of self-ordering permitted to a Delaware corporation through the certificate of incorporation or by-laws by reason of the provisions in [DGCL] §§102, 109, and 141(a). Moreover, in addition to such mechanisms, a stockholder intending to buy into a minority position in a Delaware corporation may enter into definitive stockholder agreements, and such agreements may provide for elaborate earnings tests, buy-out provisions, voting trusts, or other voting agreements. *See, e.g.,* [DGCL] §218;....

The tools of good corporate practice are designed to give a purchasing minority stockholder the opportunity to bargain for protection before parting with consideration. It would do violence to normal corporate practice and our corporation law to fashion an ad hoc ruling which would result in a court-imposed stockholder buy-out for which the parties had not contracted.

In 1967, when the Delaware General Corporation Law was significantly revised, a new Subchapter XIV entitled "Close Corporations; Special Provisions," became a part of that law for the first time. While these provisions were patterned in theory after close corporation statutes in Florida and Maryland, "the Delaware provisions were unique and influenced the development of similar legislation in a number of other states...." *See* Ernest L. Folk, III, Rodman Ward, Jr., and Edward P. Welch, 2 *Folk on the Delaware General Corporation Law* 404 (1988). Subchapter XIV is a narrowly constructed statute which applies only to a corporation which is designated as a "close corporation" in its certificate of incorporation, and which fulfills other requirements, including a limitation to 30 on the number of stockholders, that all classes of stock have to have at least one restriction on transfer, and that there be no "public offering." [DGCL] §342. Accordingly, subchapter XIV applies only to "close corporations," as defined in section 342. "Unless a corporation elects to become a close corporation under this subchapter in the manner prescribed in this subchapter, it shall be subject in all respects to this chapter, except this subchapter." [DGCL] §341. The corporation before the Court in this matter, is not a "close corporation." Therefore it is not governed by the provisions of Subchapter XIV.[19]

One cannot read into the situation presented in the case at bar any special relief for the minority stockholders in this closely-held, but not statutory "close corporation" because the provisions of Subchapter XIV relating to close corporations and other statutory schemes preempt the field in their respective areas. It would run counter to the spirit of the doctrine of independent legal significance, and would be inappropriate judicial legislation[22] for this Court to fashion a special judicially-created rule for minority investors when the entity does not fall within those statutes, or when there are no negotiated special provisions in the certificate of incorporation, by-laws, or stock-

---

19. [S]tatutory close corporations have not found particular favor with practitioners. Practitioners have for the most part viewed the complex statutory provisions underlying the purportedly simplified operational procedures for close corporations as legal quicksand of uncertain depth and have adopted the view that the objectives sought by the subchapter are achievable for their clients with considerably less uncertainty by cloaking a conventionally created corporation with the panoply of charter provisions, transfer restrictions, by-laws, stockholders' agreements, buy-sell arrangements, irrevocable proxies, voting trusts or other contractual mechanisms which were and remain the traditional method for accomplishing the goals sought by the close corporation provisions.

David A. Drexler, Lewis S. Black, Jr., and A. Gilchrist Sparks, III, *Delaware Corporation Law and Practice* §43.01 (1993).

We do not intend to imply that, if the Corporation had been a close corporation under Subchapter XIV, the result in this case would have been different.

22. *Providence & Worcester Co. v. Baker*, 378 A.2d at 124.

holder agreements. The entire fairness test, correctly applied and articulated, is the proper judicial approach.

Nixon v. Blackwell, 626 A.2d 1366 (Del. 1993) (Veasey, C.J.)

c. ...to More Remedies

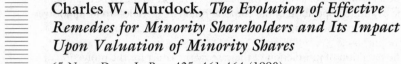

Charles W. Murdock, *The Evolution of Effective Remedies for Minority Shareholders and Its Impact Upon Valuation of Minority Shares*
65 Notre Dame L. Rev. 425, 461-464 (1990)

The concept of alternative remedies to dissolution is not new. In 1941, California broadened its grounds for involuntary dissolution by adding a provision that would permit liquidation when it was "reasonably necessary for the protection of the rights or interests of any substantial number of the shareholders, or of the complaining shareholders."[243] The legislature also enacted, in 1941, a provision providing for a buy-out of the complaining shareholder by the majority if the majority so elected. If the parties could not agree on price, the court would determine the fair cash value of the shares.

However, even though the courts were decrying dissolution as a drastic remedy, there was no rush by legislatures to provide alternative remedies, at least in the form of a buy-out option, until the 1970s. At least seven states enacted buy-out provisions in the 1970s and at least three additional states enacted such provisions in the 1980s. The statutory schemes range from simple to detailed and from a focus solely upon buy-outs to a multi-remedy approach. [See MBCA §14.34.]

Complementing these statutes are decisions in several jurisdictions in which the courts have recognized that the general equitable powers of a court suffice to order a remedy other than dissolution when the grounds for dissolution exist.

The focus of alternative relief typically has been upon buy-outs of minority shareholders. Accordingly, it cannot be gainsaid that minority shareholder buy-outs are firmly established throughout the states as alternative relief to dissolution when such shareholders have been subject to oppressive actions by those in control. The availability of alternative remedies, in turn, has had a substantial impact on the recognition of reasonable expectations as the basis for determining whether oppressive conduct exists.

The MBCA, in §14.34, provides that a defendant in an action for dissolution may irrevocably elect to purchase the plaintiff's shares for "fair value." The DGCL does not grant the Court of Chancery specific powers in this regard but, because the Court of Chancery has the full panoply of a traditional court of equity, the court could, conceivably, impose a wide range of remedies, including a forced or optional buy-out.

The courts of some states take great pride in listing the miscellaneous equitable powers they have found to remedy oppression. The following list is typical, I'm afraid.

We [identified] ten recognized alternatives to outright corporate dissolution when oppressive conduct has been proven:

---

243. 1941 Cal. Stat. 2057-58 (codified as amended at Cal. Corp. Code §1800(b)(5) (West 1977)).

"(a) The entry of an order requiring dissolution of the corporation at a specified future date, to become effective only in the event that the stockholders fail to resolve their differences prior to that date."

"(b) The appointment of a receiver, not for the purposes of dissolution, but to continue the operation of the corporation for the benefit of all of the stockholders, both majority and minority, until differences are resolved or 'oppressive' conduct ceases."

"(c) The appointment of a 'special fiscal agent' to report to the court relating to the continued operation of the corporation, as a protection to its minority stockholders, and the retention of jurisdiction of the case by the court for that purpose."

"(d) The retention of jurisdiction of the case by the court for the protection of the minority stockholders without appointment of a receiver or 'special fiscal agent.'"

"(e) The ordering of an accounting by the majority in control of the corporation for funds alleged to have been misappropriated."

"(f) The issuance of an injunction to prohibit continuing acts of 'oppressive' conduct and which may include the reduction of salaries or bonus payments found to be unjustified or excessive."

"(g) The ordering of affirmative relief by the required declaration of a dividend or a reduction and distribution of capital."

"(h) The ordering of affirmative relief by the entry of an order requiring the corporation or a majority of its stockholders to purchase the stock of the minority stockholders at a price to be determined according to a specified formula or at a price determined by the court to be a fair and reasonable price."

"(i) The ordering of affirmative relief by the entry of an order permitting minority stockholders to purchase additional stock under conditions specified by the court."

"(j) An award of damages to minority stockholders as compensation for any injury suffered by them as the result of 'oppressive' conduct by the majority in control of the corporation."

Masinter [*v. WEBCO Co.*, 262 S.E.2d 433 (W. Va. 1980)], at 441-42, n. 12 (quoting *Baker v. Commercial Body Builders, Inc.*, 507 P.2d 387, 395-96 (Or. 1973) and citations omitted).

State ex rel. Smith v. Evans, 547 S.E.2d 278, 283-84 (W. Va. 2001).

C. TERMS OF ART IN THIS CHAPTER

Cumulative voting	Preemptive right	Straight voting
Deadlock	Reasonable expectations	Supermajority
Oppression	test	Superquorum
Pooling agreements	Statutory voting	Voting trusts

17

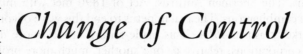

Change of Control

In this chapter we take up a central dynamic in corporate life: the transfer of control. This aspect is cognate, in many ways, to our discussion of dividends and our discussion of restrictions on stock transfers in Chapter 7. You might remember that a business owner has two ways to realize the increase in the business's fortunes: (1) by taking a portion of the cash that passes through the business, whether denominated salary, profits, interest, or dividends; and (2) by selling some or all of the ownership interest. Here, the concern is with transfers that constitute a shift of a controlling interest. That interest usually, but not always, constitutes the entire ownership interest of the transferor.

We will consider several aspects of this topic. First, we will take a step back and ask why anyone would want to transfer or acquire control. The various motivations will drive your clients' business decisions so you should pay some attention to them. You might also want to re-read Chapter 3 on how economic decisions are made. Second, we will work through the mechanics of transferring control. Third, and relatedly, we will see factors that influence your clients' choice of the appropriate acquisition technique. Fourth, we will explore the process of acquiring control from beginning to end. That is, we will focus on the temporal aspects of negotiating, documenting, and effecting a change of control. Fifth will be a consideration of the corporate law issues that most often arise in change of control settings. This chapter bookends the corporate law topics with background and context sections. The first limns the history of mergers and acquisition activity in America. The second deals with hostile takeovers. Finally, we see the federal securities regulations applicable to changes of control.

A. BACKGROUND AND CONTEXT

As you saw in Chapter 2, one way businesses become large is by combining with others. The advantages are usually ones of vertical integration (i.e., combining with a supplier or a customer) or horizontal integration (i.e., combining with enterprises engaged in substantially the same business). Although changes in corporate control happen all the time, and for a variety of reasons, changes in control of large American corporations tend to occur in waves. The first such wave began in the late 1880s when large businesses typically desired to expand horizontally. They frequently saw such acquisitions as a way to eliminate competition and, thus, to move toward monopoly positions. The Sherman Antitrust Act of 1890 met with mixed success in preventing these combinations. The real impetus to end this wave of combinations, though, was a market crash in 1904. This made raising money more difficult and made the value of corporations, relative to one another, much more problematic.

The second period of intense combination among large corporations ran from the end of World War I until the market crash of 1929. This period saw more vertical combinations than horizontal ones, at least among consumer goods manufacturers and retailers. Banks and utility companies also combined in great numbers. In response to the crash, Congress passed the Glass-Steagall Act that effectively required banks that accepted money from the public ("commercial banks") to engage in less risky investments such as secured loans to businesses and mortgage loans to individuals. Banks that did not accept deposits from the public ("investment banks") were free to invest in more uncertain enterprises such as investing in stocks. These restrictions remained in place until 1999.

The Great Depression, which followed the 1929 crash, World War II, which followed on the heels of that depression, and the post–War recovery, effectively stifled large-scale corporate combinations. As the American economy expanded and its growth prospects seemed stable, companies again began to combine. Starting in the early 1960s, these "go-go years," as they are embarrassingly called, were largely informed by a powerful intellectual idea that had recently been rigorously developed. That idea was diversification. We saw in Chapter 3 that an investor who diversifies his or her wealth by owning a variety of unrelated assets has an expected return equal to the weighted average of the investments but at much less risk.

The economic elaboration of that theory took place in the 1950s and corporate leaders of the next decade put that theory into practice. Corporations could diversify as well as individual investors could. That is, a corporation could purchase control of other corporations in unrelated businesses. The corporation's (and hence its shareholders') expected return could increase if the acquired business had a higher expected return than the acquirer, but the overall risk was reduced. Hence, a vogue for *conglomeration* began. The hunt was on for corporations that were profitable and that could stand alone — that is, businesses that did not have to be integrated in operations or management with the acquiring business. At the top of these new conglomerates, senior managers monitored the corporation's various businesses and looked for new businesses to acquire. Each business operated separately, and its head was, in effect, the CEO. The passion for conglomeration was cooled by a combination of an economic recession in 1973 and the rise in popularity of mutual funds and pension funds. The recession dampened stock prices, which made conglomerate shares less useful to fund new acquisitions. With mutual funds, individual investors could diversify for themselves; they no longer needed to invest in a conglomerate. Pension funds performed similar diversification functions for investors who were also employees.

Within ten years of the 1973 recession, acquisition activity among large corporations returned with a vengeance. The 1980s were the quintessential years for corporate combinations in America. Again, much of the impetus was provided by economic theories. These theories had the effect of encouraging changes of control over the objection of the acquired company's management and board. These changes could be effected by a *hostile tender offer* in which the acquiring company offered shareholders of the target company a premium to the prevailing market price. Because the decision whether to accept the offer rested with each shareholder, the boards of target companies were unable to defeat a hostile tender offer directly. Nonetheless, directors of likely target companies did not take the advent of hostile tender offers lying down. We will see the corporate law responses to target directors' efforts to defeat tender offers. You might note that nearly all of modern corporate fiduciary duty law comes from the period between 1985 and 1995. The hostile tender offer era came to an end in 1990 when Michael Milken, who had been instrumental in assembling much of the capital with which hostile tender offers were financed, was indicted for violating the securities laws.

Between the mid-1990s and 2000, corporate combinations, at least in certain areas such as Internet technology and health care, were common. With the bursting of the dot-com bubble in early 2000, such activity was reduced considerably.

B. THE CURRENT SETTING

1. Motivations for Changing Control

Let's begin with the seller's motivation. Why would someone who owns a corporation transfer control? For many closely held small businesses, a major motivation is that the expected returns, including noneconomic returns, are no longer sufficiently large. This may be because the owners have become disenchanted with the noneconomic benefits of ownership or because the business's economic performance is insufficient. In effect, owning the entity that owns the business is no longer "worth it." If there is more than one owner, they may have a falling out that ultimately results in a sale of the business.

Another major motivation to transfer control is the age of the owners. The owners reach a point in their life cycles when they prefer to retire. A related motivation is where control rests in a family and the controlling family members wish to assure a smooth transition of control to the next generation.

Another motivation, especially for sophisticated owners, is that the underlying business has reached some size milestone such as sales, cash flow, or profits, that the owners established as the point at which they would transfer control. This may be because their own talents are particularly suited for building businesses rather than tending more mature businesses. It may also be that the owners have estimated the point at which the business's growth will slow, such that the expected annual increase in value will drop to a level the owners find unacceptable. Whatever the trigger, the owners established an *exit strategy* when they acquired ownership and that strategy now dictates that control change hands. Finally, control may change when the owners receive an offer they can't refuse. In economic terms, the owners have been offered a price at or above their *reservation price*, even if they hadn't planned on selling.

Why do acquirers want to acquire control of a particular corporation? One motivation is the flip side of senior family members wanting to pass control to the next generation. Those younger family members may have varying degrees of enthusiasm for acquiring control, but a desire to continue a family business is often a strong motivation.

A very common reason to acquire control of a corporation is that the acquirer already owns assets that connect in some way with the acquired corporation's assets. We talked a bit in Chapter 2 about economies of scale that can be achieved by vertical or horizontal integration. In other words, there may be operational benefits from controlling both sets of assets.

Although it is currently out of fashion, an acquirer may be motivated by a desire to diversify. That is, the acquirer already owns assets that are exposed to substantially different risks than the acquired corporation's assets. By combining both sets of assets under common control, the expected returns of each set should be relatively unaffected while the risk of owning both sets of assets is less than the risk of owning either asset separately.

Regardless of whether the acquirer's primary motivation is operational benefit or diversification, that motivation may be affected by the quality of the acquired corporation's management. Where the acquired corporation's management is strong, the acquirer's costs of operating the newly acquired assets may be lower than otherwise. On the other hand, where the acquired corporation's management is weak, the acquirer may find another financial benefit. The present management's skills may have depressed the value of the corporation's assets, thus leading to a lower sales price. Further, by replacing management, the acquirer can increase the acquired assets' economic value and, presumably, increase the price at which the acquirer could resell them later.

2. Techniques for Combining Entities

In all of the combination techniques that follow, we will talk about an exchange of something for consideration. In this context consideration takes one of three forms. First, of course, is money. Nuff sed. Second is stock of the acquiring entity. Third is debt of the acquiring entity. Sometimes these forms are combined and sometimes the acquired assets' owners have a choice between types of consideration. Note that if stock is the consideration, sufficient authorized but unissued shares must be available. The acquiring corporation may have to amend its articles to increase the number of authorized shares. This probably requires a shareholder vote. So careful planning for an acquisition suggests that you, as the acquiring corporation's lawyer, must ensure that sufficient authorized but unissued shares or treasury shares are available.

a. Purchase of Assets

Perhaps the most intuitive method of acquiring a business is simply to purchase its assets. This is, indeed, a common approach. The primary benefit is that the acquirer can purchase the assets without taking the liabilities. Remember, though, that the doctrine of successor liability might result in the liabilities of the selling entity (sometimes called the *target corporation*) following the assets even where the acquisition agreement specifically excludes liabilities. See Chapter 8.

As a matter of corporate law, acquiring assets simply requires the purchaser's board to adopt a resolution. The seller's board likewise can sell the assets via a board resolution *unless* the assets of a Delaware corporation to be sold are "all or substantially all" of the corporation's assets. In that case the DGCL requires that an absolute majority of the stockholders approve the transaction. See DGCL §271.

"All" is pretty easy, but what is "substantially all" and why is that standard included in section 271?

Hollinger Inc. v. Hollinger International, Inc.
858 A.2d 342 (Del. Ch. 2004)

STRINE, V.C.

Hollinger Inc. (or "Inc.") seeks a preliminary injunction preventing Hollinger International, Inc. (or "International") from selling the *Telegraph* Group Ltd. (England).... The key question addressed in this decision is whether Inc. and the other International stockholders must be provided with the opportunity to vote on the sale of the *Telegraph* Group because that sale involves "substantially all" the assets of International within the meaning of [DGCL] §271. The sale of the *Telegraph* followed a lengthy auction process whereby International and all of [its] operating assets were widely shopped to potential bidders. As a practical matter, Inc.'s vote would be the only one that matters because ... it ... controls 68% of the voting power. [Inc. cannot exercise control over International's management, however, because of an agreement reached to settle charges related to the misconduct of Inc.'s controlling shareholder.]

I. FACTUAL BACKGROUND

International regularly acquired and disposed of sizable publishing assets. [F]or example, International engaged in the following large transactions:

- The 1996 and 1997 sales of the company's Australian newspapers for more than $400 million.
- The 1998 acquisition of the *Post-Tribune* in Gary, Indiana, and the sale of approximately 80 community newspapers, for gross cash proceeds of approximately $310 million.
- The 1998 acquisitions of *The Financial Post* (now *The National Post*), the *Victoria Times Colonist,* and other Canadian newspapers for a total cost of more than $208 million.
- The 1999 sale of 78 community newspapers in the United States, for more than $500 million.
- The 2000 sale of other United States community newspapers for $215 million.
- The 2000 acquisition of newspapers in and around Chicago, for more than $230 million.
- The 2000 sale of the bulk of the company's Canadian newspaper holdings to CanWest for over $2 billion.

The last of the cited transactions is particularly notable for present purposes. As of the year 2000, the so-called "Canadian Newspaper Group" — most of its metropolitan and community newspapers were in Canada — accounted for over 50% of International's revenues and EBITDA.[6] The EBITDA measure is significant because it is a measure of free cash flow that is commonly used by investors in valuing newspaper companies.

---

6. That is, earnings before interest, taxes, depreciation and amortization.

International Operating Units After the CanWest Sale

The CanWest sale left International with the set of operating assets it now controls. These operating assets fall into four basic groups... The Groups operate with great autonomy and there appear to be negligible, if any, synergies generated by their operation under common ownership.

THE JERUSALEM GROUP

The Jerusalem Group owns four newspapers that are all editions of the *Jerusalem Post,* which is the most widely read English-language newspaper published in the Middle East and is considered a high-quality, internationally well-regarded source of news about Israel. The Jerusalem Group makes only a very small contribution to International's revenues. In 2003, it had revenues... amounting to only around 1% of International's total revenues, and its EBITDA was nearly $3 million in the red.

THE CANADA GROUP

The Canada Group is the last of the Canadian publishing assets of International. It operates... 29 daily and community newspapers in British Columbia and Quebec... dozens of trade magazines, directories and websites... 17 community newspapers and shopping guides in Alberta.... The Canada Group is expected to generate over $80 million in revenues this year, a figure similar to last year.

THE CHICAGO GROUP

The Chicago Group is one of the two major operating asset groups that International controls. The Chicago Group owns more than 100 newspapers in the greater Chicago metropolitan area. Its most prominent newspaper is the *Chicago Sun-Times,* a daily tabloid newspaper that might be thought of as the "Second Newspaper in the Second City." That moniker would not be a slight, however, when viewed from a national or even international perspective.

Even though it ranks behind the *Chicago Tribune* in terms of overall circulation and readership, the *Sun-Times* has traditionally been and remains one of the top ten newspapers in the United States in terms of circulation and readership. Its sports coverage is considered to be excellent, its film critic Roger Ebert is nationally prominent, and its pages include the work of many well-regarded journalists. [T]he *Sun-Times* has generated very healthy EBITDA for International on a consistent basis during the recent past, producing $40 million in EBITDA in 2003, out of a total of nearly $80 million for the entire Chicago Group.

The Chicago Group also owns a valuable group of community newspapers that are published in the greater Chicago metropolitan area. These community papers have important economic value to the Chicago Group and to International. Their revenues and EBITDA, taken together, are roughly equal to that of the *Sun-Times.* In recent years, the Chicago Group as a whole has run neck-and-neck with the *Telegraph* Group in terms of generating EBITDA for International.

THE TELEGRAPH GROUP

The *Telegraph* Group includes the Internet site and various newspapers associated with the *Daily Telegraph,* including the *Sunday Telegraph,* as well as the magazines *The Spectator* and *Apollo.* The *Spectator* is the oldest continually published English-language magazine in the world and has an impressive reputation as a journal of opinion for the British intelligentsia, but it is not an economically significant asset. Rather, the *Telegraph* newspaper is the flagship of the *Telegraph* Group economically.

The *Telegraph* is a London-based newspaper but it is international in importance and readership, with a reputation of the kind that U.S. papers like the *New York Times*, the *Washington Post*, and the *Wall Street Journal* enjoy. It is a high-quality, broadsheet newspaper that is noted for its journalistic excellence, with a conservative, establishment-oriented bent. Its daily circulation of over 900,000 is the largest among English broadsheets but it trails the *London Sunday Times* in Sunday circulation by a sizable margin. Several London tabloids also outsell the *Telegraph* by very large margins. London may be the most competitive newspaper market in the world and that market continues to involve a vigorous struggle for market share that has existed since the early 1990s, when the *Times*' owner, Rupert Murdoch, initiated a price war. On balance, however, there is no question that the *Telegraph* Group is a profitable and valuable one. In the year 2003, it had over a half billion dollars in revenues and produced over $57 million in EBITDA.

II. LEGAL ANALYSIS

1. The Legal Standards to Measure Whether the Telegraph Group Comprises Substantially All of International's Assets

The origins of §271 did not rest primarily in a desire by the General Assembly to protect stockholders by affording them a vote on transactions previously not requiring their assent. Rather, §271's predecessors were enacted to address the common law rule that invalidated any attempt to sell all or substantially all of a corporation's assets without unanimous stockholder approval. According to leading commentators, the addition of the words "substantially all" was "intended merely to codify the interpretation generally accorded to the language of the pre-1967 statute that the word 'all' 'meant substantially all,' so that the statute could not be evaded by retaining a small amount of property not vital to the operation of the business."[44]

There are various metrics that can be used to determine how important particular assets are in the scheme of things. Should a court look to the percentage of the corporation's potential value as a sales target to measure the statute's application? Or measures of income-generating potential, such as contributions to revenues or operating income? To what extent should the flagship nature of certain assets be taken into account?

> The Supreme Court has long held that a determination of whether there is a sale of substantially all assets so as to trigger section 271 depends upon the particular qualitative and quantitative characteristics of the transaction at issue. Thus, the transaction must be viewed in terms of its overall effect on the corporation, and there is no necessary qualifying percentage.[51]

In other words,

> Our jurisprudence eschewed a definitional approach to §271 focusing on the interpretation of the words "substantially all," in favor of a contextual approach focusing upon whether a transaction involves the sale "of assets quantitatively vital to the operation of the corporation and is out of the ordinary and substantially affects the existence and purpose of the corporation." *Gimbel v. Signal Cos., Inc.*, 316 A.2d 599,

---

44. 1 R. Franklin Balotti & Jesse A. Finkelstein, *Delaware Law of Corporations & Business Organizations* §10.1, at 10-4 (3d ed. Supp. 2004) (quoting *Cottrell v. Pawcatuck Co.*, 128 A.2d 225 (Del. 1956));....

51. *Winston v. Mandor*, 710 A.2d 835, 843 (Del. Ch. 1997) (footnotes omitted).

606 (Del. Ch. 1974), *aff'd*, 316 A.2d 619 (Del.). This interpretative choice necessarily involved a policy preference for doing equity in specific cases over the value of providing clear guidelines for transactional lawyers structuring transactions for the corporations they advise. *See* 1 David A. Drexler, et al., *Delaware Corporation Law And Practice* §37.03 (1999) ("[*Gimbel*] and its progeny represent a clear-cut rejection of the former conventional view that 'substantially all' in Section 271 meant only significantly more than one-half of the corporation's assets.").[52]

It would be less than candid to fail to acknowledge that the §271 case law provides less than ideal certainty about the application of the statute to particular circumstances. This may result from certain decisions that appear to deviate from the statutory language in a marked way and from others that have dilated perhaps longer than they should in evaluating asset sales that do not seem to come at all close to meeting the statutory trigger for a required stockholder vote. In the morass of particular percentages in the cases, however, remain the key principles articulated in *Gimbel*, which were firmly rooted in the statutory language of §271 and the statute's history. As has been noted, *Gimbel* set forth a quantitative and qualitative test designed to help determine whether a particular sale of assets involved substantially all the corporation's assets. That test has been adopted by our Supreme Court as a good metric for determining whether an asset sale triggers the vote requirement of §271.[55]

The test that *Gimbel* articulated — requiring a stockholder vote if the assets to be sold "are quantitatively vital to the operation of the corporation" and "substantially affect [ ] the existence and purpose of the corporation" — must therefore be read as an attempt to give practical life to the words "substantially all." It is for that reason that *Gimbel* emphasized that a vote would never be required for a transaction in the ordinary course of business and that the mere fact that an asset sale was out of the ordinary had little bearing on whether a vote was required.

2. Is the Telegraph Group Quantitatively Vital to the Operations of International?

The first question under the *Gimbel* test is whether the *Telegraph* Group is quantitatively vital to the operations of International. The short answer to that question is no, it is not quantitatively vital within the meaning of *Gimbel*.

Why?

Because it is clear that International will retain economic vitality even after a sale of the *Telegraph* because it is retaining other significant assets, one of which, the Chicago Group, has a strong record of past profitability and expectations of healthy profit growth.

Now, it is of course clear that the *Telegraph* Group is a major quantitative part of International's economic value and an important contributor to its profits. I am even prepared to decide this motion on the assumption that the *Telegraph* Group is the single most valuable asset that International possesses, even more valuable than the Chicago Group.

Let's consider the relative contribution to International's revenues of the *Telegraph* Group and the Chicago Group. When considering this and other factors the reader must bear in mind that the contribution of the Canada Group dropped steeply

---

52. *In re General Motors Class H Shareholders Litig.*, 734 A.2d 611, 623 (Del. Ch. 1999).
55. *Oberly v. Kirby*, 592 A.2d 445, 464 (Del. 1991)....

after the 2000 CanWest sale. Bearing that fact in mind, a look at the revenue picture at International since 2000 reveals the following:

	Revenue ($MM)							
Operating Unit	2000	%	2001	%	2002	%	Unaudited 2003	%
Telegraph Group	$562.1	26.8	486.4	42.4	481.5	47.9	519.5	49.0
Chicago Group	401.4	19.2	442.9	38.6	441.8	43.9	450.8	42.5
Canada Group	1,065.2	50.8	197.9	17.3	69.6	6.9	80.5	7.6
Jerusalem Group	67.3	3.2	19.1	1.7	13.2	1.3	10.4	1.0
Other	0.0	0.0	0.0	0.0	0.0	0.0	0.0	0.0
Total	2,096.0	100.0	1,146.3	100.0	1,006.2	100.0	1,061.2	100.0

Put simply, the *Telegraph* Group has accounted for less than half of International's revenues during the last three years and the Chicago Group's contribution has been in the same ballpark.

In book value terms, neither the *Telegraph* Group nor the Chicago Group approach 50% of International's asset value because the company's other operating groups and non-operating assets have value:

	Book Value of Assets ($MM)							
Operating Unit	2000	%	2001	%	2002	%	Unaudited 2003	%
Telegraph Group	$542.0	19.8	533.2	25.9	568.3	26.0	629.8	35.7
Chicago Group	613.7	22.4	595.9	29.0	557.9	25.5	537.9	30.5
Canada Group	551.6	20.2	448.7	21.8	214.0	9.8	262.0	14.9
Jerusalem Group	61.2	2.2	69.6	3.4	28.9	1.3	30.1	1.7
Other	968.8	35.4	410.5	19.9	819.1	37.4	302.8	17.2
Total	2,737.2	100.0	2,058.0	100.0	2,188.1	100.0	1,762.6	100.0

In terms of vitality, however, a more important measure is EBITDA contribution, as that factor focuses on the free cash flow that assets generate for the firm, a key component of economic value. As to that important factor, the Chicago Group is arguably more quantitatively nutritious to International than the *Telegraph* Group. Here is the picture considering all of International's operating groups:

	EBITDA — All Operating Units ($MM)							
Operating Unit	2000	%	2001	%	2002	%	Unaudited 2003	%
Telegraph Group	$106.7	30.3	50.7	85.3	61.4	54.7	57.4	57.4
Chicago Group	59.8	17.0	47.6	80.1	72.1	64.2	79.5	79.4
Canada Group	190.5	54.1	(21.1)	(2.5)	(0.8)	(0.7)	(3.3)	(3.3)
Jerusalem Group	9.6	2.7	(1.5)	(2.5)	(2.8)	(2.5)	(5.3)	(5.3)
Other	(14.3)	(4.1)	(16.3)	(27.4)	(17.5)	(15.6)	(28.3)	(28.3)
Total	352.3	100.0	59.5	100.0	112.4	100.0	100.0	100.0

The picture that emerges is one of rough equality between the two Groups — with any edge tilting in the Chicago Group's direction. Importantly, the record evidence regarding the future of both Groups also suggests that their cash flow-generating potential and sale value are not greatly disparate.

The evidence therefore reveals that neither the *Telegraph* Group nor the Chicago Group is quantitatively vital in the sense used in the *Gimbel* test. International is not a human body and the *Telegraph* and the Chicago Group are not its heart and liver. International is a business. Neither one of the two groups is "vital" — i.e., "necessary to the continuation of [International's] life" or "necessary to [its] continued existence or effectiveness."[72] Rather, a sale of either Group leaves International as a profitable entity. . . .

3. Does the Telegraph Sale "Substantially Affect the Existence and Purpose of" International?

The relationship of the qualitative element of the *Gimbel* test to the quantitative element is more than a tad unclear. If the assets to be sold are not quantitatively vital to the corporation's life, it is not altogether apparent how they can "substantially affect the existence and purpose of" the corporation within the meaning of *Gimbel,* suggesting either that the two elements of the test are actually not distinct or that they are redundant. In other words, if quantitative vitality takes into account factors such as the cash-flow generating value of assets and not merely book value, then it necessarily captures qualitative considerations as well. Simply put, the supposedly bifurcated *Gimbel* test . . . simply involves a look at quantitative and qualitative considerations in order to come up with the answer to the single statutory question, which is whether a sale involves substantially all of a corporation's assets. Rather than endeavor to explore the relationship between these factors, however, I will just dive into my analysis of the qualitative importance of the *Telegraph* Group to International.

Inc.'s demand for a vote places great weight on the qualitative element of *Gimbel.* In its papers, Inc. stresses the journalistic superiority of the *Telegraph* over the *Sun-Times* and the social cachet the *Telegraph* has. If you own the *Telegraph,* Inc. notes, "you can have dinner with the Queen."[73] To sell one of the world's most highly regarded newspapers and leave International owning as its flagship the Second Paper in the Second City is to fundamentally, qualitatively transform International. Moreover, after the *Telegraph* sale, International's name will even ring hollow, as it will own only publications in the U.S., Canada, and Israel, and it will own only one paper of top-flight journalistic reputation, the *Jerusalem Post,* which has only a modest readership compared to the *Telegraph.*

The argument that Inc. makes in its papers misconceives the qualitative element of *Gimbel.* That element is not satisfied if the court merely believes that the economic assets being sold are aesthetically superior to those being retained; rather, the qualitative element of *Gimbel* focuses on economic quality and, at most, on whether the transaction leaves the stockholders with an investment that in economic terms is qualitatively different than the one that they now possess. Even with that focus, it must be remembered that the qualitative element is a gloss on the statutory language "substantially all" and not an attempt to identify qualitatively important transactions but ones that "strike at the heart of the corporate existence."

The *Telegraph* sale does not strike at International's heart or soul, if that corporation can be thought to have either one. During the course of its existence, International has frequently bought and sold a wide variety of publications. Thus, no investor in International would assume that any of its assets were sacrosanct. In the words of *Gimbel,* it "can be said that . . . acquisitions and dispositions [of independent branches of International's business] have become part of the [company's] ordinary course of business."[75]

---

72. American Heritage Dictionary 1924 (4th ed. 2000).
73. Healy Dep. at 206.
75. *Gimbel,* 316 A.2d at 608.

Even more importantly, investors in public companies do not invest their money because they derive social status from owning shares in a corporation whose controlling manager can have dinner with the Queen. Whatever the social importance of the *Telegraph* in Great Britain, the economic value of that importance to International as an entity is what matters for the *Gimbel* test, not how cool it would be to be the *Telegraph*'s publisher. The "trophy" nature of the *Telegraph* Group means that there are some buyers . . . who are willing to pay a higher price than expected cash flows suggest is prudent, in purely economic terms, in order to own the *Telegraph* and to enjoy the prestige and access to the intelligentsia, the literary and social elite, and high government officials that comes with that control.

Although stockholders would expect that International would capitalize on the fact that some potential buyers of the *Telegraph* would be willing to pay money to receive some of the non-economic benefits that came with control of that newspaper, it is not reasonable to assume that they invested with the expectation that International would retain the *Telegraph* Group even if it could receive a price that was attractive in light of the projected future cash flow of that Group. [T]he qualitative element of the *Gimbel* test addresses the rational economic expectations of reasonable investors, and not the aberrational sentiments of the peculiar (if not, more likely, the non-existent) persons who invest money to help fulfill the social ambitions of inside managers and to thereby enjoy (through the ownership of common stock) vicariously extraordinary lives themselves.

After the *Telegraph* Sale, International's stockholders will remain investors in a publication company with profitable operating assets, a well-regarded tabloid newspaper of good reputation and large circulation, a prestigious newspaper in Israel, and other valuable assets. While important, the sale of the *Telegraph* does not strike a blow to International's heart.

4. Summary of §271 Analysis

When considered quantitatively and qualitatively, the *Telegraph* sale does not amount to a sale of substantially all of International's assets. This conclusion is consistent with the bulk of our case law under §271. Although by no means wholly consistent, that case law has, by and large, refused to find that a disposition involved substantially all the assets of a corporation when the assets that would remain after the sale were, in themselves, substantial and profitable. In the cases when asset sales were deemed to involve substantially all of a corporation's assets, the record always revealed great doubt about the viability of the business that would remain, primarily because the remaining operating assets were not profitable. But, "if the portion of the business not sold constitutes a substantial, viable, ongoing component of the corporation, the sale is not subject to Section 271."[78] By any reasonable interpretation, the *Telegraph* sale does not involve substantially all of International's assets as substantial operating (and non-operating) assets will be retained, and International will remain a profitable publishing concern.[79]

---

78. 1 R. Franklin Balotti & Jesse A. Finkelstein, *Delaware Law of Corporations & Business Organizations* §10.2, at 10-7 (3d ed. Supp. 2004).

79. As International points out, the MBCA now includes a safe harbor provision that is intended to provide a "greater measure of certainty than is provided by interpretations of the current case law." [MBCA] §12.02 cmt. 1 (2002). The safe harbor is an objective test involving two factors:

> If a corporation retains a business activity that represented at least 25 percent of total assets at the end of the most recently completed fiscal year, and 25 percent of either income from continuing operations before taxes or revenues from continuing operations for that fiscal year, in each case of

Notes and Questions

1. Reality Check

a. Why does it matter whether the proposed sale by International is covered by DGCL §271?

b. Why was the phrase "substantially all" added to the statute?

c. How does Vice Chancellor Strine interpret that phrase?

d. What are the two parts of the Delaware test?

2. Suppose

a. If International were incorporated in an MBCA state, would the analysis or result be different?

b. Suppose International had never sold an operating division before. Would the analysis or result be different?

3. What Do You Think?

a. Is the MBCA's approach really different from Delaware's?

b. Which of the two approaches is better?

c. How would you define "substantially all"?

d. Do you believe that the two parts of the Delaware test are really separate from one another?

e. Do you believe it makes sense to measure "substantially all" by the expectations of an economically rational investor?

4. You Draft It

a. Draft a statute that appropriately defines the transactions upon which shareholders should vote.

> Every corporation may at any meeting of its board of directors or governing body sell, lease or exchange all or substantially all of its property and assets, including its goodwill and its corporate franchises, upon such terms and conditions and for such consideration, which may consist in whole or in part of money or other property,

---

the corporation and its subsidiaries on a consolidated basis, the corporation will conclusively be deemed to have retained a significant continuing business activity.

Id. §12.02(a).

Moreover,...the MBCA...usefully turn[s] the "substantially all" inquiry on its head by focusing, as *Gimbel* does in a more oblique way, on what remains after a sale. *See* [MBCA] §12.02 cmt. 1 (2002) (stockholder vote required if asset sale would "leave the corporation without a significant continuing business activity");...The MBCA, in particular, recognizes that while the "significant continuing business activity" test differs verbally from the "substantially all" language employed in many state corporation statutes, adoption of the MBCA provision would not entail a substantive change from existing law, because "[i]n practice,...courts interpreting these statutes [using the phrase 'substantially all'] have commonly employed a test comparable to that embodied in 12.02(a)." [MBCA] §12.02 cmt. 1 (2002). The commentary specifically cites several Delaware judicial decisions as examples of cases employing such a test. *Id.* These approaches support the conclusion I reach.

Although not binding on me, these interpretative approaches provide a valuable perspective on §271 because they are rooted, as is *Gimbel,* in the intent behind the statute (and statutes like it in other jurisdictions). Indeed, taken together, a reading of §271 that: 1) required a stockholder vote for any sales contract to which a parent was a party that involved a sale by a wholly owned subsidiary that, in economic substance, amounted to a disposition of substantially all the parent's assets; combined with 2) a strict adherence to the words "substantially all" (à la the MBCA), could be viewed as the most faithful way to give life to the General Assembly's intended use of §271. That is, §271 would have substantive force but only with regard to transactions that genuinely involved substantially all of the corporation's assets.

including shares of stock in, and/or other securities of, any other corporation or corporations, as its board of directors or governing body deems expedient and for the best interests of the corporation, when and as authorized by a resolution adopted by the holders of a majority of the outstanding stock of the corporation entitled to vote thereon....

DGCL §271(a)

No approval of the shareholders of a corporation is required, unless the articles of incorporation otherwise provide:

(1) to sell, lease, exchange, or otherwise dispose of any or all of the corporation's assets in the usual and regular course of business;

MBCA §12.01(1)

A sale, lease, exchange, or other disposition of assets, other than a disposition described in section 12.01, requires approval of the corporation's shareholders if the disposition would leave the corporation without a significant continuing business activity. If a corporation retains a business activity that represented at least 25 percent of total assets at the end of the most recently completed fiscal year, and 25 percent of either income from continuing operations before taxes or revenues from continuing operations for that fiscal year, in each case of the corporation and its subsidiaries on a consolidated basis, the corporation will conclusively be deemed to have retained a significant continuing business activity.

MBCA §12.02(a)

Under the MBCA, but not the DGCL, if an asset sale requires shareholder approval, the shareholders who disapprove of the sale also have appraisal rights. This is the right to require the corporation to purchase the dissenting shareholder's shares for fair value. This right is described in more detail below.

Purchasing assets has several drawbacks, though, that may make other acquisition techniques preferable. One drawback is where transferring title to the assets requires a change in registration. Suppose, for example, that control of a package delivery service were to change. Such a company doubtless has many motor vehicles, title to each of which must be changed into the name of the purchaser. Another drawback is where some of the assets require third-party approval before they may be transferred. If the assets include real estate leases, for example, the leases may prohibit transfer or subleasing. Where such assets are few in number or are not critical to the business a sale of assets may be feasible. Often, though, these restrictions make an asset sale impracticable.

b. Purchase of Stock

If purchasing all the assets of the seller is unattractive, another technique is to purchase the target corporation's stock instead. A corporation acquired in this way becomes a *subsidiary* of the acquiring corporation. This has the virtue of transferring control of all of the seller's assets and liabilities at once without worrying about identifying each asset or having to reregister the title to some assets. Another advantage is that the liabilities of the acquired company and those of the acquiring corporation are kept separate. The only difference is that ownership of the acquired corporation has passed to the buyer.

An important aspect of acquiring control by purchasing stock is that target board action is not required. If the target board is in favor of the transaction, this quality is of no consequence. However, if the target board is, or seems likely to be, opposed to the transaction (perhaps because the target board will be replaced) then this quality is of great importance.

An additional benefit is that an acquirer that wishes to obtain control over the seller's assets but does not want to acquire the entire ownership interest of the assets may easily do so by buying stock. The acquirer negotiates to purchase more than 50 percent of the voting stock and thereby acquires control without entirely owning the assets.

From the acquirer's perspective, purchasing stock requires the same corporate action as purchasing assets. The board must pass a resolution and, if the consideration is purchaser's stock, must assure that sufficient authorized but unissued shares (or treasury shares) are available.

From the seller's perspective, selling stock might be easier than selling assets because shares are usually more easily transferred than assets. Further, a sale of stock does not trigger appraisal rights. From the standpoint of public policy, the decision to sell one's stock is an indirect way of "voting" on whether to sell all the corporation's assets. If a selling corporation shareholder does not believe the transfer to be advantageous, he or she can refuse to sell.

This power of a selling corporation's shareholder to retain his or her ownership interest is a bit illusory as we will see below. An acquirer can combine two techniques, purchasing stock and merging, to eliminate recalcitrant target corporation shareholders. The MBCA, though not the DGCL, provides a more streamlined version of acquiring all a selling corporation's stock by providing that all such stock is automatically converted into the consideration if the transaction is recommended by the target board and approved by a majority of the shareholders. See MBCA §§11.03, 11.04, and 11.07.

c. Merger

Perhaps the most well-known acquisition device is a *merger*. In fact, many people loosely refer to any change of control transaction as a merger. Like a purchase of stock, a merger ensures that all assets and liabilities automatically pass to the acquirer. Like a purchase of assets, a merger requires a shareholder vote (and triggers appraisal rights) but does not leave the possibility of minority shareholders who refuse to give up their ownership interest. Conceptually, when two corporations merge, one disappears as a legal entity and its assets and liabilities automatically pass to the surviving corporation.

The boards of both corporations (called the *constituent corporations*) must approve a *plan of merger*. This plan sets out the terms and conditions of the merger. Most importantly from our perspective, the plan must set out the effect of the merger on the capital structure of the constituent corporations. Usually the plan of merger provides that every share of the surviving corporation remains outstanding. Each share of the target corporation becomes the consideration (i.e., cash, debt, or shares of the surviving corporation). The plan of merger must also set out the Articles of Incorporation of the surviving corporation.

After both boards approve the plan of merger, they must recommend the transaction to their shareholders. An absolute majority of shares of each corporation must be voted in favor of the transaction. The corporations file articles of merger with the secretary of state and the merger becomes effective. See DGCL §§251 and 259 and MBCA §§11.02, 11.04, 11.06, and 11.07.

When the merger becomes effective,

> all property owned by, and every contract right possessed by, each corporation ... that merges into the survivor is vested in the survivor without reversion or impairment; [and]
> all liabilities of each corporation ... that is merged into the survivor are vested in the survivor;
>
> MBCA §11.07(3) and (4). See also DGCL §259

Note that all shares are affected by the merger including those of target corporation shareholders who do not wish to receive the consideration. As we suggested above, a merger can be combined with a purchase of stock to eliminate recalcitrant target corporation shareholders. Here is how minority target shareholders are eliminated. An acquiring corporation purchases a majority of shares in the target. Then the acquirer causes the two corporations to merge, if necessary replacing the target corporation's board if those directors do not believe the merger to be in the best interest of the target corporation. The plan of merger provides that all target company shares will be converted into the consideration. The acquirer's ownership of a majority of target corporation shares guarantees that the plan will be approved by the target shareholders.

We turn now to two exceptions to the merger paradigm requiring both boards and both sets of shareholders to approve the merger. First, where the acquiring corporation already owns at least 90 percent of the target's stock, the statutes permit a merger upon only the resolution of the parent corporation's board of directors. Neither corporation's shareholders vote, although the target corporation shareholders have appraisal rights. See DGCL §253 and MBCA §11.05. This is called a *short form merger*. Second, the acquiring corporation's shareholders do not vote and do not have appraisal rights, if the acquiring corporation will not be significantly changed by the merger. More precisely, if the acquiring corporation's Articles of Incorporation will remain essentially unchanged and if the stock to be issued in the merger will be less than 20 percent of the outstanding premerger shares, then the surviving corporation's shareholders do not vote and do not have appraisal rights. See DGCL §251(f) and MBCA §11.04(g).

The merger technique does have some drawbacks. First, the assets of the constituent corporations are not kept separate, which subjects all assets to the claims of both constituent corporations' creditors. Second, a merger requires the vote of the *acquiring* corporation's shareholders, unlike a purchase of assets or stock. A merger also triggers appraisal rights for the shareholders of both corporations.

d. Reverse Triangular Mergers

This is not an Olympic diving event. It's an acquisition technique. Acquiring corporations want to acquire targets with as few hurdles as possible. That means that acquiring corporation managers would prefer a transaction that

1. Does not require a vote of, and does not trigger appraisal rights for, the acquiring corporation's shareholders;
2. Allows the acquiring corporation to eliminate the ownership interests of recalcitrant target shareholders;

3. Keeps the assets of each corporation separate; and
4. Does not *require* target board approval.

None of the techniques we have seen up to now has all these qualities. A purchase of assets allows 1 and 2 but not 3 or 4. A purchase of stock allows 1, 3, and 4 but not 2. A merger permits 2 and 3 but not 1 or 4. A stock purchase followed by a merger allows 2 and 4 but not 1 or 3.[1] The solution has become known as a *reverse triangular merger*. This technique involves these steps:

a. The acquiring corporation forms a wholly owned subsidiary that issues all its stock to the acquiring corporation in return for what will be the acquisition consideration. That is, the only assets of the subsidiary are cash, acquiring corporation shares, or acquiring corporation debt.
b. The subsidiary purchases at least a majority of target corporation stock.
c. The subsidiary merges with the target and the *target* survives. Target shares not owned by the subsidiary[2] are converted into the consideration, thus eliminating the remaining target shareholders. Subsidiary shares are then converted into target shares. The acquiring corporation then owns all shares of the target corporation.

In this way the acquiring corporation has effected a corporation that has 1, 2, 3, and 4. This technique is called a *triangular* merger because three corporations are involved: acquiring, subsidiary, and target. It is a *reverse* merger because formally the target (i.e., the acquired company) is the survivor rather than the subsidiary. If this seems convoluted to you, get used to it. This is an extremely common technique.

Note, though, that if the acquiring company is publicly held and if the consideration is shares of acquiring company stock, the acquiring corporation's shareholders may be involved in the transaction after all. Stock exchange rules require the vote of an acquiring corporation's shareholders if the amount of shares to be issued in the transaction exceeds 20 percent of the pretransaction shares outstanding. Even if acquiring company shareholders vote, they do not have appraisal rights.

3. Choosing the Appropriate Acquisition Technique

Non-tax considerations typically revolve around minimizing the process required and minimizing disapproving shareholders' appraisal rights. In the public company setting, a shareholder vote is almost always favorable to the acquisition unless the consideration is widely perceived as inadequate. In the majority of instances, where the result of the shareholder vote is not in serious doubt, planners nonetheless consider the cost of sending notice, sending proxy materials, holding the meeting, and tabulating the vote in deciding whether some acquisition forms are preferable to others. Further, even where the result and cost of a shareholder vote are acceptable to the planners, the delay required to notice and hold a shareholder meeting, which is on the order of three weeks, at least, may militate against structuring the transaction in a way that requires the shareholders to vote.

---

1. In this two-step method the target board's approval is legally required but, once control of the target has passed to the acquirer, this approval is a formality.
2. Target shares held by the subsidiary are simply cancelled.

Careful planners likewise calculate the likely number of shareholders who will seek appraisal rights and the likely cost of resolving those claims. Sometimes the transaction is made contingent upon no more than a certain number of shareholders exercising dissenters' rights.

In the abstract, tax considerations are the most important factor in choosing an acquisition technique. In any particular transaction, though, other considerations may outweigh the tax consequences. Because tax considerations are always important, we will elaborate on them here.

Particularly acute is the question of the tax consequences of the transaction on the target corporation (if it is to survive the transaction) and its shareholders. The core concept is *recognition*. That is, will the transaction be one that causes the target and its shareholders to report their gains (or losses)? If not, the transaction is said to be "tax free," although a better way to describe this is to say it is tax "deferred."

The animating idea is that Congress believes that a transaction in which a business's owners simply change the form of their ownership should not trigger taxation of gains or losses. Where a transaction exhibits two qualities, continuity of target shareholder ownership and continuity of target corporation business, whether conducted by the target or acquirer corporation, Congress believes that the target corporation and its shareholders should not recognize any gain or loss.

The most paradigmatic setting is a merger in which the consideration is surviving corporation stock. The target shareholders have gone from owning 100 percent of the target corporation to owning a proportionate interest of the surviving corporation, which owns the target corporation's assets. Target shareholders receive shares in the survivor corporation without paying any tax. In tax lingo, this is an *A reorg* because it falls within the Internal Revenue Code (IRC) §368(a)(1)(A).[3]

Building on this exclusion, Congress also exempted other transactions that seemed similar to a merger in that the target owners continue to own a proportionate share of an entity that controls the target corporation assets. A transaction in which the acquiring corporation purchases all target corporation stock in exchange for acquirer corporation voting stock has the same functional result as a merger. Congress exempted these transactions, which are called *B reorgs*.

A *C reorg* is just a bit more complex. A transaction will not result in recognition if the acquirer purchases all the target assets, again using acquirer stock for consideration, and the target corporation dissolves and distributes all its assets (i.e., acquirer stock) pro rata to its shareholders. The ultimate result is that the target shareholders own a proportionate interest in the acquirer corporation, which owns all target corporation assets. IRC §368(a)(1) has other exemptions from recognition but they don't concern us here.

Where the acquirer is using only cash or debt, the entire consideration is taxable. In many instances the target shareholders have such a low basis (essentially the price they paid for their target shares) and are united enough to pose a realistic threat of defeating the transaction so that a taxable transaction is out of the question. At other times, the typical shareholder basis is high, relative to the consideration, or the shareholders are so widely dispersed (as in a public corporation) that they do not pose a credible threat to effecting the transaction. In those settings a taxable transaction is feasible.

---

3. The term *reorganization*, or *reorg*, is used in tax law to mean the types of transactions we're talking about in this chapter. The same term is also used in the non-tax setting to mean a corporate reorganization under the bankruptcy code. The context should make clear which of these two uses is meant.

Notes and Questions

1. Notes

a. The courts in a very few states may recharacterize a transaction, at the request of a shareholder, under the *de facto merger* doctrine. Thus a transaction structured as a sale of assets will be recharacterized as a merger, or a reverse triangular merger will be recharacterized as a merger between the target and the acquiring company rather than the acquiring company's subsidiary. The consequence of recharacterizing a transaction is to grant shareholders greater rights than the ostensible transaction provides. Typically this means providing appraisal rights and possibly a shareholder vote. The Delaware courts have rejected the de facto merger doctrine, on the policy ground that the legislature, in providing for alternative forms of transactions, intended to give planners choices that would be respected. This policy is referred to as the *equal dignity doctrine*, meaning that the Delaware courts regard the various statutory provisions for transactions as being of equal dignity with one another.

2. What Do You Think?

a. The ultimate result of all of the acquisition techniques is substantially the same: placing the target assets under the control of the acquiring corporation. Do you think corporate planners should be able to choose techniques that provide less shareholder protection?

b. Do you think corporate planners should be able to choose techniques that provide greater tax benefits?

c. If planners should, as a matter of public policy, be able to choose transaction forms that will be respected by the courts, are there ethical issues that should constrain transaction lawyers from selecting some forms over others?

4. The Acquisition Process

It will be helpful to give you an overview of the process by which control of one corporation passes to another. Because the vast majority of such transactions are negotiated between the corporations' managements, we will discuss that model here. The model in which target management opposes the change of control transaction is discussed below under the rubric *hostile takeovers*.

There are three watershed events in the acquisition process. As you might expect with legal matters, each of these watersheds is memorialized by a particular kind of document or documents. These documents are mainly contracts, although some are corporate documents such as board resolutions, plans of merger, and amendments to the Articles or bylaws. If you are curious as to what the documents actually say, the most convenient place to view exemplars is on the SEC's EDGAR database. These documents are typically filed as part of the disclosure obligations of public companies.

In the first period, the parties begin preliminary negotiations with one another. Often the personal chemistry between the principals will have great consequences for the success or failure of the proposed transaction. If the preliminary negotiations progress as far as agreement (however tentative it may be) on the price and form of consideration and, possibly, the form of the transaction, the parties may execute a *letter of intent*.

In contract categories, this is a contract with open terms. It is probably phrased as an agreement between the parties to negotiate with one another in good faith looking toward the acquisition of one entity by the other. It may contain confidentiality agreements and may or may not provide that, should negotiations end, one side will pay certain expenses (usually out-of-pocket expenses) of the other.

Although the parties will have investigated one another to some extent, once the letter of intent is executed, investigation begins in earnest. The purpose is to give comfort to one party that the other is bona fide. That is, that it owns what it claims to own, it owes what it claims to owe, that it can authorize the proposed transaction, and that, in general, the financial, operational, and regulatory qualities are as the corporation represents them to be. The target is always the object of scrutiny, but the acquirer may not undergo rigorous examination if the consideration is cash rather than acquirer stock or debt. This investigative process is known as *due diligence*.

If the due diligence reveals no insurmountable issues, the parties will execute a *definitive agreement*. This will probably run between 20 and 100 pages of often dense prose. Usually the definitive agreement addresses at least eight issues. First, the agreement identifies the *parties*. Second, it describes the *transaction* (e.g., is this a merger? Asset purchase? Stock purchase?). Third, the agreement specifies the *consideration* from each party. Sometimes this description is simple, sometimes complex. Fourth, the agreement describes the *closing* — that is, when, where, and how the consideration will pass. This aspect of the agreement often reads like the protocol for a Cold War exchange of spies.

The next four areas are the most delicate and most fervently negotiated. Each party makes *representations and warranties* about itself. Essentially, each party describes itself as a legal entity (e.g., a Delaware corporation in good standing) with a particular capital structure; describes the state of its finances (including potential liabilities to lenders and other creditors); and asserts that it can legally enter into the contemplated transaction.

Although in theory it may be possible to execute a definitive agreement and transfer the consideration at one time, as a practical matter there is a gap, which may be several months long, between the execution of the definitive agreement and the closing. It may seem to you that this gap period is anticlimactic. After all, the parties have bound themselves by presumably enforceable legal documents. The only thing that remains is to swap the consideration.

In reality, the gap period is one of particular uncertainty. A party may have a change of heart about the advisability of the transaction. This change of heart might, indeed, come from the entreaties of a third party — a *raider* — who attempts to convince the target corporation to agree to be acquired by the raider rather than the original acquiring corporation.

Relatedly, because the target management controls the target during the gap, the buyer faces a moral hazard in that the target may be operated opportunistically — thus reducing the value of the target when it changes hands. Moreover, approval of the transaction is frequently legally dependent on a vote of shareholders or on approval by a regulatory agency, neither of which can be guaranteed with certainty. Other predicates to closing require the parties themselves to take actions during the gap period, such as adopting resolutions or reducing assets to cash to pay the consideration. *Covenants* in the acquisition agreement address these concerns. At bottom, these are promises to assure that the target remains in status quo and that both parties use their best efforts to ensure that all predicate actions necessary to the closing are completed.

As we just noted, completing the transaction may become unpalatable to one side or the other. The *conditions* section of the definitive agreement spells out the conditions precedent to each party's obligation to close. If those conditions are not met, and if compliance is not waived, one party or both has the option to decline to close. These conditions closely track the representations and warranties and the covenants. In effect, each party, as a condition to being able to require the other party to close, must show that what it represented about itself was true when the agreement was signed *and* is true at the closing, as well. Further, the parties usually negotiate conditions that permit one or both parties to refuse to close if certain fundamental assumptions underlying the transaction have changed. These sorts of changes, referred to as *material adverse change* clauses, cover things like a major decline in the stock market or a major change in the economics of the target company's industry.

In the end, the transaction may not close for any number of reasons. Most starkly, one side may simply breach. Alternatively, the parties may mutually agree to end the deal. Definitive agreements usually contain a date by which the transaction must close or else either party may decline to continue. Another cause of the failure to close is that one or more conditions have not been met. A material adverse change may have occurred. Finally, the target board may find that it has a fiduciary duty not to close the transaction because closing would not be in the best interest of the corporation.

The *termination* section deals with the consequence of the failure of the transaction to close. One consequence might be that no rights or duties arise from the termination — a "no fault" setting. Another consequence is to require one party to make the other financially whole by reimbursing the other party's out-of-pocket costs. Another consequence might be to penalize the party responsible for termination. Usually the termination section provides that some provisions, such as a confidentiality agreement, continue after the closing.

5. Corporate Law Issues

a. Deal Protective Measures

A number of common provisions in the definitive agreement are the result of the parties' concern with the possibility that the transaction may not close. The acquirer, in particular, may have invested a great deal of money to put the deal together. If it doesn't close, the acquirer may not be able to recover those costs. If the target is publicly held, it may find itself the object of unwanted acquisition offers if the initial deal falls through. These offers may be at prices below the initial deal price. Despite the target board's opposition, the public shareholders may tender their shares to the new suitors and the unwanted acquisition will occur anyway.

Acquisition agreement clauses that are designed to ensure that the transaction closes are often called *deal protective measures*. Although in some ways these terms seem to be of ancillary interest, in fact, these terms present the most difficult issues of corporate law in change of control settings.

One deal protective measure was implied when we described the termination provisions above. A *break-up fee* is a termination provision that makes the target liable to the acquirer if the transaction fails to close. This provision helps to ensure that the transaction closes because the break-up fee is set high enough to dissuade the target from lightly changing its mind about the deal. Typically these break-up fees run up to 5 percent of the total value of the transaction, which easily can run into hundreds of millions of dollars for a major acquisition. A similar economic incentive is a *topping fee*. This provides for an additional payment to the acquirer if the transaction does not close and if, within a specified time such as two years, the target is acquired by another entity.

Another economic incentive is provided by *asset lock-up* clauses. These give the acquirer the option to purchase certain key target assets if the transaction does not close. This provision both increases the acquirer's certainty that it can gain control of the assets it most desires and helps to ensure that the original transaction will close because the asset lock-up discourages raiders from attempting to derail the deal.

Other deal protective measures are designed to cabin the parties' range of actions so as to heighten the likelihood that the transaction will close. A *no-shop* provision prevents the target board from actively seeking other potential acquirers. A *no-talk* clause prevents the target board from negotiating with, or providing nonpublic information to, any other party. No-talk clauses are often narrowed to permit target boards to share information if the third party makes, or is likely to make, a bona fide offer for the target. Sometimes the clause provides that the target must keep the acquirer informed about any such talks, provide to the acquirer any information also provided to the third party, or require the target to permit the acquirer to match any third-party offer.

None of these deal protective measures is objectionable under contract law, although some break-up fees might be questioned under liquidated damages doctrines. The corporate law issues revolve around whether the target board has met its fiduciary duties in agreeing to the measures. The Delaware Supreme Court described the underlying tensions in the next excerpt. Although the case involved a merger, the Court's description would apply equally to sales of assets under §271, which also require stockholder approval.

> The Delaware corporation statute provides that the board's management decision to enter into and recommend a merger transaction can become final only when ownership action is taken by a vote of the stockholders. Thus, the Delaware corporation law expressly provides for a balance of power between boards and stockholders which makes merger transactions a shared enterprise and ownership decision. Consequently, a board of directors' decision to adopt defensive devices to protect a merger agreement may implicate the stockholders' right to effectively vote contrary to the initial recommendation of the board in favor of the transaction.
>
> It is well established that conflicts of interest arise when a board of directors acts to prevent stockholders from effectively exercising their right to vote contrary to the will of the board. The "omnipresent specter" of such conflict may be present whenever a board adopts defensive devices to protect a merger agreement. The stockholders' ability to effectively reject a merger agreement is likely to bear an inversely proportionate relationship to the structural and economic devices that the board has approved to protect the transaction.
>
> There are inherent conflicts between a board's interest in protecting a merger transaction it has approved, the stockholders' statutory right to make the final decision to either approve or not approve a merger, and the board's continuing responsibility to effectively exercise its fiduciary duties at all times after the merger agreement is executed. These competing considerations require a threshold deter-

mination that board-approved defensive devices protecting a merger transaction are within the limitations of its statutory authority and consistent with the directors' fiduciary duties.

Omnicare, Inc. v. NCS Healthcare, Inc., 818 A.2d 914, 930-931 (Del. 2003) (Holland, J.)

From a duty of loyalty approach, the target board, in agreeing to deal protective measures, might not believe that the transaction was in the best interest of the corporation. Even though in most transactions there is no self-dealing, the directors, which may include senior managers, may be concerned about retaining their positions after the transaction. They may have negotiated for such positions.

Turning to the duty of care, it is unlikely that target directors would not have all material information reasonably available when approving deal protective measures. Using the MBCA approach, director approval of deal protective measures would ordinarily be within "the care that a person in a like position would reasonably believe appropriate under similar circumstances." MBCA §8.30(b).

A more pointed duty of care problem arises when the board agrees to no-talk provisions. In the excerpt that follows, Asarco and Cyprus Amax had executed a definitive acquisition agreement with mutual no-talk provisions. Phelps Dodge wanted to enter into negotiations to purchase both Asarco and Cyprus Amax but the Cyprus Amax board desired to continue the original transaction. Phelps Dodge sought an injunction declaring the no-talk provision unenforceable. Chancellor Chandler described the duty of care problem that no-talk provisions present:

> Under our law, a board of directors must be informed of all material information reasonably available. The defendants properly argue that Cyprus Amax and Asarco are under no duty to negotiate [with Phelps].... Nevertheless, even the decision not to negotiate, in my opinion, must be an informed one. A target can refuse to negotiate..., but it should be informed when making such refusal.
>
> No-talk provisions, thus, in my view, are troubling precisely because they prevent a board from meeting its duty to make an informed judgment with respect to even considering whether to negotiate with a third party.
>
> Now, here, despite the presence of publicly exchanged information, the no-talk provision has apparently prevented either Cyprus or Asarco from engaging in non-public dialogue with Phelps. Now, this should not be understood to suggest that Cyprus or Asarco were legally required to or even should have negotiated, privately or otherwise, with Phelps Dodge. It is to say, rather, that they simply should not have completely foreclosed the opportunity to do so, as this is the legal equivalent of willful blindness, a blindness that may constitute a breach of a board's duty of care; that is, the duty to take care to be informed of all material information reasonably available.

Phelps Dodge Corp. v. Cyprus Amax Minerals Co., 1999 WL 1054255 (Del. Ch.) (Chandler, Ch.)

Note that the Delaware legislature, in reaction to some Delaware case law, has provided a deal protective measure in DGCL §146. The definitive agreement can provide that the transaction must be submitted to one or both sets of shareholders, even where a board determines during the gap period that the transaction is no longer in the corporation's best interest.

b. Sale of Control

We saw in the last chapter that courts impose heightened duties on controlling share-holders. The following excerpt discusses those duties in the specific setting in which a controlling shareholder desires to transfer control.

M. Thomas Arnold, *Shareholder Duties Under State Law*
28 Tulsa L.J. 213, 242-257 (1992)

SALE TO A LOOTER

A controlling shareholder is under a duty not to transfer control to another where the circumstances surrounding the proposed transfer are sufficient to put the shareholder on notice that the purchaser may loot the corporation. A controlling share-holder is under no duty to investigate a prospective purchaser of his or her shares absent circumstances that put him or her on notice that the purchaser intends or is likely to loot the corporate assets. Circumstances which may put the seller on notice of the purchaser's intent to defraud the corporation include . . . : (1) facts suggesting that the purchaser intends to finance the purchase or to secure the purchase price with corporate accets; (2) the knowledge that the corporation was the subject of looting in the past; (3) a request by the purchasers that assets of the corporation be converted into cash prior to the closing on the sale of shares and/or that the purchasers have access to its liquid assets immediately after closing; ([4]) the payment of an excessive price for the shares given the nature of the corporation's assets; ([5]) unfavorable credit reports on the purchaser or businesses controlled by the purchaser; and ([6]) prior frauds committed by the buyer on the seller. Evidence of facts that a reasonable investigation would reveal are not relevant to the question of whether the seller is on notice of facts suggesting that the buyer intends to or is likely to loot the corporation since no duty to investigate exists absent such notice. Generally more than one of these factors is present in the cases in which a seller of control is held to be on notice that the purchaser intends or is likely to loot the corporation.

Some scholars argue that a controlling shareholder should have a duty to investigate a prospective purchaser of his or her shares regardless of the absence of suspicious circumstances. Arguments supporting the imposition of such a duty include the possibility of substantial harm to the minority from a transfer of control, the fact that an investigation is unlikely to be very costly or difficult, and the fact that such investigations are already commonly done because sellers are concerned about the financial ability of the parties with whom they are negotiating. Thus, a strong argument can be made that the cost of imposing a duty on a seller of control to investigate the reputation and financial ability of a prospective purchaser of his or her control is outweighed by the potential harm such sales can cause to the minority.

On the other hand, some scholars question the wisdom of cases imposing liability for sale of control to a looter, arguing that it is difficult to detect potential looters, that looters acquire a reputation that prevents them from looting again, that most refusals to sell after a reasonable investigation are "false positives," and that the best way to deter looting is to punish looters very severely. These scholars conclude that a duty to investigate potential purchasers of control is costly and deters many beneficial transactions.

SALE AT A PREMIUM

Absent special circumstances, a controlling shareholder may sell his or her shares in a private sale at a premium price without any obligation to share the premium with other shareholders or to offer them an equal opportunity to participate in the sale of shares. A potential purchaser of controlling shares... will pay a premium for the opportunity to manage the firm's assets. Under current law this premium belongs to the seller of the controlling interest, is not a corporate asset, and need not be shared with other shareholders. In addition, the purchaser in a private sale of controlling shares has no duty to purchase all shares at the same price.

Arguably, allowing controlling shareholders to obtain a premium increases shareholder wealth by encouraging the sale of controlling shares to purchasers who will manage the corporate assets more efficiently. Under this view, a rule requiring a controlling shareholder to share the premium with other shareholders discourages the sale of controlling interests to such persons. On the other hand, even assuming that sale of control produces gains, the purchaser of a controlling interest might not share those gains with the minority shareholders, preferring instead to increase management perquisites while placing the shareholders on "starvation returns." Indeed, a potential purchaser of a controlling interest might be motivated by the belief that current management is inefficient in obtaining perks and may be willing to pay a premium for the opportunity to enjoy increased perks. Some scholars argue that the minority shareholders should share pro rata in any premium which a purchaser of a controlling interest is willing to pay, although the courts have consistently held that minority shareholders have no right to share in the premium.

Notes and Questions

1. Notes

a. Frequently a target corporation has a shareholder (or cohesive group of shareholders) that has enough stock to control the corporation but not a majority. In connection with the acquisition transaction, the acquirer may contract separately with that shareholder to obtain either the shares, an option to acquire the shares, or an irrevocable proxy to vote the shares in favor of the transaction. In such an instance the execution and enforceability of such a side agreement may be a condition to closing the transaction. This agreement with shareholders is also called a *lock-up* or a *shareholder lock-up*.

As you may intuit, these shareholder lock-up provisions both are deal protective measures, analyzed under contract law, and raise fiduciary duty issues for the controlling shareholders under a duty of loyalty.

b. It frequently happens that a merger is used by a controlling shareholder (often another corporation) to eliminate minority shareholders. As we saw from Chapter 16, controlling shareholders have a fiduciary duty to the minority at least when they use their control for their own benefit. In Delaware, and many other states, such a merger triggers the entire fairness standard, which requires the controlling shareholder to demonstrate its utmost good faith *and* the most scrupulous inherent fairness of the bargain.

Concomitantly, the subsidiary corporation's directors frequently face duty of loyalty issues because they may well have focused on their own continued employment or the controlling shareholder's best interest when they approved the merger terms.

2. What Do You Think?

a. Professor Arnold further discusses two different theoretical approaches to sale of control:

The Equal Opportunity Theory

A number of scholars argue that minority shareholders should have an equal opportunity to participate in any sale of a controlling interest in a corporation. They argue that an equal opportunity rule discourages sales of controlling interests where there is a risk of harm to the corporation through looting or mismanagement. Unless all shares are purchased, the controlling shareholder is a minority shareholder after the sale of control and therefore will be hesitant to sell to someone who will injure the value of the shares he or she retains. In addition, the sale of controlling shares in a corporation is analogized to a sale of corporate assets with a portion of the purchase price financed by the minority shareholders. Proponents of the theory urge that the sale of controlling shares is essentially a "corporate transaction" in which all shareholders should participate equally.

A number of scholars challenge the equal opportunity theory on the grounds that it would deter many beneficial transactions. Some controlling shareholders will not want to become minority shareholders in the corporation; perhaps some purchasers will not want a substantial minority shareholder to remain after the purchase. Further, some purchasers will be unwilling or unable to buy all the corporate shares in order to avoid these problems. [A] leading proponent of the equal opportunity theory, argues that beneficial transactions generally will not be deterred since: (1) if the purchaser is optimistic about the possible gains from a change in management he or she will agree to buy all the shares; (2) if the controlling shareholder is optimistic about possible gains he or she will agree to retain some of his or her shares; and (3) if the minority shareholders are optimistic about possible gains they will waive their right to participate in the sale.

M. Thomas Arnold, *Shareholder Duties Under State Law*, 28 Tulsa L.J. 213 (1992)

Do you think the equal opportunity doctrine is preferable to the current approach?

c. Appraisal

The right of appraisal, often called dissenters' rights, is the right of a shareholder to surrender his or her shares to the corporation in return for fair value. This right attaches only when the corporation undertakes certain fundamental actions such as merging. The underlying philosophy of appraisal rights is that where a corporation has truly changed in important ways the disapproving shareholders should have the right to end their investment in the enterprise. The principal questions we will take up surrounding dissenters' rights are, which transactions trigger them? And what is "fair value"?

i. Which Transactions Trigger Appraisal Rights? The MBCA, but not the DGCL, provides appraisal rights to shareholders of a corporation that sells substantially all its assets under §12.02. Both the DGCL and MBCA provide appraisal rights as the norm for the shareholders of the constituent corporations in any merger (and, under the MBCA, a forced share exchange). This norm is varied in two settings. First, where stockholders own publicly traded stock they could obtain substantially the same relief by selling as by seeking appraisal. So, such shareholders have no appraisal rights *if* the merger consideration (i.e., the shareholder's alternative to selling) is "traditional" consideration. In Delaware, this means stock in the survivor or stock in a nonconstituent company that is publicly traded. Under the MBCA, this means either publicly traded stock or cash. Note that stockholders of a public Delaware company *have* appraisal rights where the consideration is cash or debt and stockholders of an MBCA corporation *have* appraisal rights where the consideration is survivor stock that is not publicly traded.

Second, stockholders should not have appraisal rights if their corporation and their ownership interest in it will not be significantly different after the merger. The DGCL provides that stockholders of the parent corporation in a short form merger and stockholders not entitled to vote in a merger under DGCL §251(f) (stockholders' ownership interest will not be significantly diluted) do not have appraisal rights. Note that minority stockholders of the *subsidiary* in a short form merger *do* have appraisal rights.

The MBCA describes essentially the same rule more straightforwardly by providing that no appraisal rights attach to shares that will remain outstanding after a merger. The MBCA also provides that corporations may, in the Articles of Incorporation, opt out of appraisal rights. It also grants appraisal rights (despite any restrictions discussed above) to shareholders of corporations that merge with a controlling shareholder or with an entity controlled by one of its own senior executives. See DGCL §262(b), MBCA §13.02.

ii. What Is "Fair Value"?   The next case discusses one of the most contentious issues concerning appraisal rights. Shareholders and corporations nearly always disagree about the fair value to which the shareholders are entitled. The following case discusses the statutory standard and its application. Note that the case also talks about two related but separate conceptual questions. First, where the target corporation had a controlling shareholder, should the fair value of the dissenting shareholders' shares be discounted (reduced) to reflect the fact that those shares have little management power? This is the *minority discount* question. Second, where the target corporation is not publicly traded, should dissenting shareholders' shares be discounted to reflect the fact that the shares are illiquid? This is the *marketability discount* question.

Matthew G. Norton Company v. Smyth
51 P.3d 159 (Wash. App. 2002)

KENNEDY, J.

Matthew G. Norton Company (MGN)... held and managed a portfolio of commercial real estate, investments in certain private companies and venture capital funds, and a diversified portfolio of marketable stocks.

In early 1999, the Boards of Directors of MGN and Northwest Building Corporation (NWBC) proposed a corporate reorganization under which MGN would be merged into NWBC.... Each MGN shareholder would exchange his or her respective shares...for the same number of shares of NWBC stock.... The name of [NWBC] would then be changed to Matthew G. Norton Company.

MGN had 43 individual shareholders, all of them related in some way to Matthew G. Norton. None of the shareholders held a majority interest in MGN. The average ownership interest of all the shareholders of MGN was approximately 3 percent.

Stephen G. Clapp, who is one of the respondents to this appeal, was the only share-holder of MGN to dissent to the proposal. He held 25,016 shares of stock in MGN, 3.1 percent of the outstanding shares. NWBC had only two shareholders, MGN and Theodore H. Smyth.... MGN owned 99.65 percent of the outstanding stock of NWBC. Smyth owned the remainder, which amounted to 142 shares. Smyth, who is the other respondent to this appeal, also dissented.

Matthew G. Norton Company hired the accounting firm of Arthur Andersen to conduct valuations of MGN and NWBC for purposes of determining "fair value" of the dissenters' shares...as of the date of the merger. Arthur Andersen employed a "net asset" valuation method, which, in the simplest of terms, [reflects] current market values of assets and liabilities as of the valuation date. All of this indicated a net asset value of $170.246 million for MGN and $99.446 million for NWBC.

[A]rthur Andersen noted that the shareholders are severely restricted in their ability to transfer or sell their shares. Arthur Andersen opined that it was appropriate to discount the net adjusted value of MGN by 35 percent and to discount the net adjusted value of NWBC by 40 percent. This discount had the stated purpose of reflecting the lack of marketability of each and every share in the company, and not the minority status of the shares of the dissenting shareholders.

Arthur Andersen concluded that as of March 31, 1999, the value of one share in MGN was $138 and that the value of one share of NWBC was $1,451. As is con-templated by [MBCA §13.24], Matthew G. Norton Company paid Mr. Clapp $3,509,146 (including accrued interest) for his shares in MGN, and paid Mr. Smyth $208,050 (including accrued interest) for the shares of NWBC.... Mssrs. Clapp and Smyth notified the Company that they were dissatisfied with these amounts. As permitted by [MBCA §13.26], Clapp demanded a total amount of $6,858,928 for his shares and Smyth demanded a total amount of $458,864....

Matthew G. Norton Company, being unwilling to pay the dissenting share-holders any more money, filed its Petition for Determination of Fair Value of Shares of Dissenting Shareholder, pursuant to [MBCA §13.30]. In due course, Mssrs. Clapp and Smyth filed a motion for (partial) summary judgment, asking the court to rule that...the lack of marketability discount...is [not] available in a dissenter's rights valuation as a matter of law. The "fair value" of the shares of the dissenting shareholders has not yet been determined by the trial court.

At common law, unanimous shareholder approval was required in order to under-take major corporate actions. This made it possible for an arbitrary minority to estab-lish a nuisance value for its shares by refusing to cooperate. To resolve this problem, state legislatures, such as Washington's, authorized corporate action by majority vote. To avoid unfair treatment of shareholders, legislatures granted dissenting share-holders the right to obtain "fair value" for their shares.

"Fair value" is defined for purposes of the dissenters' rights statute as "the value of the shares immediately before the effective date of the corporate action to which the dissenter objects, excluding any appreciation or depreciation in anticipation of the corporate action unless such exclusion would be inequitable." The term "value" is inherently ambiguous. It is clear, however, that our Legislature's use of the term "fair value" was not a slip of the pen — the Legislature did not intend to say "fair market value," instead. All of the states and the District of Columbia have dis-senters' rights statutes. Forty-six states use the "fair value" standard or one of its iterations, exclusively. Only four states, California ("fair market value"), Louisiana ("fair cash value"), Ohio ("fair cash value") and Kansas ("value") use another term. The District of Columbia statute contains both "fair value" and "fair market value."

The statutory definition of "fair value" leaves to the parties, and ultimately the courts, the details by which fair value is to be determined, and leaves intact accumulated case law.... Proof of value may be made by any techniques or methods that are generally acceptable in the financial community. Official Comment to [MBCA §13.02], citing *Weinberger v. UOP, Inc.,* 457 A.2d 701 (Del. 1983). Determining fair value requires consideration of all relevant factors involving the value of a company, and may include elements of future value, excluding, however, the speculative elements of value that may arise from accomplishment or expectation of the transaction giving rise to the dissenters' rights. *Weinberger,* 457 A.2d at 713.

When Washington adopted its version of the Model Business Corporation Act in 1989, the Model Act was silent as to the propriety of discounts in determining "fair value." In 1999, the Model Act was amended to redefine "fair value" as follows:

> "Fair value" means the value of the corporation's shares determined:
> (i) immediately before the effectuation of the corporate action to which the shareholder objects;
> (ii) using customary and current valuation concepts and techniques generally employed for similar businesses in the context of the transaction requiring appraisal; and
> (iii) without discounting for lack of marketability or minority status[.]
>
> **Model Act §13.01(4) as amended effective April 15, 1999.**

[A] number of courts had already rejected lack of marketability discounts before the Model Act was revised, and, for that matter, before Washington adopted its version of the Model Act. A number of states have rejected such discounts since the revisions to the Model Act, without benefit of amendments to their statutes. We conclude that the fact that our Legislature has not amended [the Washington Business Corporation Act] to conform to the most recent revisions to the Model Act does not preclude the courts of this state from disapproving such discounts as may be inappropriate in ascertaining "fair value."

As noted by the *Weinberger* court:

> The basic concept of value under [Delaware's dissenters' rights statute] is that the stockholder is entitled to be paid for that which has been taken from him, viz., his proportionate interest in a going concern. By value of the stockholder's proportionate interest in the corporate enterprise is meant the true or intrinsic value of his stock [that] has been taken by the merger.
>
> *Weinberger,* 457 A.2d at 713....

And in *Cavalier Oil Corp. v. Harnett,* 564 A.2d 1137, 1144-45 (Del. 1989), the court held that a minority shareholder in fair value cases is entitled to a proportionate interest in the corporation appraised as an entity and rejected application of a marketability discount, reasoning that such a discount is contrary to the requirement that the company be valued as a going concern.

In *Swope v. Siegel-Robert, Inc.,* 243 F.3d 486, 491-94 (8th Cir. 2001), the court reviewed decisions from Missouri, New Jersey, Delaware, Maine, South Dakota, Oregon and Kansas wherein the courts rejected lack of marketability discounts.... Based on the reasoning of those courts, the *Swope* court concluded:

> The marketability discount is incompatible with the purpose of the appraisal right, which provides dissenting shareholders with a forum for recapturing their complete investment in the corporation after they are unwillingly subjected to substantial corporate changes beyond their control....
>
> ...
>
> [T]he market for minority stock in a dissenting shareholders' appraisal proceeding, absent extraordinary circumstances, is not a relevant fact or circumstance to consider when determining fair value.
>
> *Swope,* 243 F.3d at 493-94.

> "'[F]air value' in minority stock appraisals is not equivalent to 'fair market value.' Dissenting shareholders, by nature, do not replicate the willing and ready [sellers] of the open market. Rather, they are unwilling sellers with no bargaining power."
>
> *Swope,* 243 F.3d at 492-93. . . .

As the *Swope* court also noted, the American Law Institute concludes that the proper interpretation of "fair value" is the proportionate share of the value of 100 percent of the equity in the company, without any discount for minority status, or, absent extraordinary circumstances, lack of marketability. *See Standards for Determining Fair Value,* Principles of Corporate Governance: Analysis and Recommendations (ALI) §7.22(a) and ALI §7.33 cmt. *e* (1994).

[T]hose courts that generally will not apply such a discount do not support a blanket rule that, "as a matter of law," a marketability discount should *never* be considered. *See Swope,* 243 F.3d at 494 ...; *Atlantic States Const., Inc. v. Beavers,* 314 S.E.2d 245 (Ga. App. 1984) ...; *Weigel Broadcasting Co. v. Smith,* 682 N.E.2d 745, 751 (Ill. App. 1996) ...; *Ford v. Courier-Journal Job Printing Co.,* 639 S.W.2d 553 (Ky. App. 1982) ...; *Advanced Communication Design, Inc. v. Follett,* 615 N.W.2d 285 (Minn. 2000) ...; *Lawson Mardon Wheaton, Inc. v. Smith,* 734 A.2d 738, 749 (N.J. 1999) ...; *Balsamides v. Protameen Chemicals, Inc.,* 734 A.2d 721 (N.J. 1999) ....

[I]t is our task to establish guidelines for courts, litigants and appraisers in Washington that deal with our dissenters' rights statute. We conclude that the most logical starting place is to determine what it is that needs to be measured. As stated by the American Law Institute in its treatise on corporate governance:

> A focus on measurement technique is ... meaningless absent agreement on what is to be measured. This is essentially a definitional problem, and it involves significant normative issues that cannot be resolved simply by reference to the "customary valuation concepts" then in use in the relevant market.
>
> ...
>
> [Section] 7.22(a) focuses on what a buyer would pay for the firm as an entirety.... In focusing on the value of the firm, rather than the value of specific shares, §7.22(a) thus adopts the principle, long recognized by the Delaware courts, and more recently by the New York courts, that the appraisal remedy should award each shareholder a proportionate share of the firm's value. As a result, once an aggregate value for the firm is obtained, the court under §7.22(a) normally has only to prorate this value equally among all shares of the same class.
>
> 2 Principles of Corporate Governance §722 *Standards for Determining Fair Value.*

We agree. [O]ur Legislature did not adopt "fair market value" as the standard in granting dissenters' rights to shareholders for the "fair value" of their shares. The Arthur Andersen valuation reports for MGN and NWBC inappropriately equate "fair value" of the shares with "fair market value" — that being the very purpose for which lack of marketability discounts (as well as minority discounts) are applied, after all.

[T]o the extent that the trial court's order was intended to declare that, absent extraordinary circumstances, no such discount can be applied at the shareholder level, we affirm.

The parties have not had the opportunity to brief the extraordinary circumstances exception, and should be given opportunity to do so, following our remand, if either side believes any such circumstances to be applicable in this case.

Notes and Questions

1. Notes

a. Now that you've had more exposure to the idea of appraisal rights, you may wish to rethink your response to the question we posed earlier about whether corporate planners should be able to select a transaction form specifically to minimize shareholder rights.

b. The availability of appraisal rights is often more theoretical than real because the number of shareholders that perfect their appraisal rights is usually small, the costs of prosecuting an appraisal action is usually borne by each party, and attorneys' fees are not awardable against the corporation.

c. You should note that there is a significant strategic element in choosing to seek appraisal rights. First, to perfect the rights takes some diligence on the part of both the shareholder and the corporation. Second, once the shareholder has perfected appraisal rights, he or she has no power to discontinue the action. That is, unless the corporation agrees, the shareholder will get "fair value" rather than the merger consideration even if the court finds that "fair value" is less than the consideration, which is a not infrequent occurrence.

2. Reality Check

a. What was the dispute between the corporations and the dissenting shareholders?

b. How did the corporation determine its version of "fair value"?

c. How does Judge Kennedy resolve the disputes? Do you agree with the result?

3. What Do You Think?

a. Do you think that either the minority discount or the marketability discount should be routinely applied?

b. Should "fair value" be the standard? If not, what should be?

4. You Draft It

a. Draft an appraisal statute that describes the value to which a dissenting shareholder is entitled. The relevant DGCL and MBCA provisions follow.

MBCA §13.01 current version:
  (4) Fair value means the value of the corporation's shares determined:
     (i) immediately before the effectuation of the corporate action to which the shareholder objects;

(ii) using customary and current valuation concepts and techniques generally employed for similar businesses in the context of the transaction requiring appraisal; and

(iii) without discounting for lack of marketability or minority status...

MBCA §13.01 pre-1999 version:

(3) "Fair value," with respect to a dissenter's shares, means the value of the shares immediately before the effective date of the corporate action to which the dissenter objects, excluding any appreciation or depreciation in anticipation of the corporate action unless exclusion would be inequitable.

DGCL §262(h):

[T]he Court shall appraise the shares, determining their fair value exclusive of any element of value arising from the accomplishment or expectation of the merger or consolidation, together with a fair rate of interest, if any, to be paid upon the amount determined to be the fair value. In determining such fair value, the Court shall take into account all relevant factors. In determining the fair rate of interest, the Court may consider all relevant factors, including the rate of interest which the surviving or resulting corporation would have had to pay to borrow money during the pendency of the proceeding.

C. BACKGROUND AND CONTEXT—HOSTILE TAKEOVERS

As mentioned earlier, the 1980s saw an explosion of change of control activity among public companies, much of it despite the opposition of the target company's board of directors. Such a transaction is known as a *hostile takeover*. In a typical transaction, the acquiring company, or *raider*, approaches the target management to see whether a friendly transaction can be negotiated. Sometimes the target has executed a definitive agreement with another entity; the raider attempts to acquire the target out from under the other party.

If the raider is rebuffed, it may launch a *tender offer*. This is an offer to the target's shareholders to sell their shares to the raider at a premium to the current market price. Tender offers are highly regulated, but nearly all the regulation is contained in the federal securities laws rather than in state corporate laws.

The tender offer is nearly always made by a wholly owned subsidiary of the raider formed for the express purpose of acquiring the target. Usually the tender offer is conditioned on the raider's subsidiary being able to purchase more than 50 percent of target company shares. If the tender offer is successful, the raider promptly replaces the target's board and effects a reverse triangular merger. At the end of the process, the target is a wholly owned subsidiary of the raider.

Much of the law of directors' fiduciary duties in Delaware comes from these hostile takeovers. In this section we will look at four legal facets of these takeovers. First we will list some of the governance structures that corporations may adopt that deter unwanted changes of control. These structures can stand alone or they can be used in conjunction with deal protective measures if the target has agreed on a transaction with another party. Target boards may also take other actions to stave off a raider once a hostile raid has begun. Our second focus will be on the standards of review courts use in evaluating target board reactions. Third, we will see that sometimes target boards are under an obligation to maximize shareholder value in the short term. Finally, we will see that many states have enacted antitakeover laws.

1. Corporate Structures That Deter Hostile Changes of Control

Many corporations want to ensure that any change of control transaction is approved by the board. Several corporate governance structures, sometimes called *shark repellents*, keep unwanted suitors from effecting a takeover. One technique is to require a supermajority shareholder vote for takeover transactions. This requirement must appear in the Articles of Incorporation. A second device is to stagger the board so that a raider must, in theory at least, wait for two annual meetings of target shareholders before being able to elect a majority of directors. In practice, if the raider has purchased a majority of shares, the target board often capitulates and resigns in favor of the raider's nominees. Under the DGCL, directors on a staggered board can only be removed for cause unless the Articles of Incorporation provide otherwise. See DGCL §141(k). Where the board is not staggered or where the target is incorporated outside of Delaware, the Articles can be amended to provide that directors can only be removed for cause.

The corporation's Articles or bylaws can contain an *advance notice provision* that requires a shareholder to notify management several months in advance of a shareholders' meeting if the shareholder intends to nominate an alternative slate of directors or to propose an action for shareholder vote.

Under the DGCL the Articles can prohibit shareholders from acting by consent but cannot prohibit the shareholders from amending the bylaws. See DGCL §§109 and 228. Under the MBCA the shareholders' power to act by consent cannot be taken away by the Articles. A similar provision is an Article provision prohibiting shareholders from calling a special meeting. Under the DGCL the default rule is that stockholders do not have the power to call a special meeting. See DGCL §211(d).

The final two shark repellents are more complex. The first involves putting a significant percentage of the company's stock in friendly hands. The second involves enduing the company's stock with latent rights designed to make a hostile takeover economically unfeasible.

Where a corporation wishes to provide pension benefits to its employees it can establish an employee stock ownership plan (*ESOP*). An ESOP is a separate entity from the corporation and is heavily regulated under federal law. Leaving the intricacies of ESOPs to other courses, suffice it to say here that the principal asset of an ESOP is frequently the employer corporation's stock. A typical ESOP may hold 10 or 15 percent of the corporation's stock, making it one of the largest stockholders. The idea is that the trustees of the ESOP and the current and retired employees, who are the ESOP beneficiaries, are likely to support incumbent management and will vote the ESOP shares as management recommends.

The final structural device to thwart raiders is the so-called *poison pill*, more formally known as a *shareholders' rights plan*. Corporate statutes permit corporations to issue options on their stock. A poison pill is implemented by authorizing the issuance of options (usually called "rights") on the target's stock. Shareholders receive one right for each share of stock and the rights are not separately tradable; all transfers of stock include the transfer of the associated right. The rights are not represented by separate certificates. The right gives the stockholder the option to buy a new series of preferred stock; the exercise price is set so that no economically rational shareholder would exercise the option.

The rights' potency in warding off raiders is hidden in the antidilution provisions. You may recall that an option usually contains language that adjusts the amount and price of the option if the corporation changes its capital structure. (See Chapter 7.) The poison pill's provisions allow the stockholder to purchase half-price stock if a raider acquires a particular percentage of shares, usually between 10 and 20 percent, and thereafter effects a merger, such as the typical merger to eliminate minority shareholders.

If the target will be the surviving company, as in a reverse triangular merger, the shareholders may purchase half-price stock in the target (a *flip in* provision). If another company will be the survivor the stockholders may buy half-price stock in the acquiring company (a *flip over* provision). The target board has the power to redeem the rights at a nominal price before the raider purchases more than the triggering percentage of stock. Thereafter, the rights are not redeemable.

The economic effect of a poison pill is to deter raiders from purchasing shares in a tender offer unless the target board redeems the rights. The target board thus becomes a central negotiator in the change of control transaction. The Delaware courts have upheld poison pills but courts in other states have on occasion held them to be invalid, usually on the ground that the rights are not really options (because they are not intended to be exercised) on the target's stock but simply are a structural device to entrench the target company's board.

2. Standard of Review of a Target Board's Actions When Responding to a Hostile Tender Offer

In addition to the structural safeguards described above and the deal protective measures included in most acquisition agreements, target corporations can take actions to ward off raiders *after* a raid has begun. The actions taken in the heat of battle, as it were, are frequently called *defensive measures.* As the great wave of hostile takeovers began in the 1980s, the Delaware courts found themselves dealing with case after case involving a legal challenge to a corporate structure, a deal protective measure, or a target board's defensive actions.

At the core of these cases was the raider's assertion that the target board breached its duty of loyalty by taking measures that secured the directors' positions rather than furthering the best interest of the corporation (i.e., accepting the raider's offer). The raider/plaintiffs argued that the entire fairness test ought to apply because the entire board was tainted by the duty of loyalty problem. Director/defendants argued that the business judgment rule should apply because the conflict between the corporation's best interest and the directors' entrenchment was not sufficiently strong to warrant the entire fairness standard. The Delaware courts' view was that preraid structural safeguards and deal protective measures are entitled to the business judgment rule presumption. Even though these measures increase the board's power, often at the expense of the shareholders' power to accept a tender offer, the courts saw the motivation of board entrenchment to be too weak to impose the entire fairness test.

However, that deference to board actions changes once a hostile transaction appears to be a real possibility. The Delaware Supreme Court developed a test of *enhanced* or *intermediate scrutiny* for defensive actions. This standard is sometimes called the *Unocal* test from the case that first articulated this new standard. See *Unocal Corp. v. Mesa Petroleum Co.*, 493 A.2d 946 (Del. 1985). The intention is to apply a standard more strict than the business judgment rule but less strict than entire fairness.

Theoretically, the *Unocal* test is a predicate to the business judgment rule rather than an alternative to it. In practice, it is a third standard along with the business judgment rule and entire fairness. *Unocal* applies whenever the target board takes defensive measures in response to a perceived threat to corporate policy and effectiveness that touches upon issues of control. In the next case Justice Holland both describes the intermediate scrutiny test and applies it to a typical takeover fact setting.

Unitrin, Inc. v. American General Corp.

651 A.2d 1361 (Del. 1995)

[American General (the raider) announced a tender offer for any and all shares of Unitrin (the target). The consideration was cash and was 30% higher than the Unitrin market price. The Unitrin board recommended that its shareholders reject the tender on the grounds that the price was inadequate compared to Unitrin's long-term prospects and that the combination of American General and Unitrin might pose antitrust problems. Unitrin's Certificate of Incorporation contained a supermajority provision requiring 75% of the shares to approve a merger with a shareholder that owned more than 15% of the stock. The Unitrin board members collectively held 23% of Unitrin's stock.

In response to American General's offer, the Unitrin board adopted a poison pill and a Repurchase Program. The Repurchase Program authorized Unitrin to purchase up to 19% of its own shares and the company announced that its directors would not sell their own shares. American General sued Unitrin seeking to enjoin the poison pill and the Repurchase Program.]

HOLLAND, J.

In *Unocal*, this Court reaffirmed "the application of the business judgment rule in the context of a hostile battle for control of a Delaware corporation where board action is taken to the exclusion of, or in limitation upon, a valid stockholder vote." *Stroud v. Grace*, 606 A.2d 75, 82 (Del. 1992). This Court has recognized that directors are often confronted with an "'inherent conflict of interest' during contests for corporate control '[b]ecause of the omnipresent specter that a board may be acting primarily in its own interests, rather than those of the corporation and its shareholders.'" *Id.* (quoting *Unocal*, 493 A.2d at 954). Consequently, in such situations, before the board is accorded the protection of the business judgment rule, . . . the board must carry its own initial two-part burden:

> First, a *reasonableness test*, which is satisfied by a demonstration that the board of directors had reasonable grounds for believing that a danger to corporate policy and effectiveness existed, and
> Second, a *proportionality test*, which is satisfied by a demonstration that the board of directors' defensive response was reasonable in relation to the threat posed.

Unocal, 493 A.2d at 955.

The common law pronouncement in *Unocal* of enhanced judicial scrutiny, as a threshold or condition precedent to an application of the traditional business judgment rule, is now well known.

The first aspect of the *Unocal* burden, the reasonableness test, required the Unitrin Board to demonstrate that, after a reasonable investigation, it determined in good faith, that American General's Offer presented a threat to Unitrin that warranted a defensive response. This Court has held that the presence of a majority of outside independent directors will materially enhance such evidence.

The Unitrin Board identified two dangers it perceived the American General Offer posed: inadequate price and antitrust complications. The Court of Chancery characterized the Board's concern that American General's proposed transaction could never be consummated because it may violate antitrust laws and state insurance regulations as a "makeweight excuse" for the defensive measure. It determined, however, that the Board reasonably believed that the American General Offer was inadequate and also reasonably concluded that the Offer was a threat to Unitrin's uninformed stockholders.

The Court of Chancery then noted, however, that the threat to the Unitrin stockholders from American General's inadequate opening bid was "mild," because the Offer was negotiable both in price and structure. The court then properly turned its attention to *Unocal*'s second aspect, the proportionality test....

The second aspect or proportionality test of the initial *Unocal* burden required the Unitrin Board to demonstrate the proportionality of its response to the threat American General's Offer posed. The record reflects that the Unitrin Board considered ... as defensive measures: the poison pill ... and the Repurchase Program.

The Unitrin Board ... apparently feared that its stockholders did not realize that the long term-value of Unitrin was not reflected in the market price of its stock.

The Court of Chancery concluded that Unitrin's Board believed in good faith that the American General Offer was inadequate and properly employed a poison pill as a proportionate defensive response to protect its stockholders from a "low ball" bid.

The Court of Chancery concluded that ... the additional defensive response of adopting the Repurchase Program was unnecessary and disproportionate to the threat the Offer posed. Therefore, the Court of Chancery held that the plaintiffs proved a likelihood of success on that issue and granted the motion to preliminarily enjoin the Repurchase Program.[18]

The Court of Chancery's determination that the Unitrin Board's adoption of the Repurchase Program was unnecessary constituted a substitution of its business judgment for that of the Board, contrary to this Court's "range of reasonableness" holding in [*Paramount Communications, Inc. v. QVC Network, Inc.*, 637 A.2d 34, 45-46 (Del. 1994)].

In *Unocal*, ... this Court held that the board "does not have unbridled discretion to defeat any perceived threat by any Draconian means available." *Unocal* 493 A.2d at 955. Immediately following those observations in *Unocal*, this Court held that "the directors may not have acted *solely* or *primarily* out of a desire to perpetuate themselves in office" (preclusion of the stockholders' corporate franchise right to

---

18. We note that the directors' failure to carry their initial burden under Unocal does not, *ipso facto*, invalidate the board's actions. Instead, once the Court of Chancery finds the business judgment rule does not apply, the burden remains on the directors to prove "entire fairness."

vote) and, further, that the [response] must not be inequitable. *Unocal*, 493 A.2d at 955 (emphasis added).

An examination of the cases applying *Unocal* reveals a direct correlation between findings of proportionality or disproportionality and the judicial determination of whether a defensive response was draconian because it was either coercive or preclusive in character.

In the modern takeover lexicon, it is now clear that since *Unocal*, this Court has consistently recognized that defensive measures which are either preclusive or coercive are included within the common law definition of draconian.

If a defensive measure is not draconian, however, because it is not either coercive or preclusive, the *Unocal* proportionality test requires the focus of enhanced judicial scrutiny to shift to "the range of reasonableness." *QVC* at 45-46. Proper and proportionate defensive responses are intended and permitted to thwart perceived threats. When a corporation is not for sale, the board of directors is the defender of the metaphorical medieval corporate bastion and the protector of the corporation's shareholders. The fact that a defensive action must not be coercive or preclusive does not prevent a board from responding defensively before a bidder is at the corporate bastion's gate.

The *ratio decidendi* for the "range of reasonableness" standard is a need of the board of directors for latitude in discharging its fiduciary duties to the corporation and its shareholders when defending against perceived threats. The concomitant requirement is for judicial restraint. Consequently, if the board of directors' defensive response is not draconian (preclusive or coercive) and is within a "range of reasonableness," a court must not substitute its judgment for the board's.

We begin, therefore, by ascertaining whether the Repurchase Program, as an addition to the poison pill, was draconian by being either coercive or preclusive.

A selective repurchase of shares in a public corporation on the market, such as Unitrin's Repurchase Program, generally does not discriminate because all shareholders can voluntarily realize the same benefit by selling. Here, there is no showing on this record that the Repurchase Program was coercive.

[A] proxy contest remained a viable (if more problematic) alternative for American General even if the Repurchase Program were to be completed in its entirety. Nevertheless, the Court of Chancery must determine whether Unitrin's Repurchase Program would only inhibit American General's ability to wage a proxy fight and institute a merger or whether it was, in fact, preclusive because American General's success would either be mathematically impossible or realistically unattainable. If the Court of Chancery concludes that the Unitrin Repurchase Program was not draconian because it was not preclusive, one question will remain to be answered in its proportionality review: whether the Repurchase Program was within a range of reasonableness?

In considering whether the Repurchase Program was within a range of reasonableness the Court of Chancery should take into consideration whether: (1) it is a statutorily authorized form of business decision which a board of directors may routinely make in a non-takeover context; (2) as a defensive response to American General's Offer it was limited and corresponded in degree or magnitude to the degree or magnitude of the threat, (*i.e.*, assuming the threat was relatively "mild," was the response relatively "mild?"); (3) with the Repurchase Program, the Unitrin Board properly recognized that all shareholders are not alike, and provided immediate liquidity to those shareholders who wanted it.

The Unitrin Board had the power and the duty, upon reasonable investigation, to protect Unitrin's shareholders from what it perceived to be the threat from American General's inadequate all-cash for all-shares Offer. *Unocal*, 493 A.2d at 958. The adoption of the poison pill *and* the limited Repurchase Program was not coercive and the Repurchase Program may not be preclusive. Although each made a takeover more difficult, individually and collectively, if they were not coercive or preclusive the Court of Chancery must determine whether they were within the range of reasonable defensive measures available to the Board.

The interlocutory judgment of the Court of Chancery, in favor of American General, is REVERSED. This matter is REMANDED for further proceedings in accordance with this opinion.

Notes and Questions

1. Reality Check

a. Why does Justice Holland not apply either the business judgment rule or the entire fairness standard?

b. What are the elements of the *Unocal* test?

c. What do "draconian," "coercive," and "preclusive" mean in this context?

d. Do you think the Unitrin board met the *Unocal* test?

e. In applying *Unocal*, how does Justice Holland reach the ultimate result?

2. Suppose

a. Suppose Unitrin had adopted only the poison pill or only the Repurchase Program. Would the court's analysis or the result be different?

b. Note that it is unusual for the board of a public company to control such a large percentage of shares as the Unitrin board did. Suppose the Unitrin board collectively owned a very small percentage of Unitrin stock. Would the court's analysis or the result be different?

3. What Do You Think?

a. Do you think corporate law needs an intermediate standard like *Unocal*? If so, why? If not, would you apply the business judgment rule or the entire fairness standard to target board defensive actions?

b. How easy do you think it is for target boards to demonstrate that they reasonably perceive a threat to corporate policy and effectiveness?

c. How easy do you think it is for target boards to demonstrate that their defensive actions are reasonable in relation to the threat posed?

d. As a practical matter, is *Unocal* more like the business judgment rule or more like entire fairness? Is *Unocal* significantly different from either of them?

3. The Target Board's Obligation to Maximize Shareholder Value

As the Delaware courts focused on the question of the standard of review in takeover settings they also imposed a substantive obligation on target boards. That is, when certain predicates are met, a target board's actions must be designed to further a particular end. The next case discusses the rationale behind what has become known as *Revlon duties*. See Revlon, Inc. v. MacAndrews & Forbes Holdings, Inc., 506 A2d 173 (Del. 1986).

Paramount Communications Inc. v. QVC Network Inc.

637 A.2d 34 (Del. 1994)

[Paramount (the target) agreed to be acquired by Viacom (the acquirer) through a tender offer to Paramount's shareholders, which Paramout's board recommended to its shareholders. The completed tender offer would be followed by a merger of Paramount into Viacom that would eliminate the remaining Paramount shareholders. The consideration was a combination of Viacom Class A voting stock, Class B non-voting stock, and cash. Thus the Paramount shareholders would continue to have an ownership interest in the combined entity. Viacom is controlled by Sumner M. Redstone (Redstone) who controls 85.2% of Viacom's voting stock. After Viacom's acquisition of Paramount Redstone will still control the combined entity. Paramount and Viacom executed a definitive agreement (the Original Merger Agreement).]

VEASEY, C.J.

The Original Merger Agreement also contained several provisions designed to make it more difficult for a potential competing bid to succeed . . . : a "no-shop" provision (the "No-Shop Provision"), the Termination Fee, and the [Topping Fee].

QVC filed this action and publicly announced a . . . cash tender offer for 51 percent of Paramount's outstanding shares (the "QVC tender offer"). Each remaining share of Paramount common stock would be converted into . . . QVC common stock in a second-step merger. The tender offer was conditioned on, among other things, the invalidation of the [Topping Fee], which was worth over $200 million by that point.

Confronted by QVC's hostile bid, which . . . offered over $10 per share more than the consideration provided by the Original Merger Agreement, Viacom realized that it would need to raise its bid in order to remain competitive. In effect, the opportunity for a "new deal" with Viacom was at hand for the Paramount Board. With the QVC hostile bid offering greater value to the Paramount stockholders, the Paramount Board had considerable leverage with Viacom.

[T]he Paramount Board approved [an] Amended Merger Agreement [with Viacom]. . . . The Amended Merger Agreement was, however, essentially the same as the Original Merger Agreement, except that it included a few new provisions.

Although the Amended Merger Agreement offered more consideration to the Paramount stockholders . . . than did the Original Merger Agreement, the defensive measures designed to make a competing bid more difficult were not removed or modified. In particular, there is no evidence . . . that Paramount sought to use its newly acquired leverage to eliminate or modify the No-Shop Provision, the Termination Fee, or the [Topping Fee] when the subject of amending the Original Merger Agreement was on the table.

QVC responded to Viacom's higher bid . . . by increasing its tender offer. . . . [T]he Paramount Board determined that the new QVC offer was not in the best interests of the stockholders. The purported basis for this conclusion was that

QVC's bid was excessively conditional. The Paramount Board did not communicate with QVC regarding the status of the conditions because it believed that the No-Shop Provision prevented such communication in the absence of firm financing. Several Paramount directors also testified that they believed the Viacom transaction would be more advantageous to Paramount's future business prospects than a QVC transaction.

When a majority of a corporation's voting shares are acquired by a single person or entity, or by a cohesive group acting together, there is a significant diminution in the voting power of those who thereby become minority stockholders. Under the statutory framework of the [DGCL], many of the most fundamental corporate changes can be implemented only if they are approved by a majority vote of the stockholders. Such actions include elections of directors, amendments to the certificate of incorporation, mergers, consolidations, sales of all or substantially all of the assets of the corporation, and dissolution. Because of the overriding importance of voting rights, this Court and the Court of Chancery have consistently acted to protect stockholders from unwarranted interference with such rights.

In the absence of devices protecting the minority stockholders,[12] stockholder votes are likely to become mere formalities where there is a majority stockholder. For example, minority stockholders can be deprived of a continuing equity interest in their corporation by means of a cash-out merger. Absent effective protective provisions, minority stockholders must rely for protection solely on the fiduciary duties owed to them by the directors and the majority stockholder, since the minority stockholders have lost the power to influence corporate direction through the ballot. The acquisition of majority status and the consequent privilege of exerting the powers of majority ownership come at a price. That price is usually a control premium which recognizes not only the value of a control block of shares, but also compensates the minority stockholders for their resulting loss of voting power.

In the case before us, the public stockholders (in the aggregate) currently own a majority of Paramount's voting stock. Control of the corporation is not vested in a single person, entity, or group, but vested in the fluid aggregation of unaffiliated stockholders. In the event the Paramount-Viacom transaction is consummated, the public stockholders will receive cash and a minority equity voting position in the surviving corporation. Following such consummation, there will be a controlling stockholder who will have the voting power to: (a) elect directors; (b) cause a break-up of the corporation; (c) merge it with another company; (d) cash-out the public stockholders; (e) amend the certificate of incorporation; (f) sell all or substantially all of the corporate assets; or (g) otherwise alter materially the nature of the corporation and the public stockholders' interests. Irrespective of the present Paramount Board's vision of a long-term strategic alliance with Viacom, the proposed sale of control would provide the new controlling stockholder with the power to alter that vision.

Because of the intended sale of control, the Paramount-Viacom transaction has economic consequences of considerable significance to the Paramount stockholders. Once control has shifted, the current Paramount stockholders will have no leverage in the future to demand another control premium. As a result, the Paramount stockholders are entitled to receive, and should receive, a control premium and/or protective devices of significant value. There being no such protective provisions in the Viacom-Paramount transaction, the Paramount directors had an obligation to

12. Examples of such protective provisions are supermajority voting provisions, majority of the minority requirements, etc.

take the maximum advantage of the current opportunity to realize for the stock-holders the best value reasonably available.

The consequences of a sale of control impose special obligations on the directors of a corporation. In particular, they have the obligation of acting reasonably to seek the transaction offering the best value reasonably available to the stockholders. The courts will apply enhanced scrutiny to ensure that the directors have acted reasonably. The obligations of the directors and the enhanced scrutiny of the courts are well-established by the decisions of this Court. The directors' fiduciary duties in a sale of control context are those which generally attach. In short, "the directors must act in accordance with their fundamental duties of care and loyalty." *Barkan v. Amsted Indus., Inc.*, 567 A.2d 1279, 1286 (Del. 1989).

In the sale of control context, the directors must focus on one primary objec-tive — to secure the transaction offering the best value reasonably available for the stockholders — and they must exercise their fiduciary duties to further that end. The decisions of this Court have consistently emphasized this goal. *Revlon*, 506 A.2d at 182 ("The duty of the board . . . [is] the maximization of the company's value at a sale for the stockholders' benefit."); *Macmillan*, 559 A.2d at 1288 ("[I]n a sale of corporate control the responsibility of the directors is to get the highest value reasonably attainable for the shareholders."); *Barkan*, 567 A.2d at 1286 ("[T]he board must act in a neutral manner to encourage the highest possible price for shareholders.").

In pursuing this objective, the directors must be especially diligent. Moreover, the role of outside, independent directors becomes particularly important because of the magnitude of a sale of control transaction and the possibility, in certain cases, that management may not necessarily be impartial.

Barkan teaches some of the methods by which a board can fulfill its obligation to seek the best value reasonably available to the stockholders. These methods are designed to determine the existence and viability of possible alternatives. They include conducting an auction, canvassing the market, etc. Delaware law recognizes that there is "no single blueprint" that directors must follow.

In determining which alternative provides the best value for the stockholders, a board of directors is not limited to considering only the amount of cash involved, and is not required to ignore totally its view of the future value of a strategic alliance. Instead, the directors should analyze the entire situation and evaluate in a disciplined manner the consideration being offered. Where stock or other non-cash consideration is involved, the board should try to quantify its value, if feasible, to achieve an objec-tive comparison of the alternatives. In addition, the board may assess a variety of practical considerations relating to each alternative, including:

> [an offer's] fairness and feasibility; the proposed or actual financing for the offer, and the consequences of that financing; questions of illegality; . . . the risk of non-consum [m]ation; . . . the bidder's identity, prior background and other business ven-ture experiences; and the bidder's business plans for the corporation and their effects on stockholder interests.

> *Macmillan,* 559 A.2d at 1282 n.29.

These considerations are important because the selection of one alternative may permanently foreclose other opportunities. While the assessment of these factors may be complex, the board's goal is straightforward: Having informed themselves of all material information reasonably available, the directors must decide which alternative is most likely to offer the best value reasonably available to the stockholders.

The realization of the best value reasonably available to the stockholders became the Paramount directors' primary obligation under these facts in light of the change of control. That obligation was not satisfied, and the Paramount Board's process was deficient. The directors' initial hope and expectation for a strategic alliance with Viacom was allowed to dominate their decisionmaking process to the point where the arsenal of defensive measures established at the outset was perpetuated (not modified or eliminated) when the situation was dramatically altered. QVC's unsolicited bid presented the opportunity for significantly greater value for the stockholders and enhanced negotiating leverage for the directors. Rather than seizing those opportunities, the Paramount directors chose to wall themselves off from material information which was reasonably available and to hide behind the defensive measures as a rationalization for refusing to negotiate with QVC or seeking other alternatives. Their view of the strategic alliance likewise became an empty rationalization as the opportunities for higher value for the stockholders continued to develop.

[The] Order of the Court of Chancery has been AFFIRMED, and this matter has been REMANDED for proceedings consistent herewith....

Notes and Questions

1. Notes

a. It was unclear for quite some time after the original *Revlon* decision exactly when the special obligations of *Revlon* would apply. Eventually the Delaware courts seem to have reached a consensus on this matter:

> The directors of a corporation "have the obligation of acting reasonably to seek the transaction offering the best value reasonably available to the stockholders," *Paramount Communications, Inc. v. QVC Network, Inc.*, 637 A.2d 34, 43 (Del. 1994), in at least the following three scenarios: (1) "when a corporation initiates an active bidding process seeking to sell itself or to effect a business reorganization involving a clear break-up of the company," *Paramount Communications, Inc. v. Time Inc.*, 571 A.2d 1140, 1150 (Del. 1990)...; (2) "where, in response to a bidder's offer, a target abandons its long-term strategy and seeks an alternative transaction involving the break-up of the company," *id.;* or (3) when approval of a transaction results in a "sale or change of control," *QVC*, 637 A.2d at 42-43, 47. In the latter situation, there is no "sale or change in control" when "'[c]ontrol of both [companies] remain[s] in a large, fluid, changeable and changing market.'" *Id.* at 47 (citation and emphasis omitted).

Arnold v. Society for Savings Bancorp, Inc., 650 A.2d 1270, 1289-1290 (Del. 1994)

2. Reality Check

a. What aspects of this case triggered the *Revlon* analysis?

b. What are the elements of *Revlon*?

c. Why did the chief justice hold that the Paramount board violated its *Revlon* duties? Do you agree?

3. Suppose

a. Would the analysis or result have been different if Redstone were not to have a majority of the postacquisition Viacom voting stock?

b. Would the analysis or result have been different if Paramount had had a controlling shareholder before the agreement with Viacom?

4. What Do You Think?

a. Does the *Revlon* standard make any sense, given that the court has the business judgment rule, entire fairness test, and *Unocal* at its disposal?

4. State Antitakeover Statutes

Many state legislatures, in response to pleas from local public companies, adopted statutes that were designed to preclude takeovers without target board approval. These statutes took various forms and raised constitutional issues, both because tender offers are pervasively regulated by federal securities laws and because every public company is engaged in interstate commerce. In *CTS v. Dynamics Corp. of America*, 481 U.S. 69 (1987), Justice Powell upheld one such statute, in Indiana, against both a Supremacy Clause argument and a Commerce Clause argument. In so doing the Court may have made the internal affairs doctrine (see Chapter 5) a constitutional requirement under the Commerce Clause.

After *CTS* many states, including Delaware, adopted what are known as *control share acquisition acts*. See DGCL §203. In brief, these statutes prohibit certain control transactions, such as mergers or sales of all assets, between a corporation and an entity controlling more than a certain amount (15% in Delaware) of shares. Such a controlling entity is sometimes called an *interested person* in the statutes. These prohibitions end a few years (three in Delaware) after the interested person becomes such. The prohibitions also end if: (1) the board approves the transaction by which the entity became an interested person (e.g., the board approves of the acquirer's tender offer); (2) the board and a supermajority of shareholders (unaffiliated with the raider or the board) approve the control transaction after the interested person has become such; or (3) the transaction by which the interested person becomes such results in the interested person acquiring a large percentage (85% in Delaware) of the voting shares. The idea is that a raider that buys a substantial majority of stock in the initial tender offer should be able to exercise control immediately. The acquirer should also be able to proceed if the board has approved the initial control transaction. This is the case where the target has negotiated to be acquired or where the target board is capitulating to a raider, possibly because the raider has increased the consideration to a level the target board believes is advantageous to its shareholders. Acquisition agreements for Delaware corporations contain a waiver of DGCL §203's restrictions. Otherwise, a raider will either have to wait for a relatively long period of time to eliminate the minority shareholders or offer enough consideration to induce a substantial majority of minority shareholders to approve such a transaction. The MBCA does not contain a control share acquisition provision.

D. FEDERAL SECURITIES REGULATIONS

The federal securities laws loom large in change of control situations. They obviously are dominant when a corporation is the subject of a tender offer. But the federal securities laws also have an effect on many change of control transactions that do not involve tender offers. In this section we will see the federal securities issues that are most likely to be germane to negotiated acquisitions and then look briefly at the regulation of tender offers, including the restrictions on insider trading in tender offer contexts.

1. "Groups" under Section 13(d)

We saw at the end of the last chapter that any person or group that owns more than 5 percent of the equity of a public company must file a Schedule 13D. One set of issues, that even experienced lawyers may overlook, is the definition of *group* and other related concepts under Section 13(d) of the '34 Act. Section 13(d)(1) requires any "person" to file after "*acquiring*" the "beneficial ownership" of any public company equity. Section 13(d)(3) says that if two or more people "act as a . . . group for the purpose of acquiring, holding, or disposing of" equity of a public company, such group shall be deemed a "person" for the purposes of Section 13(d). Thus any time more than one shareholder agrees to act in concert regarding ownership of securities, they are a group. The group needn't be planning any purchases or sales; it is enough that the group is acting in concert even to continue ownership.

The SEC deems a group to have "acquired" its shares at the moment the group is formed, even though no shares have changed hands. So, if more than one shareholder agree to act together regarding a public company's equity, they are a "group" and the group "acquired" all shares already owned by any of the group's members. See Rule 13d-5(b)(1). To bring these rules back to the change of control context, where an acquisition involves a public company, the acquirer, the target, the principal shareholders (if they are involved in the negotiations), and the officers and directors (assuming they own at least some shares) must be careful to realize whether they have formed a "group" at some point during the negotiations and, if so, whether the group has "acquired" more than 5 percent of the public company's equity. If so, a Schedule 13D must be filed promptly.

2. Going Private Transactions

Another area in which federal securities laws affect a change of control transaction is where the target corporation is publicly held, but the change of control transaction involves the repurchase of shares by the corporation such that the shares will no longer be publicly traded. Where this transaction is not regulated under the tender offer rules, it will be considered a *going private transaction* subject to Section 13(e). This sort of transaction is often undertaken by the corporation's managers who will remain shareholders after the going private transaction is complete. As an overview, a going private transaction requires the company to file a Schedule 13E-3, which contains detailed disclosure of the transaction, the company's owners after the transaction, and the source of funds used to eliminate the public shareholders' ownership. At bottom, the going private rules are meant to ensure that such transactions involve the same kinds of investor protection (e.g., full disclosure and sufficient time to make an informed decision) as would be provided in a tender offer.

3. Tender Offers

Perhaps the most pervasive and best-known federal securities rules in the change of control setting are the tender offer rules. These are promulgated under §§14(d) and 14(e) of the '34 Act. Speaking broadly, 14(d) prohibits any person from making a tender offer for more than 5 percent of a public company's equity without complying with SEC regulations. Section 14(e) prohibits any person from committing fraud in connection with a tender offer, in contravention of any SEC rules. Although both sections are rather detailed, the SEC has the power to promulgate additional rules and those rules have, effectively, superseded the statutory provisions in terms of providing the substantive regulation of tender offers.

Any sort of detailed look at the tender offer rules would take far too much time and space here, so what follows is a précis of the way the rules work. Perhaps the most surprising and, some would say, pernicious aspect of these regulations is that "tender offer" is not defined. The SEC's rationale has been that if it defined "tender offer," then people could easily structure transactions that skirt the regulations. This hasn't convinced many non–SEC lawyers. In any event, case law has provided a standard definition of *tender offer*. For over 25 years courts and commentators have looked to the eight-factor "*Wellman* test" enunciated by Judge Carter in a 1979 district court case, *Wellman v. Dickinson*.[4] These factors are: (1) active and widespread solicitation of public shareholders for the shares of an issuer; (2) solicitation made for a substantial percentage of the issuer's stock; (3) offer to purchase made at a premium over the prevailing market price; (4) terms of the offer are firm rather than negotiable; (5) offer contingent on the tender of a fixed number of shares, often subject to a fixed maximum number to be purchased; (6) offer open only a limited period of time; (7) offeree subjected to pressure to sell his stock; and (8) public announcements of a purchasing program that precedes or accompanies a rapid accumulation of stock.

The SEC rules prohibit the commencement of a tender offer without filing a Schedule TO. As you may imagine, the Schedule TO is a detailed disclosure document containing information about the bidder, its source of funds, the consideration for the tender offer, and the target company. The rules also define commencement as being the transmission to target shareholders of the means to tender their shares. So, a bidder can announce a tender offer without filing a Schedule TO so long as a filing is made before the actual method of tendering is provided to shareholders.

The target shareholders are protected in several ways by the SEC rules. The target company must either supply the bidder with its shareholder list or must transmit the bidder's tender offer material to its shareholders (at the bidder's cost). This is to ensure that target management cannot stymie the shareholders' choice by keeping information from them. The target management must publicly announce its position on the tender offer, although that position could be simply neutrality. To ensure that target shareholders are not stampeded into tendering, the tender offer rules

4. *Wellman v. Dickinson*, 475 F. Supp. 783 (S.D.N.Y. 1979).

provide that a tender offer must remain open for at least 20 business days (and an additional 10 business days if the consideration changes), shareholders may withdraw tendered shares at any time before the bidder purchases them. If the tender offer is for a limited amount of the target company shares, such as where the bidder only seeks 51 percent of the shares, intending to eliminate the remaining shareholders by merger, and more shares are tendered, the bidder cannot purchase the shares on a first-come-first-served basis but must prorate the purchases among all shareholders who tendered during the tender offer period. The SEC rules also require that tender offers be open to all target shareholders and that all tendering shareholders receive the highest price paid by the bidder to any shareholder.

The '34 Act and SEC rules prohibit fraud in connection with a tender offer. The most salient for our purposes are the prohibition against announcing a tender offer without the intention of "commencing" a tender offer within a reasonable time, making a false or misleading statement of material fact in connection with a tender offer, and buying or selling target or bidder shares while in possession of material nonpublic information. This last prohibition is the *insider trading* proscription for tender offers. Outside of the tender offer setting, a similar proscription on trading on the basis of material nonpublic information is implied under Rule 10b-5.

E. TERMS OF ART IN THIS CHAPTER

Advance notice provision	Fair value	Raider
Appraisal right	Flip in	Recognition
Asset lock-up	Flip over	Reservation price
Break-up fee	Going private transaction	Reverse triangular
Conglomeration	Group	merger
Constituent corporations	Hostile tender offer	*Revlon* duties
Control share acquisition acts	Insider trading	Shareholder lock-up
Deal protective measures	Interested person	Shareholders' rights plan
Defensive measures	Intermediate scrutiny	Shark repellents
Definitive agreement	Letter of intent	Short form merger
Dissenter's right	Marketability discount	Subsidiary
Due diligence	Material adverse change	Target corporation
ESOP	Merger	Tender offer
Exit strategy	Minority discount	Topping fee
	No-shop	*Unocal* test
	No-talk	
	Poison pill	

Part IV.
UNINCORPORATED ENTITIES

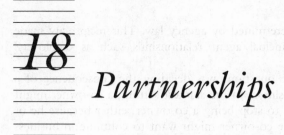

18

Partnerships

A. GENERAL PARTNERSHIPS

1. Background and Context

At its most essential, a partnership can be thought of as a business owned by more than one person. Partnerships first became commercially important in the late eighteenth and early nineteenth centuries when trading firms first became widespread. Recall that Ebenezer Scrooge and Jacob Marley were partners. Shortly after, courts and scholars began to deal with the legal consequences of common ownership of a business. Justice Joseph Story's *Commentaries on the Law of Partnership* (1841) had a major effect on the development of partnership principles. At bottom, the legal issues were ones of contract and agency. The co-owners (i.e., partners) could contract among themselves relatively freely. They could, for example, contract about how much money each would contribute, how the profits (or losses) would be divided, how the business was to be managed, and how the net assets were to be divided when one partner ceased to be a co-owner.

What the courts in England and America added to this was a system of presumptions; default rules to fill the areas in which the parties had neglected to agree. Courts created a presumption of symmetry, a presumption of equality, and a presumption that the contracts are personal such that another person could not be substituted for, or added to, the original owners. Thus, in the absence of an explicit agreement of the partners, losses would be divided in the same proportion as profits (symmetry). Each partner would have an equal right to manage the business; disputes among partners would be decided by a majority of partners, regardless of their ownership interests (equality). A partner's powers could not be transferred, and no one could become a partner without unanimous consent (personal contract).

As you see, the relation between partners was largely contractual. The relation between the partners and third parties involved agency. Obviously a business owner who contracted with, or committed a tort against, a third party would be bound under ordinary common law precepts. Courts applied agency law to allow third parties to recover against partners who had not themselves contracted or committed torts. In so doing, partners became agents of one another. In a co-owned business, then, each co-owner had the power to bind the other co-owners and, in turn, was bound by his or her co-owners' actions all as determined by agency law. This reciprocity made partners different from other principal/agent relationships such as employer/ employee.

One of the most troublesome questions was deciding the consequence of a change in the co-owners of the business. In the starkest setting, a co-owner might die. A co-owner might also decide to stop being a co-owner, either because he or she wanted to retire or because the co-owner might want to continue in business alone or with others who were not currently co-owners. Finally, the co-owners might unanimously decide to allow a new person to be a co-owner. One corollary of the personal nature of a partnership was the rule that any partner had the absolute right to end the co-ownership, even though such ending might violate a contract with the other co-owners. As between the partners themselves, a default rule developed that when a partner ceased to be a co-owner, the partnership's assets would be liquidated and each partner paid his or her interest. Because liquidating a going concern typically resulted in a depressed sale price (because the assets were sold under compulsion to achieve a quick sale) partners often agreed in advance that the partnership's assets would not be liquidated when a partner ceased to be a co-owner. Rather, the remaining partners would continue the business and the partner who left would receive the value of his or her interest.

Regardless of the partners' agreement among themselves, agency law provided that a partner who ceased to be a co-owner nonetheless remained liable to third parties for existing obligations of the business. In symmetrical fashion, where all partners agreed to admit a new person as a co-owner, the new partner was only liable to third parties for subsequent business obligations. Thus a partner, as agent, could only bind those persons who were currently partners.

By the early twentieth century there was a strong movement to codify partnership law. This movement stemmed both from a more general turn-of-the-century impetus to codify the common law and from a particular sense that commercial areas, such as partnership law, should be uniform among jurisdictions to provide the predictability necessary for a national economy. Increasingly, partnerships conducted business in more than one state and partners were resident in several states. In 1902 the Conference of Commissioners on Uniform State Laws began a project to draft a uniform partnership act. After a dozen years of work, the original Uniform Partnership Act (UPA (1914)) was promulgated. The UPA (1914) was one of the most successful of the uniform acts, being adopted in every state except Louisiana (which, nonetheless, adopted most of the underlying principles of the act). Nonetheless, after 70 years, an ABA subcommittee recommended that the commissioners (now known as the National Conference of Commissioners on Uniform State Laws) draft a replacement act. That project resulted in a new Uniform Partnership Act, which went through several important amendments and finally emerged as the current Uniform Partnership Act in 1997 (UPA). The vast majority of states have adopted the UPA and usually have provided that that act will apply even to existing partnerships after a transition period of a few years. While the UPA changes the UPA (1914) in several respects, it most profoundly changes the consequence of a change in the co-ownership of the partnership. This change is a result of a shift in the conception of the partnership.

The description of partnership law so far has been phrased to suggest that partnership is really a shorthand term for a set of agreements, some actual and some implied, rather than an artificial "entity" itself (such as a corporation, a state, or a law school). In that sense, a partnership is simply a collection of the partners (the classic simile is that a partnership is like a friendship — a set of relationships but not a separate thing). But, as a consequence of the axioms from agency law that each partner can only bind the people who are currently co-owners (and not past or future co-owners), the partnership can be seen as an entity itself. Thus any change in the co-owners ended the entity. Where an additional person was added as a partner, the original partnership (an entity) was immediately succeeded by a second partnership. Where a partner ceased to be a co-owner, the original partnership ended (after a kind of twilight winding-up period) and the underlying economic business might be sold off piecemeal or sold as a going concern to a single person, another partnership (often consisting of the remaining original partners), or another entity such as a corporation. Under the Law Merchant, the legal principles applied throughout the Western world to commercial disputes, which was accepted in England from the sixteenth century, partnerships were thought of as entities separate from their partners. Thus there was frequently a tension between the common law conception of a partnership as an aggregate of individuals and the commercial law idea of a partnership as an entity. The UPA (1914) melded both the aggregate and the entity theories of the partnership, often with unhappy results. The reason for this meld was that the original drafter, the great James Barr Ames, dean of the Harvard Law School, was a proponent of the entity approach. He died during the drafting process and his successor, William Draper Lewis, dean of the University of Pennsylvania Law School, continued the draft on the aggregate theory.

At this point the discussion may seem more than a tad abstract. After all, does it really make a difference whether a partnership is thought of as a collection of co-owners or as a separate thing that is co-owned? You may also be thinking that this is a typical academic dustup between two law professors arguing over how many angels can dance on the head of a dean. Perhaps the most important differences between an entity approach and an aggregate approach are in title to property and in litigation. Because the partnership under the UPA is an entity, a change in membership does not destroy the old partnership or create a new one. Thus there is no need to reconvey property (or other contract rights) from one partnership to the other. Second, if the partnership is thought of as an aggregate, every partner must be served in a lawsuit. Not only is this often impractical, but if the lawsuit is in federal court, diversity is defeated if one partner is a citizen of the same state as the plaintiff. Both these problems were largely ameliorated under the UPA (1914) either by the courts or by specific statutes (which typically provided that a partnership could sue and be sued under a common name without naming and serving each partner). Nonetheless, the UPA's entity approach seems better suited to the modern setting in which partnerships exist.

The use of the partnership as the dominant form for business entities ended shortly after the Civil War when the business corporation took its place. Nonetheless, many businesses were and are conducted as partnerships for several reasons. One reason is, as you will see in the next section, that a partnership can be formed inadvertently. That is, the parties might not realize they are forming a partnership. A related reason for partnerships is that some people deliberately choose the partnership form but do so without seeking legal advice as to the most advantageous business form. A third reason for doing business as a partnership is a lack of alternative forms.

Until the 1970s, the learned professions (including law) were prohibited by state law from practicing as corporations. The reason for this limitation was rooted in protecting the public. Corporations have limited liability and it was widely believed that it would be unethical for a professional such as a lawyer or doctor to limit his or her liability for malpractice to a client or patient. Further, because partners have unlimited personal liability for the debts of the partnership, each partner in a professional partnership has a strong economic incentive to monitor the professional actions of the other partners. Thus one lawyer in a partnership has a distinct motivation to be sure that another partner has not missed a filing deadline or is not commingling firm funds with client funds; one doctor has a distinct motivation to be sure another doctor is not covering up medical negligence. This monitoring function would be diminished if one partner were not liable for the malpractice of another partner. From the late 1970s onward these restrictions were reduced or eliminated.

A fourth reason for choosing the partnership form is that, until the late 1990s, certain tax advantages could only be effectively obtained by partnerships. It is not unusual for new businesses to operate at a loss because start-up costs are high and revenues are low. Further, some businesses, such as drilling oil wells or making motion pictures, incur the vast majority of their (usually large) costs at the beginning and only later see any revenues. The Internal Revenue Code taxes partnerships as aggregates rather than entities. That is, the partnership itself does not pay tax; it merely files an informational return with the Internal Revenue Service. All profits or losses are reported by the partners. By contrast, a corporation is usually taxed as an entity; it reports income on its own return. Its shareholders only report income if and when the corporation distributes dividends. But losses cannot be distributed to shareholders. If a business incurs losses, its owners would ordinarily prefer to include those losses on their own income tax returns because the losses offset any income the owner has from other sources. Hence many businesses were organized as partnerships, at least until steady profits were anticipated. Since 1996 taxation as a partnership can also be obtained by an LLC. The LLC has several advantages over partnerships and is thus the form of choice for entities seeking partnership taxation. Nonetheless, many entities that were created as partnerships for tax purposes before 1996 still exist.

Notes and Questions

1. What Do You Think?

a. Do you think professional entities such as law firms and physician groups should be required to be formed as partnerships rather than as corporations or LLCs? Are there other ways to address the concerns for the public's protection than by restricting the form of the enterprise?

2. The Current Setting

The Uniform Partnership Act (UPA) was promulgated in the mid-1990s and has been adopted in the vast majority of states. It replaces a uniform act drafted in the early twentieth century (UPA (1914)). In most respects the UPA continues the substantive rules of the UPA (1914). In the cases that follow, citations to state codes have been replaced with citations to the UPA contained in square brackets.

a. Formation

We begin with the question of how a partnership is formed. This issue is not an abstraction. Whether a partnership has been formed greatly affects the parties' rights and liabilities. In the next case, if a partnership exists, the plaintiff will receive about triple what she is entitled to if no partnership exists.

Tondu v. Akerley
855 P.2d 116 (Mont. 1993)

NELSON, J.

Mary M. Tondu (Mary) and Walter S. "Pete" Akerley (Pete) met in late 1988. They had similar interests in raising cattle and soon verbally agreed to enter into business together to raise purebred registered cattle. Each of the parties contributed assets, monetary and otherwise, to begin the enterprise. Both parties contributed their knowledge, skills, and experience toward the management and operation of the business. They were to have equal one-half interests in the business.

Mary and Pete also entered into a domestic relationship, living together and conducting their business in a rental property in Sheridan. During this time, each party also devoted time to separate pursuits and other employment.

Wages from these other income sources were added to monies from the business. Mary and Pete also took out joint loans to finance their operation. Mary and Pete had a joint checking account, a joint savings account, and two separate checking accounts, owned individually. In fact, monies from all income sources were commingled within the 4 accounts and used to pay business and personal expenses.

Although they shared their incomes and their business interests, they filed separate income tax returns during their venture together, instead of a partnership tax return. Mary indicated that the couple's accountant advised her that filing separately was the appropriate method for filing their returns.

In the spring of 1991, the personal relationship was terminated and in April, Mary moved to Arizona. The parties tried to terminate their business relationship as well, but they encountered problems, and Mary filed this action on January 27, 1992.

The trial court concluded that no partnership was established. Mary was entitled to the sum of $2,750, together with her share of the allocated interest. Brian Barragree, who performed some work for the couple, was owed $1,000, and the remainder of the money from the sale of the business assets sold at the termination of the relationship and deposited with the Clerk of Court, was awarded to Pete. The total account was approximately $14,000. Mary appeals.

In her complaint, Mary asserts that she and Pete formed a partnership and at its dissolution, Pete must make an accounting and pay her for her share of the partnership assets. Pete contends that they had a cooperative business relationship and he has fully compensated Mary for her share of the assets.

[UPA §202(a)] defines a partnership as "an association of two or more persons to carry on as co-owners a business for profit." *Barrett v. Larsen*, 846 P.2d 1012 (Mont. 1993), provides the following elements as indicative of a partnership:

> To establish . . . a partnership, it is necessary to determine the intent of the parties: such business relationships arise only when the parties intend to associate themselves as

such. There must be some contribution by each co-adventurer or partner or some-thing promotive of the enterprise. There must be joint proprietary interest and a right of mutual control over the subject matter of the enterprise or over the property engaged therein, and there must be an agreement to share the profits. The intention of the parties has to be clearly manifested, and must be ascertained from all the facts and circumstances and actions and conduct of the parties. (Citations omitted.)

Barrett, 846 P.2d at 1015.

A. CLEAR MANIFESTATION OF INTENT TO ESTABLISH A PARTNERSHIP

The element of intent to associate as partners in this instance is highly debatable. Pete testified that "I wouldn't have considered a partnership." He also asserted, when asked why by the court, "Your Honor, I think a partnership has to be equal donations and equal service. I've been in comparably the same situations previous, and I've never seen them work. And I wasn't about to get into another one." In this case, there is direct testimony that one of the alleged partners did not wish to be associated in a partnership.

Moreover, there is other evidence to support Pete's argument that he did not want to form a partnership with Mary. Although the two parties used the Diamond Dot brand, owned by Pete, it was never transferred to the partnership. Mary was a signer on the brand, not a co-owner.

Although Mary stated that they conducted business under the name of "Akerley and Tondu" or Akerley and Tondu d/b/a "Diamond Dot Ranch" or "Diamond Dot Angus," they never registered the name of their partnership with the Secretary of State. They also never put into writing their desire to associate in a partnership.

Further, they filed separate tax returns instead of partnership returns. The inten-tion of the parties to form a partnership is not clearly manifested as required.

B. CONTRIBUTION AND/OR PROMOTION OF THE ENTERPRISE

Each party made a contribution to start the business. The trial court stated that Mary contributed about $12,000 and some of her shorthorn cattle to the enterprise and Pete contributed about $3,000 in cash and "his knowledge and experience in the unique business of transplants and artificial insemination." The parties obtained joint loans and jointly purchased cattle and necessary equipment to facilitate their operation. Both parties were involved in the operation and management of the busi-ness. From the testimony elicited, it is clear that both parties put considerable effort into promoting this enterprise.

C. RIGHT OF MUTUAL CONTROL

In the pre-trial order, the agreed statement of facts states that "[b]oth of the parties actively participated in purchasing and marketing their livestock." For instance, during the Labor Day weekend of 1991, Pete and Mary met with Walter Perkins and Floyd Fredrickson about the sale of some of their cattle. Pete had earlier arranged the meeting with Walter Perkins. Mary arranged to have some of the cattle cared for and taken to the winter fair for show by some Sheridan high school students for possible sale at a later date.

When Mary's attorney asked Floyd whether he was dealing with *both* Mary and Pete concerning the sale of cattle, Mr. Perkins stated, "Yes." From the testimony presented, Mary and Pete maintained mutual control over the animals.

D. AGREEMENT TO SHARE PROFITS

The trial court's findings of fact concerning sharing of profits stated:

> The parties had no agreement expressed or implied as to the sharing of the financial benefits of their business relationship. Indeed there was little, if any profit as the term is commonly used in a joint business venture. It is apparent from the record that the enterprize (sic) was aesthetically mutually satisfying, and supplemented their individual incomes, providing them a good living during the short-lived association. Even Mary's daughter was advanced money and otherwise benefited from the relationship. Repeatedly the parties withdrew money from the business accounts for their respective personal use. In November, 1989, Mary actually repaid a $4,500 loan which had been negotiated by Pete, from her own personal account. Pete contributed $1,700 from his personal account to purchase a tractor and horse. Once Mary withdrew $775 from joint funds to supplement the purchase by her of an automobile. Neither party ever objected to this co-mingling [sic] and joint personal use of these assets.

Mary and Pete both stated that they had no agreement as to sharing profits. When asked about any agreement to share profits, Pete testified, "No. Just pool our money. It was just an oral agreement. We would pool and just go on." Further testimony revealed that money from cattle sales would be deposited into any account at any time and may have been used by Mary or Pete or jointly by the two. This is a second element of a partnership that the Tondu-Akerley business relationship cannot meet; there was no agreement between the parties to share profits.

The burden of establishing a partnership is on the party claiming one. We conclude that Mary has failed in her burden of proof, and we hold that the cooperative business association entered into by Mary Tondu and Walter "Pete" Akerley does not contain the elements necessary to establish a partnership.

This Court notes that a side issue existed which reflected upon Mary's credibility and her contention that she and Pete had established a partnership. There were a number of checks written on Pete's individual checking account which purportedly contain Pete's signature but do not appear to be in Pete's handwriting. Mary repeatedly denied signing these checks but the trial court concluded that:

> Mary wrote checks on Pete's account, signing his name. While Mary now denies that she did this, the evidence was persuasive that she did. Pete now denies that he authorized these checks, the evidence however convinces the Court that he at least knew or should have known about it. In any case the so called unauthorized checks amounted to less than $2,000.

The trial court was in the best position to determine whether Mary was credible, and we give its decision due regard.

In conclusion, the findings of fact are supported by substantial evidence, the trial court did not misapprehend the effect of the evidence and the findings are not clearly erroneous. AFFIRMED.

TURNAGE, C.J., and HARRISON, WEBER and TRIEWEILER, JJ., concur.

Notes and Questions

1. Notes

a. As you see from this case, partnerships may be formed inadvertently. The UPA emphasizes this by providing that, if the statutory test is met, a partnership is formed, "whether or not the persons intend to form a partnership." UPA §202(a). When this happens, the UPA default rules take on heightened importance because the parties have often not agreed on a wide range of issues. For this reason, you should pay particular attention to the mechanics of the UPA.

b. Arguments for the existence of a partnership are frequently made by a member of an unmarried domestic couple (or a member's estate) who seeks ownership rights in a business. Dissolution law or trust and estate law generally govern the division of a business when a married couple divorces or one spouse dies regardless of the kind of entity in which the business is conducted.

2. Reality Check

a. The court says that, a partnership is "an association of two or more persons to carry on as co-owners a business for profit." Which of these elements did the court find was lacking? Do you agree with the court's analysis?

b. Doesn't Mary's signing Pete's checks with his acquiescence if not prior approval make it *more* likely that Mary and Pete were co-owners?

3. Suppose

a. Would the court have been more likely to find a partnership if Pete and Mary had written down their agreement? Why?

b. What if the parties had written down their agreement and explicitly characterized it as a partnership? What if the written agreement explicitly said no partnership existed?

c. If someone such as Walter Perkins or Floyd Fredrickson, with whom Mary or Pete had done business, sued both of them as a partnership, would the court's analysis or result have been different?

4. What Do You Think?

a. How much weight do you think the courts should give to the parties' testimony regarding their intent? Do you think a party's answer to the question "did you intend to form a partnership?" is helpful? If not, how would you rephrase the question?

b. Do you think Mary and Pete had the same understanding of their business relationship? If not, whose understanding should control? Can there be a partnership without a common understanding?

c. Does the fact that Pete and Mary were a domestic couple make it more likely or less likely that they formed a partnership?

The UPA standard is straightforward: "[T]he association of two or more persons to carry on as co-owners a business for profit forms a partnership, whether or not the persons intend to form a partnership." UPA §202(a). Some state courts have added additional requirements to the core definition. Montana, in which both *Tondu* and *MacArthur Co.* were decided, is one such state. In addition to such required elements, the UPA provides a series of presumptions to be applied in certain fact settings. First, joint ownership of property does not, without more, establish a partnership. Second, the sharing of gross returns does not, without more, establish a partnership. Third, receiving profits creates the presumption that the receiver is a partner in a partnership unless the profits are payment for such things as principal or interest on a debt, compensation as an employee, or rent. See UPA §202(c). The comments to the UPA elaborate:

> [T]he attribute of co-ownership distinguishes a partnership from a mere agency relationship. A business is a series of acts directed toward an end. Ownership involves the power of ultimate control. To state that partners are co-owners of a business is to state that they each have the power of ultimate control. On the other hand, . . . passive co-ownership of property by itself, as distinguished from the carrying on of a business, does not establish a partnership.

UPA §202, cmt. 1.

Under UPA §101(1), "'Business' includes every trade, occupation, and profession." In *Tondu*, whether a partnership existed determined the rights of the "partners" between themselves. In the next case, if a partnership exists, the defendant must pay about $40,000. If no partnership exists, he will pay nothing. As you read this case, be aware that, unlike corporations, partnerships do not shield owners from personal liability. If a partnership's assets are insufficient to satisfy its creditors, the partners are personally liable jointly and severally. See UPA §306.

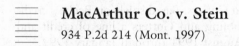

MacArthur Co. v. Stein
934 P.2d 214 (Mont. 1997)

TRIEWEILER, J.

FACTUAL BACKGROUND

Karl Stein has operated Midland Roofing in Billings since 1974. Midland Roofing was a sole proprietorship owned solely by Stein.

In the summer of 1991, several hail storms occurred in the Billings area. As a result, the demand for roofing services increased significantly in the late summer and fall of 1991. Stein recognized an opportunity to increase his profits because of the sudden demand for roofing services. He sought to take advantage of the business opportunity by seeking a line of credit at a local financial institution, but was unable to secure financing.

John L. Potter and Jesse Beebe approached Stein in late June or early July 1991 with the idea of expanding Stein's business to take advantage of the increase in roofing demand. Both Potter and Beebe were out-of-state businessmen who engaged in "storm tracking" — the business of traveling to areas where there was increased roofing activity due to storm damage. In early negotiations, Potter asserted that he could handle the general operation of a roofing business and that a third party, Bill Evans, could handle sales and material acquisition. In addition, Beebe represented that he had the ability to secure credit for the expanded business.

In early July, the parties entered into an agreement, some of which was in writing and some of which was not, but which was confirmed by subsequent actions of the parties. Pursuant to the agreement, Stein, Beebe, and Potter agreed to create a new entity which would operate under the name of Midland Roofing and Gutters. The parties expressly intended that the business name would be so similar to Stein's business name, Midland Roofing, that the public and customers would be unable to distinguish between the two businesses. In addition, both Midland Roofing and the new entity, Midland Roofing and Gutters, were to use the same telephone number and all calls to that number were to be answered by employees of Midland Roofing and Gutters. The parties agreed that a record would be made of all telephone calls and that Stein would be given a first right to accept any potential roofing job. Midland Roofing and Gutters had the option to complete any other jobs.

As part of the parties' initial written agreement, Stein's compensation was equal to three percent of total gross charges for all "nail-on roofing" jobs and ten percent of gross charges for "hot roofing" jobs performed by Midland Roofing and Gutters. Midland Roofing and Gutters also agreed to pay one of Stein's employees a portion of his salary for inspection work and to set aside $.50 per roofing square to be set up in a two-signature account, which would bear the signatures of Stein and Beebe, to cover any warranty work necessary after Midland Roofing and Gutters ceased operation.

In August 1991, Jesse Beebe arranged a line of credit for Midland Roofing and Gutters from MacArthur Company. Stein had previously been denied credit by the company. His purchases from MacArthur were on a "cash only" basis. On the credit application, Beebe listed Midland Roofing and Gutters as the company seeking credit, and named himself as the "principal or officer." Neither Stein nor Midland Roofing was mentioned on the credit application, and MacArthur was not advised of Stein's association with Midland Roofing and Gutters. Based solely on Beebe's credit references, MacArthur granted Midland Roofing and Gutters a line of credit and supplied the company with materials from August 1991 through January 1992.

In January 1992, Jesse Beebe, John Potter, and Bill Evans departed the Billings area without notice, and left an unpaid balance to MacArthur Company in the amount of $39,875.27. On May 12, 1994, MacArthur Company filed a complaint . . . against Karl Stein, Midland Roofing, Midland Roofing and Gutters, and John Does 1 and 2. MacArthur alleged that each of the defendants, as partners in Midland Roofing and Gutters, was jointly and severally liable for the outstanding debt to MacArthur.

DISCUSSION

The issue in this case is whether the District Court erred when it concluded that Karl Stein was a partner in Midland Roofing and Gutters and was therefore liable for the partnership's debt to MacArthur Company.

This Court established the elements for the determination of the existence of a partnership in *Bender v. Bender*, 397 P.2d 957, 962 (Mont. 1965): (1) the parties must clearly manifest their intent to associate themselves as a partnership; (2) each party must contribute something that promotes the enterprise; (3) each party must have a right of mutual control over the subject matter of the enterprise; and (4) the parties must agree to share the profits of the enterprise. We have consistently held that each of the four *Bender* requirements must be established in order to prove the existence of a partnership.

The initial test for the determination of whether a partnership exists is the intent of the parties. At trial, Stein testified that he did not intend to create a partnership through his negotiations with Beebe and Potter. However, as this Court noted in

Truck Insurance Exchange v. Industrial Indemnity Co., 688 P.2d 1243, 1244-45 (Mont. 1984):

> [I]f the facts bring the arrangement within the definition of a partnership, the parties cannot escape liability incident to that relationship merely by saying that no such thing exists. If the intended action of the parties creates a partnership in fact, what the parties call their arrangement or intend their arrangement to be is irrelevant.
>
> (Citation omitted.)

Therefore, where intent cannot be directly ascertained, it must be established from all the facts, circumstances, actions, and conduct of the parties. In this case, then, it is not necessary that Stein intended to be a partner in Midland Roofing and Gutters; it is only necessary that he intended his actions and that his actions created a partnership in fact.

In this case, the District Court found that, regardless of Stein's intentions, the parties had created a partnership in fact through their actions and conduct. Specifically, the court found that the remaining three elements of *Bender*—contribution, joint interest and control, and the right to share profits—had been proven and were indicative of the parties' intent to establish a partnership.

Pursuant to *Bender,* in addition to the requirement of intent, each of the purported partners must contribute something that promotes the enterprise. In this case, the District Court found that each of the parties had made a contribution to Midland Roofing and Gutters sufficient to indicate the creation of a partnership. Specifically, the court found that Stein had contributed to Midland Roofing and Gutters the name of his business, his business license, and his goodwill in the community. In addition, the court noted that Stein had agreed to warrant work completed by Midland Roofing and Gutters. The other parties, the court found, had contributed roofing skills, start-up revenue, and sales skills. Based on the substantial contributions of each of the parties, the District Court found that the element of contribution had been established.

The uncontroverted evidence at trial established that Stein lent his business name, his telephone number, his business leads, his goodwill, his business license, and his expertise to Midland Roofing and Gutters. We hold that such contribution was promotive of the enterprise of Midland Roofing and Gutters. We therefore conclude that the District Court's finding that the element of contribution had been established is supported by substantial, credible evidence and is not clearly erroneous.

A further requirement of *Bender* is that each party to an enterprise have a joint proprietary interest in, and right of control over the subject matter of the enterprise. In this case, the District Court found that Stein did have such interest and control. Specifically, the court found that, pursuant to the parties' agreement, Stein had the right to exercise quality control over the work performed by Midland Roofing and Gutters and, after inspection, could have required that the work conform with his standards. In addition, the court found that Stein had agreed to perform future warranty work for Midland Roofing and Gutters and had established a joint account for the payment for that work. Finally, the court found that Stein had reserved the right to discontinue the parties' arrangement and prohibit Midland Roofing and Gutters from using his telephone number and business license. Although the court noted that Stein did not specifically hire the employees of Midland Roofing and Gutters or arrange for their work schedule or payment, the court found that "there are sufficient indices of control and proprietary interest to determine that he was in fact a partner."

In addition..., the record reflects that Stein was involved in the oversight of the day-to-day workings of Midland Roofing and Gutters. Stein testified at trial that he visited Midland Roofing and Gutter job sites and gave advice on local building code requirements. In addition, Stein testified that he was in the offices of Midland Roofing and Gutters on a daily basis and answered the phones for that entity. Moreover, the evidence presented at trial established that Stein and Midland Roofing and Gutters worked together to contact the general public. This evidence was clearly indicative of Stein's interest in and control of Midland Roofing and Gutters. We therefore hold that the District Court's finding of Stein's right of mutual control and joint proprietary interest is supported by substantial credible evidence and is not clearly erroneous.

The final element of *Bender* requires that there must be an agreement to share profits in order to establish a partnership. In this case, the District Court found that Stein was entitled to receive a percentage of Midland Roofing and Gutters' profit. Specifically, the court noted that both the written agreement formalizing the parties' arrangement and its subsequent modification entitled Stein to a percentage of the gross revenue on all work done by Midland Roofing and Gutters. In addition, the court noted that, according to testimony at trial, Stein earned between $75,000 and $92,000 in both cash and materials from his agreement with Midland Roofing and Gutters. Based on the evidence at trial, which clearly established that Stein was entitled to share the profits of Midland Roofing and Gutters, we hold that the District Court's finding that the final element of *Bender* had been satisfied is not clearly erroneous.

Because we uphold the District Court's findings regarding the establishment of the four elements of a partnership, we hold that the court's conclusion that Stein, Beebe, Potter, and Evans had created a partnership is correct. The only remaining question, then, is whether Stein is liable, as a partner, for Midland Roofing and Gutters' debt to MacArthur Company.

In this case, because we hold that Stein was a partner in Midland Roofing and Gutters, we further conclude he was jointly liable for the partnership's debt to MacArthur Company. Furthermore, we reject Stein's contention that he is not liable to MacArthur because MacArthur was not aware of his relationship with Midland Roofing and Gutters when it extended credit to the company. Reliance is...not necessary to the establishment of liability of a partner in fact. Therefore, we hold that the District Court was correct in its conclusion that, pursuant to [UPA §306(a)], Stein was jointly liable for the partnership's debt to MacArthur Company.

We affirm the judgment of the District Court.

TURNAGE, C.J., and NELSON, GRAY and LEAPHART, JJ., concur.

Notes and Questions

1. Notes

a. *MacArthur Co.* and *Tondu* were decided by the Supreme Court of Montana within four years of one another. Both are unanimous decisions and three of the five Justices in *Tondu* also participated in *MacArthur Co.*

2. Reality Check

a. Does the court use a different standard in this case from the standard it used in *Tondu*?

b. How was MacArthur Co. hurt by Stein?

c. What is the consequence for Stein of the court's holding that he was a partner with Beebe and Potter?

d. In what way or ways did Beebe and Potter have control of the enterprise?

3. Suppose

a. Would the result or analysis be different if this were a suit by Beebe or Potter against Stein to divide the profits of the business?

b. Suppose Beebe and Potter had used a name that was clearly different from Midland Roofing?

c. What if Beebe and Potter had run up a debt of $400,000 to MacArthur Co.? $4,000,000? Would it matter that the debt was owed to several creditors rather than one?

4. What Do You Think?

a. Given the UPA's definition of a partnership, do you think the additional elements applied in these two cases are helpful? Why did the courts adopt those standards originally, do you think?

b. Do you think it is fair to let MacArthur Co. recover from Stein even though MacArthur Co. did not know Stein was involved in the venture?

c. Was Stein's intention and understanding of his business relationship with Beebe, Potter, and Evans different from Pete's intention and understanding of his business relationship with Mary? If so, does that difference explain the difference in result? If not, why are the results in the two cases different?

d. Didn't the parties explicitly agree that two entities existed: Stein's sole proprietorship and Beebe and Potter's Midland Roofing and Gutters? If so, why is there a partnership? How could the parties have drafted their agreement to avoid a finding of partnership?

Even where the parties intend to create a partnership, questions involving partnership formation can arise.

≡ **Mims, Lyemance, & Reich, Inc. v. UAB**
≡ **Research Foundation**
≡ 620 So. 2d 594 (Ala. 1993)

SHORES, J.

The plaintiff appeals from a summary judgment entered in favor of the defendant, UAB Research Foundation ("UABRF"), on claims arising out of an alleged breach of a partnership agreement between UABRF and the plaintiff, Mims, Lyemance, & Reich, Inc. ("MLR"). We affirm.

FACTS

In 1988, representatives of MLR met with representatives of the University of Alabama at Birmingham ("UAB") to explore the concept of developing a geriatric-retirement research center ("the project"). A...confidentiality agreement between UABRF and MLR was signed on February 27, 1989. Those parts of the confidentiality agreement pertinent to this appeal state:

> "The UAB Research Foundation and [MLR] hereby establish a confidentiality agreement for the purpose of protecting unto each other the information exchanged and/or developed in the course of exploring, evaluating the feasibility, and developing a facility or facilities (the 'Project') for older adults....
>
> "Information subject to this agreement...is to be held in the strictest confidence by UAB RF and MLR and their employees and representatives. Neither Party shall disclose the content of the information without the specific written consent of the other Party.
>
> "A mutually acceptable and agreeable form of entity (the 'Entity'), e.g. partnership, joint venture, or other to be identified, will be created between UAB RF and MLR to define, create, and develop the Project....
>
> "This Agreement shall extend for a term of 24 months beginning on the date of this Agreement, but may be extended for additional terms of one year upon the mutual agreement of the Parties. However, this Agreement shall be automatically terminated at any time upon (a) the creation of the Entity or (b) a determination by both Parties that the Project is not feasible or desirable (which determination shall not be unreasonably withheld by either Party)."

At a meeting on May 30, 1989, between MLR and senior UAB officials, the parties determined that if the financial and market feasibility studies on the project proved positive, then it would be desirable to pursue the evolving partnership between UABRF and MLR.

On July 25, 1989, MLR and UABRF signed an agreement to form a general partnership[:]

> This will confirm our agreement to form a general partnership under the laws of the State of Alabama under the name of The University Group, a general partnership (the "Partnership"). The initial partners of the Partnership are UAB Research Foundation and Mims, Lyemance and Reich, Inc. (the "Partners").
>
> The Partnership is organized for the purpose of exploring and evaluating the feasibility of the facility or facilities (the "Project") for older adults as contemplated under the terms and conditions of the Confidentiality Agreement between UAB Research Foundation and [MLR] (the "Confidentiality Agreement"). The Partnership shall undertake to complete a feasibility study for the Project on or before September 30, 1989. Upon completion of the feasibility study for the Project, the Partnership shall elect, with the consent of the Partners, to either (i) develop the Project on such terms as shall be mutually acceptable to the Partners; or (ii) abandon the Project and terminate the Partnership.
>
> The Partners shall not be required to make any capital contribution to the Partnership on its formation. The Partners may agree to contribute funds to the Partnership in such amounts and at such times as may be mutually agreed upon by the Partners.
>
> The Partners' interests in the Partnership shall be divided equally between the Partners: 50% to UAB Research Foundation and 50% to Mims, Lyemance and Reich, Inc. All distributions from the Partnership shall be made in accordance with such percentage interest.
>
> The Partners shall be jointly responsible for the management of the business of the Partnership. Decisions with respect to Partnership business will require consent of both Partners. All Partners shall be required to execute obligations that are binding upon the Partnership.

Except as otherwise provided herein, the Partners agree that their relationship with each other and with creditors and other persons doing business with the Partnership shall be governed by the Alabama Partnership Act. . . .

The . . . Partners agree to be bound by the terms and conditions of said Confidentiality Agreement. The formation of the Partnership shall not cause the termination of the Confidentiality Agreement notwithstanding the provision in the Confidentiality Agreement which provides that the formation of the Entity shall cause its termination. In the event the Partnership elects to develop the Project, the Partners will engage legal counsel to prepare an amended restated partnership agreement which will more clearly define our relationship as Partners in connection with the development of the Project. The execution of such amended and restated Partnership Agreement shall be deemed to constitute the "formation of the Entity" under the terms of the Confidentiality Agreement.

On November 1, 1989, the working group members of UABRF and MLR presented a progress report to senior UAB officials; that report indicated that the project was feasible at that time. [T]he president of UAB, indicated that further exploration into several areas was needed before a final decision on the project was possible.

The record shows that continued meetings and preparation of economic models reflected positively on the project's market feasibility, although there were some unanswered questions about its financial feasibility.

Representatives of UAB, UABRF, and MLR held a meeting in early November [1990] to examine continued participation in further evaluation of the project. In response to that meeting, Dr. Roozen, as executive director of UABRF, . . . informed MLR that UABRF did not consider it feasible or desirable to continue its participation in the geriatric project; that it wanted to dissolve the partnership created by the July 25, 1989, agreement; and that the parties should release each other from the confidentiality agreement dated February 27, 1989. Representatives of UABRF and MLR continued to discuss the feasibility of the project until February 6, 1991, when Dr. Roozen informed Reich that UABRF considered the partnership with MLR "dissolved due to the termination of the particular undertaking of the partnership." Roozen further informed Reich that UABRF considered the feasibility study to have been completed and that UABRF was abandoning the envisioned project.

On May 24, 1991, MLR sued UABRF for $50,000,000 in damages, based on claims arising out of an alleged breach of the confidentiality agreement; breach of the parties' partnership agreement; fraud and misrepresentation by UABRF; and breach of the obligation of good faith and fair dealing. MLR also sought to recover expenses and to recover the value of services rendered, under the theory of quantum meruit. UABRF moved for summary judgment against all claims. [T]he trial court . . . entered a final summary judgment in favor of UABRF. MLR appeals.

I.

MLR alleged that UABRF breached the parties' partnership agreement by failing to go forward with the development of the geriatric center project. Because the trial court implicitly viewed this issue as dispositive of all the claims made by MLR, we shall address this issue first. The trial court's summary judgment described the July 25, 1989, partnership agreement as, "at best, an agreement to agree."

Careful review of the record indicates that there were, in fact, two separate partnerships under consideration. The first partnership, a "feasibility partnership," was created by the July 25, 1989, agreement "for the purpose of exploring and evaluating the feasibility of the [geriatric research] facility." The evidence shows that it was through this partnership that the parties examined the feasibility of the project and that it was pursuant to this partnership that UAB began to purchase land at the site of the proposed geriatric center.

A second partnership, a "development partnership" for the purpose of developing and constructing the project once it was found to be feasible, was expressly contemplated in the July 25 partnership agreement. The July 25 agreement indicates that this development partnership, if created, would be based on "an amended and restated Partnership Agreement," and would constitute the "formation of the Entity" under the terms of the confidentiality agreement. MLR's claims for damages arise out of the failure to develop the geriatric facility, and are, thus, based on the existence of this second partnership. However, there is no substantial evidence in the record that MLR and UABRF ever formed this second partnership to develop the project.

In Alabama, formation of a partnership rests on the intention of the parties, and the agreement to become partners "may be derived from the expressions of the parties or from the facts and circumstances surrounding their business relationships." *Dutton v. Dutton,* 446 So. 2d 615, 617 (Ala. Civ. App. 1983). "There is no settled test for determining the existence of a partnership. That determination is made by reviewing all the attendant circumstances, including the right to manage and control the business." *Vance v. Huff,* 568 So. 2d 745, 748 (Ala. 1990).

The acts of the parties and all the attendant circumstances do not indicate . . . that UABRF and MLR ever formed a partnership to develop and build the geriatric center. The language of the July 25 agreement indicates that the parties intended, at some time in the future, to become partners for the development of the center. This language specifically stated that if MLR and UABRF elected to develop the project, then an "amended and restated partnership agreement which will more clearly define [their] relationship as Partners in connection with the development of the Project" would be prepared. We can find in the record no evidence that an amended and restated partnership agreement was ever created, nor is there any indication from the attendant circumstances that the parties acted in the manner necessary to establish such a partnership. Although UAB began to buy land near the tentative site for the geriatric center, the university stopped these land purchases pending the outcome of this action, and there is no evidence that UAB completed the purchase of all the land that would have been required for the project. No bonds were ever issued to finance the project, and no construction ever began. Because development and construction of the geriatric research center never began, the partnership upon which MLR bases most of its claims in this suit never came into existence.

Because the July 25 agreement was an agreement to form a partnership for the purpose of developing the project, "[b]ut the essentials necessary to the real purpose of the partnership were never completed and its operation never begun," *Higgins* [*v. Higgins,* 97 So. 2d 812 (Ala. 1957)] at 812, we hold that the trial court correctly concluded that the partnership agreement was an agreement to agree. Because the executory agreement was never consummated, there was no partnership agreement for the development of the project upon which to base a claim of breach; the trial court correctly entered the summary judgment as to the claim alleging breach of a partnership agreement.

AFFIRMED.

HORNSBY, C.J., and MADDOX, HOUSTON and KENNEDY, JJ., concur.

Notes and Questions

1. Notes

a. Business people often characterize prospective business opportunities as options. Doing so has two advantages. First, it allows the business person to highlight the fact that the business has a choice but not an obligation to undertake a future course of action. Second, modern finance theory provides methods to approximate the value of an option. Option theory is among the more complex topics in corporate finance but suffice it to say that many agreements in modern business cannot be appropriately valued (and hence may result in suboptimal choices) without the use of option pricing theory. Generally, these business options can be divided into three kinds. First is the option to discontinue a particular aspect of a business's operations, for example by selling off the machinery piecemeal. If the machinery can readily be used by other businesses for other purposes, the owner has, in effect, an inexpensive option to discontinue. On the other hand, if the machinery is custom built and can only be used for a particular purpose, the business's option to discontinue is much more expensive because it will receive only scrap value for the machinery it no longer needs.

The second kind of business option is the option to make additional investment in a line of business. This may mean that the business undertakes investment today that will undoubtedly lose money in the near term. However, the strategic advantage of starting today (gaining market share or having access to cheap supplies because other businesses do not want the necessary raw materials) may outweigh the expected initial losses if, in the future, the business is so profitable that the owner can expand easily. This kind of option is sometimes called a "follow on option." Finally, a business may use an option in a more traditional contract sense to reserve to itself the power, but not the obligation, to enter into a continuing business agreement with others. This option is useful when a business opportunity is particularly risky but is expected to become less risky (as more information becomes available) in the near future. This type of option allows the business to time its decision whether to invest with more precision and, in theory, more chance of success.

Reconsider the underlying business agreements among the parties in this case and decide what kind of options are involved for each party.

2. Reality Check

a. What standard did the court use to determine whether a partnership existed? Is it the same standard as in *Tondu* and *MacArthur Co.* or a different standard?

b. According to Justice Shores, how many partnerships did the parties intend to form? How was each partnership evidenced?

c. Why did the court find that the development partnership was not formed?

3. Suppose

a. Suppose the agreements were embodied in a single document. Would the court be more willing to find that a single entity was formed and that UABRF was liable to plaintiffs?

4. What Do You Think?

a. Do you think there were two separate partnerships or one partnership with two related purposes?

b. Is this case similar to *MacArthur Co.* in that two separate entities agreed to operate jointly? If so, did the courts analyze the question of partnership in the same way? Do you think the analysis should be the same?

c. Do the facts that the parties were both sophisticated and the agreements were drafted by counsel make a difference in the legal analysis? Should those facts make a difference in the way the court characterizes the parties' intent?

d. Should the court here give more weight to the parties' statements about whether a partnership exists than the parties' statements in *Tondu* and *MacArthur Co.*?

5. You Draft It

a. Redraft the July 25, 1989, agreement between MLR and UABRF to make it clear what would happen if, after the feasibility study, the two partners could not agree on whether to develop the project.

b. Redraft the agreement to make it clear that the parties intended the feasibility and development functions to be undertaken by only one partnership.

c. Redraft the agreement to make it clear that the parties intended to have one partnership undertake the feasibility study and a second partnership undertake the development functions.

The original language reads as follows:

> This will confirm our agreement to form a general partnership under the laws of the State of Alabama under the name of The University Group, a general partnership (the "Partnership"). The initial partners of the Partnership are UAB Research Foundation and Mims, Lyemance and Reich, Inc. (the "Partners").
>
> The Partnership is organized for the purpose of exploring and evaluating the feasibility of the facility or facilities (the "Project") for older adults as contemplated under the terms and conditions of the Confidentiality Agreement between UAB Research Foundation and [MLR] (the "Confidentiality Agreement"). The Partnership shall undertake to complete a feasibility study for the Project on or before September 30, 1989. Upon completion of the feasibility study for the Project, the Partnership shall elect, with the consent of the Partners, to either (i) develop the Project on such terms as shall be mutually acceptable to the Partners; or (ii) abandon the Project and terminate the Partnership.
>
> The Partners shall not be required to make any capital contribution to the Partnership on its formation. The Partners may agree to contribute funds to the Partnership in such amounts and at such times as may be mutually agreed upon by the Partners.
>
> The Partners' interests in the Partnership shall be divided equally between the Partners: 50% to UAB Research Foundation and 50% to Mims, Lyemance and Reich, Inc. All distributions from the Partnership shall be made in accordance with such percentage interest.

The Partners shall be jointly responsible for the management of the business of the Partnership. Decisions with respect to Partnership business will require consent of both Partners. All Partners shall be required to execute obligations that are binding upon the Partnership.

Except as otherwise provided herein, the Partners agree that their relationship with each other and with creditors and other persons doing business with the Partnership shall be governed by the Alabama Partnership Act....

The... Partners agree to be bound by the terms and conditions of said Confidentiality Agreement. The formation of the Partnership shall not cause the termination of the Confidentiality Agreement notwithstanding the provision in the Confidentiality Agreement which provides that the formation of the Entity shall cause its termination. In the event the Partnership elects to develop the Project, the Partners will engage legal counsel to prepare an amended restated partnership agreement which will more clearly define our relationship as Partners in connection with the development of the Project. The execution of such amended and restated Partnership Agreement shall be deemed to constitute the "formation of the Entity" under the terms of the Confidentiality Agreement.

Once a partnership is formed, questions often arise as to whether another person has been admitted as a partner. Because one of the central tenets of partnership law is that the partners have equal power, the default rule is that no one can be admitted as an additional partner (i.e., no one may become a co-owner) without unanimous consent of the existing partners. See UPA §401(i). Of course, the partners may unanimously agree in advance that new partners may be admitted by less than unanimous action or by action of a subgroup of partners. The converse setting is governed by a similar rule: when a partner ceases to be a co-owner of a business for profit, that person is no longer a partner. The UPA's treatment of this situation is much simpler than under the UPA (1914) and is treated below under section *f. Dissociation*.

b. Financing and Partners' Ownership Interests

i. Partner Contributions. *Tondu* and *MacArthur Co.* suggest that some courts insist that each partner contribute something to form a partnership. The UPA, however, simply defines a partnership as *co-ownership*. A person can acquire an ownership interest without making any contribution, and in the real world it does occasionally happen that a person is made a partner (i.e., given an ownership interest in a business that is co-owned with others) gratuitously. Remember that in *Mims*, the partnership agreement explicitly provided for no contribution by either partner. More typically, that interest is in return for past contributions to the business or in the expectation of future contributions. This will become plainer when we look at the ways in which a person may contribute to a business.

The most intuitive contribution is, of course, money. Another kind of contribution is property that the business will find useful or necessary. A lease on favorable terms or in a favorable location may, for example, be a valuable contribution to a partnership and may justify, as an economic matter, an ownership interest to the person contributing the lease. Other property, such as vehicles or inventory, may be useful though not uniquely valuable. Finally, intangible property such as intellectual property, whether protected by copyright or not, may be contributed to a business in return for an ownership interest.

In addition to money and other property, a person may contribute services such as working in the business's operations or providing professional services such as legal or accounting services in return for an ownership interest. Further, a person may contribute an agreement to provide services in return for an ownership interest in the business. When a person is given a partnership interest for "no contribution," often the reason is to recognize the person's past contribution to the partnership. For example, a partnership in which an employee makes a sustained or particularly valuable contribution (such as a law firm in which a associate performs well for a decade or more) may reward the employee with an ownership interest for which the person has made no contribution. There may in fact be no contribution in the sense of consideration (because the employee was remunerated through a salary for his or her past efforts) and the ownership interest may come with no explicit agreement to contribute additional services (although such additional contribution would surely be an expectation). Nonetheless, an economist might characterize the business as one in which the employee received an ownership interest in exchange for past service and the agreement to provide future services.

Another typical setting involving services is where one partner provides all, or almost all, the money and property for a new business and another partner provides the knowledge and skill, through providing services, to the partnership. A new restaurant is a paradigm of this setting. A talented but impecunious chef may find financial backers (possibly well-heeled patrons of the restaurant where the chef is currently employed) and open a new restaurant. The chef will contribute nothing but an agreement to provide future services while the other partners will provide all the necessary cash.

Not only may some partners put in cash, others property, others services, and still others nothing, but the division of the partners' ownership interests may be completely unrelated to the relative value of their contributions. This quality is fundamentally different from the corporate law norm. Remember, in corporate law shareholders who purchase identical shares contemporaneously must pay the same amount per share (even though they may pay in different kinds of consideration such as cash, property, or services). This aspect of partnership law is described in section *d* below.

ii. Partnership Property.   Under UPA (1914) the nature of partnership property and, even more, the nature of a partner's ownership interest in the partnership were rather muddled. The current UPA makes these concepts more rational, or at any rate more modern. Because a partnership is now definitely an entity separate from its partners, partnership property belongs to the partnership rather than to the partners collectively. See UPA §§203, 501. In practice, the question frequently arises whether a particular piece of property (which may well be intangible) was contributed to, or purchased by, the partnership from a partner (often in return for the partner's ownership interest) or whether the property was simply being used by the partnership with the consent of its owner, the partner.

This question is important when the partnership is insolvent and creditors seek to seize whatever partnership assets exist. The question also is important when the partnership is successful and one partner claims that key property is personal, not partnership, property. After Kurt Cobain died, his widow was engaged in litigation with the two other members of Nirvana. Much of the dispute rested upon whether Mr. Cobain owned either all of Nirvana (making the other members employees) or at least nearly all of the songs that the band performed. Mr. Cobain's widow took the view that Nirvana belonged to Mr. Cobain, while the other members believed a partnership had been formed and that the partnership owned all the assets. While resolution of this question is frequently important, the legal standard is relatively simple: UPA §203 defines partnership property as "[p]roperty acquired by a partnership. . . ." The ultimate question is the intent of the parties. See UPA §204, cmt. 3.

UPA §204 provides rules and presumptions for determining whether property is partnership property.

> Property becomes partnership property if acquired (1) in the name of the partnership or (2) in the name of one or more of the partners with an indication in the instrument transferring title of either (i) their capacity as partners or (ii) of the existence of a partnership, even if the name of the partnership is not indicated. . . . [UPA] sets forth two rebuttable presumptions that apply when the partners have failed to express their intent. First, . . . property purchased with partnership funds is presumed to be partnership property, notwithstanding the name in which title is held. . . . Second, . . . property acquired in the name of one or more of the partners, without an indication of their capacity as partners and without use of partnership funds or credit, is presumed to be the partners' separate property, even if used for partnership purposes. In effect, it is presumed in that case that only the use of the property is contributed to the partnership.

UPA §204, cmts. 2 & 3

In keeping with the ethos that every partner is equal unless otherwise agreed, every partner has an equal right to possess and use partnership property for partnership purposes but not otherwise. UPA §401(g).

iii. Partners' Interest in the Partnership. UPA §101(9) contains a not entirely helpful definition of the partners' ownership interests. It says that a partner's interest "means all of a partner's interests in the partnership"[!]. Good to know. UPA §101(9) continues, "including the partner's transferable interest," which suggests that, as we will see, some interests are not transferable, and "all management and other rights." Scattered throughout the rest of the UPA are sections that flesh out this definition. A partner has only two transferable rights: First is the right to an allocation of profits and losses, which is simply the right to have a certain percentage of the profits and losses credited to the partner's account. Second is the right to receive distributions from the partnership. See UPA §502. A fuller description of allocation and distribution is set out below in section iv. A partner has no transferable interest in the use or possession of partnership property. UPA §501. Each partner has an equal right to manage the partnership, (UPA §401(f)) but such right is nontransferable. See UPA §503(a)(3). Section *d* below details the management rights among partners. Whether there are other rights that are nontransferable and nonmanagement is not explicit in the UPA. While UPA §101(9) suggests that there are such rights (". . . *all* of a partner's interests . . . *including* . . . transferable . . . and . . . management *and other rights.*" emphasis added), the UPA does not describe any other rights than have been discussed in this paragraph.

A partner can transfer all or a portion of his or her transferable interest, although a partnership may impose reasonable restrictions on transfer that will be binding on a transferee with notice. A transferee does *not* become a partner, even where the transferee receives all of a partner's transferable interest. In addition to the rights explicitly transferred by a partner, a transferee also gains the right to seek a winding up of the partnership's business on the ground that such a course of action would be equitable. See UPA §503(b)(3). A partner's transferable interest in the partnership can also be involuntarily seized by a judgment creditor of the partner. This seizure is called a *charging order* and works like a lien. It may be foreclosed upon and sold at a judicial sale. See UPA §504.

iv. Allocations and Distributions to Partners. The economic rights of a corporation's owners are determined by the percentage of outstanding shares he or she owns. By contrast, partners' economic interests are a matter of agreement among them, need not be equal, and may change over time. The next case shows some of the problems that can arise from this quality of partnership law.

Starr v. Fordham
648 N.E.2d 1261 (Mass. 1995)

NOLAN, J.

In 1984, the plaintiff [Ian M. Starr] was a partner in the Boston law firm Foley, Hoag & Eliot (Foley Hoag). The plaintiff specialized in corporate and business law. Although the plaintiff had become a partner at Foley Hoag in 1982, he was actively seeking to leave the firm in early 1984. During this time, the founding partners [Fordham and Starrett] were also partners at Foley Hoag. Both men enjoyed outstanding professional reputations among their colleagues. Nevertheless, they agreed that they would withdraw from Foley Hoag in early 1985 in order to establish a new law firm with another established Boston attorney, Frank W. Kilburn.

Fordham invited the plaintiff to join the new law firm Kilburn, Fordham & Starrett in January, 1985. At first, the plaintiff was somewhat hesitant to accept the offer because he was not known as a "rainmaker" (i.e., an attorney responsible for significant client origination) at Foley Hoag. Fordham, however, assured the plaintiff that business origination would not be a significant factor for allocating the profits among the partners.

Prior to executing the partnership agreement, the plaintiff informed Fordham that certain provisions in the agreement disturbed him. The source of the plaintiff's disquiet was Paragraph 1 of the partnership agreement which vested in the founding partners and Kilburn, the authority to determine, both prospectively and retrospectively, each partner's share of the firm's profits. Despite his concern, the plaintiff did not claim at this time that the agreement contradicted Fordham's representations to him that rainmaking would not be a significant factor in distributing the firm's profits. Fordham summarily dismissed the plaintiff's concerns, telling him, in effect, to "take it or leave it." On March 5, 1985, the founding partners, Kilburn, and [partner Brian W.] LeClair each executed the partnership agreement for Kilburn, Fordham & Starrett. The plaintiff also signed the agreement without objection and without making any revisions. The defendant Barry A. Guryan joined the new firm on March 11, 1985. In August of 1985, Kilburn withdrew from the firm. Subsequently, the firm assumed the name Fordham & Starrett.

The founding partners had divided the firm's profits equally among the partners in 1985. Each of the five partners received $11,602. In 1986, the firm's financial fortunes improved significantly. On December 31, 1986, the firm's profits were

$1,605,128. In addition, the firm had $1,844,366.59 in accounts receivable and work in progress.

The plaintiff withdrew from the firm on December 31, 1986. The partners remaining in the firm were the founding partners, LeClair, and Guryan. When the plaintiff withdrew from the firm, the sum of the plaintiff's accounts receivable and work in process was $204,623. The firm eventually collected $195,249 of the plaintiff's total receivables. The founding partners determined the plaintiff's share of the firm's profits for 1986 to be 6.3% of the total profits. In allocating the firm's profits among the partners, the founding partners did not consider any of the firm's accounts receivable or work in process.

The founding partners argue that the judge's conclusion that they had violated both their fiduciary duties and the implied covenant of good faith and fair dealing when they allocated only 6.3% of the firm's profits for 1986 to the plaintiff was clearly erroneous. We disagree.

An implied covenant of good faith and fair dealing exists in every contract. Thus, an unfair determination of a partner's respective share of a partnership's earnings is a breach not only of one's fiduciary duty, but also of the implied covenant of good faith and fair dealing. A court has the power to determine whether a partner's share of the profits is fair and equitable as a matter of law. *Noble v. Joseph Burnett Co.*, 94 N.E. 289 (Mass. 1911). In the present case, the judge "vigorously scrutinized" the founding partners' determination of the plaintiff's share of the profits. The judge then made extensive findings concerning the fairness of the plaintiff's share of the profit distribution. The judge found that the plaintiff had produced billable hour and billable dollar amounts that constituted 16.4% and 15%, respectively, of the total billable hour and billable dollar amounts for all of the partners as a group. The judge noted, however, that the founding partners distributed only 6.3% of the firm's 1986 profits to the plaintiff. Meanwhile, the other partners received substantially greater shares of the profits.[4] The judge concluded, therefore, that the founding partners had decided to exclude billable hour and billable dollar totals as a factor in determining compensation. The judge determined that this decision to exclude billable hour figures was unfair to the plaintiff and indicated that the founding partners had selected performance criteria in order to justify the lowest possible payment to the plaintiff.[5] The judge also noted that Fordham had fabricated a list of negative factors that the founding partners had used in determining the plaintiff's share of the firm's profits. As a result, the judge concluded that the founding partners had violated their respective fiduciary duties to the plaintiff as well as the implied covenant of good faith and fair dealing. The judge also concluded that the plaintiff was entitled to 11% of the firm's profits for 1986 and awarded the plaintiff $75,538.48 in damages.[7]

---

4. The plaintiff received $101,025.60. Meanwhile, the defendants Guryan and LeClair each received 18.75% ($301,025.60) of the firm's total profits. As a result, each of the managing partners kept for himself a 28.1% share of the profits, or $451,025.60 each. The judge did note, however, that the founding partners were not unfair in allocating to the plaintiff 7.2% of the firm's expenses in 1986.

5. The judge compared the plaintiff's work performance directly to the work performance of the defendants Guryan and LeClair. The judge concluded that the plaintiff's "billable hours by working attorney" were 85% of the total billable hours that Guryan had worked and 77% of the total billable hours that LeClair had worked. The plaintiff's share of the profits, however, was only 34% of the amount which Guryan and LeClair each had received.

7. The judge found that 11% of the profits was a more accurate reflection of the plaintiff's contribution to the firm's 1986 profits after considering the plaintiff's billable hour and billable dollar totals. In addition, the judge noted that Starrett had recommended that the plaintiff receive an 11% profit share in the fall of

Having examined the record, all 127 exhibits, and the judge's own findings of fact and rulings of law, we conclude that the judge's ultimate finding of liability was not clearly erroneous. We cannot conclude that the judge committed a mistake in finding that the founding partners had violated both their fiduciary duties to the plaintiff and the implied covenant of good faith and fair dealing. Judgment affirmed.

Notes and Questions

1. Reality Check

a. Why does the court use the standard of fairness in scrutinizing the plaintiff's share of the 1986 profits?

b. Was the partnership agreement vague or ambiguous about the plaintiff's share of the profits? If not, why does the court not enforce the agreement?

c. If the partners had made no agreement regarding profits, what solution would the UPA provide? Did the court consider the UPA default rule? Should it have done so?

2. Suppose

a. If the partnership agreement had explicitly stated that the plaintiff was to receive 6.3 percent of the profits, would the court have enforced the agreement?

b. Suppose the founding partners had awarded the plaintiff 10 percent of the profits? Would the court award anything further?

c. Would this case come out differently if the partnership agreement had listed factors such as number of hours billed and collected that the founders agreed to take into account in determining the plaintiff's share of the profits?

3. What Do You Think?

a. Do you think the plaintiff should prevail given that he was an experienced corporate law attorney, explicitly identified the question of how his share of the profits was to be determined, and voluntarily entered into the partnership agreement?

b. In many new business ventures it is difficult to forecast the value each owner will provide and the profits (if any) the venture will generate in the near term. Could the founders have retained sufficient discretion to make compensation decisions and still have assuaged the concerns of the other partners if the partnership agreement had been drafted with more care?

4. You Draft It

a. Draft an enforceable provision for the partnership agreement that gives the founding partners and Kilburn the authority to determine each partner's profit share.

The UPA default rule for allocating profits and losses is quite an important one because so many partnerships are formed inadvertently with no explicit agreement for sharing profits or losses. "Each partner is entitled to an equal share of the partnership profits and is chargeable with a share of the partnership losses in proportion to the partner's share of the profits." UPA §401(b). Three aspects of this rule are worthy

---

1986 when the plaintiff first had informed his partners of his intention to withdraw from the firm. Eleven percent of the firm's total profits for 1986 amounted to $176,564.08. The judge then subtracted the 6.3% of the profits, which the plaintiff had already received, from $176,564.08 to arrive at $75,538.48.

of particular note. First, in keeping with the personal nature of partnership law, each partner is equal, regardless of the amount of money contributed. That is, if one partner puts up 60 percent of the money and the other partner puts up 40 percent, each is entitled to receive 50 percent of the profits (unless they agree otherwise).

Second, notice that the language describing losses is a bit curious: a partner is allocated losses "in proportion to the partner's share of the profits." The effect of the UPA rule is that if the partners make no agreement as to profits or losses, both are allocated per capita. If the partners explicitly agree about dividing profits but not losses, the losses mirror the profits. The reason why the rule is stated this way is because partners, particularly those who begin business without legal advice, frequently agree upon an allocation of profits but are silent about losses because they do not anticipate losing money! Of course, the partners may agree to allocate losses and may do so in a proportion different from the allocation of profits. This sort of agreement is quite frequent. For example, one partner may be particularly necessary for the venture to succeed because of that partner's background, knowledge, or contacts. This partner may be unwilling to participate unless he or she receives a larger share of the profits and a smaller share of the losses.

The final point worth noting is that "entitled to an equal share" is not the same as being entitled to receive money. See UPA §401, cmt. 3. Whether to distribute profits to the partners is a business decision to be decided in the ordinary course of the partnership's operation. Note, though, that for federal income tax purposes, a partner who is allocated a profit must report that profit as income on his or her tax return. This raises the distinct possibility that a partner will recognize income for the year from the partnership but will not have received any cash distribution with which to pay the taxes on that profit.

Each partner has an account that is credited with the amount, if any, the partner contributes and with the partner's profits. Conversely, the account is debited ("charged" is the word used in the UPA) for any money actually distributed to the partner and with the partner's losses. See UPA §401(a).

"Profits" and "losses" typically mean the money remaining (or the shortfall resulting) after the expenses of the business are subtracted from the revenues. Expenses include wages paid to employees of the partnership. What if a partner works for the partnership? The default rule is that a partner is not entitled to remuneration for working for the partnership, except when the partnership is being dissolved. See UPA §401(h). The reason for this rule is that the partners, as owners, are remunerated by the profits, and each expends efforts in the partnership on behalf of all. It frequently is the case, however, that the partners will agree that one or more partners should receive remuneration in the form of salary for efforts on behalf of the partnership. These wages are then subtracted from the partnership's revenues before profits or losses are computed. An example is the situation in which a chef opens a restaurant with capital supplied by other partners. The chef will likely contribute little or no cash but will likely be the only partner employed in the restaurant. The partners may well agree that the chef should receive a wage in addition to a share of the profits.

c. Personal Liability

One of the key consequences of the partnership form is that the partners have unlimited personal liability for the debts of the partnership. Every other business entity covered in this course provides limited liability for at least some participants. In the inadvertent partnership setting, the spectre of unlimited personal liability can be devastating. In *MacArthur Co.* for example, Stein is personally liable for the entire debt to MacArthur Co. and, doubtless, for any other debts of the partnership with Potter and Beebe. The UPA provides that a partnership creditor cannot levy on the assets of the partners until the assets of the partnership are exhausted and the creditor obtains a judgment against the partner. See UPA §307. Typically a partnership creditor will bring suit against both the partnership and its partners in one lawsuit so that, if successful, the plaintiff can levy on the partnership assets first and then seek satisfaction against the partners without having to return to court for an additional judgment.

The UPA provides that partners are jointly and severally liable for all partnership obligations. UPA §306(a). This means that a judgment creditor entitled to proceed against the partners may seek payment from some partners but not others. This will happen when one or more partners have substantial assets that are easily seized. If a partner pays more than the partner's share of partnership debts, measured by the proportion of losses each partner is to bear, he or she may recover contribution from other partners when the partnership is dissolved. See UPA §807(c).

An exception to personal liability is made in the case of new partners and dissociated partners. Under the UPA, a newly admitted partner is not personally liable for preexisting partnership debts but, in practice, such partners may be required to assume those liabilities as a condition to being made a partner. See UPA §306(b). Conversely, a dissociated partner remains personally liable for partnership obligations incurred before dissociation and, in limited circumstances, may be liable for partnership obligations incurred after dissociation. See UPA §703(a). A dissociated partner remains liable for partnership obligations incurred within two years after dissociation to persons who reasonably believed at the time of the obligation that the dissociated partner was a partner and who is not deemed to have had notice that the partner was dissociated. UPA §703(b). A dissociating partner or the partnership can file a statement of dissociation, which cuts off postdissociation liability after 90 days. UPA §704.

d. Management

The UPA continues the traditional default rule that every partner has an equal right to participate in the management of the partnership. See UPA §401(f). This management right includes a concomitant right to receive information from the partnership and other partners and a corresponding duty to render information to other partners. See UPA §403(b), (c). In keeping with the partnership norm that all partners are equal, the default rule is that matters in the "ordinary course of business" are decided by a majority of partners (regardless of their relative contributions or shares in the profits or losses) but that other matters, including amending the partnership agreement, require unanimity. See UPA §401(j). Where the partners are evenly divided on an issue, courts generally hold that a change from the status quo operation of the partnership has not been approved by a "majority."

"Each partner is an agent of the partnership for the purpose of its business." UPA §301(1). Clearly, then, every partner has actual authority to take actions that further the partnership's business. Every partner also has actual authority to do anything outside the partnership's business that all of the partners authorize. Can the partnership ever be bound by a partner's actions that are outside the partnership's business *and* have not been authorized by the partners? Can the partners limit the authority of a partner to take actions within the partnership's business? The *Kansallis* case, which follows, nicely describes the power of a partner to bind the partnership under the agency doctrine of apparent authority and under UPA §301.

Kansallis Finance Ltd. v. Fern
659 N.E.2d 731 (Mass. 1996)

Fried, J.

The United States Court of Appeals for the First Circuit has certified to this court the following [question] of State law:

"1. Under Massachusetts law, to find that a certain act is within the scope of a partnership for the purpose of applying the doctrine of vicarious liability, must a plaintiff show, *inter alia*, that the act was taken at least in part with the intent to serve or benefit the partnership?"

Kansallis Fin. Ltd. v. Fern, 40 F.3d 476, 481-482 (1st Cir. 1994).

I.

We summarize the facts.... Stephen Jones and the four defendants were law partners in Massachusetts when, in connection with a loan and lease financing transaction, the plaintiff sought and obtained an opinion letter from Jones. In the order of certification, the Court of Appeals states that the letter, executed in Massachusetts and issued on "Fern, Anderson, Donahue, Jones & Sabatt, P.A." letterhead, "contained several intentional misrepresentations concerning the transaction and was part of a conspiracy by Jones and others (though not any of the defendants here) to defraud Kansallis." Although Jones did not personally sign the letter, he arranged for a third party to do so, and both the District Court judge and the jury found that Jones adopted or ratified the issuance of the letter. Jones was later convicted on criminal charges for his part in the fraud, but the plaintiff was unable to collect its $880,000 loss from Jones or his co-conspirators.

In an effort to recover its loss, the plaintiff brought suit in the United States District Court for the District of Massachusetts seeking compensation from Jones's law partners on the theory that the partners were liable for the damage caused by the fraudulent letter. Advancing the claim on essentially three grounds, the plaintiff asserted that defendants are liable for the letter because: (1) the defendants gave Jones apparent authority to issue the letter; (2) Jones acted within the scope of the partnership in issuing the letter; and (3) the issuance of the letter violated [Massachusetts's consumer protection act], under which the partners are vicariously liable. The District Court submitted the first two common law claims to the jury and reserved the [consumer protection act] count to itself. Both the judge and jury, for different reasons, decided that defendants were not liable for Jones's conduct. The Court of Appeals affirmed both the judge's and the jury's factual findings and certified [the question] to this court in order to resolve the legal issues.

On plaintiff's common law claims, the jury based their verdict on their findings that (1) Jones did not have apparent authority to issue the opinion letter and (2) that his action in issuing the opinion letter was outside the scope of the partnership. On appeal to the Court of Appeals, the plaintiff contended that the jury based their second finding on an erroneous instruction directing that, to find Jones's actions within the scope of the partnership, the issuance of the letter must satisfy a three-prong test. It must have: (1) been "the kind of thing a law partner would do"; (2) "occurred substantially within the authorized time and geographic limits of the partnership; and" (3) been "motivated at least in part by a purpose to serve the partnership." Although the jury did not indicate which prong the plaintiff failed to satisfy, the plaintiff objected to the addition of the third prong, and it is on the correctness of including this third prong in the test that the Court of Appeals now seeks guidance. The Court of Appeals found our law on this issue unclear because it found that two decisions . . . appeared to pull in opposite directions. The Court of Appeals therefore certified this question to us.

II.

A.

[T]he issue of vicarious liability has engendered somewhat divergent formulations in the several different contexts in which it has arisen. In the context of a partnership, the person acting and the persons who might be held liable for his actions usually stand on an equal footing and may be thought of as equally implicated in a joint enterprise. By contrast, the law of the vicarious liability of a master for the acts of his servant grew up in circumstances where the actor was often in a subordinate position and had a limited interest in the enterprise which he assists. Yet both servants and partners are categorized as agents of their principals. See [UPA §301(1)] (partners are agents of the partnership); . . . *Restatement of Agency (Second)* §14A comment a (1957) (partner is general agent for copartners and liable to copartners for any breach of fiduciary obligation). . . .

Standing behind these diverse concepts of vicarious liability is a principle that helps to rationalize them. This is the principle that as between two innocent parties—the principal . . . and the third party—the principal . . . who for his own purposes places another in a position to do harm to a third party should bear the loss.

Where there is actual authority to transact the very business or to do the very act that causes the harm, . . . the case for vicarious liability is clear. Where the authority is only apparent, vicarious liability recognizes that it is the principal who for his own purposes found it useful to create the impression that the agent acts with his authority, and therefore it is the principal who must bear the burden of the misuse to which that appearance has been put. But there is little fairness in saddling the principal with liability for acts that a reasonable third party would not have supposed were taken on the principal's behalf.

In the case before us here, the jury instructions required the jury to consider both routes [i.e., partnership and agency] to vicarious liability. The jury found that Jones acted without actual or apparent authority, presumably because the form and circumstances of the letter were such that they concluded that no reasonable person in the plaintiff's position would have believed that the letter was issued with the partnership's authority. But then they were asked in the alternative whether Jones "acted in the scope of the partnership." This further question was taken to ask whether writing this opinion letter was the *kind of thing* that the partnership did—even if there was no apparent authority for this particular letter. This is the alternative theory, which the District Court labeled "vicarious liability," and under this alternative the defendants might yet be liable if the jury found all three of the conditions set out above in its charge on that issue. The rationale for this possibly more extended liability recognizes an authority in each partner to take the initiative to enlarge the partnership enterprise even without the authority — actual or apparent — of his partners, so long as what he does is within the generic description of the type of partnership involved. Whatever the harshness may be of such a rule extending vicarious liability past apparent authority, it is mitigated by the third factor, requiring that the unauthorized but law partner-like act be intended at least in part to serve the partnership. Since there is then some possibility that the partnership will benefit from the errant partner's act, then as between two innocent parties it is not unfair that the one whom the wrongful act may have and was meant to benefit must bear the burden of the harm.

B.

The Uniform Partnership Act provides as general principles that: the law of agency shall apply under that chapter, [UPA §104(a), com.]; the act of every partner apparently carrying on in the usual way the business of the partnership binds it, [UPA §301(1)]; and an act of the partner which is not apparently for the carrying on of the business of the partnership in the usual way does not bind it unless authorized, *id.* Where, however, by any wrongful act of a partner acting in the ordinary course of the business of the partnership, *or* with the authority of the copartners, loss or injury is caused to a third person, or a penalty is incurred, the partnership is liable therefore, [UPA §305].

The District Court derived the second theory of liability, which it labeled vicarious liability and on which it instructed the jury regarding the scope of the partnership business, from §228(1) of the *Restatement (Second) of Agency.* Section 228(1) provides in relevant part that conduct of a servant is within the scope of his employment, if but only if the conduct is . . . (c) actuated, at least in part, by a purpose to serve the master. Subsection (2) states the complementary proposition that conduct is not within the scope of employment if it is . . . too little actuated by a purpose to serve the master.

C.

[U]nder our law — and the law of partnership and agency generally — there are two routes by which vicarious liability may be found. If the partner has apparent authority to do the act, that will be sufficient to ground vicarious liability, whether or not he acted to benefit the partnership. It is only where there is no apparent authority, which is what the jury found on the common law counts here, that there may yet be vicarious liability on the alternative ground requiring such an intent to benefit the partnership. Since there is no evidence that Jones was acting to benefit the partnership, the District Court's judgment for the defendants on the common law counts accords with our statutes and precedents. The jury instructions on the common law claims were correct.

Notes and Questions

1. Notes

a. UPA §301(1) reads in part, "An act of a partner, . . . , for apparently carrying on in the ordinary course the partnership business *or business of the kind carried on by the* *partnership* binds the partnership. . . ." (emphasis added). The italicized portion of the act broadens the power of a partner to bind the partnership and resolves an uncertainty under the UPA (1914). See UPA §301, com. 2. Section 301(2) reads, "An act of a partner which is not apparently for carrying on in the ordinary course the partnership's business or business of the kind carried on by the partnership binds the partnership only if the act was authorized by the other partners." Under the UPA, then, a partnership is liable for an action in furtherance of what a paradigmatic partnership of this kind would do, even where this particular partnership explicitly does not do that thing.

2. Reality Check

a. Isn't rendering a legal opinion in connection with a secured financing transaction something that is done in "the ordinary course" of a law partnership's business? If so, why does that not end the court's analysis here?

b. Why could the jury have found that no apparent authority existed?

3. Suppose

What if the law firm had a policy against rendering legal opinions in financing transactions on the ground that such opinions require the firm to predict accurately (under penalty of a malpractice claim) whether a court will enforce a particular contract, which is simply impossible to do in every instance? Would the firm's policy affect the court's analysis?

4. What Do You Think?

a. What is the effect of the court's imposing the requirement that an act outside actual or apparent authority be motivated in part to benefit the partnership? Does this rule expand or contract potential partnership liability?

b. Both the UPA and the *Restatement (Third) of Agency* provide that the partnership/principal is liable for acts by a partner/agent that have not been authorized. Is the expansion of liability identical? Should it be? Compare UPA §301(1) with *Restatement (Third) of Agency* §§2.03 and 3.03.

Kansallis describes the power to bind the partnership given to each partner under the UPA and the doctrine of apparent authority. It also considers the question whether the partnership is bound by a partner's torts or other wrongful conduct. UPA §305(a) makes the partnership liable for a partner's actions "in the ordinary course of business of the partnership or with authority of the partnership." UPA §305(b) makes the partnership strictly liable "for the misapplication of money or other property received by a partner in the course of the partnership's business or otherwise within the scope of the partner's actual authority." See UPA §305, cmt.

The partnership may file a statement of authority with the secretary of state that grants or limits a partner's authority. See UPA §303. If the statement grants authority to a partner, a third party may bind the partnership for an action in accordance with the grant, even though the third party did not know of the statement on file. But, if the statement limits the authority of a partner, a third party is bound only if the third party had actual knowledge of the limitation or if the action involved the transfer of real estate. In the real estate setting, purchasers and sellers will normally undertake a title search and the UPA provides that a third party is deemed to know of (i.e., will be estopped to deny) a limitation on authority in a filed statement. Such statements of authority are often useful to third parties who anticipate entering into significant transactions with a partnership and who want added assurance that the partners with whom they deal are authorized to take actions on behalf of the partnership.

e. Fiduciary Duties

Partners have long been held to be fiduciaries for one another and the partnership itself. The UPA (1914) contained the following statement of partners' duties:

> Every partner must account to the partnership for any benefit, and hold as trustee for it any profits derived by him [or her] without the consent of the other partners from any transaction connected with the formation, conduct, or liquidation of the partnership or from any use by him [or her] of its property.

UPA (1914) §21(1)

Perhaps the most controversial part of the UPA revision concerned a change in partners' fiduciary duties. The pertinent UPA section is 404. The next case is an icon; *the* classic statement of partner fiduciary duties.

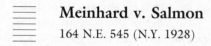

Meinhard v. Salmon
164 N.E. 545 (N.Y. 1928)

CARDOZO, C.J.

On April 10, 1902, Louisa M. Gerry leased to the defendant Walter J. Salmon the premises known as the Hotel Bristol at the northwest corner of Forty-Second street and Fifth avenue in the city of New York. The lease was for a term of 20 years, commencing May 1, 1902, and ending April 30, 1922. The lessee undertook to change the hotel building for use as shops and offices at a cost of $200,000. Alterations and additions were to be accretions to the land.

Salmon, while in course of treaty with the lessor as to the execution of the lease, was in course of treaty with Meinhard, the plaintiff, for the necessary funds. The result was a joint venture with terms embodied in a writing. Meinhard was to pay to Salmon half of the moneys requisite to reconstruct, alter, manage, and operate the property. Salmon was to pay to Meinhard 40 per cent. of the net profits for the first five years of the lease and 50 per cent. for the years thereafter. If there were losses, each party was to bear them equally. Salmon, however, was to have sole power to "manage, lease, underlet and operate" the building. There were to be certain pre-emptive rights for each in the contingency of death.

They were coadventurers, subject to fiduciary duties akin to those of partners. As to this we are all agreed. The heavier weight of duty rested, however, upon Salmon. He was a coadventurer with Meinhard, but he was manager as well. During the early years of the enterprise, the building, reconstructed, was operated at a loss. If the relation had then ended, Meinhard as well as Salmon would have carried a heavy burden. Later the profits became large with the result that for each of the investors there came a rich return. For each the venture had its phases of fair weather and of foul. The two were in it jointly, for better or for worse.

When the lease was near its end, Elbridge T. Gerry had become the owner of the reversion. He owned much other property in the neighborhood, one lot adjoining the Bristol building on Fifth avenue and four lots on Forty-Second street. He had a plan to lease the entire tract for a long term to some one who would destroy the buildings then existing and put up another in their place. In the latter part of 1921, he submitted such a project to several capitalists and dealers. He was unable to carry it through with any of them. Then, in January, 1922, with less than four months of the lease to run, he approached the defendant Salmon. The result was a new lease to the Midpoint Realty Company, which is owned and controlled by Salmon, a lease covering the whole tract, and involving a huge outlay. The term is to be 20 years, but successive covenants for renewal will extend it to a maximum of 80 years at the will of either party. The existing buildings may remain unchanged for seven years. They are then to be torn down, and a new building to cost $3,000,000 is to be placed upon the site. The rental, which under the Bristol lease was only $55,000, is to be from $350,000 to $475,000 for the properties so combined. Salmon personally guaranteed the performance by the lessee of the covenants of the new lease until such time as the new building had been completed and fully paid for.

The lease between Gerry and the Midpoint Realty Company was signed and delivered on January 25, 1922. Salmon had not told Meinhard anything about it. Whatever his motive may have been, he had kept the negotiations to himself. Meinhard was not informed even of the bare existence of a project. The first that he knew of it was in February, when the lease was an accomplished fact. He then made demand on the defendants that the lease be held in trust as an asset of the venture, making offer upon the trial to share the personal obligations incidental to the guaranty. The demand was followed by refusal, and later by this suit. A referee gave judgment for the plaintiff, . . . The case is now here on an appeal by the defendants.

Joint adventurers, like copartners, owe to one another, while the enterprise continues, the duty of the finest loyalty. Many forms of conduct permissible in a workaday world for those acting at arm's length, are forbidden to those bound by fiduciary ties. A trustee is held to something stricter than the morals of the market place. Not honesty alone, but the punctilio of an honor the most sensitive, is then the standard of behavior. As to this there has developed a tradition that is unbending and inveterate. Uncompromising rigidity has been the attitude of courts of equity when petitioned to undermine the rule of undivided loyalty by the "disintegrating erosion" of particular exceptions. *Wendt v. Fischer*, 154 N.E. 303. Only thus has the level of conduct for fiduciaries been kept at a level higher than that trodden by the crowd. It will not consciously be lowered by any judgment of this court.

The owner of the reversion, Mr. Gerry, had vainly striven to find a tenant who would favor his ambitious scheme of demolition and construction. Baffled in the search, he turned to the defendant Salmon in possession of the Bristol, the keystone of the project. He figured to himself beyond a doubt that the man in possession would prove a likely customer. To the eye of an observer, Salmon held the lease as owner in his own right, for himself and no one else. In fact he held it as a fiduciary, for himself and another, sharers in a common venture. If this fact had been proclaimed, if the lease by its terms had run in favor of a partnership, Mr. Gerry, we may fairly assume, would have laid before the partners, and not merely before one of them, his plan of reconstruction. The pre-emptive privilege, or, better, the pre-emptive opportunity, that was thus an incident of the enterprise, Salmon appropriated to himself in secrecy and silence. He might have warned Meinhard that the plan had been submitted, and that either would be free to compete for the award. If he had done this, we do not need to say whether he would have been under a duty, if successful in the competition, to hold the lease so acquired for the benefit of a venture then about to end, and thus prolong by indirection its responsibilities and duties. The trouble about his conduct is that he excluded his coadventurer from any chance to compete, from any chance to enjoy the opportunity for benefit that had come to him alone by virtue of his agency. This chance, if nothing more, he was under a duty to concede. The price of its denial is an extension of the trust at the option and for the benefit of the one whom he excluded.

No answer is it to say that the chance would have been of little value even if seasonably offered. Such a calculus of probabilities is beyond the science of the chancery. Salmon, the real estate operator, might have been preferred to Meinhard, the woolen merchant. On the other hand, Meinhard might have offered better terms, or reinforced his offer by alliance with the wealth of others. Perhaps he might even have persuaded the lessor to renew the Bristol lease alone, postponing for a time, in return for higher rentals, the improvement of adjoining lots. We know that even under the lease as made the time for the enlargement of the building was delayed for seven years. All these opportunities were cut away from him through another's intervention. He knew that Salmon was the manager. As the time drew near for the expiration of the lease, he would naturally assume from silence, if from nothing else, that the lessor was willing to extend it for a term of years, or at least to let it stand as a lease from year to year. Not impossibly the lessor would have done so, whatever his protestations of unwillingness, if Salmon had not given assent to a project more attractive. At all events, notice of termination, even if not necessary, might seem, not unreasonably, to be something to be looked for, if the business was over and another tenant was to enter. In the absence of such notice, the matter of an extension was one that would naturally be attended to by the manager of the enterprise, and not neglected altogether. At least, there was nothing in the situation to give warning to any one that while the lease was still in being, there had come to the manager an offer of extension which he had locked within his breast to be utilized by himself alone. The very fact that Salmon was in control with exclusive powers of direction charged him the more obviously with the duty of disclosure, since only through disclosure could opportunity be equalized. If he might cut off renewal by a purchase for his own benefit when four months were to pass before the lease would have an end, he might do so with equal right while there remained as many years. He might steal a march on his comrade under cover of the darkness, and then hold the captured ground. Loyalty and comradeship are not so easily abjured.

We have no thought to hold that Salmon was guilty of a conscious purpose to defraud. Very likely he assumed in all good faith that with the approaching end of the venture he might ignore his coadventurer and take the extension for himself. He had given to the enterprise time and labor as well as money. He had made it a success. Meinhard, who had given money, but neither time nor labor, had already been richly paid. There might seem to be something grasping in his insistence upon more. Such recriminations are not unusual when coadventurers fall out. They are not without their force if conduct is to be judged by the common standards of competitors. That is not to say that they have pertinency here. Salmon had put himself in a position in which thought of self was to be renounced, however hard the abnegation. He was much more than a coadventurer. He was a managing coadventurer. For him and for those like him the rule of undivided loyalty is relentless and supreme. A different question would be here if there were lacking any nexus of relation between the business conducted by the manager and the opportunity brought to him as an incident of management. For this problem, as for most, there are distinctions of degree.

If Salmon had received from Gerry a proposition to lease a building at a location far removed, he might have held for himself the privilege thus acquired, or so we shall assume. Here the subject-matter of the new lease was an extension and enlargement of the subject-matter of the old one. A managing coadventurer appropriating the benefit of such a lease without warning to his partner might fairly expect to be reproached with conduct that was underhand, or lacking, to say the least, in reasonable candor, if the partner were to surprise him in the act of signing the new instrument. Conduct subject to that reproach does not receive from equity a healing benediction.

ANDREWS, J., (dissenting):

It may be stated generally that a partner may not for his own benefit secretly take a renewal of a firm lease to himself. Yet under very exceptional circumstances this may not be wholly true.

Where the trustee, or the partner or the tenant in common, takes no new lease but buys the reversion in good faith a somewhat different question arises. Here is no direct appropriation of the expectancy of renewal. Here is no offshoot of the original lease. The issue, then, is whether actual fraud, dishonesty, or unfairness is present in the transaction. If so, the purchaser may well be held as a trustee.

Some time before 1922 Mr. Elbridge T. Gerry became the owner of the reversion. He was already the owner of an adjoining lot on Fifth avenue and of four lots adjoining on Forty-Second Street, in all 11,587 square feet, covered by five separate buildings. Obviously, all this property together was more valuable than the sum of the value of the separate parcels. Some plan to develop the property as a whole seems to have occurred to Mr. Gerry. He arranged that all leases on his five lots should expire on the same day as the Bristol Hotel lease. Then in 1921 he negotiated with various persons and corporations seeking to obtain a desirable tenant who would put up a building to cover the entire tract, for this was the policy he had adopted. These negotiations lasted for some months. They failed. About January 1, 1922, Mr. Gerry's agent approached Mr. Salmon and began to negotiate with him for the lease of the entire tract. Upon this he insisted as he did upon the erection of a new and expensive building covering the whole. He would not consent to the renewal of the Bristol lease on any terms. This effort resulted in a lease to the Midpoint Realty Company, a corporation entirely owned and controlled by Mr. Salmon. For our purposes the paper may be treated as if the agreement was made with Mr. Salmon himself.

In many respects, besides the increase in the land demised, the new lease differs from the old. Instead of an annual rent of $55,000 it is now from $350,000 to $475,000. Instead of a fixed term of twenty years it may now be, at the lessee's option, eighty. Instead of alterations in an existing structure costing about $200,000 a new building is contemplated costing $3,000,000. Of this sum $1,500,000 is to be advanced by the lessor to the lessee, "but not to its successors or assigns," and is to be repaid in installments. Again no assignment or sale of the lease may be made without the consent of the lessor.

This lease is valuable. In making it Mr. Gerry acted in good faith without any collusion with Mr. Salmon and with no purpose to deprive Mr. Meinhard of any equities he might have. But as to the negotiations leading to it or as to the execution of the lease itself Mr. Meinhard knew nothing. Mr. Salmon acted for himself to acquire the lease for his own benefit.

I assume that where parties engage in a joint enterprise each owes to the other the duty of the utmost good faith in all that relates to their common venture. Within its scope they stand in a fiduciary relationship. I assume prima facie that even as between joint adventurers one may not secretly obtain a renewal of the lease of property actually used in the joint adventure where the possibility of renewal is expressly or impliedly involved in the enterprise. I assume also that Mr. Meinhard had an equitable interest in the Bristol Hotel lease. Further, that an expectancy of renewal inhered in that lease. Two questions then arise. Under his contract did he share in that expectancy? And if so, did that expectancy mature into a graft of the original lease? To both questions my answer is "No."

The one complaint made is that Mr. Salmon obtained the new lease without informing Mr. Meinhard of his intention. Nothing else. There is no claim of actual fraud. No claim of misrepresentation to any one. Here was no movable property to be acquired by a new tenant at a sacrifice to its owners. No good will, largely dependent on location, built up by the joint efforts of two men. Here was a refusal of the landlord to renew the Bristol lease on any terms; a proposal made by him, not sought by Mr. Salmon, and a choice by him and by the original lessor of the person with whom they wished to deal shown by the covenants against assignment or under-letting, and by their ignorance of the arrangement with Mr. Meinhard.

What then was the scope of the adventure into which the two men entered? It is to be remembered that before their contract was signed Mr. Salmon had obtained the lease of the Bristol property. Very likely the matter had been earlier discussed between them. The $5,000 advance by Mr. Meinhard indicates that fact. But it has been held that the written contract defines their rights and duties. Having the lease, Mr. Salmon assigns no interest in it to Mr. Meinhard. He is to manage the property. It is for him to decide what alterations shall be made and to fix the rents. But for 20 years from May 1, 1902, Salmon is to make all advances from his own funds and Meinhard is to pay him personally on demand one-half of all expenses incurred and all losses sustained "during the full term of said lease," and during the same period Salmon is to pay him a part of the net profits. There was no joint capital provided.

It seems to me that the venture so inaugurated had in view a limited object and was to end at a limited time. There was no intent to expand it into a far greater undertaking lasting for many years. The design was to exploit a particular lease. Doubtless in it Mr. Meinhard had an equitable interest, but in it alone. This interest terminated when the joint adventure terminated. There was no intent that for the benefit of both any advantage should be taken of the chance of renewal — that the adventure should be continued beyond that date. Mr. Salmon has done all he promised to do in return for Mr. Meinhard's undertaking when he distributed profits up to May 1, 1922. Suppose this lease, nonassignable without the consent of the lessor, had contained a renewal option. Could Mr. Meinhard have exercised it? Could he have insisted that Mr. Salmon do so? Had Mr. Salmon done so could he insist that the agreement to share losses still existed, or could Mr. Meinhard have claimed that the joint adventure was still to continue for 20 or 80 years? I do not think so. The adventure by its express terms ended on May 1, 1922. The contract by its language and by its whole import excluded the idea that the tenant's expectancy was to subsist for the benefit of the plaintiff. On that date whatever there was left of value in the lease reverted to Mr. Salmon, as it would had the lease been for thirty years instead of twenty. Any equity which Mr. Meinhard possessed was in the particular lease itself, not in any possibility of renewal. There was nothing unfair in Mr. Salmon's conduct.

I might go further were it necessary. Under the circumstances here presented, had the lease run to both the parties, I doubt whether the taking by one of a renewal without the knowledge of the other would cause interference by a court of equity.

So far I have treated the new lease as if it were a renewal of the old. As already indicated, I do not take that view. Such a renewal could not be obtained. Any expectancy that it might be had vanished. What Mr. Salmon obtained was not a graft springing from the Bristol lease, but something distinct and different — as distinct as if for a building across Fifth avenue. I think also that in the absence of some fraudulent or unfair act the secret purchase of the reversion even by one partner is rightful. Substantially this is such a purchase. Because of the mere label of a transaction we do not place it on one side of the line or the other. Here is involved the possession of a large and most valuable unit of property for 80 years, the destruction of all existing structures and the erection of a new and expensive building covering the whole. No fraud, no deceit, no calculated secrecy is found. Simply that the arrangement was made without the knowledge of Mr. Meinhard. I think this not enough.

POUND, CRANE, and LEHMAN, JJ., concur with CARDOZO, C.J., for modification of the judgment appealed from and affirmance as modified.

ANDREWS, J., dissents in an opinion in which KELLOGG and O'BRIEN, JJ., concur. Judgment modified, etc.

Notes and Questions

1. Notes

a. Louisa M. Gerry acquired the fee in 1891. At the time, it was subject to an 1860 lease to William H. Webb, who had constructed the Hotel Bristol. Mrs. Gerry died in 1920, and the property passed to her widower, Elbridge T. Gerry, then in his late 80s. See *City of New York v. Gerry*, 165 N.Y.S. 659 (Sup. Ct. 1917).

b. A description of some of the tenants in the building and of Mr. Salmon's actions as landlord may be found in *Waldorf-Astoria Segar Co. v. Salomon*, 95 N.Y.S. 1053 (App. Div. 1905); *Moses v. Salomon*, 135 N.Y.S. 408 (App. Div. 1912); and *New York v. Gerry*, 165 N.Y.S. 659 (Sup. Ct. 1917).

c. As the judges point out, the lease was commercially successful. For a year-by-year breakdown of revenues, expenses, and net profits on the lease, see *Appeal of Salmon*, 3 B.T.A. 723, 724 (Bd. Tx. App. 1926). Part of the reason for the success was an increased demand for office space in what is now midtown Manhattan:

> For many years prior to 1910, the retail business section in New York City had centered around Sixth Avenue and Twenty-third Street [about one mile south of the Hotel Bristol — Ed.]. The establishment of manufacturing industries in that section made it undesirable for retail businesses; they first located at Twenty-third Street and Broadway and moved up first to Thirty-fourth Street between Broadway and Fifth Avenue and spread north to Fifth Avenue up to Forty-second Street, and certain of the specialty shops moved up between Forty-second Street and Forty-eighth Street.
>
> All of these factors centered the attention of the real estate interests in New York City upon the locality of Forty-second Street and Fifth Avenue. Tenants on that street, in the vicinity of Fifth Avenue, were offered good bonuses for their leases. There were

many deals pending in 1913 and 1914, and long-term leases on desirable properties were in great demand.

Appeal of Salmon, 3 B.T.A. 723, 724 (Bd. Tx. App. 1926)

The total rent went from about $148,000 in 1910 to $194,000 in 1914 and the profits for those years went from $36,000 to $65,000.

A further reason for the profitability of the lease was that rents skyrocketed with the end of World War I. For example, in 1918, the last year of the war, rents were $237,000 and profits were $73,000. Two years later, rents were $317,000 and profits were $140,000. See *Appeal of Meinhard*, 3 B.T.A. 612 (Bd. Tx. App. 1926).

d. Apparently this litigation delayed the razing of the Bristol building. As soon as the decision of the Court of Appeals was final, the parties began the new project. Salmon elected to have Meinhard participate as a joint venturer rather than as a shareholder of Midpoint Realty. The new building, known as 500 Fifth Avenue, was designed by Shreve, Lamb & Harrison, which was then involved in designing the Empire State Building. The building was completed in 1930 and the delay cost the parties dearly. The Great Depression following the October 1929 stock market crash made the building unprofitable to operate. The construction of the building had been financed by $7,000,000 of bonds secured by the lease from Gerry. A $1,000 bond (a typical denomination for a bond like this) was trading as low as $110 in September 1932. By the end of World War II, the lessee was $1,500,000 behind in interest on the bonds and $400,000 behind in its rent. Meinhard died in 1931 and his interest was purchased by Salmon. Salmon died in the 1950s, his son died in 1986, and the building was then sold for $124,000,000.

e. The UPA (1914) was in effect in New York at the time of this case, although neither judge found the statute to be directly applicable. Section 21(1) provided, "Every partner must account to the partnership for any benefit, and hold as trustee for it any profits derived by him [or her] without the consent of the other partners from any transaction connected with the formation, conduct, or liquidation of the partnership or from any use by him [or her] of its property."

2. Reality Check

a. Do you agree with Chief Judge Cardozo that Meinhard "would naturally assume from silence, if from nothing else," that Mr. Gerry would extend the lease? Before the lease expired, did Meinhard ever inquire from Salmon or Gerry whether the lease was going to be renewed?

b. Chief Judge Cardozo writes, "A different question would be here if there were lacking any nexus of relation between the business conducted by the manager and the opportunity brought to him as an incident of management." How strong a "nexus of relation" must there be between the current lease and the new venture to impose fiduciary duties? Chief Judge Cardozo writes, "If Salmon had received from Gerry a proposition to lease a building at a location far removed, he might have held for himself the privilege thus acquired, or so we shall assume." This observation seems to conflate two qualities. The more salient is geographical. How far away from Fifth and 42d must the new venture be before Salmon is free to accept without Meinhard? The second quality is the identity of the offeror. If the adjoining properties were owned by someone other than Gerry could Salmon have proposed to Gerry and the other property owner to construct a building on both parcels without including Meinhard?

In this regard, consider the following facts:

In August 1901, eight months before the lease from Mrs. Gerry to Salmon, Salmon purchased the property at 19 W. 42d street, virtually next door to the Hotel Bristol. See *Stevens v. Salomon*, 79 N.Y.S. 136 (N.Y. Sup. Ct. 1902).

In 1903 Salmon purchased the property on the northwest corner of Sixth and 42d street, one block away from the Bristol. See *New York v. De Peyster*, 105 N.Y.S. 612 (App. Div. 1907).

In 1919 Salmon leased an apartment building called the Nevada at the corner of Broadway and 69th, about one and one-half miles from the Hotel Bristol. In 1925 Salmon purchased the land under the Nevada. See *Kentucky Farm & Cattle Co. v. C.I.R.*, 30 T.C. 1355 (1958).

By 1927 Salmon owned the land at 11 W. 42d street, directly next door to the Gerry property and had constructed a building on that land, called Salmon Tower, which was designed by the same architects that built the new building on the corner. Salmon Tower was used as the headquarters of Salmon's real estate holdings. See *Levy v. C.I.R.*, T.C.-Memo. 1960-22; *www.lookingforspace.com*.

By 1928 Salmon also owned the Bryant Park building at 55 W. 42d street, at the opposite end of the block from the Hotel Bristol. See *Levy v. C.I.R.*, T.C.-Memo 1960-22.

c. Does it make a difference that Salmon was an experienced real estate developer in New York, while Meinhard, "was in the woolen business and was entering upon his first venture in real estate"? See *Meinhard v. Salmon*, 229 N.Y.S. 345 (App. Div. 1928).

d. Does the way in which the parties describe their relationship determine the scope of the venture? The intermediate appellate court described a 1908 disagreement between the parties that resulted in a minor modification of the agreement:

> In correspondence that passed between the parties at the time, the defendant Salmon agreed, in consideration for such compensation, "to devote such time and attention as may be necessary for furthering our *joint interests* in the building," and in this same communication, dated February 8, 1908, the defendant stated that "this agreement shall bind both of us for the remainder of our *ownership of the lease* of the said premises." This letter also provided that, except as modified, the original agreement should continue in force.

Meinhard v. Salmon, 229 N.Y.S. 345, 348 (App. Div. 1928)

e. Does it matter that the industry practice, apparently a practice followed by Salmon, was and is to have each piece of property owned by a separate entity (typically a corporation)? This facilitates transfer (because only the stock of the owning corporation need be transferred rather than title to the real estate) and keeps each property's liabilities relegated to the assets of that property. It also allows each property to be separately financed and permits a developer such as Salmon to have different additional investors in each property. Thus an investor who participates with a developer in property *A* would not necessarily expect to participate with the same developer in property *B*.

3. Suppose

a. Suppose the court had used UPA (1914) section 21? Would the analysis or result have been different?

b. If this case arose today and a court applied UPA §404, would the result be clearer? See §404(b)(1) and cmt. 2. See also UPA §403(c).

c. What if this case were decided under contract principles? Would the implied covenant of good faith and fair dealing help Salmon? Meinhard? See UPA §404(d).

d. Suppose Meinhard based his claim on agency law rather than partnership law? See *Restatement (Third) of Agency* §§8.01, 8.02, 8.04, 8.10, and 8.11. Cf. §8.06.

The next case was decided under the UPA.

Baltrusch v. Baltrusch

83 P.3d 256 (Mont. 2004)

JAMES C. NELSON, J.

FACTUAL AND PROCEDURAL BACKGROUND

Otto and William are brothers who formed Baltrusch Land and Cattle Company around 1940. They expanded their company into several other businesses as the years progressed (all of which are hereinafter collectively referred to as "the Farm Partnership").

William devoted his time to managing the construction companies of the Farm Partnership, while Otto devoted his time to managing the farming enterprises of the Farm Partnership.

Also over the years, the Farm Partnership obtained the Connolly and Graham Leases (the Leases). These farm plots were small in comparison to the Farm Partnership's remaining acres. Otto's sons, Gary Baltrush (Gary) and Greg Baltrush (Greg) helped farm the Leases and knew the land well.

However, as years past, Otto realized that his leasing options on the Leases were no longer economically advantageous, so Otto asked Gary whether he and Greg would be interested in acquiring the Leases.

At that point, Gary asked the owner of one of the Leases about his prospects for acquiring the Leases. This owner testified that she was "satisfied to have Gary and Greg" farm the Leases.

After consulting with his attorney, Otto transferred the Leases to Gary and Greg, who formed G & G Corporation.

In forming G & G, Gary and Greg needed a tractor, amongst other equipment. Otto transferred a tractor owned by the Farm Partnership to G & G with the agreement that G & G would pay for it by paying Otto's hired hand's wages. G & G did so. In addition to running their business, both Gary and Greg continued to work on the farming enterprises of the Farm Partnership.

As William and Otto's relationship began to deteriorate, the Farm Partnership did as well and this litigation ensued. During this litigation, William and Otto entered into a Partial Settlement Agreement, whereby both agreed that the Farm Partnership properties would be divided equally between them, subject to their respective claims.

The District Court made many findings, ultimately ordering that the Farm Partnership properties, both real and personal, owned jointly by William and Otto be sold, with the proceeds divided equally.

Both Otto and William raised several issues and cross-issues on appeal based on the District Court's judgment. As they become applicable, additional facts will be discussed in accordance with each issue raised.

DISCUSSION

Did the District Court err in not finding Otto liable for (1) his conversion of Farm Partnership equipment; (2) his failure to charge rent for his sons' use of Farm Partnership equipment; and (3) personal credit card expenses for which the Farm Partnership paid?

While both parties raised the following arguments separately, because we hold that each argument targets a duty of loyalty owed, we address the following arguments together.

William argues that Otto's transfer of certain Farm Partnership equipment without receipt of any consideration constituted an act of self-dealing, which was a violation of Otto's duty of loyalty and duty of care. In support of this contention, William argues that specifically Otto had a duty to disclose the transfer and secure William's consent under [UPA §404(b)].

William further argues that Otto was obligated to account for the personal expenses he charged to the Farm Partnership. He maintains that Otto must prove that various charges were not for Otto's personal benefit. In so doing, William contends that the District Court erred in finding that assessment of Otto's obligation could not be accurately based on random accounting samples because the law only mandates that damages be proven with a reasonable degree of certainty.

Otto argues that he only transferred a tractor, for which he received compensation in the form of payment of a hired hand's wages and other services. All other purportedly transferred equipment, Otto maintains, were retained by the Farm Partnership and were never titled over to or used by G & G.

Otto further argues that the District Court properly refused to allow sampling of all of the invoices in the middle of the trial because William could have analyzed these invoices before and did not.

Partners owe a duty of loyalty and a duty of care to the partnership. [UPA §404(a)]. Specifically, a partner's duty of loyalty is limited to:

> account to the partnership and hold as trustee for it any property, profit, or benefit derivedf . . . from a use or appropriation by the partner of partnership property; and . . . refrain from competing with the partnership in the conduct of partnership business before the dissolution of the partnership without the consent of the other partners.

> [UPA §404(b)(1), (c)].

We hold that Otto did not breach his duty of loyalty, as his duty was to account to the Farm Partnership for any property or benefit he received from use or appropriation of Farm Partnership property and that he did just that. The record reflects that G & G paid for the tractor it received from Otto by paying the wages of Otto's hired hand. Further, to the extent that G & G used Farm Partnership equipment in performing B & B tasks, such use was minimal in comparison to the work G & G also provided the Farm Partnership. In addition, Otto's wife testified that she separated personal credit card charges from those of the Farm Partnership. Because William had ample opportunity to inspect the credit card invoices, we conclude that the District Court did not err in finding random sampling insufficient to charge Otto for all of the years of credit card expenses. Under Otto's duty of loyalty, he needed to account for the personal credit card expenses. He did that. Therefore, we hold that the District Court did not err in not finding Otto liable for: (1) the conversion of Farm Partnership equipment; (2) his failure to charge his sons rent for use of Farm Partnership equipment; and (3) personal credit card expenses paid by the Farm Partnership. Affirmed.

Notes and Questions

1. Reality Check

a. What was the breach of fiduciary duty alleged?

b. Why did the court find no violation?

2. Suppose

a. Suppose *Baltrusch* had been decided by the court that decided *Meinhard*. Would the analysis or result be different?

b. Suppose *Meinhard* had been decided by the court that decided *Baltrusch*. Would the analysis or result be different?

3. What Do You Think?

a. Should the UPA narrow the fiduciary duties among partners? Should it allow the partners to tailor the scope of those duties? Do you believe the UPA does these things? See UPA §§404(a), (b), (c), and (e), and 103 (b)(3), (4), and (5). Compare UPA (1914) §21(1) which states,

> Every partner must account to the partnership for any benefit, and hold as trustee for it any profits derived by him [or her] without the consent of the other partners from any transaction connected with the formation, conduct, or liquidation of the partnership or from any use by him [or her] of its property.

b. Do you think the standard of appropriate behavior should depend on the business context? Do some businesses have different (or higher or lower) customs than others? Note that at about the same time as the *Meinhard v. Salmon* litigation was commenced, Salmon was embroiled in a lawsuit concerning the property at the northwest corner of Sixth and 42d street, one block west of the property involved in *Meinhard v. Salmon*. Much of the other litigation turned on Salmon's strategic ownership of a strip of land 20 feet long and *1 inch wide*. See *Finch v. Unity Fee Co., Inc.*, 208 N.Y.S. 369 (App. Div. 1925). Do you suppose the Court of Appeals was aware of *Finch* and, if so, should it have informed their view of the equities in *Meinhard v. Salmon*?

f. Dissociation

Under UPA (1914), when any partner ceased to be a co-owner, the partnership itself ended. This created significant difficulties. One of the central advantages of the UPA is a consequence of treating a partnership as an entity separate from its partners. Now, when a partner ceases to be co-owner the partner is said to be *dissociated*.[1]

---

1. Those of you who have studied psychology may think that the UPA's drafters' choice of the term *dissociation* is especially ironic.

We will consider two main questions. First, when is a partner dissociated? In other words, when is a partner no longer a co-owner? See UPA §601. Second, what are the consequences of dissociation? See UPA §603.

A partner is dissociated in five settings. First, a partner is dissociated upon the happening of an agreed-upon event, such as repayment of a loan from the partner or the passage of time. Second, a partner is dissociated upon becoming a debtor in bankruptcy. This causes dissociation because partners are individually liable for the partnership's debts and if a partner is bankrupt, the partnership's creditors are hindered.

Third, a partner may be expelled. This power of expulsion is limited because partners have equal management rights and a power to expel would generally be considered antithetical to that equality of partners. The partners can unanimously agree in advance to vary the default rule against expulsion. Further, the partners can unanimously expel a partner where it is unlawful to continue the business with that partner or where a partner that is a corporation has dissolved. Finally, the partners can unanimously expel a partner who has transferred *all* of his or her transferable interest in the partnership. A court may also order a partner's expulsion on equitable grounds because the partner has "engaged in wrongful conduct that adversely and materially affected the partnership business" or the partner has "willfully or persistently committed a material breach of the partnership agreement or of a duty owed to the partnership or the other partners" or where the partner has "engaged in conduct relating to the partnership business which makes it not reasonably practicable to carry on the business in partnership with the partner." UPA §601(5). This last ground is also cause for the court to dissolve the partnership. See UPA §801(5)(ii).

Fourth, a partner's death causes dissociation. This is so because of the personal nature of the partnership relationship. The *partner* is no longer a co-owner, although the partner's estate and then the partner's heirs succeed to the partner's transferable interest. The final method for dissociation is, as death is, rooted in the personal nature of the partnership relationship. Any partner may become dissociated simply by express will. Note that this power *cannot* be contracted away by agreement. Even if the partners agree that they will not dissociate, any partner may do so by express will. UPA §§103(b)(6), 601(1), 602(a).

What happens when a partner is dissociated? Unless dissociation causes dissolution of the partnership (see section *g. Dissolution* below), the dissociated partner's interest is bought out by the partnership. The price is based upon a hypothetical value of the dissociating partner's account as if the partnership had dissolved on the date of dissociation and the assets sold for the greater of (1) liquidation value or (2) value as a going concern without the dissociated partner. UPA §701(b). The UPA's comments elaborate:

> The terms "fair market value" or "fair value" were not used because they are often considered terms of art having a special meaning depending on the context, such as in tax or corporate law.
>
> Liquidation value is not intended to mean distress sale value. Under general principles of valuation, the hypothetical selling price in either case should be the price that a willing and informed buyer would pay a willing and informed seller, with neither being under any compulsion to deal. The notion of a minority discount in determining the buyout price is negated by valuing the business as a going concern. Other discounts, such as for a lack of marketability or the loss of a key partner, may be appropriate, however.

Since the buyout price is based on the value of the business at the time of dissociation, the partnership must pay interest on the amount due from the date of dissociation until payment to compensate the dissociating partner for the use of his interest in the firm.

The Section 701 rules are merely default rules. The partners may, in the partnership agreement, fix the method or formula for determining the buyout price and all of the other terms and conditions of the buyout right. Indeed, the very right to a buyout itself may be modified, although a provision providing for a complete forfeiture would probably not be enforceable. *See* Section 104(a).

UPA §701, cmt. 3

This price is reduced by any amount the dissociating partner owes the partnership even if payment on that obligation is not presently due.

This has the effect of accelerating payment of amounts not yet due from the departing partner to the partnership, including a long-term loan by the partnership to the dissociated partner. Where appropriate, the amounts not yet due should be discounted to present value. A dissociating partner, on the other hand, is not entitled to an add-on for amounts owing to him by the partnership. Thus, a departing partner who has made a long-term loan to the partnership must wait for repayment, unless the terms of the loan agreement provide for acceleration upon dissociation.

UPA §701, cmt. 4

The buyout price is also reduced by any damages the partnership suffers if dissociation is wrongful. See UPA §§701 (c) and 602(c).

Dissociation by an individual partner is wrongful only if it breaches an express agreement or if, prior to the end of a term partnership, the partner dissociates by express will, by becoming a debtor in bankruptcy, or by expulsion by a court order. A wrongfully dissociating partner is liable for damages for wrongful dissociation (and may be additionally liable for other damages such as breaching the partnership agreement) and cannot participate in the winding up of the partnership if it is dissolved. UPA §§602(b) and 803.

Moreover, a dissociating partner's rights and duties toward the partnership change upon dissociation, regardless of whether the partner is dissociating rightfully or wrongfully. The dissociating partner's right to participate in the management of the partnership ends unless the partnership itself is being dissolved. Also, although the partner's duty of care and loyalty continue as to events prior to dissociation, the partner is under no further fiduciary obligation and, most pertinently, can enter into competition with the partnership.

g. Dissolution

It is imperative to keep in mind the distinction between the end of the partnership as a legal entity and the end of the business as a going concern. Typically the business of the partnership will continue even when the partnership itself ceases. In that case the business is transferred to another entity (i.e., another partnership or a corporation, LLC, or individual) and continues to do business. On occasion, though, the business will cease and the assets will be sold off piecemeal. The partnership may continue in a different business or it may end.

Under the UPA, a partnership *dissolves* (i.e., ceases to exist) in six instances. First, and most obviously, is where it becomes unlawful to continue all or substantially all of the partnership's business. See UPA §801(4). Second, the partnership dissolves if all the partners agree (UPA §801(2)(ii)). Third, if the partnership was formed for a particular length of time or for a particular undertaking (sometimes called a *term partnership*), dissolution occurs upon the expiration of that time or the completion of the undertaking (UPA §801(2)(iii)). Fourth, if a partner in a term partnership ceases to be a partner for certain reasons (essentially death, bankruptcy, or wrongfully withdrawing from the partnership) half the remaining partners may opt to dissolve the partnership. UPA §801(2)(i).

Fifth, courts have equitable power to dissolve a partnership on several grounds. The court may dissolve if "the economic purpose of the partnership is likely to be unreasonably frustrated" UPA §801(5)(i) or where "it is not otherwise reasonably practicable to carry on the partnership business in conformity with the partnership agreement" UPA §801(5)(iii). Turning from the partnership and its business to a problematic partner, the court may dissolve where it is "not reasonably practicable to carry on the business in partnership with that partner." UPA §801(5)(ii). Note that the court also has the power, in that instance, to remove the problematic partner (i.e., dissociate that partner) rather than dissolve the entire partnership. See UPA §601(5)(iii). The court also has the equitable power to dissolve the partnership at the behest of a transferee of a partner's interest. UPA §801(6).

Finally, the UPA gives each partner in a partnership at will (i.e., a partnership that is not a term partnership, see UPA §101(8)), the absolute right to compel the partnership's dissolution at any time. UPA §801(1). This preserves the partnership ethos that, absent an agreement otherwise, a partnership is a voluntary association of two or more people and hence may be ended when one of those people is no longer associated with the others. This power is of particular strategic importance because it gives each partner the ability to raise the possibility that the partnership's business may be sold off against the wishes of the other partners. As with most other default rules, this power can be varied or eliminated by agreement.

The next case involves the UPA provisions governing dissolution and liquidation.

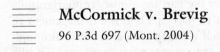

McCormick v. Brevig
96 P.3d 697 (Mont. 2004)

Jim Rice, J.

FACTUAL AND PROCEDURAL BACKGROUND

Joan [McCormick] and Clark [Brevig] are the children of Charles and Helen Brevig (hereinafter, "Charles" and "Helen"). In 1960 Charles purchased the Brevig Ranch outside of Lewistown from his parents.

Clark and his father owned the ranch in equal shares, and began operating the ranch as Brevig Land, Live & Lumber, a partnership, pursuant to a written agreement.

On October 28, 1982, Charles died unexpectedly after a short illness. Thereafter, pursuant to Charles' Last Will and Testament, Clark and Joan were appointed co-personal representatives and probated Charles' estate. Clark and Joan each received one-half of Charles' estate, which principally consisted of his 50 percent interest in the ranch and Partnership. As a result of the distributions, Clark then owned

75 percent of the ranch assets, and Joan 25 percent. A written partnership agreement was thereafter executed by Clark and Joan reflecting their respective 75/25 percent interests in the Partnership.

After Charles' death, Joan . . . made financial contributions to the new Partnership. She also maintained the Partnership's books and records. Meanwhile, Clark assumed responsibility for the day-to-day affairs of the ranch. Clark and Joan made management decisions together.

In 1984, Joan obtained an additional 25 percent in the Partnership, fully paying for this interest by the following year. For his share of the sale, Clark received a capital credit of approximately $60,000. From 1984 to 1993, Joan was listed as a 50/50 partner on all the tax returns for the Partnership.

Disagreements concerning management of the ranch, and particularly, management of the debt load on the ranch, caused Clark and Joan's relationship to deteriorate. By the early 1990s, cooperation between Clark and Joan regarding the operation of the ranch and securing of loans necessary to fund the ranch had essentially ceased, and they began looking for ways to dissolve the Partnership.

In 1995, Joan brought suit against Clark and the Partnership, alleging that Clark had converted Partnership assets to his own personal use, and sought an accounting of the Partnership's affairs. She also requested a determination that Clark had engaged in conduct warranting a decree of expulsion. Alternatively, Joan sought an order dissolving and winding up the Partnership.

[T]he District Court issued findings of fact and conclusions of law, finding that neither Clark nor Joan had dissociated from the Partnership, that Joan was a 50 percent partner and should be credited for any excess capital contributions she made to the Partnership, and that Clark was not entitled to receive compensation as a partner. The court further concluded that the Partnership should be dissolved and its business wound up. . . .

[T]he District Court ordered the value of Joan's interest in the Partnership to be determined following an appraisal conducted and paid for by the Partnership. Following such determination, Clark would have sixty days in which to purchase Joan's interest, or the Partnership assets would be liquidated and the net assets distributed to the partners.

[T]he District Court entered findings of fact and conclusions of law, accepting Blakely's findings and valuing Joan's interest in the Partnership at $1,107,672. Clark thereafter tendered this amount to Joan for the purchase of her interest, which Joan rejected. This appeal followed.

DISCUSSION

After ordering dissolution of the Partnership, did the District Court err by failing to order liquidation of the Partnership assets, and instead granting Clark the right to purchase Joan's Partnership interest at a price determined by the court?

Joan contends that when a partnership is dissolved by judicial decree, Montana's [UPA], requires liquidation by sale of partnership assets and distribution in cash of any surplus to the partners. In response, Clark asserts that there are other judicially acceptable methods of distributing partnership assets upon dissolution besides liquidating assets through a forced sale. For the reasons set forth below, we conclude that the [UPA] requires liquidation of partnership assets and distribution of the net surplus in cash to the partners upon dissolution entered by judicial decree when it is no longer reasonably practicable to carry on the business of the partnership.

We begin our analysis by reviewing the law of partnerships as it pertains to the issues in this case. [S]tatutory rules are merely default rules, which apply only in the absence of a partnership agreement to the contrary. [UPA §103]. In the present case, the parties do not dispute that the partnership agreement did not apply to situations involving a court ordered dissolution of a partnership.

Partnership law in Montana and throughout the United States has been primarily derived from the Uniform Partnership Act ("UPA (1914)"), which was originally promulgated by the Uniform Law Commissioners in 1914. Under the [UPA (1914)], the law of partnership breakups was couched in terms of dissolution. A partnership was dissolved and its assets liquidated upon the happening of specific events, the most significant of which was the death of a partner or any partner expressing a will to leave the partnership.

In 1993, our legislature significantly amended the [UPA (1914)] by adopting the [UPA]. Unlike the [UPA (1914)], [UPA] now provides two separate tracks for the exiting partner. The first track applies to the dissociating partner, and does not result in a dissolution, but in a buy-out of the dissociating partner's interest in the partnership. [UPA §601]. The term "dissociation" is new to the act, and occurs upon the happening of any one of ten events specified in [UPA §601]. Examples of events leading to dissociation include bankruptcy of a partner and death, [UPA §601(6)(i), (7)(i)], but does not include a judicially ordered dissolution of the partnership.

The second track for the exiting partner does involve dissolution and winding up of the partnership's affairs. [UPA §801] sets forth the events causing dissolution and winding up of a partnership, and includes the following:

Events causing dissolution and winding up of partnership business.

. . .

> (5) a judicial decree, issued upon application by a partner, that:
>
> (i) the economic purpose of the partnership is likely to be unreasonably frustrated;
>
> (ii) another partner has engaged in conduct relating to the partnership business that makes it not reasonably practicable to carry on the business in partnership with that partner; or
>
> (iii) it is not otherwise reasonably practicable to carry on the partnership business in conformity with the partnership agreement[.]

In this case, the District Court dissolved the Partnership pursuant to [UPA §801(5)]. In so doing, it recognized that, in the absence of a partnership agreement to the contrary, the only possible result under [UPA] was for the partnership assets to be liquidated and the proceeds distributed between the partners proportionately. The court reasoned, however, that the term "liquidate" had a variety of possible meanings, one of which was "to assemble and mobilize the assets, settle with the creditors and debtors and apportion the remaining assets, if any, among the stockholders or owners." Applying this definition, which the court had obtained from *Black's Law Dictionary,* the court concluded that a judicially ordered buy-out of Joan's interest in the Partnership by Clark was an acceptable alternative to liquidation of the partnership assets through a compelled sale.

It is true that this Court has previously utilized dictionaries when seeking to define the common use and meaning of terms. However, in this case, we conclude that it was not necessary for the District Court to resort to such devices. [UPA §807(a)] clearly provides that "[i]n winding up a partnership's business, the assets of the partnership must be applied to discharge its obligations to creditors, including partners who are creditors. Any surplus must be applied to pay *in cash* the net amount distributable to partners in accordance with their right to distributions pursuant to subsection (b)." (Emphasis added.) Furthermore, subsection (b) of the statute provides:

> Each partner is entitled to a settlement of all partnership accounts upon winding up the partnership business. In settling accounts among the partners, the profits and losses that result from the *liquidation of the partnership assets* must be credited and charged to the partners' accounts. The partnership shall make a distribution to a partner in an amount equal to that partner's positive account balance.

> (Emphasis added.)

Thus, the common purpose and plain meaning of the term "liquidation," as it is used in [UPA §807(b)] is to reduce the partnership assets to cash, pay creditors, and distribute to partners the value of their respective interest. This is all part of the process of "winding up" the business of a partnership and terminating its affairs.

Clark invites this Court to take a liberal reading of [UPA §807] and cites *Creel v. Lilly*, 729 A.2d 385 (Md. 1999), in support of the proposition that judicially acceptable alternatives exist to compelled liquidation in a dissolution situation.

However, of critical distinction between the facts in *Creel* and the case *subjudice* is the manner in which the partners exited the entity. In *Creel* one of the partners had died. Here, Joan sought a court ordered dissolution of the Partnership. Under [UPA], the death of a partner triggers the provisions of [UPA §701] which allows for the purchase of the dissociated partner's interest in the partnership, much like what was ordered in *Creel*. Conversely, a court ordered dissolution pursuant to [UPA §801(5)] as in this case, results in the dissolution and winding up of the partnership. Thus, *Creel* is both legally and factually distinguishable.

Accordingly, we conclude that when a partnership's dissolution is court ordered pursuant to [UPA §8-1(5)], the partnership assets necessarily must be reduced to cash in order to satisfy the obligations of the partnership and distribute any net surplus in cash to the remaining partners in accordance with their respective interests. By adopting a judicially created alternative to this statutorily mandated requirement, the District Court erred.

Affirmed in part, reversed in part, and remanded for further proceedings consistent with this opinion.

B. OTHER PARTNERSHIP FORMS

1. Joint Ventures

Up until now we have been concerned with what are sometimes called *general partnerships* to distinguish them from the entities we are about to discuss. In ordinary lawyer parlance, "partnership" and "general partnership" are synonymous. Four other entities are related to general partnerships and merit mention, at least briefly, here. First, a *joint venture* has both a business connotation and a more legal denotation. Business people (and lawyers as well) often refer to a joint venture as a narrowly focused business opportunity undertaken by a handful (quite often only two) established businesses. These preexisting businesses might be in unrelated fields or might even be competitors. The reason for their cooperation may be that a particular undertaking may be too expensive or too risky for one to take alone. Or, it may be that one of the participants has a contractual right to develop an opportunity (such as the right to certain intellectual property or the right to develop natural resources in a particular geographical area) but lacks the expertise to do so. In this popular description, a joint venture refers to the business opportunity itself rather than the entity through which the opportunity is developed. Even where the participants form a jointly owned corporation or LLC that undertakes the new business, that business may be called a joint venture.

A (slightly) more precise legal description of a joint venture is a partnership (i.e., two or more people co-owning a business for profit) formed for a limited time or for a limited purpose. In this sense, a joint venture is a kind of term partnership. The difference between a joint venture and a term partnership is, then, essentially one of degree with a joint venture being formed for a shorter time or more sharply defined purpose than a term partnership. Frequently, as well, a term partnership is distinguished from a joint venture by the number of partners. As the number grows much beyond three or four, courts are more likely to find that the entity is a term partnership rather than a joint venture.

So what? Once we have successfully identified an entity as being a joint venture and not a term partnership what difference does that make? Typically there are two kinds of differences. First, courts tend to give a narrower construction to the scope of the enterprise if they declare it to be a joint venture. This means that the participants' fiduciary duties are more circumscribed than if a term partnership were involved. This difference, as you may intuit, is largely circular: courts see a narrower purpose and declare it to be a joint venture; because it is a joint venture, the court will view its purpose or duration as being relatively narrow. Obviously courts do not need a separate term — joint venture — to make that kind of distinction. The second difference the characterization "joint venture" makes is a bit more substantive. Some courts find that a joint venture is not subject to all the strictures of the UPA. Which UPA rules do not apply to joint ventures? It depends upon which rules are in contention between the parties in the litigation. Mostly the courts find joint ventures make a difference when one party argues that a UPA default rule applies in its favor and where the court finds that applying such a rule would not be equitable. Declaring an entity to be a joint venture and, therefore, not subject to all of the UPA's scheme, allows the court to impose a result it finds fairer than the UPA rule in the particular instance. Note that the UPA states that it applies to joint ventures that meet the basic statutory definition of a partnership. See UPA §202, cmt. 2.

In the end, then, a joint venture is a somewhat chimerical entity. Labeling a business a joint venture may simply be a description or may be a way to ameliorate a strict application of the UPA.

2. Limited Partnerships

a. Background and Context

As you may recall from Chapter 2, before the mid-nineteenth century, states generally did not adopt corporations acts as we know them. Rather, each corporation had to obtain a charter from the state legislature. These were often expensive to obtain, and success in obtaining a charter frequently depended upon the entrepreneurs' having (or acquiring) sufficient political support in the state legislature. But in 1822, New York became the first state to enact a limited partnership act, which served some of the same purposes as incorporation. A limited partnership is a general partnership in which additional owners, called *limited partners,* invest money in return for interests that are different from those of the general partners. First, the limited partners' interests were freely transferable. Second, the limited partners had no management rights. Indeed, they were prohibited from taking part in the management of the business. They were strictly *silent partners.* Third, in recognition that the limited partners had no say in how their money was used or how the business was run, their liability was limited to the amount of their investment.

The underlying economic problem that limited partnerships (and corporations) solved was how to finance businesses that required more capital than a typical small business or trading firm. With the rise of factories in the early nineteenth century, the number of such businesses increased greatly. Raising sufficient capital in a general partnership was problematic because money was needed from a large number of individuals. Giving each a say in the partnership quickly became unwieldy, yet investors were reluctant to place all their assets at risk (as each general partner must do) in return for little or no management authority. The limited partnership allowed money to be raised from a small group of general partners, who would manage the enterprise, and from a much larger group of limited partners. An additional advantage was that a limited partnership could be formed simply by filing with the appropriate governmental authorities (usually a county clerk) rather than going to the expense of obtaining a charter from the legislature.

The Uniform Limited Partnership Act was first adopted in 1916. It was modernized a bit in 1976 and 1985 and was completely rethought in 2001. From the beginnings of limited partnerships until ULPA (1976), one of the most often-litigated questions was whether a limited partner had exercised sufficient control in the business so that he or she should be treated as a general partner and, hence, subjected to unlimited personal liability for partnership debts. The case law until 1976 was relatively strict that nearly any management activity by a limited partner (with the exception of voting to remove a general partner, which was a common right vested in the limited partners) was sufficient to subject the limited partner to personal liability. The 1976 and 1985 amendments broadened significantly, and controversially, the management powers of limited partners, while at the same time narrowing the instances in which limited partners would be held personally liable. A second trend in limited partnership law was the quest to find ways to insulate the general partner from liability. This was most frequently accomplished by having the general partner be a corporation, often with no other business purpose than to serve as the general partner. The corporation/general partner was, of course, controlled by the individuals who would otherwise have been the general partner. Thus, for all practical purposes, an entity was created in which all participants had limited liability. The advent of the limited liability limited partnership (see below) has made this status more secure.

Until the mid-1990s, limited partnerships were frequently used for enterprises that were expected to generate losses. Their use in this setting was because limited partnerships were taxed as partnerships, which allowed losses, to be passed through to the partners, unlike a corporation's losses, which must be carried over from year to year. After 1996 the LLC could serve the same functions as a limited partnership—limited liability for all participants and pass-through taxation—and so quickly supplanted the limited partnership as the entity of choice for new ventures.

b. The Current Setting

A limited partnership is similar to a general partnership but with one or more additional investors called limited partners. Unlike a general partnership, a limited partnership cannot be formed inadvertently but must be created through a simple filing with the secretary of state, much like a corporation is formed. Each limited partnership must have one or more general partners who function just as general partners in a general partnership do. The limited partners have curtailed governance powers and are not agents of the partnership. Their liability is limited to the amount of their investment and, ordinarily, their interests are freely transferable.

Today, the limited partnership is used primarily in two settings. First, it is used in a few very sophisticated commercial settings in which the participants find that mandatory corporate or LLC provisions require or prohibit agreements that the parties desire. An example is a venture capital firm that seeks to raise a large amount of money to invest in start-up enterprises. Such firms typically do not raise all the capital at once, but rather do so as each investment opportunity is found. One potential hazard of such an entity is the possibility that some investors will refuse or be unable to contribute additional funds. This will hamper the ability of the venture capital fund to make necessary investments, and so the venture capital firm's managers wish to ensure that the other investors have sufficient motivation to contribute when necessary. While, of course, such a provision can be created by contract, a more effective *in terrorem* method would be to make the investors' ownership interest *assessable* so that a failure to contribute on demand results in a forfeiture of the investor's entire ownership interest. Partnerships are a more reliable vehicle in which to provide for assessable interests than are corporations or LLCs, both of which have a presumption against assessability. It may also be easier, as a practical matter, to make those interests nontransferable in a limited partnership than in a corporation or LLC, which eliminates the possibility that recalcitrant investors will attempt to shirk their obligation to contribute more money by transferring their interest to someone else.

Second, limited partnerships are used as an estate-planning device. For example, parents establish a limited partnership to which the family business is contributed in return for all the ownership interest. The parents serve as general partners and are allocated 1 percent of the ownership interest. The parents serve as the limited partners, as well, at first and, over time, give portions of their limited partnership interests to their children. The limited partnership interests have strict restrictions on transfer (typically transfer is allowed only to other family members) and only the bare minimum of statutorily required governance interest. Because of the restrictions on transfer and the lack of management power, the value of each limited partnership interest should legitimately be discounted, often by as much as 30 or 40 percent, below the value of a similar economic interest without such restrictions. For example, suppose a family business is worth $1,000,000. Assume further that the business is owned by a family limited partnership as we have just described and that the general partnership interest is entitled to 1 percent while the limited partnership interest is divided into 99 portions, each entitled to 1 percent of the equity. If the parents give a

1 percent limited partnership interest to a child, the value of that gift is not $10,000 (i.e., 1% of $1,000,000) but probably closer to $6,000 to $7,000 because the child has no governance or management rights and cannot transfer the interest outside the family. In this way, the parents can effect an orderly transfer of family wealth to future generations (obviously the gifts can be made to grandchildren as easily as to children) while retaining complete control (which may or may not be a good thing from society's viewpoint but is almost always a good thing from a parent's viewpoint) and at a lower tax cost (because taxes are assessed based upon the legitimately discounted value of the interests transferred). While the Internal Revenue Service closely scrutinizes such family limited partnerships (because the tax savings reduce the public fisc), they have been largely upheld by the courts.

3. Limited Liability Partnerships and Limited Liability Limited Partnerships

Stop! Don't we have enough business entities, what with partnerships, limited partnerships, corporations, and LLCs, not to mention sole proprietorships? Well, for your information, we don't have enough business entities. We have to talk about two more, and that doesn't include such things as Massachusetts business trusts and joint stock companies, which are so arcane they're ignored altogether in this book.

The principal drawback of partnerships and limited partnerships, at least from the general partners' perspective, is unlimited personal liability for entity debts. The remaining two entities furnish limited liability to participants who otherwise would be personally liable. Limited liability partnerships (LLPs — NOT to be confused with LLCs) are general partnerships that have made an election to be treated as LLPs and that file a form with the secretary of state. See UPA §1001. The effect of becoming an LLP is to shield all partners from personal liability for all partnership debts. Partners remain liable for their own actions as partners. For example, a lawyer who is a partner in a law firm LLP remains liable to clients for his or her own malpractice. The partnership itself also remains liable for such malpractice. If, however, the assets of the malpracticing partner and the assets of the partnership are insufficient to cover the partnership's debts, the effect of the LLP election is to shield the other partners from liability for the shortfall. See UPA §306(c). The same liability shield is provided to general partners in a limited partnership that elects to become a limited liability limited partnership (LLLP); the limited partners, of course, already have limited liability.

The impetus to create LLPs and LLLPs came before LLCs were widely available. Since 1996, LLCs have supplanted LLPs and LLLPs. Nonetheless, LLPs and LLLPs remain niche entities that serve a particular, though narrow, purpose.

C. FEDERAL SECURITIES LAWS

If a partnership interest is a security then the federal registration requirements (and various exemptions) and the antifraud provisions of Rule 10b-5 all apply. Further, the periodic reporting requirements for public companies and the federal regulation of proxy solicitations may also apply if a partnership is a security. None of the federal statutes specifically names partnership interests, which may suggest that Congress did not intend them to be securities because partnerships were certainly well-known business entities when Congress was adopting the Securities Act of 1933 and the Securities Exchange Act of 1934. No Supreme Court case has decided the question. The Supreme Court would almost certainly apply the test from *SEC v. W.J. Howey Co.*, 328 U.S. 293 (1946). Under the cases interpreting *Howey*, the court must decide whether there was (1) an investment of money, (2) in a common enterprise in which the investor was led to expect profits, (3) primarily from the efforts of the promoter or a third party. In analyzing partnerships, the key element will be the "efforts of the promoter or a third party."

The principal case analyzing general partnerships under the securities laws is *Williamson v. Tucker*, 645 F.2d 404 (5th Cir.) *cert. denied*, 454 U.S. 897 (1981), in which the court held that a partnership interest is a security under *Howey* only if the investor can establish one of three elements:

1. That the agreement among the parties leaves so little management power in the investor's hands that the investor is analogous to a limited partner; or
2. The investor is so inexperienced and unknowledgeable in business affairs that he or she cannot intelligently exercise his or her managerial powers; or
3. The investor is so dependent upon some unique entrepreneurial or managerial talent of the promoter that the investor cannot replace the promoter or otherwise meaningfully exercise his or her managerial powers.

Very few cases have held that interests in a general partnership are securities. On the other hand, the *Williamson* court's first factor suggests that it considered limited partnership interests to be included in the definition of "security." In general, courts have held limited partnerships to be subject to the securities laws. One question that remains open is whether, with the expansion of limited partner power under the 1976, 1985, and especially under the 2001 revisions of the Uniform Limited Partnership Act, courts will hold that limited partners have sufficient management power that they should be considered analogously to general partners and thus denied the protection of the securities laws. This rationale seems especially likely where the limited partners are sophisticated commercial entities or investors rather than in the family limited partnership setting.

D. TERMS OF ART IN THIS CHAPTER

At-will partnership	General partnerships	Silent partners
Charging order	*Howey* test	Term partnership
Dissociated	Joint venture	*Williamson* test
Dissociation	Limited partnership	
Dissolution	Partnership	

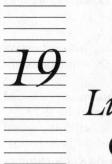

19

Limited Liability Companies

A. BACKGROUND AND CONTEXT

The final business entity we will consider is the limited liability company (LLC). It is probably the most popular choice for newly formed businesses. The reason is that it combines limited liability for the firm's owners and managers with pass-through taxation. Corporations also provide limited liability but are taxed as separate entities, leading to a double taxation of corporate profits, once at the corporate level and again when the corporation pays dividends to its shareholders. Partnerships provide pass-through taxation (i.e., profits are not taxed at the partnership level; profits and losses are reported directly by each partner) but, classically, do not provide limited liability. While Subchapter S corporations, limited partnerships with a corporate general partner, limited liability partnerships, and limited liability limited partnerships can all approximate the advantages of LLCs, none is as flexible and all are more cumbersome than the LLC. Chapter 20 will treat in greater detail the question of choosing the appropriate form for doing business.

The following excerpt explains why the LLC was developed. Professor Hamill sees three threads in the story. In her view, the motivation for developing the LLC began with the disparate tax treatment of corporations and partnerships. Second, certain kinds of businesses perceived a need in the 1970s for an entity that combined complete limited liability and pass-through tax treatment. Finally, lawyers representing those and other businesses brought their drafting and lobbying skills to bear in convincing the states and the IRS to permit the LLC.

Susan Pace Hamill, *The Origins Behind the Limited Liability Company* *
59 Ohio St. L.J. 1459 (1998)

The explanation behind the LLC's birth boils down to innovative professionals creating solutions when the current legal system fails to meet client needs. The particular client whose needs sparked the invention of the LLC was an independent oil

---

* The material in this excerpt has been rearranged from the original. ED.

explorer experiencing increased opportunities in international oil and gas exploration during the turbulent 1970s, when the major producers struggled with problems related to the Middle Eastern oil supply.

[T]he LLC's...roots can be traced to the first modern income tax, enacted within months of Congress' ratification of the Sixteenth Amendment in 1913.... Corporations, as well as unincorporated organizations deemed associations, would bear an entity level tax just like individuals while partnerships would bear no tax, creating flow-through taxation to the partners. Congress viewed the corporation as an appropriate target for an income tax due to its formal creation by and recognition as a separate entity by state issued charters. The ordinary general partnership, viewed as an inappropriate target for the tax, involved no state law filing and constituted a mere aggregate of the partners, each facing personal liability exposure with management and dissolution powers over the partnership.

The increasing level of dependence on foreign oil throughout the last half of the twentieth century, followed by the abrupt and severe reduction of that supply by the early 1970s, forced the major oil producers and other participants in the oil industry to seek crude oil from alternative sources. This need for oil outside traditional Middle Eastern sources created a market for greater numbers of independent oil producers than had ever existed in prior years. In order to secure the necessary capital to conduct drilling operations, many of these independent producers sold [limited] partnership interests to investors....

In the mid-1970s, a few entrepreneurial-minded attorneys and accountants representing a U.S. independent oil and gas company invented the LLC, [and] successfully persuaded the Wyoming legislature in 1977 to enact the first LLC statute.... Armed with the enacted LLC legislation, the Hamilton Brothers Oil Company...filed a request with the IRS ... asking for a favorable partnership classification ruling. The IRS, reluctant to allow a domestic entity with corporate limited liability partnership classification, predictably stalled the ruling process. After a great deal of correspondence between Hamilton Brothers Oil Company's representatives and the IRS, an additional request for a ruling filed by the Wyoming Secretary of State and supported by the Governor, as well as another correspondence involving the Commissioner of the IRS and Wyoming Senators, the IRS finally issued a favorable private letter ruling to Hamilton Brothers Oil Company regarding its Wyoming LLC [in] 1980, more than three years after the initial request.

Florida enacted an LLC statute in 1982, presumably to lure capital into the state.... [T]he IRS...stated that it would study the effect limited liability should have on entity classification. That study took over five years and predictably, while its tax status remained in limbo, further growth in LLC legislation and businesses using LLCs stopped; no other states enacted statutes and few businesses (less than one hundred) chose to become LLCs. As long as its ability to be taxed as a partnership remained questionable, the LLC stood no chance of expanding throughout the country.

[In] 1988, the IRS issued Revenue Ruling 88-76, a public interpretation of the law all taxpayers can rely upon, permitting the Wyoming LLC to secure partnership classification despite the presence of limited liability. Although a clear watershed in the LLC's development, the Wyoming Revenue Ruling's requirements, rendering interests in an LLC very difficult to transfer and the LLC itself highly dissolvable, limited the practical use of LLCs to small, closely held businesses and joint ventures.

After the IRS's landmark decision to recognize the LLC's right to be taxed under the partnership provisions, the states slowly and cautiously started to enact legislation allowing for the formation of LLCs. It took until 1990 — the year Colorado and Kansas both passed LLC statutes — for any states to step forward and recognize the creation of LLCs in light of the IRS's revenue ruling.

The Tax Reform Act of 1986, in addition to destroying the market for [limited] partnership syndications, materially increased the tax burden imposed on corporations.... Business ventures expecting significant taxable income, which also wished to obtain direct statutory limited liability without facing the restrictions inherent in a Subchapter S election, had, for the first time, strong reasons to support the LLC. On behalf of many clients conducting business in ventures recognizing substantial taxable income, the second group of LLC proponents pushed for more flexibility on the partnership classification front and encouraged the states to enact statutes.

From 1992 through 1996, LLC legislation swept across the country. By the end of 1994, [o]nly three remaining states were without LLC legislation, and by the close of 1996, they had passed statutes establishing the LLC in all U.S. jurisdictions. In an incredible stampede that took less than twenty years, most of it occurring from 1990 through 1996, LLCs traveled from an obscure unknown business form in 1977 to a well-recognized alternative for doing business.

[In] 1995, the IRS announced a proposal to eliminate the partnership classification rules by allowing certain unincorporated businesses, including domestic LLCs, to elect partnership or corporate taxation, and the rise of the LLC contributed greatly to this development. The public overwhelmingly favored the proposal. [In] 1996, the final regulations, dubbed the "Check-the-Box" regulations, permanently eliminated all partnership classification considerations for LLCs and all other domestic unincorporated entities. All persons filing under an LLC statute automatically receive partnership taxation. The elimination of all partnership classification issues allows those using LLCs the freedom to craft the dissolution, transferability and management provisions to satisfy business goals alone.

NOTES AND QUESTIONS

1. Reality Check

a. What were the tax and non-tax motivations that led to the development of the LLC?

b. Why did states become eager to enact LLC statutes in the early 1990s?

c. What advantages do LLCs have over other entities?

2. What Do You Think?

a. Much of the debate surrounding LLCs has centered on whether business entities that offer limited liability should also receive pass-through tax treatment. Do you think the two concepts should be related? Why have these two concepts been linked?

b. In another part of her article, Professor Hamill suggests that the success of the LLC form has led to other new entities such as the LLP and LLLP and that this fragmentation is confusing and unnecessary. Do you agree? Do you think business firms need so many entity choices? If change is needed, what change should be imposed? Who should impose such changes? The states? The federal government? The bar?

B. THE CURRENT SETTING

1. Introduction

The limited liability company (LLC) is an entity that has important elements of both corporations and partnerships. The formation requirements are similar to those of corporations, involving a public filing of a brief document. The LLC also provides limited liability both for owners and managers, as in a corporation. On the other hand, the default governance provisions of LLCs give management rights to all owners, in similar fashion to a partnership. As with partnership statutes, LLC statutes anticipate that the parties will typically supplement or supplant the default provisions with a written agreement. Many if not most operating agreements create a management structure similar to that of a corporation, giving the owners circumscribed management powers and giving control to managers who need not be owners. LLCs are treated like partnerships under the Internal Revenue Code, although the parties could elect to be taxed as a corporation (under the so-called check the box provision of the Code) instead.

The philosophy of one of the most important LLC statutes, that of Delaware, is discussed in the following excerpt:

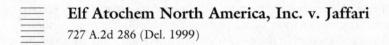

Elf Atochem North America, Inc. v. Jaffari
727 A.2d 286 (Del. 1999)

VEASEY, C.J.

The certificate of formation is a relatively brief and formal document that is the first statutory step in creating the LLC as a separate legal entity. The certificate does not contain a comprehensive agreement among the parties, and the statute contemplates that the certificate of formation is to be complemented by the terms of the [limited liability company agreement ("Agreement")].

GENERAL SUMMARY OF BACKGROUND OF THE ACT

The phenomenon of business arrangements using "alternative entities" has been developing rapidly over the past several years. Long gone are the days when business planners were confined to corporate or partnership structures.

The Delaware Act was adopted in October 1992.... The Delaware Act has been modeled on the popular Delaware LP Act. In fact, its architecture and much of its wording is almost identical to that of the Delaware LP Act. Under the Act, a member of an LLC is treated much like a limited partner under the LP Act.

In August 1994, nearly two years after the enactment of the Delaware LLC Act, the Uniform Law Commissioners promulgated the Uniform Limited Liability Company Act (ULLCA). Despite its purpose to promote uniformity and consistency, the ULLCA has not been widely popular. In addition to the ULLCA, a Prototype Limited Liability Company Act ("Prototype Act") was drafted by the Subcommittee on Limited Liability Companies of the ABA Section of Business Law. The Prototype Act was released in the Fall of 1993 and has formed the basis for several LLC statutes enacted since that time.

POLICY OF THE DELAWARE ACT

The basic approach of the Delaware Act is to provide members with broad discretion in drafting the Agreement and to furnish default provisions when the members' agreement is silent. The Act is replete with fundamental provisions made subject to modification in the Agreement (*e.g.* "unless otherwise provided in a limited liability company agreement....").

For example, members are free to contract among themselves concerning management of the LLC, including who is to manage the LLC, the establishment of classes of members, voting, procedures for holding meetings of members, or considering matters without a meeting.

Although business planners may find comfort in working with the Act in structuring transactions and relationships, it is a somewhat awkward document for this Court to construe and apply.... To understand the overall structure and thrust of the Act, one must wade through provisions that are prolix, sometimes oddly organized, and do not always flow evenly.

FREEDOM OF CONTRACT

Section 18-1101(b) of the Act provides that "it is the policy of [the Act] to give the maximum effect to the principle of freedom of contract and to the enforceability of limited liability company agreements." Accordingly, the following observation relating to limited partnerships applies as well to limited liability companies:

> The Act's basic approach is to permit partners to have the broadest possible discretion in drafting their partnership agreements and to furnish answers only in situations where the partners have not expressly made provisions in their partnership agreement. Truly, the partnership agreement is the cornerstone of a Delaware limited partnership, and effectively constitutes the entire agreement among the partners with respect to the admission of partners to, and the creation, operation and termination of, the limited partnership. Once partners exercise their contractual freedom in their partnership agreement, the partners have a great deal of certainty that their partnership agreement will be enforced in accordance with its terms.

> Martin I. Lubaroff & Paul Altman, *Delaware Limited Partnerships* §1.2 (1999) (footnote omitted).

In general, the commentators observe that only where the agreement is inconsistent with mandatory statutory provisions will the members' agreement be invalidated. Such statutory provisions are likely to be those intended to protect third parties, not necessarily the contracting members....

The two model or uniform LLC statutes mentioned in *Elf Atochem North America, Inc.*, have not been widely adopted. Some states, such as Delaware and New York, created their LLC statute essentially by modifying their limited partnership acts (which are typically based on the Revised Uniform Limited Partnership

Act). Other states, such as California, Illinois, Texas, and Ohio, created their LLC statute by amalgamating their limited partnership act with their corporations statute. Nonetheless, there is much more substantive uniformity among the states than the variety of LLC statutes would suggest. Virtually every LLC statute has common elements such as: (1) a minimal filing requirement to create an LLC; (2) default management and capital structures giving each owner voting rights and rights to distributions; (3) free transferability of an owner's financial interest but not his or her management interest; and (4) a specific grant of power to the participants to vary most of the default rules by written agreement.

2. Formation

a. Statutory Requirements

To create an LLC, every state requires the promoters to file a brief document with the secretary of state. This document is usually called the articles (or certificate) of organization or the articles (or certificate) of formation. The articles require the promoters to state the name of the LLC, which must include the words or abbreviations, *Limited Liability Company* or *LLC* and, in some states, *LC Limited* or *Ltd.* are permissible. The articles also require a statement of the LLC's purposes. The purpose can include any lawful business, except those expressly prohibited or subject to other governmental regulation such as banking and insurance. The LLC statute of most states uses the term *purpose* rather than *business* to permit LLCs to engage in not-for-profit enterprises. Because the LLC is an artificial entity, the statutes uniformly require the articles to state the registered office and registered agent for service of process. Many state statutes require the articles to state the LLC's duration although increasingly the trend is to require such a statement only where the duration is not perpetual.[1] The articles of organization also are required to state whether the LLC will be managed by the owners (usually called "members") or by managers (who need not be members) and, in either case, the articles must state the names of the people who will manage the LLC initially. LLC statutes usually specify that the LLC comes into existence upon filing of the articles or upon a later date specified in the articles.

b. Promoter Liability and Defective Formation

A promoter who incurs personal liability prior to the formation of an LLC should not be relieved of that liability simply because the LLC comes into existence later. Nonetheless a promoter and another party should be able to agree in advance to a novation when the LLC is formed and accepts a liability or should be able to agree that the promoter will remain primarily or secondarily liable after the LLC is formed and accepts a liability. The underlying policy seems analogous to that of promoters of corporations. See Chapter 5 for a more detailed discussion of promoter liability.

---

1. Most state LLC statutes were adopted at a time when partnership tax treatment was available only where the LLC's duration was, at least in theory, not perpetual. Since 1996 LLCs may have perpetual duration and still receive pass-through taxation.

On occasion, a promoter will contract with another party on behalf of the LLC even though the LLC has not yet come into existence. Where both parties know that the LLC has not been formed should the agreement be treated as an agreement that binds the promoter? Should it be treated as an agreement that the promoter will use best efforts to form the LLC and cause the LLC to accept an offer from the other party? Should the answer turn on the parties' intention? What if their intentions differ from each other? What if their intention is not clear? Are there larger interests that should override the parties' intention?

What about the setting where the promoter knows that the LLC has not been formed but the other party does not know? Should the promoter be personally liable on the agreement? Where both parties believe, erroneously, that the LLC has been formed, the de facto entity doctrine and the estoppel doctrine might govern by analogy to the defective incorporation settings. Almost no state has a provision in its LLC statute analogous to §2.04 of the MBCA, which covers defective incorporation. See Chapter 5 for a more detailed discussion of defective incorporation.

P.D.2000, L.L.C. v. First Financial Planners, Inc.
998 S.W.2d 108 (Mo. App. 1999)

ROBERT E. CRIST, SENIOR JUDGE.

The relevant facts are that Ray Sulka, a resident of California, developed information systems and implemented computer technology advancements for individuals and companies in various industries. He was also a financial planner, who in February 1996 became a registered agent of defendant, First Financial Planners, Inc. (hereinafter FFP), a Missouri corporation founded and controlled by Roy Henry. In June 1996, Sulka and Henry entered into an agreement for Sulka to evaluate FFP's computer needs and to structure a plan for technological improvements. Sulka fully performed under this agreement and submitted a report to Henry.

On July 21, 1996, Sulka and Henry executed a second agreement on behalf of their respective corporations, P.D.2000, L.L.C. (hereinafter P.D.2000) and FFP. Henry signed as president of FFP and Sulka signed as president of P.D.2000. The agreement was titled "INDEPENDENT CONTRACTOR AGREEMENT" and provided for P.D.2000 to develop a security system and a financial planning system for FFP as well as an intranet communication structure for FFP branch offices and certain clients (hereinafter the contract). The contract provided that P.D.2000 would receive $25,000.00 per month for services performed and P.D.2000 would pay all expenses incurred in performing the contract out of that amount.

The contract stated that FFP "acknowledges that [P.D.2000] was in the process of forming an LLC in the state of Nevada."

Sulka began performing services for FFP immediately after entering into the contract in July 1996. FFP made two payments under the contract, making the checks payable to "Sulka West." On September 26, 1996, FFP terminated the contract with P.D.2000 without paying the termination fee.

On October 7, 1996, the articles of incorporation for P.D.2000 were filed with Nevada. On that same date, P.D.2000 executed a formal ratification of Sulka's pre-incorporation activities.

P.D.2000 then brought the present action against FFP for breach of contract and sought the termination fee pursuant to the contract. At trial, FFP's defense was that P.D.2000 did not have the capacity to enforce the contract. The jury found in favor of P.D.2000 and assessed damages at $300,000.00. The trial court entered judgment in accordance with the verdict in the amount of $359,744.80, which consisted of damages plus court costs and prejudgment interest.

In its sole point on appeal, FFP contends the trial court erred in denying its motions for directed verdict and for judgment notwithstanding the verdict, because P.D.2000 lacked the capacity to contract or to enforce the contract. It argues that the *Restatement (Second) of Agency* section 88 (1958) precludes an action on a pre-organization agreement by a subsequently formed entity, i.e. P.D.2000, when the other party to the contract, i.e. FFP, has withdrawn from the contract prior to its ratification.

Bader Automotive & Industrial Supply Co. Inc., v. Green, 533 S.W.2d 695 (Mo. App. 1976), is on point. In that case, in 1971, plaintiff, Richard Bader and defendant, Glynn Green, entered into an employment agreement containing a covenant not to compete. *Id.* at 696-697. At the time the agreement was executed, Bader had not incorporated his business and signed the agreement in his own name. *Id.* at 697. Green worked as an employee selling auto body supplies for Bader until 1973 and received his income on checks issued by the corporation during that time. *Id.* at 697-698. Green attempted to avoid the terms of the agreement, particularly the covenant not to compete, by claiming that the corporation could not ratify a contract that had been executed before the date of incorporation. *Id.* at 699. This court responded, "It is a well settled principle that '[w]here one contracts with a body assuming to act as a corporation or by a name distinctly implying a corporate existence, both parties in a suit upon the contract are usually estopped from denying such corporate existence.'" *Id.* (quoting *Schneider v. Best Truck Lines, Inc.*, 472 S.W.2d 655, 659 (Mo. App. 1971)).

Here, after it was incorporated, P.D.2000 ratified the contract between Henry and Sulka. The fact that the contract was signed by Sulka, who was the organizer of the corporation was sufficient to bind the corporation. *See Bader*, 533 S.W.2d at 699. Thus, although the contract was executed by the parties prior to P.D.2000's formal corporate birth, it became the contract between FFP and P.D.2000 after formation of the corporation and upon its adoption by the corporation. *See id.*

FFP relies on *Davane, Inc. v. Mongreig*, 550 N.E.2d 55 (Ill. App. 1990), for the proposition that if a party enters into a contract with an agent, who is unauthorized because its principal does not exist at the time of contracting, that party may withdraw from the contract.

Davane, however, is distinguishable from the case before us. Here, unlike the defendants in *Davane*, FFP had full knowledge of the corporate status of P.D.2000 at the time of contracting. FFP was aware that P.D.2000 was not incorporated and the contract specifically stated that P.D.2000 was in the process of incorporating in Nevada. FFP also knew that Sulka was the agent of P.D.2000 when he signed the contract and that he would be the person to perform services under the contract. In addition, similar to the employment situation in *Bader*, P.D.2000 had partly performed under the contract when FFP repudiated it. Sulka began working pursuant to the contract immediately after its execution and was issued two paychecks by FFP. He moved to St. Louis and signed a one-year lease for an apartment. He took the requisite steps to incorporate in Nevada. In contrast, in *Davane*, when the defendants withdrew, the contract was executory in nature because title to the property had not been transferred. Thus, we find the *Davane* decision is not controlling.

Given the facts of this case, FFP is estopped to deny the existence of P.D.2000. The trial court did not err in refusing to grant FFP's motions for directed verdict and for judgment notwithstanding the verdict.

The judgment of the trial court is affirmed.

JAMES A. PUDLOWSKI, P.J. and CLIFFORD H. AHRENS, J.: Concur.

Notes and Questions

1. Reality Check

a. What two facts were central to the court's holding?

b. The court notes that the contract said that "[P.D. 2000] was in the process of forming an LLC in the state of Nevada." Is that accurate?

2. Suppose

a. Suppose both parties believed the LLC had been formed. What if only Henry believed the LLC had been formed? Finally, suppose only Sulka believed the LLC had been formed. Would the result in each of these settings be different from the result in the opinion?

b. Would the result have been different if Sulka had not partially performed? Why?

c. Imagine that Sulka's partial performance had been damaging to Henry. Could Henry recover from Sulka personally or would Henry have been limited to recovering only from the LLC?

d. Suppose the LLC had been formed and had adopted the contract shortly before Henry terminated the contract. Would the result or analysis be different?

e. Could Sulka personally have enforced the contract if the LLC had never been formed?

3. What Do You Think?

a. The court chose between two rules. One rule estops a party who knowingly contracts with a nonexistent entity from terminating the contract. The other rule prohibits enforcement of a contract with a nonexistent entity where the other party has terminated the agreement prior to the entity's creation. How did the court choose between the two rules? Do you think it made the right choice?

4. You Draft It

a. Draft a contract clause that makes it clear that FFP is bound immediately upon executing the contract.

b. Draft a contract clause that makes it clear that FFP is only bound if an LLC is formed and ratifies the contract.

c. Operating Agreements

An LLC's operating agreement is the detailed agreement among all the members and sometimes all the managers. It deals with such matters as the names of the members and their respective economic interests; the managers (if any) and how power will be allocated between members and managers and, among the managers, whether there will be particular officers with delegated duties. An LLC's operating agreement is analogous to a partnership agreement. Sometimes the LLC itself is a party to the agreement. The operating agreement must be distinguished from other agreements that some members or managers may have with one another. These agreements, while they may have important consequences for the operation of the LLC, are not binding on LLC participants who are not parties. Therefore, these nonunanimous agreements are like shareholder agreements in the corporate setting. Only the articles of organization and the operating agreement officially control the LLC.

3. Financing

a. Capital Contributions

The LLC statutes do not require any minimum amount to be contributed before an LLC may begin doing business. The members are free to decide among themselves how much money will be contributed in total and how much of that total each member will contribute. The members need not contribute equal amounts. The LLC statutes also provide that any form of consideration can be accepted by the LLC. This means that cash, tangible and intangible property, promissory notes, services rendered, and agreements to render services in the future can all be valid consideration.

b. Allocations and Distributions to Members

Allocation and distribution are two different, though related, concepts. Allocation refers to assigning the LLC's profits and losses among its members. Distribution refers to the transfer of LLC property (usually cash) to members. A distribution may reflect a share of members' profits or an advance to the members of anticipated profits, or it may reflect a repurchase of some or all of a member's interest. Because the promoters of LLCs usually elect to have the LLCs taxed as partnerships, which pass through to the owners both profits and losses, the members must decide how to allocate losses as well as profits among themselves. Frequently losses are allocated differently than profits because of differing motivations among the participants. For example, a member who also intends to be the primary manager of an LLC may agree with the other members that he or she will receive more of the profits and less of the losses than the other members in recognition of the efforts he or she will expend in running the business. LLC statutes typically provide as a default rule that profits shall be allocated in proportion to each member's contribution and that losses shall be allocated in proportion to each member's share of the profits.

Allocation is principally important only to the LLC's members. By contrast, distribution is also important to the LLC's creditors because property distributed to members is obviously unavailable to satisfy creditors' claims. For this reason, and also because property in the hands of members becomes difficult or impossible to retrieve for the creditors' benefit, LLC statutes restrict an LLC's power to make distributions. Most states use the "equity insolvency" test, which prohibits distributions if, afterward, the LLC will be unable to pay its debts as they become due. Most states also combine that test with some version of the "bankruptcy insolvency" test under which the LLC is prohibited from making a distribution if afterward its assets are less than its liabilities. A good faith analysis of the LLC's financial position and the effect a distribution will have on that position should insulate the LLC decision makers from liability under these statutes.

Members have no statutory right to compel a distribution. The operating agreement sometimes sets out a rule such as one that requires the LLC to distribute the maximum amount permissible under the statute. Another common rule requires the LLC to distribute cash sufficient to cover members' tax liability on the profits allocated to them. Alternatively, the operating agreement frequently leaves the question of distributions to the discretion of the managers. Both the drafter of the operating agreement (typically a lawyer) and the persons who control the LLC (whether members or managers) must be careful when deciding on a distribution policy for the LLC. Not only must the LLC comply with the statutory restrictions on paying distributions, but the tax consequences of distributions to the members must be taken into account as well. If the LLC will show a loss for the year (as is typical of many businesses in their early years), the loss is allocated to the members in accordance with the operating agreement or default rule. In the normal setting, these losses are advantageous to the members because they reduce each member's taxable income. However, where the LLC losses are so large that they are greater than the member's taxable income from every other source, the best the taxpayer can do is carry over his or her losses to the next tax year. In other words, the taxpayer cannot take full advantage of the LLC's losses because the Internal Revenue Code does not permit taxpayers to receive "negative income tax."

If the LLC generates a profit for the year, the analysis becomes more complicated. As with losses, profits are allocated to the members in accordance with the operating agreement or default rules. But remember that *allocation* is different from *distribution*. The allocation of profits increases the member's taxable income, but without a distribution there is no increase in the member's bank account. The danger is that the member will have an increased tax liability but no extra cash to meet that liability. Obviously the effect of an allocation without a distribution will vary from member to member. Some members may have substantial wealth outside the LLC and will easily be able to pay the tax liability on the LLC's profit allocation. Other members, though, may not have significant wealth beyond their LLC interest, and meeting the tax liability on their allocation of profits will be a great hardship.

The solution from the members' personal tax standpoint is for the LLC to distribute the maximum amount permissible under the statute each year. However, many business entities have a chronic need for capital both during their early years and often later as well. A struggling entity may not be able to borrow additional capital at all or may not be able to borrow at interest rates it considers fair. Attracting additional investors may be unacceptable to the current investors because of the dilution of their ownership and management interests. Obtaining additional capital from the present investors may be unpalatable for the same reason; some investors may not want the resulting dilution of their interests. Further, some current investors may simply be unable to invest additional money. For these reasons, a business entity's best source of capital is often simply the money its business generates in excess of the money needed for its direct expenses. Thus it may not always be possible for the LLC's operators to distribute cash, even though the members will be disadvantaged by a profit allocation without a corresponding distribution. Both those who are planning an LLC's structure and those charged with running an LLC must be aware of these tax and finance dynamics, the members' differing distribution preferences, and the capital needs and financing options of the LLC.

If a distribution is declared, the LLC statutes provide as a default rule that members have no right to receive LLC property rather than cash.[2] The converse of this default rule is not true, however. A member can be forced to accept property instead of cash as a distribution if all members are receiving the same proportion of the distribution in property. A distribution of property can be a distinct disadvantage for members where the property is difficult to value or where there is no ready market for the property. The LLC and the members will have different incentives for valuing the property and, regardless of valuation, where no ready market for the property exists, disposal is at best protracted and may be decidedly cumbersome.

4. Members' Interest

a. Financial

A member's financial interest consists of the right to receive an allocation of the profits and losses, in accordance with the operating agreement or the statute, and the right to receive assets (after creditors have been paid) upon the dissolution of the LLC. In most LLCs the operating agreement contains the parties' agreement for distributing assets on dissolution. Often these agreements provide that assets will be distributed in accordance with the members' share of the profits. Sometimes the operating agreement provides that assets shall be used for the partial or complete return of members' initial contribution and only then will they be distributed in accordance with the profit allocation. Where the operating agreement is silent about distributing assets on dissolution, the statutory default rule applies. The statutes in the various states contain a variety of default rules in this regard, and no single system can be said to be typical. In general, the default systems mirror the variations that are typically found in operating agreements.

Every LLC statute provides that the members and managers shall not be personally liable for the LLC's debts. This provision is one of the key advantages of the LLC form over partnerships. Members are, of course, liable to the LLC and its creditors to pay their agreed-upon contribution and some operating agreements provide that members may be required to contribute additional money in the future. As you will remember from Chapter 8 above, equitable principles of corporate law suggest that in some circumstances the business form should be disregarded and liability should be imposed on the entity's owners. This is usually called "piercing the corporate veil" and is based in common law rather than in statute. In the LLC setting, though, several states (including, for example, California) have statutes specifically imposing personal liability on LLC members "under principles of common law of this state that are similar to those applicable to business corporations and shareholders in this state." In states without such a statutory provision, it seems likely that courts

---

2. It may seem unlikely that a member would prefer property (which could be a machine the LLC uses in its business or raw or partially finished materials, or items in inventory) to cash, but a distribution of property and one of cash can have different tax consequences for the member. The transfer of property from the LLC to a member is not usually a taxable event, while the transfer of money usually is.

would impose similar results in any event on the same policy grounds used in deciding whether to pierce the corporate veil.

New Horizons Supply Cooperative v. Haack
590 N.W.2d 282 (Wis. App. 1999)

DEININGER, J.

BACKGROUND

On May 30, 1995, Haack signed a "CARDTROL AGREEMENT" whereby the "Patron" agreed "to be responsible for payment of all fuel purchased with" the "Cardtrol Card" issued under the agreement by a predecessor to New Horizons. "Kickapoo Valley Freight, LLC" is shown as the "Patron" in the first paragraph of the form agreement, and it is signed by "Allison Haack," with no designation indicating whether her signature was given individually or in a representative capacity on behalf of Kickapoo Valley.

An employee of New Horizons testified at trial that in September 1997, when the Kickapoo Valley account was in arrears, she contacted Robert Koch about the bill. Koch referred her to his sister, Haack, who apparently took care of paying the bills for the company. When contacted, Haack told the New Horizons employee that she would start paying $100 per month on the account. When no payment was received in October, Haack was contacted again, and she then informed New Horizons that Kickapoo Valley had dissolved, "that she was ... a partner, that Robert had moved out of state, and that she planned to assume responsibility and would again start to make a hundred dollars per month beginning in October." The employee also testified that during the October telephone conversation, Haack told her she had the assets of the business: a truck, which was secured by the bank; and some accounts receivable "that they were trying to collect." When contacted in November, Haack again promised a payment, but in December, Haack told the New Horizons employee "not to call her at work anymore."

When attempts to contact Haack at her home phone number proved unsuccessful, New Horizons commenced this action to collect the account balance, $1,009.99, from Haack "DBA KICKAPOO VALLEY FREIGHT." Haack testified that Kickapoo Valley had been organized as a limited liability company, but she did not introduce articles of organization or an operating agreement into evidence.[3] Haack did offer as exhibits a Wisconsin Department of Revenue registration certificate, as well as some correspondence from the department, showing the enterprise identified as "Kickapoo Valley Freight LLC." Haack stated her defense to New Horizons' claim was that the account was in the business name, that she was not personally liable for debts of the limited liability company, and that she had not personally guaranteed the obligation.[4]

---

3. Haack testified that a Mount Horeb attorney had drafted and filed the necessary papers to establish Kickapoo Valley as a limited liability company, but that she did not receive copies of those documents. She also testified that she had drafted the operating agreement herself, but that she did not bring a copy of the operating agreement to court with her.

4. New Horizons' witness conceded on cross-examination that "I don't have a personal guarantee other than the signature on your agreement for purchases."

According to Haack, her brother, Robert Koch, had suffered a nervous break-down and left the state; the truck was sold, with all proceeds going to the bank who held the lien on it; and there were "no additional assets," but that she was "left with quite a lot of debt that I had signed for." She acknowledged that she told New Horizons that she "would try to take care" of the account "several times" after the business ceased operations. Finally, Haack testified that she had not filed articles of dissolution or notified creditors of the termination of the business when it ceased operations in the fall of 1997.

In response to questions from the court regarding her investment in the company, and the limits of her liability and that of Mr. Koch, Haack answered that both of them had "lost" their investments in the company. She also testified that the company was taxed as a partnership, and that she had with her copies of a sale agreement whereby "the assets" of the company were sold and the pro-ceeds were given to the bank in order to release the lien on the truck. None of those documents were introduced as exhibits, however, and they are not a part of the record. Haack later testified that the assets that were sold consisted of a "truck, a pallet jack and the customer list." She did not testify as to the disposi-tion of any cash or accounts receivable remaining at the time the business was dissolved.

ANALYSIS

[T]he gravamen of Haack's appeal is that the court erred in applying the law to the largely undisputed facts of record. Thus, we are called upon to decide a legal question: Were Haack's testimony and exhibits sufficient to establish a defense under §183.0304, STATS., which provides that "a member or manager of a limited liability company is not personally liable for any debt, obligation or liability of the limited liability company"?

New Horizons seeks to defend the trial court's judgment, and its rationale of "piercing the corporate veil," by noting that ch. 183, Stats., expressly permits the importation of concepts such as "piercing the veil" from business corporation law:

> Notwithstanding sub. (1) [which sets forth the limitation on member liability], noth-ing in this chapter shall preclude a court from ignoring the limited liability company entity under principles of common law of this state that are similar to those applicable to business corporations and shareholders in this state and under circumstances that are not inconsistent with the purposes of this chapter.
>
> Section 183.0304(2), Stats.

The cooperative argues that the court properly applied the concept of "piercing the veil" to the facts adduced at the trial of this matter. We disagree, and con-clude, as Haack contends, that the court's comments imply that it erroneously deemed Kickapoo Valley's treatment as a partnership for tax purposes to be conclusive. There is little in the record, moreover, to support a conclusion that Haack "organized, controlled and conducted" company affairs to the extent that it had "no separate existence of its own and [was Haack's] mere instrumentality," which she "used to evade an obligation, to gain an unjust advantage or to commit an injustice." *See Wiebke v. Richardson & Sons, Inc.*, 265 N.W.2d 571, 573 (1978).

Notes and Questions

1. Notes

a. The trial court held Haack personally liable on the grounds that the evidence was insufficient to establish Kickapoo Valley Freight's formation as an LLC and further that the entity was taxed as a partnership. On those facts, the trial court held that Haack would be treated as a general partner of a general partnership.

b. The court went on to consider New Horizon's argument that Haack was personally liable because the LLC was not dissolved properly. That portion of the opinion is printed below.

2. Reality Check

a. Haack described herself as a "partner" to New Horizons. Laypeople in business often describe themselves as "partners" in an entity or as "partners" with other entity owners. Such a description could be a trap in litigation when it is uncertain whether another kind of entity has been formed or where it is uncertain whether the speaker is a co-owner with others rather than a principal or agent. In either setting such a self-description could open the speaker up to unintended personal liability. How should clients be counseled to avoid such possibilities?

b. The body of the contract names the LLC as a party but Haack signed the contract in her own name without indicating that she was acting as an agent. Should that inconsistency have resulted in a finding either that no agreement was reached (in which case might Haack be liable on a quantum meruit theory?) or that both New Horizons and Haack intended Haack to be personally liable?

3. Suppose

a. Would Haack be personally liable if New Horizons had believed that Kickapoo Valley Freight was a partnership and that Haack was, as she described herself, a partner?

b. Suppose New Horizons had believed that Kickapoo Valley Freight was a partnership but had no knowledge of Haack's status. Personal liability for Haack?

c. Assume New Horizons knew Kickapoo Valley Freight was an LLC. Would Haack's self-description as a "partner" be sufficient to impose liability on her as a partner? Would it be sufficient to impose liability on her as a guarantor of the LLC's debt? See footnote 4 of the opinion.

4. What Do You Think?

a. Do you think LLC statutes should explicitly import "piercing the veil" concepts from corporate law? Suppose the state supreme court radically changes the law of piercing the corporate veil after the LLC statute is adopted? Should a trial court automatically apply the new piercing law to LLCs?

b. Do you think corporation statutes should codify piercing principles? Do you think corporation statutes should reference LLC piercing principles?

b. Managerial

Almost all LLC statutes provide as a default rule that the LLC will be managed by the members. Many of the statutes provide that members' managerial power will be exercised in proportion to each member's contribution. In other words, in an

LLC where *A* contributes $60,000, *B* contributes $35,000, and *C* contributes $5,000, the parties' voting power would be *A* 60 percent, *B* 35 percent, and *C* 5 percent. In other states, the members' managerial power is per capita. In the example just given, the parties' voting power would be *A* one-third, *B* one-third, and *C* one-third, even though their contributions were unequal. In every state the default management scheme can be varied by the operating agreement and many if not most operating agreements make at least some change from the default rule. Typical management structures and issues are discussed in more detail below.

c. Additional Members, Transferability, and Dissociation

After an LLC has been formed, additional members may be admitted. In many states the default rule requires unanimous consent of the members. In many LLCs, though, the operating agreement permits additional members to be admitted either by the managers or by a majority or supermajority of the members.

As originally drafted, most LLC statutes distinguished between a transfer of a member's economic interest and a transfer of that member's management interest. A member's economic interest was freely transferable, but the transferee did not become a member unless specifically admitted under the operating agreement, which typically required the approval of a majority of other members. Management interests could not be transferred. The only method of transferring a member's entire economic and management interest to another person was for the member to dissociate (discussed below), and for the assignee to be admitted as a new member, a process that was often cumbersome and, in any event, did not relieve the original member from every obligation to the LLC. This distinction between economic and management interests was required so that LLCs could be taxed as partnerships. Since 1996, however, an LLC can be taxed as a partnership even though both the economic and management interests can be transferred. LLC statutes now provide that the operating agreement can permit a transfer of both the economic and management interest. As with a corporation or limited partnership, good reasons often exist for the parties to prohibit or limit the transferability of an owner's interest. Even where both economic and management interests are transferable, the transferring member remains liable for additional contributions, if any, under the operating agreement. A creditor of a member can usually obtain a charging order, which acts as a lien on the member's economic interest. This charging order is analogous to a charging order on a partner's interest and can be foreclosed in the same manner.

Dissociation is the term used by LLC statutes to mean that a member is no longer a member. Because members are not liable for LLC debts but only for their agreed-upon contribution, dissociation usually poses little economic risk to the LLC or its creditors. For this reason, there seems to be no compelling reason today to restrict a member's ability to dissociate. Until 1996 such restrictions were necessary to ensure that an LLC could be taxed as a partnership. Today, most LLC statutes permit a member to dissociate at will, subject to a restriction in the operating agreement. LLC statutes also generally provide that a member is dissociated upon the transference of all of his or her economic interest. Most LLC statutes also retain an older rule providing for dissociation upon the occurrence of certain events, largely tracking those that cause dissociation of a limited partner. These events include the death or bankruptcy of a member. As with some other statutory provisions, these were required before 1996 to ensure that LLCs were taxed as partnerships. A dissociated member is usually not entitled under the statute to any payment from the LLC, but some operating agreements provide for the return of some or all of a member's contribution upon dissociation.

A member who transfers his or her economic interest or dissociates by selling his or her interest back to the LLC may face the problem of later determining exactly what interests were transferred, the value of those interests, and what rights and obligations the member retains. The following case illustrates some of these issues.

Five Star Concrete, L.L.C. v. Klink, Inc.

693 N.E.2d 583 (Ind. Ct. App. 1998)

STATON, J.

We affirm in part, reverse in part and remand.

On June 14, 1994, Klink, Inc. ("Klink") and four other corporations, all engaged in supplying ready-mix concrete, formed Five Star, a limited liability company ("LLC"), in order to furnish concrete to large construction projects. Klink contributed $38,500.00, 12.5% of the initial total capitalization, and was issued 12.5 ownership units.

In a letter dated October 13, 1995, Klink formally notified Five Star of its intent to withdraw from membership effective October 10, 1995. The remaining members decided to purchase Klink's ownership units and to continue the business. To accomplish this end, Five Star members met on October 23, 1995 and agreed that Klink would receive $61,047.22 for the value of its "units."

After Five Star's fiscal year ended December 31, 1995, Klink was allocated $31,889.02 of income, representing its share of the LLC's profits for the approximate ten-month period of 1995 when Klink was a member. The allocation did not result in a monetary distribution to Klink. Instead, the allocation was made only for the purpose of properly determining Klink's tax liability. After receiving notification of the allocation, Klink filed a complaint against Five Star claiming that it was entitled to a distribution of cash in the sum of $31,889.02. Klink moved for summary judgment on its claim, and Five Star responded with its own motion for summary judgment, asserting that Klink had already been paid for its entire interest. Following a hearing, the trial court granted Klink's motion, finding that Klink had a legal right to receive a distribution of $31,889.02. The court also denied Five Star's cross-motion. Five Star appeals both rulings.

I. DISTRIBUTION OF $31,889.02

Here, there is no dispute that the allocation, Klink's portion of Five Star's income, was proper. Five Star was being taxed as a "pass-through" entity, and the allocation was required by tax law as well as by the Operating Agreement. However, Klink insists that when there is an allocation to a dissociating member there is a corresponding obligation to make a cash distribution of income equal to the allocation. We do not agree.

Nowhere does the Indiana Business Flexibility Act (the "Act") provide that allocation of income to members for income tax purposes creates an automatic legal right to receive a distribution in the amount of that income, even when a member is withdrawing from the LLC. Indeed, there are times that such a distribution would be unlawful. See Ind.Code §23-18-5-6.[4]

The Operating Agreement is also silent regarding the timing and amount of distributions; thus, under the Act, these decisions are to be made by the majority of the members. The evidence construed in favor of Five Star shows that Five Star made a distribution to all members in July of 1995; Klink's share was approximately $12,500.00. However, neither this distribution nor any other was made based upon the amount of income allocated to a member. Further, since that date no distributions were made to any members.

We conclude that the allocation of profits for tax reporting purposes did not provide Klink with a legal right under either the Act or the Operating Agreement to receive a distribution in the same amount. Summary judgment in favor of Klink was improvidently granted.

It does not follow, however, that Klink's interest in Five Star's profits for the ten-month period of 1995 should be ignored. Here, the member's share of Five Star's profits and losses is part of the total economic interest transferred in the buy-sell agreement. However, in this case, we cannot value that interest as a matter of law. This brings us to Five Star's next argument.

II. DIVESTMENT OF ECONOMIC INTEREST

The minutes of the October 23, 1995, meeting memorializing the Five Star members' buy-sell agreement states that Klink would receive $61,047.22 for the value of its "units." Five Star contends that it is entitled to summary judgment because, when Klink sold its "units" to Five Star for $61,047.22, Klink divested itself of its entire economic interest, including its right to profits. Klink counters that the use of the term "units" proves that it sold less than all its interests for that amount.

Pursuant to the Operating Agreement, "unit" refers to "an interest in the Company representing a contribution to capital." This supports Klink's argument that it sold less than all of its economic rights in Five Star when it accepted the $61,047.22. However, as Five Star points out, under the same Operating Agreement, the members' interests are represented by the units held by each member. Thus, each unit generally entitled the members to one vote and to a proportionate share of the LLC's net income, gains, losses, deductions and credits. "Units," as used in the minutes, could reasonably denote either all or only part of Klink's economic interests in Five Star.

The designated evidence supports an inference that the parties entered into the contract with materially different meanings attached to the word "unit." The trial court recognized the factual dispute and properly denied Five Star's motion for summary judgment.

III. VALUATION METHOD

Five Star maintains that the valuation method chosen by the parties demonstrates that Klink actually received the fair market value of its entire interest. We analyze this as a separate argument.

4. A distribution may not be made if after giving effect to the distribution: (1) the limited liability company would not be able to pay its debts as the debts become due in the usual course of business; or (2) the limited liability company's total assets would be less than the sum of its total liabilities plus, unless the operating agreement permits otherwise, the amount that would be needed if the affairs of the limited liability company were to be wound up at the time of the distribution to satisfy any preferential rights that are superior to the rights of members receiving the distribution. IC 23-18-5-6 (1993).

Here, the parties determined fair market value by examining Five Star's September 30, 1995, balance sheet. Liabilities of $104,495.42 were subtracted from assets valued at $592,873.16, leaving $488,377.74. That amount was then multiplied by 12.5%, Klink's percentage of ownership, resulting in the agreed sum of $61,047.22. Five Star claims that, . . . by using this valuation method, Klink received the amount upon which its complaint is based.

Valuing the interest of a member is a "complex task," more of a business matter than a legal one. . . . There is no best method for valuation and much depends on the nature of the business. . . . We do not agree with Five Star that resolution of this matter is appropriately decided as a matter of law. Five Star is not entitled to summary judgment on this ground.[5]

Affirmed in part, reversed in part and remanded.

GARRARD and RUCKER, JJ., concur.

Notes and Questions

1. Note

a. Under most LLC statutes at the time this case was decided, a member who had the power to dissociate ("withdraw" is a synonym used in the opinion) could cause the LLC to dissolve unless the other members elected to continue the business, as the remaining members of Five Star did in this instance.

2. Reality Check

a. What did Klink believe it transferred to the LLC when it sold its "units"? What did Five Star believe it received when it bought Klink's "units"?

b. On remand, how will the trial court decide what was transferred? How will it value that transfer?

3. Suppose

a. If the operating agreement clearly defined "unit" as a member's entire economic interest would Klink or Five Star have a better argument for relief?

b. Suppose Klink had sold its units in October 1995 to Alpha, a third party, for the same price, $61,047.22? If Five Star had computed its profits only for the entire calendar year of 1995, how should the profits be allocated between Klink and Alpha?

c. Assume some profits are allocated to Alpha, but no distribution is made. Can Alpha seek money from Klink to cover its tax liability? If some profits are allocated to Klink, can it seek money from Alpha? What if there are losses instead?

d. If a distribution is made shortly after the sale to Alpha, is Alpha entitled to all the distribution? None? If Five Star dissolved soon after, and had enough net assets to repay the members' original contribution, would Klink or Alpha be entitled to Klink's original $38,500 contribution?

---

5. Upon remand, the buy-out provision in the Operating Agreement may become relevant. It provides that, if Five Star elects to purchase the interest of a "Former Member" and no pre-determined purchase price of a "unit" had been established within a two-year period: [t]he fair market value shall be determined by a certified public accountant selected by the selling Member and a certified public accountant selected by the Company or purchasing Member, although all Members may select the same accountant. If the two accountants cannot agree as to the fair market value, the value shall be determined by a majority vote of said accountants and a third certified public accountant selected by said accountants.

4. What Do You Think?

a. Apparently Klink representatives attended the October 23, 1995, meeting at which Klink's units were valued and agreed with the valuation. Do you think Klink should be estopped from seeking further compensation?

b. Do you think the ambiguity in the term *unit* was foreseeable? If so, which party should have the ambiguity resolved in its favor? Why? If the ambiguity was foreseeable, how could the parties' lawyers have prevented the ambiguity before it resulted in this dispute?

c. Five Star began business in June 1994. The opinion does not state whether distributions were made in 1994, nor whether the LLC had profits or losses for that year. In 1995, though, Klink received a $12,500 distribution and $61,047.22 for the sale of its units for a total of $73,547.22. Its allocation of the 1995 profit was $31,889.02, which suggests a maximum federal tax liability of about $11,000. Do you think that, as a matter of fairness, Klink has been amply compensated for its investment?

d. In footnote 5 the court quotes the operating agreement language for valuing a Member's interest. Do you think the procedure is a workable one?

5. You Draft It

a. Draft a clause for the buy-sell agreement that supports Klink's position.
b. Draft a clause for the buy-sell agreement that supports Five Star's position.

5. Management

a. Statutory Default Rules

In almost all states member-managed LLCs are the default rule. Most states require any variation from this rule to be stated in the articles of organization, but some states permit variations to be stated only in the operating agreement. A majority vote is required for action to be approved (although, of course, the members may validly change that rule to require a supermajority or even unanimous vote on some or all issues), but the states are divided as to the default voting power of members. In roughly half the states, voting power is a function of each member's contribution to the LLC's capital. A member who contributed 20 percent of the LLC's total capital would have 20 percent of the vote. In the remaining states, voting is per capita with each member having one vote regardless of economic contribution. Although a few states require member meetings and have corporatelike provisions for call, notice, and quorum, most statutes are silent, leaving the question of when and how member meetings are to be conducted entirely in the hands of the members themselves.

Under agency rules, the members of a member-managed LLC can give actual authority to any member to act on behalf of the LLC. In addition to such an explicit grant of actual authority by the members, most statutes provide as a default rule that all members have equal management power. This provision may be construed to create a kind of apparent authority, allowing a member to bind an LLC to acts outside its business, and even to acts specifically forbidden by the other members, if a third party reasonably believes the act is within the LLC's business and has no notice of the restrictions on a member's authority. Most statutes permit limitations on a member's or all members' authority to be stated in the articles of organization filed with the secretary of state, but such restrictions are probably not binding on third parties who are unaware of them.

b. Manager-Managed Structures

As an alternative to the default rule of member-managed LLCs, many operating agreements provide for management by managers. As noted above, managers need not be members, although in the closely held entity setting they often are members. In theory, the operating agreement could allocate power among members and managers in an infinite variety of ways. Few states have explicit statutes regarding the division of power in manager-managed LLCs, preferring to leave the decisions to the parties to be embodied in the operating agreement. In practice, though, most LLC operating agreements that effect a manager-managed structure create a division of power that replicates that of a corporation. Under this scheme the members vote once each year for the election of managers. Members usually have the right to remove managers during their term even without cause. Often members are required to vote on proposals for extraordinary transactions involving the LLC, such as mergers or dissolution.

In a manager-managed LLC, the operating agreement could provide for a hierarchy of managers; some managers being in charge of others. Mostly, though, operating agreements reflect a corporate model in which the managers are analogous to the board of directors. In that setting the managers are co-equal. They probably have the power to appoint persons to be agents of the LLC, much as corporate officers and employees are agents of a corporation. Most LLC statutes provide a default rule that managers have the same authority to bind the LLC as members in a member-managed LLC do. That is, each manager has the power to bind the LLC to any action that is apparently for carrying on in the usual way the business of the LLC. This power is, of course, in addition to any actual authority the manager possesses.

The operating agreement will suffice to divide power between members and managers. However, because the default LLC rule is typically for a member-managed entity, apparent authority or estoppel concepts may allow third parties to bind LLCs for unauthorized actions by members in manager-managed LLCs. Most LLC statutes require the articles of organization to state whether the LLC will be member or manager managed, and every statute permits the articles of organization to contain statements that limit the authority of members or managers or particular individuals. Such disclosure is probably not sufficient to preclude third parties without actual knowledge of the provisions from asserting apparent authority or estoppel arguments. A special rule sometimes applies in transferring LLC real estate. A few statutes provide that grants or limitations of authority contained in the articles of organization are sufficient to bind third parties, even without actual notice, as to the authority of members or managers to effect a real estate transfer.

6. Fiduciary Duties

Fiduciary duties in LLCs divide into three settings. First are duties owed by members to one another when the LLC is manager managed. Second are fiduciary duties owed by managers to the entity or to members. Finally, are duties owed by members to one another when the LLC is member managed. As to the first situation, a few states have statutory provisions stating that members have no fiduciary duties in manager-managed LLCs, but most statutes are silent. It seems likely that members in manager-managed LLCs do not owe one another any fiduciary duties. Rather, they probably owe only the standard contract duty of good faith and fair dealing. This obligation is one that would probably be imposed in most states given the contractual nature of LLCs and given that the typical manager-managed LLC analogizes members to corporate shareholders. Nonetheless, courts in some states may impose higher duties on members, at least to the extent that those duties have not been expressly modified by the operating agreement. In those states members may be analogized to partners in a partnership rather than shareholders in a corporation. In such a situation, members would owe each other a duty of the highest trust and loyalty. Which model will apply in any particular state will depend upon whether the state legislature (or courts) sees LLCs as being closer to partnerships or closer to corporations.

In the second setting, the manager-managed LLC, managers probably owe fiduciary duties of care and loyalty, analogous to those of corporate directors. As to the duty of care, state statutes are split roughly equally between those that contain no provision, those that require managers to act as a reasonably prudent person would act, and those that impose liability only for gross negligence or bad faith. Managers (and managing members) also have a duty of loyalty to the LLC. This duty seems likely to be analogous to the duty corporate directors owe. In outline, managers must act solely in the best interest of the LLC and its members. Transactions in which the manager has an interest or transactions that the manager takes for himself or herself rather than offering to the LLC should raise the question of whether the manager has violated the duty of loyalty, and the manager would probably have the burden of proving that the transaction did not violate that duty.

In the final setting, where the LLC is member managed, some statutes explicitly state that members have the same fiduciary duties that managers would have. Where only some members have management power under the operating agreement, only those members should have fiduciary duties. Again, while some states would impose duties on member managers that are analogous to corporate directors, other states would impose higher, partnerlike duties of utmost good faith and loyalty. Remember that this difference can have important consequences because states provide, as a default rule, that LLCs are to be member managed.

The following case raises issues about the duties owed in an LLC. The LLC in this case was member managed.

McConnell v. Hunt Sports Enterprises

725 N.E.2d 1193 (Ohio App. 1999)

TYACK, J.

On June 17, 1997, John H. McConnell and Wolfe Enterprises, Inc. filed a complaint for declaratory judgment . . . against Hunt Sports Enterprises, Hunt Sports Enterprises, L.L.C., Hunt Sports Group, L.L.C. ("Hunt Sports Group") and Columbus Hockey Limited ("CHL"). CHL was a limited liability company formed under R.C. Chapter 1705. A brief background of the events leading up to the formation of CHL and the subsequent discord among certain of its members follows.

In 1996, the National Hockey League ("NHL") determined it would be accepting applications for new hockey franchises. In April 1996, Gregory S. Lashutka, the mayor of Columbus, received a phone call from an NHL representative inquiring as to Columbus's interest in a hockey team. As a result, Mayor Lashutka asked certain community leaders who had been involved in exploring professional sports in Columbus to pursue the possibility of applying for an NHL hockey franchise. Two of these persons were Ronald A. Pizzuti and McConnell.

Pizzuti began efforts to recruit investors in a possible franchise. The deadline for applying for an NHL expansion franchise was November 1, 1996. On October 31, 1996, CHL was formed when its articles of organization were filed with the secretary of state pursuant to R.C. 1705.04. The members of CHL were McConnell, Wolfe Enterprises, Inc., Hunt Sports Group, Pizzuti Sports Limited, [Ameritech,] and Buckeye Hockey, L.L.C. CHL was subject to an operating agreement that set forth the terms between the members. Pursuant to section 2.1 of CHL's operating agreement, the general character of the business of CHL was to invest in and operate a franchise in the NHL.

On or about November 1, 1996, an application was filed with the NHL on behalf of the city of Columbus. In the application, the ownership group was identified as CHL. . . . Also included within the application package was Columbus's plan for an arena to house the hockey games. There was no facility at the time, and the proposal was to build a facility that would be financed, in large part, by a three-year countywide one-half percent sales tax. The sales tax issue would be on the May 1997 ballot.

On May 6, 1997, the sales tax issue failed. The day after, . . . Dimon McPherson, chairman and chief executive officer of Nationwide Insurance Enterprise ("Nationwide"), met with [Lamar] Hunt, and they discussed the possibility of building the arena despite the failure of the sales tax issue. Hunt was interested, and Nationwide began working on an arena plan. On or about May 9, 1997, the mayor spoke with [NHL Commissioner Gary] Bettman and let him know that alternate plans would be pursued, and Mr. Bettman gave Columbus until June 4, 1997, to come up with a plan.

By May 28, 1997, Nationwide had come up with a plan to finance an arena privately and on such date, Hunt Sports Group did not accept Nationwide's lease proposal. On May 29, 1997, Nationwide representatives again met with representatives of Hunt Sports Group. Again, Hunt Sports Group indicated that the lease proposal was unacceptable. . . . The June 4, 1997, NHL deadline was discussed. Hunt Sports Group stated that it would continue to evaluate the proposal, and it wanted the weekend to do so. Nationwide informed appellant that it needed an answer by close of business Friday, May 30.

On May 30, 1997, McPherson called McConnell and requested that they meet and discuss "where [they] were on the arena." McConnell testified that the conversation was "totally out of the blue. [McPherson] said that Nationwide was going to finance and build an arena, and that he had offered the Hunt group the opportunity to pick up the lease and bring a franchise in." McPherson told McConnell about appellant's rejection of the lease proposal and discussed the NHL's June 4 deadline. McConnell stated that if Hunt would not step up and lease the arena and, therefore, get the franchise, McConnell would. Hunt Sports Group did not contact Nationwide on May 30, 1997.

Hunt Sports Group told Nationwide that it still found the terms of the lease to be unacceptable. On June 3 or June 4, McConnell, in a conversation with the NHL, orally agreed to apply for a hockey franchise for Columbus. On June 4 . . . Hunt informed McPherson that he was still interested in pursuing an agreement with Nationwide.

On June 4, 1997, the NHL franchise expansion committee met. The expansion committee recommended Columbus to the NHL board of governors as one of four cities to be granted a franchise.

On June 5, 1997, the NHL sent Hunt a letter requesting that he let them know by Monday, June 9, 1997, whether he was going forward with his franchise application. Hunt responded that CHL intended to pursue the franchise application. Hunt indicated that the application was contingent upon entering into an appropriate lease for a hockey facility.

On June 9, 1997, a meeting took place at Pizzuti's office. The NHL required that the ownership group be identified and that such ownership group sign a lease term sheet by June 9, 1997. Brian Ellis, president and chief operating officer of Nationwide, presented the lease term sheet. . . .

Hunt indicated the lease was unacceptable. Ameritech and Buckeye Hockey, L.L.C. indicated that if Hunt found it unacceptable then they too found it unacceptable. Pizzuti and Wolfe agreed to participate along with McConnell. McConnell then signed the term sheet as the owner of the franchise. Christie [a McConnell family representative] faxed the signed lease term sheet to Bettman that day along with a cover letter and a description of the ownership group. Such ownership group was identified as: John H. McConnell, majority owner, Pizzuti Sports, L.L.C., John F. Wolfe and "[u]p to seven (7) other members."

On June 17, 1997 . . . , the complaint in the case at bar was filed. On or about June 25, 1997, the NHL board of governors awarded Columbus a franchise with McConnell's group as owner.[2] Hunt Sports Group, Buckeye Hockey, L.L.C. and Ameritech have no ownership interest in the hockey franchise.

[C]ount one of the first amended complaint sought a declaration that section 3.3 of CHL's operating agreement allowed members to compete against CHL to obtain an NHL franchise.

Section 3.3 of the operating agreement states:

> Members May Compete. Members shall not in any way be prohibited from or restricted in engaging or owning an interest in any other business venture of any nature, including any venture which might be competitive with the business of the Company.

Appellant [Hunt Sports Group] emphasizes the word "other" in the above language and states, in essence, that it means any business venture that is different from the business of the company. Appellant points out that under section 2.1 of the operating agreement, the general character of the business is "to invest in and operate a franchise in the National Hockey League." Hence, appellant contends that members may only engage in or own an interest in a venture that is not in the business of investing in and operating a franchise with the NHL.

Appellant's interpretation of section 3.3 goes beyond the plain language of the agreement and adds words or meanings not stated in the provision. Section 3.3, for

---

2. The ownership group is now formally known as COLHOC Limited Partnership ("COLHOC"). Portions of the record indicate COLHOC was formed before the June 9, 1997, meeting. JMAC, Inc. [the investment entity for the McConnell family] is the majority owner, and JMAC. Hockey L.L.C. is the general partner of COLHOC.

example, does not state "[m]embers shall not be prohibited from or restricted in engaging or owning an interest in any other business venture that is different from the business of the company." Rather, section 3.3 states: "any other business venture *of any nature*." (Emphasis added.) It then adds to this statement: "including any venture which might be competitive with the business of the Company." The words "any nature" could not be broader, and the inclusion of the words "any venture which might be competitive with the business of the Company" makes it clear that members were not prohibited from engaging in a venture that was competitive with CHL's investing in and operating an NHL franchise. Contrary to appellant's contention, the word "other" simply means a business venture other than CHL. The word "other" does not limit the type of business venture in which members may engage.

Hence, section 3.3 did not prohibit appellees from engaging in activities that may have been competitive with CHL, including appellees' participation in COL-HOC. Accordingly, summary judgment in favor of appellees was appropriate, and appellees were entitled to a declaration that section 3.3 of the operating agreement permitted appellees to request and obtain an NHL hockey franchise to the exclusion of CHL.

[A]ppellant contends the trial court erred in excluding evidence that would have shown appellees breached fiduciary duties. For the reasons that follow, we find the trial court did not err in excluding certain evidence.

Before we can review the propriety of the directed verdict in this case, the law on fiduciary duty and interference with a prospective business relationship must be addressed. The term "fiduciary relationship" has been defined as a relationship in which special confidence and trust is reposed in the integrity and fidelity of another, and there is a resulting position of superiority or influence acquired by virtue of this special trust. In the case at bar, a limited liability company is involved which, like a partnership, involves a fiduciary relationship. Normally, the presence of such a relationship would preclude direct competition between members of the company. However, here we have an operating agreement that by its very terms allows members to compete with the business of the company. Hence, the question we are presented with is whether an operating agreement of a limited liability company may, in essence, limit or define the scope of the fiduciary duties imposed upon its members. We answer this question in the affirmative.

A fiduciary has been defined as a person having a duty, created by his or her undertaking, to act primarily for the benefit of another in matters connected with such undertaking. A claim of breach of fiduciary duty is basically a claim for negligence that involves a higher standard of care. In order to recover, one must show the existence of a duty on the part of the alleged wrongdoer not to subject such person to the injury complained of, a failure to observe such duty, and an injury proximately resulting therefrom. These principles support our conclusion that a contract may define the scope of fiduciary duties between parties to the contract.

Here, the injury complained of by appellant was, essentially, appellees competing with CHL and obtaining the NHL franchise. The operating agreement constitutes the undertaking of the parties herein. In becoming members of CHL, appellant and appellees agreed to abide by the terms of the operating agreement, and such agreement specifically allowed competition with the company by its members. As such, the duties created pursuant to such undertaking did not include a duty not to compete. Therefore, there was no duty on the part of appellees to refrain from subjecting appellant to the injury complained of herein.

We find further support for our conclusion in case law concerning close corporations and partnerships. *Cruz* [*v. S. Dayton Urological Assoc., Inc.*, 700 N.E.2d 675 (Ohio App. 1997)] stands for the proposition that close corporation employment agreements may limit the scope of fiduciary duties that otherwise would apply.... The same principle has been applied in situations involving partnerships that are subject to partnership agreements.

"Operating agreement" is defined in R.C. 1705.01(J) as all of the valid written or oral agreements of the members as to the affairs of a limited liability company and the conduct of its business. R.C. 1705.03(C) sets forth various activities limited liability companies may engage in and indicates such are subject to the company's articles of organization or operating agreement. Indeed, many of the statutory provisions in R.C. Chapter 1705 governing limited liability companies indicate they are, in various ways, subject to and/or dependent upon related provisions in an operating agreement.... Here, the operating agreement states in its opening paragraph that it evidences the mutual agreement of the members in consideration of their contributions and promises to each other. Such agreement specifically allowed its members to compete with the company.

Given the above, we conclude as a matter of law that it was not a breach of fiduciary duty for appellees to form COLHOC and obtain an NHL franchise to the exclusion of CHL. In so concluding, we are not stating that no act related to such obtainment could be considered a breach of fiduciary duty. In general terms, members of limited liability companies owe one another the duty of utmost trust and loyalty. However, such general duty in this case must be considered in the context of members' ability, pursuant to operating agreement, to compete with the company.

Judgment affirmed in part and reversed in part.

BOWMAN, J., concurs.

PEGGY L. BRYANT, J., concurring in part and dissenting in part.

Notes and Questions

1. Reality Check

a. What was the main disagreement between the Hunt faction and the McConnell faction?

b. Was the court's result based more upon contract law or fiduciary duty law?

2. Suppose

a. If Hunt had not objected to the lease terms and if McConnell had obtained the franchise for COLHOC anyway, would the court's analysis and result have been the same?

b. Suppose the operating agreement had been silent about the members' duties toward one another? Would the analysis or result have differed?

c. Assume the operating agreement explicitly said that the members owed each other no fiduciary duties. Would the court have enforced that provision?

d. Assume the operating agreement explicitly said that the Members owed each other the same fiduciary duties as partners in a general partnership? How would the court have analyzed this dispute?

3. What Do You Think?

a. Do you think the Hunt group or the McConnell group acted in a more inappropriate way? Both groups? Neither group?

b. Do you think this case is analogous to *Meinhard v. Salmon* in that a key issue is the scope of the enterprise? What are the differences between the two cases?

c. Do you think states should impose no fiduciary duties on LLC members as a default rule, as in Delaware? If states should impose fiduciary duties on LLC members, how should those duties be defined? Do you think members should be able to contract out of some or all of such default duties?

7. Dissolution

Dissolution means the end of the LLC as an entity. As with the dissolution of any other business entity, you must be careful to distinguish between the dissolution of the entity and the cessation of the business it operates. Generally, even when a business entity dissolves, its business continues and is sold or transferred as a going concern to another owner. In outline, when an LLC dissolves, it ceases to operate its business, its assets are disposed of (if the business is not transferred as a going concern, its assets may be sold off piecemeal), usually for cash, and the proceeds are applied to creditors' claims. If cash remains after the creditors have been satisfied, the members share it according to the statutory default rule or the operating agreement. If, as is much more typical, the LLC has insufficient money to satisfy the creditors, the entity usually files for bankruptcy, and the creditors divide the assets according to the federal bankruptcy laws, but cannot seek additional assets from the members.

When LLC statutes were initially adopted, they usually provided that dissolution was triggered by a variety of occurrences, including the dissociation of a member. In many states dissociation could happen by the member's express will even though in violation of the operating agreement, a member's death, or the bankruptcy of a member. The provision for LLC dissolution upon a member's dissociation was necessary to ensure that the LLC could be taxed as a partnership. Since 1996, though, such provisions are unnecessary for tax purposes. With tax considerations irrelevant, no other social policy supports a default rule that requires dissolution upon a member's dissociation. Accordingly, most LLC statutes have been amended to provide that dissociation does not automatically cause dissolution.

Typically, LLC statutes provide for dissolution in three settings. The first is where all the members vote to dissolve. This provision might be invoked where the business is not as successful as the members had anticipated or where the parties have had a significant falling out with one another. The second setting is dissolution in accordance with the operating agreement. A common provision in the operating agreement is to require dissolution whenever approved by a majority (or often a supermajority) of members.

Although no longer required for tax purposes, some LLCs may permit a single member or a minority of members to force the LLC's dissolution. This agreement is likely to occur in very small LLCs where each member is active and where each member's contribution is considered so important that the character of the LLC would be destroyed if the member left. Other operating agreements may specify that the LLC dissolves upon the expiration of a certain time period or upon the achievement of a particular event such as completing the business project for which the LLC was formed. Again, this is relatively unusual but not completely unknown. It is safe to say that most operating agreements today either provide that the LLC shall have perpetual existence (subject to the members' vote to dissolve) or are silent.

Third, LLC statutes provide that a court may order dissolution. As with dissolution of corporations, this power is equitable, which means that a petitioning party must not only show that the statutory requirements for dissolution are met but that justice would be best served by dissolution. The statutes usually provide for dissolution in three situations. An LLC's creditor may petition for dissolution. In effect, this action seeks to stop the LLC from continuing to do business. Second, any member (or in some states members holding at least 10% of the ownership interests) may petition for dissolution on the ground of illegality, waste, or oppression. Finally, such member or members may petition for dissolution on the ground that it is "not reasonably practicable" to continue the LLC. The reasons why it may no longer be reasonably practicable to carry on the business of the LLC tend to fall into three categories: (1) the relatively unusual setting in which the business becomes regulated or prohibited; (2) one or more of the members may have taken such actions that, while not constituting illegality, waste, or oppression, nonetheless make it impracticable to continue the business; and (3) the relationship between the parties may simply have deteriorated to the point where it is no longer reasonably practicable to carry on the LLC's business. In this final instance, dissolution is something in the nature of a "no fault" remedy.

Typically the persons charged with operating the LLC (whether members or managers) are charged with winding up the entity. If the parties are in substantial disagreement either over who may wind up the LLC or how the winding up should proceed, they may petition the court, which may either make rulings in the matter or, more frequently, appoint a receiver to oversee the winding up. Once the assets of the LLC have been reduced to cash, the statutes all require that creditor claims be satisfied in full before any cash is paid to the members. Members who are also LLC creditors are treated as creditors for this purpose, at least in the absence of unfairness. When the assets of the LLC are sufficient to satisfy the creditors in full and additional assets remain, the LLC statutes contain default rules for distributing the money to members. The statutes in most states provide that money be distributed first to satisfy distributions declared but not already paid. Second, money is distributed pro rata until each member's initial contribution is repaid. Finally, money is distributed pro rata in accordance with the LLC's profit allocation rule. In all states the operating agreement may vary the default rule but may not, of course, change the requirement that, in dissolution, creditors be satisfied in full before assets are distributed to members. A typical operating agreement variation is to provide that assets will be distributed strictly in accordance with the members' profit allocation, ignoring their capital contributions.

If there is insufficient cash to satisfy the creditors in full, a common occurrence, the members' limited liability means that the creditors bear the loss. As you might imagine, where the amount is sufficiently large, creditors will attempt to hold the members personally liable on one of three grounds. First is outright fraud, second is disregarding the entity (i.e., piercing the veil), and third is failing to follow the statutory requirements for dissolution. In the *New Horizons Supply Cooperative* case above, you will recall that the creditor attempted unsuccessfully to persuade the court to disregard the LLC entity and hold the member, Ms. Haack, personally liable. The creditor made a second argument for Ms. Haack's personal liability:

New Horizons Supply Cooperative v. Haack

590 N.W.2d 282 (Wis. App. 1999)

DEININGER, J.

[The facts are stated in the excerpt above].

[W]e conclude that entry of judgment against Haack on the New Horizons' claim was proper because she failed to establish that she took appropriate steps to shield herself from liability for the company's debts following its dissolution and the distribution of its assets.

[A] fact-finder could have inferred from Haack's testimony and from her exhibits showing that the Department of Revenue apparently recognized Kickapoo Valley as a "LLC," that Haack and her brother had properly formed a limited liability company.

The record is devoid, however, of any evidence showing that appropriate steps were taken upon the dissolution of the company to shield its members from liability for the entity's obligations. [T]he order for distributing the company's assets following dissolution is fixed by statute, and the company's creditors enjoy first priority, see §183.0905, STATS. A dissolved limited liability company may "dispose of known claims against it" by filing articles of dissolution, and then providing written notice to its known creditors containing information regarding the filing of claims. See §183.0907, STATS. The testimony at trial indicates that Haack knew of New Horizons' claim at the time Kickapoo Valley was dissolved. It is also clear from the record that articles of dissolution for Kickapoo Valley Freight LLC were not filed, nor was the cooperative formally notified of a claim filing procedure or deadline.

Section 183.0909, Stats., provides in relevant part as follows:

> A claim not barred under §§183.0907 or 183.0908 may be enforced under this section against any of the following: . . .
> (2) If the dissolved limited liability company's assets have been distributed in liquidation, a member of the limited liability company to the extent of the member's proportionate share of the claim or to the extent of the assets of the limited liability company distributed to the member in liquidation, whichever is less, but a member's total liability for all claims under this section may not exceed the total value of assets distributed to the member in liquidation.

It appears from the record that certain of Kickapoo Valley's assets were sold, and that the proceeds from that sale were remitted to the bank which held a lien on the company's truck. There is nothing in the record, however, showing the disposition of other company assets, such as cash and accounts receivable. New Horizons' witness testified that, in October 1997, Haack had claimed to be attempting to collect the accounts of the dissolved company and hoped to pay the instant debt from those proceeds. We do not know the value of the accounts receivable in question, however, or the amounts of any other company debts to which the proceeds of the accounts may have been applied, because Haack presented no testimony on the issue.

In this regard, we agree with the trial court's comments regarding the lack of evidence in the record to show that Kickapoo Valley's affairs were properly wound up following its dissolution occasioned by Robert Koch's dissociation from the enterprise. Although Kickapoo Valley Freight LLC may have been properly formed and operated as an entity separate and distinct from its owners, Haack did not establish that she distributed the entity's assets in accordance with §183.0905, STATS., following Kickapoo's dissolution. Her failure to employ the procedures outlined in §§183.0906 and .0907, STATS., left her vulnerable to New Horizons' claim under §183.0909(2), STATS., absent proof that the value of any assets of the dissolved company she received were exceeded by the cooperative's claim.

Thus, although Haack correctly contends that the judgment cannot be sustained on the ground relied upon by the trial court, we "nevertheless . . . look to facts in the record 'in favor of respondent which [seem] to be insurmountable.'" *See State v. Alles*, 316 N.W.2d 378, 388-89 (1982) (citation omitted).

By the Court. — Judgment affirmed.

Notes and Questions

1. Note

a. The provision in the Wisconsin statute for shielding members from personal liability in dissolution by giving notice of dissolution to known creditors is a common one.

2. Reality Check

a. What assets did Kickapoo Valley possess? What became of them?

3. Suppose

a. Suppose Haack only received $500 in distributions from the LLC. How much could New Horizons Supply Cooperative have recovered?

4. What Do You Think?

a. While an LLC is operating as a going concern, its members have limited liability (subject to piercing, of course). When the LLC dissolves, though, members have limited liability only if they follow the notice procedure, as demonstrated in this case. Do you think the distinction between the two settings is justified? Why?

b. Becase state statutes provide a method of imposing personal liability in dissolution settings where the entity does not notify known creditors (as in this case), do you think creditors of a dissolving LLC should be able to make piercing the veil arguments as well or do you think the statutory method should be exclusive?

c. Most states have a provision like the Wisconsin statute that limits members' personal liability where the dissolving LLC does not notify known creditors to the lesser of the creditor's claim or the amount distributed to the member. Do you think this statutory limit makes sense, especially given that personal liability under the piercing the veil theory is not limited?

C. FEDERAL SECURITIES LAWS

If an ownership interest in an LLC is a security, then LLCs and their legal counsel must be concerned with the federal registration requirements (and various exemptions), the periodic reporting requirements for public companies, the federal regulation of proxy solicitations, and the antifraud provisions of SEC Rule 10b-5, among other legal issues. None of these problems applies, however, if LLC interests are not "securities." None of the federal statutes specifically names interests in LLCs as securities and no Supreme Court case has decided the question. The Supreme Court would almost certainly apply the test from *SEC v. W.J. Howey Co.*, 328 U.S. 293 (1946). Under the cases interpreting *Howey*, the court must decide whether there was (1) an investment of money, (2) in a common enterprise in which the investor was led to expect profits, (3) primarily from the efforts of the promoter or a third party. In analyzing LLCs under this test the key element will be the "efforts of the promoter or a third party." The *Howey* analysis for LLCs should be similar to that for general partnerships because the management structure of an LLC can vary, as it can in a partnership, from entities in which all members participate equally to entities in which all management power is delegated to a nonmember manager.

The principal case analyzing general partnerships under the securities laws is *Williamson v. Tucker*, 645 F.2d 404 (5th Cir.), *cert. denied*, 454 U.S. 897 (1981), in which the court held that a partnership interest is a security under *Howey* only if the investor can establish one of three elements:

1. That the agreement among the parties leaves so little management power in the investor's hands that the investor is analogous to a limited partner; or
2. The investor is so inexperienced and unknowledgeable in business affairs that he or she cannot intelligently exercise his or her managerial powers; or
3. The investor is so dependent upon some unique entrepreneurial or managerial talent of the promoter that the investor cannot replace the promoter or otherwise meaningfully exercise his or her managerial powers.

The few lower-court cases that have considered the question have applied the *Williamson* test to LLCs. In *Keith v. Black Diamond Advisors, Inc.*, 48 F. Supp. 2d 326 (S.D.N.Y. 1999) the court found that the investment in the LLC was not a security because the operating agreement provided for member management. In *SEC v. Parkersburg Wireless LLC*, 991 F. Supp. 6 (D.D.C. 1997) the court found that the investment in the LLC was a security because the investors could not, as a practical matter, exercise any significant management control.

D. TERMS OF ART IN THIS CHAPTER

Allocation	Limited liability company	Member
Dissolution	Manager	Member managed
Distribution	Manager managed	Operating agreement

Part V.
CHOICE OF FORM

20
Choice of Entity

This chapter covers a very practical question: What kind of entity should own a particular business? Too many practitioners have a very easy answer: an LLC. The problem is not that the answer is wrong, but that it isn't *always* right. The answer also is insidious because the disadvantageous consequences of choosing the wrong entity may not become apparent for years. For that reason lawyers believe that they can get away with making unthinking choices about the business entities that are appropriate for their clients' businesses.

There is another perennial answer to the choice of entity question: whatever the client wants. This answer is always "right" in that, except for illegality, a lawyer should effect the client's desires even when not in the client's best interest. Clients occasionally have eccentric views of the type of entity they desire for their businesses. When the client insists upon an inappropriate entity choice, you must make certain that the client understands the possible consequences of his or her choice. This is best done with a letter that spells out the scope of your engagement, the counsel you have given your client as to the appropriate form, and the fact that the client insists upon a different form.

Our approach in this chapter is straightforward. We will begin with the most salient considerations in choosing the appropriate business form. Then, we will explore a method for choosing the appropriate business form. Finally, we'll look at the "problem" of the plethora of entity forms.

I have been keeping something from you for several hundred pages now, and it's time you knew the truth. A corporation can be taxed in one of two ways for purposes of federal income tax. The shareholders of a corporation that has 75 or fewer shareholders and has one class of stock can unanimously elect to be taxed under Subchapter S of the Internal Revenue Code. Ingeniously, these entities are called "S corporations." Generally speaking, entities cannot be shareholders of S corporations. Further, shares of S corporation stock may differ as to voting rights but must be identical in other respects. Corporations whose shareholders have not elected, or could not elect, Subchapter S treatment are taxed under IRC Subchapter C. Throughout this chapter you may assume that a corporation is a C corporation unless otherwise stated.

A C corporation is taxed as a separate entity, just as individuals are, though there are differing rules for corporations and individuals. This means that income of a business owned by a corporation is taxed twice, once at the corporate level and

again when the income is distributed to shareholders as dividends. Depending upon
the relative rates of taxation, this *double taxation* characteristic can be extremely
problematic or essentially a nuisance. By contrast, S corporations are not taxed separately. Rather, profits and losses are allocated directly to the shareholders who include
those profits or losses on their own income tax returns. As we will see, this *pass-through
taxation* is essentially similar to the way partnerships and most LLCs are taxed.

A. VARIABLE CHARACTERISTICS IMPORTANT IN CHOOSING AN ENTITY

It may not be obvious, but the criteria one uses in selecting an entity form are a
function of the differences between the entities. If a particular characteristic is identical
across every entity, it can't be a criterion for choosing between them. Thus the
focus here is on characteristics that differ among the entities and that might make
a practical difference to clients.

In this section we identify and organize the differences among business entities
that may be important in deciding which entity is most appropriate for a particular
new business. Many discussions of choice of entity issues divide these differences
into tax issues and non-tax issues, but we will use a different thematic approach
that recognizes that the important characteristics may concern the relationship
between investors as well as the tax consequences of contemplated actions for the
entity and for its investors.

We will start by looking at the differences most relevant to the initial organization
of the entity. Many clients and their lawyers begin and end with these considerations
without taking a longer view. Then we will look at the differences in operating
the enterprise. We further divide these into financial operation and managerial operation. Finally, we look at the differences germane to transferring ownership interests in
the entity.

1. Organizational Differences

The differences between entities that pertain to the area of initially organizing the
entity are few. When the entity's organization is more broadly conceived as encompassing the entity's financing, both at start-up and over time, then the differences
are more important. Creating an entity and drafting the initial operative documents
and side agreements takes about the same amount of lawyer and client time and
money.

One of the major differences among forms has to do with the entity's capitalization. In general, any kind of entity can give the parties the mix of economic and
managerial rights they desire. However, where the parties anticipate that within a
few years they will solicit equity capital from more than about 20 others who will
not be active in day-to-day management, then there are differences among the entities.
The only realistic ownership interest for such investors is stock in a corporation.
Further, in many instances the parties' desire for differing managerial or financial
rights may rule out an S corporation.

The other major difference among forms is that S corporations have restrictions on the number and kind of owners. These restrictions do not apply to the other forms.

2. Operational Differences

a. *Financial*

Business entities differ from one another in their financial operation in three ways. First, when planning the financial rights each investor will get, you may remember that shares of the same class or series of stock must be identical. So, all investors holding the same kind of shares will receive the same per-share right to dividends. Also, you may remember that shareholders purchasing stock contemporaneously must pay the same price per share. In effect, the economic rights a shareholder receives are proportional to his or her investment relative to that of other investors. While these rules ensure equal treatment of shareholders (proportionate to their shareholdings), they inhibit the planner's ability to tailor financial rights to each investor. By contrast, partnerships and LLCs need not make the investors' economic rights proportionate to their relative investment.[1]

The second financial difference is that the profits and losses of C corporations are recognized only by the entity, not by its shareholders. The profits and losses of S corporations, partnerships, and LLCs are allocated to their owners, pursuant to the owners' agreement. C corporation shareholders, then, do not recognize income until the corporation pays dividends, which gives the owners at least some control over the timing of their income. Owners of the other entities do not have such control over the timing of their income.

Finally, the entities vary as to the tax consequences of distribution of property or money from the entity to its owners. Remember, allocation means assigning profits or losses to owners; it is not synonymous with the distribution of assets to owners. Distributions by partnerships, S corporations, and LLCs, are generally not taxed because the owners have already paid tax when the profits were allocated to them. Dividends by C corporations are taxed as ordinary income to the shareholders. Further, a C corporation cannot allocate or "distribute" its losses to its shareholders. This means that shareholders of a C corporation that experiences losses cannot take advantage of those losses through reducing their own income, as partnership, S corporation, and LLC owners can.

b. *Managerial*

The differences in this area are not so much bright-line ones as practical differences in the default provisions. Generally, any kind of plan for allocating management

---

1. You may remember that at the end of Chapter 18 we discussed partnership forms more exotic than the general and limited partnerships. Specifically, we adverted to the existence of limited liability partnerships (LLPs) and limited liability limited partnerships (LLLPs). Both forms are taxed as partnerships as LLCs are. Both also provide limited liability for all participants much like that afforded to LLC members and managers and to corporate shareholders. Be aware that the differences in limited liability provisions vary among the states. Also, some states treat LLCs as entities for state income tax purposes but not LLPs or LLLPs. Thus depending upon state law, LLPs and LLLPs are essentially equivalent to LLCs or may be different in important ways. Because, in general, LLPs and LLLPs are equivalent to LLCs, we will not mention them again.

power can be effected in any of the entities, although with varying degrees of ease and efficacy.

The division of managerial power between the entities must be very clear to you by now. In corporations, all power is in the board subject to an annual referendum of the shareholders. In partnerships, every partner has equal management power. In LLCs the default rule is the partnership model (although some states provide that default power is proportional to the capital contributed rather than per capita among the members). As with the financial operation of the entity, disparate treatment of the parties, especially treatment that is not proportional to the amount invested, is easier to accomplish in noncorporate entities.

The entities also vary in the default power of an owner to bind the enterprise in the absence of actual authority. Shareholders have no power to bind the corporation but every partner is an agent of the partnership and can bind the partnership even beyond the partnership's business if the action is consistent with the kind of business in which the partnership is engaged. See UPA §301. LLC members have the same presumptive power to bind the entity as partners do, but that presumption may be more easily overcome in the LLC setting because (a) there's no equivalent of section 301 expansion of authority beyond the actual business conducted by the entity, and (b) many LLCs are manager managed so a third party's expectations should be different as to members than as to partners.

Perhaps the most salient difference between the entities is in the personal liability of owners. General partners are jointly and severally liable for the entity's debts.[2] Limited liability exists in varying degrees in the other entities. Shareholders are not liable for the corporation's debts in the absence of piercing the corporate veil settings. Limited partners are similarly not liable for a limited partnership's debts. Members' limited liability is the same as that of shareholders or limited partners, but the settings in which the entity will be pierced are more uncertain. Some state statutes explicitly provide that corporate piercing doctrine be applied to LLCs. Other statutes are silent and little case law exists at present. We looked at this issue in Chapter 19.

Many planners view limited liability in start-up businesses as an illusory quality because creditors (either lenders of capital or trade creditors) will typically require the principals to agree to personal liability as a condition of extending credit. Nonetheless, where the enterprise is likely to face tort claims rather than contract claims, limited liability is a genuine distinction between the forms.

3. Differences Regarding Transferred Ownership Interest

Here again the primary non-tax differences between the forms are not typically mandatory provisions but rather default rules that can be altered more or less satisfactorily. The tax consequences of transfer are significantly different among the forms, however, and cannot be completely eliminated.

Stock is freely alienable unless the Articles of Incorporation provide otherwise. The transferee has complete ownership of the shares and the transferor retains none. Further, the shareholders themselves may have contracted to restrict the transfer-

---

2. Where the partners are not individuals but rather limited liability entities, there may be no human who is personally liable. Still, the principle is the same.

ability of shares. Remember, however, that an agreement that separates the economic interest from the managerial interest may be invalid if the result is a voting trust that does not comply with the statute.

A companion issue to transferability is that of *guaranteed exit*. That is, do owners have a right to relinquish their ownership interest at will and receive money from the entity? Stock can be made redeemable, but at least some stock must not be redeemable or callable. Again, the parties may contract to purchase an owner's interest in certain settings but in the absence of such agreements a shareholder has no guaranteed exit.

Only the economic portion of a partnership or LLC interest is freely transferable. The management portion remains with the original partner or member. Further, even though a partner has transferred all his or her economic interest, he or she remains personally liable for the partnership's liabilities. The transferee does not become a partner or member but merely has certain economic rights in the entity. In both the partnership and LLC setting, the parties can agree that an owner's full interest may be transferred and may also provide that such new owner automatically becomes a partner or member. Especially in the partnership context, however, such provisions would be unusual because of the intertwined nature of partners' interests. As to exit, the default partnership (and under some LLC statutes) rule is that a partner or member may dissociate at any time and receive the value of his or her ownership interest in cash, unless the dissociation was wrongful. That is, partners and possibly members have guaranteed exit. This rule is frequently but not always negated by agreement among the parties.

The differing tax consequences of ownership transfer among the entities make this area particularly important. The tax consequences of stock are easy. Such transfer has no effect on the corporation or other stockholders. The transferor recognizes gain or loss and the transferee's basis is the fair value of the stock at the time of transfer. Dividends are recognized as income by the stock's owner on the record date; this bright-line rule makes it easy to know whether the transferor or transferee receives the gain. If the entity is an S corporation, the buyer and seller prorate the year's profits and losses.

Partnership and LLC transfers raise much more complex issues. The entity and thus the other owners are affected as well as the buyer and seller. To give you just an outline of the difficulties, imagine a partnership or LLC with four equal owners. The entity has one asset, which was purchased for (i.e., the entity's basis is) $100,000. Several years later the asset's value is $1.1 million. One owner transfers his or her entire financial interest for fair value to a new owner for $275,000. The transferor has a capital gain of $250,000 (i.e., $275,000 consideration less $25,000 basis). If the entity now sells the asset for $1.1 million, each partner has income of $250,000 (one-fourth of the $1 million gain). This is unfair to the new owner who just paid $275,000 for an asset (the ownership interest) worth $275,000. The new owner's basis should be $275,000 rather than $25,000. This is called an "inside basis" problem and the Internal Revenue Code permits the partnership to solve the problem by letting the new owner (but not the continuing owners) increase ("step up") his or her basis to $275,000. Thus on the sale the three original owners have income of $250,000 and the new owner has no income. If the entity is anticipating many transfers of ownership interests, keeping track of the owners' differing bases quickly becomes a nightmare. As a practical matter, then, a partnership or LLC is infeasible for entities in which there are likely to be many changes of ownership.

B. HOW TO CHOOSE THE APPROPRIATE ENTITY

Having surfaced the important differences among the various business entities, we now come to choosing the most appropriate entity for a particular business, recognizing that no entity may be perfect. What follows is one protocol for achieving the goal. Among the information you will want to obtain from your clients, the questions that bear on the choice of entity can be divided into those that require or eliminate certain forms and those that only militate toward or away from certain forms. As you gather this information you might want to press your clients particularly hard about their answers to ensure they understand the consequences of their preferences. You should be aware that state and local regulations might change this protocol. For example, some states treat all LLCs as entities for income tax purposes rather than following the federal default rule of pass-through taxation. Another common variation among states is in the kind of limitations on liability that partners in LLPs enjoy. Thus you must be particularly attentive to the vagaries of the jurisdiction in which you practice.

Client choices that require or eliminate certain forms:

Will the owners be restricted to 75 or fewer individuals (or certain trusts)?

If not, an S corporation is unavailable.

Is it important to control the timing of income receipt and recognition for the owners? Relatedly, is income anticipated with such certainty and magnitude that the timing question is genuinely important?

If so, a C corporation or LLC electing to be taxed under Subchapter C is required.

Is it important for the owners to recognize losses? Relatedly, are losses anticipated with such certainty and at such a magnitude that the question of recognizing losses is genuinely important?

If so, an S corporation, partnership or LLC is required.

Is the possibility of uninsurable tort liability such that the owners must be protected from personal liability?

If so, a partnership is unavailable.

Do the owners anticipate that there will be multiple transfers of ownership interests?

If so, a corporation or LLC electing to be taxed under Subchapter C are the only realistic entities.

Client choices that militate toward or away from certain forms:

Do the owners anticipate raising capital from many owners?

If so, a C corporation or LLC electing to be taxed under Subchapter C is more appropriate.

Do the owners anticipate that their financial rights will not be proportional to their investment or managerial interests?

If so, a partnership or LLC is more appropriate.

Will management of the entity be permanently allocated with little or no owner power to change that management?

If so, a limited partnership or LLC is more appropriate.

Will management of the entity be allocated with some (e.g., annual) owner power to change that management?

If so, a corporation or LLC is more appropriate.

Will management of the entity be shared among the owners?

If so, a partnership or LLC is more appropriate.

Will the owners have the power to bind the entity?

If so, a partnership or LLC is more appropriate. If not, a corporation is more appropriate.

Is free transferability of economic and managerial ownership important?

If so, a corporation is more appropriate.

Do the owners want to ensure they may exit the business?

If so, a general partnership or LLC is more appropriate.

C. FIXING THE PROBLEM

OK, *what* problem? The "problem" of too many, and too indistinct, entities. As you know, until the mid-1990s corporations, general partnerships, and limited partnerships were the only significant entity choices. More importantly, the differences between the entities were not amenable to significant amelioration. With the spread of the LLC and, to a lesser extent the LLP and LLLP, and with the increased power of planners to vary entity default rules, the current system evolved.

But the current system need not persist. In recent years academics and thoughtful practitioners have focused on the question whether the current system is desirable and, if not, how it might be changed. Below are observations from two of the most thoughtful commentators. The first article describes the landscape of entities and suggests reform.

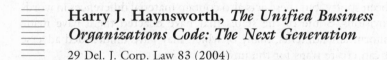

Harry J. Haynsworth, *The Unified Business Organizations Code: The Next Generation*

29 Del. J. Corp. Law 83 (2004)

In 1990 only two states had statutes authorizing LLCs. By the end of 1996, all fifty states and the District of Columbia had LLC statutes. In 2002, forty percent of all new businesses in the United States were formed as LLCs and in at least twenty-eight states more LLCs than corporations were formed. In the period between 2000 and 2002, the number of new businesses formed as corporations declined from fifty-nine percent in 2000 to forty-eight percent in 2002.

The increase in the number of business forms is bewildering to practicing lawyers, judges, law professors, and legislators. Almost every year, a new type of entity or a major revision to an existing business organization statute is promulgated or enacted. Frequently, the cause of the statutory modifications have been precipitated by changes in federal tax law. LLC legislation in the 1990s is an example. In 1996 the IRS approved the so-called check-the-box regulations which eliminated many of the prior requirements necessary for partnership taxation. This change was followed by [a] nationwide flurry of LLC statutory amendments.

The differences between the various state business organization statutes are significant and the problems resulting from these differences are growing. In many respects, Delaware is ahead of most states in trying to maintain reasonable consistency between the statutory provisions that govern each type of organizational format. When a change is made in one business entity statute, the practice in Delaware is to enact parallel statutory language in all the other business entity statutes that have similar provisions. This is not an easy task because the various statutory provisions are currently in four separate titles of the Delaware Code.

The Model Business Corporation Act (MBCA), which also includes special supplements for close corporations and professional corporations, has been amended extensively in the past twenty years to take into account developments in corporate law. Approximately twenty-four states have adopted all or substantially all of the MBCA. Most of the Model Act states have not, however, adopted all the various amendments to the Model Act approved by the ABA Committee on Corporate Laws. Twenty-nine states adopted the 1964 version of the Model Nonprofit Corporation Act but only two states have adopted the 1987 Revised Model Nonprofit Corporation Act.

The National Conference of Commissioners on Uniform State Laws, which has traditionally drafted uniform acts governing unincorporated organizations, has promulgated new versions of the Uniform Partnership Act and the Uniform Limited Partnership Act and has approved two new uniform unincorporated organizations acts in the past decade. The Revised Uniform Partnership Act . . . was approved in 1997. It has been adopted in thirty states including Delaware . . . but the remaining states still have the 1914 version of the Uniform Partnership Act. The Uniform Limited Partnership Act . . . was extensively revised and reapproved in 2001. Most states, however, still have the 1985 version of the ULPA. The two new uniform acts governing unincorporated organizations are the Uniform Limited Liability Company Act (1996), adopted in eight states, and the Uniform Unincorporated Nonprofit Association Act (1996), adopted in ten states.

Not only has the enactment of the recently promulgated uniform unincorporated organization acts been spotty, but these acts also contain material differences in wording for similar provisions. Some of the states that have enacted them have made significant non-uniform amendments, many of which may have unintended adverse consequences that can create traps for the unwary.

The lack of uniformity in style, format and substance is particularly acute with respect to limited liability company legislation. In many cases, amendments that fundamentally change the basic rights of the LLC members have been enacted at the insistence of a small group of lawyers. Several states, for example, have amended their statutes at the request of estate planning lawyers to provide that a member cannot sell or dispose of his or her interest unless the operating agreement otherwise provides. This will supposedly reduce the valuation of ownership interests with resulting favorable tax consequences for inter-family transfers of LLC ownership interests. The Uniform Limited Liability Company Act, however, which uses the Uniform Partnership Act as its model, provides that a member can dispose of his or her economic interest (but not the governance rights) unless otherwise agreed in the operating agreement. In states that have adopted the no-exit default rule, a serious trap for the unwary lawyer who might assume that because LLC statutes are based on a partnership model the partnership exit rights, or something similar, can exist. The lock-in created by this change in the default exit rule can lead to the same problems that have faced minority shareholders in closely held corporations who have no market for their shares. Most corporate codes, however, now contain involuntary dissolution provisions and buy-out rights that provide reasonable remedies from arbitrary and oppressive action by the minority shareholders. Members of LLCs in states that have the no-exit default rule may not, however, have these same exit rights, unless the lawyer representing the members is astute enough to draft them in the operating agreement.

My suggestion for reform is to create a unified business organizations code. The idea of a unified business organizations code is not new. The perplexing question has always been what such a code would look like. At one extreme are hub-and-spoke proposals that would attempt to eliminate all the non-essential differences between the various organizational forms leaving a single formulation for each major element, for example, the fiduciary duties of equity owners. The end result would presumably be a business organizations code having a large core that applied to all the various forms and separate rather short chapters for each of the different forms that continue to exist. Another type of hub-and-spoke proposal seeks to harmonize and compile all of the common basically administrative provisions in the various organizational statutes such as definitions, filing of documents, and other formalities of formation, permissible names, purposes and powers, required records and inspection rights, registered agents and registered offices, service of process, indemnification, registration of foreign entities and the administrative powers of the Secretary of State in one article of the unified code and then have separate articles for each of the organizational forms. These articles would be basically the same as before consolidation into a single code, except for the omission of definitions and other provisions that would be moved to the general provisions article. The basic difference between these two hub-and-spoke proposals is in the amount and scope of material that is in the hub.

Other proposals for a unified code have focused on eliminating some of the existing forms. These proposals generally advocate retaining the traditional corporate code designed for large, publicly held corporations, and a separate code for small or closely held businesses with limited liability for the equity owners, broad contractual flexibility for matters relating to the owners rights inter se, and pass-through tax consequences.

The plethora of new business entity forms in recent years has spawned renewed interest in this approach.

A legitimate question that might be asked is: if all existing businesses can continue to operate under the statutes governing them before the new consolidated code was adopted, what positive purpose does the new code serve? The most logical response is that the new code will govern all new businesses established after it is enacted, and if it truly meets their needs, most, if not all, of the existing businesses will, over a period of time, convert to the new form or forms. This conversion process, however, could take innumerable years.

A counter argument is that a great deal of convergence of the various forms has already taken place and the consolidation code will speed up a process that is well underway. Therefore, the conversion and transition issues may not be that difficult to resolve. The proponents of this line of reasoning will point to the many cases where courts have applied partnership fiduciary duty principles to close corporations on the basis that they are really partnerships in a corporate form. Many state corporate codes also specifically authorize shareholder management agreements that can allow shareholders in a close corporation to eliminate the board of directors and have a management system similar to a partnership. Moreover, many partnership and limited liability company acts increasingly contain provisions formerly found only in corporate codes.

The convergence that has taken place, however, is not necessarily a good thing. For example, the attempt to apply partnership fiduciary duties to close corporations has not been universally praised as a positive development. More importantly, convergence does not necessarily lead to consolidation. In short, convergence may occur while leaving all the various business forms intact.

A more telling argument against eliminating one or more of the existing organizational forms is the fact that the business organization marketplace provides empirical evidence of the demand for each of the existing forms. The number of limited partnerships, for instance, continues to increase despite the growing popularity of limited liability companies. Moreover, corporations, including close corporations, continue to be formed at a somewhat reduced but nevertheless brisk rate.

Another argument against undertaking a business organizations code with the objective of elimination of some of the existing organizational formats is the role federal tax policy has played in the development of the various types of business organizations. The rapid development of limited liability companies after . . . authorizing limited liability companies to be taxed as partnerships is only the most recent example.

Finally, statutes and regulations other than tax law also impact on the choice of business form decision. Some states prohibit certain types of businesses from operating in a particular form. In Oklahoma, for example, it is not permissible for a liquor store to operate as an LLC. Moreover, regulations of professional firms in many states may make one type of organizational format either more or less desirable than other possible forms. There are many other state and federal statutes that can have major impact on which organization form best fits the needs of a particular business. The elimination of one or more forms could have the unintended consequence of causing significant adverse regulatory problems for existing businesses that have been organized in a format that complies with (or successfully avoids) these regulations.

Notes and Questions

1. Reality Check

a. Why is entity reform necessary?
b. What are the arguments against entity reform?
c. What is Dean Haynsworth's vision for reform?

2. Suppose

a. Suppose entity rationalization became a reality. Would this book be 400 pages shorter? Would this course have two fewer credits?

3. What Do You Think?

a. Why have so many different business entities developed?
b. Do you think entity reform is necessary or desirable?
c. Is Dean Haynsworth's vision realistic?

≡ **Richard A. Booth, *Form and Function in***
≡ ***Business Organizations***
≡ 58 Bus. Law. 1433 (2003)

Lawyers and academics who deal with the law of business organizations on a regular basis tend to minimize the differences between partnerships, corporations, and other forms of business organization. It is possible—perhaps even quite easy—to set up a corporation that works like a partnership or a partnership that works like a corporation. Some of us even question whether the law matters in this realm other than in connection with taxes—and now it may not matter much there. The question that naturally arises is why not get rid of this ever expanding alphabet soup of corporations, partnerships, limited partnerships, limited liability companies (LLCs),...and replace it with a unified system? In other words, is it not time for entity rationalization?

The standard response is that not every lawyer specializes in the law of business organizations. Indeed, not everyone who sets up a business organization is a lawyer. In other words, there are certain efficiencies inherent in off-the-rack forms of organization. Standard form firms reduce transaction costs and therefore make it cheaper and easier to form a business. Standard form firms mean that it is not necessary to reinvent the wheel every time one forms a business organization.

This answer—which might well be the first to occur to most lawyers—is strikingly parochial. It assumes that law is for lawyers in that it focuses on the convenience of those who design business organizations. But what about those who work with or within the structure of a corporation or partnership? How are they affected by the difference in structures? Does it matter to a junior partner or a lower level officer in a corporation that he or she is working in a partnership or corporation? And what about investors, suppliers, and customers? Does it matter to them whether they deal with a corporation or partnership?

It seems clear that there are fundamental differences between forms. Viewed from within, a corporation is a hierarchy with the chief executive officer (CEO) at the top of the pyramid. It is essentially a vertical form of organization. A partnership, on the other hand, is basically a horizontal form of organization. Of course, most businesses are somewhat mixed. Division heads within a corporation may have considerable freedom. And a managing partner may have considerable authority. It seems clear, however, that those within an organization may have a strong preference for one form or the other, and that one form or the other may be better for certain lines of business. For example, banks, investment banks, and brokerage firms were once invariably partnerships. Now they are primarily corporations, but many are still essentially partner-owned as a result of massive stock option plans. Law firms are still primarily partnerships.... Accounting firms have become more like corporations. And medical practices have become even more like corporations with the advent of health maintenance organizations. There are also examples of migration in the other direction. [T]he heavy use of stock options as compensation in technology firms, together with the relatively small percentage of shares typically offered to the public, is...reminiscent of a partnership. These examples all suggest that choice of form may affect the culture of a firm, and indeed that choosing the wrong form or mixing and matching elements may be harmful.

Why do people choose the business forms that they do? And why do they modify some default rules but not others? Presumably, one would want to know the answer before tinkering too much with existing forms as they have evolved over the years. To be sure, I assume here that entity rationalization means simplification to some degree and not just codification. I do not necessarily assume that the goal of entity rationalization is a single form of organization. My point is that even if entity rationalization only involves the designation of certain features of the law or procedures that will be common to all forms of organization, we need to be sure that those features are not linked in some special way to other form-specific features. On the other hand, if entity rationalization means that businesspeople will have more choice (generally a good thing), we need to think about what we should do (if anything) to steer them away from choices that, like certain drugs, may not interact well with each other.

WHY PEOPLE FORM FIRMS

Before attempting to answer this question, one must deal with a still more fundamental question. Who cares? Why does it matter? Is it not enough simply to observe that people do form firms, whatever the reason may be? The answer is that if individuals form firms for a variety of reasons, it may be appropriate to have a variety of forms. Moreover, we should not limit our focus to formation. An equally important question is why do people join firms? Some forms of organization may be more attractive to recruits than others.

I have identified at least five general reasons: (i) delegation and specialization, (ii) diversification, (iii) separation and legitimacy, (iv) managing competition, and (v) discipline and incentives. There may be more.

Delegation and Specialization

People often retain agents because they do not have the time or expertise to conduct their own business. In other words, it may be cheaper to hire someone to do some tasks than it is to do them yourself, whether in terms of out-of-pocket expenses or in terms of opportunity costs. And if you need someone to perform a particular task repeatedly, it may be cheaper still to hire one or more employees.

But why would an employee take a job in such a pyramid scheme in which the employer keeps the profits? One answer is that a firm may be able to generate more business opportunities than could a self-employed individual. Moreover, the firm may have other resources or tools that the employee needs in order to do the work — tools that the employee could not afford to acquire individually.

Diversification

[P]articipants in a firm may also benefit from diversification in a variety of ways. A firm may be able to generate a more regular stream of business opportunities than could an individual. Also, the firm may be able to smooth out the income stream for individuals. Similarly, by joining a firm, one may be able to call on others to fill in if one is too busy or even simply to manage one's schedule and get in a round of golf. A firm may also provide a form of insurance by absorbing the costs of accidents through vicarious liability.

Separation and Legitimacy

In some cases, people form a firm simply to separate business from self. Of course, one of the primary motivations here is limited liability and the insulation of assets from unrelated liabilities. But limited liability aside, forming a corporation (for example) may give the business more legitimacy than doing business under one's own name as a sole proprietor. It suggests to the world that the business is something more than (and different from) the individual who owns it. And indeed this separation of business from participants is what allows a corporation to raise equity capital from outside investors.

A related, but somewhat more substantial reason for forming a firm is that when two or more people have joined together to conduct a business, it suggests that the business may be better thought out and therefore more trustworthy than a business that has been started by a single individual who may have idiosyncratic ideas. Similarly, it may be easier to attract others to join a firm than it is to retain the services of an independent contractor or free-lance agent to provide some needed input. Or association with a firm may add value to an agent's contribution. My basic point here is that there is a tendency to view firms primarily in terms of internal control structure. But external appearance may also matter. To sum up, people sometimes form firms simply to gain status for the enterprise or to define status to the world.

Managing Competition

In some cases, people form firms to reduce competition. In other words, two or more competitors might form a partnership in order to split the available profits, while saving the costs of competing (such as advertising). Of course, by eliminating competition, a firm may also be able to raise prices or restrict output. Although this may be illegal under the antitrust laws for very large businesses, it is fairly clear that it is an important reason for some smaller businesses. Whatever one might think of such tactics, and whether or not such agreements are ultimately enforceable, it is quite clear that non-competition is a motive. In any event, it is far easier to achieve the same result by forming a firm....

Although it is clear that businesspeople might form a firm to reduce competition, it is also possible that forming a firm may increase competition. In some cases, consumers are more likely to seek out a department store or supermarket than a boutique or specialty shop. Of course, the opposite is true as well. The point is that a firm with a wider array of products and services may sometimes be more attractive to consumers. Or the firm may serve to concentrate talent in such a way that it produces a better product. For example, a law firm (or a law faculty for that matter) may produce better services or written product because the various members are able to have their work reviewed, checked, or commented on by others.

Discipline and Incentives

One final motivation for forming a firm (or joining one) is that association with a group may generate additional motivation, perhaps particularly for people who are not self-starters. In other words, it may be that people form or join firms to force themselves to work harder or to impose discipline that may be difficult to self-impose.

To sum up, there are several distinct reasons why people form firms. Curiously, most of those reasons seem to turn more on the relationship of active participants to each other or on the relationship of the firm to various third parties (including creditors), than on the relationship between participants and investors. Of course, investors are interested in how well managers work with each other, but not too interested. A diversified investor cares little about the fortunes of individual companies. It may be, therefore, that we lawyers, judges, and academics have given short shrift to how well the rules work for those who toil day to day in the trenches of partnerships and corporations. Moreover, the recent spate of corporate scandals strongly suggests we should focus more on internal controls than we have in the past, particularly in connection with firms that do not have a large, involved shareholder. External monitors may not be nearly as important as we have made them out to be.

Does Form Follow Function?

The fact that there seem to be several discrete reasons for forming firms suggests the possibility that there may be a need for several discrete firm forms or — assuming complete freedom of contract — that several distinct forms are likely to evolve.

In summary, . . . if one were to eliminate the arguably artificial incentives of limited liability and differing tax treatment from the mix of reasons for choosing a particular form, there would still be good reasons for choosing one form over another.

It almost goes without saying that managers and investors may have a distinct preference for one form over another. Indeed, most people would likely say that organization law is primarily about the relationship between investors and managers. But suppliers and customers may also care about organizational form. In other words, it also seems quite possible that third parties may have a preference for dealing with a particular kind of firm.

It is difficult to believe that an entrepreneur does not think about how choice of entity will help the business succeed. Indeed, many say that venture capital firms prefer to deal with corporations. Although there are several technical reasons offered for this preference (such as worries about unrelated business income for nonprofit investors), most have been debunked. In the end, however, it may be that investors are simply worried that there may be too many surprises lurking in the customized structure of alternative forms such as LLCs. Thus, it may be that one function of the corporate form is to provide a more or less standardized package of rights (or at least parameters) that can be more easily and reliably understood by potential investors and other third parties. As it turns out, this is nothing new. The stock exchanges have always imposed listing standards, presumably for similar reasons. And recent events notwithstanding, one of the essential functions of generally accepted accounting principles (GAAP) is to foster comparability across companies. Although one might question the need for standardization, it seems clear that in a world of innumerable investment opportunities, a firm can compete better for capital if it is more easily understood by potential investors. In other words, it costs less for investors to invest in a familiar form of organization. That is not to say that a new control feature of some sort might not be attractive and indeed afford the firm an edge from time to time. But that does not mean that it makes sense to reinvent the wheel with every deal. Boilerplate has its value.

There is probably less bureaucracy in a partnership and more choice of who will handle your business. Indeed, it is clear in a partnership that each partner has the authority to bind the firm. With a corporation, on the other hand, there is an ultimate authority and it is fairly clear that all of the assets of the business are pledged in connection with each transaction undertaken. As I have argued elsewhere, the ultimate rationale for limited liability is that it facilitates bargaining with creditors. In the absence of limited liability, entrepreneurs would be presumed to risk all of their wealth in connection with each and every venture. With limited liability, an entrepreneur must agree to assume any risk beyond her investment in the venture. In other words, creditors are forced to negotiate for additional security.

IMPLICATIONS FOR ENTITY RATIONALIZATION

The fact that form follows function and the fact that certain features of organization law tend to be found together, living in symbiosis as it were, suggest that firm form matters. But the fact that discrete forms exist and persist does not necessarily imply that we should maintain rigid or even prototypical firm forms. And it certainly does not imply that we should return to the days of mandatory rules and the traditional corporate norm. After all, businesspeople and business lawyers might easily negotiate their way to the proper combinations even in the absence of a statute. Perhaps it would be more efficient for the law to provide a menu of provisions from which the parties may choose, though it is unclear whether such a creature would be a statute or law in any traditional sense.

On the other hand, if organization law is essentially contractual, then why do we need it at all? Although it may be somewhat extreme to suggest the repeal of organization law altogether, it is not self-evident that we should bother to rationalize the system. It is not clear that these contracts are any more important than others. For example, franchising is an important form of business organization, but there is no general franchise law designed to relieve the parties of the need to specify the terms. For some reason, the law leaves franchising almost entirely to negotiation, albeit a rather one-sided negotiation. Then again there are many forms of contractual arrangements that are the subject of fairly elaborate efforts to set down some standard terms, for example, the Uniform Commercial Code (UCC) and the *Restatement of Agency*. It bears noting that neither of these emanated in the first instance from a governmental authority. Both were the work of the American Law Institute (ALI), and the UCC was a joint effort with the National Conference of Commissioners on Uniform State Laws (NCCUSL). Similarly, most jurisdictions have standard forms for very common contracts, such as retaining a real estate broker or conveying residential real estate. So it may be that rationalization will come not from above but from convention. Or it may be that the first authoritative source of law tends to remain authoritative. Why does the law come from so many different sources and take so many different forms? What belongs in a statute and what should be left to contract? Organization law itself comes from multiple sources: state law, federal law, the American Bar Association (ABA), NCCUSL, the ALI, the various stock exchanges, and maybe even the Financial Accounting Standards Board (FASB). Undoubtedly, we should think hard about why a particular rule comes from a particular authority before we undertake to rationalize the system.

The ultimate question, however, is why do we have organization law at all? The easy answer is that it is cheap and convenient. But that is not a good enough answer. If it were, then no one would object to the notion that it is essentially a contract that may be varied at will. There are at least two ways in which organization law differs from a simple standard form contract.

First, organization law provides a set of default rules for individuals who fail to plan. This may be a good enough reason to worry about getting it right. Indeed, the common law of partnerships and later corporations, from which modern statutory law evolved, was (by definition) all about controversies, that is, sorting out the rights of various business constituencies. Statutes arose slowly and section by section as various common controversies were settled by legislative fiat. It is important to remember also that failure to plan may be intentional. Businesspeople often fail to plan because they sense that they are unlikely to reach an agreement with each other or because it is just too expensive to specify each detail. Thus, choosing a form is about choosing the preferred set of default rules. In addition, organization law may also be about reserving power to change these complex contracts without renegotiation among parties, whether by changing the law, or effectively agreeing to have the courts supply the missing terms through such vague concepts as fiduciary duty. The courts have traditionally been very reluctant to reform contracts except in the context of mutual mistake, and even then it is more likely that the contract will be voided. To be sure, contract law generally implies a duty of good faith. RUPA now explicitly incorporates a duty of good faith among partners. And corporation case law has recognized a duty of good faith. But the duty of good faith has seldom made a difference even though it has been repeatedly cited by bondholders.

Second, organization law provides a catalyst of sorts that makes it easier to reach an agreement in a complex multilateral setting. There are at the very least three parties to most businesses: participants, investors, and third parties, including creditors as well as suppliers and customers. All of these groups must negotiate somehow over both control and financial return. Needless to say, such a negotiation can be exceedingly complex and, like a game of rock-paper-scissors, may not — indeed probably will not — have a single stable solution. In the absence of well-crafted default rules, it may often be impossible to reach an agreement at all. In other words, prepackaged firms may be designed to solve complex bargaining problems involving multiple constituencies.

As I noted earlier, the best explanation for limited liability is that it facilitates bargaining between investors and creditors. Others have argued recently that partnership law may perform a similar function by setting default rules where the most deals are likely to end up anyway. For example, it has been argued that the default rule that partners are entitled to equal financial return may have evolved because those who are willing to agree to such a deal are more likely in the end to make deals and form firms (and ultimately succeed in making money). Thus, those who agree to equal shares will prosper, and those who insist on a greater share or are willing to accept a lesser share will evolve away. It has also been argued that partnerships are much more popular in the UK because they are somewhat more difficult to dissolve.

Although the foregoing arguments suggest that organization law matters, they do not really speak to the question of whether it is important to rationalize or unify the extant system. The jury is still out on this question. Clearly rationalization would have some benefits, but it would also have some costs. Perhaps the most obvious benefit is statutory simplification. It is far from clear, however, that this can be achieved.

A more concrete benefit may come from the identification and elimination of conflicting statutory provisions. For example, corporation law specifies the consequences of defective incorporation — joint and several liability for knowing participants. But presumably a non-corporation is also a partnership by default, the consequences of which are very different. In many situations, it is not at all clear which of these two provisions should apply. Presumably, a unified statute would eliminate such problems.

A subtler benefit arises from the fact that the law may sometimes confuse organizational rules with rules designed to regulate certain businesses that gravitate to a given form. For example, personal liability for partners may be more a function of attitudes toward professional malpractice than of partnership law. Clearly, such concerns weighed heavily in the evolution of the LLP. Similarly, limited liability for shareholders may be more a function of team production than of corporation law. Entity rationalization may help clarify these rules. For example, withdrawing such crutches as the prohibition on practicing law in the corporate form will force regulators to say what they mean.

On the other hand, some issues that appear to be matters of professional ethics, or otherwise outside the realm of organization law, may in fact properly be part of organization law. For example, the enforceability of non-competition agreements has been viewed as a matter of professional rules in some cases, simple contract in other cases, and fiduciary duty in still other cases. If in fact controlling competition is a proper reason for forming a firm, it may be that non-competition agreements should be viewed as part of organization law. Clearly, corporation law views competition as within its purview. But partnership law is essentially silent on the subject.

This raises the more general question of what should be included in organization law and what should not. For example, some states have recently added provisions relating to divisive reorganizations. Perhaps we should also consider statutory provisions relating to poison pills, tracking stock, or the terms of compensatory stock options. Such additions to statutory law, are not clearly necessary. These devices have arisen without benefit of legislative clergy. Still, most states have fairly elaborate provisions outlining the most common terms of preferred stock, even though with a few exceptions these provisions must be reiterated with specificity in the articles of incorporation in order to be enforceable. Is it really necessary that they be in the statute? Indeed, the rights of various ownership units in partnerships are often far more complex than those of preferred stock. Yet partnership law is almost totally silent about the ways in which financial rights may be varied.

One of the distinct risks of entity rationalization—at least under a menu approach that permits relatively free mixing and matching of terms—is that businesspeople will overplan and choose terms that do not work well together. The default rules for a particular organization may be internally coordinated in ways that are difficult to sort out. Mixing and matching rules from different organizations may be dangerous. The challenge is to determine which elements are safely modified and which are not. Too much freedom of contract, or making it too easy to mix and match terms, may also confuse the courts about which rules go together. Both phenomena are illustrated by the Massachusetts experience.

In *Donahue v. Rodd Electrotype Co.*, the court ruled that in a closely held corporation shareholders owe each other duties similar to those that partners owe each other because they are effectively locked in by the lack of a liquid market through which they might be able to exit (cash out). The result was that a minority shareholder was able to force the corporation to repurchase her shares because the majority shareholder had sold a block of his own shares back to the corporation. Although this rule seems sensible enough given the facts of the case, it quickly led to a series of unintended consequences. In a sense, it gave the minority shareholder exit rights similar to those in a partnership without considering the concomitant right to force dissolution of the firm.

The unintended consequences were quick to follow. In *Wilkes v. Springside Nursing Home*, the plaintiff minority shareholder argued in effect that he could not be fired from his positions as director, officer, and salaried employee, a position that is clearly consistent with the status of partner. In *Smith v. Atlantic Properties*, the four shareholders retained veto power over fundamental business decisions and fell into deadlock (and tax troubles) as a result of their inability to choose between dividends and reinvestment. In *Merola v. Exergen Corp.*, the plaintiff claimed that he had become a partner as a result of buying stock and hence could not be fired. And the question remains open whether the shareholder-to-shareholder duties created in *Donahue* mean that a minority shareholder can sue directly (rather than derivatively) when a controlling shareholder uses his power to the disadvantage of the minority. In short, Massachusetts bought into a multistep rejiggering of its corporation law prompted, at least in part, by shareholder opportunism in the wake of new found rights. And majority shareholders found that they did not have the power (or wealth) they may have thought they had.

On the other hand, Delaware and Maryland have more or less resisted the temptation to develop a special body of case law for close corporations. Indeed, it is well settled in Delaware that shareholders have no duty to each other. But it is also well settled that a controlling shareholder may not use that control to exact a benefit to the detriment and exclusion of the remaining shareholders. In any event, Delaware and Maryland have seen relatively little close corporation litigation. Moreover, it may well be that failure to appreciate the subtle interconnections between default rules may explain why the close corporation election has proved to be unpopular.

CONCLUSION

Business organization law matters. The fact that one can bargain around the law does not mean that most people do so. Indeed, it may be that the law is vital to getting any negotiation going. Bargaining happens in the shadow of the law. Thus, there is every reason to try to get the default rules right and to take great care in making sure that the rules are right in relation to each other. To the extent that entity rationalization eliminates unintentional conflicts between forms, it is a good thing. But simplification for its own sake is risky business.

Notes and Questions

1. Notes

a. We dealt with the Massachusetts rule announced in *Donahue* and *Wilkes* in Chapter 16 when we looked at the fiduciary duties of shareholders.

2. Reality Check

a. What is Professor Booth's assessment of entity rationalization?

b. How should entity rationalization be brought about, according to Professor Booth?

c. How is Professor Booth's vision of entity rationalization different from that of Dean Haynsworth?

3. What Do You Think?

a. Do you think that entity reform is necessary or desirable?

b. Do you think entity reform is more likely to come about from intentional efforts or from practical evolution?

D. TERMS OF ART IN THIS CHAPTER

| C corporation | Enterprise rationalization | Pass-through taxation |
| Double taxation | Guaranteed exit | S corporation |

Glossary

Absolute majority A majority of all the voting power, regardless of whether that power is present at the meeting; thus, absent votes are no votes. Chapter 15.

Accounting statements Independent accountants review the accounting records of their clients and prepare standardized reports, *accounting statements*, based on that review. Chapter 3.

Accredited investors A term of art that refers to rich people who invest in corporations. Chapter 6.

Actual authority A principal is bound to third parties by anything the agent does that is in accordance with the principal's "manifestation" to the agent. Chapter 4.

Adjustment and anchoring In many situations, people make estimates by starting from an initial value that is adjusted to yield the final answer. Adjustments are typically insufficient. That is, different starting points yield different estimates, which are biased toward the initial values. We call this phenomenon *anchoring*. Chapter 3.

Advance notice bylaw A clause that requires a shareholder to give the board notice of his or her intention to move a proposal or nominate directors at a meeting. Chapter 15 and Chapter 17.

Adverse selection Principals choosing suboptimal agents, or agents choosing suboptimal principals. Chapter 4.

Affiliated corporations Corporations under common control, whether parent-subsidiary or sibling corporations. Chapter 8.

Affirmative covenants Things that a borrowing corporation agrees to do or refrains from doing in order to make a loan less risky, such as maintaining certain financial ratios or agreeing to make all payments of other loans in a timely fashion. Chapter 6.

Agency costs The total of the expenditures made in ameliorating the moral hazard plus the residual loss resulting from moral hazard and risk differences between agent and principal. Chapter 4.

Agent In economics, one who uses some degree of judgment in performing a service for a principal's benefit. In law, one who agrees to act on behalf of another and subject to the other's control. Chapter 4.

All purpose clause A clause in the articles of incorporation that grants the corporation the power to pursue any lawful business. Chapter 10.

Allocation Assigning a partnership's or LLC's profits and losses among its members. Chapter 18 and Chapter 19.

Amotion The power of the shareholders to remove directors during their term. Chapter 9 and Chapter 15.

Angels Rich individuals who provide venture capital. Chapter 6.

Annual meeting Shareholder meeting that occurs once a year during which shareholders elect directors and engage in other valid shareholder action. Chapter 15.

Antidilution provision A provision that prevents a shareholder's ownership interest from being reduced by change in capital structure. Chapter 7.

Apparent authority An agent's power to bind the principal stemming from a third party's belief, traceable to the principal's manifestation, that the agent is authorized to act for the principal. Chapter 4.

Appraisal right A right, available in certain fundamental corporate changes, to require the corporation to purchase a dissenting shareholder's shares for fair value. Chapter 17.

Asset lock-up These clauses give the acquirer the option to purchase certain key target assets if the transaction does not close. Chapter 17.

At-will partnership A partnership that continues and exists indefinitely. Chapter 18.

Availability Situations in which people assess the frequency or probability of an event by the ease with which instances or occurrences can be brought to mind. Chapter 3.

Bacon Money.

Balance sheet An accounting statement that divides things you own on a particular date into assets and liabilities. It further divides both assets and liabilities into those that are liquid and those that are illiquid. Chapter 3.

Barristers British lawyers who had the exclusive right to appear in court on behalf of clients and derive their title from having been admitted to the bar. Chapter 1.

Beans Money.

Berle and Means type of corporation In corporate law scholarship, the paradigm of the large, publicly held corporation that is run by senior managers. Chapter 2.

Blank (or blank check) stock Stock authorized in the Articles of Incorporation as noncommon stock, the terms of which have not been determined. The characteristics of the stock are set by the board of directors. Chapter 6.

Board of directors The group of people that manages the business and affairs of every corporation and exercises all corporate power. Chapter 9.

Bonding An assurance, such as an insurance policy or a financial penalty clause in an agency agreement, that assures principals that agents will not shirk or behave opportunistically. Chapter 4.

Bonds Debt securities issued by a corporation that are typically secured by the corporation's assets. Chapter 6.

Book entry system System whereby an entity, the Depository Trust Company, credits or debits a brokerage house's account with the net number of shares of each corporation owed or owing to other brokerage houses at the end of each trading day. Shares are not actually transferred. Chapter 15.

Brass Money.

Bread Money.

Break-up value The value of a business comprising assets that would be worth more if operated separately. Chapter 3.

Break-up fee A termination provision that makes the target liable to the acquirer if the transaction fails to close. Chapter 17.

Broker overvote When a brokerage house inadvertently executes proxies (on behalf of shareholders) for more shares than it is entitled to vote. Chapter 15.

Bucks Money.

Business A business engages in sustained activities intended to generate more wealth than they use. Chapter 2.

Butter Money.

Buy-sell agreement A restriction on the transfer of shares in which both sides are required to effect a transaction. Chapter 7.

C corporation A corporation that is taxed as a separate entity, meaning the corporation's income is taxed twice, once at the corporate level and again when distributed to shareholders as dividends. Chapter 20.

Call The decision to hold a meeting at a particular time and place, and often, for a particular reason. Chapter 9 and Chapter 15.

Call option A real option that permits a business to do something. A financial option that connotes the standard right sold by a person other than the corporation to purchase securities of the corporation from that person. Chapter 6.

Callable Stock that the corporation has the power to require the shareholder to return for a predetermined price. Chapter 6.

Capital For no-par value shares, capital is some portion of the consideration paid for those shares. For par-value shares, capital is, at minimum, the par value of the shares. Chapter 7.

Capital expense An expense for an asset that is expected to last longer than one year. Chapter 3.

Capital formation The method by which a corporation gets money into the corporation. Chapter 6.

Capital gain The gain that an equity holder realizes when he or she sells equity in a corporation. Chapter 6.

Capital structure A corporation's choice of how much debt and equity it should have. It also refers to how much common stock and noncommon stock a corporation should issue. Chapter 6.

***Caremark* claim** When the plaintiff alleges a failure to establish and monitor information systems within the corporation. Chapter 13.

Cede & Co. A partner of DTC that holds the actual shares of stock to facilitate transfer when necessary; the shareholder of record for shares traded under the book entry system. Chapter 15.

Charging order A court order seizing a partner's transferable interest for the benefit of a judgment creditor of that partner; similar to a lien. Chapter 18.

Charter limitation A provision in the articles of incorporation that caps or eliminates monetary liability of directors for breach of their duty of care. Chapter 13.

Check kiting A fraud in which the perpetrator, having control over checking accounts at different banks, deposits checks drawn on one bank in the other bank to create the appearance of an increase in the balance in the other bank account. Chapter 12.

Class of stock Common stock or preferred stock. Chapter 6.

Classified board A board in which the power to elect at least one director is vested in, or denied to, at least one class or series of stock. Chapter 9.

Close (or closely held) corporations A corporation owned by few shareholders, or even by one person. Chapter 6.

Collar A loan with a minimum and maximum variable rate. Chapter 6.

Commercial paper market Loans to corporations that are good credit risks and need to borrow large amounts of money on a regular cycle. Chapter 6.

Common stock Shares that have (1) one vote per share on any matter submitted to the shareholders, (2) the right to its proportionate amount of any dividend, and (3) the right to its proportionate amount of the corporation's assets upon dissolution. Chapter 6.

Conflict of interest An incentive for a director or officer to act other than in the best interest of the corporation. Chapter 11.

Conglomeration A corporation's strategy of purchasing unrelated business that can stand alone. Chapter 17.

Constituent corporations Corporations that are parties to a merger. Chapter 17.

Continuity of enterprise exception An exception to the rule that a corporation is not liable for liabilites of a corporation from which it has purchased all assets. The transferee corporation is liable if the transferor's business itself is continued as a going concern even when there is no continuation of ownership between the transferor and transferee corporations. Chapter 8.

Control share acquisition acts Statutes that prohibit certain control transactions, such as mergers or sales of all assets, between a corporation and an entity controlling more than a certain amount (15% in Delaware) of shares. Chapter 17.

Convergence In corporate law scholarship, the theory that the forces of global competition will lead nations to adopt a single efficient form of corporate governance. Chapter 2.

Convertible Stock that may be exchanged for other securities of the corporation. Chapter 6.

Coping Efforts to manage specific demands (and conflicts between them) that are appraised as taxing or exceeding a person's resources. Chapter 3.

Corporate lawyer as conciliator A lawyer who is called upon to help resolve a conflict between the client and another, often regarding a potential transaction. Chapter 1.

Corporate lawyer as counselor A lawyer who gives advice to the client. Chapter 1.

Corporate lawyer as facilitator A lawyer who negotiates the substantive elements of a transaction such as price, quantity, and other essential points; ensures that the transaction complies with applicable regulations; or drafts writings that both accurately capture the agreed-upon terms and legally effect the anticipated transaction. Chapter 1.

Corporate lawyer as guardian A lawyer who protects the client and the public against some contemplated actions by persons acting on the client's behalf. Chapter 1.

Corporate opportunity A business opportunity presented to an officer or director that is so closely associated with the corporation's current business activities that the officer or director may not accept the opportunity for himself or herself in place of the corporation. Chapter 11.

Corporate social responsibility The corporate law theory that requires corporate managers and directors to take into account the needs not only of shareholders but of workers, consumers, and communities when making business decisions. Chapter 10.

Corporate survival statute Statutes designed to protect shareholders and corporate creditors when a solvent corporation dissolves. The statute permitting a soon-to-be dissolved corporation to notify its known creditors and to give notice to the public of the impending dissolution and thereby cut off future liability. Chapter 8.

Corporation by estoppel An equitable defense to individual liability predicated on defective incorporation. A third party can be estopped from denying the existence of the corporation when

it reasonably believes it is dealing only with an existing corporation. Chapter 5.

Counterparty risk The possibility that the other side of a transaction will not perform, either because of unwillingness or inability. Chapter 3.

Coupled with an interest A form of agency relationship that is irrevocable because of the agent's heightened interest in the subject of the agency relationship. Chapter 4.

Credit rating agencies Agencies that rank corporations by their perceived credit worthiness. Chapter 14.

Cumulative Preferred stock as to which the dividends, if not declared and paid, accumulate. The corporation is prohibited from paying dividends on other stock until the accumulated dividends have been paid in full. Chapter 6.

Cumulative voting A method of voting for directors in which each shareholder has the number of votes equal to the number of shares owned multiplied by the number of director slots to be filled. The shareholder may cast those votes for one candidate or distribute them among several candidates. Chapter 16.

Currency risk The possibility that exchange rates may change during the course of a transaction resulting in more or less home currency than was anticipated. Chapter 3.

DCF *See* Discounted cash flow. Chapter 3.

De facto An equitable defense to individual liability predicated on defective incorporation. A de facto corporation exists when an individual makes a good faith but ineffective attempt to incorporate. Chapter 5.

De jure A corporation that has substantially complied with all mandatory provisions that are intended to be conditions precedent to incorporation. Chapter 5.

Deadlock An impasse among directors or among shareholders. Chapter 16.

Deal protective measures Acquisition agreement clauses that are designed to ensure that a transaction closes. Chapter 17.

Debentures Debt securities issued by a corporation that are typically unsecured. Chapter 6.

Debt A temporary investment in a corporation that entails mandatory periodic interest payments and a return of the investment. A loan. Chapter 6.

Declared A dividend is declared when the board of directors authorizes the corporation to pay it. Chapter 7.

Default *See* Counterparty risk. Chapter 3.

Defeased A loan that the corporation repays out of a trust in which sufficient assets have been set aside to repay the loan in full. Chapter 6.

Defective incorporation The situation in which obligations are incurred in the name of a corporation that has not yet been formed. The corporation's promoter may be individually liable for such obligations. Chapter 5.

Defensive measures Actions taken by a target corporation's board to defeat raiders after a raid has begun. Chapter 17.

Definitive agreement The written acquisition contract between corporations. Chapter 17.

Delist A stock exchange's action that prohibits further trading in a particular company's securities. Chapter 7.

Demand excused Shareholder-plaintiff may file a derivative suit without making demand on the board if he or she can demonstrate that prior demand would have been "futile" because the board could not have evaluated the demand fairly. Chapter 15.

Demand refused A board's refusal to grant a shareholder's demand that the corporation redress harm caused to it. If the refusal was wrongful, the shareholder can file a derivative suit. Chapter 15.

Derivative action A lawsuit filed by shareholders on behalf of the corporation to redress harm to the corporation that the board will not redress. Chapter 15.

Diluted A reduction in a shareholder's ownership interest caused by the issuance of more shares. Chapter 6.

Disclosed principal A principal whose identity is known to a third party. Chapter 4.

Discount rate The rate used to calculate the present value of future money. The discount rate is an interest rate in reverse. Chapter 3.

Discounted cash flow A method of valuing an asset that will generate money in the future. It involves projecting net cash flows for a determined period, setting a terminal value of the asset at the end of the projected period, and then discounting those values at a set rate to determine the net present value. Chapter 3.

Discounting to present value The process of determining how much money one needs to invest today to receive a given amount at a certain time in the future. Chapter 3.

Dissenter's right The right of a dissenting shareholder to sell his or her shares to the corporation for fair value when the corporation engages in certain fundamental changes such as a merger or sale of all assets. Chapter 17.

Dissociated When a partner ceases to be a co-owner of a partnership. Chapter 18.

Dissociation The process by which a partner ceases to be a co-owner of a partnership, and his or her interest is bought out by the partnership. Chapter 18.

Dissolution The process by which a partnership or an LLC ceases to exist. All assets are disposed of, all creditors are paid, and the partners or members receive distributions of the any remainder. Chapter 18 and Chapter 19.

Distribution The transfer of partnership or LLC property (usually cash) to partners or members. Chapter 18 and Chapter 19.

Diversification Investing in assets that respond differently to particular risks. Diversification can reduce overall risk while preserving the assets' expected return. Chapter 3.

Dividend A distribution of the increased value (or part of it) of a corporation to its shareholders. Chapter 7.

Domestic corporation A corporation incorporated within the state. Chapter 5.

Double taxation Income earned by a corporation is taxed twice. Once when earned by the corporation and again when distributed to shareholders as a dividend. Chapter 20.

Dough-ray-mi Money.

DTC Depository Trust Company; an entity that acts as a custodian of shares and credits or debits the accounts of brokerage houses. Chapter 15.

Ducats Money.

Due diligence The acquiring corporation's investigation of a corporation to be acquired. Chapter 17.

Duty of care The fiduciary duty of a director to act on an informed basis or with the care that a person in a like position would reasonably believe appropriate under similar circumstances. Chapter 12.

Duty of loyalty The fiduciary duty of a director to take and approve only those actions the director believes to be in the corporation's best interest. Chapter 11.

Economic realities test An inquiry used by the IRS and courts to recharacterize debt as equity, when an unrelated third party would not have been willing to make a loan of similar size on similar terms to the corporation. Chapter 6.

Employee An agent whose principal controls or has the right to control the manner and means of the agent's performance of work. Chapter 4.

Enterprise liability A doctrine that allows a creditor to seek repayment not only from the debtor corporation but from related entities, as well. Chapter 8.

Enterprise rationalization A proposal that the multiple forms of entities be replaced by a unified system with one entity form complemented by a menu of options and choices. Chapter 20.

Entire fairness The standard of review of a directors' action in which the burden is on the defendants to demonstrate their utmost good faith and the most scrupulous inherent fairness of the bargain. It has two components: fair dealing and fair price. Chapter 13.

Equitable subordination A doctrine that protects creditors of a bankrupt corporation. The bankruptcy court may subordinate (i.e., give a lower preference to) debt that the court deems to resemble a shareholder's ownership interest more that a debt. Chapter 6 and Chapter 8.

Equity Ownership interest in a corporation. Chapter 6.

ESOP Employee stock ownership plan, which provides pension benefits to a corporation's employees through a trust that holds the corporation's stock. Also, a method of deterring hostile takeovers. Chapter 17.

Estoppel A theory under which a principal is liable for an agent's action, even if neither authorized nor apparently authorized, if third parties have changed their position in reliance upon their belief that the action was authorized and the principal caused (intentionally or carelessly) the belief, or if the principal, knowing of the belief, did nothing to notify the third parties of the facts. Chapter 4.

Event of default A significant or sustained violation of negative covenants by a debtor corporation. Chapter 6.

Exchange Act (or the '34 Act) One of two principal acts of Congress in the area of federal securities regulation. Chapter 6.

Exit strategy A motivation for changing control of a corporation that is triggered by some previously determined plan. Chapter 17.

Expected return The expected return of an investment is the sum of the value of each possible outcome multiplied by each outcome's likelihood. Chapter 3.

Fair value The value a dissenting shareholder is entitled to for his or her shares. Chapter 17.

Family capitalism Firms in which the entrepreneur and his or her close associates (and their families) who built the enterprise continue to hold the majority of stock, maintain a close personal relationship with their managers, and retain a major say in top management decisions. Chapter 2.

Financial capitalism Firms in which the financial institutions providing the corporation's capital are represented on the firm's board. The corporation's managers share top management decisions, particularly those involving the raising and spending of large sums of capital, with the representatives of the financial institutions. Chapter 2.

Flip in A provision, related to a poison pill, that allows shareholders to purchase half-price stock in the target if it will be the surviving entity in a merger. Chapter 17.

Flip over A provision, related to a poison pill, that allows shareholders to purchase half-price stock in the acquiring company if it will be the surviving entity in a merger. Chapter 17.

Floating interest rate A loan with an interest rate that varies over the life of the loan, possibly with a minimum or maximum rate. Chapter 6.

Foreign corporation A corporation that has been incorporated in another U.S. state. Chapter 5.

Foreign investment risk When investing assets in another country, the possibility that the other country might change its rules regarding foreign investment. Chapter 3.

Form S-1 A form required by the SEC to register a corporation's securities for sale to the public. Chapter 6.

Fraudulent conveyance A doctrine designed to protect a corporation's creditors. If a corporate debtor transfers assets for less than fair value at a time when it was insolvent and for the purpose of harming its other creditors, those other creditors can trace the transferred assets into the hands of the transferees. Chapter 8.

GAAP Generally Accepted Accounting Principles. The rules that tell accountants how to present the results of an audit. Chapter 3.

General partnerships Synonym for partnership used to distinguish an entity from other partnership forms such as limited partnerships. Chapter 18.

General proxy A proxy in which the agent is authorized to use his or her discretion in voting. Chapter 15.

Go public To sell securities of a corporation to the public for the first time. Chapter 6.

Going concern value The value of an asset operated as a discrete business. Chapter 3.

Going private transaction A transaction such as a merger or tender offer by which a public corporation becomes a private one. Chapter 17.

Greenmail The premium price that a corporation pays to to an obstreperous shareholder to reacquire the shareholder's shares. Chapter 7.

Group More than one shareholder agreeing to act in concert regarding ownership of publicly traded securities. Chapter 17.

Guaranteed exit An agreement by which a shareholder has a right to require the corporation to repurchase the shareholder's interest. Chapter 20.

Happy cabbage Money.

Hay Money.

Heuristics Short-cuts that people routinely employ in deciding how much information to get, how to analyze information, and how to make decisions. Chapter 3.

Holdover A director who has continued in office after the expiration of his or her term because no successor has been elected. Chapter 9 and Chapter 15.

Horizontal integration A combination of businesses engaged in the same enterprise. Chapter 2.

Hostile tender offer An offer to shareholders at a premium price for at least a majority of the shares, which offer is opposed by the corporation's board. Chapter 17.

Howey **test** Test to determine whether an investment is an investment contract and therefore a security. The elements are (1) an investment of money, (2) in a common enterprise, (3) in which the investor was led to expect profits (4) primarily from the efforts of the promoter or a third party. Chapter 18.

Ice Money.

Indemnification An agreement to pay a director's (or agent's) expenses incurred in defending a third party's claim against the defendant. Chapter 13.

Indenture A document that sets out the terms of the loan and is executed by the borrowing company and an investment bank, acting as trustee for the ultimate lenders. Chapter 6.

Inflation risk The possibility that inflation will be different than anticipated thus increasing or decreasing the value of money to be received in the future. Chapter 3.

In-house lawyer A lawyer who works as an employee *of* the client rather than as an employee of a law firm that is hired *by* the client. Chapter 1.

Initial public offering (IPO) The sale of a corporation's securities to the general public for the first time. Chapter 6.

Insider trading Buying or selling publicly traded securities while in possession of material nonpublic information. Chapter 7.

Insolvency test A test to determine whether a corporation has lawfully declared a dividend. The elements are whether, after the dividend, the corporation's assets will exceed its liabilities and whether the corporation can pay its debts as they come due. Chapter 7.

Inspection right A shareholder's right to examine certain corporation documents in certain circumstances. Chapter 15.

Interested person An entity controlling a certain percentage of a target corporation's shares. Chapter 17.

Intermediate scrutiny Standard of review in Delaware that applies to a board's defensive actions during a hostile takeover; in between the business judgment rule and the entire fairness standard. Chapter 17.

Internal affairs The relations inter se of the corporation, its shareholders, directors, officers, and agents. The internal affairs doctrine is a choice of law rule that provides that a corporation's interal affairs are governed by the law of the state of incorporation. Chapter 5.

Intrastate exemption An exemption from the registration requirements of the federal securities laws for securities that are offered and issued only to the residents of the state in which the issuing corporation is incorporated and doing business. Chapter 6.

Investment contract An investment of money in a common enterprise in which the investor has an expectation of profit to come solely from the efforts of others. Chapter 6.

Issued Shares that a corporation has exchanged for consideration. Chapter 6.

Joint venture A partnership formed for a limited time or for a limited purpose. Chapter 18.

Kale Money.

Legal capital test A test to determine whether a corporation may declare dividends. Dividends can be paid only if the corporation's legal capital is unimpaired. Chapter 7.

Letter of intent An agreement between the parties to negotiate with one another in good faith looking toward the acquisition of one entity by the other. Chapter 17.

Lettuce Money.

Limited liability company An entity that combines limited liability for the firm's owners and managers with pass-through taxation. Chapter 19.

Limited partnership A partnership with one or more general partners, who manage but have unlimited liability, and one or more limited partners, who do not manage but have limited liability. Chapter 18.

Limited proxy A proxy in which the shareholder authorizes the agent to vote in a particular way. Chapter 15.

Liquidity The relative ease with which an asset can be transferred. Chapter 3 and Chapter 6.

Lolly Money.

Long green Money.

Manager A person, either member or nonmember, selected to run an LLC. Managers have actual authority to bind the LLC and have fiduciary duties. Chapter 19.

Manager managed An LLC managed by managers rather than members. Chapter 19.

Managerial capitalism Firms in which ownership is widely scattered, salaried managers dominate top as well as lower and middle management, and in which those managers determine long-term policy as well as manage short-term operating activities. Chapter 2.

Marketability discount Discount applied to the value of a dissenting shareholder's shares in a close corporation to reflect the lack of marketability. Chapter 17.

Material adverse change Clause that permits a party to refuse to close a transaction if certain fundamental assumptions underlying the transactions have changed. Chapter 17.

Member A person with an ownership interest in the LLC. Chapter 19.

Member managed An LLC managed by its members rather than by managers. Chapter 19.

Mere continuation exception A successor liability doctrine in which the key element is whether there is a common identity of the officers, directors, and stockholders among the selling and purchasing corporations. Chapter 8.

Merger A transaction in which the assets and liabilities of one corporation are transferred by operation of law to another corporation and the first corporation ceases existence. Chapter 17.

Middle manager Supervises managers below and reports to managers above. Chapter 2.

Minority discount The discount applied to the value of a dissenting shareholder's shares, when the corporation has a majority shareholder, to reflect the lack of managerial power. Chapter 17.

Monitor A method used to decrease the costs of the agency relationship. It can include watching the agent work, measuring the agent's efforts, or contractual limitations on the agent's discretion. Chapter 4.

Moolah Money.

Moral hazard The risk that a party with discretion to act will choose an action that decreases the expected value of the transaction to the other party in a way that the other party cannot effectively prohibit. Chapter 4.

Negative covenants Agreements between a debtor corporation and a lender that prohibit the debtor from taking certain actions that may disadvantage the lender. Chapter 6.

Net cash flow The cash generated by an asset net of the cash used to acquire or maintain the asset. Chapter 3.

Net present value The cost of an asset minus its present value. Chapter 3.

Nexus of contract A theory that views the corporation as an aggregate of various inputs acting together to produce goods or services. Chapter 10.

NOBO list A list of nonobjecting beneficial owners of a corporation's stock who do not object to the disclosure of their names and addresses to the corporation for the limited purpose of allowing direct communication on corporate matters. Chapter 15.

No-shop A clause in an acquisition agreement that prevents the target board from actively seeking other potential acquirers. Chapter 17.

No-talk A clause in an acquisition agreement that prevents the target board from negotiating with, or providing nonpublic information to, a party other than the acquirer. Chapter 17.

Notice The requirement that the board or shareholders must become aware that a meeting has been called. The time and content requirements of the notice are different for board and shareholder meetings. Chapter 9 and Chapter 15.

Officer An officer is a person who holds a corporate position to which particular kinds of duties or powers are attached. The term includes a president, vice president, secretary, principal financial officer, principal accounting officer, or any person routinely performing corresponding functions Chapter 9.

Oil of palm Money.

Oof Money.

Operating agreement The detailed LLC governance agreement among all the members, and sometimes all the managers, that sets forth the names of the members and their respective economic interests, the managers (if any) and how power will be allocated between members and managers and, among the managers, and whether there will be particular officers with delegated duties; analogous to a partnership agreement. Chapter 19.

Operating expenses Expenses for assets that are expected to be used up in within one year. Chapter 3.

Oppression A cause of action by minority shareholders. Under one approach, oppression is conduct that substantially defeats the minority shareholders' reasonable expectations. Under a second approach, oppression is inequitable conduct by the majority. Chapter 16.

Option The power but not the obligation to do something, or a power granted by a corporation to a particular person to purchase securities. Chapter 3 and Chapter 6.

Option writer The seller of a standardized right to purchase securities from, or sell securities to, the writer. Chapter 6.

Ordinary income Income from such sources as wages, dividends, or interest income that is taxed at a higher rate than capital gains. Chapter 6.

Outstanding Authorized and issued shares that remain in the hands of some entity other than the corporation itself. Chapter 6.

Overissue Shares issued in excess of the number of shares authorized in the articles of incorporation. Chapter 6.

Par value An arbitrary value, usually nominal, for a class or series shares, which is stated in the articles of incorporation. Shares may not be issued for less than par value. Chapter 6.

Participating Preferred stock that receives dividends along with the common stock after it has received its preferential dividend. Chapter 6.

Participation theory of liability A theory under which a corporate officer is personally liable for a tort committed by the corporation when the officer is sufficiently involved in the commission to the tort. Chapter 8.

Partnership The association of two or more persons to carry on as co-owners a business for profit. Chapter 18.

Pass through taxation Tax treatment of an entity, such as a partnership or LLC, in which income and losses realized by the entity are allocated to the entity's owners. Thus the entity itself does not pay income tax. Chapter 20.

Peanuts Money.

Periodic reporting The requirement that a public company provide certain information to its shareholders annually and quarterly. Chapter 15.

Pewter Money.

Piercing the corporate veil An equitable doctrine that holds a corporation's shareholders liable for the corporation's debts if the corporation is unable to pay. Chapter 8.

Plurality The largest percentage of votes cast, even if less than a majority. Chapter 15.

Poison pill An anti-takeover device by which the target shareholders have the right to purchase half-price stock in a raider if the raider acquires a particular percentage of shares, usually between 10 percent and 20 percent, and thereafter effects a merger. Chapter 17.

Pooling agreements An agreement among shareholders that states how shareholders themselves will vote their own shares; these agreements are not subject to voting trust statutes. Chapter 16.

Potatoes Money.

Precatory motion Motion at a shareholders meeting that would constitute only a recommendation to the board. Chapter 15.

Preemptive right The equitable right of shareholders to purchase shares proposed to be issued so that their respective economic and managerial interests will be preserved. Chapter 16.

Preferred stock A class of stock that has a priority or preference over other stock (common stock) in either the payment of dividends, the distribution of assets on dissolution, or both. Chapter 6.

Price The actual consideration for a particular investment. Price may be determined by active negotiation between the parties or it may be determined by reference to a market. Cf. Value. Chapter 3.

Principal The person or entity (1) for whom an agent has agreed to act and (2) who has the right to control the agent. Chapter 4.

Private benefits The goods or services that an agent has obtained opportunistically through the agency relationship and for which the agent bears only a part (or none) of the cost. Chapter 4.

Private placement exemption An exemption from the federal registration requirements given to securities sold by a corporation in transactions not involving a public offering. Chapter 6.

Product line exception A successor liability doctrine in which the key is whether the successor corporation produces essentially the same products as the transferor corporation. Chapter 8.

Progressive corporate law The school of corporate law scholarship that espouses the view that the corporation should be viewed as a community comprising shareholders, creditors, directors, managers, employees, and possibly customers. Corporate law scholars seek to impose on the corporation a responsibility not to society in general, but to those groups that make up the corporate community. Chapter 10.

Promoters The persons who organize a new corporation. Chapter 5.

Proper purpose A shareholder, when exercising certain inspection rights, must establish that the purpose for inspection is reasonably related to such person's interest as a shareholder. Chapter 15.

Proxy An agency relationship in which a shareholder appoints another person to attend a shareholders meeting on the shareholder's behalf and to vote the shareholder's shares. Chapter 15.

Put option A real option that permits the owner to cease an activity. A standardized right sold by someone (the option writer) other than the corporation to sell securities of the corporation to the writer. Chapter 3 and Chapter 6.

Quorum The minimum amount, typically a majority, of voting power that must be present at a meeting for actions to be valid. Chapter 9 and Chapter 15.

Raider An entity that seeks to obtain control of another entity against the wishes of the other entity's management. Chapter 17.

Ratcheting The risk that a principal will increase an agent's work without increasing the agent's recompense. Chapter 4.

Ratification A doctrine under which a principal is liable for an agent's actions, when no actual or apparent authority exists. Ratification occurs when the principal manifests assent to the agent's actions, thus electing to treat the action as authorized. Chapter 4.

Rational self-interest The paradigm of human behavior in classical economics. It posits that people, in economic settings, act logically to acquire as much for themselves as possible. Chapter 3.

Real options A business's relations with others, viewed as options. Real options are distinguished from financial options and hedges. See Option. Chapter 3.

Reasonable expectations test A test for shareholder oppression. It focuses on the minority shareholders's reasonable expectations in committing their capital to the particular enterprise. If conduct by the majority substantially defeats those expectations, the minority have been oppressed. Chapter 16.

Receivables skim A financial fraud in which the perpetrator diverts money customers pay to the business before that money is recorded by the business. Chapter 12.

Recognition An event such as a sale that requires a taxpayer to report gain or loss. Chapter 17.

Record date The date on which the shareholders entitled to receive a dividend or to vote at a meeting are fixed. Chapter 7.

Redemption The right of the corporation, contained in the articles of incorporation, to repurchase shares of a particular class or series. Chapter 6.

Registration statement The statement required to be filed with the SEC before a corporation may offer securities to the public. Chapter 6.

Regular meeting A periodic (e.g., monthly) meeting of a board of directors. Chapter 9.

Regulation D An SEC regulation that exempts certain stock sales by a corporation from registration requirements. Chapter 6.

Regulatory risk The possibility that a government might impose unanticipated regulations. Chapter 3.

Reinvestment risk The possibility that a lender will not be able to reinvest the loan principal at equally favorable terms when the principal is repaid. Chapter 6.

Renounce An agent's unilateral ending of the agency relationship. Chapter 4.

Representativeness A heuristic in which the likelihood of *A* being related to *B* is determined by how closely *A* resembles *B*. Chapter 3.

Reputational intermediaries A person or entity that vouches for one entity's merits to another entity. Chapter 14.

Reservation price The lowest price at which a seller would sell an asset or the highest price at which a buyer would buy an asset. Chapter 17.

Respondeat superior The doctrine by which a principal is liable for an employee's tort committed within the scope of employment. *See* Vicarious liability Chapter 4.

Restitution The doctrine by which a principal is liable to third parties when (1) the principal is unjustly enriched by the agent's actions and (2) those actions

are not within the agent's actual or apparent authority. Chapter 4.

Restrictions on transfer Limitations on a shareholder's power to sell, give, bequeath, or retain ownership of shares. Chapter 7.

Retired Reacquired shares that are not held as treasury shares. Chapter 7.

Reverse stock split An amalgamation of shares at a fixed ratio into fewer shares. Chapter 7.

Reverse triangular merger A merger of an acquiring corporation subsidiary with and into the target corporation. Chapter 17.

***Revlon* duties** The directors' duty, imposed by *Revlon, Inc. v. MacAndrews & Forbes Holdings, Inc.,* 506 A.2d 173 (Del. 1985), to act reasonably to seek the transaction offering the highest value reasonably obtainable in the sale of corporate control. Chapter 17.

Revoke The principal's unilateral termination of the agency relationship. Chapter 4.

Rhino Money.

Risk The possibility that something different than expected will happen. Chapter 3.

Round lot The typical trading unit of 100 shares. Chapter 7.

S corporation A corporation that has elected to be taxed under Subchapter S of the Internal Revenue Code. S corporations are not taxed separately. Profits and losses are allocated directly to the shareholders who include those profits or losses on their own tax returns. Chapter 20.

Sales skim A fraud in which the perpetrator sells company products ostensibly on behalf of the company, but diverts the proceeds to himself or herself. Chapter 12.

Salvage value The value of a nonoperating asset derived from the value of its components. Chapter 3.

Sarbanes-Oxley Act of 2002 A federal act that constrains public corporation board power first, by requiring that the corporation have an audit committee of independent directors who retain and oversee the corporation's independent accounting firm; and second, by requiring senior officers to certify the corporation's financial statements and to certify that the corporation has a *Caremark* system of effective internal controls. Chapter 14.

Scienter The element of Rule 10b-5 liablity that requires a defendant to have intended to deceive. Chapter 7.

Scope of employment An employee acts within the scope of employment when performing work assigned by the employer or engaging in a course of conduct subject to the employer's control. Chapter 4.

Scrap value *See* Salvage value. Chapter 3.

Scratch Money.

Secondary trading market Markets such as the New York Stock Exchange or NASDAQ that permit securities to be traded among participants who are not issuing corporations. Chapter 6.

Securities The standardized rights granted by a corporation in return for money investments. Stock, bonds, and debentures are typical securities. Chapter 6.

Securities Act (or the '33 Act) One of two major federal acts that regulate the public issuance and trading of securities. Chapter 6.

Securities analyst Securities analysts investigate a particular industry and its businesses and write analytical assessments of both the industry and the businesses that compete. These analyses are used by brokerage houses to recommend stock to their clients. Chapter 14.

Securities and Exchange Commission (SEC) An independent federal agency that has regulates publicly held companies and stock exchanges. Chapter 6.

Self-dealing Self dealing occurs when a director or officer enters into a contract with the corporation, usually to buy something from, or sell something to, the corporation. Chapter 11.

Series of stock A subset of a class of stock. Chapter 6.

Settled When a securities trade becomes complete, meaning the seller gets the

money and the buyer gets the shares. Chapter 15.

Share A unit of ownership in a corporation. Chapter 6.

Shareholder The owner of stock. Chapter 6.

Shareholder lock-up A side agreement between an acquirer and a target's controlling shareholder by which the shareholder agrees to sell its shares, or agrees to give a proxy, to the acquirer. Chapter 17.

Shareholder primacy The idea that, because shareholders own the corporation, directors and officers are required to act in the shareholders' interest. Chapter 10

Shareholders' rights plan Formal term for a poison pill. Chapter 17.

Shark repellents Corporate governance structures that keep unwanted suitors from effecting a takeover. Chapter 17.

Shirking A moral hazard faced by principals, in which the agent chooses to perform less well than the parties anticipated. Chapter 4.

Short form merger Where the acquiring corporation owns at least 90 percent of the target's stock, the statutes permit a merger upon only the resolution of the acquiring corporation's board of directors. Chapter 17.

Shrapnel Money.

Signaling Tactics used by both principals and agents to convince others that they will perform well in an agency relationship. Signaling may include such actions as providing references or obtaining educational degrees. Chapter 4.

Silent partners Partners who do not take part in the management of the business. Chapter 18.

Simoleons Money.

Simple majority A majority of votes cast. Votes not present and votes present but not voting are not included in calculating the denominator. Chapter 15.

Sinking fund Money segregated by a borrowing corporation to ensure that it can make loan payments when due. Chapter 6.

Soap Money.

Solicitors British lawyers who were not admitted to the bar and could not be heard in court. They undertook all other legal work, however, including what today would be called corporate work. Chapter 1.

Special committee A committee of non-implicated directors assigned to evaluate a shareholder's demand for litigation against other directors. Chapter 15.

Special litigation committee A committee of nondefendant directors assigned to investigate the allegations against the defendant directors who are being sued for breach of fiduciary duties. The committee also recommends whether pursuing those allegations is in the best interest of the corporation. Chapter 13.

Special meeting A board meeting other than a regular meeting. A shareholder meeting other than the annual meeting. Chapter 9 and Chapter 15.

Special purpose clause A clause in the article of incorporation that states the single purpose for which the corporation was formed. Chapter 10.

Spinach Money.

Spondulicks Money.

Staggered terms A corporate governance device in which the directors are divided into two or three classes, with each class holding terms of two or three years, so that only one class of directors is elected each year. Chapter 9.

Statement of cash flows A financial statement that presents the net cash used in three areas over a period of time. Chapter 3.

Statement of income A financial statement that presents revenues and expenses over a period of time. Chapter 3.

Statutory voting *See* Straight voting. Chapter 16.

Stock Collective ownership interests in the corporation, used interchangeably with shares. Chapter 6.

Stock right Rights given to the holders of stock, such as the right to vote or receive dividends. Chapter 6.

Stock split The division of outstanding shares into more shares, such that the ownership interests are not affected. Chapter 7.

Stockholder Someone who owns shares of stock. Chapter 6.

Straight voting A system of shareholder voting for directors. A shareholder may cast one vote for every share he or she owns for each director slot. Thus each shareholder may cast votes equaling the number of his or her shares for as many different candidates as there are slots. Also called Statutory voting. Chapter 16.

Street name Shares of stock as to which the record holder has no ownership interest but holds the stock on behalf of a brokerage house that also has no ownership interest but that, in turn, holds the stock for a customer, which is the beneficial owner. Chapter 15.

Subordinated Debt that has a lower priority for repayment than other debt. Chapter 6.

Subscription agreements Contracts to purchase shares, usually in a corporation that has not yet been formed. Chapter 6.

Subsidiary A corporation that has the majority of its voting stock owned by another corporation. Chapter 17.

Successor liability A doctrine that holds a corporation liable for the debts of a second corporation that sold all its assets to the first corporation. Chapter 8.

Sugar Money.

Supermajority A provision in the articles of incorporation or bylaws that requires a greater than majority vote at either the board or the shareholder level. Chapter 16.

Superquorum A provision in the articles of incorporation or bylaws that increases the quorum requirements above the default statutory rule, for board meetings or shareholder meetings. Chapter 16.

Surplus A corporation's net assets less its capital. Chapter 7.

Syndicate A group of investors that makes a joint investment to a corporation, either by making a loan or by underwriting the corporation's public offering. Chapter 6.

Synergy value The value of operating an asset in conjunction with other assets the investor already owns. This conjoined operation might produce more profits than operating the assets separately. Chapter 3.

Target corporation The corporation that is purchased in a change of control transaction. Chapter 17.

Team production An economic endeavor in which multiple actors are required and in which the results are not easily attributable to the efforts of particular actors. Chapter 4.

Tender offer An offer to the target's shareholders to sell their shares to the raider at a premium to the current market price. Chapter 17.

Term partnership A partnership formed for a particular length of time or for a particular undertaking. Chapter 18.

Terminal price The likely sales price of an asset at the end of its holding period. Chapter 3.

Time value of money The increased value of a unit of money in the present over the value of the same unit of money in the future. Chapter 3.

Topping fee A contract clause that requires additional payment to the acquirer if an acquisition transaction does not close and if, within a specified time such as two years, the target is acquired by another entity. Chapter 17.

Traditional logic of property The idea that a corporation should be run for the benefit of shareholders because they own the corporation and hence, indirectly, the corporation's property. Chapter 10.

Transaction reporting The requirement that a public company provide certain information to its shareholders with respect to a contemplated financial transaction. Chapter 15.

Transfer agent A corporation's agent in charge of reissuing shares from sellers to buyers and noting such transfers on the shareholder list. Chapter 15.

Treasury stock Shares that have been reacquired by the issuing corporation but that have not been retired. Chapter 7.

Ultra vires A doctrine that limits corporate action to the ends and means stated in the articles of incorporation or corporation statute and validly approved by the corporation. Chapter 10.

Underwriter An investment banker that facilitates the public offering of a corporation's securities by buying securities from the issuer and reselling them to the investing public. Chapter 6.

Undisclosed principal A principal is undisclosed where a third party has no knowledge that the agent is acting on behalf of any principal. Chapter 4.

Unidentified principal A principal is unidentified when a third party knows that the agent is acting on behalf of a principal, but does not know the principal's identity. Chapter 4.

Units Stock and warrants sold as a package. Chapter 6.

***Unocal* test** A standard of review that applies to a target board's defensive actions during a hostile takeover. It is intermediate in strictness between the business judgment rule and the entire fairness standard. It takes it name from *Unocal Corp. v. Mesa Petroleum Co.*, 493 A.2d 946 (Del. 1985). Chapter 17.

Utility The economic and noneconomic worth of an asset to its owner. Chapter 3.

Value The economic worth of an investment to an owner. The wealth an asset will likely produce for its owner. Chapter 3.

Venture capital Money invested in nonpublic corporations by entities unconnected with the corporation with a view to preparing the corporation to go public. Chapter 6.

Vertical integration A combination of a business with its suppliers or customers. Chapter 2.

Vest The ability of an option holder to exercise the option. Chapter 6.

Vicarious liability A doctrine under which a principal is liable for an agent's torts. See Respondeat superior. Chapter 4.

Voidable preferences Corporate property transferred to certain corporate insiders within one year prior to the corporation's bankruptcy if the transfer was for an antecedent debt, had the effect of giving the insiders more than they would have received in bankruptcy, and was made while the corporation was insolvent. Voidable preferences may be recovered for the benefit of the corporation's creditors. Chapter 8.

Voting trusts Stock as to which (1) the voting rights are separated from the other attributes of ownership; (2) the voting rights granted are intended to be irrevocable for a definite period of time; and (3) the principal purpose of the grant of voting rights is to affect voting control of the corporation. Chapter 16.

Warrant A long-term option (i.e., over one year) to purchase securities. Chapter 6.

Waste An exchange of corporate assets for consideration so disproportionately small as to lie beyond the range at which any reasonable person might be willing to trade. Chapter 10 and Chapter 13.

Williamson **test** Test to determine whether a partnership interest is an investment contract and hence is a security. The test is whether (1) The agreement among the parties leaves so little management power in the investor's hands that the investor is analogous to a limited partner; or (2) the investor is so inexperienced and unknowledgeable in business affairs that he or she cannot intelligently exercise his or her managerial powers; or (3) the investor is so dependent upon some unique entrepreneurial or managerial talent of the promoter that the investor cannot replace the promoter or otherwise meaningfully exercise his or her managerial powers. See *Williamson v. Tucker*, 645 F.2d 404 (5th Cir. 1981). Chapter 18.

Working capital Cash needed to run a business on a day-to-day basis. Chapter 6.

Table of Cases

Italic type indicates principal cases.

Abercrombie v. Davies, 606
Adlerstein v. Wertheimer, 333
Alaska Packers Assn. v. Industrial Accident Commn., 122
Allied Chem. & Dye Corp. v. Steel & Tube Co. of Am., 619, 621
American Vending Servs., Inc. v. Morse, 136
Andrews v. Southwest Wyo. Rehab. Ctr., 346
Anheuser-Busch Cos. v. Summit Coffee Co., 300
Appeal of _____. *See* name of party
Aprahamian v. HBO & Co., 547, 553
Arnold v. Society for Sav. Bancorp, Inc., 679
Aronson v. Lewis, 425
Associated Vendors, Inc. v. Oakland Meat Co., 283

Baker v. Commercial Body Builders, Inc., 638
Baltrusch v. Baltrusch, 725, 727
Barkan v. Amsted Indus., Inc., 401
Baron v. Allied Artists Pictures Corp., 207
Basic, Inc. v. Levinson, 252, 253
Basile v. H & R Block, Inc., 91, 94-95
Beam v. Stewart, 577
Beckett v. H & R Block, Inc., 94
Benjamin Plumbing, Inc. v. Barnes (456 N.W.2d 628), 108
Benjamin Plumbing, Inc. v. Barnes (470 N.W.2d 888), 106, 109
Berkey v. Third Ave. Ry. Co., 276
Bossier v. Connell, 324-325
Brane v. Roth, 442
Brehm v. Eisner, 426, 445, 476, 482

Brevet Intl., Inc. v. Great Plains Luggage Co., 280
Brown Bros. Equip. Co. v. Michigan, 277
Broz v. Cellular Info. Sys., Inc., 388, 390

Cady, Roberts & Co., In re, 260, 261, 264
Campbell v. Loew's, Inc., 324-325
Caremark Intl., Inc. Derivative Litig., In re, 409, 410, 417, 421, 423, 426-427, 443-444, 507-508, 541
Cede & Co. v. Technicolor, Inc., 381, 401, 409, 420, 426
Chiarella v. United States, 261, 264, 268, 272
Cinerama, Inc. v. Technicolor, Inc., 443
Citron v. Fairchild Camera & Instrument Corp., 425
City of _____. *See* name of city
Compaq Computer Corp. v. Horton, 567
Crown v. Hawkins Co., 403, 410, 417, 420
CTS Corp. v. Dynamics Corp. of Am., 121-122, 680

Dawson, In re Estate of, 225
Derdiger v. Tallman, 552
Detter v. Schreiber, 140
Dirks v. SEC, 264
Dobler v. Montgomery Cellular Holding Co., 54
Doft & Co. v. Travelocity.Com, Inc., 55
Donahue, In re Estate of, 212-213
Donahue v. Rodd Electrotype, 615, 617, 790

Dura Pharms., Inc. v. Broudo, 248, 252

Elf Atochem N. Am., Inc. v. Jaffari, 742
Emerald Partners v. Berlin (787 A.2d 85),
  465, 468
Emerald Partners v. Berlin (2003 WL
  21003437), 468
Enron Corp., In re, 500, 509
Eshleman v. Keenan, 207

Farm Indus., Inc., In re, 605
F.B.I. Farms, Inc. v. Moore (769 N.E.2d
  688), 242
F.B.I. Farms, Inc. v. Moore (798 N.E.2d
  440), *237*
Finch v. Unity Fee Co., 727
Fisher v. Townsends, Inc., 101, 104
Five Star Concrete, L.L.C. v. Klink, Inc., 755
Fought v. Morris, 614
Francis v. United Jersey Bank, 442

Gabelli & Co., Inc., Profit Sharing Plan v.
  Liggett Group, Inc., 208
Gagliardi v. TriFoods Intl., Inc., 421, 445
Gaylord Container Corp., In re, 401
Geller v. Allied-Lyons PLC, 396
Gimbel v. Signal Cos., 444-445
Goldberg v. Lee Express Cab Corp. (634
  N.Y.S.2d 337), *293,* 295
Goldberg v. Lee Express Cab Corp. (642
  N.Y.S.2d 292), 295
Greater Kan. City Roofing, NLRB v.,
  277-278
Green v. H & R Block, Inc., 94
Grimes v. Donald, 315, 318, 321
Grobow v. Perot, 425
Guth v. Loft, Inc., 381, 388-390

Hall v. Woods, 207
Harbor Fin. Partners v. Huizenga, 360, 361
Harris v. Looney, 133
Harrison v. NetCentric Corp., 229, 235
H-D Irrigating, Inc. v. Kimble Props., Inc.,
  340
Henry v. Delaware Law Sch. of Widener
  Univ., Inc., 333
Herby's Foods, Inc., Debtor, In re, 296
Hewlett v. Hewlett-Packard Co., 609
Hill v. County Concrete Co., 130
HMG/Courtland Props., Inc. v. Gray, 434

Hofeller v. General Candy Corp., 207
Hollinger, Inc. v. Hollinger Intl., Inc., 643
Hoschett v. TSI Intl. Software, Ltd., 325,
  328-329
Hoye v. Meek, 442

IXC Communications, Inc., Shareholders
  Litig., In re, 608
In re _____. *See* name of party

Kahn v. Lynch, 464
Kaiser Aluminum Corp. v. Matheson, 157
Kalageorgi v. Victor Kamkin, Inc.,
  186, 323
Kalb, Voorhis & Co. v. American Fin.
  Corp., 120
Kansallis Fin., Ltd. v. Fern, 713, 716
Kansas Gas & Elec. Co. v. Ross, 278,
  282-283
Kavanaugh v. Ford Motor Co., 284
Keith v. Black Diamond Advisors, Inc., 769
Kentucky Farm & Cattle Co. v. C.I.R.,
  724
Kiriakides v. Atlas Food Sys. & Servs., Inc.,
  626
Kramer v. Western Pac. Indus., Inc., 576

Lehrman v. Cohen, 605
Levy v. C.I.R., 724
Lynam v. Gallagher, 214, 225

MacArthur Co. v. Stein, 694, 695, 698,
  703-705, 712
Malone v. Brincat, 564
Malpiede v. Townson, 466, 468
Man o' War Rests., Inc. v. Martin, 233, 235-
  236
Masinter v. WEBCO Co., 638
Matthew G. Norton Co. v. Smyth, 664
McConnell v. Hunt Sports Enters., 760
McCormick v. Brevig, 730
McDermott Inc. v. Lewis, 122
McDuffie, In re, 96, 97
McIlvaine v. AmSouth Bank, NA, 211
McKesson Corp. v. Derdiger, 546
Meinhard, Appeal of, 723
Meinhard v. Salmon (164 N.E. 545), 379,
  717, 727, 765
Meinhard v. Salmon (229 N.Y.S. 345),
  724

Mims, Lyemance, & Reich, Inc. v. UAB Research Found., 699, 705
Mobridge Cmty. Indus. v. Toure, 277
Moneywatch Cos. v. Wilbers, 115
Moses v. Salomon, 722
Moskowitz v. Bantrell, 207

NCS Healthcare, Inc., Shareholders Litig., In re, 438
New Horizons Supply Coop. v. Haack, 751, 766-767
New York, City of, v. Gerry, 722
New York v. De Peyster, 724
NLRB v. Greater Kan. City Roofing, 277-278
Northeast Harbor Golf Club, Inc. v. Harris (661 A.2d 1146), *382*
Northeast Harbor Golf Club, Inc. v. Harris (725 A.2d 1018), 388

Oceanic Exploration Co. v. Grynberg, 605
O'Hagan, United States v., 268, 272
Omnicare, Inc. v. NCS Healthcare, Inc., 442, 660
Orman v. Cullman, 427

Pancratz v. Monsanto Co., 302, 305
Paramount Communications, Inc. v. QVC Network, Inc., 676, 679
Paramount Communications, Inc. v. Time, Inc., 679
Parkersburg Wireless, LLC, SEC v., 769
Parsons v. Jefferson-Pilot Corp., 571
P.D.2000, LLC v. First Fin. Planners, Inc., 745
Peterson v. H & R Block Tax Servs., Inc., 94
Peyton v. William C. Peyton Corp., 604
Phelps Dodge Corp. v. Cyprus Amax Minerals Co., 660
PSE&G Shareholder Litig., In re, 583

Ralston Purina Co., SEC v., 201
Ray v. Alad Corp., 305
Reddy v. Electronic Data Sys. Corp., 469
Reiss v. Financial Performance Corp. (715 N.Y.S.2d 29), 218
Reiss v. Financial Performance Corp. (764 N.E.2d 958), 222

Reves v. Ernst & Young, 200
Revlon, Inc. v. MacAndrews & Forbes Holdings, 676, 679-680
Riblet Prods. Corp. v. Nagy, 622
Richardson, State of Del. ex rel., v. Swift, 565
Robert's Hawaii Sch. Bus, Inc. v. Laupahoehoe Transp. Co., 284
Romanik v. Lurie Home Supply Ctr., Inc., 207

Sadler v. NCR Corp., 120
Salmon, Appeal of, 722-723
Saltiel v. GSI Consultants, Inc., 307
Schein v. Northern Rio Arriba Elec. Coop., Inc., 567
Schreiber v. Carney, 607-608
SEC v. Parkersburg Wireless, LLC, 769
SEC v. Ralston Purina Co., 201
SEC v. W.J. Howey Co., 200, 738, 769
Shapiro v. Greenfield, 457
Shaw v. Agri-Mark, Inc., 566
Sinclair Oil Corp. v. Levien, 425, 444
Singer v. Magnavox Co., 621
Smith, State of W. Va. ex rel., v. Evans, 638
Smith v. McLeod Distrib., Inc., 285, 295
Smith v. Van Gorkom, 442
Snukal v. Flightways Mfg., Inc., 349, 354
Solomon v. Armstrong, 464
Starr v. Fordham, 708
State Farm Mut. Auto. Ins. Co. v. Superior Court, 207
Sterling v. Mayflower Hotel Corp., 621
Stevens v. Salomon, 724
Superwire.com, Inc. v. Hampton, 325
Swift v. State of Del. ex rel. Richardson, 565

Taylor v. Standard Gas & Elec. Co., 172
Telcom-SNI Investors, L.L.C. v. Sorrento Networks, Inc., 178
Tomaino v. Concord Oil of Newport, Inc., 391, 395
Tondu v. Akerley, 691, 694-695, 698-699, 703-705
Tracey v. Franklin, 605
Turner v. Bituminous Cas. Co., 305

U-Haul Intl., Inc., In re, 290
United Housing Found. v. Forman, 200
United States v. *See* name of opposing party

Unitrin, Inc. v. American Gen. Corp.,
  672
Unocal Corp. v. Mesa Petroleum Co., 672,
  675, 680

Waldorf-Astoria Segar Co. v. Salomon,
  722
Walkovszky v. Carlton, 276
Wallace v. Wood, 283
Walt Disney Co. Derivative Litig., In re
  (2005 WL 2056651), 489
Walt Disney Co. Derivative Litig., In re
  (731 A.2d 342), 464

Walt Disney Co. Derivative Litig., In re
  (825 A.2d 275), *476, 482*
Weinberger v. UOP, Inc., 621
Wellman v. Dickinson, 682, 694
Western Airlines, Inc. v. Sobieski,
  121
Whetstone v. Hossfeld Mfg. Co., *595, 611,
  613*
Wilkes v. Springside Nursing Home, Inc.,
  618, 790
Williamson v. Tucker, 738, 769
W.J. Howey Co., SEC v., 200, 738, 769
WorldCom, Inc., In re, 514

Index

ABA. *See* American Bar Association
  (ABA)
Absolute majority, 554
Accounting, 73-82
  accrued income taxes, 77
  accrued liabilities, 77
  balance sheet, 77
  capital expenses versus operating
    expenses, 76, 77
  cash flow from financing activities, 78
  cash flow from investing activities, 78
  cash flow from operations, 78
  checkbook method, 76
  costs, 79
  depreciation, 77
  financial statement, 78
  fraud, categories of, 497
  Generally Accepted Accounting Practices
    (GAAP). *See* Generally Accepted
    Accounting Practices (GAAP)
  Generally Accepted Auditing Standards
    (GAAS). *See* Generally Accepted
    Auditing Standards (GAAS)
  income method, 76
  net income, 80
  net revenues, 79
  net sales, 79
  net worth, 77
  operating profit, 79
  operating versus capital expenses, 76, 77
  overhead, 79
  partners' equity, 77
  prepaid expenses, 77
  research and development, 79
  retained earnings, 77
  shareholders' equity, 77
  statement of cash flows, 78, 79
  statement of income, 79
Accounting statements, 73

Accredited investor, 202
Accrued income taxes, 77
Accrued liabilities, 77
Acknowledgment of signature, 126
Acquisition of business, 642-654
  acquisition agreement, 657. *See also*
    Contract terms
  choice of appropriate technique, 654-656
  process, 656-658
Actual authority, 95-96, 343
  members of member-managed LLCs,
    758
  termination of, 110-111
Ad hominem situations, 322
Adjustment, 66
Advance notice
  bylaw, 557
  provision, 670
Adverse selection, 85
Affective component of decision making,
  67-69
Affiliated corporations, aggregation of, 284
Affirmative covenants, 163
Agency, 85-111
  agent. *See* Agent
  costs, 88
  creation of, 91-94
  defined, 85, 90-91
  economic concept of, 85-88
  moral hazard, 86
  powers coupled with an interest, 110
  principal. *See* Principal
  renunciation of, 110
  revocation of, 110
  signaling, 85
  termination of, 110-111
Agent. *See also* Principal
  actual authority of, 95-96, 99, 343
  apparent authority of, 96-99, 343

Agent (continued)
  bonding actions, 88
  capability of, 85
  contract, liability on, 105-109
  death or incapacity of, 111
  defined, 90
  director as, 379
  duties of, 109-110
  liability on contract of, 105-109
  monitoring of, 88
  moral hazard, 86
  motivation of, 85
  officer versus, 344
  other sources of liability to third party,
      105-109
  principal, relation to, 109-110
  private benefits, 86
  ratcheting, 86
  risk averse, 87
  scope of employment, actions within,
      104-105
  shirking, 86, 88
  third parties, relation to, 105-109
  tort of agent, liability of principal for,
      100-105
Aggregation
  affiliated corporations, 284
  horizontal, 284
  vertical, 284
Agreement, 44
ALI. See American Law Institute (ALI)
Allocation versus distribution, LLCs, 749
All purpose clause, 359, 361
Altruism, 62-63, 534
  pure, 62
American Bar Association (ABA), 787
American Law Institute (ALI), 16, 787
  corporate opportunity doctrine and, 385
Amote, 544
Amotion, 323
Anchoring, 66
Angels, 177
Annual meeting
  agenda for, 588
  failure to hold, 325-329
  of public corporation, 556-558
  of shareholders, 545
Annual report, 508
Antidilution provision, 223, 671
Antifraud provisions, 590. See also Federal
      securities laws
Antitakeover statutes, 680
Antitrust laws, 357
Apparent authority, 95, 96, 343, 348
  of members of member-managed LLCs,
      758

of partner, 713-717
  termination of, 110-111
Appraisal remedy, 598
Appraisal rights, 654, 663-669
  fair value, 664, 667
  triggers for, 663-664
A reorg, 655
Articles of Incorporation, 124
  limitations in, 465
Asset lock-up clauses, 659
Assets, purchase of, 642-651
At-will partnership, 730
Audit, risk-based, 514
Audit committees, 507
Auditors, corporate fraud and, 512-514
Availability, 65-66

Bad debts, 408
Balance sheet, 75, 77, 81
Bankruptcy, 522, 538
  commercial doctrines and, 296-301
Bankruptcy insolvency test, 749
Banks, 124
  commercial, 640
  investment, 640
Barristers, versus solicitors, 8
Berle and Means type of corporation, 31
Biases, 64-66
Big Four accounting firms, 512, 514
Blank check stock, 185
Blank stock, 185
Board of directors. See Directors
Bonding, 88
Bonds, 163
Book entry system, 561
Breaking a quorum, 332
Break-up fee, 658, 659
Break-up value, 48
B reorg, 655
Broker overvote, 563
Business, 19
  big, development of, 25-32
Business entities
  acquisition of. See Acquisition of
      business
  choice of. See Choice of entity
  combination of. See Combination of
      entities
  corporation. See Corporation
  types, 15
Business judgment rule, 426, 434
  prevailing despite application of, 444-455
Business lawyer, 10
Buy-sell agreement, 228
Bylaws, 545

Callable stock, 156
Call of meeting, 545
Call option, 60, 164
Capability of agent, 85
Capital, 209
Capital expenses, 76, 77
Capital formation, 151-203
    common stock, 153-154
    corporate securities, 153-165
    debt, 160-163, 166
    derivatives, 164
    excessive debt, 168-172
    getting money into the business, 151-198
    going public, 176-184
    issuance of stock, mechanics of, 185
    leverage, 166-168
    options, 164
    preferred stock, 154-156
    relative rights, 156-160
    rights, 164
    start-up corporation, 174-176
    venture capital, 177
    warrants, 164
    working capital, 151
Capital gain, 173
Capitalism
    entrepreneurial, 29
    family, 29, 30
    financial, 29, 30
    managerial, 31
Capital structure, 151
    planning of, 165-184
    start-up corporation, 174-175
    thin capitalization, 171
    top-heavy, 171
Care, duty of. *See* Duty of care; Fiduciary
        duties
Caremark claim, 426
Cash flows
    from financing activities, 78
    from investing activities, 78
    from operations, 78
    statement of, 78
    typical statement, 79
C corporation, 773. *See also* Corporation
Cede & Co., 562
Certificate of Incorporation, 124, 126
    contents of, 362
Chance, misconceptions of, 65
Change of control, 639-683
    acquisition process, 654-658
    appraisal rights. *See* Appraisal rights
    combinations. *See* Combination of
        entities
    federal securities regulations, 681-683
    going private transactions, 681-682

"groups" under Section 13(d), 681
    hostile, 669-680
    merger. *See* Merger
    purchase of assets, 642-651
    purchase of stock, 651-652
    reorganization. *See* Reorganization
    takeover. *See* Hostile takeover
Character, 534
Character building, 69-72
    defining moments, 69-72
Charging order, 708
Charter limitations, 465
Check-kiting scheme, 408
Check register, 74
Check-the-box provisions of IRC, 742
Choice of entity, 773-791
    factors militating against certain forms,
        778-779
    factors requiring or eliminating certain
        forms, 778
    financial differences, 775
    how to choose, 778-779
    managerial differences, 775-776
    operational differences, 775
    organizational differences, 774-775
    transferability of interest, 776-777
    variable characteristics, 774-777
    why people form firms, 784-787
Class-action clients, 143
Classified board, 322
Class of stock, 154
Client, defined, 4
Client-lawyer relationship, formation of,
        143-144
Close corporation, 176, 610, 636
Closely held corporations, 176
Close of business, 210
Closing, 657
CoI Safe Harbor statutes, 456
    effect of compliance with, 462-463
    eligible transactions, 457-462
    procedural or substantive prerequisites,
        462
Collar, 163
Combination of entities, 640
    horizontal, 640
    techniques, 642-654
    vertical, 640
Commercial and bankruptcy doctrines,
        296-301
Commercial banks, 640
Commercial paper market, 162
Common enterprise, 200
Common stock, 151, 153-154
Comparable company approach, 54
Comparable transactions approach, 54

Compensation
  of directors, 400
  of senior officers, 400
Comprehensive Environmental Response,
        Compensation and Liability Act
        (CERCLA), 358
Conditions in agreement, 658
Confidentiality agreements, 657
Confidentiality of information, 146
Conflict of interest, 395, 526
  current clients, 146-147
Conflict of interest transactions
  shareholder ratification, 463-465
  statutory safe harbor, 456-465. *See also* CoI
        Safe Harbor statutes
Conglomeration, 640
Conjunctive events, 66
Consent solicitation, 559
Consideration, 194, 195-196, 657
  noncash, 196
Consolidation of financial performance, 75
Constituent corporations, 652
Continuing education, 527-534
Continuity of enterprise exception, 305
Contract terms
  asset lock-up clause, 659
  break-up fee, 658-659
  closing, 657
  conditions, 658
  confidentiality agreement, 657
  deal protective measures, 658-660
  expenses, payment of, 657, 658
  material adverse change clause, 658
  no-shop provision, 659
  no-talk clause, 659, 660
  representations and warranties, 657
  termination, 658
Contra proferentem, 159
Control
  change of, 639-683. *See also* Change of
        control
  sale of, 660-663
Control premium, 55
Control share acquisition acts, 680
Convergence, 39-41
Convertible debt, 163
Convertible stock, 156
Cooperators, 534
Coping with stress, 68
Corporate accounting scandals, 491
Corporate action versus board action, 357
Corporate formalities, observation of, 279
Corporate governance law, 531
Corporate governance quotient, 528
Corporate governance rules, cost of, 535-536
Corporate lawyer

  as conciliator, 5
  as counselor, 5
  defined, 3
  demographics, 13-15
  as facilitator, 5
  as gatekeeper, 6
  as guardian, 6
  in-house lawyers, 11-12
  knowledge, areas of, 15-17
  in large firm, 11
  in medium-sized firm, 11
  professional responsibility to multiple
        clients/entity clients of, 139-149
  statistics, 13-15
Corporate opportunity, 381, 382
  defined, 386
Corporate opportunity doctrine, 381-390
Corporate power
  board of directors. *See* Directors
  effect of, 362-363
  in-house attorneys, 509-510
  internal auditors, 509-510
  officers. *See* Officers
  restrictions on board's power. *See*
        Restrictions on board's power
  structural constraints, 497
Corporate social responsibility, 373-377
Corporate survival statutes, 305-306
Corporation, 229
  advantages of incorporation, 34-36. *See
        also* Incorporation
  Berle and Means type of, 31
  board of directors. *See* Directors
  capital formation. *See* Capital formation
  creation of, 115-149. *See also*
        Incorporation
  creditors, payment of, 275-310
  de facto, 128, 130-136
  de jure, 127-130, 131, 133
  distributions to shareholders, 205-273
  domestic, 119
  as dominant legal entity for businesses,
        32-36
  by estoppel, 136-139
  finances of, 151-311
  foreign, 119
  globalization, 39-41
  incorporation process, 115-149. *See also*
        Incorporation
  large corporations, management in, 28-32
  limitations on power to purchase own
        shares, 243-244
  management patterns, 28-32
  officers. *See* Officers
  as purchaser of own shares, 243-246
  purposes of, 362

S corporation, 773, 774
start-up corporation, capital structure for, 174-175
Corporation by estoppel, 136-139
Costs, 79
Counterparty risk, 46
Coupled with an interest, 110, 556
Covenants
    in acquisition agreement, 657
    affirmative, 163
    negative, 163
Creditors, liability to, 275-311
    bankruptcy doctrines, 296-301
    commercial doctrines, 296-301
    enterprise liability, 284-296
    equitable subordination, 296, 298
    fraudulent conveyances, doctrine of, 296
    individual shareholder liability, 276-284
    officer liability, 306-310
    participation theory of liability, 307
    piercing corporate veil, 276-284
    shareholder liability, 276-284
    successor liability, 301-306
    voidable preferences, 296
Credit-rating agencies, 517-521
Creditworthiness
    of companies, 517-521
    of consumers, 519
C reorg, 655
Cumulative dividends, 155
Cumulative voting, 599-603
Currency risk, 46

DASHs. See Deal approval sheets (DASHs)
DCF. See Discounted cash flow (DCF) analysis
Deadlock, 611-612
    breaking, 622
    of directors, 623
    of shareholders, 623
Deal approval sheets (DASHs), 499
Deal protective measures, 658-660
Debentures, 151, 163
Debt, 160-163
    consequences of, 166-168
    convertible, 163
    costs of, 170-171
    defeased, 163
    excessive debt, economic risks of, 168-170
    excessive debt, legal dangers of, 171-172
    interest on, 169
    long-term, 162-163
    short-term, 161-162
    subordinated, 163
    traditional common stock versus, 160
Debt/equity ratio, 171

Decision making
    affective component of, 67-69
    ethical component of, 69-72
Declared dividends, 206
Deed of trust, 97
De facto corporations, 128, 130-136
De facto merger doctrine, 656
Default, event of, 163
Default risk, 46
Defeased debt, 163
Defective incorporation, 126-139
Defensive measures, 671
Defining moments, 69
    for executives, 71-72
    for individuals, 70
    for work groups, 71
Definitive agreement, 657
De jure corporation, 125-128, 129, 131
Delaware, 36
    special role of, 122-123
Delisting of company, 217
Demand excused cases, 585
Demand refused cases, 585
Depository Trust Company (DTC), 561
Depreciation, 77
Derivative, 164
Derivative action, 507, 577
Derivative litigation, 576, 583
Diluted interest, 152
Directors, 313-340
    as agents, 379
    beneficiaries, identification of, 363
    board action versus corporate action, 357
    board power, restraints on, 357-378, 491-541
    business judgment rule, 426
    classified board, 322, 323
    compensation of, 400
    conduct, standards of, 426
    continuing education of, 527-534
    de jure authority of, 192
    duty of care of. See Duty of care
    duty of loyalty of. See Duty of loyalty
    education of, 527-534
    election of, 322-328
    federal securities regulation, 354-355
    fiduciary duties of. See Fiduciary duties
    holdover, 323
    intentionality, 527-534
    knowing violations of, 209
    legislation that restricts power, 357-359
    liability of, 209
    mechanics of board action, 330-340
    meeting of. See Meeting of directors
    negligent violations of, 209
    as nexus of contract, 370-371

Directors *(continued)*
  number of initial directors, 322
  removal of, 323-325
  removal for cause, 324, 325
  removal without cause, 324
  restrictions on, 357-378, 491-541
  review of board actions, 425-489
  role of, 313-322
  selection of initial directors, 322
  staggered terms, 323
  standards of review of actions of. *See*
      Standards of review of board action
  term of, 322-323
  ultimate beneficiaries and, 363-377
  ultra vires, 359-363
Disclosed principal, 99
Disclosure controls and procedures, 422
Disclosure of material information, 589.
      See also Federal securities laws
Discounted cash flow (DCF) analysis, 54-55,
      56, 82
Discounting to present value, 50-51
Discount rate, 51
Disinterest, defined, 462
Disinterested directors, 462
Disjunctive events, 66
Dissenters' rights. *See* Appraisal rights
Dissociation, 754
Dissociation of partner, 727-729
Dissolution
  of LLC, 765-768
  of partnership, 729-733
Distributions
  allocation versus distribution, LLC, 749
  dividends. *See* Dividends
  LLCs, 748-750
  sale of stock by shareholders, 227-246. *See*
      also Transfer restrictions
  to shareholders, 205-273
Diversification, 47
Divestment, 579
Dividends, 205, 206-227
  board discretion in declaring, 206-208
  mechanics of paying, 210-213
  statutory restrictions on, 208-210
  stock dividend, 214
  stock splits, 213-217. *See also* Stock splits
Documents, incorporation documents,
      124-125
D&O insurance policy, 475
Domestic corporations, 119
Double taxation, 774
DTC. *See* Depository Trust Company (DTC)
Due diligence, 657
Duty of care, 437-444, 660
  charter limitations, 465

directors and officers, 402, 403-423
disclosure controls and procedures,
      422-423
federal securities regulation, 422-423.
      See also Federal securities regulations
limitations in Articles of Incorporation,
      465
monitoring of corporate operations, 414
tort, analogy of duty of care to, 420
Duty of good faith, 400-402, 421
Duty of loyalty, 402, 427-437, 507, 660,
      671
  compensation of directors and senior
      officers, 400
  conflict of interest. *See* Conflict of
      interest; Conflict of interest
      transactions. *See also* CoI Safe
      Harbor statutes
  corporate opportunity doctrine,
      381-390
  directors and officers, 379-402
  good faith and, 400-402
  ratification by shareholders, 463-465
  safe harbor for conflict of interest
      transactions, 456-465
  self-dealing. *See* Self-dealing
Duty of trust or confidence, 272

Earnings, retained, 77
Earnings before interest, taxes, depreciation,
      and amortization (EBITDA),
      55, 58
EBITDA. *See* Earnings before interest, taxes,
      depreciation, and amortization
      (EBITDA)
Economic decision making, 61-73
  affective component of, 67-69
  ethical component of, 69-72
  rational self-interest, 61-73, 82
Economic rationality, 63
Economic realities test, 171
Economics
  accounting, 73-82
  agency concepts. *See* Agency
  biases, 64-67
  heuristics, 64-67
  making economic decisions, 61-73. *See also*
      Economic decision making
  risk, 43-48
  valuation, 48-61
EDGAR database, 656. *See also* Federal
      securities laws
Education, reform through, 527-534
Effective managers, 71
Effective tax rate, 173

Emotional competence, 67-69
Employee, 103
Employee stock ownership plan (ESOP), 670
Employer-employee relationship, 103
Employment, scope of, 104-105
Enhanced scrutiny, test of, 672
Enron, 491-493
    directors. *See* Enron board of directors
    in-house attorneys, 509
    officers, 508
Enron board of directors, 498-504
    Audit Committee, 502-503
    committees of, 498
    compensation of members, 500
    explanations for failure of, 503-504
    Finance Committee, 501-502
    transaction approval policies, 500-501
Enterprise liability, 284-296
Entire fairness analysis, 467
Entire fairness standard, 434-437
Entity rationalization, 783, 784, 787-790
Entrepreneurial capitalism, 29
Environmental regulations, 357
Equal dignity doctrine, 656
Equitable subordination, 172, 296, 298
Equity, 153
    defined, 153
    factors that make equity attractive, 172-174
    of partners, 77
    of shareholders, 77
Equity insolvency test, 748
Equity security, 181, 182
ESOP. *See* Employee stock ownership plan (ESOP)
Estoppel, 99-100, 128, 343
    corporation by, 136-139
Ethical component of decision making, 69-72
Ethics
    business ethics, course on, 529-530
Event of default, 163
Ex ante, 85
Executive directors, training of, 528
Exit strategy, 641
Expectation, 44
Expectation of profit, 200
Expected return, 44
Expenses
    advancement of, 468-469
    capital, 76, 77
    operating, 76, 77
    other revenues and, 79
    prepaid, 77

Ex post, 86
Ex post facto claims, 421

Fair dealing, 435
Fair market value, 236
    of partnership interest, 728
Fairness, 462
Fair price, 435-437
Fair value, 236
Family capitalism, 29, 30
Family resemblance test, 200
FASB. *See* Financial Accounting Standards Board (FASB)
FCPA. *See* Foreign Corrupt Practices Act (FCPA) of 1977
Federal law, matters requiring shareholder vote under, 588-589
Federal securities laws, 357
    antifraud provisions, 590
    board power, methods of controlling, 540-541
    change of control, 681-683
    directors and, 354-355
    disclosure of information, 422
    disclosure of material information, 589
    duty of care, 422-423
    EDGAR database, 656
    FCPA and, 377-378
    financing of corporations, 198-203
    Form 8-K, 590
    Form 10-K, 590
    Form 10-Q, 590
    Form S-1, 202
    fraud in purchase or sale of securities, 248, 252
    going private transactions, 681-682
    going public, 176-184, 202-203
    governance requirements, 354-355
    "groups" under Section 13(d), 681
    Howey test. *See Howey* test
    initial public offering (IPO), 176
    insider trading, 259-271, 683
    intrastate exemption, 201
    investment contract, 200
    LLCs and, 768-769
    material information, disclosure of, 589
    NOBO list for inspection, 572-575
    ownership reporting requirements, 590
    partnerships and, 738
    periodic reporting to shareholders, 590
    private placement exemption, 201
    Private Securities Litigation Reform Act of 1995, 251-252
    proxy solicitations, regulation of, 589-590

Federal securities laws *(continued)*
  registration. *See* Registration
  Registration statement, 201
  Regulation D, 202
  restrictions on resale, 246-272
  Rule 10b-5, 248-272, 738
  Rule 14a-8, 588
  Rule 144, 247-248
  sale of stock by stockholders, 246-272
  Sarbanes-Oxley Act of 2002. *See* Sarbanes-
    Oxley Act of 2002 (SOx)
  Schedule 13D, 590
  Schedule TO, 682
  scienter, 249, 252, 271
  Section 16(b), 246-247
  Securities Act of 1933, 199, 540, 738
  Securities and Exchange Commission
    (SEC), 177, 199
  securities, defined, 199-200
  Securities Exchange Act of 1934, 199,
    377, 738
  securities registration, 201-203
  shareholder power in public companies,
    588-590
  shareholder vote, matters requiring,
    588-589
  tender offers, 682-683
  tippee liability, 268
  Wellman test, 682
  Williamson test, 738, 769. *See also*
    Williamson test
Federal Sentencing Guidelines, 358, 423
Fiduciary duties
  breach of, 425-489, 507. *See also* Standards
    of review of board action
  duty of care. *See* Duty of care
  duty of loyalty. *See* Duty of loyalty
  of shareholders, 613-622
  violation of duties, amelioration of liability
    for, 455-475
Filing of Articles of Incorporation, 125-126
Financial Accounting Standards Board
    (FASB), 787
Financial capitalism, 29, 30
Financial expert, 507
Financial statement, 78
Financing
  going public, 176-184
  venture capital, 176-178
Fitch Ratings, 517
Fixed amount versus percentage, 153
Flip in provision, 671
Flip over provision, 671
Float, 55, 163
Floating interest rate, 163
Foreign corporations, 119

Foreign Corrupt Practices Act (FCPA) of
    1977, 377
Foreign investment risk, 46
Form 8-K, 590. *See also* Federal securities laws
Form 10-K, 590. *See also* Federal securities
    laws
Form 10-Q, 590. *See also* Federal securities
    laws
Form S-1, 202. *See also* Federal securities laws
Fraud
  categories of accounting fraud, 497
  in purchase or sale of securities, 248, 252.
    See also Federal securities laws
Fraud or inequitable consequence test, 278
Fraudulent conveyances, doctrine of, 296
Free ride, 62
Future, 164

GAAP. *See* Generally Accepted Accounting
    Practices (GAAP)
GAAS. *See* Generally Accepted Auditing
    Standards (GAAS)
Generally Accepted Accounting Practices
    (GAAP), 73, 496, 515, 786
Generally Accepted Auditing Standards
    (GAAS), 73
General partnerships, 687-733
  allocations of profits and losses, 708-711
  apparent authority of partner, 713-717
  contribution to enterprise, 692
  death of partner, 728
  dissociation, 727-729
  dissolution, 729-733
  dissolution/winding up of business, events
    causing, 732
  distributions to partners, 708-711
  equitable grounds for expulsion, 728
  expulsion of partner, 728
  fair market value of interest, 728
  federal securities laws, 738
  fiduciary duties of partners, 717-727
  financing, 705-711
  formation of, 690-705
  intent to associate as partners, 692
  liquidation value of interest, 728
  management, 712
  mutual control, right of, 692
  ownership interests of partners, 705-711
  partner contributions, 705-706
  partnership property, 706-707
  partners' interest in partnership,
    707-708
  personal liability, 711-712
  power of partner to bind partnership,
    713-717

profits, sharing of, 693
term partnership, 730
General proxy, 562
Globalization, 39-41
Going concern value, 48, 236
Going private transactions, 681-682
Going public, 176-184, 202-203. *See also*
    Federal securities laws
Good faith
    acting in, 421
    duty of. *See* Duty of good faith
Governance of corporations
    directors. *See* Directors
    officers. *See* Officers
    shareholders. *See* Shareholder governance
        powers
Greenmail, 244
Group, 681
Guaranteed exit, 777

Hedges, 60
Heuristics, 64-67
Holdover, 555
Holdover directors, 323
Home schooling for business people, 529
Horizontal aggregation, 284
Horizontal combinations, 640
Horizontal dimension, 20
Hostile takeover, 656, 669-680
    corporate structures deterring,
        670-671
    defined, 669
    state antitakeover statutes, 680
Hostile tender offer
    response to, 671-680
    standard of review of board action in
        response to, 671-675
Hostile tender rule, 640
Howey test. *See also* Federal securities laws
    LLCs, 769
    partnerships, 738

Illusion of validity, 65
Incentive compensation plans, 88
Income
    net, 78, 80
    statement of, 79
    taxable, 78
Income before income taxes, 79
Income tax, negative income tax, 749
Incorporation
    Articles of, 124
    Certificate of, 124

defective, 126-139
documents, 124-125
filing, 125-126
internal affairs doctrine, 119-122
jurisdiction, choice of, 119-123
mechanics of, 123-126
organizational meeting, 126
promoter liability, 115-119
reservation of name, 124
Indemnification by corporation, 468-475
    advancement of expenses, 468-473
    circumstances requiring, 473-474
    procedural and substantive prerequisites to,
        474-475
Indenture, 163
Independent accountants, 512-517
Independent versus disinterested, 433
Inflation risk, 46
Information, shareholders' rights to,
    564-575
In-house lawyers, 11-12, 509, 510
Initial public offering (IPO), 176. *See also*
    Federal securities laws
Insider trading, 259-271, 683. *See also* Federal
    securities laws
Insolvency test, 209
Inspection right, 565-575
Insurance, 475
Integration
    horizontal, 20, 21
    vertical, 20, 21
Intentionality, 527-534
Interest, 50
Interested person, 680
Intermediate scrutiny, 672
Internal actors below board, 507-510
Internal affairs doctrine, 119-122
Internal auditors, 509, 510
In terrorem inducement, 236
Intrastate exemption, 201. *See also* Federal
    securities laws
Intrinsic fairness test, 437
Investment, 200
    cash flow from, 78
    investment banks, 640
Investment contract, 200. *See also* Federal
    securities laws
IPO. *See* Initial public offering (IPO)
Issued stock, 185

Joint stock companies, 737
Joint ventures, 733-734
Jurisdiction, choice of, 119-123

Knowledge, actual, 351

Legal capital test, 209
Letter of intent, 656
Leverage, 166-168
Liability
    accrued, 77
    advancement of expenses, 468-473
    amelioration of, 455-475
    to creditors, 275-311
    enterprise, 284-296
    expenses, advancement of, 468-473
    indemnification by corporation, 468-475
    insurance, 475
    of officers, 306-310
    of shareholders, 276-284
    standards of, 426
    successor, 301-306
Limited liability companies (LLCs), 15,
        739-769
    actual authority, 758
    additional members, 754-758
    allocations to members, 748-750
    apparent authority, 758
    capital contributions, 748
    check-the-box provisions of IRC, 742
    default rule on management, 758-759
    default rule regarding distributions, 750
    defective formation, 744-747
    Delaware statute, 742-744
    dissociation, 754-758
    dissolution, 765-768
    distributions to members, 748-750
    divestment of economic interest, 756
    duties, 759-765
    duty of care, 760
    equity insolvency test, 748, 749
    federal securities laws, 768-769
    fiduciary duties, 760-765
    financial interests, 750-753
    financing, 748-750
    formation of, 744-748
    good faith and fair dealing, duty of, 760
    interests of members, 750-758
    management, 758-759
    managerial interests, 753-754
    manager-managed, 759
    member-managed, 758-759
    members' interest, 750-758
    operating agreements, 747-748, 759
    origins of, 739-742
    piercing the corporate veil, 750-751, 753
    promoter liability, 744-747
    statutory requirements, 744
    transferability, 754-758

    unit, meaning of, 757, 758
    valuation of interest, 756-757
    winding up of, 765-768
Limited liability limited partnerships (LLLPs),
        737
Limited liability partnerships (LLPs), 737
Limited partners, 735
Limited partnerships, 735-737
    as estate-planning device, 736
Limited proxy, 562
Line cost E/R ratio, 493
Line cost expenses, 496
Liquidation value, partnership interest, 728
Liquidity, 48, 176
Liquidity risk, 48
Listing requirements, stock exchanges, 355
LLC. See Limited liability companies (LLCs)
LLLP. See Limited liability limited
        partnerships (LLLPs)
LLP. See Limited liability partnerships (LLPs)
Loan agreement, 162
Loans to senior executives, prohibition
        against, 508
Lock-up, 662
Looter, sale to, 661
Loyalty, duty of. See Duty of loyalty;
        Fiduciary duties

Management patterns
    large corporation, 28-32
    middle manager, 28, 29
Managerial capitalism, 31, 32
Manager-managed LLCs, 759
Managers, 744
Manifestation, 95
Manufacturer, 19
Marginal tax rate, 173
Marketability discount, 664. See also Appraisal
        rights
Market cap, 55
Massachusetts business trusts, 737
Master-servant relationship, 103
Material adverse change clause, 658
Material information, disclosure of, 589
Material statement, 252
MBCA. See Model Business Corporations Act
        (MBCA)
Meeting. See also Voting
    annual meeting of public corporation,
        556-558
    of directors. See Meeting of directors
    of shareholders. See Shareholder meeting
Meeting of directors
    breaking a quorum, 332
    call of, 331

notice of, 331-332
quorum, 332
regular meetings, 331
special meetings, 331
sufficient vote, 331-333
Member-managed LLCs, 758
Members, 744
Mere continuation exception, 302-306
Merger
de factor merger doctrine, 656
plan of, 652
reverse, 654
reverse triangular mergers, 653-654
short form, 653
triangular, 654
Middle manager, 28, 29
Minority discount, 55, 664
Minority shareholders, 623-626, 637-638
remedies for, 637-638
valuation of minority shares, 623-626,
637-638
Model Business Corporations Act (MBCA),
127, 780
Model Nonprofit Corporation Act, 780
Money, investment of, 200
Monitor, 88
Moody's Investors Service, 517-518, 520-521
Moral compass, 531
Moral hazard, 86
Motivation of agency, 85
Multiple clients and entity clients, professional
responsibility of lawyer to, 139-149

Name of corporation
reservation of, 124
words or abbreviations to use, 124
NASDAQ. See National Association of
Securities Dealers Automated
Quotation (NASDAQ)
National Association of Corporate Directors,
528
National Association of Securities Dealers,
355, 539
National Association of Securities Dealers
Automated Quotation (NASDAQ),
176, 202
National Conference of Commissioners on
Uniform State Laws, 688, 780, 787
Negative covenants, 163
Negative income tax, 749
Negligence, analogy of duty of care to, 420
Net cash flow, 49
Net income, 78, 80
Net present value, 51, 53-54, 56, 82
Net revenues, 79

Net sales, 79
New York Stock Exchange, 202, 225, 355,
518
Nexus of contract, 370-371
NOBO list for inspection, 572-575. See also
Federal securities laws
Noncash consideration, 196
No-shop provision, 659
No-talk clause, 659-660
Notarization, 126
Notice of meeting, 331-332
due notice, 332
of shareholders, 546

Occupational health and safety (OSHA)
requirements, 357
Offer, defined, 201
Offer of security, 201
Officers, 340-354, 508
agents and, 340-348
agents versus, 344
apparent authority of, 348
compensation of, 400
creditors, liability to, 306-310
definition of, 343-344
direct liability of, 306-310
duty of care of. See Duty of care
duty of loyalty of. See Duty of loyalty
fiduciary duties of. See Fiduciary duties
ostensible authority of, 348
power of, 348-354
types of, 345
Operating agreement, LLC, 759
Operating expenses, 76-77
Operating profit, 79
Oppression, 622-637
shareholder oppression, 208
Option, 59-61, 164
call, 60
hedges, 60
put, 60
real options, 60
underlying, 60
valuation of, 59-61
Option writer, 164
Ordinarily prudent person, 409
Ordinary income, 173
Organizational meeting, 126
Organization clause as client, 144-146
OSHA. See Occupational health and safety
(OSHA) requirements
Ostensible authority, 348
Other-regarding behavior, 532-534
Other revenues and expenses, 79
Out-of-pocket costs, 657-658

Outside accountants, 512-517
Outside law firms, 510-512
Outstanding, meaning of, 197
Overestimation, 66
Overhead, 79
Overissue, 185
Ownership reporting requirements, 590

Pari pasu, 155
Participating, 155
Participation theory of liability, 307
Parties, identification of, 657
Partners' equity, 77
Partnership at will, 730
Partnerships, 15, 32, 687-738
    drawbacks of, 737
    federal securities laws, 738
    general. See General partnerships
    joint ventures, 733-734
    limited, 735-737
    limited liability limited partnerships
        (LLLPs), 737
    limited liability partnerships (LLPs), 737
Par value, 194-195
Pass-through taxation, 774, 778
Perfection, delayed perfection as inequitable
    conduct, 299
Periodic reporting, 564-565, 738, 769
Personality type, 534
Piercing the corporate veil, 172, 276-284
    LLCs, 750-751, 753
Plan of merger, 652
Plurality of votes, 554
Poison pill, 670, 675
Pooling agreements, 604, 606-607
Power given as security, 110-111
Power of position, 98
Precatory motions, 544
Preemptive rights, 197-198, 229, 593-595
    management component, 595
Preferred stock, 154-156
    participating preferred stock, 155
    series of, 154
Preferred stock dividends, 155
Prepaid expenses, 77
Present value, discounting to, 50-51
Price, defined, 48
Principal
    agent, relation to, 109-110
    death or incapacity of, 111
    defined, 90
    duties of, 110
    estoppel, 99-100
    liability for agent's torts, 100-103
    liability of third party to, 105

manifestation to agent, 95
    partially disclosed, 99
    ratification, 100
    respondeat superior, 104
    restitution, liability for, 100
    third parties, liability to, 95-105
    third party's liability to, 105
    tort of agent, liability for, 100-105
    undisclosed, 99
    unidentified, 99
    vicarious liability of, 100-103
Private benefits, 86
Privately held corporations, shareholder
        governance powers, 593-638
    agreements regarding shareholder voting,
        603-609
    cumulative voting, 599-603
    deadlock, 611-612, 622-634
    external restrictions, 613-638
    fiduciary duties of shareholders,
        613-622
    minority shareholders, remedies for,
        637-638
    oppression, 622-634
    pooling agreements, 604, 606-607
    preemptive rights, 593-595
    self-dealing transaction, 621
    self-imposed restrictions on governance
        rights, 593-612
    supermajority provisions, 595-599, 611
    superquorum provisions, 599
    vote buying, 607-609
    voting agreements, 603
    voting trusts, 604-606
Private placement exemption, 201. See also
        Federal securities laws
Private Securities Litigation Reform Act of
        1995, 251-252. See also Federal
        securities laws
Probabilities, insensitivity to prior probability
        of outcomes, 65
Product line exception, 305
Professional responsibility of lawyers,
        139-149
Profit
    from dividends, 205-227
    expectation of, 200
    from sale of stock by shareholders,
        227-246
Profit-sharing plans, 88
Progressive corporate law, 375-376
Promissory note, 162
Promoter
    defined, 115
    liability of, 115-119, 130, 136
Promoter liability doctrine, 136

Proper purpose, 567, 570
Property, traditional logic of, 368, 370
Proportionality test, 674
Proxy, 556
   defined, 589
   federal rules governing, 588
   form, rules concerning, 589
   general, 556
   limited, 556
   solicitations, regulation of, 589-590
Proxyholder, 556
Prudent person, 409
Public offering, transactions not involving,
   201
Public policy considerations, corporate
   fiduciaries, 397-398
Purchase of assets, 642-651
   drawbacks, 651
Purchase of stock, 651-652
Put option, 60, 164

Quorum, 332, 553-554
   breaking a, 332

Raider, 657, 669, 671
Range of reasonableness standard, 674
Ratcheting, 86
Ratification, 100
   of agent's actions, 343
Rating companies, 517-521
Rationality, limits of, 63-67
Rational self-interest, 61-73, 82
Ratio of line cost expense to revenue, 493
R&D. *See* Research and development (R&D)
Real options, 60
Reasonable expectations test, 624-626, 630
Reasonable particularity requirement, 574
Receivables skim, 408
Recognition, 655
Record date, 210, 546
Redeemable stock, 156
Redemption right, 156
Reform, 535-536. *See also* Enron; Restrictions
   on board's power; Scandals; World-
   Com
   effectiveness of, 535-540
   through intentionality, 527-534
Registration. *See also* Federal securities
   laws
   going public, 202-203
   process of, 202-203
   of securities, 201-203
Registration statement, 201. *See also* Federal
   securities laws

Regular meetings, 331
Regulation D, 202. *See also* Federal securities
   laws
Regulatory risk, 46
Reinvestment risk, 171
Relative rights, 156-157
Reliance, justifiable, 351
Renunciation of agency, 110
Reorganization
   A reorg, 655
   B reorg, 655
   C reorg, 655
   defined, 655
Reporting, up-the-ladder, 17
Reporting requirements, 590, 738, 769
Representations and warranties, 657
Representativeness, 64-65
Repurchase of shares, 243-246
   metaphysics of, 245-246
Reputational intermediaries, 510-526
   credit-rating agencies, 517-521
   independent accountants, 512-517
   outside law firms, 510-512
   securities analysts, 521-527
Research and development (R&D), 79
Reservation price, 641
Respondeat superior, 104
Restitution, 100
Restrictions on board's power, 491-541
   federal securities regulation, 377-378
   Foreign Corrupt Practices Act, 377-378
   legislation effecting, 357-359
   reputational intermediaries, 510-526
   scandals and. *See* Enron; Scandals;
     WorldCom
   structural constraints, 497-507
   ultimate beneficiaries of, 363-377
   ultra vires, 359-363
Restrictions on resale, 246-248
   Rule 144, 247-248
   Section 16(b), 246-247
Restrictions on transfer. *See* Transfer
   restrictions
Retained earnings, 77
Retired shares, 245-246
Revenues, 79
   other revenues and expenses, 79
Reverse merger, 654
Reverse stock split, 217-224
Reverse triangular mergers, 653-654
Revised Model Nonprofit Corporation Act,
   780
Revised Uniform Partnership Act, 780
Revlon duties, 676
Revocation of agency, 110
Right, 164

Right appraisal, 663-669
Rights of first refusal, 239
Risk, 43-48
    assessment of, 81
    counterparty, 46
    currency, 46
    default, 46
    foreign investment, 46
    inflation, 46
    regulatory, 46
    tax laws, 46
Risk averse, 87
Round lot, 214
Rule 10b-5, 738. *See also* Federal securities
        laws
    antifraud provisions, 248-272
    insider trading, 259-271
Rule 14a-8, 588. *See also* Federal securities
        laws
Rule 144, 247-248. *See also* Federal securities
        laws

Safe harbor, 202
Sale at premium, 662
Sale of control, 660-663
    to looter, 661
    at premium, 662
Sales skim, 408
Sale to looter, 661
Salvage value, 48
Sarbanes-Oxley Act of 2002 (SOx). *See also*
        Federal securities laws
    annual report, requirements for, 508
    audit committee, with financial expert,
        507
    board power, methods of controlling, 540
    certification of accuracy of financial
        information, 508
    conflicts of interest, disclosure of, 527
    credit-rating agencies, regulation of, 521
    disclosure controls and procedures, 422
    ethics code for CFOs, 508
    financial reporting, 422
    governance rules, 355, 535
    internal controls, 508
    loans to senior executives, prohibition
        against, 508
    obligations of senior officers of public
        companies, 508
    securities analysts, 527
    up-the-ladder reporting, 17
Scandals, 17, 355, 491, 538, 539-540. *See also*
        Enron; Restrictions on board's
        power; WorldCom

Schedule 13D, 590. *See also* Federal securities
        laws
Schedule TO, 682. *See also* Federal securities
        laws
Scienter, 249, 252, 271. *See also* Federal
        securities laws
Scope of employment, 104-105
S corporation, 773, 774
Scrap value, 48
Secondary trading market, 176
Secretary of corporation, 344
Section 16(b), 246-247. *See also* Federal
        securities laws
Secured transactions, 16
Securities, 151, 153
    defined, 199-200. *See also* Federal
        securities laws
    exotic, 164-165
    meaning of, 11
    registration of, 201-203. *See also* Federal
        securities laws
Securities Act of 1933, 199, 540, 738. *See also*
        Federal securities laws
Securities analysts, 521-527
Securities and Exchange Commission (SEC),
        177, 199. *See also* Federal securities
        laws
Securities Exchange Act of 1934, 199, 377,
        738. *See also* Federal securities laws
Securities laws. *See also* Federal securities
        laws
Self-dealing, 390-394, 395, 400
    full disclosure of, 398-399
Self-dealing transaction, 621
Self-interest, 61, 62-63
Sentencing Guidelines. *See* Federal Sentencing
        Guidelines
Series of stock, 154, 185
Settled trades, 560
Shareholder, 154, 229
    liability for corporate debt, 276-284
    power to redress harm to corporation,
        575-588
    rights to information, 564-575
    sale of stock by, 227-246
Shareholder action
    by consent in lieu of meeting, 558-559
    as group, 544-545
    in meeting, 545-558
Shareholder fiduciary duties, 613-622
Shareholder governance powers. *See also* Vote;
        Voting
    consent in lieu of holding meeting, action
        taken by, 325-329, 558-559
    derivative action, 576-588
    federal securities regulation, 588-590

group, actions taken as, 544-545
inspection right, 565-575
matters requiring shareholder vote under
    federal law, 588-589
meeting, action taken in. *See* Shareholder
    meeting
ownership reporting requirements, 590
periodic and transaction reporting,
    564-565, 590
in privately held corporations, 593-638. *See
    also* Privately held corporations,
    shareholder governance powers
proxy solicitations, regulation of, 589-590
in public companies, 543-591
redressing harm to corporation, 575-588
rights to information, 564-575
shareholder agreements affecting, 609-611
Shareholder governance questions, privately
    held corporation, 593-638
Shareholder governance rights
external restrictions on, 613-638
self-imposed restrictions on, 593-612
Shareholder inspection right, 565-575
Shareholder lock-up, 662
Shareholder meeting, 545-558. *See also*
    Voting
advance notice bylaw, 557
annual meeting of public corporation,
    556-558
call of meeting, 545-546
notice of, 546, 557
presence at meeting, importance of,
    555-556
quorum, 553-554
sufficient vote, 554-555
voting power, 553, 555
Shareholder primacy model, 368
Shareholder ratification, 463
Shareholders' equity, 77
Shareholders' rights plan, 670
Shareholder value, target obligation to
    maximize value, 675-676
Shareholder voting. *See also* Voting
agreements regarding, 603-609
matters requiring shareholder vote,
    588-589
who counts the vote, 562-564
whose vote counts, 559-562
Shares. *See also* Stock
canceled, 245
defined, 153, 154
outstanding, 197
ownership versus receipt, 214
repurchase of, 244-246
retired, 245-246
Shark repellents, 670

Sherman Antitrust Act of 1890, 640
Shirking, 86
Short form merger, 653
    subsidiary in, 664
Signaling, 85
Significant events, 590
Silent partners, 735
Simple majority, 554
Sinking fund, 163
Size of sample, insensitivity to, 65
Skimming, 408
Snake pit, 564
Social responsibility, corporate, 373-377
Solicitation, defined, 589
Solicitors, versus barristers, 8
SOx. *See* Sarbanes-Oxley Act of 2002 (SOx).
    See also Federal securities laws
Special committee, 583
Special litigation committee, 456
Special meetings, 331
    of shareholders, 545
Special purpose entities (SPEs), 492
SPEs. *See* Special purpose entities (SPEs)
Staggered terms, 323
Standard & Poor's, 517, 519, 521
Standards of review of board action,
    425-489
amelioration of liability for violation of
    duties, 455-475
business judgment rule, 426, 444-455
duty of care, 437-444
duty of loyalty, 427-437
entire fairness standard, 434-437
fair dealing, 435
fair price, 435-437
summation of issues, 476-489
Start-up corporation, capital structure for,
    174-175
Starvation returns, 662
State antitakeover statutes, 680
Statement of cash flows, 78
Statement of income, 79
Statute of Frauds, 399
Statutory voting, 599
Stock, 153. *See also* Shares
blank check stock, 185
blank stock, 185
board authorization, 186
callable, 156
cancelled shares, 245
common, 151, 153-154
consideration, 194-197
convertible, 156
defined, 153-154
dividend. *See* Stock dividend
fully paid, 186

Stock *(continued)*
    issuance at inadequate price, 196
    issuance of, 185-198
    issued, 185
    nonassessable, 186
    noncash consideration, 196
    outstanding, 197
    overissue, 185
    ownership versus receipt, 214
    par value, 194-195
    preemptive rights, 197-198
    preferred, 154-156
    redeemable, 156
    repurchase of, 244-246
    retired shares, 245-246
    splits. *See* Stock splits
    statutorily authorized stock, 185
    statutory authorization, 185
    subscription agreements, 194
    validly issued, 186
    watered, 196
Stock dividend, 214. *See also* Dividends
    stock split versus, 224-227
Stock exchanges, listing requirements, 355
Stockholder, 154
Stock right, 151
Stock splits, 213-217
    reverse stock splits, 217-224
    stock dividend versus, 224-227
Straight voting, 599
Street name, 561
Stress, coping with, 68
Structural constraints, 497-534
Subordinated debt, 163
Subordination, degree of, 300
Subscription agreements, 194
Subsidiary, 651
    in short form merger, 664
Successor liability, 301-306
Supermajority, defined, 597
Supermajority provisions, 595-599, 611
Supermajority vote, 595
Superquorum provisions, 599
Surplus, 209
Syndicate, 163
Synergy value, 48
System failure, 536-537
Systemic problem versus cyclical anomalies,
    536-540

Takeover, hostile, 656
Target corporation, 642
Tax deferred, 655
Taxes, accrued income taxes, 77
Tax laws risk, 46

Tax rate
    effective, 173
    marginal, 173
Team production model, 88
Tender offers, 669, 682-683
    hostile tender offer. *See* Hostile tender offer
Terminal price, 49
Termination section of agreement, 658
Term partnership, 730
Thin capitalization, 171
Time value of money, 49-50
Tippee liability, 268. *See also* Federal securities
    laws
Topping fee, 659
Tort, analogy of duty of care to, 420
Trader, 19
Traditional logic of property, 368, 370
Transaction, description of, 657
Transaction causation, 252
Transaction reporting, 564-565
Transfer agent, 561
Transfer of control. *See* Change of control
Transfer restrictions, 238-241
    blood members of the family, 240
    with board approval, 239-240
    involuntary transfers, 240-241
    restrictions on, 228, 236
Treasury stock, 246
Triangular merger, 654

UCC. *See* Uniform Commercial Code
    (UCC)
UCC-1, 162
Ultra vires, doctrine of, 359-363
Uncertainty, and risk, 43
Undercapitalization, 298-299
Underestimation, 66
Underlying, 60
Underwriter, 177, 202
Undisclosed principal, 99
Unidentified principal, 99
Uniform Commercial Code (UCC), 16,
    787
Uniform Limited Liability Company Act,
    780
Uniform Limited Partnership Act, 91, 735,
    780
Uniform Partnership Act (UPA), 15, 91,
    688, 690, 780
Uniform Unincorporated Nonprofit
    Association Act, 780
Unit, 164
Unocal test, 672, 674, 675
UPA. *See* Uniform Partnership Act (UPA)
Utility, 54, 56, 57

Validity, illusion of, 65
Valuation, 48-61
    break-up value, 48
    defined, 48
    as discounted cash flow, 49-54. *See also*
        Discounted cash flow (DCF)
        analysis
    discount rate, 51
    going concern value, 48, 236
    interest, 50
    methods of valuation, 54-55
    of options, 59-61
    present value, discounting to, 50-51
    price, 48
    salvage value, 48
    scrap value, 48
    synergy value, 48
    time value of money, 50
Veil piercing, 172, 276-284
    LLCs, 750-751, 753
Venture capital, 176-178
Venture capital firms, 177
Vertical aggregation, 284
Vertical combinations, 640
Vertical dimension, 20
Vest, 164
Vicarious liability, 100
Voidable preferences, 296
Vote. *See also* Shareholder governance powers
    absolute majority, 554
    "no" vote, 554
    plurality of votes, 554
    simple majority, 554
    sufficiency of, 554-555
    supermajority vote, 559
    tabulation of votes, 559-564

who counts votes, 562-564
    whose vote counts, 559-562
Vote buying, 607-609
    rule against, 607-609
Voting. *See also* Shareholder governance
        powers
    cumulative, 599-603
    selling stock as indirect way of voting,
        652
    shareholder. *See* Shareholder voting
    statutory, 599
    straight, 599
    tabulation of votes, 559-564
Voting agreements, 603-609
Voting power, 553
Voting trusts, 604-606
    defined, 605

Warrant, 164
Warranties, 657
Waste, 359-362
Watered stock, 196
Wellman test, 682. *See also* Federal securities
        laws
Williamson test. *See also* Federal securities laws
    LLCs, 769
    partnerships, 738
Worker, 19
Working capital, 151
WorldCom, 493-497
    bankruptcy, 522
    board of directors, 504-507
    independent auditor and, 514-516
    internal auditors, 510
    securities analysts, interactions with,
        523-526